HANDBOOK OF THE ECONOMICS OF GIVING, ALTRUISM AND RECIPROCITY
VOLUME 2

EHEHEHEHEHEHEHEHEHEHEHEHEHEHEHEHEHEHEHEHEHEHE

HANDBOOKS IN ECONOMICS

23

Series Editors

KENNETH J. ARROW
MICHAEL D. INTRILIGATOR

AMSTERDAM • BOSTON • HEIDELBERG • LONDON
NEW YORK • OXFORD • PARIS • SAN DIEGO
SAN FRANCISCO • SINGAPORE • SYDNEY • TOKYO
North-Holland is an imprint of Elsevier

EHEHEHEHEHEHEHEHEHEHEHEHEHEHEHEHEHEHEHEHEHEHE

HANDBOOK OF THE ECONOMICS OF GIVING, ALTRUISM AND RECIPROCITY

APPLICATIONS

VOLUME 2

Edited by

SERGE-CHRISTOPHE KOLM
Paris, France

and

JEAN MERCIER YTHIER
University of Metz

AMSTERDAM • BOSTON • HEIDELBERG • LONDON
NEW YORK • OXFORD • PARIS • SAN DIEGO
SAN FRANCISCO • SINGAPORE • SYDNEY • TOKYO
North-Holland is an imprint of Elsevier

North-Holland is an imprint of Elsevier
Radarweg 29, PO Box 211, 1000 AE Amsterdam, The Netherlands
The Boulevard, Langford Lane, Kidlington, Oxford OX5 1GB, UK

First edition 2006

Library of Congress Cataloging-in-Publication Data
A catalog record for this book is available from the Library of Congress

British Library Cataloguing in Publication Data
A catalogue record for this book is available from the British Library

ISBN-13: 978-0-444-52145-3
ISBN-10: 0-444-52145-3

ISSN: 0169-7218 (Handbooks in Economics series)
ISSN: 1574-0714 (Handbook of the Economics of Giving, Altruism and Reciprocity series)

For information on all North-Holland publications
visit our website at books.elsevier.com

Printed and bound in The Netherlands

06 07 08 09 10   10 9 8 7 6 5 4 3 2 1

INTRODUCTION TO THE SERIES

The aim of the *Handbooks in Economics* series is to produce Handbooks for various branches of economics, each of which is a definitive source, reference, and teaching supplement for use by professional researchers and advanced graduate students. Each Handbook provides self-contained surveys of the current state of a branch of economics in the form of chapters prepared by leading specialists on various aspects of this branch of economics. These surveys summarize not only received results but also newer developments, from recent journal articles and discussion papers. Some original material is also included, but the main goal is to provide comprehensive and accessible surveys. The Handbooks are intended to provide not only useful reference volumes for professional collections but also possible supplementary readings for advanced courses for graduate students in economics.

KENNETH J. ARROW and MICHAEL D. INTRILIGATOR

CONTENTS OF THE HANDBOOK

VOLUME 1

PREFACE TO THE HANDBOOK

Field and methods

The field of the Handbook is the analysis of non-market voluntary transfers of scarce resources, of the reasons for their existence including notably the motives of the agents involved, and of their relations and interactions with market allocation and public finance. It includes the measurement of the magnitude and share of non-market voluntary transfers and their evolution over time; and the assessment of the importance of moral conducts in market exchange for the good functioning of markets. It also includes the developing, and systematic use for the purposes of economic analysis, of descriptions and abstract representations of the "social man" significantly more realistic, accurate and complete than the conventional representation of the "economic man" often assumed in the economics of the nineteenth and twentieth centuries. From this latter aspect, the Handbook extends and renews a continuous tradition of economic science, notably represented in the works of most of the founders, from the late eighteenth century (Adam Smith) to the early twentieth (notably Pareto). Applications include family transfers, gift-giving and volunteering in charities and other non-profit organizations, cooperation and reciprocity in labor relations, social transfers, public redistribution and international aid. Methods cover a wide spectrum, in relation to the variety of considered phenomena, notably: psychological and normative analysis, including the relevant branches of moral and political philosophy; models of economic equilibrium and growth; game theory, including its evolutionary variants; laboratory experiments in psychology and game interactions; and econometric and statistical assessment of transfers and transfer motives.

Purpose

The *Handbook of the Economics of Giving, Altruism and Reciprocity* aims to provide a definitive source, reference guide, and teaching supplement for its field. It surveys, as of the early 2000's, the state of the art of the economic theory and of the econometric and statistical study of its object, and it also provides extensive reviews of the contemporary contributions of the other disciplines concerned by the domain, such as anthropology, psychology, philosophy, political science, sociology, biology and socio-biology. In addition to its use as a reference guide, the Editors hope that this Handbook will assist researchers and students working in a particular branch of this vast field to become acquainted with other branches. Each of the chapters can be read independently.

Organization

The Handbook includes 26 chapters on various topics in the field. Chapter 1 introduces the subject and proposes a first overview of the field. The following chapters are arranged into four parts. *Part I* treats *Foundations*, including reviews of economic theories and empirical findings relative to gift-giving, reciprocity and their motives, and also surveys of similar contributions from within anthropology, philosophy, psychology and evolutionary theory. The next three parts concentrate on applications to the three sectors of society where non-market voluntary transfers are particularly significant: the family, with *Part II* relative to *Family Transfers*, including microeconomic and macroeconomic theories of family transfers and of their taxation, and corresponding econometric analyses; the third sector, with *Part III* on *Third Sector and Labour*, including theoretical and empirical analyses of philanthropy, non-profit organizations, cooperatives and co-operation in labor relations, and organ donations; and the State, with *Part IV* covering *The Political Economy of Voluntary Transfers*, including reviews of the theoretical and empirical analyses of the welfare state and of international aid.

Level

All the topics presented are treated at an advanced level, suitable for use by economists and social scientists working in the field, or by graduate students in both economics and the social sciences.

Acknowledgements

First of all, we would like to make a special mention of gratitude to Louis-André Gérard-Varet, who participated as editor to the initial conception of the Handbook, and who unfortunately died shortly after the launching of the project. These two volumes would not have existed without him. They are dedicated to his memory. Our other principal acknowledgements are to Kenneth Arrow and Michael Intriligator for their friendly advice as general editors of the series, and to the authors of chapters in the present Handbook, who not only prepared their own chapters but also provided advice on the organization and content of the volumes and reviewed other chapters. We are also most grateful to Valerie Teng, senior publishing editor in charge, and her team, for their very helpful assistance and their patience. The authors' conference that we organized at Marseilles in January 2002 was an important step in the preparation of the volumes. We are indebted to the Institut d'Economie Publique, the Université de la Méditerranée, and the Ecole des Hautes Etudes en Sciences Sociales for providing us with the necessary financial and organizational support on this occasion. Finally, we are grateful to the Université de Metz and the Equipe de Recherche en Anthropologie et Sociologie de l'Expertise for providing us with financial support for the editing of substantial parts of the volumes.

The editors

CONTENTS OF VOLUME 2

PART 3: THIRD SECTOR AND LABOR

PART 2

FAMILY TRANSFERS

Chapter 13

MICROECONOMIC MODELS OF FAMILY TRANSFERS*

ANNE LAFERRÈRE

INSEE (Institut National de la Statistique et des Etudes Economiques) and CREST (Centre de Recherche en Economie et Statistiques), Paris, France
e-mail: anne.laferrere@insee.fr

FRANÇOIS-CHARLES WOLFF

LEN-CEBS University of Nantes, CNAV and INED, Paris, France
e-mail: wolff@sc-eco.univ-nantes.fr

Contents

* Thanks are due to our referee Jean-Pierre Vidal, to the editors, and to Francis Kramarz, Mohamed Jellal, Guy Laroque, David le Blanc, Bernard Salanié for discussions and reading all or part of previous versions. Remaining errors are ours.

Handbook of the Economics of Giving, Altruism and Reciprocity, Volume 2
Edited by Serge-Christophe Kolm and Jean Mercier Ythier

DOI: 10.1016/S1574-0714(06)02013-6

Abstract

Standard *homo economicus* lives in a world of complete markets and maximizes utility which is a function of his personal consumption. This approximation cannot account for parents making transfers to adult children, children taking care of old parents, nor for gifts, inheritance and many other services exchanged within families. Such behavior can be derived from three main mechanisms. Firstly, in the so-called pure altruism model, the parent's utility is augmented by the utility of his child. This leads to transfers from the parent to his child. An important feature of this model is the strong property of redistributive neutrality: since parents and child pool their income, any government transfer to one will be undone by the other adjusting his transfer. In a second model, altruism is impure as the parents want the child to behave in a certain way: exchange and strategic considerations enter the picture, as both parents' and child's income become endogenous. Thirdly, in a non-altruistic setting, with imperfect credit market, transfers to children and to old parents correspond to a reciprocity contract and are an investment for old age. Families embody long term and widespread commitments: born as a needy child, one becomes a parent and ultimately a (perhaps) needy grandparent. Moreover for much of what is exchanged within families, there is no market substitute. These features explain why the network of reciprocities can be large both in time and space, why those transfers change but do not disappear as market or public insurance develop, and why displacing them can have perverse side effects.

Family transfers influence intra- and inter-generational inequality, hence the importance to assess their motivation. Tests usually conclude that the income pooling predicted by pure altruism is not observed, but family transfers are also far from being entirely motivated by direct exchange considerations.

Keywords

altruism, exchange, reciprocity, intergenerational transfer, redistribution

JEL classification: D1, D64, J14, J22, R2

More blessing come from giving than from receiving
Acts, 20:35.

1. What families are made of

Transfers are the very fabric of families. The English word 'relative', for family members, stresses the primacy of relationship. The means and ways of transferring within families are varied. They go from bequests, *inter vivos* gifts or presents, to education and all kind of help and services flowing between parents and children. There is a continuum of actions, from making a child's bed, lodging a would-be child-in-law for months, to lending a summer house to grand-children, paying the rent of a student, temporarily housing a divorced son, lending money for a downpayment, helping fix the kitchen cabinets or visiting an ailing parent. What is really a transfer to a different household and what is just part of the household's consumption?

Family transfers are different from those taking place on the market in that there is no immediate or defined counterpart. Services, such as child care or loans between generations, may have market substitutes. But their exchange within families takes place 'outside the market'. The exchange may not be perceived as such (on receiving a present, the rule is not to give back immediately but later and differently, and one may never give back), or is very indirect (an entrepreneur marries a public servant 'in order to' mitigate their income variability). Usually there is no written contract,[1] as would be the case with market insurance for example, although some internal favor may be expected: parents invest in education, expecting that the children will eventually become independent, or hoping further that they will help them when they are old. But no parent would ever go to court to make a child reimburse his tuition fees. In some instances, there is no market for those services because they have many dimensions: the grand-mother who looks after her grand-child would not do it for a neighbor's. What is 'bought', and at what price, is not known exactly. Finally those transfers include goods such as affection, caring, which clearly have no market substitutes.

Moreover, family transfers are loaded with more or less hidden characteristics. Even if the exchange is explicit, such as in a family credit operation with an interest rate and schedule of payment, the very fact that it takes place within a family may create gratitude, sentiment of duty, but also envy, jealousy that would not exist between banker and clients.

Thus intergenerational transfers, while sometimes closely resembling market transactions, are essentially different in their non-written, non-formalized, unpredictable

[1] This is also the case in many day-to-day market transactions between non-family members: turning to the legal system is a rare event. However it remains a possibility when social norms of cooperation are absent. This possibility is much rarer between parents and children.

nature. This makes the study of their economic motivations more difficult to grasp and model. It is nevertheless what is attempted in this chapter.[2]

The economic motivations of family transfers may be seen through three main types of models. Firstly, according to the pure altruism model, the welfare of an individual, the parent, is influenced by the utility level of another one, the child, which is an argument of his own utility function. The parent is then said to be altruistic (section 2). The main prediction is that of 'income pooling' or 'redistributive neutrality': an increase in the non-altruistic child's income, matched by a decrease in his altruistic parent's income, does not change parent's and child's consumption. This has important consequences in terms of the effect of public redistribution between generations. We shall follow the Ariadne's thread of the redistributive neutrality prediction along the whole chapter. In particular we show that it only holds under very restrictive assumptions. Secondly, altruism becomes 'impure' as soon as the altruist is interested not only in his child's utility but in a particular element of his consumption vector, leisure time for instance; then exchange considerations enter the picture (section 3). Thirdly, in a non-altruism setting, called here the mutuality model, transfers to children and to old parents correspond to explicit reciprocities, for instance they are an investment for old-age (section 4). Then the effects of public redistribution are very different than under redistributive neutrality. Since all three types of models rely on different forms of more or less inter-related preferences, and since families are the very place where tastes are transmitted, we devote a section to preference formation (section 5). The models are archetypes, that go along with specific assumptions. We try to make them explicit, along with the mechanisms that allow them to work. The testable predictions of the models are finally summarized, along with the most conclusive empirical tests (section 6).

2. Altruism, or the power of families

We start from the basic one-sided pure altruism model. There are only one commodity and one period; transfer goes from a single altruistic parent to a single non-altruistic child,[3] incomes are exogenous (section 2.1). These assumptions are then gradually relaxed. The child will be allowed to be simultaneously altruistic toward his parent (section 2.2). Allowing for multiple recipients introduces the possibility of unequal transfers (section 2.3.1); multiple donors turn the recipient into a 'public good' (section 2.3.2).

[2] Relations within couples and exchanges between non-related households are left aside. Masson and Pestieau (1991, 1997) provide a review of inheritance models. Laitner (1997) also reviews intergenerational and inter-households economic links. Bergstrom (1997) encompasses both nuclear and extended family economic theories. Laferrère (1999, 2000) are short surveys on which the present chapter draws. In this Handbook, Arrondel and Masson (2006) is closely related.

[3] The conclusions obviously apply to the case of an altruistic child and non-altruistic (presumably old) parents, or to relationships between siblings.

Table 1
The eight pillars of the pure altruism model

Assumption	Basic pure altruism	Extended pure altruism
A1	One parent, one child	Relaxed in section 2.3
A2	Utility normal good	Not relaxed
A3	Perfect information of parent	Relaxed in section 2.4
A4	One good (monetary transfers only)	Relaxed in section 2.4
A5	One period	Relaxed in sections 2.4 and 3
A6	Child non altruist	Relaxed in section 2.2
A7	Parent leads the game	Relaxed in sections 2.2 and 3
A8	Exogenous income	Relaxed in sections 2.4 and 3

Finally, a second commodity, time, will be introduced and the exogenous income assumption will be relaxed (section 2.4).[4]

2.1. *The eight pillars of pure one-sided altruism, and redistributive neutrality*

The altruism model was made famous by Barro (1974) and Becker (1974, 1991). There are two generations (assumption A1), one parent labeled with subscript p and one child labeled with subscript k. The parent is a pure altruist, that is the child's utility is a normal good for him (assumption A2). Let U be the parent's utility function and V the child's (both monotonous and strictly quasi-concave), V is perfectly known to the parent (assumption A3).[5] There is only one normal good (or equivalently, transfers are only monetary) (assumption A4) and one period, thus no uncertainty (assumption A5).

Table 1 summarizes the main assumptions of the pure altruism model with two generations: only assumption A2 on the form of utility is necessary for the model to remain altruist. However, as will become clear below, all assumptions are necessary to draw the main conclusions of the Beckerian altruism model.

The parent maximizes his utility, an increasing weakly separable function of his own consumption denoted by C_p and of the child's utility:

$$\max_{C_p} U(C_p, V(C_k)) \tag{1}$$

with $U_c > 0$. The intensity of altruism is measured by the derivative U_v, such that $0 < U_v < 1$, also called the caring parameter. The child is not altruist, his utility $V = V(C_k)$ is only an increasing function of his consumption C_k and does not depend on U (assumption A6).

[4] Parental investment in the children's education is left out. The interactions between human capital investment and financial transfers are thoroughly discussed in Behrman (1997) and Laitner (1997).

[5] Next to one's own preferences, the best known are likely to be one's child's. Preferences are here exogenous. Sections 2.5, 3, and especially 5, briefly deal with endogenous altruism.

This specification means that individuals are not isolated: one cares for another separate entity, and knows his utility function. The other may receive a transfer from a separate entity for which he does not care. Note that pure altruism refers to a model where the child's well-being, and not only one element of the child's consumption vector, is an argument of the parent's utility.[6] The parent is assumed to be in a dominant position (assumption A7). This assumption about the mechanism by which parent and child interact, the game they are playing, is important. The parent observes the child's income and then decides on a transfer. The child is passive and accepts without bargaining his parent's transfer.

Here, the term altruism has no moral connotation. An altruistic person maximizing her utility behaves as 'selfishly' as any *homo economicus*. To put it bluntly, she consumes her child's utility. Following Becker (1991), the aim of the model is just to explain consumption decisions within the family, with no pretension to attain their real motives.[7] Pollak (2003) recently suggested to drop the term altruism and call this form of preferences *deferential*. This rightly stresses the characteristics of altruism, from an economist's point of view.

Each generation is endowed with an exogenous income (assumption A8), Y_p for the parent, and Y_k for the child. Let T be the amount of financial transfer from parent to child. This transfer cannot be negative: the parents cannot commit their child to make them a transfer, even if his income is high compared to theirs. The budget constraints are given by:

$$C_p = Y_p - T \tag{2}$$

$$C_k = Y_k + T \tag{3}$$

$$T \geq 0 \tag{4}$$

At each date, knowing his own income and the child's, the parent chooses his own consumption, thus the transfer to the child, and the child's consumption, by maximizing (1) under the constraints (2) to (4), that is he maximizes:

$$\max_{T \geq 0} U(Y_p - T, V(Y_k + T)) \tag{5}$$

which yields the first-order condition:

$$-U_c + U_v V_c \leq 0 \tag{6}$$

[6] With only one commodity, the distinction does not make much formal difference here, but will be important below. In a simpler model the parent's level of satisfaction is only function of the quantity and/or quality of the children. Such a framework is also called altruism by Becker (1991). For instance parents maximize the child's human capital or earnings (Behrman, 1997).

[7] A parent reluctantly settling on a long and difficult journey to help nursing a sick child is altruistic if he is compensated in terms of utility, even if he does it more on the grounds of moral responsibility than enthusiastic love.

Two cases are to be considered. First, when there is a positive transfer (constraint (4) on T is not binding, for instance when the parental income is high enough compared to the child's), the optimal transfer equalizes the parent's and the child's marginal utilities of consumption, as seen from the parental point of view:

$$U_c = U_v V_c \tag{7}$$

where U_v indicates the rate at which the parent is ready to give up his consumption for the child's. Altruism improves welfare without any change in total income. In that case, the two budget constraints can be pooled into one:

$$C_p + C_k = Y_p + Y_k \tag{8}$$

and the levels of consumption C_p and C_k can be written as functions of total family income $(Y_p + Y_k)$:

$$C_p = c_p(Y_p + Y_k)$$
$$C_k = c_k(Y_p + Y_k).$$

A key feature of the model is the effects of income on the optimal transfer. They can be easily derived by rewriting (3) as $T = c_k(Y_p + Y_k) - Y_k$, and noting that the function c_k is increasing in income, and that the good is normal. Then:

$$\frac{\partial T}{\partial Y_p} = c_k' > 0 \tag{9}$$

$$\frac{\partial T}{\partial Y_k} = c_k' - 1 < 0 \tag{10}$$

Hence, the parent is expected to partially compensate the child for a decrease in income. For example, in case of child's unemployment that would cut his income by half, the parent would raise his transfer to partially compensate his child's loss of income, by diminishing his own consumption C_p. Conversely, a rise in the child's income is beneficial for an altruistic parent, even when the child is absolutely not altruistic, because the parent is able to lower the amount of transfer to the child, thus raising his own consumption. In the same vein, the gift value is positively related with the parent's income. Subtracting (10) from (9) gives:

$$\frac{\partial T}{\partial Y_p} - \frac{\partial T}{\partial Y_k} = 1 \tag{11}$$

This result is known as income pooling, or as the difference in transfer-income derivatives restriction, or else as the redistributive neutrality property.[8] It is the core of most

[8] Or simply as the derivative restriction (McGarry, 2000). It was mentioned for the first time by Cox (1987, p. 514). Others mention the compensatory nature of altruistic transfers.

empirical tests of altruism.[9] Consider a small change in the income distribution such that $dY_p = -dY_k$, with $dY_p > 0$. The parent adjusts his transfer T to cancel the decrease in the child's income. The rise in the parent's income is also cancelled, he does not increase his own consumption. A change in the distribution of income between individuals linked by altruism does not modify their consumption, *if* there is an effective transfer from parents to child. This neutrality property is the basis of Ricardian equivalence: in a world where families are linked by positive monetary transfers, government monetary redistribution between them is neutralized by family action. More precisely, a government subsidy to adult children, say a housing subsidy, raises Y_k, and benefits the altruistic parent if he was previously paying for his child's rent by a transfer T. He is able to lower his transfer. Then the public transfer (the housing subsidy) is said to crowd out the family transfer. If the subsidy is exactly financed by a tax on the parent's income, the parent will exactly reduce his transfer by the tax amount, and the public redistribution has no effect, thus the term neutrality for the property. It also lies at the root of Becker's Rotten Kid theorem by which the selfish child has an incentive to maximize total family income.

The second case to be considered is when $T = 0$. Then,

$$U_c > U_v V_c \tag{12}$$

While the parent and the child pooled their resources in case of positive transfers, each generation consumes its own income in case of corner solutions characterized by $T = 0$. Two remarks are in order. First, from the parent's point of view, there might be cases when it would be optimal to receive a transfer from the child ($T < 0$). However, as the child is not altruistic, he does not make any transfer to his parent. Second, altruism can make the parent worse off. If the child has an exogenous negative income shock when the parent is at a corner, the child's utility is lowered, and so is the parent's.

Cox (1987) notes that the parent decides in two steps: first, whether he makes a transfer, second, given the transfer occurs, what amount he transfers. As shown by the previous first-order condition, the first decision is taken by comparing the marginal utility of own consumption $(U_{c_p})_{T=0}$ to the marginal utility of child's consumption $(U_{c_k})_{T=0}$, at the point where $C_p = Y_p$ and $C_k = Y_k$ (with $U_{c_k} = U_v V_c$). A transfer will occur if the latent variable $t = (U_{c_p})_{T=0} - (U_{c_k})_{T=0}$ is negative. Assuming diminishing marginal utility of consumption for parent and child implies that

$$\frac{\partial t}{\partial Y_k} < 0$$

and

$$\frac{\partial t}{\partial Y_p} > 0$$

[9] It stems from the mathematical properties of the problem: the fact that consumption only depends on the sum $(Y_p + Y_k)$.

The existence of a transfer increases with Y_p and decreases with Y_k. Individual incomes Y_p and Y_k have the same impact on both the occurrence of a transfer and its value.

Using a separable logarithmic utility function and an intensity $0 < \beta_p < 1$ for the strength of the altruistic feelings[10] allows to explicitly compute the transfer and consumption levels. Given the utility function

$$U(C_p, V(C_k)) = \ln C_p + \beta_p \ln C_k \tag{13}$$

the altruistic maximization program leads to the transfer value:

$$T = \max\left(0, \frac{\beta_p}{1+\beta_p} Y_p - \frac{1}{1+\beta_p} Y_k\right) \tag{14}$$

The transfer is an increasing function of the degree of altruism parameter ($\partial T/\partial \beta_p > 0$) and the transfer is positive only if $Y_p > Y_k/\beta_p$, that is parent's income is high enough.[11] The optimal transfer is more sensitive to the child's income than to the parental income (because $\beta_p < 1$). When $T > 0$, $C_p = \frac{1}{1+\beta_p}(Y_p + Y_k)$, $C_k = \frac{\beta_p}{1+\beta_p}(Y_p + Y_k)$, and the child's consumption is a fraction of the parent's:

$$C_k = \beta_p C_p \tag{15}$$

2.2. *Two-sided altruism*

A straightforward way to enlarge the model is to assume that altruism can be two-sided and that the child is also an altruist (relaxing assumption A6). This seemingly small change, just two individuals caring for each other, leads to some puzzles. Some examples are given at the end of this section.[12] Moving one step further, it seems natural to assume that the parent p not only cares for the child k, but also for his own parent gp; symmetrically, the child k cares not only for his parent p, but for his own child gk. Thus generations become linked together to infinity both to their offsprings and to their parents. The case was examined by Kimball (1987) and Hori and Kanaya (1989).[13] The main conclusion is that inefficiency cannot be eliminated in the dynamic of models that

[10] If $\beta_p \geq 1$, the altruistic parent would give more or equal weight to his child's marginal utility than to his own. While this can surely happen (for instance in the extreme case when a parent is ready to die for his child), it is left aside here. In a dynamic setting, it would lead to non-bounded dynastic utility (Barro and Becker, 1988).

[11] Or the parent is very altruistic, $\beta_p > Y_k/Y_p$. For instance if the child's income is half the parent's, β_p has to be above $1/2$.

[12] According to Hori (1999), the first formal analysis of utility interdependence is due to Edgeworth (1881). Collard (1975) revives Edgeworth's results.

[13] Kimball (1987) considers the linear utility case. Hori and Kanaya (1989) extend it to non-linear utility. Bergstrom (1999) also looks at the same kind of models. The seminal paper on dynastic altruism is due to Barro (1974), who proves that the neutrality result holds as long as a chain exists, whatever the direction of altruistic feelings. He does not however consider both backward and forward altruism.

incorporate externalities due to two-sided altruism.[14] This is because of recursiveness, what Becker calls infinite regress, and Kimball a 'Hall of Mirrors Effect': the translation from my preferences into a set of optimal allocations is complicated by your reaction to my allocation through your own preferences, making me react though my preferences which are linked to yours.[15] We stick here to a simple model, where time does not play any role, as analyzed by Bergstrom (1989b) and Stark (1993). Note that assumption A3 of perfect information on mutual preferences holds.[16]

There is again one parent p and one child k, but now each generation is altruistic towards the other. Let U and V be the utility functions of parent and child respectively. For simplification, we assume additive utilities and that u and v are the corresponding felicity (instantaneous utility, or sub-utility) functions, and that the altruism parameters β are not too high.[17] Preferences are then given by:

$$\begin{cases} U(C_p, V) = u(C_p) + \beta_p V(C_k, U) \\ V(C_k, U) = v(C_k) + \beta_k U(C_p, V) \end{cases} \tag{16}$$

where the $\beta_i \in]0;1[$ are the parent's and child's degree of altruism. System (16) can be put in the following equivalent form:

$$\begin{cases} U = \dfrac{1}{1-\beta_p\beta_k} u(C_p) + \dfrac{\beta_p}{1-\beta_p\beta_k} v(C_k) \\ V = \dfrac{\beta_k}{1-\beta_p\beta_k} u(C_p) + \dfrac{1}{1-\beta_p\beta_k} v(C_k) \end{cases} \tag{17}$$

Each generation maximizes its utility function given a fixed level of family income $\overline{C} = C_p + C_k$. Assuming logarithmic utilities ($u = v = \ln(C)$), the optimal consumption from the parent's point of view is:

$$C_p = \frac{C_k}{\beta_p} > C_k$$

as found before in (15) under one-sided altruism.[18] From the child's point of view, it is:

$$C_k = \frac{C_p}{\beta_k} > C_p$$

[14] Even when one simplifies the situation by assuming that all generations have the same utility function, and that each parent has only one child.

[15] Bramoullé (2001) shows that the mathematical property of contraction of the utility functions helps having non-multiple and non-infinite solutions. The intuition of contraction is that a change in the utility of others translates into a proportionally smaller change in one's own utility.

[16] One has to know the others' preferences in order to defer to them. Hori (1999) rightly insists on this being a strong assumption. It is more likely to hold within the family context.

[17] When altruism is too strong, it leads to a conflict in the optimal allocation since each generation wants the other to have a larger share of family income. See for instance Bergstrom's reflections on Romeo, Juliet and spaghetti (Bergstrom, 1989b).

[18] The above logarithmic utilities are the same as (13), but for a multiplication by a constant $(1-\beta_p\beta_k)^{-1}$, which does not change the transfer and consumption levels.

Thus two-sided altruism does not eliminate a possible conflict. Each, in spite of altruism, wants to consume more than the other. If there is a transfer, either it is from parent to child, or from child to parent. The parental transfer T_p is again given by (14). It is positive if parent's income is high enough compared to the child, i.e. $Y_p > \frac{\overline{C}}{1+\beta_p} = \underline{Y}_p$, or child's income low enough, $Y_k < \frac{\beta_p \overline{C}}{1+\beta_p} = \overline{Y}_k$. Symmetrically, the child transfers $T_k = \frac{\beta_k}{1+\beta_k} Y_k - \frac{1}{1+\beta_k} Y_p$ if his income is high enough: $Y_k > \frac{\overline{C}}{1+\beta_k} = \underline{Y}_k$, or the parent's income is low enough: $Y_p < \frac{\beta_k \overline{C}}{1+\beta_k} = \overline{Y}_p$. It can be shown that those conditions give income zones where there is a transfer from parent to child, or from child to parent, and also zones where nobody transfers. But a case with two transfers, from child to parent and from parent to child, can never occur. To fix the ideas, assume that $\beta_p > \beta_k$, the parent is more altruistic than the child. Then it follows that: $\overline{Y}_k < \overline{Y}_p < \underline{Y}_p < \underline{Y}_k$. When parent's income is higher than $\overline{Y}_p$ and lower than $\underline{Y}_p$ there is no transfer, whatever the altruism parameters.

Or to put it in an even simpler way, if we have at point (Y_p, Y_k),

$$\frac{u_c}{v_c} < \beta_p$$

the parent is willing to transfer $T_p > 0$. Conversely, if at the point (Y_p, Y_k),

$$\frac{u_c}{v_c} > \frac{1}{\beta_k}$$

the child is willing to transfer $T_k > 0$. The parent is better off than when the child is not altruistic. But he would like a transfer as soon as $u_c/v_c > \beta_p$ which is sooner than the child wants, since $1/\beta_k > \beta_p$. In terms of income (in the logarithmic case), the parent wants to receive a transfer as soon as $Y_p < Y_k/\beta_p$ but the child waits for $Y_p < \beta_k Y_k$.[19]

Comparing the two-sided case with altruism going in one direction only, it is clear that the area with positive transfers is larger (since they can be either upward or downward), thus both generations reach a higher utility level. And the more altruism, the less conflict on allocations. However, there is still a zone of conflict where both generations would prefer a higher share of consumption. Hence, while two-sided altruism reduces conflict, it does not eliminate it altogether.

Bernheim and Stark (1988) and Stark (1995, chap. 1) wonder what happens in terms of *utility* (and not only of allocation of consumption) if the parent's degree of altruism increases, for instance following an exogenous event. They take the derivative of (17) with respect to β_p.[20] It turns out that it is a function of parent's and child's felicity. Thus in some cases a higher β_p can lower both parent's and child's levels of satisfaction. The intuition for this first paradox is that altruism makes one feel unhappy from the other's

[19] The only way to reconcile them is for β_p and β_k to be close to 1, which would mean that parent and child are but one entity, and eliminate transfers, and our problem altogether.

[20] In the logarithmic case, but they claim the results are robust.

unhappiness. Consider a child whose parent's felicity level is high enough compared to his own. Then, the child would rather have a less altruistic father, who would rejoice more in his own felicity rather than be sad of the low level of the child's felicity. The same situation happens when the altruistic child faces a low enough felicity level: the more altruistic the parent, the lower his utility.

Second paradox, transfers are an increasing function of the intensity of altruism, but the level of well-being does not necessarily increase with transfer received. This happens in a setting where both father and son engage in an on-going relationship (which forces to relax assumption A5). Indeed, in response to higher transfers, the possibility of exploiting the partner arises: altruism limits the credible retorting measures since threats by an altruistic and indulgent parent are not taken seriously (see the discussion in Bernheim and Stark, 1988). Therefore altruism entails possible exploitation, and the occurrence of mutual beneficial arrangements is reduced.

Thirdly, in a slightly modified context, where for instance the child's utility would be convex at low level of parent's utility and concave at high levels of parent's utility, and where $\overline{C}$ is low, both parent and child can be stuck in a misery trap where they are worse off than without altruism.[21]

Finally, there are three regimes for transfers ($T_p > 0$ and $T_k = 0$, $T_p = 0$ and $T_k > 0$, $T_p = 0$ and $T_k = 0$), therefore for a given case, two-sided altruism is analogous to the one-sided model. Hence, the redistributive neutrality or income pooling property remains valid. It is even more likely to be verified than in the case of one-sided altruism because more transfers can take place. However, it holds for a specific flow of transfers, either upward or downward. As pointed out by Altonji et al. (1992), a marginal redistribution of resources between the generations is likely to affect the direction of private transfers, with shifts from interior solutions to corner solutions with zero transfers, thereby involving a local breakdown of the neutrality property.

2.3. Multiple recipients or multiple donors

So far, the issue was *inter-generational* redistribution of income between one parent and one child. With more than one child or more than one parent, relaxing assumption A1, the issue of *intra-generational* redistribution enters the picture.

2.3.1. Where altruistic fairness leads to inequality, and the Rotten Brother theorem

We focus first on the case of several potential recipients. For the sake of simplicity, we assume there are one parent and two children i, $i = 1, 2$ (extension to the case with n children leads to analogous conclusions). Individual consumption and income are respectively C_{ki} and Y_{ki}, and there is a specific utility function V_i for each child, again perfectly known to the parent (assumption A3). The parent maximizes the following

[21] See the discussion in Bramoullé (2001).

utility:

$$\max_{T_1 \geq 0, T_2 \geq 0} U(C_p, V_1(C_{k1}), V_2(C_{k2})) \tag{18}$$

with $U_c > 0, U_{v_1} > 0$, and $U_{v_2} > 0$. The exogenous altruism parameters may be different for each child ($U_{v_1} \neq U_{v_2}$). There are now three budget constraints, one for the parent, $C_p = Y_p - T_1 - T_2$, and one for each child, $C_{ki} = Y_{ki} + T_i$, along with the two non-negativity constraints, $T_i > 0$. When both are non-binding, the pooled budget constraint is the following:

$$C_p + C_{k1} + C_{k2} = Y_p + Y_{k1} + Y_{k2}$$

According to the first-order conditions, $U_c = U_{v_1} V_{1c}$ and $U_c = U_{v_2} V_{2c}$, the parent's marginal utility from transferring resources is equal to each child's marginal benefit, from the parent's point of view. Hence, at the optimum:

$$U_{v_1} V_{1c} = U_{v_2} V_{2c} \tag{19}$$

This important result means that the parent adjusts his transfers T_1 or T_2 to compensate the inequalities of resources between siblings from his own point of view.[22]

As in the only-child case, the consumption of each family member is a function of total family income (as long as $T_1 > 0$ and $T_2 > 0$). Thus, the transfer received by each child not only depends on the parent's income and the own child's income, but is also affected by his sibling's. The transfers can be written as:

$$T_i = c_{ki}(Y_p + Y_{k1} + Y_{k2}) - Y_{ki} \tag{20}$$

Hence, assuming that consumption is normal,

$$\frac{\partial T_i}{\partial Y_p} = c'_{ki} > 0$$

$$\frac{\partial T_i}{\partial Y_{ki}} = c'_{ki} - 1 < 0$$

which means that the transfers are compensatory. It follows that $\partial T_i / \partial Y_p - \partial T_i / \partial Y_{ki} = 1$, the redistributive neutrality result is still valid. Intergenerational variations in resources between the parent and one of the children are perfectly compensated by changes in transfer amount, even when the parent cares for many children, as long as he can make a transfer to this child.

Given the interplay between all the incomes, the multiple-recipients framework leads to three additional comparative statics results. First, the transfer to one child is an increasing function of the other child's income since

$$\frac{\partial T_i}{\partial Y_{kj}} = c'_{ki} > 0 \quad (i \neq j)$$

[22] It is only if $U_{v_1} = U_{v_2}$ (same level of altruism towards the two children) that $V_{1c} = V_{2c}$. Then the marginal utilities of children's consumption are made equal through T_i. It could be that $U_{v_1} > U_{v_2}$ (the parent prefers child 1), then the transfers will be adjusted so that $V_{1c} < V_{2c}$.

Starting from a situation with transfers T_1 and T_2, if child 1's income increases, the parent will lower T_1, so that he can devote more resources to child 2: T_2 increases.

Second, the difference in transfer-children's income derivatives is equal to minus one:

$$\frac{\partial T_i}{\partial Y_{ki}} - \frac{\partial T_i}{\partial Y_{kj}} = -1 \quad i \neq j \tag{21}$$

The interpretation is as follows. For a fixed family income $(Y_p + Y_{k1} + Y_{k2})$, when one euro is taken away from the first child and given to the second child, the parent perfectly adjusts their transfers, so that the first child who is poorer receives one additional euro. This result may be seen as an intra-generational neutrality result, and complements the previous intergenerational neutrality result. Even if the children are not altruistic towards each other, it is as if they pooled their resources: this can be labeled the Rotten Brother theorem, a natural corollary of the Rotten Kid.

A third result is that a shift of resources between the parent and one of the children does not affect the optimal transfer to the other child. Indeed, we observe that $\partial T_i/\partial Y_p = \partial T_i/\partial Y_{kj}$ which implies that the difference in derivatives $\partial T_i/\partial Y_p - \partial T_i/\partial Y_{kj}$ is nil. Hence, when redistributing money, the parent accounts both for the individual and relative economic position of his children.[23]

With many recipients, the transfers to each child are substitutes since $\partial T_i/\partial Y_{kj} > 0$ and $\partial T_i/\partial Y_{ki} < 0$. As siblings can be expected to have different levels of income, the model predicts the prevalence of unequal transfers or unequal sharing of inheritance. For instance, in the case of additive logarithmic utility, and equal altruism, $T_2 - T_1 = -(Y_2 - Y_1)$ and the children consumption levels are equalized. If parents' altruism is different for each child, it can also lead to unequal transfers (or mitigate inequality). This, as before, holds only in the very specific context of perfect information, passive siblings, non-constrained parent, and exogenous children's incomes.

Psychological costs may limit the occurrence of unequal transfers (Menchik, 1988; Wilhelm, 1996). For instance, if the children are not convinced that their income is the exogenous fruit of the lottery of genetics, but feel it is the endogenous result of their personal hard work, the ground of the equalizing purpose of unequal sharing may be lost to them.[24] Then the parent may choose an equal sharing, in spite of his altruism. This is likely to be the case with bequests. First they occur at a dramatic moment when family ties may be fragile;[25] second they are more public than gifts: if social norms command

[23] As before, the validity of the neutrality result, both from an intergenerational and intra-generational perspective, remains only local. The non-negativity constraints are more likely to bind if income redistribution takes place within a larger family.

[24] This is linked to the merit goods and the deserving poor questions. Here the parent would be convinced that all children are deserving, but some of the children would not be. See section 2.5 of this chapter and Bowles et al. (2006) in this Handbook for more.

[25] When asked, parents say that they help their children according to their needs (that is altruistically) *when they are alive*, but an overwhelming majority condemns unequal inheritances (Laferrère, 1999). Empirically, *inter vivos* gifts are found to be more unequal than inheritances (Laferrère, 1992; Dunn and Phillips, 1997).

equal sharing of bequests, the parent will comply, to save his *post mortem* reputation (Lundholm and Ohlsson, 2000). Besides, the income inequality between children may not be public knowledge, and family pride may command to hide it. Finally if the division of bequests is interpreted by the children as a sign of parental affection, the parent will be induced to divide equally (Bernheim and Severinov, 2003). Stark and Zhang (2002) imagine a situation with two children receiving transfers from an altruistic parent. One child is an efficient investor, the other is not. The more efficient child invests the gift received from parents, and pays back to them with interest, allowing them to give more *net* transfer to the less well endowed. Such behavior makes it more difficult to test for altruism in the absence of empirical data on all lifetime transfers, to and from all family members. In the first period the parent may give more to the better endowed child.[26]

Note also that unequal transfers equalize marginal utilities, from the parent's viewpoint, not consumption levels. Imagine two brothers, for a given C, one is of the 'easily happy' type, the other 'always unhappy' ($V_{1c} > V_{2c}$). To equalize marginal utilities the parent makes unequal transfers; the children may resent it, even if made to equalize marginal utilities. Their final happiness is likely to depend on their knowledge of their brother's preference, and how they feel about it.

2.3.2. Free-riding on the other's altruism

There can also be more than one donor. In real life the 'parent' is often a father and a mother. A child and her spouse can have as many as four parents and in-laws, or many more, if grandparents, or step-parents are included. Each may be more or less altruistic, and know more or less about the others' income and transfer behavior. Symmetrically an elderly parent is likely to receive help from more than one altruistic child. The case of multiple donors is more complicated than the above case of multiple beneficiaries, because there are several decision makers in the game instead of one.

Suppose one child and two altruistic parents p_1 and p_2, with separate income Y_{p_1} and Y_{p_2}, each having a utility of the form (1). Assume further that the two parents know the child's utility and income. Let us first focus on the timing of the intergenerational game. There can be many situations. First, both altruistic parents can move at the same time, not knowing that the other is an altruist. This is not unrealistic if one thinks of divorced parents, and fully grown-up children. If the parents observe only Y_k, the child can get either zero (both parents are constrained), one (only one parent is constrained) or two transfers (no parent constrained), expressed as functions $T_1(Y_{p_1}, Y_k)$ and $T_2(Y_{p_2}, Y_k)$. In that case the parents do not know the real final income of the child and assumption A3 may be considered violated. Since the (non-altruist) child may get two transfers instead of one he has no incentive to tell one parent about the other's altruism.

[26] When one considers a model where altruism is endogenous, the predictions may also be modified. See section 5.2.2.

Second, let us change the situation by assuming one parent, p_2, knows the existence of the other and the fact that he may be altruistic. Conversely, the other parent p_1 is not aware of it. Let us further assume that p_1 acts first. Observing Y_k, he decides on the same transfer $T_1(Y_{p_1}, Y_k)$ as in case 1. Then the parent p_2 enters the picture. She observes (Y_k+T_1), the child's real income, and, being altruistic, she decides on a transfer $T_2(Y_{p_2}, Y_k + T_1)$. Again, this is not unrealistic: a severe father decides on a level of allowance for a student child, an indulgent mother supplements it, without the father's knowing. Obviously parent p_2 gives less than in the first situation and she gives less if parent p_1 has given more $(\partial T_2/\partial T_1 < 0)$.[27] Also the child cannot receive less than in the case of only one altruistic parent. Straightforward calculations (in the case of additive logarithmic utilities) show that in general the total transfer received by the child depends on which parent moves first. For identical levels of altruism (or identical levels of income), the child will get more if the richest parent (or the more altruistic) moves last.[28] Only if both parents have the same income, and the same level of altruism, or if one's high altruism compensates for the other's low income (for instance, p_1's income is half of p_2's but his altruism is twice p_2's), is total transfer not modified by who moves first.

But imagine a third case, where both potential donors are aware of the other's existence. For instance, the severe altruistic father knows about the indulgent altruistic mother. The parent who moves first, knowing that the child will receive another transfer, has an incentive to give less, and even to wait for the second parent to start first. The situation evokes the provision of a public good, and the possibility of multiple contributions leads to standard free-riding problems. As usual in the public good literature, the optimal choices of transfer depend on the donors' behavior and the game they are playing (see Lam, 1988). The outcome differs if they play a Nash non-cooperative equilibrium or cooperate to reach a Pareto efficient situation.

In a Nash non-cooperative equilibrium, each parent independently chooses the amount of money that he provides to the child, taking as given the transfer made by the other parent. The maximization program for each parent is given by:

$$\max_{T_i} U_i(C_i, V(C_k)) = U_i(Y_i - T_i, V(Y_k + T_i + T_j))$$
$$\text{s.t.} \quad T_i \geq 0 \quad i = 1, 2 \quad i \neq j \tag{22}$$

What they will give depends on their relative incomes and altruism parameters. Thus, each parent is induced to choose the level of full transfer $T_1 + T_2$ since he takes into account the transfer made by the other parent. The non-negativity constraint $T_i \geq 0$ means that a parent can never lower the global contribution to the public good. Thus,

[27] For instance, in the case of additive logarithmic utilities, she subtracts $\frac{T_1}{1+\beta_2}$ from her former transfer of case 1.

[28] The difference between T_1 (p_1 moves first) and T_2 (p_2 moves first) is given by $\frac{\beta_{p_2} Y_{p_2} - \beta_{p_1} Y_{p_1}}{1+\beta_{p_2}+\beta_{p_1}}$.

at an interior equilibrium, the marginal rate of substitution between the parental consumption and the child's consumption is equal to one since $U_{ic}/U_{iv}V_c = 1$ $(i = 1, 2)$. Two main properties characterize this problem of provision for a public good (Warr, 1983; Bergstrom et al., 1986). First, the Nash equilibrium exists and it is unique. Second, the full contribution to the public good is not affected by a small change in the redistribution of resources between the donors, even when the parents have different levels of altruism for the child.[29] With interior solutions, the pooled budget constraint is $C_{p1} + C_{p2} + C_k = Y_{p1} + Y_{p2} + Y_k$ and the optimal transfer can be expressed as $T_1 = Y_{p1} - c_{p1}(Y_{p1} + Y_{p2} + Y_k)$. It follows that $\partial T_1/\partial Y_{p1} - \partial T_1/\partial Y_{p2} = 1$ and $\partial T_1/\partial Y_{p1} - \partial T_1/\partial Y_k = 1$, which is the neutrality result. However, as emphasized in Bergstrom et al. (1986), significant changes in the distribution of family incomes are likely to modify the set of positive transfers and thus the optimal provision of the public good.[30]

What if the two parents cooperate for a Pareto efficient outcome? In a situation where the donors know each other well and have a consensus on what are all the utility functions, it may seem appropriate to think they will want to cooperate. In this situation 4, they may decide on the following weighted sum of their utilities:

$$\max_{T_1,T_2} \mu U_1(C_{p_1}, V(C_k)) + (1 - \mu)U_2(C_{p_2}, V(C_k)) \tag{23}$$

with $0 \leq \mu \leq 1$. Note that it amounts to a form of horizontal two-sided altruism between the donors. The situation is radically changed. From the corresponding first-order conditions for an interior solution, we now have $\mu U_{1c} = (1 - \mu)U_{2c} = (\mu U_{1v} + (1 - \mu)U_{2v})V_c$ at the equilibrium. The optimality condition is such that:

$$\frac{U_{1v}V_c}{U_{1c}} + \frac{U_{2v}V_c}{U_{2c}} = 1 \tag{24}$$

Condition (24) involves three levels of consumption, the private consumption of both potential donors C_{p1} and C_{p2} and the 'public' child's consumption C_k. It follows that the distribution of income between the donors now matters for the provision of the public good even in the presence of interior solutions. However, for special forms of the utility functions, the neutrality result may hold. Samuelson (1955) finds that income distribution is neutral with quasi-linear preferences $U_i = C_i + u_i(C_k)$, a result extended to the family of quasi-homothetic preferences $U_i = A(C_k)C_i + u_i(C_k)$ by Bergstrom and Cornes (1983). But in the general case, maximizing the weighted sum of individual utility functions no longer leads the parents to pool their resources.

[29] If both parents make a transfer, any redistribution of income between parents such that none looses more than his/her original transfer induces every parent to change the amount of his/her transfer by precisely the amount of the change in his/her income.

[30] Konrad and Lommerud (1995) show that the redistributive neutrality may cease to hold when one accounts for time allocation between market work and the family public good. In particular, lump-sum redistribution between participants in a Nash game are no longer neutral in a situation where each has a different productivity in contributing to the public good. But this is dropping assumption A4 of a single good.

The public good aspect of intergenerational relationships may occur in various contexts. Schoeni (2000) studies the case where altruistic parents and parents-in-law make transfers to their adult children. Wolff (2000a) considers grandparents and parents providing money to young adults. Jellal and Wolff (2002a) examine how altruistic siblings care for their elderly parents when parental needs are random.[31] In Hiedemann and Stern (1999), the altruistic siblings and their elderly parent play a two-stage non-cooperative game. Each child first announces whether he offers care for the parent, then the parent chooses his preferred arrangement. The framework is extended to bargaining among children and side payments by Engers and Stern (2001). Comparing monetary transfers and transfers in the form of co-residence, Eckhardt (2002) also accounts for financial compensation of the sibling living with the elderly parent. Konrad et al. (2002) study the residential choice of siblings who are altruistic towards their parents. Location choices become endogenous: transfers take the form of a service, measured by the distance to the parent's home. In this setting, the eldest sibling, choosing first, shifts part of the burden of caring for the parents to the younger sibling who locates nearer to the parents.

2.4. Extending the model to endogenous incomes

Starting with the pure one-sided altruism model and its correlative assumptions we relaxed, in turn, A6 by introducing two-sided altruism, and A1 by allowing more than one giver or beneficiary. But we stuck to the crucial assumptions that incomes were exogenous, that the beneficiary is passive, takes the transfer as given, and does not change his behavior as a consequence of the gift (A4, A8), that his utility function is perfectly observed (A3) and accepted without discussion by the 'blind' deferential or altruistic parent (A2). We now relax the assumption that the child's income is exogenous and perfectly observed by the parent. This is a first step towards introducing time into the picture (relaxing A5). The problem was raised by Bergstrom (1989a) who first stated the necessary assumptions to Becker's Rotten kid theorem. The theorem is an attractive reformulation of the neutrality property (11) and states that no matter how selfish, the child acts to maximize the family income. Bergstrom[32] points that it holds if there is only one commodity, money (all goods are 'produced') (A4), if the child's consumption is a normal good for the parent (A2); the model is static (A5); the parent chooses after the child in a two-stage game (A8); and he makes positive transfers.

The other face of the Rotten kid is the Samaritan dilemma (Buchanan, 1975). In the Gospel parable a traveler, attacked by robbers, is rescued by a foreigner to the country, a Samaritan. There is no hint that the victim organized the attack and robbery himself in the hope of being taken care of by the passing Samaritan. However if it turns out that

[31] Comparing the Nash non-cooperative equilibrium to the case when all altruistic children maximize the sum of each child's utility, they show that each contributes more under cooperation, because it offers no possibility of free-riding. In addition, while the more donors, the less each transfers under a Nash equilibrium, the effect can be either positive or negative under the Pareto efficient solution.

[32] And Becker in his introduction to the *Treatise on the Family* (1991, p. 9).

he enjoyed the care, he may be less prudent in his next journey, knowing that passers-by are helpful and generous. In families, a child may become rotten or prodigal, should the parent be known as a passive pure altruist.[33]

This sub-section is divided into three parts. In the first, a second commodity, time, is introduced in the child's utility and budget constraint, under the form of child's effort e to earn wage w_k (section 2.4.1). Then we mention some related considerations on future uncertainty, in which it is not the child who reacts but the parent who lacks information on Y_k (section 2.4.2). The partly symmetric situation where time is introduced in the parent's budget constraint and in the child's utility, under the form of a service S given by the parent (whose wage is w_p) to the child is addressed in section 2.4.3.

2.4.1. *Where the child may become rotten*

Assume that the child's income is no more exogenous, but a function of his choice of working hours; in other words, there are now two goods in the economy: money and leisure time (A4 is dropped). This simple and natural extension changes the model significantly, because of the new importance of timing.

The parent now maximizes:

$$U_p = U(C_p, V(C_k, e)) \tag{25}$$

where e is the child's effort level, $U_c > 0$, $U_v > 0$, $V_c > 0$ and $V_e < 0$. The budget constraints are:

$$C_p = Y_p - T, \quad T \geq 0 \tag{26}$$

$$C_k = Y_k + w_k e + T, \quad e \geq 0 \tag{27}$$

We start from a situation where the parent knows Y_p, Y_k, V, and w_k. He decides on the optimal values of T and e from his own viewpoint. Assuming separability for U (to simplify the presentation), the parent's program is:

$$\max_{T,e} U = U(Y_p - T) + \beta_p V(Y_k + w_k e + T, e)$$

Let us assume both T and e positive, then the first-order condition $\beta_p V_c = U_c$ defines the transfer function $T = T(Y_p, Y_k + w_k e)$. The optimal effort level $e^1 = e^1(Y_k, T)$, from the parent's point of view is defined from:

$$V_e = -w_k V_c \tag{28}$$

$T(Y_p, Y_k, w_k)$ and $e^1(Y_p, Y_k, w_k)$ can be computed. If the parent is able to impose on the child to exert effort e^1, he will transfer T, and the situation is exactly the same as when the child's income is exogenous. The parent, by making a transfer induces his

[33] This is also the dilemma of benevolent governments designing transfers to the poor. See Besley and Coate (1995) among others.

(perhaps) rotten kid to share his extra wage income through a smaller T. Of course, as before, if $T = 0$, the parent cannot commit his child to make *him* a transfer even if $\beta_p V_c \leq U_c$. Thus the neutrality conditions holds, if the parent is able to endogenize the child's new source of income, namely if he is making the transfer after the child has decided on his effort level. The parent is 'having the last word', as Hirschleifer (1977) puts it.

Is e^1 the effort level that would be spontaneously chosen by a child knowing that his parent is altruistic, that is, knowing the transfer function? The child's program is the following:

$$\max_e V_k = V(Y_k + w_k e + T(Y_p, Y_k + w_k e), e) \tag{29}$$

If $e > 0$, the child's optimal work effort e^k, from his own viewpoint, is given by the first-order condition:

$$V_{e^k} = -w_k V_c \left[1 + \frac{\partial T}{\partial e}\right] \tag{30}$$

It is easy to check that $V_{e^k} > V_{e^1}$.[34] The marginal cost of effort as seen from the child's viewpoint is higher than as seen from the parent's viewpoint. This is because the parent lowers his transfer when the child's revenue increases, thus taxing away part of the child's effort. If the parent announces his transfer *function* before the child has decided on his effort level *and* if his transfer is a function of the effort level the child will not choose effort e^1 but $e^k < e^1$.[35] He would definitely behave 'rotten'.[36] And the Samaritan would like to be able to induce him to work more. The neutrality condition does not hold.[37]

Thus there might be a conflict between parents and child, even in the pure altruism setting. Either the parent is able to impose the first-best solution and choose both positive transfer and effort level e^1, and we are still in the neutrality property world where

[34] Because $\partial T / \partial e < 0$, from the parent's first-order condition defining T.

[35] It is the case as long as the parent is a blind altruist, or a blind Samaritan, who is altruist enough or rich enough to transfer, and as long as the child knows the parent's utility function.

[36] The situation is different in Chami (1996), where the parent announces a level of transfer that is not a function of the child's effort level. Chami sees the child's situation as a chance event, a good or bad draw of income. In that case the child works harder when he moves last, because the parent does not compensate him.

[37] Kotlikoff et al. (1990) change the rules of the game relaxing A7 and assume that parent (who is no longer dominant) and child each have a threat point $\overline{U}$ and $\overline{V}$ and negotiate. Parent and child maximize:

$$\max[U(C_p, V(C_k)) - \overline{U}][V(C_k) - \overline{V}]$$

under a collective budget constraint. There is no child's effort, but they show that the neutrality condition never holds under this Nash bargaining solution. As often in this kind of game, the definition of the threat-point is problematic. They define the threat by a going-alone strategy. However, it seems difficult to imagine a menacing altruistic parent. How an altruist can credibly threaten not to make a transfer?

rotten kids are well-behaved, or the parent has to yield to the child who is going to work less than the optimum. The situation will depend on the relative marginal utilities of effort and consumption for the child and the parent, and on their bargaining power. Problems are likely to arise when the parent gets close to a corner solution where he is no more able to make a transfer and exert a pressure on the child.

A solution for the parent would be to hide his altruism, or to announce a transfer as computed in his first-best solution and stick to it ($\partial T/\partial e = 0$) even if the child chooses his own favorite effort level in the (false) hope that the parent will yield. In the next period, the child would realize that he would have the same utility level by complying. But it might be difficult for a pure altruist to punish his child even for one period and, again, he may not be able to do so if his income is not high enough.

This is still under assumptions A3 (perfect information of parent) and A7 (the parent dominates the game). As soon as the child's income is endogenous, two things can happen. First the child has an incentive to hide from his parent the real amount of his income in order to get a higher transfer. If w_k varies, $\partial e/\partial w_k > 0$, the child exerts more effort if his wage rate increases, and $\partial T/\partial w_k < 0$. Then it is natural to think that the parent does not fully observe w_k and cannot decide on an efficient transfer scheme. The child has an inventive to hide the information, trading-off effort for a parental transfer. Second, the child may have an incentive to work less, in order to get the protective transfer from his altruistic parent.

Some recent papers have formally developed this idea and explicitly stated the consequence of the introduction of leisure on the neutrality conditions in this imperfect information setting. Gatti (2000) introduces endogenous child effort and incomplete information of parents. The parent faces a trade-off between the insurance and the disincentive to work that his transfer provides the child. If he can pre-commit to a level of transfer, he chooses not to compensate as much as predicted by pure altruism. When there are many children, this is another instance where the parent can choose to compensate only partially or not at all for earning differences. In Fernandes (2003), part of the child's income is exogenous, part is endogenous, through his choice between consumption and leisure, and, again his choice is not always part of the information set of parents. This allows her to prove that the neutrality result does not hold in all cases. Kotlikoff and Razin (1988) and Villanueva (2001) raise the same questions. For Villanueva, the endogenous part of income is likely to come from children who have a high labor supply elasticity, for instance from the secondary earner in a couple, while the exogenous part is income of the primary earner. There are two goods, money, and leisure of the secondary earner. Parents observe incomes, and know the child's preference. Thus they know all about exogenous income (that of the primary earner), but they do not observe the market opportunity, nor the effort of the secondary earner. He shows that altruism may distort the effort decision of the child's household, so that the altruistic parent provides transfers that do not respond much to the earnings of the secondary earner but more to those of the primary earner who has a lower labor supply elasticity.

2.4.2. The Samaritan dilemma and future uncertainty

Others have considered the Samaritan dilemma in a two-period framework, with saving or human capital accumulation. There might be more in child's effort than leisure foregone. Becker (1991) and Lindbeck and Weibull (1988) put forward the negative effect of early inheritance on human capital formation and accumulation. A child who relies on parental transfer may put less energy in his education, or not save enough, knowing that his parents will provide. The same intuition was already present in Blinder (1988) who pointed that bequests may affect labor supply in the context of imperfect capital market. If transfers are postponed or made in kind, children cannot shirk at the expenses of their parents and are less likely to waste their talents.[38] This may explain why parents' (and governments') largest transfer to children is in the form of education, or why parents often provide loans or collateral to buy a house rather that money for vacations, or for drugs. Inheritance may be a chain which entraps the spirit of enterprise.[39] Not to make a poisonous gift may be one of the reasons for tardy inheritance. Bruce and Waldman (1990) show that government debt policies (redistributing from parent to child) may not be neutral in a two-period framework where child's action influences both his and his parent's income, and where the parent can choose to make a transfer after the child has decided on his income, but before he has decided on his consumption. This happens if there are capital market imperfections and because the government transfer, unlike second-period parent's transfer, cannot be manipulated by the child's first-period consumption decision. Much hinges on the child's anticipations.

The possibility of a reaction of the child's income is formally close to another real world feature which we have overlooked up to now, namely future uncertainty. Altonji et al. (1997) extend the pure altruism model in a two-period framework. In McGarry (2000) the parents, not knowing their child's second period income, are caught between the desire to postpone transfer until they really know about their child lifetime income (assumption A3 of perfect information of parent) and the necessity to help liquidity constrained children in the first period. When the parents know only about the distribution of the child's future income, she shows that the derivative restriction does not hold, when the child's second period income Y_{k2} depends on the first period income Y_{k1}. Then a low Y_{k1} not only increases the first period transfer T_1, but the probable need of T_2, the second period transfer, thus inducing the parent to save more, and increase T_1 less than he would otherwise. Actually what she shows is not so much the failure of the restriction, as, again, the strong assumptions underlying it, which are not likely to be met in real life. In the basic model, the altruistic parent wants to take into account the

[38] Cremer and Pestieau (1996, 1998) rely on adverse selection and moral hazard arguments to explain why parents postpone their transfers.

[39] See Stark (1995, chap. 2). On the other hand, some have found that parental transfers help credit-constrained individuals to start new enterprises (Blanchflower and Oswald, 1990).

life-time income of his child, and his own life-time income, when deciding on a life-time transfer. In real life-time course, future uncertainty makes assumption A3 shaky, and assuming only one period (A5) seems restrictive.[40]

2.4.3. *Parents can't be rotten, but two goods complicate the picture*

If time is used by the parent to provide a service to the child, instead of being used by the child to augment his income, the conclusions are close. However the underlying problem is slightly more complex since the service is at the same time a source of disutility to the parent and of satisfaction to the child.

Assume that the child's utility increases both with the private monetary consumption C_k and with the amount of services S that only the parent can perform (money cannot buy it). The two forms of transfers, money T and service S, are separate arguments of the child's utility $V(C_k, S)$. Transfers are normal goods ($V_c > 0$ and $V_s > 0$). The parent is indifferent between the two forms of support and maximizes the following utility function (Sloan et al., 2002):

$$\max_{T,S} U = U(C_p, V(C_k, S)) \tag{31}$$

Since services are non-marketable, the child's budget constraint is still given by (3):

$$C_k = Y_k + T.$$

But parental resources are the sum of an exogenous income Y_p and labor income. Assuming that the parent is endowed with one unit of time, $(1 - S)$ is time devoted to the labor market at wage rate w_p and his budget constraint is:[41]

$$C_p = Y_p + w_p(1 - S) - T \tag{32}$$

There are now two first-order conditions. For financial transfers, we again find condition (6) and $U_c = U_v V_c$ holds. For time-related transfers, the condition is:

$$-w_p U_c + U_v V_s = 0 \tag{33}$$

meaning that the marginal utility of attention received by a child from the parental perspective equals the parent's weighted marginal utility of consumption at the equilibrium. Combining (7) and (33), the child's marginal utility from financial transfer equals his marginal utility from services, in terms of the parental wage:

$$V_c = \frac{1}{w_p} V_s \tag{34}$$

[40] It could however hold for myopic parents. Feldstein (1988) also shows that in a world where second period incomes are uncertain, so are the second period transfer, and that it is a contradiction to Ricardian equivalence.

[41] Note the paradoxical situation: the service has no market substitute (for instance, in the case of baby-sitting, nothing comes close to what happens between grandparent and grandchild) but it has a market value to the grandparent in terms of lost income. This is central to many models of family transfers. See section 3, and Cox (1996).

When this equality does not hold, at least one generation can reach a higher level of well-being by reallocating the two types of transfers.

This extension leads to interesting comparative statics conclusions, with different effects of endogenous and exogenous incomes on financial and time transfers. Using the pooled budget constraint and taking S as a parameter,

$$C_k + C_p = Y_p + w_p(1 - S) + Y_k \tag{35}$$

the consumption C_k is a function of total family income, and the transfer T is:

$$T = c_k(Y_p + w_p(1 - S) + Y_k) - Y_k \tag{36}$$

Again, only the total income $Y_p + Y_k$ matters for the allocation of resources between parent and child and the predictions of the altruism model with only one good are retrieved (given S). A wealthy or high wage rate parent provides higher financial transfers to the child ($\partial T/\partial Y_p > 0$, $\partial T/\partial w_p > 0$). Also, a rise in the child's income diminishes the transfer ($\partial T/\partial Y_k < 0$), at least when consumption and service are assumed to be complements (see Sloan et al., 2002). Finally, the redistributive neutrality holds only for the exogenous non-labor income and $\partial T/\partial Y_p - \partial T/\partial Y_k = 1$. Indeed, when his wage changes, the parent adjusts his labor force participation, thus the service to the child, and his consumption does not remain constant.

Predictions are different for the service S. A wealthier parent transfers more time-related resources to the child,

$$\partial S/\partial Y_p > 0$$

but the effect of his wage rate is ambiguous, $\partial S/\partial w_p$ may be positive or negative because there are two offsetting effects. On the one hand, an increase in the wage rate increases the parent's income, and thus the service value. On the other hand, it also increases the parental opportunity cost of time, which reduces the contribution to the child. Also, a richer child is expected to receive more services from the parent:

$$\partial S/\partial Y_k > 0$$

In response to a larger child's income, the parent lowers his financial help and provides more services to complement the rise in the child's consumption. Finally, when there are interior solutions for both S and T, comparative statics lead to what we call the redistributive invariance result.[42] It stems from the pooled budget constraint (35), which implies:

$$S = 1 - \frac{C_p + C_k - Y_p - Y_k}{w}$$

Recalling that when T is positive, C_p and C_k depend on the aggregate family income ($Y_p + Y_k$), it follows that the marginal effects of the parental and child's income on the

[42] This prediction is mentioned for the first time in Cox (1987), in a different context, see our section 3.1.

level of services are equal:

$$\frac{\partial S}{\partial Y_p} - \frac{\partial S}{\partial Y_k} = 0 \tag{37}$$

When T and S are positive, the distribution of intergenerational exogenous income should not affect the amount of time-related resources provided to the child, which only depends on total family income. Let us consider a change in the exogenous income distribution. From the neutrality result, when $T > 0$, we know that taking one euro from the parent and giving it to the child is compensated by a decrease of exactly one euro in the initial transfer. This means that for a fixed family non-labor income $(Y_p + Y_k)$, both parent's and child's level of consumption remain constant, which also imply a constant level of services (see Cox, 1987, p. 514). That the provision of family services is not affected by modifications in the distribution of (exogenous) family incomes, has so far never been tested. When $T = 0$, (37) does not hold because the two generations do not pool their exogenous resources.

2.5. *Daddy knows best*

At this stage, one is lead to reflect on the essence of the altruist's utility function. Even if he is a (benevolent) dictator, the parent of model (1) is somewhat blind. On the one hand, he is assumed to know his child's utility function perfectly, but on the other how can he remain an altruist if he disapproves of the child's preferences? The model of section 2.4.1 took the example of child's effort, but it could also be the child's smoking, drinking, becoming a drug addict or a terrorist. There might be limits to the parent's deference. It soon does not make sense to assume pure altruism. A discussion of Adam Smith's notion of sympathy/empathy is found in Khalil (1990, 2001). He translates Smith's idea of altruism into the following maximization problem:

$$\max_{C_p, C_k} W_{exo} = W(U(C_p), V(C_k))$$

The new function W_{exo} expresses the altruist's empathy, that is his capacity to step out of his shoes and see the situation from a third exo-centric station. Khalil stresses three conditions for this kind of altruism to exist: familiarity, propriety, and approval. In the terms of this survey, familiarity amounts to a knowledge of the child's preference. Propriety is the fact that the beneficiary's response to the gift is adequate. In the family context, approval means the parent has to approve of the child's choice. The child has to deserve the transfer.[43] It could go to the point of a parent knowing better than the child what is good for him. Without the negative connotation of paternalism, the altruist may give in kind, rather than the monetary equivalent which would be dissipated in smoke, because he knows best. Becker and Murphy (1988) mention college education

[43] We already mentioned this question of deserving in the context of multiple beneficiaries. In order for altruism to be accepted by the siblings, they have to approve of it.

or down-payment on a home (see also Pollak, 1988). Not only, as in section 2.4.1, does the child react to the transfer, but the parents want a particular reaction. Such reflections naturally lead to leave pure altruism (assumptions A2, A4) for impure altruism or the endogenous formation of altruism (section 3). Before that, let us summarize the main results of section 2.

1. Redistributive neutrality: providing parent and child are linked by positive transfers, redistributing at the margin income from parent to child or from child to parent is neutralized by a family transfer in the opposite direction, under pure altruism. In that (restrictive) case public transfer may totally crowd-out private family transfers. The occurrence of a transfer and its size are positively related to parent's income and negatively related to child's income.
2. Two-sided altruism raises the occurrence of intergenerational transfers but does not automatically eliminate conflict over consumption allocation. Nor does a higher altruism intensity unambiguously increase well-being.
3. In case an equal altruism is directed towards many children, transfers will be more important towards the one with the lower income. When the parents make positive transfers to all children, a transfer to one is an increasing function of the other child's income, and redistributing income from one sibling to the other does not change their consumption, since the transfers adjust in consequence.
4. Results (1) and (3) lead to an important effect of altruism on inequality. Private transfers can reduce inequality between individuals linked by altruistic relations: within a cohort, since they tend to benefit those whose level of utility is the lowest; between cohorts, since they flow from rich to poor. However the reduction occurring within families may be small compared to the inequality existing between families or groups that are not related by altruism.
5. In the case of many altruistic parents, there could be free-riding on the others' altruism.
6. When the child's income reacts to the transfer, the redistributive neutrality property may or may not break down, depending on the information of parent and child about each other's preferences and endowment. It is also the case when there is more than one period and when second period income is uncertain or with credit market imperfection.
7. Invariance: in the pure altruism model, redistributing exogenous income from parent to child or child to parent does not change the non-monetary transfer provided to the child by the parent.

3. Impure altruism: merit good and transfers as a means of exchange

The parent's utility function is now changed slightly, by introducing again a second commodity 'produced' by the child, which directly influences parental utility level and can be viewed as time (effort e or service S provided by the child). We take two examples. In both the parent's utility function is of the following form:

$$U = U(C_p, e, V(C_k, e)) \tag{38}$$

with $U_v > 0$, $U_e > 0$, $V_e < 0$. The first case is exposed in Chami (1998). The only formal difference with model (25) above is that e appears twice in the parent's preferences, both directly and indirectly through its effect on the child's utility. The parent is an altruist, but his altruism is impure: it is polluted by an interest in an element of the child's consumption vector, his effort e, that is costly to the child. This is what Becker calls a merit good. In our first example, taken from Chami's model (Chami, 1996), the cost to the child of introducing a merit good is mitigated because effort increases his income, as shown by the child's budget constraint, the same as (27). In the second example, drawn from Cox (1987), the merit good is the child's service S that the parent wants to enlist.[44] It does not enter the budget constraint.

3.1. *Child's effort as a merit good*

The budgets constraints are still given by (26) and (27). With separable utility and assuming the parent is a benevolent and omniscient dictator, he maximizes:

$$\max_{T,e} U(Y_p - T, e) + \beta_p V(Y_k + w_k e + T, e)$$

From the first-order conditions, the transfer function is as before $\beta_p V_c = U_c$ (note however that parent's preferences have been altered). However, the condition on effort level is different from (28):

$$V_{e^m} = -w_k V_c - \frac{U_e}{\beta_p} \tag{39}$$

The marginal disutility of effort e^m (m standing for merit good) is lower for the child than in the case with no merit good (V_{e^1}), from the parent's viewpoint, because his effort raises the parent's utility. He gets less transfer as a compensation for a higher level of effort. The parent's impure altruism induces his child to exert effort, in other words the child knows that the parent will not be carried away by his altruism. But let us stress that the parent's preferences have changed.

This is still under assumptions A3 (perfect information of parent) and A7 (the parent dominates the game). As above, as soon as the child's income is endogenous, he has an

[44] In Hobbes' *Leviathan* and in many traditional societies, the following contract is found: P makes a transfer to K on the condition that K will give it to GK, the grand-child. This would apply to a capital, such as land, to be maintained and to be handed down from generation to generation, because it was received (not made) in the first place. This way of tyeing the transfer to a particular action of the recipient (here, transmitting it in turn) can be seen as a merit good entering the altruist's utility function. In that case the child lowers his consumption (formally isolated here by S in (43)), in order to increase his parent's utility. What Arrondel and Masson (2006, in this Handbook) call indirect reciprocity seems close to this model of impure altruism, and may have the same predictions.

incentive to hide the real amount of his income in order to get a higher transfer, and to work less, take risk, squander, etc. Information may be imperfect in the case of more than one child, if one cries louder than the others.

In this first example of a merit good, the child benefits from his own effort through a higher income, even if this income is taxed by parental impure altruism.[45] We take now a second example, where effort e becomes a service S flowing from the child to the parent, as in the model originally proposed by Cox (1987). This service is not 'produced', in the sense that it does not enter the budget constraints. It can be seen as extra leisure time of the child, which could not be used to increase its earnings, but can be turned into non-market services, such as attention or visits to the parents. There is a natural development of the market at the expense of non-market activities as people become better off. From barter to money, from family help to salaried services, from village loans to sophisticated credit system, the progress and progression seem inevitable. But some non-market goods may become more important at a higher level of development, being richer leaves more time for affection.[46] Besides the development of leisure time could lead to a revival of the exchange of non-produced goods. In our model, the child could not sell his services to anyone else, and the parent could not buy them elsewhere.[47] But they may find it mutually beneficial to 'trade'.

3.2. Buying or extorting the child's services or the parent's inheritance

The parent's utility remains the same as in (38), replacing e with S, but the child's budget constraint is the same as in (3), the effort/service level does not enter it. The child's utility is as before $V(C_k, S)$, with $V_s < 0$: helping his parent is costly, as was effort. The parent maximizes:

$$\max_{T,S} U(Y_p - T, S) + \beta_p V(Y_k + T, S) \tag{40}$$

His transfer function does not change, but again the child's marginal cost of effort/service is modified:

$$V_s = -\frac{U_s}{\beta_p} \tag{41}$$

It is obviously even higher than before (V_{e^m}), because the child does not derive any income from his effort.

A game is played between the parent, who wants the child's time consuming services, and the child, who receives a transfer of money in exchange of his service. Three

[45] On the top of the usual tax on a higher income through a lower transfer (but it leaves the child's on the same utility level), there is this second tax of the merit good.

[46] See for instance Zeldin (1995) on affection for children appearing at the turn of the 20th century in the US among the poorest classes of the population.

[47] In that the model differs slightly from the above endogenous parent's income model (section 2.5) where his time was used to produce consumption, via earnings.

main cases may be considered. In the first, the parent is an (impure) altruist and the non-altruistic child is more than compensated for his effort in helping the parent. In the second, the child is just paid for his effort: neither parent nor child is altruistic, the child exchanges his service for a transfer. In the third case the child is altruistic towards his parent. The first two cases are considered in Cox (1987), the second and third by Victorio and Arnott (1993). The second case, where both parent and child are non-altruists, is also studied by Bernheim et al. (1985). They assume that the parent uses the threat to disinherit to extort attention from his children. The structure of the game between parent and child is important: the leader can extract the gains from the exchange.

3.2.1. From transfer to transaction

Let us start with the first case: an altruistic parent wants his non-altruistic child to render some services S. Cox (1987) introduces an incentive compatibility constraint: the child enters the relationship only if it does not lower his utility. Denoting by $V^0 = V(Y_k, 0)$ the child's utility when no exchange takes place ($T = 0$, $S = 0$), his threat point, the participation constraint is:

$$V(Y_k + T, S) \geq V(Y_k, 0) \tag{42}$$

Assuming that the parent is dominant in the game (A7 again, along with A3), the problem viewed from the parent's perspective can be expressed as:

$$\max_{T,S} U(Y_p - T, S, V(Y_k + T, S)) \tag{43}$$

under the participation constraint (42). If λ is the associated Lagrange multiplier, the first-order conditions for T and S are:

$$-U_c + U_v V_c + \lambda V_c \leq 0$$
$$U_s + U_v V_s + \lambda V_s \leq 0$$

with equality if $T > 0$ or $S > 0$. Assuming that the parent is effectively altruistic, let us consider the case where the participation constraint is not binding ($\lambda = 0$); the child derives some satisfaction when effectively helping the parent and receiving some money. For interior solutions, $T > 0$ and $S > 0$, the first-order conditions are:

$$U_c = U_v V_c$$
$$U_s = -U_v V_s$$

As before, the transfer equates the parent's and child's marginal utility of consumption; the level of service equates the parent's marginal utility and his child's marginal disutility of service. The neutrality property is retrieved and so are all the properties of the model of section 2.1 for financial transfers.

However comparative statics in terms of the level of attention S yield different results (see Cox, 1987). There is no definite prediction concerning the sign of $\partial S/\partial Y_p$ nor that of $\partial S/\partial Y_k$. But the difference in services to income derivatives is equal to zero:

$$\frac{\partial S}{\partial Y_p} - \frac{\partial S}{\partial Y_k} = 0$$

The level of upward service does not depend on the intergenerational distribution of family income: this is the invariance result (37) of section 2.4.2. The parent's motivation is purely altruistic since the child is more than compensated for the disutility incurred by the time he devotes to his parent. As already mentioned, service to the parent exists, but has no market value and does not enter the child's budget constraint. The fact that the parent transfers and the child helps is not part of any reciprocity mechanism, there is no direct link between the two decisions.

Assume now that the participation constraint is binding: there is no altruistic parent-to-child transfer. This situation is more likely to occur when the child's income is high compared to the parent's or when the parent is not altruistic enough. Financial transfer from the parent is exchanged for the child's services. The parent can no longer influence the child's utility, and the marginal financial help no longer equalizes the marginal utilities of consumption ($U_c > U_v V_c$). When the parent leads the game, he is the only beneficiary from the gains of exchange, since the child has the same utility level whether he participates in the exchange or not. The fact that the child receives no benefit from the family exchange may seem problematic. If he derives no satisfaction, there is no clear reason for him to devote time to the parent.

In this second case, called the exchange regime by Cox, the parent's two decisions, whether to transfer or not, and how much to transfer, are not taken in the same manner as in the first altruism regime. Strictly speaking, the decision is not one of transfer, but one of transaction. It occurs when the difference in parent's and child's money-services marginal rates of substitution is strictly positive. The demand price of the parent's first unit of services is greater than the supply price of the child's first unit of services. Thus, the *existence* of a transaction is positively related to the parent's income, but negatively related to the child's income, as was the existence of transfer in the altruism case. Indeed, the compensation for the child's disutility has to be higher for a richer child, and thus the exchange is less likely. The transfer/transaction value, T, perfectly compensates for the services S given by the child.

The comparative statics results are as follows. First,

$$\frac{\partial S}{\partial Y_p} > 0$$

and

$$\frac{\partial S}{\partial Y_k} < 0$$

the child's supply of services is an increasing function of the parent's income, but it is lowered when the child's income is higher. A richer child is characterized by an increased disutility when he devotes time to his parent. Since

$$\frac{\partial T}{\partial Y_p} > 0$$

the parental income exerts a positive impact on the service payment to the child. Again, this prediction is a common feature of the altruism framework. But the effect of the child's income on T is unclear. It depends on the pseudo elasticity of the parent's demand for services, thus it can be positive or negative (see Cox, 1987). However, remember there is by assumption no market substitute for the child's attention, so that the demand for services by the parents is likely to be inelastic; thus the relationship between the child's income and the payment is likely to be positive (Cox and Rank, 1992; Cox, 1996).[48]

That the transfer amount can rise with the child's income in the case of exchange stands in contrast to the altruism model, where a richer child receives a lower gift. While a negative derivative $\partial T/\partial Y_k$ is compatible both with the exchange and altruism motives, the empirical finding of a positive effect of Y_k on T indicates the existence of exchange, or reciprocity, within the family. Indeed, if the child's income increases, so does his threat point $V(Y_k, 0)$ and the parent may have to increase his payment to get the same level of services.[49]

Note that at the limit $U_v = 0$ (the parent is not only a constrained altruist, but a non-altruist) and this second regime of non-altruism can be written in the following way:

$$\max_{T,S} U = U(Y_p - T, S) \tag{44}$$

under the participation constraint (42). If λ is the associated Lagrange multiplier, the corresponding first-order conditions for T and S are:

$$-U_c + \lambda V_c = 0$$

$$U_s + \lambda V_s = 0$$

Hence,

$$U_s/U_c = -V_s/V_c \tag{45}$$

At the optimum, the marginal cost of attention from the child equals the marginal benefit of attention to the parent.[50]

[48] To show why Cox (1987) writes the optimal payment as $T = PS$, where P may be seen as the price of a unit of services. Then $\frac{\partial T}{\partial Y_k} = S\frac{\partial P}{\partial Y_k}(1 + \frac{\partial S}{\partial P}\frac{S}{P})$. This derivative can be either positive or negative. But when S is fixed, $\frac{\partial T}{\partial Y_k} = S\frac{\partial P}{\partial Y_k} > 0$.

[49] This is more likely to occur for personal attention (such as contact and visits) than for other types of time-related services with closer market substitutes and cheaper to get on the market. It is an additional prediction of the exchange model.

[50] Feinerman and Seiler (2002) extend the model to the case of two children and a parent who does not observe the children's cost of service. Jellal and Wolff (2003) also considers an exchange model with financial transfers, services and co-residence, where the parents do not observe the privacy cost of children.

3.2.2. The case of a dominant child

To solve the paradox of the passive child entering in this game with his parent, one has to drop assumption A7 of a dominant parent. One could assume a Nash bargaining solution. This is what is done by Cox (1987, p. 517 and note 11). He defines the parent's and child's threat points as $U^0 = U(Y_p, 0, V(Y_k, 0))$ and $V^0 = V(Y_k, 0)$. In this setting, both the parent and the child seeks to maximize the joint product $(U - U^0)(V - V^0)$. Then the child can be above his threat point utility. The comparative statics results are the same as under the exchange regime with A7, but the child gets a share of the joint 'production'.

What if one assumes that the child is the leader in the game and keeps the parent at his threat-point utility $U(Y_p, 0)$? The child's program is the following:

$$\max_{T,S} V = V(Y_k + T, S) \tag{46}$$

under the parent's participation constraint:

$$U(C_p, S) \geq U(Y_p, 0) \tag{47}$$

The child is not altruistic in the strict sense, yet he does not want his parent's level of well-being to fall below a certain threshold. We assume $T > 0$. If λ is the Lagrange multiplier associated to the parent's participation constraint (47), the corresponding first-order conditions for T and S are:

$$V_s + \lambda U_s = 0$$
$$V_c - \lambda U_c = 0$$

Condition (45) is verified at the optimum.

However, the comparative statics results are somewhat different from the dominant parent case. We still find that $\partial T/\partial Y_p > 0$ (if a richer parent demands more attention, i.e. if attention is a normal good to him, he pays more for it) but $\partial S/\partial Y_p > 0$ or < 0, contrary to the dominant parent case, where a richer parent would attract more attention. Here a richer parent could attract less attention from an egoistic dominant child. This is because attention is a normal good to the parent and an inferior good to the child. A richer parent demands more service and offers a higher remuneration: since the child gets a higher transfer, he is richer. Thus he increases his supply price (the marginal cost of attention is higher to him).[51] There can be a negative relationship not only between parent's income and service, but between financial transfer and service.

Finally one can consider a third case where the child is altruistic and maximizes:

$$\max_{T,S} V = V(C_k, S, U(C_p, S)) \tag{48}$$

[51] Also, $\partial T/\partial Y_k$ can be positive or negative, as in the dominant parent case, but $\partial S/\partial Y_k$ can be positive.

under (47) and parent's and child's budget constraints.[52] If the child is sufficiently altruistic so that his parent's participation constraint does not bind, the child's program is:

$$\max_{T,S} V = V(Y_k + T, S, U(Y_p - T, S)) \tag{49}$$

The first-order conditions are:

$$V_s + V_u U_s = 0$$
$$V_c - V_u U_c = 0$$

This case is considered by Victorio and Arnott (1993). Comparative statics give:

$$\partial T/\partial Y_p > 0$$

but

$$\partial S/\partial Y_p \gtrless 0$$

An altruistic child does not always devote more attention to a poorer parent (if money was needed, the altruistic child would give more money to a poorer parent).

This money-service model can be extended. Ioannides and Kan (2000) assume two-sided altruistic feelings within the family, so that financial help and time-related resources can flow both upward and downward.[53] This leads to three regimes of family redistribution. In the pure altruism case, the price of both parent's and child's attention is null and financial transfer does not depend on the receipt of service. In the altruistic exchange regime, there is still two-sided altruism and a financial transfer includes both an altruism component and a pure payment of services. Finally, in the pure exchange model, the generations are no longer altruistic and the transfer is the exact payment of the service provided to the other generation. Transfer has become a transaction.

As this series of models shows, a crucial point is the distribution of power between parent and child. Despite its importance, the issue of decision within the family is often neglected. If there is no *a priori* on who is dominant in the transfer game, it could be useful to consider a general Nash setting $(U - U_0)^\delta (V - V_0)^{1-\delta}$ and try to recover the parameter δ that measures the parent's power in the transfer decisions.

Table 2 summarizes the results; it is easy to see that to draw any conclusion on the alternative motives of children's attention to their parents or parents' transfer to their children demands detailed data on family types and resources.

[52] This case is half way between impure altruism, and altruism with two goods, as in section 2.4.2. The money transfer is negative (as seen from the altruist's point of view), and the time transfer does not enter the altruist's budget constraint.

[53] Under a Nash equilibrium, each generation takes as given the other's level of well-being. In this setting, both the parent and the child may derive utility from a family exchange.

Table 2
Impure altruism: comparative statics predictions

	Transfer T from p to k		Transfer S from k to p	
	$\partial T/\partial Y_p$	$\partial T/\partial Y_k$	$\partial S/\partial Y_p$	$\partial S/\partial Y_k$
Altruistic parent $V > V_0$ $U_p = U(C_p, S, V(C_k, S))$	> 0	< 0	?	?
Non-altruistic dominant parent $V = V_0$ $U_p = U(C_p, S, V(C_k, S))$	> 0	?	> 0	< 0
Non-altruistic dominant child $U = U_0$ $V_k = V(C_k, S)$	> 0	?	?	?
Non-altruism Nash bargaining $(U_p - U_0)(V_k - V_0)$	> 0	?	> 0	< 0
Altruistic child (see note 52) $U > U_0$ $V_k = V(C_k, S, U(C_p, S))$	> 0	< 0	?	> 0

3.2.3. A strategy to buy the children's services

Bernheim et al. (1984, 1985) suggest that attention or services provided by the children to a parent are motivated by their expecting an inheritance. The parent gets his desired level of attention by threatening to disinherit his children if they do not comply. The amount of the bequest and a sharing rule between the children are fixed in advance by a non-revocable will. By this threat, the parent plays the children out against each other, letting them know he will leave more or all of his wealth to the siblings who best take care of him.

The differences with the previous model of exchange with a dominant parent are the explicit timing of the transfers (the exchange is not simultaneous), and the information sets of the parent and children (the sharing rule is written down).

The parent's utility U is defined over private consumption C_p and the different amount of services provided by each child S_i $(i \in \{1, \ldots, n\})$. The parent's wealth Y_p finances C_p and a global bequest T to the n children. The maximization program for the parent is:

$$\max_{S_1, \ldots, S_n, T} U = U(C_p, S_1, \ldots, S_n) \quad \text{s.t. } C_p = Y_p - T \tag{50}$$

The parent manipulates his children and uses the promised inheritance to influence *ex ante* their decisions (Hoddinott, 1992). When the children's incomes are exogenous,[54] each potential heir accounts for the costly provision of services and maximizes his utility V_i:

$$\max_{S_i} V_i = V_i(C_{ki}, S_i) \quad \text{s.t. } C_{ki} = Y_{ki} + \rho_{ki} T \tag{51}$$

with $V_S < 0$. Each child i receives a fraction ρ_{ki} of T in exchange of the attention devoted to the parent. The sharing rule ρ_{ki} may be expressed as:

$$\rho_{ki} = \rho_{ki}(S_1, \ldots, S_n), \quad \sum_{i=1}^{n} \rho_{ki} = 1 \tag{52}$$

There are two periods in this game (a Stackelberg equilibrium). First, the parent chooses his level of consumption C_p, thus what is left for bequest T, and the sharing rule ρ_{ki}. Second, conditional on ρ_{ki}, each child chooses his optimal attention S_i and receives the predetermined financial transfer at the death of the parent.

Again, it is easy to show that a child who accepts the parent's contract derives no satisfaction and $V_i^0 = V_i(Y_{ki}, 0)$. The parent extracts all the surplus. Bernheim et al. (1985) expect a positive relationship between parental wealth and the mean level of attention provided by the children. However, as shown above, there may be offsetting effects since a higher expectation of inheritance increases the child's price of services (see Table 2, and Victorio and Arnott, 1993).

At first glance, the strategic mechanism may seem clever. By giving early to the children, a parent loses a means of getting attention and affection from them.[55] Nevertheless, the main focus in the strategic model is not so much the early transmission as the rivalry established between siblings by the means of the sharing rule. Like an altruistic parent compensating unequal exogenous income draws of his children, the strategic parent compensates unequal services from the children. But the risk is that the children forget about the unequal income draws, or unequal services, and only remember the unequal bequest, thus becoming rivals. It is likely that a child takes part in the game not only because he receives money in exchange of his attention, but also because inheritance is shared between his siblings if he does not comply. The issue of jealousy is not directly raised in the model, but because of it (and for the reasons exposed at the end of section 2.3.1), a parent is rather unlikely to leave unequal inheritances, be it for fear of destroying the family or his reputation.

[54] It is important to know whether the child's supply of attention only affects leisure time, as in the previous model (Cox, 1987), or his labor supply (Lord, 1992). If labor supply is fixed, attention only decreases the leisure time and the child's income remains exogenous. If the child works less to care for his parent, his income becomes endogenous, the expected inheritance may be seen as a delayed income. The delay would be especially harmful to liquidity constrained children.

[55] From an historical perspective, the 19th century is full of parliamentary discussions (especially in France), which saw in the mere existence of the hereditary reserve and of equal sharing prescribed by the Civil Code, the end of fathers' authority and the decline in old age status (Gotman, 1988).

There is also a possibility of coalition among siblings deciding to share equally the parental inheritance. In that case, the level of service received from children is not set at its maximum value. Also, the strategy does not work for parents with only one child (as mentioned by Bernheim et al., 1985), neither for parents who do not leave any inheritance, or for parents whose children do not need any inheritance.[56] In addition, a benevolent parent may find it hard to stick to his threat of disinheritance, and the freedom to testate is limited in certain countries. Finally, the assumption that the size of the sibship is exogenous is questionable. Cremer and Pestieau (1991) show that if the parents only care about total attention (and not about the care received by a particular child) they will want as many children as possible.

The question of care to old parent is an important one both in countries with no pension system, and in modern societies where life expectancy has risen and a higher income makes individuals more demanding in care. The models presented so far do not seem fully satisfactory. Before we turn to other kind of models, let us reflect a little more on the timing of transfers, in the altruism setting. So far, the timing of transfer has no explicit role, except in the last strategic model. Obviously, if capital markets are perfect, both parents and child are indifferent about the timing of the transfer.[57] It is the same to receive a punctual help to pay for a consumption good, the means to attend college, or an inheritance at the parent's death. We now definitely relax assumption A5 (one period) and attempt to shed light on the role of age and time on the structure of family reciprocities.

3.3. *Transfers as family loans*

In the same setting with one commodity and two transfers, one upward and the other downward, we now examine the situation in which the parents give money to the child, who pays them back in a second period. Interestingly, the fact that transfers flow in both directions does not preclude altruism. When the child is constrained on the borrowing credit market, he is induced to enter into the exchange.[58] The model also applies to the case where parents cannot save for retirement because there is no capital market. In fact, it is very similar to the one in which parents bought the child's services. The effect of liquidity constraints can be described in a pure altruism framework (see Cox and Raines, 1985; Kan, 1996), but we present instead the mixed model of transfers

[56] High-income children have less time-related resources to devote to their parents. Hence, parents may expect to receive more attention from poorer children with more leisure time, who would have cared for their parents even in the absence of strategic considerations ($\partial S/\partial Y_k < 0$ according to the dominant parent model of section 3.2).

[57] We already mentioned that in the presence of merit good, the altruistic parent had an incentive to make a tied transfer to its child. As we now see in more details, it is directly related to the introduction of dynamics into the model.

[58] The role of the child's liquidity constraint on the provision of parental transfer is further examined by Laitner (1993, 1997). Cox and Jappelli (1993) and Guiso and Jappelli (1991) point to the important share of parental transfers in children's resources at young age.

proposed by Cox (1990) and Cox and Jappelli (1990), in which the motives are either altruism or exchange.[59]

In an inter-temporal framework, the altruistic parent takes into account the well-being of his child at each of the two periods 1 and 2. He maximizes the following time-separable utility function:

$$\max U = U_1(C_{p1}, V_1(C_{k1})) + \frac{1}{1+\delta} U_2(C_{p2}, V_2(C_{k2})) \tag{53}$$

where δ is a fixed family discount rate. The parent has access to the capital market, and his lifetime budget constraint may be expressed as:

$$C_{p1} + \frac{C_{p2}}{1+r} + T_1 + \frac{T_2}{1+r} = Y_{p1} + \frac{Y_{p2}}{1+r} \tag{54}$$

where r is the market interest rate and $T_1 \geq 0$ and T_2 are the first and second-period transfers. The child cannot borrow against his future income, hence his two budget constraints, one per period:

$$C_{k1} = Y_{k1} + T_1 \tag{55}$$

$$C_{k2} = Y_{k2} + T_2 \tag{56}$$

The second period transfer T_2 may be positive or negative if the child pays back T_1. Hence T_1 is either a subsidy or a loan. The participation constraint for the child can be described in two different ways, over utilities or over transfer value, without affecting the conclusions on the impact of income on transfers. In Cox (1990), the child accepts the parental loan only if it raises his utility above what it would be without transfers, his reservation level V^0:[60]

$$V_1(C_{k1}) + \frac{1}{1+\delta} V_2(C_{k2}) \geq V_1^0(Y_{k1}) + \frac{1}{1+\delta} V_2^0(Y_{k2}) \equiv V^0 \tag{57}$$

Under (57), the credit constrained child may want to borrow at a family interest rate above that of the financial market, for instance when he is impatient enough ($\delta > r$). There are again two regimes, altruism or exchange, depending on the comparison of V and the reservation utility. When the participation constraint is not binding, the parental transfer increases the child's utility and the transfer is altruistic. Conversely, in the exchange case, the parental transfer T_1 is a loan reimbursed in period 2 by the means of a negative transfer T_2. Both under altruism and exchange, the Euler condition holds for the parent who can access to the capital market:[61]

$$U_{1c} = \frac{1+r}{1+\delta} U_{2c} \tag{58}$$

[59] See also Cox et al. (1998) for a two-sided altruism model of family loans.

[60] Alternatively, in Cox and Jappelli (1990), the child participates in the family exchange when the inter-temporal sum of transfers is non-negative: $T_1 + T_2/(1+r) \geq 0$.

[61] Additive separability between U_1 and U_2 is not required for the Euler condition to hold.

The Euler equality also holds for the child, if the parental altruism parameter is constant over time ($U_{1v_1} = U_{2v_2}$). At the optimum, the transfer also ensures proportionality between each period child's marginal utilities of consumption:

$$V_{1c} = \frac{1+r}{1+\delta} V_{2c} \tag{59}$$

When the child is constrained, the financial transfer occurs when the difference in the child's marginal utilities of consumption per period $(\frac{\partial V_1}{\partial Y_{k1}})_{T=0} - \frac{(1+r)}{(1+\delta)}(\frac{\partial V_2}{\partial Y_{k2}})_{T=0}$ is strictly positive. From the concavity of V_i it follows that the occurrence of a transfer, whatever the regime, is positively related to Y_p and Y_{k2}, but negatively related to Y_{k1}. The amount of the loan/gift is also positively related to the child's second period income. The more liquidity constraints, the higher the amount transferred to the child to finance the optimal first-period consumption.

To discriminate between altruism and exchange, the effect of the child's current income on the transfer amount has again to be examined. While a poorer child receives a higher amount of money under altruism, the relationship between T and Y_{k1} can be negative or positive under exchange, at least when the participation constraint is defined by (57). A rise in Y_{k1} increases the child's threat point V^0, so that the first-period transfer has to be higher in order to make the participation constraint binding. In addition, a richer child benefits from more attractive borrowing opportunities since the family interest rate is a decreasing function of Y_{k1}. Conversely, for a fixed permanent income $(Y_{k1}+Y_{k2}/(1+r))$, the child becomes less liquidity constrained as Y_{k1} rises, which leads to a lower parental transfer. Finally, depending on the strength of these two effects, the effect of Y_{k1} on T_1 remains unclear.[62]

This model may be seen as a generalization of the exchange mechanism proposed by Cox (1987). In the exchange regime, if the child pays back the parental loan with services, then the loan model is analogous to the money for services model, with two periods instead of one. However, under altruism, there is a possibility that no transfer ever flows from child to parent in period 2, if the parent is rich enough. The main problems are the enforcement of the child's repayment, and uncertainty. While the parent is induced to lend money, since he may benefit from an above-market rate of return, there is no clear reason for the child to honor his debt in period 2. Relying on altruistic family values and care of good reputation, Cox (1990, p. 191, note 7) assumes that the child will pay back. The side-issue of uncertainty is linked to endogenous child's income and merit good and has been discussed above: the safety-net provided by parents' altruism may have adverse effect on child's work effort or his human capital investment (see Laitner, 1997, pp. 222–227).

[62] The negative impact through the child's permanent income is more important when Y_{k1} is low. If altruistic parents use the first period income to predict the second period income and if they save, the altruist's reaction to first period income may be somewhat mitigated (McGarry, 2000). This makes it difficult to distinguish between altruism and exchange motives.

3.4. Family insurance and banking

In the presence of altruism, exogenous income shocks are smoothed by transfers from (to) altruistic (selfish) parents toward (from) selfish (or altruistic) children. Altruism acts as a means of insurance within families.[63] We have also seen that the altruistic family can function as a bank.

Why would family arrangements be adequate? Are not they deemed to disappear as market insurance and banking develop or as public social insurance gets more common? It could be argued that mutualizing risk over a larger population (for example a village, a country, or the whole world) is more efficient that doing it over a family. Besides, a positive correlation between all family members' income (or ability) makes family insurance less effective. Moreover, families are not always stable structures, and may become less and less so. Geographical mobility may also weaken family ties. The more conflict and instability within families, the less efficiency as compared to market insurance. The correlatives of love and affection are envy and jealousy, that are not likely to exist between a banker or an insurance company and their customers, or between government and citizens, but could plague family relationships. Finally, love and affection themselves can sustain exploitation and free-riding. Despite all this, the family offers other advantages.

First, the family incurs less transaction costs than the market since many arrangements remain informal. Second, it has more complete information on the real situation of its members, more mutual supervision and trust, thereby reducing agency problems such as moral hazard and adverse selection (see Ben-Porath, 1980; Pollak, 1985). Consumption is hard to hide among people living close by, even if, as we have shown, the Rotten kid theorem does not always hold. This stems from the fact that family relationships are durable, freedom of entry and exit is limited. This provides opportunities to sanction and reward, and lowers the cost of information. Family is also partly the fruit of a choice: one does not choose one's parents, but one chooses one's spouse. The fact that families are likely to be homogeneous in tastes facilitates day to day interactions.[64] Finally as already mentioned, some goods have no market equivalent, and moreover some risks are not (or not yet) covered by insurance.[65] One may think of weather fluctuations and their consequences on agricultural income in less developed agrarian societies. Even in rich countries, widows (or orphans) are still poorly protected against the loss of a spouse's (or a parent's) income, and divorce has adverse consequences on income that cannot be insured on the market. The uncertainty about the length of life leads to the risk of outliving one's resources in absence of an efficient annuity market.

[63] It is even a perfect insurance, since the optimal transfer perfectly compensates any change in the distribution of family income (for a fixed family income).

[64] See Bowles (1998) on what he, following biologists, terms segmentation in the context of evolution of traits in a population.

[65] Stark (1995) stresses the fact that it is not only because market institutions do not exist that families engage in altruistic transfers, but that it is because of the efficiency of those transfers that market transactions or insurance do not necessarily emerge.

Kotlikoff and Spivak (1981) present a model where non-altruistic individuals protect themselves against the risk of poverty in old age by an implicit or explicit contract of transfers. When a market for annuities exists such protection can be done efficiently, otherwise involuntary transmissions due to precautionary savings may be important. The gain in risk sharing may be large, in particular when pooling income with a spouse. Such an insurance system seems especially suitable for analyzing marriage (with the mutual care it yields) and marriage contracts, that define the surviving spouse's portion. But it is less likely to apply in an intergenerational context, since parents and children have different probabilities of surviving and thus face non-symmetric risks. Then, the key issue is to find a successful mechanism to induce a child to take care of his parents in old age. The problem is solved in Kotlikoff and Spivak (1981) by altruism, combined with trust and honesty. Although each generation does not care about the partner's utility and just wants insurance, its purely selfish motive needs an altruistic mechanism in order to work.

Foster and Rosenzweig (2000, 2001) also stress that the Pareto efficient allocation of risk must overcome some information and enforcement problems. How family members can commit to insure one another when they cannot enter into binding contracts? In their model, transfers respond both to contemporary income shocks and to the history of previous transfers, and the response varies with the degree of altruism. As in a market credit transaction, a past debt to the family affects current borrowing possibility from the family.[66] To Foster and Rosenzweig (2001, p. 405) 'commitment issues may also play a role in childbearing and parental investment in human capital in developing countries to the extent that children cannot commit to provide parents with a secure source of support in old age'. This is precisely the question to which we turn in section 4. We aim to show that it is far from being only a developing countries issue.

3.5. Decisions within the family: altruism and collective models

The use of altruism to explain family transfers has been attacked on two fronts: from within and from outside. We have dwelt so far on the inside attack. It hangs mainly around merit goods. The outside attack comes from using the word altruism in the context of the so-called collective (or bargaining) models. Since collective models sometimes involve bargaining (usually between spouses, but it could be between parent and child), and parent and child can bargain when merit goods are introduced in the altruism model, there is ground for confusion. Therefore, before leaving altruism, we try to clarify the two approaches.

[66] Attanasio and Rios-Rull (2000) imagine an isolated village, where self-enforcing contracts partly insure the villagers. Introducing an institution that would insure them against a common shock affecting village income seems likely to improve welfare. They show however that such well-intended policy interacts with the functioning of private markets and can destroy the social fabric that weaved the village arrangements, and reduce welfare. See Docquier and Rapoport (2006) in this Handbook for more.

Table 3
Collective models and altruism: a comparison

Collective model C	Pure altruism A
2 individuals p and k Live together	2 individuals p and k Live apart
$U_p = U_p(C_p, L_p)$, $U_k = U_k(C_k, L_k)$ 2 goods: private consumption and leisure Exogenous non-labor income y Only $y = Y_p + Y_k$ observed	$U_p = U_p(C_p, V_k)$, $V_k = V_k(C_k)$ 1 good: private consumption Y_p and Y_k exogenous observed
Only $C = C_p + C_k$ observed w_p, L_p, w_k, L_k observed Cooperative solution	C_p and C_k observed Non-cooperative equilibrium, last word to p
Exogenous bargaining or power index Sharing rule on non-labor income Pareto efficiency	Exogenous altruism parameter Transfer T from p to k Efficiency only if $T > 0$

The altruism model A was developed as a reaction against a purely individualistic view of utility. The idea was to go from $U(C_p)$ to $U(C_p, V(C_k))$. We have seen that, under some (restrictive) hypotheses, it leads to income pooling *between* two households. The collective approach C started as a reaction against the assumption of income pooling *within* one household. The idea of altruism is to link separate households, whereas collective models were created to individualize and separate utility functions, consumption and decisions within a household. Table 3 summarizes some of the differences. Bargaining models were initiated by Manser and Brown (1980) and McElroy and Horney (1981), but we follow here the collective approach developed in Chiappori (1992).

Models A focus on the transfer function, models C focus on choice of leisure and on the sharing rule. We have seen that model A is quite transformed if choice of leisure is introduced, but it can be accommodated. Collective models assume Pareto efficiency: p and k always share. The altruism model may lead to inefficiency if the parent is 'at a corner' and $T = 0$, or if he would like $T < 0$.

In the collective model C, the maximization program for a person p can be written as follows:

$$\max U_p(L_p, C_p) + \beta(w_p, w_k, y)U_k(L_k, C_k)$$
$$\text{s.t. } C_p + C_k = w_p(1 - L_p) + w_k(1 - L_k) + y$$

where U is separable over consumption and leisure, y is an exogenous non-labor income, w_p and w_k are the wage rates of p and k, 1 is the total time endowment and β, the pre-determined non-observable bargaining rule or power index, is a function of the environment (w_p, w_k and y).

This program can be given a sharing rule ϕ interpretation and written as (Chiappori, 1992):

$$\max_{L_i, C_i} U_i(L_i, C_i)$$
$$\text{s.t. } C_i = w_i(1 - L_i) + \phi_i(y, w_p, w_k)$$

for $i = p$ and $i = k$, with $\phi_p = \phi_i$ and $\phi_k = y - \phi_i$. For the comparison, the altruism model A can be expressed as:

$$\max U_p(L_p, C_p) + \beta U_k(L_k, C_k)$$
$$\text{s.t. } \begin{cases} C_p = w_p(1 - L_p) + Y_p - T \\ C_k = w_k(1 - L_k) + Y_k + T \end{cases}$$

We introduce leisure in the altruism model to stress the similitude, but as we have seen, the choice of leisure is not well accommodated by the model, except when p is a benevolent dictator. Model A could also accommodate two-sided altruism. What should be stressed is the difference in β, the degree of altruism: it is fixed in the altruism model (the parent's taste makes him more or less altruistic), whereas it may depend on wages (prices) in the collective model.[67] If it is fixed, the two models look very much alike.

The collective model will aim at getting the sharing rule ϕ and its partial derivatives from the observation on leisure choices, under certain conditions. In model C, ϕ may increase with w_i (i has more power) or decrease (i has less need). In model A, T increases with w_p (p richer) and decreases if w_k increases (k has less need). An increase with w_k is the sign of an exchange regime (assimilating here w_i to Y_i).

We have shown that model A predicts income pooling when $T > 0$. Model C typically predicts that the partial derivatives $\phi_y, \phi_{w_p}, \phi_{w_f} \neq 0$, that is to say the share of an extra euro gained by p at the expense of k could be different from 0. Actually it could be one, or even negative, that is, k could get less than before.[68]

In the context of pure altruism (and positive transfer) a government transfer to p or k is welfare neutral, when under the collective model a transfer to p has not the same welfare effect as a transfer to k (see Ward-Batts, 2003, and Attanasio and Lechene, 2002, for recent applications). If empirically one does not find a one to one neutrality, is it because altruism is impure (in all the ways we underlined: endogenous child's or parent's income, uncertainty about the future, merit goods...) or because individuals collectively bargain? In other words, the empirical finding of imperfect income pooling is interpreted as a rejection of pure altruism by those studying inter-households relationship; it is interpreted as a rejection of the unitary model in favor of the collective

[67] Section 5 introduces a model where altruism is endogenous and depends on prices, to a certain extent.

[68] In a simplified (yet complicated enough) setting, Blundell et al. (2002) find that an extra pound gained by p (the husband) is totally consumed by p, an extra pound gained by k (the wife) means 0.1 pound less for p (she gets 1.1 out of it), and an extra pound of non-wage income increase p's consumption by 0.24 and k's by 0.76. In the case $dw_k = -dw_p$ it would mean the husband consumes 1.1 $(1 + 0.1)$ more when he earns 1 more and his wife 1 less.

model by the growing body of those studying intra-household relationship. It is often interpreted as a rejection of altruistic preferences in favor of a collective model. However when one finds that giving child benefit to the mother rather than to the father, increases expenditure on children's clothes (Lundberg et al., 1997) and decreases those on father's tobacco (Ward-Batts, 2003), is it more interesting to conclude that father and mother do not pool their income, or that mothers are more altruistic towards children than towards husband, and fathers are less altruistic than mothers towards children? We mentioned free-riding problems in the presence of more than one altruistic parent. It seems collective models could be applied to inter-household relationships (when they are close enough), as have been done by McElroy (1985) to study the nest-leaving behavior of young adults, and impure altruism model could be applied to intra-household relationships (when individuals are individualistic enough).

On the one hand, model C seems to include model A. On the other, it cannot look at inefficient outcomes since it assumes efficiency (an issue linked to transferable utility and binding commitment); and it overlooks multi-period games when altruism is most interesting: the life cycle of a family where one starts as k and then becomes p.[69] In any cases, there is still room for models encompassing at the same time inter-related preferences, endogenous choices of leisure and some form of game between households.

3.6. *Pure and impure altruism*

We finally summarize the main results of section 3, contrasting pure altruism (one good and exogenous income) with impure altruism (two goods, endogenous income or merit good) (Table 4). We have shown in section 2 that as soon as child's income becomes endogenous, the child has an incentive to become rotten (work less, hide his income from the parent). In that case,

1. The parent has an incentive to become an impure altruist, that is impose the consumption of a merit good to the child.
2. As soon as the parent becomes an impure altruist (interested in the child's consumption of a merit good), family transfers may turn into family transactions, resembling market transactions.
3. If the parental transfer is positively related to the child's income, the relationship is no more altruistic, but one of reciprocity or exchange (therefore, it is more a transaction than a transfer). Then the neutrality property breaks down. In this context, the introduction of a public transfer may have no effect on the private transfer and could even increase it. Suppose that the giver is paying a service, at the current wage rate, and consider a tax on the young, that diminishes his net wage, to the benefit of the old generation: the donor parent may now compensate the beneficiary child at a lower rate.
4. If the parent transfer is negatively related to the child's income, the relationship may be either altruistic or one of reciprocity or exchange.

[69] For dynamic models of collective choices, see Ligon (2002).

Table 4
Main assumptions and results of the pure and impure altruism models

One sided altruism		
Parent's utility and [information set]	Child's utility	Budget constraints
Pure altruism, one good, exogenous incomes		
$U_p = U(C_p, V(C_k))$	$U_k = V(C_k)$	$C_p = Y_p - T, T \geq 0$
$U_c > 0, U_v > 0$	$V_c > 0$	$C_k = Y_k + T$
$[Y_p, Y_k, V]$	$\frac{\partial T}{\partial Y_p} - \frac{\partial T}{\partial Y_k} = 1$	After exogenous shock
	Redistributive neutrality	on exogenous incomes
Pure altruism, two goods, one non-produced, endogenous child's income [Villanueva (2001)]		
$U_p = U(C_p, V(C_k, e))$	$U_k = V(C_k, e)$	$C_p = Y_p - T, T \geq 0$
$U_c > 0, U_v > 0$	$V_e < 0, V_c > 0$	$C_k = Y_k + w_k e + T, e \geq 0$
$[Y_p, Y_k, V, w_k e]$	Redistributive neutrality	May not hold
		(endogenous income)
Pure altruism, two goods, one non-produced, endogenous parent's income [Sloan et al. (2002)]		
$U_p = U(C_p, V(C_k, S))$	$U_k = V(C_k, S)$	$C_p = Y_p + w_p(1 - s) - T, T \geq 0$
$U_c > 0, U_v > 0$	$V_S > 0$	$C_k = Y_k + T, S \geq 0$
$[Y_p, w_p, Y_k, V]$		
$V_c > 0$	$\frac{\partial T}{\partial Y_p} - \frac{\partial T}{\partial Y_k} = 1$	$\frac{\partial S}{\partial Y_p} - \frac{\partial S}{\partial Y_k} = 0$
	Redistributive neutrality	Redistributive invariance
	on exogenous incomes	
Impure altruism, two goods, one non-produced, exogenous income [Cox (1987)]		
$U_p = U(C_p, S, V(C_k, S))$	$U_k = V(C_k, S)$	$C_p = Y_p - T, T \geq 0$
$U_c > 0, U_v > 0, U_s > 0$	$V_c > 0, V_s < 0$	$C_k = Y_k + T, e \geq 0$
$[Y_p, Y_k, V]$		
	$\frac{\partial T}{\partial Y_p} - \frac{\partial T}{\partial Y_k} = 1$	$\frac{\partial s}{\partial Y_p} - \frac{\partial s}{\partial Y_k} = 0$
	Redistributive neutrality	Redistributive invariance
Impure altruism, two goods, one merit good, endogenous child's income [Chami (1996)]		
$U_p = U(C_p, e, V(C_k, e))$	$U_k = V(C_k, e)$	$C_p = Y_p - T, T \geq 0$
$U_c > 0, U_v > 0, U_e > 0$	$V_c > 0, V_e < 0$	$C_k = Y_k + w_k e + T, e \geq 0$
	$\frac{\partial T}{\partial Y_p} - \frac{\partial T}{\partial Y_k} = 1$	
	Redistributive neutrality	
	on exogenous incomes	

4. Non-altruism: transfers as old-age security

Parental altruism may seem natural. After all, the adult child has been taken care of when he was an infant and altruism may stem partly from the fact that babies are born as dependent who cannot survive without parental care. Helping grown-up children would come out of the habit of having taken care of them as infants. There is nothing of the sort with old-age support. Hence the fifth biblical commandment demanding to honor one's parents, while there is no need of an equivalent command to honor one's children.[70] The exchange models presented above awkwardly tackled with this issue of parental support, and the mechanisms behind them are not fully convincing. A model of family transfers that could do without exogenous altruism would seem stronger. We now consider such an inter-temporal exchange model. Time is introduced more explicitly: the parent remembers that he has been a child in the past, and, more important, he knows that he will be a grandparent in the future. There are three generations instead of two.

4.1. The mutuality model or how to glue the generations together

The context is one of need of the old grandparents, either because there is no capital market to save, no pensions of a pay-as-you-go type, or because they demand care or attention without market substitute. In all cases, the family acts as a substitute or a complement to the credit market and transfers are a means of improving the inter-temporal allocation of resources. But the mechanism is different from the exchange that was previously discussed. Transfers are no longer a substitute for private consumption as in the altruism model, where the child's consumption is a normal good to the parent. They are instead a form of investment, like a portfolio-choice operation. Each family member has a credit when deciding to make a transfer, while the debt is reduced when paying back.

The model is known as the 'child as old-age security' or 'family constitution' model; we call it the mutuality model to stress the system of reciprocity and solidarity it implies. Samuelson (1958), Shell (1971) and Hammond (1972) propose a game involving retirement benefits paid by one generation to its predecessor, that requires a kind of social contract between generations.[71] However, there is no explicit investment of one generation in the next. While Shubik (1981) and Costa (1988) present a general solution, for glueing the generations together (as Shubik puts it), a detailed analysis is due to Cigno (1991, 1993, 2000), who examines the sustainability of selfish transfers within three-generation families.[72]

In an overlapping generation model, egoistic individuals live for three periods and only derive satisfaction from their own consumption. An individual born at date t receives an exogenous income in the middle age period 2, but has no resources during the childhood and retirement periods. Denoting by C_1^t, C_2^t and C_3^t the consumption levels

[70] Another dissymmetry is the following: a parent transfers to a child (young adult), hoping that the child will be able to become independent, that is, not needing a transfer any more (and therefore survive when the parent is dead). A parent transferring to a grandparent has no such hope. The transfer stops, not when the beneficiary is self-sufficient, but when he is no more.

[71] Such family contracts were effectively written among peasants in Europe up to the 20th century. The demographic consequences of the old-age security model are examined by Lee (2000).

[72] Ehrlich and Lui (1991) is close. For a detailed exposition, especially for a comparison with the Barro and Becker (1988) altruism model with endogenous fertility, which we have left aside her, see Cigno's chapter in this Handbook.

of each period, his utility function is:

$$U^t = U(C_1^t, C_2^t, C_3^t) \tag{60}$$

Since U is supposed to be strictly quasi-concave, the individual can be better off transferring resources from period 2 to periods 1 and 3. What happens when there is no credit market? The structure of the model is as follows (subscripts d and u respectively stand for downward and upward). In period 1, the child who cannot borrow receives a fixed amount of transfer T_d^{t-1} from his parent. In period 2, the adult earns the income Y^t, transfers $n^t T_d^t$ to his n^t children, and makes a transfer T_u^t to pay back the loan previously received from the parent. The number of children per individual from generation t is endogenous. Finally, in period 3, the retiree receives the transfer $n^t T_u^{t+1}$ from the next generation $t+1$.

The family transfers T_d^{t-1}, T_d^t, T_u^t and T_u^{t+1} are fixed, and the only choice is of the number of children.[73] The maximization for an adult may be expressed as $\max_{n^t} U^t$ subject to the fertility constraints $0 \leq n^t \leq \bar{n}$ and the following budget constraints:

$$C_1^t = T_d^{t-1} \tag{61}$$

$$C_2^t = Y^t - n^t T_d^t - T_u^t \tag{62}$$

$$C_3^t = n^t T_u^{t+1} \tag{63}$$

Noting ρ^t the rate of return of the parent-to-child transfer such that $\rho^t T_d^{t-1} = T_u^t$, the inter-temporal budget constraint becomes:

$$C_1^t + \frac{C_2^t}{\rho^t} + \frac{C_3^t}{\rho^t \rho^{t+1}} = \frac{Y^t}{\rho^t} \tag{64}$$

From the corresponding first-order conditions, the ratios of marginal utilities of consumption equal the family interest factor at the optimum (Cigno, 1991):

$$\frac{U_2^{\prime,t-1}}{U_3^{\prime,t-1}} = \frac{U_1^{\prime,t}}{U_2^{\prime,t}} = \rho^t \tag{65}$$

This system of selfish family loans leads to Pareto efficiency. The central assumption is the existence of a family constitution which prescribes at each date t the transfers T_d^t to young children and the transfer T_u^t to the parent. The rule of the constitution is that defectors, and defectors only, are punished. If the adult does not transfer to his parent ($T_u^t = 0$), and decides to go it alone instead of complying to the family constitution, he is punished and his children are exempted from transferring to him in the next period ($T_u^{t+1} = 0$); the children are not punished themselves since they have rightly punished a defector in the family game. Under certain conditions, the family constitution defining

[73] If one assumes that both the transfers and fertility are endogenous, there is an infinity of solutions. It would be equivalent for an adult to have n children and give each child a transfer T_d, or to invest nT_d in only one child.

all transfers and the rule of the game is self-fulfilling and the optimal strategy is a Nash subgame perfect equilibrium (see Cigno, 1993). The following assumptions are made: parents and children have the same preferences; when the contract is violated, the result is that all siblings punish the defecting parent; the consumption of young and adults are sufficiently non-substitutable; and the horizon is infinite. Either all generations are interested in complying with the family rules, or else the system of transfers breaks down (and thus the family, since consumption in youth and in old-age is only made of transfers). If one generation anticipates the family credit network to break down in the future, no generation would have a reason to transfer resources. Guttman (2001, pp. 143–144) points that no optimal rule can be implemented if changes in future economic conditions (for instance the market interest rate) are foreseen. Much depends on the probability of those exogenous future shocks for the current deciding generation.[74] Moreover, nothing prevents the constitution to be made environment-conditional.

If a credit market is introduced in the model, an adult has the choice between having children and lending to them at the family interest rate $\rho^{t+1} - 1$ or investing on the market at the interest rate $r^{t+1} - 1$. In that case, the family interest rate must be above the market rate of interest. There is a fixed cost because the adult's income is diminished by his debt to the parents, therefore the family interest rate must be set a very high value. When an adult decides not to have any children, the family mutualization breaks down and the inter-temporal budget constraint becomes:

$$C_2^t + \frac{C_3^t}{r^{t+1}} = Y^t \tag{66}$$

When a family member complies with the contract between generations, his budget constraint is:

$$C_2^t + \frac{C_3^t}{r^{t+1}} = Y^t - T_u^t - n^t T_d^t + \frac{n^t T_u^{t+1}}{r^{t+1}} \tag{67}$$

It follows that an adult will comply only if the following inequality holds:

$$\rho^{t+1} > \frac{T_u^t + n^t T_d^t}{n^t T_d^t} r^{t+1} > r^{t+1} \tag{68}$$

In order to invest in children, what they will repay must outweigh what has been discharged to one's own parents instead of being invested in the market at the interest rate $r^{t+1} - 1$.

Lagerlöf (1997) notes that interior solutions to the utility maximization program can yield lower utility than corner solutions. In particular, fertility and saving cannot be

[74] In fact, there are two different decision units in the mutuality model. On the one hand, the rule of transfers is set by the whole family, which includes all the succeeding generations. On the other hand, a particular generation decides to accept or refuse the family contract with its fixed amount of transfers. In a steady-state equilibrium, the family is able to implement an optimal system of family transfers which maximizes the well-being of all the generations. See Cigno (2006) in this handbook, on the selection of a constitution, and Cigno (2000) on heterogeneity and the consequence of a changing environment.

positive in an optimal steady state. However, the model may apply even when interest rate is high or retirement benefits comfortable, if one assumes that what the elders expect from their children is care and attention for which no market exists (Cigno and Rosati, 2000). In Ehrlich and Lui (1991), parents invest in their children's human capital not only because it brings them material security in old age but because they will need their companionship.[75] Therefore, the parent receives both material transfers that depend on the children's human capital, which is an investment, as in Cigno (1991), and affection that is a function of the number of surviving children. Here, the child's probability of survival is a function of the parents' investment. The selfish parent invests so that the child repays in the next period. As material transfers and affection coexist, the family constitution is even more efficient. If a parent can do without material transfers from the children by saving, there is no market substitute for affection. The physiological ceiling on fertility and future uncertainty (such as the premature death of a child) are also a reason to save. Besides, there obviously are other reasons to have children than old age support.

Some testable predictions of the mutuality/constitution model are different from those of altruism (Cigno et al., 1998). First, financial assistance should be little affected by the incomes of the donors and the recipients. This result stems from the exchange motive and the fixed cost of participating in the family network. Even if a donor is poor, he has to give money to his children if he wants to be paid back during old-age.[76] If both money and services are exchanged, individuals are more likely to give money if they have a high income, and to render personal services if their time is less valuable (low wage rate), which is the same prediction as the exchange model. But another prediction is unique to the mutuality model. Parents facing credit market constraints are more likely to give assistance to the children, a paradox due to the high value of the family interest rate. Investing in children lowers the donor's present consumption, but allows a higher consumption in the next period when the children discharge their debt, hence globally a higher inter-temporal utility (Cigno, 1993). Finally, there is a chain of solidarity between the generations. The receipt of a parental transfer increases the occurrence of help to the children, and transfers made by the parents to the grand-parents are a condition of transfers received in the next period from the children (except if the grand-parent was a defector). Finally a person without children would not make any upward transfer since she may defect without being punished.

An interesting feature of the model is its macroeconomic predictions. The introduction of an actuarially fair pension system (or the development of the credit market), that had no effect on the consumption of households linked by altruistic transfers, changes

[75] Ehrlich and Lui (1991) call such a need conditional altruism. But strictly speaking there is no altruism here, since the children's utility is not an argument of the parent's satisfaction. As in Cox, services given by children are an argument of the parent's utility function, and attention is not included in the budget constraint.

[76] In addition, a small positive variation of the transfer in period 2 is rather offset by saving than by consumption.

the behavior of mutualistic families. Some will be induced to default and not comply with the family constitution, because the family rate of return is not large enough to recover the fixed cost of complying. The number of children will also diminish as public transfers take care of old age support, except if non-monetary need remain important.[77]

4.2. Old age support: other mechanisms

To account for old age support, the family mutuality model with its family constitution stresses the importance of parents paying back the grand-parents, and the necessity for their children to be aware of it. Otherwise they could opt out of the system without being punished. But some other mechanisms can be thought of. They hang around the formation of preferences: since childhood is the time for education, there might be externalities to the parents' actions if being altruists they induce their child to become so.

In the case of upward-altruism, the trick is that the middle-aged altruist will become old and needy, and has a self-interest in his child being an upward altruist in the future. The altruist is not only, as we said before, maximizing his own utility (that happens to be of an altruistic form), but in the case of ascending altruism he may also take into account the fact that his own utility will enter his child's utility function *in the future*. Parents may invest to make their child altruistic towards themselves. Becker (1996) suggests they teach their children the desired behavior by instilling in them culpability if they do not conform to the norms. A small g, for *guilt*, is introduced in the child's utility function and makes it costly for him not to help his parents. Providing they invest properly in this 'education', the parents gain. The child feels less guilty when making more upstream transfers. Another suggestion is that parents invest in their old parents' care because there is an exogenous probability that their children will imitate and do the same for them in the future (Cox and Stark, 1996, 1998b). The parent's investment in the child's preference takes the form of setting an example. We dwell on this 'demonstration' mechanism in section 5.1.

In the case of descending altruism, the parent may be aware that a gift creates gratitude or sentiment of obligation towards the giver, which might be useful *in the future*. There is a positive externality to being an altruist, when time enters the picture. In Stark and Falk (1998), the very transfer to the child modifies the child's preferences. He will help his parents in the future out of gratitude. This is in line with the huge anthropology literature on gift-giving, initiated by Mauss (1923). The prediction of the model is

[77] On the economic value of children see Caldwell (1976). Balestrino (1997) studies education policy in a mutuality/constitution model with endogenous fertility. Anderberg and Balestrino (2003) extend the model by accounting for endogenous education, assuming an exogenous growth rate of the population n. Middle-aged adults provide financial transfers to elderly parents and support the education of children. Wages in the second period are no longer exogenous, but depend on education received. They find that self-enforceable education transfers can be achieved if and only if $n > r$. However, lack of commitment may cause too little family provision for education.

the same as the pure altruism model $\partial T/\partial Y_k < 0$, whereas it was more likely to be $\partial T/\partial Y_k > 0$ in the exchange model. This is because the altruistic parent is not buying a service from the child in the period he is making the transfer (as in the exchange model) but 'inadvertently' buying *future* gratitude. This could be called the 'upward altruism as a side-effect of downward altruism', or the reciprocal altruism model. We show below that those mechanisms are not always observationally different from the family mutuality model, making the clear empirical distinction between altruism, exchange and reciprocity somewhat blurred.

To summarize, not only is the rotten kid well-behaved, but he will become a parent in due time. The interaction between parents and children is the place and time for preferences formation or transmission (be they genetic or acquired) and it opens the door to the literature on endogenous preferences.

5. The formation of preferences

We begin by describing the mechanism of what is called the demonstration effect (section 5.1). Then, we give examples of dynamic probability models of preference formation (section 5.2). A characteristic a (for altruism) has a given exogenous frequency in the population at the beginning of time. Individuals mate, reproduce, exchange, according to their type. The models predict the prevalence of the a type after some generations. The results depend heavily on the rules of transmission and on the relative advantage of altruism over egoism in reproduction (section 5.2.1). Finally, a model where the degree of altruism β is endogenous is presented (section 5.2.2).

5.1. To imitate or to demonstrate?

In the basic model, selfish parents P take care of their elders G in order to elicit the same support from their children K in the future (Bergstrom and Stark, 1993; Cox and Stark, 1996, 1998a). They set an example of good conduct, hoping they will be imitated by their children. Contrary to the exchange model of section 3, the parents do not help the grandparents in the hope of a future inheritance, but, as in the mutuality model, they do so in order to be helped in the future. In a direct exchange, the giver is paid back by the beneficiary. Here, the mechanism involves the extended family and the exchange is indirect: there is a time to give, when adult to the old parent, and a time to receive, when old, from one's adult children. As in the mutuality model, the idea of a demonstration precludes upward transfers from parents to grandparents when there are no children around. Hence the predictions that individuals will have contacts with their parents when they have young children around by the virtue of the importance of early childhood experiences on future attitudes, and that the donor will favor transfers which his own children will be aware of: time-related help rather than hidden cash gifts, visits rather than discreet letters or phone calls.[78]

There are three generations, one passive grandparent G, one parent P and n children K. In the basic model the children are clones, supposed to behave all in the same manner. They blindly reproduce the observed parental actions with an exogenous probability π $(0 \leq \pi \leq 1)$, but they may also adopt a different maximizer attitude, with probability $1 - \pi$. The parent P is characterized by a twice-differentiable, strictly quasi-concave utility function $U(X, nY)$, where X indicates the transfer from P to G and nY the transfers from K to P. The parent maximizes the expected value $EU(X, Y, \pi, n)$:

$$\max_X \; EU(X, Y, \pi, n) = \pi U(X, nX) + (1 - \pi)U(X, nY) \tag{69}$$

Let $U^I \equiv U(X, nX)$ be the utility of the parents if the children are imitators and $U^S \equiv U(X, nY)$ their utility if the children are short-sighted maximizers. Providing care is costly, but expected care from K increases the level of satisfaction ($U_1 < 0$, $U_2 > 0$, $U_{22} < 0$). The optimal value for X is such that:

$$-\left[\pi U_1^I + (1 - \pi)U_1^S\right] = n\pi U_2^I \tag{70}$$

meaning the marginal cost $-[\pi U_1^I + (1 - \pi)U_1^S]$ of transfers from P to G is equal to the marginal expected benefit $n\pi U_2^I$ of the symmetric assistance from K to P, at the equilibrium. It is easy to show that X is positively correlated with the exogenous probability of imitation since $\partial \overline{X}/\partial \pi = U_1^S/\pi EU_{XX} > 0$. Jellal and Wolff (2000) extend the model by introducing uncertainty in the life expectancy of the parent, and a time discount rate. They prove that the longer the parents' life expectancy (or the higher the rate of time discount), the more they can expect to reap from their children. In many societies, wives are younger than their husbands and outlive them. Thus they have a lower rate of time preference, higher need for old-age support than their husbands who in addition can rely on their wife for assistance (see Browning, 2000), and will be induced to transfer more to their parents. This suggests that individuals with an important expected need of old-age support, whether female, isolated or disabled, have an incentive to provide more assistance to their elderly parents.

Contrary to intuition,[79] the demonstration is not necessarily more productive in the presence of more children (Jellal and Wolff, 2005). This stems from the assumption that all children behave in the same way. On the one hand, the marginal benefit of the expected reciprocity is greater with many children. But on the other hand, investing in elders' care may be seen as a risky investment, and the loss, in case the children behave

[78] Parents also know that they will be able to rely on the support of their children only if the latter themselves have children. Cox and Stark (1998b) suggest that parents make tied transfers to their children in order to encourage the production of grandchildren.

[79] And the claim of Stark (1995) and Cox and Stark (1996).

as selfish maximizers, increases in n.[80] The more risk adverse the parent, the more he fears not to be helped in turn by the children ($dX/dn \leq 0$). Conversely, a risk-lover parent with more children is expected to provide more help because he gives a higher weight to the expected utility from imitative behaviors ($dX/dn \geq 0$). If the assumption of clone children is relaxed, the model becomes more realistic and the parent's expected gain is in general higher if they have more children.

The assumption that the probability of imitation is exogenous also seems problematic, since setting an example is precisely intended to induce the children to imitate. Jellal and Wolff (2005) suggest a dynamic model with an endogenous likelihood of imitation, growing with the stock of assistance provided by the parent in the past. Then, the parent invests more in the demonstration.

The demonstration mechanism is open to at least one strong criticism. Each generation solves an optimization problem but the possible child's incentive to induce imitation in his own children is left out. Thus even if he does not imitate, he may nevertheless help in order to be helped (be a far-sighted rather than a short-sighted maximizer). However, not helping the parent may also be optimal. After all, there is always a chance that the grandchildren will start the game again and help. The third generation has exactly the same incentive to start setting a good example as the second. Thus, an agent will be better off not helping his parent and this should not affect his children's behavior. If one generalizes this free-riding attitude, the whole intergenerational sequence of transfers breaks down. There is a logical puzzle: it is optimal to help and not to help.

Cigno's mutuality model circumvents this problem with the family constitution. Children are allowed not to help their parents only if they (the parents) have defected, and this will not prevent them (the children) from being helped in the future, since only defectors are punished. There is no demonstration in the sense of a probability of imitation, but parent's action leads to similar children's action, by demonstrating the value of the family mutualization. That the parents behaved in a certain way informs the child about the consequences of certain types of actions and increases his and the family social capital (Becker, 1996).[81] Thus the efficiency of the demonstration mechanism may stem from the fact that it is an information device.

Finally, the process of imitation remains to be explained. Selfish maximizers act as if they were altruists, so that their children be altruistic. Why should not they be altruistic in the first place (Kapur, 1997)? If imitating individuals have truly become altruistic,

[80] The sign of the derivative dX/dn may be positive or negative since $U_2^I > 0$, but $U_{22}^I < 0$:

$$\frac{dX}{dn} = -\frac{\pi U_2^I + n\pi X U_{22}^I + \pi X U_{12}^I + Y(1-\pi)U_{12}^S}{EU_{XX}}$$

Clearly, dX/dn is negatively related to relative risk aversion $\sigma_r = -nXU_{22}^I/U_2^I$. For instance, with $U_{12}^I = 0$ and $U_{12}^S = 0$, one obtains $dX/dn = -\pi U_2^I(1-\sigma_r)/EU_{XX}$.

[81] For instance, the relative price for a loan made by parents to the children would be lower because parents have themselves received such a loan in the past, so that both parents and children know how to behave.

they should devote resources to the grandparents without evoking a further demonstration effect. In that case, they will help even if they do not have children of their own. Demonstrating and imitating are intertwined and there is a positive externality in being or pretending to be an altruist. Indeed, true altruists may be more efficient than pure selfish maximizers in transmitting their altruistic preferences to their children. Again, as in the insurance model of Kotlikoff and Spivak (1981), the mechanism is unlikely to hold with egoistic agents: the selfish motive requires some form of altruism to perform properly.

5.2. Cultural transmission and endogenous preferences

In his Nobel Lecture, Becker (1993) argues that economists have excessively relied on altruism to explain family behavior when discussing how to enforce contracts between generations. He suggests instead to account for the rational formation of preferences within the family (Becker, 1993, 1996). The key feature of the preference shaping theory is that parents attempt to influence their children during the formative early years because of the correlation between childhood experiences and adult behaviors.

But the idea of parents instilling a sentiment of culpability into their children if they do not conform to the norms seems slightly ad hoc. Besides, Becker (1993) indicates that the rational formation of preferences replaces altruism by feelings of obligation and affection. But the final objective of preference shaping is that children behave as altruists toward their parents as they grow older. Chased by the door, altruism comes back by the window. The issue seems the necessity to account for endogenous altruism. This is not really a new argument. For instance, Akerlof (1983) and Frank (1988) claim that the best way to appear altruistic is to actually behave like one, and such genuine altruism is likely to rub off on children. The mutuality model seems to fare better because it does not need any altruism. As Cigno (2000, p. 239) puts it: 'an altruistic parent will endow his descendants with just such a (efficient self-enforcing family) constitution. It is not that self-interested individuals behave as if they were altruists in a repeated game (as rotten kids do), but rather that altruists behave as if they were self-interested in a game played only once'.

The issue of the transmission of preferences is tackled more by biologists than by economists. Cavalli-Sforza and Feldman (1981) study cultural transmission and evolution and compare it to genetic transmission and evolution. To simplify a complicated subject, while genetic transmission is only vertical (from mother and father[82] to child), cultural transmission is also horizontal (one learns from peers) and oblique (from teacher to pupil). Thus cultural evolution can be more rapid than genetic evolution. Another difference is that it is not always easy to see how cultural changes increase

82 With the added complication of assortative mating.

Darwinian fitness, that is, how they prove an advantage in survival probability.[83] Going back to altruism, the main questions are:

1. is altruism a genetic innate trait or a cultural learned trait?

2. is there an evolutionary advantage to being an altruist?

3. what is the equivalent of a genetic mutation for the evolution of altruism?

The answer to the first question seems to be that altruism of parents towards children is at least partly innate if 'the genes are selfish' (Dawkins, 1976). Altruism toward children is then a means to increase one's genes survival probability. A parent 'naturally' wants to help a child who carries half of his genes. The so-called Hamilton rule would then predict a value of $1/2$ for the altruism parameter between parent and child.[84] But altruism is also partly cultural, thus the education effort of parents and society.[85]

Several models have been suggested to assert the evolutionary advantage of altruism. The most convincing hang around the advantage of cooperation in games of the prisoner's dilemma type (Axelrod, 1984; Bergstrom and Stark, 1993). A related question is how altruism is transmitted. We refer the reader to Bergstrom's chapter in this book, but give a flavor of such models through section 5.2.1. The tenants of the demonstration or of the gratitude effect feel that parents shape their children's preferences to obtain commitment in the absence of family contracts. Then altruism is not important *per se*, but acts like oil in the mechanics of family relationships. It is as if the family mutuality/constitution model was sufficient, but altruism made it easier to apply in real life. Also if altruism is found to prevail in family relationships, one can bet that maximizing an altruistic form of utility both gives pleasure (a tautological way of saying that it maximizes utility), and increases selection fitness (the non-altruists have been eliminated). 'Utility mirrors fitness' (Hansson and Stuart, 1990, quoted by Mulligan, 1997, p. 261). Put differently it is hard to distinguish between teaching altruism to children (demonstration, guilt), and their acceptance of altruism.

The third question may be the most interesting to an economist. Becker (1996, p. 18) refers to Karl Marx and Adam Smith and their belief that the economic process affects preferences.[86] In that classical view, for instance, governments transfer more to the old than in the past because countries are richer (an external positive shock in productivity is redistributed through pensions), with the side-effect that it diminishes 'altruistic' ties:

[83] Besides, the notions of mutation, or random drift, usual in biology and natural selection, pose problem in cultural evolution and selection. See Sethi and Somanathan (2003) for a survey on the evolutionary game theoretic literature on reciprocity in human interactions.

[84] The parameter would be $1/4$ between parent and nephew, or grand-parent and grand-child [Hamilton (1964)]. On this and related topics, see for instance Hirschleifer (1977), Bergstrom (1996), and Bergstrom (2006) in this volume. Case et al. (2000) study resource allocation in step-households, and empirically find strong influence of blood relationships on benevolence.

[85] See Lévy-Garboua et al. (2006) in this Handbook for more on psychology.

[86] Bowles (1998) also suggests that economic institutions influence motivation and values.

parents have less need of their children, thus invest less in them, therefore children feel less gratitude or imitate less, thus they take less care of their parents; therefore their own children get less altruistic imprinting, etc. An exogenous economic shock induces a cultural change: altruism is endogenous. And the whole mechanism is reinforced by the fact that behaving altruistically increases altruism and vice-versa. Sociologists would rather see a decline in altruism as a cultural change, that forces the governments to step in and take care of the old, or induces individuals to save more through banks than through their children. Mulligan (1997) addresses the question of endogenous altruism.

5.2.1. *Cultural transmission*

Models of cultural transmission of altruism have recently been developed by economists (Bergstrom and Stark, 1993; Jellal and Wolff, 2002b). They distinguish between a vertical transmission where children learn from their parents, and an oblique transmission where they learn from other members of the parents' generation (see Bisin and Verdier, 1998, 2001; Boyd and Richerson, 1985; Cavalli-Sforza and Feldman, 1981).

Consider an overlapping generation model with a continuum of agents for each generation. Each individual lives for three periods, young, adult and elderly, and decisions of transfers are only made by adults. Each adult has one child. Individuals are either altruistic or non-altruistic. As in Jellal and Wolff (2002b), altruistic adults k of type a care about their parents' utility and make financial transfers T^a to them. They maximize the utility function $U^a = U(Y_k - T^a, V(Y_p + T^a))$. Conversely, adults of type s are selfish and maximize $U^s = U(C_k)$ with $C_k = Y_k$. Then only adults of type a provide financial resources to the parents ($T^a > 0$) and may be seen as cooperators, while egoistic agents are defectors, as in Bergstrom and Stark (1993).

The rules of transmission of preferences are the following. First, there is a possible vertical transmission. The child adopts parental preferences of type a or s with probability π^i $(i = a, s)$, which is a function of parental attitude such that $\pi^a = \pi(T^a)$, with $\pi'(T^a) > 0$ and $\pi^s(T^s) = \pi^s(0) = 0$. Second, there is some horizontal transmission. With probability $(1 - \pi^i)$, the child does not inherit the parental attitude and adopts the preferences of an adult with whom he is randomly matched. How do preferences for filial care evolve in such a society? If n_t is the proportion at time t of altruistic adults, the transition probabilities P_t^{ij} that a type-i adult has a child adopting the type-j of preferences are:

$$\begin{cases} P_t^{aa} = \pi^a + (1 - \pi^a)n_t \\ P_t^{as} = (1 - \pi^a)(1 - n_t) \\ P_t^{ss} = 1 - n_t \\ P_t^{sa} = n_t \end{cases} \tag{71}$$

The altruistic parent's child is altruistic with probability π^a (the child imitates his altruistic parent), plus $(1 - \pi^a)n_t$ (the child imitates an altruistic adult), etc. The dynamics of behavior for an agent of type a is defined by:

$$n_{t+1} = n_t P_t^{aa} + (1 - n_t)P_t^{sa} \tag{72}$$

so that the long term dynamic equilibrium is given by:

$$n_{t+1} - n_t = n_t(1 - n_t)\pi(T_t^a) \tag{73}$$

Hence the cultural system converges in the long run to an homogeneous population characterized by ascending altruism[87] and, in this special case, only the altruistic preferences endogenously survives evolutionary selection. This occurs because the probability of cultural transmission increases in T^a, parents who make more transfers are more likely to have altruistic children and to be helped by them. Importantly, the model predicts an intergenerational correlation in the transfer behavior, not because of a family contract as in the mutuality model, nor because of pure probability of imitation, but because altruism is inherited. While the focus is here on child-to-parent altruism, the same model could be applied to downward transfers.

The model can be enriched so that both cooperators and defectors coexist in the long run (see Bergstrom and Stark, 1993; Bergstrom, 1995). A similar conclusion is reached and cooperation is likely to persist and flourish over time. For instance, Bergstrom and Stark (1993) consider models in which behavior is acquired by imitation. In a setting where each individual has two siblings and plays prisoners' dilemma games with each of them, they assume that reproduction depends on the average payoff received in the games played with siblings. Parents can be a two-cooperator couple, a cooperator-defector couple, or a two-defector couple, and it can be shown that the number of surviving individuals for each generation increases with the number of cooperators in the parents' generation. Thus, cooperative behavior is more likely to prevail when children have a high probability to imitate their parents.

In Bisin and Verdier (1998, 2001) intergenerational transmission of preferences is the result of deliberate inculcation by rational parents, who evaluate ex ante the well-being of their children by using their own preferences (imperfect empathy). Their model assumes what they call cultural substitution, that is, the vertical and oblique transmissions are substitutes, which amounts to $\pi^i(n_t)$ being a strictly decreasing function in n_t and $\pi^i(1) = 0$. Parents belonging to the population minority will devote more energy than those belonging to the majority in the transmission of their own traits to their children because the children are less likely to catch the trait obliquely. They show that this substitutability is sufficient (but non-necessary) to assure heterogeneity in the long run stationary distribution of preferences in the population.

5.2.2. *Endogenous altruism, prices and interest*

We already mentioned that altruism could be endogenous. First, when evoking Adam Smith's notion of approval as a condition for empathy, then when drifting from pure

[87] There are two steady states for the dynamics of the preferences distribution, $n = 0$ and $n = 1$, but $n = 0$ is locally unstable since $\frac{d(n_{t+1} - n_t)}{dn}\mid_{n=0} > 0$.

blind altruism to merit goods, finally when filial altruism grew out of parental altruism, or when cooperation proved to be a long-term winning strategy. Now, we turn to Mulligan's idea that the formation of altruism is a function of income and prices.

Instead of considering the spreading of altruism as the result of an evolutionary game, Mulligan (1997) concentrates on the degree of altruism (our U_v or β) and remarks that the intergenerational inequality in earnings depends on parents' human capital investments (and their sensitivity to parental income) and on the intergenerational transmission of ability. If altruism differs across families and especially if it is related to income, it changes the dynamic of inequality.

In Mulligan's model, parents accumulate altruism β by consuming child-oriented resources, for instance spending time with their children. Their incentives to do so depend on three parameters: the total family resources A, the interest rate r, and the price p_t of child-oriented resources. Altruism β depends on the amount of resources q_t devoted to altruism accumulation. The model includes three goods: parents' and child's consumption, and the resources devoted to children. The intergenerational budget constraint is the following (in a dynamic setting):

$$C_t + \frac{C_{t+1}}{1+r} + p_t q_t \equiv A = (1+r)X_t + Y_t + \frac{Y_{t+1}}{1+r} \tag{74}$$

where t is the period when the parent consumes, and $t+1$ is the period when the child consumes, X_t is the parental inheritance. The objective function of the parent is

$$\max_{\beta, C_t, C_{t+1}} U_P(C_t, C_{t+1}, \beta) = \min(f(\beta)C_t, g(\beta)C_{t+1}) \tag{75}$$

$f(\beta)$ and $g(\beta)$ are functions that determine the effect of altruism on preferences. For a given degree of altruism β, indifference curves in the C_t, C_{t+1} plane are L-shaped. To study the formation of altruism, he writes the quantity of child-oriented resources as a function of altruism $q_t = \theta(\beta)$.[88] At the equilibrium, the marginal cost of accumulating altruism $p\theta'(\beta)$ equals the willingness to pay for altruism. The model predicts that altruism is positively related to the resources A of parent and child, but negatively related to the price p_t of child-oriented resources, that is mainly with cost of time. This negative 'substitution' effect offsets the positive resource effect, a parent with a high wage rate invests less in the formation of altruism. Finally, a high interest rate increases altruism. It lowers the price of the child's consumption C_{t+1}, thus lowers the price of the complementary child-oriented resources. The model is silent on the return to altruism for parents in terms of old age resources.[89]

[88] For the precise assumptions of the model see Mulligan (1997, chapter 4, appendix B, p. 124). His appendix C, p. 134, generalizes the utility function to $U_P(C_t, C_{t+1}, \beta) = U(C_t) + \beta(q_t)U(C_{t+1})$. The same results obtain under the assumption of a constant elasticity of substitution of parental consumption for child consumption.

[89] Only descending altruism is considered. To account for both upward and downward transfers, a tri-generational framework is required.

That altruism is endogenous modifies some of the conclusions of the preceding sections. For instance the neutrality result may not hold. A positive exogenous shock on the parent's wage increases his value of time. Therefore the cost of accumulating altruism increases, relative to the increase in total family resources and parents may allocate a smaller fraction of their resources to their children.[90] What if the positive exogenous shock affects the child's income? Total family resources are increased, the cost of accumulating altruism is constant, parental altruism increases and parents devote a larger fraction of total family resources to the child. Parent's consumption increases less than in the exogenous altruism model. Thus when altruism is endogenous it may not provide full insurance for the family members.

Endogenous altruism also gives an additional incentive for parents to treat their children differently. Mulligan mentions four reasons; only two of them seem specific to his model. First children may differ in ability: this will change the price of giving through different rates of return to human capital investment. This can be accommodated within the exogenous altruism model, that assumes a perfect knowledge of the child's resources by the parent. Y_k has to be understood as total lifetime resources of the child. In a multi-period model where the child invests the transfer with more or less ability (be it in human capital or on the stock market), the omniscient altruist parent may well give more to the better endowed child. This is close to Stark and Zhang (2002). Second, children may differ in the price of their consumption (for instance some live in the city, others in the country, thus the same transfer would not buy the same quantity of housing for each). Again this question of quantity and price is accommodated in the exogenous altruism model where parents equalize children's marginal utilities (and not consumption). Thirdly, children may differ in the price of child oriented resources: for instance some children live close by and it is cheap to spend time with them, thus increase altruism toward them. This clearly could explain a difference in U_{v_1} and U_{v_2} in the model of section 2.3.1. Fourthly the parental willingness to pay for child oriented resources increases in child's happiness, therefore parents will be more altruistic towards a happier child and make him more transfer.[91] In terms of the merit good model, a child consuming more merit goods lowers the price of merit goods to his parents, which encourages parents to accumulate altruism.

What about the effect of government transfers to families in such a model? To the extent that they increase family resources, they will increase altruism. But if they are financed by taxes on the same families, the net effect may be to decrease altruism. In the Barro world, that is under the neutrality condition, a transfer such as pay-as-you-go social security taxing the young to give the proceed to the old, will have no

[90] In the pure exogenous altruism with two goods, $\partial T/\partial w > 0$ but $\partial S/\partial w$ could be negative because of an increase in the parental cost of time. The child could suffer, not through less altruism (altruism was exogenous), but through less total transfers (see section 2.4.3).

[91] We have seen that Becker (1991) mentions the case of child's merit goods that may affect the parental utility. But Mulligan's model goes further. Going in the opposite direction but with the same result, a child could make his parent altruistic by being a nuisance: the transfer is then made to silence him.

effect on family resources, therefore no effect on altruism. However, more tax by the young decreases their value of time (they want to work less), so decreases the price of child-oriented resources, so may encourage the formation of altruism, thus savings and long-term growth.[92]

Note that this conclusion runs counter to that of the family mutuality model, where selfish parents treat their children well because they need them. In that model, government transfers to the old lower the transfer to the child because the parents have less need of them. Therefore they may have adverse effect on the parent's treatment of children, an idea also suggested by Becker (1996, p. 128). Then government transfers are not neutralized by family actions, but government transfers may neutralize family transfers, by destroying their necessity.[93]

6. Tests of family transfer models

We announced three main types of models, three branches of a tree, but on the way we also followed some smaller ramifications. So let us trim the boughs and summarize. In the pure altruism model (1), altruist P gives to K without condition, providing P cares enough for K's well-being or P's income is high enough compared to K's. K does not bargain. The gift becomes an exchange (2) if P gives to K on the condition that K will give back to him, sooner or later, something equivalent in value or in utility. Time has an influence only in that it induces P or K to enter the game, for instance P is old (and needs care) or K is credit constrained. In the mutuality model (3), time is crucial, G is P's parent and K's is P's child. Then, P gives to G and to K, because he received from G (when he was a child) and wants to receive from K in the future.

To test the models, one needs to specify who is giving, what is given, and to whom. As stated in our introduction, there are many types of transfers and the tests require precise measurement. In this section, we first dwell on measurement issues and the importance of observing both family and institutional context, then turn to the main empirical tests of altruism and non-altruism models.

6.1. Who gives what, and to whom?

For a transfer to exist, there have to be separate entities. If parents live with their young children and feed them spaghetti (to borrow the image from Franco Modigliani) they are no separate entities (or one would enter the field of collective bargaining models) and therefore no transfer occurs. However, in real life, the separation from parents takes

[92] If taxes are payed by rich families and government programs are targeted to poor families, then the government transfer will increase both consumption and altruism of poor families and decrease altruism and consumption of rich families. Thus the effect of targeted programs may be large.

[93] In reality it strongly depends on the way the public pensions are financed. See Cigno's chapter (Cigno, 2006) in this Handbook.

place gradually, and the bulk of intergenerational *inter vivos* transfers occurs around the time when the household splits, when the children leave home. Around that period, spaghetti eating gradually becomes receiving a transfer (think of college tuition in the USA or student housing in countries where tuition is free). Besides, the widespread practice of providing children with pocket money has been found in line with transfer models (Furnham, 1999, 2001; Barnet-Verzat and Wolff, 2002). And did not parents giving an allowance to their 20 year old student child, prepare her to use it properly by providing her with pocket money when she was younger, and still at home? Is then pocket money a transfer, when spaghetti was not? Are students really separate?

Later in life, the student marries, maybe she divorces. She temporarily comes back to live with her parents. Co-residence provides her with a transfer, which has much in common with the parents paying her rent, but is also different. She marries again, gets a collateral from her parents when she buys a house, she begets children who spend the school vacations at their grand parents. Her father dies, all the family comes to live in the parent's home and take care of her invalid mother. She inherits the house at her mother's death. This simple example (two parents, one child, no in-laws) shows the difficulty of defining the actors (the 'whos') and the direction of the transfers (the 'what'). Clearly, there exists a continuum, from pocket money to bequest, through financial gifts, services, care and co-residence, and one of the main empirical issue is to observe and record the transfers, and evaluate them in a common unit.

Economists have first focused on bequests. Challenging the altruism explanation developed in Becker (1974), Bernheim et al. (1985) suggest that bequests correspond to the payment of the child's attention. However, transfers at death are not necessarily voluntary.[94] If bequests arise only because of uncertainty on life expectancy, they are accidental (Davies, 1981). However, parents who do not want the children to inherit have the option to make a will. Since the vast majority do not disinherit their children, this is *a contrario* a proof if not of active altruism, then at least of passive acquiescence to altruism towards children: there is no outside preferred option for benevolence. By contrast, *inter vivos* transfers are always voluntary. But their empirical study may be difficult, since they are generally smaller in value than bequests and not always registered.

Some suggested to infer about the motive from the way the gifts or bequest were shared between siblings, since altruistic parents should provide more to their less well-off children. In the United States of America, bequests tend to be equally shared among siblings, while gifts rather go to poorer children (Dunn and Phillips, 1997; McGarry, 1999, 2001; Wilhelm, 1996). It could be that parents can be more altruistic with *inter vivos* gifts because they can handle siblings jealousy more easily while they are alive. Besides as we have shown (see section 2.3.1), several theoretical models can accommodate equal sharing of bequests and altruism.

Bequests and formally registered *inter vivos* gifts are important masses, but are less frequent than other smaller money transfers. In survey data, parents may be tempted to

[94] For a survey on bequest motive, see Laitner and Ohlsson (2001) and Masson and Pestieau (1997).

report only large transfers, that occur only rarely. Thus, for a given year, the probability to observe a transfer is low. A solution would be to record the transfers over a longer period of time. But retrospective questions have to be carefully phrased to overcome memory problem (and the models require information about the donor's and recipient's characteristics at the date of each transfer), and diaries kept over shorter periods usually yield better results. It is also necessary to induce the individual to recall all forms of monetary transfers, including loans and their rate of interest, down-payments, the paying of a rent, etc. Some transfers may be in-kind: food, meals, the lending of a house, etc. Time-related services (visits, telephone calls, baby-sitting, letters, care, help, support...) may seem easier to record because they occur fairly frequently, but they are so varied that few surveys can combine information on all types of transfers, both given and received, by all the members of a household. Besides, time and money transfers are difficult to evaluate in a common unit.[95]

Measuring time spent together may not provide the right information on who is really the recipient of assistance. For instance, both in the United States of America and in France, parents of young children are more likely to have contact and to visit their parents than childless couples. Cox and Stark (1996) interpret this as attention given to the parents, according to their demonstration mechanism. However, Wolff (2001) shows that adults with children are more likely to visit their parents because the latter look after the grandchildren. Then visits to parents are not an upward transfer of leisure time, but a downward help to grandchildren's which benefits their parents and the interpretation in terms of demonstration is misleading. Even when the true recipient of time transfers is not questionable (as for care given to an old parent), parents and children may have the double role of donor and recipient.[96] How should the net transfer be measured, if both gain from the exchange?

In home-sharing (McElroy, 1985; Rosenzweig and Wolpin, 1993; Ermisch and Di Salvo, 1997), who benefits, parents or children, may be unclear. Co-residence is different from other transfers in many aspects. First, do parents and children share all expenses? Home-sharing is likely to go along with many services flowing in both directions. Second, it is a cheaper than paying for another independent home because of the public good nature of housing. This is linked to the question of the price of transfer, that is overlooked in models with one consumption good.[97] Finally, home sharing entails a privacy cost for both generations. If poorer children are found to stay longer at the parental home (Dunn and Phillips, 1998; Wolff, 1999), it is compatible with altruism toward the less well-off child, but also to his having a lower privacy cost than his siblings, if privacy is a normal good.

[95] The true value of a gift to the beneficiary may anyway be problematic (see Prendergast and Stole, 2001).

[96] Taking care of an old cantankerous person is surely a high valued time transfer. If this person is full of wisdom and interesting stories, it may be a pleasure to push her wheelchair.

[97] If parents are reactive to the tax system, it proves that they take into account the price of transfer. Arrondel and Laferrère (2001) find that *inter vivos* gifts and bequests strongly react to change in taxation. See also Poterba (2001).

Not only transfers are to be recorded, but the model requires good control variables, especially on incomes of both givers and potential beneficiaries. If most surveys inform about the income of the respondent, few ask about relatives living outside, be they children who left, old parents or in-laws. It is the very nature of models of inter-related utilities or family reciprocities to be very demanding on the data. Many tests are not conclusive for lack of contextual information.

6.2. Institutions and family transfers

Our section 5.2 on cultural transmission and endogenous preferences raised the questions of the influence of the exogenous institutions (credit, pension, insurance) on family transfers motives and of the possible endogeneity of those institutions. Families, public and market services interact. In other words, when differences in altruism are found between countries, do they stem from differences in preferences (for instance a Japanese is less altruistic than an American, see Horioka et al., 2000) or from differences in constraints and institutions?

In countries without public pension schemes, there are no alternative forms of support for the elderly than relying on their children's assistance. In those with little unemployment insurance for the young, parents provide a safety net. If there is no possibility to borrow to buy a house, children stay home longer. In developed countries, the living standard is higher for the older generations than for the youths, transfers flow downwards and no financial repayment from middle-aged adults to the elderly is observed. The latter receive care and services from their children but no money transfers. But the presence of market substitutes for care tends to decrease the provision of attention. Looking at monetary transfers, one is likely to find altruism or family insurance mechanism in poor countries, and not in rich ones. On the other hand, the reverse may be true for transfers in care and visits if being richer leaves more time for such activities, more demand for goods with no market substitutes, and more leverage to buy the children's attention.

For instance, comparing Spain and Italy (the South) to Germany, Britain and the US (the North), Bentolila and Ichino (2000) find that an increase in the duration of unemployment spells of male household heads is associated with smaller consumption losses in the South. Given that both social welfare institutions and credit and insurance markets are more developed in the North, the result is puzzling. They conclude that extended family networks are stronger in the South than in the North and provide insurance against unemployment in Southern countries.

There are interactions between preferences, constraints, institutions and behavior. It may be that preferences are the same, but that endowment constraints yield different behaviors, either geographically between countries with different institutions, within a country between families with different wealth levels, or along the life-cycle for a given family. A change in institution may affect the very pattern of private transfers, thus apparently the preferences. As altruism is a morally loaded word, before ruling it out, or concluding to its prevalence, one should be aware of the institutional context where families evolve.

6.3. The limited scope of pure altruism

The most clear-cut prediction of the pure altruism model is the neutrality result, the difference in transfer-income derivatives:[98]

$$\frac{\partial T}{\partial Y_p} - \frac{\partial T}{\partial Y_k} = 1$$

It provides an effective way to test the presence of altruism. However, it is not straightforward to implement. First, it requires information on the amount given, the current incomes of both the parents and the beneficiary child, and non-beneficiary siblings, and also the levels of their permanent income if they enter the parent's information set at the time of the transfer decision.[99] Altonji et al. (1997) mention that not controlling properly for the income of one generation may introduce a bias against altruism. Two datasets provide (at least part of) the necessary information: the Panel Study of Income Dynamics (PSID) for the US, and the cross-sectional Trois Générations CNAV survey for France (on a sub-sample of middle-aged households with old parents and adult children). Second, the test itself raises some econometric problems (Altonji et al., 1997). One is due to the non-observability of the altruism parameter, the distribution of which influences the existence of positive transfers (through the ratio of incomes Y_p/Y_k, in a logarithmic setting). Not taking it into account, leads to a bias against altruism since families with richer children have to be relatively more altruistic for transfers to appear (see section 2.1). The problem can be solved by integrating over the intensity of altruism.[100] Another econometric problem stems from the fact that the transfers have to be positive for the test to be valid (the parent is not 'at a corner'). Altonji et al. (1997) propose a sophisticated way to correct the selectivity bias, using a selection-corrected derivative estimator for non-separable limited dependent variables (see also Altonji and Ichimura, 1999). Thus, the econometrician evaluates the expectation of the difference $E(\partial T/\partial Y_p - \partial T/\partial Y_k \mid T > 0)$. Ideally, to test the neutrality result, one should use data providing 'derivatives' across time: how a *change* in parent's income matched by a *change* in child's income coincides with a *change* in transfer. It could be likely that significant changes in incomes affect the decision of transfers, with new families engaging

[98] Compensatory gift probabilities are compatible with both altruism and exchange motive.

[99] This question of possible imperfect information of parent is a problem, both in theory, and empirically (what are the right variables to 'control for'?). See our section 2.4.1 and also the discussion in Villanueva (2001). Note that in-laws could also enter the picture. And should an annualized value of expected bequest be added to the current measure of *inter vivos* parent-to-child transfers?

[100] As the difference in derivatives is always equal to one whatever the degree of altruism, the equality still holds when the caring parameter is above the threshold value corresponding to interior solutions (see Altonji et al., 1997).

in private redistribution, others becoming constrained. Instead of such 'within' family derivatives (that could be obtained from natural experiment or from panel data), one only uses cross-section data and compares 'between' households derivatives of income.

The first measure of the difference in transfer-income derivative is due to Cox and Rank (1992) who find a very low value (around 0.003), but use an imputed measure for parental income. Using the PSID, Altonji et al. (1997) find a positive but low difference estimate. With regard to the child's income, the transfer derivative is equal to −0.09, while it is 0.04 for the parent's income. This leads to a difference of 0.13, far from the unitary value requested by pure altruism. Following the same econometric method on French data, Wolff (2000c) finds a selection-corrected transfer derivative equal to 0.009 for the parent's income and to 0.012 for the child's income, so that the difference is negative and of very low magnitude (−0.003).[101] Parents seem not to react much to variations of their own and their children's income. This finding is consistent with evidence that American parent's and child's households do not pool their resources for (food) consumption (Altonji et al., 1992). However, a third test conducted by Raut and Tran (2005) on Indonesian data, in a totally different institutional context, estimates a difference of 0.956 which is consistent with altruism of children towards their parents.

As shown in McGarry (2000), a small or negative difference in the transfer-income derivative can be compatible with altruism in a dynamic setting where parents are not fully informed about their child's future income. Villanueva (2001) shows using simulation that not only imperfect information but an endogenous child's effort could also explain why parents provide transfers that do not respond much to both child's and parent's incomes. He finds that for the household of a married child the probability to receive a transfer is higher if the primary earner looses some income than if the more flexible secondary earner does. This is consistent with parental imperfect information or endogeneity of the secondary earner's income.

The empirical conclusions of Altonji et al. (1997) are similar to the results of many other less econometrically precise tests. In general, the strong predictions of pure altruism are not supported, but evidence of impure altruism can be found. Using an estimated income for the potential donor, Cox (1987) finds a positive relationship between the recipient's income and the transfer amount after controlling for selectivity bias: this rules out altruism. Cox and Rank (1992) go one step further, by showing that not only do earnings affect positively the gift received, but that the probability to receive a transfer is positively related to measures of child's services. Even if the validity of the test is challenged by Altonji et al. (1997), these results are more consistent with exchange than altruism. Cox (1990) reflects on the recipient's permanent income. While the transfer decision only depends on the marginal utility of consumption from current income under altruism, the gift value should be negatively related to the child's current income

[101] In both studies, accounting for non-linearities in incomes, child's endogenous income or changing the econometric specification (using least absolute deviations for instance) does not affect the result and the unitary value is always rejected.

and positively to his future income if the exchange mechanism is motivated by liquidity constraints of the child. Empirically, the decision to transfer seems strongly linked to liquidity constraints of the beneficiary, but the amount of the transfer is not (Cox, 1990; Cox and Jappelli, 1990).

The timing of transfers is closely related to the motive. For instance, under altruism, the parents should transfer when the children are in a needy position, especially when entering the adult life. However, bequests are larger than *inter vivos* transmissions. Besides, Poterba (2001) and McGarry (2001) find that Americans do not take full advantage from the legal tax-avoiding device of *inter vivos* gifts, that could reduce the price paid for transferring their wealth. This could be explained by precaution for old-age long term care, but also by concern about the adverse effect of gift on the children. This would mean the pure altruism model is mitigated by consideration of endogenous child's work incentives problem, and merit goods.

Rather than relying on these income effects, which leads to an apparent rejection of altruism, some authors incorporate both time and money transfers, and in both directions. Using the PSID, Ioannides and Kan (2000) find that parents' and adult children's behavior is consistent with altruism, but that there is a significant dispersion of the altruism parameter among parents. Altonji et al. (2000) and Schoeni (1997) also find that transfers decrease income inequality, poorer family members receiving higher amounts of transfers. In addition, time transfers are neither related to income, nor to financial assistance. Such a result rules out the strategic exchange motive. In the United States, time-related assistance to the elderly is mainly devoted to those in poor health, thus comforting altruism (see Sloan et al., 1996, 2002). Perozek (1998) finds that the sensibility to the parent's wealth is very dependent on the econometric specification and the available control variables. But she finds no effect of parent's wealth on care. Again, children's services do not seem to be made in order to get the parents' bequests.

Another empirical strategy is to focus on the distribution of transfers among siblings. McGarry and Schoeni (1995) assign each child a ranking based on his relative income position among siblings and one based on the parental gift value, and show that the correlation between the two ranks is negative. After controlling for unobserved heterogeneity in parental altruism, McGarry and Schoeni (1995) and Dunn (1997) find that the child's income is negatively related to the magnitude of gift value, and that liquidity constrained children are more likely to be recipient (McGarry, 1999).[102] This negative relationship also holds for specific family sizes. In addition, McGarry and Schoeni (1997) provide additional evidence that intra-family financial gifts to the less well-off children are not linked to an exchange of upstream care, controlling for unobserved differences across families. That parents give more either to the less well-off children or elderly parents is consistent with altruism.

[102] Family fixed effects control for the time invariant characteristics of the parents and home environment that do not vary for all the siblings within the family, and provide an unbiased estimate of the effect of the recipient's income.

In France however, cross-section data cast doubt on the altruistic motive. For instance, Arrondel and Masson (1991) and Arrondel and Wolff (1998), controlling for selectivity bias, show that richer children receive higher amount of donations from parents. However, the gifts add all transfers received up to the date of the survey, and the beneficiary's characteristics at the date of survey are not necessarily those at the date of the gift. This timing problem is corrected in Arrondel and Laferrère (2001) who use adequate measures of both current and permanent beneficiary's income. Again they exhibit non-compensatory effects for the child's resources. But they use only proxies for the parents' income and wealth. Wolff (2000c) controls both for the parent's and the child's income and wealth. He finds that the occurrence of a gift is compensatory, but that young and middle-aged children receive significantly higher amounts of transfer when they are richer. Jürges (1999) reaches the same conclusion in Germany, with a small positive effect of the child's income on gift value.

With numerous co-authors, Cox tests altruism on microeconomic data from various poorer countries. Family transfers are large and widespread in Eastern Europe during the transition to capitalism. Focusing on Russia in 1992 and 1993, Cox et al. (1996) find that private transfers help to equalize the income distribution within families and significantly diminish poverty. In Poland, private transfers act as safety nets and flow from high to low-income households, even if the response slightly declines over time (Cox et al., 1997). In Vietnam, private transfers tend to be targeted towards vulnerable low-income households. However they are also disproportionately given to the well-educated family members (Cox et al., 1997), and in Peru transfers received increase with the recipient's pre-transfer income (Cox et al., 1998). All in all family transfers seem more altruistic (in the sense that they benefit less well-off recipients) in poorer economies, but they are also compatible with family insurance mechanism.[103]

As pointed out by Cox et al. (2004), non-linearities income may lead to an erroneous rejection of altruism. Altruism should be present when the beneficiary is poor. But as soon as the child's income rises above a certain threshold, transfers are likely to be an exchange. Treating the knot point as an unknown parameter, Cox et al. (2004) find such a non-linear relationship between transfers and recipients' incomes for the Philippines. In France, Wolff (1998) also finds such non-linearities: the gift value received by adult children first decreases when their income increases, then the transfer derivative for the recipient becomes positive. These findings suggest that altruism is not the only motivation for family transfers.

Different motives are likely to coexist in the course of the life cycle or across different populations. Various forms of help respond to specific parental purposes. Arrondel and Laferrère (1998) show that wealth transfers of the moderately wealthy conform to 'family models', but the transfer behavior of the very affluent neither is altruistic, nor

[103] In France, a survey of homeless shows that the early absence of all family ties and roots is a strong factor of marginalization, which a contrario proves that family economic links are important, if no proof that they are altruistic (Marpsat and Firdion, 1996).

motivated by exchange, nor stems from a mutuality model.[104] Studying pocket money, Barnet-Verzat and Wolff (2002) reject the assumption of a unique motive. Regular allowances fit in an inter-temporal framework, irregular payments depend on the need of the recipient and are closer to altruistic motives. But among them, some are a means of payment of services while others reward the children for their results at school (merit goods). School effort is then endogenous and parents may shape their children preferences (Weinberg, 2001). Dustmann and Micklewright (2001) note that children are likely to reduce their willingness to participate in the labor market when parental cash transfers increase.

6.4. *Tests of family mutuality models*

According to the mutuality model, family transfers from parents are a form of investment that the children pay back later. The fact that transfers flow from the middle-aged adults both to the elderly and to the young is compatible with the model. However, it is also consistent with two-sided altruism if parents are richer than both their children and the grandparents. Conversely if the transfers only flow from the old to the young generations it is problematic for an inter-temporal exchange since the previous receipt of assistance would never be repaid. Finally, if family transfers are only ascending, they may be interpreted as preference shaping of the young generation. But as one attempts to combine monetary help, services and affection, the interpretation is less clear.

Although the family constitution model needs both upward and downward assistance, some tests only focus on transfers from parents to children. Using cross-sectional data from Italy, Cigno et al. (1998) point to three results consistent with the self-interest hypothesis of parents investing in young adult children. First, the probability of transferring resources is positively related to the parents' level of income, either transitory or permanent, but the marginal effects are very low (the beneficiary's income is not controlled for). This low sensitivity contradicts altruism. Second, having received cash transfers from one's parents at any time in the past significantly influences the probability of making a transfer to one's child. This may be seen as a credit network used by all the succeeding generations. Thirdly, they find a positive influence of being credit constrained on the probability of *making* a transfer to somebody outside the household, which clearly is not a prediction of altruism but is compatible with a high family rate of return.[105]

Looking at transfers in kind (providing a house, acting as collateral) or in cash (paying for the rent, making money gifts or loans) to non-co-resident children in France,

[104] Tax considerations, dynastic motives or firm survival are relevant factors. The strong reaction to tax incentives of inheritance and gifts is compatible with a simple joy of giving model (Arrondel and Laferrère, 2001). The affluent hold a large proportion of the wealth, therefore their behavior has a strong influence on some empirical tests.

[105] See the discussion in Cigno and Rosati (2000), and also Cigno et al. (2004). Rather than using household data, Cigno and Rosati (1996) focus on macroeconomic time series on fertility, interest rate, savings and public deficit, with results in favor of the mutuality model.

Laferrère (1997) finds that each form of transfers corresponds to a different motive. Helping an adult child with housing is not linked to credit constraints of the helping parents, and may stem from altruism. While similar in certain respects, money transfers are made more frequently by parents who are or have been constrained in the credit market, which is in line with the family mutuality model. Finally, loans and collaterals are closer to a family credit system.[106]

Do middle-aged adults ever repay their parents for transfers received earlier? A brief look at aggregate data reveals that upstream flows of money remain rare. For example, in France, the sum of inheritance, gifts and financial help to children is more than ten times greater than upward monetary assistance (Laferrère, 1999, Table 1, p. 21). Either ascending altruism is low, or the repayment of the parental transfers in the family self-interested network does not exist, or upstream assistance takes a non-monetary form. Because the current level of retirement benefits make the parental income high compared to the children's, elderly parents are more likely to need services without market substitutes such as affection and attention than money. Clearly, survey data shows the importance of time-related assistance compared to upstream financial transfers (Soldo and Hill, 1993; Attias-Donfut, 1995).

In a joint study of downstream and upstream transfers, Wolff (2000b) shows that financial help from middle-aged adults to children mainly corresponds to investment in human capital. Thus, if the mutuality model holds, one should observe that more educated adults provide more care to their elders. However, education has no significant effect on upstream transfers (either financial or time-related).[107] Similar results are found for the United States (McGarry and Schoeni, 1997; Schoeni, 1997; Sloan et al., 2002), so that the presence of a repayment is not warranted. As already mentioned, care is mainly devoted to parents in poor health and characterized by low incomes. That less well-off parents receive more is rather consistent with child's altruism. In the mutuality model, the situation of the elderly recipient should not really matter in the transfer decision.[108]

However, the well-documented strong heritability of transmission practices is not predicted by altruism nor exchange models, but more in accordance with the existence of family constitutions of some demonstration or education mechanism (Arrondel and Masson, 1991; Laferrère, 1997; Arrondel and Wolff, 1998; Cigno et al., 1998). Parents help their children when they have been helped in the past by their own parents and the result holds when both the donor and recipient's incomes are controlled for (Jellal and Wolff, 2002c). In the upward direction, parents are more likely to care for their elders

[106] Using the same data, Arrondel and Wolff (1998) separate wealth transfers between generations (inheritance, donations, some of the gifts and help) from education spending. Different motives are also associated to different types of assistance.

[107] Others results for descending transfers are rather consistent with the mutuality model: individuals who suffered from financial difficulties in their youth are more likely to help their children (Wolff, 2000b).

[108] Such an empirical strategy is used by Cigno et al. (1998, 2004) who however only account for the donor's characteristics when explaining family transfers.

when the latter have themselves provided care to their own parents (Jellal and Wolff, 2002b). In the family mutuality model, care-giving is a signal to the children that the family contract is accepted, so that they will go on with their own children. For the parents, the belief that investing in the children is better than investing on the market is encouraged by the fact that they have been helped themselves by their parents, so that family investment looks less risky than other options. Preferences are thus shaped by the receipt of a transfer and information goes along with transmission.

There is some evidence that people act towards their parents as they would like their children to act towards themselves: in France, women and adults in poor health are more likely to provide time-related assistance to their parents.[109] Finally, a way of repaying the parents is to do it through one's own children, the grand-children (Rosati, 1996). If an adult is not able to repay the parents because of a premature death or a too high parental income, the debt would be paid by transfers to the grandchildren in the very way the parents had behaved when the adult was in the child's position.

Using data on time and money transfers between generations in Malaysia, Bommier (1995) wonders whether children can be relied on to look after their parents in their old age. The data do not support the strategic model: for a given child, the decision to transfer money to the parents does not depend on the other siblings' choices. He and Lillard and Willis (1997) find evidence that children are an important source of old-age security. Clearly, children repay for earlier parental investment in education in countries with no pension system. Also, parents and children engage in the exchange of time help for money. However, as noted by Bommier (1995), it is difficult to reject altruism since the transfers are directed towards the parents who need them most. One has to keep in mind that the altruism and insurance motives lead to similar predictions.

Thus, while some predictions of the exchange motive and of the self-interest model fit with the data according to some authors, the stronger test of pure altruism seem rejected, especially for financial transfers. However less stringent implications of altruism are clearly verified. The altruistic model may be a victim of its simplicity, the other models offering less clear cut testable predictions. Table 5 offers a summary of empirical results, concentrating on evidence on transfer amounts in developed countries.

7. Conclusion: homo reciprocans, or living in a world of externalities

Identifying the motives of family intergenerational transfers is important because of their potential effect on inequality,[110] their relation to public transfers (whether they

[109] Arrondel and Masson (2001), Wolff (1998), Kotlikoff and Morris (1989). However, Byrne et al. (2002) find no sex differences in the care for old parents, once individual wages (thus the opportunity cost of time) have been taken into account. Another result is that the number of children increases the probability that parents make cash gifts to their elders, and they are also more likely to expect money from their children if they themselves make financial transfers to their parents (Cox and Stark, 1998a; Arrondel and Masson, 2001).

[110] See Cremer and Pestieau (2006) in this Handbook on the optimal taxation of family wealth transfers.

Table 5
Motives for *inter vivos* transfers in developed countries: evidence from transfer amounts

Authors	Date	Data	dT/dY_d	dT/dY_r	Δ (dT/dY)	dS/dY_d	dS/dY_r	Econometric model	Transfer motive
United States									
Altonji et al.	1997	PSID	+	−	0.1			Non-linear	Reject altruism
Altonji et al.	2000	PSID	+	−		n.s.	n.s.	Tobit	Reject exchange
Bernheim et al.	1985	LRHS					+	Two-stage least squares	Strategic exchange
Cox	1987	PCPP	+	+				Two-step selectivity	Exchange
Cox	1990	PCPP	+	+				Two-step selectivity	Exchange (liquidity constraint)
Cox and Jappelli	1990	SCF		−	−			Tobit	Exchange (liq. const.)
Cox and Raines	1985	PCPP		−				Tobit	Altruism
Cox and Rank	1992	NSFH	n.s.	+	0.003			Generalized Tobit	Exchange (payment of services)
Cox and Stark	1996	NSFH				−		OLS	Demonstration (grandchil-dren)
Dunn	1997	NLS	+	−				Tobit	Altruism
Hochguertel and Ohlsson	2003	HRS	+	−				Tobit	Altruism
Ioannides and Kan	2000	PSID	+	+		−	+	Tobit	2-sided altruism
McGarry	2000	HRS		−				OLS	Altruism (lagged and future incomes)
McGarry and Schoeni	1995	HRS	+	−				OLS	Altruism
McGarry and Schoeni	1997	AHEAD	+	−				OLS	Altruism
Perozek	1998	NSFH					n.s.	Two-stage least squares	Reject strategic exchange
Schoeni	1997	PSID	+	−		−	n.s.	Tobit	Altruism
Sloan et al.	1997	NLTCS				−	n.s.	Two-step selectivity	Reject strategic exchange
Sloan et al.	2002	HRS	+	−		n.s.	n.s.	Tobit	Altruism
Villanueva	2001	PSID	+	−	0.22			Non-linear	Altruism (asymmetric information)

Table 5
(*Continued*)

Authors	Date	Data	dT/dY_d	dT/dY_r	$\Delta (dT/dY)$	dS/dY_d	dS/dY_r	Econometric model	Transfer motive
France									
Arrondel and Laferrère	2001	Actifs Financiers		+				Two-step selectivity	Reject altruism
Arrondel and Masson	1991	Actifs Financiers		+				Two-step selectivity	Reject altruism
Arrondel and Wolff	1998	Actifs Financiers		+				Two-step selectivity	Reject altruism
Jellal and Wolff	2002a	3 Générat.				n.s.	+	Tobit	Cultural transmission of altruism
Wolff	2000b	3 Générat.	+	+	−0.003			Non-linear	Reject altruism
Germany									
Bhaumik	2001	GSOEP		−				Tobit	Altruism
Croda	2000	GSOEP	+					OLS	Altruism
Jürges	1999	GSOEP	+	n.s.				Generalized Tobit	Reject altruism
Italy									
Cigno et al.	1998	Bank of Italy	+					Two-step selectivity	Reject altruism and exchange
Cigno et al.	2004	Indagine Multiscopo	+					Tobit	Mutuality model (credit rationing)

Note: PSID: Panel Study of Income Dynamics. LRHS: Longitudinal Retirement History Study. PCPP: President's Commission on Pension Policy. SCF: Survey of Consumer Finances. NSFH: National Survey of Families and Households. NLS: National Longitudinal Survey; HRS: Health and Retirement Survey. AHEAD: Assets and Health Dynamics of the Oldest-Old. NLTCS: National Long-Term Care Survey; Actifs Financiers: French National Institute of Statistics and Economics Studies survey on wealth. 3 Générations: Caisse Nationale d'Assurance Vieillesse Survey. GSOEP: German Socio-Economic Panel.

crowd-out, crowd-in or have no effect on private transfers), and the link between the services and credit provided by the family and those provided by the market. To those reasons, which are mostly analyzed from the point of view of the giver, or the passive beneficiary, another should be added: the effects of the gift on a reactive beneficiary. The most recent developments of the models are concerned with the reactions of the object of philanthropy. Especially how he modifies his time allocation, work effort or human capital investment. It is not only government transfers that may or may not be displaced by private transfers, but effort and other time use, that can be 'displaced' by both private and public transfers. This is particularly important at the beginning of an adult life, when a new household, i.e. a new potential recipient of transfer, is created, and at the very end of life, when elders need help that the market cannot provide, and do not want to be a burden on their children. The question of incentives, or in biblical terms, the Samaritan dilemma, becomes central in the study of intergenerational transfers.

The insight of sociology, psychology and anthropology that any transfer implies reciprocity (the gift and counter-gift of Marcel Mauss) is absent from altruism models. In that sense, the exchange or mutuality models seem more satisfactory. Without taking directly into account phenomena such as the power of the giver over the receiver, these models can incorporate reciprocal actions. Their insight into the timing of exchange, and the long term investment characteristics of help, conforms to intuition. Helping is a form of insurance to be helped in return if and when needed. A precious good is stored. And this good, a part of social capital, is transferable to a third party member of the network.[111] What is put forward by the inter-temporal exchange model is also the sequence of generations, with the successive roles everybody occupies: as a beneficiary child, as a giving parent, then as helped grandparent. The coexistence of three generations is crucial to the model. In comparison, altruism needs only two generations or two partners, and one does not have to occupy each of the different roles.

However the intuition of altruism that 'each of us is made of a cluster of appartenances', as Henry James wrote, has a very strong appeal. How could it be denied that our utility is influenced by others' utility, and not only by what they can give or ask from us? And the sign of the derivative of U, the altruist's utility, with respect to V, the non-altruist's utility, is, without doubt, not always positive. Envy, jealousy, the desire to protect oneself, and altruism, are intertwined. Thus in spite of the many reasons for altruism to be impure, the simple basic model remains an interesting benchmark.

The models are simplistic. However, with simple specifications, they provide different predictions, that are testable to a certain extent. In an age of crisis, of both family and public transfers, be it of the retirement system facing the demographic pressure of the baby-boomers, rising life expectancy and lower fertility, or of the health benefit systems faced with the costs of care to the very old, or of unemployment insurance, it is important to know how private, market and public transfers between the generations are connected.

References

Akerlof, G.A. (1983). "Loyalty filters". American Economic Review 73, 54–63.

Altonji, J.G., Hayashi, F., Kotlikoff, L.J. (1992). "Is the extended family altruistically linked? Direct tests using micro data". American Economic Review 82, 1177–1198.

Altonji, J.G., Hayashi, F., Kotlikoff, L.J. (1997). "Parental altruism and inter vivos transfers: Theory and evidence". Journal of Political Economy 105, 1121–1166.

[111] 'Can you give me some information on this school for my niece', (*hinting*, 'you remember I gave you a good address for your vacation)'.

Altonji, J.G., Hayashi, F., Kotlikoff, L.J. (2000). "The effects of income and wealth on time and money transfers between parents and children". In: Mason, A., Tapinos, G. (Eds.), Sharing the Wealth. Oxford University Press, New York, pp. 306–357.

Altonji, J.G., Ichimura, H. (1999). "Estimating derivatives in nonseparable models with limited dependent variables", mimeo, University of Northwestern.

Anderberg, D., Balestrino, A. (2003). "Self-enforcing intergenerational transfers and the provision of education". Economica 70, 55–71.

Arrondel, L., Laferrère, A. (1998). "Succession capitaliste et succession familiale: Un modèle économétrique à deux régimes endogènes". Annales d'Économie et de Statistique 51, 187–208.

Arrondel, L., Laferrère, A. (2001). "Taxation and wealth transmission in France". Journal of Public Economics 79, 3–33.

Arrondel, L., Masson, A. (1991). "Que nous enseignent les enquêtes sur les transferts patrimoniaux en France ?". Économie et Prévision 100–101, 93–128.

Arrondel, L., Masson, A. (2001). "Family transfers involving three generations". Scandinavian Journal of Economics 103, 415–443.

Arrondel, L., Masson, A. (2006). "Altruism, exchange or indirect reciprocity: What do the data on family transfers show?". In: Kolm, S.C., Mercier-Ythier, J. (Eds.), Handbook on the Economics on Giving, Reciprocity and Altruism. North-Holland.

Arrondel, L., Wolff, F.C. (1998). "La nature des transferts inter vivos en France: Investissements humains, aides financières et transmission du patrimoine". Économie et Prévision 135, 1–27.

Attanasio, O.P., Lechene, V. (2002). "Tests of income pooling in households decisions". Review of Economic Dynamics 5, 720–748.

Attanasio, O.P., Rios-Rull, J.V. (2000). "Consumption smoothing in island economies: Can public insurance reduce welfare?". European Economic Review 44, 1225–1258.

Attias-Donfut, C. (1995). Les Solidarités Entre Générations. Vieillesse, Familles, État. Nathan, Paris.

Axelrod, R. (1984). The Evolution of Cooperation. Basic Books, New York.

Balestrino, A. (1997). "Education policy in a non-altruistic model of intergenerational transfers with endogenous fertility". European Journal of Political Economy 13, 157–169.

Barnet-Verzat, C., Wolff, F.C. (2002). "Motives for pocket money allowances and family incentives". Journal of Economic Psychology 23, 339–366.

Barro, R.J. (1974). "Are government bonds net wealth?". Journal of Political Economy 82, 1095–1117.

Barro, R.J., Becker, G.S. (1988). "A reformulation of the economic theory of fertility". Quarterly Journal of Economics 98, 371–400.

Becker, G.S. (1974). "A theory of social interactions". Journal of Political Economy 82, 1063–1093.

Becker, G.S. (1991). A Treatise on The Family. Harvard University Press, Cambridge.

Becker, G.S. (1993). "Nobel Lecture: The economic way of looking at behavior". Journal of Political Economy 101, 385–409.

Becker, G.S. (1996). Accounting for Tastes. Harvard University Press, Cambridge.

Becker, G.S., Murphy, K.M. (1988). "The family and the state". Journal of Law and Economics 31, 1–18.

Behrman, J.R. (1997). "Intrahousehold distribution and the family". In: Rosenzweig, M.R., Stark, O. (Eds.), Handbook of Population and Family Economics, vol. 1A. North-Holland, Amsterdam, pp. 125–187.

Ben-Porath, Y. (1980). "The F-connection: Families, friends, and firms and the organization of exchange". Population and Development Review 6, 1–30.

Bentolila, S., Ichino, A. (2000). "Unemployment and consumption: are job losses less painful near the Mediterranean?". CESifo Working paper 372.

Bergstrom, T.C. (1989a). "A fresh look at the Rotten-Kid theorem—and other household mysteries". Journal of Political Economy 97, 1138–1159.

Bergstrom, T.C. (1989b). "Love and spaghetti, the opportunity cost of virtue". Journal of Economic Perspectives 3, 165–173.

Bergstrom, T.C. (1995). "On the evolution of altruistic ethical rules for siblings". American Economic Review 85, 58–81.

Bergstrom, T.C. (1996). "Economics in a family way". Journal of Economic Literature 34, 1903–1934.
Bergstrom, T.C. (1997). "A survey of theories of the family". In: Rosenzweig, M.R., Stark, O. (Eds.), Handbook of Population and Family Economics, vol. 1A. North-Holland, Amsterdam, pp. 21–79.
Bergstrom, T.C. (1999). "Systems of benevolent utility functions". Journal of Public Economic Theory 1 (1), 71–100.
Bergstrom, T.C. (2006). "Evolution and social behavior: individual and group". In: Kolm, S.C., Mercier-Ythier, J. (Eds.). Handbook on the Economics on Giving Reciprocity and Altruism. North-Holland.
Bergstrom, T.C., Blume, L., Varian, H. (1986). "On the private provision of public goods". Journal of Public Economics 29, 25–49.
Bergstrom, T.C., Cornes, R.C. (1983). "Independence of allocative efficiency from distribution in the theory of public goods". Econometrica 51, 1753–1765.
Bergstrom, T.C., Stark, O. (1993). "How altruism can prevail under natural selection". American Economic Review 83, 149–155.
Bernheim, B.D., Severinov, S. (2003). "Bequests as signals: An explanation for the equal division puzzle". Journal of Political Economy 111, 733–764.
Bernheim, B.D., Shleifer, A., Summers, L.H. (1984). "Bequests as a means of payment". NBER Working Paper 1303.
Bernheim, B.D., Shleifer, A., Summers, L.H. (1985). "The strategic bequest motive". Journal of Political Economy 93, 1045–1076.
Bernheim, B.D., Stark, O. (1988). "Altruism within the family reconsidered: Do nice guys finish last?". American Economic Review 78, 1034–1045.
Besley, T., Coate, S. (1995). "Group lending, repayment incentives and social collateral". Journal of Development Economics 46, 1–18.
Bhaumik, S.K., (2001). "Intergenerational transfers: The ignored role of time", mimeographed, Max Planck Institute.
Bisin, A., Verdier, T. (1998). "On the cultural transmission of preferences for social status". Journal of Public Economics 70, 75–97.
Bisin, A., Verdier, T. (2001). "The economics of cultural transmission and the dynamics of preferences". Journal of Economic Theory 97, 298–319.
Blanchflower, D., Oswald, J. (1990). "What makes an entrepreneur?". Manuscript, Dartmouth College, N.B.E.R. and the Centre for Economic Performance.
Blinder, A.S. (1988). "Comments on Chapter 1 and Chaper 2". In: Kessler, D., Masson, A. (Eds.), Modelling the Accumulation and Distribution of Wealth. Clarendon Press, Oxford, pp. 68–76.
Blundell, R., Chiappori, P.A., Magnac, T., Meghir, C. (2002). "Collective labor supply: Heterogeneity and non-participation", mimeographed, University of Chicago.
Bommier, A. (1995). "Peut-on compter sur ses enfants pour assurer ses vieux jours ? L'exemple de la Malaisie". Économie et Prévision 121, 75–86.
Bowles, S. (1998). "Endogenous preferences: the cultural consequences of markets and other economic institutions". Journal of Economic Literature 36, 75–111.
Bowles, S., Fong, C., Gintis, H. (2006). "Reciprocity, redistribution, and the welfare state". In: Kolm, S.C., Mercier-Ythier, J. (Eds.), Handbook on the Economics on Giving, Reciprocity and Altruism. North-Holland.
Boyd, R., Richerson, P. (1985). Culture and The Evolutionary Process. University of Chicago Press, Chicago.
Bramoullé, Y. (2001). "Interdependent utilities, preference indeterminacy, and social networks", mimeographed, University of Maryland.
Browning, M. (2000). "The saving behaviour of a two-person household". Scandinavian Journal of Economics 102, 235–251.
Bruce, N., Waldman, M. (1990). "The Rotten-Kid theorem meets the Samaritan's dilemma". Quarterly Journal of Economics 105, 155–165.
Buchanan, J.M. (1975). "The Samaritan's dilemma". In: Phelps, E.S. (Ed.), Altruism, Morality and Economic Theory. Russel Sage, New York, pp. 71–85.

Byrne, D., Goeree, M.S., Hiedemann, B., Stern, S. (2002). "Long-term care, formal home health care, and informal care", mimeographed, University of Virginia.

Caldwell, J.C. (1976). "Toward a restatement of demographic transition theory". In: Population and Development Review. Reprinted as chapter 4 of his Theory of Fertility Decline, Academic Press, 1982, pp. 113–180.

Case, A., Lin, I.F., McLanahan, S. (2000). "How hungry is the selfish gene?". Economic Journal 110, 781–804.

Cavalli-Sforza, L., Feldman, M. (1981). Cultural Transmission and Evolution: A Quantitative Approach. Princeton University Press, Princeton.

Chami, R. (1996). "King Lear's dilemma: Precommitment versus the last word". Economics Letters 52, 171–176.

Chami, R. (1998). "Private income transfers and market incentives". Economica 65, 557–580.

Chiappori, P.A. (1992). "Collective labor supply and welfare". Journal of Political Economy 100, 437–467.

Cigno, A. (1991). Economics of the Family. Oxford University Press, Oxford.

Cigno, A. (1993). "Intergenerational transfers without altruism: Family, market and state". European Journal of Political Economy 9, 505–518.

Cigno, A. (2000). "Saving, fertility and social security in the presence of self-enforcing intra-family deals". In: Mason, A., Tapinos, G. (Eds.), Sharing the Wealth. Oxford University Press, New York, pp. 232–255.

Cigno, A. (2006). "The political economy of social transfers". In: Kolm, S.C., Mercier-Ythier, J. (Eds.), Handbook on the Economics on Giving, Reciprocity and Altruism. North-Holland.

Cigno, A., Giannelli, G., Rosati, F.C. (1998). "Voluntary transfers among Italian households: Altruistic and non-altruistic explanations". Structural Change and Economic Dynamics 9, 435–451.

Cigno, A., Giannelli, G., Rosati, F.C., Vuri, D. (2004). "Is there such a thing as a family constitution? A test based on credrationing", mimeographed, IZA Working Paper, p. 1116.

Cigno, A., Rosati, F.C. (1996). "Jointly determined saving and fertility behaviour: Theory, and estimates for Germany, Italy, UK and USA". European Economic Review 40, 1561–1589.

Cigno, A., Rosati, F.C. (2000). "Mutual interest, self-enforcing constitutions and apparent generosity". In: Gérard-Varet, L.A., Kolm, S.C., Mercier-Ythier, J. (Eds.), The Economics of Reciprocity, Gift-giving and Altruism. MacMillan Press, London, pp. 226–247.

Collard, D. (1975). "Edgeworth's propositions on altruism". Economic Journal 85, 355–360.

Costa, G. (1988). "On linking generations together: The overlapping generations economy as a non-cooperative game", mimeographed.

Cox, D. (1987). "Motives for private income transfers". Journal of Political Economy 95, 508–546.

Cox, D. (1990). "Intergenerational transfers and liquidity constraints". Quarterly Journal of Economics 104, 187–218.

Cox, D. (1996). "Comment on James Davies: Explaining intergenerational transfers". In: Menchik, P.L. (Ed.), Household and Family Economics. Kluwer Academic, Boston, pp. 83–90.

Cox, D., Eser, Z., Jimenez, E. (1996). "Family safety nets during economic transition: A study of inter-households transfers in Russia". In: Klugman, J. (Ed.), Poverty, Policy and Responses: The Russian Federation in Transition. World Bank.

Cox, D., Eser, Z., Jimenez, E. (1998). "Motives for private transfers over the life cycle: An analytical framework and evidence for Peru". Journal of Development Economics 55, 57–80.

Cox, D., Fetzer, J., Jimenez, E. (1997). "Private safety nets through inter-household transfers". In: Dollar, D., Glewwe, P., Litvack, J. (Eds.), Household Welfare and Viet Nam's Transition to a Market Economy. World Bank.

Cox, D., Hansen, B.E., Jimenez, E. (2004). "How responsive are private transfers to income? Evidence from a laissez-faire economy". Journal of Public Economics 88, 2193–2219.

Cox, D., Jappelli, T. (1990). "Credrationing and private transfers: Evidence from survey data". Review of Economics and Statistics 72, 445–454.

Cox, D., Jappelli, T. (1993). "The effect of borrowing constraints on consumer liabilities". Journal of Money Credand Banking 25, 197–213.

Cox, D., Raines, F. (1985). "Interfamily transfers and income redistribution". In: David, M., Smeeding, T. (Eds.), Horizontal Equity, Uncertainty, and Measures of Well-Being. University of Chicago Press, Chicago, pp. 393–421.
Cox, D., Rank, M.R. (1992). "*Inter vivos* transfers and intergenerational exchange". Review of Economics and Statistics 74, 305–314.
Cox, D., Stark, O. (1996). "Intergenerational transfers and the demonstration effect", mimeographed, Boston College.
Cox, D. Stark, O. (1998a). "Financial transfers to the elderly and the demonstration effect", mimeographed, Boston College.
Cox, D., Stark, O. (1998b). "On the demand for grandchildren, tied transfers, liquidity constraints, and the demonstration effect", mimeographed, Boston College.
Cremer, H., Pestieau, P. (1991). "Bequests, filial attention and fertility". Economica 58, 359–375.
Cremer, H., Pestieau, P. (1996). "Bequests as a heir discipline device". Journal of Population Economics 9, 405–414.
Cremer, H., Pestieau, P. (1998). "Delaying inter vivos transmissions under asymmetric information". Southern Economic Journal 65, 322–330.
Cremer, H., Pestieau, P. (2006). "Wealth transfer taxation: A survey of the theoretical literature". In: Kolm, S.C., Mercier-Ythier, J. (Eds.), Handbook on the Economics on Giving, Reciprocity and Altruism. North-Holland.
Croda, E. (2000). "Sharing the wealth: Income shocks and intra-family transfers in Germany", mimeographed, UCLA.
Davies, J.B. (1981). "Uncertain lifetime, consumption, and dissaving in retirement". Journal of Political Economy 89, 561–577.
Dawkins, R. (1976). The Selfish Gene. Oxford University Press, New York.
Docquier, F., Rapoport, H. (2006). "Economics of migrants' remittances". In: Kolm, S.C., Mercier-Ythier, J. (Eds.), Handbook on the Economics on Giving, Reciprocity and Altruism. North-Holland.
Dunn, T.A. (1997). "The distribution of intergenerational income transfers across and within families", mimeographed, Maxwell Center for Demography and Economics of Aging.
Dunn, T.A., Phillips, J.W. (1997). "The timing and division of parental transfers to children". Economics Letters 54, 135–138.
Dunn, T.A., Phillips, J.W. (1998). "Intergenerational coresidence and children's incomes", mimeographed, Maxwell Center for Demography and Economics of Aging.
Dustmann, C., Micklewright, J. (2001). "Intra-household transfers and the part-time work of children". CEPR Discussion Paper 2796.
Eckhardt, S. (2002). "Stratégies familiales et négociations entre conjoints : les choix de contraception, les choix migratoires et le soutien aux parents âgés en Indonésie". PHD Thesis (Thèse nouveau régime), IEP de Paris, 305 p.
Edgeworth, F.Y. (1881). Mathematical Psychics. Kegan Paul, London.
Ehrlich, I., Lui, F.T. (1991). "Intergenerational trade, longevity, and economic growth". Journal of Political Economy 99, 1029–1059.
Engers, M., Stern, S. (2001). "Long term care and family bargaining". International Economic Review 43, 73–114.
Ermisch, J.F., Di Salvo, P. (1997). "The economic determinants of young people's household formation". Economica 64, 627–644.
Feinerman, E., Seiler, E.J. (2002). "Private transfers with incomplete information: A contribution to the altruism-exchange motivation for transfers debate". Journal of Population Economics 15, 715–736.
Feldstein, M. (1988). "The effects of fiscal policies when incomes are uncerta: a contradiction to Ricardian equivalence". The American Economic Review 78, 14–23.
Fernandes, A. (2003). "Altruism with endogenous labor supply", mimeographed, CEMFI Working Paper.
Foster, A.D., Rosenzweig, M.R. (2000). "Financial intermediation, transfers, and commitment: Do banks crowd out private insurance arrangements in low-income rural areas?". In: Mason, A., Tapinos, G. (Eds.), Sharing the Wealth. Oxford University Press, New York, pp. 211–231.

Foster, A.D., Rosenzweig, M.R. (2001). "Imperfect commitment, altruism and the family: Evidence from transfer behavior in low-income rural areas". Review of Economics and Statistics 83, 389–407.

Frank, R.H. (1988). Passions Within Reason: The Strategic Role of The Emotions. Norton, New York.

Furnham, A. (1999). "The saving and spending habits of young people". Journal of Economic Psychology 20, 677–697.

Furnham, A. (2001). "Parental attitudes to pocket money allowances for children". Journal of Economic Psychology 22, 397–422.

Gatti, R. (2000). "Family altruism and incentives", mimeographed, World Bank.

Gotman, A. (1988). Hériter. PUF, Paris.

Guiso, L., Jappelli, T. (1991). "Intergenerational transfers and capital market imperfections. Evidence from a cross section of Italian households". European Economic Review 35, 103–120.

Guttman, J.M. (2001). "Self-enforcing reciprocity norms and intergenerational transfers: Theory and evidence". Journal of Public Economics 81, 117–151.

Hamilton, W.D. (1964). "The genetical evolution of economic behavior, I and II". Journal of Theoretical Biology 7, 1–52.

Hammond, P. (1972). "Charity: Altruism or cooperative egoism?". In: Phelps, E.S. (Ed.), Altruism, Morality and Economic Theory. Russel Sage Foundation, New York, pp. 115–131.

Hansson, I., Stuart, C. (1990). "Malthusian selection of preferences". American Economic Review 80, 529–544.

Hiedemann, B., Stern, S. (1999). "Strategic play among family members when making long term care decisions". Journal of Economic Behavior and Organization 1999, 29–57.

Hirschleifer, J. (1977). "Shakespeare vs. Becker on altruism: The importance of having the last word". Journal of Economic Literature 15, 500–502.

Hochguertel, S., Ohlsson, H. (2003). "Compensatory inter vivos gifts", mimeographed, Goteborg University.

Hoddinott, J. (1992). "Rotten kids or manipulative parents: Are children old age security in Western Kenya?". Economic Development and Cultural Change 40, 545–565.

Hori, H. (1999). "Altruism and voluntary gift giving", mimeographed, Tohoku Economics Research Group.

Hori, H., Kanaya, S. (1989). "Utility functionals with non-paternalistic intergenerational altruism". Journal of Economic Theory 49, 241–265.

Horioka, C.Y., Fujisaji, H., Watanabe, W., Kuno, T. (2000). "Are Americans more altruistic than the Japanese? A US–Japan comparison of savings and bequests motives". International Economic Journal 14 (1), 1–31.

Ioannides, Y.M., Kan, K. (2000). "The nature of two-directional intergenerational transfers of money and time: An empirical analysis". In: Gérard-Varet, L.A., Kolm, S.C., Mercier Ythier, J. (Eds.), The Economics of Reciprocity, Gift-giving and Altruism. MacMillan Press, London, pp. 314–331.

Jellal, M., Wolff, F.C. (2000). "Shaping intergenerational relationships". Economics Letters 68, 255–261.

Jellal, M., Wolff, F.C. (2002a). "Altruisme, coopération et transferts familiaux". Revue Economique 53, 863–885.

Jellal, M., Wolff, F.C. (2002b). "Cultural evolutionary altruism: Theory and evidence". European Journal of Political Economy 18, 241–262.

Jellal, M., Wolff, F.C. (2002c). "Altruistic bequests with inherited tastes". International Journal of Business and Economics 1, 95–113.

Jellal, M., Wolff, F.C. (2003). "Leaving home as a self-selection device". Economica 70, 423–438.

Jellal, M., Wolff, F.C. (2005). "Dynamique des transferts intergénérationnels et effet de démonstration". Annales d'Economie et de Statistique 77, 81–107.

Jürges, H. (1999). "Parent-child transfers in Germany: A study of magnitude and motivations". Zeitschrift für Wirtschafts und Socialwissenschaften 119, 429–453.

Kan, K. (1996). "Empirical evidence on consumption smoothing and intergenerational transfers". Southern Economic Journal 63, 76–94.

Kapur, B.K. (1997). "Book review: Oded Stark, Altruism and Beyond". Journal of International Trade and Economic Development 6, 113–116.

Khalil, E.L. (1990). "Beyond self-interest and altruism, a reconstruction of Adam Smith's theory of human conduct". Economics and Philosophy 6, 255–273.

Khalil, E.L. (2001). "A pure theory of altruism", mimeographed, University of Chicago.

Kimball, M.S. (1987). "Making sense of two-sided altruism". Journal of Monetary Economics 20, 301–366.

Konrad, K.A., Künemund, H., Lommerud, K.E., Roberto, J.R. (2002). "Geography of the family". American Economic Review 92, 981–998.

Konrad, K.A., Lommerud, K.E. (1995). "Family policy with noncooperative families". Scandinavian Journal of Economics 97, 581–601.

Kotlikoff, L.J., Morris, J.N. (1989). "How much care do the aged receive from their children?". In: Wise, D. (Ed.), The Economics of Aging. Chicago, University of Chicago Press.

Kotlikoff, L.J., Razin, A. (1988). "Making bequests without spoiling children: Bequests as an implicoptimal tax structure and the possibility that altruistic bequests are not equalizing", NBER Working Paper 2735 and chapter 8 of Kotlifoff, L.J., Essays on Saving, Bequests, Altruism and Life-Cycle Planning, The MIT Press, 2001.

Kotlikoff, L.J., Razin, A., Rosenthal, R. (1990). "A strategic altruism model in which Ricardian equivalence does not hold". Economic Journal 100, 1261–1268.

Kotlikoff, L.J., Spivak, A. (1981). "The family as an incomplete annuity market". Journal of Political Economy 89, 372–391.

Laferrère, A. (1992). "Inheritances and gifts inter vivos: Unequal division between siblings in France". Continuity and Change 7, 377–404.

Laferrère, A. (1997). "Help to children's households: Testing their motivations on French data", mimeographed, Insee.

Laferrère, A. (1999). "Intergenerational transmission model: A survey". Geneva Papers on Risk and Insurance 24, 2–26.

Laferrère, A. (2000). "Intergenerational transmission model: A survey". In: Gérard-Varet, L.A., Kolm, S.C., Mercier Ythier, J. (Eds.), The Economics of Reciprocity, Giving and Altruism. MacMillan Press, pp. 207–225.

Lagerlöf, N.P. (1997). "Endogenous fertility and the old-age security hypothesis: A note". Journal of Public Economics 64, 279–286.

Laitner, J. (1993). "Long-run equilibria with borrowing constraints and altruism". Journal of Economic Dynamics and Control 17, 65–96.

Laitner, J. (1997). "Intergenerational and interhousehold economic links". In: Rosenzweig, M.R., Stark, O. (Eds.), Handbook of Population and Family Economics, vol. 1A. North-Holland, Amsterdam, pp. 189–238.

Laitner, J., Ohlsson, H. (2001). "Bequest motives: A comparison of Sweden and the United States". Journal of Public Economics 79, 205–236.

Lam, D. (1988). "Marriage markets and assortative mating with household public goods". Journal of Human Resources 23, 462–487.

Lee, R. (2000). "A cross-cultural perspective on intergenerational transfers and the economic life cycle". In: Mason, A., Tapinos, G. (Eds.), Sharing the Wealth. Oxford University Press, New York, pp. 17–56.

Lévy-Garboua, L., Meidinger, C., Rapoport, B. (2006). "The formation of individual social preferences". In: Kolm, S.C., Mercier-Ythier, J. (Eds.), Handbook on the Economics on Giving, Reciprocity and Altruism. North-Holland.

Ligon, E. (2002). "Dynamic bargaining in households", mimeographed, University of California, Berkeley.

Lillard, L.A., Willis, R.J. (1997). "Motives for intergenerational transfers. Evidence from Malaysia". Demography 34, 115–134.

Lindbeck, A., Weibull, J.W. (1988). "Altruism and time consistency: The eEconomics of fait accompli". Journal of Political Economy 96, 1165–1182.

Lord, W.A. (1992). "Saving, wealth, and the exchange-bequest motive". Canadian Journal of Economics 25, 742–752.

Lundberg, S., Pollak, R.A., Wales, T.J. (1997). "Do husbands and wives pool their resources? Evidence from the United Kingdom child benefit". Journal of Human Resources 32, 463–480.

Lundholm, M., Ohlsson, H. (2000). "Post mortem reputation, compensatory gifts and equal bequests". Economics Letters 68, 165–171.

Manser, M.E., Brown, M. (1980). "Marriage and household decision-making: A bargaining analysis". International Economic Review 21, 31–44.

Marpsat, M., Firdion, J.M. (1996). "Devenir sans-domicile: ni fatalité, ni hasard". Population et Société 313.

Masson, A., Pestieau, P. (1991). "Types et modèles d'héritage et leurs implications". Économie et Prévision 100–101, 31–71.

Masson, A., Pestieau, P. (1997). "Bequests motives and models of inheritance: A survey of the literature". In: Erreygers, G., Vandevelde, T. (Eds.), Is Inheritance Legitimate? Springer-Verlag, Berlin, pp. 54–88.

Mauss, M. (1923). "Essai sur le don, forme et raison de l'échange dans les sociétés archaïques". In: l'Année sociologique, 2de série, 1923–24, tome 1. Reprinted in Sociologie et anthropologie, PUF, 1950, 1993.

McElroy, M.B. (1985). "The joint determination of household membership and market work: The case of young men". Journal of Labor Economics 3, 293–315.

McElroy, M.B., Horney, M.H. (1981). "Nash-bargained decisions: Toward a generalisation of the theory of demand". International Economic Review 22, 333–349.

McGarry, K. (2000). "Testing parental altruism: Implications of a dynamic model". NBER Working Paper 7593.

McGarry, K. (1999). "Inter vivos transfers and intended bequests". Journal of Public Economics 73, 321–351.

McGarry, K. (2001). "The cost of equality: Unequal bequests and tax avoidance". Journal of Public Economics 79, 179–204.

McGarry, K., Schoeni, R.F. (1995). "Transfer behavior in the Health and Retirement Study. Measurement and the redistribution of ressources within the family". Journal of Human Resources 30, S185–S226.

McGarry, K., Schoeni, R.F. (1997). "Transfer behavior within the family: Results from the asset and health dynamics survey". Journal of Gerontology: Social Sciences 52B, 82–92.

Menchik, P.L. (1988). "Unequal estate division: Is altruism, reverse bequests, or simply noise?". In: Kessler, D., Masson, A. (Eds.), Modelling the Accumulation and Distribution of Wealth. Oxford University Press, pp. 105–116.

Mulligan, C.B. (1997). Parental Priorities and Economic Inequality. University of Chicago Press, Chicago.

Perozek, M.G. (1998). "A reexamination of the strategic bequest motive". Journal of Political Economy 106, 423–445.

Pollak, R.A. (1985). "A transaction cost approach to families and households". Journal of Economic Literature 23, 581–608.

Pollak, R.A. (1988). "Tied transfers and paternalistic preferences". American Economic Review 78, 248–250.

Pollak, R.A. (2003). "Gary Becker's contributions to family and household economics". Review of Economics of the Household 1, 111–141.

Poterba, J. (2001). "Estate and gift taxes and incentives for *inter vivos* giving in the US". Journal of Public Economics 79, 237–264.

Prendergast, C., Stole, L. (2001). "The non-monetary nature of gifts". European Economic Review 45 (10), 1793–1810.

Raut, L.K., Tran, L.H. (2005). "Parental human capital investment and old-age transfers from children: Is a loan contract or reciprocity for Indonesian families?". Journal of Development Economics 77, 389–414.

Rosati, F.C. (1996). "Social security in a non-altruistic model with uncertainty and endogenous fertility". Journal of Public Economics 60, 283–294.

Rosenzweig, M.R., Wolpin, K.I. (1993). "Intergenerational support and the life-cycle incomes of young men and their parents: Human capital investments, coresidence, and intergenerational financial transfers". Journal of Labor Economics 11, 84–112.

Samuelson, P.A. (1955). "Diagrammatic exposition of a theory of public expenditures". Review of Economics and Statistics 37, 350–356.

Samuelson, P.A. (1958). "An exact consumption loan model of interest with or without the social contrivance of money". Journal of Political Economy 66, 467–482.

Schoeni, R.F. (1997). "Private interhousehold transfers of money and time: New empirical evidence". Review of Income and Wealth 43, 423–448.

Schoeni, R.F. (2000). "Support networks within the family as a public good problem", mimeographed, Rand Labor and Population Program.

Sethi, R., Somanathan, E. (2003). "Understanding reciprocity". Journal of Economic Behavior and Organization 50, 1–27.
Shell, K. (1971). "Notes on the economics of infinity". Journal of Political Economy 79, 1002–1011.
Shubik, M. (1981). "Society, land, love or money: A strategic model of how to glue the generations together". Journal of Economic Behavior and Organization 2, 359–385.
Sloan, F.A., Hoerger, T.J., Picone, G. (1996). "Effects of strategic behavior and public subsidies on families saving and long-term care decisions". In: Eisen, R., Sloan, F. (Eds.), Long Term Care. Economics Issues and Policy Solutions. Kluwer Academic, Dordrecht, pp. 45–78.
Sloan, F.A., Picone, G., Hoerger, T.J. (1997). "The supply of children's time to disabled elderly parents". Economic Inquiry 35, 295–308.
Sloan, F.A., Zhang, H.H., Whang, J. (2002). "Upstream intergenerational transfers". Southern Economic Journal 69, 363–380.
Soldo, B.J., Hill, M.S. (1993). "Intergenerational transfers: Economic, demographic and social perspectives". Annual Review of Gerontology and Geriatrics 13, 187–216.
Stark, O. (1993). "Non-market transfers and altruism". European Economic Review 37, 1413–1424.
Stark, O. (1995). Altruism and Beyond. An Economic Analysis of Transfers and Exchanges Within Families and Groups. Cambridge University Press, Cambridge.
Stark, O., Falk, I. (1998). "Transfers, empathy formation, and reverse transfers". American Economic Review 88, 271–276.
Stark, O., Zhang, J. (2002). "Counter-compensatory inter vivos transfers and parental altruism: Compatibility or orthogonality". Journal of Economic Behavior and Organization 47, 19–25.
Victorio, A.G., Arnott, R.J. (1993). "Wealth, bequests and attention". Economics Letters 42, 149–154.
Villanueva, E. (2001). "Parental altruism under imperfect information: Theory and evidence", Economics working papers 566, Universitat Pompeu Fabra.
Ward-Batts, J. (2003). "Out of the wallet and into the purse: Modelling family expenditures to test income pooling", mimeographed, Claremont College, Working Paper 2003-10.
Warr, P. (1983). "The private provision of a public good is independent of the distribution of income". Economic Letters 13, 207–211.
Weinberg, B.A. (2001). "An incentive model of the effect of parental income on children". Journal of Political Economy 109, 266–280.
Wilhelm, M.O. (1996). "Bequest behavior and the effect of heir's earnings: Testing the altruistic model of bequests". American Economic Review 86, 874–892.
Wolff, F.C. (1998). Altruisme, échange et réciprocité. Les transferts inter vivos entre deux et entre trois générations, Ph. Dissertation, University of Nantes.
Wolff, F.C. (1999). "Altruisme et corésidence en France". Cahiers Économiques de Bruxelles 164, 457–488.
Wolff, F.C. (2000a). "Transferts et redistribution familiale collective". Revue Économique 51, 143–162.
Wolff, F.C. (2000b). "Les transferts versés aux enfants et aux parents : altruisme ou échange intertemporel ?". Économie et Prévision 142, 67–91.
Wolff, F.C. (2000c). "Transferts monétaires inter vivos et cycle de vie". Revue Économique 51, 1419–1452.
Wolff, F.C. (2001). "Private intergenerational contact in France and the demonstration effect". Applied Economics 33, 143–153.
Zeldin, T. (1995). Les Françaises, une histoire intime de l'humanité. Fayard, Paris.

Chapter 14

ALTRUISM, EXCHANGE OR INDIRECT RECIPROCITY: WHAT DO THE DATA ON FAMILY TRANSFERS SHOW?

LUC ARRONDEL AND ANDRÉ MASSON*

Pse-Cnrs, ENS-Pse, 48 bd. Jourdan, 75014 Paris, France
e-mail: arrondel@pse.ens.fr; masson@pse.ens.fr

Contents

* We would like to thank Alessandro Cigno, Michael Hurd, Serge-Christophe Kolm, Jean Mercier-Ythier, Muriel Roger and especially François-Charles Wolff for their very helpful and stimulating remarks on successive versions of this paper. We are also grateful to Jim Ogg for his careful rereading of the paper.

Handbook of the Economics of Giving, Altruism and Reciprocity, Volume 2
Edited by Serge-Christophe Kolm and Jean Mercier Ythier

DOI: 10.1016/S1574-0714(06)02014-8

Abstract

Most models of family transfers consider only two generations and focus on two motives: altruism and exchange. They also assume perfect substitution between inter vivos financial transfers and bequests to children. On the contrary, this survey of recent developments in the literature emphasizes the strong *heterogeneity* of downward financial transfers and motives for these transfers over the life-cycle. In face of the empirical failure of standard models in developed countries (these models may perform better in less developed countries or in old Europe), it also advocates "*mixed*" motivations of transfers, such as strategic altruism, models with endogenous heterogeneous behavioral regimes (Becker, Cigno), and especially *indirect reciprocities* between three generations, which lead to the replication of the same type of transfer from one generation to the next. Indirect reciprocities appear able to accommodate several empirical puzzles: they are thus compatible (against altruism) with small compensatory effects of transfers both between and within generations, and (against exchange) with the lack of parents' observable counterpart to financial or time support given by their children. They also predict "3rd generation effects"—transfers between parents and children being determined by grandparents' transfers or again grandchildren's characteristics—which appear corroborated by (mainly French or U.S.) available evidence. We thus face the challenge of innovative modelling of indirect reciprocities within the framework of individual forward-looking rationality.

Keywords

intergenerational transfers, intergenerational redistribution, wealth transmission motives, family altruism, family exchange, 3-generations indirect reciprocities

JEL classification: D10, D31, D63, D64, J14

1. Introduction

The economic literature on intergenerational transfers within the family has considerably developed since the last thirty years, or so. "Standard" models in this field emphasize two main competing motives for *inter vivos* transfers (i.e. between living members of the family):

- *altruism* towards children, especially in a Barro-Becker form: parents care for the well-being of their offspring;
- self-interested (inter-temporal) *exchange* between parents and children, meaning that the implicit contract where (e.g.) parents trade prior education, or the promise of future inheritance, for children's support in their old age, is expected to be mutually advantageous—if enforceable.

Moreover, bequests (post-mortem transfers) may also reflect a *precautionary* motive against lifetime uncertainty in the absence of efficient annuity markets (the ownership of durable, illiquid, indivisible assets, such as homes, is another reason).

There are several theoretical and/or empirical surveys of this literature, which distinguish various forms of altruism and exchange—as well as their recent extensions based upon processes of imitation or cultural transmission (such as children's "preference shaping")—, and compare the predictions derived with observed transfer behavior in the U.S. and elsewhere. Their general conclusions tend to emphasize the poor empirical performances of altruistic and exchange-motivated models, regarding equally the determinants of *inter vivos* transfers and those of bequests.[1]

In comparison with these studies, our own review, which focuses on modern developed countries, does not intend to be exhaustive and may look slightly oriented. Its main objective is threefold. First, we try to grasp better *why* the predictions of standard models of altruism or exchange fail to apply in previous tests. A key reason is the perfect substitution that these models assume between financial help, various gifts and bequests to children: it does not accord at all with the observed strong heterogeneity of downward financial transfers and motives for these transfers over the life-cycle (see section 3).

Second, we show more precisely *where* models of altruism and exchange fail, empirically, using new (French) data to design more powerful tests and to underline stylized facts about transfers which are generally overlooked or unexplained (see sections 5 and 7).

Third, to solve the empirical puzzles encountered by standard models, we advocate "mixed" motivations for transfers, including "strategic altruism", Becker's or Cigno's models with several endogenous behavioral regimes (section 5.4) and, especially, *indirect (serial) reciprocities* between *three* generations, which lead to the replication of the same type of transfer from one generation to the next (see sections 6 and 7). In the absence of satisfactory economic models of indirect reciprocities, the important part of the paper devoted to these mechanisms is bound to be more tentative and to have a dominant

[1] See Masson and Pestieau (1997), Arrondel et al. (1997), or Laferrère and Wolff (2006).

empirical orientation; one of its objective, however, is to make a link between the models of family intergenerational transfers and the approaches to *reciprocity* developed, in other contexts, in this handbook.

1.1. Motivations: transfers governed by indirect reciprocities

Standard models of transfers rely indeed on a simplistic view of the intergenerational family: either no apparent family, for the selfish life-cycler who leaves "accidental" bequests owing to random life duration; or the unified Beckerian family, headed by a benevolent patriarch driven by altruism towards his progeny; or even pure self-interested family relations, where intergenerational exchanges act as (imperfect) substitutes for private exchanges or contracts that should exist on ideal markets. Drawing on anthropology, the concept of reciprocity, based upon the gift-return-gift relation, should lead to a more satisfactory view of family linkages, providing new motivations for transfers and more realistic norms of behavior between kin generations.[2]

More specifically, we shall try to convince the reader that *indirect* forms of reciprocity between generations may be viewed as appropriate dynamic syntheses of altruism and exchange allowing, with minimal deviations, the introduction of "intermediate" motivations for transfers which better fit the data.

Note first that our approach to reciprocity will be quite specific by comparison with other analyses in this handbook. Instead of being applied to general human sociality, or to explain reciprocity between strangers by a norm of "fairness" leading to retaliation behavior in experimental games,[3] or again to foster cooperation within small communities,[4] it concerns family and kinship, i.e. blood relationship and asymmetric links between parents and children. Moreover, the concept must be adapted to the succession of generations, taking a particular form which has been introduced by the French anthropologist Mauss (1968): namely, indirect (serial) reciprocity, involving three successive generations at a time and leading to infinite endless chains of descending or ascending transfers between parents and children.

Reciprocity differs from market exchange in that it proceeds from a set of "internal" obligations—to give, to receive, and to give back—, whether driven by norms or collective values, group or social pressure (Kolm, 2000). Moreover, if direct reciprocity looks still like standard *quid pro quo* exchange between two parties, *indirect* reciprocity implies either that the beneficiary generation gives back to a *third* generation (e.g., provides bequests to one's children "in return" for inheritance received from one's parents),

[2] If central to anthropology, the concept of reciprocity has in fact an earlier and broader origin: as shown by Kolm (1984), it was already introduced by philosophers of the 18th and 19th centuries, and has been used by sociologists (Sorokin, Gouldner), and also by economists since the 1970s.

[3] See Fehr and Schmidt (2006).

[4] In an evolutionary perspective, *strong reciprocity* corresponds, thus, to a pro-social norm that aims at the survival of small communities in case of crisis: the individual applies a *tit-for-tat* strategy in all cases—independently of the probability of extinction of the community—, that is even against her own interest, when rewards and punishments become costly to her (see Fong et al., 2006).

or that the giving generation will be paid back by a third generation (e.g., will receive support given by her children in return to past support given to own parents):[5] in each case, it leads to the replication of the *same* type of transfer along the intergenerational chain. For instance, the way to pay back my parents for the education I received is to give myself proper education to my own children, and so on; of course, this process will often work through imitation or transmission of norms.

Our initial motivation for extending exchange or reciprocity to three generations within this encompassing framework came from French evidence on parent-to-child transfers: strong and highly significant *retrospective effects*, both qualitative and quantitative, have been systematically found for downward transfers and transmission practices on different data sets by different authors (Arrondel et al., 1997). Hence, what is left in bequest (and declared gifts) to children appears commensurate to what has been received from parents, the life propensity to bequeath out of inheritance being much higher than the one out of human resources. Moreover, transmission patterns and behaviors tend to be reproduced from one generation to the next: everything being equal (especially the amount of wealth owned), inheritance received through a will increases the probability to make a will, recipients are more likely to become donors, etc. (sections 7.1 and 7.2).

These results refer to transmission practices and downward transfers influenced by corresponding behaviors of the previous generation. For that reason, they will be interpreted as a *backward-looking* (i.e. retrospective) and *downward* indirect reciprocity. Likewise, Barro-Becker dynastic altruism—where parents care about their child's utility *and* expect their children to exhibit a comparable degree of altruism and to adopt a similar bequeathing behavior towards their own children, and so on—may be seen as a particular variant of *forward-looking* downward indirect reciprocity, where agents are endowed with an infinite horizon.[6] Four types of these reciprocities will then be considered, according to the orientation of time (backward or forward), and the direction of the transfer considered: upward (child-to-parent) or downward. Thus, examples of upward and forward-looking ones are so-called "demonstration effects", where effective

[5] The first case is a form of (what we shall call) the *propagation effect*—or "helping behavior" in Kolm's (Kolm, 1984) terminology; the second case is a form of the *rebound effect*—or "Descartes effect" for Kolm, see section 6.

[6] This interpretation of dynastic altruism as indirect reciprocity is in line with the view of Barro (1974, p. 1100): parents' choice of bequest takes into account not only the effect of children's attainable utility on their own utility, but also the "chain dependence" of children's utility on grandchildren's attainable utility, of grandchildren's utility on great-grandchildren's attainable utility, etc. The problem is that dynastic altruism is an equilibrium concept: it says nothing about the process of transmission of altruistic preferences, or about bequest choices when the "chain dependence" is broken—e.g., when there is no grandchild or when children will leave no bequests (see section 6.3).

support of elder parents is assumed to favor, by one way or another, later support by own children during one's old age.[7,8]

1.2. Outline of the paper

Section 2 provides a quick reminder of theoretical models of family transfers, relying on three main explanations: precautionary savings against lifetime uncertainty, leading only to accidental bequests; altruism and exchange, in different forms, that should also account for the determinants of *inter vivos* transfers, whether from parents to children or, especially in the case of exchange motivations, from children to parents.

A major source of misunderstanding and confusion in the literature comes from the lack of a proper definition and classification of *inter vivos* transfers. Section 3 claims that this identification problem is of central importance for *parent-to-child, financial* transfers. Their strong heterogeneity is not enough acknowledged, as if college fees to a 20-year old child and major (official, declared) gifts received some 25 or 30 years later as anticipated inheritance were perfect substitutes. We propose a typology of transfers according to their timing and their objective (whether they add to child's income, consumption or wealth). This typology has an obvious bearing on the lively Kotlikoff–Modigliani debate concerning the share of received wealth in total existing accumulation, as well as on the related issue about the quantitative importance of inter vivos transfers with respect to bequests.

Section 4 sums up existing tests of standard transfer models, with rather negative conclusions for developed countries: in particular, pure altruism cannot account for the observed absence, or limited importance, of *compensatory* effects for parent-to-child transfers, either between generations, or among siblings.[9] Indeed, we emphasize the dominant feeling of disillusion in the profession about the explanatory power of these models.

Section 5 adds to previous empirical studies in several directions. Most models of transfers, including recent ones based on values transmission or preference formation, assume a unique family composition of either two or three generations: data show, however, that the most frequent one is rather with *four* overlapping generations (with two working ones); also, there is no such thing as a "representative" family but a large *diversity* of compositions—a result which has implications for policy design and inequality of well-being between families.

[7] See for instance Cox and Stark (1996, 1998). In this demonstration process, children may as well be simple imitators as rational choosers, trying to induce grandchildren to adopt similar helping behavior (see Bergstrom and Stark, 1993, and section 6.3).

[8] In this new field, the terminology may vary a lot from one author to another. Thus, Ribar and Wilhelm (2002), who follow the Anglo-Saxon literature on social exchange, call "downward tit-for-tat chains of reciprocity" our backward-looking indirect reciprocities...

[9] The fact that *equal sharing* seems the dominant pattern, even in countries where there is freedom to bequeath, appears especially difficult to reconcile with altruism, but also with exchange.

Furthermore, while adopting a restrictive definition of *time* transfers and using richer data sets, with detailed information on services and financial support given to old parents, we show precisely at which steps most forms of exchange fail empirically in modern occidental countries—and incidentally why exchange motivations might be more relevant in old Europe or in less developed countries. First, support of old parents by their children appears the only significant (time or financial) upward transfer in developed countries. Second, the latter transfers cannot be explained—in French or U.S. data—by any observable, past, present or expected *counterpart*, from parents to children: helpers have not received more than non helpers, and do not expect higher inheritances, but smaller ones. This empirical puzzle is solved by two *non-standard* forms of exchange and altruism, with heterogeneous behavioral regimes: the self-enforcing family constitution model (Cigno, 1993); and the model of either free or constrained altruism (Becker and Tomes, 1986).[10] It can also be explained by *indirect reciprocity*: in helping children expect then to be paid back not by parents, but by similar help received later from their own children.

Section 6 first emphasizes that reciprocity encompasses mixed or intermediate ("other-oriented") motivations between (strategic) exchange and pure altruism, while allowing for richer relations within the family, especially through the notion of gift "ambivalence": a gift is *both* a positive act of sharing, and a negative one of domination exerted on the receiver. Indirect reciprocity is then introduced as a form of "general" reciprocity, a concept already analyzed at length by Kolm (1984), who has identified its two basic ingredients: the "rebound effect"—one gives to the givers—and the "propagation effect"—the helped help in turn. Applied to family transfers between three generations, this analysis leads to four types of serial reciprocities: backward- or forward-looking ones, for upward or downward transfers. Upward transfers are governed by the rebound effect, downward ones by the propagation effect; whatever the specific motivation at work (imitation, habits, education, social approval, etc.), backward-looking reciprocities typically reflect the obligation to comply to the relevant effect, and forward-looking ones the intentional desire to provoke it.[11]

Section 7 reports preliminary tests, performed on French or U.S. data, concerning specific predictions of indirect reciprocities, i.e. "3rd generation effects": transfers between parents and children depend on grandparents' or grandchildren's characteristics/behavior. Parent-to-child transfers appear strongly influenced by the corresponding behaviors or transmission practices of the previous generation. In fact, estimated retrospective effects appear not only very significant and robust but also highly *selective*: thus, wealth gifts bestowed on children depend specifically upon wealth gifts received, not so much upon other receipts, whether inheritance or financial help. Moreover, in

[10] Both Cigno's and Becker's models predict that child's support goes preferably to *less* well-off parents, as empirically observed. Albeit somewhat ad hoc, *reverse* (child-to-parent) *altruism* might also explain support of old parents: but it should lead to crowding out effects that neither French nor U.S. evidence confirm (if anything, public and private transfers to the elderly appear rather complementary, see section 5.4).

[11] The same typology of chain reciprocities appears already in Kolm (2000, p. 30).

favor of demonstration and related effects, observed (time or financial) support given to old parents could be motivated by the expectation of receiving comparable assistance from one's own children during old days—although the possibility of alternative interpretations of the findings cannot be ruled out.

Section 8 deals briefly with the macroeconomic and policy implications of alternative motivations of transfers, including: Cigno's self-enforcing family "constitutions", where the agent has the choice to "go-it-alone" (life-cycle saving) or to "comply" to a family norm of extended exchange between three generations; Becker's parental altruism with investment in a child's human capital under two regimes, either free with operative transfers *a la* Barro that crowd-out public transfers, or constrained by the interdiction of negative bequests; and indirect reciprocities, introducing specific links between three successive generations. We consider in turn the impact of government redistribution policy on growth, saving and education; the interaction effects between public and private transfers; and distributive issues, such as the effect of transfers on income inequality, on wealth concentration and inter-generational mobility. In particular, altruism may paradoxically give complementary roles to the family and the State, since more public transfers towards the elderly—pensions, health—should entail *more* private transfers to (grand) children—education, gifts, bequests.[12]

Section 9 sums up the main conclusions drawn in this survey and indicates some directions for future research. Especially welcome would be a more thorough comparison of the features and motives of family upward and downward transfers in modern developed countries and in less developed countries (*LDCs* thereafter), or in old Europe.

2. Altruism, exchange, and other motives: a quick reminder

A theorist not familiar with the topic might be scared by the impressive blossoming of miscellaneous models and motivations introduced in the literature in order to explain bequests and other family transfers between generations: capitalist (or entrepreneurial) bequests; precautionary (or accidental) bequests; transfers motivated by parental altruism, using different specifications—pure (Beckerian) altruism, retrospective (or golden-rule) bequests, paternalistic, "joy of giving" or "warm glow" bequests; models of upward or mutual altruism; transfers motivated either by pure or by "strategic" exchange (in different forms); intergenerational risk sharing; and so on...

A brief historical perspective may help to understand why there has been such an accumulation of different ideas, leading to a real patchwork of bequest models, and also to explain the shift of interest towards inter vivos transfers: being "voluntary"—i.e. presumably due to a *family* bequest motive—, the latter allow an emphasis on only two main competing motives, namely altruism and (self-interested) exchange.

[12] A general lesson, however, is that economic and policy implications will not only depend on the motivation of transfer, but also on other elements in the model, as well as "non-economic" factors, such as the externalities engendered by family transfers, as well as mating patterns, fertility differentials, estate sharing rules, etc.

2.1. *"Involuntary" transfers: accidental or entrepreneurial bequests*

To quote Modigliani (1988), "in the early Keynesian period [...], although there was little concern as to what led people to save, whether to increase income, to increase their power, or to leave bequests, the basic view of the saving process unavoidably implied that all of the accumulation, or nearly all, would finally wind up as bequeathed wealth". This view led to *wealth*-motivated, capitalist or entrepreneurial bequests, usually made by well-to-do people, whose prime saving motive is neither retirement needs nor family considerations, but accumulation for its own sake, prestige, power, control...[13] On the other hand, such bequests have a significant economic importance, owing to the high degree of wealth concentration: the typical figures for developed countries show that the top one percent of wealth holders own roughly a quarter of total national wealth, and the top 0.1% still more than one tenth.

The life-cycle model introduces another motive for accumulation, namely *hump saving*, when wealth is run down during retirement. Extensions to a random age of death have shown that a risk-averse consumer, who cannot purchase fair annuities on imperfect private insurance markets in order to cope with lifetime uncertainty, may leave considerable accidental or precautionary bequests (Davies, 1981; Kotlikoff and Spivak, 1981). The latter represent deferred consumption, had he lived longer: in other words, there are *consumption*-motivated bequests made by presumably less well-off individuals, who do not want to trade with their children (if they have any) and do not want to make inter vivos transfers. Such bequests are determined only by personal characteristics or situation: their amount should be proportional to life resources (with homothetic preferences), should decrease with age, pension coverage or private annuities, but be independent of the existence and income of children, as well as of the level of estate taxation.[14]

This dichotomy between entrepreneurial and accidental bequests was reminiscent of a two-class approach, featuring the "perpetual saver" of the capitalists' class, and the pure wage-earner of the working class (see Brezis, 2000). The development of the economics of the family in the seventies has modified the picture by introducing *family*-motivated transfers—by altruism or exchange.

[13] Since it does not take into consideration the social dimensions of large fortunes—an example would be Veblen's conspicuous motives for accumulation—, the assumption that wealth has direct, present utility may seems a bit ad hoc, but see Hurd (1990) or Caroll (2000): the marginal utility of consumption is assumed to decrease sharply at high levels of consumption, or at least more rapidly than the marginal utility of wealth (relative satiation of consumption needs).

[14] These conclusions need further qualification: Friedman and Warshawsky (1988, 1990) have shown that a pure life-cycler should still fully annuitize her wealth, despite the unfavorable terms offered by the thin market of private annuity. Other capital market imperfections, such as the illiquidity and indivisibility of durables and homes, may be part of the answer. Moreover, parents may not have a bequest motive, but may still desire not to deprive one's children from any inheritance *intentionally*: for the actual low level of estate taxation, precautionary savings is the dominant motive at the margin; but much heavier taxation (such as partial or total confiscation of inheritance) could actually lead to the purchase of additional life annuities and to a reduction of bequests.

2.2. Altruism

Pure altruism assumes that parents care about the well-being of their progeny, using bequests and other gifts to obtain the desired distribution of resources within the family, between themselves and their children, as well as among their children: altruistic transfers have thus a double *compensatory* effect, both between and within generations (Becker, 1991). Moreover, when transfers are "operative", the model leads to Ricardian equivalence and full neutralization of public policy: in particular, a rise in social security benefits should lead to an equivalent increase in altruistic parent-to-child transfers (Barro, 1974).

From a theoretical perspective, pure altruism is a very efficient working hypothesis. It is a clear-cut alternative to self-interest, assumed to prevail on the market. Besides, another form of neutrality, the "rotten kid" theorem, allows consideration of only single-headed families and implies "income pooling", as if the head of the family held all the resources of its members (Becker, 1974): whenever the transfers of the *pater familias* are operative—i.e. when he owns enough of the family resources not to want to *receive* transfers from other family members—the selfish child has no better way than to maximize total family income, which determines her own income. Moreover, "dynastic" altruism, when parents expect their children to care *in turn* about their offspring in a comparable way (a form of indirect reciprocity), allows to endow agents with an infinite horizon: consumption smoothing and Ricardian equivalence then concern all future generations of the family. And last but not least, many economists think that altruism towards one's progeny is essential in order to obtain optimal high levels of parental investments in the human capital of their children.

At this stage, some extensions or variants of pure and operative altruism are already worth mentioning, since their predictions agree better with empirical observation, and especially with three challenging stylized facts relative to parent-to-child transfers.

2.2.1. Zero bequests and inter vivos transfers

The fact that a significant fraction of the population does not seem to make significant transfers to their progeny can be explained by *constrained* altruism and non operative transfers. Liquidity or borrowing constraints prevent altruistic parents to borrow against child's expected income, leaving then *negative* bequests: they wish to, but cannot die in debt, so they leave no (planned) bequests at all—an inefficient solution. To determine which families will be constrained requires the analysis of the trade-off faced by parents between a child's education and material transfers—a hallmark of Beckerian altruism (see section 5.4). But in any case, the fact that bequests are a luxury and that zero-bequests leavers are concentrated among low-income families, is clearly in favor of this constrained regime of altruism.

2.2.2. The limited importance of inter-vivos transfers relative to bequests

Altruistic parents should transfer their wealth mainly in the forms of gifts, when liquidity-constrained children need them most, rather than much later, through bequests. But notwithstanding the fact that their quantitative importance has been for a long time underestimated, inter vivos transfers do not appear to strongly dominate bequests in developed countries (see section 3.4). To account for this deferred transmission of wealth, other extensions of the altruistic model build on the rotten kid theorem, considering the possibility of child's shirking. To cope with "lazy" or "prodigal" rotten kids, as well as with the uncertainty about child's future income, parents want to have the last word and have a preference for delaying transfers as long as possible, in order to prevent the child from overconsuming.[15]

2.2.3. Altruism and the "equal division puzzle"

Finally, proponents of altruism have tried to cope with the puzzle of estate equal sharing, which appears to be the overwhelmingly dominant behavior, even in countries like the U.S. where there is freedom to bequeath with a non distortionary estate tax (see section 4.2). The puzzle comes from the substantial income inequality between siblings, meaning that bequests are not at all compensatory. A lot of tricks have been used to overcome this difficulty, and we shall review them more throughly.

Some specifications try to minimize deviations from pure altruism. Behrman et al. (1982) propose a somewhat ad hoc "separable earnings-bequest" model, where parental utility depends separately on the human capital of each child and on the amount of inheritance she will receive much later: decreasing marginal utility of bequest received by each child implies equal sharing. Wilhelm (1996) invokes the costs of unequal division, either financial (unequal sharing requires making a will) or psychic, due to a kind of parents' aversion to the inequality of bequests; his use of a constant fixed cost to represent the disutility derived from unequal division seems again a bit arbitrary. More recently, McGarry (1999) has drawn on the interaction effect between inter vivos compensatory transfers and later bequests: assumed to be targeted towards liquidity-constrained children, inter vivos transfers should be negatively related to the current income of children; but altruistic bequests, depending solely on the permanent income of the child, could be positively correlated to the child's *current* income.[16]

Impure forms of altruism, implying more substantial departures from Becker's formulation, have also been proposed. "Joy of giving" or "warm glow" models, for instance,

[15] See, among others, Bruce and Waldman (1990), Lindbeck and Weibull (1988), Altonji et al. (1997).

[16] If the child's income increases, implying that she is less liquidity-constrained, parents will make lower inter vivos transfers to her, so that they will have more resources left both for their own consumption and for bequests.

assume that parents obtain satisfaction, not from the well-being of children per se, but from the very act of giving, their utility rising with the (post-tax?) amount given.[17]

We shall concentrate, however, on two other routes used to resolve the equal sharing puzzle, because they introduce new insights developed at large in this survey. Both assume still that original preferences are purely altruistic, but rely on additional considerations, concerning imperfect information, transfer observability, or incentives.

In so-called *retrospective* or golden rule bequests, of which Bevan and Stiglitz (1979) propose a variant, parents have only an approximate knowledge of the income of children (and even less so with grand-children...), knowing only the process of intergenerational regression towards the mean in income. It follows that bequeathing patterns tend to be *reproduced* from one generation to the next: what is left is commensurate to what has been received. This implicit rule "do unto your children as you would have liked your parents to have done unto you" appears rooted in norms of (backward-looking) *indirect reciprocity*, as if bequests were made to one's children "in return" for received inheritance from one's parent. In equilibrium, such family norms lead in general to social optimality, if not the golden rule; otherwise, they may be interpreted as a form of *limited* rationality (see section 6.3 and Masson and Pestieau, 1997).

2.2.4. *Equal bequests but compensatory gifts?*

A more recent track, usually with a game theoretic component, addresses a stronger version of the puzzle: if bequests are most often equally divided, inter vivos gifts of financial or tangible property are *not*, advantaging the less well-off children—even if the compensation is quantitatively modest. In order to explain this differential treatment, the only way out is to introduce a source of *heterogeneity* between gifts and bequests. The main issue invoked is *observability*: gifts are more likely to be private information to the donor and the recipient, while bequests are public information known to all siblings. Laitner (1997) and Lundholm and Ohlsson (2000) thus interpret estate equal sharing as a way, for parents, to insure post mortem "reputation" and to preserve family links while avoiding conflicts between children. Bernheim and Severinov (2003) view rather estate equal division as a "signal" about parents' indifferent altruistic preferences: even if it is not true, parents wish children to believe that they love them equally, in order not to hurt the feelings of the less cherished child...

Besides observability, however, there may be other, perhaps better ways to separate inter vivos transfers from bequests.[18] If directed towards children in need, gifts

[17] This type of altruism allows an escape from the free-riding problem raised by pure altruism, where the consumption of a common descendent is a public good (Bernheim and Bagwell, 1988; Andreoni, 1989; Kolm, 2000).

[18] Indeed, transfer observability is not always a relevant issue. In France, unequal estate division occurs mainly through declared gifts which are yet public information: a lot of them concern *indivisible* professional assets.

are potentially distortionary owing to a child's response (reduced labour supply, underreporting...), while bequests come too late in life to be an efficient redistributive tool. It could be also that financial gifts are compensatory because they are substitutes to downward *time* transfers (e.g. caring for grandchildren), which are more likely to benefit higher-income siblings.[19] All in all, our essential argument will be that early gifts and bequests, made and received at very distant dates over the life-cycle, do not simply serve the same purposes (section 3.2).

2.3. Exchange

Among other considerations, the predicted substantial size of "wasted" accidental bequests and the lack or limited importance of estimated compensatory effects for downward financial transfers (see section 4.2), prompted the development of transfer models alternative to altruism, based upon an (intertemporal) exchange between self-centered parents and children. There is a large variety of models, according to the nature of each transfers: as well as education, parents may use previous help or gifts, loan or insurance given to their offspring, or again the promise of an inheritance, as a payment for child's services—whether insurance, support or "attention"—expected to be received mainly during their old age.

Different forms of exchange have also been considered. *Pure* exchange concerns "fair" transactions run to the mutual advantage of parents and children (e.g., Kotlikoff and Spivak, 1981). *Strategic* types of exchange characterize bargaining or even manipulative relations between family members, between parents and children, but also between spouses having different propensities to bequeath—as assumed by the "collective" approach to household's behavior—, or again between siblings striving for a larger share of education or inheritance or for a smaller share of parental support (see e.g. Lee et al., 1994, for references). In each case, a key issue concerns the possibility of credible and enforceable commitments.

In the case of strategic parental transfers, the generic assumption is that parents reap entirely the gain from trade (Cox, 1987). A noteworthy variant of strategic bequests is the model of Bernheim et al. (1985). Parents use the threat of disinheritance to manipulate their children, playing each one off against the other in order to get the maximum of *attention*, mainly in the form of non pecuniary services; of course, there must be at least two children. Parents are assumed to prevent the formation of any coalition between siblings, and to successfully pre-commit to a publicly known rule of division of their "locked-in" bequeathable wealth, according to the level of attention provided by each

[19] This rather straightforward explanation does not seem to be supported by the (U.S.) data. In the 1988 PSID, Altonji et al. (2000) find that parents who provide money transfers also tend to provide time transfers; but time transfers do not preferably go to higher-income children, and there is little sign that time and money transfers are substitutes (in particular, *distance* has a strong negative effect *only* on time transfers).

child.[20] Moreover, since having the last word is absolutely crucial for them, parents make only bequests, not gifts, to their children.

Anyhow, an important contribution of these models has been to draw the attention of economists on *child-to-parent* transfers—more often *time* transfers rather than cash—which had been largely ignored before, perhaps also owing to data limitations and to the difficulty in evaluating, empirically, the quantitative importance of time transfers and services.

Besides the obvious fact that they need the presence of children, models of exchange-motivated transfers have often *ambiguous* and perhaps too flexible predictions, depending on the specific type of exchange considered and, moreover, on the nature of children's services, their implicit price as well as the substitutes or complements existing on the market or in the public sector. Thus, bequests may well be a necessity (their share decreases with the size of life resources), if the service provided by children, such as "attention", is assumed to be so. Likewise, the effect on transfers of a rise in social security benefits is not clear, depending notably on the degree of substitutability or complementarity between parental consumption and children's services.[21]

On the other hand, models of bequests as a mean of exchange generally predict that *richer* parents should get *more* reverse transfers, since they have more to offer in return. In addition, transfers may be often *anti-compensatory*, perhaps among siblings but especially between parents and children. According to Cox and Rank (1992), for instance, "public transfers need not 'crowd out' private ones [and indeed] can actually reinforce rather than offset the effects of public income redistribution"; more precisely, public redistribution will have a negative impact on the probability of *existence* of a transfer (as in the altruistic case), but a positive one on the *amount* of the transfer, whenever the implicit price of child's services provided in exchange increases with child's pre-transfer income.

Finally, the observed prevalence of estate equal division is again difficult to reconcile with models of bequests-as-exchange (see Menchik, 1988): since the share received by each child will depend on her personal characteristics, equal division should be again considered, as Bernheim and Severinov (2003) put it, a knife-edge, "measure zero" event.

2.4. *Summing up: distinctive predictions of basic transfer models*

Table 1 summarizes the predictions of the basic models of transfers—accidental bequests; pure altruism; "warm glow"; retrospective bequests; exchange—concerning the

[20] The hypothesis that parents can prevent any coalition between children is crucial. Cigno (1991) makes the point that children could agree among themselves that only one of them will give (minimal) attention to parents and then pre-arrange, contractually, the distribution of bequests. As the only heir, the helping child would keep a given, pre-agreed part of the inheritance for himself and share the rest equally with his siblings. In this case, it is the children who would extract the whole surplus from the game—not the parents, as in Bernheim et al. (1985).

[21] The reader will get additional insights on these issues in Laferrère and Wolff (2006).

Table 1
Predictions of basic models: determinants of parent-to-child transfers

Type of transfers or bequests	Effect on transfers of...			Form of transfers (gift/bequest)	Counterpart to transfers given (existence/nature)
	Givers' income (necessity/luxury)	Children			
		Presence	Quality		
Accidental	Proportionality	None	None Equal sharing	Bequests only	None
Altruistic (pure form)	Luxury good	Positive	Prob.: – Size: – Unequal sharing	Gifts and bequests Gifts: needy child	None
'Warm glow' (paternalistic)	Luxury good	Positive	None Equal sharing	Gifts and bequests	None
Retrospective[1]	Luxury good	Positive	Prob.: (–) Size: (–) Equal sharing	Gifts and bequests	Transfers received from own parents
Exchange	May be a necessity	Positive	Prob.: – Size: + or – Unequal sharing	Strategic: no gifts Pure: also gifts	Some child's counterpart

[1](–): limited compensation.

individual determinants of parent-to-child transfers (for policy implications, see Table 6).

With respect to the level of parental resources, bequests are normally a luxury good for the different forms of altruism (pure, warm glow, retrospective), most likely a necessity in exchange models, and proportional to resources if they are accidental.[22] Except when they are accidental, family transfers presuppose the existence of children, but only those motivated by pure altruism or exchange should also depend on each child's characteristics, which implies that estate equal division is obtained—by default—in all other cases.[23]

[22] We shall not go into details here, but it should be noted that models of accidental or altruistic bequests can explain elasticities inferior to 1 for *less wealthy* households. The income elasticity of bequests will thus be nil for constrained altruistic parents leaving no bequests. And it will remain small for accidental bequests whenever the latter result more from capital market than annuity market imperfections, that is to say for life-cycle savers whose wealth is mainly held in homes and durables.

[23] Only (pure or retrospective) altruism requires transfers to be compensatory in amount as well as in probability. But retrospective altruism predicts equal sharing and only *limited* intergenerational compensation, since parents' choices are solely based on expectations of children's incomes—inferred from own income and the degree of intergenerational regression towards the mean in income (see Bevan and Stiglitz, 1979). Note finally that no basic model predicts that the probability of a transfer could increase with child's current income.

Accidental bequests and strategic exchange do not allow for the existence of inter vivos transfers, all other basic models do; pure altruism even predicts that inter vivos transfers, directed towards children in need (being liquidity-constrained, insufficiently insured against risks of unemployment, etc.), should be the dominant form of transmission. Finally, only retrospective and exchange-motivated transfers require a counterpart given to parents, in the former case by grandparents, in the latter by children.

3. Heterogeneity of (financial downward) transfers

The shift of interest in the literature from bequests to *inter vivos* transfers has created a difficulty: as opposed to the former, the latter encounter theoretical and empirical problems of definition and typology which are far from innocuous but have been largely overlooked so far. We shall first give a general idea of these conceptual pitfalls before focusing on the case of parent-to-child financial transfers, which has the most important implications.

3.1. *Foreword: how to define "transfers" between living generations?*

In order to identify and classify inter vivos transfers in an appropriate way, one has to answer three kinds of intertwined questions at the same time, namely:

• *To whom?* Intergenerational transfers may go downwards, from parents to children, or upwards, from children to parents. They may also skip a generation, and occur between grandparents and grandchildren in both directions.

As far as downward transfers are concerned, an important preliminary issue deals with the relevant dividing line between transfers to children as such and outlays required to bring up young kids at home. It is generally assumed that the beneficiary child must be an *adult*, both for theoretical and empirical reasons: inter vivos transfers must be free, resulting—to a certain extent—from a parental choice (the baby must be fed and taught to talk and walk...); and they must be relatively easy to observe and to evaluate.

However, the definition of an "adult" child—whether she must be above a minimum age of 18 or 22 and/or living in an independent household, for instance—varies from one author to another.[24] In any case, one should remember that the inevitable separation introduced between kids' education and formation process on the one hand, and inter vivos transfers per se on the other, is in part arbitrary.[25]

• *What?* Inter vivos transfers may as well consist of financial or time transfers.

[24] Assuming that any child aged 18 or over is an adult, as does Cox (1987), is thus bound to increase the frequency of inter vivos transfers, which additionally include food, accommodation and pocket money provided to late teenagers.

[25] One convention is still required: the care of young grandchildren (generation skipping) is exceptionally considered as a (time) transfer, which is however assumed to benefit her parents (see below section 5.2).

Financial transfers, especially those from parents to children, cover a large range of transactions. They may take the form of gifts of various assets, cash transfers made once or regularly, alimony, and so on. But they also include in kind transfers, such as the payment of a rent, free disposal of a home, college fees, loans, co-signature for home mortgage, etc., which may not have an obvious equivalent cash value. Moreover, there is considerable variation in the literature as to the minimal amount required for the transfer to be recorded.[26]

Time transfers, which concern a priori any non financial help or services, including co-residence, raise greater problems of identification. They seem too loosely defined in the literature, incorporating as well anecdotal, temporary or infrequent services (such as occasional gardening...). Also, the alleged *direction* of some time "transfers" may be questionable. For instance, contacts and visits and other similar parent-child relations, which are generally considered as "attention" given to elderly parents, may rather represent simultaneous, mutually profitable exchanges, or even services going by and large in the opposite (downward) direction: as shown by Wolff (2001) on French data, many contacts and visits are first motivated by grandchildren care—to the benefit of children...[27] Co-residence of adult generations may create similar difficulties, regarding the very direction of the transfer.

• *When?* This is the most neglected question on which we shall concentrate below. In short, financial gifts received at distant dates over the life-cycle, e.g. while a student and when close to retirement, do not take the same form, nor do they lead to comparable implications.

3.2. Three types of financial inter vivos transfers

Most models of parent-to-child transfers assume indeed that various inter vivos transfers (made and received at different stages of the life-cycle), as well as inter vivos transfers and bequests are quasi-perfect *substitutes*: besides the choice of the right *timing*, only the present total value of these financial transfers has to be taken into consideration.[28]

3.2.1. Theoretical considerations

While making modelling and predicting far easier, this view appears quite unrealistic owing to the strong *heterogeneity* of inter vivos transfers. Free disposal of a home or

[26] A related issue concerns the choice of the *period* of reference over which transfers are collected: the shorter it is, the smaller the average size of transfers recorded.

[27] Bernheim et al. (1985) go as far as to include into "attention" given to parents *letters* which are written to them. To take an extreme example, this means that letters asking parents repeatedly for money help should be considered as transfers given to them!

[28] Altruistic parents face thus a trade-off between the desire to help liquidity-constrained children when young and a preference for *flexibility* which induces them to postpone transfers and avoid irreversible decisions.

payment of college fees for a 20 years old independent child may be substitutes for co-residence with parents. But major gifts, received some twenty or thirty years later, play the role of an anticipated inheritance and are more likely to be substitutes for bequests. The two types of transfers have different determinants and may correspond to altogether different motives, even for the same parents.

This heterogeneity of inter vivos transfers leads us to propose a division into three types according to the main objective pursued: education, assistance or transmission.

(a) *Education transfers*. Investments in the human capital of the adult child, such as college fees, are received at the very beginning of her economic life; as a close substitute for parental earlier investment in a pre-adult child's human capital, these transfers add presumably to her present and future *income*.

(b) *Financial assistance*, often due to imperfect capital or insurance markets. Parents help liquidity-constrained children by increasing their present resources or extending their access to credit, especially for the purchase of a home; they may offer a partial insurance against their offspring's risks of unemployment, divorce, etc.; they may also care for their young grand-children. These transfers, which are mainly received by children still in the first part of their working life, add primarily to the *consumption* (including services of durables) of their household.

(c) *Wealth gifts*. Inter vivos transfers that are part of the wealth transmission process are often received later in life, and take most often the form of official, declared, and taxable stocks rather than regular flows. Generally interpreted as anticipated inheritances, they add presumably to child's *wealth*.

A number of predictions allowing us to disentangle the three types of transfers are worth mentioning. First, since one of the parents' motivations is to reduce taxation, the probability of wealth gifts should increase with their wealth, or better still, *taxable* wealth (Poterba, 2001); but this latter variable should have little bearing on other transfers.

Consider next the distribution of transfers *among siblings*. Being more likely to be substitutes for bequests, wealth gifts should be, most of the time, shared equally among siblings; moreover, exceptions should be concentrated among self-employed, having to transmit an indivisible asset, and rich parents, who will be more willing to pay the financial and other costs associated with a testate unequal division (especially in countries like France where taxation is highly distortionary). On the other hand, *unequal* sharing is likely to be more common for education transfers, which depend on child's relative ability, and financial assistance, which in turn depends on children's respective needs—and in this latter case, only wealthy parents will be able to afford equal division between grown-up children.

Third, consider the effect of a *child's current income* on the *probability* of transfers. This effect appears dubious for education transfers, owing to income endogeneity (reflecting reverse causation). If our typology has any economic relevance, the probability of financial assistance, given to children in need, is the most likely to be compensatory, almost by definition. But the effect for wealth gifts remains undetermined, depending on the alleged dominant motive of transmission: it will be negative under pure altruism or exchange (Cox, 1987), nil under paternalistic or retrospective transfers, and could be positive if other motivations prevail (e.g. advantaging well-endowed children in order to perpetuate the family social rank or enterprise: see Chu, 1991).

3.2.2. French and U.S. evidence in favor of the heterogeneity of financial transfers

A reexamination of French and U.S. data gives some empirical support to this ternary division of inter vivos transfers.

French household surveys (Insee in 1992 and 1997, Cnav in 1992) provide complementary cross-sectional and recall information on a wide scope of financial transfers, made or received over a minimum of the last five years—or even over the entire past life-cycle for (wealth) gifts: typically, they do not allow for a precise test of intergenerational compensation, which requires reliable estimates of *both* parents' and child's incomes *at the time of the transfer*—a difficult challenge for gifts received or given more than ten years ago.[29] Most of the empirical literature on inter vivos transfers in developed countries is based on several U.S. household surveys (PSID, HRS, AHEAD...), where such information is available; but the period of reference considered is usually *short*—concerning transfers given or received during the last year or so—, and the minimum threshold moreover quite low (100, 200 or 500$).[30] On the other hand, estate data in both countries give information about bequests and declared (wealth) gifts.

French household surveys record parents' transfers in the following categories: significant (wealth) gifts on the one hand, and "financial help" on the other, divided into four items: *housing*, i.e. payment of a rent or providing a separate home rent-free; *money*, including regular payments or financial help for an important purchase; *loan*, meaning a money loan; *co-signature* for a mortgage and other help for its repayments. Arrondel and Masson (2001) find that housing and money transfers correspond more often than not to education transfers: their probability of occurrence increases with the levels of a child's and parents' education, and is higher for non-working, compared to wage-earning children. Loans and co-signatures are more likely to correspond to financial assistance: the probability of these transfers neither increases with a child's education, nor with parents' education, but is significantly higher if the child is self-employed (especially farmers), who need a back up for professional investments. Finally, the probability of gifts (presumably a component of wealth transmission) has very different determinants: education variables and parental income have no effect at all, whereas

[29] There is one exception, however: both parents' and child's *current* incomes are available in the Cnav survey, allowing to test for compensatory effects of transfers other than wealth gifts (see Wolff, 2000, and section 4.2).

[30] Cox (1987), on the PCPP, considers any payment made during January–August 1979 between "family units", where any child above 18 forms a separate family unit. Altonji et al. (1997, 2000), Dunn (1997), McGarry (1999), on the PSID, define as transfers total financial help over 100$ given to non-coresident children in the past year; the same definition is used in AHEAD and in the HRS, but with a threshold of 500$. Only Cox and Rank (1992), on the NSFH, consider transfers (above 200$) made during the last five years.

wealth, and even more taxable wealth have, as predicted, a strong and significant positive influence;[31] gifts are more often made by self-employed parents to self-employed children (including farmers and professionals), being used as a privileged means of ensuring an efficient transmission of professional assets; also, the highly positive effect of being a widow shows that a lot of gifts are made as anticipated inheritances, after the death of the first spouse.

In U.S. households surveys, financial transfers, being recorded over a short period and above a low minimum threshold, correspond mainly to *financial assistance*.[32] The usual findings in the U.S. of rather compensatory inter vivos transfers (see section 4.2), benefiting more (often) less well-off children, should be interpreted with these qualifications in mind: they do not apply to major, declared gifts.

To the extent that wealth gifts coincide with *taxed* or *taxable* inter vivos transfers, the recent strand in the literature concerning the effect of gift and estate taxation on the timing of transfers has also some bearing on our typology. Both in France (Arrondel and Laferrère, 2001) and in the U.S. (Bernheim et al., 2004), estate data show that the frequency or amount of gifts with respect to inheritance is highly sensitive, over the short run, to the relative tax advantage granted to gifts relative to bequests or inheritance; yet, Poterba (2001) and McGarry (2001) claim that most U.S. households fail by a substantial margin to exploit the advantages of gifts to the full extent permitted by law. This is evidence that wealth gifts and bequests are considered by parents as substitutes, but only as *partial* substitutes, for a number of reasons: uncertainty concerning future health or longevity, desire to monitor children and to have the last word, etc. Anyhow, it is significant that no study has tried, to our knowledge, to evaluate the effect of the rate of gift and estate taxation on other, *untaxed*, parent-to-child transfers (i.e. financial assistance or education transfers), as if it was agreed that the possibility of substitution between the former and the latter transfers were negligible.[33]

Finally, sharing practices among siblings depend, as predicted, on the nature of the transfer. In France, registered gifts, when mentioned in the estate, are equally shared in more than 90% of the cases, unequal sharing concerning mainly the rich and the self-employed. For financial help, French results in households surveys are, on the contrary, quite in agreement with Hochguertel and Ohlsson (2000) conclusions on American data (Health and Retirement Survey): equal sharing remains the exception and is concentrated among wealthy parents.

[31] France has an inheritance tax with an exemption threshold, so that taxable wealth depends on the amount of wealth but also on marital status and on the total number of children (see Arrondel and Laferrère, 2001).

[32] One may hope that they do not too often correspond to "education transfers" (otherwise, the endogeneity of child's income would become a main issue).

[33] Yet, contrary to this view, one explanation often given for typically small rates of estate or inheritance taxation is that an increase of these tax rates would make parents shift to untaxed inter vivos transfers (see Lundholm and Ohlsson, 2000).

3.3. The importance of "inherited" wealth in total wealth accumulation

This ternary division of financial inter vivos transfers has an obvious bearing on the Kotlikoff–Modigliani debate, relative to the share of "inherited wealth" in total existing accumulation.[34] Kotlikoff and Summers (1981) claim and Kotlikoff (1988) maintains that this share is close to 80% in the U.S., while Modigliani (1988) estimates the same ratio below 20%—it would be equal to zero if there was only saving for retirement. How does one account for such a huge discrepancy which shows that empirical measures are "theory laden"? There are two main sources of disagreement: the first one concerns the definition of an inter vivos (financial) transfer, the second the way to evaluate the actual contribution to wealth accumulation of a transfer received in the past (see Kessler and Masson, 1989; Kessler et al., 1991).

On the first point, Modigliani retains only inheritance and "major" gifts (that "add to children's wealth, not to consumption") between independent households, that is to say wealth gifts (case (c)), whereas Kotlikoff wants to add all transfers received above 18 years of age, including "minor" gifts (case (b)) as well as college education fees and other parents' spending (case (a)), which means for the U.S. *twice* as much transfers.[35] Although the dividing line drawn by Modigliani between "minor" and "major" gifts seemed somewhat artificial, most authors side here with his position, advocating the limited degree of substitutability between financial help, on the one hand, and wealth gifts, on the other.

On the second point, Modigliani imputes to the contribution of bequests only the sum in real terms of received transfers, whereas Kotlikoff adds to this the accumulated interest on transfers—once again *doubling* the figures (hence the discrepancy in the results, in the order of one to four). Who is right? Apparently no one since each convention relies on an arbitrary, *accounting* decomposition of wealth in inherited and self-accumulated shares (Blinder, 1988). Moreover, each solution begs the question of the importance of the bequest motive since it is only appropriate when a specific motive for accumulation dominates: thus, Kotlikoff's convention is best suited for Rockefellers. On the other hand, if a pure life-cycle saver has received, at the eve of retirement, an inheritance equal in amount to self-accumulated savings, one would like to say that transfer-wealth

[34] Not surprisingly, when asked directly about the approximate share of received gifts and inheritance in current net worth (Insee 1997), French households tend to *underestimate* the contribution of capital receipts: even among those who have lost their parents, nearly 40% claim to have received almost nothing, and only a good third of the others declare a share of received wealth superior to 25% (and 17% more than half).

[35] Kotlikoff considers that all transfers received after 18 years of age, from pocket money or college fees up to bequests, are perfect substitutes. Against this overall aggregation, Blinder (1988, p. 70) argues that the relevant issue is the origin of non-human wealth and that college fees presumably build *human* wealth: if the latter is included into the accounts, then many more expenses on child rearing should be taken into consideration, so that 100% of wealth could well be inherited: 'Where would I be without my genes?'. But this does not mean that Modigliani's conception is entirely satisfactory: e.g., according to a "neo-Marshallian" view (shared by Becker, among others), parents' investments in children's human capital remain the most productive form of "saving" and are partially substitutable to investments in non-human wealth.

and life-cycle wealth are equal during her retirement: in this case, both authors will overestimate transfer wealth...

Using Modigliani's conventions, estimates of the contribution of bequests are now available for a number of developed countries. Laitner and Ohlsson (1997) find a share of inherited wealth of 51% in Sweden (in 1981), but only of 19% in the U.S. (in 1984). Cigno et al. (1998) estimate a share up to 58% for Italy (in 1991). Using different waves of the Survey of Consumer Finances, Gale and Scholz (1994) find that transfer wealth accounts for approximately half of aggregate U.S. wealth in 1986, but Brown and Weisbenner (2002) reduce this figure to 20–25% in 1998 while correcting for the wealth–mortality correlation.

Yet, the right question to ask would concern the reduction of total saving engendered by a confiscation of bequests, or a uniform reduction of $x\%$ of their amounts. To perform such a thought experiment, one needs a behavioral and "comprehensive" simulation model of accumulation, that is capable of reproducing the aggregate level and the distribution of wealth over time, from one generation to another. Estimates derived with this method are comprised between 35 to 40% for France (Kessler and Masson, 1989). Davies and St. Hilaire (1987), applying a comparable method to Canadian data, find a 35% share for inherited wealth.

All in all, the contribution of bequests and wealth gifts to wealth accumulation appears therefore substantial but not overwhelming; moreover, it should be more important in most countries in continental Europe and in Canada than in the U.S.[36]

3.4. The importance of "gifts" (inter vivos transfers) relative to bequests

Differences of definition and coverage help also to explain the conflicting estimates concerning the importance of inter vivos transfers relative to bequests; but there are, obviously, other sources of discrepancy.

The topic has been a controversial issue in the U.S. Tomes (1988) thinks that gifts are only of minor importance, with the possible exception of the wealthiest individuals. Bernheim et al. (1985) see "the apparent insignificance of gifts" as an element supporting strategic bequests. But Cox (1987) and Cox and Raines (1985) claim that an enlarged conception of inter vivos transfers, including in kind or in cash transfers received by any "adult" child (above 18) even in the same household, make them more important than inheritance (in the ratio of 3 to 2). More surprisingly, Gale and Scholz (1994), considering only inter-household transfers worth more than $3000, find yet that inter vivos transfers "account for at least 20 percent of U.S. wealth and possibly more" (and inheritances for roughly 30%).

[36] It is likely that the contribution of bequests has declined over time in France (presumably a representative example of continental Europe). In the 19th century, it was more difficult to build a fortune without a sizeable inheritance. Things changed after the destruction caused by the first World War and the steady growth following the second one, although the last twenty years may have altered this secular trend.

In France, estate duty statistics indicate that the total amount of *declared* (wealth) gifts represented approximately one third of the one of *declared* inheritances during the 1970s and 1980s (or one quarter of total transfers); but there was clearly an upward trend.[37] The reinforcement of tax advantages of gifts since the 1990s led to a sharp increase of the ratio, the gifts/inheritance trade-off being highly sensitive to changes in taxation, especially among the rich who make a very large proportion of gifts. The most recent figures, including financial help (education transfers and financial assistance), concern 1994: in billions of French Francs, the aggregate amount of financial help was then around 100, wealth gifts rose to 111, and inheritances amounted to 122. In interpreting these figures, one should remember that small inheritances are excluded, and that the year was very favorable to declared gifts (the main tax reform occurred in 1992). But all in all, recent French figures seem to show that total inter vivos transfers, of which perhaps half are wealth gifts, may have become quantitatively more important today than bequests, a result not too far from recent U.S. estimates.[38]

4. Previous tests of transfer models

Keeping in mind this heterogeneity and distribution of financial parent-to-child transfers, we may now give a brief appraisal of existing empirical tests, which have been performed (for a large majority of them) on various U.S. data sets, including panel data. French and other European evidence will also be considered for comparison. These tests lead to rather jaundiced conclusions for the three broad types of transfer models considered in the literature: precautionary savings against lifetime uncertainty, (pure) altruism, and exchange, mainly considered on an intertemporal basis, when parents want to secure old age needs.

4.1. Accidental bequests do not apply to the richer part of the population

The model of accidental bequests leads to three striking, almost unique, predictions: transfers do not depend on the existence of children; there should be only bequests, no inter vivos transfers; finally, bequests should never be a luxury good (see Table 1).

[37] See Arrondel and Laferrère (2001). Note that small inheritances are not declared; many "gifts", especially those handed over directly, get also unreported, but these correspond mainly to financial help—not wealth gifts.

[38] In the Insee 1997 survey, the ratio of gifts to inheritance is in the order of 1 to 3.5 for households with no more inheritance expectations. This low measure should be corrected for the fact that gifts rose sharply in the nineties. More importantly, households surveys typically miss the top 1% of wealth holders, who make some 20% of total bequests but up to 50% of official gifts. Correcting for the higher degree of concentration of gifts leaves a ratio of cumulated gifts to inheritance in the right range of magnitude, between (say) one half and two thirds.

4.1.1. *Do bequests depend on the existence of children?*

Surprisingly enough, few studies deal specifically with the effect on transfers of the *existence* of children, although most authors would agree that this effect is presumably positive (against accidental bequests), once the cost of bringing up children has been appropriately taken care of. There is one noticeable exception. On the Longitudinal Retirement History Survey (LRHS), Hurd (1987, 1989) finds that most people *dissave* at old age, leaving typically small amounts of "desired" (i.e. not accidental) bequests, and, more importantly, that couples with independent children dissave on average during retirement proportionally *more* than childless couples—everything being equal, including the amount of wealth and annuities at retirement eve.

These striking conclusions in favor of accidental bequests are not entirely warranted, however, for three possible reasons: first, the LHRS panel survey excludes rich households; second, couples without children may continue to save for precautionary motives against major catastrophes (illness, invalidity), whereas children may provide a "safety net" in other families; third, altruistic parents could decumulate more rapidly during their retirement period because they make (partly unobserved) inter-vivos transfers to their liquidity-constrained children rather than passing on their wealth only at death (Bernheim, 1991).

4.1.2. *Inter vivos transfers and the precautionary motive*

The fact (for a long time neglected) that inter vivos transfers could be at least of the same quantitative importance as bequests runs clearly against the existence of precautionary motives. The high sensitivity of the timing of transfers to changes in taxation is also bad news: actual bequests decrease significantly with the relative tax advantage given to gifts, whereas accidental bequests are predicted independent of the level of estate or gift taxation. On the other hand, the very high concentration of the amount of declared (wealth) gifts among wealthy households means that accidental bequests still have their chance for the remaining bulk of the population.

4.1.3. *Are bequests a luxury good?*

The question amounts to assessing whether the elasticity of bequests (or of received inheritance) with respect to parental life resources is superior or inferior (or equal) to one.

For the U.S., estimates of this elasticity are fairly scattered but generally superior to one: on household cross-sectional data, 1.3 for Adams (1980), 1.7 for Tomes (1981), who both compare the amount of inheritance received to a proxy for parental permanent income; a wide range from 0.9 to 2.9 for Tomes (1982)—depending on the functional form used to evaluate intergenerational savings. Using estate data statistics, Menchik (1980b) finds a higher elasticity of 2.5 for intergenerational savings, while on the LRHS panel data, Kotlikoff (1989), who substitutes bequeathable wealth for bequests, is the only one to find a much lower elasticity, in the range of 0.5 to 0.8 (depending on permanent income estimation).

Methodological and empirical pitfalls aside, such a difference in estimates seems to reflect the heterogeneity in income of the populations studied: e.g., Kotlikoff focuses on the middle class to the exclusion of the well-off, while only the latter are represented in Menchik's sampling. Hence the idea that the elasticity of bequests may *increase* along the income scale. Menchik and David (1983), the most reliable study in this field, do corroborate this hypothesis while merging estate duty files and social security files: in each cohort, bequests are of a limited amount and of an elasticity inferior to one for the 80% lower incomes, but become much larger for the top 20% in permanent income, with an elasticity comprised between 2 and 3. A similar procedure has been applied for French data, with comparable, although less striking results.[39]

Interestingly enough, these results may receive different interpretations. They are roughly compatible with (free or constrained) altruistic behaviors throughout the entire population (see section 2.4), but could also reveal heterogeneity in accumulation patterns, as suggested by Modigliani (1986): the bottom 80% in income would be mainly life-cycle savers, whereas the top 20% would have a longer horizon that extends to future generations.

All in all, the dominant view in the profession is that accidental bequests in occidental developed countries should be mainly concentrated among lower and middle-income, self-centered households.[40]

4.2. Parental altruism cannot explain non-compensatory gifts or bequests

As far as models of parent-to-child altruism are concerned, the main empirical issues are twofold. The first one focuses on the predicted *compensatory* effects of downward transfers, especially bequests, both between generations, i.e. parents and children, and within generations, i.e. among siblings; the second issue deals more specifically with inter vivos transfers that should dominate bequests and be primarily given to children in need, whether liquidity-constrained, jobless, etc. We shall just underline the main conclusions here, according to the type of financial transfer distinguished in section 3.2, and refer to other surveys for further details and comments (Arrondel et al., 1997; Laferrère and Wolff, 2006).

[39] Estimates have been derived both on a sample survey (Arrondel and Masson, 1991) and on estate data (Arrondel and Laferrère, 1991). In this latter case, the dividing line obtained is again between the 80% lower incomes and the top quintile of bequest leavers, with an elasticity of bequests between 0.6–0.7 for the first group, and around 1.6 in the second one.

[40] On the other hand, accidental bequests may have gained diffusion in LDCs, following the loosening of traditional (extended) family networks—the lack of appropriate data does not allow to check this conjecture.

4.2.1. Compensatory bequests?

In several papers, Tomes (1981, 1988)—see also Becker and Tomes (1986)—obtains strong and consistent results in favor of altruistic compensatory bequests, either between or within generations. But most other authors, whether in the U.S. or elsewhere, reach opposite conclusions, finding no evidence of significant compensations by bequests, to the contrary.

Consider first *inter*-generational compensation. Do bequests—or bequeathable wealth at old age—decrease with a child's income, or more precisely with the average pre-transfer income of children? On U.S. estate data, Tomes (1981) finds a significant compensatory effect, both for the probability of (a minimal) bequest and its amount: however, the negative correlation between bequest and children's average earnings depends crucially on the (not very reliable) proxy used to estimate parents' income. Wilhelm (1996) is the only study to have direct information on current incomes of the deceased as well as of all his or her children. Dealing with well-to-do families with several children, he concludes that the amount of bequests is actually more likely to increase with the average level of children's resources, but estimated effects are small and often not significant. Laitner and Ohlsson (2001) also find limited support for the altruistic model, both in Sweden (LLS) and in the U.S. (PSID): inheritances are positively related to the donors' lifetime resources and negatively related to the heirs' earning potentials, but the magnitude of the estimated effects is again much smaller than the theory would predict.

French studies, using sample surveys as well as estate data, reach a uniform conclusion: as far as intergenerational differences in resources are concerned, bequests or bequeathable wealth are (slightly) *anti-compensatory*: for given parents' income, the latter increase with the average level of education or income of children.[41]

Consider next *intra*-generational redistribution. As we have seen, it is quite difficult to reconcile altruism with the observed dominant practice of *equal sharing* of bequests, in the U.S. as well as in France. It remains to be seen whether, in the infrequent cases of unequal estate division, the less privileged child gets advantaged. In the U.S, there is some indication that girls, assumed to receive less education or to care more for parents, are slightly advantaged (Menchik, 1980a; Bennet, 1990). Otherwise, evidence is again two-sided: Tomes (1981, 1988) obtains significant compensatory effects, but other authors (Menchik, 1988; Wilhelm, 1996) find no correlation between children's *observable* characteristics and the relative amount of inheritance received,[42] a conclusion shared by Arrondel and Laferrère (1992) working on estate French data. Indeed, French and American studies—apart from Tomes'—can explain why unequal estate division occurs illiquid or indivisible bequests, professional assets, etc.), but much less the rationale underlying the distribution observed.

[41] See Arrondel and Laferrère (1991) or Arrondel and Masson (1991).

[42] More precisely, Wilhelm does find that large earnings differentials between siblings make an unequal estate division more likely and, moreover, that unequal inheritances may provide some compensation to children with low earnings, but both effects are not always significant and in any case very small.

4.2.2. *Wealth gifts and taxation*

As an intermediate step, consider then declared *wealth gifts*. Their responsiveness to tax schemes favoring inter vivos transfers, in France and in the U.S., is at least evidence of "voluntary" transfers. They are, however, highly concentrated among the rich. Moreover, they are bestowed only a limited time span before inheritance (seven years on average in France, with mean ages of reception of 38 for gifts and 45 for bequests): households fail to exploit a large proportion of the tax advantages associated with gifts (for the U.S., see section 3.2). Although parents may have reasons to postpone transfers—so as to have the last word or to cope with unforeseen future contingencies—, altruistic motivations should lead to an earlier timing of transfers, not only to take better advantage of tax avoidance but also to help children when they need it most, being liquidity-constrained or still insecure in their professional carrier.

Wealth gifts appear most often equally shared among siblings, albeit to a lesser extent than bequests.[43] Regarding the effect of (average) child's income, few U.S. studies deal with wealth gifts *per se*, but the guess is that the probability of such transfers is slightly compensatory (e.g., Cox and Rank, 1992). French results appear even less clear cut: depending upon households surveys, the correlation between the probability of a transfer and a child's income may be slightly negative (Arrondel and Masson, 1991), or rather positive, meaning anti-compensation against both exchange and altruism predictions (Arrondel and Laferrère, 2001); moreover, the amount bestowed is generally anti-compensatory.

4.2.3. *Financial assistance leads at best to limited compensatory effects*

We have noted that most household U.S. data on *inter vivos* transfers are typically candidates for financial assistance, acting as a proxy for missing credit or insurance markets for children; moreover, the short span of reception considered allows the use of parents' and children's *current* incomes for a test of compensatory effects (section 3.2). A distinctive prediction of pure altruism is that *both* the probability and the amount of transfers should be negatively correlated with the level of child's resources, with moreover *strong* compensatory effects.

Most U.S. studies find a negative income correlation in the probit model, but evidence on amounts is *mixed*. Cox (1990) and Cox and Japelli (1990) claim that transfers are meant for liquidity-constrained children, insofar as their *permanent* income (i.e. consumption needs) exceeds their current resources (income or assets): for a given permanent income of the child, the probability of receiving a transfer decreases both with current income and the ratio of financial assets to income; but these variables have no significant effect on the amount of the transfer received. However, when there is no control for a child's permanent income, Cox (1987), and Cox and Rank (1992) conclude

[43] In France, for instance, unequal estate division, which concern less than 8% of the estate declarations, occurs in 80% of the cases only through unequal previous gifts, bequests remaining equally divided.

that the transfer decision is compensatory, but the transfer amount anti-compensatory, increasing with child's current income.

On the other hand, McGarry and Schoeni (1995, 1997) find using HRS data that parents give *more* to less well-off children. Likewise, Hochguertel and Ohlsson (2000), using the same data set, conclude that transfers are compensatory "in the sense that a child is more likely to receive a gift if she works fewer hours and has lower income than her siblings, and that the results carry to the amounts given". What then about the quantitative importance of these compensatory effects on amounts (when transfers are positive)? Altonji et al. (1997), using PSID data, give the most reliable estimates, correcting for different biases against the altruism hypothesis: "redistributing one dollar from a recipient child to donor parents leads to less than a 13-cent increase in the parents' transfer to the child, far less than the one-dollar increase implies by [pure] altruism".

French results show even less evidence of compensatory effects for financial assistance. In some cases (loans, co-signatures), parents may give more often to better-off children (Arrondel and Wolff, 1998). Moreover, Wolff (1998, 2000), replicating Altonji et al. (1997) method on the Cnav 1992 survey, finds that shifting one unit incurrent income from the parents (of the middle generation) to their child leads to no reduction, but rather to a small increase in the transfer.

To conclude, how to interpret these mixed results? If one admits that altruism is a reasonable and necessary hypothesis to explain large investments in children's human capital, a bold answer would be that the explanatory power of altruism decreases gradually with the age of children: if it is still working fairly well for undeclared, untaxed inter vivos transfers, its performances deteriorate in the case of wealth gifts, and become poor for bequests, which do not appear at all compensatory, either between or within generations.

Surprisingly enough, its typical field of application—which are the typical altruistic families in the population?—remains also a controversial issue. Cox et al. (2004) claim that altruism works best for poorer households in LDCs with limited public redistribution, but far less in developed countries with substantial public transfers.[44] But a majority of authors hold opposite views. For Becker and his colleagues, operative altruistic transfers are concentrated among richer families. Indeed, for a "neo-Marshallian" view, parental altruism should have risen over time with "civilization" and the increase of well-being, the development of the welfare state and higher investments in education; presumably, it was much lower in old Europe—when children were mainly considered as a resource for retirement, education remained low, and child labor was quite wide spread—, and remains limited in poor LDCs.

[44] Cox et al. (2004) advocate a non-linear (Spline) relationship between the amount of private transfers received and the resources of the beneficiary household. They find that crowding out effects created by government public redistribution—a major implication of altruism—are very small in developed countries, like the U.S., but more important in developing countries with extremely limited public redistribution, such as the Philippines; moreover, in the latter country, they find strong crowding out effects only among the poorest households.

4.3. Parent-child exchange: non specific predictions, weak attention-bequest correlation

Empirical tests of models of exchange have concerned two different kinds of predictions. The first are often ambiguous and do not appear specific to these models, but play a strategic role insofar as they may accommodate stylized facts which run against the altruistic view of transfers. On the contrary, the other predictions concern the existence of a specific *quid pro quo* (intertemporal) exchange, where parents trade expected bequests or gifts for children's earlier support during their old days, whether insurance, financial or time assistance.

4.3.1. Can exchange motivations be a remedy to the failures of altruism?

A first difference in predictions between altruism and exchange concerns the way the beneficiary's income should affect received transfers: while the probability of a transfer is compensatory in both types of models, the amount of the transfer should decrease with a child's income if altruism prevails, but is more likely to be anti-compensatory under exchange, provided that the implicit price of a child's services increases with her earnings—which will be the case if they are time consuming, or if the market offers only poor substitutes. Thus, Cox and colleagues have interpreted (somewhat too hastily) "in favor" of exchange their findings of anti-compensatory amounts of financial assistance, notwithstanding the fact that other U.S. studies reach opposite conclusions. In fact, the small size of estimated effects of a child's income, whatever their sign, can only be viewed as clear evidence against the full compensation predicted by pure altruism.

On the other hand, as Menchik (1988) emphasizes, the prevalence of estate equal division is, if anything, *more* difficult to reconcile with exchange than with altruism, where several ways out have been proposed in the recent years (section 2.2).

Consider next the parents' income elasticity of bequests. The fact that bequests appear a necessity for lower incomes and a luxury good for higher incomes—often interpreted in favor of the existence of (free and constrained) altruism (section 4.1)—may be reconciled with the flexible predictions of exchange models, albeit in an ad hoc way, while assuming that attention and other services desired by old people are altogether different goods according to their financial means: they should be a necessity for low-income parents, but a luxury for richer parents looking for more specific personal services, such as affection or respect, which cannot be provided by the market or the State.

Finally, models of (self-interested) intertemporal exchange predict a later timing of parental transfers than altruism, i.e. a smaller importance of inter vivos transfers relative to bequests: enforcement problems and children's potential ingratitude make it essential for parents to have the last word if they want to be looked after during old age—the strategic bequests of Bernheim et al. (1985) being just an extreme example, allowing for no gifts at all. In view of the observed substantive but not overwhelming importance of gifts, it may then well be that altruism predicts too many inter vivos transfers, but most forms of exchange too little.

4.3.2. Are levels of aid/attention to parents and gift/inheritance expectations positively correlated?

Exchange-motivated models predict a specific relation between the amount of services provided to parents and the size of inheritance and gifts received or still expected. A preliminary distinction should be made between strategic bequests, left in return for "attention", and insurance bequests, left in exchange for "aid" at old-age. Strategic inheritance aims at obtaining attention *today*, in return for expected inheritance, i.e. *bequeathable* wealth; moreover, in the extreme case of Bernheim et al. (1985), it is only truly operative if there are several children (there should be virtually no link between attention and inheritance expectations if there is a sole presumed heir). Insurance bequests occur in families with one heir as well as many, but guarantee only *potential* aid (whether financial or in kind), should parents be in need: for that reason, they may be more difficult to test.

Up to recently, results were available only for the U.S. and for bequests or bequeathable wealth, but not for inter vivos transfers. As far as "aid" is concerned, Menchik et al. (1986) recall that the NLS survey asked households whether they thought they could call on their children in case of need for financial or other assistance. The authors obtain no relation between "the intention to bequeath" and the fact of counting on one's children for financial or other help. This result seem to contradict the insurance model but should be confirmed on more reliable data.

Consider next the case of "attention". In Tomes (1981), the frequency of visits has a significant *negative* effect both on the amount of the inheritance received and on the child's human capital income. Similarly, an equation which attempts to explain the number of visits by the characteristics of both the deceased and the beneficiary reveals that the amount of the inheritance received by the child enters with a negative but not significant coefficient. On the other hand, Menchik et al. (1986) obtain, in favor of exchange-motivated bequests, a positive correlation between the parents' intention to bequeath and the frequency of their children's telephone calls and visits; yet, these results do not directly pertain to the (extreme version of) strategic bequest model, since they do not distinguish between single and multiple heirs.[45]

The reference study on strategic bequests is that of Bernheim et al. (1985) on the LRHS panel. The authors compare the average amount of attention provided by children, in the form of telephone calls or visits, with parents' bequeathable and non bequeathable wealth, while controlling for the age and state of health of parents and whether they were retired or not. In families with two or more children, bequeathable

[45] Moreover, Menchik et al. (1986) point out that a positive correlation between the volume of attention and the intent to bequeath may be given an entirely different interpretation (than that of an exchange), based upon the heterogeneous quality or intensity of relations within families: the intent to bequeath and the attention received would then only be the concomitant signs of harmonious and close families. Anyhow, comparing behaviors in families of one and more than one child would allow for a more convincing test of strategic exchange.

wealth is found to have a decisive positive influence on the amount of such attention, while the effect of (non bequeathable) retirement or pension rights is negative but not significant. In one-child families, the effect of the size of bequeathable wealth on the level of attention is on the contrary not significant (and negative).

These conclusions are very favorable to the strategic model but have been questioned since. Perozek (1998), replicating Bernheim et al. (1985) test on richer American data (1987 NSFH: National Survey of Families and Households), finds thus that bequeathable wealth looses any significant effect on attention when additional child and family characteristics are included in the specification and/or a more comprehensive measure of attention is used.

More recently, Altonji et al. (2000), using the 1988 wave of the PSID panel, have focused on *inter-vivos* time and money transfers running both ways between parents and children. Their thorough study allows thus for an alternative test of exchange models of transfers. The conclusions are worth mentioning (see section 5.3): "in contrast to simple exchange models of transfers, there is little evidence that parental income or wealth raises time transfers from children, or that time transfers from the children are exchanged for money transfers from the parents, and vice versus". Time transfers decrease sharply with geographical distance but are otherwise weakly related to income differences within the family or to the existence of money transfers from parents. On the other hand, money transfers do not depend on distance; they are not an implicit payment for services but tend to reduce inequality in household incomes ("richer siblings give more to parents and receive less"). But the authors claim once again that these equalizing effects are *too small* to fit a simple (and unidirectional) altruism model.[46]

In conclusion, it appears fair to say that standard models of (dual) exchange have not proved fully convincing as an alternative explanation to altruism of private transfers in modern, developed countries. This does not mean, however, that the introduction of a component of trade or bargaining in the relations between altruistic parents and children would not help (see previous note).[47]

4.4. Negative conclusions on the empirical front?

At this stage, it may be useful to check whether our overall jaundiced assessment about existing tests (in developed countries) of standard transfer models of private transfers

[46] Among the alternative models that may account for such limited compensatory responses of transfers to differences in incomes, Altonji et al. (2000) advocate a so-called "*strategic altruism*", which would incorporate the problems of information and control faced by parents who are uncertain about their own future and the needs of their children, and who want to have the last word while preventing conflict or jealousy among siblings (see also Bernheim et al., 2004). Using the same 1988 wave of the PSID, Ioannides and Kahn (2000) point, likewise, to the absence of an exchange motive in intergenerational transfers; they suggest, rather, a kind of mutual but unbalanced altruism between parents and children.

[47] On the other hand, it is still possible that exchange models work better for extended families in old Europe or in less developed countries (see section 5).

does not reflect too personal views. As a matter of fact, many economists studying the determinants and the role of bequests and other family transfers, seem to adopt today quite skeptic views about the predictive power of altruism, exchange and precautionary savings—as well as about the empirical knowledge accumulated over the years on these topics.[48]

4.4.1. Skeptic views today in the profession?

Just for illustration's sake, consider the informal opinion poll obtained by a selection of statements made by representative experts in the field at a recent conference, edited by Munnell and Sunden (2003).

Gale and Potter (2003), reviewing the Kotlikoff–Modigliani debate (section 3.3), conclude that "estimates of the magnitude of life-cycle wealth have proven difficult to pin down empirically. [...] The methodology used appears to be unlikely to resolve current disputes concerning the motivation for household saving and transfers, nor those regarding the impact of government policies on wealth accumulation."[49] Kopczuk and Slemrod (2003) consider the effects of taxation on the timing of transfers in the U.S. (section 4.2): "The responsiveness of estate planning to the price of intergenerational transfers is consistent with altruism. But some of the new evidence deepens the puzzle over why, if transfers are motivated by altruism, they seem to be postponed to an extent that, for tax reasons, significantly reduces the eventual after-tax transfer". Pestieau (2003), comparing the role of gifts and bequests in the United States and in Europe, regrets that "there are very little precise findings [...]. Even in the United States, where the academic debate over the motives and the implications of inheritance is more intense than anywhere else, most questions are still widely open". And E. Wolff (2003), using data of the U.S. Survey of Consumer Finances, is somewhat puzzled by his finding "that inheritances and other wealth transfers tend to be *equalizing* in terms of the distribution of household *wealth* [...]. These results are counter-intuitive...".

If our evaluation of existing tests of transfer models may seem at times as pessimistic as this sample of disillusioned assessments, it remains nevertheless clear to us that significant progress has been made, both on empirical and theoretical grounds, since (say) the early seventies. No one can thus claim today, like Tomes (1981) or Bernheim et al. (1985), who had little information on that matter, that U.S. gifts to children are "apparently insignificant". And upward transfers, especially in a non-financial form, have been introduced in models, so that family links between overlapping generations are now more fully taken into consideration.

[48] Evidence on transfers appears inconclusive even in the macroeconomic literature: in a debate relative to the consequences of public deficits, Bernheim (1989) asserts not to know of any test favorable to the altruistic Ricardian model, while Barro (1989) considers that the Ricardian equivalence principle is borne out by American data, even if the latter do not lead to definitive conclusions...

[49] The last argument is justified by the fact that the effects of government policies depend mainly on the motives for transfers *at the margin*, not so much on the aggregate level of different wealth components.

4.4.2. *Opposite views on transfers or heterogeneous transmission motives along the wealth scale?*

There are indeed lessons to be learned from the failures of standard exchange and altruistic models. We know more precisely what we are looking for: bluntly stated, a model with an altruistic component that leads, nevertheless, to small compensatory effects of transfers—be it an extended form of either exchange or altruism (see section 5.4), or an elaborate mixture of both motives (such as 3-generations indirect reciprocities). Also, more attention given to the *heterogeneity* and *timing* of financial parent-to-child transfers has helped to resolve several puzzles, such as the existence of unequal gifts and equal bequests (section 2.2), the relationship between the timing of transfers and taxation (section 4.2), and the large discrepancies in empirical estimates of the quantitative importance of gifts and bequests (sections 3.3 and 3.4).

To illustrate further, consider the following exchange. Hurd (2003), at the same conference, tries to assess whether American AHEAD data are more consistent with accidental bequests or with the existence of large planned bequests—whether driven by altruism or by exchange. Looking at the determinants of households wealth accumulation patterns, he concludes that:

> "the results here and the prior results [he has] reviewed in this paper show no evidence for an important bequest motive for saving".[50]

On the other hand, Bernheim et al. (2004), using American SCF data to evaluate the effect of estate and gifts taxes on the timing of transfers, claim that:

> "the responsiveness of transfers [...] provides additional evidence that bequests arise intentionally [among high-wealth households] and are likely due to altruism, strategic interplay between family members, or some combination of the two".

These two statements seem at first hard to reconcile and to convey a distressing, inconclusive message. But Bernheim et al. (2004) conclusion concerns potential donors of wealth gifts, that is to say only the top five percent or so of the richest households in the U.S. (the proportion is markedly higher in continental Europe); on the other hand, this privileged subgroup owns almost *half* of total bequeathable wealth. Hence, the two statements appear both important and roughly compatible whenever one makes the reasonable hypothesis of *heterogeneous motives* of bequests and other transfers along the income or wealth ladder (see section 4.1). Moreover, Hurd's quotation applies only to bequests: otherwise, this author claims that *inter vivos* parent-to-child transfers are partly compensatory (both in probability and amount) in the U.S., being driven by some

[50] Hurd attributes the existence of large estates to wealth-motivated bequests, not to a (family) bequest motive. Incidentally, Arrondel and Laferrère (1998) find on French estate data that the presence and/or the number of children do not explain the size of bequests only among the *very rich* (see also section 5.4, empirical statement 5).

altruism, thus assuming that not only transfers, but also *motives* for transfers are heterogeneous over the life-cycle—a position that was not common until recent years but has since gained many adepts in the profession (see section 3.2).

5. More on inter vivos transfers in developed countries

In order to pinpoint further specific shortcomings of standard models and to decide which extensions may better work, we shall take a closer look at three characteristics of observed family transfers (section 3.1): their *timing*—at which stage of the life-cycle are they received or given; their *direction*—the relative diffusion and quantitative importance of upward and downward transfers; their *nature*—whether in financial form or time transfers: the ultimate goal would be to get an overall picture of the "*circulation*" of private transfers between generations. The analysis leads to several so-called "empirical statements" (*ES*) of imprecise status, some of them being merely stylized facts: they are expected to be valid in most modern and developed countries, but do not seem to apply in less developed countries, neither in old Europe. The extended 3-generations variants of exchange (Cigno, 1993) and altruism (Becker, 1988), each composed of two behavioral regimes, appear already more compatible with these empirical statements than standard models of transfers.

5.1. *New demographic insights*

An adequate treatment of the timing of inter vivos downward financial transfers would in fact lead to a typical division of the life-cycle in *four* periods, rather than the usual ternary decomposition (childhood, activity, retirement). Would it be worthwhile to introduce a family with four overlapping generations in an OLG model? The question leads first to assess the degree of realism and representativeness of this specific family intergenerational composition.

5.1.1. *A four-period life-cycle (three overlapping adult generations)*

A key difference in the different types of financial downward transfers—education transfers, financial assistance, wealth gifts and bequests—is their timing (section 3.2): the grown-up child is expected to receive education transfers, or even financial assistance, much earlier in life than wealth gifts; however, even wealth gifts and inheritance are most often received largely before retirement. Hence, the idea to divide working life in two stages, C (Child) and P (Parent): education transfers and most of financial assistance are received at age C, when you become independent; wealth gifts, and even more inheritances, may be received at age P, when your parents are already old and retired.

The "representative" life-cycle is thus appropriately divided in *four* periods, according to a *KCPG* scheme. G represents old age (Grandparent) and K (Kid) pre-adult childhood at parents' home, two periods of economic dependency. C corresponds to the beginning of adult life, when you leave parents, start to work and create your own family, and have the highest probability to be liquidity-constrained; P represents mature age, with no more births, where the bulk of saving for retirement—"hump saving"—takes place for the typical consumer.[51]

Families will have four overlapping generations, with three adult ones and a *middle generation* at stage P, which may give (receive) transfers both to (from) her old parents and adult children: Altig and Davies (1993), Ribar and Wilhelm (2002) use this composition.

5.1.2. *The diversity of family intergenerational compositions*

We have thus two candidates for a theoretical description of the family in OLG models: either three overlapping generations, *KPG*, where P represents total working life, or four, *KCPG*, where P is restricted to mature age (K may be omitted). The choice is first empirical: what are, at a given time, the relative frequencies of these two intergenerational compositions, and of other existing ones, in order to get an idea of how "representative" they are. This is often a neglected issue. When studying intergenerational transfers, it is still important to know, for instance, the proportion of childless individuals or couples.

Moreover, models of transfers rely often, if implicitly, on the existence of *specific* family compositions. The model of strategic bequests (Bernheim et al., 1985), which brings parents at the beginning of retirement face to face with their children starting their working life, assumes a *(K)PG* family composition—the existence of kids K to children does not matter. But Cox and Stark (1998) specific "demonstration effect" requires a complete *KPG* composition for the mechanism of preference formation to work: parents (P) help their own parents (G) *in the presence* of their young child (K), in order to set an example for her, the idea being to inculcate in her the values or feelings—guilt, obligation, filial love or respect...—that would later secure their old-age support; but this "preference" shaping process can only work if the child is *young enough* to be modeled, i.e. in position K, not C.

To assess the relative frequencies of family compositions, consider, e.g., the French case depicted on Table 2. The reference individual, *ego*, is in position P, around fifty years old. A family *branch* to which *ego* belongs may then have any of the following eight compositions: *KCPG*: four generations; *CPG*: idem, but *ego* has no grand-children on the branch considered; and so forth for *KPG, PG, KCP, CP, KP* and finally *P*—*ego* has no living ascendants or descendants. But *ego* may belong to several family branches of different composition owing to the spacing of her children, some being of age C,

[51] To illustrate, Gokhale et al. (2001) use such a four-period life-cycle, with age K before 22 years old, age C from 22 to 43, age P from 44 to 65, age G thereafter (until 88 at the most). Note that this division is more appropriate for the U.S., with a legal retirement age of 65, than for France, where this age is only 60...

Table 2
Relative frequencies (%) of family generational compositions for individuals of age P between 49 and 53

Composition	%	%
One 3 adult generations branch (CPG):		
– $KCPG$	17.2	
– CPG*	31.9	
Total $(K)CPG$**		49.1
Parent(s), no adult child (no C):		
– KPG	8.8	
– PG*	6.8	
Total $(K)PG$**		15.6
No parents, adult child (no G):		
– KCP	9.6	
– CP*	16.9	
Total $(K)CP$**		26.5
No parents, no adult child (no G, no C):		
– KP	5.1	
– P*	3.7	
Total $(K)P$**		8.8
Total cohort age 49–53	100.0	100.0
Parent(s), one kid at home (KPG):	35.7	

Source: French survey: Insee "Patrimoine 1997".
*No K: only this composition.
**(K): may or may not have grandchildren.

others of age K: if she has living parents, she may thus belong to three types: *KPG*, *CPG* and *KCPG*.

Derived from the Insee 1997 wealth survey, Table 2 shows that 35.3% (26.5 + 8.8) of 49 to 53 years old *egos* have lost their two parents, 24.4% (15.6 + 8.8) have no adult child, 10.5% (6.8 + 3.7) no child at all. The three-adult generations compositions *(K)CPG*—with or without grand-children K—are clearly the *most frequent one*, concerning almost *half* of *egos* (49.1%). By comparison, only 8.8% of the 49–53 years old cohort belong to a *KPG* family branch while having no adult child; however, there are 35.7% who are members of a *KPG* branch (a majority of them having therefore also an adult child). Hence, there is still a good third of the families where the Cox and Stark pure demonstration effect could *potentially* work; but in a majority of cases, children are already all adults when parents face the choice whether to help or not their own parents...[52]

[52] Results were similar in the Insee 1992 wealth survey (see Arrondel and Masson, 2001).

In any case, these figures mean that there is no such thing as a *representative* family with n overlapping generations. Indeed, the multiplicity of intergenerational compositions constitutes another factor of inequality in family support, besides the level of income or wealth, the geographical distance between family members, or the heterogeneity in preferences and family links: some individuals are thus "lucky" to be early orphans, not having to spend a lot of time and money, of energy and stress, in order to support their old and dependent parents... This multi-dimensional heterogeneity should be taken into account when designing new family policies or when contemplating a withdrawal of the welfare state.

5.2. The asymmetry of (financial) transfers given mainly to younger generations

The dominant direction of financial and time transfers, that is to say the relative diffusion and amounts of upward and downward transfers, is by itself quite informative about the motivations of household behaviors and may help to rule out specific models of transfers, especially in the context of a long period of economic growth.

Whether we use, as the family composition of reference, a 3-generation one, *KPG*, or a 4-generation one, *KCPG*, *P* represents the *middle generation*. Remember also, from section 3.1, that we consider only transfers between adult generations, *K* being never the direct beneficiary (the care of young grandchildren is, in any case, considered as a time transfer benefiting the child).

5.2.1. A restrictive definition of time transfers

In this perspective, however, time transfers raise serious problems of identification that may greatly influence the conclusions obtained, e.g. concerning the dominant direction of intergenerational flows. Time transfers may include co-residence as well as various services and non financial help between independent households. But clearly, love and affectionate relations between members of the family, which are time-consuming, are not "transfers".

Contrary to Bernheim et al. (1985) and other authors, we shall thus not include "attention" given to parents in the form of *contacts* and *visits*, unless parents have health or invalidity problems: as emphasized in section 3.1, these family links often represent simultaneous exchanges, going both ways, or even *downward* transfers. Other time transfers present similar pitfalls, albeit to a smaller degree, or appear too anecdotal. Also, decisions concerning time transfers are heavily constrained, depending strongly on the distance between family members...

For all these reasons, we have decided to retain only those time transfers of significant diffusion and importance, which benefit pre-adult grandchildren and other (physically or economically) *needy* individuals—as this is especially the case with disabled or ill old parents.

5.2.2. *The only significant upward transfers are received by old retired parents from their children*

With these restrictive qualifications, upward *time* transfers received by the middle generation from an adult child should be of negligible importance in most occidental, modern societies. In any case, this result is warranted on French data (Cnav 1992 survey): C to P time transfers are quite seldom, and also limited. American data seem to convey a comparable message.[53] Moreover, among other possible upward time transfers, child-to-grandparent (C to G) support seems of a much smaller diffusion and magnitude than parent-to-grandparent (P to G) support; only the latter seems to have a significant quantitative importance.[54]

Consider then *financial* upward transfers. French (Cnav) data show again that we can safely disregard those given by the young adult generation (C). Less than 2.7% of adult children report to have given financial help to their parents of the middle generation—and even fewer parents report to have received one: this is only one fourth of the proportion of middle generation households helping their own parents (10.8%), and the amounts given are also much smaller. Furthermore, only 0.3% of children help(ed) their grandparents (C to G transfers). Similar conclusions can be drawn for the U.S. and Germany.

Provided that comparable results—which need much further qualifications—can be derived elsewhere in modern and developed occidental countries, we thus obtain:

EMPIRICAL STATEMENT 1 (*ES*1). *The only upward transfers of economic importance, whether in time or financial form, are given to the old, retired generation (G) by their children of the middle generation (P): adult children (C) do not make any significant transfers.*

Apparently, this conclusion *ES*1 does *not* extend to less developed countries: the best counter-example is perhaps given by the development of the economics of migrants' remittances, sent to their parents by grown-up children who have left home to work in urban areas, i.e. C to P transfers (see Lucas and Stark, 1985; Rapoport and Docquier, 2006). Neither was *ES*1 valid in France a century ago: especially in working classes

[53] On German data, Kohli (1999) finds more important C to P time transfers, but uses a very different definition: time transfers correspond to "any help with household tasks" (instrumental support), excluding care-giving.

[54] Consider French evidence. The Cnav 1992 survey contains similar information as the PSID survey about time transfers received or given over the last five years, but considers only *(K)CPG* families. A quarter of middle generation households give support to their elderly parents (or parents-in-law), but only 5.7% of the young generation declare to help their grand-parents. Moreover, the help given by the middle generation is much more important: when the spouse is not the "principal" helper, the latter is a child (P) in more than 90% of the cases, but a grand-child C in less than 2% of the cases (the remaining 8% being friends, neighbours, or other relatives). Comparable findings are found in the U.S. and in Germany, albeit with different definitions of time transfers.

(e.g. in the coal mine industry), young adult children had to "pay back" their parents for their upbringing.[55]

5.2.3. The overwhelmingly downward direction of financial transfers

Surprisingly, most studies on the U.S. do not much enlighten a major stylized fact: the very strong downward direction of financial transfers.[56] One noticeable exception is Lee and Miller (1994), who evaluate the (undiscounted) balance sheet of all interhousehold gifts and transfers between parents and children, in both directions, as well as bequests. Using CES 1987 data, they find that the average *net* payments in transfers from parents to *adult* children amount to about $25 000 per child, one reason for this unbalance being that young households at phase C "make no transfers at all but receive a considerable amount"—that is to say $ES1$. In addition, Lee and Miller estimate average child rearing costs at $81 000 per child.

Surveys of three adult generations—$(K)CPG$—families in European countries bring related evidence on the relative importance of upward and downward flows of transfers. On the German Aging Survey, Kohli (1999) obtains that among 40–55 years old respondents (P generation), with at least one living kin in the respective group considered below, more than 40% have made a financial transfers to adult children, but less than 12% to their parents(-in-law).

This asymmetry is even more striking in the French (Cnav 1992) survey: in 28% of the three-generational "family units"—composed of the interviewed adult child, her parents, and her (up to) four grandparents—, there was no financial transfers; in 10.8% of the cases, the P generation made a financial transfer to parents(-in-law) during the last five years—but more than half of these givers also made a financial transfer to their children; finally, only downward transfers (G to P, P to C, or G to C) occurred in the remaining 61.2% families.[57]

Hence, the following conclusion, assumed to hold in most industrial nations:

[55] On the logic of family transfers in different social classes in France in the 19th century, see Brezis (2000).

[56] According to McGarry (1999), 29% of the families in the HRS (51–61 years old) have made a cash transfer (of $500 or more) to an adult child during the past 12 months, and 25% in the AHEAD survey (70 years old and over); on the 1988 wave of the PSID, Altonji et al. (2000) report similar figures: 24% of parents made money transfers to their children (average amount: $1850), whereas only 1.8% of adult children made money transfers to their parents (average amount: $1320); on the same data, Ioannides and Kahn (2000) find comparable, although less striking results (22.4% of parents made downward money transfers, only 4.1% of children made upward money transfers). Both studies, using a loose definition for *time* transfers, find a much more balanced distribution: 30% of parents made time transfers and 27% of children.

[57] All in all, G-to-P and P-to-C financial transfers are roughly twice as frequent (concerning around 45% of the beneficiary generation) than G-to-C transfers (22% of children); as expected, wealth gifts are mainly (G-to-P) transfers (see Arrondel and Masson, 2001). Moreover, French Insee 1994 data give the following rough decomposition for the amount of 100 billion francs (or so) given to the next generations in the form of financial help (not wealth gifts): 50 billion from P to C, 30 billion from G to C, but also 20 billion from G to P—each type of transfers having thus significant diffusion and quantitative importance (Barry et al., 1996).

EMPIRICAL STATEMENT 2 (*ES*2). *There is a very large asymmetry in inter vivos financial transfers between generations: the bulk of these transfers goes downwards, towards children and grandchildren. (On the other hand, time transfers are surely more balanced).*

If true, these empirical findings already cast doubt on views of generalized, undifferentiated risk sharing, credit expansion and/or redistribution between generations, which cannot easily explain that family upward financial transfers are far less frequent than downward ones, despite past sustained economic growth benefiting younger generations in developed countries. They give weight to the idea of a strong asymmetry of altruism, being much more powerful from parents to children than in the reverse direction.

This conclusion *ES*2 is related to the debate raised by Caldwell (1978) conjecture about the *inversion* of net intergenerational wealth flows (including a child's upbringing) after the demographic transition: previously an overall profitable investment, children should have become costly. Although controversial (see Bergstrom, 1996; Lee, 2000), this hypothesis shows at least that net intergenerational—private—transfers between *adult* generations might have run from younger to older generations in old societies, such as hunter-gatherer groups or peasant agricultural societies, and could still do so in less developed countries with low social protection at old age and limited accessibility to borrowing and lending markets.[58] In industrial nations such as the U.S., on the contrary, family transfers run downwards, but may be now, according to Lee (2000), "more than offset by capital accumulation which reallocates consumption to older ages, and by strong upward transfers through the public sector".

5.3. *Time or financial assistance to elderly parents: not a dual exchange*

The result *ES*1 allows for a more precise test of models of family exchange. We have found that significant upward (time or financial) transfers go only from middle generation P to G. The question is then to know if the motivation of these transfers could be to repay their parents for the education or transfers previously received from them, or for expected gifts and bequests. The test will thus concern the existence of such past or expected G to P *counterparts* to actual transfers given to their old parents by the middle generation: it refines and extends previous tests of "dual" exchange, between the same two generations over their life-cycle (see section 4.3).

Table 3 gives the answer, the dependent variable being the probability of time or financial transfers given by the middle generation (P) to their old parents (G). Figures on the left hand side concern the French (Cnav 1992) data—see Arrondel and Masson (2001) for details. Columns on the right hand side reproduce the results of Cox and

[58] Lucas and Stark (1985) emphasize the existence of substantial remittances made by young migrants in traditional African societies. Lee et al. (1994) find evidence in Taiwan of a widespread pattern of financial support to elders, including both cash and in-kind gifts, from adult sons and daughters.

Table 3
Probability of transfers given to elderly parents

Arrondel and Masson (2001) Wolff (1998)	Time transfer[b]	Financial transfer[c]		Cox and Stark (1998)	Financial transfer	
Variables	Coef.[a]	Coef.[a]	Coef.[a]	Variables	Coef.[a]	Coef.[a]
Old generation's characteristics				Old generation's characteristics		
Support of own parents in the past	(+)			—		
Woman alone	+	0	0	—		
Professional help	++			—		
Bad health	++	0	0	No. of parents with health problems	+	+
Wealth	−−	−	(−)	—		
Income (Log.)	(+)	0	0	Number of low-income parents	++	++
				Number of high-income parents	−−	−−
Number of children alive	−−	0	0	Number of siblings	0	0
Gift to children	0			—		
Past grandchildren care	0	0	0	—		
Distance from children	−−			—		
Middle generation's characteristics				Middle generation's characteristics		
Sex (female: 1)	++	0	0	Single female	−	+
In couple	−	0	0	Married	−−	−−
Years of education	0	0	+	Years of education	+	++
Number of children at home	0			—		
Number of children not at home	0			—		
Number of children		0	+	*Number of children*	0	++
Children × education			−	*Children × education*		−−
Some health problems	+			—		
—				Percent female earnings	(+)	(+)
Income (Log.)	0	+	(+)	Household income	++	++
Wealth	0	(+)	0	Net worth	+	+

Source: French survey: Cnav survey 1992; US survey: Health and Retirement Survey.
[a]++ or −−: coefficient statistically significant at 1%; + or −: coefficient statistically significant at 5%; (+) or (−): coefficient statistically significant at 10%.
[b]Time transfer: Help given to parents owing to health problem or old age.
[c]Financial transfers include inter vivos gift, alimony, regular payments, money help, loan and housing help.

Stark (1998) for financial transfers, which are derived from the U.S. Health and Retirement Survey. In the French case, the two first columns concern a bivariate probit model for time and financial transfers (with our restrictive definition of time transfers), and the last one the results for financial transfers of the bivariate probit, when adding a cross-effect between the education level of the middle generation and the number of her children—a specification explained below (section 7.4). In the U.S. case, the two columns represent the results of a simple probit for financial transfers: the difference concerns the introduction of the mentioned cross-effect.[59]

Can transfers to old parents be explained in France either by education and transfers received in the past, or by the expectation of future gifts and inheritance? The answer is clearly negative. In particular, helped grandparents, whether in financial or non financial form, have actually *less bequeathable wealth*, meaning that their children have lower inheritance expectations: the result is the opposite to the one of Bernheim et al. (1985). Gifts and other financial transfers made to children of the middle generation do not increase the probability of being helped, neither does past care of grandchildren. Finally, helpers are not any better educated—as long as the cross-effect (children × education) is not introduced in the regression. There is therefore no sign, whatsoever, of a dual exchange, to the contrary.

The U.S. data for financial transfers reveal that grandparents are more likely to be helped if they have a low income: their wealth being not recorded, low income may actually be a proxy for *low wealth*. Anyhow, there is again no evidence of a bequest-as-exchange motivation. On the other hand, the fact that more educated children are more often helpers could be interpreted as preliminary evidence reflecting an exchange mechanism. Finally, as in the French case, the probability of financial help to parents increases with the level of available resources, whether earnings or net worth. All in all, these HRS results appear in line with those derived from other American data (section 4.3): Perozek (1998), on NSFH data, Altonji et al. (2000) or Ioannides and Kahn (2000), on the PSID, reject the hypothesis of a *quid pro quo* intertemporal trade between parents and children; Ioannides and Kahn conclude typically that "children's decisions are determined only by their parents' needs and their own ability to make transfers".

From these French and U.S. studies, we draw the following conclusions, which need further qualification and should be replicated for other modern occidental countries:

EMPIRICAL STATEMENT 3 (*ES*3). *Financial and time transfers made to old parents cannot be explained by any observable (past, present, or future) counterpart, given or promised to their children: helpers have not received more than others and do not expect higher inheritances—helped retired parents are actually poorer in (bequeathable) wealth and in income.*

On the other hand, the conclusions of *ES*3 do *not* seem to apply so much in less developed countries. There is thus ample evidence of bequests as a mean of exchange,

[59] In both cases, some explanatory variables, generally with no significant effect, are not reported in Table 3.

inheritance being used as an enforcement device in securing remittances (Rapoport and Docquier, 2006). Likewise, the implications of several "natural-as-if experiments" reveal a kind of family intergenerational bargaining contract, as for the black community in South Africa, where sizeable public transfers have been suddenly given to retirees (Duflo, 2003): having gained in power through received social security payments, old black parents were able to attract additional family transfers (such as increased co-residence with children); but grandmothers—if not grandfathers—also helped, in return, to finance grandchildren's education.

Moreover, it is likely that bilateral exchange between parents and children was much more widespread in old Europe, especially in the form of gifts or bequests given as a "payment" for old age support. In France, past official contracts of gifts allowed precisely this: parents alienated most of their property, dividing it between siblings; in return, the latter had to fulfill a number of obligations carefully specified in the contract (food, shelter, wood for the fire in winter, etc.)—if not, the gift was cancelled. Such contracts, which tried to avoid King Lear's blunders, are not available any more today.

5.4. Introducing extended 2-regimes forms of altruism and intertemporal exchange

If true, *ES*3 cast doubt on the relevance of any kind of simple exchange between parents and children in modern occidental countries, and call for alternative motives of transfers. To simplify, we shall concentrate on the last proposition in *ES*3: how to explain that, ceteris paribus, children tend to give time or financial transfers more often to *poorer*, especially lower-wealth parents?

An obvious candidate is *reverse*, child-to-parent *altruism*, or again mutual (two-sided) altruism. Such hypotheses remain nevertheless somewhat ad hoc (but see Kimball, 1987; Stark, 1993); also, they do not easily account for the dominant downward direction of co-residence and financial transfers (*ES*2), especially under sustained economic growth. Finally, if upward altruism prevailed, formal care, either professionally or publicly provided, should "crowd out" informal, familial care. This prediction does not seem warranted. On French data, the existence of professional help increases the probability that the older generation will benefit from child's support, as if professional and family helps are "complementary".[60] Cox and Stark (1998) report similar evidence for the U.S., claiming that "large increases in publicly provided home care for disabled elderly in the United States from 1982 to 1985 resulted in practically no reduction in familial care" (see also Pezzin et al., 1996).

While being more realistic, the following two extended versions of downward altruism and exchange also predict that transfers preferably go to less well-off old parents. Both of them use a three-generations framework and lead to two heterogeneous behavioral regimes.

[60] See Table 3, first column: this conclusion needs much further qualification, however, since the specific conditions required to obtain professional help are likely to create a selectivity bias.

5.4.1. *Parental altruism, liquidity constraints, and investments in child's education*

The existence of liquidity constraints prevent parents leaving *negative* bequests: they cannot borrow against a child's expected income, nor are available private intergenerational contracts which would allow to pre-commit the young child to reimburse the education received from parents by offering assistance or insurance during their old age. This so-called "generation dilemma" leads to two regimes of altruism: *free* altruism, with a Barro–Becker "operative" system of positive transfers to children, neutralizing any intergenerational public redistribution; and *constrained* altruism, inducing parents, for lack of anything better, to leave no (voluntary) bequests at all, so that public policy may become effective again.

Following a neo-Marshallian vein, Becker (1988, 1991) extends this analysis of the two regimes of altruistic transfers, while introducing parents' investments in child's human capital in a three *KPG* periods framework. Parents have now two ways of raising child's resources: either human capital transfers or material transfers to adult children. The two types of transfers being assumed to be perfectly substitutable, parents always choose the most efficient one at the margin: since human capital transfers are furthermore assumed to have initially very high but decreasing (marginal) rates of return, they first invest in child's education up to a given *threshold*, X^*, which depends only, for a given market rate of interest, on child's endowed ability and the level of parental efficiency—often proxied by their level of education; when this threshold is reached, they make inter vivos transfers and bequests.

In this setting, constrained altruism means that the level of investment X in a child's human capital will be lower than X^* and will depend also on family size and the level of resources and degree of altruism of parents. The gap $(X^* - X)$ measures the loss occurring for constrained families, who fail to fully exploit the *surplus* generated by efficient human transfers: parents underinvest in the human capital of children and get suboptimal protection when old. Hence, there is room for public intervention, any policy allowing parents to reach X^* being welcome. By contrast, unconstrained families make optimal transfers, stopping human investments at X^* and giving additional material transfers.[61]

Consider now the implications of the two regimes of altruism for upward transfers. In the free regime, parents planned to leave positive bequests; if the latter are large enough, Becker and Murphy (1988, p. 369) claim that "parents get excellent protection against

[61] Tomes (1981) tests the implications of this 2-regimes model on U.S. estate data, comparing the determinants of parental human capital investments according to whether material transfers are positive or zero. Tomes (1982) looks at the hypothesis of substitutable human capital and material transfers: since they are more efficient at producing learning or earning skills in their children, "more educated parents, holding income constant, are predicted to make lower material wealth transfers to them". Becker and Tomes (1986) focus on the predictions regarding the level of intergenerational mobility in earnings, consumption and wealth. Empirical results obtained in these studies give support to the extended altruistic model but have not been replicated by other authors.

[old-age and other] hazards through the opportunity to reduce bequests [...]; in effect, children [indirectly] help support their parents in old age, although their support is not fully voluntary". Liquidity-constrained parents, leaving no bequests, do not have such an opportunity: hence, the prediction that the probability of being helped at old age should increase with *lower* (bequeathable) *wealth*. This is precisely what French data show (see Table 3).

Constrained altruism and "inoperative" transfers may however lead to strong inefficiencies in the allocation of family resources. Public intergenerational redistribution is one possible remedy for these failures (Becker and Murphy, 1988). The other solution available to parents is the—unfortunately costly—formation of child's preference, used as a commitment device to secure support in old age. When Becker claims in his Nobel lecture that "many economists, including me, have excessively relied on altruism to tie together the interests of family members", he has precisely in mind this process of intergenerational transmission of family values or norms, in particular during early childhood.[62]

The extended 2-regimes model of altruism, incorporating investments in children's education, brings thus new realistic insights into the understanding of upward family transfers, as well as downward ones. Still, it does not solve several empirical puzzles concerning, e.g., the small compensatory effects, the heterogeneity and the timing of parent-to-child inter-vivos transfers and bequests. Incorporating the suggestions made earlier to cope with these shortcomings (in sections 2.2, 4.2 and 4.3), one may conclude this analysis of altruism by the following, albeit too vague statement, that should apply to modern developed countries:

EMPIRICAL STATEMENT 4 (*ES*4). *The 2-regimes model of parental altruism is a good start to explain downward family transfers—large investments in children's education, especially—as well as upward ones. But it should incorporate new elements regarding uncertainty and imperfect information (about transfers or children's needs), the formation and control of children's preferences, costs of unequal sharing, etc.*

In any case, this model of altruistic transfers appears less adapted to past or present traditional societies, since the latter appear notably characterized by: low investments in a child's *general* human capital; early child labor and specific training, so as to ensure the survival of the family and/or its business (Brezis, 2000); closer (economic and other) family links, allowing parents to commit more successfully children to helping them out in old age; low social protection in old age (health, pensions).

5.4.2. Self-enforcing family constitutions of three-generations exchange

Cigno's 2-regimes model of extended exchange with endogenous fertility involves three presumably self-interested generations. In the basic version, which does not consider

[62] See Becker (1993, p. 400): "parents worried about old-age support may try to instill in their children feelings of guilt, obligation duty, and filial love that [...] can commit children to helping them out".

human capital investments nor bequests, the third generation is already grown up, so that the reference framework is a *(K)CPG* one. Instead of altruism or simple *quid pro quo* exchanges, the existence of inter vivos transfers is assumed to depend on a crucial choice, made at period C, in order to circumvent the generation dilemma and to secure old-age: namely, whether to enter or not into the "round dance" of a full system of family obligations and expectations; i.e., whether to obey a set of rules or norms of transfers, or to stay out and manage on one's own. Cigno calls the two available options the "comply" and "go-it-alone" strategies.

In the "comply" case, where you rely on family intergenerational "solidarity", the contract takes the form of a self-enforcing *constitution* (Cigno, 1993): after having been brought up, you first receive transfers from your parents at age C, mainly in a financial form; then, as the middle generation (P), you give transfers and services both to children and old parents; otherwise, you will not receive support at old age G from your children—mainly through personal services. Transfers to parents are a fixed entry cost, insofar as they depend only on parents' previous transfer behavior; and you provide for old age by investing optimally in children, according to the marginal rate of return of this implicit investment (in Cigno, 1993, you choose only the number of children, transfers per capita being fixed).

In the "go-it-alone" case, you simply use borrowing and lending markets to self-finance your retirement consumption by life-cycle saving—planned bequests normally being ignored in that model; consequently, you should have few children (in principle none).

The model has a straightforward implication regarding upward transfers. Old parents with less wealth are more likely to be compliers than life-cycle savers; consequently, their probability of receiving a transfer should be *higher*, in agreement with *ES*3.

Two other series of predictions of this type of model are worth mentioning (Cigno et al., 2001). The first ones deal with the effects of public upward redistribution or funded pension schemes. An increase in benefits makes complying less profitable, inducing a number of agents, who no longer recover the fixed cost of complying, to shift from family networks and transfers to life-cycle self-accumulation: hence, even an actuarially fair, non distortionary pension system will have a macroeconomic impact—increasing total saving).

The second set of predictions concern relations to borrowing or lending markets: the more limited the accessibility to credit, the more attractive the comply strategy. They have immediate bearing in LDCs with strongly imperfect markets, but have also striking implications in highly developed market economies: credit rationed households (in position P) may have a *higher probability of making transfers* to parents and children, family solidarity acting as a remedy for market failures. Standard exchange or altruistic models predict, on the contrary, a negative effect of rationing on transfers given.

Cigno et al. (2001) provide a test of the latter prediction on Italian data. The Bank of Italy survey has information both on money transfers given—although the beneficiary is *not* known—and on credit rationing: i.e., whether any household member was denied (or believes that would have been denied if she tried) credit by a financial institution.

Since transfers are made in the family constitution essentially during the P-stage, the authors divide the sample in two: the first sub-sample includes households with children and head under the age of 65 (a proxy for the P-stage), the second childless and/or above 65 years old households. Their results give strong support to the constitution model: on the P-sample, the effects of credit rationing are positive and large, both for the probability and for the amount of transfers; on the other sub-sample, they are not significant. Moreover, the effects of the donor's resources are small on the P-sample, once again as predicted by the constitution hypothesis.

We have replicated this test on French data (Insee 1997 wealth survey) with some adjustments. Dependent variables are the probabilities of making different types of transfer to children, distinguishing wealth gifts and four forms of financial help—housing; "money"; loans; co-signature and other non monetary help (see section 3.2). Probit regressions are run on two sub-samples of households with independent children, according to whether the head is under 60 years old (P-sample) or over. Information on credit rationing is similar to that used in the Italian study.[63]

French results are not so in favor of the family constitution model. A dummy variable for credit rationing is *never* significant in the P-sample (the coefficient is positive at 11% only for the probability of co-signature), but has positive significant effects on the other sample for the probability of financial help altogether, and for two forms of help (loans and co-signature). When the credit ration variable is instrumented, results get worse for the model: in the P-sample, being credit rationed has now a negative impact on the probability of giving "money" and for financial help altogether—but still no effect for wealth gifts. Moreover, the probability of giving money (cash transfers) increases strongly with donor's income—although less in the P-sample. On the other hand, the fact that credit rationing has often *no* significant effect at all on the probability of making transfers to children may be already interpreted as an encouraging sign for the constitution hypothesis.

5.4.3. Different models of transfers for different incomes (again)?

That the constitution model works better in Italy, where family (intergenerational) solidarity is likely to be much stronger than in France, should not come as a surprise, however. And, in any case, this type of results reminds us that intra-family transfers are not always luxury goods—indeed, they appear to play a major role in developing

[63] The French survey allows for a rich set of explanatory variables, concerning both parents' and children's characteristics. The two questions about credit rationing—whether the consumer is a "discouraged borrower" or a "turned down applicant"—, are those used in the SHIW Italian survey (Guiso et al., 1996). In the P-sample, 15% of the French households declare to be credit rationed, compared with only 6% in the Italian case. To correct for a potential endogeneity bias, the instrumental procedure first estimates the probability to be liquidity-constrained, as in Cigno et al. (2001). The results are unpublished but can be obtained upon request.

countries. Even in highly developed countries, there may be a wide range of transfer motives and behaviors according to available resources, preferences and binding constraints, as illustrated by the 2-regimes models of extended exchange (Cigno) and of altruism (Becker).

"Combining" in a loose way the predictions of these two models and previous discussion (see sections 4.1 and 4.2) leads hence to the following suggestions:

EMPIRICAL STATEMENT 5 (*ES*5). *There is likely to be a large heterogeneity in motivations for private transfer and in observed behaviors, especially along the income scale: at the bottom, most transfers might obey rules of family constitution; then life-cycle saving and accidental bequests might prevail; then altruistic, policy neutralizing transfers—and at the top, wealth-motivated, entrepreneurial bequests.*

Of course, this summary is a simplification: in the constitution and altruistic models, the transition between the two regimes depends on other factors than the level of family resources. Moreover, the implicit assimilation of constrained altruism with autonomous life-cycle saving and accidental bequests is not entirely warranted.

In fact, this large heterogeneity of transfer motivations and behaviors seems likely to prevail not only within occidental countries, but also across time and between societies. Hence, in less developed countries and in old Europe, transfers might be often determined by family rules of exchange, although the type of intergenerational exchange enforced by family norms might differ from Cigno's self-enforcing constitutions: in particular, C-to-P transfers, from young adults to their middle age parents, would be quite common (against *ES*1); moreover, transitions to other stages would be made easier by the development of financial markets, the expansion of social security, and higher investments in general human capital.

5.4.4. The two extended models of exchange and altruism linked to particular forms of reciprocity

As a description of family transfers in developed countries, the two models of Becker and Cigno perform much better than simple exchange or altruism: they are more compatible with facts *ES*1 to *ES*3; and still more elaborate versions of these models could accommodate *ES*4 and *ES*5. Also, the two models appear, in a sense, "complementary": Cigno's model does not treat parental investments in child's education, which are at the center of Becker's analysis; on the other hand, downward altruism pays limited attention to upward transfers towards old parents, which play a key role in the constitution hypothesis.

The constitution model pictures a "general" form of family intergenerational *reciprocity*. In essence, the constitution is a system of obligations and expectations that you are *free*, however, to accept or to refuse: you may feel an "internal" obligation to return the gift, but you are under no "external" obligation to "comply", as is the case in a market exchange when agreed (Kolm, 2000, p. 8). Moreover, in the comply strategy, you first have to make it even with the previous generation: this represents the fixed cost of entry into the constitution; then, you may trade in the optimal way with the next generation in order to secure old age. Therefore, a central implication is that an increase in social security or pension coverage, or better financial markets, should weaken family ties (substitution effect).

Dynastic altruism *a la* Barro–Becker relies on a mechanism of transmission that can be viewed as a specific form of downward and forward-looking *indirect reciprocity*: I do for my kids what I expect them to do in turn for their own kids. As a matter of fact, the (early) formation of child's preferences appears a hidden but crucial issue in both altruistic regimes: dynastic altruism presupposes that the benevolent patriarch is fully able to model children's preferences and control their transfer behavior—as if they were his clones; and liquidity-constrained altruistic parents have to resort to a costly process of transmission of family values and norms in order to secure old-age needs.

6. Indirect reciprocities between generations: theory

Cigno's and Becker's 2-regimes models represent one way to remedy for major empirical failures of standard exchange and altruistic models, while only introducing a few changes or extensions. In the same spirit, *indirect reciprocities* between generations constitute another, also with minimal deviations from standard models.

At the theoretical level, they can be seen as a reconciliation of exchange and altruism, that blur somewhat the distinction between the two generic motivations for transfers: they are norms of three-generational exchange but require, in the case of education and transfers to children, some kind of altruism in order to be self-enforcing. Moreover, they bear *some* relation to the burgeoning literature on imitation, transmission of norms and cultural traits, education and preference formation (Becker, 1993, 1996), but some relation *only*: again, they must first be viewed first as a reciprocal exchange, where the replication from one generation to the next of the same kind of transfer or action contributes to the perpetuity of the family *chain* and "values", while enhancing mutually beneficial cooperation.

From an empirical point of view, indirect reciprocities present a number of advantages. Against altruism, they are compatible with small or non-existent compensatory effects, since their prime objective is not income pooling and consumption smoothing between generations, but the participation to chains of transfers, perceived as systems of obligations (towards previous generations) and expectations (towards following ones). Also, they can explain the lack of any bilateral counterpart for the support of elderly parents (section 5.3): the return-gift should come not from their parents but from their children. Finally, they allow to introduce *new explanatory variables* of observed transfers between parents and children, which are relative to a *third* generation, and we shall see that these variables show significant predictive power: transfers given to children appear strongly influenced by transfers received from own parents (so-called "retrospective" effects), and support or help given to parents depend upon expectations of similar transfers, received at old age from one's children (e.g., "demonstration effects").[64]

We shall first recall some basic features of reciprocal behavior as such, especially when applied to generations within the family. Following Kolm's approach, we shall then introduce *general* reciprocity, which is bound to have some holistic component. This analysis will be used to propose a typology of intergenerational indirect reciprocities (see Table 4).

6.1. Reciprocity between generations in the family

Up to now, most economists of the family tend to explain transfers between parents and children, either by the existence of a counterpart, already given or expected by the donor generation [exchange], or directly by the psychological gain that the donor gets from the gift itself or the increased well-being of the beneficiary [altruism]. *Reciprocity*, the touchstone of anthropology, offers a third route.

6.1.1. Homo reciprocans

Loosely speaking, "reciprocal exchange" means some chain of gifts and return-gifts encapsulated in a full system of expectations and sanctions (and "internal" obligations), where affectivity, "emotions", a sense of justice, etc. play important roles, and where failure to comply with the rules may place oneself in an intolerable position, especially in a family context: "opting out" may not always be an acceptable option, and group survival is often a crucial issue.

A central theme of this handbook concerns the ways economists have imported and adapted this concept, especially in experimental games and relations. Very bluntly stated, a *Homo reciprocans* will follow tit-for-tat strategies of "cooperation", even when the folk theorem (valid in indefinitely repeated, non cooperative games) does not apply: an extreme case occurs between "strangers" playing only once. Agents are assumed to share a similar sense of justice, or rather *fairness*, indicating which behaviors or responses can be considered "benevolent", and which behaviors "malevolent": the first ones should be rewarded, and the second ones punished, even if these rewards and sanctions appear *costly* and thus against pure self-interest (see Fehr and Schmidt, 2006). Of course, in the specific context of strangers meeting once, a *Homo oeconomicus* would not give any weight to her "emotions" and would not embark in such expensive reactions that bring nothing to her.

[64] See section 7. It should be noted that Cigno's and Becker's models have indirect ways to accommodate these "3rd generation effects", although the predicted effects would be too small and not enough selective.

This schematic example shows why reciprocity introduces an intermediate, hybrid motivation between altruism and exchange, as clearly pointed out by the French anthropologist Mauss (1950) through his concept of *échange-don* (gift-exchange): costly rewards bear some similarities with (reciprocal) generous altruism, whereas costly retaliation (when it is not simply motivated by revenge) seems at first due to a form of elaborate strategic or manipulative exchange.

But there is more than this: generally overlooked by economists, two key lessons can be learnt from (especially French) anthropological studies: they have a specific bearing on the analysis of transfers and relations between generations within the family.

6.1.2. *The "ambivalence" of gifts*

The first one, which has been underlined by Mauss (1950) in his famous *Essay on Gift*, concerns the inherent ambivalence of any gift, which induces a double relation between donor and recipient: a *positive* relation of sharing and solidarity on the one hand; but also, a *negative* relation of superiority, domination, coercion or violence, the recipient becoming *in debt* to the giver and, to a certain extent, subordinate to her.[65]

This statement has strong implications in the case of parent-to-child gifts. Their primary objective should be to favor and speed up wealth transmission, while strengthening family links. Instead, they have been repeatedly accused, through history, of destroying family links and generating conflicts, with children showing ingratitude, or parents wanting to manipulate and control children—all the more so when the gift was, like a will, revocable (see below). Economic models of transfers use to tackle this issue only incidentally—the "rotten kid" is first an ungrateful child. Bernheim et al. (1985) introduce manipulative transfers only in the form of strategic *bequests* (for parents to have the last word), and refer to King Lear's strategic *gifts* as the "King Lear's blunder", as if it was meaningless or insane behavior.[66]

This pessimistic view about gifts however accords with the historical change concerning its legislation (Toubiana, 1988). Thus, up to the 16th century in France, a declared gift was *reversible*, leading to many abuses and pressures on children. The law had to be changed, making now gifts irrevocable, except in very specific cases (when the child is *too* ungrateful): consequently, their number decreased very significantly.[67]

This latent violence in family relations could still explain other "puzzles" in transfer behavior that will not be pursued here. Hence, the dominant practice of estate equal sharing could be interpreted as a way to avoid conflict between siblings and to preserve harmonious family links (see section 2.2). Likewise, the increased popularity of

65 See, e.g., Godelier (2000). Incidentally, a gift may also correspond to a relation of *inferiority*, being a way to show one's submission to the beneficiary, to ask for her protection, etc. (see Kolm, 1984, p. 79–81).

66 But King Lear had personal reasons to act the way he did. His gift to his three daughters is generally interpreted as a disguised "incestuous" proposal to his youngest and preferred daughter, Cordelia, still a virgin, who had to choose between her two suitors the very same day... (Toubiana, 1988).

67 Anyhow, French parents are still trying to make only "partial" or half-reversible gifts: they often keep the usufruct of the asset given, or else give only the usufruct of the asset (see Arrondel and Laferrère, 2001).

"gifts to the surviving spouse" (in France at least) may be due, in part, to the limited reliability parents attach to children's support in modern nuclear families. Also, the fact that old household owners *rarely* sell their homes on an installment payment to be provided with a life annuity cannot be entirely explained by the well known drawbacks of annuity markets: the operation would often remain profitable *both* to parents and liquidity-constrained children. Here again, the family taboo not to deprive children from one's inheritance may be part of the answer.

As we have seen, a recent move in the literature tries to incorporate more fully such elements in an altruistic framework in order to account for empirical puzzles, such as estate equal division, or the significant but limited effects of taxes on the timing of parent-to-child transfers (Bernheim et al., 2004); Altonji et al. (2000) also invoke a kind of parents' "strategic altruism" in order to explain limited compensatory effects of inter vivos transfers (section 4.3).

6.1.3. Negative reciprocities between family generations

The second lesson taught by anthropology comes from the importance of *harmful* reciprocal behaviors that cannot be interpreted as sanctions or retaliation in response to failures to comply but correspond, on the contrary, to the very observance of rules. This is especially true in the case of indirect reciprocities. According to Mauss (1968), the best illustrations of indirect reciprocities, which occur often between generations, deal with ragging, hard *rituals of initiation* and the like, "to which we must very often comply, even nowadays". These are examples of negative downward forms where, typically, it is impossible to "give back" to the malefactor, i.e. to get even with him.

Negative, upward forms of indirect reciprocity may seem less common. But consider the following quotation from Montaigne's *Essais* (book I, chapter XXIII):

> "He that was seen to beat his father, answered that it was the custom of their family: that his father had beaten his grandfather, his grandfather his great-grandfather, and pointing to his son: 'and this will beat me when he comes to age' ".

Of course, a *Homo oeconomicus* will try to break this tradition. How then to interpret this equilibrium of abusive chain behaviors? Imitation effects, endless retaliation, the prevalence of (unconsciously instilled) habits, the transmission of social norms, etc. are only part of the answer. Apparently, in the society considered, there was no cheaper way to guarantee the succession of generations, i.e. the passage of *authority* from father to son: in other words, this harmful tradition aimed at reproducing the symbolic murder of the father, and should be interpreted as a kind of reverse ragging, a *transition ritual* to elders' retirement. Yet, the ritual appeared a crucial condition of the functioning and reproduction of that society.

6.2. General reciprocity: "rebound" and "propagation" effects

Indirect reciprocity is a form of *general* reciprocity, which involves more than two agents. Gifts and return-gifts are still driven by a process of *debt* creation and payment, but the principle at work has now some "holistic" dimension, referring to the *group* within which reciprocal exchanges take place (strangers to the group are excluded from this game of reciprocity). Namely, by making a gift to *B, A* acquires a claim on the group and expects one of its member (not necessarily B) to pay it back to her; likewise, the beneficiary B becomes in debt to the group, and will be "obliged" to redeem it while giving, in turn, to another member (not necessarily A), and so forth. This is how links of reciprocal debts and claims, escaping the prison of dual relations, can spread all over the group and strengthen solidarity ties, all the more so that return-gifts can now be made in a visible comparable form.

Such a possibility is especially important in our case, where the group is assimilated to the family lineage and relations between generations are strongly *asymmetric*, implying that *quid pro quo* exchanges between parents and children may not be always appropriate. Thus, an heir becomes in debt to the family, with an obligation to give back that cannot be fulfilled to the deceased: the only way to redeem the debt is to pay it back to one's children, *as if* bequests were made *in return* for received inheritance from one's parents. Likewise, in the Cox and Stark demonstration effect, parents, by helping their own parents, acquire a *claim* on their children, as if they could pre-commit their offspring to support them in their old days (as in pay-as-you-go retirement systems).

If we want to remain within the framework of methodological individualism, we have to determine how these mechanisms of general reciprocity can work at the level of *personal motivations*. Kolm (1984) addressed this issue already some twenty years ago, bringing to light the existence of two human (universal-?) features:

(i) experimental studies and observations by socio-psychologists find that people tend to give to a third party when they have been given to, even when they do not know their benefactor or the beneficiary—an effect labeled "helping behavior" by Kolm;

(ii) also, people tend to give to those who have given (to a third party)—a phenomenon already emphasized by Descartes, and hence referred to as the "Descartes effect".[68]

We will briefly comment on these two *basic ingredients* of general reciprocity, while using other denominations and emphasizing the fact that such effects may take the form of *malevolent* as well as benevolent behaviors. The problem may be stated simply as follows. A gives to B. The direct return-gift should be: B gives back to A, but B may have little incentive to do so, especially in games with sequential players (such as generations). How can, then, a third party (X or Y) be introduced in the return gift. There are only two possibilities, which rely on the holistic dimension of reciprocity through the Maussian obligation to give back (see Table 4):

- Having received from A, B becomes in debt to the group, and redeems it by giving in turn to a third party X, and so on. Call this the *propagation effect* (helping

[68] The quotation of Descartes (*Œuvres complètes*, Paris, Vrin, 1964, IV, p. 316) is reproduced in Kolm (1984, p. 108–109).

effect), which modifies and extends the responsibility of one's deeds: for better or for worse, one's actions may have far-reaching chain consequences, beyond the effect on the situation of the initial beneficiary. On the positive side, this means that "helped people will help in turn", whereas the negative side corresponds rather to "evil engenders evil" or more precisely: "torturers are often former victims", e.g., parents beating children have often been beaten by their parents.

- Having given to B, A has acquired a claim on the group, which will be reimbursed by a third party Y, giving in turn to A, and so on. This *rebound effect* (Descartes effect) expresses a norm of immanent justice: "you shall reap what you have sown", meaning, in positive variants: "one gives to the givers", and in negative ones: "unkind people get punished".

Well documented by socio-psychologists and anthropologists, the propagation effect provides the rationale for ragging and many rituals of initiation: Godelier (1982) gives the example, in the Baruya tribe (in New Guinea), of elder young men, still unmarried and virgin, giving their "uncontaminated" sperm in the mouth of younger—unrelated—men (this transmission between successive male generations is meant to get rid, symbolically, of any previous female influence, and to deprive women of their initial power, i.e. to make children).

The strange custom reported by Montaigne—sons beating fathers in turn – has clearly the structure of a rebound effect. Yet, anthropologists have not paid much attention to this effect, although Ekeh (1974), building on Lévi-Strauss' work, describes a kind of generalized social exchange which has close relations with a linear rebound effect.[69]

This discussion leads to a primary classification of general reciprocities in four categories, according to whether they rely on the rebound or on the propagation effect, and according to their position in the gift-return-gift process (see Kolm, 2000, p. 30):

- reciprocities will be called *backward-looking*, when they entail a *final obligation to give back*, i.e. an obligation to comply to the relevant effect, to respond to a third party behavior: for instance, in the case of the propagation effect, I should help people if I have been previously helped;
- reciprocities will be called *forward-looking*, if they entail an *initial obligation to give* in order to provoke the desired effect, to "force" the return-gift in one's own favor (rebound), or in favor of somebody else (propagation): according to Kolm (1984, p. 109), Descartes was thus well aware that by acting generously, one could gain others' favor and profit in the end from the whole operation—in other words, selfish people may behave as if they were altruistic in order to take advantage of the rebound effect.

[69] Ribar and Wilhelm (2002) provide an analysis of Ekeh's work on social exchange. Many anthropologists, such as Lévi-Strauss (1958), come to rebound effects only in *circular* indirect reciprocities: A gives to B, who gives to X ... who gives to Y, who gives back to A.

6.3. Four types of intergenerational indirect "serial" reciprocities

Four types of serial reciprocities between generations have been introduced in section 1.1, concerning upward or downward transfers, and being either "backward-looking", when transfer decisions are influenced by parents' behavior, or "forward-looking", when transfers are made in expectation of similar behavior on behalf of the next generation. Clearly, the two approaches of backwardness and forwardness are equivalent, and the two typologies coincide: rebound effects apply to upward transfers, and propagation effects to downward transfers.

Table 4 reproduces the main characteristics of each of the four types. As expected, forward-looking types will appear more familiar to economists: pay-as-you-go retirement schemes follow a forward and upward reciprocity (type II); forward and downward forms allow an endowment of agents with a longer, if not infinite horizon, as with dynastic altruism (type IV). Of course, in dynamic equilibrium, types I and II should be viewed as the two connected phases (backward and forward) of the rebound effect, and likewise, types III and IV as the two moments of the propagation effect. In each case, the act of transfer represents the entry cost into the indefinite chain of beneficial cooperation—do as your predecessor did—, *and* gives, at the same time, the right to expect the same treatment from successor(s).

To achieve optimality, such norms of reciprocity should follow *Rawlsian* rules of justice between generations: the initial obligation to give corresponds then to the choice of a principle, such that you *would like* all succeeding generations to adopt it in turn; and the final obligation to give back comes to the choice of a principle, such as you *would have liked* all previous generations to have followed it. Yet, the second rule relies on a pious hope, since it is not possible to rewrite history: enforcement conditions are more severe in the case of backward reciprocities, requiring some kind of "generosity".

The problems of modelling and enforcement of these four types of indirect reciprocities is clearly beyond the scope of this paper. We shall only, on given examples, underline typical pitfalls encountered by each type.

Hammond (1975) "pension game" is an example of a backward and upward type, which anticipates some elements of Cigno's family constitution model. It is a non-cooperative game of sequential players representing selfish overlapping generations who have to decide whether or not to give a (fair) pension to the previous generation. A *history* dependent rule allows to reach an equilibrium of mutually beneficial cooperation where each generation gives a pension *as if* she was altruistic. The rule considers the number n of periods in which no (or an unfair) pension has been paid, since a (fair) pension was last paid: if n is odd, the present generation gives no pension to punish ascendants; if n is even or nil, she rewards the previous generation by giving her a fair pension.

This model points out two revealing difficulties. First, a tit-for-tat strategy is hard to adapt to a chain of generations: if I cooperate generously although my father did not, my son cannot punish me or he will not receive himself a pension. Also, what should be done if the five previous generations have not paid any pension: to punish my father,

Table 4
Types of serial indirect reciprocities between family generations

Direction of transfers	Time orientation: *Backward-looking* Final obligation to give back	*Forward-looking* Initial obligation to give
Upward (Child-to-parent transfers)	*Type I*	*Type II*
Objective: Self-survival		
Rebound effect[1] Descartes–Montaigne (+): "One gives to the givers" (−): "Unkind people get punished"	Backward–upward	Forward–upward
⇒ example	Hammond: The pension game	Cox-Stark: The demonstration effect
Downward (Parent-to-child transfers)	*Type III*	*Type IV*
Objective: Perpetuation of the family		
Propagation effect[2] Mauss–Godelier (+): "The helped ones help in turn" (−): "Evil engenders evil"	Backward–downward	Forward–downward
⇒ example	Bevan-Stiglitz: Retrospective (or golden-rule) bequests	Barro-Becker: Dynastic (Ricardian) altruism

[1]Rebound effect or "Descartes effect" (Kolm). Ritual: transition to retirement, loss of (economic) power.
[2]Propagation effect or "helping effect" (Kolm). Ritual: initiation, passage to adulthood (hazing...).

I should be able to distinguish between disguised defections and genuine sanctions... The second difficulty comes from the fact that cooperation requires that every generation holds *appropriate beliefs* about all future generations: no one, including herself, should have a better choice than to comply to the rule. Of course one may wonder how such common beliefs can be sustained in a family context in the absence of institutional obligations, i.e. how collective norms may emerge.

Cox and Stark's demonstration effect, where adults help their parents in the presence of their young children in order to imprint on them a corresponding behavior pattern, is a forward and upward type. The problem of enforcement concerns the appropriate mean, by one way or another, to pre-commit future generations in a long-term contract. The model has interesting predictions: people with (several) young kids should give more help to their parents; children will give more help if they expect to need themselves more support, when old; and grandparents will have a strong incentive to subsidize the birth and education of grandchildren.

The demonstration effect encounters, however, several difficulties. First, it works well only in a *KPG* context: in a *CPG* context, the adult child *C* is too mature to be modeled when grandparents need support (see section 5.1). More importantly, the intergenerational chain of upward transfers has key features of a *public good*: every generation is better off if the chain of transfers has always existed, but would prefer the chain just to begin with her (i.e. to be the first to receive support), all the more so that her children will have, anyhow, to use the demonstration effect for their own children. This creates problems of free-riding and time inconsistency.[70]

Bevan and Stiglitz's (Bevan and Stiglitz, 1979) retrospective (or golden rule) bequests, where bequeathing patterns tend to be reproduced from one generation to the next, can be interpreted as a form of backward and downward indirect reciprocity. As a matter of fact, they correspond to altruism under imperfect information and, especially, limited rationality (see section 2.1).

Finally, Barro-Becker dynastic altruism may be viewed as a variant of forward and downward indirect reciprocity, whenever one considers identical preferences and transmission behavior from one generation to the next, not just as a simplifying assumption but rather as the outcome of parents' formation of children's preferences, of the education and transfers given to their offspring. Yet, if this is the case, one may question the universal success of this transmission process of tastes and assets, and wonder why each generation does not have to struggle to make up her mind in the trade-off between received "family values" and multi-dimensional inheritance on the one hand, and own projects and personal desires on the other.

These illustrative examples lead to a preliminary conclusion. Apparently, to explain mechanisms of indirect reciprocity between generations, economic models have to invoke some form of limited rationality and/or imperfect knowledge. One solution to these problems of enforcement could be to combine upward and downward indirect reciprocities together, or else to combine direct and indirect reciprocities together, e.g. adding child's education in Hammond's model (to get a pension, people should first give one to their own parents and properly educate their children). Such views are developed in Cigno's (Cigno, 1993) constitution model or in Ribar and Wilhelm's (Ribar and Wilhelm, 2002) approach to the transmission of intergenerational assistance attitudes.

7. Indirect reciprocities: preliminary French and U.S. evidence

Precise predictions of indirect reciprocities are difficult to formulate because of the lack of completely specified and articulated models. Nevertheless, three kinds are easy

[70] One way out would be to assume that the current generation consciously chooses how to help parents while her offspring simply *copy* their parents, a problematic solution indeed. Bergstrom and Stark (1993) resolve the difficulty by assuming that, with given probabilities, a child will either copy its parents' actions or choose rationally on its own self-interest. The helping decision of the current generation will then depend, in equilibrium, upon the proportions of imitators and choosers (see also Bergstrom, 1996).

to state and have been already emphasized: the first two ones give indirect reciprocities an empirical advantage over altruism and exchange; the last ones—"3rd generation effects"—provide *specific* tests of these reciprocities.

First, contrary to pure altruism, indirect reciprocities should entail at most *limited* compensatory effects, since the prime motivation for the (downward) transfer is not to increase relatives' well-being, but to keep on the intergenerational chain in order to benefit in turn from it. Thus, retrospective bequests lead to equal sharing of estate and only to partial compensation between generations, since parents are assumed not to know the actual level of children's resources and to base their choice only on expectations on that level (derived from their own income and the degree of intergenerational regression towards the mean in income).

Second, contrary to simple (dual) *quid pro quo* exchange, the payment for services or financial assistance to parents comes, in a comparable form, from one's own children.

Third, indirect reciprocities predict strong 3rd generation effects, meaning that transfers between parents and children depend on the characteristics or transfer behavior of either grandparents or grandchildren. In what follows, we shall concentrate on preliminary tests of:

- "retrospective effects" (backward-looking reciprocities): financial transfers to children, as well as time and money transfers to old parents, should be largely influenced by corresponding behaviors of own parents (probability, form or amount of the transfer);
- "expectations effects" (forward-looking reciprocities): transfers to children should advantage siblings more able to continue the family chain of transfers (e.g., having children); likewise, support given to parents should be motivated by demonstration and related effects, which depend both on the characteristics of, and specific demands on one's own children.

7.1. "Retrospective effects" on parent-to-child inter vivos transfers and bequests

Consider first "quantitative" effects. French and U.S. results, albeit quite tentative, show that the propensity to bequeath out of capital receipts is significantly *higher* than the one out of life earnings. Hence, on the basis of somewhat flimsy composite data, Menchik (1980b) obtains an elasticity of bequests with respect to human resources of approximately 2.5, compared with an elasticity of 0.33 to 0.38 with respect to inheritance received; since the total wealth received represents typically less than 10% of human resources—even for the rich American sub-population considered—, complete substitutability between the two components of resources would lead to an inheritance elasticity of bequests below 0.25, much lower than the one observed. Arrondel and Masson (1991) have applied the same methodology on French household data, using bequeathable wealth in old age as a proxy for bequests. They find an elasticity of wealth with respect to inheritance and gifts of 0.5 to 0.6 for all households—and still between 0.35 and 0.4 for households with children—, whereas the corresponding one with respect to human resources is only 1.5: the first elasticity appears at least twice as high as the one that would be obtained under complete substitutability.[71]

More convincingly, Arrondel et al. (1997) systematically report, on various French data sets, strong and significant retrospective effects on a "qualitative" basis. In addition, the latter appear highly *selective*: i.e., the existence of transfers received from one's parents increases above all the probability to make the *same* kind of transfer to one's children. Thus, heirs have not only a higher propensity to bequeath, but also to make a will if their parents have made one; likewise, having benefited from a given form of financial help increases the probability to make the same form of help, but not so much, or not at all, the probability of making other transfers (i.e. gifts or bequests) to children.

To document further the high degree of selectivity of qualitative retrospective effects, we have analyzed the differential rates of intergenerational reproduction of specific transfer patterns, distinguishing financial help from wealth gifts, and again various forms of financial help: "housing", "money", and "loan". Using the Insee 1992 wealth survey, Arrondel and Masson (2001) find strong and selective retrospective effects on the probabilities of making *each* type of these transfers to children (see also Wolff, 1998, on French Cnav data).

As a further illustration, Tables 5a and 5b report similar Probit results obtained from the more recent Insee "Patrimoine 1997" survey. The top of Table 5a compares the estimated probabilities of giving financial help and wealth gifts to children, using dummies for the existence of various transfers received. The estimated probability of making a wealth gift is twice higher for recipients (10.9%) than for non beneficiaries (5%), whereas it does not depend on the existence of financial help received, and less on inheritance received (7.4% against 5.3%). The probability of helping (or having helped) children is 61.1% for households who have been themselves helped by their parents, but only 46.4% among non helped households—a 15% gap compared with a 5% or so difference in the probability of helping between beneficiaries and non-beneficiaries of other receptions (gifts or inheritance).

Table 5b gives equivalent results for the probability of making different forms of financial help. Once again, the probability of a given form of help depends strongly on the existence of the *same* form of help received, whereas the effects of the reception of other transfers are less important and not always significant.

7.2. Discussion: robustness of retrospective effects on parent-to-child transfers

These striking observed effects of the existence of a given transfer received on the probability of making the same kind of transfer could prove an important empirical

[71] Once again, a ratio of capital receipts to life resources of 10% can be considered an upper bound. Data of the more recent Insee survey ("Patrimoine 1997") give a smaller elasticity of (bequeathable) wealth with respect to inheritance, around 0.15. For the top decile of wealth, the elasticity of wealth with respect to income is 1.2; for the 90% lower incomes, this elasticity is 0.7. In any case, the elasticity of wealth with respect to inheritance remains markedly higher than the one that would be obtained if there were complete substitutability.

Table 5a
Parent-to-child transfers: retrospective effects; any help or wealth gift

Effect of transfers received	Probability of helping (in %)		Probability of making a wealth gift (in %)	
	Non beneficiary	Beneficiary	Non beneficiary	Beneficiary
	• With dummy variables (0–1) for transfers received			
Inheritance	46.4	52.6	5.3	7.4
Gift	48.1	52.6	5.0	10.9
Financial help	46.4	61.1	Non pertinent variable	
Average probability	49.6		5.9	
	• With instrumental variables for wealth			
Inheritance	Non pertinent variable		5.6	8.4
Gift	Non pertinent variable		5.6	10.5
Financial help	46.4	64.1	Non pertinent variable	
Average probability	49.7		6.4	
	• With instrumental variables for transfers received*			
Inheritance	Non pertinent variable		Non pertinent variable	
Gift	Non pertinent variable		4.4	12.0
Financial help	42.9	69.4	Non pertinent variable	
Average probability	49.9		5.7	

Source: French survey: Insee "Patrimoine 1997".
Note: probabilities are calculated everything being equal (other individual characteristics are fixed to their average value: age, social status, education, income, wealth, marital status, children's characteristics...).
*Probabilities of helping or giving for beneficiary are calculated for a maximum (instrumented) probability of receiving a transfer.

Table 5b
Parent-to-child transfers: retrospective effects; different forms of help

Effect of transfers received	Probability of helping in housing (in %)		Probability of giving money (in %)		Probability of making a loan (in %)	
	Non beneficiary	Beneficiary	Non beneficiary	Beneficiary	Non beneficiary	Beneficiary
Gift	Non pertinent variable		43.6	45.7	Non pertinent variable	
Inheritance	Non pertinent variable		43.1	47.0	Non pertinent variable	
Same help	6.6	11.7	42.3	58.0	5.6	14.6
Other help	6.4	8.9	43.6	51.0	Non pertinent variable	
Average probability	6.8		44.4		6.0	

Source: French survey: Insee "Patrimoine 1997".
Note: probabilities are calculated everything being equal (other individual characteristics are fixed to their average value: age, social status, education, income, wealth, marital status, children's characteristics...).

contribution to the understanding of the motives for parent-to-child transfers. However, they have been obtained mainly on French data and, with a few exceptions, have not been replicated elsewhere. It is therefore worthwhile to check, at least on French data, whether they are not a pure artifact. Indeed, such estimated effects could be spurious (being due to omitted variables) or again not robust, for a series of different reasons that we examine briefly in turn.

(i) *Measurement error in the household declaration of receipts*. The information used regarding the existence of transfers received from parents is built on the declaration of the possible *beneficiary*. But those households which actually give a transfer in a specific form to their own children may have a better recall of similar transfers received earlier from parents, or may be more willing to acknowledge such receipts. The Cnav "three-generations" survey, where both parents' and children's declarations about transfers given or received are available, allow a check on the importance of this potential bias.

Replacing children's by parent's declaration shows that this bias is likely to be small: although there are differences in declarations between generations, neither the size nor the degree of significance of retrospective effects change much in the Probit regressions.

(ii) *Mismeasurement of other variables (wealth)*. The coefficient for transfer receipts could capture in part the effects of other quantitative explanatory variables that are often underestimated, such as the value of net worth. There are two simple ways of controlling for these measurement errors.

First, omitting altogether in the regressions variables concerning transfers receipts does not greatly modify the estimated effects of other factors, especially of parents' net worth.

Second, results shown at the bottom of Table 5a show that retrospective effects are robust to the instrumentation of wealth or of transfer receipts (replacing dummy variables by estimated probabilities of reception). Indeed, retrospective effects on the probability of helping become quantitatively more important and "perfectly" selective, the existence of *other* types of transfers received being no longer significant.[72] The same happens for the probability of gifts with instrumented transfer receipts: the probability of making a gift is almost three times more important for recipients (12%) than for other households (4.4%).

(iii) *Intergenerational correlation in heterogeneous preferences*. Suppose that parents making transfers have a higher degree of altruism towards children and that tastes are (partially) transmitted to children. In this case, households having benefited from parent transfers would have a higher probability of making transfers to their own children simply because they are *more altruistic* towards their progeny.

[72] The significant effects of "other" transfers that are obtained without instrumentation seem indeed to capture part of the wealth and retrospective effects.

An indirect way to test for this alternative scenario is to check whether transfer recipients are more altruistic than non recipients. In the Insee "Patrimoine 1997" survey, an additional questionnaire has allowed us to build a qualitative (ordinal) "score of altruism" for a sub-sample of interviewees. We find only a weak—although significant—positive correlation between the score and the existence of transfer received, that cannot account for the quantitative importance and the selectivity of estimated retrospective effects.[73]

(iv) *Heterogeneity in family values and "culture"*. Instead of the heterogeneity in individual parameters of preferences such as the degree of altruism, sociologists and anthropologists will rather invoke the heterogeneity in family values or *culture*, a "holistic" concept that involves a whole set of do's and don'ts concerning a large range of behaviors and practices besides transfer decisions (relative to marriage, children, etc.)—the idea being to secure the socio-economic and symbolic survival of the family across generations. Economic household data are not really tailored for a test of this hypothesis which appears, however, largely inoperative in accounting for the high selectivity of qualitative retrospective effects.

In short, retrospective effects obtained on French data appear compatible with indirect reciprocities, where transfers received and given are part of an extended "balanced" exchange between three generations (possibly due to bounded rationality or imperfect information). Other explanations are of course conceivable, but we have been able to rule out or limit the most obvious ones.

7.3. Dynastic transmission behavior (forward-downward type)

Forward-looking and downward indirect reciprocities appear less obvious to test: here especially, we lack specific predictions derived from explicit models. Unequal sharing gives some indication of such reciprocities, however.

Arrondel and Laferrère (1992) have analyzed the rare cases of unequal sharing of French estates (8%), which occur mainly in rich or self-employed families, and through gifts rather than inheritance (in more than 80% of the cases). They find that the only registered variable that explains the discrepancy between the amounts received by siblings is demographic: namely, the advantaged children are the ones who have themselves children. Presumably, these privileged beneficiaries will be more able to perpetuate the family lineage or enterprise and to replicate the same transmission process in favor of their own offspring.

On U.S. data, corresponding evidence is mixed. On the Estate Income Tax Match, Wilhelm (1996), who has information only on bequests (not on gifts), finds a positive correlation between the amount of inheritance received and the fact of being married;

[73] The main determinants of the score of altruism are income level, level of education and number of children; it has a slightly positive effect on the probability of making transfers to children (see Arrondel et al., 2004). A full test of this scenario would have to measure the intergenerational correlation in the degree of altruism (or in attitudes towards transmission), a correlation for which we know of no empirical evidence.

however, unequal sharing does not appear to be explained by the presence of grandchildren. And Tomes (1988), analyzing a sample of probate records from Cleveland, obtains with a similar econometric specification opposite results regarding the effect of marital status...

7.4. Child-to-parent transfers: demonstration effects and other indirect reciprocities

Let us turn again to regressions, such as those in Table 3, concerning the probability of time or financial transfers given by P-households to old G-parents. What happens if one adds, beside traditional explanatory variables (including income and wealth of the two generations), the existence of support given in the past by the old generation (G) to her own parents—a positive correlation being predicted by backward-looking forms of indirect reciprocity? Or if one adds relevant characteristics of the young generation (K or C) to test, especially, for various forms of (forward) demonstration effects?

We will address these two questions in turn on French and American data, looking successively at the determinants of time transfers and at those of financial transfers.

7.4.1. Time transfers

For a test of backward-looking indirect reciprocities, consider the first column of Table 3, which concerns, on French data, the determinants of upward time transfers other than co-residence. The retrospective effect is almost significant at a 10 percent level: grandparents who helped their own parents tend to receive more support during their old days. But this effect does not appear robust to alternative specifications (see Arrondel and Masson, 2001).

On the other hand, the retrospective effect concerning *co-residence* with old (needy) parents is much more significant and robust, according both to French and U.S. evidence. On the French Cnav survey, Wolff (1998) finds that aged respondents whose own parents had moved in with them in the past, have a significantly higher probability to be now part of a child's household. Similar findings have been emphasized by Cox and Stark (1998) on U.S. data: "the incidence of sharing housing with parents was 27 percent higher for respondents whose grandparents had moved in when the respondents were children."

Consider next variables relevant for a test of forward-looking indirect reciprocities. In the first column of Table 3, the number of children, and in particular the number of those still at home, has no influence whatsoever (notwithstanding upbringing and education costs) on the probability of helping old parents: this can already be interpreted as a weak sign of the presence of a demonstration effect.

More importantly, the probability of transfers is higher for *egos* who are daughters, single children, or those who have some health problems. These results may be viewed as indirect evidence in favor of Cox and Stark's demonstration effect: those helpers are more likely to themselves need support in their old days, respectively because they have a longer life expectancy, are alone, or have already some health problems. But other explanations are possible. Social norms may account for the fact that daughters give more of their time to their parents—in fact most often to their widowed mothers.[74] Single persons may have more free time and are more sensitive to parental pressure. And helpers, undergoing painful physical and psychological stress, are more likely to have some health problems (reverse causation).

Also, especially in the case of demonstration effects, estimated results are likely to be *less* robust than those found for downward transfers. There is thus no satisfactory correction for the endogeneity of the number of children, which could be an indicator of the degree of household altruism towards children... but also towards parents. Moreover, as acknowledged by Cox and Stark (1998) themselves, "cultural forces might be expected to play a greater role in determining transfers from young to old [than for parent-to-child transfers]", but it is indeed difficult to control for heterogeneity in family values or culture.[75]

7.4.2. Financial transfers

Interestingly enough, tests of backward-looking reciprocities appear rather inconclusive. In French (Cnav) data, the old generation (in position G) has apparently a very bad recall of financial transfers given to their parents. For Mexican-Americans (S3GM survey), Ribar and Wilhelm (2002) find almost no significant intergenerational correlation in attitudes regarding the provision of financial assistance to old parents.

Table 3 sums up French and U.S. Probit results regarding demonstration effects relative to financial transfers given to parents. In both countries, the coefficient of the number of *ego*'s children is positive, though small and imprecisely estimated. Cox and Stark (1998) argue that it is already favorable to their demonstration effect, owing to child rearing costs. In order to take these costs into account, these authors suggest that better educated *egos* will "commit more resources to their children's human capital, leaving less to give to parents". Hence the prediction that, holding income constant, *ego*'s education "will interact negatively with children, reflecting budget constraints", while the coefficient of children will be positive, reflecting the demonstration effect. This is precisely what the results of Table 3 show, both in the U.S. and in France. This is preliminary evidence "in favor" of the demonstration effect; but, once again, much more will have to be done to check its robustness.

This analysis of French and U.S. evidence leads to our last empirical statement:

EMPIRICAL STATEMENT 6 (*ES*6). *Transfer motives seem driven in part by indirect reciprocities. Co-residence with old parents tends to be reproduced from one generation*

[74] In favor of this interpretation, the probability of helping remains significantly higher for *working* daughters.

[75] No wonder, then, that interpretations in terms of indirect reciprocities cannot be easily disentangled from other close explanations, based upon a socialization process that would ensure the transmission of assistance attitudes towards one's parents. On a survey of three generations of Mexican-Americans, Ribar and Wilhelm (2002) do indeed find for women a positive intergenerational correlation of attitudes regarding co-residence with parents.

to the next. Each form of parent-to-child financial transfers appears strongly influenced by, and only by, the same form of transfer received. There is also (less robust) evidence that upward transfers are explained by demonstration effects made in expectation of similar support at old age.

Together with *ES*2—the dominant downward direction of (financial) transfers—, *ES*6 means that simple forms of undifferentiated intergenerational risk sharing or redistribution, that may prevail in some LDCs, do not apply (anymore?) in modern developed countries. Some of the empirical findings in *ES*6 can be accounted for, or at least accommodated with, several models existing in the literature: e.g., Cox and Stark (1998) demonstration effect, Bevan and Stiglitz (1979) golden rule bequests. But there is apparently no way that these models can explain our most striking results, i.e. the high selectivity and robustness of strong retrospective effects relative to financial parent-to-child transfers. Obviously, more has still to be done on this issue, both at the empirical and theoretical levels.

8. Economic implications of family transfers (prolegomena)

The theoretical and empirical analysis of the motivations for private intergenerational transfers is not only of interest for family micro-economists. These motivations are even more important for their economic implications concerning the interactions between public and private transfers and the effects of public policies on growth, saving and education, as well as distributive issues, such as the effect of transfers on income inequality or on the concentration and intergenerational immobility of wealth.

These economic implications of transfer models will be very briefly tackled in this study.[76] The central message of this literature is that key policy issues, such as the future of social security and the debate between pay-as-you-go retirement schemes and private pension funds, cannot be analyzed only by comparing the relative efficiency of the State and the market in securing old-age needs: *family* intergenerational relations and specific motives for transfers do also matter when assessing the effects of government transfer policies. Although partially warranted, this view needs, however, much further qualification: economic and policy implications of private transfers do not depend only on their motivation, but also on *other elements* considered in the model (e.g., capital market imperfections, heterogeneity of agents, behavior towards risk...), as well as other demographic and socioeconomic factors, such as fertility differentials, mating patterns, estate sharing rules, etc.

We first recall the basic policy implications of standard transfer models—altruism, exchange, accidental bequests—that will soon appear in textbooks. We then consider the

[76] In this handbook, Cigno analyses the political economy of intergenerational public and private transfers; Cremer and Pestieau deal especially with transfer taxation.

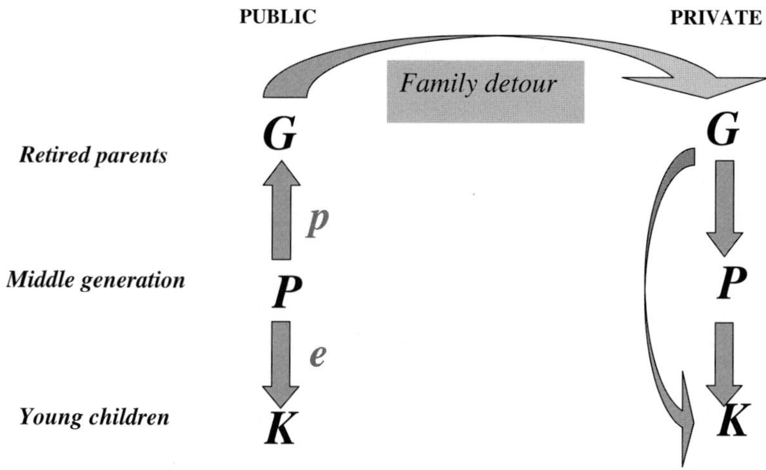

Figure 1. The circuit of intergenerational public and private transfers.

economic implications of more elaborate and realistic models: Cigno's family constitution model; Becker and Murphy 2-regimes of parental altruism; and indirect reciprocities.

A *KPG* three-overlapping generations framework is best suited for this purpose: public transfers go from the middle generation P to its retired parents G (health, pensions) and its young children K (education), raising crucial issues concerning their total amount but also the relative shares of upward and downward transfers. Family downward transfers (including children's upbringing) may go as well from G to P, P to K, and from G to K (see Figure 1).

8.1. Standard views

Table 6 sums up the main policy implications of standard models of transfers: accidental bequests; unconstrained altruism; and intertemporal exchange, when parents trade education or promised bequests for a child's services in old age (see section 2).

An *increase in estate taxation* should have no bearing on accumulation patterns when bequests are accidental. If behaviors are driven by unconstrained altruism, parents will try to share the burden of the tax between themselves and their children, so that both parents' and children's consumption will be similarly reduced: the before-tax transfer will then increase, but the after-tax inheritance will be reduced. Finally, the tax increase is likely to be most distortionary if bequests are motivated by exchange: the before-tax

Table 6
Policy implications of standard models of parent-to-child transfers

Type of transfers or bequests	Unexpected increase of the estate tax rate	Public transfers to poor (adult) children	Rise in social security benefits
Accidental	No effect on given (before-tax) bequests	No effect on bequests	Negative effect on bequests
Altruistic (operative transfers)	• Positive effect on given (before-tax) transfers • Negative effect on received (after-tax) transfers	Negative effects on Parent-to-child transfers (crowding-out effect)	Positive effect on transfers (Ricardian equivalence)
Exchange	Possibly negative effect on before-tax transfers	• Negative effect on the probability of a transfer • Likely positive effect on the amount of the transfer	Ambiguous effect (depending on the form and nature of exchange)

transfer may actually decrease if parents can now find cheaper ways on the market to secure old-age needs.

A welfare transfer program *targeted at indigent grown-up children* should, likewise, have no impact on accidental bequests driven by precautionary motives. Altruistic parents would cut transfers to indigent children who can tap government aid (crowding-out effect). But the effect on exchange-motivated gifts or bequests would be ambiguous: private transfers, being more likely anti-compensatory (especially if the price of child's services increases with her income), may reinforce public income redistribution (see section 2.3).

Finally, an unexpected *rise in social security benefits* would reduce precautionary needs and accidental bequests, but increase the amount of transfers made by altruistic parents in order to neutralize public redistribution (Ricardian equivalence). And one can show that the effect on exchange-motivated transfers or bequests would, once again, be ambiguous, depending on the specific forms of exchange or of child's services considered.

In each scenario, the effects of government policy on private transfers could in principle allow a discrimination between the three alternative models. Note especially the implications of operative altruism regarding the interactions between private and public transfers: i.e., complete substitution for transfers received by the *same* beneficiary (as in the case of a social program targeted to indigent children); but perfect *complementarity* between public pensions and family downward transfers—generating the frictionless "circuit" of intergenerational transfers depicted in Figure 1 (see section 8.3).

8.2. Social security, education and growth (more elaborate transfer models)

In order to analyze the policy implications of more appropriate motivations for transfers, we shall adopt a three overlapping generations *KPG* framework both for public and private transfers, thus assuming—despite the empirical findings in section 5.1—the existence of a "representative" family with a *KPG* intergenerational composition.

8.2.1. Family constitutions

Self-enforcing family constitutions and public redistribution appear directly competing ways of insuring old-age consumption needs. Therefore, a common implication of constitution models is that an increase in social security should lead to a reduction of family inter vivos transfers, meaning that public pensions and *all* private transfers are substitutes (see section 5.4).

This is not the end of the story, however: the precise formulation of the model still matters. Cigno's (Cigno, 1993, 2000) original model has endogenous fertility, two regimes (life-cycle saving and family constitution), and no specific investment in a child's human capital. A rise of public pensions has two effects: it reduces the saving of *already* life-cycle savers, but makes also complying less profitable, so that the number of parents who self-finance retirement needs rises. Cigno has shown that the outcome of these opposite effects is an increase in total savings. In addition, fertility is reduced. If you further believe in the positive externalities of investments in *non human* capital, the rise in old-age security increases per capita income and "is likely to be of stimulus, rather than hindrance, to economic growth".

On the other hand, Anderberg and Balestrino (2003) propose an adapted version of the constitution model which focuses on investments in children's human capital. However, to avoid analytical difficulties, fertility is *exogenous* and only the determinants of transfers in the "comply" case are considered (for stationary equilibria). A rise of public pension coverage will still reduce the efficiency of family informal constitutions, but the consequence will be now a decrease in private financing of human capital. If you hold the neo-Marshallian view that (general) education is the main contributor to technical progress and, moreover, that the family plays an essential role in the accumulation of human capital, it follows that an expansion of the social security system is *bad* for per capita income and growth, the exact opposite of Cigno (2000) conclusions.[77]

[77] Incidentally, Anderberg and Balestrino raise another important issue: in their *KPG* framework with purely self-interested generations, family transfers are likely to be *sub-optimal*, because the children (in position K) have no bargaining power. Indeed, each generation makes her transfer decisions when an adult (in position P), having already received education, an incorporated human capital which is difficult to take away from her! She will then have a permanent temptation to renegotiate the contract with the old generation (of age G), and to reduce education transfers to the detriment of the young generation. In a way, this caveat shows that parental altruism constitutes a *necessary* condition for optimal investments in children's education.

8.2.2. Two altruistic regimes with educational investments

Becker and Murphy (1988) adopt such a neo-Marshallian approach of inter-generational redistribution that does not only rely on (free and constrained) altruism but shares also the two general views on education just mentioned: education is the supreme good, the main engine for endogenous growth, with (initially) increasing rates of return on human capital investments; and these investments must be done in part by parents—the family cannot be entirely replaced by the market, the State or any social organization (e.g., Kibbutz).

Moreover, constrained altruism, leading parents to underinvest in children education, is likely to prevail in highly developed countries, where such human investments become costly, owing to the high levels of education required by sustained technical progress, the limited possible gains in productivity in this time consuming activity, and the rising costs of opportunity linked to the increased (female) wage rate. In other words, the likely importance of liquidity constraints (preventing parents to leave negative bequests), "inoperative" transfers and incentives problems (to pay back old parents) gives room for State intervention, with public intergenerational transfers "mimicking" optimal arrangements on ideal perfect markets. Becker and Murphy (1988) indeed claim that:

> "Taxes on adults help finance efficient investments in children. In return, adults receive pensions and medical payments when old. This social compact tries to achieve for poorer and middle level families what richer families tend to achieve without government help; namely, efficient levels of investments in children and support of elderly parents".

In that representative agent framework, public redistribution between generations, which is assumed to be innocuous for unconstrained, usually richer families (Ricardian equivalence), appears thus both Pareto-improving and more equitable, and also favorable to economic growth—a real *jackpot*...

8.2.3. Indirect reciprocities between three generations

Policy implications of indirect reciprocities as well as predicted interaction effects between public and private transfers remain largely an open question in the absence of well-articulated reference models. However, some general guesses can be made, especially in comparison with altruism.

For instance, the specific links introduced between three successive generations imply that neutrality and Ricardian equivalence do not hold any longer: households reactions to policy measures or changing environments should be slower and more limited than under Barro–Becker compensatory altruism, indirect reciprocities leading to a partial *inertia* in family transfer behavior. Hence, in the Cox and Stark framework, transfers to old parents will not be sensitive to short term changes in (retirement or health) policies, the middle generation reacting only to expected changes in the long run which concerns herself. Likewise, transfers to children, strongly influenced by family background, will not fully respond to policy changes and may only adapt with long lags.

On the other hand, policy reforms could have unintended far-reaching consequences in the very long run, especially on young and future generations, if they contribute to disrupt family intergenerational links and "solidarity" (whether it should be welcomed or deplored).

More generally, in an anthropological perspective, (indirect) reciprocity needs to take also into consideration the intrinsic *ambivalence* of any family gift or bequest, while analyzing their impact on family relations and vice versa—as in the case of "strategic altruism" (section 6.1). This is another reason why neutrality does not apply, that we further explore below.

8.3. The circuit of intergenerational private and public transfers: which Welfare State?

There is a potential flaw in the Becker and Murphy (1988) altruistic model, whenever the latter is taken too literally: the level of public pensions could be as high as desired, since parents will give back sums of excess (at no costs) to their descendants through increased private inter vivos transfers and bequests to children and grandchildren. Albeit a caricatured implication of Ricardian equivalence, this frictionless circuit of upward public redistribution and downward private transfers, represented in Figure 1, raises nevertheless an important issue: instead of giving directly to the young through the State, what are the advantages and drawbacks of this *detour arrangement* via the family, public transfers to the elderly being (optimally) channeled back to the young trough private transfers (see Kohli, 1999).

Let us ignore obvious causes of frictions or losses in this circuit of transfers, making the detour via the family costly or inefficient, such as administrative and information costs of policy redistribution, distortions engendered by non lump-sum public transfers, or even the high diversity of family intergenerational compositions (how can the young generation get back the surplus of pensions given to rich and childless old people?). A first way out is to question the overall relevance of compensatory altruism, allowing for heterogeneous transfer motives. Thus, if transfer decisions include an exchange component, old parents may still increase transfers to their descendants in response to a rise in public pensions; however, they will probably ask their children for something in return, e.g. increased attention or co-residence. Also, if indirect reciprocities prevail, old parents' responses to an increase in social security are likely to be somewhat delayed or limited.

The *ambivalence* of family transfers offers an alternative, complementary solution. Under Ricardian equivalence, the two ways of redistribution—giving directly public transfers to the young children, or giving to the old and using the detour via the family—are indeed equivalent. But few family sociologists or anthropologists will believe that this detour via the family is such a blank operation: the increase in private transfers to children and grandchildren is likely to have a specific impact on the relations within the family, i.e. to engender positive or negative *externalities*, concerning family cohesion, the status and bargaining power of each generation, etc. Following Barro (1974), most economists have been, until recently, rather agnostic (in their models) on this issue, letting the field be treated by others...

Indeed, in the French version of his book, *The Three Worlds of Welfare Capitalism*, Esping-Andersen (1999, p. 293) does claims that this detour via the family is "a perverse, second-order, redistribution system [...] which favors rich families and disadvantages poorer ones". On the other hand, Kohli (1999) minimizes these anti-redistribution effects and sees, otherwise, only positive effects in the resulting increase of family "solidarity".[78] Deserted by economists, this debate has yet immediate bearing on the issue concerning the optimal relative shares of upward and downward public transfers. But it is also important to see that the position of each author depends on his preconceptions regarding the welfare state.

Just to give an idea, consider in an intergenerational setting Esping-Andersen's well-known division into "neo-liberal", "social-democratic" and "familial-corporatist" welfare states. A *neo-liberal*, who believes in the free market, may be indifferent between the two options: giving directly to the young through the State, or indirectly via the family. A *social-democrat*—such as Esping-Andersen himself—, who believes in equality of opportunity engendered by a generous welfare state, but trusts neither the market (and its unequal property rights) nor the traditional family (and its authoritarian male "head"), wants to give less to old people and more to young children and also to young working women, in order to help them to reconcile a professional career and a family life. Finally, proponents (like Kohli) of a *familial-corporatist* view favor "Birmarkian" social insurance and "social acquired rights", and want to enhance "solidarity" at different levels, within the family, the corporation, the nation...: no wonder, then, that they will first trust "family heads" or parents to do the best for their children, a paternalistic attitude justifying high levels of public transfers targeted towards the elderly (see Masson, 2001).

8.4. Distributive issues

Distributive issues, such as the effect of family transfers on income inequality within and between families, or the role of inheritance and major gifts on the concentration and intergenerational immobility of wealth, are clearly beyond the scope of this paper—see, e.g., Davies and Shorrocks (1981) for developments on the distribution of wealth.

A key question would be to know whether the main results obtained (for developed countries) in this survey, such as the strong heterogeneity of the types and motivations of financial parent-to-child transfers, the quantitative importance of inter vivos transfers, the high diversity of family intergenerational compositions, and the dominant part

[78] The detour will improve the position of the elderly in the family and allow them to exert additional control over the young, all welcome changes since the parents know best what is good for their children and hold private information not available to the State...

attributed to indirect reciprocities among transfer motives, could help for a revaluation of these hot issues.

For instance, the fact that financial or time assistance to old parents is made by higher income households and appears targeted towards needy, poorer parents, means that family *upward* transfers may lead to a positive intergenerational redistribution of resources—all the more so if public and private transfers to parents are complements, as preliminary evidence seems to show. On the other hand, the observed high diversity of family compositions is a potential source of inequality between (helping and not helping) children.

Moreover, motivations governed by indirect reciprocities are likely to create a dichotomy between two heterogeneous types of families: those making sizeable chain transfers, and those who do not make any, or only small ones. Hence, *downward* transfers, especially, could strengthen intra-generational inequalities, between "heirs" and "non heirs", and also through the specific link introduced between what is received from parents and what is left to children (see Arrondel et al., 1997).

In any case, much more work would be needed to assess the relevance of our contribution for the debate on the role of inheritance on income and wealth inequality. According to the "received" view, inheritance was income unequalizing; appeared a major factor of wealth concentration among the top-wealth holders but played a more limited role for the remaining part of the wealth distribution; and strongly reinforced the degree of wealth immobility (predicted significantly higher than that of income).[79]

But this view has been challenged since. Thus, Becker and Tomes (1986) claim that altruistic bequests could well be income *equalizing*, mainly because they act, among richer families, as a "buffer" against the intergenerational regression towards the mean in income. Other authors still maintain the opposite: e.g., Atkinson (1988) advocates the view of inheritance of the "man in the street [who] thinks of the Rockefellers, the Rothschilds, and the Dukes of Westminster"—whose dynastic accumulation behavior could be captured by a variant of downward and forward-looking indirect reciprocity. In any case, it is now largely acknowledged that the role of inheritance depends strongly on demographic and other factors, such as estate sharing rules, mating patterns, fertility differentials, or even spacing of children, which require extensive micro-simulation techniques.[80]

[79] See Davies and Shorrocks (1981) for references.

[80] The issue is even more tricky than this. Take thus a life-cycle model with homothetic preferences and purely *accidental* bequests, which presumably underestimates the unequalizing effects of inheritance on income and wealth distributions. Yet, the model could lead in certain cases to *income* equalizing inheritance, simply owing to the intergenerational regression towards the mean in income (inheritance expectations decrease with the level of income). Moreover, Gokhale et al. (2001) claim that, in such a model, inheritance could well be (slightly) *wealth equalizing*: the main reason for their findings is that they use quasi-Leontief preferences which lead to very high precautionary savings and complete ignorance in savings choices of inheritance expectations (since the latter have a positive probability to be nil). Of course, the model may appear too unrealistic for the richest households, who make sizeable inter vivos transfers, own mainly stocks and shares, and owe their fortunes at least partly to risk-taking behavior and entrepreneurial activity.

9. Conclusions

To conclude this empirical survey devoted to the types and motives of family intergenerational transfers in developed countries, five points are worth being (re)emphasized.

9.1. Heterogeneity of transfers and motives for transfers

The multiplicity of intergenerational transfers, post-mortem or inter-vivos, financial or time transfers, upward or downward ones, etc. is bound to create problems of typology and definition. We have argued that the *timing* of transfers is another relevant dimension: e.g., financial transfers received at a young age and later wealth gifts or bequests are likely to have different determinants and to serve different purposes. Another crucial issue concerns the identification of *time* transfers (including co-residence with old parents or young adult children): we have retained only services or assistance given to *needy* individuals—such as pre-adult grandchildren or unhealthy old parents—because the existence and direction of the transfer can be clearly stated in these cases.

Other methodological choices are of course possible. This is why studies of family transfers should indicate right from the start, besides the type of data used (estate statistics or household surveys; cross-sectional, recall or panel data), precisely *which* inter vivos transfers do they retain—including the period of reference for transfers given or received, the minimum amount for cash transfers, etc. This will allow a better assessment of the usual conclusions obtained—"that such or such model is corroborated or rejected by the data".

All in all, the heterogeneity of the characteristics and *motives* of transfers, both along the income or wealth scale and over the life-cycle, is more and more acknowledged. Heterogeneous inter vivos transfers and bequests to children could thus help to solve several *empirical puzzles*, such as: bequests seem "involuntary" (accidental) for many households, although gifts are of a significant importance and tend to be compensatory; bequests are most often equally shared whereas inter vivos gifts are not, advantaging once again the less well-off children; the timing of financial transfers does not fully respond to changes in relative tax advantages of gifts over bequests.

9.2. Looking for models of mixed motivations

Considering the overall failure, in developed countries, of standard models of transfers based on simple exchange or altruism, these puzzling facts call for new theoretical developments. A promising direction is the introduction of so-called "mixed" motivations, accounting for the fact that family relations are neither totally harmonious (altruism) nor totally self-interested (exchange).

Variants of *strategic altruism*, where parents care about the well-being of their progeny but may face problems of reputation, incentives, imperfect information on children, uncertainty regarding one's own or children's future, control and monitoring of children, etc., have thus been proposed in recent years, precisely in order to account for previous puzzles as well as for the observed limited size of compensatory effects of transfers.[81]

Models with *several endogenous regimes* offer another route. In Becker's model of free and constrained altruism, the control of a child's behavior remains a crucial issue: in the constrained (inefficient) regime, especially, parents have to resort to a costly and risky process of formation of child's preferences. In Cigno's constitution model, extended exchange between three generations is governed by a self-enforcing norm of cooperation: the latter leads to an efficient allocation of resources while urging self-interested generations to behave—to a certain extent—*as if* they were altruistic.

Indirect reciprocities, such as retrospective bequests or demonstration effects, may be seen as a further attempt in the same direction. Their purpose is to enforce indefinite chains of mutually beneficial cooperation between generations through the replication of the same kind of transfers. Hence, they offer a middle way between altruism and exchange that tends to blur the distinction between these two basic motivations. Moreover, they emphasize the ambivalence of any gift, implying at the same time an act of sharing and solidarity and a relation of domination or violence.

9.3. Reproducing the circulation of private transfers between generations

As part of an agenda for future research, a worthwhile goal would be to obtain a full picture of the "circulation" of private transfers between generations in different countries, that would inform of the frequency and quantitative importance of transfers, according to their direction (from who to whom?), their timing (when, over the life-cycle?), their nature (financial or time transfers), as well as their likely dominant motivation.

To begin with, one has to choose a representative intergenerational family composition: we argue that a *four*-generation composition with three adult ones (corresponding to a four-periods life-cycle) is best suited for modern *developed* countries. We then obtain a number of empirical results—or rather conjectures—expected to be valid in these countries, such as:

- upward time or financial transfers are of significant importance only from mature age households to their old retired parents, and cannot be explained, contrary to simple exchange, by any observable counterpart already given or promised by old parents;
- the bulk of financial flows goes downwards, towards children and grandchildren;
- granted that some form of altruism may be necessary to explain large and costly investments in children's education and some earlier assistance to adult children, and notwithstanding the high heterogeneity of motives according to age or to the level of resources, most transfers seem driven, at least in part, by indirect reciprocities: co-residence with old parents tend to be reproduced from one generation to

[81] In the related literature on migrants' remittances, Lucas and Stark (1985) also invoke mixed motivations of "tempered altruism or enlightened self interest", which lead to a "far richer array of predictions".

the next; each form of financial downward transfers appears strongly and selectively determined by the same form of transfer received earlier; and demonstration effects play a role in securing support during old age.

9.4. *What about family transfers in less developed countries?*

A striking remark, only alluded in this paper in often too vague or impressionistic paragraphs or footnotes, is that most if not all of these results do *not* seem to apply in the majority of less developed countries—nor in old Europe.

In particular, simple forms of exchange and/or bargaining between parents and children seem to work much better in LDCs than in occidental industrial nations. Of course, these differences can be partially explained by the existence, in developed countries, of more elaborate financial and insurance markets, of a higher level of education and social protection, and especially, of large public transfers to the elderly. But this is only part of the story, and a detailed comparison of the determinants and the "circulation" of intergenerational private transfers in the two types of nations should be really welcome.

In any case, it implies that transfer policies may have quite different effects in occidental countries and in LDCs. Against Caldwell's hypothesis, Lee (2000) for instance claims that the resulting sum of *all* (public and private) transfers goes *upwards* in industrial nations (such as the U.S.), but still *downwards* in previous times and in the Third World, and emphasizes the implications of these differences "for capital accumulation, for fertility theory, for externalities to child bearing, and for the consequences of population aging".

9.5. *Intergenerational indirect reciprocities as an outcome of individual rationality?*

Indirect reciprocities seem to bring a valuable contribution to the understanding of family transfer behavior observed in developed countries such as France or the U.S. They are compatible (against altruism) with small compensatory effects of transfers both between and within generations, and (against exchange) with the lack of parents' counterpart to financial or time support given by their children. They presuppose a given ambivalence of transfers and the existence of tensions in family relations that help to explain other puzzles, such as the equal division of estate, or the low degree of annuitization of private wealth. And they predict "3rd generation effects"—transfers between parents and children being determined by grandparents' transfers or again grandchildren's characteristics—which appear corroborated by available evidence in France or in the U.S.

The fact that economists for a long time have been reluctant to consider indirect reciprocities is not surprising: at first sight, the latter simply imply the replication of the same transfer behavior from one generation to the next, leaving the field to psychologists (and their concept of imitation) or to sociologists (and their notion of social reproduction). But indirect reciprocities imply much more than this: their prime issue concerns the participation to, and the perpetuation of endless intergenerational chains of transfers, which may as well involve the formation of preferences, the emergence of norms, the transmission of family values or cultural traits, evolutionary imperatives... They may also include more specific prerequisites: e.g., for the demonstration effect to work best, grandparents should devote time and money to subsidy grandchildren's birth and education.

This paper will be most useful if it helps to convince more economists of the field to face the *challenge* of innovative modelling of indirect reciprocities within the framework of individual forward-looking rationality—a key issue being that the mutually advantageous chain of transfers must be viewed much alike a public good between generations. In any case, the ultimate goal will be to produce more precise and specific predictions, allowing for more powerful tests.

References

Adams, J.D. (1980). "Personal wealth transfers". Quarterly Journal of Economics 95, 159–179.

Altig, D., Davies, S.J. (1993). "Borrowing constraints and two-sided altruism with an application to social security". Journal of Economics Dynamics and Control 17, 467–494.

Altonji, J.G., Hayashi, F., Kotlikoff, L.J. (1997). "Parental altruism and *inter vivos* transfers: theory and evidence". Journal of Political Economy 105, 1125–1166.

Altonji, J.G., Hayashi, F., Kotlikoff, L.J. (2000). "The effects of income and wealth on time and money transfers between parents and children". In: Mason, A., Tapinos, G. (Eds.), Sharing the Wealth: Demographic Change and Economic Transfers between Generations. Oxford University Press, Oxford, pp. 306–357.

Anderberg, D., Balestrino, A. (2003). "Self-enforcing intergenerational transfers and the provision of education". Economica 70 (1), 55–71.

Andreoni, J. (1989). "Giving with impure altruism: application to charity and Ricardian equivalence". Journal of Political Economy 97, 1447–1458.

Arrondel, L., Laferrère, A. (1991). "Successions et héritiers à travers les données fiscales". Economie et Prévision 100–101, 137–159.

Arrondel, L., Laferrère, A. (1992). "Les partages inégaux des successions entre frères et sœurs". Economie et Statistique 250, 29–42.

Arrondel, L., Laferrère, A. (1998). "Succession capitaliste et succession familiale: un modèle econométrique à deux régimes endogènes". Annales d'Economie et de Statistique 51, 187–208.

Arrondel, L., Laferrère, A. (2001). "Taxation and wealth transmission in France". Journal of Public Economics 79, 3–33.

Arrondel, L., Masson, A. (1991). "Que nous enseignent les enquêtes sur les transferts patrimoniaux en France?". Economie et Prévision 100–101, 93–128.

Arrondel, L., Masson, A. (2001). "Family transfers involving three generations". Scandinavian Journal of Economics 103, 415–443.

Arrondel, L., Masson, A., Pestieau, P. (1997). "Bequest and inheritance: empirical issues and French–U.S. comparison". In: Erreygers, G., Vandevelde, T. (Eds.), Is Inheritance Legitimate? Springer-Verlag, Heidelberg, pp. 89–125.

Arrondel, L., Masson, A., Verger, D. (2004). "Préférences de l'épargnant et accumulation patrimoniale". Economie et Statistique, 374–375.

Arrondel, L., Wolff, F.C. (1998). "Les transferts *inter vivos* en France: investissements humains, aides financières et transmission du patrimoine". Economie et Prévision 135, 1–27.

Atkinson, A.B. (1988). "Comments on redistribution, inheritance and inequality: an analysis of transitions of J. Davies and P. Kuhn". In: Kessler, D., Masson, A. (Eds.), Modelling the Accumulation and Distribution of Wealth. Oxford University Press, Oxford, pp. 144–145.

Barro, R.J. (1974). "Are government bonds net wealth". Journal of Political Economy 82, 1095–1117.
Barro, R.J. (1989). "The Ricardian approach to budget deficits". Journal of Economic Perspectives 3, 37–54.
Barry, C., de Eneau, D., Hourriez, J.M. (1996). "Les aides financières entre ménages". Insee Première, (441), 1–4.
Becker, G.S. (1974). "A theory of social interactions". Journal of Political Economy 82 (6), 1063–1093.
Becker, G.S. (1988). "Family economics and macro behavior". American Economic Review 78 (1), 1–13.
Becker, G.S. (1991). A Treatise on the Family, enlarged edn. Harvard University Press.
Becker, G.S. (1993). "The economic way of looking at behavior". Journal of Political Economy 101 (3), 385–409.
Becker, G.S. (1996). Accounting for Tastes. Harward University Press.
Becker, G.S., Murphy, K.M. (1988). "The family and the state". Journal of Law and Economics 31, 1–18.
Becker, G.S., Tomes, N. (1986). "Human capital and the rise and fall of families". Journal of Labor Economics 4 (part 2), S1–S39.
Behrman, J., Pollack, R., Taubman, P. (1982). "Parental preferences and provision for progeny". Journal of Political Economy 90 (1), 52–73.
Bennet, S.K. (1990). "Economic and non-economic factors motivating bequest patterns", mimeo, Trinity University.
Bergstrom, T.C. (1996). "Economics in a family way". Journal of Economic Literature XXXIV, 1903–1934.
Bergstrom, T.C., Stark, O. (1993). "How altruism can prevail in an evolutionary environment". American Economic Review 83 (2), 149–155.
Bernheim, B.D. (1989). "A neoclassical perspective on budget deficits". Journal of Economic Perspectives 3, 55–72.
Bernheim, B.D. (1991). "How strong are bequest motives? Evidence based on estimates on the demand for life insurance and annuities". Journal of Political Economy 99, 899–927.
Bernheim, B.D., Bagwell, K. (1988). "Is everything neutral?". Journal of Political Economy 96 (2), 308–338.
Bernheim, B.D., Lemke, R.J., Scholz, J.K. (2004). "Do estate and gift taxes affect the timing of private transfers?". Journal of Public Economics 88 (12), 2617–2634.
Bernheim, B.D., Severinov, S. (2003). "Bequests as signals: an explanation for the equal division puzzle ". Journal of Political Economy 111 (4), 733–764.
Bernheim, B.D., Shleifer, A., Summers, L.H. (1985). "The strategic bequest motive". Journal of Political Economy 93, 1045–1076.
Bevan, D.L., Stiglitz, J.E. (1979). "Intergenerational transfers and inequality". Greek Economic Journal 1 (1), 8–26.
Blinder, A.S. (1988). "Comments on Modigliani (chap. 1) and Kotlikoff and Summers (chap. 2)". In: Kessler, D., Masson, A. (Eds.), Modelling the Accumulation and Distribution of Wealth. Oxford University Press, Oxford, pp. 68–76.
Brezis, L. (2000). "Population, social classes, and economic growth during industrialization", mimeo, Bar-Ilan University.
Brown, J.R., Weisbenner, S.J. (2002). "Is a bird in hand worth more than a bird in the bush? Intergenerational transfers and savings behavior", NBER Working Paper No. 8753.
Bruce, N., Waldman, M. (1990). "The Rotten Kid theorem meets the Samaritan dilemma". Quarterly Journal of Economics 105, 1165–1182.
Caldwell, J. (1978). "A theory of fertility: from high plateau to destabilization". Population, Development Review 4 (4), 553–577.
Caroll, C.D. (2000). "Why do the rich save so much". In: Slemrod, J.B. (Ed.), Does Atlas Shrug? The Economic Consequences of Taxing the Rich. Harvard University Press, pp. 463–485.
Chu, C.Y.C. (1991). "Primogeniture". Journal of Political Economy 99 (1), 78–99.
Cigno, A. (1991). Economics of the Family. Clarendon Press, Oxford.
Cigno, A. (1993). "Intergenerational transfers without altruism: family, market and state". European Journal of Political Economy 7, 505–518.

Cigno, A. (2000). "Self-enforcing family constitutions: implications for saving, fertility and intergenerational transfers". In: Mason, A., Tapinos, G. (Eds.), Sharing the Wealth: Demographic Change and Economic Transfers between Generations. Oxford University Press, Oxford, pp. 232–255.

Cigno, A., Giannelli, G.C., Rosati, F.C. (1998). "Voluntary transfers among Italian households". Structural Change and Economics Dynamics 9, 435–451.

Cigno, A., Giannelli, G.C., Rosati, F.C. (2001). "Is there a family constitution? A test based on credit rationing", mimeo, University of Florence.

Cox, D. (1987). "Motives for private income transfers". Journal of Political Economy 95 (3), 508–546.

Cox, D. (1990). "Intergenerational transfers and liquidity constraints". Quarterly Journal of Economics 104, 187–217.

Cox, D., Japelli, T. (1990). "Credit rationing and private transfers: evidence from survey data". Review of Economics and Statistics 72, 445–453.

Cox, D., Raines, F. (1985). "Interfamily transfers and income redistribution". In: David, M., Smeeding, T. (Eds.), Horizontal Equity, Uncertainty, and Measures of Well-being. University of Chicago Press, Chicago.

Cox, D., Rank, M.R. (1992). "Inter vivos transfers and intergenerational exchange". Review of Economics and Statistics 74, 305–314.

Cox, D., Stark, O. (1996). "Intergenerational transfers and the demonstration effect", mimeo, Boston College–Harvard University.

Cox, D., Stark, O. (1998). "Financial transfers to the elderly and the "Demonstration effect", mimeo, Boston College–Harvard University.

Cox, D., Hansen, B., Jimenez, E. (2004). "How responsive are private transfers to income? Evidence from a Laissez-Faire economy ". Journal of Public Economics 88, 2193–2219.

Davies, J.B. (1981). "Uncertain lifetime, consumption and dissaving in retirement". Journal of Political Economy 89 (3), 561–577.

Davies, J.B., Shorrocks, A.F. (1981). "The distribution of wealth". In: Atkinson, A.B., Bourguignon, F. (Eds.), Handbook of Income Distribution, vol. 1. North-Holland, Amsterdam, pp. 605–675.

Davies, J.B., St. Hilaire, F. (1987). "Reforming capital income taxation in Canada", Minister of Supply and Services of Canada, Ottawa.

Duflo, E. (2003). "Grandmothers and granddaughters: old age pension and intra-household allocation in South Africa". World Bank Economic Review 17 (1), 1–25.

Dunn, T.A. (1997). "The distribution of intergenerational income transfers across and within families", mimeo, Syracuse University.

Eheh, P.P. (1974). Social Exchange Theory: The Two Traditions. Harvard University Press, Cambridge.

Esping-Andersen, G. (1999). Les trois mondes de l'Etat-providence. PUF, Paris. French translation of: The Three Worlds of Welfare Capitalism, Cambridge, Polity Press, 1990.

Fehr, E., Schmidt, K.M. (2006). "The economics of fourness, reciprocity and altruism: experimental evidence", this volume.

Fong, C., Bowles, S., Gintis, H. (2006). "Strong reciprocity and the welfare state", this volume.

Friedman, B.M., Warshawsky, M. (1988). "Annuity prices and savings behavior in the United States". In: Bodie, Z., Shoven, J., Wise, D. (Eds.), Pensions in the US Economy. University of Chicago Press, Chicago, pp. 53–77.

Friedman, B.M., Warshawsky, M. (1990). "The cost of annuities: implications for saving behavior and bequests". Quarterly Journal of Economics 94, 135–154.

Gale, W., Potter, S. (2003). "The impact of gifts and bequests on aggregate saving and capital accumulation". In: Munnell, A.H., Sunden, A. (Eds.), Death and Dollars: The Role of Gifts and Bequests in America. Brookings Institution Press, Washington. Chapter 9.

Gale, W.J., Scholz, J.K. (1994). "Intergenerational transfers and the accumulation of wealth". Journal of Economic Perspectives 8, 145–160.

Godelier, M. (1982). La production des Grands Hommes. Pouvoir et domination masculine chez les Baruya de Nouvelle Guinée. Fayard, Paris.

Godelier, M. (2000). "Things you don't give or sell but which you keep: valuable and social objects". In: Gérard-Varet, L.A., Kolm, S.C., Mercier-Ythier, J. (Eds.), The Economy of Reciprocity, Giving and Altruism. MacMillan, London, pp. 182–195.

Gokhale, J., Kotlikoff, L.J., Sefton, J., Weale, M. (2001). "Simulating the transmission of wealth inequality via bequests". Journal of Public Economics 79, 93–128.

Guiso, L., Jappelli, T., Terlizzese, D. (1996). "Income risk, borrowing constraints and portfolio choice". American Economic Review 86, 158–172.

Hammond, P. (1975). "Charity: altruism or cooperative egoism?". In: Phelps, E.S. (Ed.), Altruism, Morality and Economic Theory. Russel Sage Foundation, New-York.

Hochguertel, S., Ohlsson, H. (2000). Compensatory inter vivos gifts. Dept. of Economics, Göteborg University. Working Paper No. 31.

Hurd, M.D. (1987). "Savings of the elderly and desired bequests". American Economic Review 77, 298–312.

Hurd, M.D. (1989). "Mortality risk and bequests". Econometrica 57, 779–813.

Hurd, M.D. (1990). "Research on the elderly: economic status, retirement, and consumption and saving". Journal of Economic Literature 28, 565–637.

Hurd, M.D. (2003). "Bequests: by accident or by design?". In: Munnel, A.H., Sunden, A. (Eds.), Death and Dollars: The Role of Gifts and Bequests in America. Brookings Institution Press, Washington. Chapter 4.

Ioannides, Y.M., Kahn, K. (2000). "The nature of two-sided altruism in intergenerational transfers of money and time: an empirical analysis". In: Gérard-Varet, L.A., Kolm, S.C., Mercier-Ythier, J. (Eds.), The Economy of Reciprocity, Giving and Altruism. MacMillan, London, pp. 314–331.

Kessler, D., Masson, A. (1989). "Bequest and wealth accumulation: are some pieces of the puzzle missing?". Journal of Economic Perspectives 3, 141–152.

Kessler, D., Masson, A., Pestieau, P. (1991). "Trois vues sur léritage: la famille, la propriété, l'Etat". Economie et Prévision 100–101, 1–29.

Kimball, M.S. (1987). "Making sense of two sided altruism". Journal of Monetary Economics 20 (2), 301–326.

Kohli, M. (1999). "Private and public transfers between generations: linking the family and the state". European Societies 1 (1), 81–104.

Kolm, S.C. (1984). La bonne économie: la réciprocité générale. PUF, Paris.

Kolm, S.C. (2000). "Introduction: the economics of reciprocity, giving and altruism". In: Gérard-Varet, L.A., Kolm, S.C., Mercier-Ythier, J. (Eds.), The Economy of Reciprocity, Giving and Altruism. MacMillan, London, pp. 1–44.

Kopczuk, W., Slemrod, J. (2003). "Tax Consequences on Wealth Accumulation and Transfers of the Rich". In: Munnell, A.H., Sunden, A. (Eds.), Death and Dollars: The Role of Gifts and Bequests in America. Brookings Institution Press, Washington. Chapter 7.

Kotlikoff, L.J. (1988). "Intergenerational transfers and savings". Journal of Economic Perspectives 2, 41–58.

Kotlikoff, L.J. (1989). What Determines Savings. Cambridge, MIT Press.

Kotlikoff, L.J., Spivak, A. (1981). "The family as an incomplete annuities market". Journal of Political Economy 89, 372–391.

Kotlikoff, L., Summers, L. (1981). "The role of intergenerational transfers in aggregate capital accumulation". Journal of Political Economy 89, 706–732.

Laferrère, A. Wolff, F.-C. (2006). "Microeconomic models of family transfers", this volume.

Laitner, J. (1997). "Intergenerational and interhousehold economic links". In: Rosenzweig, M.R., Stark, O. (Eds.), Handbook of Population and Family Economics, vol. 1A. North-Holland, Amsterdam, pp. 189–238.

Laitner, J., Ohlsson, H. (1997). "Equality of opportunity and inheritance: a comparison of Sweden and the U.S.", Paper presented at the conference "Wealth, Inheritance and Intergeneration Transfers" 22–23 June 1997, University of Essex, U.K.

Laitner, J., Ohlsson, H. (2001). "Bequest motives: a comparison of Sweden and the United States". Journal of Public Economics 79, 205–236.

Lee, R. (2000). "A cross-cultural perspective on intergenerational transfers and the economic life cycle". In: Mason, A., Tapinos, G. (Eds.), Sharing the Wealth: Demographic Change and Economic Transfers between Generations. Oxford University Press, Oxford, pp. 17–56.

Lee, R., Miller, T. (1994). "Population age structure, intergenerational transfers, and Wealth". Journal of Human Resources 29 (4), 1027–1063.

Lee, Y.J., Parish, W.L., Willis, R.J. (1994). "Sons, daughters, and intergenerational support in Taiwan". American Journal of Sociology 99 (4), 1010–1041.

Lévi-Strauss, C. (1958). Anthropologie Structurale. Plon. In English: Structural Anthropology, 1958 publ. Allen Lane, The Penguin Press, 1968.

Lindbeck, A., Weibull, J.W. (1988). "Altruism and time consistency: the politics of fait accompli". Journal of Political Economy 96, 1165–1182.

Lucas, R.E.B., Stark, O. (1985). "Motivations to remit: evidence from Botswana". Journal of Political Economy (1985) 93, 901–918.

Lundholm, M., Ohlsson, H. (2000). "Post mortem reputation, compensatory gifts and equal bequests". Economics Letters 68 (2), 165–171.

Masson, A. (2001). "Economie du débat intergénérationnel: points de vue normatif, comptable, politique". In: Véron, J., Legaré, J., Pennec, S., Digoix, M. (Eds.), Le contrat social à l'épreuve des changements démographiques. In: Dossiers et Recherches de l'Ined, vol. 104, pp. 15–51.

Masson, A., Pestieau, P. (1997). "Bequests motives and models of inheritance: a survey of the literature". In: Erreygers, G., Vandevelde, T. (Eds.), Is Inheritance Legitimate?, pp. 54–88.

Mauss, M. (1950). Sociologie et anthropologie. PUF, Paris.

Mauss, M. (1968). Essais de sociologie. Editions de Minuit, Paris.

McGarry, K. (1999). "Inter vivos transfers and intended bequests". Journal of Public Economics 73, 321–351.

McGarry, K. (2001). "The cost of equality: unequal bequest and tax avoidance". Journal of Public Economics 79, 179–204.

McGarry, K., Schoeni, R.F. (1995). "Transfer behavior in the health and retirement study: measurement and the redistribution of resources within the family". Journal of Human Resources 30 (Supplement), S185–S226.

McGarry, K., Schoeni, R.F. (1997). "Transfer behavior within the family: results from the asset and health dynamics survey". Journal of Gerontology 52B, 82–92.

Menchik, P.L. (1980a). "Primogeniture, equal sharing and the U.S. distribution of wealth". Quarterly Journal of Economics 94, 299–316.

Menchik, P.L. (1980b). "Effect of material inheritance on the distribution of wealth". In: Smith, J.D. (Ed.), Modelling the Distribution and Intergenerational Transmission of Wealth. University of Chicago Press, Chicago, pp. 159–185.

Menchik, P.L. (1988). "Unequal estate division: is it altruism, reverse bequests, or simply noise". In: Kessler, D., Masson, A. (Eds.), Modelling the Accumulation and Distribution of Wealth. Oxford University Press, London, pp. 105–116.

Menchik, P.L., David, M.H. (1983). "Income distribution, lifetime savings, and bequests". American Economic Review 73, 672–690.

Menchik, P.L., Irvine, F.O., Jianakoplos, N.A. (1986). "Determinants of intended bequests", Discussion Paper A-197, Michigan State University.

Modigliani, F. (1986). "Life cycle, individual thrift and the wealth of nations". American Economic Review 76, 297–313. (Nobel Lecture).

Modigliani, F. (1988). "The role of intergenerational transfers and life cycle saving in the accumulation of wealth". Journal of Economic Perspectives 2, 15–40.

Munnell, A.H., Sunden, A. (Eds.) (2003). Death and Dollars: The Role of Gifts and Bequests in America. Brookings Institution Press, Washington.

Perozek, M.G. (1998). "A reexamination of the strategic bequest motive". Journal of Political Economy 106, 423–445.

Pestieau, P. (2003). "The role of gift and estate transfers in the United States and in Europe". In: Munnell, A.H., Sunden, A. (Eds.), Death and Dollars: The Role of Gifts and Bequests in America. Brookings Institution Press, Washington. Chapter 3.
Pezzin, L., Kemper, P., Reschovsky, J. (1996). "Does publicly provided home care substitute for family care? Experimental evidence with endogenous living arrangements". Journal of Human Resources 31, 650–676.
Poterba, J. (2001). "Estate and gift taxes and the incentives for inter vivos giving in the united states". Journal of Public Economics 79, 237–264.
Rapoport, H., Docquier, F. (2006). "The economics of migrant's remittances", this volume.
Ribar, D.C., Wilhelm, M.O. (2002). "Socialization, exchange and the intergenerational transmission of elder support attitudes: evidence from three generations of Mexican-Americans", mimeo.
Stark, O. (1993). "Nonmarket transfers and altruism". European Economic Review 37, 1414–1424.
Tomes, N. (1981). "The family, inheritance and the intergenerational transmission of inequality". Journal of Political Economy 89, 928–958.
Tomes, N. (1982). "On The intergenerational saving function". Oxford Economic Papers 34, 108–134.
Tomes, N. (1988). "Inheritance and inequality within the family: equal division among unequals or do the poor get more?". In: Kessler, D., Masson, A. (Eds.), Modelling the Accumulation and Distribution of Wealth. Oxford University Press, London, pp. 79–104.
Toubiana, E. (1988). L'héritage et sa psychopathologie. PUF, Paris.
Wilhelm, M.O. (1996). "Bequest behavior and the effect of heirs' earnings: testing the altruistic model of bequests". American Economic Review 86, 874–892.
Wolff, E.N. (2003). "The impact of gifts and estates on the distribution of wealth". In: Munnell, A.H., Sunden, A. (Eds.), Death and Dollars: The Role of Gifts and Bequests in America. Brookings Institution Press, Washington. Chapter 10.
Wolff, F.C. (1998). Altruisme, échange et réciprocité, Thèse, Nantes.
Wolff, F.C. (2000). "Transferts monétaires inter vivos et cycle de vie". Revue Economique 51 (6), 1419–1452.
Wolff, F.C. (2001). "Private intergenerational contact in France and the demonstration effect". Applied Economics 33, 143–153.

Chapter 15

INTERGENERATIONAL ALTRUISM AND NEOCLASSICAL GROWTH MODELS*

PHILIPPE MICHEL

GREQAM, Univ. Aix-Marseille II and EUREQua, Univ. Paris I, France

EMMANUEL THIBAULT

GREMAQ, University Toulouse I, Toulouse, France

JEAN-PIERRE VIDAL

European Central Bank[1]*, Frankfurt am Main, Germany*

Contents

* We thank Sabrina Buti, Bertrand Crettez, Louis Gevers, Nicola Giammarioli, Pierre-André Jouvet, Serge-Christophe Kolm, Jean Mercier-Ythier, Pierre Pestieau, Gilles Rotillon and an anonymous referee of the ECB Working Paper Series for their comments and suggestions.

[1] The views expressed in this chapter are those of the authors and do not necessarily reflect those of the European Central Bank.

Handbook of the Economics of Giving, Altruism and Reciprocity, Volume 2
Edited by Serge-Christophe Kolm and Jean Mercier Ythier

DOI: 10.1016/S1574-0714(06)02015-X

Abstract

This chapter surveys intergenerational altruism in neoclassical growth models. It first examines Barro's approach to intergenerational altruism, whereby successive generations are linked by recursive altruistic preferences. Individuals have an altruistic concern only for their children, who in turn also have altruistic feelings for their own children. Through such a recursive relation all generations of a single family (a dynasty) are linked together by a chain of private intergenerational transfers, countervailing any attempt by the government to redistribute resources across generations. This offsetting of public by private transfers operates only if bequests are positive. This is an important qualification to Barro's debt neutrality result. The conditions under which the Ricardian equivalence (debt neutrality) theorem applies are specified. The effectiveness of fiscal policy is further analysed in the context of an economy populated by heterogeneous families differing with respect to their degree of intergenerational altruism.

We also examine other forms of dynastic altruism consistent with Barro's recursive definition of altruism, ascending altruism and two-sided altruism. These forms could be expected to deliver debt neutrality unconditionally, as families leaving zero bequests could be families characterised by child-to-parent gift under ascending altruism. We find that this is not the case and no form of dynastic altruism therefore ensures debt neutrality without condition. Even under two-sided altruism there are cases, in which both bequests and gifts are constrained and fiscal policy remains effective. We then review ad hoc forms of altruism and their implications for the debt neutrality results. Only one specific form of ad hoc altruism always guarantees debt neutrality; this form departs from the recursive approach underpinning dynastic altruism, with its objective function being formally equivalent to that of the social planner. Extensions to the fields of education and environmental are presented in a final section.

Keywords

neoclassical general aggregative models, altruism, fiscal policy, Ricardian equivalence

JEL classification: C60, D64, E13, E62

1. Introduction

How do altruistic sentiments in the family affect economic outcomes and policies? This largely self-contained chapter surveys the macroeconomic literature on intergenerational altruism, examining the assumptions underpinning altruistic growth models and their consequences for both the macroeconomic equilibrium and fiscal policy.

Private sector's reaction to fiscal policy is a key determinant to the effectiveness of fiscal policy in stimulating economic activity and growth. Modern macroeconomic theory is based on the assumption of highly rational and reactive economic agents, who are farsighted and rely on rather complex calculations to take their consumption-saving decisions. However, the two main macroeconomic paradigms—the overlapping generations model and the infinitely lived agent model—entail opposite conclusions regarding the impact of fiscal policy on economic activity. Whereas public debt crowds out private savings and results in a lower level of capital accumulation in the Allais (1947)–Samuelson (1958)–Diamond (1965) overlapping generations model, it is neutral in the Ramsey (1928) infinitely lived agent model. Key to the neutrality result is the overlap between the period of time over which the government reimburses public debt by levying taxes and the period of time over which the consumer's budget constraint extends. If consumers die before public debt is redeemed, the financing of a given level of public expenditure from the issuance of public bonds increases their net wealth compared with an equivalent financing from taxation, as death allows them to escape future taxation and to leave the tax burden to future generations. More generally, Buiter (1988) and Weil (1989) proved that the cornerstone of the neutrality result is whether or not new agents enter the economy. Infinitely lived individuals would not support the entire tax burden associated with increases in public debt, were new individuals to be born tomorrow, regardless of their life span. The set of taxpayers must remain the same over time for the neutrality result to apply.

Intergenerational altruism reconciles finite lifetimes and infinite horizons. Family affections extend one's economic decision making beyond one's finite lifetime. The view that wealth is stored up for the purposes of enhancing children's welfare has been advocated by neoclassical economists. In his *Principles of Political Economy*, Marshall points to the concern for children as the main reason for saving. This concern is mainly expressed by intergenerational transfers, such as bequests. Altruistic families or dynasties, exactly as infinitely lived agents, are able to counter the effects of fiscal policy. If a government takes one euro from children and gives it to their parents, it affects neither parents' nor children's consumption profiles, since the parents compensate for this transfer by increasing their bequests to their beloved children by exactly one euro. This offsetting of public by private transfers is at the heart of the debt neutrality debate, which dates back to Ricardo and has been revived by Barro (1974). Barro's approach to intergenerational transfers is in line with Becker's (Becker, 1974) theory of social interactions, according to which redistribution between family members is neutral, when the head of the family makes positive gifts to all the members of the family. Barro applies the same logic to the complete sequence of descendants.

Barro's analysis of debt neutrality is based on an assumption that individuals are motivated by a special form of intergenerational altruism, which we refer to as dynastic altruism. Individuals have an altruistic concern for their children, who also have altruistic feelings for their own children, and so on. Through this recursive relation, all generations of a single family—or a dynasty—are linked together by a chain of private intergenerational transfers. This view of altruism is consistent with the succession of generations within a dynasty and therefore fully reconciles finite life and infinite horizon. In this respect, dynastic altruism seems to provide a fully fledged microeconomic foundation for the infinitely lived agent model, insofar as the infinitely lived agent can be interpreted as a dynasty of altruistically linked individuals. A dynasty, however, clearly differs from an infinitely lived agent, insofar as it is a succession of distinct—albeit altruistic—individuals, who are endowed with their own preferences and freedom of choice. This entails serious qualifications to the debt neutrality result—also known as the Ricardian equivalence theorem.[1] Assume for instance that parents are so poor that despite their strong altruistic feelings they cannot afford to leave bequests to their children. If the government takes one euro away from these now relatively wealthy children and gives it to their needy parents, the parents would use this sum to increase their consumption, not to increase their bequests, and the children would end up with a lifetime income lower than prior to the policy intervention. Importantly, this suggests that parents fully agree with this redistributive scheme and would even implement it themselves in the family by leaving debt—negative bequests—to their children, if inherited debt were enforceable.

The non-negative bequest constraint plays a crucial role in the definition of the economic equilibrium and in the analysis of fiscal policy in the dynastic model. Even though it formally resembles a liquidity constraint in the infinitely lived agent model, there is a clear distinction between non-negative bequest conditions and liquidity constraints. While there is no reason for forbidding individuals to borrow over their lifecycle, using future earnings as collateral, children's future labour income—or human capital—is no valid collateral for parents' private borrowing. Altruistic feelings do not always trigger positive transfers between generations. Poor parents love their children but may leave no bequests, which has direct implications for the effectiveness of fiscal policy. Fiscal policy is effective, when successive generations are not linked by a chain of positive private transfers.

Modelling the bequest motive requires several crucial assumptions in a dynastic framework, as described by Barro (1974). When presenting the altruistic individual's utility function in Section 2, we pay particular attention to the modelling of expectations and to the first individual of the altruistic dynasty, two aspects which are usually disregarded in the literature. The behaviour of altruists is illustrated in the case of a

[1] The Ricardian view has often been associated to Barro, whose seminal paper has rejuvenated the debt neutrality debate. See Seater (1993) and Elmendorf and Mankiw (1999) for an excellent analysis of this both theoretical and empirical debate.

small open economy. In Section 3 we examine the closed economy version of altruistic models and characterise the intertemporal equilibrium, which generically features either zero bequests (bequest-constrained equilibrium) or positive bequests (bequest-unconstrained equilibrium). We also compare the intertemporal equilibrium with the social optimum. In Section 4 we characterise the steady state equilibria of the dynastic model, focusing on existence and multiplicity. The neutrality of fiscal policy—public debt, social security and estate taxation—is thoroughly analysed in Section 5, where we provide a theoretical exposition of the Ricardian equivalence theorem.

The baseline altruistic model of economic growth presented in Sections 2–5 is built upon the assumption of a representative family or dynasty, in this respect very much similar to the infinitely lived representative agent model. The coexistence of bequest-constrained and bequest-unconstrained families is worth enquiring and seems to be a more appropriate abstraction of real economies, where heterogeneity of behaviours clearly prevails. In Section 6 we consider the altruistic growth model with heterogeneous individuals. It is shown that Ricardian equivalence still holds from a macroeconomic viewpoint, as capital accumulation, which is driven by the saving behaviour of the more altruistic individuals, is not affected by fiscal policy, but that there are important distributional effects of fiscal policy.

Other forms of altruism, which have been investigated in the literature, are also reviewed in Section 7. First, we review models of ascending altruism and models of two-sided altruism, which stretch Barro's intuitive formulation of dynastic or pure altruism towards its limits. Second, we survey other forms of altruism, which we refer to as *ad hoc* altruism. They are *ad hoc* to the extent that the benefactor's utility does not directly depends on the beneficiary's utility, in contrast to Barro's description of family affections. Extensions of the baseline altruistic growth model to the fields of education and of environmental economics are provided in Section 8. A brief conclusion is gathered Section 9.

2. The behaviour of altruistic households

The overlapping generations model is appropriate for the analysis of intergenerational transfers, owing to its demographic structure. Altruistic transfers are therefore investigated in a dynastic framework underpinned by the baseline two-period overlapping generations model, in which a new generation is born in each period, so that two generations are alive in each period. First, we briefly outline the two-period overlapping generations model, a thorough exposition of which is provided by de la Croix and Michel (2002). Second, we introduce the bequest motive in this model, setting out the utility function of altruistic individuals. Third, we characterise the optimal decisions taken by altruistic individuals. Finally, we consider the small open economy case with a view to illustrating the behaviour of altruists.

2.1. The two-period overlapping generations model

Consider an economy where time is discrete. Individuals who are identical within as well as across generations are indexed by their date of birth, t. An individual's life-cycle consists of two periods, which we refer to as youth and old-age. The number of individuals born in period t is $N_t = (1+n)N_{t-1}$, where $n > -1$ is the exogenous population growth rate.

Young agents born in period t supply one unit of labour, receive the market wage w_t, consume c_t and save s_t, therefore facing the budget constraint: $w_t = c_t + s_t$. When old, they consume the proceeds of their savings, $d_{t+1} = R_{t+1}s_t$, where R_{t+1} is the factor of interest.

Agents are selfish and maximise their life-cycle utility[2] $U_t = U(c_t, d_{t+1})$. Their saving function s^D is given by:

$$s_t = \arg\max_s U(w_t - s, R_{t+1}s) \equiv s^D(w_t, R_{t+1})$$

Their optimal consumptions are:

$$c_t = w_t - s^D(w_t, R_{t+1}) \equiv c^D(w_t, R_{t+1})$$
$$d_{t+1} = R_{t+1}s^D(w_t, R_{t+1}) \equiv d^D(w_t, R_{t+1})$$

With a neoclassical production sector, the equilibrium of the overlapping generations economy may be dynamically inefficient (see Diamond, 1965). Saving decisions are decentralised and individuals may save more than necessary to maintain the golden rule capital stock, defined as the stock of capital maximising net output. In such a case, the economic equilibrium is not Pareto-optimal. There is then room for fiscal policies such as public debt financing or pay-as-you-go social security, which improve welfare by absorbing saving in excess of the golden rule, thereby increasing net output. Regarding the long-run equilibria of the overlapping generations model, standard assumptions on the utility and production function are not sufficient to ensure uniqueness or even existence of positive steady states. Galor and Ryder (1989) have shown that, under fairly standard assumptions, this model can experience no or more than one positive steady state.

2.2. Modelling the bequest motive

Young altruists born in period t supply one unit of labour, receive the market wage w_t, inherit x_t, consume c_t and save s_t. When old, they consume part of the proceeds of their savings, d_{t+1}, and bequeath the remainder, $(1+n)x_{t+1}$, to their $1+n$ children. The

[2] We assume that the function $U(c,d)$ is strictly concave and twice continuously differentiable over the interior of the set $\mathbb{R}_+^\star \times \mathbb{R}_+^\star$. Moreover: $U_c'(c,d) > 0$, $U_d'(c,d) > 0$, $\lim_{\varrho\to 0} U_c'(\varrho, d) = +\infty$ and $\lim_{\varrho\to 0} U_d'(c,\varrho) = +\infty$. We also assume that the Hessian of U is negative definite, i.e. $U_{cc}''U_{dd}'' - U_{cd}''^2 > 0$, which ensures the differentiability of saving functions.

budget constraints that individuals face over their life are therefore:

$$x_t + w_t = c_t + s_t \tag{1}$$

$$R_{t+1}s_t = d_{t+1} + (1+n)x_{t+1} \tag{2}$$

Bequests[3] are private intergenerational transfers from the old to the young. Since children are exempted by law from responsibility for parental debts, credit institutions do not accept children's future earnings as collateral for parents' private borrowing. Inherited debt are not enforceable. In bequest models, it is therefore assumed that parents face the following non-negativity constraint:

$$x_{t+1} \geq 0 \tag{3}$$

If this constraint is binding, bequests are zero and bequest motive said to be inoperative. Altruistic households behave as if they were selfish, when the non-negative bequest constraint is binding. The evolution of bequests is obtained by eliminating s_t in the budget constraints (1) and (2):

$$x_{t+1} = \frac{1}{1+n}[R_{t+1}(x_t + w_t - c_t) - d_{t+1}] \tag{4}$$

Parents are assumed to have an altruistic concern for their children. According to Barro's (Barro, 1974) recursive definition of altruism,[4] parents care about their children's welfare by weighting their children's utility in their own utility function V_t. Denoting with V_{t+1} the well-being of each of their $1+n$ children, the utility of individuals born in period t is given by:

$$V_t = U_t + \gamma V_{t+1} \tag{5}$$

where $U_t = U(c_t, d_{t+1})$ is the utility from life-cycle consumption.[5]

Parents have two sources of utility: (i) they derive (selfish) utility from consumption; (ii) they derive (altruistic) utility from the welfare of their children. We refer to the parameter γ as the degree of intergenerational altruism.[6] Equation (5) relates the utility of

[3] The structure of the model is such that parents' and children's life-cycles overlap. It results that bequests could also be interpreted as *inter vivos* gifts. In the absence of incentive and information problems, there is no difference between both types of transfers and we shall only refer to them as bequests.

[4] Most authors, including Bevan and Stiglitz (1979), Buiter (1979) and Carmichael (1982), who examine Barro's formulation of dynastic altruism, assume separability with respect to the attainable level of children's utility.

[5] Initially Barro (1974) proposed the following compact formulation of altruism: $V_t = G(U_t, V_{t+1})$. This intuitive formulation leads to complex mathematical problems (for example, non convergence of V, non optimality of first order conditions,...). On these issues, see Hori and Kanaya (1989) and Hori (1992) or the survey of Bergstrom (1999). To avoid these mathematical problems, economists usually assume separability of Barro's (Barro, 1974) recursive definition of altruism ($V_t = U_t + \gamma V_{t+1}$).

[6] An alternative specification consists in writing $\tilde{\gamma}(1+n)$, where $\tilde{\gamma}$ is the factor of pure altruism and $1+n$ the number of children. These two formulations are equivalent, when the number of children per family is exogenous (Buiter and Carmichael, 1984). A refinement of this approach considers that altruism influences fertility (Barro and Becker, 1988).

parents to the utility of each of their children. Although parents have altruistic feelings only for their own children, these children are also concerned for their own children, i.e. $V_{t+1} = U_{t+1} + \gamma V_{t+2}$. It results that parents' utilities depend—albeit not directly—on the utilities of their grand-children, i.e. $V_t = U_t + \gamma U_{t+1} + \gamma^2 V_{t+2}$. We can substitute children's utilities forward for all $T > t$:

$$V_t = \sum_{j=t}^{T-1} \gamma^{j-t} U_j + \gamma^{T-t} V_T$$

If the following condition holds,

$$\lim_{T \to +\infty} \gamma^{T-t} V_T = 0$$

we can express V_t as a weighted infinite sum of the life-cycle utilities of current and future generations:

$$V_t = \sum_{j=t}^{+\infty} \gamma^{j-t} U_j \tag{6}$$

Altruistic individuals take into account the infinite stream of their descendants' utilities. Their altruistic utility is equal to the discounted sum (with a discounting factor γ) of their own life-cycle utility and the life-cycle utilities of all their descendants. The degree of intergenerational altruism γ is assumed to be smaller that 1. This reflects weights diminishing with the social distance between the altruists and those to whom they are altruistically related, as parents discounts less the utility of their children than that of their grand-children. This also implies that the infinite sum (6) is convergent, when life-cycle utilities are bounded.

2.3. Expectations and optimal choices

Individuals belonging to generation $\theta \geq t$ choose c_θ, s_θ, $d_{\theta+1}$ and $x_{\theta+1}$, take prices w_θ, $R_{\theta+1}$ as given and maximise their utility V_θ subject to their budget constraints (1) and (2) and to the non-negative bequest condition (3) evaluated in period $t = \theta$. To decide how much to leave to their children, they need to forecast the choices of all their descendants, whose decisions and utility levels hinge on the bequests they will receive. Individual choices are therefore based on forecasts of all current and future prices.

In each period t, an individual's information set is denoted with $\mathcal{P}_t = \{(w_\theta, R_{\theta+1}); \theta \geq t\}$. This notation makes clear that the expectations of all successive cohorts are compatible, since we have $\mathcal{P}_t = \mathcal{P}_{t+1} \cup (w_t, R_{t+1})$. By definition the maximum utility of an individual is given by the following recursive relation:

$$V_t^\star(x_t, \mathcal{P}_t) = \max_{c_t, s_t, d_{t+1}, x_{t+1}} \left\{ U(c_t, d_{t+1}) + \gamma V_{t+1}^\star(x_{t+1}, \mathcal{P}_{t+1}) \right\} \tag{7}$$

subject to (3) and (4).

$V_t^\star(x_t, \mathcal{P}_t)$ stands for the maximum level of utility that can be attained by individuals who have inherited x_t from their parents. Importantly, this level depends on the sequence of all current and future prices, $\{w_\theta, R_{\theta+1}\}_{\theta=t}^{+\infty}$, which is the individual's information set. This is the level of utility individuals attain by maximising the sum of the utility they derive from their life-cycle consumption and the utility, $\gamma V_{t+1}^\star$, they derive (out of altruism) from leaving a bequest x_{t+1} to each of their $1+n$ children. Equation (7) is a recursive relation, the solution of which $\{V_t^\star(.)\}_{t\geq 0}$ is the sequence of utilities of all members of the altruistic dynasty. This is also the Bellman equation of an infinite horizon problem, relating the value function of parents, $V_t^\star$, to the value function of children, $V_{t+1}^\star$. Two remarks are here in order. First, the value function is generally not independent from the period where it is evaluated, and is therefore indexed by time. Second, recursive utilities are well defined only if the expectations of all generations are compatible. Compatibility of the expectations of successive generations is a crucial assumption of the altruistic model, which is usually not stated in an explicit manner.

2.3.1. *The associated infinite horizon optimisation problem*

Consider the following infinite horizon problem with an initial state $x_0 \geq 0$ and an exogenously given sequence of positive prices $\mathcal{P}_0 = \{w_t, R_{t+1}\}_{t\geq 0}$:

$$\max_{\{c_t, d_{t+1}, x_t\}_{t=0}^{+\infty}} \sum_{t=0}^{+\infty} \gamma^t U(c_t, d_{t+1}) \tag{8}$$

$$\text{subject to:}\quad \forall t \geq 0,\quad x_{t+1} = \frac{1}{1+n}[R_{t+1}(w_t + x_t - c_t) - d_{t+1}]$$
$$\forall t \geq 1,\quad x_t \geq 0$$

To characterise the solution of this maximisation problem,[7] we set up the Lagrangean $\mathcal{L}_t$ of period t, which is equal to the sum of the life-cycle utility $U(c_t, d_{t+1})$ and the increase in the shadow value (in terms of utility) of x_t over one period,[8] $\gamma p_{t+1}x_{t+1} - p_t x_t$:

$$\mathcal{L}_t = U(c_t, d_{t+1}) + \frac{\gamma}{1+n} p_{t+1}[R_{t+1}(x_t + w_t - c_t) - d_{t+1}] - p_t x_t$$

For all $t \geq 0$, maximising the Lagrangean with respect to c_t and d_{t+1} gives:

$$U_c'(c_t^\star, d_{t+1}^\star) = \frac{\gamma}{1+n} p_{t+1} R_{t+1} \tag{9}$$

$$U_d'(c_t^\star, d_{t+1}^\star) = \frac{\gamma}{1+n} p_{t+1} \tag{10}$$

[7] For a thorough presentation of discrete time optimisation, see Mc Kenzie (1986).

[8] The current shadow price p_{t+1} of bequest x_{t+1} in period $t+1$ is discounted by the factor γ in order to calculate the increase in the shadow value in period t.

For all $t \geq 1$, maximising $\mathcal{L}_t$ with respect to x_t subject to the non-negative bequest condition gives:

$$-p_t + \frac{\gamma}{1+n} p_{t+1} R_{t+1} \leq 0 \quad (= 0 \text{ if } x_t^\star > 0) \tag{11}$$

The transversality condition states that the limit of the shadow value of bequests tends to zero when time goes to infinity:

$$\lim_{t \to +\infty} \gamma^t p_t x_t^\star = 0 \tag{12}$$

These conditions, along with equations (3) and (4), are necessary and sufficient conditions for optimality.[9] Equivalently, in addition to (3) and (4), the following conditions are necessary and sufficient:

$$\forall t \geq 0,\ U_c'(c_t^\star, d_{t+1}^\star) = R_{t+1} U_d'(c_t^\star, d_{t+1}^\star) \tag{13}$$

$$\forall t \geq 1,\ U_c'(c_t^\star, d_{t+1}^\star) - \frac{1+n}{\gamma} U_d'(c_{t-1}^\star, d_t^\star) \leq 0 \quad (= 0 \text{ if } x_t^\star > 0) \tag{14}$$

$$\lim_{t \to +\infty} (1+n)\gamma^{t-1} U_d'(c_{t-1}^\star, d_t^\star)\, x_t^\star = 0 \tag{15}$$

Equation (13) is obtained by merging equations (9) and (10) and eliminating the shadow price p_{t+1}. Equation (14) results from plugging (10) into (11). The transversality condition (15) is also obtained by substitution of p_t.

Equations (13) and (14) characterise the optimal life-cycle consumptions and the optimal bequest $x_t^\star$. In period t, old individuals can reduce their own consumption by one unit, suffering a utility loss of $U_d'(c_{t-1}^\star, d_t^\star)$ and can increase their bequest $x_t^\star$ to each of their children, increasing the utility of their children by $U_c'(c_t^\star, d_{t+1}^\star)/(1+n)$. This increase in the utility of their children raises their own utility by $\gamma U_c'(c_t^\star, d_{t+1}^\star)/(1+n)$. If bequests are positive ($x_t^\star > 0$), the utility loss from a reduction in parental consumption equals the utility gain from increased bequests. If the utility loss from reduced consumption exceeds the utility gain from increased bequests, altruists leave no bequests ($x_t^\star = 0$). Lastly, the transversality condition (15) means that the limit of the shadow value of bequests is equal to zero.

If the optimisation problem (8) has an optimal solution from any date t onwards and any level of x_t, the associated sequence of value functions, $V_t(x)$, which is by definition the maximum of the objective function (8) from t to $+\infty$ starting at $x_t = x$, satisfies the Bellman equation.[10] Thus, this sequence of value functions[11] is the solution to the altruistic problem (7).

[9] The necessary condition is satisfied when the objective is finite along a path with zero bequests. See assumption A.2 in Michel (1990a).

[10] The Bellman equation, which defines the behaviour of altruistic individuals, corresponds to an infinite number of optimisation problems.

[11] Standard assumptions ensure that these functions exist; see de la Croix and Michel (2002).

2.3.2. The dynasty's founding father

Despite the fact that the bequest left by the first old generation, x_0, is usually considered as given and treated as an initial condition of the economic dynamics, it is actually an economic decision taken by the first old generation born in period $t = -1$. The N_{-1} first old agents receive the proceeds of their savings $R_0 s_{-1}$, which they use to consume d_0 and leave the remainder $(1+n)x_0$ to their children. In period $t = 0$, the first-period consumption of the first old individual c_{-1} is given, as it belongs to the past. Old individuals in period 0 therefore solve the following maximisation problem:

$$\max_{d_0, x_0} \{U(c_{-1}, d_0) + \gamma V_0^\star(x_0, \mathcal{P}_0)\} \tag{16}$$

$$\text{subject to:} \quad R_0 s_{-1} = d_0 + (1+n)x_0 \quad \text{and} \quad x_0 \geq 0$$

Previously, we have resorted to the optimisation problem (8) to solve (7). Similarly, we set up a new optimisation problem to solve (16), the objective function of which, $\sum_{t=-1}^{+\infty} \gamma^t U(c_t, d_{t+1})$, is maximised under the following set of constraints (c_{-1}, s_{-1}, R_0 and $\mathcal{P}_0$ are given):

$$x_0 = \frac{1}{1+n}[R_0 s_{-1} - d_0]$$

$$\forall t \geq 0 \quad x_{t+1} = \frac{1}{1+n}[R_{t+1}(w_t + x_t - c_t) - d_{t+1}]$$

$$\forall t \geq 0 \quad x_t \geq 0$$

The Lagrangeans of periods $t > 0$ are unchanged and the first-period Lagrangean $\mathcal{L}_0$ is:

$$\begin{aligned}\mathcal{L}_0 = {} & \gamma^{-1} U(c_{-1}, d_0) + U(c_0, d_1) + p_0[R_0 s_{-1} - d_0 - x_0] \\ & + \frac{\gamma}{1+n} p_1 [R_1(x_0 + w_0 - c_0) - d_1]\end{aligned}$$

By maximising $\mathcal{L}_0$ with respect to d_0 and x_0 subject to $x_0 \geq 0$, we obtain:

$$U_d'(c_{-1}, d_0^\star) = \frac{\gamma}{1+n} p_0 \tag{17}$$

$$-p_0 + \frac{\gamma}{1+n} p_1 R_1 \leq 0 \quad (= 0 \text{ if } x_0^\star > 0)$$

Note that the first condition corresponds to equation (10) evaluated in period $t = -1$ and the second to equation (11) evaluated in period 0. Eliminating the shadow prices in these two conditions, which characterise the optimal behaviour of the first old altruists, gives equation (14) for $t = 0$.

2.4. Small open economy

It is more difficult to characterise the behaviour of altruists than that of selfish individuals, as an altruist's economic decision making requires relatively sophisticated expectations. In this section, altruistic behaviour is illustrated in the simple case of a small open economy with a constant world interest rate or, alternatively, of an economy where production occurs according to a linear technology. Such an assumption simplifies the maximisation problem a great deal, since (given the wage rate w and the interest factor R) the value function $V_t(x)$ is independent from time:

$$V(x_t) = \max_{c_t, d_{t+1}, x_{t+1}} \{U(c_t, d_{t+1}) + \gamma V(x_{t+1})\}$$

$$\text{subject to:} \quad x_{t+1} = \frac{1}{1+n}[R(x_t + w - c_t) - d_{t+1}] \quad \text{and} \quad x_{t+1} \geq 0$$

The maximisation problem faced by each generation is the same, which should come as no surprise, since it is assumed that the dynasty's macroeconomic environment is stationary. For any bequest $x \geq 0$, the optimal consumptions $\tilde{c} = \tilde{c}(x)$ and $\tilde{d} = \tilde{d}(x)$, and the bequest passed on to the next generation $\tilde{z} = \tilde{z}(x)$ are the solutions to:

$$V(x) = \max_{c,d,z} \{U(c, d) + \gamma V(z)\}$$

$$\text{subject to:} \quad z = \frac{1}{1+n}[R(x + w - c) - d] \quad \text{and} \quad z \geq 0.$$

Let us further assume that the value function is concave and differentiable.[12] For an interior solution (with positive bequests $\tilde{z} > 0$), the two following optimality conditions are obtained by differentiation:

$$U'_c(\tilde{c}, \tilde{d}) = \frac{\gamma R}{1+n} V'(\tilde{z}) \tag{18}$$

$$U'_d(\tilde{c}, \tilde{d}) = \frac{\gamma}{1+n} V'(\tilde{z}) \tag{19}$$

Comparing these two conditions with the optimality conditions (9) and (10) shows that the shadow price p_{t+1} is equal to the marginal value of bequests $x^\star_{t+1}$. The optimality analysis with the Lagrangean $\mathcal{L}_t$ corresponds to a "marginal form" of the Bellman equation applied to one particular solution. The Lagrangean method is more powerful, because it requires no assumption on the (unknown) value function. Moreover, providing an analytical form of the value function is feasible only in very special cases. In the following example, we calculate a closed-form solution of the value function in the case of log-linear life-cycle utilities.

[12] For the concavity and the differentiability of the value function, see Stokey and Lucas (1989) and de la Croix and Michel (2002).

Indeed, in the case of a log-linear utility $U(c_t, d_{t+1}) = \ln c_t + \beta \ln d_{t+1}$ with $\beta > 0$, we prove that, under some conditions, there are positive constants a, b, m such that $V(x_t) = a + b\ln(x_t + m)$ is the unique solution of the Bellman equation. With this form of the value function, equations (18) and (19) imply:

$$\tilde{c} = \frac{(1+n)(\tilde{z}+m)}{\gamma b R} \quad \text{and} \quad \tilde{d} = \frac{(1+n)\beta(\tilde{z}+m)}{\gamma b}$$

By substitution, the maximum $\tilde{M}$ of $U(c, d) + \gamma V(z)$ satisfies:

$$\tilde{M} = (1 + \beta + \gamma b)\ln(\tilde{z} + m) + \gamma a - (1 + \beta)\ln b + \xi$$

where $\xi = (1 + \beta)\ln((1 + n)/\gamma) - \ln R$ and $\tilde{z}$ is given by:

$$\tilde{z} + m = \frac{\gamma b R}{(1+n)(1+\beta+\gamma b)}\left[x + w + \frac{(1+n)m}{R}\right]$$

The condition $\tilde{M} = V(x) = a + b\ln(x + m)$ is then equivalent to the three following conditions, which pin down m, b and a:

(1) $\ln(x + m) = \ln(x + w + \frac{(1+n)m}{R})$ implies $m = \frac{Rw}{R-(1+n)}$.
(2) $b = 1 + \beta + \gamma b$ implies $b = \frac{1+\beta}{1-\gamma}$.
(3) The identification of the constant term gives:

$$a = \frac{1}{1-\gamma}[b\ln\left(\frac{\gamma R}{1+n}\right) - (1+\beta)\ln b + \xi]$$

b is positive ($\gamma < 1$), and m is positive[13] if and only if $R > 1 + n$. In addition, the condition for an interior solution ($\tilde{z}(x) > 0$ for all $x > 0$) is equivalent to $\gamma R \geq 1 + n$. One can show that, under these assumptions, the value function $V(x) = a + b\ln(x + m)$ is the unique solution to the Bellman equation. When $\gamma R = 1 + n$, the optimal bequest is always equal to the received bequest,[14] $\tilde{z}(x) = x$. When the degree of altruism γ is greater than $(1 + n)/R$, $\tilde{z}(x)$ is greater than x. When it is smaller than $(1 + n)/R$, the optimal bequest is necessarily equal to zero from a finite date t onwards.

3. The intertemporal equilibrium

Until now we have focused on the behaviour of altruists, considering prices as given. In this section, we examine the intertemporal equilibrium of the dynastic model, assuming that production occurs according to a neoclassical production function. After characterising the competitive intertemporal equilibrium in the general case, we thoroughly

[13] The function V is defined for $x \geq 0$ and the consumptions $\tilde{c}$ and $\tilde{d}$ are positive for $\tilde{z} \geq 0$ if and only if m and b are positive.

[14] As we shall see in Section 3.2, where prices are endogenous, the steady-state equilibrium is characterised by $\gamma R = 1 + n$ (the modified golden rule) when the bequest motive is operative.

analyse the economic dynamics under the assumption of a Cobb–Douglas production function. We then consider the social optimum and its decentralisation. We finally spell out the main differences between the infinitely lived agent and the dynastic model.

3.1. Definitions

3.1.1. Production and firms

Production occurs according to a neoclassical technology $F(K, L)$ using two inputs, capital K and labour L. Homogeneity of degree one of the function F allows us to write output per young as a function[15] of capital per young: $f(k) = F(k, 1) + (1 - \mu)k$ where $k = K/L$ is the capital stock per young (or worker) and $\mu \in [0, 1]$ the depreciation rate of capital.

In each period, there is one representative firm, producing one good, which is either consumed or invested. For given prices, wage rate w_t and interest factor R_t, the maximum of profits, $\Pi_t = F(K_t, L_t) - w_t L_t - R_t K_t$, is obtained when marginal products are equal to prices. The factor prices are given by:

$$\begin{aligned} w_t &= F'_L(.) = f(k_t) - k_t f'(k_t) \equiv w(k_t) \\ R_t &= F'_K(.) + 1 - \mu = f'(k_t) \equiv R(k_t) \end{aligned} \tag{20}$$

3.1.2. Intertemporal equilibrium

Given the initial capital stock K_0 and the initial wealth of the first old altruists $s_{-1} = K_0/N_{-1}$, an intertemporal equilibrium with perfect foresights is a sequence of prices $\{w_t, R_t\}_{t\geq 0}$, of value functions $\{V_t^\star\}_{t\geq 0}$, of individual quantities $\{c_t, s_t, d_t, x_t\}_{t\geq 0}$ and of aggregate quantities $\{K_t, L_t, Y_t, I_t\}_{t\geq 0}$ such that in each period t:

- Firms maximise their profits (equation (20)).
- Individuals maximise their utility (equation (16) for the first old and equation (7) for the individuals born in period $t \geq 0$).
- The next period's capital stock K_{t+1} is equal to investment I_t or the sum of individual savings $N_t s_t$:

$$K_{t+1} = I_t = N_t s_t$$

- The labour and the good markets clear:

$$L_t = N_t \qquad \text{and} \qquad Y_t = F(K_t, N_t) = N_t c_t + N_{t-1} d_t + I_t$$

[15] The function f is assumed continuous on $\mathbb{R}_+$ and twice continuously differentiable on $\mathbb{R}_+^\star$. Moreover, we assume that for all positive k: $f(k) > 0$, $f'(k) > 0$ and $f''(k) < 0$.

In an economy with dynastic altruism, the assumption of perfect foresights is more stringent than in models with selfish individuals, such as the Diamond (1965) model, where individuals only need to forecast next period's prices, namely the rate of interest. As altruistic individuals have to forecast all future prices to take decisions today, the characterisation of the economic equilibrium entails an infinite dimensional fixed point of the sequence of prices $\{w_t, R_t\}_{t\geq 0}$. Sequences of value functions $\{V_t^\star\}_{t\geq 0}$ and of individual optimal decisions $\{c_t^\star, d_t^\star, s_t^\star, x_t^\star\}_{t\geq 0}$ are associated with the sequence of prices, while the aggregation of individual optimal decisions determines the macroeconomic variables and ultimately the sequence of prices.

3.1.3. *Characterisation of the intertemporal equilibrium*

Assuming that an intertemporal equilibrium with perfect foresights exists, a simple method of characterisation consists in replacing the equilibrium prices with their expressions ($w_t = w(k_t)$ and $R_t = R(k_t) = f'(k_t)$) in the individual optimality conditions.[16] Under standard assumptions, equations (9) and (10), together with $R_{t+1} = f'(k_{t+1})$, define the optimal consumptions as a function of the capital stock and of the shadow price of bequests:

$$c_t^\star = \mathcal{C}(k_{t+1}, p_{t+1}) \qquad \text{and} \qquad d_{t+1}^\star = \mathcal{D}(k_{t+1}, p_{t+1})$$

We also have $d_0^\star$ as a function of p_0 and the initial conditions (see equation (17)). Plugging the optimal consumptions into the equation describing the evolution of bequests and that driving the dynamics of capital, we obtain the two following relations:

$$(1+n)k_{t+1} = s_t^\star = x_t^\star + w(k_t) - \mathcal{C}(k_{t+1}, p_{t+1})$$
$$(1+n)x_{t+1}^\star = f'(k_{t+1})s_t^\star - \mathcal{D}(k_{t+1}, p_{t+1})$$

Bequests thus are a function of the capital stock and the shadow price:

$$x_{t+1}^\star = f'(k_{t+1})k_{t+1} - \frac{\mathcal{D}(k_{t+1}, p_{t+1})}{1+n} \equiv \mathcal{E}(k_{t+1}, p_{t+1})$$

Using this equation in period t, we obtain the dynamic equation of capital:

$$(1+n)k_{t+1} = \mathcal{E}(k_t, p_t) + w(k_t) - \mathcal{C}(k_{t+1}, p_{t+1}) \tag{21}$$

When characterising the intertemporal equilibrium, we must distinguish two cases depending on whether or not the optimal bequest in period t is positive.

If the optimal bequest $x_t^\star$ is positive in period t, the optimality condition (11) implies:

$$p_t = \frac{\gamma}{1+n} f'(k_{t+1}) p_{t+1} \tag{22}$$

[16] Since these optimality conditions are necessary and sufficient, the conditions obtained by substitution are also necessary and sufficient for an intertemporal equilibrium.

Equations (21) and (22) implicitly define a two-dimensional dynamics of k_t and p_t. The initial capital stock k_0 is given, but not the shadow price p_0. These equations define the forward–backward dynamics of the dynastic model. The same expressions hold in each period, provided that bequests are positive all along the transition path. In this case, the following transversality condition pins down the optimal path:

$$\lim_{t\to+\infty} \gamma^t p_t \, \mathcal{E}(k_t, p_t) = 0 \tag{23}$$

If the optimal bequest is equal to zero in period t, the dynamics in period t can be described by a one-dimensional dynamic equation. Indeed, when $x_t^\star = 0$, the equation $\mathcal{D}(k_t, p_t) = (1+n) f'(k_t) k_t$ implicitly defines p_t as a function π of k_t, and we obtain:

$$(1+n)k_t = x_{t-1}^\star + w(k_{t-1}) - \mathcal{C}(k_t, \pi(k_t)) \tag{24}$$

We can distinguish two cases depending on whether or not $x_{t-1}^\star$ is positive.

If $x_{t-1}^\star$ is positive, equation (22) in period $t-1$ gives:

$$p_{t-1} = \frac{\gamma f'(k_t)}{1+n} \pi(k_t) \equiv \sigma(k_t)$$

Together with $x_{t-1}^\star = \mathcal{E}(k_{t-1}, \sigma(k_t))$, equation (24) implicitly defines (for one period) a one-dimensional dynamic equation.

If bequests are not positive in period $t-1$ ($x_{t-1}^\star = 0$), equation (24) defines (for one period) a one-dimensional dynamic equation, which is similar to the dynamics of the baseline overlapping generations model—the Diamond model presented in Section 2.1. To check whether this occurs along the dynamic path of the altruistic economy, one must examine equation (11):

$$-p_t + \frac{\gamma}{1+n} p_{t+1} f'(k_{t+1}) \leq 0$$

which holds when $x_t^\star = 0$.

In practice, it is only possible to characterise either intertemporal equilibria along which bequests are always positive or equilibria along which bequests are always zero. Analysing dynamics switching between a temporary equilibrium with positive bequests and a temporary equilibrium with zero bequests is an issue for future research.

3.2. The Cobb–Douglas case

We analyse the dynamics of the altruistic model in the Cobb–Douglas case. We look for a solution satisfying (21) and (22) in all periods (i.e., a dynamic path along which bequests are positive) and the transversality condition (23). With a Cobb–Douglas production function $f(k_t) = Ak_t^\alpha$ ($A > 0$ and $\alpha \in (0,1)$) we have:

$$w_t = w(k_t) = (1-\alpha)Ak_t^\alpha \qquad \text{and} \qquad R_t = f'(k_t) = \alpha A k_t^{\alpha-1}$$

With a log-linear utility function $U(c_t, d_{t+1}) = \ln c_t + \beta \ln d_{t+1}$ ($\beta > 0$) we obtain, according to (9) and (10), the following functions $\mathcal{C}(k_{t+1}, p_{t+1})$ and $\mathcal{D}(k_{t+1}, p_{t+1})$:

$$c_t^\star = \mathcal{C}(k_{t+1}, p_{t+1}) = \frac{1+n}{\gamma p_{t+1} f'(k_{t+1})}$$

$$d_{t+1}^\star = \mathcal{D}(k_{t+1}, p_{t+1}) = \frac{(1+n)\beta}{\gamma p_{t+1}}$$

We can then calculate $x_t^\star$:

$$x_t^\star = \mathcal{E}(k_t, p_t) = \alpha A k_t^\alpha - \frac{\beta}{\gamma p_t}$$

By multiplying equation (21) by p_t we obtain:

$$(1+n) p_t k_{t+1} = A p_t k_t^\alpha - \frac{\beta}{\gamma} - \frac{(1+n) p_t}{\gamma p_{t+1} \alpha A k_{t+1}^{\alpha-1}} \tag{25}$$

When the bequest motive is operative, condition (22) holds:

$$p_t = \frac{\gamma \alpha A k_{t+1}^{\alpha-1} p_{t+1}}{1+n}$$

Substituting the expression of p_t in equation (25) gives:

$$\alpha \gamma A k_{t+1}^\alpha p_{t+1} = A p_t k_t^\alpha - \left(1 + \frac{\beta}{\gamma}\right)$$

Let us define $v_t = A p_t k_t^\alpha$, the implicit value of output (for the dynasty). The previous equation is linear in this new variable:

$$v_{t+1} = \frac{1}{\alpha\gamma}\left(v_t - 1 - \frac{\beta}{\gamma}\right)$$

This equation admits a unique bounded solution, the constant solution:

$$v_t = \bar{v} = \frac{1}{1-\alpha\gamma}\left(1 + \frac{\beta}{\gamma}\right)$$

It is the unique solution satisfying the transversality condition $\lim_{t\to+\infty} \gamma^t p_t x_t^\star = 0$. Indeed, we have:

$$p_t x_t^\star = \alpha A p_t k_t^\alpha - \frac{\beta}{\gamma} = \alpha v_t - \frac{\beta}{\gamma}$$

Since $p_t = \bar{v}/(A k_t^\alpha)$, we obtain:

$$x_t^\star = \left(\alpha - \frac{\beta(1-\alpha\gamma)}{\gamma+\beta}\right) A k_t^\alpha$$

Thus, bequests are positive if and only if the degree of altruism γ is sufficiently high:

$$\gamma > \frac{\beta(1-\alpha)}{\alpha(1+\beta)} \equiv \bar{\gamma}$$

Here again we must distinguish two cases depending on whether or not bequests are positive. In the Cobb–Douglas case, the condition for positive bequests only depends on parameters characterising preferences and technology.

Positive bequests ($\gamma > \bar{\gamma}$)

When bequests are positive, the dynamics (k_t, x_t) of the economy can be fully characterized analytically.

$$\text{If } \gamma > \bar{\gamma}, \text{ then for all } t \geq 0, \text{ we have: } \begin{cases} k_{t+1} = \dfrac{\alpha\gamma}{1+n} A k_t^{\alpha} \\ x_t = \left(\alpha - \dfrac{\beta(1-\alpha\gamma)}{\gamma+\beta}\right) A k_t^{\alpha} \end{cases}$$

These dynamics converge to the capital stock $\hat{k}$ and the level of bequests $\hat{x}$:

$$\hat{k} = \left(\frac{\alpha\gamma A}{1+n}\right)^{\frac{1}{1-\alpha}} \quad \text{and} \quad \hat{x} = A\left(\alpha - \frac{\beta(1-\alpha\gamma)}{\gamma+\beta}\right)\left(\frac{\alpha\gamma A}{1+n}\right)^{\frac{\alpha}{1-\alpha}}$$

When $\bar{\gamma}$ is larger than 1 or individuals are not sufficiently altruistic to leave bequests ($\gamma \leq \bar{\gamma}$), optimal bequests are zero, and we have $\mathcal{D}(k_t, p_t) = (1+n) f'(k_t) k_t$ and $p_t = \pi(k_t) = \beta/(\alpha\gamma A k_t^{\alpha})$. The intertemporal equilibrium with altruistic individuals is then equivalent to that of an economy consisting of selfish individuals, consuming entirely their life-cycle income. When individuals leave zero bequests, the dynamics of the economy can also be expressed in an explicit manner.

$$\text{If } \gamma \leq \bar{\gamma}, \text{ then for all } t \geq 0, \text{ we have: } \begin{cases} k_{t+1} = \dfrac{(1-\alpha)A\beta}{(1+n)(1+\beta)} k_t^{\alpha} \\ x_t = 0 \end{cases}$$

The capital stock capital converges to k^D:

$$k^D = \left[\frac{(1-\alpha)A\beta}{(1+n)(1+\beta)}\right]^{\frac{1}{1-\alpha}}$$

To conclude this example, note that the possibility to switch from a temporary equilibrium with positive bequests to a temporary equilibrium with zero bequests along the transition path is excluded in the Cobb–Douglas economy.

3.3. Comparison with the social optimum

3.3.1. The central planner's problem

Consider a social planner with a utilitarian objective, that is a discounted sum of generational utilities, with the discount factor reflecting social time preference. What should be the objective function of a central planner in an economy with altruistic individuals? When individuals are altruistic, one faces the issue of whether or not the social planner should ignore this dimension in designing the social objective. In other words, the question is whether or not the social planner should ignore individuals' altruistic feelings, and simply adopt as social objective the discounted sum of generational utilities, after laundering their altruistic components.

In studies on dynastic altruism,[17] the social objective usually only includes the selfish component of each generation's utility. If this were not the case, there would be double counting and the social weights would increase over time, thereby leading to a time-inconsistent optimisation problem (see Bernheim, 1989). The most usual specification assumes that the central planner mimics the founding father of the dynasty, but without taking account of non-negative bequest constraints. It is equivalent to the problem of a central planner combining life-cycle utilities. Hence, the central planner problem can be interpreted in two ways. It can be considered either as the command optimum of an economy with selfish agents or as the command optimum of an altruistic economy.

We consider the problem of a benevolent planner, who can allocate the resources of the economy between capital accumulation, consumption of the young and consumption of the old. The resource constraint $F(K_t, L_t) = N_t c_t + N_{t-1} d_t + K_{t+1}$ can be expressed in intensive form $f(k_t) = (1+n)k_{t+1} + c_t + d_t/(1+n)$. The objective of the social planner is to maximise the discounted sum of the life-cycle utilities of all current and future generations with the social discount factor γ under the resource constraints of the economy:

$$\max_{\{c_t, d_{t+1}\}_{t=-1}^{+\infty}} \sum_{t=-1}^{+\infty} \gamma^t U(c_t, d_{t+1})$$

$$\text{subject to:} \quad \forall t \geq 0 \quad f(k_t) = (1+n)k_{t+1} + c_t + \frac{d_t}{1+n}$$

$$k_0 \text{ and } c_{-1} \text{ given}$$

[17] As noted by Michel and Pestieau (2004), the same approach can be adopted with other types of altruism, in line with Harsanyi (1995) who wants to "*exclude all external preferences, even benevolent ones, from our social utility function*". Using a model where bequests are motivated by joy of giving, Michel and Pestieau (2004) compare the case where utilities are purged from their altruistic component with the case where they are unaltered. Social discounting may also result from uncertainty. See the discussion of social discounting in Arrow and Kurz (1970) and in Michel (1990b).

To characterise the optimal solution, we make use of the method of the infinite Lagrangean:[18]

$$\mathcal{L} = \sum_{t=-1}^{+\infty} \gamma^t U(c_t, d_{t+1}) + \sum_{t=0}^{+\infty} \gamma^t q_t \left[f(k_t) - (1+n)k_{t+1} - c_t - \frac{d_t}{1+n} \right]$$

For all $t \geq 0$, the maximum with respect to c_t, d_t and k_{t+1} is attained when:

$$U_c'(c_t^\star, d_{t+1}^\star) = q_t \tag{26}$$

$$U_d'(c_{t-1}^\star, d_t^\star) = \frac{\gamma q_t}{1+n} \tag{27}$$

$$q_t = \frac{\gamma q_{t+1} f'(k_{t+1})}{1+n} \tag{28}$$

The transversality condition is:

$$\lim_{t \to +\infty} \gamma^t q_t k_{t+1} = 0 \tag{29}$$

We can now compare these optimality conditions with those of the altruistic problem ((9)–(12)), thereby analysing the decentralisation of the social optimum.

3.3.2. Decentralisation of the social optimum

The social optimum can be decentralised in a market economy with non-altruistic individuals by means of lump-sum taxes and transfers. This is the Second Welfare Theorem applied to the overlapping generations model—see Atkinson and Sandmo (1980). The optimal transfer τ_t to each young individual in period t is financed by a tax equal to $(1+n)\tau_t$ paid by each old at the same period. Since old individuals consume the profit net of taxes, the condition for decentralisation,

$$d_t^\star = R_t s_{t-1} - (1+n)\tau_t = f'(k_t)(1+n)k_t - (1+n)\tau_t,$$

defines the optimal lump-sum tax:

$$\tau_t = f'(k_t)k_t - \frac{d_t^\star}{1+n}$$

If all optimal taxes τ_t paid by the old are non-negative, the optimal path is the intertemporal equilibrium of an economy with altruistic individuals; the level of bequests is equal to the lump-sum tax $x_t^\star = \tau_t$.

To prove this result, assume that for all t, $x_t^\star = \tau_t \geq 0$ and $p_t = q_t$. Hence, the optimality conditions (9)–(11) are satisfied. Moreover, $x_{t+1}^\star = f'(k_{t+1})k_{t+1} -$

[18] The two consumptions c_t and d_{t+1} appear in two different resource constraints (in t and $t+1$). In order to apply the method of the Lagrangean $\mathcal{L}_t$ of period t, one can define a modified state variable as in Michel and Venditti (1997).

$d^{\star}_{t+1}/(1+n) < f'(k_{t+1})k_{t+1}$. Since we have $0 \le p_{t+1}x^{\star}_{t+1} < p_{t+1}f'(k_{t+1})k_{t+1} = (1+n)p_t k_{t+1}/\gamma = (1+n)q_t k_{t+1}/\gamma$, the transversality condition (29) of the planner's problem implies the transversality condition (12) of the altruist's maximisation problem. Hence, the solution of the planner problem is an intertemporal equilibrium of an altruistic economy with positive bequests.

The intuition of this result is simple. When τ_t is always positive, altruistic agents, who have the same utility as the social planner, choose to leave bequests equal to the transfers implemented at the command optimum.

If all bequests are positive and if the transversality condition (29) is satisfied, the intertemporal equilibrium of the dynastic model coincides with the planner's optimal solution. Indeed, since the intertemporal equilibrium satisfies $x^{\star}_t > 0$ in every period, replacing q_t by p_t allows to obtain equations (26)–(28) from equations (9)–(11).

Since $\{c^{\star}_t, d^{\star}_t, k_{t+1}\}_{t=0}^{t=+\infty}$ is the optimal allocation chosen by the planner with a social discount factor γ, the founding father of the dynasty behaves as a family planner, reallocating the resources of the dynasty across generations. A dynasty in which individuals are altruistic and are linked to future generations through a chain of positive bequests can be interpreted as an infinitely lived individual. Alternatively, the altruistic model can be thought of as a realistic interpretation of the infinite horizon representative agent model.

3.3.3. *Infinitely lived agents versus altruistic agents*

Even though the overlapping generations model with dynastic altruism can be thought of as a microfoundation for the infinite horizon representative agent model, four significant differences between these two models need to be stressed.

First, bequests must be positive. The old generation can never take resources away from future generations; they could do so if inherited debt were enforceable. Such a restriction does not make much sense in a model with infinitely lived agents. In the absence of credit constraints, one can borrow against one's own future labour income, thus shifting resources from the future to the present. It is not always possible to interpret an infinitely lived agent as a dynasty of altruists.

Second, there is the condition that the indirect utility functions of each generation (the value functions) must be defined, as each generation takes their life-cycle decisions, being aware of the effects of their bequests on the welfare of the next generation. In contrast, infinitely lived agent determine their entire consumption path at the outset of their lives, taking prices as given.

Third, in contrast to the standard assumption of time-additively separable utility functions in models of infinitely lived agent, we consider a more general formulation of preferences, which are represented by a non-separable life-cycle utility function. This has implications for the intertemporal substitution effects, which are reinforced, when the current marginal utility depends on future consumption. As shown by Michel and Venditti (1997), this difference may have important consequences for the equilibrium dynamics.

The fourth difference relates to the transversality condition. In the altruistic model, the discounted value of bequests tends to zero. In the infinitely lived agent model, the discounted value of wealth tends to zero. The wealth of a representative infinitely lived agent includes all the assets of the economy. On the contrary, the bequest of an altruistic agent, who lives a finite number of periods, only includes the wealth transmitted to the next generation. Whereas the transversality condition (29) of an infinitely lived agent implies the transversality condition of an altruist (12), the converse is not true.[19]

4. Steady state

In this section we confine the analysis to steady states. There are two types of steady states: steady state with positive bequests and steady state with zero bequests. After spelling out the steady state equilibrium conditions, we specify the condition under which bequests are positive and address the issue of existence and multiplicity of steady states in the model of dynastic altruism.

In steady state, the marginal utility $U'_d(c, d)$ can be eliminated in equation (13) and the optimality condition (14) becomes $\gamma R \leq 1 + n$ ($=$ if $x > 0$). The following conditions are necessary and sufficient for a steady state equilibrium:

$$x + w = c + s \quad \text{and} \quad Rs = d + (1 + n)x \tag{30}$$

$$U'_c(c, d) = RU'_d(c, d) \tag{31}$$

$$\gamma R \leq 1 + n \quad (= \text{if } x > 0) \tag{32}$$

$$(1 + n)k = s \tag{33}$$

$$w = w(k) \quad \text{and} \quad R = R(k) \tag{34}$$

These conditions fully characterise the steady states of the dynastic model.[20] The transversality condition is fulfilled, since the degree of altruism γ is smaller than 1. In a steady state with positive bequests ($x > 0$), the interest factor R is equal to $\hat{R} = (1 + n)/\gamma$. The steady state capital intensity k is the so-called modified golden rule, $k = \hat{k} = f'^{-1}((1 + n)/\gamma)$.

4.1. Steady state with positive bequests

When bequests are positive, the intertemporal equilibrium is Pareto-optimal, since it coincides with the social optimum (see Section 3.3). As the condition for non-negative bequests plays an important role in the effectiveness of fiscal policy, many economists

[19] See, for example, Michel and Thibault (2006).

[20] These conditions imply the equilibrium condition of the good market, since we have: $f(k) = R(k)k + w(k)$, $R(k)k = R(k)\frac{s}{1+n} = \frac{d}{1+n} + x$ and $w(k) = c + s - x = c + (1 + n)k - x$.

have investigated the determinants of bequests. In his seminal paper, Barro (1974) mentioned the factors that are likely to influence bequests, and pointed to the need for further analysis:

> *"The derivation under which the solution for intergenerational transfer would be interior appears to be a difficult problem and would seem to require some specialization of the form of the utility functions in order to make any headway. However it seems clear that bequests are more likely to be positive the smaller the growth rate of the wage rate, the higher the interest rate ..."*

However, Barro considered an overlapping generations model with exogenous wage and interest rate (see also Drazen, 1978), thereby disregarding significant general equilibrium effects. Carmichael (1982) analysed a model of dynastic altruism with a neoclassical production sector and emphasised the role of the underlying utility function in the bequest behaviour. Abel (1987) and Weil (1987) were the first to establish a formal condition for the existence of a steady state with positive bequests. Both of them assume[21] that the underlying overlapping generations economy—the Diamond model—has a unique and stable positive steady state capital intensity k^D. The dynamics of the Diamond model are:

$$k_{t+1} = s^D\big(w(k_t), R(k_{t+1})\big)$$

where $s^D(.,.)$ is defined Section 2.1.

Abel (1987) and Weil (1987) show that bequests are positive if and only if the steady-state equilibrium of the Diamond model, k^D, is smaller than the modified golden rule capital stock $\hat{k}$. Since $\hat{k}$ is equal to $f'^{-1}((1+n)/\gamma)$, the Abel–Weil condition can be stated as follows: $\gamma > (1+n)/f'(k^D)$, i.e. bequests are positive if the bequest motive is sufficiently strong. This condition implies that over-accumulation of capital in the Diamond model[22] rules out positive bequests in the model of dynastic altruism.

Although the Abel–Weil condition is intuitive, it is obtained under some restrictive assumptions on the Diamond model. Importantly, the characterisation of equilibrium is based on the assumptions of existence, uniqueness and stability of the steady state of the Diamond model. According to Abel (1987, p. 1042) and Weil (1987, footnote 8–p. 385), these assumptions seem sufficient to avoid counterintuitive results. However, Thibault (2001) shows with a simple example that an increase in the degree of altruism can result in a decrease in the steady state level of bequests even under the assumptions made by Abel and Weil. To rule out this counterintuitive result, an assumption on the curvature of the production function is needed.[23]

[21] Weil (1987) assumes that the life-cycle utility function $U(c,d)$ is additively separable.

[22] Over-accumulation of capital occurs when k^D is greater than the golden rule $k^G = f'^{-1}(1+n)$, and thus also greater than the modified golden rule: $k^D > k^G > \hat{k}$.

[23] When $f''(\hat{k})$ is sufficiently close to 0, a small increase in $\hat{k}$ results in no significant change in the interest factor and an increase in the market wage. Children's labour income increases, while parents' saving income $\hat{R}s$ remains broadly constant. Therefore, parents reduce their bequests, although they are more altruistic (see Thibault, 2001).

Thibault (2000) has established a necessary and sufficient condition for the existence of a steady-state equilibrium with positive bequests, which holds regardless of the number and the stability property of steady states in the Diamond model. This condition is obtained by expressing savings as a function of bequests. The steady-state conditions (30) and (34) imply:

$$c + \frac{d}{\hat{R}} = w(\hat{k}) + \left(1 - \frac{1+n}{\hat{R}}\right)x = w(\hat{k}) + (1-\gamma)x \equiv \Omega$$

The consumptions only depend on the disposable-for-consumption life-cycle income Ω, and satisfy the arbitrage condition (31), i.e. $U_c' = \hat{R}U_d'$. Thus, the first-period consumption can be expressed as follows: $c = \Omega - s^D(\Omega, \hat{R})$. This leads to an expression of savings as a function of bequests:

$$s = w(\hat{k}) + x - c = s^D\big(w(\hat{k}) + (1-\gamma)x, \hat{R}\big) + \gamma x \equiv \phi(x)$$

An equilibrium with positive bequests exists if and only if $\phi(x) = (1+n)\hat{k}$ admits a positive solution $\hat{x}$. Assuming that the second-period consumption d is a normal good, $s^D(w, R)$ is increasing with respect to w and, therefore, $\phi(x)$ is increasing. The existence of a positive $\hat{x}$ solution to $\phi(\hat{x}) = (1+n)\hat{k}$ is then equivalent to $\phi(0) < (1+n)\hat{k}$, or:

$$s^D\big(w(\hat{k}), \hat{R}\big) < (1+n)\hat{k} \tag{35}$$

This condition means that, at the modified golden rule, savings in the underlying overlapping generations economy would not be sufficient to maintain the capital stock of the golden rule modified by the degree of altruism γ. Given a level of bequests $\hat{x}$, the steady-state consumptions are determined by (30):

$$\hat{c} = \hat{x} + w(\hat{k}) - (1+n)\hat{k} \qquad \text{and} \qquad \hat{d} = (1+n)\big(\hat{R}\hat{k} - \hat{x}\big)$$

A graphical rule can be used to determine whether or not bequests are positive. Altruists choose to leave positive bequests in the long run if and only if, evaluated at the modified golden rule $\hat{k}$, the curve representing the saving function in the Diamond model divided by $1+n$ (i.e. $k \to S^D(k) = \frac{1}{1+n}s^D(w(k), R(k)))$ lies below the 45° line.

To illustrate the graphical rule, let us consider four degrees of altruism γ_1, γ_2, γ_3 and γ_4 arranged in ascending order. For each degree of altruism γ_i, we define $\hat{k}_i = f'^{-1}((1+n)/\gamma_i)$, the capital stock of the golden rule modified by the degree of altruism γ_i. Let us further assume that Figure 1 depicts the saving function in the Diamond model.

The graphical rule indicates that the model of dynastic altruism does not experience a steady state with positive bequests if the degree of altruism is γ_1 or γ_3. Since $S^D(\hat{k}_2)$ and $S^D(\hat{k}_4)$ are respectively smaller than $\hat{k}_2$ and $\hat{k}_4$, the dynastic model has an equilibrium with positive bequests when the degree of altruism is either γ_2 or γ_4. Interestingly, if the Diamond model has no positive steady state, the dynastic model has a steady state

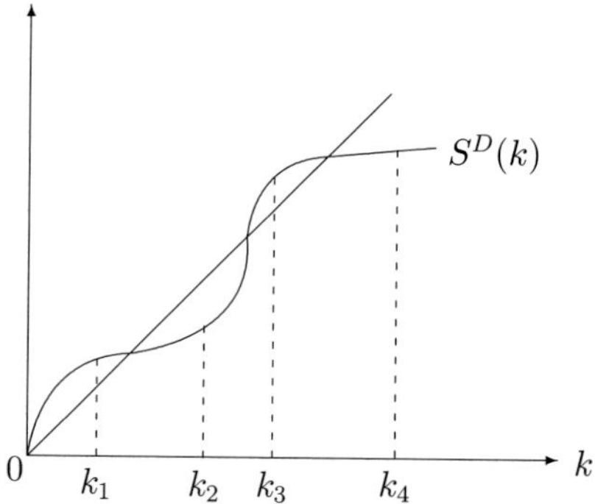

Figure 1. The graphical rule.

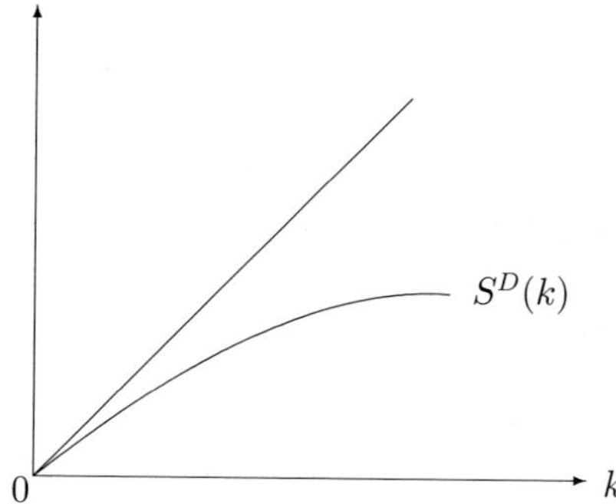

Figure 2. No positive steady state in the Diamond model.

with positive bequests, as the Diamond savings function always lies below the 45° line (see Figure 2).

Furthermore, we remark that the necessary and sufficient condition (35) on s^D for the existence of a steady state with positive bequests can be equivalently expressed using the life-cycle utility function. This condition is equivalent to $\gamma > (1+n)U'_d(c,d)/U'_c(c,d)$, where the marginal utilities are evaluated at $c = w(\hat{k}) - (1+n)\hat{k}$ and $d = (1+n)\hat{R}\hat{k}$. As the function $\varphi(s) = U'_c(w(\hat{k}) - s, \hat{R}s) - \hat{R}U'_d(w(\hat{k}) - s, \hat{R}s)$ is increasing in s because of the strict concavity of U, $\varphi((1+n)S^D(\hat{k})) = 0$ and (35) are equivalent to $\varphi((1+n)\hat{k}) > 0$.

4.2. *Steady state with zero bequests*

Altruists who are not sufficiently wealthy to leave a bequest to their children behave as if they were selfish. Any steady state with zero bequests of the economy with dynastic altruism, therefore, is a steady state of the Diamond economy. The zero-bequest steady

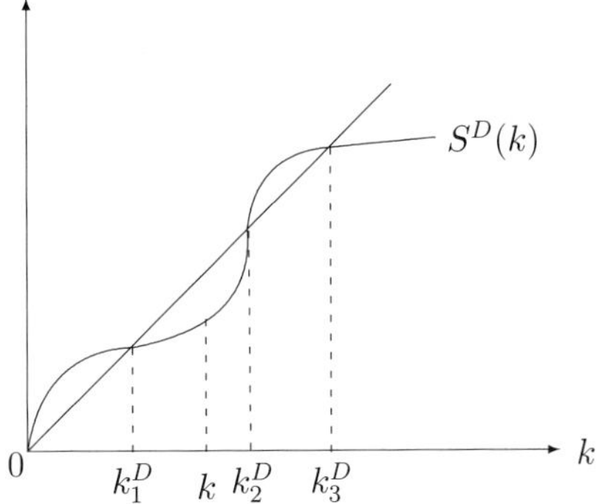

Figure 3. Multiplicity of equilibria.

states of the model of dynastic altruism feature a capital stock which is greater than that of the modified golden rule, since equations (32) and (34) imply that a steady state with zero bequests satisfies the following inequality: $\gamma f'(k) \leq 1 + n$, or equivalently $k \geq \hat{k}$. Since the modified golden rule capital stock $\hat{k}$ is smaller than that of the golden rule $k^G = f'^{-1}(1 + n)$, regardless of the degree of altruism, dynamically-inefficient equilibria of the Diamond model are equilibria with zero bequests of the dynastic model. The only dynamically-efficient Diamond equilibria, which are also equilibria of the dynastic model, are located between the modified golden rule capital stock $\hat{k}$ and the golden rule capital stock k^G. According to the graphical rule, the zero-bequest equilibria of the dynastic model are the Diamond equilibria located on the right-hand side of the modified golden rule, $\hat{k}$. Whereas the steady state with positive bequests is unique, there can be a multiplicity of steady states with zero bequests.

4.3. Existence and multiplicity of steady states

The steady state with positive bequests can coexist with bequest-constrained equilibria, which are formally equivalent to those of the Diamond model.[24] To illustrate multiple equilibria, let us assume that the function $S^D(k)$ is represented in Figure 3.

The economy depicted in Figure 3 experiences three steady states. The equilibrium with positive bequests $\hat{k}$ coexists with two bequest-constrained equilibria k_2^D and k_3^D. The steady-state equilibrium k_1^D, which would be a steady state of the Diamond model, is not an equilibrium of the dynastic model, as it is smaller than the modified golden rule ($k_1^D < \hat{k}$). In contrast to the Diamond model, the model of dynastic altruism always experiences at least one steady state with positive capital. We consider two cases. First, if the Diamond model has no positive steady state, we have proved in Section 4.1 (see Figure 2) that the dynastic model has a unique steady state, the modified golden rule

[24] Aiyagari (1992) obtains a similar result in a pure exchange economy.

$\hat{k}$. Second, if the Diamond model has several positive steady states, either the highest of these equilibria, k^D_{max}, is greater than, or equal to, $\hat{k}$ and it is a steady state with zero bequests, or k^D_{max} is smaller than $\hat{k}$ and the dynastic model has a steady state with positive bequests, because (35) is satisfied.[25]

This result can be extended to a more general setting with endogeneous labour supply, where the population consists of individuals endowed with heterogeneous degrees of altruism. In this setting, Thibault (2004) establishes that the presence of an agent with altruistic preferences (but not necessarily leaving positive bequests) is sufficient to guarantee the existence of at least one non-trivial steady state.

Finally, using the graphical rule, it is straightforward to establish that the dynastic model has a unique positive steady state only in two cases:

- If the Diamond model has no positive steady state greater than $\hat{k}$, the dynastic model has a unique steady state, the modified golden rule.
- If the Diamond model has a unique steady state k^D greater than $\hat{k}$ and if (35) is not satisfied, k^D is the unique equilibrium of the dynastic model.

5. Fiscal policy

Any dynamic path of the economy with dynastic altruism coincides with the social optimum, provided that bequests are positive all along the equilibrium path (see Section 3.3). This means that fiscal policies aimed at redistributing resources between generations have no impact on the intertemporal equilibrium, as long as fiscal policy choices remain compatible with the existence of an equilibrium with positive bequests. Public debt is neutral, as public intergenerational transfers resulting from the issuance and redemption of government bonds are offset by private intergenerational transfers of an equivalent amount. In this section, we illustrate the neutrality of fiscal policies by analysing their effects on the steady state of the dynastic model. First, we present the debt-neutrality result. Second, we extend the neutrality result to unfunded or pay-as-you-go social security schemes. Third, we analyse the effects of estate taxation on the equilibrium of the dynastic model. Finally, we reconsider public debt and its neutrality property, when the bequest motive is inoperative before, but not after government intervention.[26]

5.1. Neutrality of government debt

We consider a public debt scheme along the lines of Diamond (1965). The relation between savings and capital accumulation is modified, as savings finance both physical

[25] We have $\lim_{k\to+\infty} \frac{S^D(k)}{k} = 0$ (since $S^D(k) < \frac{w(k)}{1+n}$). Thus, for $k > k^D_{max}$ we have $S^D(k) < k$.

[26] Bernheim and Bagwell (1988) criticise dynastic altruism, arguing that it is not a suitable assumption for analysing redistributive policies. They point out that family linkages result in complex networks, where each individual may belong to many different families. These linkages give rise to additional neutrality results, including the irrelevance of redistribution.

capital and government bonds:

$$K_{t+1} + B_t = N_t s_t$$

In each period the government reimburses the capital and interest of the outstanding debt by issuing new bonds and levying taxes on the young. The government budget constraint is:

$$B_t = R_t B_{t-1} - N_t \tau_t$$

B_t denotes the total level of debt and τ_t is a lump-sum tax paid by each young. We further assume that the debt issued in period 0 was distributed to the old in period 0 and that there is no public spending. We define the debt per young individual $b_t \equiv B_t / N_{t-1}$ and assume that it is constant, $b_t = b$. The path of taxes necessary to maintain this constant debt ratio is given by: $\tau_t = (R_t - (1+n))b$. Henceforth, we restrict the analysis to steady state with a view to explaining the debt neutrality result in a simple framework. In steady state, we have:

$$\tau = [R - (1+n)]b$$

In the absence of government intervention ($b = 0$), $\{c, d, x, k\}$ is a steady state of the dynastic model if and only if the optimality conditions (30), (31), (32), (33) and (34) are satisfied (see Section 4). When bequests are positive ($x > 0$), equation (32) pins down the steady state capital stock, the modified golden rule $k = \hat{k}$, and the long-run equilibrium is $\{\hat{c}, \hat{d}, \hat{x}, \hat{k}\}$. To extend the baseline model to public debt, only two optimality conditions have to be modified in steady state.

- The first-period budget constraint becomes:

$$w + x - \tau = c + s \qquad \text{where} \quad \tau = [R - (1+n)]b$$

- The relation between the capital stock and savings reads now:

$$s = (1+n)(k+b)$$

Given $k = \hat{k}$ and $x = \hat{x} + \hat{R}b$, the consumptions are $c = \hat{x} + w(\hat{k}) - (1+n)\hat{k} = \hat{c}$ and $d = \hat{R}s - (1+n)x = \hat{d}$. The condition for positive bequests $x > 0$ results from $\hat{x} > 0$, when debt is positive.[27] Hence, consumption and production are not modified in the long run with a constant debt per young individual. The Ricardian equivalence theorem applies to the model of dynastic altruism, when the bequest motive is operative before debt is issued. The only changes concern the decision variables s and x. Altruists counter the government intervention by reallocating their bequests and their savings. Increasing their bequests by $\hat{R}b$ allows them to leave their consumption path and their utility unaffected, when the government issues public bonds amounting to b.

[27] Neutrality is also obtained with a negative debt, i.e. public investment, as long as $\hat{x} + \hat{R}b$ is positive.

5.2. Neutrality of pay-as-you-go social security

An increase in social security benefits makes parents richer and children poorer, since children pay taxes to finance the social security system. Altruistic parents, who leave bequests to their children before the increase in the scale of the social security programme, are aware of the transfer of resources operated by the pension system and react to this policy change by increasing their bequests. Any increase in the scale of the social security programme is thereby offset by an equivalent increase in bequests, provided that bequests are positive before the policy change.

To simplify the exposition, we consider the steady state of an economy without a pay-as-you-go social security system ($\tau = 0$), which we denote with $\{\hat{c}, \hat{d}, \hat{x}, \hat{k}\}$. In steady state, the optimal bequest $\hat{x}$ satisfies equation (31):

$$U_c'\big(w(\hat{k}) + \hat{x} - \hat{s}, \hat{R}\hat{s} - (1+n)\hat{x}\big) = \hat{R}U_d'\big(w(\hat{k}) + \hat{x} - (1+n)\hat{s}, \hat{R}\hat{s} - (1+n)\hat{x}\big)$$

where $\hat{s} = (1+n)\hat{k}$ is the level of savings at the modified golden rule.

Let us consider an unfunded pension scheme consisting of a payroll tax τ paid by the workers and a pension benefit θ given to the retirees. The budget of the public pension system is balanced in each period:

$$\theta = (1+n)\tau$$

If bequests are positive, the steady state capital stock is given by the modified golden rule. The incomes of the young and the old are $x+w-\tau$ and $Rs+(1+n)\tau$, respectively. The steady-state bequest x must then satisfy the optimality condition:

$$\begin{aligned} &U_c'(x + w - \tau - s, Rs + (1+n)\tau - (1+n)x) \\ &\quad = RU_d'(x + w - \tau - s, Rs - (1+n)x + (1+n)\tau) \end{aligned} \tag{36}$$

When $k = \hat{k}$, $w = w(\hat{k})$, $R = \hat{R}$ and $s = \hat{s}$, $x = \hat{x} + \tau$ is the solution to equation (36). Given a level of bequests $x = \hat{x} + \tau$, the consumption of parents, $d = \hat{R}\hat{s} + (1+n)\tau - (1+n)x = \hat{R}\hat{s} - (1+n)x = \hat{d}$, as well as the consumption of children, $c = w(\hat{k}) - \tau + x - \hat{s} = w(\hat{k}) + \hat{x} - \hat{s} = \hat{c}$, are not affected by the pension system.

The neutrality of a pay-as-you-go system is valid in the dynastic model, provided that bequests are positive before its introduction. The private intergenerational transfers from parents to children exactly offset the public intergenerational transfers operated by the pension system, and the optimality conditions defining the consumption path of the dynasty remain unchanged. Altruistic agents increase their bequests exactly by the amount of taxes paid by the young to finance the social security scheme.

5.3. Nonneutrality of estate taxation

Estate taxation affects the intertemporal equilibrium, since it distorts individual choices. A proportional tax rate τ_e applies to bequests, and the tax revenue is redistributed in a lump-sum manner, θ_e, to the young individuals. Thus, the first-period budget constraints are modified as follows:

$$(1-\tau_e)x + w + \theta_e = c + s$$

The optimality condition regarding bequests (i.e. equation (32)) becomes:

$$R - \frac{1+n}{(1-\tau_e)\gamma} \leq 0 \quad (= \text{ if } x > 0)$$

If bequests are positive, the steady-state capital stock $\hat{k}_e$ is given by:

$$\hat{k}_e = f'^{-1}\left(\frac{1+n}{(1-\tau_e)\gamma}\right)$$

Assuming that the government budget is balanced in each period, we have: $\theta_e = \tau_e x$. Estate taxation reduces the capital stock ($\hat{k}_e < \hat{k}$), while increasing the interest factor (i.e. $R(\hat{k}_e) > R(\hat{k})$). As the net product per young agent (available for consumption) $f(\hat{k}_e) - (1+n)\hat{k}_e$ is diminished, estate taxation reduces the steady state welfare of altruistic individuals.

5.4. Neutrality of high debts

The neutrality of government debt or public pension hinges on the assumption that bequests are positive all along the equilibrium path. If bequests are constrained before government intervention, the Ricardian equivalence theorem does not hold, and fiscal policy affects the economic equilibrium. Let us reconsider the case of public debt. The steady-state equilibrium with a constant debt ratio, b, is characterised by the following equations:

$$x^b + w^b - \tau = c^b + s^b \qquad \text{and} \qquad R^b s^b = d^b + (1+n)x^b$$
$$U'_c(c^b, d^b) = R^b U'_d(c^b, d^b)$$
$$\gamma R^b \leq 1+n \quad (= \text{ if } x^b > 0)$$
$$(1+n)(k^b + b) = s^b$$
$$w^b = w(k^b) \qquad \text{and} \qquad R^b = R(k^b)$$
$$\tau = [R^b - (1+n)]b$$

There are two possibilities depending on whether x^b is positive or equal to zero.

- If $x^b = 0$, the steady state $\{c^b, d^b, x^b = 0, k^b\}$ is a steady state of the Diamond economy.
- If x^b is positive, the steady state is given by the modified golden rule, with $k^b = \hat{k}$, $R^b = \hat{R}$, $w^b = w(\hat{k})$ and $s^b = (1+n)(\hat{k} + b)$.

The optimal solution $\{\hat{c}, \hat{d}, \hat{k}\}$ corresponds to the steady state obtained by ignoring the non-negative bequest condition $x \geq 0$. When there is no debt, we denote with:

$$\tilde{x}^0 = \frac{\hat{R}\hat{s} - \hat{d}}{1+n}$$

the transfer (positive or negative) which is desired by the parents. Taking into account the non-negative bequest condition, the optimal bequest chosen by an altruist is given by:

$$x^0 = \max\{0, \tilde{x}^0\}$$

Given a debt level b, the transfer (positive or negative) which is desired by a parent becomes:

$$\tilde{x}^b = \frac{\hat{R}(1+n)X(\hat{k}+b) - \hat{d}}{1+n} = \tilde{x}^0 + \frac{1+n}{\gamma}b$$

When the government issues a positive debt b, the optimal bequest chosen by an altruist is:

$$x^b = \max\{0, \tilde{x}^b\}$$

To examine the effects of public debt, we distinguish different cases depending on the level of debt and the degree of altruism γ. When the desired parent-to-child transfer is non-negative ($\tilde{x}^0 \geq 0$), a positive debt implies $\tilde{x}^b > 0$ and we obtain the neutrality result showed in Section 5.1. When the desired intergenerational transfer is negative ($\tilde{x}^0 < 0$) in the absence of public debt, altruists choose to leave no bequests (i.e. $x^0 = 0$). Altruists then behave as pure life-cyclers and fiscal policy—public debt or social security—is effective.

When fiscal policy is effective, its effects depend on the size of public debt, b. Consider the threshold level of debt $\bar{b}$ equal to $-\gamma\tilde{x}^0/(1+n)$. When the size of debt b is sufficiently low ($b \leq \bar{b}$), public debt does not affect bequests. As bequests are constrained before and after the government intervention, the effect of public debt is the same as in the Diamond model.

However, when b is greater than $\bar{b}$, bequests x^b become positive. The bequest motive is inoperative before the introduction of debt but not afterwards. Importantly, an increase in b from above $\bar{b}$ has no further effect on the equilibrium. This property has been studied by several authors in voting models (see, e.g., Cukierman and Meltzer, 1989). In this framework, the amount of debt preferred by old agents is the level $\bar{b}$, which makes individuals free from the non-negative bequest constraint.

6. Heterogenous altruistic dynasties

Mankiw (2000a) has highlighted several empirical findings, supporting the view that neither the Barro (1974) model of intergenerational altruism nor the Diamond (1965) model are consistent with available empirical evidence. In place of these two standard models, Mankiw (2000a, 2000b) puts forward a macroeconomic framework, also advocated by Michel and Pestieau (1998), which seems to be more attune to empirical heterogeneity in consumers' behaviours. Some altruistic people (the savers) have long time horizons, which is consistent with the great concentration of wealth and the importance of bequests in aggregate capital accumulation. Others (the spenders) have short time horizons, as evidenced by the failure of consumption smoothing and the prevalence of households with near zero net worth. The savers-spenders theory, writes Mankiw (2000b), takes a small step toward including this microeconomic heterogeneity in macroeconomic theory. As we shall see, this setting which combines both agents *à la Diamond* and agents *à la Barro* yields new conclusions regarding the effectiveness of fiscal policy (see also Smetters, 1999).

In line with this approach, we consider an economy consisting of two types of altruistic agents. They have the same life-cycle utility function $U(c, d)$, but different degrees of altruism: $\gamma_1 > \gamma_2$. In each dynasty, all agents have the same degree[28] of intergenerational altruism γ_i, $i \in \{1, 2\}$. We denote with p_i the exogenous proportion of individuals of type i. First, we study the steady state of this economy. Second, we characterise the effects of fiscal policy.

6.1. *Steady state*

In steady state, the optimality conditions (30), (31) and (32) apply to both types of individuals with x_i, c_i, s_i, d_i and γ_i. The equilibrium prices satisfy (34), but the relation between the capital stock and savings needs to be amended to take account of individuals' heterogeneity:

$$(1 + n)k = p_1 s_1 + p_2 s_2 \tag{37}$$

As we have $\gamma_2 < \gamma_1$, the optimality conditions imply $\gamma_2 R < \gamma_1 R \leq 1 + n$. Since condition (32) holds for both types, a positive bequest in the less altruistic dynasty ($x_2 > 0$) is ruled out. Only individuals belonging to the dynasty endowed with the higher degree of altruism can leave bequests. In steady state, the less altruistic individuals leave no bequests ($x_2 = 0$) and their saving function is similar to that of selfish individuals: $s_2 = s^D(w(k), R(k))$.

If bequests are positive in the more altruistic dynasty ($x_1 > 0$), condition (32) implies: $\gamma_1 R(k) = 1 + n$. The steady-state capital–labour ratio is that of the modified golden rule corresponding to the degree of altruism of the more altruistic agents ($k = \hat{k}_1 = f'^{-1}((1 + n)/\gamma_1)$). The steady state capital–labour ratio is determined by the degree of altruism of the more altruistic individuals, regardless of their relative number. The society is divided into two classes: those who are linked with their children through bequests and those who behave as if they were selfish.

[28] In this chapter we assume that each dynasty is characterised by a given degree of altruism: children are as altruistic as their parents. Another approach referred to as imperfect altruism assumes that there are two possible types of children within each family: altruistic or selfish (see Dutta and Michel, 1998 or Gevers and Michel, 1998).

When interpreting (see Mankiw, 2000a, 2000b) the degree of altruism as a degree of patience or a propensity to save,[29] this result is consistent with Ramsey (1928) and Becker (1980). If different individuals discount future utility at different rates, equilibrium, writes Ramsey (1928), would be attained by a division of society into two classes, the thrifty enjoying bliss and the improvident at the subsistence level. In an economy with heterogeneous infinitely lived agents,[30] the most patient ones drive the long-run capital accumulation. Vidal (1996a) extends this result to heterogeneous dynasties in a closed economy, while Vidal (2000) studies capital mobility under the assumption that degree of intergenerational altruism differs across countries. When labour supply is endogeneous, the most altruistic individuals who inherit can behave as rentiers, provided they choose not to work. Thibault (2005) establishes the conditions under which rentiers emerge and analyses their characteristics (proportion, wealth, propensity to save).

Let us calculate the savings of the more altruistic individuals, s_1, in the case of positive bequests $x_1 > 0$. In steady state, the life-cycle budget constraint of the more altruistic individuals is:

$$c_1 + \frac{d_1}{R(\hat{k}_1)} = w(\hat{k}_1) + \left(1 - \frac{1+n}{R(\hat{k}_1)}\right)x_1 = w(\hat{k}_1) + (1-\gamma_1)x_1 \equiv \Omega_1$$

In addition to their wages, altruists consume the difference between the bequest they receive from their parents and the bequest they leave to their children. This, along with condition $U'_c(c_1, d_1) = R(\hat{k}_1)U'_d(c_1, d_1)$ implies: $c_1 = \Omega_1 - s^D(\Omega_1, R(\hat{k}_1))$. Their consumptions only depend on their disposable-for-consumption life-cycle income. By substitution in the first-period budget constraint, we obtain:

$$s_1 = w(\hat{k}_1) + x_1 - c_1 = s^D\big(w(\hat{k}_1) + (1-\gamma_1)x_1, R(\hat{k}_1)\big) + \gamma_1 x_1 \equiv \phi_1(x_1)$$

Under the assumption that the second-period consumption is a normal good, $s^D(w, R)$ is increasing in w, and thus $\phi_1(x_1)$ is increasing in x_1. Moreover, ϕ_1 increases from $\phi_1(0) = s^D(w(\hat{k}_1), R(\hat{k}_1))$ to $+\infty$, when x_1 increases from 0 to $+\infty$. The equilibrium condition (37) is at the steady state $\hat{k}_1$:

$$p_1\phi_1(x_1) = (1+n)\hat{k}_1 - p_2 s^D\big(w(\hat{k}_1), R(\hat{k}_1)\big)$$

and there exists a solution $x_1 > 0$ if and only if the right-hand-side of this expression is greater than $p_1\phi_1(0)$:

$$(1+n)\hat{k}_1 > s^D(w(\hat{k}_1), R(\hat{k}_1))$$

This is exactly the condition we would have in the model of homogenous altruistic agents with degree of altruism γ_1. At the modified golden rule $\hat{k}_1$ the Diamond saving

[29] Falk and Stark (2001) analyse the roles of altruism and impatience in the evolution consumption and bequests. See also Drugeon (2000) on the role of long-run endogeneous impatience in homothetic growth path.

[30] Nourry and Venditti (2001) study the determinacy of perfect foresight equilibrium near the steady state of the model with heterogeneous dynasties.

function lies below the modified golden rule capital stock. In this case, there exists a unique steady state with positive bequests x_1 in the economy with heterogeneous altruists. The more altruistic individuals' bequests compensate for the less altruistic individuals' insufficient savings. This clearly appears when studying the effect of p_1 on the equilibrium. Even though the capital-labour ratio $\hat{k}_1$ of the modified golden rule does not depend on the share of more altruistic individuals in the population, the level of bequests does. Interestingly, x_1 is a decreasing function of p_1, as well as the life-cycle income Ω_1. The lower the proportion of the more altruistic agents, the more they consume and the higher their utility.

6.2. Government debt

We consider the case of a government debt b that is constant per young individual. The first-period budget constraint of individuals of type i needs to be amended to take account of taxation:

$$w + x_i - \tau = c_i + s_i$$

Physical capital and government bonds are financed by savings of both types of individuals:

$$(1+n)(k+b) = p_1 s_1 + p_2 s_2 \tag{38}$$

The analysis developed in Section 6.1 still applies. We have $x_2 = 0$, $s_2 = s^D(w - \tau, R)$ and if bequests are positive in the more altruistic dynasty ($x_1 > 0$), we obtain $k = \hat{k}_1$, $\Omega_1^b = w(\hat{k}_1) - \tau + (1-\gamma_1)x_1$ and:

$$\tau = \big(R(\hat{k}_1) - (1+n)\big)b \equiv \varepsilon(\hat{k}_1)b$$

The savings of the more altruistic individuals are:

$$s_1 = \phi_1(x_1, b) \equiv \gamma_1 x_1 + s^D\big(w(\hat{k}_1) - \varepsilon(\hat{k}_1)b + (1-\gamma_1)x_1, R(\hat{k}_1)\big)$$

Equation (38) becomes:

$$p_1\phi_1(x_1, b) = (1+n)(\hat{k}_1 + b) - p_2 s^D\big(w(\hat{k}_1) - \varepsilon(\hat{k}_1)b, R(\hat{k}_1)\big)$$

Bequests x_1 are positively related to government debt b. When x_1 is positive, public debt is neutral from the aggregate point of view, since it does not modify capital, output and total consumption. In the economy with heterogeneous agents, it has redistributive implications, reducing the income, consumptions and welfare of the less altruistic individuals. Since total consumption is unchanged, increasing public debt results in higher levels of consumption and welfare for the more altruistic individuals. This stems from the increase in the bequests of the more altruistic individuals x_1, compensating for the lower savings of the less altruistic individuals. Public debt has no redistributive implications only in the case of homogenous agents ($p_1 = 1$), provided that bequests are positive.

6.3. Pay-as-you-go social security and estate taxation

A pay-as-you-go social security system with lump-sum taxes and benefits entails the same effects as government debt. When bequests are positive in the more altruistic dynasty ($x_1 > 0$), the economy is in a situation of under-accumulation of capital with $k = \hat{k}_1$. The life-cycle income Ω_2^τ of the less altruistic individuals is reduced by an increase in the scale of the social security programme. With a lump-sum tax τ paid by the young, the benefits received by retirees amount to $\theta = (1+n)\tau$, and the steady-state life-cycle income of the less altruistic individuals is given by:

$$\Omega_2^\tau = w(\hat{k}_1) - \tau + \frac{\theta}{R(\hat{k}_1)} = w(\hat{k}_1) - (1-\gamma_1)\tau < w(\hat{k}_1) = \Omega_2$$

Aggregate variables and prices are unchanged in the long run, whereas there is a welfare loss for the less altruistic individuals and a welfare gain for the more altruistic individuals.

Estate taxation with heterogeneous individuals has been studied by Michel and Pestieau (1998).[31] A proportional tax rate τ_e applies to bequests and the tax revenue is redistributed in a lump-sum manner θ_e to young individuals. Thus, the first-period budget constraints are modified as follows:

$$(1-\tau_e)x_i + w + \theta_e = c_i + s_i$$

The optimality condition regarding bequests (32) becomes:

$$R - \frac{1+n}{(1-\tau_e)\gamma_i} \leq 0 \quad (= \text{if } x_i > 0)$$

This implies that the less altruistic individuals do not leave bequest ($x_2 = 0$), and if x_1 is positive, the steady-state capital stock $\hat{k}_e$ is given by:

$$\hat{k}_e = f'^{-1}\left(\frac{1+n}{(1-\tau_e)\gamma_1}\right)$$

Assuming that the government budget is balanced in each period, we have: $\theta_e = \tau_e p_1 x_1$. Estate taxation reduces the capital stock (i.e. $\hat{k}_e < \hat{k}_1$), while increasing the interest factor (i.e. $R(\hat{k}_e) > R(\hat{k}_1)$). The net product per young agent (available for consumption) $f(\hat{k}_e) - (1+n)\hat{k}_e$ is diminished.

Estate taxation has three effects on the welfare of the less altruistic individuals who do not leave bequests: a negative effect on their labour income $w(\hat{k}_e)$, a positive effect resulting from the redistribution of estate tax revenues $\theta_e = p_1\tau_e x_1$ and a positive effect stemming from the decrease in the relative price $1/R(\hat{k}_e)$ of old-age consumption. For the more altruistic individuals, there are two additional effects, the tax on bequests and

[31] They consider the case in which the less altruistic individuals are pure life-cyclers (i.e., $\gamma_2 = 0$). The value of γ_2 ($< \gamma_1$) has no impact on the steady-state equilibrium; see Vidal (1996a).

the induced changes in bequests. Michel and Pestieau (1998) show in a simple case with a log-linear utility and a Cobb–Douglas production function that the negative effects dominate for a sufficiently low level of the estate tax rate τ_e, and that estate taxation worsens the steady-state welfare of both types of agents.

7. Other forms of altruism

The neutrality of fiscal policy hinges on individual reactions. The motive for intergenerational transfers is therefore crucial in analysing the effects of fiscal policy. Dynastic altruism guarantees the neutrality of fiscal policy when bequests are positive, but results are less clear cut, when other motives underpin intergenerational transfers. In this section we present several models of intergenerational altruism and analyse fiscal policy in each of them, thereby making clear the conditions for the neutrality of fiscal policy.

We distinguish two strands of models. In the first one, the utility of the beneficiary is an argument of the utility of the benefactor. Since we have already examined the model of descending dynastic altruism, we focus on others forms of pure altruism: ascending and two-sided altruism. In the second one, altruism is said to be *ad hoc*. Either the altruistic argument in the benefactor's utility function is only some part of the utility of the beneficiary (Burbidge, 1983; Abel, 1987) or some other variables such as the level of bequests (paternalistic altruism) or the level of income (family altruism).

7.1. Others forms of pure altruism

7.1.1. Ascending altruism

Barro (1974) stresses that the neutrality result depends on the existence of positive transfers between parents and children. These transfers can be from parents to children (descending) or from children to parents (ascending). The model of ascending intergenerational altruism is formally similar to the model of descending altruism. Children have an altruistic concern for their parents and face the following budget constraints:

$$c_t + s_t + g_t = w_t$$

$$d_{t+1} = R_{t+1} s_t + (1+n) g_{t+1}$$

where g_t denotes the gift that individuals born in period t give to their parents and $(1+n)g_{t+1}$ the gifts that they receive in period $t+1$ from their $1+n$ children. Gifts are private intergenerational transfers from the young to the old and are restricted to be non-negative in each period:

$$g_t \geq 0$$

We again consider a recursive definition of altruism. Children care about their parents' welfare by weighting their parents' utility in their own utility function v_t. Denoting with v_{t-1} the well-being of their parents, we assume that the utility of individuals born in period t is given by:

$$v_t = U(c_t, d_{t+1}) + \delta v_{t-1}$$

where $\delta \in (0, 1)$ is the degree of ascending altruism. This formulation is based on several implicit assumptions. We can substitute parental utilities backwards to obtain an infinite sequence of past life-cycle utilities (from $t = 0$ to $t = -\infty$). The optimality conditions are therefore similar to those prevailing in the case of descending altruism ((13) and (14)). Equation (13) is the arbitrage condition driving consumption choices, whereas reversing the direction of transfers leads to replacing (14) with the following condition:

$$-U_c'(c_t, d_{t+1}) + \delta(1+n)U_d'(c_{t-1}, d_t) \leq 0 \quad (= \text{ if } g_t > 0) \tag{39}$$

Since ascending altruism is based on calculations regarding past utilities, this formulation raises some modelling concerns:

- Past variables are given and cannot be modified. In this context, what is the significance of a backward dynamics of the capital stock?
- Assuming that all generations have the same behaviour, the intertemporal equilibrium goes from $t = -\infty$ to $t = +\infty$ and has no initial condition.
- From (13), (20) and (39), the steady state capital stock of the economy with positive gifts satisfies: $f'(k) = R = (1+n)\delta$. The steady state with positive gifts is characterised by over-accumulation of capital.[32]

Along the same lines as those we developed when analysing descending altruism, one can show that government debt or pay-as-you-go social security do not affect steady-state consumptions, when long-run gifts are positive. Individuals can counter fiscal policies by adjusting gifts. Ricardian equivalence holds, as long as the chain of positive intergenerational transfers is not broken. Since public debt is an ascending public transfer between generations, an increase in the level of public debt is offset by an equivalent decrease in gifts. There therefore exists a level of public debt, such that gifts are driven down to zero. When public debt is sufficiently high, parents become so wealthy that there is no longer a need for gifts. As gifts are no longer positive, families cannot counter fiscal policy, which then becomes effective.

7.1.2. *Two-sided altruism*

Neither descending nor ascending altruism can ensure debt neutrality, which holds only if bequests or gifts are positive. Some authors have therefore combined both ascending and descending altruism, leading to a new form of altruism known as two-sided or reciprocal altruism.

[32] O'Connell and Zeldes (1993) analyse the model of ascending altruism under the assumption of strategic behaviours. When parents save less to receive more, the steady state may be characterised by under-accumulation of capital.

Since intergenerational transfers operate in both directions, from children to parents (gifts g_t) and from parents to children (bequests x_t), an individual born in t faces the following budget constraints:

$$c_t + s_t + g_t = w_t + x_t$$

$$d_{t+1} + (1+n)x_{t+1} = R_{t+1}s_t + (1+n)g_{t+1}$$

In each period, private intergenerational transfers are assumed to be non-negative:

$$g_t \geq 0 \quad \text{and} \quad x_t \geq 0 \tag{40}$$

Assuming that individuals have an altruistic concern for both their parents and their children, one can represent their utility function as follows:

$$v_t = \delta v_{t-1} + U(c_t, d_{t+1}) + \gamma v_{t+1}$$

where $\delta \in (0, 1)$ and $\gamma \in (0, 1)$ are the degree of ascending altruism and the degree of descending altruism, respectively.

The formulation of two-sided altruism deserves some comments:

- Analysing two-sided altruism is difficult, because the life cycle utility $U(c_t, d_{t+1})$ is both in v_{t-1} and in v_{t+1}, and two key questions therefore arise. When does a solution exist? What is the relation between the degree of ascending altruism and the degree of descending altruism? Kimball (1987) shows that strong assumptions on the degrees of altruism are required to guarantee that an infinite sum of life-cycle utilities is the solution to the functional equation defining the utility of altruists.[33] Some parametric restrictions are also necessary to ensure that intergenerational transfers are positive.
- Since the intertemporal equilibrium goes from $-\infty$ to $+\infty$, there are no initial conditions.
- In a model where individuals leave bequests to their children and support their parents, three types of steady-state equilibrium are possible. Because of the two inequality constraints (40), there are two first-order conditions (14) and (39), which are not mutually compatible in steady state. The steady state cannot therefore be characterised by both positive bequests and positive gifts. Either bequests are positive and gifts zero, or bequests are zero and gifts positive, or both are zero. There is a wide range of parameters leading to zero intergenerational transfers (see Vidal, 1996b).

Concerning fiscal policy the results are straightforward extensions of those obtained under one-sided altruism. The neutrality of government debt is again guaranteed only if the same type of transfers (either gifts or bequests) is positive both before and after the change in the level of government debt.

[33] Kimball (1987) shows that the sum of both degrees of altruism must be smaller than 1, i.e. $\delta + \gamma < 1$.

7.2. Ad hoc *altruism*

There always are restrictions to the neutrality of public debt in models of dynastic altruism. In the literature there is only one specification of altruism ensuring that Ricardian equivalence always holds. This specification departs from the recursive definition of altruism proposed by Barro and belongs to *ad hoc* forms of the altruistic utility function, which we review in this section. First, we examine the specification of the altruistic utility function ensuring debt neutrality and highlight its caveats. Second, we present paternalistic altruism, whereby bequests are broadly equivalent to consumption goods in the utility of parents. Third, we briefly expound family altruism, which departs from paternalism, but still does not assume that families are infinitely lived decision makers.

7.2.1. *A model with debt neutrality*

Burbidge (1983) has proposed a particular form of altruism, which always results in government debt neutrality. He suggests adding a term of ascending altruism, which relates to an altruistic concern for parents, to a term of descending altruism:

$$v_t = \frac{1}{\gamma}U(c_{t-1}, d_t) + U(c_t, d_{t+1}) + \sum_{j=1}^{+\infty} \gamma^j U(c_{t+j}, d_{t+1+j})$$

This utility function is the sum of the utility of dynastic altruists born in t (see expression (5)) and the life-cycle utility of their parents, which is weighted by an altruistic factor $1/\gamma$. Given c_{t-1}, this implies that the welfare function of the young in t coincides with the central planner's objective:

$$v_t = \sum_{i=-1}^{+\infty} \gamma^i U(c_{t+i}, d_{t+1+i})$$

The intertemporal equilibrium of this model coincides with the social optimum. Transfers to the young are interpreted as bequests and transfers to the old as gifts. Fiscal policy, therefore, is ineffective. Importantly, note that the component of descending altruism appears in the central planner's objective, but not the component of ascending altruism of future generations.

Abel (1987) has extended Burbidge's analysis by assuming that the altruistic concern for parents is weighted by δ, which can differ from $1/\gamma$. For $\delta \neq 1/\gamma$, fiscal policy is not always neutral, because the objective of an altruist, $v_t = \delta U(c_{t-1}, d_t) + \sum_{j=1}^{+\infty} \gamma^j U(c_{t+j}, d_{t+1+j})$, differs[34] from that of the social planner.

This form of *ad hoc* altruism strongly departs from the notion of dynastic altruism. Both Burbidge and Abel make a distinction between the concern for parents and the concern for children, as if future generations had no concern for their parents.

[34] In contrast to the model of two-sided dynastic altruism, it is sufficient to assume that the product $\gamma\delta$ is smaller than 1 to guarantee that optimal decisions made by two successive generations are mutually consistent.

7.2.2. Paternalistic altruism

We examine one of the most popular specification of *ad hoc* altruism. Bequests are said to be paternalistic, when parents derive utility not from their children's utilities, but from the size of the estate they leave to them. The utility function of a paternalistic altruist, who is born in t and consume c_t and d_{t+1}, can be represented by the following function:

$$v_t = U(c_t, d_{t+1}) + \Phi(x_{t+1}) \tag{41}$$

where x_{t+1} is the level of bequests and separability is assumed for the sake of simplicity. Φ is defined on the set of non-negative values of x_{t+1} and the non-negative bequest constraint still applies to this model. With an infinite marginal utility of zero bequests (i.e., $\lim_{x \to 0} \Phi'(x) = +\infty$), optimal bequests are always positive. As the objective function (41) does not depend on the decisions and budget constraints of children, fiscal policy (government debt or pay-as-you-go social security) is effective.

Paternalistic bequests are related to altruistic bequests. Paternalistic parents also accumulate savings for the purposes of leaving bequests to their children. Nevertheless the amount and structure of bequests are not related to their children's preferences, but rather to parental views on what is good for their children, or to the pleasure they derive from giving. Models dealing with paternalistic bequests are therefore often referred to as "bequest-as-consumption models" or "joy-of-giving models", because bequests enter in the parental utility function as a consumption good (see, for example, Abel and Warshawsky, 1988 or Andreoni, 1989).

Since paternalistic altruism is analytically more tractable than dynastic altruism, it is often used to study inequality, wealth distribution or social mobility (see, for example, Galor and Zeira, 1993, Aghion and Bolton, 1997 or Benabou, 2000).

7.2.3. Family altruism

Models of dynastic altruism consider the family as an infinitely lived entity. By contrast, models of pure life-cyclers feature another extreme view on the family, according to which parents and children are fully distinct economic units. Following Becker (1991), one can envisage a less drastic approach to modelling economic relations within the family.

Models of family altruism assume that a family is neither a dynasty nor an isolated household. Each individual starts a new household, when he becomes adult. In turn, each of an individual's children will also establish a new household, and so on. Individuals are members of two family units: the family founded by their parents and their own household. They play a different role in these two households. They belong to the former during both their childhood and adulthood, where they play the role of children, and to the latter when adult and old, where they play the role of parents. In the former they make no decision, being completely passive when young and being only a descendant and possibly heir when adult. In the latter they are fully fledged decision makers.

Family altruism refers to the sentiments between these two successive households. Altruists born in t take account of their children's adult disposable income denoted with ω_{t+1}. The budget constraints of individuals born in t are the following:

$$\omega_t = w_t + x_t = c_t + s_t$$

$$R_{t+1}s_t = d_{t+1} + (1+n)x_{t+1}$$

$$\omega_{t+1} = x_{t+1} + w_{t+1}$$

$$x_{t+1} \geq 0$$

The utility of altruists depends on three arguments: their first-period consumption c_t, their second-period consumption d_{t+1} and their children's disposable income ω_{t+1} during adulthood:

$$v_t = U(c_t, d_{t+1}) + \Psi(\omega_{t+1})$$

Altruists can influence the starting position of their grown-up children. They are non-paternalistic, since intergenerational transfers aim at providing children with a good starting position in life. The idea[35] behind family altruism is that parents only care about the income of their children and not about how they use their income.

The concept of family altruism leads to interesting fiscal policy conclusions. It can be shown that the introduction of a pay-as-you-go social security system has no real effects, when bequests are positive. In contrast to the model of dynastic altruism, such a neutrality property does not hold for public debt.

To illustrate the neutrality of a pay-as-you-go pension system, we assume that the government levies a social contribution τ_{t+1} on each young and distributes revenues to the old, born in t, who receive θ_{t+1}. Balancing the pension system in every period implies $N_t\theta_{t+1} = N_{t+1}\tau_{t+1}$, or $\theta_{t+1} = (1+n)\tau_{t+1}$. Following the method developed in Section 5.2, the new optimal bequest is $x'_{t+1} = x_{t+1} + \tau_{t+1}$.The consumption of parents and the income of children are not altered by the social security scheme, as we have:

$$d'_{t+1} = R_{t+1}s_t + (1+n)\tau_{t+1} - (1+n)x'_{t+1} = R_{t+1}s_t - (1+n)x_{t+1} = d_{t+1}$$

$$\omega'_{t+1} = w_{t+1} - \tau_{t+1} + x'_{t+1} = w_{t+1} + x_{t+1} = \omega_{t+1}$$

This proves that bequests exactly offset intergenerational transfers operated by the pay-as-you-go social security system.

The non-neutrality of government debt is straightforward. Assume that government bonds, issued in period $t+1$, are distributed to the old in $t+1$ and is reimbursed by the young in $t+3$. Since altruists born in t do not take into account the utility of their descendants, they do not care about the situation of individuals born in $t+3$. As in

[35] Some growth models with human capital are based on a similar concept of altruism. For example, the preference of altruists in Glomm and Ravikumar (1992) depends on the quality of schools. This variable is directly linked to the adult disposable income of children (see Section 8).

the Diamond model, but in contrast to models of dynastic altruism, public debt has real effects.

The model with family altruism[36] leads to conclusions regarding the effectiveness of fiscal policy, which are less clear-cut and more realistic than those obtained with either the standard overlapping generations model or the model of dynastic altruism.

8. Extensions

Intergenerational altruism significantly influences the economic equilibrium and the effectiveness of fiscal policy. It is worth enquiring, as it most likely underpins a wide range of economic decisions. Selfishness is certainly not a fully satisfactory assumption for the analysis of bequests, gifts, or private education. Altruistic behaviours may also drive economic decisions which have an impact on future generations, such as environmental policy. In this section, we consider two issues that can be analysed under the assumption of altruistic behaviours. First, we consider a model of education, where parents' educational choices are driven by altruism. Second, we turn to environmental economics and present a model, where there is an intergenerational external effect of pollution.

8.1. Altruism and education

In growth models, education is closely related to the concept of human capital, which represents a quantity of efficiency units of labour. The production function, F, uses two inputs, physical capital K_t and efficient labour or human capital H_t. This function is assumed to be linearly homogenous and each production factor is paid its marginal product:

$$R_t = F'_K(K_t, H_t) = f'(k_t) \qquad \text{where} \quad f(k) = F(k, 1) \quad \text{and} \quad k_t = K_t/H_t$$

$$w_t = F'_L(K_t, H_t) = f(k_t) - k_t f'(k_t) = w(k_t)$$

The labour income of an individual that supplies h_t efficiency units of labour is equal to $w_t h_t$. The human capital of individuals born in t depends on their parents' human capital, h_t, and their parents' educational spending, e_t:

$$h_{t+1} = \varphi(h_t, e_t)$$

[36] Lambrecht et al. (2006) analyse the equilibrium dynamics of the model with family altruism and show that its dynamical properties are halfway between the overlapping generations model with pure life-cyclers (Diamond, 1965) and the model of dynastic altruism (Barro, 1974). For an analysis of pay-as-you-go social security in a model of family altruism, see Lambrecht et al. (2005).

Altruistic parents, who maximise $V_t = u(c_t, d_{t+1}) + V_{t+1}$, choose how much to spend on their children's education, along with their consumptions, c_t and d_{t+1}, and the bequest they leave to their children, x_{t+1}. We can then write the altruistic maximisation problem as follows:

$$\begin{aligned} V_t^*(x_t, h_t) = & \max_{c_t, e_t, d_{t+1}, x_{t+1}} U(c_t, d_{t+1}) + V_{t+1}^*(x_{t+1}, h_{t+1}) \\ \text{subject to:} \quad & x_t + w_t h_t = c_t + (1+n)e_t + s_t \\ & R_{t+1} s_t = d_{t+1} + (1+n)x_{t+1} \\ & h_{t+1} = \varphi(h_t, e_t) \end{aligned}$$

Parents take into account the impact of their educational spending on the welfare of their children, which depends on their level of human capital, h_{t+1}, and their bequests. This model has two state variables and is therefore more intricate than the baseline model of dynastic altruism. Most authors have assumed that there is no physical capital or that parents have an altruistic concern only for the level of human capital of their children.

Glomm and Ravikumar (1992) have for example developed a simplified altruistic model of education, in which parents are only concerned for their children's human capital, focusing on the distribution of income in the economy. Parents decide on the education of their children. In each period t, children devote u_t units of their time endowment to educate themselves, whereas their parents pay e_t for their education. They also benefit from the level of human capital of their parents, h_t, so that their own level of human capital in period $t + 1$ is:

$$h_{t+1} = A u_t^{\alpha} e_t^{\beta} h_t^{1-\beta} \qquad \text{with} \quad \alpha > 0 \quad \text{and} \quad 0 < \beta < 1 \tag{42}$$

With their income in period $t + 1$ (h_{t+1}) individuals finance their consumption and the education of their children:

$$h_{t+1} = c_{t+1} + e_{t+1} \tag{43}$$

The life-cycle utility is assumed to be log-linear:

$$U_t = \ln(1 - u_t) + \ln c_{t+1} + \ln e_{t+1} \tag{44}$$

Individuals choose u_t, c_{t+1} and e_{t+1} so as to maximise (44) subject to the constraints (42) and (43). In period t, h_t and e_t are given. The solution to this maximisation problem is:

$$\begin{aligned} u_t^* &= \frac{\alpha}{\alpha + 1/2} \\ c_{t+1}^* &= e_{t+1}^* = \frac{1}{2} h_{t+1} \end{aligned}$$

By substituting the optimal decisions into (43), we obtain the dynamics of human capital:

$$\ln h_{t+1}^* = b^* + \ln h_t^* \qquad \text{where} \quad b^* = \ln\left(A \left(\frac{\alpha}{\alpha + 1/2} \right)^{\alpha} \left(\frac{1}{2} \right)^{\beta} \right)$$

If human capital is initially distributed according to a log-normal distribution of mean μ_0 and variance σ_0^2, human capital in period t is distributed according to a log-normal distribution of mean μ_t and variance σ_t^2:

$$\mu_{t+1} = b^* + \mu_t \qquad \text{and} \qquad \sigma_{t+1}^2 = \sigma_t^2 = \cdots = \sigma_0^2$$

The average level of human capital, $\bar{h}_t$, is defined by:

$$\ln \bar{h}_t = \mu_t + \frac{1}{2}\sigma_t^2$$

When education is publicly financed, all individuals benefit from the same level of educational spending, $\bar{e}_t$, which is financed by a wage tax, τ_t:

$$\bar{e}_t = \tau_t \bar{h}_t$$

The utility of an individual born in t is then the maximum of (44) under the constraints:

$$c_{t+1} = (1 - \tau_{t+1})h_{t+1} \qquad \text{and} \qquad \bar{e}_{t+1} = \tau_{t+1}\bar{h}_{t+1}$$

Individuals make less effort to educate themselves under a public education system. Given τ_{t+1} and $\bar{h}_{t+1}$, they maximise $\ln(1 - u_t) + \ln h_{t+1}$ under the constraint $h_{t+1} = Au_t^\alpha \bar{e}_t^\beta h_t^{1-\beta}$. Under a public education regime, the optimal effort is $u_t^P = \frac{\alpha}{1+\alpha} < u_t^*$. The optimal effort is smaller than under a private education regime, because individuals can no longer directly influence the education level of their children.

The public educational spending and therefore the level of taxation are the result of a voting equilibrium. The derivative of an individual's utility with respect to τ_{t+1} is equal to $\frac{1}{1-\tau_{t+1}} + \frac{1}{\tau_{t+1}}$ and the maximum level of utility is obtained for $\tau_{t+1} = 1/2$. The result of the voting equilibrium is given by:

$$\tau_{t+1}^P = 1/2, \qquad c_{t+1}^P = \frac{1}{2}h_{t+1}^P \qquad \text{and} \qquad \bar{e}_{t+1}^P = \frac{1}{2}\bar{h}_{t+1}^P$$

Hence,

$$\begin{aligned}\ln h_{t+1}^P &= \ln A + \alpha \ln u_t^\alpha + \beta \ln \bar{e}_t^P + (1-\beta)\ln h_t^P \\ &= b^P + \beta \ln \bar{h}_t^P + (1-\beta)\ln h_t^P\end{aligned}$$

where $b^P = \ln(A(\frac{\alpha}{1+\alpha})^\alpha(\frac{1}{2})^\beta) < b^*$. With a log-normal distribution $(\mu_t^P, (\sigma_t^P)^2)$ we have:

$$\begin{aligned}\mu_{t+1}^P &= b^P + \frac{\beta}{2}\left(\sigma_t^P\right)^2 + \mu_t^P \\ \left(\sigma_{t+1}^P\right)^2 &= (1-\beta)^2\left(\sigma_t^P\right)^2\end{aligned}$$

We can conclude from this model that:

- A public education system reduces inequality ($\lim_{t\to+\infty}(\sigma_t^P)^2 = 0$), whereas a private education system maintain inequality ($\sigma_t^2 = \sigma_0^2$).

- In the long run, the mean of the logarithm of human capital grows at a lower rate under a public education regime ($\mu_{t+1}^P - \mu_t^P \simeq b^P$) than under a private education regime ($\mu_{t+1}^* - \mu_t^* = b^* > b^P$). The same conclusion applies to the average level of human capital, since we have: $\ln \bar{h}_{t+1}^P - \ln \bar{h}_t^P = b^P - \frac{1}{2}(1-\beta)\beta(\sigma_t^P)^2$ and $\ln \bar{h}_{t+1}^* - \ln \bar{h}_t^* = b^*$.

In the model of Glomm and Ravikumar, the effect of taxation on growth is negative, because taxation reduces educational efforts. In another formulation of this model, the educational effort is made by parents, who devote time l_t to the education of their children. Individuals then face the following budget constraints:

$$w_t(1-l_t) = c_t + e_t$$

Human capital evolves according to:

$$h_{t+1} = A l_t^\alpha e_t^\beta h_t^{1-\beta}$$

In this model, taxation and public education exert opposite effects, because time devoted to the education of children is free from taxation. The growth rate is then higher under a public education regime (see Wigniolle, 1994).

8.2. *Altruism and environment*

Dynamic issues relating to the environment, pollution or the depletion of natural resources, have mainly been analysed in the framework of optimal growth models. The main feature of environmental externalities is their double dimension, intra- and intertemporal, as they affect today's generation as well as future generations. Altruistic individuals are concerned for the quality of the environment over their life-cycle, as they directly suffer from pollution or poor environmental quality, but also for the quality of the environment in the future, as they are altruistically linked to their children. Along with physical capital (here bequests), the environment is an asset which is passed on to future generations. Altruistic individuals therefore devote resources to abate pollution and to preserve the quality of the environment. Even individuals who leave zero bequests can contribute to pollution abatement and environmental quality.

Clearly, the environment is a public good shared within as well as between generations. Private contributions to finance public goods typically result in underprovision, as subscription equilibria are non-cooperative. There is a case for public intervention in spite of the altruistic tendencies of private individuals (see Howarth and Norgaard, 1995), as subsidies to private contributions can restore efficiency. If pollution stems from industrial activities, there is a tradeoff between the accumulation of physical capital and the quality of the environment. The private return of physical capital differs from its social return, thereby leading to a second inefficiency. In contrast to results obtained in the baseline altruistic model, the market equilibrium is no longer Pareto-optimal, when taking account of environmental externalities.

Jouvet et al. (2000) examine these aspects in a model consisting of altruistic individuals, who only consume during their second period of life, but whose utility is negatively affected by the level of pollution. They can voluntarily contribute to environmental quality. There is no population growth. The utility of individuals born in period t can be written as follows:

$$V_t = U(d_{t+1}, P_{t+1}) + \gamma V_{t+1}$$

$$\text{subject to:} \quad x_t + w_t = s_t$$
$$R_{t+1}s_t = d_{t+1} + z_{t+1} + x_{t+1}$$
$$x_{t+1} \geq 0 \quad \text{and} \quad z_{t+1} \geq 0$$

where the main difference with respect to the maximisation problem set up in Section 2 is the voluntary contribution to pollution abatement z_{t+1} and the pollution term in the utility function. The emission of pollutants in period t is a linear function of the output level, aY_{t+1}, and pollution abatement occurs according to a linear technology, $-bZ_{t+1}$ (where Z_{t+1} is the total contribution to environmental cleaning), whereas pollution absorption takes place linearly, $(1-h)P_t$. The dynamics of pollution are therefore given by:

$$P_{t+1} = (1-h)P_t + aY_{t+1} - bZ_{t+1}$$

When choosing their personal contribution z_{t+1}, individuals take other individuals' contributions as given. We have:

$$P_{t+1} = (1-h)P_t + aY_{t+1} - b(z_{t+1} + \overline{Z}_{t+1})$$

where $\overline{Z}_{t+1}$ is the sum of other individuals' contributions. It is further assumed that the technology of pollution abatement is efficient,[37] $b > a$.

In steady state, four types of equilibria are possible, depending on whether or not bequests are positive and on whether or not voluntary contributions to pollution abatement are positive. To illustrate these equilibria, we consider the following utility function: $U(d, P) = \ln d + \lambda \ln(\overline{P} - P)$, where $\overline{P}$ is an upper limit on the level of pollution and λ the relative weight of environmental quality, $\overline{P} - P$, in the utility. Figure 4 shows the steady-state equilibria in the plane (λ, γ).

When individuals are not sufficiently altruistic (low γ), the bequest motive is inoperative and we have: $k_{t+1} = w_t = f(k_t) - k_t f'(k_t)$. If the steady state $\tilde{k}$ is unique, the condition for positive bequests is:

$$\gamma > \tilde{\gamma} = 1/f'(\tilde{k})$$

If bequests are positive, the steady state is the modified golden rule $k_\gamma = f'^{-1}(1/\gamma)$. In the absence of voluntary contributions, the steady-state level of pollution is $\widetilde{P}(\gamma) =$

[37] Each unit produced devoted to pollution abatement has a negative net effect, $a - b$, on the increase in pollution.

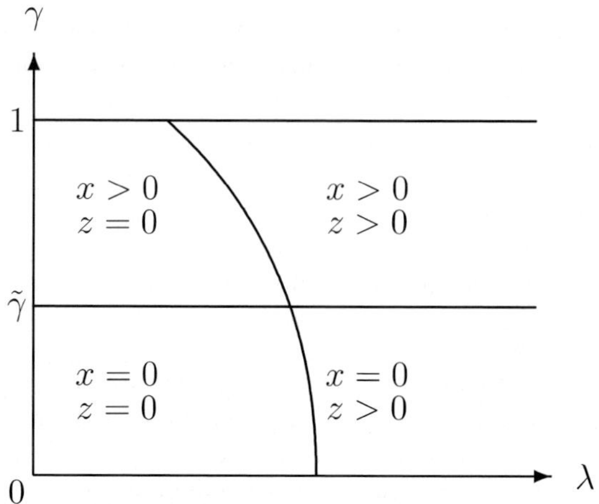

Figure 4. Steady state equilibria.

$aNf(k_\gamma)/h$. There is a threshold[38], $\tilde{\lambda}(\gamma)$, on the weight of pollution in the utility function above which contributions are positive. Alternatively, when the bequest motive is inoperative, contributions are positive if the weight of pollution in the utility λ exceeds a threshold $\tilde{\lambda}_0(\gamma)$. In both cases, the thresholds triggering positive contributions are lower, the higher the degree of intergenerational altruism.

The competitive equilibrium is suboptimal, because of the two externalities prevailing in the economy. The first externality is well-known in public economics; the Cournot-Nash decision process is inefficient, and individuals under-contribute to pollution abatement. The second externality affects the economy through the production process: altruistic individuals do not take into account the effect of production on pollution, thereby leading to a level of capital that is higher than socially desirable. The central planner takes into account these two externalities and maximises the following social welfare function:

$$\sum_{t=0}^{+\infty} \gamma^t U(d_t, P_t)$$

$$\text{subject to:} \quad f(k_t) = d_t + z_t + k_{t+1}$$

$$P_t = (1-h)P_{t-1} + aNf(k_t) - bNz_t$$

$$k_0 \text{ and } P_{-1} \text{ given}$$

In the long run, the marginal productivity of capital, which characterises the social optimum, is:

$$f'(k^S) = \frac{1}{\gamma(1 - a/b)}$$

[38] The expression of this threshold is derived in Jouvet et al. (2000).

This is the genuine modified golden rule that takes into account the environmental externality of capital accumulation. The social planner chooses to accumulate less capital than altruistic individuals, $f'(k^S) > 1/\gamma$. This is because the social value of capital differs from its private value, as altruistic individuals fail to internalise the impact of production on the environment. Furthermore, the social planner takes into account the social willingness to pay for pollution abatement, leading to higher spending on pollution abatement than in the competitive equilibrium.

Since two externalities have to be internalised by altruistic individuals, the decentralisation of the social optimum can be achieved by using two policy instruments. First, to attain an efficient allocation of resources between consumption, a private good, and the quality of the environment, a public good, the government has to subsidise contributions to pollution abatement. Second, the government has to limit capital accumulation, for instance by reducing savings, since private altruistic individuals do not take into account the adverse consequences of pollution on environmental quality. This can be done by setting a tax on the return of savings.

9. Conclusion

Altruism is the appropriate microeconomic foundation underpinning the possible ineffectiveness of fiscal policy in stimulating economic activity, referred to as Ricardian equivalence. Our review of altruistic growth models shows that the Ricardian equivalence theorem does not always hold in dynastic models. The debt neutrality result hinges on positive private transfers between successive generations (bequests or gifts). When these transfers are zero, fiscal policy is effective. Barro's intuitive formulation of altruism in macroeconomic models does not always deliver Ricardian equivalence, when taking account of all general equilibrium linkages. Even extending his intuition to two-sided altruism is not enough to ensure debt neutrality without conditions, as fiscal policy is effective when both bequests and gifts are zero.

Dynastic altruism features the view of highly rational economic agents, who are farsighted and see through the government budget constraint, thereby possibly countering the effects of fiscal policy. A specific *ad hoc* form of altruism is needed to deliver the debt neutrality results without conditions. The altruistic utility proposed by Burbidge (1983) is formally equivalent to a central planner's objective and, not surprisingly, delivers Ricardian equivalence, but as any *ad hoc* formulation it suffers from weak theoretical foundations. The model of dynastic altruism remains the benchmark for discussing debt neutrality, as it offers a fully consistent framework to analyse fiscal policy in an intertemporal framework.

As argued by Ricardo, the neutrality result is a point of theory, insofar as individuals certainly suffer from myopia, leaving some room for fiscal policy. Extending the basic framework to heterogeneous individuals provides some insights in this respect. The steady state equilibrium is still a modified golden rule, which depends on the degree of altruism of the more altruistic individuals, but fiscal policy entails important redistributive effects between heterogeneous dynasties. Models consisting of both short-sighted or selfish individuals and far-sighted or altruistic individuals certainly represent a better abstraction of real world economies, and further progress in the characterisation of the effects of fiscal policy on economic activity requires a better understanding of individual heterogeneity in macroeconomic models. Analysing transition dynamics of heterogeneous economies is key to understanding both the long term and the short term effects of fiscal policy.

References

Abel, A.B. (1987). "Operative gift and bequest motives". American Economic Review 77, 1037–1047.

Abel, A.B., Warshawsky, M. (1988). "Specification of the joy of giving: insights from altruism". Review of Economics and Statistics 70, 145–149.

Aghion, P., Bolton, P. (1997). "A theory of trickle-down growth and development". Review of Economic Studies 64, 151–172.

Aiyagari, S.R. (1992). "Co-existence of a representative agent type equilibrium with a non-representative agent type equilibrium". Journal of Economic Theory 57, 230–236.

Allais, M. (1947). Economie et Intérêt. Imprimerie nationale, Paris.

Andreoni, J. (1989). "Giving with impure altruism: applications to charity and Ricardian equivalence". Journal of Political Economy 96, 1447–1458.

Arrow, K.J., Kurz, M. (1970). Public Investment, the Rate of Return and Optimal Fiscal Policy. The Johns Hopkins Press, Baltimore.

Atkinson, A.B., Sandmo, A. (1980). "Welfare implications of the taxation of savings". Economic Journal 90, 529–549.

Barro, R. (1974). "Are government bonds net wealth?". Journal of Political Economy 82, 1095–1117.

Barro, R., Becker, G. (1988). "A reformulation of the economic theory of fertility". Quarterly Journal of Economics 103, 1–25.

Becker, G. (1974). "A theory of social interaction". Journal of Political Economy 82, 1063–1091.

Becker, G. (1991). A Treatise on the Family, enlarged edition. Harvard University Press, Cambridge, MA; London.

Becker, R. (1980). "On the long run steady state in a simple dynamic model of equilibrium with heterogeneous households". Quarterly Journal of Economics 95, 375–382.

Benabou, R. (2000). "Unequal societies: income distribution and the social contract". American Economic Review 90, 96–129.

Bergstrom, T. (1999). "System of benevolent utility functions". Journal of Public Economic Theory 1, 71–100.

Bernheim, B.D. (1989). "Intergenerational altruism, dynastic equilibria and social welfare". Review of Economic Studies 56, 119–128.

Bernheim, B.D., Bagwell, K. (1988). "Is everything neutral?". Journal of Political Economy 96, 308–338.

Bevan, D.L., Stiglitz, J.E. (1979). "Intergenerational transfers and inequality". Greek Economic Review 1, 8–26.

Buiter, W.H. (1979). "Government finance in an overlapping generations model with gifts and bequests". In: Social Security Versus Private Saving. Ballinger, Cambridge.

Buiter, W.H. (1988). "Death, birth, productivity growth and debt neutrality". Economic Journal 98, 279–293.

Buiter, W.H., Carmichael, J. (1984). "Government debt: comment". American Economic Review 74, 762–765.

Burbidge, J.B. (1983). "Government debt in an olverlapping generations model with bequests and gifts". American Economic Review 73, 222–227.

Carmichael, J. (1982). "On Barro's theorem of debt neutrality: the irrelevance of net wealth". American Economic Review 72, 202–213.

de la Croix, D., Michel, Ph. (2002). A Theory of Economic Growth: Dynamics and Policy in Overlapping Generations. Cambridge University Press.

Cukierman, A., Meltzer, A. (1989). "A political theory of government debt and deficits in a neo-Ricardian framework". American Economic Review 79, 713–732.

Diamond, P.A. (1965). "National debt in a neoclassical growth model". American Economic Review 55, 1126–1150.

Drazen, A. (1978). "Government debt, human capital, and bequests in a life cycle model". Journal of Political Economy 86, 505–516.

Drugeon, J.P. (2000). "On the roles of impatience in homothetic growth paths". Economic Theory 15, 139–161.

Dutta, J., Michel, Ph. (1998). "The distribution of wealth with imperfect altruism". Journal of Economic Theory 82, 379–404.

Elmendorf, D.W., Mankiw, N.G. (1999). "Government debt". In: Taylor, J., Woodford, M. (Eds.), Handbook of Macroeconomics, vol. 1C. North Holland, pp. 1615–1669.

Falk, I., Stark, O. (2001). "Dynasties and destiny: on the roles of altruism and impatience in the evolution of consumption and bequests". Economica 68, 505–518.

Galor, O., Ryder, H. (1989). "Existence, uniqueness, and stability of equilibrium in an overlapping generations model with productive capital". Journal of Economic Theory 49, 360–375.

Galor, O., Zeira, J. (1993). "Income distribution and macroeconomics". Review of Economic Studies 60, 35–52.

Gevers, L., Michel, Ph. (1998). "Economic dynasties with intermissions". Games and Economic Behavior 25, 251–271.

Glomm, G., Ravikumar, B. (1992). "Public versus private investment in human capital: endogenous growth and income inequality". Journal of Political Economy 100, 818–834.

Harsanyi, J. (1995). "A theory of social values and a rule utilitarian theory of morality". Social Choice and Welfare 12, 319–344.

Hori, H. (1992). "Utility functionals with nonpaternalistic intergenerationnal altruism: the case where altruism extends to many generations". Journal of Economic Theory 56, 451–467.

Hori, H., Kanaya, S. (1989). "Utility functions with nonpaternalistic intergenerationnal altruism". Journal of Economic Theory 49, 241–255.

Howarth, R.B., Norgaard, R.B. (1995). "Intergenerational choices under global environment change". In: Handbook of Environmental Economics. Basil Blackwell.

Jouvet, P.A., Michel, Ph., Vidal, J.P. (2000). "Intergenerational altruism and the environment". Scandinavian Journal of Economics 102, 135–150.

Kimball, M.S. (1987). "Making sense of two-side altruism". Journal of Monetary Economics 20, 301–326.

Lambrecht, S., Michel, Ph., Thibault, E. (2006). "Capital accumulation and fiscal policy in an OLG model with family altruism". Journal of Public Economic Theory, in press.

Lambrecht, S., Michel, Ph., Vidal, J.P. (2005). "Public pensions and growth". European Economic Review 49, 1261–1281.

Mc Kenzie, L.W. (1986). "Optimal economic growth, turnpike theorems and comparative dynamics". In: Handbook of Mathematical Economics, vol. 3. North Holland.

Mankiw, G. (2000a). "The savers–spenders theory of fiscal policy". NBER Working Paper n. 7571.

Mankiw, G. (2000b). "The savers–spenders theory of fiscal policy". American Economic Review 90, 120–125.

Michel, Ph. (1990a). "Some clarifications on the transversality condition". Econometrica 58, 705–723.

Michel Ph. (1990b). "Criticism of the social time-preference hypothesis in optimal growth". Working Paper 9039, CORE, Université Catholique de Louvain.

Michel, Ph., Pestieau, P. (1998). "Fiscal policy in a growth model with both altruistic and nonaltruistic agents". Southern Economic Journal 64, 682–697.

Michel, Ph., Pestieau, P. (2004). "Fiscal policy in an overlapping generations model with bequest as consumption". Journal of Public Economic Theory 6, 397–408.

Michel, Ph., Thibault, E. (2006). "The failure of Ricardian equivalence under dynastic altruism". GREMAQ Working Paper.

Michel, Ph., Venditti, A. (1997). "Optimal growth and cycles in overlapping generations models". Economic Theory 9, 511–528.

Nourry, C., Venditti, A. (2001). "Determinacy of equilibrium in an overlapping generations model with heterogeneous agents". Journal of Economic Theory 96, 230–255.

O'Connell, S.A., Zeldes, S.P. (1993). "Dynamic efficiency in the gift economy". Journal of Monetary Economics 31, 363–379.

Ramsey, F.P. (1928). "A mathematical theory of saving". Economic Journal 38, 543–559.

Samuelson, P.A. (1958). "An exact consumption–loan model of interest with and without the social contrivance of money". Journal of Political Economy 66, 467–482.

Seater, J. (1993). "Ricardian equivalence". Journal of Economic Literature 31, 142–190.

Smetters, K. (1999). "Ricardian equivalence: long-run leviathan". Journal of Public Economics 73, 395–421.

Stokey, N., Lucas, R. (1989). Recursive Methods in Economic Dynamics. Harvard University Press.

Thibault, E. (2000). "Existence of equilibrium in an OLG model with production and altruistic preferences". Economic Theory 15, 709–716.

Thibault, E. (2001). "Bequests and the intergenerational degree of altruism". Louvain Economic Review 67, 131–138.

Thibault, E. (2004). "The power of love". Economic Letters 84, 183–189.

Thibault, E. (2005). "Existence and specific characters of rentiers. A savers-spenders theory approach". Economic Theory 25, 401–419.

Vidal, J.-P. (1996a). "Altruisme et hétérogénéité". Annales d'Economie et de Statistiques 43, 57–71.

Vidal, J.-P. (1996b). "L'altruisme dans les modèles à générations imbriquées". Louvain Economic Review 62, 21–42.

Vidal, J.-P. (2000). "Capital mobility in a dynastic framework". Oxford Economic Papers 52, 606–625.

Weil, P. (1987). "Love thy children. Reflections on the Barro debt neutrality theorem". Journal of Monetary Economics 19, 377–391.

Weil, P. (1989). "Overlapping families of infinitely lived agents". Journal of Public Economics 38, 183–198.

Wigniolle, B. (1994). "Capital humain, innovation et hétérogénéité dans une économie en croissance". Ph.D. Thesis, Paris I University.

Chapter 16

WEALTH TRANSFER TAXATION: A SURVEY OF THE THEORETICAL LITERATURE*

HELMUTH CREMER

GREMAQ and IDEI, University of Toulouse, Toulouse, France

PIERRE PESTIEAU

CREPP, University of Liège, Liège, Belgium and CORE, University of Louvain, Belgium

Contents

* We are grateful to Ravi Kanbur and S.Ch. Kolm for suggestions.

Handbook of the Economics of Giving, Altruism and Reciprocity, Volume 2
Edited by Serge-Christophe Kolm and Jean Mercier Ythier

DOI: 10.1016/S1574-0714(06)02016-1

Abstract

The purpose of this paper is to survey the theoretical literature on wealth transfer taxation. The focus is normative: we are looking at the design of an optimal tax structure from the standpoint of both equity and efficiency. The gist of this survey is that the optimal design crucially depends on the assumed bequest motives. Alternative bequest motives are thus analyzed either in isolation or combined. Even though there are as many results as models and as many models as combinations of bequest motives, the general conclusion is that the case for a zero taxation of inheritance is very weak.

Keywords

inheritance taxation, capital income tax, altruism

JEL classification: D64, H20, H21

1. Introduction

Nobody likes paying taxes, especially when he is dead. More today than yesterday it would seem. A number of countries are without an inheritance or an estate tax and some, including the United States, contemplate to phase it out in the near future. Opponents of the "death tax" as they have dubbed it claim that it is unfair and immoral. It adds to the pain suffered by mourning families and it prevents small business from passing from generation to generation. Because of many loopholes, people of equivalent wealth pay different amounts of tax depending on their acumen at tax avoidance. It hits families that were surprised by death (and it is therefore sometimes called a tax on sudden death). It penalizes the frugal and the loving parents who pass wealth on to their children, reducing incentive to save and to invest.

Supporters of the tax, in contrast, retort that it is of all taxes the most efficient and the most equitable. They assert that it is highly progressive and counterweight existing wealth concentration. They also argue that it has few disincentive effects since it is payable only at death and that it is fair since it concerns unearned resources. For a number of social philosophers and classical economists, estate or inheritance taxation is the ideal tax.

Clearly, death taxation more than any other generates controversy at all levels: political philosophy, economic theory, political debate and public opinion. The truth probably lies between these two opposite camps. For economists this tax like all taxes should be judged against the two criteria of equity and efficiency to which one could add that of simplicity and compliance.

In this survey, we focus on the criteria of equity and efficiency. Equity is hard to gauge. It has inter- and intragenerational aspects which can only be measured by relying on some normative criterion. Efficiency implies minimizing distortions to economic activity with an important dynamic dimension. Inheritance taxes affect incentive governing the choice between consuming now and bequeathing. The gist of this survey is that inheritance taxation cannot be analyzed separately from other taxes and that its implications in terms of efficiency and equity depend on why people leave assets when they die.

As a benchmark, we consider a dynamic model without bequest and study the optimal structure of taxation in the absence of bequests. Assuming that taxes can be levied on saving and labor income and are distortive, we want to see how this tax structure is affected when bequests are introduced and can be taxed as well.

As it will appear, the resulting tax structure depends on the bequest model chosen. One model states that bequests are simply an accident. People do not know how long they will live and so they keep more money than they turn out to need. If bequests are accidental, estate taxation is quite efficient. However, if people are motivated to work and to save by the idea of leaving their families an inheritance, the tax will be distortionary. The impact of the distortion will depend on the bequest motive. If people have a specific amount they wish to leave to their children regardless of their needs and their behavior, the outcome will be different from what it would be if the amount bequeathed is determined by a concern for the welfare of the heirs.

The survey deliberately adopts a theoretical and normative view.[1] It studies how transfers between generations ought to be taxed along with other tax tools and according to some welfare criterion. The type of tax that is thus obtained does not necessarily correspond to existing taxes.

To characterize the tax structure, one first has to distinguish taxation at death from taxation on *inter vivos* gifts which can have different rates. One also distinguishes three broad categories of death taxes. An estate tax is based on the total estate of the donor. An inheritance tax, on the other hand, is based on the share received by each donee and tax rate scales and thresholds depend on the relationship between the donor and the donee. Finally, the accession tax is based on the share received by the donee plus his other assets. One would hope that the theory will indicate which of these forms is the most desirable.

The rest of this paper is organized as follows. Section 2 presents a brief overview of alternative bequest models. Section 3 develops the optimal tax structure under alternative models. We proceed in steps. We first assume that individuals are identical but for age and generation and that the government can control the capital stock. Then we introduce restrictions to the ability of government of controlling aggregate saving and we consider individual heterogeneity. Section 4 looks at a number of theoretical issues regarding the choice between estate and inheritance taxation, differential taxation of bequests and *inter vivos* gifts, the coexistence of different bequest motives within the same society, the transmission of human capital and finally the non observability of inherited wealth.

2. Bequest motives

It is now widely agreed that to understand the importance and the role of gifts and estate transfers one needs to have a better grasp of the donor's motives, if any. Consider two examples concerning gifts and bequests. First, when the transfer takes the form of gifts it may be unclear whether they are "true gifts", due to altruism, or effectively involve some sort of exchange (the donee provides services to the donor). It is clear that a number of effects would differ under the two cases. Second, in the case of bequests we may not know whether they are left accidentally, because of the incompleteness of annuity markets, or intentionally for motives which rely on some type of altruism. Again, depending on the case, the effects of bequests on income inequality, capital accumulation, education could be quite different.

[1] For an empirical survey, see Arrondel et al. (1997), Pestieau (2003) and Gale et al. (2000). This is not the first theoretical survey. See e.g. Batina and Ihori (2000), Erregeyers and Vandevelde (1997), Aaron and Munnell (1992), Kaplow (2000), Kopczuk (2001a), Masson and Pestieau (1997).

We examine briefly a number of bequest motives that have been offered in the literature and sketch their implications focusing on those that are testable.[2]

2.1. Taxonomy of transfers motives

Pure dynastic altruism: altruistic bequest[3]

Parents care about the likely lifetime utility of their children and hence about the welfare of future generations.

Accordingly, wealthier parents make larger bequests and holding parent's wealth constant children with higher labor earnings will receive smaller bequests. There is also a tendency for parents to leave different amounts to different children in order to equalize their incomes. Finally, pure altruism typically leads to the Ricardian equivalence: parents compensate any intergenerational redistribution by the government through matching bequests.

Joy of giving: paternalistic bequest (bequest-as-last-consumption)[4]

Parents here are motivated not by altruism but by the direct utility they receive from the act of giving. This phenomenon is also referred to as "warm glow" giving. It can be explained by some internal feeling of virtue arising form sacrifice in helping one's children or by the desire of controlling their life. Formally these bequests appear in the utility function as a consumption expenditure incurred in the last period of life. *Ceteris paribus*, they are subject to income and price effects but do not have any compensatory effect, namely they are not intended to smoothen consumption across generations. A crucial element is whether what matters to the donor is the net or the gross of tax amount.

Exchange-related motives: strategic bequests[5]

In their canonical form, exchange-related models consider children choosing a level of "attention" to provide to their parents and parents remunerating them in the prospect of bequest. The exchanges can involve all sorts of non-pecuniary services and they can be part of a strategic game between parents and children. Strategic bequests as they were originally presented imply that parents extract all the surplus from their children by playing them against each other.

[2] See also on this Pestieau (2000), Cox (1987).

[3] Among the classical references, one has Barro (1974), Becker and Tomes (1979, 1986). See also Altonji et al. (1992).

[4] Andreoni (1990), Bevan and Stiglitz (1979), Glomm and Ravikunar (1992).

[5] Bernheim et al. (1985), Cremer et al. (1993, 1994), Cremer and Pestieau (1991, 1996, 1998), Kotlikoff and Spivak (1981).

Strategic or exchange bequests depend on the wealth and the needs of the donor; they are not compensatory between parents and children and they don't need to be equal across children.

No bequest motive: accidental bequests[6]

Up to this point, we have considered planned bequests. Whatever the underlying motive they were voluntary. We now consider unplanned or accidental bequests which result from a traditional life-cycle model. Accordingly, people save during their working lives in order to finance consumption when retired. Bequests occur solely because wealth is held in bequeathable form due to imperfections in annuity markets or the need to have precautionary savings. The main implication of that form of bequests is that even a 100% estate tax rate should not have any disincentive effect on the amount of bequest.

In this survey we will show that the tax structure depends crucially on the type of bequest motive considered. Table 1 gives an overview of some of the expected implications of wealth transfers for each of these alternative models. It summarizes the results of the existing literature on the subject.

One clearly sees that there are two dividing lines. The first division is between pure altruism and the other motives; it concerns intra and intergenerational redistribution. The second is between unplanned and planned bequest, the former being indifferent to any restriction including taxation while the latter is affected by any obstacle to the freedom to bequeath.

2.2. Canonical model

We use a Diamond-style overlapping generation model. Identical individuals are assumed to live two periods, consuming in both, providing some labor in the first one.[7] Population is increasing at the rate n. The government has an exogenously given revenue requirement which has to be financed. through taxes on income from labor and capital and on estate transfer, if any. Individual can derive some utility from transferring resources to their offsprings.

The problem of the representative consumer is to maximize his utility subject to the budget constraint.

$$b_t + \omega_t \ell_t = c_t + \frac{d_{t+1} + x_{t+1}}{1 + \varrho_{t+1}}, \tag{1}$$

where b_t is inherited wealth, x_{t+1} is the amount of bequests, ω_t is the consumer wage (net of tax age), ϱ_{t+1} the consumer rate of interest (after tax interest rate), c_t, first period consumption, ℓ_t, labor supply and d_{t+1}, second period consumption. The preferences

[6] Davies (1981).

[7] Diamond (1965).

Table 1
Implications of bequests motives

	Types of bequests			
	Accidental	Altruistic	Paternalistic	Exchange
Effect on intrafamily disparity				
Disparity between parents and children	Neutral	Equalizing	Neutral	Neutral
Disparity among siblings	Neutral	Equalizing	Neutral	Neutral
Equal estate division	Yes by default	No	Yes by default	No
Effect on social inequality	Uncertain	Positive	Moderate but positive	Weak and uncertain
Effect of fiscal policy				
Public debt on consumption	Positive	Neutral	Positive	Positive
Inheritance taxation on saving	Nil	Negative	Negative or nil	Negative

are represented by the following utility function:

$$
\begin{aligned}
u_t &= u(c_t, d_{t+1}, \ell_t) + \gamma B_{t+1}, \\
&= u(c_t) + \beta u(d_{t+1}) - h(\ell_t) + \gamma B_{t+1},
\end{aligned} \tag{2}
$$

where B_{t+1} is the utility derived from bequeathing if any, β and γ are positive parameters, $u(\cdot)$ is strictly concave and $h(\cdot)$ strictly convex. The additive specification is used for the sake of simplicity.

Consider now five models:

1. No bequests: $\gamma = 0, b = x = 0$.
2. Accidental bequests: $\gamma = 0, \beta = \tilde{\beta}\theta$, where $\tilde{\beta}$ is the factor of time preference and θ is the survival probability. There is a probability θ that the individual will live till the end of the second period and $(1 - \theta)$ that he will die at the end of the first period. In the latter case, $b_{t+1} = d_{t+1}/(1 + n)$ for a fraction $(1 - \theta)$ of children whose parents decease prematurely.
3. Paternalistic bequests: $B_{t+1} = h(x_{t+1})$ and $b_{t+1} = x_{t+1}/(1 + n)$.
4. Altruistic bequests: $B_{t+1} = u_{t+1}$ and thus by recursion:

$$u_t = \sum_{s=0}^{\infty} \gamma^s u_{s+t},$$

with again $b_{t+1} = x_{t+1}/(1 + n)$.

5. Exchange-based bequests:

$$B_{t+1} = h(a_{t+1}) \qquad \text{and}$$
$$u_t = u\big(c_t - v\big(a_t^g\big), \ell_t, a_{t+1}\big) + \beta u(d_{t+1}) - h(\ell_t),$$

where a_{t+1} is attention received, a_t^g is attention given representing a monetary cost of $v(a_t^g)$ that is paid by a bequest b_t. In the strategic bequest vein, we assume that $b_t = v(a_t^g)$.

We have three tax instruments: τ^w, τ^r, τ^x, namely a proportional tax on earnings, interest income, inherited wealth. The government budget constraint is:

$$\tau_t^w \ell_t + \frac{\tau_t^r s_{t-1} + \tau_t^x x_t}{1+n} = R,$$

where R is the (per capita) revenue requirement, w_t and r_t (ω_t and ϱ_t) are the producer (consumer) factor prices ($\tau^w = w - \omega$; $\tau^r = r - \varrho$) and s_{t-1} is saving.

3. Optimal taxation of factor income and wealth transfer

3.1. The overlapping generation model[8]

In the Diamond (1965) model each generation lives for two periods, consuming in both and working in the first. There are no bequests and the lifetime budget constraint for the representative household born in period t may be written:

$$c_t + \frac{d_{t+1}}{1 + \varrho_{t+1}} = \omega_t \ell_t. \tag{3}$$

It is clear that endowing the government with two instruments, taxes on labor income ($\tau^w = w - \omega$) and capital income ($\tau^r = r - \varrho$) is equivalent to allowing the government to tax first- and second-period consumption at possibly different rates. A zero-tax on capital income—a labor income tax—would result in uniform taxation of consumption in the two periods.[9]

We now characterize the optimal steady-state taxes resulting from a utilitarian objective

$$\sum \delta^t u_t, \tag{4}$$

where $0 < \delta < 1$ is the factor of social time preference and

$$u_t = u(c_t, d_{t+1}, \ell_t) \tag{5}$$

[8] See Ihori (1996).

[9] See Atkinson and Sandmo (1980), Pestieau (1974).

is the individual utility function. Two general results have been obtained. First with the government able to redistribute resources across generations through debt policy, pay-as-you-go social security or any other devices the marginal product of capital converges to the population growth rate divided by the factor of time preference $((1+n)/\delta)$, namely the modified golden rule. Second, optimal taxes on labor and capital should follow the standard analysis of static optimal tax theory.

Maximizing (5) subject to (1) yields the demand function for $c(\omega_t, \varrho_{t+1})$, $d(\omega_t, \varrho_{t+1})$ and $\ell(\omega_t, \varrho_{t+1})$ which substituted back in the utility function yields the indirect utility function:

$$v_t = v(\omega_t, \varrho_{t+1}),$$

with

$$\frac{\partial v_t}{\partial \omega_t} = \alpha_t \ell_t \qquad \text{and} \qquad \frac{\partial v_t}{\partial \varrho_{t+1}} = \frac{\alpha_t d_{t+1}}{(1+\varrho_{t+1})^2} = \frac{\alpha_t s_t}{1+\varrho_{t+1}},$$

where α is the marginal utility of income $\alpha = \partial u/\partial I$ and s is saving. We use I to denote non labor income, if any.

There is a production sector represented by a CRS production function relating output Y_t to capital K_t and labor L_t:

$$Y_t = F(K_t, L_t),$$

or

$$y_t = F\left(\frac{K_t}{L_t}, 1\right) = f(k_t),$$

with $y = Y/L$ and $k = K/L$. With perfect competition factor payments equal the value of marginal products:

$$w_t = F_L'(K_t, L_t) \qquad \text{and} \qquad 1 + r_t = F_K'(K_t, L_t).$$

We assume total depreciation after one period and $L_t = \ell_t N_t$, where $N_t = N_{t-1}(1+n)$ is the size of generation t.

In this simple economy, the dynamics is conducted by the capital accumulation equation:

$$K_{t+1} = N_t s_t,$$

where $s_t = \sigma(\omega_t, \varrho_{t+1}) = \omega_t - c(\omega_t, \varrho_{t+1})$.

Under some assumptions, one can show that k_{t+1} converges to a unique steady-state k^* which can be compared to the steady-state value $\hat{k}_\delta$ which is consistent with the modified golden rule and defined by:

$$f'(\hat{k}_\delta) = \frac{1+n}{\delta}.$$

For the time being we assume that the economy is on the modified golden rule growth path through some appropriate intergenerational transfers by the government. So doing we focus on the optimal tax structure abstracting from dynamic efficiency considerations.

The government's budget constraint is simply:

$$\tau_t^w \ell_t + \tau_t^r \frac{d_t}{(1+\varrho_t)(1+n)} = R, \tag{6}$$

where R is given. The second term on the left is the revenue from capital income taxation which concerns the previous generation ($s_{t-1} = d_t/(1+\varrho_t)$).

We solve this problem by differentiating the Lagrangean expression,

$$\pounds = \sum \delta^t \left\{ v(\omega_t, \varrho_{t+1}) + \mu\left(\tau_t^w \ell_t(\omega_t, \varrho_{t+1}) + \tau_t^r \frac{d_t(\omega_{t-1}, \varrho_t)}{(1+\varrho_t)(1+n)} - R \right)\right\},$$

with respect to ω_t and ϱ_t. This yields:

$$\frac{\partial \pounds}{\partial \omega_t} = \delta^t \left(\alpha_t \ell_t + \mu \left[\tau_t^w \frac{\partial \ell_t}{\partial \omega_t} - \ell_t + \tau_t^r \frac{\partial d_{t+1}}{\partial \omega_t} \frac{\delta}{(1+n)(1+\varrho_{t+1})} \right] \right), \tag{7}$$

$$\begin{aligned} \frac{\partial \pounds}{\partial \varrho_{t+1}} &= \delta^t \left(\alpha_t \frac{d_{t+1}}{(1+\varrho_{t+1})^2} + \mu \left[\tau_t^w \frac{\partial \ell_t}{\partial \varrho_{t+1}} + \frac{\delta}{1+n} \right.\right. \\ &\quad \left.\left. \times \left(\tau_{t+1}^r \frac{\partial d_{t+1}}{\partial \varrho_{t+1}} \frac{1}{1+\varrho_t} - \frac{d_{t+1}(1+r_{t+1})}{(1+\varrho_t)^2} \right) \right] \right). \end{aligned} \tag{8}$$

Evaluating (7) and (8) in the steady-state, while adding and subtracting the income effect times ℓ for $\partial \pounds/\partial \omega$ and times $d/(1+\varrho)^2$ for $\partial \pounds/\partial \varrho$ yields:

$$\left(\frac{\alpha}{\mu} - 1 - \Delta \right) \ell + \tau^w \frac{\partial \tilde{\ell}}{\partial \omega} + \tau^r \frac{\partial \tilde{d}}{\partial \omega} \frac{\delta}{(1+n)(1+\varrho)} = 0, \tag{9}$$

$$\begin{aligned} &\left(\frac{\alpha}{\mu} - 1 - \Delta \right) \frac{d}{(1+\varrho)^2} - \frac{1+n-\delta(1+r)}{1+n} \frac{d}{(1+\varrho_t)^2} \\ &\quad + \tau^w \frac{\partial \tilde{\ell}}{\partial \varrho} + \tau^r \frac{\partial \tilde{d}}{\partial \varrho} \frac{\delta}{(1+n)(1+\varrho)} = 0, \end{aligned} \tag{10}$$

where

$$\Delta = \tau^w \frac{\partial \ell}{\partial I} + \tau^r \frac{\partial d}{\partial I} \frac{\delta}{(1+n)(1+\varrho)},$$

and the ˜ denotes the compensated effects. Given our assumption on the modified golden rule, this can be further simplified:

$$\tau^w \frac{\partial \tilde{\ell}}{\partial \omega} + \tau^r \frac{\partial \tilde{d}}{\partial \omega} \frac{\delta}{(1+n)(1+\varrho)} = \left(\tau^w \frac{\partial \tilde{\ell}}{\partial \varrho} + \tau^r \frac{\partial \tilde{d}}{\partial \varrho} \frac{\delta}{(1+n)(1+\varrho)} \right) \frac{\ell(1+\varrho)^2}{d}. \tag{11}$$

This equation characterizes the relative levels of the tax rates on earnings and capital income with the absolute levels being determined by the government's revenue requirement R. As usual this characterization depends on compensated and not gross derivatives. Assume for simplicity of interpretation that the cross effects are zero. Then we can have:

$$\frac{\tau^w/\omega}{\tau^r/\varrho} = \frac{\tilde{\varepsilon}_{d\varrho}}{\tilde{\varepsilon}_{\ell w}} \frac{1+\varrho}{\varrho(1+r)}, \tag{12}$$

where the $\tilde{\varepsilon}$ are the compensated elasticities. If labor is completely inelastic along the compensated supply curve, the optimal tax on interest income is zero because the tax on earnings is equivalent to a lump-sum tax. The argument is reversed when the demand for future consumption is inelastic. In general however there is no particular reason to believe that either tax will be zero nor that both taxes are the same.

Let us come back to the assumption that the economy is on the modified golden rule path, that is, on the assumption that the government can control capital. From (10) one can see that if $1 + n \neq (1 + r)\delta$ we have an additional term in either (11) or (12). In other words these taxes are not only used to finance R but also to foster or discourage capital accumulation depending on whether the rate of interest is higher or lower than the rate of population growth divided by the discount factor.

As shown by Atkinson and Sandmo (1980) too little capital may call for a *lower* taxation of *earnings* and a *higher* tax on *interest income* than when the modified golden rule holds. This apparent paradox can be explained by noting that with a log-linear utility function saving depends only on earnings and not on the interest rate.

We shall now introduce transfers into this model and successively consider the motives discussed in Section 2.1. Within each setting we study the design of factor income and wealth transfer taxes. To do so it is convenient to distinguish the case where the government has the instruments to secure the modified golden rule from the case where the government cannot fully control the capital stock.

3.2. Accidental bequest

The accidental bequest case is not much different from the case without bequest. Saving is affected by survival probabilities. Accidental transfers are taxed at 100%, without affecting the supply of saving. The part of public spending (if any) which exceeds the proceeds of the transfer tax is financed through labor and capital income taxes designed *à la Atkinson–Sandmo*.

3.3. Pure altruism[10]

To keep things relatively simple, we assume that $\beta = 0$ so that $d = 0$. In other words, people live only one period and only save for bequeathing. This assumption implies that

[10] The classical papers on this are Chamley (1986) and Judd (1985).

the tax on saving is also the tax on wealth transfer.[11] Then, the social planner's problem at time 0 is to maximize:

$$\sum_{t=0}^{\infty} \gamma^t u(c_t, \ell_t),$$

subject to the resource constraint

$$F(k_t, \ell_t) = (1+n)k_{t+1} + c_t + R,$$

and to the revenue constraint

$$(1+n)z_{t+1} = (1+\varrho_t)z_t + (1+\varrho_t)k_t + \omega_t \ell_t - F(k_t, \ell_t) + R,$$

where z denotes per worker public debt. Recall that k is the per worker capital stock while R per worker public spending and that the production function exhibits constant returns to scale.

Chamley (1986), Judd (1985) and Coleman (2000) show the following:

- if one could tax as much as possible initial wealth k_0, one could do without using any distortionary tax;
- if this first-best solution is not accessible, one will have initially a tax on both earnings and saving (that is bequests);
- in the long run the tax on saving tends to 0.

We restrict ourselves to proving the last point which represents the main result. The government's objective is the same as that of the representative individual ($\gamma = \delta$). It maximizes the Lagrangean:

$$\pounds = \sum_{t=0}^{\infty} \gamma^t [u(c_t, \ell_t) + \lambda_t (F(k_t, \ell_t) - c_t - (1+n)k_{t+1} - R)]$$
$$+ \mu_t [(1+n)z_{t+1} - (1+\varrho_t)z_t - (1+\varrho_t)k_t - \omega_t \ell_t + F(k_t, \ell_t) - R],$$

where λ and μ are the Lagrange multiplier associated with the resource and the revenue constraint respectively. The FOC with respect to z and k in the steady-state are:

$$(1+\varrho)\gamma = 1+n, \tag{13}$$

and

$$-(1+n)\lambda + \gamma\lambda(1+r) + \mu\gamma(r-\varrho) = 0. \tag{14}$$

[11] We have the following equality between saving and bequest:

$$s_t = x_{t+1} = (1+n)k_{t+1}.$$

Combining these two equations give:

$$-\lambda(1+\varrho)+\lambda(1+r)+\mu(r-\varrho)=0.$$

This yields $(\lambda+\mu)(r-\varrho)=0$ and thus $\tau^r=0$, so that (13) implies $(1+r)\gamma=1+n$. In words, we have the modified golden rule and most notably, a zero tax on savings which correspond to bequests in our setting. Consequently, wealth transfers are not taxed in the steady state.[12]

Chamley–Judd's result has become the standard rule for a number of public economists and particularly macroeconomists. However, it has also been challenged on various grounds. It relies on a set of strong assumption which have been questioned. In any case the zero tax result only applies to the steady-state; during the transition period, wealth transfers along with capital income are subject to taxation.

In a recent paper, Saez (2002) introduces a progressive tax on capital income (initial of a linear one) in the Chamley–Judd model. Under some plausible assumption, he shows that such a tax is desirable; it drives all the large fortunes down a finite level and produces a truncated long-run wealth distribution.

3.4. *Joy of giving*

Unlike in the case of pure altruism, the objective of individuals and that of the social planner may now diverge. Each individual maximizes:

$$u(c_t,d_{t+1},\ell_t)+\gamma v(x_{t+1}),$$

subject to

$$x_t+\omega_t\ell_t=c_t+\frac{d_{t+1}+(1+n)(1+\tau^x)x_{t+1}}{1+\varrho_{t+1}}.$$

In a *laissez-faire* equilibrium, each individual chooses ℓ_t, c_t, d_{t+1} and x_{t+1} given factor prices ω_t and ϱ_t and inherited wealth x_t. As to the social optimum, one faces the issue of whether or not laundering individual utilities. Harsanyi (1995) and Hammond (1988) have advocated "excluding all external preferences, even benevolent ones, from our social utility function". Advocates of a utilitarian approach, on the other hand, argue that the social planner cannot paternalistically modify individuals' preferences.

We shall use a generalized objective which admits the two approaches as special case. Denoting the social factor of time preference by δ, social welfare is given by

$$U_t=\sum_{s=1}^{\infty}\delta^s[u(c_s,d_{s+1},\ell_s)+\varepsilon\gamma v(x_{s+1})],$$

[12] This result generalizes to the case where $\beta>0$ and $d>0$. However, the proof becomes much more complicated.

where $0 \le \varepsilon \le 1$ with $\varepsilon = 0$ for the non utilitarian and $\varepsilon = 1$ for the utilitarian case.

With this setting, the steady-state rule of optimal capital accumulation is the modified golden rule. The key issue is the treatment of x_t. For $\varepsilon = 1$ the first-best optimal value of x is that for which $v'(x) = 0$. In other words without laundering out utilities the social planner will push for a very high value of x (that could be infinity). In a first-best world, such a solution could be implemented through a subsidy on x financed by public debt. It is clearly not reasonable and such a pathological outcome provides an argument in favor of laundering out the joy of giving from the donors' welfare.

In the second-best, with linear taxes on earnings, capital income and bequests, the revenue constraint is given by:

$$R = \tau_t^w \ell_t + \tau_t^r s_{t-1} + \tau_t^x (1+n) x_t,$$

which can also be written as:

$$R = \tau_t^w \ell_t + \tau_t \frac{d_t}{1+\ell_t} + \theta_t^x (1+n) x_t,$$

where

$$\theta_t^x = \frac{\tau_t^r (1+\tau_t^x)}{1+\varrho_t} + \tau_t^x$$

is the total (or effective) tax on transfers. Observe that bequests are subject to a double tax: first, the tax on savings, τ^r, and then the specific tax on transfers τ^x. The total tax on bequest is higher than that on second period consumption if $\theta^x > \tau^r/(1+\varrho_t)$, which occurs when $\tau^x > 0$.

Michel and Pestieau (2006) show that with no laundering the tax structure is not much different from (11). Taxes on earnings, on second period consumption and on bequests only depend on compensated elasticities and on the revenue requirement when the capital stock is directly controlled. In the case of zero cross elasticities, the tax on second period consumption (τ^r) may be higher than the estate tax (θ^x) if the own compensated elasticity of second period consumption is lower than that of bequests. When there is laundering, bequest loses its direct social utility and is thus subject to a relatively higher tax.

3.5. *Exchange*

We will use an exchange model of the strategic type in which parents obtain attention from their children in exchange of some bequests. By playing their children against each other they control the exchange to their full benefit.

The utility function of an individual belonging to generation t is given by:

$$u\big(c_t - v\big(a_t^g\big), d_{t+1}, \ell_t, a_{t+1}\big), \tag{15}$$

where a_{t+1} denotes attention received and a_t^g attention given which requires some effort. The disutility of attention given is expressed in monetary terms. First and second period budget constraints are:

$$\omega_t \ell_t + b_t = c_t + s_t, \tag{16}$$

$$(1+\varrho_{t+1})s_t = \left(1+\tau_{t+1}^x\right)x_{t+1} + d_{t+1}. \tag{17}$$

In addition, we have

$$x_{t+1} = (1+n)b_{t+1}, \tag{18}$$

and

$$v\left(a_t^g\right) = b_t. \tag{19}$$

Equation (18) gives the straightforward relation between bequest and inherited wealth. Equation (19) results from our strategic bequest assumption: parents extract all the surplus from their children who are just paid for the disutility of their effort.

Substituting (16)–(19) into (15) shows that each member of generation t maximizes the following expression

$$u\left(\omega_t \ell_t - \frac{(d_{t+1})}{1+\varrho_{t+1}} - \frac{v(a_{t+1})(1-\tau_{t+1}^x)}{1+\varrho_{t+1}}, d_{t+1}, \ell_t, a_{t+1}\right).$$

The indirect utility is given by:

$$V_t = V\left(\omega_t, \varrho_{t+1}, \tau_{t+1}^x\right).$$

The problem for the social planner is to maximize the discounted sum of utilities, $\sum \delta^t V_t$, subject to the revenue constraint:

$$R = \tau^w \ell + \frac{\tau^r d_t}{(1+\varrho_t)(1+n)} + \frac{\tau_t^r + \tau_t^x(1+r_t)}{(1+\varrho_t)(1+n)} v(a_t).$$

We continue to assume that capital accumulation is socially optimal (i.e., $1+r = (1+n)/\delta$). The FOC in the steady-state can be written as:

$$\tau^w \frac{\partial \tilde{\ell}}{\partial \tau^w} + \frac{\tau^r}{(1+r)(1+\varrho)} \frac{\partial \tilde{d}}{\partial \tau^w} + \frac{\tau^r + \tau^x(1+r)}{(1+r)(1+\varrho)} v'(a) \frac{\partial \tilde{a}}{\partial \tau^w} + \left(\frac{\alpha}{\mu} - 1 - \Delta\right)\ell = 0,$$

$$\tau^w \frac{\partial \tilde{\ell}}{\partial \tau^r} + \frac{\tau^r}{(1+r)(1+\varrho)} \frac{\partial \tilde{d}}{\partial \tau^r} + \frac{\tau^r + \tau^x(1+r)}{(1+r)(1+\varrho)} v'(a) \frac{\partial \tilde{a}}{\partial \tau^r} + \left(\frac{\alpha}{\mu} - 1 - \Delta\right)\frac{d}{(1+\varrho)^2} = 0,$$

$$\tau^w \frac{\partial \tilde{\ell}}{\partial \tau^x} + \frac{\tau^r}{(1+r)(1+\varrho)} \frac{\partial \tilde{d}}{\partial \tau^x} + \frac{\tau^r + \tau^x(1+r)}{(1+r)(1+\varrho)} v'(a) \frac{\partial \tilde{a}}{\partial \tau^x}$$

$$+\left(\frac{\alpha}{\mu}-1-\Delta\right)\frac{v(a)}{1+\varrho}=0.$$

For same reasons as developed above (Subsection 3.4), the overall tax on bequests, $\tau^r + \tau^x(1+r)$, may or may not be higher than that on future consumption. In other words, there is no particular reason to believe that the wealth transfer tax τ^x is positive. This will depend on the relative magnitude of the compensated derivatives which determine the overall tax on bequests and the tax on future consumption through Atkinson and Sandmo type rules.

To illustrate this point in the simplest possible way, assume again that the cross elasticities are zero. Then, we have:

$$\frac{\tau^r+\tau^x(1+r)}{\tau^r}=\frac{v(a)\dfrac{\partial\tilde{d}}{\partial\tau^r}(1+\varrho)}{v'(a)\dfrac{\partial\tilde{a}}{\partial\tau^x}d}.$$

Clearly if the demand for attention is much more elastic than that for future consumption, the tax on inheritance, τ^x, is negative.

3.6. Inequality and wealth transfer taxation

Up to now most of the discussion has focused on the restricted case of a representative individual and of full control of capital by the social planner.

On the latter issue, we have to note that with pure altruism and equality between the individuals rate of altruism and the social planner's time preference factor, the modified golden rule is achieved without the government intervening. With the other bequest motives there is no guarantee that the optimal accumulation of capital is achieved. Then if the government does not have direct control of capital, it has to use tax policy to affect the capital labor ratio. As already alluded to, if there is a need of additional capital accumulation, because $(1+r)\gamma > (1+n)$, this will not necessarily push for lesser taxation of capital income and wealth transfer and more taxation of labor income. What matters is aggregate saving and with a log-linear function saving depends on net of tax earnings relatively more than on the rate of interest.

Let us now consider individuals who differ in ability but have the same utility. As shown by Atkinson and Stiglitz (1972, 1976)[13] in the presence of weak separability between consumption and leisure, there is no need of taxation of capital within the standard OLG model. The Atkinson–Stiglitz theorem assumes that all households have identical utility functions and differ in their wage rates reflecting abilities or productivities, the government maximizes a quasi-concave (welfarist) objective function, applies a non-linear income tax and could also apply linear excise taxes. Thus if the utility function is weakly separable in goods and labor so that $u(c,d,\ell)=u(g(c,d),\ell)$ a tax

[13] See also Stiglitz (1987).

on capital income (alternatively on d) should not be used. This result can be readily extended to the model with exchange (strategic bequest), granted that the government controls the rate of capital accumulation.[14] Naturally if the economy does not converge to the modified golden rule, then the result does not hold anymore: capital income and wealth transfers will be taxed or subsidized depending on their effect on aggregate saving. This extension of the Atkinson and Stiglitz to estate taxation has been discussed by Kaplow (2000) and Kopczuk (2001a).

The reason why the Atkinson and Stiglitz proposition applies to the strategic bequest model presented above is that bequest has no effect on the next generation. Each individual regardless of his ability and of his generation receives from his parents exactly what he pays for.

The case of joy of giving is quite different. Individual heterogeneity makes a difference in the case of "joy of giving". The reason is rather simple. Even though the donor is not interested by the impact of his gift on the next generation's welfare the social planner cannot ignore this incidence. A non-linear income tax on generation t does not make redundant a linear or a non-linear tax on what we can call a distributive externality.

The difficulty is how to express this externality, how to represent the effect of paternalistic gifts on the next generation's welfare. A convenient shortcut is to reduce individual heterogeneity to two levels of productivity, low and high, with endogenous probability. Suppose that the level of bequest has the effect of increasing the probability that the child's donor has a higher productivity. In other words, we assume that inherited wealth has the sole effect of fostering heirs' earning capacity.[15] With such a specification we can show that with an optimal non-linear income tax it makes sense to have a tax or a subsidy on bequest. If there is no laundering out, a subsidy is desirable: fostering bequests implies increasing the probability of being more productive and thus the average level of human capital.

In case of laundering out the social planner may want to tax bequests as the joy of giving *per se* has no social value. We then have two opposite forces: one in favor of subsidizing bequests because of their positive externality on human capital and the other in favor of taxing bequests because they have no direct value for the social planner.

Note that the role of the tax-subsidy is not to redistribute income but to correct for some positive or negative externalities. In that respect it does not invalidate the Atkinson and Stiglitz proposition.

Let us now turn to the remaining bequest motives. In the model with pure altruism, the zero capital income tax result holds with different individuals without further assumptions. See on this Chamley (1986).

[14] It is paradoxal that with a single individual the zero taxation of capital income does not apply with weak separability (you need strong separability *à la Stone–Geary*) and it does with heterogeneous individuals and optimal non-linear tax. The reason is that the equivalent of a non-linear income tax in a one-individual setting is the lump-sum tax (which is ruled out). See Atkinson and Stiglitz (1980).

[15] We use the argument given by Cremer and Pestieau (2006).

Table 2
Wealth transfer tax

	With control of capital and a representative agent	Without control of capital and a and heterogenous agent	With control of capital representative agents but with a non-linear income tax
Accidental bequest	1	1	<1
Joy of giving	$\pm$	$\pm$	$\pm$
Pure altruism	0	0	0
Exchange	$\pm$	$\pm$	0

With accidental bequest, on the other hand, heterogeneity of individuals makes a difference. Indeed one can argue that under some conditions it is not anymore desirable to have a 100% tax on accidental bequests. Blumkin and Sadka (2004) show that a 100% estate tax can interfere with the redistributing role of labor income taxation. This is the case when individuals with higher ability tend to spend a lower fraction of their marginal wealth on leisure than individuals with lower ability. As a result estate taxation would result in a reduction in aggregate labor earnings. Kopczuk (2001b) correctly points out that accidental bequests result from some imperfections in the annuity markets and the first-best solution is not necessarily to tax them but rather to eliminate them.

Table 2 presents the main results obtained so far. Note that one cannot sign the tax on wealth transfer with joy of giving and with exchange regardless of whether or not the government controls capital.

With individuals differing in ability but with non-linear income tax, the Atkinson–Stiglitz result applies to the cases of joy of giving and exchange. The Atkinson–Stiglitz theorem assumes that the government can use a wide range of instruments. The literature contains a number of models exploring the consequences of restricting the policy environment.

For example, for administrative reasons, one can assume that the government cannot use non-linear tax schedules. If it is restricted to using linear income taxes, the case for a zero tax on capital income and wealth transfers (with accidental and exchange based bequests) is weakened. Another line of concern is that the government may very well observe labor earnings but not bequests. In that case, on which we come back below, a linear tax on capital income might be desirable; see Subsection 4.4.

There is clearly the possibility that the government cannot control capital accumulation by debt policy. Then the Atkinson–Stiglitz proposition does not apply. While it may remain true that taxes on savings and bequests have not redistributive role, they may be useful for other reasons (e.g., to foster or limit capital accumulation). Similarly, these taxes are not redundant when there is a conflict between individual and social preferences as it is the case when the social planner decides to launder the out of the parents' welfare the offspring's welfare.

Choosing between the two canonical models, the infinite lived individuals model and the OLG model and even more between their implications is not obvious. Both have in common to tell little about the nature of optimal tax schedules in transition. Except through numerical simulation (see e.g. Coleman, 2000) we know little about the linkage between transition and long run policy. Chamley's model and his finding of a zero tax on capital income in the long run is striking and powerful. It quickly attracted a majority of economists concerned by the highly distortionary nature of such a tax. It however rests on the implausible assumption that agents live forever or behave in an equivalent manner with respect to their heirs. Without infinite lifetime no such result holds. This does not necessarily mean that a positive tax on capital income and on wealth transfer is the rule. We have seen that we could also have a subsidy. Note that the sign of the tax then depends on a number of factors including the revenue requirement and whether or not there is under-accumulation.

4. Miscellaneous issues

4.1. Estate taxation or inheritance taxation

There exists two main types of wealth transfer taxes:[16] the estate and the inheritance taxes which correspond to two contrasting views of inheritance.

To differentiate these alternative views, the Anglo-Saxon and the Continental one, toward taxation and regulation of bequests one may focus on their respective view of family and state.[17] In the Continental (Napoleonic) view, the government makes good decisions, particularly regarding families of different incomes; families are suspected of biases in the way they allocate resources among their children. As a consequence, equal sharing among children is mandatory; the tax base is the amount received by each heir, and the tax rate is related to consanguinity (for example, higher for a nephew than for a son). This is the inheritance tax.

According to the Anglo-Saxon view, parents make unbiased bequests and adjust them to the needs of each heir. We have the so-called estate tax, with its rate being independent of the number of heirs and degree of consanguinity. With an estate tax, parents can disinherit their children or at least devote an important share of it to a charity, which is not possible in many European countries for households with children.

The issue of wealth transfer taxation cannot be reduced to just designing a tax schedule; it also includes non-tax regulations.

These views are part of a nation's culture but can also be explained by its history. For example, in England equal division of estate was made mandatory at time when there were a lot of remarriages together with mistreatment of stepchildren by stepparents.[18]

[16] The accession tax is another type but that has never been applied in any country.

[17] This is a summary of Pestieau (2000). These issues are also discussed in Erregeyers and Vandevelde (1997).

[18] This has been labeled the *Cinderella effect*. See Brenner (1985), Pestieau (2000), Cremer and Pestieau (2001).

Table 3

	Anglo-Saxon	Continental
Freedom of bequeath	Free will	Equal sharing among children
Tax base	Aggregate estate	Share of estate
Tax rate	Neutral	Consanguinity-related

For an economist, it would be interesting to see which of these two taxes correspond best to an optimal tax. In a first-best perfect information setting wealth transfer taxes can be designed along with the other taxes to achieve optimal redistribution within and across families. In an asymmetric information setting, this is less clear.

In a recent paper, Cremer and Pestieau (2001) adopt a second-best setting in which families are better informed than the tax authorities.[19] Well to do families can be induced to leave lower bequests to avoid a too heavy tax burden. The paper studies the optimal design of a possibly non-linear wealth transfer tax. This problem encompasses the joint determination of the tax rates, the tax base and the sharing rules. In particular, sharing restrictions can be implemented through non-linearities in the tax function.[20]

Basically it appears that the optimal tax is different from existing tax regimes. When the social planner and the parents weight the children in the same way, an estate tax, that is a tax based on aggregate bequest suffices. When they adopt different weights, then one needs to use a progressive tax formula that depends on individual bequests. In other words, we have something which resembles the inheritance tax but without compulsory equal sharing. Finally, when there is a possibility of the parent disinheriting their less endowed child, the government may find it optimal to impose a tax schedule which implies equal sharing along with a progressive tax.

4.2. *Inter vivos gifts versus bequests*

In most countries *inter vivos* gifts are subject to lower tax rates than bequests. Furthermore, gifts being made informally and in several installments they lend themselves to tax avoidance and tax evasion more easily than bequests. Also, in countries with inheritance taxation and mandatory equal sharing gifts are viewed as the only way to treat children differently according to needs, talents or preferences.

From a theoretical viewpoint one can ask whether differential taxation of gifts and bequests is consistent with social optimality. There are some reasons which plead in favor of such a policy.

[19] Tax authorities observe the transfer to each of the children, but do not observe parent's wealth and children's ability.

[20] Another issue is that of differential tor treatment depending on the relation between the donor and the donee. Typically rates are higher for strangers than for children. See Cremer and Pestieau (1988).

1. Assume that the bulk of bequests is of accidental nature and that planned transfers are made much before the donor's death as *inter vivos* gifts. Then it makes much sense to discriminate in favor of *inter vivos* gifts.
2. Such a differential tax treatment fosters *inter vivos* gifts which are a more effective form of transfer in the case where heirs are liquidity constrained.
3. In countries where it applies, gifts cannot be subject to the same strict equal sharing rule as bequests. Therefore they hopefully can be used for compensating for difference in luck or in talent among children. For that reason they ought to benefit from tax breaks.

However, there are also arguments against a heavier taxation of bequests. In particular, Cremer and Pestieau (1996, 1998) have shown that bequests as opposed to gifts can be used to induce children to reveal their ability and to provide a desirable amount of effort, which they would not do if they were given outside resources too early in their lifetime. In that respect, a tax break for *inter vivos* gifts is not necessarily desirable.

4.3. Mixed motives

The theoretical literature on wealth transfer taxation tends to assume that individual have only one type of bequest motives. The purpose of this section is to suggest that such an approach is deficient and it proposes to consider a society consisting of individuals with different motives. We first turn to a society consisting of individuals who combine different motives, namely who leave both altruistic and accidental bequests. Then we consider a society where individuals are all either altruistic or pure "life-cyclers".

4.3.1. A mix of accidental and paternalistic bequest[21]

It is widely believed that actual bequests are an hybrid of canonical types analyzed above and in particular of accidental bequests (related to imperfect annuity markets) and of paternalistic bequests (related to some joy of giving). In such a case, the estate consists of two components: an amount intended by altruistic parents and an amount which results from the "premature" death of parents and which represents intended second period consumption in one overlapping generations framework. We have seen that these two types of bequests have totally different implications. Determining the relative importance of the time is thus crucial to design an optimal estate tax.

To illustrate this, we use an isoelastic utility function:

$$u(c,d,x) = \left(c^{1-1/\sigma} + \beta\theta\, d^{1-1/\sigma} + \gamma\, x^{1-1/\sigma}\right)\left(1 - \frac{1}{\sigma}\right)^{-1},$$

with $\sigma > 1$ to make sure that an estate taxes τ^x has a depressive effect on x. Isoelasticity implies homotheticity, a property that we shall use below. Labor supply in the first

[21] This section follows Michel and Pestieau (2002). On this subject see also Blumkin and Sadka (2004).

period is inelastic. One shows that

$$d_{t+1} = \delta(1 + r_{t+1})\tilde{s}(r_{t+1})(w_t + h_t),$$

and

$$(1 + n)x_{t+1}\left(1 + \tau_t^x\right) = (1 - \delta)(1 + r_{t+1})\tilde{s}(r_{t+1})(w_t + h_t),$$

where h_t is inherited wealth, with

$$h_t = x_t + \left(\frac{1 - \theta}{1 + n}\right)\left(1 + \tau_t^\theta\right)d_t + R_t,$$

while δ is the share of saving devoted to second period consumption, $\tilde{s}(r)$ is the saving ratio, τ^x and τ^θ are respectively the tax on voluntary and accidental bequests respectively, and R_t is a uniform lump-sum payment financed by wealth transfer taxes. Clearly if $\gamma = 0$, ($\delta = 1$) there is no intended bequest. If $\bar{\theta} = 1$, (longevity is certain) there is no accidental bequests. In this approach inherited wealth varies across individuals. It depends on one's parent's intended bequest x_t, second period consumption d_t and longevity θ_t. At each period, the revenue constraint is simply:

$$R_t = \frac{(1 + r_t)\bar{s}_{t-1}}{1 + n}\left(\frac{\tau_t^x(1 - \delta)}{1 + \tau_t^x} + \delta\tau_t^\theta(1 - \bar{\theta})\right),$$

where the upper-bar denotes average values. If the social planner's objective is to minimize the steady-state coefficient of variation of inherited wealth, one can easily show that $\tau^\theta = 1$ and τ^x is likely to be between 0 and 1 for $\sigma \geq 1$. Note that here R_t is not a fixed amount of public spending but an endogenous lump-sum transfer. In the normal case when one cannot distinguish bequest motives and there is a single rate of taxation $\tau^\theta = \frac{\tau^x}{1+\tau^x}$ then one shows that the optimal value of this unique rate represents a compromise between the equity objective and the desire of not discouraging wealth accumulation. The closer δ is to 1, the closer the tax to 1.

In this very simple model the only source of inequality is longevity θ. When $\bar{\theta} = 1$ or when $\tau^\theta = 1$, then there is no inequality. Introducing a second source of heterogeneity, e.g., different productivities, is surely more realistic. In that case, as shown by Blumkin and Sadka (2004) even when there is only accidental bequest a 100% tax is not necessarily desirable.

4.3.2. Altruists and life-cyclers

For long economists have rejected the idea of heterogeneous preferences. Differences in behavior had to be explained by differences in ability, inherited wealth or by random shocks. Over the last years, there is an increasing awareness that to better understand the world and analyze economic policy it is important to admit that society consists of individuals with different preferences in terms of altruism and time preference. In his celebrated paper, Ramsey (1928) already indicated that within a society consisting of individuals differing in time preferences, the most patient would end up with all the wealth in the long run.

In this section we address the question of wealth transfer tax in a society with two types of individuals, pure life-cyclers and altruistic savers. Formally, their utility function is:

$$u_t^i = u(c_t^i, d_{t+1}^i) + \gamma^i u_{t+1}^i,$$

with $i = L$ for life-cyclers and thus $\gamma^L = 0$ and $i = A$ for altruists and thus $\gamma^A = \gamma > 0$. The technology is the same as above: CRS production function and we have competitive profit maximization. Population grows at a uniform rate n and preferences are dynastic. In other words, there is a fixed fraction π of altruistic dynasties and a fraction $1 - \pi$ of non-altruistic dynasties.

It can easily be shown that government debt does not affect the steady-state capital stock and national income.[22] As in Ramsey, the altruistic (the more patient) households hold the entire capital stock. Moreover, government debt though neutral in aggregate terms increases steady-state inequality. A higher level of debt means a higher level of taxation to pay for the interest payments. The taxes fall on both life-cyclers and altruists but the interest payments go entirely to the altruist. Consequently, a higher level of debt, or alternatively of pay-as-you-go social security, raises the steady-state consumption and income of the altruists and lower the steady-state consumption and income of the life-cyclers.

For the purpose at hand we are interested by the incidence of a wealth transfer tax which in the present setting is only paid by altruistic dynasties. Assuming that the proceeds of the tax are redistributed uniformly to everyone, it can be shown that the tax may lower the utility of not only the altruists but also that of the life-cyclers. This paradoxical result was already obtained by Stiglitz (1978) in a slightly different setting.[23] When capital is taxed the quantity falls which in turns depresses the real wage. This effect may be large enough to make any tax on wealth transfer undesirable even from the standpoint of people who own no wealth, pay no tax and indeed benefit from a transfer.

One should recall that this result is obtained in the steady-state. In the short run life-cyclers could be tempted to tax inheritance and enjoy a utility boost. If they have to vote they will vote for such a tax without being concerned by the fate of their descendance. The political economy of wealth transfer thus yields a result different from steady-state social welfare maximization. It explains why a tax that would be undesirable from the steady-state standpoint can be voted on when life-cyclers hold a majority.

[22] See Michel and Pestieau (1998, 1999, 2000, 2005), Mankiw (2000).

[23] See also Stiglitz (1977).

Table 4
Wealth transfer taxes as a percentage of total revenues and GDP (%) in 1998

	Share of GDP (%)	Share of total tax revenue (%)
United States	0.36	1.16
Belgium	0.39	0.86
France	0.51	1.13
Germany	0.13	0.34
Italy	0.08	0.17
Netherlands	0.32	0.78
Spain	0.20	0.57
United Kingdom	0.21	0.57

Source: OECD (2000), Revenue Statistics 1965–1999, Paris, OECD.

4.4. Unobservability of inherited wealth

Regardless of the type of wealth transfer taxation, inheritance or estate tax, its actual yield is uniformly poor.[24] Table 4 provides the relative yield of wealth transfer taxation for a sample of OECD countries.

From Table 4 it is clear that such taxes are not successful, if their primary objective has been to reduce reliance on other taxes. This poor yields have led some countries to seriously consider abandoning the tax. In any case, from a theoretical viewpoint, it is interesting to see how other taxes should be adjusted if wealth transfers could not be taxed anymore.

Boadway et al. (2000) and Cremer et al. (2001, 2003) have addressed the question of the optimal taxation of labor and interest income in an economy where not only ability but also inheritance were not observed.[25] In such a setting, even with separability between leisure and consumption, Atkinson and Stiglitz proposition does not apply and there is a good case for taxing capital income.[26] Intuitively, the additional instrument of capital income taxation now improves screening for the unobservable characteristics. Roughly speaking its role is to indirectly tax inherited wealth.

This bring us back to the old public finance debate between a comprehensive income tax and an expenditure tax.[27] For the latter to be desirable one needs to be sure that inheritance can be effectively taxed. When this is not possible, one must rely on an income tax which involves double taxation of capital income.

[24] See Kessler and Pestieau (1991).

[25] As a matter of fact, one only needs to assume that a fraction of inherited wealth cannot be observed. In this quite realistic case, the same results hold true.

[26] Because of the two-dimensional heterogeneity, a tax on capital income is an effective way of relaxing an otherwise binding self-selection constraint. This is because even under separability, mimicker and mimicking individual do not have the same marginal rate of substitution between first and second period consumption.

[27] See on this Simons (1938) and Bradford (1986).

4.5. Investment in the human capital of children

In most societies there are two main ways of transferring financial resources to ones's children: human and physical capital. Human capital makes indeed a large bulk of voluntary intergenerational transfer in most families but the very rich.

As argued by Becker and Tomes (1979, 1986), parents tend to devote resources on behalf of their children, first to education and then to physical bequest. We are not thinking of time and attention but of financial spending. Becker and Tomes consider two transfers: e for education and $x \geq 0$ for bequest. The overall transfer is $e + x$ whereas inherited resources are $wh(et) + (1 + r)x$ where h is the (strictly concave) human capital function and r the rate of interest. Accordingly parents have to devote their saving to their own second period consumption, to e ant to x. Take a simple two period model; their utility function is

$$u(c, d, wh + x) = u\left(wh(\bar{e}) - s, (1 + r)s - e - \frac{x}{1 + r}, wh(e) + (1 + r)x\right),$$

where $\bar{e}$, w and r are given and the bequest motive is an extended form of joy of giving. Parents are concerned by the life-cycle income of their only child.[28] There are two possible types of solution to this problem. For some individuals: $x = 0$ and $e < e^*$ where e^* is defined by: $wh'(e^*) = 1 + r$. These individuals would like to finance high educational expenditures through a negative bequest which is not possible. Hence, the non-negativity constraint on x is binding. For others $e = e^*$ and $x > 0$. Whether parents are constrained by the assumption that $x \geq 0$ and thus leave $0 \leq e < e^*$ depends on their wealth, their degree of (imperfect) altruism and on the relative returns of both types of transfers (r versus $wh'(e)$).

The question at hand is whether these two types of transfer ought to be taxed (or subsidized) differently. Even in the simple framework adopted here both types have different economic implications. For pure efficiency reason there is a good case for subsidizing e up to the level e^* even if this requires taxing financial bequests. Furthermore in a dynamic setting of endogenous growth a number of papers have more or less explicitly shown that education ought to be subsidized and/or supplied collectively. This holds particular true when an optimal income tax is available. See Glomm and Ravikunar (1992), Benabou (2002).

Cremer and Pestieau (2006) consider a model of successive generations wherein parents provide education out of some joy of giving and with the knowledge that it increases the probability that their child(ren) be highly productive. Individual are only differentiated by their degree of productivity. The paper shows that when a non-linear income tax is available and when there is no laundering, there is a good case for subsidizing private education and possibly for providing some public education.

[28] We have $n = 0$.

5. Conclusion

Even though our survey was limited to the normative aspects of wealth transfer taxation there are a number of questions that we have not dealt with. There are indeed a number of issues that explain why estate taxation is today so unpopular that in some countries the political system is considering abolishing it.

There is first the issue of avoidance and evasion which not only leads to poor tax yields but also leads to strong departure from both vertical and horizontal equality.[29] Related to that, there is the issue of tax competition within countries and among countries. In federal states one observes a real race to the bottom regarding estate taxation. In an economic union such as the European one there is an increasing tax competition for financial wealth and this includes estate taxation. Another issue pertains to alleged adverse effect of estate taxation on family businesses.

Those three issues have a real political impact and yet there is little evidence on how important is their effect. It is thus not surprising that there exists little theoretical work taking them into account.

References

Aaron, H.J., Munnell, A.H. (1992). "Reassessing the role for wealth transfer taxes". National Tax Journal 45 (2), 119–143.

Altonji, J.G., Hayashi, F., Kotlikoff, L.J. (1992). "Is the extended family altruistically linked? Direct tests using micro data". American Economic Review 105 (6), 1121–1166.

Andreoni, J. (1990). "Impure altruism and donations to public goods: a theory of warm-glow giving?". Economic Journal 100 (401), 464–477.

Arrondel, L., Masson, A., Pestieau, P. (1997). In: Erreygers, G., Vandevelde, T. (Eds.), Bequests and Inheritance: Empirical Issues and French–US Comparison. Springer-Verlag, Berlin, pp. 89–125.

Atkinson, A.B., Sandmo, A. (1980). "Welfare implications of the taxation of savings". Economic Journal 90, 529–549.

Atkinson, A.B., Stiglitz, J.E. (1972). "The structure of indirect taxation and economic efficiency". Journal of Public Economics 1, 97–119.

Atkinson, A.B., Stiglitz, J.E. (1976). "The design of tax structure: direct versus indirect taxation". Journal of Public Economics 6 (1–2), 55–75.

Atkinson, A.B., Stiglitz, J.E. (1980). Lectures in Public Economics. McGraw Hills, New York.

Batina, R., Ihori, T. (2000). Consumption Tax Policy and the Taxation of Capital Income. Oxford University Press.

Barro, R. (1974). "Are government bonds net wealth?". Journal of Political Economy 82, 1095–1117.

Becker, G.S., Tomes, N. (1979). "An equilibrium theory of the distribution of income and intergenerational mobility". Journal of Political Economy 87, 1153–1189.

Becker, G.S., Tomes, N. (1986). "Human capital and the rise and fall of families". Journal of Labor Economics 4 (part 2), S1–S39.

Benabou, R. (2002). "Tax and education policy in an heterogenous agent economy: what levels of redistribution maximize growth and efficiency?". Econometrica 70, 481–517.

[29] See Kopczuk and Slemrod (2000).

Bernheim, B.D., Shleifer, A., Summers, L.H. (1985). "The strategic bequest motive". Journal of Political Economy 93 (6), 1045–1076.
Bevan, D.L., Stiglitz, J.E. (1979). "Intergenerational transfers and inequality". Greek Economic Review 1 (1), 8–26.
Blumkin, T., Sadka, E. (2004). "Estate taxation". Journal of Public Economics 88, 1–21.
Boadway, R., Marchand, M., Pestieau, P. (2000). "Redistribution with unobservable bequests: a case for capital income tax". Scandinavian Journal of Economics 102, 1–15.
Bradford, D. (1986). Untangling the Income Tax. Harvard University Press, Cambridge.
Brenner, G.A. (1985). "Why did inheritance laws change?". International Review of Law and Economics 5, 91–106.
Chamley, Ch. (1986). "Optimal taxation of capital income in general equilibrium with infinite lives". Economica 54, 607–622.
Coleman, W.J. (2000). "Welfare and optimum dynamic taxation of consumption and income". Journal of Public Economic 76, 1–39.
Cox, D. (1987). "Motives for private income transfers". Journal of Political Economy 95 (3), 508–546.
Cremer, H., Pestieau, P. (1988). "A case for differential inheritance taxation". Annales d'Economie et de Statistiques 9, 167–182.
Cremer, H., Pestieau, P. (1991). "Bequest, filial attention and fertility". Economica 58, 359–375.
Cremer, H., Kessler, D., Pestieau, P. (1993). "Education for attention: a Nash bargaining solution to the bequest-as-exchange model". Public Finance 48 (supplement), 85–97.
Cremer, H., Kessler, D., Pestieau, P. (1994). "Public and private intergenerational transfers: evidence and a simple model". In: Ermisch, J., Ogawa, N. (Eds.), The Family, the State and the Market in Aging Societies. Clarendon Press, Oxford, pp. 216–231.
Cremer, H., Pestieau, P. (1996). "Bequests as a heir "discipline device"". Journal of Population Economics 9, 405–414.
Cremer, H., Pestieau, P. (1998). "Delaying inter vivos transmission under asymmetric information". Southern Economic Journal 65, 322–331.
Cremer, H., Pestieau, P. (2001). "Non-linear taxation of bequests, equal sharing rules and the trade-off between intra- and inter-family inequalities". Journal of Public Economics 79, 35–54.
Cremer, H., Pestieau, P. (2006). "Intergenerational transfer of human capital and optimal income taxation." Journal of Public Economic Theory, in press.
Cremer, H., Pestieau, P., Rochet, J.-C. (2001). "Direct versus indirect taxation: the design of the tax structure revisited". International Economic Review 42, 781–789.
Cremer, H., Pestieau, P., Rochet, J.-C. (2003). "Capital income taxation when inherited wealth is not observable". Journal of Public Economics 87, 2475–2490.
Davies, J.B. (1981). "Uncertain lifetime, consumption and dissaving in retirement". Journal of Political Economy 89, 561–577.
Diamond, P. (1965). "National debt in a neoclassical growth model". American Economic Review 58, 1126–1150.
Erregeyers, G., Vandevelde, T. (1997). Is Inheritance Legitimate? Ethical and Economic Aspects of Wealth Transfers. Springer-Verlag, Berlin.
Gale, W.G., Hines, J.R., Slemrod, J. (Eds.) (2000). Rethinking Estate and Gift Taxation. Brookings Institution, Washington, DC.
Glomm, G., Ravikunar, R. (1992). "Public versus private investment in human capital: endogenous growth and income inequality". Journal of Political Economy 100, 818–834.
Hammond, P. (1988). In: Altruism in the New Palgrave: a Dictionary of Economics. Eatwell, J., Milgate, M., Newman, P. (Eds.). Macmillan Press, London.
Harsanyi, J. (1995). "A theory of social values and a rule utilitarian theory of morality". Social Choice and Welfare 12, 319–344.
Ihori, T. (1996). Public Finance in an Overlapping Generation Economy. St Martin's Press, New York.
Judd, K.L. (1985). "Redistributive taxation in a simple perfect foresight model". Journal of Public Economics 28, 59–83.

Kaplow, L. (2000). "A framework for assessing estate and gift taxation". In: Gale, W.G., Hines, J.R., Slemrod, J. (Eds.), Rethinking Estate and Gift Taxation. Brookings Institution, Washington, DC.
Kessler, D., Pestieau, P. (1991). "Wealth taxes in the EEC". Canadian Public Policy 17, 309–321.
Kopczuk, W., Slemrod, J. (2000). "The impact of the estate tax on the wealth accumulation and avoidance behavior of donors". In: Gale, W.G., Hines, J.R., Slemrod, J. (Eds.), Rethinking Estate and Gift Taxation. Brookings Institution, Washington, DC.
Kopczuk, W. (2001a). "Optimal estate taxation in the steady-state", unpublished.
Kopczuk, W. (2001b). "The trick is to live. Is the estate tax social security for the rich?" unpublished.
Kotlikoff, L.J., Spivak, A. (1981). "The family as an incomplete annuities market". Journal of Political Economy 89 (2), 372–391.
Mankiw, G. (2000). "The savers–spenders theory of fiscal policy". AEA Papers and Proceedings 90, 120–125.
Masson, A., Pestieau, P. (1997). "Bequests motives and models of inheritance: a survey of the literature". In: Erreygers, G., Vandevelde, T. (Eds.), Is Inheritance Justified? Springer-Verlag, Berlin, pp. 54–88.
Michel, Ph., Pestieau, P. (1998). "Fiscal policy in a growth model with both altruistic and non-altruistic agents". Southern Economic Journal 64, 682–697.
Michel, Ph., Pestieau, P. (1999). "Fiscal policy in a growth model where individuals differ with regard to altruism and labor supply". Journal of Public Economic Theory 1, 187–203.
Michel, Ph., Pestieau, P. (2000). "Tax-transfer policy with altruists and non-altruists". In: The Economics of Reciprocity, Giving and Altruism. Gérard-Varet, L.A., Kolm, S.C., Mercier-Ythier, J. (Eds.). International Economic Association, Macmillan, London, pp. 275–284.
Michel, Ph., Pestieau, P. (2002). "Wealth transfer taxation with both accidental and desired bequests," unpublished.
Michel, Ph., Pestieau, P. (2005). "Fiscal policy with agents differing in altruism and in ability". Economica 72, 121–136.
Michel, Ph., Pestieau, P. (2006). "Fiscal policy in an overlapping generations model with bequest-as-consumption". Journal of Public Economic Theory, in press.
Pestieau, P. (1974). "Optimal taxation and discount rate for public investment in a growth setting". Journal of Public Economics 3, 217–235.
Pestieau, P. (2000). "Gifts, wills and inheritance law". In: Bouckaert, B., De Geest, G. (Eds.), Encyclopedia of Law and Economics, vol. 3. Edward Edgar, pp. 888–906.
Pestieau, P. (2003). "The role of gift and estate transfers in the United States and in Europe". In: Munnell, A., Sunden, A. (Eds.), Death and Dollars. The Brookings Institution Press, Washington, DC.
Ramsey, F.P. (1928). "A mathematical theory of saving". Economic Journal 38, 543–559.
Saez, E. (2002). "Optimal progressive capital income taxes in the infinite horizon model". NBER Working Paper No 9046.
Simons, H.C. (1938). Personal Income Taxation. University Press of Chicago, Chicago.
Stiglitz, J.E. (1978). "Notes on estate taxes, redistribution and the concept of balanced growth path incidence". Journal of Political Economy 86 (2), 137–150.
Stiglitz, J.E. (1977). "Equality, taxation and inheritance". In: Krelle, W., Shorrocks, A. (Eds.), Personal Income Distribution. North-Holland, Amsterdam, pp. 271–303.
Stiglitz, J.E. (1987). "Pareto efficient and optimal taxation in the new welfare economics". In: Auerbach, Feldstein, M. (Eds.), Handbook of Public Economics, vol. 2. North-Holland, Amsterdam, pp. 991–1042.

Chapter 17

THE ECONOMICS OF MIGRANTS' REMITTANCES

HILLEL RAPOPORT*

Department of Economics, Bar-Ilan University, Ramat Gan, 52900 Israel

SCID, Department of Economics, Stanford University, USA

CADRE, Université de Lille 2, France
e-mail: hillel@mail.biu.ac.il

FRÉDÉRIC DOCQUIER

National Fund for Scientific Research, IRES,

Université Catholique de Louvain, Belgium

Contents

* Corresponding author. For the most part this chapter was written while the first author (Hillel Rapoport) was visiting research fellow at the Center for Research on Economic Development and Policy Reform (CREDPR)—now the Stanford Institute for International Development (SCID) at Stanford University's Department of Economics, in 2001–03. He wishes to express his gratitude to Anne Krueger, Nick Hope and Roger Noll, the Center's past, former and current Directors, for their hospitality, and to Cosima Schneider for excellent research assistance. The study benefited from comments by, and interaction with Flore Gubert, Anjini Kochar, David McKenzie, Alice Mesnard and Jackie Wahba. Special thanks to Sylvie Lambert for her accurate reading of the preliminary version of this chapter and her many useful suggestions. The usual disclaimer applies.

Handbook of the Economics of Giving, Altruism and Reciprocity, Volume 2
Edited by Serge-Christophe Kolm and Jean Mercier Ythier

DOI: 10.1016/S1574-0714(06)02017-3

Abstract

This chapter reviews the recent theoretical and empirical economic literature on migrants' remittances. It is divided between a microeconomic section on the determinants of remittances and a macroeconomic section on their growth effects.

At the micro level we first present in a fully harmonized framework the various motivations to remit described so far in the literature. We show that models based on different motives share many common predictions, making it difficult to implement truly discriminative tests in the absence of sufficiently detailed data on migrants and receiving households' characteristics and on the timing of remittances. The results from selected empirical studies show that a mixture of individualistic (e.g., altruism, exchange) and familial (e.g., investment, insurance) motives explain the likelihood and size of remittances; some studies also find evidence of moral hazard on the recipients' side and of the use of inheritance prospects to monitor the migrants' behavior.

At the macro level we first briefly review the standard (Keynesian) and the trade-theoretic literature on the short-run impact of remittances. We then use an endogenous growth framework to describe the growth potential of remittances and present the evidence for different growth channels. There is considerable evidence that remittances (in the form of savings repatriated by return migrants) promote access to self-employment and raise investment in small businesses, and there is also evidence that remittances contribute to raise educational attainments of children in households with migrant members. Investigation of the effects of remittances on outcomes such as children's education and health raise identification issues, however, as we explain below. Finally, the relationship between remittances and inequality appears to be non-monotonic: remittances seem to decrease economic inequality in communities with a long migration tradition but to increase inequality within communities at the beginning of the migration process. This is consistent with different theoretical arguments regarding the role of migration networks and/or the dynamics of wealth transmission between successive generations.

Keywords

migration, remittances, growth, development, inequality

JEL classification: D1, D64, F22, O1

1. Introduction

During the last two decades, the economic analysis of remittances has experienced a dramatic renewal, applying and sometimes initiating the development of new economic tools and approaches. First of all, the microeconomics of remittances has focused since the early 1980s on the role of information and social interactions in explaining transfer behavior. This resulted in a deep change in the way economists look at the determinants of remittances, with familial and strategic motives being increasingly acknowledged for alongside more traditional motivations. From a macroeconomic perspective, new growth theories have also profoundly altered the directions for research on the impact of migration and remittances. While previous research in the 1970s and 1980s was centered on the short-run effects of international transfers, mainly within the framework of static trade models, the focus gradually shifted to long-run considerations, notably the role of remittances in the dynamics of inequality and development.

To the best of our knowledge, there is no comprehensive survey on the economic analysis of remittances, at least no recent survey that would cover the new theoretical and empirical findings mentioned above.[1] These findings provide answers to questions such as: Who transfers? Why? How much? And, most importantly, what are the economic consequences of remittances for developing countries? The answers to the first three questions do not necessarily differ from those exposed elsewhere in this handbook for other types of private transfers. However, the context in which remittances take place, that of developing countries, makes them unique in many respects. First, developing countries are characterized not only by high levels of poverty, but also high levels of inequality and income volatility (which, in turn, make access to credit and insurance so crucial); since remittances have an effect on each of these dimensions, their overall economic impact—and, hence, the marginal value of a dollar of remittances—is likely to be quite large. Second, developing countries are also characterized by pervasive capital markets imperfections, offering no market response to the needs for credit and insurance of the majority of the population; therefore, despite being voluntary and altruistic to a large extent, remittances differ from most private transfers observed in Western countries in that additional motives (insurance, investment, and exchanges of various types of services) are central to explaining transfer behavior. Third, with few exceptions, private transfers in the Western countries either take place "anonymously"—in the sense that donors do not necessarily know the identity of the beneficiaries (e.g., charity, philanthropy)—or within a very restricted familial group; by contrast, remittances are increasingly recognized as informal social arrangements within extended families and communities. Finally, while most public and private transfers tend to reduce economic inequality, this needs not be the case for remittances: the presence of liquidity constraints that impinge investment in migration and education, combined with the use of inheritance procedures to monitor the migrants' behavior, sometimes generate patterns of remittances that tend to increase inter-household inequality.

[1] Early descriptive surveys include Russell (1986).

Another challenging aspect of the study of remittances is related to data collection and analysis. At a macro level, it is not always possible to test appropriately for the macroeconomic impact of remittances because of poor data quality; at a micro level, it is extremely difficult to discriminate between competing theories of remittances, which often share similar predictions as to the impact of the main right-hand-side variables, implying that truly discriminative tests have to rely on additional variables for which details are not always available. In spite of these limitations, there is a lot to learn from existing data on remittances. For example, international data reveal that workers' remittances often make a significant contribution to GNP and are a major source of foreign exchange in many developing countries. For some countries, it is not uncommon to observe flows of remittances that equal about half the value of their exports or 10% of their GDP (see Table 1). This is or was the case for relatively small Caribbean and Pacific countries, but also for traditional labor-exporting countries such as Egypt, Turkey, or Pakistan.[2] In the case of Mexico, it has been estimated that remittances received in 1989 amounted to 10% of merchandise exports, 65% of earnings from tourism, were equivalent to agricultural exports, and sufficient to cover three times the balance of payments deficits (Durand et al., 1996); more recently, the Bank of Mexico estimated that Mexican migrants remitted in 1998 about 1.5% of Mexico's GDP, with remittances reaching as much as 10% of GDP in one Mexican State (Michoacan). These figures exclude internal (mainly urban-rural) remittances and informal international remittances and are therefore probably well below the actual figures.[3]

A maybe more meaningful way to assess the economic role of remittances is to rely on household surveys and estimate the proportion of households for which remittances are an important source of income. Such surveys tend to show that remittances are often a crucial element of survival and livelihood strategies for many (typically rural) poor households. For example, Rodriguez (1996) reports that 17% of Philippines' households receive income transfers from abroad, representing 8% of national income. Similarly, Cox et al. (1998) found that 25% of Peruvian households receive private transfers (mainly remittances), representing 22% of their incomes. On a more reduced scale, de la Brière et al. (2002) show that approximately 40% of the households in the Dominican Sierra, a poor rural region of the Dominican Republic, have migrant members, 52% of

[2] It is also striking that in some places remittances are a relatively new phenomenon and are still gaining in magnitude (especially in Central America) while in other places (e.g., Morocco, Turkey), the magnitude of remittances has decreased sharply since the 1970s. See Table 1.

[3] The number of internal migrants itself is unknown. To give a very crude element of comparison, the number of international migrants in 1981 was estimated at 95 millions and has increased threefold since then, whereas India alone had about 200 millions internal migrants for that same year (Zlotnik, 1998). See Lucas (1997) for a survey of economic research on internal migration in developing countries. Russell (1986) suggested that official international flows of remittances account for less than half of the total amount (internal and informal remittances included) actually remitted. Official statistics exclude small transfers (moreover, the thresholds above which bank transfers are reported differ from country to country), but also transfers in-kind, transfers directly carried by the migrants themselves, and unofficial transfers (which are likely to be substantial where transaction costs are high and there is a high black-market premium on foreign exchange).

Table 1
International remittances as a share of exports and GDP (selected countries and years, in%)

Selected countries	1980		1990		1995		1999	
	Exports	GDP	Exports	GDP	Exports	GDP	Exports	GDP
Albania					127.2	15.5	85.1	9.7
Algeria	2.8	1.0	2.4	0.6	9.7	2.7	7.1	2.0
Bangladesh	27.0	1.1	40.4	2.5	28.9	3.2	28.1	3.7
Benin	34.7	5.5	33.7	4.8	22.8	4.6	18.4	3.1
Burkina	87.1	8.8	39.7	5.1	29.0	3.8	22.9	2.6
CapeVerde			130.1	16.5	110.7	21.2	50.9	11.8
Comoros	15.1	1.3	27.9	4.0	26.7	5.7	24.4	6.4
Dominic. R.	14.4	2.8	13.2	4.5	21.5	6.7	28.7	8.7
Ecuador			1.4	0.5	3.2	0.9	15.4	5.7
Egypt	38.6	11.8	43.3	8.7	24.3	5.5	26.4	4.2
El Salvador	0.9	0.3	40.1	7.4	51.6	11.2	44.5	11.0
Eritrea					69.4	20.7	194.1	19.7
Guatemala			6.6	1.4	12.8	2.4	13.4	2.6
Honduras			4.5	1.6	6.9	3.0	13.8	5.9
India	24.7	1.5	7.2	0.5	18.1	2.0	21.3	2.6
Jamaica	3.7	1.9	6.2	3.2	23.0	12.7	20.2	9.9
Jordan	37.7	15.0	20.1	12.4	35.7	18.3	47.3	20.6
Lebanon			355.7	64.0	182.9	21.5		
Mali	22.6	3.3	25.8	4.4	21.5	4.5	13.1	3.3
Morocco	32.2	5.6	29.4	7.8	21.8	6.0	18.4	5.5
Nepal	13.3	1.5	16.0	1.7	9.5	2.3	13.2	3.0
Nicaragua					11.2	4.0	39.3	13.2
Pakistan	59.1	7.4	31.2	4.9	19.1	3.1	12.0	1.8
Samoa	66.8	16.7	96.2	29.4		25.3		25.3
Sri Lanka	11.7	3.8	16.5	5.0	17.3	6.2	18.8	6.6
Turkey	58.3	3.0	16.2	2.2	9.8	2.0	10.5	2.4
Yemen, R.			195.5	32.2	82.3	26.9	46.9	18.1

Source: World Bank (2001).

whom are sending remittances. For El Salvador, Cox-Edwards and Ureta (2003) find that 14% of rural and 15% of urban households received remittances from friends and relatives abroad in 1997. These studies, as well as many others detailed below, show that remittances are instrumental to achieving mutual insurance, consumption smoothing, and alleviation of liquidity constraints.

As to their economy-wide consequences, it is clear that remittances may have a short-run macroeconomic impact through their effects on price or exchange rate levels. The long run implications of remittances, however, would seem to be more significant. First, remittances impinge on households' decisions in terms of labor supply, investment, education, migration, occupational choice, fertility, etc., with potentially important aggregated effects. Secondly, another channel through which remittances may affect a country's long-run economic performance is through their distributional effects and impact on economic inequality, a key issue from an endogenous growth perspective. Once we know that the amounts at stake are important and their potential economic impact is significant, it is worth trying to understand the determinants of remittances. This is the purpose of section 2 on the size and motives of remittances. Section 3 details the macroeconomic consequences of remittances, and distinguishes between short-run and long-run effects. Section 4 offers concluding remarks.

2. The microeconomics of remittances

Is the study of remittances in essence distinct from that of migration? To answer this question, we refer to Edward Funkhouser's (Funkhouser, 1995) comparative study on remittances to the capital cities of El Salvador and Nicaragua. In this study, Funkhouser noted that while the number of migrants and the general economic conditions prevailing in the two countries during the 1980s were quite similar, twice as many households received remittances from relatives abroad in San Salvador than in Managua; moreover, for those who received remittances, the average transfer received in San Salvador was twice as high as that in Managua. To explain this apparent puzzle, two possible directions may be suggested: is it that migrants self-select differently in the two countries? Or is it that, among those who emigrated, "remitters" self-select differently?

Using micro data on both migrants and receiving households, Funkhouser (1995) concluded in favor of the latter explanation. Indeed, the data revealed many similarities between the two pools of migrants with respect to age, education, gender, and, to a lesser extent, number of years since emigration.[4] In other words, differences in remitting behavior could not be accounted for by differences in households' or migrants' observed characteristics, including the timing of migration. By contrast, the estimation of remittance functions revealed substantial differences in remitting behavior between the two samples, allowing to conclude that differences in unobserved characteristics (i.e., how remitters self-select within the pool of migrants) are central to explaining inter-country differences in remittance behavior. Two insights from Funkhouser's study tend to confirm this. First, remitters were negatively selected out of the pool of emigrants, but in a more pronounced way for Nicaragua, meaning that educated Salvadorans tend to be less detached from their family and/or more "patriotic". Secondly, it was striking that while in the case of El Salvador, the likelihood and level of remittances reacted ambiguously to the time spent in the US (negatively for non-family members, and positively

[4] For both countries, neither gender nor age were significantly correlated with the probability or level of remittances, education decreased the likelihood of remittances but increased the amount remitted conditional on remitting, and both the likelihood and level of remittances were positively affected by "proximity" (blood or marriage relations). Funkhouser (1995) used probit estimates of the probability of remittances and a linear functional form for the estimation of the remittance function, while self-selection was accounted for using a Heckman-type two-stage procedure.

for close family members), they were negatively correlated to years since emigration for both immediate family members and other relative emigrants in the case of Nicaragua, suggesting higher propensities to return among Salvadorans.

Of course, such behavioral differences may simply be due to the different political contexts prevailing in the two countries and the "repulsive" effect the Sandinist government may have had on wealthy Nicaraguans emigrants. Still, Funkhouser (1995) study remains exemplary in that it highlights that migration and remittance decisions, although interdependent, are generally influenced by different sets of determinants. In other words, remittance behavior is not simply predicted by the migrants' characteristics, and its analysis requires specific attention. In particular, the "behavioral differences" put forward by Funkhouser are nothing but another wording for different motivations to remit.

Obviously, the most common motivation to remit is simply that migrants care of those left behind: spouses, children, parents, and members of larger kinship and social circles. Until recently, however, this altruistic inclination to remit was more frequently assumed than tested against competing theories. Alongside altruism, and notwithstanding self-rewarding emotions associated with remitting behavior (e.g., warm-glow), the very fact that donors and beneficiaries of remittances are spatially differentiated creates room for additional motives. First of all, remittances may just "buy" a wide range of services such as taking care of the migrant's assets and relatives at home, with the likelihood and size of remittances depending on whether and when the migrant intends to return. Secondly, it is clear that migration is primarily (but not only) driven by wage differentials, implying that people are ready to incur substantial moving costs in order to access to international migration. Such migration costs, however, are beyond the possibilities of many prospective migrants and, given capital markets imperfections, must be financed through informal family loans repaid later (with interest) in the form of remittances. Even when wage differentials are not significant enough to compensate for migration costs, it may still be optimal for some families to have migrant members. This is the case, in particular, for rural households whose agricultural income is highly volatile due to changing climatic conditions and other idiosyncratic risks. When the market does not allow for a trade-off between a lower mean and a reduced variance, migration by some members may become a straightforward way to achieve mutual insurance; for this to occur, wages at destination need not be higher providing that incomes at home and destination are not positively correlated.

Migration is now recognized as an informal familial arrangement, with benefits in the realms of risk-diversification, consumption smoothing, and intergenerational financing of investments, and remittances are a central element of such implicit contracts. The small number of members, however, limits the size of the insurance pool and the degree of risk diversification that can be attained. This is somehow compensated by families' comparative advantage in obtaining reliable information on individual members (their skills, degree of trustworthiness, etc.), and their enforcement power. Should intrafamilial altruism be insufficient to make the contract self-enforcing, families may sanction opportunistic behavior through inheritance procedures and social sanctions.

Despite these informational and enforcement advantages, familial arrangements are not immune to strategic behavior: distance renders the migrants' resources—and the needs of the family—imperfectly observable, thus creating informational problems that are more pervasive—and, therefore, make strategic behavior more likely—than in many other transfer situations.

As we shall see, remittances combine an altruistic component, a repayment-of-loans component, an insurance component, an inheritance component, and exchange of a variety of services, this complex mixture of motives being best described using fuzzy concepts such as "impure altruism" (Andreoni, 1989) or "enlightened selfishness" (Lucas and Stark, 1985). However, it is extremely difficult to empirically discriminate between these different motives: most empirical studies regress remittances on a set of variables (which typically includes pre-transfer incomes of both senders and recipients), but any sign for these relations may be interpreted in a number of ways, and the additional information needed to implement more discriminative tests (e.g., longitudinal data on the timing of remittances, information on the migrant's education, the recipient household's assets and number of heirs, etc.) is rarely available in a sufficiently detailed manner.

These two characteristics of the microeconomics of remittances—coexistence, at the theoretical level, of a variety of motives that are not exclusive one of the other, and, at the empirical level, difficulties inherent to the implementation of truly discriminative tests and to identify the effects of remittances—provide the structure for this section. We first present the different motivations to remit suggested so far in the literature in a unified theoretical framework, with an emphasis on their testable implications so as to contrast them, when possible, by their predictions (section 2.1). We then review the evidence from selected empirical studies (section 2.2).

2.1. Theory

To keep the general model as simple as possible, and unless specified differently, we consider only two decision units: one migrant (m), and one recipient household (h), which can consist of one or more individuals. Utility is denoted by U, pre-transfer incomes by I, consumption by C, and T stands for the amount remitted by m to h. Additional variables will be introduced gradually.

2.1.1. Altruism

To present the altruistic motive, we borrow from Stark (1995, chapter 1) a model that is convenient to account for both unilateral and mutual (or two-sided) altruism. Each agent's utility U^i, $i = m, h$, is assumed to be affected by the felicity (or ophelimity) derived from his or her own consumption, $V(C^i)$, with $V' > 0$ and $V'' < 0$, and the utility of the other. Utility may be expressed as a weighted average of these two elements, with $0 \leq \beta^i \leq 1/2$ denoting the individual's degree of altruism:

$$U^m(C^m, C^h) = (1 - \beta^m)V^m(C^m) + \beta^m U^h(C^h, C^m) \tag{2.1}$$

$$U^h(C^h, C^m) = (1-\beta^h)V^h(C^h) + \beta^h U^m(C^m, C^h). \tag{2.2}$$

Solving these two equations in terms of $V(C^i)$ gives:

$$U^m(C^m, C^h) = (1-\gamma^m)V(C^m) + \gamma^m V(C^h) \tag{2.3}$$

$$U^h(C^h, C^m) = (1-\gamma^h)V(C^h) + \gamma^h V^m(C^m), \tag{2.4}$$

where

$$0 \leq \gamma^m = \frac{\beta^m(1-\beta^h)}{1-\beta^m\beta^h} \leq 1/2 \quad \text{and} \quad 0 \leq \gamma^h = \frac{\beta^h(1-\beta^m)}{1-\beta^m\beta^h} \leq 1/2.$$

The migrant's utility function may thus be rewritten as:

$$U^m(C^m, C^h) = (1-\gamma^m)V(I^m - T) + \gamma^m V(I^h + T). \tag{2.5}$$

Maximizing (2.5) with respect to T gives the first order condition:

$$-(1-\gamma^m)\frac{\partial V}{\partial C^m} + \gamma^m \frac{\partial V}{\partial C^h} \leq 0, \quad \text{with equality for T} > 0.$$

Ruling out the possibility of negative transfers from m to h, and with $V(.) = ln(.)$, it is straightforward to see that the optimal remittance is given by:

$$T^* = Max\{\gamma^m I^m - (1-\gamma^m)I^h, 0\}, \tag{2.6}$$

with $\partial T^*/\partial I^m > 0$, $\partial T^*/\partial I^h < 0$, $\partial T^*/\partial \beta^m > 0$, and $\partial T^*/\partial \beta^h < 0$.

That is, the altruistic transfer increases with the migrant's income and degree of altruism, and decreases with the recipient's income and, more interestingly, degree of altruism.[5] Since the altruistic parameters β^m and β^h are not observable, and that other possible motives predict that the amount transferred would increase with the migrant's income, as we shall see, the main testable implication of the altruistic model is that transfers cannot increase with the recipient's income. This is by contrast to other motives, as will be detailed below. Another interesting prediction of the pure altruism hypothesis is that an increase by one dollar in the income of the migrant, coupled with a one-dollar drop in the recipient household's income, should raise the amount transferred exactly by one dollar. Formally, the transfer-income derivatives should satisfy the following condition:

$$\frac{\partial T}{\partial I^m} - \frac{\partial T}{\partial I^h} = 1.$$

An important implication of this is that the distribution of consumption should be independent of the distribution of income; this is a very strong testable implication of the altruistic motive (see section 2.2 below).

[5] This is the classical result where, since m knows that h, being altruistic towards him, is harmed when m's income is decreased, there are less transfers under mutual than unilateral altruism (in other words, the less altruistic is h towards m, the more he receives).

As already mentioned, the altruistic motive for remittances has been more commonly assumed than contrasted to other possibilities. To illustrate this, we again refer to Funkhouser (1995), who proposed a behavioral model of remittances based on altruism, with the following testable implications:

(a) emigrants with higher earnings potential remit more;
(b) low-income households receive more;
(c) remittances should increase with both the degree of proximity between the migrant and the remaining household members and the migrant's intentions to return;
(d) remittances by a given migrant should decrease with the number of other emigrants from the same household;
(e) the time profile of remittances should depend on the comparison between the migrants' time-discount factor and their earnings profile abroad.

As the discussions below will show, predictions (a) and (b) are compatible with a number of other possible motives, predictions (c) and (e) are extremely general, while prediction (d) is also consistent with the investment hypothesis and the inheritance hypothesis.

2.1.2. *Exchange*

There are many situations of Pareto-improving exchanges involving remittances. The most natural way to think of these situations is to assume that remittances simply "buy" various types of services such as taking care of the migrant's assets (e.g., land, cattle) or relatives (children, elderly parents) at home. Such motivations are generally the sign of a temporary migration, and signal the migrants' intention to return. Another intuitive way to think of such exchanges is to consider the case where, due to market imperfections, transaction costs may be saved on through non-market interpersonal agreements. For example, migrants' remittances may be viewed as repayments of loans used to finance the migrant's investments in human capital or the expenditures incurred in the course of migration (we will analyze this particular type of intertemporal exchanges in section 2.1.5 on the "investment" motive). In such exchanges, there is a participation constraint determined by each partner's external options, with the exact division of the pie (or surplus) to be shared depending on their bargaining power. For example, when remittances buy services such as taking care of the migrant's assets or relatives, the amount transferred must lie somewhere between the market price for such services (or their marginal value for the buyer if these are not traded) and the opportunity cost of the recipient. As to the partners' respective bargaining powers, these may be determined by local labor markets conditions (e.g., more unemployment raises the migrant's bargaining power). Similarly, the implicit interest rate for the repayment of loans must lie somewhere between the market rate for debtors and creditors.[6]

[6] Since the difference between the two is a possible measure of the degree of market imperfection, one conceives that such exchanges are more likely in the context of developing countries.

In the following we use an exposition of the exchange motive based on Cox (1987), which we adapt by considering the case of non-altruistic agents only and a fixed amount of service. Assume that remittances buy a fixed quantity of service $\bar{X}$. The sides' utility functions are now given by $V^i(C^i, \bar{X})$, $i = m, h$, with $V_{\bar{X}}^{m'} > 0$, $V_{\bar{X}}^{h'} < 0$ and $V_{\bar{X}}^{m''} < 0$, $V_{\bar{X}}^{h''} > 0$ to account for the increasing disutility of effort.

Suppose that the surplus is entirely appropriated by the migrant, who transfers the minimal compensation required for the service to be provided.[7] It follows that the remaining resident would accept to provide the service would the compensating transfer be such that:

$$V^h(I^h + T, \bar{X}) \geqslant V^h(I^h, 0). \tag{2.7}$$

Solving this participation constraint for equality, T may be expressed as: $T = T(\bar{X}, I^h)$. Then, the implicit function theorem gives:

$$\frac{\partial T}{\partial I^h} = -\frac{\partial V^h(I^h + T, \bar{X})/\partial C^h - \partial V^h(I^h, 0)/\partial C^h)}{\partial V^h(I^h + T, \bar{X})/\partial C^h} \gtrless 0$$

$$\frac{\partial T}{\partial \bar{X}} = -\frac{\partial V^h(I^h + T, \bar{X})/\partial \bar{X}}{\partial V^h(I^h + T, \bar{X})/\partial C^h} > 0.$$

This shows that the amount transferred increases with the quantity of service to be offered but reacts ambiguously to an exogenous increase in the recipient's pre-transfer income. Indeed, the sign of $\partial T/\partial I^h$ depends on the effect of X on the marginal utility of consumption. Intuitively, if X has no effect on the marginal utility of income (as is the case, for example, for an additive and separable utility function), this is higher at T equal zero than at T positive; then, the sign of the numerator is negative and the sign of the derivative is positive. However, if there exists some complementarities between X and I, the opposite may hold so that a negative sign for the derivative is also consistent with the exchange hypothesis.

Note that a similar participation constraint could be derived for the migrant, the maximal amount he would accept to transfer being such that: $V^m(I^m - T^{\max}; \bar{X}) = V^m(I^m; 0)$. Applying the same techniques as above, it could be shown that this maximal transfer increases with the migrant's income. The central prediction of the exchange model, therefore, is that in contrast to the altruistic model, an increase in the recipient's income may raise the amount transferred.[8]

[7] A more general (but more complex) model with egoistic agents (e.g., Cox et al., 1998) would allow for different possible divisions of the pie. However, we neglect this aspect as it does not affect the central predictions of the exchange model.

[8] This is best shown using a logarithmic example: $V^h(C^h, \bar{X}) = \ln C^h + \ln(a - \bar{X})$. In this case, the household participation constraint becomes: $\ln(I^h + T) + \ln(a - X) = \ln I^h + \ln a$, so that the minimal compensating transfer is given by: $T = \frac{\bar{X}}{a - \bar{X}} I^h$, showing that the amount remitted is proportional to the recipient's income.

To be operating, however, the exchange motive requires the recipient's minimal compensation to be lower than the maximal amount the migrant is ready to offer: $T < T^{\max}$. Hence, another interesting difference in the predictions between the altruistic and the exchange motives concerns the likelihood of remittances: as shown by Cox et al. (1998), in the altruistic case, the *probability* of transfer decreases with recipients' incomes, meaning that the effects of an increase in the recipient's income on the likelihood of transfers, on the one hand, and the amount transferred, on the other hand, are of identical signs. However, since this needs not be the case for the exchange motive, this introduces a supplementary difference in the predictions of the two models: while in the altruistic case, the probability for a given household to receive a transfer should be positively correlated to the average amount received, inverse correlations between these two variables could be the sign that an exchange motivation is at work.

The two models may be further contrasted; in particular, as mentioned above, a more general exchange model would allow for different possible contractual arrangements reflecting the parties' bargaining powers. In such a setting, higher unemployment at home should affect negatively the transfer received (since the recipient's bargaining power is thereby decreased), while the unemployment *rate* should not affect remittances received by a given household when altruism applies. More generally, the exchange model—especially its bargaining version—implies that threat-points matter. Hence, an interesting policy-implication of this approach is that, contrarily to the neutralization of public redistribution that is known to characterize altruism, in the case of exchange-motivated transfers, it may well be that public transfers, instead of crowding out private transfers, induce an increase in the amounts privately received by the recipients of public transfers (since their bargaining power is thereby increased).[9]

Until now, we have considered situations without information imperfections. In the real world, various types of informational asymmetries may arise in the context of migration. A first imperfection concerns the way employers at destination evaluate the migrants' productivity. Since individual skills are imperfectly observable, it may be that, during a given period, the migrants' wage is fixed according to a crude evaluation of their average productivity. To the extent that the migrants' may influence these beliefs, remittances may be used strategically and aim at positive selection among migrants. A second imperfection concerns the fact that, once the migrant is abroad, an informational asymmetry is created in favor of the non-migrants with respect to the economic conditions at home. Since remittances provide those left behind with an insurance against bad economic times, such informational asymmetries may also give rise to moral hazard.

2.1.3. A strategic motive for remittances

By contrast to the first two motives just exposed, the "strategic" motive is specific to the context of migration where it has first been developed (Stark, 1995, chapter 4). As

[9] On this possibility, see Cox and Jimenez (1992) and Cox et al. (1998).

underlined above, remittances may be both the cause and the consequence of migration; therefore, it is necessary to treat those two interdependent decisions in an encompassing framework. Among various plausible comprehensive approaches, Stark suggested that remittances may be part of a strategic interaction aiming at positive selection among migrants. The rationale is approximately the following: when migrants are heterogeneous in skills and individual productivity is not perfectly observable on the labor market of the host country (at least for a given period of time), employers apply statistical discrimination so that migrant workers are paid the average productivity of the minority group to which they belong. In such a context, there is room for cooperative arrangements between skilled and unskilled migrants: the former can act cohesively and "bribe" the latter in order to maintain them home; in addition, the community of those left behind must also control potential free riders (since any given unskilled worker would have a strong incentive to be the first to emigrate once positive selection is achieved).

To illustrate this, consider the case where m and h are potential migrants but h is less skilled than m. More precisely, assume that h's productivity is only a proportion π, $0 < \pi < 1$, of m's productivity. If both remain home, there is no information problem: h earns I^h and m earns a higher wage, I^h/π. If m alone emigrates, she is paid her marginal product in the destination country, I^m. If both h and m migrate, however, they are paid according to their average productivity, $\frac{1+\pi}{2}I^m$, at least until individual skills are revealed. There is a fixed migration cost c. The interaction is summarized using the following payoff matrix:

		Player h	
		Migrate	Not Migrate
Player m	Migrate	$\left(\frac{1+\pi}{2}I^m - c, \frac{1+\pi}{2}I^m - c\right)$	$(I^m - c, I^h)$
	Not Migrate	$\left(\frac{I^h}{\pi}, \pi I^m - c\right)$	$\left(\frac{I^h}{\pi}, I^h\right)$

Formally, the strategic motive operates when two conditions hold. First, in the game without transfers, (Migrate, Migrate) must be a Nash equilibrium. This requires:

$$\frac{1+\pi}{2}I^m - c > \frac{I^h}{\pi}. \tag{2.13}$$

Second, assuming that condition (2.13) holds, strategic remittances must make both players better off. For this to hold true, we must have simultaneously:

$$I^m - T \geq \frac{1+\pi}{2}I^m \tag{2.14}$$

and

$$I^h + T \geq \frac{1+\pi}{2} I^m - c, \tag{2.15}$$

with strict inequality for at least one of the two players.

From (2.15), and consistently with our presentation of the exchange motive, one may derive the minimal optimal transfer:

$$T^* = \frac{1+\pi}{2} I^m - I^h - c. \tag{2.16}$$

Substituting (2.16) into (2.14) gives:

$$I^h > \pi I^m - c, \tag{2.17}$$

meaning that efficiency may be achieved through side-payments if and only if unskilled workers have no interest in emigration unless they are pooled with skilled workers. Under the above conditions, remittances may be effective in achieving positive selection, and should be viewed as side-payments taking place in the course of a strategic interaction between migrants and non-migrants.

Before we turn to the predictions of this model, we would like to point out some of its potential weaknesses, such as the tendency for each migrant to free ride on others' efforts to achieve positive selection, and the low gains at stake when the revelation of individuals' skills does not take too long.[10] In addition, Docquier and Rapoport (1998) suggested that this theory requires from the employers at destination a "knowledge in anthropology" that they are unlikely to possess. Indeed, information on group affiliations is not shared symmetrically between employers and migrant workers. The former can associate a given community of migrants to a wider group of foreigners; the result would be that the selection undertaken by one particular group would benefit the whole group it is identified with. For example, if the Mossi from Burkina Faso who are working, say, in France, are successful in preventing the migration of their unskilled brothers but that, at the same time, French employers do observe the average productivity of the African people altogether, strategic transfers will definitely not be a sustainable means for promoting wealth among the Mossi.

Notwithstanding the different arguments above, the strategic motive hypothesis generates a number of interesting predictions listed by Stark (1995, p. 97–99) as follows: "First, [...], migration will be selective right from the start. [...] Selectivity and remittances are positively related. [...] Second, remittances will be targeted to those at home who have earning power since there would be no need to "bribe" those who would not credibly threaten to engage in labour migration. [...] Fourth, remittances come to an end once the high-quality workers are identified. [...] Fifth, the formation of groups is more

[10] Assessing a "high-productivity reputation" among Philippine's nurses or among Bangladeshi construction workers in the Gulf countries have been suggested as possible illustrations for this strategic motive; in these examples, the free rider problem is solved by governmental control over the whole emigration process.

likely when the [intercountry] differential in wage is large". More formally, from (2.16), it is straightforward to see that, as in the case of altruistic transfers, the level of remittances is expected to rise with the migrant's pre-transfer income and to decline with the recipients' pre-transfer income ($\partial T^*/\partial I^m = (1+\pi)/2 > 0$, $\partial T^*/\partial I^h = -1 < 0$). However, by contrast to the altruistic case, it is clear that the strategic motive predicts a stronger transfer response to pre-transfer income inequality, given that:

$$\frac{\partial T}{\partial I^m} - \frac{\partial T}{\partial I^h} = \frac{3+\pi}{2} > 1.$$

According to Stark, therefore, the omission of the strategic motive for remittances could be the reason why the degree of altruism inferred from empirical studies is generally biased upward. However, the relevancy of the theory is difficult to assess: some of its predictions are similar to those of the altruistic model (e.g., selectivity and remittances are also positively related when altruism prevails; furthermore, selectivity may be obtained as a byproduct of altruistic transfers—see section 2.1.7 below) or are not easily testable (e.g., recipient households are themselves composed of heterogeneous individuals and even if targeting towards members who are both low-skill and potential migrants would take place, it would hardly be observable). Indeed, we are not aware of an empirical study specifically designed to test for the presence of a strategic motive for remittances.

Until now, we have considered migration and remittances as individual decisions; another fruitful possibility is to think of migration and remittances as resulting from social and familial interactions. Notably, in a context of imperfect capital markets, remittances may be part of an implicit migration contract between the migrant and his or her family, allowing the familial entity to access to higher and/or less volatile incomes.

2.1.4. Insurance and moral hazard

"There are six important environmental and technological characteristics of many rural areas in low-income countries that must be incorporated in any useful analysis of institutions in such settings: (a) an important production input (weather) is stochastic, its realization during the course of production being unpredictable and exogenous; (b) the intertemporal distribution of weather outcomes is characterized by stationarity; (c) positive correlations in weather outcomes diminish with distance; (d) another important production input, land, is immobile; (e) the technology of production is stable; (f) and costs of acquiring information are high" (Rosenzweig, 1988a, p. 1150). Such characteristics make income volatility a salient attribute of agriculture in the rural regions of most developing countries; in the quasi-absence of credit and insurance markets, this gives rise to a variety of informal inter- and intrafamilial coinsurance arrangements. Interfamilial arrangements include traditional manifestations of reciprocity between producers of a given village, with cooperation emerging from their repeated interactions (Fafchamps, 1992; Coate and Ravallion, 1993). As to intrafamilial arrangements, and given the characteristic c) above, these often imply allocating some members outside of agriculture, via urban or foreign migration (Stark and Levhari, 1982; Rosenzweig, 1988a, 1988b; Lambert, 1994; Chen and Chiang, 1998).[11]

Urban and foreign jobs are generally subject to risks uncorrelated with those impeding on agricultural activities at home (e.g., crop failure, cattle disease, etc.). Hence, migrants would insure the remaining members of the family against drops in rural incomes, and receive assistance in case of unemployment or for retirement, with the exact terms of the insurance contract depending on the relative bargaining power of the sides. To be operating, however, such Pareto-improving arrangements must also be self-enforcing. This is generally achieved because a sufficient degree of altruism prevails within the family, or, more prosaically, because families detain reliable information on individuals' types and, thus, may be "picky" in selecting the right migrants (i.e., those who combine high income potentials and degrees of loyalty).[12] Should this not be sufficient, families can ultimately sanction opportunistic behavior using a variety of retaliation strategies. Alongside reputation (loss of prestige), or ostracism, default to remit may also be sanctioned by denying the migrant rights to future family solidarity (this is the "mutual" aspect of the contract), inheritance, or return to the village for retirement, an option that most migrants want to keep open. This also implies that, ceteris paribus, rich families that can monitor the migrants' behavior through inheritance procedures would tend to rely on migration more than poor families (Hoddinott, 1994). We discuss the role of inheritance in more details in section 2.1.6 below.

For the sake of simplicity, we neglect hereafter the insurance provided by the family to the migrant in case of economic "failure" of the latter. The risks that impinge on urban (or foreign) activities are kept implicit; would these materialize, it is simply assumed that the migrant would be delivered from his obligation to remit. However, reverse transfers may be observed in "good rural times" in some conditions. Besides, the insurance described below is not perfect since the volatility of familial income, although decreased, remains positive.

Consider a family with two members living for two periods. Each member receives a given first-period wage, I^0, and the second-period rural wage is random, amounting to $\underline{I}^h$ with probability p and $\bar{I}^h$ with probability $1 - p$, and $\underline{I}^h < \bar{I}^h$. This is an aggregate uncertainty, which affects all individuals in the same way. The utility function is identical for all agents and is additively separable. Agents' expected utility is therefore given by:

$$E(V^0) = v(I^0) + pv(\underline{I}^h) + (1 - p)v(\bar{I}^h), \tag{2.18}$$

[11] Another possibility is to allocate members in (sufficiently) distant villages through intra-rural migration and marriage (Rosenzweig and Stark, 1989).

[12] This could account for the fact that it is not always the members with the highest wage potential that are sent, but sometimes those considered as providing more secure sources of remittances. This is the argument raised by Lauby and Stark (1988) to explain the higher migration propensities of daughters in the context of rural–urban migration in the Philippines.

with $v' > 0$ and $v'' < 0$ to account for risk-aversion.

Suppose now that agents have the possibility to migrate to a destination where there is no uncertainty, and earn a wage I^m during the second period. Migration is costly and implies financing a fixed migration cost (c) at the beginning of the second period. Assume moreover than all agents are credit constrained, so that no individual member is able to finance the migration cost alone, meaning that migration requires a familial arrangement:

$$I^0 < c < 2I^0. \tag{2.19}$$

During the first period, agents may agree on an informal contract specifying how migration costs are shared and the amounts to be remitted in bad and good states of nature. The set of Pareto-efficient contracts is given by:

$$\underset{\xi, T_p, T_{1-p}}{Max} \quad E(V^m) + \lambda[E(V^h) - \bar{V}^h], \tag{2.20}$$

where T_p and T_{1-p} are the amounts to be remitted in the bad and the good state, respectively, ξ is the share of the migration cost supported by the migrant, λ is the relative weight of the remaining agent in the bargaining process, $\bar{V}_h$ is a given utility level for h, and $E(V^m)$ and $E(V^h)$ denote the expected levels of utility for the migrant and the remaining household, respectively, with:[13]

$$\begin{aligned} E(V^m) &= v(I^0 - \xi c) + pv(I^m - T_p) + (1-p)v(I^m - T_{1-p}) \\ E(V^h) &= v(I^0 - (1-\xi)c) + pv(\underline{I}^h + T_p) + (1-p)v(\bar{I}^h + T_{1-p}). \end{aligned} \tag{2.21}$$

The first order conditions are given by:[14]

$$\begin{aligned} &-cv'(I^0 - \xi c) + \lambda cv'(I^0 - (1-\xi)c) = 0 \\ &-pv'(I^m - T_p) + \lambda pv'(\underline{I}^h + T_p) = 0 \\ &-(1-p)v'(I^m - T_{1-p}) + \lambda(1-p)v'(\bar{I}^h + T_{1-p}) = 0. \end{aligned}$$

To illustrate this interaction, we assume that $\lambda = 1$ and $I^m = E(I^h)$. In this simple case, $\xi^* = 1/2$, migration reduces uncertainty by one half, and expected utilities are

[13] Note that while T_p is necessarily positive, T_{1-p} can in principle take any sign.

[14] Using a simple utility function such as $v(.) = \ln(.)$ gives the following solutions:

$$\xi^* = \frac{(\lambda-1)I^0 + c}{(\lambda+1)c}; \qquad T_p^* = \frac{\lambda I^m - \underline{I}^h}{\lambda+1}; \qquad T_{1-p}^* = \frac{\lambda I^m - \bar{I}^h}{\lambda+1}.$$

Substituting these solutions into (2.20) gives:

$$\begin{aligned} E(V^m) &= \ln\left(\frac{2I^0 - c}{\lambda+1}\right) + p\ln\left(\frac{I^m + \underline{I}^h}{\lambda+1}\right) + (1-p)\ln\left(\frac{I^m + \bar{I}^h}{\lambda+1}\right) \\ E(V^h) &= \lambda\ln\left(\frac{2I^0 - c}{\lambda+1}\right) + p\lambda\ln\left(\frac{I^m + \underline{I}^h}{\lambda+1}\right) + (1-p)\lambda\ln\left(\frac{I^m + \bar{I}^h}{\lambda+1}\right). \end{aligned}$$

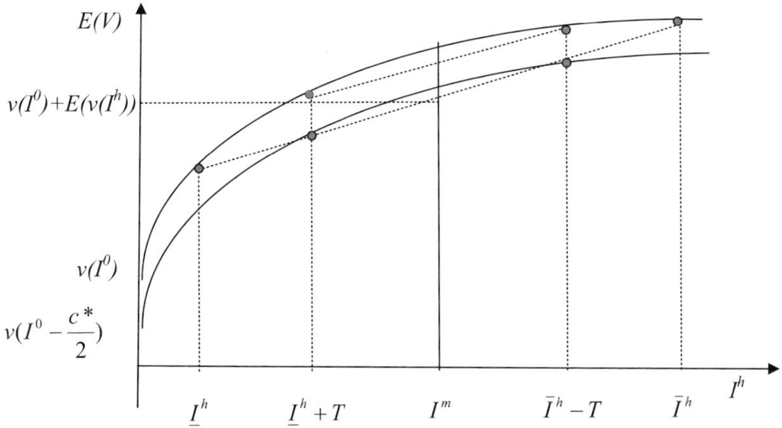

Figure 1. Migration, remittances and insurance.

equalized. Migration is worthy, however, only if migration costs are sufficiently low, i.e., below a critical threshold c^* that depends on the degree of risk-aversion. This is apparent from Figure 1, where migration reduces uncertainty by one-half, generating a gain in utility that exactly compensates for the migration cost incurred in the first period.

The insurance and the altruistic motives share similar predictions with respect to the sign of the effects of pre-transfer income levels on the amounts remitted. However, they differ with respect to the predicted timing of remittances and, to a lower extent, the predicted effect of familial wealth on the size of remittances. As to the timing of remittances, the insurance model predicts that migration and attached remittances are more likely where income at origin is more volatile, and that remittances should be sent on a relatively irregular basis. Moreover, if one admits that altruism is solvable in distance and time, the altruistic model should imply a gradual decrease of remittances over time, while the insurance motive should imply no decrease during a given period (if specified contractually), and a sharp decline after a while. Another difference between the two hypotheses is that while purely altruistic models predict higher remittances to lower-income households, ceteris paribus, the bargaining model of insurance could imply the opposite for two reasons: first, recall that migration is more worthy—and, hence, more likely—for families holding sizeable (and relatively risky) assets; in addition, we know from the bargaining-cum-exchange model that greater familial wealth increases the family's bargaining power. Therefore, with an insurance rationale, the prediction according to which the likelihood and size of remittances should decrease with recipients' incomes may be true for a given household (as in the case of altruism) but not necessarily so across households (in contrast to altruism).

In addition, the number of migrants within a given household may also provide a basis for discrimination between altruism and insurance. As pointed out by Agarwal and Horowitz (2002), the number of migrants is expected to reduce altruistic transfers by any particular migrant as all sources of transfers (whether public or private) are perfect substitutes under the pure altruistic hypothesis. By contrast, if each migrant individually subscribes an insurance contract, no such negative effect is expected. This argument is essentially correct but neglects two aspects that must be kept in mind regarding the exogeneity of the number of migrants, on the one hand, and of the recipients' income, on the other hand. The exogeneity of the number of migrants may be questioned as households living in more volatile environments (or with higher degrees of risk aversion) have an incentive to send more migrants out and further diversify their portfolio of income sources; at the same time, liquidity constraints may prevent poor households from attaining optimal diversification, an issue we explore in more details below. The exogeneity of the recipients' income may also be questioned since, as agents become insured against risks, they may reduce their level of effort (moral hazard).

To illustrate this problem, we present a simple model adapted from Azam and Gubert (2005). Assume that there is no altruism, and the household's pre-transfer income depends on its productive effort and on the realization of an idiosyncratic risk that impede on local production. Assuming an increasing marginal disutility of effort, and using an additive-separable form, the household's utility function may be written as:

$$V^h(E(C^h), e) = E(C^h) - \frac{\omega}{2}e^2, \tag{2.22}$$

where the parameter ω is positive and e denotes the household's level of effort.

Assume that there are only two states of nature, and that it is only in the "good" state of nature, which occurs with probability p, that local production is conditioned upon the household's productive effort. In the "bad" state of nature, on the other hand, local production is brought to a minimum regardless of the household's effort. Without loss of generality, we normalize this minimal level to zero so that we have:

$$I^h = \begin{cases} \alpha e & \text{with probability } 0 < p < 1, \\ 0 & \text{with probability } (1-p), \end{cases} \tag{2.23}$$

where α is the marginal productivity of the household's effort.

Assume moreover that the insurance contract specifies that the migrant guarantees a minimal consumption level to the household, $I^{\min}$. Remittances are then given by:

$$T = Max\{I^{\min} - I^h, 0\}. \tag{2.24}$$

The household's expected utility is, therefore:

$$E(V^h) = p[\alpha e + Max\{I^{\min} - \alpha e; 0\}] + (1-p)I^{\min} - \frac{\omega}{2}e^2, \tag{2.25}$$

which gives the first-order conditions and the corresponding levels of effort:

$$\frac{\partial E(V^h)}{\partial e} = \begin{cases} p\alpha - \omega e \leq 0 & \text{if } \alpha e \geq I^{\min} \Rightarrow e_1^* = \dfrac{p\alpha}{\omega}, \\ -\omega e \leq 0 & \text{if } \alpha e < I^{\min} \Rightarrow e_2^* = 0. \end{cases} \tag{2.26}$$

The household chooses its effort level so as to maximize its expected utility; the optimal solution is derived from a comparison between:

$$E\left[V^h(e_1^*)\right] = \frac{1}{2}\frac{p^2\alpha^2}{\omega} + (1-p)I^{\min} \tag{2.27}$$

and

$$E\lfloor V^h(0)\rfloor = I^{\min}. \tag{2.28}$$

The condition required to obtain a positive level of effort is, therefore:

$$\begin{aligned} E\left[V^h\left(e_1^*\right)\right] > E[V^h(0)] &\Leftrightarrow \frac{1}{2}\frac{p^2\alpha^2}{\omega} + (1-p)I^{\min} \\ > I^{\min} &\Leftrightarrow \frac{1}{2}\frac{p\alpha^2}{\omega} > I^{\min}, \end{aligned} \tag{2.29}$$

which will be referred to as the "no moral hazard condition". If condition (2.29) holds, then, we have:

$$\begin{aligned} E(C^h) &= \frac{p^2\alpha^2}{\omega} + (1-p)I^{\min} \\ E(T) &= (1-p)I^{\min} \\ E(C^m) &= I^m - (1-p)I^{\min}. \end{aligned}$$

It should be noted that the migrant has the possibility to fix the minimal consumption level to avoid opportunistic behavior. For example, choosing $I^{\min} = \frac{1}{2}\frac{p\alpha^2}{\omega}$ rules out the possibility of a moral hazard equilibrium. In this particular case, the expected amount of transfer becomes $E(T) = \frac{(1-p)p\alpha^2}{2\omega}$: it is a quadratic function of α, the marginal productivity of effort (which may also be seen as an indicator of the household's level of productive assets).

There are, however, theoretical as well as empirical justifications to focus on cases where condition (2.29) does not hold. At an empirical level, some studies provide evidence of opportunistic behavior on the recipients' side (e.g., Azam and Gubert, 2005 in the case of rural Mali—see section 2.2 below). At a theoretical level, it may seem too optimistic to assume that all the parameters in (2.29) are known to the migrant. Alternatively, one may view the minimal level of consumption as resulting from a collective decision taken before migration. It could also be argued that any amount satisfying (2.29) falls below the optimal altruistic transfer decided by the migrant himself. In all of these cases, the condition (2.29) does not hold and a moral hazard equilibrium emerges; it is defined by:

$$\begin{aligned} E(C^h) &= I^{\min} \\ E(T) &= I^{\min} \\ E(C^m) &= I^m - I^{\min}. \end{aligned}$$

Note that without insurance (remittances), the level of effort would be chosen so as to maximize:

$$E(\tilde{V}^h) = p\alpha e - \frac{\omega}{2}e^2, \tag{2.30}$$

which would yield:

$$\tilde{e}^* = e_1^* = \frac{p\alpha}{\omega}, \tag{2.31}$$

and

$$E(\tilde{V}^h) = \frac{p^2\alpha^2}{2\omega}. \tag{2.32}$$

One can see that under the "no moral hazard condition" (2.29), the insurance contract does not distort individual effort (this is of course by definition, and is apparent from the comparison between (2.26) and (2.31)) but generates an increase in the recipient's expected utility, which may be interpreted as the value of the insurance contract from the recipient's standpoint:

$$E\big[V^h\big(e_1^*\big)\big] - E[\tilde{V}^h] = (1-p)I^{\min}. \tag{2.33}$$

In the case where condition (2.29) is not satisfied, the insurance contract induces a moral hazard equilibrium characterized by a minimal level of effort; in this case, the expected value of the insurance contract becomes:

$$E[V^h(0)] - E[\tilde{V}^h] = I^{\min} - \frac{p^2\alpha^2}{2\omega}. \tag{2.34}$$

An interesting implication of this analysis is that if the household is ready to finance a migration cost higher than (2.33), this signals its intention to adopt an opportunistic behavior and reduce its effort. Figure 2 represents the case where the "no moral hazard condition" (2.29) holds. The dotted line depicts the ex-ante budget constraint (i.e., before the state of nature is realized) without insurance contract. The solid line represents the ex-ante budget constraint with insurance (recall that the expected income cannot be lower than $I^{\min}$). The "no moral hazard conditions" requires that the expected utility level with a positive effort must be higher than without effort (i.e., $V_1^h > V_2^h$): in this case, the equilibrium is at point N. Otherwise (i.e., if $V_1^h < V_2^h$), the insurance contract has a distorting effect on effort, and the equilibrium is at point D.

2.1.5. Family loan arrangements: the investment motive

The same kind of rationale may be used to explain remittances as repayments of loans on investments in education and/or migration. In this case, the familial implicit contract aims at increasing family income rather than at reducing uncertainty. Implementing such loans may require complex decision procedures as to the amount to be financed, the various sources to be solicited for fund-raising, and the recipients of the loans. The

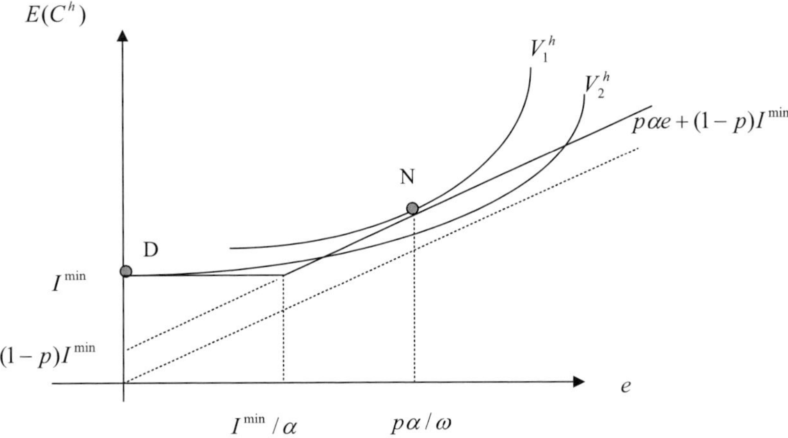

Figure 2. Insurance and moral hazard.

investment motive may be seen as a particular exchange of services in a context of imperfect credit markets, following the general lines we presented in our exposition of the exchange motive, but within a framework containing social as well as intergenerational elements.

The idea that remittances consist at least partly of repayments of loans has long been present in the remittance literature, especially in the empirical studies on the determinants of remittances. However, to the best of our knowledge, it is only recently that it has explicitly been modeled theoretically.[15] A relatively neglected aspect of the debate on remittances as dividends from investments concerns the interplay between migration, remittances, and the distribution of income and wealth among rural households. Indeed, if investments are the underlying familial motivation for sending migrants away, this implies that the family will keep on sending migrants as long as family income is thereby increased. Since migration is costly, however, this also implies that liquidity constraints limit the number of migrants that can be sent by a given family, and that richer families are more likely to take advantage of such investment opportunities. In the following, therefore, we discuss the implications of the investment hypothesis on the size and likelihood of remittances in connection with inter-household economic inequality. We neglect enforcement problems, since these are identical to those detailed above for the insurance motive. Besides, we focus on the level of familial assets, although it is clear that the composition of such assets could also be of importance.

[15] For example, Lucas and Stark (1985) refer to the investment hypothesis, but, as they put it, just offer outlines for the underlying theory. Cox and Jimenez (1992) seem to be the first to provide a theoretical framework for the investment hypothesis, followed by Cox et al. (1998) and Ilahi and Jafarey (1999). One should also mention Poirine (1997), who derives many interesting implications from his simple diagrammatic model.

Consider a family of unitary size, making its living from agriculture. Total familial output in agriculture is represented by a quadratic production function, $\alpha(\ell - \frac{\beta}{2}\ell^2)$, where ℓ is the number (or proportion) of workers employed in the domestic activity (typically, one minus the proportion of migrants), α is a technological parameter capturing the quantity and quality of familial land, and $0 < \beta < 1$ accounts for the decreasing marginal productivity of labor.

Since we are interested in inter-household inequality and not in the intra-familial distribution of income, for the sake of simplicity, we assume that income is equally shared between the members of a given family. Agents live for two periods. Without migration, income per member at each period is given by:

$$I_1^h = I_2^h = \alpha - \frac{\alpha\beta}{2}. \tag{2.35}$$

Assume that there is a migration possibility to a high-wage destination at a fixed cost c per migrant. In the absence of credit markets, this cost—which may include education expenditures—must be financed using first-period savings. Migration occurs in the second period, so that $\ell = 1$ in the first period. We denote by m the number (or proportion) of family members who migrate in the second period, and the migrants' wages by I^m. The labor force employed in the domestic activity is thus $\ell = 1 - m$. Utility is linear in income since we assume no risk-aversion and there is no inter-temporal discounting of income. Moreover, we assume that there is a minimal level of subsistence, $I^{\min}$, which must be kept for consumption at each period, but this minimum level could be set at zero without loss of generality.

The effect of familial wealth (captured by the technological parameter α) on the number of migrants is a priori unclear. On the one hand, migration incentives would seem to be greater for members of poor families, since their foregone earnings are lower than those of members of rich families (or, in other words, the wage differential is higher for poor families). On the other hand, poor families are likely to be liquidity constrained and hence unable to finance every profitable migration. That is, for each family, there may be a difference between the maximal number of migrants that the family can afford and the number of migrants that is optimal from its perspective.

To find how binding the liquidity constraint is, let us first determine the maximal number of migrants for a given family. The constraint may be written in the following form:

$$\alpha\left(1 - \frac{\beta}{2}\right) - mc \geq I^{\min} \Leftrightarrow m \leq \frac{\alpha}{c}\left(1 - \frac{\beta}{2}\right) - \frac{I^{\min}}{c} \equiv m^c(c, \alpha). \tag{2.36}$$

Clearly, this maximal proportion of migrants increases with the technological parameter α but decreases with the migration cost and the minimum of subsistence.

As to the optimal (unconstrained) proportion of migrants, it is derived from the maximization of total family income:

$$\underset{m}{Max}\, \alpha - \frac{\alpha\beta}{2} - mc + \alpha(1 - m) - \frac{\alpha\beta}{2}(1 - m)^2 + mI^m. \tag{2.37}$$

This gives:

$$m^* = \begin{cases} 0 & \text{if } -\alpha + \alpha\beta + I^m - c < 0 \\ 1 & \text{if } -\alpha + I^m - c > 0 \\ \dfrac{I^m - c}{\alpha\beta} - \dfrac{1-\beta}{\beta} & \text{otherwise.} \end{cases} \tag{2.38}$$

The actual proportion of migrants is the minimum between the optimal and the constrained proportions: $m^{eff} = Min\{m^*; m^c\}$. Clearly, for interior solutions, the constrained migration rate increases with α while the optimal rate decreases with α. Note also that m^* is a linearly decreasing function of c and m^c is a decreasing and convex function of c.

In keeping with the equal sharing rule assumed above, the amount received by each remaining resident is given by the difference between the average familial income, $I^m m^{eff} + \alpha(1 - m^{eff}) - \frac{\alpha\beta}{2}(1 - m^{eff})^2$, and the domestic income per remaining member, $\alpha - \frac{\alpha\beta}{2}(1 - m^{eff})$. This gives:

$$T = m^{eff}\left[I^m - \alpha + \frac{\alpha\beta}{2}(1 - m^{eff})\right], \tag{2.39}$$

which is a concave function of the migration rate.

The total derivative of remittances with respect to the technological parameter α, $\frac{dT}{d\alpha} = \frac{\partial T}{\partial m^{eff}}\frac{dm^{eff}}{d\alpha} + \frac{\partial T}{\partial \alpha}$, may be positive or negative depending on the volume of migration as well as on the regime observed (constrained or unconstrained migration).

Hence, given (2.36), (2.38) and (2.39), this familial model of investment in migration provides interesting predictions on the relationship between the amount of remittances received by each remaining household member and the level of his/her pre-transfer income. More precisely, for interior solutions, the model predicts an inverse U-shaped relationship between remittances and family income. To illustrate this, we present numerical simulations, with the following values of the parameters: $\beta = 0.8$, $I^{\min} = 0$, $I^m = 30$, $c = 10$ and $10 < \alpha < 30$. The results are apparent from Figure 3: for $\alpha < 18.7$, migration is constrained and the relationship between the amount of remittances received and the recipient's pre-transfer income is concave; for higher values of α, migration is unconstrained and the relationship between remittances and income is always decreasing. These results are robust to the choice of the values of the parameters (provided that an interior solution for m^* holds).

Such an inverted U-shaped relationship between remittances received and average pre-transfer income, which is the main prediction of our investment model, is confirmed by a number of empirical studies on migration and inequality (see the macroeconomic section below).

As emphasized above, the migration cost to be financed by the family may include physical and informational migration costs as well as education expenditures. With this latter case in mind, Poirine (1997) concluded that if the "loan" element is more important than the "altruistic" and the "insurance" elements, three consequences should

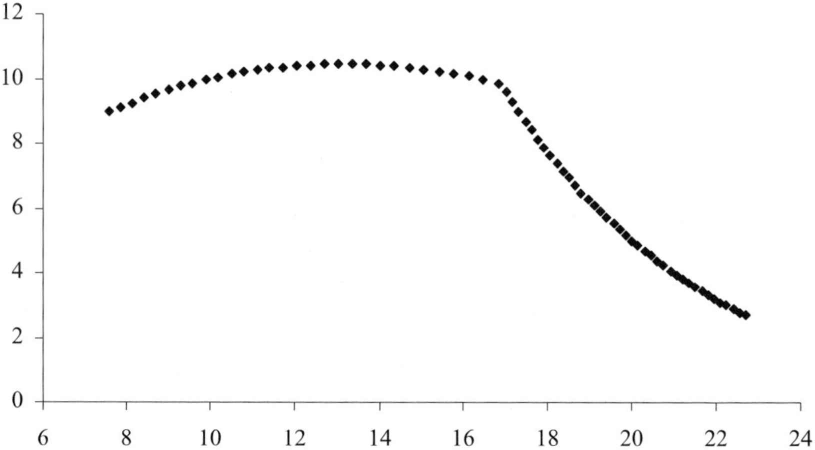

Figure 3. Volume of remittances per remaining household member (y-axis) and average pre-transfer income (x-axis), with $10 < \alpha < 30$.

follow: first, remittances should not be used for capital investment by the receiving family; second, they should be a regular payment, with no tendency to decay over time; and third, their amount should depend on the magnitude of the loan received.

Finally, the "investment" motive may be distinguished from the broader exchange motive with respect to the effects of unemployment on remittances. In our presentation of the exchange motive, we indicated that unemployment at home, in lowering the bargaining power of the recipient, tends to decrease the amount transferred. On the contrary, since education provides at least partly an insurance against unemployment, higher unemployment at home increases the value of education and, therefore, should positively affect the contractual terms for the family and translate into higher remittances (Stark and Bloom, 1985).

2.1.6. Inheritance as an enforcement device

When remittances and compensations occur at different periods of time, there is a strong incentive to deviate from the contractual terms. For example, if remaining households first cover the migrants' migration costs and then expect to receive compensating transfers in the future, how may such an arrangement be enforced?

Two basic mechanisms generally serve as enforcement devices to make family arrangements incentive compatible: punishment, and social norms (however, social norms themselves may be viewed as a trigger of social sanctions, i.e., punishments imposed by society at large). At a family level, the most obvious threat that may be used to secure remittances is the possibility of depriving the migrants of their rights to inheritance and/or return. From an economic perspective, this is reminiscent of the theory of strategic bequest initiated by Bernheim et al. (1985). The central premise of this theory is that parents use bequests to monitor the behavior of their children, allocating bequests among siblings according to their relative attention. Using U.S. data, Bernheim, Shleifer and Summers found supportive evidence of their theory. Hoddinott (1994), Subramanian (1994), and de la Brière et al. (2002) applied a similar approach to the case of developing countries. Instead of developing a formal model, we provide a sketch of the main assumptions and summarize the predictions of these studies.

Following Hoddinott (1994), assume that there is a benchmark, minimal amount of money that each migrant is expected to remit. Hoddinott argues that parents can encourage transfers above this benchmark level by offering a "reward" in the form of land or any other inheritable asset. According to that view, remittances may be seen as a pure strategy of investment in inheritance on the side of the migrant and as an enforcement device to secure remittances on the side of the family. A natural extension of this model would be to allow for multiple migrants competing for inheritance within a given family; from the rent-seeking contests literature,[16] we would expect remittances per migrant to first increase and then decrease with the number of other migrants as the effect of competition is offset by the decrease in one's probability of inheritance. Recently, de la Brière et al. (2002) summarized the main predictions of this inheritance motive (which they called the investment hypothesis) as follows: the amount of remittances increases with (a) the remaining household's assets and income, (b) the probability of inheriting (which depends on the age of the parents, the number of siblings, etc.), (c) the migrant's wealth and income, and decreases with (d) the degree of risk aversion, providing that inheritance is more risky than other available forms of savings.

2.1.7. Mixed motives

Obviously, one should not expect remittances to be driven by a single motive. In reality, a combination of different motives applies, with the exact mixture varying over times and places. In our presentation of the different motives above, we insisted that discriminative tests are not always available. Were they, it would still be quite presumptuous to infer from their results that a particular motive is dominant in explaining remittance behavior. It is not only that different individuals may be heterogeneous in their motivations to remit, but also that different motivations to remit may coexist within the same individual. For example, informal family contracts may contain a loan repayment as well as an insurance contract, the enforcement of which depend on loyalty and trustworthiness, these concepts being somehow related to altruism. Such complex interdependencies have long been recognized in the empirical literature (e.g., Lucas and Stark, 1985) and, more recently, in the theoretical literature. For example, Cox et al. (1998) or Feinerman and Seiler (2002) combine altruism and exchange,[17] Foster and Rosenzweig (2001) combine altruism and mutual insurance, and Docquier and Rapoport (2000) combine

[16] See Nitzan (1994) for a theoretical survey.

[17] Feinerman and Seiler (2002) extend the framework developed by Cox and his co-workers to describe the interaction between an altruistic donor (a parent seeking attention from children) and multiple selfish ben-

altruism and the strategic motive. These approaches have in common that altruism may hide the existence of other underlying motives. For example, altruistic transfers tend to smooth interpersonal consumption levels, thus rendering the need for insurance less urgent; besides, altruistic transfers may also induce counter-gifts in the form of services provided under the rule of reciprocity.

To illustrate this complexity—and the difficulty inherent to the design of appropriate empirical tests—, we give a simple diagrammatic exposition of a situation where altruistic transfers induce a particular "service" in return. More precisely, we show that altruistic remittances bring about a specific by-product consisting in the achievement of positive selection among migrants. We choose this example for its heuristic properties, but the same argument could apply to other types of services. Assume that the conditions required for strategic transfers to be observed apply, and, for simplicity, that the migrant only is altruistic toward the non-migrant. Using our previous notations and a logarithmic utility function (see the previous section on altruism), this means that we have $\beta^m = \gamma^m > 0$, $\beta^h = \gamma^h = 0$, and the migrant's utility is maximal when $\frac{C^h}{C^m} = \frac{\gamma^m}{1-\gamma^m}$. In this setting, it is clear that the altruistic remittance from m to h may be high enough to prevent unskilled workers' migration without having to rely on strategic side-payments. This is the case when the "spontaneous" altruistic transfer is higher than the amount required for positive selection to be obtained. This is illustrated on Figure 4.

As apparent from Figure 4, if both m and h migrate, each agent receives $\frac{1+\pi}{2} I^m - c$. If m alone migrates, total income is increased to $I^m - c + I^h$. The minimal strategic transfer (or side-payment) required to prevent h's migration, T_{str}, is lower than the altruistic remittance that m would choose if migrating alone, T_{alt}. Anticipating this, h would rationally choose not to migrate.

2.1.8. Summary of predictions

Before we discuss the empirical evidence on migrants' remittances, let us first summarize the predictions derived from the different models just exposed. In an attempt to clarify whether a given prediction is distinctive of a particular theory, Table 2 presents the six motives for remittances in the columns, including the four individualistic motives (altruism, exchange, inheritance, and the strategic motive) and two types of familial agreements (on insurance and investment) reviewed so far. For each theory, the table indicates the sign of the marginal effect of nine explanatory variables on the amount of remittances. We restrict the analysis to explanatory variables: (i) for which panel data can reasonably be collected, and (ii) that potentially allow for discriminating between

eficiaries of different types (children for which time devoted to visit parents is more or less costly), with imperfect information on the latter's types. In this context they explore how parental altruism affects selection into the pool of beneficiaries as well as the amounts transferred and the volume of services received. They notably contrast their results to the case of symmetric information and show that under imperfect information, increases in parental altruism towards one given child raises the volume of trade (attention time versus transfers) with that child at the expenses of the other, ceteris paribus.

Table 2
Remittances' sensitivity to various explanatory variables—a summary

Motives	Individual motives				Familial arrangements	
Expl. variables	Altruism	Exchange	Inheritance	Strategic motive	Insurance	Investment
Migrant's income	>0	>0	>0	>0	nde *	>0
Migrant's education	nde	<0 *	nde	>0	nde	>0 *
Time since arrival	≤ 0	nde	nde	≤ 0	nde	nde
Distance from family	≤ 0	nde	<0	nde	nde	>0
Number of migrants/heirs	<0	nde	Inverse U-shape effect	nde	nde	nde
Recipient's long run income	<0	$\gtrless 0$	nde*	<0	nde *	$\gtrless 0$
Adverse short run shocks in recipients' income	>0	$\gtrless 0$ *	nde	>0	>0	>0
Recipient's assets (land, cattle, etc.)	nde	nde	>0 *	nde	nde	nde
Specific predictions	$\frac{\partial T}{\partial I^m} - \frac{\partial T}{\partial I^h} = 1$	It is possible that $\frac{\partial T}{\partial I^h} > 0$	Role of parental assets and number of heirs	(i) $\frac{\partial T}{\partial I^m} - \frac{\partial T}{\partial I^h} > 1$ (ii) $\frac{\partial T}{\partial I^h} = -1$	(i) Irregular basis (ii) No effect of I^h in the long run	Inverse U-shaped effect of I^h

Note: nde = no direct effect (after controlling for migrants' and/or recipients' incomes).
*Specific prediction.

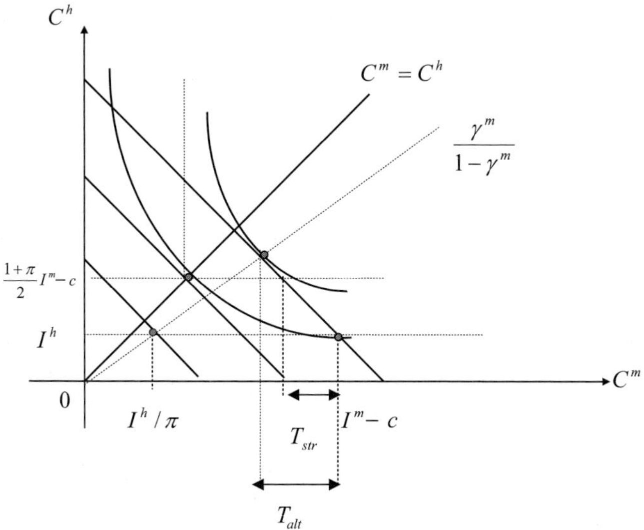

Figure 4. When altruism makes a particular exchange motive irrelevant.

competing theories. The mention "no direct effect" (nde) means that the parameters associated to the corresponding variable are expected to be non-significant, at least if the other relevant controls are introduced. For example, once the migrants' incomes are taken into account, their education level should not play any role under the altruistic hypothesis but is expected to impact negatively on remittances under the exchange hypothesis (as educated migrants have lower propensities to return) and to have a positive impact on remittances under the investment hypothesis. Note also that the last line of the table (as well as the cells marked with a *) signals the predictions that are specific to a particular approach and as such provide a basis for the conception of discriminative tests.

As can be seen from the table, pure altruism can be singled out as a motivation to remit thanks to the specific prediction on the transfer-income derivative. In addition, and assuming that altruism decreases with time and familial distance, the size of remittances should be negatively related to these two variables in the altruistic case. The possibility of a positive impact of recipients' income on transfers is a specific prediction of the exchange motive (although a negative relationship is also compatible with exchange, as we have seen); to a lower extent, a negative effect of education levels could also be seen as supportive evidence of exchange motivations. Under the inheritance hypothesis, the amounts remitted should in principle be independent of the recipients' incomes (once their wealth is introduced) but are expected to be closely related to the probability of receiving inheritance; in turn, this probability depends on the quantity of assets held by the remaining household members as well as on the number of heirs (the sign of the latter variable, however, would seem to be ambiguous: on the one hand, sharing the parental assets with the other heirs should reduce the incentives to remit, but competition among heirs could well stimulate remittances).[18]

The strategic motive may easily be contrasted to altruism as it predicts: (i) a transfer response to changes in pre-transfer incomes higher than one, and (ii) a one-to-one substitution effect of recipients' income; moreover, strategic transfers are likely to come to an end once individuals' productivity is revealed. The insurance mechanism, on the other hand, implies that transfers should not depend on migrants' and recipients' long-run incomes; it may further be contrasted to the inheritance motive in that in the case of insurance, short-run income shocks on the recipient's side are key determinants of remittances, which should be observed on an irregular basis and be correlated with aggregate productivity indicators such as drought indices. Finally, under the investment motive, remittances have a loan repayment component and should therefore be related to the amounts invested by the family in the migrant's education and/or moving costs: remittances are therefore expected to increase with the migrant's education and with geographic distance; in addition, from an exchange-bargaining perspective, the investment motive (and, to some extent, the insurance motive) may give rise to an inverse U-shaped relationship between transfers and recipients' incomes.

Discriminating between these different motives requires collecting panel data on a large number of variables. Such a time-series dimension is required to distinguish between the effects of "permanent" changes in income (typically proxied by a moving average of past and present income levels) and those of short-run income shocks. Moreover, a time-series dimension is obviously necessary to capture the exact timing of transfers; this is critical, in particular, to discriminate between insurance and inheritance, as explained above. The number of variables is also important in its own right. For example, the migrants' education (even if correlated with income) is required to discriminate between the investment motive and all the other motives. Controlling for the recipients' wealth (even if this is clearly correlated with income) is necessary as well, notably to test for the presence of an inheritance motive. As the above discussion makes clear, working with a limited data set makes it impossible to reach any decisive conclusion regarding the underlying motives for remittances.

2.2. Evidence

The theoretical models presented above have highlighted the role of a number of critical variables in explaining remittance behavior: levels of current and expected pre-transfer income of migrants and recipients, income volatility at home and destination, or current and expected levels of unemployment at home and destination. Individual characteristics obviously play a role that cannot be overstated: first of all whether the migrant's

[18] Intuitively, one may expect a non-linear relationship, with the competition effect dominating when the number of heirs is small and the sharing effect becoming dominant when the number of heirs is relatively large.

immediate family is living back in the country of origin, and also the migrant's education and gender,[19] the number of heirs and migrant members within a given household, the assets hold by the remaining household, etc. Other variables (e.g., marital status, gender of the household's head, etc.) may also play a role and will be mentioned in the course of the presentation of the empirical studies.

The main issue addressed in most empirical studies concerns the degree of altruism that may be inferred from the migrants' behavior. Before we detail the results from selected studies on remittances, it may be worth keeping in mind that similar studies on the determinants of private transfers in developed countries have generally rejected the pure altruism hypothesis. Using American data on interpersonal private transfers (and controlling for uncertainty and liquidity constraints, number of siblings, etc.), Altonji et al. (1997) rejected the altruistic hypothesis (at least for transfers between parents and children). They estimated a transfer-income derivative in the 0.04–0.13 range, far from the unitary value predicted by the pure altruism model. This result confirmed their previous findings (Altonji et al., 1992), which showed that the distribution of consumption within the family was dependent on the distribution of income.

The first empirical study to accurately discriminate between various motivations to remit is the important work of Lucas and Stark (1985) on Botswana. In this pioneering study, Lucas and Stark found that remittances rise steadily with the migrants' earnings, which is consistent with a variety of motives, as explained above, including altruism. However, pure altruism would imply that remittances are primarily directed to low-income households, while Lucas and Stark's estimates show a positive relationship between the level of remittances received and households' pre-transfer income. This suggests that exchange, investment and inheritance could play a key role in determining remittance flows.

To discriminate between these different possibilities, Lucas and Stark (1985) first established that remittances rise significantly with the migrant's years of schooling, but more so among the recipient household's "own young" (children, grandchildren, nephews and nieces, as opposed, e.g., to sons and daughters in law), showing that remittances are likely to result from an understanding to repay initial educational investments. When interacted with a dummy for "own young", however, the coefficient on years of schooling turned out to be positive but not highly significant. In addition, as we mentioned earlier, intrahousehold bargaining models could also potentially account for this result. Another direction was then explored to control for inheritable assets. Botswana's inheritance customs and laws are quite diverse, but sons are roughly more likely to inherit than daughters or other household members. Since most agricultural lands are common property, cattle are the dominant form of inheritable wealth. The authors thus added a dummy variable for whether the household holds a cattle herd larger

[19] Recall that we indicated that daughters are often thought to be more trustworthy and caring than sons. This seems to be a rational belief since a number of studies (e.g., Lucas and Stark, 1985, for Botswana, and Kaufmann and Lindauer, 1986, for El Salvador) show a positive relationship between remittances and female status.

than 20 beasts. The results showed that indeed, sons remit more to families with larger herds while the associated coefficient is weakly negative for daughters and their spouses. Hence, sons behave significantly differently from daughters and other relatives in that they remit more to households with large herds, which is consistent with a strategy to secure inheritance. However, it is also common for sons to keep their cattle with those of the household, so it may also be that, along the lines suggested by the "exchange" hypothesis, remittances compensate the recipients for maintaining and expanding the sons' own cattle.

In short, the three potential explanations for the positive relation between remittances and the household's income were all shown to be consistent with the evidence from Botswana. This is not sufficient, however, to disqualify an altruistic-based rationale for remittances. From a dynamic perspective indeed, this pattern of remittances may be reconciled with altruism if, for example, past remittances sent with an altruistic intent have contributed to raise today's income. Testing for such possibilities would require longitudinal data that were not available to Lucas and Stark.

Lucas and Stark also tested for the insurance hypothesis, which implies that remittances should increase during bad economic times in the rural sector and be directed to households who possess assets with volatile returns. The context of Botswana, situated in a semi-arid tropical region, and the time span covered by the data, allowed for such an inquiry since 1978–79 was a drought year whose severity varied across villages. For each village sampled, the severity of drought was indexed and included in the remittance equation both separately and interacted with (the logarithm of) two familial assets, namely agricultural land and cattle owned. When omitting the interaction terms, the coefficient on the drought index alone proved significantly positive, a finding that could be interpreted as suggestive of either altruism or insurance. Yet, with interactions terms included, existence of drought conditions or possession of more drought-sensitive assets did not stimulate greater remittances per se, but the interactions of drought with these drought-sensitive assets did. This is consistent with rural households sending members to the city for the prospect of insurance.

The work of Lucas and Stark (1985) has generated further empirical work on remittances in different contexts. In particular, positive relationships between transfer amounts and recipients' incomes have repeatedly been uncovered in developing countries, notably by Donald Cox and his co-workers (Cox, 1987; Cox and Rank, 1992, Cox et al., 1998). The latter study was dedicated to the analysis of private transfers in Peru, which consist for the most part of remittances. As distinct from Lucas and Stark (1985), whose study encompassed a number of possible motivations, Cox et al. (1998) concentrated on altruism versus exchange and tested the effect of recipient households' pre-transfer incomes on the size and probability of remittances. Recall that a negative sign is consistent both with altruism and exchange, but a positive sign is in principle incompatible with altruism and consistent with exchange. More precisely, the type of exchange envisioned in their study is a loan repayment of educational investments. This implies that liquidity constraints matter, and that the non-market implicit interest rate reflected in remittances depends on the sides' respective bargaining power.

Cox et al. (1998) tested these two motives for both ascending (from children to parents) and descending (from parents to children) private transfers in Peru in the mid-1980s, and controlled for social security benefits, gender, marital status, household size, home ownership, education, and for whether transfers were transitory or permanent. Analyzing the timing of transfers, they established that transfer receipts and earnings move in opposite directions over the life-cycle (i.e., net recipients are either very young or very old), suggesting that liquidity constraints indeed matter. Probit results for transfers from child-to-parent (which consist mostly of remittances) indicate that the probability of transfer is inversely related to parental income, a finding which is consistent with both altruism and exchange. But the effect of income on the amount transferred, conditional on receiving a transfer, is first positive, then negative (i.e., inverse-U shaped), as suggested by the bargaining-exchange hypothesis. The same pattern applies to parent-to-child transfers, leading the authors to conclude that the bargaining-cum-altruism framework appears more powerful than the strong form of the altruistic model. Besides, Cox et al. (1998) also found that private transfers are targeted toward the unemployed and the sick, a finding consistent with both altruism and insurance; however, public pension transfers and private transfers from children to parents are shown to be complements instead of substitutes, a finding which makes sense in a bargaining framework but is incompatible with altruism. In contrast, Jensen (2003) finds evidence that public pensions crowd out private transfers in South Africa, but only partially (by about a quarter to a third).

The "loan repayment" or "investment" theory is also supported by the study of Ilahi and Jafarey (1999) on Pakistan, with an emphasis on loans aimed at financing international migration costs rather than education. Their argument is that international migration costs are quite substantial and above the financial possibilities of the migrants' close family, requiring financing from larger kinship networks (the extended family). And indeed, retrospective surveys of return migrants in Pakistan show that 58% of them borrowed from relatives to finance the initial costs of their migration, with loans from relatives financing half of the migration expenses (4/5 for those migrants who did rely on relatives from the extended family). However, the loan repayment hypothesis cannot be tested directly since the data on remittances between migrants and households other than their immediate family are generally not available from existing surveys. To circumvent this difficulty, Ilahi and Jafarey (1999) propose an indirect method for tracing such remittance flows, the main testable implication of their model being that remittances to the immediate family and retained savings overseas should fall with the size of the loan received from extended relatives. Using data from Pakistan, they find support for this hypothesis, implying that the initial loan from relatives calls for subsequent repayment. Their econometric tests also reveal the existence of an upper threshold in pre-migration borrowing.

A number of empirical studies have also focused on inheritance as an enforcement device in securing remittances. Hoddinott (1994) provides strong evidence supporting this theory using data from Western Kenya. Hoddinott estimated a remittance function after controlling for two sources of selection bias: (i) the fact that migrants are a non-random group, and, (ii) the fact that remittance behavior depends on the parents' information about migrants' earnings abroad (since migrants with uninformed parents would tend to remit less). Both sources of selectivity-bias were controlled for, using an extension of the Heckman procedure. An interesting implication of this approach is that since rich families only may secure remittances through inheritance, migration tends to increase inter-household inequality.[20] A limit to this approach may be the fact that many resources are collectively-owned in the rural communities rather than family-owned, thus limiting the scope for inheritance-seeking through remittances; however, Osili (2004) finds that the same behavior seems to apply at a community level, with migrants investing more in wealthier communities so as to secure their membership rights.

It has already been mentioned that evidence of an insurance mechanism was found in contexts as different as Botswana (Lucas and Stark, 1985) or Peru (Cox et al., 1998). Similar results were found for West African countries, notably by Lambert (1994) in the case of Cote d'Ivoire and by Gubert (2002) for Western Mali. The first study showed that risk-aversion positively influences migration, and the second study showed that remittances were instrumental in providing insurance to the remaining household members, but in a way that depends on the nature of the shock (e.g., climatic change, sickness of a household member, etc.). In contrast, Agarwal and Horowitz (2002) found a negative effect of the number of migrants on remittances sent to Guyana; building on their argument on multiple-migrant households, they took this finding as supportive evidence of altruism instead of insurance.

The study by de la Brière et al. (2002) explores whether remittances to a poor rural region of the Dominican Republic are better explained by reference to insurance or inheritance, two motives for remittances that are not exclusive one of the other. Their data reveal that remittances should be treated as censored data (remittances in small amounts are frequently observed) and that more than 75 percent of households with migrants have more than one migrant. Four alternative estimation procedures are compared: OLS, a random-effect model (to account for the clustering effect of the presence of a sibling from the same household), a standard tobit, and a censored remittance model. They show that the relative importance of each motive is affected by the migrant's destination (U.S. or Dominican cities), the migrant's gender, and the composition of the receiving household. Interestingly, insurance appears as the main motivation to remit for female migrants who emigrated to the U.S.; the same result holds true for males, but only when they are the sole migrant member of the household and when parents are subject to health shocks. Investment in inheritance, on the other hand, seems to be gender neutral and only concerns migrants to the U.S.

As already explained, the enforcement constraint generally limits the degree of insurance (or whatever is looked for) that may be attained through implicit migration contracts; this, in turn, often implies a sub-optimal migration rate. Obviously, altruism

[20] This is consistent (but differently motivated) with the prediction of our investment model; see infra, section 3.2, for discussions on migration and inequality.

tends to mitigate such inefficient outcomes in that it decreases the cost of enforcement, thereby expanding income-pooling opportunities. This was recently confirmed by Foster and Rosenzweig (2001), who first proposed a theoretical model of risk sharing under imperfect commitment, and then estimated linear approximations of transfer functions using three panel data sets from different rural regions of South Asia. Their results show that, when remittances play an insurance role but do not allow for full insurance due to informational barriers (which give rise to commitment problems), the amounts transferred depend both on contemporary income shocks and on the history of previous transfers (which themselves arose in that same context of impossibility for the members to commit to make first-best state-contingent transfers). On the whole, they demonstrated that altruism reduces but does not eliminate the commitment constraint.

Another potential problem related to asymmetric information raised in the theoretical section concerns the possibility of moral hazard on the recipients' side. Using panel survey data on migration, production and income of Soninke households from the Kayes region in Western Mali, Azam and Gubert (2005) tested the effect of familial insurance on the domestic productivity of remaining households, after controlling for other determinants such as the number of remaining individuals, their skills, the type of domestic activity, the size of the cultivated plot, ethnic affiliation, etc. They first constructed a measure of total household productivity by estimating a plot level production function with household-specific fixed effects, and then used this measure to test how productivity is affected by the ratio of the number of migrants to the total number of family members (a ratio interpreted as an indicator of the reliability of the migration-based insurance mechanism). Their results show that recipients' productivity is lower for the ethnic group for which migration is an old tradition and a relatively widespread phenomenon (i.e., for which transfers prospects are the highest), a finding that would seem to provide evidence of opportunistic behavior (moral hazard) on the recipients' side. This is by contrast to Cox et al. (1998), who found no such evidence in the case of Peru (i.e., private transfers have no impact on labor-supply decisions) or to Joulfaian and Wihelm (1994) who found no significant impact of inheritance prospects on labor-supply incentives in the U.S.

A neglected aspect in this review of the evidence concerns the "social determinants" of remittance behavior. Obviously, most studies control for individual characteristics of both migrants and receiving households, but tend to disregard the social context in which remittances take place. Community characteristics are generally absent from remittance regression analysis, except in very specific cases (e.g., when data on rainfalls or other climate variables at the village level are used to account for the volatility of individual incomes). Two examples will serve as a demonstration of the potential benefits from broadening the analysis to include social determinants of remittances. The first example is from the above-cited study by Azam and Gubert (2005) on the Kayes region in Western Mali. According to Azam and Gubert (2005), it is the fact that the migrants internalize the effect of their transfers on the social prestige of their clan that renders the implicit insurance contract enforceable.

The second example is borrowed from Massey and Basem (1992), who used data from four Mexican communities to study the determinants of savings, remittances and spending patterns among Mexican migrants. The intriguing result was that dummy variables for community membership explained a large share of the variance in the propensity to repatriate and invest foreign earnings. In the words of Durand et al. (1996, p. 250), who commented on this study, "whatever factors governed migrants' decisions, they operated at the community level, but with only four communities, the investigators could not say what these factors were." This challenging question has been partly answered by Durand et al. (1996) for the "spending" side (see section 3.3.3 below); however, it is clear that further research is required on the social determinants of remittances, possibly in connection with the social networks literature.

On the whole, the evidence from micro surveys confirms that patterns of remittances are better explained as familial inter-temporal contracts than as a result of altruism or other purely individualistic considerations. This is not to deny the importance of individualistic motives, however, since altruism, intentions to return, and prospects for inheritance explain why implicit migration contracts emerge mainly if not exclusively within a familial context.

3. The macroeconomics of remittances

Before we begin the analysis of the macroeconomic impact of migrants' remittances, a terminological disclaimer may be required. In the microeconomic section, remittances were defined as an interpersonal transfer between the migrant and his or her relatives in the home country. Accordingly, we did not include temporary migration—understood as a strategy aimed at accumulating enough savings abroad to start an investment project upon return at home—among the different motivations to remit reviewed in that section. At a macro level, however, there are only minor differences between remittances *stricto sensu* and repatriated savings upon return.[21] The money saved abroad may be either sent regularly to relatives, deposed on a saving account at home, or repatriated upon return, depending on a host of personal circumstances and on existing financial infrastructures in the home country.[22] But from a macroeconomic perspective, the relevant questions are: How much income earned abroad is repatriated to the home country? What kind of households (belonging to what segments of the income distribution) are the most affected? And, are the amounts repatriated used for investment or consumption? On all these aspects, there is no difference in essence between remittances and repatriated

[21] Moreover, the two are generally mixed together in international statistics.

[22] For example, in the case of Mexico, Durand et al. (1996, p. 259) note that "sending monthly remittances to Mexico and returning home with savings are interrelated behaviors and represent different ways of accomplishing the same thing: repatriating earnings from the United States". They also report that migrants are more likely to remit when they are married, and more likely to return with savings if they come from communities with good road connections to the highways, and in periods of high inflation.

savings; in the following, therefore, we use the term "remittances" as a generic label for both.

This section is divided between the short-run and the long-run effects of remittances on migrants' home economies. While the short-run effects (e.g., on activity and price levels, trade and relative prices, etc.) were the main focus of macroeconomic research on remittances until the end of the 1980s, the emergence of new growth theories has since then given rise to an important body of research on the growths effects of remittances, notably through their impact on economic inequality and on other outcomes of interest (such as children's human capital) that affect origin countries growth prospects. However, since migration is likely to impact on inequality and human capital formation through channels other than remittances and that most determinants of remittances are also determinants of migration, there is a growing tendency for empirical studies to investigate the overall impact of migration instead of just looking at remittances (see McKenzie, 2005).

3.1. Short-run approaches

Using static demand-oriented models with sticky prices and wages, traditional short-run macroeconomics have focused on the effect of international transfers on the aggregate expenditure and the national output. Alongside this standard approach, an important trade-theoretic literature on remittances has developed during the 1980s; based on two-sector (traded and non-traded goods) general equilibrium models, this strand of the literature concentrates on the impact of remittances on relative prices and welfare.

3.1.1. The standard macroeconomic view

When remittances constitute a significant source of foreign exchange, they may clearly affect the equilibrium level of the gross national product and other macroeconomic variables. The pure Keynesian model is the oldest model that tries to capture the short-run macroeconomic impact of international transfers. Under the assumptions of sticky prices, fixed exchange and interest rates, and in the absence of supply constraints, this model shows that any shock on the demand side has a disproportionate effect on the national output. Obviously, the magnitude of this impact depends on the Keynesian multiplier (which, itself, depends on several parameters such as the marginal propensity to import), and on the size of the transfer shock (which itself depends on the amounts received and on the recipients' marginal propensity to consume remittances). As is well known from the works of Modigliani or Friedman, the propensity to consume must be related to the agents' expectations regarding future income streams (including remittances).

Based on this rationale, Glytsos (2002) proposed a very simple macro-econometric estimation of the aggregate effect of remittances for seven Mediterranean countries.[23]

[23] The results must be taken with extreme caution given the non-stationarity of some time-series.

Using data for 1969–93, he shows that the impact of remittances on consumption, investment, imports, and output varies over time and across countries. For Egypt and Jordan, remittances have a strong influence on output, while evidence of a moderate impact is found for the other countries. In a similar vein, using annual data on Egypt for 1967–91, El-Sakka nad McNabb (1999) found that imports financed through remittances have a very high income elasticity, implying that remittances may have low multiplying effects. This is by contrast to Adelman and Taylor (1992), who developed a "Social Accounting Multiplier" matrix to account for the direct and indirect changes in income stemming from remittances to Mexico in the late 1980s. They estimated that each dollar of remittances increased output by a multiplier of 3 when successive rounds of indirect effects were taken into account; this seems quite high indeed, and subject to methodological qualifications clearly exposed in their paper.

An alternative framework for analyzing the short-run economy-wide consequences of remittances is the Mundel–Flemming model of an open economy with fixed prices and a single composite good. In this framework, the effect of international transfers on GDP depends on the assumptions made about the degree of capital mobility and the exchange-rate regime. Let us consider the case of perfect capital mobility: in a pure flexible exchange-rate regime, the equilibrium level of GDP is fully determined on the money market and, hence, is unaffected by international transfers. A rise in the aggregate amount of remittances may stimulate the national expenditure, but this effect is fully compensated by a currency appreciation. Indeed, the purpose of the flexible exchange rate regime is to protect countries against real shocks. In a pure fixed exchange-rate regime, on the other hand, the equilibrium of the balance of payments is obtained through variations in the money supply. It is only in this case that a rise in the aggregate amount of remittances may induce an increase of the national income. The Mundel–Flemming model, therefore, provides a very simple framework to account for the complex interactions between the balance of payments constraints and short-run macroeconomic shocks. The overall effect of any demand shock (e.g., a shock induced by remittances) depends on the degree of capital mobility and on the exchange-rate regime.

Modern short-run macroeconomics, however, are based on a systematic exploration of the endogenous determination of wages and prices, a process in which expectations play a critical role. If expenditure shocks (e.g., induced by international remittances) are perfectly expected by wage-setters, the effect on the level of activity would then depend on the extent to which wages and prices are flexible. If prices are fully flexible, there should be no effect on output (in such a setting, only unexpected shocks may generate departures from the natural output level). If prices or wages adjustments are sluggish, however, temporary real effects could be obtained.

To the best of our knowledge, there is no study on the short-run effects of remittances applying the most recent econometric techniques to these modern macroeconomic approaches. Although this could in principle be a useful step, the reason why it has not been attempted so far may be due to the limits inherent to the context of developing countries. A first limit is that the tools of non-stationary econometrics require the construction of long time-series for each macroeconomic variable, and this is generally beyond the statistical coverage of most developing countries. A second limit, in the same spirit, is that this also requires time-series data for the "remittances" account of the balance of payments, a variable which is very difficult to measure given the variety of legal and illegal transmission channels.[24] A third limit is intrinsic to the economic structure of developing countries; since standard macroeconomic models generally abstract from the informal sector, the degree of financial development, and other institutional (e.g., political instability, ethnic divisions) factors, they are likely to offer a very biased description of developing countries. In any event, their application should be restricted to the analysis of countries at intermediate stages of development and for which the statistical apparatus is sufficiently developed (e.g., Turkey, or Mexico).

3.1.2. Trade, relative prices and welfare

Assuming perfect price flexibility and full employment, international trade theory has been applied to the analysis of the impact of international transfers on relative prices and trade flows. The historical controversy on the "German transfer problem" is a well-known paradox in international trade theory. Its essence is that a positive transfer may deteriorate the terms of trade of the receiving country when transfers are mostly spent on imports; a possibility of impoverishing transfers then emerges if the terms-of-trade effect dominates the positive income effect. This is similar (but differently motivated) to the "Dutch disease" syndrome, as presented for example in Corden and Neary (1982) or Corden (1984). Nevertheless, it has been shown that the conditions required for impoverishing transfers to materialize are extremely restrictive (Bhagwati et al., 1983) so that, on the whole, the idea that international transfers benefit to the receiving countries remains largely accepted.

For the most part, the trade-theoretic literature on international transfers is based on models with homogenous agents. However, it is clear that the welfare effects of international remittances critically depend on the identity of the recipients. Consider, therefore, a small open economy with two factors of production (capital and labor) that are perfectly mobile between two sectors for traded (T) and non-traded goods (N). Agents have identical homothetic preferences. Without remittances, Rivera-Batiz (1982) has shown that emigration adversely affects the welfare of the remaining residents when the economy's capital-labor ratio changes. This is due to the fact that emigration deprives the remaining residents from the opportunity to trade with the migrants in the market for non-traded goods. Introducing heterogeneity in the form of two types of agents characterized by different capital endowments into a similar two-sector model, Quibria (1997) showed that emigration does not affect all categories of residents symmetrically. More precisely, there are winners and losers, with the total welfare effect depending on the particular social welfare function adopted. However, Quibria (1997) argues that emigration is always welfare-improving (irrespective of the welfare criteria adopted) if it is

[24] See the discussion on this point in the introduction.

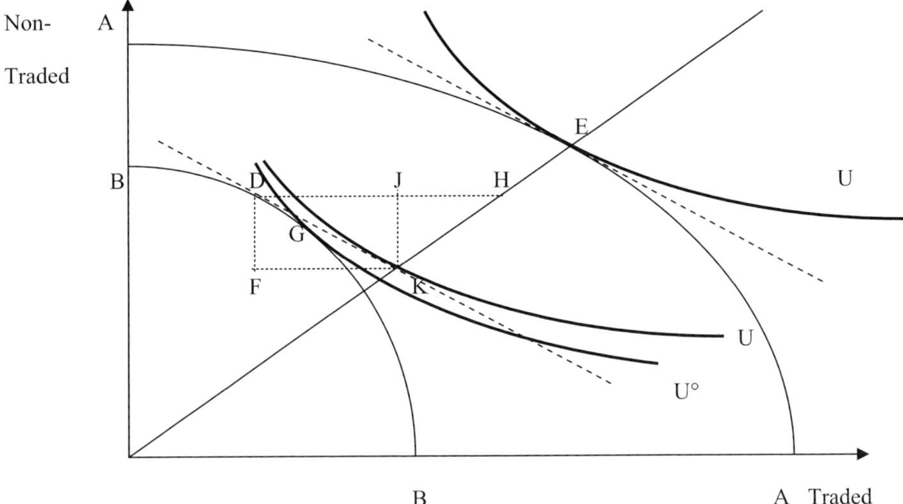

Figure 5. Remittances and welfare in a static trade model.

accompanied by enough remittances. The division between losers and winners depends on the volume of remittances, the type of migration (who emigrates, i.e., with how much capital?), and the distribution of factor endowments. The latter variable helps explaining the conflicting attitude of workers (emigration raises real wages) and capitalists (emigration reduces the return to capital) toward emigration.

The distinction between losers and winners is also central in the analysis of Djajic (1986). If migrants remit a fraction of their income to the source country, obviously, one has to distinguish between two distinct groups, those who receive the transfers (the related remaining residents—RRR) and those who do not (the unrelated remaining residents—URR), the intuition being that RRR should be better off while URR should be worse off. In fact, what Djajic (1986) demonstrates is that even the URR may benefit from their countrymen's emigration if the flow of remittances is sufficiently large. This case is obtained when the size of the transfer gives rise to an excess demand for non-traded goods by the RRR. This pushes the relative price of non-traded goods upwards and stimulates the purchasing power of the URR.

The diagrammatic representation of this model is given in Figure 5, in which we consider the case where Unrelated-Remaining-Residents are net suppliers of non-traded goods. Let AA be the production-possibilities frontier before migration occurs. Given the preferences of domestic agents, the pre-migration equilibrium for this economy is, say, at point E, the point of tangency between AA and a social indifference curve U. Assume now that the frontier moves to BB as migrants are leaving the country. At constant prices, the new production solution would be D while the optimal consumption bundle would be K, keeping consumption (and, thus, utility) constant for the remaining residents. Clearly, K is not an equilibrium since it is characterized by an excess demand for traded goods (remaining residents want to sell DF units of non-traded goods against FK units of traded goods). The relative price of non-traded goods therefore decreases, as does the welfare of the remaining residents (for example, G may be the new equilibrium).

What happens if migrants send back remittances? Suppose that DH units of traded goods are remitted to the RRRs. At constant prices, this allows them to consume traded and non-traded goods in the pre-migration proportion by exchanging DJ units of traded goods against JK units of non-traded goods with the URRs. This can be achieved at the pre-migration price-system and gives the optimal bundle K: if the flow of remittances is exactly DH, therefore, both the structure of relative prices and the utility level of remaining residents are kept constant. A larger transfer would increase the relative price of non-traded goods, thus leading to an improvement of the URRs' utility (since the latter are net suppliers of non-traded goods). In this configuration, the URRs experience a positive price effect while the RRRs experience a positive income effect and a negative price effect; since the former is likely to dominate the latter, migration and subsequent remittances altogether are Pareto-improving. Alternatively, a smaller transfer would reduce the price of non-traded goods and decrease the welfare of the URRs. This shows that, on the whole, the net effect of migration on the welfare of remaining residents depends on the size of remittances.

The main criticism that could be addressed to this strand of the literature is that remittances are analyzed for a given level of migration, treated as exogenous. In an attempt to analyze the welfare consequences of remittances and the determinants of international migration (and unemployment) in a unified framework, McCormick and Wahba (2000) recently proposed a model where migration and remittances are jointly determined. They show that for certain values of the parameters, the model exhibits multiple equilibria corresponding to different levels of emigration and associated remittances. Interestingly, the high-migration equilibrium Pareto dominates the low-migration equilibrium, showing that both the URRs and the RRRs may be better off with higher migration rates if lump-sum transfers between residents are available.

3.2. *The long-run view*

It has long been recognized that remittances affect the long-run performance of receiving economies in a way that depends on whether remittances are used for consumption or investment. This issue was central in the controversy on the effects of migration on development during the 1970s; for example, Böhning (1975) or Rempel and Lobdell (1978) explained that, for the most part, remittances were financing consumption and housing expenditures, with limited dynamic effects. At the same time, most socioeconomic studies presented a strongly negative view of remittances; it was argued that remittances were used for conspicuous consumption, thus increasing frustration and resentment among non-migrants; furthermore, remittances were allegedly discouraging labor-supply and effort on the side of the recipients, thus increasing dependency and delaying rural development and change. By contrast, Griffin (1976) or Stark (1978) tried to promote a more optimistic view of remittances, explaining that their negative effects were often unclear or exaggerated and that in fact remittances were often financing productive investments, especially in the rural sector. As Stark (1991, chapter 14) rightly explained, the additional income from remittances is fungible and investments may well increase even if the actual cash remitted is not invested; moreover, in providing coinsurance to household members, migration in and of itself may allow some households to engage in risky activities (e.g., increased investments in production, adoption of new technologies) with no need for remittances to occur.

About a decade later, during the 1980s, the core of the debate on the growth effects of remittances shifted from productivity to inequality (Stark et al., 1986; Taylor and Wyatt, 1996). These studies emphasized that remittances actually reduced economic inequality in the origin communities and contributed to alleviate liquidity constraints, thus promoting investments in new agricultural techniques, education, and further migration. However, despite this considerable evidence (detailed in the next section) and the strong emphasis put by new growth theories on the interplay between inequality and growth, it is only very recently that the long-run impact of remittances has been reformulated in an endogenous growth framework. In this section, we adopt the view that the growth effects of remittances cannot be dissociated from their distributive effects. We first present two simple models where remittances encourage investment in physical and human capital and may therefore modify the long-run steady-state of the domestic economy. We then present a dynamic extension of the investment model of section 2.1.5 to discuss the impact of remittances on inequality more broadly.

3.2.1. Liquidity constraint 1: entrepreneurship[25]

Following Mesnard (2001), we extend Banerjee and Newman (1993) for migration, and adopt the simplified model and notations of Ray (1998, chapter 7). More precisely, we extend Ray's model of occupational choice, inequality and growth to the case where, in addition to existing domestic occupations, individuals may also choose to migrate to a high-wage destination. This migration possibility is subject to a liquidity-constraint, as is the case for accessing to entrepreneurship. In addition to the introduction of a migration possibility, the main departure from Ray (1998) is that we assume the collateral required for accessing to credit markets to be exogenously given (instead of depending on domestic wages). The model is basically a simplification of Mesnard (2001): as distinct from her model, we assume only one type of domestic firms (instead of the individual and corporate types), and the entrepreneurial activity is assumed to involve no risk; with these understandings, we obtain the same qualitative results, but in a much simpler model. We first present the benchmark model based on Ray (1998); the model is then extended to allow for possible migrations and we explore the conditions under which, starting from an initial underdevelopment trap, migration and subsequent remittances allow for a shift towards the efficient long-run equilibrium.

[25] This section is based on Rapoport (2002).

3.2.1.1. The closed economy benchmark case Consider an economy consisting of a continuum of one-period lived individuals distributed over a continuum of wealth, Ω. The distribution of wealth is denoted by $G(\Omega)$, and the size of the population is normalized to unity. Agents may work in the subsistence sector (in this case they receive a fixed minimal wage, $\underline{w}$) or work as salaried workers in the industrial sector (in this case they receive a wage w, endogenously determined on the domestic labor market), or become entrepreneur. Becoming an entrepreneur implies incurring a start-up cost I to be repaid with interest r at the end of the period; production requires hiring a given number of workers, m, whose total output value is given by q. Profits, therefore, depend only on domestic wages, w, and on the parameters I, q, m, and r:

$$\pi = q - mw - I(1+r). \tag{3.1}$$

A central assumption is that for most individuals, the initial wealth inherited from the previous generation is lower than the start-up cost required for becoming an entrepreneur. Consequently, most individuals (without loss of generality, we assume this is the case for all individuals) must rely on the credit market to finance their entrepreneurial projects. To prevent default in repayment, however, loan contracts stipulate the wealth threshold to be put as collateral before the loan is transferred. This means that individuals with insufficient wealth to be put as collateral cannot access to credit markets and, thus, to entrepreneurship. To determine the critical collateral, one has to compare the amount to be repaid (and gained in case of default), $I(1+r)$, to the cost of defaulting, which includes the value of the lost collateral, $\Omega(1+r)$, and the expected value of a legal or social sanction, *E(S)*. Therefore, credit suppliers know that borrowers would honor the loan repayment if:

$$\Omega > I - \frac{E(S)}{1+r} \equiv \Omega^*. \tag{3.2}$$

This condition determines the critical wealth threshold below which individuals have no access to entrepreneurship.

The dynamics of this model is extremely simple. Suppose that, at the end of his life, each agent gives birth to one child, bequeaths a fraction b and consumes a fraction $1-b$ of his life-time income, $\Omega(1+r)+y$, where y denotes the income earned over the period. The dynamics of wealth within a given dynasty is then governed by:

$$\Omega_{+1} = b[\Omega(1+r)+y], \tag{3.3}$$

where $b < (1+r)^{-1}$ may be interpreted as the prevailing degree of intergenerational altruism. This latter assumption ensures that individual wealth converges toward a long-run steady-state:

$$\Omega^{ss} = \frac{by}{1-b(1+r)}. \tag{3.4}$$

The endogenous determination of wages is a central element in this model. When the economy is closed to migration, the labor demand is given by:

$$LD = \begin{cases} [1 - G(\Omega^*)]m & \text{if } w < \bar{w} \\ 0 & \text{if } w \geq \bar{w} \end{cases}, \tag{3.5}$$

with $\bar{w} \equiv \frac{q-I}{1+m}$, the wage rate such that individuals are indifferent between being an entrepreneur or a salaried worker. For any higher rate indeed, the number of entrepreneurs and, therefore, the demand for labor, would fall to zero, while for any lower rate, the demand for labor is proportional to the number of entrepreneurs, which depends on the distribution of wealth.

As to the labor supply, it is positive only when the equilibrium wage rate is higher than, or equal to, the subsistence wage, $\underline{w}$, and is determined by the proportion of agents having no access to credit markets when w lies between $\underline{w}$ and $\bar{w}$. Finally, when w is higher than $\bar{w}$, everybody wants to be a salaried worker. This gives:

$$LS = \begin{cases} 0 & \text{if } w < \underline{w} \\ G(\Omega^*) & \text{if } \underline{w} \leq w < \bar{w} \\ 1 & \text{if } w \geq \bar{w}. \end{cases} \tag{3.6}$$

As apparent from Figure 6,[26] there are two possible labor-market equilibria. An efficient equilibrium obtains if the degree of prevailing inequality is relatively limited. In this case, the proportion of agents without access to entrepreneurship is sufficiently low so that $G(\Omega^*) < \lfloor 1 - G(\Omega^*) \rfloor m$, implying that the equilibrium wage rate is $\bar{w}$ and the economy is in an efficient state (Figure 6). A second possible equilibrium emerges when the initial distribution of wealth is characterized by a high degree of inequality. In this case, the proportion of constrained agents is high, so that $G(\Omega^*) > \lfloor 1 - G(\Omega^*) \rfloor m$. The equilibrium wage rate is then equal to the subsistence wage, $\underline{w}$, and the economy is in an inefficient state (Figure 6).

The initial distribution of wealth fully determines the type of equilibrium observed in the short-run. In the long run, the initial distribution of wealth matters only if social mobility is limited: notably, a poor (inefficient) economy will be stuck in a poverty trap if the following condition holds:

$$b\lfloor \Omega^*(1+r) + \underline{w} \rfloor < \Omega^* < b\lfloor \Omega^*(1+r) + q - \underline{w}l - I(1+r) \rfloor. \tag{3.7}$$

3.2.1.2. The effects of migration and remittances Consider now a poor economy for which condition (3.7) holds, but where individuals face a possibility of emigration to a high-wage destination at a fixed cost c. Assuming that wages at destination are unaffected by immigration, without loss of generality, the foreign wage is set at $\bar{w}$, with $\bar{w} - c > \underline{w}$. Since the migration cost has to be incurred at the beginning of the period, candidates to emigration are subject to a liquidity constraint, $\Omega > c$. If c is higher than

[26] For diagrammatic convenience, we assume in Figure 6. that $m = 1$.

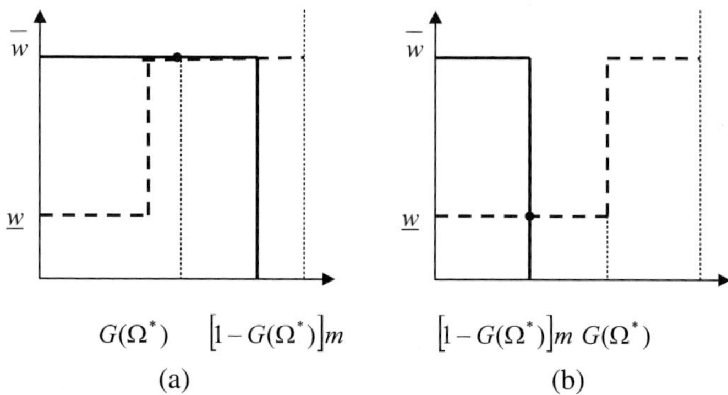

Figure 6. The labor market equilibrium. (a): The efficient equilibrium. (b): The inefficient equilibrium.

Ω^*, emigration is not a relevant option since an individual of wealth Ω^* would choose to become an entrepreneur in the home country rather than emigrate. If c is lower than Ω^*, however, some workers would opt for emigration and subsequently transfer a given fraction, b, of their foreign income (net of migration cost). A first and immediate (although not interesting) effect of emigration, therefore, consists in a reduction of the labor supply, which becomes $G(c)$; we neglect this first effect, which is likely to be minute, and concentrate on the more realistic (and more interesting) case where emigration has no direct impact on labor-market outcomes but, rather, an indirect impact through migrants' intergenerational transfers. To evaluate their dynamic effects, three cases have to be distinguished, depending on the extent of social mobility generated by remittances:

- If $b\lfloor\Omega^*(1+r)+\bar{w}-c\rfloor < \Omega^*$, there is no mobility since intergenerational transfers have no dynamic effects; the steady-state wealth of a migrant's offspring remains below the critical threshold required for accessing to entrepreneurship;
- If $b\lfloor\Omega^*(1+r)+\bar{w}-c\rfloor > \Omega^*$ and $b[c(1+r)+\underline{w}] > c$, there is full mobility in that migrants' descendents gain access to entrepreneurship and domestic workers' descendents gain access to migration and ultimately, to entrepreneurship. The economy then converges to the efficient solution. However, the same efficient outcome may be obtained with less intergenerational mobility; more precisely:
- If $b\lfloor\Omega^*(1+r)+\bar{w}-c\rfloor > \Omega^*$ and $b[c(1+r)+\underline{w}] < c$, there is partial mobility in that migrants' descendents progressively become entrepreneurs while domestic workers' descendents remain in their origin condition. This is the case apparent on Figure 7, which depicts the dynamics of wealth within dynasties in the case of partial mobility.

In this configuration, remittances induce a change in the long-run equilibrium of the economy providing that an excess demand of labor appears at the wage rate $\underline{w}$. Formally, this is realized if $G(c) < [1-G(c)]m$. In this case, the economy converges to its long-run efficient equilibrium, and emigration eventually comes to an end.

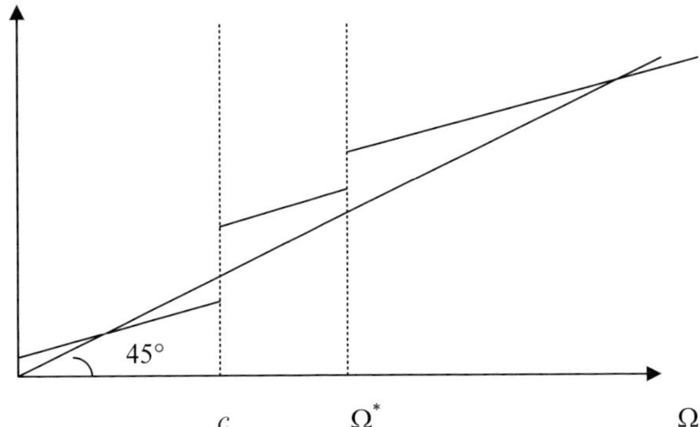

Figure 7. The dynamics of wealth within dynasties.

3.2.2. Liquidity constraint 2: human capital

Assume now that human capital is the engine of growth, and that liquidity constraints impinge on human capital formation. In the same spirit as above, we explore how international remittances may modify the long-run steady-state of a developing economy initially stuck in a poverty trap. We consider an economy where individuals live for two periods. In the first period, they earn a minimal wage (w_m), receive a transfer (T) from the previous generation, and have the possibility to participate in an education program at a given cost normalized to unity. As in Perotti (1993), the decision to invest in education, e, is taken subject to a liquidity constraint: savings cannot be negative at the end of the period. This gives:

$$e = \begin{cases} 1 & \text{if } T \geq 1 - w_m \\ 0 & \text{if } T < 1 - w_m. \end{cases} \tag{3.8}$$

The parental transfer fully determines the educational investment. The initial distribution of transfers is denoted by *F(T)*.[27] In the second period, income is endogenous and given by $w_{+1}(1 + Re)$, where w_{+1} is the wage rate at time $t + 1$ and R is the return to education. As is commonly assumed in this literature, we assume a threshold intragenerational externality such that the wage rate depends on the proportion of educated workers in the home country. Denoting that critical proportion by $\tilde{\mu}$, we write:

$$w = \begin{cases} \bar{w} & \text{if } \mu \geq \tilde{\mu} \\ \underline{w} & \text{if } \mu < \tilde{\mu}. \end{cases}$$

As in the previous model on entrepreneurship, we assume that each old agent transfers a fraction b of his second period income to his child. The evolution of the economy, therefore, depends on two main factors: the equilibrium wage rate, and the distribution

[27] Time subscripts are eliminated to simplify the notations.

of transfers. Since the wage rate can only take two values, the dynamics of the model can easily be expressed in terms of T. In the closed economy, only two types of equilibrium can emerge, and the dynamics of transfers is given by:

$$T_{+1} = \begin{cases} bw_{+1} & \text{if } T \leq 1 - w_m \\ bw_{+1}(1+R) & \text{if } T > 1 - w_m. \end{cases} \tag{3.9}$$

A poverty trap is a situation in which $\mu < \tilde{\mu}$ and $w = \underline{w}$. It is obtained if those who do not have access to education do not transfer enough to allow their children to invest in education ($b\underline{w} < 1 - w_m < b\underline{w}(1 + R)$) and if the proportion of educated is low ($F(1 - w_m) > 1 - \tilde{\mu}$). A high-income solution with $\mu = 1$ and $w = \bar{w}$ obtains if, at the high-wage equilibrium, all agents opt for education ($b\bar{w} > 1 - w_m$). In the following, we consider the case of a developing economy that is initially stuck in a poverty trap.

Assume now that people may migrate in the second period to a rich country, characterized by a high-income equilibrium (i.e., the foreign wage is $\bar{w}$). At the end of the second period, migrants return to their home country and transfer their accumulated savings to the next generation. Migration involves two types of costs: a fixed cost c, which has to be financed through first-period savings, and, given the fact that people generally prefer living in their country of origin, a subjective cost such that one dollar earned abroad is discounted to k, $0 < k < 1$. Assume moreover that the migration cost is lower than the cost of education (for if it was not, migration prospects would have no impact): $c < 1$. In this configuration, the population in the home country may be split between four distinct groups characterized by different amounts of intergenerational transfers received: group A has no access to education or migration, group B has access to migration but not to education, group C has access to education or migration but not to both, and group D has access to both education and migration. This is apparent from the next graph:

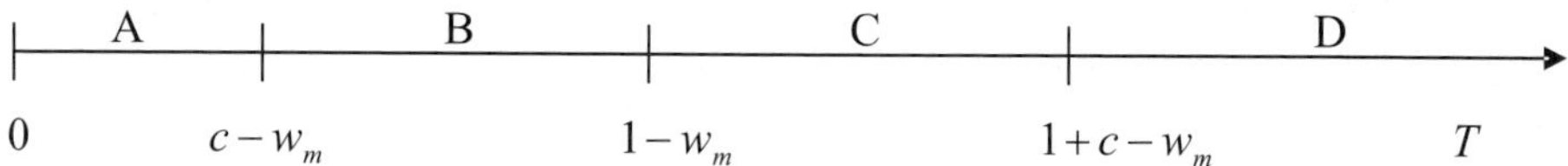

The dynamics of transfers within each group is then governed by:

$$\begin{aligned}
&\text{Group A}: && T_{+1} = b\underline{w} \\
&\text{Group B}: && T_{+1} = bMax\{\underline{w}; \bar{w}k\} \\
&\text{Group C}: && T_{+1} = bMax\{\underline{w}(1+R); \bar{w}k\} \\
&\text{Group D}: && T_{+1} = bMax\{\underline{w}(1+R); \bar{w}(1+R)k\}.
\end{aligned}$$

It should be noted that the poorest group (A) is unable to extract itself from poverty unless the proportion of educated becomes high enough to modify the wage rate from $\underline{w}$ to $\bar{w}$. Since groups C and D always have access to education, the potential for an increase in the proportion of educated is concentrated within group B. Depending on how intergenerational transfers impact on educational investments within this group, the whole picture may or may not be modified. More precisely, if $1 - F(c - w_m) < \tilde{\mu}$, the increase in the number of educated within group B is not significant enough to impact on the determination of the wage rate. However, if $1 - F(c - w_m) \geq \tilde{\mu}$, changes in educational choices within group B have an impact on the determination of the wage rate.

Formally, three cases must be distinguished:

- if $\bar{w}k < \underline{w}$, migration costs are so high that there is no migration at all and, consequently, no departure from the initial equilibrium;
- if $\underline{w} < \bar{w}k < \underline{w}(1 + R)$, groups B and D opt for migration.[28] The proportion of educated within the younger generation increases if the children from Group B gradually gain access to education, i.e., if $b\bar{w}k > 1 - w_m$;
- if $\underline{w} < \underline{w}(1 + R) < \bar{w}k$, groups B, C and D emigrate and their transfers allow for the next generation to invest in education.

Intuitively, the possibility of an economic take-off depends on the proportion of migrants in the middle-income group and on the amounts remitted. More precisely, the size of group B must be sufficiently large (formally, we must have $1 - F(c - w_m) \geq \tilde{\mu}$), the members of group B must opt for migration (formally, $\underline{w} < \bar{w}k$) and intergenerational transfers within this group must be such that they allow future generations to access to education (formally, $b\bar{w}k > 1 - w_m$). If these three conditions hold simultaneously, then the economy converges to its long-run efficient steady-state.

3.2.3. Migration, remittances and inequality: a dynamic approach

The two simple models above analyzed how the initial distribution of wealth conditions the long-run steady-state of the economy in the presence of capital market imperfections. In such a context, we exposed the basic mechanisms through which migration and subsequent remittances may represent a private solution to overcome liquidity constraints. A central assumption in these models is that familial wealth is an asset accumulated over time and transmitted across generations. In the rural regions, this asset generally takes the form of a plot of land, the quality and quantity of which determines the family's income potential. As explained in the microeconomic section, migration incentives are stronger for poor families, but rich families are less constrained; as a result, the exact composition of migration flows in terms of social origin is a priori unclear. In addition, migration decisions may also be affected by the level of information on job opportunities at destination, which may be related to skills and income, or by incentive compatibility constraints (e.g., wealthy households have a stronger enforcement power to secure remittance through inheritance).

In this discussion, migration costs play a critical role since they determine the wealth threshold at which a given family may or may not access to migration. Until now, these costs have been treated as exogenous; this may be adapted to situations where migration costs mainly include transportation and border crossing expenditures. However,

[28] This change on the supply-side may be sufficient to raise the wage rate up to $\bar{w}$ (formally, this would be the case if $C/(C+A) > \tilde{\mu}$, with C and A denoting the respective sizes of the eponymous groups). However, in the same spirit as in the previous section, we neglect that possibility since it would make remittances irrelevant.

this may not be adapted when information costs (e.g., search process for a destination, and for a job at destination) are significant; in this case, we know thanks to an impressive body of sociological literature that migration costs tend to decrease as the size of the relevant network at destination increases.[29] Such network effects have also been recognized more recently in the economic literature (e.g., Carrington et al., 1996; Bauer et al., 2002; Munshi, 2003; McKenzie and Rapoport, 2004). An immediate implication is that the impact of remittances on economic inequality is likely to vary over time since migration can be viewed as a diffusion process with decreasing information costs. This question has been analyzed in a number of empirical studies detailed below, suggesting that the dynamics of migration and remittances may be characterized by a "trickle down" effect: in the presence of liquidity constraints and initially high migration costs, high-income groups only can access to higher income opportunities abroad and, hence, remittances tend to increase inter-household inequality at origin; as the number of migrants increases, however, migration costs tend to decrease, thus making migration affordable to low-income households; ultimately, economic inequality decreases.

To show this formally, we extend our investment model of section 2.1.5 to the case where migration costs are endogenously determined in the presence of network effects. In doing so, we derive some conditions under which remittances may increase or decrease inequality at origin; interestingly, the model generates the possibility of a Kuznets-type relationship between economic inequality and migration history. For the sake of simplicity, we use a very simple measure of income dispersion, namely, the income ratio between the richest and the poorest household. We denote by $\bar{\alpha}$ and $\underline{\alpha}$ the technological characteristics of rich and poor households, respectively (with $\bar{\alpha} > \underline{\alpha}$). Given equation (2.37) and with $m = 0$, the closed economy income ratio is simply $\sigma_{cl} = \bar{\alpha}/\underline{\alpha}$; we hereafter refer to this ratio as to the "intrinsic technological ratio".

In an economy open to migration, this ratio becomes:

$$\sigma_{op} = \frac{\bar{\alpha} - 0.5\bar{\alpha}\beta - \bar{m}^{eff}c + \bar{\alpha}(1-\bar{m}^{eff}) - 0.5\bar{\alpha}\beta(1-\bar{m}^{eff})^2 + \bar{m}^{eff}I^m}{\underline{\alpha} - 0.5\underline{\alpha}\beta - \underline{m}^{eff}c + \underline{\alpha}(1-\underline{m}^{eff}) - 0.5\underline{\alpha}\beta(1-\underline{m}^{eff})^2 + \underline{m}^{eff}I^m}, \tag{3.10}$$

where $\bar{m}^{eff}$ and $\underline{m}^{eff}$ are the actual numbers of migrants sent by rich and poor households, respectively (obviously, this is determined by the minimum between the optimal and constrained numbers—see equations (2.36) and (2.38) above).

Depending on the size of migration costs, the regime in which rich and poor households operate, and the "intrinsic technological ratio", migration and induced remittances may modify the income range positively or negatively. A simple simulation illustrates this result. We use the same set of parameters as in section 2.1.5, except that: (i) $\underline{\alpha} = 3$ and $\bar{\alpha}$ varies from 4.5 to 31.5 (i.e., the intrinsic technological ratio varies from 1.5

[29] Among the contributions to this literature, the work of Douglas Massey and his co-workers on Mexican immigrant networks has been particularly influential. See Massey et al. (1994), Durand et al. (1996), or Massey and Espinoza (1997).

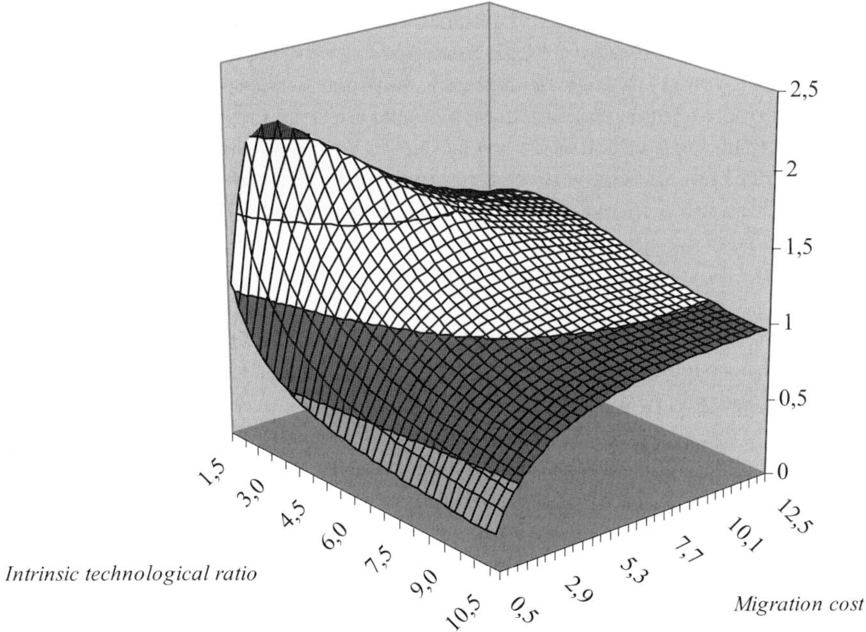

Figure 8. Remittances and inequality—a numerical simulation.

to 10.5), and, (ii) the migration cost varies from 0.5 to 12.5. Figure 8 represents the open economy income ratio in deviation from the intrinsic technological ratio, i.e., the endogenous variable σ_{op}/σ_{cl}. A value above 1 (respectively below 1) indicates an increase (respectively, a decrease) in economic inequality as a result of the migration process. Clearly, for low migration costs, both types of households are unconstrained so that migration and remittances reduce the income range at origin whatever the initial income gap. The opposite result, however, is not necessarily true. For high migration costs, poor households are definitely more constrained so that inequality should increase ceteris paribus. However, it may also be optimal for some rich households to reduce migration from among their ranks, so that the overall effect of migration costs on economic inequality is ambiguous.

The dynamic extension of this discussion is obvious. Consider a constant level of intrinsic technological gap, and suppose that past migration is such that migration costs are relatively high. At an early stage of the diffusion process, remittances are concentrated on high-income classes and inequality increases. In the long run, a decrease in inequality obtains if migration costs decrease sufficiently, as apparent from Figure 8. However, Docquier and Rapoport (2003) demonstrated that the same prediction of an inverse U-shaped relationship between migration and inequality may result from the interplay between remittances, the evolution of wages on the local labor market (a notable features of their model is to capture the impact of migration on the domestic supply and demand of labor), and the intergenerational transmission of wealth, with no need for migration costs to decrease over time thanks to network effects. In particular, in their model with exogenous migration costs, they show that while migration and remittances always contribute to reduce wealth inequality, they may first increase income inequality before a trickle-down effect is observed; for this to occur, migration incentives must be sufficiently high for relatively affluent households, a situation which requires initial inequality to be sufficiently low.

3.3. *Evidence on the growth effects of remittances*

Given the poverty of comparative macroeconomic data on remittances (cf. the introduction to this chapter), the evidence presented below is all from case studies based on micro data. The only recent cross-country study based on macroeconomic statistics we are aware of is the recent IMF study by Chami et al. (2005). Building on the idea that remittances take place under asymmetric information and are likely to generate moral hazard problems (see section 2.1.4), they argue that remittances can have a negative effect on economic growth in receiving countries. They test this prediction using aggregated panel data for 113 countries and, applying various econometric techniques, find a negative effect of remittances on growth after controlling for the investment/GDP ratio, regional dummies and other control variables. However, Chami et al. (2005) disregard the possibility that, due to liquidity constraints, remittances could affect investments (thus making the investment/GDP ratio endogenous) and human capital formation, the latter variable being completely absent from their analysis.

3.3.1. *Migration, remittances and inequality*

We know from the theoretical discussion above that migration and remittances have an ambiguous impact on inequality at origin; and indeed, the results from empirical studies are mixed. Early efforts to measure the impact of remittances on inequality treated remittance income as an exogenous transfer, and compared Gini coefficients with and without the inclusion of remittance income. Following this approach, Stark et al. (1986) analyzed household data from two Mexican villages, one with a relatively recent Mexico-to-U.S. migration experience, and one with a longer history of migration. Their findings indicate that the distributional impact of remittances strongly depends on the village's migration history, which in fact captures the magnitude of migration costs. They showed that income dispersion was decreased when migrants' remittances were taken into account in both villages, but more so in the second village, characterized by a longer migration tradition. From these observations, they derived the general conclusion that "the effect of remittances on inequalities over time depends critically upon how migration-facilitating information and contacts become diffused through the village population. If contacts and information are not household specific, that is, if there is a tendency for them to spread across household units, then migration and receipt of remittances by households at the lower end of the income distribution is likely to occur.

This would erode and possibly reverse any initially unfavorable effects of remittances on income inequality" (Stark et al., 1986, p. 724). Following similar methods, Milanovic (1987) also tested for the possibility of such a "trickle down" effect using panel data from the 1973, 1978, and 1983 Yugoslavian household surveys. He found no empirical support for this hypothesis; instead, his results showed that remittances tend to raise inequality, although their effects differed over the periods and social categories considered (it was mainly for agricultural households that an inequality-enhancing effect was found).

Noting that migrant workers would otherwise be working and earning income at home, Adams (1989) predicts what income would have been without remittances. Using a sample of three villages in Egypt, he finds that the inclusion of remittances from abroad worsens inequality. In contrast, following the same approach with households from 4 districts in Pakistan, Adams (1992) concludes that remittances have an essentially neutral impact on the rural income distribution. Taylor (1992) and Taylor and Wyatt (1996) note that in addition to the direct immediate impact on income, remittances can ease credit constraints for liquidity constrained households. Using a sample of 55 households from one part of Michoacan in Mexico, they find evidence that remittances translate into greater increases in income for rural households with illiquid assets. By allowing poorer households access to credit, remittances also finance the accumulation of productive assets, increasing future income. These indirect effects of remittances act to equalize incomes, and they find that remittances reduce inequality, with a greater effect once the indirect effects are included. Barham and Boucher (1998) follow on from Adams, in treating remittances as a substitute to home production. Using data from three neighborhoods in Bluefields, Nicaragua, they estimate a double-selection model to allow for the counterfactual of no migration and no remittances to impact on the participation decisions and earning outcomes of other household members. Treating remittances as exogenous would lead them to conclude that remittances reduce income inequality, whereas treating them as a substitute for home earnings results in remittances increasing inequality.

Finally, McKenzie and Rapoport (2004) examine the overall impact of migration on inequality in a large number of Mexican rural communities.[30] This impact is composed of the direct and indirect effects of remittances, multiplier effects of remittances through their spending on products and services produced by other community members (Adelman and Taylor, 1992) and other potential spillover and general equilibrium effects; this also includes the network effects of migration on the costs and benefits of migration for other community members. Using two detailed data sets (the Mexican Migration Project (MMP), a survey consisting of data from 57 rural communities typically located in areas of high migration, and the national demographic dynamics survey (ENADID), which consists of a representative sample of 97 rural communities in Mexico), they confirm that Mexican immigrants to the United States come from the middle

[30] Results for economy-wide studies suggest that Mexico–U.S. immigration worsens wage-inequality in both countries (Chiquiar and Hanson, 2005).

of the asset wealth distribution, with the migration probability displaying an inverse-U shaped relationship with wealth. The presence of migration networks, both at the family and at the community level, is found to increase the likelihood of migration, which accords with their ability to raise the expected benefits and lower the costs of migration, and to generate a Kuznets-type relationship between migration and inequality. Indeed, at high levels of migration prevalence, such as occur in many of the MMP communities, they find that migration leads to a reduction in inequality, with asset inequality declining more than consumption or income inequality; however, for the communities with a more diverse migration experience, as those surveyed as part of the ENADID project, migration appears to increase inequality at lower levels of migration stock and then to reduce inequality as one approaches the migration levels prevailing in the MMP communities.

3.3.2. *Remittances and human capital formation*

In section 3 we analyzed a first possible link between remittances and education through the "repayment of loans" hypothesis, and detailed a number of empirical studies confirming that in many instances, remittances may be seen as repayment of informal loans used to finance educational investments. A natural interpretation is that it is the prospect of migration (rural–urban or international) that makes education a profitable investment for the family; hence, migration fosters human capital formation provided that not too many educated individuals emigrate out of the country.[31] This first link may be referred to as a "backward" linkage as remittances are targeted toward the generation that preceded the migrant himself. Along the lines suggested in the theoretical model of remittances and liquidity constraints in section 3.2.2 above, a second possible link between remittances and education must be considered as remittances also finance education for the next generation (thus creating a "forward" link as well). Since dollars are fungible and education has a relatively high income-elasticity, one would expect remittances to have significant positive effects on the educational attainments of children from households with migrant members. And indeed, recent empirical research has emphasized the potential for remittance transfers to alleviate credit constraints and improve access to education for the poor. For example, in El Salvador, Cox-Edwards and Ureta (2003) found that remittances significantly contribute to lower the hazard of leaving school. Their estimates of "survival functions" show that remittances significantly contribute to lower the hazard of leaving school. This effect would seem to be greater in urban areas, but the mere fact of receiving remittances (irrespective of amounts) is shown to have a very strong effect in the rural areas. López-Córdoba (2004) uses the 2000 Mexican census to examine relationships between remittances and various outcomes at the municipality level and finds that municipalities in Mexico which receive

[31] Note however that there is a growing literature on the possibility of a beneficial brain drain. See for example Beine et al. (2001) and Docquier and Rapoport (2004).

more remittances have greater literacy levels and higher school attendance among 6 to 14 year olds. Similarly, Yang (2004) finds greater child schooling in families whose migrants receive larger positive exchange rate shocks in the Philippines.[32]

However, the implicit assumption in these studies is typically that migration only affects educational outcomes through remittances while migration of a family member may have a number of other effects on child schooling attainment. For example, parental absence as a result of migration may translate into less parental inputs into education acquisition and may also require remaining children to undertake housework or work to help meeting short-term familial labor and cash shortages. If any of these other channels operate, studies which focus just on the effect of remittances will generally be biased,[33] and therefore researchers should focus on the overall effect of migration.

Hanson and Woodruff (2002) take this approach and compare instead the education outcomes of children living in households with and without migrant members, using historical migration networks formed by 1920 as an instrument for migration seven decades later. Using the 2000 Mexican Census, they evaluate the effect of migration on "accumulated schooling" (number of school grades completed) by 10–15 year-olds and find that children in households with a migrant member complete significantly more years of schooling, with an estimated increase that ranges from 0.7 to 1.6 years, depending on age and gender. Interestingly, the gain appears highest for the categories of children traditionally at risk of being dropped out of school (i.e., girls in general, especially relatively older ones). They interpret this result as showing that remittances relax credit constraints on education investment, thus offsetting any possible negative impact on schooling of having a parent away from home.

McKenzie and Rapoport (2006) follow a similar route using a large Mexican demographic survey instead of Census data. This allows them to obtain a broader measure of household migration experience, and to examine what children are doing when they are not in school. They also include children aged 16 to 18, an age at which education is no longer compulsory and migration for work starts to become a possibility, while the absence of migrant parents may lead to children of this age being entrusted with household responsibilities which take the place of schooling. In addition, they use econometric techniques that allow for dealing with nonlinearities in the education decision and with the fact that the education data used is right-censored. In contrast to the above cited studies, they find evidence of a significant negative effect of migration on schooling attendance and attainments of 12 to 18 year-old boys and of 16 to 18 year-old girls. Their results show that living in a migrant household lowers the chances of

[32] They also point out that the effects of growing up separated from one's birth parent(s) on educational attainments have not yet been explored in the case of temporary separations motivated by economic factors.

[33] Theoretically one could separate the effect of remittances from other effects of migration through the use of a valid instrument which predicts whether or not one migrant will send more remittances than another. Such instruments are uncommon in practice, with the exchange rate shocks used by Yang (2004) coming closest in this regard among the existing literature (although as he acknowledges, these shocks also affect migrant wealth holdings).

boys completing junior high-school and of boys and girls completing high-school. The negative effect of migration on schooling is somewhat mitigated for younger girls with low educated mothers, which is consistent with remittances allowing to relax credit constraints on education investment at the lower end of the wealth and income distribution. However, for the majority of rural Mexican children, migration has a depressing effect on educational attainments. Comparison of the marginal effects of migration on school attendance and on participation to other activities shows that the observed decrease in schooling of 16 to 18 year olds is more than accounted for by current migration of boys and increases in housework for girls.

3.3.3. Remittances, return migration and entrepreneurship

Most of the empirical literature on migration and access to entrepreneurship concentrates on return migrants. One reason for this may simply be that the return migration channel is quantitatively more important than the remittances channel. Another reason has to do with data constraints: while the data sets on return migrants are relatively rich (often including information on pre- and post-migration wealth levels and on savings accumulated abroad), household surveys generally provide no information on the wealth distribution prior to self-employment and do not always track properly the exact uses of remittances. While the relative importance of self-employment is a distinctive feature of the labor force of most developing countries,[34] evidence has accumulated that the credit market only plays a minor role in financing investments in small businesses. For example, Mesnard (2004) indicates that during the 1980s, 87% of the entrepreneurial projects started by Tunisian return migrants were totally financed through accumulated savings while abroad, with only 13% receiving complementary financing from governmental programs, and none relying on private bank credits. Similarly, Dustmann and Kirchkamp (2002) show that only 1.2% of Turkish return migrants who were self-employed in 1988 did resort to bank credits as a major source of financing their start-up costs. In such a context, it is clear that for many prospective entrepreneurs, temporary migration is often the only means for accessing to self-employment.

Among the many case studies that confirm this reality, we present in more details recent studies on Tunisia, Turkey and Mexico. More evidence on return migration and occupational choice may be found in Ilahi (1999) for Pakistan, Massey and Parrado (1998) for the central-western region of Mexico, and McCormick and Wahba (2001, 2003) for Egypt. The latter studies offer additional insights in that they show that in the case of literate migrants, both the amount of savings and the migration duration have a significant positive effect on the probability of entrepreneurship upon return, while the first proposition only holds true for illiterate migrants; this suggests that skill-acquisition

[34] For example, the United Nations (2000) estimated that self-employment represents about one third of the nonagricultural labor force in North-Africa in 1990. Woodruff and Zenteno (2001) report data from Mexico's National Development Bank showing that firms with less than 15 workers provided 45% of Mexico's jobs in the manufacturing, commercial and service sectors in 1994.

may be more important for relatively educated migrants than the need to overcome liquidity constraints. In turn, the fact that skilled migrants, which often originate from the urban areas, benefit more from migration, explains why international return migration tends to deepen rural-urban inequality.

The first case study on Tunisia is due to Mesnard (2004) who uses data collected in 1986 by the Tunisian Settled Abroad Office on Tunisian workers who did work abroad at least once between 1974 and 1986 and returned to Tunisia before the survey date. The survey provides detailed information on the occupation chosen upon return as well as on the savings accumulated abroad up to 1986. The evidence shows that self-employed return migrants have accumulated more than twice as much savings as salaried return migrants, that they have stayed longer abroad, and that less than 8% of them used the skills acquired abroad after they returned. This is consistent with a story of temporary migration in order to overcome liquidity constraints in the home country where workers choose simultaneously their migration duration and saving effort in the foreign country. A formal test of the model is provided by estimating a probability model of self-employment under borrowing constraints, where potential simultaneous bias is taken into account. The main results show that savings accumulated abroad are alleviating liquidity constraints to self-employment in Tunisia. Interestingly, having a high-education level does not increase the probability to be self-employed upon return, while having a large family increases it, suggesting strong labor market imperfections in Tunisia. The model also implies that an increase in wages in the foreign country or lump sum payments offered by some host countries to migrants conditioned upon return encourage would-be self-employed return migrants to return earlier. But they also induce some workers to stay longer by encouraging them to choose self-employment after return instead of wage-employment, as they would have chosen otherwise.

In a similar line, Dustmann and Kirchkamp (2002) found that 50% of a sample of Turkish emigrants returning from Germany by 1984 started their own business within four years after resettling thanks to the savings accumulated abroad. Dustmann and Kirchkamp simultaneously tested the migration duration and the type of activity chosen upon return (self-employed, salaried or retired), their working assumption being also that these two decisions are made jointly with the decision on the amount to be saved abroad. Their results show that an increase in the host-country wage is likely to decrease the migration duration for those opting for entrepreneurship after return. Conditioned upon returning, they also show that the level of schooling (which determines the wages earned abroad) increases the probability to opt for self-employment upon return, and reduces the length of the migration duration. Both results are consistent with the idea that migration is part of a life-cycle strategy to accumulate capital so as to gain access to entrepreneurship in the origin country.

By contrast to these two studies, which relied on specific surveys on return migrants, Woodruff and Zenteno's (Woodruff and Zenteno, 2001) study on remittances and the creation of micro-enterprises in the urban areas of Mexico combines three national data sets: the 2000 population Census provides the information on migration rates, a data set from the Bank of Mexico provides an accurate and comprehensive picture of remittances receipts (including repatriated savings), and the data on enterprise investment comes from a national survey of micro-enterprises. Startup costs in Mexico are relatively low (around \$1000) but vary considerably across sectors, and are almost entirely financed through personal savings and loans from family members and friends; only 2.5% of the firms received bank credit at startup. In this context, it is clear that remittances have a potentially strong impact on access to entrepreneurship. Woodruff and Zenteno's results show that this is indeed the case, with remittances representing an important financing source for investments in micro-enterprises (i.e., thanks to remittances, more firms are created, and of a higher average size): they estimate that remittances are responsible for 20% of the capital invested in micro-enterprises throughout urban Mexico (the figure jumps to nearly one-third of the invested capital in the 10 high-migration States).[35] Interestingly, other things equal, the impact is stronger for female-owned firms; in addition, for owners for which the State of residence differs from the State of birth, networks at origin (i.e., in the region of birth) seem to be more important than those at destination. Their findings not only support the view that access to capital (and, hence, economic inequality) are crucial determinants of investments, they also show that migration is indeed instrumental in overcoming such constraints. Another important contribution of their study is to show that some—if not most—of the growth potential associated with remittances by international migrants originating from the rural areas is in fact located in the urban sector. This implies that the impact of remittances on investment tends to be largely underestimated by studies focusing exclusively on rural communities.

Finally, Mesnard and Ravallion (2001) study more closely possible non-linearities in the wealth-self-employment relationship. Using the same data set as Mesnard (2004), they estimate both a non-parametric linear probability model and a parametric nonlinear model of the choice to be self-employed amongst return migrants in Tunisia, allowing for nonlinear effects of savings accumulated while abroad. Controls for heterogeneity are included, and tests are made for selection bias and separability between wealth and the controls. Their results show that savings accumulated abroad are of over-ridding importance in explaining business start-ups by Tunisian return migrants and that their effect is concave. Interestingly, they show that there is no sign of increasing returns at low savings level, suggesting generally low start-up costs. These results indicate that the aggregate self-employment rate is an increasing function of aggregate savings accumulated abroad, but a decreasing function of savings inequality.

3.3.4. Migration, productivity and rural development

As mentioned previously, most initial studies of the impact of migration and remittances on rural development adopted a strongly pessimistic view. To put it shortly, the main

[35] Woodruff (2002) complements these results in showing that remittances seem to foster investment in micro-enterprises not only directly but also indirectly, in attracting supplementary sources of financing, especially trade credit.

criticism that many scholars initially put forward was that remittances were unproductive and mostly spent on (sometimes conspicuous) consumption. Part of the explanation for this pessimism, as Taylor et al. (1996) point out, is maybe that community characteristics leading to out-migration simultaneously discourages productive investment. This is exemplified by Durand and Massey's (Durand and Massey, 1992) study on 37 Mexican communities, in which although remittances were shown to be spent mostly on consumption in all communities, the share allocated to production investments greatly varied from village to village; this led them to suggest that, "rather than concluding that migration inevitably leads to dependency and a lack of development, it is more appropriate to ask why productive investment occurs in some communities and not in others" (p. 27).[36]

In line with this research program, Durand et al. (1996) studied 30 Mexican communities located in the States with a long tradition of emigration to the U.S., and showed that the presence in the village of an *ejido* (production cooperative) significantly increased the likelihood of having remittances spent on production. Similarly—and quite obviously—, at an individual level, the likelihood that a given household would spend a dollar of remittances for productive uses greatly increased with access to land and housing ownership, suggesting that on average, less unequal communities at origin would tend to channel remittances towards more productive uses. In a similar spirit, and again for rural Mexico, Taylor and Wyatt (1996) show that remittances are distributed almost evenly across income groups, hence inducing a direct equalizing effect in terms of economic inequality. However, remittances have the highest shadow value for households at the middle-to-low-end of the income distribution; for such households indeed, remittances allow for accessing to productive assets (land) and/or complementary inputs; a second equalizing effect is thereby obtained. This suggests that the impact of remittances on rural development depends not only on the initial distribution of wealth in the origin community (in particular, the presence or absence of an *ejido* appears critical), but also on a host of factors affecting their shadow value (e.g., degree of liquidity of land rights, costs of complementary inputs, availability of local labor, etc.).

Fortunately, the literature on the effects of migration and remittances on rural development is not limited to Mexico. In particular, two studies undertaken in very different contexts have illuminated the positive impact of remittances on rural productivity. The first study is the influential work of Robert Lucas on the outmigration to South Africa's mines from neighboring countries (Botswana, Lesotho and Malawi) and homelands within South Africa, where Lucas makes clear that the short run decline in rural production due to the loss of labor is more than offset by later increases in agricultural productivity as remittances help raise farm investments (Lucas, 1987). The second study, by Rozelle et al. (1999) on rural China, follows along similar lines; however, their results show an overall negative impact of migration on rural output; still, the decrease in output is partly offset by access to capital through remittances.

[36] The summaries of Taylor et al. (1996) and Durand and Massey (1992) are borrowed from Durand et al. (1996).

4. Conclusion

This chapter shows that in general migration and associated remittances tend to have an overall positive effect on origin countries' long-run economic performance. It is beyond the scope of this survey to evaluate whether emigration is a sustainable development strategy or to ask whether governments should try to impact on the migrants' skill composition or immigration status (e.g., temporary or permanent visas). However, two relatively modest policy issues can be briefly discussed further: (i) how to increase the amount of remittances for a given number and quality of migrants; and, (ii) how to increase the social value of a dollar of remittances.

The first objective is essentially a matter of financial development, with implications well beyond the issue of remittances. As far as remittances are concerned, however, it is clear that promoting saving accounts in foreign currency and cross-national banking would contribute to a substantial reduction in the level of transaction costs. In some extreme cases, transaction costs on remittances have been estimated at 25% of the amounts remitted for Latin America (15% in direct fees for wire-transfers or money orders, plus 10% in currency exchange). Specific financial incentives for emigrants have been designed in some countries (e.g., accounts in foreign currency in India, Sri Lanka, or Pakistan, bonus on the official exchange rate in Egypt and Turkey), but it is unclear whether the gains from increased remittances are offset by the costs of additional distortions to the financial system. An even less convincing strategy, followed by countries such as China, is to rely on mandatory transfers as a condition to issue exit permits; such policies require State control of the whole process of labor migration and have their own obvious drawbacks in terms of economic freedom and welfare.[37]

The second objective is equivalent to channeling remittances into their most productive uses. With this in mind, several countries have implemented special programs, notably for return migrants: free managerial training for prospective entrepreneurs (Korea, Sri Lanka), reduced tariffs on imported equipment goods (Pakistan), etc. On a broader scale, an alternative frequently raised within international forums (e.g., Lowell, 1997) is to create remittances-based funds, as if the core of the problem was a pure matter of intermediation. On this question—and on a final note—, simply to make ours the following statement by Durand et al. (1996, p. 261): "As they elevate a family's standard of living, contribute to business formation, and lead to community improvements, [remittances] represent a tangible accomplishment [...]. The way for policy makers to encourage productive investment is not to harangue migrants about their excessive consumption or to attempt to change their micro-level behavior. Rather, the best way is to pursue macroeconomic policies that yield a stable and propitious investment climate and to make expenditures on infrastructures [so as to] ... make investments an attractive, profitable proposition."

[37] The World Bank's "Global Economic Prospects 2006" focus on "the economic implications of migration and remittances" and discuss the policy issues raised by remittances in greater length. See World Bank (2005), especially Chapter 6 on "reducing remittance fees".

References

Adams, R. (1989). "Workers remittances and inequality in rural Egypt". Economic Development and Cultural Change 38 (1), 45–71.

Adams, R. (1992). "The impact of migration and remittances on inequality in rural Pakistan". Pakistan Development Review 31 (4), 1189–1203.

Adelman, I., Taylor, J.E. (1992). "Is structural adjustment with a human face possible? The case of Mexico". Journal of Development Studies 26, 387–407.

Agarwal, R., Horowitz, A.W. (2002). "Are international remittances altruism or insurance? Evidence from Guyana using multiple-migrant households". World Development 30 (11), 2033–2044.

Altonji, J.G., Hayashi, F., Kotlikoff, L.J. (1992). "Is the extended family altruistically linked? Direct tests using micro data". American Economic Review 82 (5), 1177–1198.

Altonji, J.G., Hayashi, F., Kotlikoff, L.J. (1997). "Parental altruism and inter-vivos transfers: theory and evidence". Journal of Political Economy 105 (6), 1121–1166.

Andreoni, J. (1989). "Giving with impure altruism: Applications to charity and Ricardian equivalence". Journal of Political Economy 97 (6), 1447–1458.

Azam, J.P., Gubert, F. (2005). "Those in Kayes. The impact of remittances on their recipients in Africa". Revue Economique 56 (6), 1331–1358.

Banerjee, A.V., Newman, A.F. (1993). "Occupational choice and the process of development". Quarterly Journal of Economics 105, 501–526.

Barham, B., Boucher, S. (1998). "Migration, remittances and inequality: estimating the net effects of migration on income distribution". Journal of Development Economics 55, 307–331.

Bauer, T., Epstein, G.S., Gang, I.N. (2002). "Herd effects or migration networks? The location choice of Mexican immigrants in the US", IZA Discussion Paper No 551, August.

Beine, M., Docquier, F., Rapoport, H. (2001). "Brain drain and economic growth: theory and evidence". Journal of Development Economics 64 (1), 275–289.

Bernheim, B.D., Shleifer, A., Summers, L.H. (1985). "The strategic bequest motive". Journal of Political Economy 93 (6), 1045–1076.

Bhagwati, J., Brecher, R., Hatta, T. (1983). "The generalized theory of transfers and welfare". American Economic Review 83, 606–618.

Böhning, W.R. (1975). "Some thoughts on emigration from the Mediterranean basin". International Labour Review 111 (3), 251–277.

Carrington, W.J., Detragiache, E., Vishwanath, T. (1996). "Migration with endogenous moving costs". American Economic Review 86 (4), 909–930.

Chami, R., Fullenkamp, C., Jahjah, S. (2005). "Are immigrant remittance flows a source of capital for development". IMF Staff Papers 52 (1), 55–81.

Chen, K.P., Chiang, S.H. (1998). "Migration as portfolio selection", mimeo, York University.

Chiquiar, D., Hanson, G. (2005). "International migration, self-selection and the distribution of wages: evidence from Mexico and the United States". Journal of Political Economy 113 (2), 239–281.

Coate, S., Ravallion, M. (1993). "Reciprocity without commitment—characterization and performance of informal insurance arrangements". Journal of Development Economics 40, 1–24.

Corden, W.M. (1984). "Booming sector and Dutch disease economics: survey and consolidation". Oxford Economic Papers 36, 359–380.

Corden, W.M., Neary, P.J. (1982). "Booming sector and de-industrialization in a small open economy". Economic Journal 92, 825–848.

Cox, D. (1987). "Motives for private transfers". Journal of Political Economy 95 (3), 508–546.

Cox, D., Jimenez, E. (1992). "Social security and private transfers in a developing country: the case of Peru". World Bank Economic Review 6 (1), 155–169.

Cox, D., Rank, M. (1992). "Inter-vivos transfers and intergenerational exchange". Review of Economics and Statistics 74, 305–314.

Cox, D., Eser, Z., Jimenez, E. (1998). "Motives for private transfers over the life cycle: An analytical framework and evidence for Peru". Journal of Development Economics 55, 57–80.

Cox-Edwards, D., Ureta, M. (2003). "Internation migration, remittances ans schooling: evidence from El Salvador". Journal of Development Economics 72 (2), 429–461.

de la Brière, B., Sadoulet, E., de Janvry, A., Lambert, S. (2002). "The roles of destination, gender, and household composition in explaining remittances: An analysis for the Dominican Sierra". Journal of Development Economics 68 (2), 309–328.

Djajic, S. (1986). "International migration, remittances and welfare in a dependent economy". Journal of Development Economics 21, 229–234.

Docquier, F., Rapoport, H. (1998). "Are migrant minorities strategically self-selected?". Journal of Population Economics 11, 579–588.

Docquier, F., Rapoport, H. (2000). "Strategic and altruistic remittances". In: Gerard-Varet, L.-A., Kolm, S.-C., Mercier Ythier, J. (Eds.), The Economics of Reciprocity, Giving and Altruism. MacMillan and St. Martin's Press, London and New York, pp. 285–297.

Docquier, F., Rapoport, H. (2003). "Remittances and inequality: a dynamic migration model", CREDPR Working Paper No 167, Stanford University, June.

Docquier, F., Rapoport, H. (2004). "Skilled migration: the perspective of developing countries", World Bank Policy Research Paper No 3382, August.

Durand, J., Massey, D.S. (1992). "Mexican migration to the United States: A critical review". Latin American Research Review 27, 3–43.

Durand, J., Kandel, W., Parrado, E.A., Massey, D.S. (1996). "International migration and development in Mexican communities". Demography 33 (2), 249–264.

Dustmann, C., Kirchkamp, O. (2002). "The optimal migration duration and activity choice after remigration". Journal of Development Economics 67 (2), 351–372.

El-Sakka, M.I.T., McNabb, R. (1999). "The macroeconomic determinants of emigrant remittances". World Development 27 (8), 1493–1502.

Fafchamps, M. (1992). "Solidarity networks in pre-industrial societies: rational peasants with a moral economy". Economic Development and Cultural Change 41 (1), 147–174.

Feinerman, E., Seiler, E.J. (2002). "Private transfers with incomplete information: A contribution to the "Altruism-echange motivation for transfers" debate". Journal of Population Economics 15 (4), 715–736.

Foster, A.D., Rosenzweig, M.R. (2001). "Imperfect commitment, altruism, and the family: evidence from transfer behavior in low-income rural areas". Review of Economics and Statistics L XXXIII (3), 389–407.

Funkhouser, E. (1995). "Remittances from international migration: a comparison of El Salvador and Nicaragua". Review of Economics and Statistics 77 (1), 137–146.

Glytsos, N. (2002). "Dynamic effects of migrant remittances on growth: an econometric model with an application to Mediterranean countries", Discussion Paper No 74, KEPE, Athens.

Griffin, K. (1976). "On the emigration of the peasantry". World Development 4 (5), 353–361.

Gubert, F. (2002). "Do migrants insure those who stay behind? Evidence from the Kayes Area". Oxford Development Studies 30 (3), 267–287.

Hanson, G.H., Woodruff, C. (2002). "Emigration and educational attainment in Mexico", mimeo, University of California at San Diego.

Hoddinott, J. (1994). "A model of migration and remittances applied to Western Kenya". Oxford Economic Papers 46, 450–475.

Ilahi, N. (1999). "Return migration and occupational change". Review of Development Economics 3 (2), 170–186.

Ilahi, N., Jafarey, S. (1999). "Guestworker migration, remittances and the extended family: evidence from Pakistan". Journal of Development Economics 58, 485–512.

Jensen, R.T. (2003). "Do private transfers 'displace' the benefits of public transfers? Evidence from South Africa". Journal of Public Economics 88, 89–112.

Joulfaian, D., Wihelm, M.O. (1994). "Inheritance and labor supply". Journal of Human Resources 29 (4), 1205–1234.

Kaufmann, D., Lindauer, D.L. (1986). "A model of income transfers for the urban poor". Journal of Development Economics 22, 337–350.

Lambert, S. (1994). "La migration comme instrument de diversification intrafamiliale des risques. Application au cas de la Cote d'Ivoire". Revue d'Economie du Développement 2, 3–38.
Lauby, J., Stark, O. (1988). "Individual migration as a family strategy: young women in the Philippines". Population Studies 42, 473–486.
López-Córdoba, E. (2004). "Globalization, migration, and development: the role of Mexican migrant remittances. Economia, in press.
Lowell, L.B. (1997). "The role of migrants' remittances in U.S. Latino communities and Latin America and the Caribbean", mimeo, Inter-American Development Dialogue and Tomas Rivera Policy Institute, December.
Lucas, R.E.B. (1987). "Emigration to South Africa's mines". American Economic Review 77 (3), 313–330.
Lucas, R.E.B. (1997). "Internal migration in developing countries". In: Rosenzweig, M.R., Stark, O. (Eds.), Handbook of Family and Population Economics, vol. 1B. North Holland, Amsterdam, pp. 721–798. Chapter 13.
Lucas, R.E.B., Stark, O. (1985). "Motivations to remit: Evidence from Botswana". Journal of Political Economy 93 (5), 901–918.
Massey, D.S., Basem, L. (1992). "Determinants of savings, remittances, and spending patterns among Mexican migrants to the US". Sociological Inquiry 62, 186–207.
Massey, D.S., Goldring, L., Durand, J. (1994). "Continuities in transnational migration: an analysis of nineteen Mexican communities". American Journal of Sociology 99 (6), 1492–1533.
Massey, D.S., Espinoza, K.E. (1997). "What's driving Mexico–U.S. migration? A theoretical, empirical and policy analysis". American Journal of Sociology 102 (4), 939–999.
Massey, D.S., Parrado, E.A. (1998). "International migration and business formation in Mexico". Social Science Quarterly 79 (1), 1–20.
McCormick, B., Wahba, J. (2000). "Overseas unemployment and remittances to a dual economy". Economic Journal 110, 509–534.
McCormick, B., Wahba, J. (2001). "Overseas work experience, savings and entrepreneurship amongst return migrants to LDCs". Scottish Journal of Political Economy 48 (2), 164–178.
McCormick, B., Wahba, J. (2003). "Return international migration and geographical inequality: the case of Egypt". Journal of African Economies 12 (4), 500–532.
McKenzie, D. (2005). "Beyond remittances: the effects of migration on Mexican households". In: Ozden, C., Schiff, M. (Eds.), International Migration, Remittances and the Brain Drain. McMillan and Palgrave, pp. 123–147. Chapter 4.
McKenzie, D., Rapoport, H. (2004). "Network effects and the dynamics of migration and inequality: theory and evidence from Mexico", BREAD Working Paper No 63, Harvard University, April.
McKenzie, D., Rapoport, H. (2006). "Can migration reduce educational attainments? Depressing evidence from Mexico", CReAM Working Paper No 01/06, University College London, April.
Mesnard, A. (2001). "Temporary migration and intergenerational mobility". Louvain Economic Review 67 (1), 59–88.
Mesnard, A. (2004). "Temporary migration and capital market imperfections". Oxford Economic Papers 56, 242–262.
Mesnard, A., Ravallion, M. (2001). "Wealth distribution and self-employment in a developing country", CEPR Discussion Paper DP3026.
Milanovic, B. (1987). "Remittances and income distribution". Journal of Economic Studies 14 (5), 24–37.
Munshi, K. (2003). "Networks in the modern economy: Mexican migrants in the US labor market". Quarterly Journal of Economics 118 (2), 549–599.
Nitzan, S. (1994). "Modeling rent-seeking contests". European Journal of Political Economy 10 (1), 41–60.
Osili, U.O. (2004). "Migrants and housing investment: theory and evidence from Nigeria". Economic Development and Cultural Change 52 (4), 821–850.
Perotti, R. (1993). "Political equilibrium, income distribution and growth". Review of Economic Studies 60, 755–776.
Poirine, B. (1997). "A theory of remittances as an implicit family loan arrangement". World Development 25 (5), 589–611.

Quibria, M.G. (1997). "International migration, remittances, and income distribution in the source country: a synthesis". Bulletin of Economic Research 49 (1), 29–46.

Rapoport, H. (2002). "Migration, credit constraints and self-employment: A simple model of occupational choice, inequality and growth". Economics Bulletin 15 (7), 1–5.

Ray, D. (1998). Development Economics. Princeton University Press, Princeton.

Rempel, H., Lobdell, R. (1978). "The role of urban-rural remittances in rural development". Journal of Development Studies 14, 324–341.

Rivera-Batiz, F. (1982). "International migration, non-traded goods and economic welfare in the source country". Journal of Development Economics 11, 81–90.

Rodriguez, E.R. (1996). "International migrants' remittances in the Philippines". Canadian Journal of Economics 29 (2), 427–432.

Rosenzweig, M.R. (1988a). "Risk, implicit contracts and the family in rural areas of low-income countries". Economic Journal 393, 1148–1170.

Rosenzweig, M.R. (1988b). "Risk, private information, and the family". American Economic Review—Papers and Proceedings 78 (2), 245–250.

Rosenzweig, M.R., Stark, O. (1989). "Consumption smoothing, migration and marriage: evidence from rural India". Journal of Political Economy 97, 905–926.

Rozelle, S., Taylor, J.E., deBrauw, A. (1999). "Migration, remittances and agricultural productivity in China". American Economic Review (AEA Papers and Proceedings) 89 (2), 287–291.

Russell, S.S. (1986). "Remittances from international migration: a review in perspective". World Development 14, 677–696.

Stark, O. (1978). Economic-Demographic Interaction in Agricultural Development: The Case of Rural-to-Urban Migration. UN Food and Agriculture Organization, Rome.

Stark, O. (1991). The migration of Labor. Basil Blackwell, Oxford and Cambridge, MA.

Stark, O. (1995). Altruism and Beyond. Basil Blackwell, Oxford and Cambridge.

Stark, O., Bloom, D.E. (1985). "The new economics of labor migration". American Economic Review—Papers and Proceedings 72 (5), 173–178.

Stark, O., Levhari, D. (1982). "On migration and risk in LDCs". Economic Development and Cultural Change 31, 191–196.

Stark, O., Taylor, J.E., Yitzhaki, S. (1986). "Remittances and inequality". Economic Journal 28, 309–322.

Subramanian, R. (1994). "A theory of remittances", CRIEF Working paper, N° 9406, University of St-Andrews.

Taylor, J.E. (1992). "Remittances and inequality reconsidered: direct, indirect and intertemporal effects". Journal of Policy Modeling 14 (2), 187–208.

Taylor, J.E., Massey, D.S., Arango, J., Hugo, G., Kouaouci, A., Pellegrino, A. (1996). "International migration and community development". Population Index 62 (3), 397–418.

Taylor, J.E., Wyatt, T.J. (1996). "The shadow value of migrant remittances, income and inequality in a household-farm economy". Journal of Development Studies 32 (6), 899–912.

United Nations (2000). The World's Women 2000: Trends and Statistics. Department of Economic and Social Affairs, New York.

Woodruff, C. (2002). "Firm finance from the bottom up: micro-enterprises in Mexico", mimeo, University of California at San Diego.

Woodruff, C., Zenteno, R. (2001). "Remittances and micro-enterprises in Mexico", mimeo, University of California at San Diego.

World Bank (2001). World Tables. The World Bank, Washington.

World Bank (2005). Global Economic Prospects 2006. Washington, DC, The World Bank.

Yang, D. (2004). "International migration, human capital, and entrepreneurship: evidence from Philippine migrants' exchange rate shocks", mimeo, Ford School of Public Policy, University of Michigan.

Zlotnik, H. (1998). "International migration 1965–96: An overview". Population and Development Review 24 (3), 429–468.

PART 3

THIRD SECTOR AND LABOR

Chapter 18

PHILANTHROPY

JAMES ANDREONI*

Department of Economics, University of California, San Diego, CA 92093, USA
e-mail: andreoni@ucsd.edu

Contents

* I would like to thank the National Science Foundation for financial support, and Molly Dahl and Joseph Guse for helpful research assistance.

Handbook of the Economics of Giving, Altruism and Reciprocity, Volume 2
Edited by Serge-Christophe Kolm and Jean Mercier Ythier

DOI: 10.1016/S1574-0714(06)02018-5

Abstract

Philanthropy is one of the enduring areas of economic research. Why would people work hard only to give their earnings away? The paper explores the theoretical foundations, as well as the empirical and policy research on philanthropy. This paper reviews over 25 years worth of economic research, and points to the many challenging new questions that remain.

Keywords

philanthropy, charitable giving, altruism, public goods, voluntarism, bequest, fund-raising

JEL classification: D4, H41

1. Introduction

While the first academic articles on philanthropy appeared in the 1960s, there has been an explosion of interest in the economics of philanthropy and charitable giving since the 1980s. Hundreds of articles have been written to explore and extend various theoretical findings, and hundreds more have pursued empirical questions. This chapter will, by necessity, address only a small subset of these papers, focussing only on the most central themes. I will do my best to acknowledge the original sources for the findings discussed, and through comments and footnotes direct the reader to the broader literature. Even then, I am afraid, this will be something of a stingy review of a rather generous literature.[1]

Philanthropy is one of the greatest puzzles for economics. A science based on precepts of self-interested behavior does not easily accommodate behavior that is so clearly unselfish. How can unselfish behavior be reconciled with self-interest?

One explanation is that charitable giving is not unselfish at all. One who gives to medical research may hope one day to benefit from its findings. A person who gives to public broadcasting may expect to enjoy improved programming. A benefactor of the opera may seek to hire more talented performers. A second justification, sometimes called "enlightened self-interest," is a step removed from pure selfishness. A comfortably employed person may give to poverty relief in order to keep the institution in place, banking on the rare event that he may himself be impoverished some day. But these clearly cannot be full explanations. What about the person who gives to famine relief on another continent? Or the environmentalist who contributes to saving a rare species that she never expects to see? And what about charitable bequests—such gifts have no chance of affecting consumption of a person while alive. These examples raise a third explanation: Altruism toward others or toward future generations may be a motivator in giving, and gifts are made to maximize a utility function that includes the benefits to others or to society in general. While these three explanations are distinct, an economic theorist would model them all the same. Since each implies a concern about the total supply of the charitable good or service, albeit for different reasons, each could be modelled identically as private gifts to a pure public good.[2]

Notice that all three of these explanations are best suited to situations in which one's own contribution has a measurable impact on the charitable good. When the good is large in scale and when donors are many, it becomes difficult to accept that people can actually experience the impact of their gifts. As a result, free riding may predominate.

[1] Pun intended.

[2] Hochman and Rodgers (1969) are credited with first noting that altruistic feelings can translate the object of those feelings into a public good, but see also Kolm (1969). Arrow (1972) provided a thoughtful discussion of the main issues for analysis, as did Boulding (1973). Becker (1974) formalized the discussion and began the modern literature on altruistic giving to charity. See the chapters in this volume by Schokkaert and by Kolm for other discussion of transfer motives.

In these cases, a fourth explanation for giving may be more attractive: People may get utility—a "warm-glow"—from the act of giving.

A fifth possibility is that our economic discipline of self-interested behavior is simply not well suited to explain philanthropy. Humans are, after all, moral beings. Perhaps our behavior is constrained by moral codes of conduct that make our choices unexplainable by neo-classical models of well-behaved preferences and quasi-concave utility functions.[3] While this argument undoubtedly has merit, it represents the last refuge for the economic theorist. Since the models we discuss below are capable of characterizing the data on giving, we hold off on considering non-utility-based models of giving.

Regardless of the reasons for its existence, there is clearly a strong public policy interest in philanthropy. First, private philanthropy can substitute for public sector provision of goods and services. With individuals to provide poverty relief or support for the arts, there is less need for the government to do so. As such, it becomes essential to understand how private charity is provided and how it interacts with public provision. Second, governments have historically treated charitable donations with tax-favored policies, such as the charitable deduction in the US. What are the effects of these policies on giving and on tax collections? Third, there are obviously enormous efficiency concerns. How is this set of public and private institutions co-existing to provide public charitable services, and is there a more efficient configuration of these institutions? What is the best policy for providing public goods?

This chapter will address these and other aspects of charitable giving. The focus will be on making readers familiar with the basic tools of analysis, and presenting them with most current state of research on these topics. Perhaps most importantly, I will try to uncover important questions, topics and themes that have not been addressed or understood, and point readers to potentially fruitful new areas of inquiry. Despite being an extensively studied and important topic, there is still a great deal to be learned about altruism, giving, charity and how government policy affects it all.

2. General facts on philanthropy

Here we will review the general facts about charitable giving. Most of what we know about philanthropy is based on data from the US. For this reason, much of our discussion will focus on American data. Later in this section we will look at evidence and data from around the world.

2.1. Giving in the USA

There are two main sources of data about individual contributions to charity. The first is household surveys. The Independent Sector, for instance, surveys about 2500

[3] Sugden (1982, 1984) suggests this interpretation. See also Sen (1977).

households by telephone every two years.[4] Surveys are valuable since they can obtain information on age, education levels, and other personal characteristics of respondents. A disadvantage is that individuals must rely on imprecise memories when answering questions, or may be reluctant to give accurate information about their incomes or donations.

A second important source is samples of tax returns. Since individuals who itemize their tax returns in the US can take a charitable deduction, we can learn about donations from this sector of the economy. The advantage to tax returns is that the information on them is precise, as long as people don't cheat on their taxes.[5] The disadvantage is that tax returns contain very little information about the personal characteristics of the filers that would be helpful in explaining giving, such as education levels or religious affiliation, nor can we learn about the giving habits of those who don't itemize their tax returns. Since no data source is perfect, we must conduct many studies on varied data sources in order to reach a consensus on charitable behavior.

Charitable donations can come from individuals, charitable foundations, corporations, or through bequests. While all are significant, by far the dominant source of giving is from individuals. Table 1 shows that in 2002 individuals gave over 183 billion dollars to charity, or 76% of the total dollars donated. The second biggest source, foundations, was responsible for 11.2% of all donations (also see Greene and McClelland, 2001).

The trends in giving over the last 30 years can be seen in Figure 1. Total giving has been on a steady rise, with temporary jumps coming in 1986, along with a pronounced rise starting in 1996 through 2001. When measured as a percent of income, however, giving seems much more stable. Since 1968 giving has varied from 1.5% to 2.1% of income. In the most recent years, however, giving has risen from 1.5% of income in 1995 to 2.1% in 2001. This rise coincided with a run up on stock-market wealth, which is the likely explanation for the latest increase in giving. Notice, however, that this latest rise in giving counteracts a longer trend of slowly falling generosity. The peak of giving in 2001 matches the former peak set back in 1963. Table 2 presents details on the characteristics of individual givers. The data, from the Independent Sector in 1995, show that 68.5% of all households gave to charity and that the average gift among those giving was $1081. Table 2 shows that the more income a household has, the more likely the household is to give to charity, and the more it gives when it does donate. This table also reveals an interesting pattern typically found in charitable statistics. Those with the lowest incomes give over 4% of income to charity. As incomes grow to about $50 000, gifts fall to 1.3% of income, but then rise again to 3.0% for the highest incomes. What could cause this "u-shaped" giving pattern? One explanation is that those

[4] See their web-site for details about the survey and information about purchasing the data: www.independentsector.org/

[5] Slemrod (1989) explored this potential problem and found that, while there is some evidence of cheating by overstating charitable deductions, the effects are small and don't appreciably affect the analysis. Joulfaian and Rider (2004), however, found that tax evasion by misreporting income can bias coefficients, as evasion and marginal tax rates tend to be correlated.

Table 1
Sources of private philanthropy, 2002

Source of gifts	Billions of dollars	Percent of total
Individuals	183.7	76.3
Foundations	26.9	11.2
Bequests	18.1	7.5
Corporations	12.2	5.1
Total for all sources	240.9	100

Source: Giving USA, 2003.

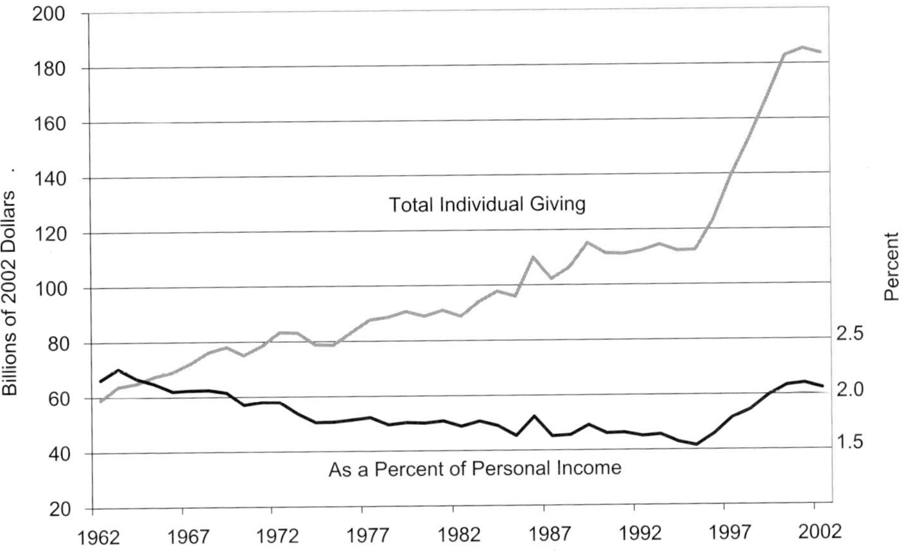

Figure 1. Trends in individual giving. Source: Giving USA, 2003.

with low incomes may be young people who know their wages will be rising, hence they feel they can afford more giving now. It may also be due to the composition of the types of charities people give to, since lower income people tend to give significantly more to religious causes. Hence, it will be important to account for all the factors that may explain giving before offering explanations for the averages seen in these tables.

Table 2 also illustrates that giving varies significantly with the age and educational attainment of the givers. As people get older they are typically more likely to give to charity and to give a greater fraction of their incomes. Likewise, those with more

Table 2
Private philanthropy by income, age, and education of the giver, 1995

	Percent of households who give	Average amount given by those who give	Percent of household income
All contributing households	68.5	1081	2.2
Household income			
under $10 000	47.3	324	4.8
10 000–19 000	51.1	439	2.9
20 000–29 999	64.9	594	2.3
30 000–39 999	71.8	755	2.2
40 000–49 999	75.3	573	1.3
50 000–59 999	85.5	1040	1.9
60 000–74 999	78.5	1360	2.0
75 000–99 999	79.7	1688	2.0
100 000 or above	88.6	3558	3.0
Age of giver			
18–24 years	57.1	266	0.6
25–34 years	66.9	793	1.7
35–44 years	68.5	1398	2.6
45–54 years	78.5	979	1.8
55–64 years	71.7	2015	3.6
65–74 years	73.0	1023	2.9
75 years and above	58.6	902	3.1
Highest education of giver			
Not a high school graduate	46.6	318	1.2
High school graduate	67.2	800	1.9
Some college	74.1	1037	2.1
College graduate or more	82.3	1830	2.9

Source: Author's calculations, data from Independent Sector, 1995.

education give more often, give more dollars, and generally give a higher fraction of income. Note that the table does not show a smooth acceleration of giving with age. Again, age, education, and income all vary with each grouping in the table and will have to be considered jointly.

In 1997 over 45 000 charitable, religious and other non-profit organizations filed with the US government (see Bilodeau and Steinberg in this volume). Table 3 attempts to categorize these charities by the types of services they provide. This reveals that, among all types, households are most likely to give to religious organizations and to give them the most money—48% of all households give to religion and 59% of all charitable dollars go to religion.

Table 3
Private philanthropy by type of charitable organization, 1995

Type of charity	Percent of households who give	Average amount given by those who give	Percent of total household contributions
Arts, culture and humanities	9.4	221	2.6
Education	20.3	335	9.0
Environment	11.5	110	1.6
Health	27.3	218	8.1
Human Services	25.1	285	9.5
International	3.1	293	1.1
Private and community foundations	6.1	196	1.4
Public or societal benefit	10.3	127	1.7
Recreation	7.0	161	1.4
Religious	48.0	946	59.4
Youth development	20.9	140	3.8
Other	2.1	160	0.3

Source: Author's calculations, data from Independent Sector, Giving and Volunteering, 1995.

2.2. International statistics

A difficult aspect of comparing data from across countries is the varied sources of information and the inconsistent definitions of charitable giving and non-profit organizations. Using data from Johns Hopkins Comparative Nonprofit Sector Project,[6] we can nonetheless attempt to gain some perspective on the differing size of the charitable sectors of various economies.

Figure 2 shows reports of cash revenues of non-profits from philanthropy. The experience varies widely around the globe. The US, however, stands out as being the most reliant on private donations, at 21 percent of all revenues. With the exception of Spain, European countries are much lower, varying from 3 to 11 percent. The South American countries of Argentina and Brazil rely heavily on philanthropy (about 18 percent), while Mexico does not (6 percent).

Figure 3 provides a different perspective by looking at the total expenditures of the non-profit sector. Here the US falls closer to the middle of the pack, at 7.5 percent of GDP. The Netherlands and Israel have the largest non-profit sectors, while Mexico and Brazil have the smallest.

[6] See their web-site, http://www.jhu.edu/~cnp/.

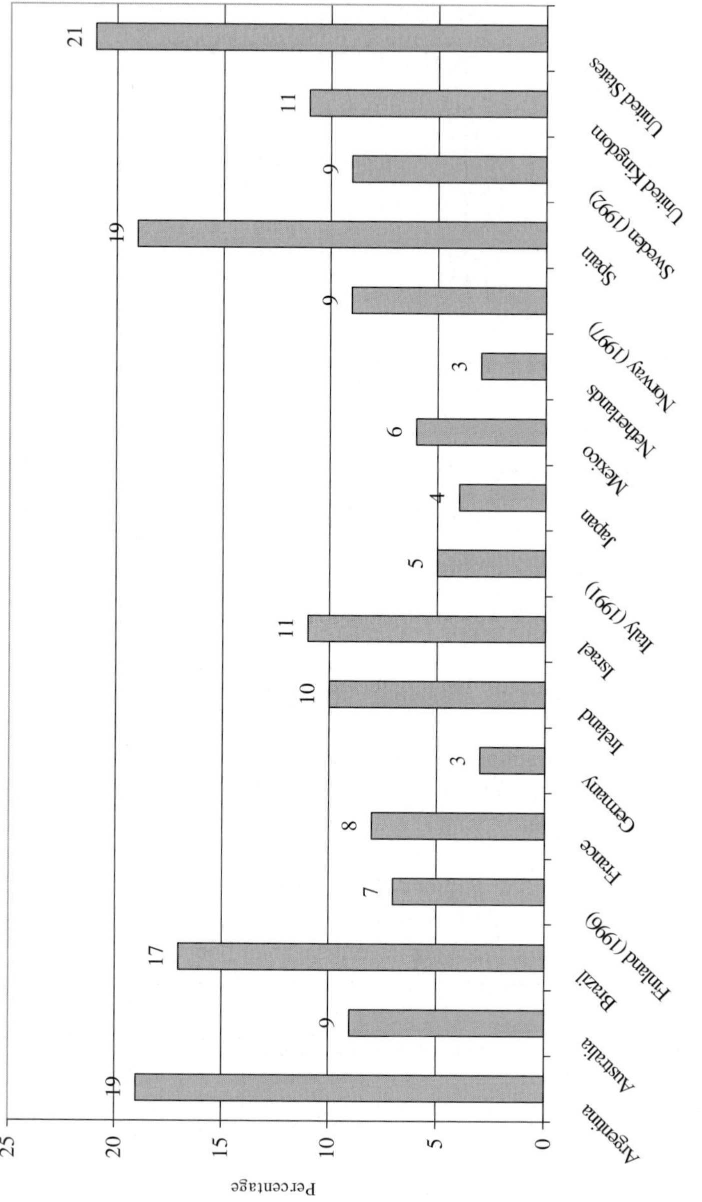

Figure 2. Percentage of cash revenues of the nonprofit sector received from philanthropy: 1995.

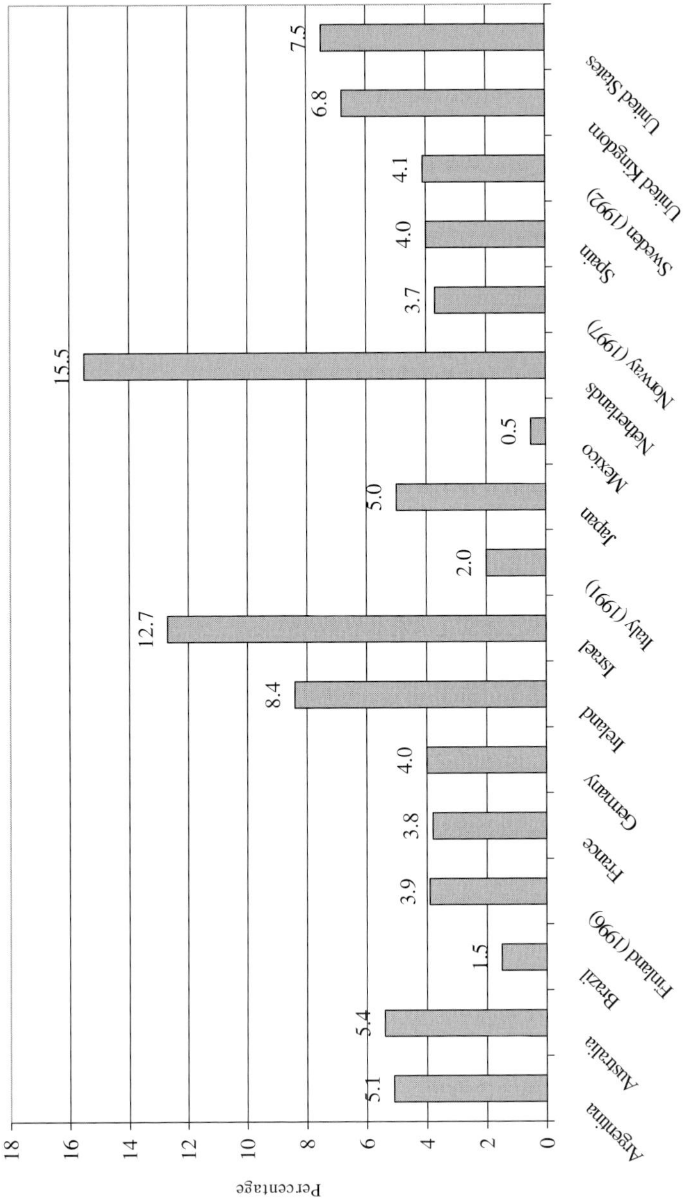

Figure 3. Nonprofit sector expenditures as a percentage of GDP: 1995.

3. Theoretical foundation

This section outlines the basic theoretical foundations for philanthropy. Hochman and Rodgers (1969) and Kolm (1969) were the first to recognize that charitable giving, motivated out of altruism, creates a public good out of charity. Even if, for instance, the recipients of the charitable services are individuals and are given private goods, such as income transfers, day care, or housing, the fact that others feel altruistically toward these individuals means that the private consumption of these charity recipients becomes a public good.

Similar arguments hold for other charities that provide private goods. Education dollars benefit the students and faculty of the institution, but because the donors also take pride in the quality of the institution, the donations act as public goods. Gifts to health care will benefit the patients of hospitals, and medical research will help those with particular maladies, but the fact that givers value these outcomes in general again makes them into public goods. Similarly with the arts. The patrons of the museum or opera will get the direct benefits of any gifts, but the fact that the giver values these benefits received by others makes the donations public goods to the donors.

We begin our theoretical analysis, therefore, with a discussion of privately provided public goods.

3.1. *A model of private giving to public goods*

Let's start with the simplest model without government or foundations, in which only individuals are providing the good through voluntary donations.[7] Assume that there are $i = 1, \ldots, n$ individuals in the economy. Each individual i consumes a composite private good x_i and a public good G. Let an individual's donation to the public good be g_i and define $G = \sum_{i=1}^{n} g_i$. Since G is a pure public good, we assume preferences are $u_i(x_i, G)$. For simplicity, assume the public good can be produced from the private good with a simple linear technology, and that both goods are measured in the same units.[8] Finally, assume each person is endowed with money income m_i. Then each person faces the optimization problem

$$\max_{x_i, g_i} u(x_i, G) \tag{3.1}$$

[7] There are many antecedents to this model, but Becker (1974) deserves the primary credit for this formulation of the problem. The most thorough treatment of this model, however, is given in the extremely important work of Bergstrom et al. (1986). Their paper is the basis for this subsection.

[8] We could, alternatively, assume a concave technology that converts x to a public good G'. For instance, $G' = F(G)$, $F' > 0$, $F'' < 0$. However, if we embed this in a quasi-concave utility function, $u = v(x_i, G') = v(x_i, F(G)) = u(x_i, G)$, this utility function can absorb the technological concavity. Hence, the assumption of a linear technology is consistent with an assumption of a public good provided with increasing marginal cost and a quasi-concave utility. However, if the function $F(G)$ exhibits a range of increasing returns, special care will be needed. See Andreoni (1998) and section 9.1 below.

$$\text{s.t.} \quad x_i + g_i = m_i$$
$$G = \sum_{j=1}^{n} g_j$$
$$g_i \geq 0$$

We solve this model by assuming a Nash equilibrium. That is, we assume each person i solves (3.1) taking the contributions of the others as given.[9] Let $G_{-i} = \sum_{j \neq i} g_j = G - g_i$ equal the total contributions of all individuals except person i. Then under the Nash assumption, each person i treats G_{-i} as independent of g_i when solving (3.1). Notice that this implies that each individual is behaving as though they are "topping up" the charitable good from G_{-i} to their own most desired level G. To see this, add G_{-i} to both sides of the budget constraint in (3.1), and to the third constraint. Then we can rewrite the optimization problem with each individual choosing G rather than g_i:

$$\max_{x_i, G} u(x_i, G) \tag{3.2}$$
$$\text{s.t.} \quad x_i + G = m_i + G_{-i}$$
$$G \geq G_{-i}$$

This formulation highlights an important implication of public goods models, first noted by Becker (1974), that each individual acts as though their "social income" were $m_i + G_{-i}$. In other words, m_i and G_{-i} have the same marginal effect on an individual's optimal G.

To write our solution, first solve (3.2) by ignoring the inequality constraint, $G \geq G_{-i}$. In this case, find a solution to (3.2) from setting the marginal rate of substitution equal to 1, that is $(\partial u_i/\partial G)/(\partial u_i/\partial x_i) = 1$. Solving this we find individual supply equations $G = f_i(m_i + G_{-i})$ or, equivalently, $g_i = f_i(m_i + G_{-i}) - G_{-i}$. However, since we assume that people can only give positive amounts to the public good, we must write the individual's best reply function as

$$g_i = \max\{f_i(m_i + G_{-i}) - G_{-i}, 0\} \tag{3.3}$$

Finally, we assume that the public good is a normal good and the private good is strictly normal for all individuals. That is, there exists a θ such that $0 < f_i' \leq \theta < 1$ for all i in the set of givers.[10] This assumption is sufficient to guarantee that there exists a unique Nash equilibrium.

DEFINITION 3.1. *A* ***Nash equilibrium*** *is a partition of the set of individuals into a set of givers S and of non-givers S', such that for all $i \in S$, $g_i = f_i(m_i + G_{-i}) - G_{-i} \geq 0$, and for all $j \in S'$, $g_j = 0$ and $f_j(m_j + G_{-j}) - G_{-j} < 0$.*

[9] As before, the pun is entirely intentional.

[10] The parameter θ is needed to show that as n goes to infinity there is an equilibrium level of the public good. Without this, there may be no bound to G in equilibrium.

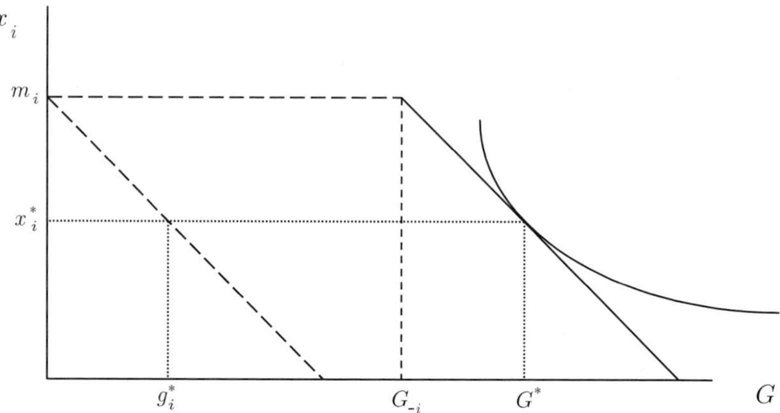

Figure 4. Nash equilibrium in the private provision of public goods.

PROPOSITION 3.2. *A Nash equilibrium exists and is unique.*

PROOF. (a) Existence. Define the set $\mathcal{B} = \{(g_1, g_2, \ldots, g_n): 0 \leq g_i \leq m_i\}$. Define $\mathcal{F} = (f_1, f_2, \ldots, f_n): (g_1, g_2, \ldots, g_n) \to (g_1, g_2, \ldots, g_n)$ as a mapping from the set $\mathcal{B}$ into itself. Since $\mathcal{F}$ is continuous, we apply Brouwer's fixed point theorem to show an equilibrium exists. [Bergstrom et al. (1986)].

(b) Uniqueness: By normal goods, $\mathcal{F}$ is a contraction mapping. Hence, the equilibrium is unique. (Fraser, 1992, and Cornes et al., 1999). □

The decision problem and Nash equilibrium can be illustrated in Figure 4. The "endowment point" can be seen where consumption $x_i = m_i$ and the public good $G = G_{-i}$. As the individual decides to give, x_i can be traded for more G along the 45-degree line. In equilibrium, all individuals consume the same G but, assuming different preferences and incomes, different x_i.[11]

This is basically the classic model of Samuelson (1954) applied to voluntary giving. Along with this is the other classic finding that private giving will not be Pareto efficient. According to the Samuelson conditions, G reaches the efficient level when the sum of the marginal rates of substitution equal the marginal cost, that is $\sum_{i=1}^{n}(\partial u_i/\partial G)/(\partial u_i/\partial x_i) = \sum_{i=1}^{n} MRS_i = 1$. However, we know that each giver is setting $MRS_i = 1$, hence $\sum_{i=1}^{n} MRS_i$ is in excess of 1 whenever at least one person is giving (and G is a good for all others), implying inefficiently low G. This inefficiency

[11] Note, however, that if all individuals have the same preferences, then all givers must also have the same consumption in equilibrium, even if they have different incomes. This is easy to show: In equilibrium all have the same G. They also are all optimizing so that the $\mathrm{MRS}(x_i, G) = 1$. But if $\mathrm{MRS}(x_i, G) = \mathrm{MRS}(x_j, G)$ then $x_i = x_j$.

can justify the involvement of the government in providing public goods. Either by direct grants or subsidies to private giving, government involvement was thought to be an efficiency-enhancing supplement to private charitable markets. This suggests a partnership between government and private donors. However, upon closer examination, natural extensions of this model call into question the assumption that the government can supplement or encourage private donations. We discuss this next.

3.2. Neutrality: crowding out

In 1984 Russell Roberts (Roberts, 1984) made a bold assertion in the *Journal of Political Economy*: The great expansion of government services for the poor since the Great Depression was accompanied by an equal decline in charitable giving for the poor, with the result that the government dollars had no net effect on alleviating poverty. The same was true, he claimed, for all public–private partnerships in providing public goods. His empirical evidence was all impressionistic, and his main basis for his assertion was theoretical.

Roberts' claims were built upon a model of Warr (1982). Warr showed that any "small" lump sum tax on donors that is contributed to the public good will completely crowd out private donations. The substitution will be dollar-for-dollar. In fact, given the set up in (3.2), this effect is trivial to show.

Begin with the case of no government intervention. Let $(g_1^*, g_2^*, \dots, g_n^*)$ be the vector of equilibrium private contributions to the public good. Now introduce taxation. Let t_i be a lump sum tax on person i, with the proceeds donated to the public good. The individual's budget constraint is then $x_i + g_i + t_i = m_i$. Now each individual's donation will be the sum of the voluntary donation g_i and the involuntary donation t_i. Call this total donation $y_i = g_i + t_i$. Likewise, define $Y = \sum_{i=1}^{n} y_i$, and $Y_{-i} = \sum_{j \neq i} y_j$. Then it is easy to see that the optimization problem (3.2) can be rewritten as

$$\begin{aligned} &\max_{x_i, Y} u(x_i, Y) \\ &\text{s.t.} \quad x_i + Y = m_i + Y_{-i} \\ &\qquad\;\; Y \geq Y_{-i} + t_i \end{aligned} \tag{3.4}$$

Notice that this optimization problem (3.4) is identical to (3.2), with two exceptions. First, G and G_{-i} have been replaced by Y and Y_{-i}. However, this is only a change in notation and not a real change in the optimization problem. Hence, as long as the solution to (3.2) without taxation is feasible in (3.4) with taxation, then it too should be an equilibrium. This is where the second difference comes in: The inequality constraint in (3.4) now includes a t_i, which guarantees that $g_i \geq 0$. When will the solution without taxation be feasible with taxation? Whenever $t_i \leq g_i^*$, that is, whenever the lump sum tax is no greater than the original equilibrium contribution. In this case the equilibrium is $y_i^* = g_i^*$, so that the new equilibrium gift, say g_i', will be $g_i' = g_i^* - t$. In equilibrium, therefore, everyone will reduce their voluntary contribution by the amount of the involuntary contribution in order to keep their total utility maximizing contribution the same. This demonstrates the next proposition, shown by Bergstrom et al. (1986).

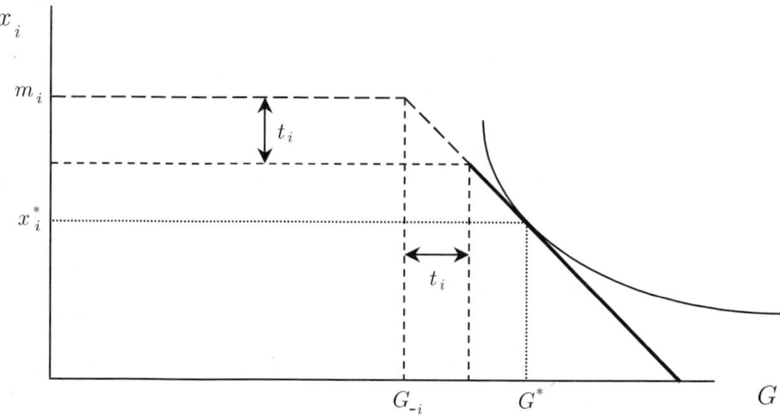

Figure 5. Complete crowding out.

PROPOSITION 3.3. ***Complete Crowding Out.*** *Let* $(g_1^*, g_2^*, \ldots, g_n^*)$ *be the Nash equilibrium donations with no government taxation. Then if lump sum taxes* $0 \leq t_i \leq g_i^*$ *for all i are donated to the public good, the equilibrium donation after taxation will be* $g_i' = g_i^* - t_i$ *for all i, and the total supply of the public good will be unchanged.*

Intuitively, the reason that crowding out is complete is that the model assumes that people are indifferent between voluntary giving g_i and involuntary giving t_i. In equilibrium, each person is acting as though they are choosing their total gift, $y_i = g_i + t_i$, so that if one element of the sum is forced to move in one direction, the other element will respond with and equal and opposite change.

This intuition is illustrated in Figure 5. This shows a lump sum tax that is completely neutral—the effect is simply to erase part of the budget set that was not being selected. Notice that if the tax were to rise to $t = g^* = m - x^*$, then this person's private contribution would be driven to zero. Any tax beyond this would be non-neutral and would force total giving to rise.

Of course, a good deal of taxation involves individuals who are not givers or for whom $t_i > g_i$. What happens to the equilibrium Y when this happens? Naturally enough, total provision will increase. Bergstrom et al. (1986) provide an elegant proof of this proposition, but the effect is intuitive enough to explain informally. Consider taxing a non-giver. This person will not be able to reduce g_i to counteract the increase in t_i. As a result, this person's y_i will be higher. This means that for all givers, Y_{-i} will be higher and, as a result, their "social income" will also be higher. Since Y is a normal good, each will demand more of it, and so the new equilibrium Y will be higher than before the tax.

These two results of complete crowding but also non-neutral taxation on non-givers can explain a lot about what we see in the real world data. However, further exploration of these models indicates that there is a lot less predictive power to these models than may at first appear. This is the topic of the next subsection.

3.3. Neutrality: reductio ad absurdum

A number of articles in the 1980s appeared which explored further implications of these models, including Sugden (1982), Warr (1983), Bergstrom et al. (1986), Bernheim (1986), Roberts (1987), Andreoni (1988), and Sandler and Posnett (1991), bringing to light an elegant model with clear analysis and stunning results. Unfortunately, many of the results seemed so absurd as to call into question the basic assumptions of the model and to undermine its usefulness in understanding philanthropy.

Consider, first, the observation that a large number of individuals give to a charity. Suppose that the government taxed non-givers by an amount τ and donated this to the public good. As we saw above, this will increase the total supply of the public good. But by how much?

Solving for the new equilibrium, each giver will satisfy the equation

$$G + \tau \equiv f_i(m_i + G_{-i} + \tau)$$

Implicitly differentiate with respect to τ to find

$$\begin{aligned}\frac{dG}{d\tau} + 1 &= f_i'\left(\frac{dG_{-i}}{d\tau} + 1\right)\\ &= f_i'\left(\frac{dG}{d\tau} - \frac{dg_i}{d\tau} + 1\right)\end{aligned}$$

This equation can be solved for $dg_i/d\tau$. This in turn can be summed across all givers to find $dG/d\tau$. Doing so, one finds

$$\frac{dG}{d\tau} = \frac{-\sum_{i=1}^{k} \frac{1-f_i'}{f_i'}}{1 + \sum_{i=1}^{k} \frac{1-f_i'}{f_i'}} > -1$$

This is as predicted by the theory of the last subsection. However, divide the numerator and denominator by k, the number of givers, and let k increase to infinity. Combine this with the assumption that $0 < f_i' \leq \theta < 1$, and it follows immediately that

$$\lim_{k\to\infty} \frac{dG}{d\tau} = -1$$

Hence, when the number of givers is large, even non-neutral taxes become approximately neutral.[12]

[12] This result was motivated by Sugden (1982) and derived by Andreoni (1988).

Another result from large economies is that as n increases, the *proportion* of the population giving shrinks to zero. This can be seen most easily by assuming identical preferences but different incomes. Imagine a probability distribution function for incomes from which the population of potential givers is drawn. Then for any population of n and equilibrium G, all givers will satisfy

$$G = f(m_i + G_{-i})$$

Invert f to get

$$\begin{aligned} f^{-1}(G) &= m_i + G_{-i} \\ &= m_i + G - g_i \end{aligned}$$

Rearrange to get

$$\begin{aligned} g_i &= m_i - f^{-1}(G) + G \\ &= m_i - m^*(G) \end{aligned}$$

This expression reveals that for each G there is a critical level of income, m^*, such that only those with incomes greater than m^* will be giving. Since $m^*(G) \equiv f^{-1}(G) - G$, it follows from normal goods that $dm^*(G)/dG > 0$. The question then is, how does m^* change as population changes?

Formal demonstration of this can be found in Andreoni (1988), but again we provide the intuition here. Let's draw another member of the economy from the probability density function of income. If we draw an $m < m^*$, then this has no effect on G but increases the proportion of non-givers. Suppose we draw an $m > m^*$. Then this person will be a giver. Can total giving then decline? A simple revealed preference argument (Andreoni and McGuire, 1993) shows it cannot—if more givers end up giving less in total, then the original set of givers could have increased utility by giving less in the first place. Hence, total giving will rise, and so m^* will rise, which also means that a smaller fraction of the population will have $m > m^*$ and so a smaller fraction will be giving. As n rises to infinity, one can show that only the richest sliver of the economy will be givers. Moreover, the result is robust to heterogeneity of types.

Another set of elegant yet unexpected findings come from extensions of the crowding out result to neutrality of income redistribution. Warr (1983) and Bergstrom et al. (1986) show that small redistributions of income among givers have no effect on either the total supply of public good, or on individual consumption. The fact that people give to a common public good will undo the effect of the redistribution.

A simple way to see this result is by sequential application of the crowding out proposition proved in the prior subsection. First take money $t \leq g_i$ from giver i and donate this to the public good. This will be neutral. Next take t from the public good and give it to giver j. This just runs the crowding out proposition in reverse, so it too will be neutral. But notice what we have done—we've taken t from giver i and transferred it to giver j. Because both i and j are giving to the same public good, the redistribution of income is neutral. No consumption has been affected.

Bernheim (1986) showed how this effect extends to the case of multiple public goods. What if person i and j in this example are giving to different public goods? Person i gives to good A and person j gives to good B. Then certainly this income transfer will not be neutral, right? Maybe not. Suppose there is a person k who gives to both A and B, and that $g_k^B > t$. Then the transfer of t from i to j can be constructed by first transferring t from i to k, then transferring again from k to j. Both of these are neutral so the transfer from i to j is neutral too. Of course, we don't need to stop here. If there are many public goods and a chain of neutral transfers between pairs of agents that can reconstruct a given redistribution, then the redistribution itself will be neutral. The greater the number of public goods, the greater the chance that any redistribution will be neutral.[13] Hence, not only will the government be helpless to affect the amount of public goods provided, but helpless to affect the distribution of income.

Bernheim (1986) and Andreoni (1988) found circumstances under which neutrality also extends to subsidies to giving, that is, even distortionary taxes can be neutral. Andreoni and Bergstrom (1996), however, showed that neutrality does not extend to all distortionary taxes. The key to whether subsidies are neutral rests on how the government chooses to make credible its promise to balance the budget, even outside of equilibrium. If, for instance, the government moves last, after individual gifts are made, and adjusts government donations or individual taxes to keep the budget in balance, then subsidies simply act like elaborate redistributions of income and, appealing to earlier results, have a neutral effect. If the government moves first, however, and offers a credible tax and subsidy scheme that balances the budget even outside of the equilibrium, the subsidies can be effective.[14]

Most readers would agree that the results reported in this subsection cast those of the prior subsection in a different light. If we are going to accept complete crowding out, we also need to believe in near complete crowding of any government gifts to charity, that only the very richest are giving, that redistributions of income are neutral as long as people are giving to charities, and that even "distortionary" taxes may be non-distortionary. Few people, I expect, are willing to adopt the full slate of predictions

[13] Bernheim and Bagwell (1988) have a related finding with respect to redistributions across generations, where transfers between families are neutralized. They draw a similar conclusion that the strength of neutrality leads to absurd conclusions.

[14] Andreoni and Bergstrom (1996) showed that any model of subsidies must also make a credible plan for balancing the government's budget (a subtlety not recognized by Warr, 1982, and Roberts, 1987). That is, even if the tax and subsidy scheme will balance the budget in equilibrium, explicit and credible plans for balancing the budget even in non-equilibrium choices must also be made. If, for instance, the government is left to be the residual claimant, that is, any imbalance in the government's budget must be made up in further taxation on individuals or reduction in government contributions to the public good, then subsidies become an incredible method for increasing giving—they amount to elaborate and neutral redistributions of income. However, if the government makes other citizens the residual claimants by, for instance, setting taxes $t_i = sG_{-i}/(n-1)$ where s is the subsidy rate, then taxes can increase giving. This holds even if non-givers are taxed. Related results are found in Boadway et al. (1989).

from a model of pure public goods—a classic *reductio ad absurdum*. How, then, can we modify the model of charitable giving to get a more realistic picture of giving to public goods?

3.4. Warm-glow giving

The model of pure public goods is an extremely natural model to turn to, so what made it such a poor predictor? Certainly the goods people are giving to are pure public goods, and certainly people have feelings of altruism that make them demand these goods. So what needs to change to make the model more realistic and more predictive?

All of the results presented in the last section rely on one feature of the pure public goods model: all else equal, individuals are assumed to be indifferent between all the *sources* of the contributions to the charity, are indifferent to the *means* by which the good is provided, and only care for the total supply of the public good. Simple introspection (an often dangerous avenue to take) reveals that there are many other considerations to giving that may make people *not* indifferent to the means of providing the good. As stated in the introduction, humans are moral—they enjoy doing what is right. They are also emotional, empathic and sympathetic—they enjoy gratitude and recognition, they enjoy making someone else happy, and they feel relieved from guilt when they become a giver. Put more simply and more generally, people may experience a "warm-glow" from giving. All of these moral compunctions and emotional exchanges mean that people are not indifferent to their own voluntary gift and the gifts of others. They strictly prefer, all else equal, that the gifts come from themselves.

A simple model that could capture these effects would be to put an individual's contribution in the utility function directly: $u_i = u_i(x_i, G, g_i)$. This means that donations will have some qualities of public goods, but also some properties of private goods. A similar model, first suggested in a footnote by Becker (1974), has been developed and analyzed by Cornes and Sandler (1984), Steinberg (1987), and Andreoni (1989, 1990).[15] Because this model contrasts with the case where giving is motivated only by a concern, perhaps altruistically, for the public good, the model with warm-glow is also sometimes referred to as *impure altruism*. More commonly, however, the model is simply referred to as one of *warm-glow giving*.[16]

[15] Note that the warm-glow model $u(x_i, G, g_i)$ is different from a model that assumes $u(x_i, G_{-i}, g_i)$, as was suggested by Becker (1974). By including g_i in *two* arguments, the warm-glow model can take advantage of added convexity in proving theoretical results, and can also contain two polar cases of pure altruism, $u(x_i, G)$, and pure warm-glow (or egoism), $u(x_i, g_i)$.

[16] Charlie Clotfelter once mentioned to me, informally, that the term "warm-glow" is somewhat pejorative, but that the tone it projects is right on the mark. First, the hint of sarcasm keeps us constantly reminded of the Stigler and Becker (1997) "De Gustibus" critique—the economic theorist cannot casually assume in preferences that the people behave as they do simply because they want to. Nonetheless, the fact that people do get a joy from giving is such a natural observation as to be nearly beyond question. Hence, the playfulness of the "warm-glow" phrase conveys the sense of "but of course, isn't it obvious?" Both aspects of the subtext here are important: when the simplest model doesn't work, turn to introspection—but do so carefully.

How will the model of warm-glow giving affect predictions of crowding out? Write the individual's optimization problem this way, assuming the inequality constraint is not binding:

$$\max_{x,g} u_i(x_i, G, g_i)$$
$$\text{s.t.} \quad x_i + g_i = m_i$$

As above, rewrite this problem so that the person is choosing G rather than g_i:

$$\max_{x_i,G} u(x_i, G, G - G_{-i})$$
$$\text{s.t.} \quad x_i + G = m_i + G_{-i}$$

Again, the solution to this will be a supply of gifts function that depends on social income, but also will have a separate argument for G_{-i}, resulting from the new third argument of the utility function:

$$g_i = f_i(m_i + G_{-i}, G_{-i}) - G_{-i}$$

Let f_i^s be the derivative with respect to social income, and let f_i^w be the derivative with respect to the second term, which is the warm-glow term. Normal goods assures us that $0 < f_i^s < 1$, and as shown in Andreoni (1989, 1990), the warm-glow term is positive, $f_i^w > 0$. Take the derivative of this function with respect to G_{-i} to get

$$\begin{aligned}\frac{dg_i}{dG_{-i}} &= f_i^s + f_i^w - 1\\ &= -(1 - f_i^s) + f_i^w\end{aligned}$$

This derivative reveals the primary difference between purely altruistic and warm-glow models of giving. With no warm-glow, increased giving by others causes people to reduce their gifts, because others' gifts are a perfect substitute for one's own. This is captured in the $-(1 - f_i^s)$ part of the expression above. However, with warm-glow the others' gifts are imperfect substitutes for one's own. Hence, with warm-glow a person is no longer as willing to reduce his own contribution in response to increased gifts by others. This is captured in the f_i^w part. Hence, warm-glow creates a "stickiness" to giving—people are no longer indifferent to the source of the gift. At the extreme where people care only for warm-glow, then $dg_i/dG_{-i} = 0$ and so $f_i^s + f_i^w = 1$.

This will, obviously, imply that crowding out will no longer be complete. But this is true only so long as warm-glow does not extend to gifts made involuntarily through taxes.[17] To see this, write the utility function $u(x_i, G + t, g_i)$. Assume that only person i is taxed. Following the steps above we get a supply function $g_i = f_i(m_i + G_{-i}, G_{-i} + t) - (G_{-i} + t)$. It is easy to see that $dg_i/dt = f_i^w - 1$. If there is no warm-glow then $f_i^w = 0$ and $dg_i/dt = -1$, which is complete crowding out. However, when

[17] For instance, if utility were $u(x_i, G + T, g_i + t_i)$ then small taxes will again be neutral.

$f_i^w > 0$, then $-1 < dg_i/dt$ which means person i will not reduce g_i enough to restore the prior equilibrium and crowding out will be incomplete.

Formally, assume only person 1 is taxed. Then totally differentiate the demand equation to get

$$dg_1 = f_1^s dG_{-1} + f_1^w(dG_{-1} + dt) - (dG_{-1} + dt)$$

Also totally differentiate the other $n-1$ equations. For each equation, substitute $dG_{-i} = dG - dg_i$. Add these n equations and solve for dG/dt to get

$$\begin{aligned}\frac{dG}{dt} &= c\frac{f_1^w}{f_1^s + f_1^w} - 1\\ &= c\omega_1 - 1\end{aligned}$$

where $c > 0$ is a function of all n responses.[18] The coefficient $\omega_1 = f_1^w/(f_1^s + f_1^w)$ can be interpreted as the relative strength of the warm-glow motive for person 1. The stronger the warm-glow motive relative to the altruism motive, that is the bigger is ω_1, the lower crowding out will be. If there is no warm-glow motive for person 1, then $f_1^w = 0$, so $\omega_1 = 0$, and again crowding out is complete.[19]

Similar results hold with respect to transfers of income. Imagine taking money from person 1 and giving it to person 2. We can construct this transfer as a simultaneous tax increase on person 1 and tax decrease on person 2. Letting $dt_1 = dt = -dt_2$ then we can repeat the steps above and solve to find

$$\frac{dG}{dt} = \frac{dG}{dt_1} - \frac{dG}{dt_2} = c(\omega_1 - \omega_2)$$

If $\omega_1 > \omega_2$, so that the warm-glow motive of the person losing income is relatively stronger than that of the person receiving income, then the level of the public good will rise.[20] Intuitively, warm-glow makes people's giving "sticky" and a poor substitute for another's giving. Thus, reducing income of the less responsive person will have the least effect on G.

We now see that the simple generalization to warm-glow preferences means that neutrality goes away. Moreover, we see that pure altruism—the absence of a warm-glow motive—is both necessary and sufficient for neutrality, and thus an extremely special case.

Putting warm-glow into the model is, while intuitively appealing, an admittedly *ad hoc* fix. Hence, it is important to find real evidence that warm-glow is an important feature of preferences. Using survey data on giving, this would be a nearly impossible

[18] In particular, $c = [1 + \sum_{i=1}^n (1 - f_i^s - f_i^w)/(f_i^s + f_i^w)]^{-1}$. See Andreoni (1989) for a more detailed derivation.

[19] See Andreoni (1989) for formal proof. Note that this discussion differs subtly from Andreoni (1989, 1990), who described $1 - \omega$ as an "altruism coefficient," rather than ω as a "warm-glow coefficient."

[20] Notice that the transfer will have a neutral affect on G if whenever $\omega_1 = \omega_2$. However, the effect on *all* consumption, including x's will only be neutral if $\omega_1 = \omega_2 = 0$. See Andreoni (1989) for details.

task. We could only indirectly test the hypothesis by finding choices consistent with predictions of the model (see Ribar and Wilhelm, 2002). However, using controlled laboratory experiments we can more accurately identify whether preferences include a warm-glow term. Fortunately, the experimental data is overwhelming in its support of warm-glow. Most notably, Andreoni (1993, 1995), Palfrey and Prisbrey (1996, 1997), and Andreoni and Miller (2002) find clear evidence of well-behaved preferences for giving that include a warm-glow motive. These provide the needed evidence to turn this *ad hoc* fix into a solid foundation of human motivation.

3.5. The dominance of warm-glow

Suppose both motives of altruism and warm-glow exist. One can show that as the economy grows large, warm-glow will become the dominant if not the exclusive motive for giving at the margin. While general arguments exist, perhaps it is most expedient to use a special example to motivate the result.[21]

Suppose the economy has n individuals with identical incomes m and identical Cobb–Douglas preferences

$$u_i = \ln x_i + \alpha \ln G + \beta \ln g_i$$

The first order conditions are then

$$-\frac{1}{m - g_i} + \alpha \frac{1}{G} + \beta \frac{1}{g_i} = 0$$

Since individuals are identical, the Nash equilibrium gifts will be the same for all i, thus $G^* = ng^*$. Substitute this into the above and find the Nash equilibrium contribution to be

$$g^* = \frac{\alpha m/n + \beta m}{1 + \alpha/n + \beta} \tag{3.5}$$

Note that if there were only altruism and no warm glow, then $g^* = \alpha m/(n + \alpha)$. In this case, as n increases, each person's equilibrium gift asymptotes to zero (while total giving asymptotes to αm). By contrast, if there were no altruism and only warm-glow, then $g^* = \beta m/(1 + \beta)$, which is independent of n. Now look again at (3.5). As n increases, the relative importance of α, the utility parameter on altruism, diminishes and, in the limit, choices are dictated solely by β, the warm-glow parameter. With this, all the implications of neutrality disappear—in the limit giving is a solely private good.[22]

Another way to see this intuitively is that, as the size of the charity grows, all giving due to altruism will be crowded out, leaving only giving due to warm-glow. This accords

[21] See Ribar and Wilhelm (2002).

[22] Ribar and Wilhelm (2002) show that for general preferences, the sufficient condition for this to be met is that the marginal rate of substitution between warm-glow and consumption, evaluated at $g = 0$, not vanish as n grows.

naturally with the observation that giving $100 to an organization that collects millions is motivated more by an admiration for the organization than for any measurable effect of the marginal donation. That does not, however, imply that altruism is not important—the two are surely tied together. Just like hunger tells a person it is *time* to eat but taste buds tells the person what they *want* to eat, it is altruism that should tell you what to give to, but warm-glow tells you how much to give.

4. Should warm-glow count in social welfare?

Now that we have explored the implications of the warm-glow assumption, demonstrated its importance, and verified the assumption on empirical grounds, we are faced with a deep and significant question: How should warm-glow giving factor into calculations of social welfare?[23]

This is as much a philosophical question as it is an economic one. Reasonable people will likely differ on the answer. On one hand, we should not question preferences. On the other hand, however, we can easily imagine cases where a (paternalistic) government would improve well-being by ignoring those preferences. Perhaps the best way to understand this question is through a series of examples and analogies.

Consider an example of time preferences and savings. Madrian and Shea (2001) have recently shown that if new employees are automatically entered into a 401(k) retirement savings plan (unless they opt out), far more of them enroll than when they are not automatically entered (and must opt in). All that differs between these two situations is the institution within which people make their savings decision. If we believe that people are revealing what is in their own best interest, then which situation is revealing the true preferences? If a social planner, with the objective to maximize social welfare, choose which institution it wanted for society, which would it choose and how would it frame the choice? Most economists would, I suspect, say that the two institutions simply provide different frames for the decision and that these frames may bias or distort behavior, preying perhaps on people's incomplete information or financial naivete, and that social welfare calculations about the optimal level of savings should be independent of these biases or frames and should assume complete information and sophisticated choices. But, conceding to these biases, frames, and naivete, economists would choose the institution that resulted in behavior closest to that selected in a hypothetical "clean" environment of no biases, no frames, and perfect information.

[23] Diamond (2006) provides a related discussion, which also inspired some of the points provided below. For a contrasting view, see Kaplow (1995, 1998) who treats gifts and warm-glow as in the realm of social welfare maximization. Thus, he argues that those who are loved more by others are also loved more by the government. He also argues that the government should subsidize gifts, and those who enjoy giving more should get greater subsidies. While, in principle, these arguments are defensible, I argue here that under greater scrutiny, their application becomes unclear.

Next, consider a laboratory experiment to provide public goods (see Andreoni, 1995). In this experiment, the exact same game is presented in two frames, one positive and one negative. In the positive frame subjects are given 100 units of money to keep, but are told they can contribute any share of it to a public good, thus creating a positive externality for other subjects. In the negative frame they are told that all the money is already given to the public good, but that they can withdraw up to 100 units to keep, thus creating a negative externality. What happens? People don't seem to be bothered that much by creating a negative externality, although they don't like the "cold-prickle" they feel, but really enjoy the warm glow of creating positive externalities. Does this mean it is socially preferred to provide more of the public good when giving donations creates a warm-glow than in the world where withdrawing donations creates a cold-prickle? What is happening in this game is that there is utility from the act of making the choice, and this "choice utility" is again biasing choices. Since the only difference in these worlds is the frame which prejudices the decisions—whether the economy is endowed with money in the public good (like a commons) or in the private good (as with charitable giving)— it seems that we would want a social criterion that would give us the same directive in both cases.

What about this hypothetical situation: Imagine two pairs of friends. Each pair meets every week for lunch at the same restaurant and always orders the same thing. Al and Andy each pay for their own meals, while Bob and Brad take turns picking up the tab. The B friends get a warm-glow from giving a gift to each other each week. Can we say they are better off than the A friends? Maybe, but maybe not. Bob and Brad are constantly in a state of having to retire a debt. So, while buying lunch for the friend is improving utility, it may be the debt they are paying off has lowered their utility in the first place. Hence, it is just as likely that the mutual gift-giving friends are actually worse off than the self-sufficient friends. As economists, we have no way of knowing.

Next, a related point on the "power of the ask." Fund-raisers know that to get money donated, you have to ask for it. And, most often you either get nothing or you get the amount you asked for. Think of how you feel when colleagues asks you to give to a cause, buy girl scout cookies, or sponsor their kids' sports teams. Although you cringe when they approach, you give because saying no would be even more painful than saying yes. Hence, giving has a marginally positive effect on your utility—but it was "the ask" that lowered it in the first place. By providing public goods through charities, we are creating obligations, guilt, and social pressure among people that they relieve by giving to charity. The giving creates warm feelings, provides social praise, and may actually build valuable relationships. But even with successful charitable fund-raising, do the positive feelings of giving outweigh the negative feelings of the burdens of obligation and guilt? Again, we have no way of knowing.

Finally, consider this experimental data collected by Kahneman and Knetsch (1992). They ask people a series of questions about how much they are willing to contribute to a public good. Each successive question they ask involves a environmental public good that embeds the public good in the prior question—environmental clean up on a local level versus regional level versus national level. Thus, stating a smaller number when moving to a larger scale would be logically inconsistent. What they find is that the answer to the first question they ask is, on average, about $25, and the answer to the second is about $50. But this is true whether the first question is about the local, regional or national good. Hence, the good itself seems not to matter for the willingness to pay. Kahneman and Knetsch instead argue that the answers to these questions are simply maintaining a self-image of being an environmentalist. What if the warm glow of giving to a public good is exactly the same as this? When a fund-raiser calls and asks for a donation, the gift is simply buying a self-image that says "I am a decent and generous person," or perhaps less positively, "I am not cold-hearted and selfish." This is a demand that, as in Say's law, would not have been generated had the supply of fund-raisers for charitable causes not emerged in the first place. So, whether and how this "spin off" good should be counted in social welfare will depend on whether the social planner has any direct interest in creating this market in the first place. That is, does society have a direct interest in creating a market for maintaining self-images? Lacking any argument that it does, then the creation of this market should not in itself affect the social welfare goals of proving the efficient level of charity.

These examples have illustrated four principles that militate against counting warm-glow in welfare:

1. Choices in the real world are distorted by the institutions within which they are made. These biases prey on decision frames, incomplete information, and naive decision makers. Optimal social policy should have as a goal decisions that would be made in an idealized world where there are no decision frames, no missing information or knowledge, and no social distortions.
2. Different institutions for providing public goods bring up different emotions or sentiments simply by creating different environmental cues. Even small or seemingly innocuous changes may have big effects on behavior. This "decision utility" does not itself represent any new consumption, but only utility gained by the process of generating consumption.[24] While such decision utility may affect society's choice of institution to reach social goals, the determination of these social goals, that is the social welfare calculations, should be independent of such decision utility.
3. Even if we were to include warm-glow, we are not sure whether it should increase or decrease welfare. If giving to charity is relieving a guilty feeling, then although it certainly increases utility to give, it does not necessarily mean utility is higher than it would be if the government had forced the contribution through taxation.
4. What if warm-glow giving is purchasing some other good that, while related, is totally separate from the charity itself, such as maintaining a self-image. What is society's interest in creating this spin-off good? If there is no compelling social interest in creating this good, it seems like its existence should have no effect on the calculation of the socially optimal level of the public good itself.

[24] The term "decision utility" is taken from Diamond (2006).

These four points present a (partial) list of the reasons why counting warm-glow in social welfare calculations is either problematic or potentially misleading. In my own view, it is most prudent and most informative to first recognize that behavior is chosen by people seeking warm-glows, but then to set the social welfare maximizing goals that makes no adjustment for warm-glow in aggregating welfare. That is, all social welfare prescriptions should be made without counting warm-glow, but should be constrained by behavior that is dictated by seeking warm-glow.[25]

Why is this important? When choosing government policy that affects giving, it is essential to know what our government's objective should be. We next explore an example of this in describing the optimal tax treatment of giving.

5. Optimal tax treatment of charitable giving

In the US and many other countries, there is a tax preference for giving to charity. This effectively reduces the price of giving. In the US, for instance, charitable giving can be deducted from taxable income, making the price inversely related to the marginal tax rate. With progressive rates, this means those with higher incomes get higher marginal subsidies. This section explores the question, can this subsidy be justified within the context of an optimal tax framework?

This question has been in the literature for a long time. Feldstein (1980) produced the first serious work on it, followed by Boadway and Keen (1993) and Kaplow (1996). A recent paper by Diamond (2006) (see also Saez, 2004), however, has made significant progress on advancing this question. Here we present a simplified version of Diamond's model.

Imagine a world with two types of people, high skilled, H, and low skilled, L. The problem for optimal income taxation is to get the types to self-select into jobs and wages that separate the types and allow the social planner to implement a progressive tax system. The binding constraint, however, is that the high skilled must be better off revealing themselves to be of the high-skilled type. That this constraint is binding makes the tax system second-best (see Stiglitz (1982) for the origins of this literature).

Suppose we add to this system a set of subsidies to giving to a public good. The intuition of Diamond is that this adds a second dimension on which to sort individuals. Suppose, for instance, that we gave a bigger subsidy to the high skilled type than the low skilled type. If a high skilled person pooled with the lower skilled, then not only would the person get less consumption, but would also get a lower subsidy to giving and, as a result, less of the public good. This makes sorting to the right type even more

[25] Note that this is not a non-welfarist argument. I am not arguing that something other than utility should matter, I am arguing that the definition of utility can be compromised for social welfare calculations. Hence the critique of Kaplow and Shavell (2001) does not quite apply. For instance, we should not think that a murder was less important because a murderer enjoyed the act of killing. Rather, we would choose to ignore this in calculating the social cost of murder.

attractive. This then relaxes the self-selection constraint, which allows the government to engage in more welfare-enhancing redistribution. Hence, moving to a situation of all-government provision to one of subsidized giving can improve welfare by relaxing the self-selection constraint on the high skilled types.

More formally, suppose individuals have warm-glow preferences $U = u(x_i) + \alpha + v(G) + w(g_i)$, where $u()$, $v()$ and $w()$ are all continuous, differentiable and concave, and α is the utility of labor. Let α_{ij} be the utility of a person of type i working in a job of skill j. We assume that a low skilled person can only work in a low skilled job, so normalize $\alpha_{LL} = 0$. Then we assume that $\alpha_{HL} > \alpha_{HH}$, that is, a high skilled person gets less disutility from working in the low skilled job. Let m_H and m_L be the production from high and low skilled jobs, and let N_H and N_L be the number of each in the economy.

Following the arguments of the prior section, we assume that choices are dictated by warm-glow preferences, but social welfare prescriptions are made without counting warm-glow.[26] Let p_i be the price of giving faced by type i. Then define c_i^* and g_i^* as the solution to the individual first order conditions:

$$\frac{v'(\sum g_j^*) + w'(g_i^*)}{u'(c_i^*)} = p_i \tag{5.1}$$

Equation (5.1) implicitly defines $g_i^* = g(c_i^*)$. Then the social welfare optimization problem becomes

$$\max_{c,G} N_H[u(c_H) + \alpha_{HH} + v(G)] + N_L[u(c_L) + v(G)]$$

subject to:

$$E + G + N_H c_H + N_L c_L = N_H m_H + N_L m_L \tag{5.2}$$

$$u(c_H) + \alpha_{HH} + v(G) + w(g_H) \geq u(c_L) + \alpha_{HL} + v(G - g_H + g_L) + w(g_L) \tag{5.3}$$

$$G \geq N_H g_H + N_L g_L \tag{5.4}$$

$$g_i = g(c_i), i = H, L \tag{5.5}$$

The first constraint (5.2) is the resource constraint of society, where E is the government expenditures other than on the public good. For simplicity, we have normalized the cost of G to be 1. The second constraint (5.3) is the self-selection constraint. This requires that the subsidy scheme is one in which the high skilled individual chooses not to act as if he were a low skilled type. Constraint (5.4) defines G in terms of private and government gifts. The inequality indicates that the government may also give directly

[26] Diamond (2006) has explicit derivations for the general case of many types, with and without warm-glow preferences, and with and without counting warm-glow in welfare. As noted above, Diamond argues that warm-glow preferences and no-warm-glow social welfare maximization are the appropriate assumptions.

to the public good, so private contributions are a lower bound on G. The final constraint (5.5) specifies the relationship between c_i and g_i that is derived from the individuals' first order conditions (5.1). It's this relation between (5.1) and (5.5) that specifies the implied subsidy to giving for each income class.

Diamond shows that, in principle, there could be two solutions to this problem, one in which the self-selection constraint binds and one in which it does not. The more interesting one is when it binds. In this case, the solution is that $c_H \geq c_L$, and $g_H > g_L$.

To see how the effect works, reserve some money from the economy to pay for G at the optimal second-best level (so we think of the problem as allocating consumption c). Then imagine the above problem with no utility for public goods, that is, without $v()$ or $w()$. Then the self-selection constraint would require $c_H > c_L$ in order to induce the high skilled to accept the more arduous job. Next add in the public good and the utility $v()$. Now the second-best c_H and c_L we found without the public good utility will leave the self-selection constraint slack, with the left-hand side strictly larger. Hence, the government can reduce c_H and raise c_L if this redistribution will improve social welfare. Finally, add in the warm-glow term, $w()$. This will make the self-selection constraint slack again, so even more redistribution is possible. How do we lower c_H and raise c_L in each step? By lowering the p_H relative to p_L, that is by subsidizing the gifts of the wealthy by more than the gifts of the poor.

Diamond shows, therefore, that a subsidy system like that inherent in the US tax code could be optimal. That is, an increasing marginal income tax rate that redistributes consumption, combined with a subsidy rate on giving (one minus the marginal tax rate) that rises with income could be about right.[27]

This then leads to a fascinating yet complex question: What happens to the second-best level of G—is it higher or lower than the first best level? The answer, it turns out, is unclear. In the case of Diamond's model, it will depend on the shape of the various components of the utility functions. It is possible that G may be either higher or lower than in the first-best case. But a deeper answer to this puzzle can be seen in relation to a parallel literature on optimal second-best level of public goods when they are provided entirely by the government, not via subsidies to private giving.

Recall the familiar Samuelson conditions for the first-best efficient level of public goods provision: the sum of the marginal rates of substitution equal to the marginal cost of the public good. When moving to a second-best world, obviously, this equation must be modified. It was first noted by Pigou (1947) that if we must raise distortionary taxes to cover the cost of this good, then these distortionary taxes are themselves adding to the cost side of this equation. As a result, the second-best level of the public good must be lower than the first-best level.

[27] Scharf (2000) offers another explanation that is rooted in some of the same incentives for redistribution. She asks why majority voting would lead to a system with subsidies to giving. She shows that the median voter can use giving subsidies to favorably affect the distribution of income, thus leading to welfare improvements over total government provision of the public good.

As with so much of second-best taxation, it's not that simple. Atkinson and Stern (1974) noted that whether the second-best G is above or below the first-best will depend on how the public good affects the marginal excess burden of the taxed goods. For instance, suppose that the public good reduces the elasticity of demand for a taxed good. Providing public broadcasting, for instance, may reduce the elasticity of demand for televisions. In this case increasing G can, at the margin, reduce deadweight loss. If the gain is big enough, the second-best G may exceed the first-best.[28]

6. Gifts of cash: price and income elasticities

As we saw in the last section, there are economic rationales for providing a tax-subsidy for charitable giving. Indeed, a tax exclusion for giving is part of the US tax system, and of other tax systems around the globe. In the US the present day income tax was first established by the 1913 Revenue Act, after the 16th amendment to the US Constitution ensured its legality earlier that same year. Just a few years later, the Revenue Act of 1917 was passed. Its main purpose was to broaden the tax base in order to raise funds for World War I, but it also introduced the deduction for charitable giving. It has been part of the tax code ever since.

The importance for policy makers of the charitable deduction is first that it reduces tax revenues—a so-called tax expenditure. This is one cost of the program. The benefit is that it also reduces the cost of giving and thus may encourage more of it. Let t be the marginal tax rate faced by an individual. A gift of g which is deductible from taxable income will reduce taxes owed by tg. Hence, the effective price of a dollar of giving is $1 - t$.

A question policy makers have often raised is whether the cost, measured in foregone tax revenues, is less than the benefit, measured by increased dollars of giving. The answer will be yes if the price elasticity of giving, ε, is less than negative one, that is, if giving is price elastic.[29] It is also true that at $\varepsilon = -1$ the policy will be revenue neutral. Hence, searching for $\varepsilon < -1$ has been the "gold-standard" for some policy analysis. But is this the appropriate benefit-cost measure? What is the appropriate counterfactual in measuring the cost? If it is that these tax dollars could be applied directly to the charity, then foregone tax revenue is an accurate cost measure only if there is no crowding out of the government grant to charity. If there is crowding out, then it is possible that

[28] Thomas Gaube (2000) provides a modern theoretical examination of this. Pigou's conjecture is correct if all goods are normal, and if all private goods are gross substitutes. Without this, counterexamples to Pigou's conjecture can be found. For a related literature on contributing to "public bads" of pollution, see the debate on the "double dividend," such as Cremer and Gahvari (2001) or Fullerton and Metcalf (2001).

[29] The benefits, g, minus the cost, tg, gives net benefits $n(t) = g - tg = (1 - t)g$. Then $\partial n(t)/\partial t > 0$ iff

$$\frac{\partial g}{\partial(1-t)} \frac{(1-t)}{g} = \varepsilon < -1.$$

a subsidy could still be more effective at raising charity dollars even when the price elasticity is greater than negative one. Moreover, this sum must be deflated to account for the distortionary cost of collecting taxes. On the benefit side, measuring the benefit by simply the dollars donated is also incomplete. The fact that gifts create externalities means measuring benefits this way is likely to understate the benefits. Both the cost and benefit side ignore the institutional responses by fund-raisers. The "gold-standard," therefore, is only an imperfect criterion of the policy evaluation.

This section will provide a brief review of the most recent and important contributions to measuring price and income elasticities of giving. Over the years there have been hundreds of studies of these effects. Not surprisingly, these studies have grown in their sophistication and value over the years. Along the way economists have learned many important lessons on measurement and inference with the charitable deduction. For that reason the next section will provide a discussion of the issues faced by the econometrician in estimating giving. We then will offer a brief historical summary of estimates and end with more detailed discussion of the most promising new developments in the area.

6.1. Econometric issues in measuring the effects of price and income

This section explores a number of issues and dilemmas that the econometrician must face when analyzing the effects of price and income on charitable giving. The section relies heavily on an excellent discussion by Robert Triest (1998).

Identification problems

By definition marginal tax rates are a function of income. This means that the two independent variables are correlated, making it difficult to identify the effects of either. For instance, suppose income enters linearly into an estimation equation. Then non-linear relations between price and income will bias the estimated effects of price. In addition, other conditioning variables like marital status and numbers of children will also affect both marginal tax rates and propensities to give, creating an omitted variable bias. This in turn complicates the identification of the effects of price and income.

What is needed to remedy this problem is variation in price that is independent of federal Adjusted Gross Income (AGI) and other conditioning variables. Feenberg (1987) points out that variation in state tax rates and deductibility rules can add extra independence. However, adjusting federal tax prices to include any state tax benefits will only improve identification if there is no systematic or endogenous effect of policies. For instance, states in which people value giving more may be more likely to have generous subsidies to giving. If this were the case, one would want to add state fixed effects to control for the heterogeneity. But adding the fixed effects eliminates the ability to use tax variation as well.

The obvious best solution is to use variation created over a panel, relying on individual variation in income to identify separate effects. The ideal data would be a panel that spans a period of tax reform, so that tax rates are also varying independently in the sample. Barring this, identification of price and income effects will rest solely on functional form specifications.

Endogenous marginal tax rates

What should we do when an individual's contribution reduces their AGI to the point that it pushes them into a lower tax bracket, thus raising the price of giving? The price of the last dollar given is the most economically meaningful, but this number is dependant upon the amount given. Can we find a suitable instrument for the last-dollar tax price? A common instrument used in this literature is to use the first-dollar tax price, that is, use the marginal tax rate that applies to the first dollar donated to charity. This is uncorrelated with the amount of charity deducted. However, the first-dollar tax price is still dependent on all other determinants of tax price. If any of these (omitted) variables are correlated with giving, then even the first-price will not be an effective instrumental variable. Again, as suggested by Feenberg (1987), state tax variation added to the federal first-dollar price can improve the independence of the instrument. Alternatively, one could calculate the effective marginal tax rate at a "predicted" level of giving, where the prediction depends on exogenous factors.[30]

Itemizers and non-itemizers

For most years under the US tax code, only filers who itemize their deductions can claim a charitable deduction.[31] If tax returns are the source of data, therefore, only information on givers who itemize is available. For this reason, studies that rely on tax returns for data must use only itemizers, and careful studies should use only itemizers who would have itemized in the absence of the charitable deduction to avoid endogeneity of the itemization status. Using only itemizers means that only a subset of all givers are in the sample. This may suggest that surveys rather than income tax returns are preferred source of data. While surveys allow information on non-itemizers, they have other serious drawbacks. First, they rely on self-reports of both giving and income, which may be biased due to faulty memories and by people overstating both income and contributions. Second, surveys usually do not include information on marginal tax rates or on whether individuals itemize. Thus, the researcher is left to use available information to guess at both itemization status and marginal tax rates.

[30] For instance, Auten et al. (2002) use one percent of income as a predicted contribution, since this is near the median gift in the sample.

[31] The term "itemize" refers to a feature of the US tax system. All filers are entitled a deduction from taxable income equal to the maximum of a "standard deduction" and an "itemized deduction" which includes charitable giving, among other things. As a result, itemizers tend to have higher incomes than nonitemizers. For the year 1985 non-itemizers could deduct 50% of their contributions, and in 1986 they could deduct 100%. This policy was later dropped, leaving non-itemizers with no charitable deduction.

After-tax income

Econometric analysis has often used either AGI or after-tax income as income measures. Both measures, however, depend on charitable giving. Hence, before applying these, they should be adjusted to the level they would be if giving were zero. If gross income is used, obviously, no adjustment need be made. Sensible arguments exist for both measures of income. After-tax income is a measure of discretionary spending, whereas gross income is broad-based and independent of tax avoidance decisions.

Appreciated assets

When giving appreciated assets, there is an extra tax incentive. Imagine giving a share of stock that was purchased for \$20 but is now valued at \$100. The taxpayer can deduct \$100 from current taxable income, avoiding $100t$ in taxes. In addition they also eliminates any capital gains tax. If t_c is the rate that applies to the capital gain, the taxpayer saves an additional $80t_c$. That makes the price of giving equal to $1-t-0.8t_c$. More generally, let θ be the discounted gain-to-value ratio of the asset. Then the price of giving appreciated property is $p_a = 1 - t - \theta t_c$. Unfortunately, data on appreciated property is often not available, and even when it is the θ is rarely observed. Some authors have attempted to account for gifts of appreciated property by arbitrarily choosing a value of θ of, say, 0.5, or by using capital gains tax filings to estimate likely gains. As seen in the next section on gifts by the wealthy, however, for most samples that do not include people with high incomes (over, say, \$200 000), the value of appreciated property is less than 20% of all gifts. As incomes rise above this level, however, appreciated property becomes an increasingly large and dominant fraction of gifts.

Kinked budgets

Consider someone who, without charitable giving, is near the point of being able to itemize deductions. Giving a few dollars extra kicks them into itemizations status, lowing their price of giving from 1 to $1 - t$. Crossing this threshold creates both an income and substitution effect that promotes giving. Failure to account for this may make giving appear more responsive to price than it actually is. Over the years, itemization has become increasingly likely, and the number of different marginal tax rates has declined. Hence, the problem of kinked budgets is less severe than it once was.

Timing of gifts

Imagine an individual whose income is variable. Her marginal tax rate varies from year to year as her income changes. Of course, she anticipates this and smooths her consumption. But it would be optimal to smooth her charitable giving as well. She should give more in years when her marginal tax rate is high and less in years when it is low.

Similar effects will be seen during a period of tax reform. If tax rate reductions are expected next year, people should move some giving forward in order to get a higher tax benefit. This means giving should spike in the year before tax cuts and drop in years after. Failure to account for this could dramatically bias estimates.

Household rather than individual decisions

Becker's (Becker, 1974) famous "unitary" model states that as long as household decisions are made by a benevolent head, then we can treat demands by households under a neo-classical utility maximization framework. However, recent work has shown that a household bargaining model—one that cannot be reduced to act a single neo-classical utility maximizer—is a better description of household decisions. Hence, household variables matter in how they affect the marital bargain. This means that not simply household income, but relative incomes of the spouses, may matter. Likewise, demographics such as age and education of the head may not be enough controls, but relative age and education and the presence of children may affect the household bargain and thus may all need to be accounted for in the analysis. A recent paper by Andreoni et al. (2003) confirms this. Men and women have different tastes for giving, and household decisions represent a compromise between husband and wife. Men, as it turns out, appear to have most of the bargaining power. The household choice is closer to men's preferences than women's.

Interdependence of preferences

We saw in the theoretical section that, for all intents and purposes, when giving to a large public good individual donations are dominated by warm-glow at the margin. As such, it is likely to be safe to ignore the aggregate gifts of others in the regressions—they can be subsumed into the constant. However, that is not to say that the gifts of others have no influence. Psychologists and sociologists who have studied giving are convinced that the actions of others in one's own environment can also influence one's acts of altruism. Giving, for instance, is not like eating—there is no natural measure of "enough." Rather, this is determined subjectively as a matter of the "socially correct" amount to give. Societies or groups of people can determine their own norms of the expected donations. Hence, the gifts of those of a similar age, education and income can act as a benchmark for one's own gift. Likewise, the gifts of others in a work-place charity drive, like the United Way, can also influence giving, as can solicitations coming from friends rather than strangers. There are two studies that confirm these effects. Andreoni and Scholz (1998), based on sociological findings, show that "peer group" effects are significant. Carman (2003), using a unique data set of work-place contributions, shows that giving by people one interacts with at work has a positive influence on one's own giving. This suggests strategic considerations by fundraisers to take advantage of these interdependent preferences, which raises the next issue.

The interactions with fund-raising

It seems that almost anyone with a telephone or mail box has experienced charitable fund-raising. Few of us, I suspect, would give in the absence of direct appeals from charitable organizations. It is likely that these organizations respond to government policy. For instance, they may increase fund-raising efforts after a reduction in marginal tax rates. This means that elasticities estimated during a period of stable tax rates may not apply after a tax reform. In addition to the issues raised under "timing" above, these responses of fund-raisers are likely to cause long-run elasticities lower than short-run elasticities as their fund-raising tactics respond to the changing environment of giving. We discuss fund-raising, both theoretically and empirically in later sections of this paper.

6.2. A brief history of empirical studies on charitable giving

There are several complete and detailed surveys of econometric studies of giving. These include Clotfelter and Steuerle (1981), Clotfelter (1985, 1990), and Steinberg (1990). See also Chapter 4 of this Handbook. Because of limited space, I refer interested readers to these authors for details. My purpose here is to give a general flavor of the findings up until 1995.

The first empirical analysis of giving was by Michael Taussig (1967), who looked at data from 47 000 tax returns in the 1962 Treasury tax file. While the results of Taussig's study are not very relevant for today's economy, he did have a lasting impact by introducing a staple of the literature: the constant elasticity, or log–log, specification. Let g_i be i's gifts to charity, y_i be income, $p_i = 1 - t_i$ be the tax price of giving by person i (as defined above) and X_i be a vector of demographic variables, such as age, education, marital status, number of children, and state of residence. Then the log–log specification is

$$\ln g_i = \alpha + \beta_1 \ln p_i + \beta_2 \ln y_i + BX_i + \epsilon_i \tag{6.1}$$

This specification is convenient because, corner solutions aside, β_1 can be interpreted as the price elasticity and β_2 as the income elasticity.[32]

Of course, there are several shortcomings of this framework. First is that many people give $g_i = 0$, and the log of 0 is undefined. For this reason many researchers adopt the compromise of adding \$10 to both g_i and y_i and then estimate (6.1) using OLS. This (approximately) preserves the interpretation of the β's as elasticities. Given the censoring of g_i at zero, however, it would more appropriate to estimate (6.1) with Tobit analysis, where $\ln g_i$ is censored at 1 rather than zero. In this case, however, the estimated β's would no longer be directly interpretable as elasticities, because we would have to weight the coefficient by the conditional probability that $g_i > 0$.

[32] To be accurate, Taussig used t_i in place of p_i in equation (6.1). Others that followed use p_i.

The first important study of this type was by Feldstein and Clotfelter (1976), who performed OLS on (6.1). Using data from a survey conducted by the Federal Reserve Board that included both itemizers and non-itemizers, they found price elasticity of -1.15 and income elasticity of 0.87. Feldstein and Taylor (1976) conducted a similar study using the 1970 Treasury tax file. Their sample consisted of 15 000 itemizers. They were also able to account for state tax laws in computing the tax price of giving. In addition, they made a serious attempt to account for gifts of appreciated assets. Under several variations of estimates, they found price elasticities of -1.1 to -1.5 and income elasticities of 0.70 to 0.80. Note that both of these early studies found price elasticities that exceed the gold-standard of -1.

These two studies are very important in this literature for two reasons. First, they cast the dye for the log–log analysis and the focus on the gold-standard elasticity. Second, the massive literature to follow did not do much to change their estimates. In Coltfelter's 1985 survey, the consensus was that price elasticities hovered around -1.3, and income elasticities around 0.7.

By the 1990s, however, this "consensus view" was being challenged. Analysis using the log–log specification began finding price elasticities spanning an extremely broad range, falling much higher and lower than -1. Moreover, studies that used specifications other than log–log were finding consistently smaller price elasticities.[33] At the same time there were several periods of tax reform that provided the independent variation in price that help identify both price and income elasticities. With these tax reforms as "natural experiments" and with more sophisticated estimation techniques, the consensus view of the effects of government policy began to erode. In the next two subsections I will review in more detail two recent contributions to this literature. Each uses the ideal data, that is, panels of tax returns that straddle periods of tax reforms. However, the two papers come to strikingly different conclusions.

6.3. *Randolph's 1995 JPE paper*

William Randolph (1995) used a panel of US federal tax returns running from 1979–89. This panel followed 12 000 filers and covered a period of two tax reforms. First was the Economic Recovery Tax Act of 1981 (ERTA) and second was the Tax Reform Act of 1986 (TRA). Each tax reform significantly reduced marginal tax rates, especially for high income tax payers, and reduced the number of different tax brackets. Randolph's data over-samples wealthy households and his sample includes only itemizers.

Randolph had two main objectives in his study. First was using the tax reforms to strengthen the identification of price and income elasticities of giving. Second was to address the issue of timing. If in a cross section people are adjusting the timing of their contributions because of fluctuations in their own marginal tax rates, this will have

[33] Most notable of these is Reece and Zieschang (1985). This also differed, however, by using data from the consumer expenditure survey rather than tax returns.

the effect of overstating the price elasticities of giving. The panel nature of his data, combined with the exogenous tax variation, will help differentiate between temporary and permanent changes in price, and thus identify short run and long run elasticities.

To illustrate, consider this two-period model. Let g be gifts and $T(y-g)$ be the tax schedule, with $T' > 0$, $T'' > 0$. Let interest rates be zero, for simplicity. Then individuals solve

$$\begin{aligned} &\max U(g_1, g_2, x_1, x_2) \\ &\text{s.t.} \quad x_1 + g_1 + x_2 + g_2 = y_1 - T(y_1 - g_1) + y_2 - T(y_2 - g_2) \end{aligned}$$

Let y^* be permanent income and y^T be transitory income, so $y_t = y^* + y^T$, $t = 1, 2$. Then note that an increase in y^* will first have a normal income effect, but will also lower the price (raise marginal tax rates) in both periods. However, an increase in transitory income will only lower price in the current period. Given convex preferences, an increase in y^T will have a bigger effect on current giving than a comparable change in y^*.

Randolph's empirical model considers the effect of both current and future prices and income. Let P_{it} and Y_{it} be current prices and income (at the *first price* calculation) and P^*_{it} and Y^*_{it} be expected future prices and income. Randolph then uses the Almost Ideal Demand System of Deaton and Muellbauer (1980) to estimate this equation:

$$\begin{aligned} \frac{P_{it} g_{it}}{Y_{it}} &= \delta_{ot} + \delta_{oi} + \mathbf{X}_{it}\beta + \delta_1 \log\left(\frac{P_{it}}{P^*_{it}}\right) + \delta_2 \log P^*_{it} \\ &\quad + \delta_3 \log\left(\frac{Y_{it}}{Y^*_{it}}\right) + \delta_4 \log Y^*_{it} + \delta_5\left[\log\left(\frac{P_{it}}{P^*_{it}}\right)\right]^2 \\ &\quad + \delta_6 \log P_{it} \cdot \log P^*_{it} + \epsilon_{it} \end{aligned} \tag{6.2}$$

This demand system is an extremely flexible generalization of Cobb–Douglas demands that allows for non-homothetic preferences and cross-price elasticities between current and future consumption. The equation includes fixed effects for both time, δ_{ot}, and individuals, δ_{oi}, as well as a vector $\mathbf{X}_{it}$ of characteristics, including age, age squared, and marital status.

Since the econometrician does not observe either permanent or transitory income, or permanent or transitory prices, instruments must be chosen. We need at least four instruments, two that are correlated with the permanent components and two with the transitory components.

Define the following: $\bar{y}_i$ is the 10 year average of income, $ERTA81$ is a dummy variable equal to 1 for the years between ERTA and TRA, and $TRA86$ is a dummy variable for years under the TRA. The instruments for P^*_{it} and Y^*_{it} used by Randolph are $\ln(\bar{y}_i)$, $ERTA81 \times \ln y_{it}$, and $TRA86 \times \ln y_{it}$. The reasoning is that the average income is similar to permanent income, and that the tax reforms are exogenous, hence income in those years will be correlated with permanent income and price.

Table 4
Randalph's estimates of permanent and transitory price and income elasticities

		Unweighted means	Weighted means
Income:	Permanent, $d(Y/Y^*) = 0$	1.30	1.14
		(0.02)	(0.01)
	Transitory, $dY^* = 0$	0.09	0.58
		(0.03)	(0.01)
Price:	Permanent, $d(P/P^*) = 0$	−0.08	−0.51
		(0.10)	(0.06)
	Transitory, $dP^* = 0$	−2.27	−1.55
		(0.13)	(0.06)

Source: Randolph (1995). Standard errors in parentheses.

The instruments for y_i^T and p_i^T are $(\ln \bar{y}_i - \ln y_{it}) \times ERTA81$ and $(\ln \bar{y}_i - \ln y_{it}) \times TRA86$. The reasoning here is that deviations from average income in the years of the tax reform will be somewhat exogenous measures of income shocks.

Table 4 shows Randolph's estimated price and income elasticities (both weighted and unweighted). As hypothesized, permanent income effects are much stronger than transitory changes, and the temporary price elasticities are much stronger than the permanent elasticities. In fact, the "consensus" elasticities of the prior literature fall between the permanent and transitory measures of Randolph. This supports the speculation that the prior literature had both understated income elasticities and overstated price elasticities. Since, as Randolph notes, "for tax policy predictions, it is often the permanent behavioral effects that matter most," these estimates by Randolph have put the preceding literature into a whole new light. A similar analysis using panel data, by Barrett et al. (1997) found results quite close to Randolph's. This research seriously undermines the consensus view on price and income elasticities and, in particular, suggests that the price elasticity that "matters most" may in fact be far closer to zero than previously believed.

6.4. *Auten, Sieg and Clotfelter's 2002 AER paper*

Gerald Auten, Holger Sieg, and Charles Clotfelter (Auten et al., 2002) tackle the same questions as Randolph (1995). Their data is basically the same, but spans five more years, 1979–1993, and includes 20 000 filers in an unbalanced panel. The file, again, over-samples high incomes, while the sample is restricted to those who are itemizers throughout and those whose marital status does not change over the sample.

Auten, Sieg, and Clotfelter's (ASC's) approach is vastly different from Randolph's. Their analysis draws on modern studies of the permanent income hypothesis. Rather than instrumenting for permanent and transitory changes in income and price, ASC recognize that the stochastic elements of income and price variation imply restrictions on the covariance matrices of income and price.

They begin with a standard log–log regression equation

$$\ln g_{it} = \alpha + \beta_1 \ln p_{it} + \beta_2 \ln y_{it} + u_i + \epsilon_{it} \tag{6.3}$$

where u_i is an individual fixed effect. For ease of notation, we drop the i subscripts and use bold to indicate variables in logs, that is $\mathbf{x}_t = \ln x_{it}$. Then rewrite (6.3) as

$$\mathbf{g}_t = \alpha + \beta_1 \mathbf{p}_t + \beta_2 \mathbf{y}_t + u + \epsilon_t$$

To control for fixed effects, the authors consider first-differences, to get the estimation equation

$$\Delta \mathbf{g}_t = \beta_1 \Delta \mathbf{p}_t + \beta_2 \Delta \mathbf{y}_t + \Delta \epsilon_t \tag{6.4}$$

The task then becomes to separate the permanent and transitory effects of income and price. Write these this way:

$$\mathbf{y}_t = \mathbf{y}_t^p + \mathbf{y}_t^t$$
$$\mathbf{p}_t = \mathbf{p}_t^p + \mathbf{p}_t^t$$

Starting with $\mathbf{y}$, assume that permanent income follows a random walk, $\mathbf{y}_t^p = \mathbf{y}_{t-1}^p + \xi_t$, where ξ's are independently and identically distributed random variables. Then write the transitory component as $\mathbf{y}_t^t = \eta_t$. This means that we can write

$$\Delta \mathbf{y}_t = \xi_t + \eta_t - \eta_{t-1} \tag{6.5}$$

This in turn implies that

$$\operatorname{var}(\Delta \mathbf{y}_t, \Delta \mathbf{y}_{t-s}) = \begin{cases} \sigma\xi^2 + 2\sigma\eta^2 & s = 0 \\ -\sigma\eta^2 & |s| = 1 \\ 0 & |s| > 1 \end{cases} \tag{6.6}$$

A similar restriction results if we follow these steps again for $\mathbf{p}$.

The authors then parametrize $\mathbf{p}_t^p$ and $\mathbf{p}_t^t$ as

$$\mathbf{p}_t^p = \mathbf{p}_{t-1}^p + \omega_t + a_1 \xi_t$$
$$\mathbf{p}_t^t = \varsigma_t + a_2 \eta_t$$

where the a_1 and a_2 reflect the fact that variability in income is a cause of variability in price. This then produces

$$\Delta \mathbf{p}_t = \omega_t + a_1 \xi_t + \varsigma_t - \varsigma_{t-1} + a_2(\eta_t - \eta_{t-1}) \tag{6.7}$$

Combining (6.4), (6.5) and (6.7) we get the ultimate regression equation

$$\Delta g_t = b_1(\omega_t + a_1 \xi_t) + b_2(\varsigma_t - \varsigma_{t-1} + a_2(\eta_t - \eta_{t-1})) \\ + b_3 \xi_t + b_4(\eta_t - \eta_{t-1}) + \psi_t + \epsilon_t - \epsilon_{t-1}$$

Table 5
Auten, Sieg and Clotfelter's estimates of permanent and transitory price and income elasticities

		Unweighted means
Income:	Permanent	0.87
		(0.01)
	Transitory	0.29
		(0.01)
Price:	Permanent	−1.26
		(0.04)
	Transitory	−0.40
		(0.04)

Source: Auten et al. (2002). Standard errors in parentheses.

Estimating this model, and calculating the relevant permanent and temporary elasticities generates the numbers reported in Table 5. These results stand in stark contrast to those of Randolph. First, the elasticity of the permanent component is more elastic in *both* the price and income terms. This challenges Randolph's claim that individuals will respond more aggressively to transitory changes in prices than in income. Second, the permanent price elasticity again exceeds the gold-standard of −1. This challenges Randolph's second main contention, that cross sectional studies were seriously overstating price elasticities by merging temporary and permanent effects. This study indicates that, instead, the consensus view of a price elasticity of −1.3 is actually quite accurate.

How do we reconcile these two studies? Should we believe price elasticities are low, as Randolph says, or high, as ASC report? We cannot attribute their disagreement to differing data—the two data sets are sufficiently similar that results are not likely to vary on this account. That leaves two remaining differences. First is the estimation method. Randolph uses instruments for permanent and temporary changes, whereas ASC gain identification through restrictions on the covariance matrix of price and income. This difference is not trivial. The second difference is the specification of the regression equation. At the heart of the ASC study is the log–log (or constant elasticity) specification, the same specification that produced high price elasticities in the prior literature. Randolph uses a flexible functional form that allows elasticities to vary across price and income. Which of these two differences is at the heart of this debate is impossible to tell simply by reading the papers. But, with the huge chasm between a price elasticity of −1.26 and −0.08 to −0.51, and the major policy implications of this difference, it seems worthwhile to invite further study on how best to measure these elasticities of charitable giving.

7. Gifts by the very wealthy

Most of the studies reported in the prior section do not include the very wealthy. However, while the very wealthy are only a small fraction of all givers, when counted in terms of dollars donated their impact is quite substantial. According to one study, the richest 400 US tax filers in the year 2000 donated over $10.1 billion to charity, accounting for about 7% of all individual giving in that year.[34] Moreover, with the expansion of wealth among the top wealth holders in the US over the recent decades, their influence is growing.

Despite their importance, there are few studies of giving by the very wealthy. This is because data is scarce. Because the rich are relatively few in number, surveys have not attempted to reach them. However, even if they did, concern for anonymity would likely keep participation low. The best way to get information on large numbers of wealthy givers is from the IRS, including both income and estate tax filings. However, the privileged nature of this data restricts its availability, often limiting it to only select employees of the US Treasury. As a result, we rely largely on government researchers to produce studies for academic journals. Fortunately, several such high quality studies exist.

Any discussion of gifts by the wealthy must include a discussion of the estate tax. In fact, a good *de facto* definition of "very wealthy" is those individuals whose heirs could have exposure to the estate tax. Some giving by the wealthy will surely be motivated by avoiding estate taxes and other taxes that fall predominately on the wealthy. However, there are other differences between wealthy givers and those of more modest means. Among the most important of these is that the wealthy can and do exert greater control over how their charitable gifts are spent. For example, large gifts may be rewarded with a seat on the governing board of a charity, and charities are more likely to tolerate conditions attached to large gifts. Finally, the very wealthy can often spurn existing charities and create new charities or foundations to suit their tastes. The explosion of private foundations in the past decade is a testament to this.

In this section we will discuss giving by the very wealthy by first discussing the different tax consequences that these philanthropists face. We then discuss several studies of giving by the wealthy. Finally, we discuss what impact the recently legislated phase-out of the estate tax may have on giving by the wealthy.

7.1. Tax consequences of gifts by the wealthy

Compared to those of more modest means, the wealthy in the US face a much more complex tax code. Income taxes and estate taxes both affect the incentives to give. Income taxes change the price of giving relative to both consumption and bequests to

[34] A report by a foundation called Newtithing calculated this based on data from the Statistics of Income. See their report at http://www.newtithing.org/content/researchreports_1.html

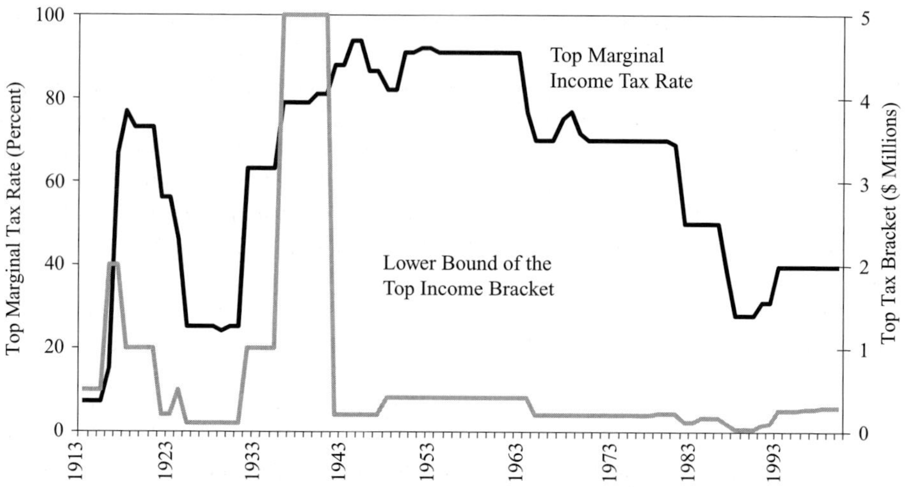

Figure 6. History of top marginal tax rates in the US. Source: US Joint Committee on Taxation, March 6, 2001, JCX-06-01.

one's heirs. Estate taxes can, of course, only affect the trade-off between charitable giving and bequests to one's heirs. Here we highlight portions of US tax code which policy analysts will need to account for in determining the effect of taxes on giving by the very wealthy.

Marginal income tax rates

As with other tax-payers, the deductibility of charitable contributions reduces the price of giving. The rates faced by the wealthy have varied dramatically since the charitable deduction was introduced in 1917. Figure 6 shows the changes in the top marginal income tax rate. The top marginal tax rate reached a high of 90% during that World War II and has more or less steadily fallen since. In particular the tax reforms of 1981 and 1986 reduced the top marginal rates significantly for wealthy families when they reached a modern day low of 28%. Tax changes instituted during the first Bush and Clinton administrations restored somewhat higher rates. However the 2001 tax cut brought the top rate back down to 33%.

Charitable deduction caps

Individuals are not allowed to deduct more than 50% of their adjusted gross income (AGI) through cash gifts to charities. Cash gifts to foundations are limited to 30% of AGI. Gifts of appreciated assets—which would have otherwise been subject to capital gains taxes—are deductible at their full market value, but only up to 30% of AGI or 20% if the asset is given to a foundation. In general, tax payers are allowed to carry over contributions made in excess of these limits for up to five years. It should be noted that wealthy donors are much more likely to run up against either of these deduction caps for charitable gifts. However, it is interesting to note that data from Joulfaian (2000) suggests that wealthy donors on average do not manage to deduct more than half of their lifetime contributions. It is not clear why this is. Perhaps large donors don't really mind "contributing" to the US. government. In any case, this fact should give pause to any researcher trying to estimate a price elasticity. For example, should one use the price of the first dollar given to charity or the last dollar, since not carrying over the entire amount of a large contribution is equivalent to paying a marginal price of one?

Overall limitation on itemized deductions

Besides the caps put on charitable deductions *per se*, there is also a limitation on the sum total of all deductions from taxable income.[35] Itemizers in tax year 2000 whose incomes are greater than roughly $129 000 are required to reduce their total deductions (with some exceptions which do not include charitable contributions) by the smaller amount of 80% of their deductions or 3% of their AGI over the threshold amount.

Alternative minimum tax

The very wealthy will very likely be subject to the Alternate Minimum Tax. This is relevant to researchers for two reasons. First, under the normal way of figuring deductions, gifts of appreciated assets to charities are deductible at current market value. However, for a period of time between 1987 and 1993, this was not necessarily the case for people exposed to the AMT. Second, the top marginal rates are lower under the AMT. Therefore the price of giving for wealthy people paying the AMT may be higher.

The estate tax

Because charitable bequests are deductible from taxable estates, the estate tax is the second source of subsidy when figuring the price of giving. An estate tax liability is set when the value of an estate, at death, exceeds a legislated exemption level. This exemption level was set at $121 000 under the 1976 Tax Reform Act which gave the estate and gift taxes their current 'unified' structure. The 1981 ERTA raised the exemption to $225 000. The 1986 TRA raised it to $600 000. The 1997 Taxpayer Relief Act put the exemption on a schedule of increases toward $1 000 000 by 2006. The 2001 tax cut accelerated the exemption level increases, as shown in Table 6, culminating in a total repeal by 2010. However, a sunset clause in the law will restore the estate tax to it pre-2001 form for 2011 decedents. Careful estate planners may therefore choose 2010 as the tax-preferred year to die.

[35] For more detail, see the US Code Title 26, Section 68.

Table 6
Effects of 2001 changes to the estate tax

Year of death	Taxable estate exemption levels
Before the change	$600 000
2003	$1 000 000
2004–2005	$1 500 000
2006–2008	$2 000 000
2009	$3 500 000
2010	No estate tax
2011 and beyond	Pre-2001 law rules

Currently the top marginal tax rate on estates is 49%, making a $1000 bequest to charity cost just $510 in one's heir's wealth. It is important to keep in mind that estate tax also lowers the price of giving for contributions made during life. For example, for an individual in the top income tax and estate tax brackets, the price of $1000 given to charity while alive is just $340 of heir's wealth—the gift first avoids the 0.33 marginal income tax rate and then also the 0.49 marginal estate tax. An unsettled question in the literature is why, given the added benefit to one's heir of giving during life, do we see the wealthy give so much in the form of bequests.

Foundations and trusts

An increasingly popular way for the wealthy to make charitable gifts is through establishing foundations and trusts. The laws regulating these are voluminous and complex. Auten et al. (2000) have an excellent overview of the regulations governing these, which I summarize here.

A foundation is typically set up by an individual or family as an intermediary that makes grants to actual operating charities. Gifts to foundations are deductible from either current income or from the estate. Foundations' actions are limited by many regulations. Among the more important ones is that a foundation must give away a minimum of 5% of its assets each year.[36]

Besides foundations, the law recognizes several forms of split-interest trusts which have both charitable and non-charitable beneficiaries. A popular form is the charitable remainder trust (CRT). A CRT pays its non-charitable beneficiary either a fixed annuity or a fixed percentage of trust assets. When the trust expires, the remaining assets are

[36] A legislative debate in the US is currently under way about whether this requirement should be raised. See the "Charitable Giving Act," H.R. 7 of the 149th Congress. In particular, if the required distribution rate falls below the growth rate of the assets of the trust, it is possible for the foundation to exist in perpetuity. Questions have been raised as to whether this is desirable for either tax or societal reasons.

transferred to a charity. The principle tax advantage is that the donor can deduct from current income the amount eventually to be given to the charitable organization. The IRS Statistics of Income reports that 85 060 returns were filed by CRTs for the 1998 tax year—a 19% increase over the number filed in 1996.

7.2. Differences in giving behavior

Virtually the only source for learning about wealthy givers is tax filings. This means, however, that information is only available for itemizers. Surprisingly, not all high income tax payers itemize their returns. Of those earning \$50–75 000 in 2000, 62.7% were itemizers. The number climbs to 81.1% for those earning \$75–100 000, but plateaus at 90.5% for those earning from \$100 000 up to \$5 million. And for those earning over \$5 million, only 95.5% are itemizers.[37] Thus, if those who fail to itemize are also making considerable charitable donations, the inferences from these tax returns may be somewhat biased.

The first question to ask about the wealthy is, are they more or less generous than middle income tax payers? Table 7 shows that this depends on the measure of overall generosity. The average level of giving as a percent of income is 2.6% for those making \$50 000, rising to 4.0% for those making \$2.5 million annually, indicating that the rich are, on average, more generous. When measured by the median giver, however, the rich appear less generous. The median \$50 000-per-year-earner gives 1.4% of income, while the median \$2.5-million-earner gives only half as much, 0.7%. What's behind this switch? The final column of Table 7 gives an answer—the variance of generosity rises dramatically with income. The 95th percentile gift is about 8–10% of income for those making less than \$1 million, but for those making over \$2.5 in 1995, the 95th percentile gift is almost 21% of income.

One could be tempted to conclude from this that some of the rich are exceptionally generous, while the majority are extremely selfish. This could be incorrect, however. The reason is that giving by the wealthy is much more sporadic over time. They may give nothing for many years and then make a major donation all in one year. A sociological study by Schervish and Havens (2003) indicates that the wealthy are looking for ways to donate money that will have the greatest impact but will retain some control by the donor. Large gifts made all at once may make this more likely. Moreover, large one-time gifts are more frequently rewarded with monuments, such as a name on a campus building, than are equivalent gifts acclimated over a number of years. Hence, once can speculate that the rich may be hoarding their money so that, when they do give it away, they get a greater personal benefit from the act of giving.

Another reason giving by the wealthy may be more sporadic and "lumpy" is that they are more likely to give gifts in kind, such as appreciated property. For instance, giving a valuable Picasso painting to a museum is, by necessity, a one-time large gift. Giving

[37] These percentages are from the author's calculations from the IRS Statistics of Income for 2000.

Table 7
Giving as percent of income, 1995

Adjusted gross income	Mean	Median	95th percentile
50K to 100K	2.6	1.4	10.0
100K to 200K	2.4	1.3	8.5
200K to 500K	2.6	1.2	9.0
500K to 1 Million	2.7	1.0	9.7
1M to 2.5 Million	3.2	0.8	14.0
2.5M and above	4.0	0.7	20.9

Source: Auten et al. (2000).

Table 8
Non-cash contributions as a percent of total contributions, tax year 2000

Adjusted gross income	Percent non-cash
$50 000 to $100 000	17.2
$100 000 to $200 000	21.0
$200 000 to $500 000	25.3
$500 000 to $1 000 000	35.2
$1 000 000 to $1 500 000	42.1
$1 500 000 to $2 000 000	44.8
$2 000 000 to $5 000 000	49.5
$5 000 000 to $10 000 000	57.1
$10 000 000 and above	73.9

Source: Tabulated by Auten et al. (2000) from IRS Statistics of Income of Individual Income Tax Return Samples.

appreciated stocks may also be lumpy because of market timing concerns. Table 8 shows that this effect grows rapidly with income.

Despite the clear tax advantage of giving during life, the rich hold a surprising fraction of giving in their estates. Joulfaian (2001) uses data built from a panel of income tax returns and subsequent estate tax returns to show this, as seen in Table 9. The preference for delaying giving until death goes against the grain of tax incentives. The price of lifetime contributions is effectively lower since one enjoys both an income tax benefit and the same estate tax savings down the road. Joulfaian speculates that this behavior among the very wealthy may represent a reluctance to part with wealth during life. Or it could be that the wealthy consider government to be as good a recipient of their assets as any charity or heir. In an interesting clue to the psychology of wealth, Avery and Rendall (1993) claim that inherited wealth is held more dear than earned wealth—they find that entrepreneurial wealth is given away at a rate six times that of inherited wealth.

Table 9
Giving in estates

Wealth at death (in $1 million)	Total giving (in $1000)	Bequest share (%)
Under 1	129	0
1 to 2.5	213	12.2
2.5 to 5	452	6.9
5 to 10	728	26.4
10 to 20	1851	28.9
20 to 50	6059	51.6
50 to 100	8533	59.5
100 and over	244 907	77.6

Source: Joulfaian (2001).

A final feature of giving by the wealthy is that they give to a dramatically different set of recipients. In particular, while religious causes are the target of a large percentage of contributions across the entire population, wealthy donors give almost nothing to religious charities. Looking at charitable bequests alone, Auten et al. (2000) calculated that estates of less that $1 million give 27% to religious causes, estates of about $5 million gave about 13% to religion, estates of about $10 million gave about 6% to religion, but estates over $20 million gave less than 1 percent to religious charities.

7.3. *Tax elasticity of gifts in life and at death*

A central question for policy makers is how does the estate tax effect giving by the wealthy, both in life and at death. As such, we define "very wealthy" as whether the taxpayer faces exposure to the estate tax. Two recent studies have made important contributions to this issue.

First, David Joulfaian (2000) notes that prior studies of the estate tax focused only on its effect on charitable bequests, ignoring the prospect that the estate tax can also affect gifts during life. Joulfaian accounts for both by employing to a 10 year panel of individual income tax returns *and* those same individuals' estate tax returns. Joulfaian limits his sample to only those with possible exposure to the estate tax.[38]

Joulfaian estimates estate-tax price elasticities, income-tax price elasticities, and income elasticities on total giving (in life and at death) under various specifications. He finds estate tax price elasticities are positive, ranging between 1.1 and 1.7. He finds income tax price elasticities around −2.8 for all specifications and wealth elasticities of roughly 1.0 for most specifications. Combining the effects, Joulfaian claims that a

[38] During the period of his sample, all estates with gross assets over $600 000 were required to file estate tax returns. These filings, including those which owe no taxes, are included in Joulfaian's sample.

repeal of the estate tax would reduce total contributions by up to over 30%, depending on the specification.

A second paper, by Bakija et al. (2003), focuses on the effect of federal and state inheritance taxes on charitable bequests. The study is notable for the scope of its data, which draws on virtually every federal estate tax return filed since 1945. The returns contain information on state of residence which they use to calculate the total tax rates faced by decedents. They estimate both price and wealth elasticities under several specifications. Under the most straightforward specification, they estimate a price elasticity of −1.62 and a wealth elasticity of 1.32. Both estimates have extremely low standard errors. Under their most inclusive specification which controls for wealth, states of residence, and years, they estimate a significantly greater price elasticity of −2.14 and an only slightly higher wealth elasticity of 1.55.

This paper is also noteworthy for its interpretation of the elasticity estimates. They argue that due to the progressivity of the estate tax, its total repeal would increase the price of charitable giving by a much greater percentage than such a repeal would increase wealth. For the average individual in their sample, the absence of the estate tax would have increased the price of charitable bequests by 77% while only increasing disposable wealth by 24%. Therefore, they argue, wealth elasticities would have to be three times greater than price elasticities in order for a repeal to have a neutral effect on charitable bequests. Since their range of estimates show wealth elasticities at most on par with price elasticities, they predict a repeal would result in a significant reduction of charitable bequests.

8. Giving time

While we have thus far focused on gifts of money, charities also benefit from substantial gifts of time. Americans are especially generous volunteers. According to a recent national survey, 44% of respondents claimed to give time to a charitable organization in the prior year, with volunteers averaging about 15 hours of volunteer time per month.[39]

These gifts of time clearly have great value to the charitable sector, and it seems important for policy makers to understand the influences of volunteering, the value of volunteering, and its interaction with gifts of money. The question of the joint determination of time and money gifts is especially important. Suppose, for instance, that time and money gifts are substitutes. Then a policy, like the charitable deduction, that increases gifts of money may have the effect of reducing gifts of time. Any policy analysis would overstate the benefits by ignoring the tradeoff between time and money. On the other hand, suppose time and money gifts are complements. Then the subsidy to money will have the added benefit of producing more time contributions as well, and the policy would be even more beneficial than thought before.

[39] Independent Sector, *Giving and Volunteering in the United States, 2001*, Washington, DC.

What can economic theory tell us about the complementarity or substitutability of gifts of time and money? It turns out, this depends critically on the assumptions we make on givers' preferences.

8.1. Theoretical framework for volunteering

Let m be an individual's money gift and v be volunteer hours. Let x be consumption, ℓ be leisure hours. Let t be the marginal tax rate applied to market wages, and t' be the marginal tax rate applied to charitable deductions. For itemizers $t = t'$, but for non-itemizers $t' = 0$. Then $w(1-t)$ is the after-tax wage the person earns in the market, and $1-t'$ is the price of giving. Let w_o be non-labor income and assume a time endowment of 1. Then all givers face the budget constraint $x+(1-t')m = w_o+w(1-t)(1-\ell-v)$. Notice that $w(1-t)$, the opportunity cost of leisure, is also the price of volunteering.[40]

Then a simple first model would assume individuals are warm-glow givers who care only about the dollars they give away and the hours they volunteer. That is, givers have the simple preferences:

Model 1: $u(x, \ell, m, v)$

Model 1 give us no guidance as to whether time and money are complements or substitutes—it all depends on preferences. Model 2 will change this.

Notice that Model 1 assumes that individuals care about their *expenditures* on different components of their donation, that is the dollars and hours they give. Since giving is motivated by some altruistic concern for the charity, it may make more sense to assume that individuals care about the *impact* of their contribution instead. That is, volunteers may ask, "What are my hours worth to the charity?" It seems reasonable that a volunteering attorney would get more satisfaction by giving free legal advice to the charity than from mopping its floors, and he would feel like each hour he gives contributes more to the charity. Let w' be the wage imputed to the activity the individual volunteers for. One can think of this as the wage the charity would have to pay to contract for these services in the market.[41] It thus makes sense to think individuals care about the total value of their contribution, both money and time. That is, they care about $c = m + w'v$. Individuals thus have preferences

Model 2: $u(x, \ell, m + w'v)$

Notice that Model 2 assumes that individuals gain no extra utility from volunteering *per se*, apart from how it increases the total value of their contribution c. Likewise,

[40] Periodically there is a call in the public press, and even among some economists, to make volunteer time "tax deductible." This budget constraint reveals that it in fact already is. By working an hour for the charity, at an opportunity cost of $w(1-t)$, there is no net impact on tax liabilities. The same is true if the hour was worked in the market and the pre-tax wage was given to charity. Hence, tax law treats time and money gifts identically—both gifts escape income taxation.

[41] Freeman (1997) offers evidence that, in fact, w and w' are highly correlated.

they get no independent warm-glow from money gifts. This assumption now makes time and money perfect substitutes—givers care about which creates more value for the charity. In fact, one can see that from a technological point of view, time and money gifts *should* be perfect substitutes. It is only preferences for giving in one form or the other that should create complementarity.

The simple observation of Model 2 creates a stark prediction. First, since m and v are perfect substitutes, people should tend to choose one or the other. But, suppose people work in a competitive labor market, and choose their labor hours optimally—they aren't constrained to work more or fewer hours than they desire, and they work in the best paying job their skills will support. Then it must be that $w \geq w'$, that is, the wage earned in the labor market exceeds the wage imputed to the volunteer activity.[42] Why? If not then the worker could switch jobs and be made better off. Stated differently, people can only volunteer for jobs that they are over-qualified for. The lawyer can volunteer his legal expertise or can mop the organization's floors, but a janitor cannot provide legal advice. Now suppose an individual is considering spending an hour volunteering, thus donating $w'v$, or spending another hour in the labor force and donating the money she earns. If gifts are fully deductible and $p = 1 - t$, then working an extra hour means she can donate the pre-tax wage w. Hence, as long as $w > w'$, this person will strictly prefer working and giving money rather than volunteering time. If people care about the total *value* of their donations, therefore, volunteering should be extremely rare among itemizers.

As noted at the top of this section, volunteering is anything but rare. So, while Model 2 captures some interesting and surely important features of the giving decision, it cannot explain much of the data. There needs to be some independent warm-glow ascribed to volunteering itself. This suggests the final model is likely to be the best guide to thinking about volunteering is

Model 3: $u(x, \ell, m + w'v, m, v)$

This model contains Models 1 and 2 as special cases. But, as shown by Andreoni et al. (2004), to the extent that people care about total value of donation, there should be a fundamental bias in the data toward giving money first. Only after the marginal warm-glow of money gifts falls should people switch to giving time. That is, we should be more likely to see time gifts follow money gifts than vice versa.[43]

8.2. Empirical studies on gifts of time and money

One of the first empirical studies of volunteering was by Menchik and Weisbrod (1987), using the 1974 National Survey on Philanthropy. They considered Model 1 above, and

[42] The payroll tax creates a wedge that may cause this to be contradicted.

[43] Why might time gifts have independent warm-glow? First is the simple joy of being involved. Second is that volunteering helps gather information about how the organization spends money, so has value as an oversight tool. Finally, Menchik and Weisbrod (1987) hypothesize that individuals volunteer to learn valuable job skills or to make contacts useful in the future. They find some weak evidence to support this view.

focused solely on hours, not dollars, given. They found volunteering is sensitive to the market wage rate, with a elasticity of -0.4. Including the price of money donations in their regression, they found that time and money are gross complements—the higher the cost of giving cash gifts, the less people give time. In the remainder of this section we will discuss the findings of three recent studies that explored the joint determinants of time and money.

Brown and Lankford (1992) are the first to look at time and money gifts in the same model. They used a special sample of Florida households in 1984. The survey asked about giving and volunteering of the respondent in the prior year. Their sample included 915 females and 717 males. Over 55% of respondents who work full time reported volunteering, and over 65% of retirees reported volunteering. All respondents averaged 7.4 hours of volunteering per month.

Brown and Lankford estimated a seemingly unrelated regression (SUR) model on time and money gifts. Because of possible differences in time gifts by sex, they estimated a three-equation model, one equation for money gifts, one for time gifts by women, and one for time gifts by men. As suggested by the theoretical model above, they find that the probability of giving time conditional on giving money is twice as high as the probability of giving money conditional on giving time (0.49 versus 0.25). This is consistent with a concern for the total value of a contribution, thus reflecting the natural tendency for time and money to be substitutes. However, they also find the correlations of the error terms in the SUR analysis to be large and positive. While this could be caused by individual heterogeneity in the cross section, it could also mean that preferences are indeed imposing a complementarity. This is also reflected in the large and negative cross price elasticities, estimated by Brown and Lankford to be -1.79.[44]

While these two studies seem to point to significant complementarity, two other studies indicate substitutability. Freeman (1997) uses 1990 survey data from Independent Sector to regress ln(volunteer hours) $-$ ln(money donations) on ln(wage). Since the wage is the relative cost of volunteering, this coefficient is an indicator of the elasticity of substitution between time and money gifts. Freeman finds a large negative coefficient, indicating substantial substitution—those with higher wages favor gifts of money.[45] Duncan (1999) uses the same data set considered by Menchik and Weisbrod (1987) and explicitly explores the hypothesis that time and money are perfect substitutes. His results are mixed, but he is unable to reject the perfect substitutes hypothesis.

[44] Brown and Lankford conduct a final interesting policy experiment. What happens to volunteerism by women if those out of the labor force suddenly begin to work full time? The reduction in time available reduces volunteering, but the income effect increases it. The net effect, they report, is that this would lead women to cut back volunteering by a little over 30 minutes per week. Similar conclusions were reported by Tiehen (2000) who studied female labor and volunteering trends from 1965 to 1993. Little of the decline in female volunteering could be attributed to labor market participation.

[45] Freeman's estimates, however, assume that the price of giving is one. In fact the price of giving should fall as the wage goes up, which should reduce this estimated elasticity of substitution and weaken his claim.

The published literature leaves open the question of whether time and money are complements or substitutes. Of course, estimation of volunteerism is hampered by all of the same difficulties discussed in the section on gifts of money. However, in this case the identification of the effect of the tax-subsidy to giving is even more severe. The marginal tax rate is also going to keenly influence the elasticity of labor supply, which will affect the propensity to volunteer. Most of the data on volunteering does not also include hours worked in the market. Although they recognized this problem, Brown and Lankford could not fully address it, and were forced to take available hours as exogenous. On the other side, Freeman's analysis made no attempt to account for the charitable deduction on volunteer hours.

In sum, the literature on time and money contributions is in great flux, and there has yet to be a definitive study to address this gap.

9. Fund-raising: charities as strategic players

Both the theoretical and empirical analysis presented thus far have assumed that charities have no active role to play in extracting donations from potential givers. In fact, fund-raising is a vibrant, innovative and highly professional industry with trade organizations and professional accreditation—one university even offers a professional degree in fund-raising. According to one estimate, about 115 000 organizations hire fund-raising staff and consultants, spending \$2 billion per year on fund-raising. In 1995 the twenty-five largest charities spent an average of over \$25 million each on fund-raising, or about 14 percent of charitable gifts.[46]

This raises several important questions. What role do fund-raisers play in affecting the gifts received by charities? How do they respond to government policy? How do they affect the efficiency of the goods provided?

Understanding the institution of fund-raising can be quite important in setting policy toward charities. Consider the following suggestive evidence. In the 1980s there were severe reductions in marginal tax rates. The economists' models predicted a steep decline in giving. However, giving over this period seemed largely to follow trends established years earlier.[47] At the same time, the popular press reported a new phenomenon called "donor fatigue." As charities faced an anticipated loss in revenues, they became more aggressive in soliciting donors, leading donors to feel tapped-out. In response, press reports account, charities were adapting to the new situation by altering their fund-raising tactics.[48] Charities, it seems, were responding strategically to changes in government policy, which in turn could have mitigated its effect. Because economic

[46] See Andreoni (1998) for more discussion of these and other facts about fund-raising.

[47] See Clotfelter (1990) for a discussion of the response to the 1980s tax reforms. See also Figure 1 in this paper.

[48] For instance, the *Wall Street Journal*, July 13, 1989 (Section 2; Page 1, Column 3), in an article entitled "Charities Shift Marketing Tactics in a Bid to Offset 'Donor Fatigue,'" reports that, "Donor fatigue has

analysis had not accounted for the strategic response of fund-raisers, it made incorrect predictions about the consequences of policy changes.

Economists have only just begun to take seriously the effects of fund-raising in understanding the strategic equilibrium of charity markets.[49] The reason, in part, is that it remains a difficult area to study. First, there is very little direct information on fund-raising. Some data sets include measures of dollars spent on fund-raising, but there is no systematic evidence on fund-raising practices. One is left to scour fund-raisers' training manuals and "how-to" books for generalizable facts about fund-raising tactics. Second, it is difficult to establish theoretically how fund-raising works. The problem is similar to that of advertising—how do these efforts alter or facilitate demands for giving?

Next I give an overview of the budding theoretical and empirical literatures on fund-raising. The theoretical literature separates fund-raising into two categories, *capital campaigns* and *continuing campaigns*. Capital campaigns characterize new charities, or major new initiatives of existing charities, such as buying expensive equipment, constructing new buildings, opening a new office, or expanding to include a new type of service. Hence, capital campaigns have two distinctive features. First is possibly large fixed costs of capitalization, and second is incomplete information about the quality or success of the project.

Continuing campaigns, by contrast, raise the operating funds for ongoing charities, funding things like salaries, direct services, supplies and maintenance. It is unlikely that continuing campaigns can be built around revealing information about the charity. As a result, models of continuing campaigns have focused on revealing information about the donors. We consider each type of fund drive in turn.

9.1. Capital campaigns

In building models, we first need to collect the stylized facts that can shape our models. Below is a partial list.

Capital campaigns have three phases: Research, Silent Phase, and General Campaign. Capital campaigns are nearly universally characterized by these three phases.[50] In the research phase the organization identifies potential donors who could give significant funds. In the silent phase the charity attempts to collect about one third of its ultimate goal from a small number of these large donors, perhaps even one. The general campaign then collects the rest in relatively small donations.

become a major marketing roadblock for charities that need to raise money steadily, year after year." They go on to report that, "Charities are revamping their marketing efforts in attempt to reach new audiences of potential donors."

49 Rose-Ackerman (1982) provides the first major theoretical model that includes fund-raising. Rather than explain how fund-raising works, she shows how free entry into a charity "market" with slight "product differentiation" can lead to socially inefficient amounts of fund-raising—a monopoly charity could raise as much revenue with lower fund-raising expense. The reason is that some fund-raising is shifting gifts across charities rather than creating new gifts.

50 See Andreoni (1988) for a discussion of sundry sources for this claim.

Capital campaigns announce gifts, especially the first gift or group of gifts. This observation is important because it defies economic reasoning—in a simple model like those of Section 3 above, announcing gifts should only encourage free riding, especially when those gifts are large.[51]

Wealthy "leadership givers" give first, and make extraordinary gifts. Large gifts, often called leadership gifts, are used to start major fund drives. Why do they come at the beginning rather than the middle or end?

Some gifts are meant as "seed grants" that spur others to give. Fund-raisers hate anonymous gifts, since they say that large publicly given gifts can be used to encourage others to donate.[52] Some philanthropists are committed to providing "challenge grants" that are meant as examples for others to follow.[53]

We have two features of capital campaigns to use as foundations for explaining these facts: potential fixed costs of capitalization, and incomplete information on the quality of the new project. Below I will introduce three classes of models and motivate how they can explain the stylized facts.

Model 1: Full information on quality, fixed costs of capitalization

This analysis is based on Andreoni (1988). Consider building a business school on campus. Unless the university can raise a minimum amount of money, the building cannot be built. However, if it exceeds this minimum, the quality of the building can rise with the dollars donated. That is, there are fixed costs (or increasing returns) of providing the public good. How does this observation affect the model of privately provided public goods?

Return to the model of Section 3 above. First, ignore the fixed cost and suppose there exists an interior equilibrium. Call this $G^* = \sum_{i=1}^n g_i^*$. Now, add in the fixed costs by redefining the level of the public good this way:

$$G = \begin{cases} \sum_{i=1}^n g_i & \text{if } \sum_{i=1}^n g_i \geq \overline{G} \\ 0 & \text{if } \sum_{i=1}^n g_i < \overline{G} \end{cases}$$

where $\overline{G}$ is the minimum amount needed before the public good can be built.

Suppose that $\overline{G} < G^*$, so that the original Nash equilibrium remains. However, this threshold $\overline{G}$ can also create a second Nash equilibrium at zero gifts. Suppose everyone is giving zero, and that $\overline{G}$ is so large that no one individual would be willing to give $\overline{G}$

[51] See, e.g., Varian (1994a) for a discussion of sequentially provided public goods.

[52] *New York Times*, November 18, 1998, "Got a Match? If Not, You Lose the Grant," by David Firestone, says "When a big (leadership giver) comes in, the smaller donors pay attention. It legitimizes a fund-raising project and puts the institution on a much faster track."

[53] Notables are Brook Atsor and foundations, like the Kresge Foundation. See Potters et al. (2005) for discussion of this evidence.

as a best reply. Then $g_i = 0$ for all i will be a Nash equilibrium. Without some efforts to get the economy over the threshold $\overline{G}$, no public goods will be provided.

What's the solution? The "silent phase" of fund-raising. If the charity can raise enough dollars to assure people that the threshold $\overline{G}$ will be met, then the interior equilibrium G^* will be attained. Let $\widehat{G}_{-i}$ be the solution to $u(m_i + \widehat{G}_{-i} - \overline{G}, \overline{G}) \equiv u(m, 0)$. Then $\widehat{G}_{-i}$ is the amount of giving by others that makes i indifferent from making a gift to cover the threshold and not. Let $\widehat{G}_S$ be the minimum among all of these $\widehat{G}_{-i}$'s. If the fund-raiser can raise $\widehat{G}_S$ in the silent phase, perhaps in the form of binding pledges,[54] then moving to the general campaign phase will be successful. Notice that $\widehat{G}_S$ is below the technological threshold $\overline{G}$, so these gifts themselves do not need to be enough to guarantee the good is built, but they must be enough to assure that the threshold $\overline{G}$ will be met.

This fixed cost of public goods now gives a purpose to fund-raising. There must be concerted and coordinated efforts to secure a significant fraction of the funds ultimately needed before a general fund drive can be announced.[55] This model can capture three of the stylized facts above: A silent phase organizes a few wealthy donors first, announces their gifts, and these spur others to give. Next we look at models that can also explain why some leadership gifts are extraordinarily large.

Model 2: Unknown quality that can be learned in advance

We now focus on incomplete information. Suppose a charity can be of two qualities. If quality is 0 then the good is "worthless" and everyone would prefer it not be built. Or the quality can be 1, in which case people would prefer to build. Assume that the probability that the good is worthless is high enough that no one is willing to build the public good without some additional confidence on the quality. Suppose that by paying a cost $c > 0$ an individual can learn the true quality. Vesterlund (2003) analyzes a model of this sort and assumes that the charity has the strategic choice of first soliciting a contribution from a particular individual, and then adopting a policy of announcing this person's contribution or not. What can a potential giver glean from a charity that chooses not to announce contributions?

Vesterlund shows that in a Bayesian–Nash equilibrium all of the high-quality charities will choose to announce gifts, and zero-quality charities will be indifferent to announcing and not. The selected first-giver will pay the cost c of learning information only if the charity announces gifts. If the gift is positive, then people will infer the quality is good. In this model the charity signals its quality by announcing gifts, and the informed first-giver signals the quality of the charity by making a large gift.

[54] The fund-raiser could employ a common mechanism for providing $\widehat{G}_S$ among a small number of rich donors. For example, the subscription mechanism of Admati and Perry (1991).

[55] They also show that governments or foundations can also provide the needed $\widehat{G}_S$. See List and Lucking-Reiley (2002) for an experimental demonstration of this effect.

Andreoni (2006) builds on this result by assuming a good charity can be of *two* possible qualities, high, H, or low, L. People prefer to build a charity of either quality, but are willing to pay more for the high quality charity. This creates an interesting dilemma for a giver who learns that the quality is only L. He prefers to fool others into thinking that the quality is H, in which case they would give more to the public good, for which the first-giver will benefit. This means that if he actually does observe quality H, he cannot simply give the amount that would be consistent with common knowledge of high quality—people would assume the quality is low. Instead, the first-giver must make a gift that separates a quality H from quality L. That means that the lead giver must give an extra-large donation, larger than he would if H were common knowledge. This explains why first givers give large gifts, but why are they also rich? This is a question of who will volunteer to move first and provide this extra-large leadership gift. Building on results of Bilodeau and Slivinski (1996a, 1996b), Andreoni (2006) shows that this war-of-attrition will lead the richest giver to be the lead giver since they have the lowest opportunity cost of providing the signal. This now explains the final stylized fact—leadership givers are the wealthy and they make extraordinarily large gifts.

Model 3: Unknown quality that can only be learned by experience

A feature of seed grants not captured by the models above is that they are sometimes in the form of experiments. Suppose the quality of the charitable project can only be learned after it is in operation. If the charity performs well, then the next year it can be expanded. The more of the good we provide this year, the faster we learn about its merit. But this means gifts have two positive externalities. First, they provide charitable services; and second, they allow us to learn about the quality of the charity. But this simply compounds the free-rider problem since now people have two reasons to let someone else give first.

Consider a world with risk averse agents with identical preferences but different degrees of income. For this case, construct a model in which public goods can grow like snowballs over time.[56] Because of decreasing absolute risk aversion, the rich will give first—they are most able to absorb the risk of a low-quality charity. If the experiment goes well and potential givers become more confident that the quality is good, the next people down the income distribution become willing to give as well. As time goes on good charities grow in both dollars donated and numbers of givers, while bad charities shrink and fade away.

9.2. Continuing campaigns

Continuing campaigns are about raising money for an established charity. The funds pay the operating expenses of the organization. Here are some of the stylized facts on continuing campaigns:

[56] See Yildirim (2003), and Bolton and Harris (1999) on strategic experimentation.

The power of the ask. Both charities and donors report that the most effective fund-raising tool is to directly ask someone to donate.

Donors are recognized. Donors see their names printed in the program for the opera or in the alumni magazine, or hear their name broadcast over public radio. Often donations are reported in broad categories rather than by exact amounts.

Charity raffles and auctions. These devices often generate surpluses when run by charities that far exceed what raffles or auctions would get in the absence of a charitable beneficiary.

The literature on continuing campaigns is organized around these stylized facts. The focus of the models is often on how charities can manipulate the incentives to provide "social rewards" to donors, such as recognition, and how charities might compete with each other for attracting donors' dollars. Again, I present summaries of the different models.

Model 4: The power of the ask: latent demands for giving

An iron law of fund-raising is that people tend not to give unless they are asked. Why would someone with a desire to give wait until they get a mailing or phone call? Andreoni and Payne (2003) build a model in which donors have latent demands to give, but transaction costs such as finding the address or simple procrastination keep them from giving. When contacted by a charity, their costs fall dramatically and so they give. The models assumes that charities differ on some dimension θ, and that each donor has a favorite θ. If contacted by several charities, donors give to the one whose θ is closest to their favorite. The closer the charity is to their ideal, the more the donor gives. Thus, solicitations increase donations for two reasons. First, they turn non-donors into donors; and second, they move givers to charities they prefer.

Andreoni and Payne (2003) then ask what happens to fund-raising efforts when a charity gets a grant from the government. The answer is fund-raising falls. This is due in part to classic crowding out, but also to the fact that any solicitation is likely to be less productive, so charities will choose to conduct fewer of them. The net effect of the grant is then to reduce donations to the recipient charity, some of which are lost altogether and some of which shift to competing charities. Hence, we can observe crowding out in part because donors give less, but also because charities ask for less. However, even if fewer dollars are given to the organization receiving the grant, some of those dollars are given instead to other firms. Analyses that ignore these two effects—the endogeneity of fund-raising and the shifting of donations to competing charities—will overstate the problem of crowding out.

Model 5: Donor recognition: signals of wealth, altruism or prestige

Charities often provide public recognition to donors. They publish names of donors or give them tokens, such as coffee mugs, to display to others. Some of this effect may be psychological—givers are showing pride, avoiding shame, or bowing to social pressure, as suggested in experiments by Andreoni and Petrie (2004) and Rege and Telle (2004). Romano and Yildirim (2001) show theoretically that if donors are affected this way, which they characterize generically as "snob-appeal," then announcing donations can produce competition among donors to appear generous. Taking a different approach, Glazer and Konrad (1996) suggest that donors may also be using charitable gifts as a way to signal their wealth to others. Giving may be an especially good form of "burning money" since it has the added benefit of helping the world and of lending some prestige to the donor.

Harbaugh (1998a) notes that a clever charity can capitalize on donors' desires for prestige by manipulating the reports of donors. For instance, rather than reporting exact dollar donations, suppose charities reported donations in categories, such as "gave \$1000 to \$2000". By carefully selecting these categories, fund-raisers can nudge people to increase their donations in order to qualify for the next higher reporting category. Of course, poorly selected categories can have the opposite effect. Harbaugh (1998b) shows the effect empirically—gifts to a law school's fund drive were almost exclusively made at the lower end of each reporting bracket.[57]

Model 6: Charity raffles: endogenous subsidies

Morgan (2000) and Morgan and Sefton (2000) ask why a charity might hold a lottery to raise money. Consider a lottery with prize P that is not connected to a charity. Let g_i be the number of lottery tickets purchased by i and $G = \sum_{i=1}^{n} g_i$. Then define $p_i = g_i/G$ as i's chance of winning the lottery. Then a risk-neutral person endowed with m_i maximizes utility

$$u_i = m_i - g_i + \frac{g_i}{G} P$$

It is easy to show that at the optimum, $G^L = P(n-1)/n$, so that profits of the lottery are $\pi = G^L - P = -P/n < 0$. The lottery will lose money.

Next consider a charity apart from the lottery. Suppose the individuals have quasi-linear utility, and that they care about the charitable services in excess of some fixed costs P, so utility is

$$u_i = m_i - g_i + \ln(G - P)$$

It is easy to show that the equilibrium donations will be $G^C = P + 1$, so that net charitable services are $G^C - P = 1$. Notice, this holds for any P, including $P = 0$, and any n.

Now couple the lottery with a charity. Individuals maximize utility

$$\begin{aligned} u_i &= m_i - g_i + \frac{g_i}{G} P + \ln(G - P) \\ &= m_i - g_i \left(1 - \frac{P}{G}\right) + \ln(G - P) \end{aligned}$$

[57] Andreoni and Petrie (2004) verify the effect in an experiment.

Notice that now the lottery acts like a subsidy on giving, with subsidy rate P/G. Rather than coming externally from a government, however, the subsidy is endogenous to the charity. It is again easy to show that the solution to this will yield $G^{CL} > P + 1 = G^C$; that is, the combination of the lottery and the charity will yield profits for the lottery and these profits will exceed the donations received without the lottery.[58] This result follows from any quasi-linear utility function.

Note the rather striking result. A lottery that would lose money by itself is profitable when coupled with a public good. Moreover, the profits exceed ordinary voluntary donations. The logic of this can be seen in the interpretation of the lottery as a subsidy to giving. Suppose $G < P$. Then the price of giving, $1 - P/G$, is actually negative—the charity essentially pays people to give. This alone guarantees the charity will break even. At $G^{CL} - P = G^C$, the lottery is still subsidizing the price for givers, further guaranteeing the success of the lottery at raising charitable revenues.

9.3. What remains to be done

Notice that in modeling fund-raising, we are describing *actual* mechanisms that are used to increase, or at least attract, donations to public goods. These models are, thus far, positive models that attempt to understand the broadest facts, and to provide a justification for fund-raisers to enter the model. Perhaps one of the most interesting aspects of charitable "markets" not captured by any of these models is that fund-raising strategies have evolved and developed in a competitive market among charities. Those with the best products and the best fund-raising strategies will be the ones to survive in the market. In this sense, the charities themselves are designing mechanisms for providing public goods, but these must satisfy an added constraint that is not common in the mechanism design literature, in particular, that their fund-raising scheme survive innovation by others. In this sense, charities practice "organic mechanism design"—they design mechanisms that must not only be incentive compatible and individually rational, but must also survive the marketplace of mechanisms used by competing charities.

Some new additions to the mechanism design literature are beginning to resemble fund-raising mechanisms. These "natural" mechanisms are simple and easily employed. Bagnoli and Lipman (1989, 1992) show how one can use repeated hill-climbing techniques to build up a public good in discrete jumps over time. Admati and Perry (1991) show that a subscription mechanism of mutually binding promises of the sort, "I'll pay X if you pay Y" can reach efficiency. In a similar vein, Varian (1994b) shows that people can offer to subsidize each other and improve efficiency. Marx and Matthews (2000), in an especially important contribution, show that repeated simultaneous contributions

58 In this case, solving for the first order conditions, summing across all i, yields

$$\frac{n-1}{n} = \frac{G}{P}\left(1 - \frac{1}{G-P}\right)$$

which can only hold if $G - P > 1$.

can, in a long enough horizon, always reach the threshold for provision of a discrete public good when it is efficient to do so. By insisting on models that reflect something in reality, these normative models can be bridges or building blocks for the literature based on the positive models above.

Perhaps the most important way models of fund-raising can affect economic analysis is in empirical studies. The empirical analysis outlined above implicitly takes the fund-raising strategies as treating people symmetrically in a cross-section, and implicitly treats them as constant in a time series. Of course, as we have seen in the models above, fund-raising strategies are likely to be affected by government policies, so neglecting how fund-raising is responding to a period of tax reform, for instance, may be leaving an important piece of the puzzle out of the model. We turn to these concerns in the next section.

10. Empirical analyses of fund-raising, government grants and crowding out

The theoretical models of the last section indicate that government grants and charitable fund-raising are likely to be jointly determined, hence when looking at the effects of one we should really also consider the other. In doing so, there are two important questions. First, do government grants crowd out private giving? The theoretical models of section 3.2 suggest they should. We call this the classic crowding out hypothesis. But if warm-glow is dominant, as section 3.5 demonstrates, then perhaps crowding out will be slight. The second question is, are charities net-revenue maximizers? If a charity is acting like a business, it should spend dollars on fund-raising until the marginal dollar spent raises an additional dollar of funds. If instead charities are "satisficers" who have revenue goals and stop when they are reached, then marginal revenues may exceed marginal costs.

This section will review the recent contributions to this literature. We begin by looking at some important studies that provide a background for later analysis.

10.1. Background studies

Two recent studies, using similar methods and data, give some insights into these two questions. Okten and Weisbrod (2000) consider panel data from charitable organizations, with data drawn from IRS Form 990 filings. Khanna et al. (1995) consider a panel of comparable data for the UK. Both use similar methods and build on their prior studies on a single cross-section (Weisbrod and Dominguez, 1986; Posnett and Sandler, 1989). The main innovation of this analysis is to assume that total donations depend on a variable they call price, P. The justification for this variable comes from the assumption that donors may suffer from a "plausible irrationality" (Rose-Ackerman, 1982) that individuals confuse marginal dollars spent on fund-raising with average dollars spent. For example, people who observe that, on average, a charity spends 20% of its revenues on fund-raising will assume that only 80% of their own dollars go to charitable services. Let f equal the ratio of fund-raising expenses to total expenditures of the charity. Then these authors define price as $P = 1/(1 - f)$. The hypothesis is that donations should be negatively related to this price.[59] Then the basic regression equation estimated is

$$C_{it} = \beta_o + \beta_1 F_{it-1} + \beta_2 P_{it-1} + \beta_3 G_{it-1} + BX_{it} + \epsilon_{it}$$

where C is total charitable contributions, F is fund-raising expenses, G is government grants, and X is other variables such other revenues and the age of the organization.[60] Note that current contributions depend on lagged exogenous variables.

While the interpretation and motivation for P can be debated,[61] the inclusion of this variable in a regression equation is important, especially when fund-raising expenses F enter the equation directly as well as indirectly in P. In particular, we can appeal to any number of explanations from the theory models above to predict that there will be a net-revenue maximizing level of fund-raising, F. This means that in the neighborhood of the optimum the contributions function should be concave, with random events putting charities sometimes to the left and sometimes to the right of the optimum. As a result, a positive coefficient β_1 on F would imply that we should also observe a negative coefficient β_2 on P, simply due to the concavity of the contributions revenue function.

These authors consider several estimation strategies, including adding fixed effects to the estimation, and both papers come to similar conclusions. First, they find that, as predicted, the relationship between contributions and fund-raising is concave; $\beta_1 > 0$ and $\beta_2 < 0$. Okten and Weisbrod find that the net effect is that charities fall short of net-revenue maximization, consistent with satisficing. By contrast, Khanna et al. find that UK charities are net-revenue maximizers.

Turning to crowding out, both find that the coefficient on G is approximately zero. In fact, the point estimates for both studies indicate β_4 is positive but insignificant. The authors interpret this as providing evidence that crowding out is not important, and that there may even be "crowding in." Both results, however, have recently been questioned, as we see next.

10.2. Endogeneity bias in grants

Payne (1998) offers an important challenge to this interpretation of crowding out.[62] She notes that the government officials who approve the grants are elected by the same people who make donations to charities. Hence, positive feelings toward a particular charity will be represented in both the preferences of givers and of the government. To

[59] Okten and Weisbrod define price as $(1 - t)/(1 - f)$ where t is the marginal tax rate applying to the charitable deduction. However, they consider ln P in their regression, making this distinction moot. Khanna et al. (1995) define price as $1/(1 - f - a)$, where a is the ratio of administrative expenses to donations. Interpreting this as a price requires the same "plausible irrationality."

[60] In Okten and Weisbrod (2000), these variables are defined as logs, while in Khanna et al. (1995) they are in levels.

[61] See Steinberg (1991) for a critique.

[62] See also Payne (2001) on crowding-in at research universities.

illustrate, consider both government and private giving to disaster relief in the year of a great tragedy, such as a hurricane, flood, or 9/11 attacks. Both private and pubic giving are going to be higher, leading to a bias against finding crowding out.[63]

To examine this, Payne used data similar to Okten and Weisbrod, a panel of 430 non-profits for 10 years. She restricts the sample to only those nonprofits that provide local services. Repeating simple OLS analysis of the sort done prior to her study, she replicates the finding—point estimates indicating near zero crowding out. She then turns to two-stage least squares analysis to address the problem of endogeneity. As an instrument for government grants she uses aggregate government transfers to individuals in the state. This is something that should be correlated with the political power of representatives in the state, but not correlated with demands for charity.

Her approach is extremely successful. She finds that estimates of crowding out now rise to around 50%—each dollar of government grants generates only 50 cents of new charity. This is a startling and important departure from the prior literature.

Payne's analysis did not account for fund-raising expenditure of the charities. If fund-raising and government grants depend on each other, as shown above, directly entering fund-raising expenses would lead to biased coefficients. For instance, a charity that applied for and won a large government grant would spend less effort on fund-raising, or conversely a charity with productive fund-raising apparatus isn't as likely to spend efforts on winning grants. In this way, Payne's efforts can be seen as a reduced form estimate of the effect of grants on giving, and it suggests this reduced-form effect is profound. However, it leaves open the question of the mechanism through which government grants cause a reduction in donations. Is the effect direct, as in classic crowding out, or is it indirect—people give less because the charity has opted to spend less effort on fund-raising? We begin to answer this question next.

10.3. What's crowded out, giving or fund-raising?

Andreoni and Payne (2003) ask the simple questions: what happens to a charity's fund-raising expenses when it gets a government grant? Does it fall, and by how much?

To answer these, they again looked at IRS 990 filings, this time on a 14-year panel of 233 arts organizations and 534 social services organizations. The two types of organizations were treated separately because of their special differences. Arts organizations typically rely heavily on fund-raising, and get relatively few government grants. Only 10% of their budget comes from grants, and over 50% from donations. By contrast, social service organizations rely heavily on the government, with 23% of their budget coming from grants and 26% from donations. The remainder of both budgets come largely from "program service revenues," such as ticket sales or service fees.

[63] A more subtle endogeneity issue is raised by Coate (1995). Because charities cannot commit to *not* help those in need, the government (conditional on a binding budget constraint) will strategically use private charity to supplement it's own provision of public goods. It is unclear how this will bias coefficients, especially in the presence of many goods.

The estimation equation of Andreoni and Payne is

$$F_{it} = \alpha_i + \gamma_t + \beta G_{it} + \mathbf{O}_{it}\eta + \mathbf{Z}_{it}\lambda + \epsilon_{it}$$

where F is fund-raising, G is government grants, $\mathbf{O}$ is a vector of organization variables, and $\mathbf{Z}$ a vector of state-specific demographic and political variables. Notice fixed effects for both the firm and year are included, and that all variables pertain to the same year.[64]

In estimating the effect of grants on fund-raising, one must again deal with endogeneity. As with Payne's (Payne, 1998) earlier observation, charities that are in high demand will likely receive government grants and engage in active fund-raising. As such, we must instrument grants to remove the positive bias in estimating β.

Andreoni and Payne first estimate the model without accounting for endogeneity. They estimate the coefficient β to be positive and significant, indicating a likely endogeneity bias. They then apply the instrumental variables analysis, and things turn around dramatically. For art organizations they find that a \$1000 increase in grants will reduce fund-raising by \$265. For social service organizations, the reduction would be \$54. Extrapolating these effects out, grants decrease fund-raising by about 52% for arts organizations and 32% for social service organizations. These reductions are clearly significant.

This study raises an interesting and important question. Do we see crowding out because people are discouraged directly by the government grants, or because charities themselves are discouraged from spending money on fund-raising? The answer to this question could make a critical difference for policy. Suppose that all of the reduced giving is due to reduced fund-raising and none is due to classic crowding out. Then it would be feasible to have a government policy that awarded grants on the condition that dollars raised through private fund-raising not fall. Such "matching grants" (or "partially matching grants") could improve the impact of grants on charitable services. A matching policy could be desirable, depending on how the "deadweight loss" of fund-raising compares to the deadweight loss of taxation (weighted by the crowding factor). Future work will be needed to sort out these important questions.

A paper by Straub (2003) has begun to look at these issues in the context of Public Broadcasting in the US. Following on work by Kingma (1989), Straub estimates a structural model on a panel of public radio stations.[65] He finds the reduction in giving after a grant is due almost entirely to reduced fund-raising, and not to classic crowding out. Moreover, he estimates a concave "revenue function" for fund-raising and finds that, by and large, most public radio stations are net-revenue maximizers, with a few notable

[64] The timing of fund-raising to donations is always unclear—do dollars spent this year yield donations this year or next year? Andreoni and Payne (2003) provide sensitivity tests, and discuss this and several other subtle measurement issues in detail.

[65] Kingma's often cited paper finds about 13% crowding out in donations to Public Radio. Manzoor and Straub (2005) fail to replicate Kingma's findings on a larger set of data, instead finding roughly no crowding out using Kingma's methods.

exceptions of both kinds. This is a very clear and compelling study. If these results also hold in more general studies with other types of charities, the results could profoundly change prevailing views of crowding out and fund-raising in providing charitable services.

11. Conclusion: the future of giving research

Philanthropy has for decades been one of the most important areas of public finance research. Millions of people and billions of dollars are devoted to charitable giving. Moreover, the government's involvement in both grants to organizations and subsidies to givers makes it a perennially important public policy topic. Each new generation of government policy makers will need to know the determinants of giving and the impacts of grants. For this reason, it will always be a productive and valued area of research.

Despite its importance, a clear understanding of philanthropy has eluded economists. One reason is the basic challenge in understanding the motives of givers—why do people give? We have argued strongly here that the model of "warm-glow giving" provides a good foundation for analysis. This, however, is just a partial answer to this question. The concept of warm-glow is only a convenient reduced-form representation for deeper and more complex considerations of givers. Future work, perhaps combined with laboratory or field experiments, can help fine-tune the model of givers.

Fine-tuning the model of givers is interesting in its own right, but it becomes especially important when we begin to analyze philanthropy as a market, with both suppliers (the givers) and demanders (the fund-raising charities). As we have argued in this chapter, both sides of this market are active and strategic, and both are likely to respond to changes in the government policy or other factors in their environment. Unfortunately, this interaction between the supply and demand for philanthropy has been largely neglected in both theoretical and empirical analysis. Clearly, however, its impact is extremely important. Failure to treat philanthropy as a market has likely led empirical work to overstate the effect of the marginal tax rate on giving. As policy changes, so do fund-raisers to counteract the change, so that in the long run the price elasticity of giving may be lower than could be estimated in a cross-section.

Failing to look at philanthropy as a market has also likely biased our estimates of crowding out. On the one hand it leads to an understatement of the response. Because the tastes of government grant-givers are positively correlated with tastes of individual gift-givers, estimates have likely been biased against crowding out. On the other hand, by looking at only the "partial equilibrium" of a single charity, we may also be overstating the effect of crowding out.

To see this, imagine charities in a "monopolistically competitive" market. For instance, there are several cancer research charities, dozens of world-hunger charities, and hundreds of environmental charities. If one charity gets a major grant or a large bequest, how do the others respond? How do givers respond? Do they move their gifts to competing charities in the same market, to charities of another variety, or do they simply give less overall? Which of these is the right answer will have a profound effect on how we view crowding out more globally, and how we asses the cost, incidence and effectiveness of government grants and subsidies.

Another potential for research is in viewing philanthropy as a dynamic market. Why, for instance, are there hundreds of environmental organizations? Which survive in the long run? How does competition for donations shape both the outputs of the charity and the fund-raising mechanisms they employ? And, perhaps most importantly, does this competition promote a sort of "organic mechanism design" that will move the economy toward efficient mechanisms for the provision of public goods?

One goal of this chapter has been to collect the state of knowledge on philanthropy and to provide a vehicle for the new entrant into this research. A second and more important goal has been to inspire and promote new interest in larger and more challenging questions about philanthropy. Despite being an active area of research for several decades, I view the literature on charitable giving as full of open questions. As I hope I have conveyed, we are on the doorstep of an exciting new era for research on philanthropy.

References

Admati, A.R., Perry, M. (1991). "Joint projects without commitment". Review of Economic Studies 58, 259–276.

Andreoni, J. (1988). "Privately provided public goods in a large economy: the limits of altruism". Journal of Public Economics 35, 57–73.

Andreoni, J. (1989). "Giving with impure altruism: applications to charity and Ricardian equivalence". Journal of Political Economy 97, 1447–1458.

Andreoni, J. (1990). "Impure altruism and donations to public goods: a theory of warm-glow giving". Economic Journal 100, 464–477.

Andreoni, J. (1993). "An experimental test of the public-goods crowding-out hypothesis". American Economic Review 83, 1317–1327.

Andreoni, J. (1995). "Cooperation in public goods experiments: kindness or confusion?". American Economic Review 85, 891–904.

Andreoni, J. (1998). "Toward a theory of charitable fund-raising". Journal of Political Economy 106, 1186–1213.

Andreoni, J. (2006). "Leadership giving in charitable fund-raising". Journal of Public Economic Theory 8, 1–22.

Andreoni, J., Bergstrom, T.C. (1996). "Do government subsidies increase the private supply of public goods?". Public Choice 88, 295–308.

Andreoni, J., Brown, E., Rischall, I. (2003). "Charitable giving by married couples: who decides and why does it matter?". Journal of Human Resources 38, 111–133.

Andreoni, J., Gale, W.G., Scholz, J.K., Straub, J. (2004). "Charitable contributions of time and money". Manuscript, University of Wisconsin.

Andreoni, J., McGuire, M.C. (1993). "Identifying the free riders: a simple algorithm for determining who will contribute to a public good". Journal of Public Economics 51, 447–454.

Andreoni, J., Miller, J.H. (2002). "Giving according to GARP: an experimental test of the consistency of preferences for altruism". Econometrica 70, 737–753.

Andreoni, J., Payne, A.A. (2003). "Do government grants to private charities crowd out giving or fund-raising?". American Economic Review 93, 792–812.

Andreoni, J., Petrie, R. (2004). "Public goods experiments without confidentiality: a glimpse into fund-raising". Journal of Public Economics 88, 1605–1623.

Andreoni, J., Scholz, J.K. (1998). "An econometric analysis of charitable giving with interdependent preferences". Economic Inquiry 36, 410–428.

Arrow, K.J. (1972). "Gifts and exchanges". Philosophy and Public Affairs 1, 343–362.

Atkinson, A.B., Stern, N.H. (1974). "Pigou, taxation and public goods". Review of Economic Studies 41, 119–128.

Auten, G.E., Clotfelter, C.T., Schmalbeck, R.L. (2000). "Taxes and philanthropy among the wealthy". In: Slemrod, J.B. (Ed.), Does Atlas Shrug? The Economic Consequences of Taxing the Rich. Russell Sage, New York.

Auten, G., Sieg, H., Clotfelter, C.T. (2002). "Charitable giving, income, and taxes: an analysis of panel data". American Economic Review 92, 371–382.

Avery, R.B., Rendall, M.S. (1993). "Estimating the size and distribution of baby boomers' prospective inheritances". In: American Statistical Associations 1993 Proceedings of the Social Statistics Section, pp. 11–19.

Bagnoli, M., Lipman, B.L. (1989). "Provision of public goods: fully implementing the core through private contributions". Review of Economic Studies 56, 583–601.

Bagnoli, M., Lipman, B.L. (1992). "Private provision of public goods can be efficient". Public Choice 74, 59–78.

Bakija, J.M., Gale, W.G., Slemrod, J.B. (2003). "Charitable bequests and taxes on inheritances and estates: aggregate evidence from across states and time". American Economic Review 93, 366–370.

Barrett, K.S., McGuirk, A.M., Steinberg, R. (1997). "Further evidence on the dynamic impact of taxes on charitable giving". National Tax Journal 50, 321–334.

Becker, G.S. (1974). "A theory of social interactions". Journal of Political Economy 82, 1063–1093.

Bergstrom, T.C., Blume, L.E., Varian, H.R. (1986). "On the private provision of public goods". Journal of Public Economics 29, 25–49.

Bernheim, B.D. (1986). "On the voluntary and involuntary provision of public goods". American Economic Review 76, 789–793.

Bernheim, B.D., Bagwell, K. (1988). "Is everything neutral?". Journal of Political Economy 96, 308–338.

Bilodeau, M., Slivinski, A. (1996a). "Toilet cleaning and department chairing: volunteering a public service". Journal of Public Economics 59, 299–308.

Bilodeau, M., Slivinski, A. (1996b). "Volunteering nonprofit entrepreneurial services". Journal of Economic Behavior and Organization 31, 117–127.

Boadway, R., Keen, M. (1993). "Public goods, self-selection and optimal income taxation". International Economic Review 34, 463–478.

Boadway, R., Pestieau, P., Wildasin, D. (1989). "Tax-transfer policies and the voluntary provision of public goods". Journal of Public Economics 39, 157–176.

Bolton, P., Harris, C. (1999). "Strategic experimentation". Econometrica 67, 349–374.

Boulding, K.E. (1973). The Economy of Love and Fear: A Preface to Grants Economics. Wadsworth Publishing Co, Belmont, CA.

Brown, E., Lankford, H. (1992). "Gifts of money and gifts of time: estimating the effects of tax prices and available time". Journal of Public Economics 47, 321–341.

Carman, K.G. (2003). "Social influences and the private provision of public goods: evidence from charitable contributions in the workplace", Manuscript, Stanford University.

Clotfelter, C.T. (1985). Federal Tax Policy and Charitable Giving. University of Chicago Press, Chicago.

Clotfelter, C.T. (1990). "The impact of tax reform on charitable giving: a 1989 perspective". In: Slemrod, J.B. (Ed.), Do Taxes Matter? The Impact of the Tax Reform Act of 1986. MIT Press, Cambridge.

Clotfelter, C.T., Steuerle, C.E. (1981). "Charitable contributions". In: Aaron, H.J., Pechman, J.A. (Eds.), How Taxes Affect Economic Behavior. Brookings Institution, Washington, DC.

Coate, S. (1995). "Altruism, the Samaritan's dilemma, and government transfer policy". American Economic Review 85, 46–57.

Cornes, R., Hartley, R., Sandler, T. (1999). "Equilibrium existence and uniqueness in public good models: an elementary proof via contraction". Journal of Public Economic Theory 1, 499–509.

Cornes, R., Sandler, T. (1984). "Easy riders, joint production, and public goods". Economic Journal 94, 580–598.

Cremer, H., Gahvari, F. (2001). "Second-best taxation of emissions and polluting goods". Journal of Public Economics 80, 169–197.

Deaton, A., Muellbauer, J. (1980). Economics and Consumer Behavior. Cambridge University Press, Cambridge.

Diamond, P. (2006). "Optimal tax treatment of private contributions for public goods with and without warm glow preferences". Journal of Public Economics 90, 897–919.

Duncan, B. (1999). "Modeling charitable contributions of time and money". Journal of Public Economics 72, 213–242.

Fraser, C.D. (1992). "The uniqueness of nash equilibrium in the private provision of public goods: an alternative proof". Journal of Public Economics 49, 389–390.

Feenberg, D. (1987). "Are tax price models really identified: the case of charitable giving". National Tax Journal 40, 629–633.

Feldstein, M. (1980). "A contribution to the theory of 'tax expenditures': the case of charitable giving". In: Aaron, J.J., Boskin, M.J. (Eds.), The Economics of Taxation. Brookings, Washington, DC.

Feldstein, M., Clotfelter, C.T. (1976). "Tax incentives and charitable contributions in the United States: a microeconometric analysis". Journal of Public Economics 5, 1–26.

Feldstein, M., Taylor, A. (1976). "The income tax and charitable contributions". Econometrica 44, 1201–1222.

Freeman, R.B. (1997). "Working for nothing: the supply of volunteer labor". Journal of Labor Economics 15, S140–S166.

Fullerton, D., Metcalf, G.E. (2001). "Environmental controls, scarcity rents, and pre-existing distortions". Journal of Public Economics 80, 249–267.

Gaube, T. (2000). "When do distortionary taxes reduce the optimal supply of public goods?". Journal of Public Economics 76, 151–180.

Glazer, A., Konrad, K.A. (1996). "A signaling explanation for charity". American Economic Review 86, 1019–1028.

Greene, P., McClelland, R. (2001). "Taxes and charitable giving". National Tax Journal 54, 433–453.

Harbaugh, W.T. (1998a). "What do donations buy? A model of philanthropy based on prestige and warm glow". Journal of Public Economics 67, 269–284.

Harbaugh, W.T. (1998b). "The prestige motive for making charitable transfers". American Economic Review 88, 277–282.

Hochman, H.M., Rodgers, J.D. (1969). "Pareto optimal redistribution". American Economic Review 59, 542–557.

Joulfaian, D. (2000). "Estate taxes and charitable bequests by the wealthy", NBER Working Paper 7663.

Joulfaian, D. (2001). "Charitable giving in life and at death". In: Gale, W.G., Hines, J.R., Slemrod, J.B. (Eds.), Rethinking Estate and Gift Taxation. Brookings Press, Washington, DC.

Joulfaian, D., Rider, M. (2004). "Errors-in-variables and estimated income and price elasticities of charitable giving". National Tax Journal 57, 25–43.

Kahneman, D., Knetsch, J.L. (1992). "Valuing public goods: the purchase of moral satisfaction". Journal of Environmental Economics and Management 22, 57–70.

Kaplow, L. (1995). "A note on subsidizing gifts". Journal of Public Economics 58, 469–477.

Kaplow, L. (1996). "The optimal supply of public goods and the distortionary cost of taxation". National Tax Journal 49, 513–533.

Kaplow, L. (1998). "Tax policy and gifts". American Economic Review 88, 283–288.

Kaplow, L., Shavell, S. (2001). "Any non-welfarist method of policy assessment violates the Pareto principle". Journal of Political Economy 109, 281–286.

Khanna, J., Posnett, J., Sandler, T. (1995). "Charity donations in the UK: new evidence based on panel data". Journal of Public Economics 56, 257–272.

Kingma, B.R. (1989). "An accurate measurement of the crowd-out effect, income effect, and price effect for charitable contributions". Journal of Political Economy 97, 1197–1207.

Kolm, S.Ch. (1969). "The optimal production of social justice". In: Margolis, J., Guitton, H. (Eds.), Public Economics: An Analysis of Public Production and Consumption and their Relations to the Private Sectors. MacMillian Press, London, pp. 145–200.

List, J.A., Lucking-Reiley, D. (2002). "The effects of seed money and refunds on charitable giving: experimental evidence from a university capital campaign". Journal of Political Economy 110, 215–233.

Madrian, B.C., Shea, D.F. (2001). "The power of suggestion: inertia in 401(k) participation and savings behavior". Quarterly Journal of Economics 116, 1149–1187.

Manzoor, S., Straub, J. (2005). "The robustness of Kingma's crowd-out estimate: evidence from new data on contributions to public radio". Public Choice 123, 463–476.

Marx, L.M., Matthews, S.A. (2000). "Dynamic voluntary contribution to a public project". Review of Economic Studies 67, 327–358.

Menchik, P.L., Weisbrod, B.A. (1987). "Volunteer labor supply". Journal of Public Economics 32, 159–183.

Morgan, J. (2000). "Financing public goods by means of lotteries". Review of Economic Studies 67, 761–784.

Morgan, J., Sefton, M. (2000). "Funding public goods with lotteries: experimental evidence". Review of Economic Studies 67, 785–810.

Okten, C., Weisbrod, B.A. (2000). "Determinants of donations in private nonprofit markets". Journal of Public Economics 75, 255–272.

Palfrey, T.R., Prisbrey, J.E. (1996). "Altruism, reputation and noise in linear public goods experiments". Journal of Public Economics 61, 409–427.

Palfrey, T.R., Prisbrey, J.E. (1997). "Anomalous behavior in public goods experiments: how much and why?". American Economic Review 87, 829–846.

Payne, A.A. (1998). "Does the government crowd-out private donations? New evidence from a sample of non-profit firms". Journal of Public Economics 69, 323–345.

Payne, A.A. (2001). "Measuring the effect of federal research funding on private donations at research universities: is federal research funding more than a substitute for private donations?". International Tax and Public Finance 8, 731–751.

Pigou, A.C. (1947). A Study in Public Finance, 3rd edn. MacMillian, London.

Posnett, J., Sandler, T. (1989). "Demand for charity donations in private non-profit markets: The case of the UK". Journal of Public Economics 40, 187–200.

Potters, J., Sefton, M., Vesterlund, L. (2005). "After you—endogenous sequencing in voluntary contribution games". Journal of Public Economics 89, 1399–1419.

Randolph, W.C. (1995). "Dynamic income, progressive taxes, and the timing of charitable contributions". Journal of Political Economy 103, 709–738.

Reece, W.S., Zieschang, K.D. (1985). "Consistent estimation of the impact of tax deductibility on the level of charitable contributions". Econometrica 53, 271–293.

Rege, M., Telle, K. (2004). "The impact of social approval and framing on cooperation in public good situations". Journal of Public Economics 88, 1625–1644.

Ribar, D.C., Wilhelm, M.O. (2002). "Altruistic and joy-of-giving motivations in charitable behavior". Journal of Political Economy 110, 425–457.

Roberts, R.D. (1984). "A positive model of private charity and public transfers". Journal of Political Economy 92, 136–148.

Roberts, R.D. (1987). "Financing public goods". Journal of Political Economy 95, 420–437.

Romano, R., Yildirim, H. (2001). "Why charities announce donations: a positive perspective". Journal of Public Economics 81, 423–447.

Rose-Ackerman, S. (1982). "Charitable giving and 'excessive' fund-raising". Quarterly Journal of Economics 97, 193–212.

Saez, E. (2004). "The optimal treatment of tax expenditures". Journal of Public Economics 88, 2657–2684.

Samuelson, P.A. (1954). "The pure theory of public expenditure". Review of Economics and Statistics 36, 387–389.

Sandler, T., Posnett, J. (1991). "The private provision of public goods: a perspective on neutrality". Public Finance Quarterly 19, 22–42.
Scharf, K.A. (2000). "Why are tax expenditures for giving embodied in fiscal constitutions?". Journal of Public Economics 75, 365–387.
Schervish, P.G., Havens, J.J. (2003). "Gifts and Bequests: Family or Philanthropic Organizations". In: Munnel, A.H., Sundén, A. (Eds.), Death and Dollars: The Role of Gifts and Bequests in America. Brookings Institution Press, Washington, DC, pp. 130–158.
Sen, A.K. (1977). "Rational fools: a critique of the behavioral foundations of economic theory". Journal of Philosophy and Public Affairs 6, 317–344.
Slemrod, J. (1989). "An empirical test for tax evasion". Review of Economics and Statistics 67, 232–238.
Steinberg, R. (1987). "Voluntary donations and public expenditures in a federalist system". American Economic Review 77, 24–36.
Steinberg, R. (1990). "Taxes and giving: new findings". Voluntas 1, 61–79.
Steinberg, R. (1991). "Does government spending crowd out donations? Interpreting the evidence". Annals of Public and Cooperative Economics 62, 591–617.
Straub, J.D. (2003). "Fund-raising and crowd-out of charitable contributions: new evidence from contributions to public radio", Manuscript, Texas A&M University.
Stigler, G.J., Becker, G.S. (1997). "De gustibus non est disputandum". American Economic Review 67, 76–90.
Stiglitz, J.E. (1982). "Self-selection and Pareto efficient taxation". Journal of Public Economics 17, 213–240.
Sugden, R. (1982). "On the economics of philanthropy". Economic Journal 92, 341–350.
Sugden, R. (1984). "Reciprocity: the supply of public goods through voluntary contributions". Economic Journal 94, 772–787.
Taussig, M.K. (1967). "Economic aspects of the personal income tax treatment of charitable contributions". National Tax Journal 20, 1–19.
Tiehen, L. (2000). "Has working more caused married women to volunteer less? Evidence from time diary data, 1965 to 1993". Nonprofit and Voluntary Sector Quarterly 29, 505–529.
Triest, R.K. (1998). "Econometric issues in estimating the behavioral response to taxation: a nontechnical introduction". National Tax Journal 51, 761–772.
Varian, H.R. (1994a). "Sequential contributions to public goods". Journal of Public Economics 53, 165–186.
Varian, H.R. (1994b). "A solution to the problem of externalities when agents are well-informed". American Economic Review 84, 1278–1293.
Vesterlund, L.D. (2003). "The informational value of sequential fund-raising". Journal of Public Economics 87, 627–657.
Warr, P.G. (1982). "Pareto optimal redistribution and private charity". Journal of Public Economics 19, 131–138.
Warr, P.G. (1983). "The private provision of a public good is independent of the distribution of income". Economics Letters 13, 207–211.
Weisbrod, B.A., Dominguez, N.D. (1986). "Demand for collective goods in private nonprofit markets: can fund raising expenditures help overcome free-rider behavior?". Journal of Public Economics 30, 83–90.
Yildirim, H. (2003). "Getting the ball rolling: voluntary contributions to a large-scale public project". Journal of Public Economic Theory, in press.

Chapter 19

DONATIVE NONPROFIT ORGANIZATIONS*

MARC BILODEAU[1] and RICHARD STEINBERG[2]
IUPUI, Indianapolis, IN, USA

Contents

* Thanks to Jean Mercier-Ythier, Myles McGregor-Lowndes, Petra Brhlikova, participants at ARNOVA and particularly Rob McClelland for helpful suggestions. Thanks also to the Centre of Philanthropy and Nonprofit Studies at Queensland University of Technology and the Myer Foundation for supporting completion of this project.

[1] Associate Professor of Economics, IUPUI, Indianapolis, IN, USA.
[2] Professor of Economics, Philanthropic Studies, and Public Affairs, IUPUI, Indianapolis, IN, USA. Visiting Professor, Centre of Philanthropy and Nonprofit Studies, QUT, Brisbane, Australia.

Handbook of the Economics of Giving, Altruism and Reciprocity, Volume 2
Edited by Serge-Christophe Kolm and Jean Mercier Ythier

DOI: 10.1016/S1574-0714(06)02019-7

Abstract

In this chapter, we explore why donations are made to nonprofit organizations instead of other institutions or directly to recipients; how such nonprofit organizations behave; and what is the appropriate public policy toward subsidizing and regulating these entities. We focus on donative nonprofits—organizations precluded from distributing their surplus revenues to those in control that receive resources in the forms of donated time and money and tend to provide private pure, distributional, or excludable public goods. First, we discuss the definition of a private nonprofit organization and delineate some immediate corollaries and consequences of that definition. Next, we summarize the dimensions of the nonprofit sector—size, scope, and revenue mix—for various countries around the world. Third, we discuss various models of the role and behavior of donative nonprofit organizations. Finally, we discuss some specific behaviors of nonprofit organizations—the ways in which they conduct fundraising campaigns, set prices, employ labor, and use capital.

The discussion of models of donative nonprofits forms the heart of our paper, and is organized as follows. First, we show that agency problems between donors (as principals) and charitable service-providing organizations (as agents) result whenever the latter are employed to provide public goods. If the organization is constrained against the distribution of profits, this agency problem is resolved. Second, we argue that a three-stage game is the most natural way to model the choices of intermediaries and donors. In this game, an intermediary makes a seed donation, collects donations from others, then can add to (but not subtract from) the total donated in previous stages. Third, we detail the choice the founding entrepreneur makes between organizing as a nonprofit or a for-profit organization, showing that it can be individually rational for the entrepreneur to constrain his future ability to distribute profits. Fourth, we show how commercial activities alter entrepreneurial decisions. Fifth, we discuss nonprofits that provide excludable public goods, such as those in the arts. Sixth, we discuss sorting of entrepreneurial types across sectors and industries. Seventh, we consider multiple public goods, which may be provided by a single or separate organizations, and the passthrough intermediaries that may support them. Eighth, we delineate a variety of internal agency problems and the ways in which nonprofit organizations cope with them. The final subsection looks at models of long-run equilibrium.

Keywords

nonprofit organizations, donations, fundraising, intersectoral competition, public policy

JEL classification: H41, L31, L33

1. Introduction

Other chapters in this volume examine the behavior of individuals, altruistic and otherwise, who engage in "other-regarding" behaviors. The mode of giving is typically unspecified in these chapters—a transfer of money or donation of time is made to help a family member, beggar on the street, or some other recipient. There is no focus on whether that transfer is made directly to the recipient or passed through some intermediary organization such as a charity. In this chapter, we look at the choice of institutions—when do individuals organize or support a formal organization to channel their donations and when do they choose the nonprofit legal form for these organizations?

For most of this chapter, we adopt the definition of "nonprofit organization" (NP) formalized and popularized by Hansmann (1980), that a NP is an organization constrained by laws, regulations, or internal structure from distributing its financial surplus to its owners. This definition, while not without faults and ambiguities (which we will discuss presently), is implicit in all of the nonprofit corporation acts in the U.S. and many corresponding provisions around the world (Salamon and Anheier, 1992). Nondistribution provides a coherent and shared analytic framework with which to examine a vast array of entities with little else in common. Soup kitchens, hospitals, universities, grant-making foundations, symphony orchestras, organized religions, labor unions, think tanks, cross-national environmental action groups, day care centers, old-age homes, political parties, and trade associations are, at least sometimes, organized in ways that restrict the distribution of financial surplus. Some, but not all, of these can be regarded as intermediaries for those with an altruistic bent, and these are the nonprofits we will focus on in this chapter. Thus, we will de-emphasize theories relating to "commercial nonprofits" (Hansmann, 1980)—organizations that derive their revenues from sales of goods and services—except when the theories relate to altruistic motives or behaviors or when the organization both receives donations and sells a product.

More specifically, we focus on those NPs that provide collective benefits, including pure public goods, distributional public goods (where a group of donors each care about the provision of an otherwise private good to some recipient), excludable nonrival goods, and private goods that provide other types of external benefits (such as vaccinations). These organizations are "donative nonprofits" (Hansmann, 1980), receiving substantial resources from donated time and/or money. We also de-emphasize labor unions and political parties because, for no clear analytic reason, these organizations are rarely discussed in terms of their nondistribution of profits.

The next section of this paper discusses the definition of a private nonprofit organization and delineates some immediate corollaries and consequences of that definition. Then, we discuss the dimensions of the nonprofit sector—size, scope, and revenue mix—for various countries around the world. The fourth section discusses various models of the role and behavior of nonprofit organizations. The fifth section discusses specific behaviors of nonprofit organizations—the ways in which they conduct fundraising campaigns, set prices, employ labor, and use capital. A final section provides our conclusions.

2. What is a private nonprofit organization?

As noted above, we define NPs by a "nondistribution constraint" prohibiting the distribution of profits to the owners. Questions arise from every part of this definition, as we must interpret, in an economically-meaningful way, what counts as "profits," what constitutes a distribution, and who is an owner. Having done so, we must then define the boundaries of the organization and distinguish private NPs from public agencies. We consider each of these issues, then the immediate consequences of defining an organization in this way. We simplify matters considerably by working with a "pure" definition that is not always consistent with the many statutes, regulations, and case law of the various governments around the world. Thus, the reader is cautioned that the set of organizations classified as nonprofit by legal and statistical authorities may differ from those that would be so classified here.

These definitional issues apply equally well to donative and commercial nonprofits. We begin to distinguish the two again in section 3.3, where we present statistics on the donative share of total revenues for various kinds of nonprofit organizations.

2.1. Nondistribution

Sometimes NPs are called organizations without owners, but this takes an overly narrow view of "ownership." Ben-Ner and Jones (1995) argue that property rights have three components: the right to control the use of an asset, the right to retain any financial surpluses generated from that use, and the right to sell the first two rights to a new owner. NP boards and executives have "attenuated property rights," enjoying the first but not the second and third components of full ownership.

Nonprofit organizations do not like to call their financial surplus "profits," but they do earn scarcity rents, however they are labeled. The definition of profit appropriate for the nondistribution constraint is probably closer to an accounting than an economic notion, but ambiguities remain in calculating explicit revenues minus explicit costs. Including revenues from sales, dues, and donations in the former, nonprofit organizations can and do make profits (defined as end-of-year surplus), and accounting rates of profit are broadly similar to those enjoyed by for-profit firms (e.g., Steinberg, 1987; Chang and Tuckman, 1990).

As long as financial surpluses are retained for "charitable purposes" (by adding them to the legally-restricted endowment or the board-restricted quasi-endowment, by making grants to other NPs, or by reinvesting them in the organization), the nondistribution constraint is not violated. It is even possible to pay something like a profit-sharing bonus, provided the bonus is linked to a component of profits rather than to their totality (either just cost reduction or just revenue enhancement but not revenues minus costs per se) (see Steinberg (1990) or Wright and Rotz (1992) for some U.S. case law and regulations regarding permissible incentive plans). NPs can own for-profit subsidiaries or create commercial divisions within a unified corporate structure, but retain their non-profit status if the net after-tax earnings from these subsidiaries and divisions are wholly devoted to charitable purposes.

In accounting terms, the value of owners' time is not included as a cost, so that any compensation paid to the owners would seem to constitute a distribution of profit. This is how nondistribution is generally interpreted with respect to the members of governing board. The executive director and other top staff members have substantial control over the organization and so may be regarded as owners. However, executive compensation appears as an accounting cost, rather than a distribution of profits, and so does not violate the nondistribution constraint if compensation is not excessive. This restriction, labeled the "fair compensation constraint" by Hansmann (1980), is a natural corollary to the nondistribution constraint, but it is hard to make the idea precise. Under one interpretation, the fair compensation constraint is violated if the NP pays more than it needs to attract an executive with given talents and motivation; under another, the constraint is violated if the executive received more than her opportunity cost. These interpretations might not lead to the same level of compensation because the market for NP executives might be imperfect. Consider two candidates who would perform equally well as executive director of a particular nonprofit, but who would have widely different productivities in their next-best opportunity as the CEO of a for-profit firm. Candidate A, who has the lower productivity in his alternative employment, could be obtained at lower cost to the NP. If instead candidate B were selected and offered compensation just sufficient to cover her opportunity costs, this would constitute a distribution of profits under the first interpretation but not under the second.

The nondistribution constraint covers distribution in the form of cash and cash equivalents, but other forms of compensation can flow to those in control of the organization. Although in practice many kinds of cash-like distribution occur (due to the difficulty in monitoring complex transactions), in theory the nondistribution constraint allows distribution only through job attributes. These can be private goods (nice offices, pleasant locales for board meetings, attractive but nonproductive staff, tenure) or the warm glow provided to those who feel that their position of power and control allows them to make the world a better place. Some authors have stressed the former (e.g., Clarkson, 1972; Glaeser and Schleifer, 2001), arguing that the nondistribution constraint forces the organization to use a higher-cost compensation package that emphasizes perks over cash (these papers differ in whether that "distortion" enhances or diminishes economic efficiency). Others follow Hansmann's [Hansmann (1980)] original suggestion by including both forms of distribution (Schlesinger, 1985; Eckel and Steinberg, 1993, 1994; Handy, 1997).

Alternative definitions are used in the literature, either substituting for or adding to the nondistribution constraint. Thus, Preston (1988), noting that most U.S. state nonprofit corporation statutes refer to permissible outputs as well as the nondistribution of profits, proposes that we include a "public benefit constraint" as part of the definition. Again, statutory formulations are hazy at best, but her formal model captures this idea by requiring that a specified minimum expenditure be made on provision of public goods. We prefer to discuss the public benefit constraint as a way to regulate NPs, rather than a definitional requisite. In contrast, Kaplan (1999) notes three problems with the notion of nondistribution: (a) monitoring compliance with the constraint is difficult for regulatory authorities and stakeholders; (b) ambiguities permeate the determination of what is and is not permissible in many applications; (c) distribution through job attributes and provision of public goods is, in any case, permissible. He proposes that instead of regarding nonprofits as organizations that cannot distribute their profits, they should be regarded as organizations in which rights to distribution are unclear and perpetually contested. This insight may prove useful in future modeling efforts, stressing the internal political dynamics of nonprofit governance.

2.2. Nongovernmental

Weisbrod (1988) noted that governments are also precluded from distributing profits, so something more is needed to distinguish private NPs from public agencies. His point is in part a matter of interpreting ownership. It is true that the elected representatives constituting most governments receive fixed compensation, rather than a share of any fiscal surplus generated by the government. However, if we regard the citizens who elect those representatives as the true owners, these citizens can certainly enjoy a tax rebate whenever government's surplus is positive. Nonetheless, distinguishing private "voluntary action for the public good" (Payton, 1988) from public action is remarkably hard.

We have found no single criterion that reliably distinguishes organizations generally regarded as private from those regarded as public. Private NP governance (by a board of directors or trustees) might be distinct from public-sector governance (by representatives answerable to an electorate). However, public sector agencies often have boards that are somewhat insulated from political control and NP board members are sometimes appointed by government officials or elected by a broad selection of citizens deemed to be members. NP boards are sometimes self-perpetuating, but so, unfortunately, are some governments.

NP finance also seems different from government; the former relies on sales and voluntary donations, whereas the latter relies on coerced payments (taxes). Again, however, the difference is not clear cut. In weak states, tax payments are essentially voluntary; in some jurisdictions (e.g., Germany) NP churches have the power to tax their members, piggybacking on the federal tax collection process. Many NPs receive some of their funds from government agencies, either through grants or purchase-of-service contracts, and some receive essentially all their revenues from this originally tax-financed source. This is particularly true in human services, where many NPs were founded and run exclusively to take advantage of contracts offered during the early years of the welfare state (Smith and Lipsky, 1993). Hence, the source of funds does not always distinguish public from private.

NPs seem private if they get to decide who is hired and fired and who is allowed to be a member. However, U.S. court rulings that some private organizations (especially country clubs) are to be regarded as "places of public accommodation" have limited the ability of these organizations to decide who can be a member. In addition, NPs may become bound by civil service rules when they accept contracts from government.

We despair of drawing any bright-line distinction between public and private, suggesting instead that some organizations are more public-like (e.g., independent commissions, quasi-governmental agencies, contract service providers) and some are more private-like (e.g., NGOs, QUANGOs (quasi-nongovernmental organizations), social movements, clubs). Organizations are more private-like if they are answerable to a special segment of the population, receive the bulk of their revenues from voluntary transactions, appoint their own directors, and have widespread latitude to hire and fire their workers.

2.3. *Organization*

What is meant by "organization," and why is an organization employed rather than some other form of nonprofit transaction? What determines the boundaries of the organization—the set of activities that occur within, rather than between, nonprofit organizations? These questions have been studied in the context of the firm (starting with Coase, 1937) and the generic organization (e.g., Arrow, 1974), but only obliquely for nonprofit organizations, and perhaps they are different. For example, Coase argued that the boundary of the firm separates market transactions (outside) from nonmarket transactions (inside), but many nonprofit outputs are given away or otherwise allocated to clients in nonmarket transactions (Steinberg and Weisbrod, 1998). We think these issues deserve further study, and present here some hints and lines of inquiry that may prove fruitful.

Beggars solicit donations directly from passers-by on the street, but many donors prefer to send their gifts to a nonprofit organization, a charitable intermediary that produces services for "clients" in accord with the wishes of donors. In this way, donors can economize on a variety of transactions costs, leaving the experts to identify and determine the "worthiness" of potential clients and the efficient way to give them services. The organization can realize economies of scale and scope in the collection of information and the production of services. These gains must be balanced against the agency costs of employing the charitable intermediary (Posnett and Sandler, 1988; Handy, 2000).

While not touching directly on these questions, Ben-Ner and Van Hoomissen (1991) detail a variety of transactions costs that impede entrepreneurs from creating new nonprofits. Entrepreneurs must first identify and assemble a collection of willing stakeholders, then determine whether collective demand is sufficient to cover costs, then organize production decisions, induce stakeholders to reveal their preferences truthfully, and establish a governance mechanism to insure stakeholder control against free-riding, agency problems, and the like. Without the formation of an organization, these transactions costs would be vastly greater. Each potential stakeholder would have to bilaterally identify and contract with each other stakeholder for each of these purposes. For example, suppose that altruistic individuals wish to help tens of thousands of victims of a natural disaster in a far away place. The transactions costs for each of them to travel to that region and meet personally every victim to make a donation would be prohibitive. Without an organization taking the initiative to set up a kettle or collection plate or a bank account into which donors could deposit their donations, and taking charge of distributing the funds collected to the intended recipients, very little of the public good would be provided. Or suppose that the altruists are paternalistic and want the victims of that disaster to receive medical care, rather than money. Those altruists who are not themselves doctors would have to individually contract with doctors in the disaster area or with local doctors willing to travel, and would have to arrange for the building and staffing of emergency clinics on site, either each buying a clinic or contracting with other altruists until collective agreement was reached on building a combined clinic.

Besides these traditional economic arguments, a variety of cultural and sociologic forces may be important. Donors and givers may prefer to act with other like-minded individuals because they enjoy the social relation and sense of community that develops through repeated interaction with the organization and its stakeholders. "Warm glow," the utility received from the act of giving rather than from instrumental accomplishments resulting from the gift, may not manifest without the organizational community setting that reifies the act. Alternatively, donors may prefer to avoid direct contact with clients, finding them distasteful or simply preferring to keep some distance in their charitable relationships. Finally, begging may be regulated or prohibited by law, raising the cost of direct giving versus gifts to charitable intermediaries.

The precise boundaries of the organization are not clear. "Organizations can be seen as bundles of long-term transactions" (Gassler, 1998, p. 102), but which transactions are within and which are among nonprofit organizations? Krashinsky (1986, p. 116) takes a contractual approach, arguing that "the law restricting the distribution of profits can be seen as a "standard contract" that firms can offer to consumers, one that commits the firm to zero—or at least undistributable—profits and guarantees that this commitment extends to all the firm's other contracts. Both this standard contract and the limited actions taken by government to enforce it reduce transactions costs." Some economic models identify the organization with a set of agents that agree to the rules of some, possibly multistage, game and call that organization nonprofit if the rules preclude the distribution of financial surplus. Thus, Easley and O'Hara (1983) view the nonprofit organization as a mechanism for solving specified agency problems, and Bilodeau and Slivinski (1998) view it as a mechanism both for solving agency problems and for the provision of public goods.

The boundaries of the nonprofit organization are even harder to define when the nonprofit engages in a repeated bundle of transactions with other organizations through a partnership or joint venture, when the organization is the sole owner of a subsidiary (for-profit or nonprofit) or is wholly-owned as a subsidiary, or when the organization is a semi-autonomous unit within a larger association or franchise structure. Analysis of transactions costs can help us to understand these hybrid organizations better, although serious analysis of the issues has only just begun (e.g., Young, 1989; Oster, 1996; Koebel et al., 1998; Sansing, 2000; Besley and Ghatak, 2001).

2.4. *Corollaries and correlates*

Organizations precluded from distributing profits differ from profit-distributing organizations in their capital structure, susceptibility to takeovers, and treatment under governmental tax and regulatory rules. These differences have immediate consequences that foreshadow the range of plausible economic theories of the behavior of nonprofit organizations, as we elaborate below.

Nonprofit organizations cannot offer conventional shares of stock to raise equity capital. Payment of dividends to stockholders or capital gains from sale of stocks would constitute a prohibited distribution of profits, so that any nonprofit stockholders would receive, at best, limited control rights in return for their supply of capital. Thus, nonprofit issuance of stock certificates is extremely rare. However, major donors act like such stockholders in that they are commonly offered a seat on the NP's governing board in return for their gratuitous supply of capital. Bilodeau and Slivinski (1998) emphasize the irreversibility of supplying equity capital through donations. Donors take their returns in the vicarious enjoyment of NP outputs (that is, they consume public goods provided by the firm), leading Wedig (1994) to model donors as stockholders who receive "dividends in kind."

Nonprofit donors and shareholders cannot profit from the sale of their control rights. If they wish to transfer control of all the NP's assets to another NP, they do so in the form of a donation. If they wish to transfer control to a for-profit entity, they must (in theory) sell the NP assets at a fair market price and donate all the proceeds from that sale to another nonprofit organization (typically a newly-created grant-making "conversion foundation"). Because NP ownership shares cannot be sold in the usual sense, the market for control of these organizations is very different from that of publicly-traded firms. NPs that wish to depart from profit-maximizing behaviors are not constrained by the threat of takeover bids (although other forces may constrain these behaviors), and so *a priori* we must consider a broad range of possible objective functions for NP organizations.

Nonprofit organizations are often granted tax and regulatory advantages over alternative organizational forms (Weisbrod, 1991). NP corporations are typically exempt, on all or part of their commercial income, from paying corporate taxes, and are often exempt from local sales, property, and value-added taxes. Those donating money to NPs often receive tax breaks that reduce the after-tax cost of their giving. In some jurisdictions, NPs receive favorable treatment in the application of bankruptcy, antitrust, tort, and labor disputes.

Finally, entrepreneurs and other key management decision-makers may sort themselves across sectors, recognizing that certain goals are best accomplished through the creation and management of NPs. This sorting can occur for any of the reasons above—difficulty in securing capital, protection of the organizational mission from future takeover bids, or the tax and regulatory advantages that accompany the selection of the nonprofit form. All of these factors allow the nonprofit organization to send distinct signals to other agents and permit the sectors to differ in the set of outcomes that can be supported in equilibrium.

3. Dimensions of the nonprofit sector

In this section, we briefly survey available statistics on the size and scope of the nonprofit sector. The first subsection details the prominent role of the nonprofit sector in national economies. The second subsection illustrates the diverse range of "industries" that contain nonprofit organizations and shows that in many of these industries, nonprofit organizations coexist with apparently similar organizations in the for-profit, household, and government sectors. The third subsection concerns the mixture of funding sources employed by nonprofits and shows the surprisingly small role played by philanthropy in many nonprofit industries. We also report on the composition of the philanthropic component of giving in more detail.

Although efforts to change this are underway (e.g., Australian Bureau of Statistics, 2002), national systems of accounts do not report on the size and scope of the nonprofit sector, at least as we understand the term. Most of what we know about cross-national comparisons (and all of the evidence summarized here) comes from the ongoing Johns Hopkins Comparative Nonprofit Sector Project directed by Lester M. Salamon, which to date has assembled 1995 statistics using consistent definitions for 35 countries. They report nonprofit employment and expenditures in each country, classified by "field of activity" (which most economists would understand as an industry group). They also report, for each country and field of activity, the composition of revenues. In each case, they report separately on paid employees/cash expenditures/cash donations and total employees/expenditures/donations including an imputation for the value of volunteer labor. Data comes from a combination of government-published statistics and special surveys, and generally represents an underestimate of the nonprofit role for two reasons. First, religious organizations are excluded from the tables reported here (except religiously-affiliated schools, hospitals, and the like). This shortcoming has been remedied for some included countries, and the reader is referred to the project web site for updated details (www.jhu.edu/~cnp). Second, smaller or more informal nonprofit organizations are vastly under-represented in most available data, even in the U.S. where data is thought to be most complete (Grønbjerg, 1994; Smith, 1997).

3.1. Size of the sector

In the first 22 countries studied, expenditures by nonprofit organizations were 4.6% of GDP in 1995. Because 28% of the citizens in these countries volunteered, the percentage of "expenditures plus imputed expenditures on volunteers" relative to "GDP plus imputation" is higher, at 5.7% (Salamon et al., 1999).

More detail is available for employment. For the 35 countries studied, the unweighted averages indicate that paid nonprofit employees circa 1995 were a bit under 3% of the economically active population (which includes an estimate for the informal economy). Adding an imputation for volunteering brings this percentage up to 4.4% (Johns Hopkins Comparative Nonprofit Sector Project, hereinafter CNSP) (CNSP, 2003). When, in addition, employment by religious organizations is included for the 16 countries where this was measured (but now comparing to the nonagricultural workforce, rather than the economically active population), this percent rises to 8.5% (Salamon et al., 1999). The variation across countries (now excluding religion, but returning to a base of the economically active population) is vast. Four countries, the Netherlands, Ireland, Belgium, and Israel exceeded what had once been thought to be the leader, the U.S., in paid nonprofit employment, whereas Mexico's nonprofit employment constituted only 0.3% of the total. Three countries exceeded the U.S. when volunteering was added to the numerator and denominator of these fractions, with the Netherlands again leading (14.4%), the U.S. near the top (9.8%) and Mexico at the bottom (0.4%).

3.2. Scope of the sector

Nonprofit organizations provide a dizzying array of services, ranging from helping the needy (soup kitchens, shelter, disaster assistance) to health care (hospitals, clinics, long-term care facilities, self-help groups), education (higher and lower), the arts (museums, orchestras, dance companies, historical societies), religion (houses of worship, denominations, missionary societies), social services (day care, nursing homes, foster care, job training), research (think tanks, medical research), advocacy (grassroots, public policy, human rights), and development (NGO's, microcredit societies, neighborhood associations). Several systems have been developed to classify nonprofit organizations by activity area or "industry." In the U.S., the National Taxonomy of Exempt Organizations (NTEE) was developed by those who felt the Standard Industrial Code (SIC) was not well-suited to the classification of nonprofits. Both systems are currently in use in the U.S. The Comparative Nonprofit Sector Program developed its own, more aggregated, classification system called the ICNPO (International Classification of Nonprofit Organizations). This system is modeled after the ISIC (International Standard Industrial Code) and classifies organizations into twelve major groups and twenty-seven subgroups.

Table 1 reports the share of paid employment in each of the ICNPO fields of activity for each of the countries. Salamon et al. (1999) summarize this data by noting five clusters of countries with similar patterns. First are the "education dominant" countries, including Argentina, Belgium, Brazil, Ireland, Israel, Mexico, Peru, and the U.K., where an average of 48% of nonprofit employment is in the Education field (countries studied later that also fit this pattern include Pakistan, the Philippines, and South Korea). In most of these countries, this reflects the prevalence of religiously-affiliated private schools; in the U.K., this reflects the prevalence of private universities. Second are the "health dominant" countries of Japan, the Netherlands, and the U.S., where an average

Table 1
Nonprofit FTE paid employment, by field, ca. 1995

	Percent of total nonprofit FTE paid employment												
	Cult.	Educ.	Health	Social svcs.	Envir.	Devel.	Civic/ Advocacy	Fdns.	Intl.	Prof.	Other	Total (000's)	Share of economy*
Argentina	15.1	41.2	13.4	10.7	0.3	5.7	0.4	0.2	1.3	6.8	4.9	395.3	4.8
Australia	16.4	23.2	18.6	20.1	0.5	10.8	3.2	0.1	0.2	4.3	2.6	402.6	6.3
Austria	8.4	8.9	11.6	64.0	0.4	0.0	4.5	0.0	0.8	1.4	0.0	143.6	4.9
Belgium	4.9	38.8	30.4	13.8	0.5	9.9	0.4	0.2	0.2	0.9	0.0	357.8	10.9
Brazil	17.0	36.9	17.8	16.4	0.2	1.1	0.6	0.0	0.4	9.6	0.0	1034.6	1.6
Colombia	9.4	26.1	17.5	14.6	0.8	13.1	1.3	0.9	0.1	15.1	1.2	286.9	2.4
Czech Rep.	31.0	14.6	13.6	11.2	3.7	7.4	3.1	2.0	1.1	12.3	0.0	74.2	2.0
Egypt	n/a	n/a	n/a	n/a	n/a	n/a	n/a	n/a	n/a	n/a	n/a	611.9	2.8
Finland	14.2	25.0	23.0	17.8	1.0	2.4	8.7	0.0	0.3	7.2	0.3	62.8	5.3
France	12.1	20.7	15.5	39.7	1.0	5.5	1.9	0.0	1.8	1.8	0.0	959.8	7.6
Germany	5.4	11.7	30.6	38.8	0.8	6.1	1.6	0.4	0.7	3.9	0.0	1440.9	5.9
Hungary	38.1	10.0	4.5	11.1	2.0	13.2	1.0	3.3	0.8	16.1	0.0	44.9	1.1
Ireland	6.0	53.7	27.6	4.5	0.9	4.3	0.4	0.1	0.3	2.2	0.0	118.7	10.4
Israel	5.9	50.3	27.0	10.9	0.8	1.0	0.4	2.0	0.1	1.8	0.0	145.4	8.0
Italy	11.9	20.3	21.6	27.5	0.5	5.1	2.0	0.1	0.2	8.9	1.8	568.5	3.8
Japan	3.1	22.5	47.1	16.6	0.4	0.3	0.2	0.2	0.4	5.0	4.3	2140.1	4.2
Kenya	4.1	12.0	4.2	22.4	4.5	19.3	5.4	0.4	0.0	1.1	26.6	174.9	2.1
Mexico	7.7	43.2	8.1	8.7	0.7	0.5	0.3	0.3	0.0	30.5	0.0	93.8	0.4
Morocco	n/a	n/a	n/a	n/a	n/a	n/a	n/a	n/a	n/a	n/a	n/a	74.5	1.5
Netherlands	4.1	27.4	42.6	18.9	1.0	2.5	0.6	0.4	0.6	1.9	0.0	661.7	14.4
Norway	13.3	25.9	10.3	25.9	0.2	2.6	2.9	0.2	1.8	16.8	0.1	60.0	7.2
Pakistan	0.3	71.9	11.3	3.0	0.0	7.6	5.1	0.0	0.0	0.9	0.0	261.8	1.0
Peru	4.0	72.7	4.1	1.2	0.6	14.2	0.8	1.4	0.0	1.1	0.0	129.8	2.5
Philippines	2.1	65.7	2.3	2.8	2.8	9.5	0.8	2.0	0.7	11.3	0.0	187.3	1.9
Poland	31.6	23.7	7.2	17.3	1.8	1.1	0.9	0.4	0.7	11.5	3.7	122.5	0.8
Romania	34.0	17.9	13.1	20.7	0.7	3.6	4.4	0.8	1.3	3.6	0.0	37.4	0.8

(continued on next page)

Table 1
(Continued)

	Percent of total nonprofit FTE paid employment												
	Cult.	Educ.	Health	Social svcs.	Envir.	Devel.	Civic/ Advocacy	Fdns.	Intl.	Prof.	Other	Total (000's)	Share of economy*
Slovakia	36.7	28.5	1.9	5.2	6.8	1.1	2.9	4.9	0.9	10.4	0.8	16.2	0.8
South Africa	9.4	8.6	13.7	31.4	7.8	19.0	8.5	0.5	0.0	1.1	0.0	298.2	3.4
South Korea	4.9	52.0	26.8	9.3	0.0	0.0	2.7	0.0	0.0	4.3	0.0	413.3	2.4
Spain	11.8	25.1	12.2	31.8	0.3	11.2	3.4	0.1	2.0	1.8	0.3	475.2	4.3
Sweden	26.9	20.8	3.3	17.8	2.0	6.1	3.7	0.6	2.7	14.8	1.1	82.6	7.1
Tanzania	9.0	15.9	14.0	11.2	8.8	12.2	7.1	7.9	4.3	3.4	6.0	82.0	2.1
Uganda	6.2	9.6	26.3	21.3	1.8	21.0	3.1	2.6	7.3	0.8	0.0	102.7	2.3
U.K.	24.5	41.5	4.3	13.1	1.3	7.6	0.7	0.7	3.8	2.6	0.0	1415.7	8.5
U.S.	7.3	21.5	46.3	13.5	0.0	6.3	1.8	0.3	0.0	2.9	0.0	8554.9	9.8

Source: Johns Hopkins Comparative Nonprofit Sector Project, 2003 (CNSP, 2003).
*Nonprofit FTE paid plus volunteer workforce as share of economically active population.

of 45% of nonprofit employment is in the Health field. In contrast, in countries with a heavy state presence in health care like the U.K., only 4.3% of nonprofit employment is in Health. Third are those countries in which Social Services are dominant, including Austria, France, Germany, and Spain, with an average of 44% of nonprofit employment in this field (South Africa also fits this category). Fourth are the "culture/recreation dominant" countries of the Czech Republic, Hungary, Romania, and Slovakia, reflecting the prior Communist suppression of other types of nonprofits and subsidization of nonprofits in this field (Poland also joins this category). Finally, we have the "balanced" model of Australia, Colombia, and Finland (and also Italy, Kenya, Norway, Sweden, Tanzania, and Uganda) in which no field predominates.

One puzzle for economic theorists is to explain the coexistence of nonprofit, for-profit, government, and household production in the same fields. For example, day care for young children is provided by informal organizations in the household sector, nonprofit organizations (religious and secular), for-profit firms, and government agencies. If the nonprofit form is superior in providing a particular good, why do other organizational forms persist? If other forms are superior, why do nonprofits persist? If organizations perform equally well, are the sectoral shares entirely arbitrary, or are there subtle differences in the products produced by the respective sectors that explain determinate market shares? Table 2 summarizes the nonprofit share of service delivery in various fields and countries.

3.3. Revenue mix

Nonprofit organizations receive a mixture of revenue streams—donations, fees for service, government grants, purchase-of-service contracts, dues, royalties, and property and investment income. This complicated revenue stream is interesting to economists for a variety of reasons discussed later in this paper, including revenue interactions, nonlinear revenue streams, and revenue-portfolio stability. Table 3 reports on the average revenue mix in a variety of countries, classified into "Government," "Philanthropy," and "Fees, Dues." Government revenues include general purpose grants, contracts in support of specific services, and third-party payments (e.g., payments for vouchers received from clients). Philanthropy includes gifts by individuals, alive or through bequests, an imputation for volunteering, gifts by corporations, foundation grants, and contributions received from other nonprofit organizations such as allocations from United Way. Fees and dues include membership dues, fees paid directly by individual clients for services rendered, investment income, and income from commercial sales of products and services. Most newcomers to the field are surprised that philanthropy is not the predominant source of income. Philanthropy accounted for less than 50% of revenues in every country studied except Pakistan (53.1%), Sweden (53.7%), Tanzania (61.9%) and Romania (66.5%). The 32-country unweighted average was 30.4%. Instead, fees and dues was the largest category (42.4%) with government in last place but still quite prominent (27.2).

Table 2
Nonprofit share of service delivery, by field and country, 1990

Field	Measure	Percent of total output						
		France	Germany	Hungary	Japan	Sweden (1992)	United Kingdom	United States
Health	Patient-days, inpatient hospitals	15.5	42.0	–	4.0	7.9	1.6	67.0
	Residents, nursing homes for the frail elderly	–	49.4	4.1	81.0	3.1	4.2	22.0
Education	Students, primary and secondary schools	17.1	5.3	0.2	2.0	1.1	21.9	11.0
	Students, universities	15.5	0.5	0.3	76.0	1.4	100.0	20.0
Social services	Residents, facilities other than nursing homes	54.9	60.3	2.9	43.0	–	14.5	19.0
	Pre-School day-care facilities	39.4	34.6	0.1	36.0	7.6	81.6	–
Housing	Dwelling units, constructed or rehabilitated	–	17.5	1.4	–	39.2	9.0	–
Culture & arts	Attendees, orchestra and opera	–	8.7	13.2	100.0	19.6	100.0	–

Source: Salamon et al. (1996).

Table 3
Nonprofit sources of revenue, ca. 1995*

	Percent of total revenues			
	Government	Philanthropy	Fees, dues	Total (millions US$)
Argentina	16.2	23.0	60.8	160.1
Australia	25.4	23.6	51.0	243.0
Austria	41.3	23.1	35.6	76.4
Belgium	65.9	18.1	16.0	297.7
Brazil	14.5	16.3	69.2	121.4
Columbia	13.1	24.9	62.0	19.5
Czech Republic	32.1	30.0	37.9	10.6
Finland	25.2	34.6	40.3	87.2
France	33.4	46.6	20.0	992.3
Germany	42.5	36.2	21.3	1428.9
Hungary	26.2	21.1	52.7	14.8
Ireland	67.6	18.6	13.8	57.3
Israel	59.1	17.0	23.9	118.4
Italy	30.2	19.7	50.1	476.5
Japan	41.5	10.7	47.8	2823.1
Kenya	4.0	29.0	67.0	4.9
Mexico	7.5	17.9	74.7	17.7
Netherlands	46.1	23.9	30.1	773.9
Norway	20.0	46.9	33.1	99.0
Pakistan	4.9	53.1	41.9	3.8
Peru	17.5	14.7	67.7	13.1
Philippines	3.1	43.2	53.7	18.8
Poland	22.8	20.1	57.1	27.7
Romania	20.5	66.5	13.0	2.8
Slovakia	21.3	25.1	53.5	3.0
South Africa	31.5	45.9	22.6	33.5
South Korea	21.6	14.9	63.5	221.9
Spain	25.2	36.3	38.5	328.3
Sweden	14.6	53.7	31.7	208.1
Tanzania	12.8	61.9	25.3	5.5
U.K.	36.4	28.8	34.8	1002.0
U.S.	25.6	26.9	47.4	6759.7

Source: Johns Hopkins Comparative Nonprofit Sector Project, 2003 (CNSP, 2003).
*Includes an imputation for the value of volunteer labor.

There is also tremendous variation across charitable fields. Table 4 summarizes the revenue mix in ten ICNPO categories, finding that philanthropy accounts for the largest share of resources only for "international." Perhaps it is surprising that the Philanthropic Organizations category (consisting mostly of foundations) derives the largest share of its income from fees and charges, but this is because earnings on endowment are treated as fee income. The picture changes a bit if an imputation for volunteering is made, which

Table 4
Sources of nonprofit revenue by field, ca. 1995

	Fees, dues	Government	Philanthropy
All fields	49%	40%	11%
Fee-dominant			
Professional	88%	7%	5%
Culture, recreational	65%	22%	13%
Development	52%	36%	12%
Philanthropic orgs.	47%	16%	37%
Environment	42%	34%	24%
Civic, advocacy	40%	38%	22%
Government-dominant			
Health	34%	55%	11%
Education	45%	47%	8%
Social Services	37%	45%	18%
Philanthropy-dominant			
International	27%	35%	38%

Source: Salamon et al. (1999, p. 27).

greatly increases philanthropy's share in the culture/recreation category, and one category not reported on (religion) is primarily funded by giving. Philanthropy's share can also be increased if governmental grants to nonprofits are reclassified as gifts. Finally, philanthropy dominates in several narrowly-defined industries, but this gets lost in the aggregation in Table 4.

The composition of philanthropy has been well-studied in several countries, but we are unaware of efforts to report this composition on a consistent cross-national basis and so report here only on one set of estimates for the U.S. (AAFRC Trust for Philanthropy, 2003). The vast majority of gifts (76.3% in 2002) were made by living individual donors. Such gifts totaled about $184 billion in that year, or 2.4% of disposable personal income. The next largest category is giving by foundations (excluding corporate foundations), which were 11.2% of the total or $26.9 billion. Gifts by bequest accounted for 7.5% of donations, or $18.1 billion. Reported corporate giving was in last place, at $12.2 billion, 5.1% of all contributions or 1.8% of corporate pretax income, but this is an underestimate because many forms of corporate philanthropy are reported in other categories (such as advertising) in the corporate tax forms used to create this estimate. By field (here using the NTEE classification instead of ICNPO), Religion received 35.0% of donations ($84.3 billion), Education 13.1% ($31.6 billion), Non-corporate Foundations 9.1% ($25.7 billion), Health 7.8% ($18.9 billion), Human Services 7.7% ($18.7 billion), Arts, Culture, and Humanities 5.1% ($12.2 billion), Public/Societal Benefit 4.8% ($11.6 billion), Environment/Animal 2.8% ($6.6 billion), International Affairs 1.9% ($4.6 billion), and Unallocated Gifts 12.6% ($30.5 billion).

4. Models of nonprofit organizations

In this section, we survey broader models of why donative organizations are organized as nonprofits. Although we consider commercial nonprofits, we do so only as far as they also seek donations and provide public goods. The models discussed here are not appropriate for analyzing purely commercial nonprofits. However, the insights derived here may also be appropriate for some government agencies that provide public goods. Notably, as argued above, the dividing line between public and private nonprofit organizations is not clear, as both are governed by a nondistribution constraint, both receive donations, and both provide, at least in part, public goods. Although government agencies may receive the bulk of their resources from tax collection (and so must be concerned with interactions between coerced and volunteered resources), we have seen above that private nonprofit agencies receive substantial resources from tax-financed grants and contracts with governments, so even this distinction is not dispositive.

First, we show that agency problems between donors (as principals) and charitable service-providing organizations (as agents) result whenever the latter is employed to provide public goods. If the organization is constrained against the distribution of profits, this agency problem is resolved. Second, we argue that a three-stage game is the most natural way to model the choices of intermediaries and donors. In this game, the intermediary makes a seed donation, collects donations from others, then can add to (but not subtract from) the total donated in previous stages. Third, we detail the choice the founding entrepreneur makes between organizing as a nonprofit or a for-profit organization, showing that it can be individually rational for the entrepreneur to constrain his future ability to distribute profits. These three subsections basically follow the logic in Bilodeau and Slivinski (1998), and provide the core model of nonprofit organizations that we will discuss. Later subsections either elaborate on this core model or use the core model as a point of departure for the discussion of alternative approaches.

Subsection 4.4 introduces commercial activities, and shows how this alters the entrepreneurial decisions. Subsection 4.5 discusses nonprofits that provide excludable public goods, such as those in the arts. Subsection 4.6 discusses the sorting of entrepreneurial types across sectors and industries. Subsection 4.7 adds multiple public goods, which may be provided by a single or separate organizations. We also discuss the role of financial intermediaries that support multiple public goods (like United Ways or community foundations). Subsection 4.8 delineates a variety of internal agency problems and the ways in which nonprofit organizations cope with them. The final subsection looks at models of long-run equilibrium.

4.1. Agency problems and the nondistribution constraint

In most real-world situations where individuals contribute voluntarily toward the provision of a public good, intermediaries are involved. Someone other than the final intended recipient collects donations and takes responsibility to produce the public good desired by the donors. This intermediary could be a single individual, but more commonly the complexity of the task of collecting money from all potential donors and physically producing the public good requires that an organization be set up. That organization might or might not fulfill the task set to it by the donors, and so we have our first agency problem with donors as principals and organizations as agents. The various principals may have a common objective or there may be conflicts among them over the nature of the public good that is to be provided. For example, if the public good is the performance of symphonies, some donors may wish to see Mozart, others Schoenberg, and the agent organization would most like to perform Zappa. In turn, most organizations have employees or subcontract various tasks to other organizations, creating a second link in the chain of agency problems if those employees fail to fulfill the tasks set by management. Sometimes the chain has additional links, when donors contribute to a united fundraising organization (such as United Way) or a community foundation, asking that intermediary to allocate their donations to other, service-providing organizations. In this section, we focus on the simplest version of the first link—the agency problem between donors that all value the same public good and the organization they choose as an intermediary to provide that public good when there is complete information. Later sections deal with internal agency problems and financial intermediaries.

Suppose that donors value increased provision of a public good and give money to an organization with the understanding that it will be used to increase provision of this public good. As pointed out by Hansmann (1980), enforcing such understandings is often difficult or impossible. He called this kind of agency problem "contract failure."[1] The public good may be provided in a distant locale, or delivered to future generations. Even if the donor can verify the total expenditures the organization devoted to providing the public good, he cannot determine whether that expenditure is higher than it otherwise would have been because of his gift unless he knows the total donated by others. Thus, the non-enforceability of contracts is inherent in the use of intermediary organizations for the provision of public goods.

More formally, consider the classic voluntary contributions model in which $n+1$ individuals simultaneously contribute toward the provision of a public good. Suppose preferences are well behaved and of the form $U_i(x_i, Z)$ where x_i is i's private consumption and Z is the public good, and each is facing a budget constraint $w_i = x_i + z_i$ where w_i is i's wealth and z_i is i's contribution to the public good. When there is no intermediary, the total level of public good provided, Z, will be the sum of the z_i's. Solving the contribution game, each individual will contribute an amount

$$z_i^* = \max\left\{0, h_i\left(w_i + \sum_{j\neq i} z_j^*\right) - \sum_{j\neq i} z_j^*\right\}$$

[1] Hansmann's (Hansmann, 1987) exposition of contract failure, designed to cover commercial as well as donative nonprofits, is somewhat broader than we need here: "where, due to (1) the circumstances under which a service is purchased or consumed or (2) the nature of the service itself, consumers feel unable to evaluate accurately the quality or quantity of a service produced for them."

where $h_i()$ is i's Engel curve in full wealth (gifts by others constitute wealth to i) and the * indicates equilibrium values. When both goods are normal, Bergstrom et al. (1986) show that the resulting equilibrium always exists and is unique. There is no role for an intermediary in this model, but it provides background and notation for models in which there is an intermediary between donors and public good provision and that intermediary can operate with or without a nondistribution constraint.

Suppose now that instead of having everyone put their money into a pile simultaneously, one individual (labeled $i = 0$) is charged with collecting money from the n others and using it to provide the public good. In the two-stage game where agents 1 through n donate simultaneously and then the zero'th person (the intermediary) provides a quantity of the public good, the intermediary would provide

$$Z = h_0\left(w_0 + \sum_{i=1}^{n} z_i\right)$$

Note that although the intermediary may value the public good, there is still an agency problem. The intermediary views incremental donations as equivalent to an increase in her income, and increases total expenditures on the public good accordingly. Total expenditures on the public good can be less than, the same, or more than the total contributed by the n first-stage donors. For example, if the slope of the Engle curve is $1/2$ and gifts by others are larger than the intermediary's own income, total expenditure on the public good will be less than total contributions by others.

The nondistribution constraint, if perfectly enforced, solves this agency problem. In the second stage, the constrained intermediary would provide

$$Z = \max\left\{h_0\left(w_0 + \sum_{i=1}^{n} z_i\right), \sum_{i=1}^{n} z_i\right\}$$

of the public good. The nondistribution constraint acts as a commitment device, guaranteeing donors that their donations will not be expropriated by the intermediary. The nondistribution constraint does not stop free-riding behavior, but it does guarantee that expenditures on the public good will be at least as large as their donations.

4.2. *Strategic investment by the intermediary*

In this section, we argue that a three-stage game in which the intermediary moves first and last is the most natural way to model voluntary contributions through an intermediary. The previous section characterized a two-stage game, in both the for-profit and nonprofit case, when the intermediary goes last. What if the intermediary could contribute first? After all, she controls the fundraising process and nothing prevents her from contributing before soliciting others. Then we would have the sequential public goods problem analyzed by Varian (1994), in which the first donor reduces her giving, knowing that other donors will replace part of it. However, as we will show below, following the conclusion of this game, the first donor would (generally) want to give again.

Absent a credible commitment by the intermediary to contribute once and only once (and we are not aware of good reasons to suppose such a commitment can generally be made), the two-stage game with the intermediary moving first has little relevance. The intermediary cannot avoid being the donor of last resort.

Now consider a three-stage game of complete information, where the intermediary moves first by making a "seed donation," other donors move simultaneously in the second stage, and the intermediary can adjust the total in the third stage. This additional stage makes little difference to a for-profit intermediary, as any first-stage donation can be undone in the third-stage, and donors know this. However, the same cannot be said for nonprofit intermediaries when the nondistribution constraint binds.

Bilodeau and Slivinski (1998) show that in any nonprofit equilibrium with positive donations, the intermediary would make a sufficiently large seed donation to insure that the nondistribution constraint would bind in the third stage. To see why, consider the contrary. Suppose that the constraint does not bind in the last stage. Then, second-stage donors recognize that the first stage is irrelevant, that they are playing in a sequential game similar to Varian's (Varian, 1994) with the intermediary as the follower. As in Varian, second-stage donors free-ride on the intermediary. The intermediary can prevent this by giving so much in the first stage that he would not wish to give again. Although he gives more initially, his total donations are lower than they would be if he made a smaller first-stage donation. The first-stage donation makes the nondistribution constraint bind, increasing second-stage donations. Bilodeau and Slivinski show that this results in higher expenditures on the public good at a lower cost to the intermediary, and hence unambiguously increases his utility.

4.3. *Choosing between sectors*

Next, we focus on the role of founding entrepreneurs, who choose whether to create an intermediary organization and whether that organization should be constrained against the distribution of profits. Because the founder sets the rules for organizational governance, it makes sense to regard the preferences of the organization as being the preferences of the founder (Young, 1983). For our purposes, we will assume that any group of founders operate as a single individual with a single set of preferences. We consider first whether an existing organization would prefer to operate as a nonprofit or a for-profit. Then we consider whether the "preferred-sector" organization should be created at all.

Why would any individual choose to permanently constrain his future option to receive a share of profits? In the previous section, we showed that self-interest suffices for organizations financed solely by donations, rather than revenues from sales. The founder does not need to be an altruist, or to care about social welfare. By committing to not expropriating the firm's net cash flow at any time in the future, the founding entrepreneur can increase donations from the public and enjoy a larger quantity of a public good. Thus, we have a natural tie between the theory of nonprofit organizations and the private provision of a public good, complementing Weisbrod's (Weisbrod, 1975) theory that nonprofits serve as an outlet for high-demanders to supplement governmental provision of public goods.

To be, or not to be? All may want to contribute to a nonprofit organization, but they will have no object for their desire unless someone finds it in her interest to create one. In particular, in the three-stage model above, Bilodeau and Slivinski show that entrepreneurship is costly in the sense that the founding entrepreneur would always prefer to remain a donor-at-large rather than founder. Founding entrepreneurs always contribute more than identical donors-at-large and enjoy the same level of public goods provision whatever their role. Why then, does anybody do it? The answer is simple. Otherwise, nobody else would. In this model, a game of chicken is played among all agents that value the public good, and there are alternative equilibria in which any one of them becomes the founder.

Having established that self-interest suffices to induce an entrepreneur to choose the nonprofit form, let us not be too cynical. This conclusion does not rely on the secret distribution of profits in the forms of hidden payments and perks. This is in contrast to the work of property rights theorists (e.g., Alchian and Demsetz, 1972; Clarkson, 1972; Frech, 1980), who argue that true nonprofits would not exist unless they are provided with tax and regulatory advantages over their for-profit competitors. Restrictions on cash payouts, they argue, would force the nonprofit to provide an inefficient compensation package, weighted toward perks. For example, Frech (1980, p. 57) states that "Imposition of nonprofit constraints necessarily leads to greater consumption of nonpecuniary goods, lower firm wealth, and thus greater managerial inefficiency or 'shirking'." Tax and regulatory breaks allow distribution of larger quantities of perks, making up for their inefficiency and allowing the nonprofit form to survive competition. More cynically, some might point to the lax enforcement of the nondistribution constraint and argue that organizations claiming to be nonprofit are really profit-distributing entities ('for-profits-in-disguise') that exploit the availability of tax and regulatory breaks. We do not deny that some nonprofits are founded for these reasons—the real insight of Bilodeau and Slivinski is to show that if public good provision is valued by founding entrepreneurs, nonprofits will be founded regardless.

4.4. Profitable nonprofits

Now consider an organization that obtains revenues from sales. Several possibilities warrant discussion. First, organizations may be selling a private good whose quality or quantity is difficult to observe, as in Hansmann's (Hansmann, 1980) examples of commercial nonprofits. Then, nondistribution of profits reduces the incentive of the firm to provide less than the promised quality or quantity (e.g., Easley and O'Hara, 1983; Glaeser and Schleifer, 2001) and offers signaling possibilities that enable the organization to provide the promised quality or quantity at lower costs than similar for-profits (Chillemi and Gui, 1991). Alternatively, the absence of a market for control may allow nonprofits to pursue distributional objectives not open to profit maximizers (Steinberg and Weisbrod, 2002). Because our paper focuses on donative nonprofits, we will not consider these models any further. Second, the organization may sell a private good in order to obtain net revenues with which to enhance its provision of a public good. This affects the entrepreneurial choice of sectors, which we discuss presently. Third, the organization may sell an excludable public good or a private good with externalities, receiving both donations and revenues from sales. Again, those entrepreneurs wishing to pursue alternative objectives may prefer the protection from takeover bids accompanying the nonprofit form, but beyond that, the literature to date has not analyzed the choice of sectors. (We do discuss these models further in the section on pricing behavior).

When the sale of the private good is profitable (due either to market circumstances or tax and regulatory preferences), this profit will crowd-out some or all donations. Sectoral choice then depends upon whether donations would remain positive in equilibrium. More specifically, Bilodeau (2000) shows that if equilibrium donations by others are positive when the nondistribution constraint is imposed, the entrepreneur will always prefer the nonprofit form.

If donations by others are completely crowded out, then sectoral choice depends upon whether the nondistribution constraint would bind in equilibrium. If it does not bind, the entrepreneur is indifferent between the two sectors, and any unmodeled tiebreaker (such as tax preferences attached to nonprofit status) would suffice. When profits are sufficiently high that the nondistribution constraint would bind, the choice of sectors is ambiguous. The entrepreneur could found a closely-held for-profit firm and devote some profits to the provision of public goods.[2] This would enable the entrepreneur to provide precisely the amount of public good she desires, given her income level. However, the firm's revenue would be higher under the nonprofit form because, as shown by (Posnett and Sandler, 1986), purchasers of the private good would be willing to pay a higher price when buying from a nonprofit organization if they know that it will use its profits to provide a public good they value. This added income provides utility to the entrepreneur despite the fact that she is constrained to devote it all to public good provision. If entrepreneurial preferences for the public good and consumer rewards to nonprofit organizations are sufficiently high, the nonprofit form will be chosen.

The legal interpretation of the fair compensation constraint restraining cash distributions to the entrepreneur also affects choice of sector. If the constraint is set far below the entrepreneur's opportunity cost, he will prefer to found a for-profit firm. There is an intermediate range where the fair distribution constraint binds and the entrepreneur chooses the nonprofit form. Finally, if the salary cap is so high that the constraint is nonbinding, there is no meaningful choice of sector—*de jure* nonprofit organizations will be *de facto* for-profit firms. Thus, the relation between the salary cap (S) and public good provision (Z) is illustrated by the following diagram (Figure 1).

The optimal salary cap level, if the policy objective is to maximize public good provision, is just sufficient to induce the entrepreneur to choose the nonprofit form. Any

[2] For example, Bilkent University in Turkey received approximately 60% of its operational budget in academic year 2000–2001 from the commercial activities of Bilkent Holding, a for-profit holding company owned by the University's founder (Yildirim, 2000).

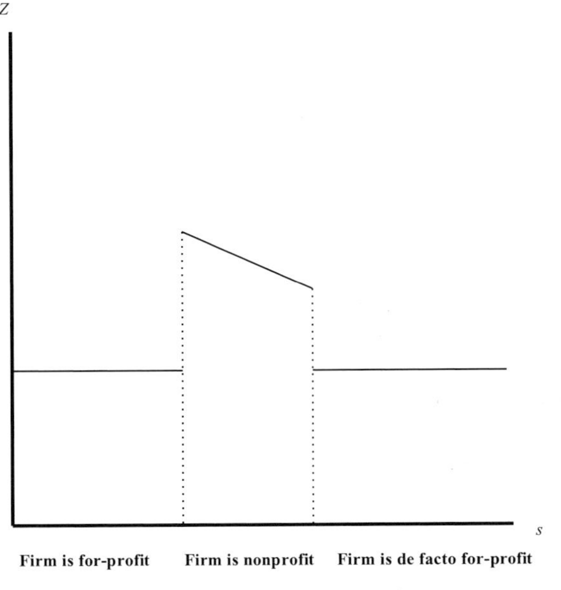

Figure 1.

higher level of permitted compensation would come at the expense of public good provision.

This approach goes a long way toward explaining the coexistence of nonprofit and for-profit providers for some services like child-, health-, or nursing-care. To the extent that the market structure is best modeled as a local monopoly or monopolistic competition, variations in potential profitability across market niches will lead to entry of either for-profit or nonprofit firms. However, this approach does not suffice to explain sectoral shares in oligopolistic markets, where except for the knife-edge level of potential profits, one sectoral choice or the other would dominate.

This approach may also help to explain intersectoral conversions. A change in expected profits from sales or in the legal interpretation and enforcement of the fair compensation constraint would change the relative merits of locating in one sector. If that change sufficed to overcome the transactions costs of conversion, conversion would occur. Goddeeris and Weisbrod (1998) detail, informally, several other factors that could lead to conversion. First, enforcing the nondistribution of profits during the conversion process is difficult—an increase in potential profits might lead nonprofit managers to risk a conversion that secretly distributes profits accrued during the nonprofit period. Second, an increase in capital needs (due either to an increase in the demand for capital or a decrease in the subsidized supply of capital to nonprofit organizations) may lead the organization to convert in order to obtain equity capital. Third, a reduction in the other tax and regulatory preferences given to nonprofits may shift the balance in favor of conversion. Fourth, conversion may be an aspect of the organizational life cycle.

They also summarize empirical evidence showing that conversions occur in both directions and appear to be motivated by the factors above (Ferris and Graddy, 1995; see also Legoretta and Young, 1986).

4.5. *Excludable public goods*

When goods are nonrival but excludable, entrepreneurs may prefer the for-profit form. Thus, rock concerts are organized as for-profit ventures, profitably supported through the sale of tickets. Nonetheless, other kinds of performing arts are provided by nonprofits through a combination of ticket sales and donations. Why do nonprofits play a role in providing some, but not other, excludable public goods? Why do these nonprofits continue to rely on donations although sales are feasible? These subjects have received limited attention, with Hansmann (1981a) playing a pioneering role.

Hansmann considers an excludable public good with high fixed costs and limited demand, so that the average total cost curve lies everywhere above the demand curve. These conditions describe the market for operas, symphony orchestras, dance companies, and other "high arts" that are commonly provided through nonprofits, but not the sorts of popular cultural experiences typically provided by for-profits. Despite high costs and limited demand, these public goods should be provided if, as often happens, the area under the demand curve exceeds total costs, but there is no single price at which producers can break even. Perfect price discrimination would allow the good to be sold profitably, but there are limits to price discrimination because tickets are resellable. Although opera companies can charge more for front-row seats, any separating equilibrium where high demanders buy front-row seats would not collect all the consumer surplus and might not suffice to allow the show to go on.

Nonprofits solve this problem, he asserts, by simply asking consumers to pay an additional amount voluntarily. Consumers do so, he argues, because they are told that absent their donations, the organizations on which they depend for their cultural experiences may disappear. In effect, their resulting donations act as a form of voluntary price discrimination. Hansmann does not develop this point formally, simply asserting it and then modeling the effect of donations on the quality and quantity of performances. This gap is filled by Bilodeau and Steinberg (1997). In their model, nonprofit managers wish to maximize the number of consumers who develop cultural appreciation by purposefully setting ticket prices below average costs. High demanders are induced to contribute in the subgame-perfect Nash equilibrium of a multistage game because they are pivotal to the solvency of the enterprise. Spiegel (1995) also provides a formal model of donations motivated by a desire to continue to consume an excludable public good, but in his model ticket prices will be higher than cost.

Market failure obtains even when for-profits provide public goods. Because there is no cost to extending consumption to an additional consumer, social welfare maximization requires that all who want to consume be allowed to do so. For-profits over-exclude unless perfect price discrimination is feasible. As noted above, consumers would not reveal their willingness to pay to for-profit firms, who would take advantage of consumer revelation to extract all their surplus. Ben-Ner (1986) argues that consumers are willing to reveal their preferences to nonprofit organizations because nonprofits can be trusted to use this information in more benign ways. Thus, nonprofits are less likely to over-exclude low-demand consumers.

4.6. Entrepreneurial sorting

The founding entrepreneur decides whether an organization is organized as for-profit or nonprofit, designs the organization's articles of incorporation and bylaws, and selects the initial set of board members and the rules for succession. This gives her considerable power over the subsequent role and behavior of the organization, and entrepreneurial preferences shape the use of that power. In Bilodeau and Slivinski (1998), entrepreneurs are selected through a game of chicken and entrepreneurial sorting does not occur. Other papers follow Young's (Young, 1983) suggestion to model how sector choice varies with entrepreneurial preferences.

Two other papers by Bilodeau and Slivinski (1996a, 1996b) model the equilibrium choice of entrepreneur as a war of attrition and discuss the characteristics of the individual most likely to volunteer to serve in this capacity. The model predicts that nonprofit entrepreneurs will be those who incur relatively low private entrepreneurial costs (due to skills, experience, connections, and the like) or value the public good relatively more. They further focus on the role of wealth when agent preferences are identical but wealth varies. If anticipated donations are sufficiently large, the wealthiest individuals will serve as entrepreneurs, but otherwise, the entrepreneur is either the richest nondonor or the poorest donor.

Steinberg and Eckel (1994) assume that potential entrepreneurs value three things: income, perks (job attributes that benefit only them), and public goods (job attributes that benefit both themselves and a group of external others). They further assume that there is a spectrum of preferences across potential entrepreneurs, with some placing more weight on perks and others placing more weight on public goods. Market opportunities and tax and regulatory preferences determine the set of entrepreneurial applicants (those whose prospective indirect utility from starting and managing a nonprofit firm exceeds their reservation level of utility). One of these applicants is selected to serve as entrepreneur. They make two alternative assumptions about the mechanism for selecting the entrepreneur—either that the winner is randomly selected from the set of applicants or that the applicant with the largest gain in indirect utility is the winner. They apply this approach to a mixed-sector duopoly, in which a nonprofit with endogenous objectives competes with a profit-maximizing for-profit. They show: (1) that although for-profit firms will, in general, support some provision of the public good (corporate philanthropy), the mixture of perks and public goods will differ across sectors; (2) that the relative price of perks to public goods is an important determinant of nonprofit behavior, both because it affects equilibrium for given entrepreneurial preferences and because it affects the selection of entrepreneurs from the preference spectrum; and (3) that public policies, such as the granting of tax exemptions of various sorts to nonprofit organizations but not their for-profit competitors, will also affect nonprofit behavior through these two channels. First, each potential entrepreneur would make a different choice when policy changes. Second, the set of applicants, and therefore the selected entrepreneur, will have different preferences when policy changes. Accounting for the second channel can reverse conclusions about the welfare effects of specified public policies. They derive many more results for a specific parameterization of the model, but it is not clear whether these generalize. One such result is that both pure public goods lovers and pure perk lovers are more likely to apply for the entrepreneurial niche than mixed types, so that the selected winners will be either among the best or among the worst.

Two papers derive entrepreneurial sorting from the assumption that nonprofit organizations must offer strictly lower levels of financial compensation than for-profit firms (Gui, 1990; Schlesinger, 1985). Preston (1992) assumes that potential managers differ (and sort) according to entrepreneurial ability, rather than preferences. Gassler (1989) and Schiff and Weisbrod (1991) assume that entrepreneurs are of two types (those valuing only profits, and those valuing other things), and demonstrate a separating equilibrium in which types sort perfectly by sector.

There is almost no empirical evidence on whether nonprofit entrepreneurs differ from for-profit entrepreneurs in observable characteristics. A study of graduates of Vanderbilt who received MBA degrees and later entered either the for-profit or nonprofit sectors (Rawls et al., 1975) found no difference across sectors in problem-solving ability, intelligence, or creativity. Those choosing nonprofit managerial careers were better at personal relations, dominance, capacity for status, social presence, and flexibility and gave higher priority to being cheerful, forgiving, and helpful. Those choosing for-profit managerial careers gave high ranking to financial prosperity, ambition, neatness, obedience, and dependability and had a greater expressed need for power and lower expressed need for security. Another study looked at the contractual incentives given to university presidents for the meeting of specified goals in academic, research, and financial performance (Ehrenberg et al., 2000). Neither is specific to founding entrepreneurs.

4.7. Multiple public goods

When there are multiple public goods, donors face a variety of problems. Donors must find appropriate nonprofit recipients, verify their compliance with donor wishes, and coordinate their allocation across charities with that of other donors. A new layer of intermediary organizations arises in response, consisting of nonprofit organizations that provide financial assistance and services to other nonprofit organizations. We refer to these intermediaries generically as *passthrough organizations* because they serve as a conduit between donors and service-providing nonprofits. In this section, we detail the difficulties donors face, describe various forms of passthrough organizations, and show how these organizations help solve some donor problems while creating other ones.

The first task for donors is to find charities that provide appropriate public goods. Providers are distinguished by the nature of the service provided, quality, ideology, and bundling of other public and private goods with the public good of interest. Search is costly, and this inhibits giving. Charities reduce donor search costs by providing information through fundraising campaigns, but these campaigns increase the costs of solicitation at rival charities, creating a "commons externality" (Rose-Ackerman, 1982).

The second donor task is to coordinate her gifts with those of other donors. In a world of incomplete information, there is no natural decentralized mechanism for assuring that individual donations are directed to achieve aggregate outcomes that the donor likes. For example, if a donor cares about both disaster relief and research efforts to cure diabetes, he would want to know whether other donors are already providing enough to disaster relief agencies that he could concentrate his donations on diabetes research. The situation is more complicated than that faced by buyers of private goods, who need only obtain information on suppliers. Public-good donors would like to obtain information on both suppliers and demanders.

Even when there is complete information and Nash equilibrium is unique, there is still a coordination problem leading to an inefficient allocation of donations across public goods (Bilodeau, 1992). A simple example illustrates the problem (this example is formally identical to that presented as Figure 16, as an example of the general model discussed in sections 2 and 5 of chapter 5, this volume). Suppose there are two individuals, identified by subscripts 1 and 2, and three public goods, whose quantities are A, B, and C respectively. Each individual is endowed with \$Y, and all public goods can be produced at a constant marginal cost, normalized to \$1. Thus, the quantity of each public good is simply the sum of the amounts purchased by each individual, that is:

$$\mathrm{X_1 + X_2 = X}; \qquad \text{for} \quad \mathrm{X = A, B, C}$$

Finally, assume that donor utility functions are Cobb–Douglas, with the following parameters:

$$\mathrm{U_1 = A^{1/4}B^{1/4}C^{1/2}}; \qquad \mathrm{U_2 = A^{1/4}B^{1/2}C^{1/4}}$$

Each donor picks a contribution level for each public good, subject to the budget constraint that total contributions equal endowment. It is easy to show that there is a unique Nash equilibrium to the simultaneous contributions game of complete information. In equilibrium, the first donor gives 1/5th of his income to A, 4/5ths to C, and nothing to B while the second donor gives 1/5th of income to A and 4/5ths of income to B so that the total provided to each of the goods is $(2/5, 4/5, 4/5)\mathrm{Y}$. This is inefficient because they would both prefer $(1/2, 3/4, 3/4)\mathrm{Y}$. Although there is no shortfall in total contributions to public goods in this example (both donate their entire endowment), the allocation of donations across public goods is inefficient because each player free rides on provision of the good to which they both contribute. Individual A reasons that if he contributed an extra dollar to good A instead of good C, individual 2 would respond by shifting 2/3rds of a dollar from A to B, which individual 1 feels is already overprovided. Individual 2 reasons symmetrically, and the Pareto-improving reallocation is not made through unilateral decisions.

Third, donors would want to know the share of incremental donations received by various nonprofit service-providing agencies that will be devoted to the public good of interest. Contract failure is always a concern in a world of imperfect enforcement of the nondistribution constraint. However, even if the constraint is perfectly enforced, donations can still "leak" to uses the donor does not approve of when organizations provide multiple public goods.

Finally, donors sometimes wish to continue giving long after their deaths. The allocation of their estate across multiple public goods could be specified precisely in a contract, but donors might prefer a more flexible arrangement that can take advantage of evolving technology, needs, and information flows.

Donors facing these problems might use a variety of pre-existing passthrough organizations or found a new one. Thus, we define various pure types of passthrough organizations below, then show how they address donor needs. The reader is cautioned that the labels we assign within this typology have particular legal definitions in some jurisdictions that do not conform with our usage, but absent an international juridical consensus, this is inevitable. There are two major types of passthroughs, and several subtypes. *United fundraising organizations*, or UFOs, receive funds from one or more donors and disburse them as grants in the year donations are received. *Foundations* receive funds periodically from one or more donors and are not constrained to disburse them in the year received.

UFOs are distinguished by the presence or absence of *donor option plans*. Early UFOs, like Community Chest or United Way, disbursed their funds only to member agencies. No organization could join the UFO without the approval of existing members. Some of these UFOs evolved plans that allow donors to specify that all or part of their donations be allocated to specific member or nonmember agencies. Regardless of the presence of donor option plans, UFO members agreed to accept a share of the funds raised by a joint effort and limit their conduct of independent fundraising campaigns.

There are several types of foundations. *Family foundations* receive their funds from a single individual or small group of individuals. Grant decisions are made by a self-perpetuating board that may include the donor and members of the donor's family. *Community foundations* receive donations from a large group of individuals and institutions (typically anyone who cares to donate) and grant decisions are made by a board that may include elected and appointed members. *Corporate foundations* receive their funds from a single for-profit firm, and grant decisions may be made by an independent board or a board controlled by the funding corporation.

UFOs reduce donor search costs (Rose-Ackerman, 1980). Instead of each donor contemplating collecting information on each nonprofit organization (and rationally choosing to make a poorly-informed allocation after collecting only a small fraction of that information), donors can trust UFOs to research organizational qualities and community needs and are therefore willing to delegate decisionmaking powers to the UFO. UFOs can develop special expertise and enjoy economies of scale in grant allocations. Finally, when individual donors are freed from the need to search for recipient nonprofit organizations, these nonprofits are freed from the need to search for individual donors (Rose-Ackerman, 1982). UFO member agencies will spend less on educating the public about their existence and need for funds, so the commons externality will be reduced.

UFOs commonly offer a convenient and relatively painless way to make donations—payroll deduction plans. Rather than incur the transactions costs of writing and mailing multiple checks, contributions to UFOs are automatically deducted from employee paychecks by mutual agreement with their employers. Most employers do not want to incur the costs of an elaborate payroll deduction plan that would make donations directly to service-providing agencies, and so agree to provide this service only for one or more UFOs.

UFOs reduce coordination problems between donors. One donor does not have to guess at what other donors are doing to decide which public goods need incremental donations—a once and for all allocation is made by the UFO and this allocation is shared with donors. UFOs can be thought of as mechanisms that enable donors to make binding commitments and so avoid the inefficient allocations resulting from the voluntary contributions mechanism. Alternatively, UFOs can be modeled as players with preferences over public good allocations, as in Bilodeau (1992). Then, UFOs face a tradeoff between total donations and the most-preferred output mix.

UFOs typically require their members to undergo periodic outside audits and share information about governance, budgetary, and operating procedures because they do not want the combined campaign to suffer from scandals involving member agencies. This helps reduce contract failure resulting from the distribution of surplus to those in control of the nonprofit organization, but cannot stop contract failure resulting from the diversion of funds from donors' preferred public goods to management's preferred public goods. On the other hand, passthroughs add another layer of bureaucracy between donors and the clients the donor cares about, perhaps worsening agency problems and leading to abuses. Finally, mistakes by UFOs affect the entire allocation of funds to public goods, whereas mistakes by individual donors would tend to cancel each other out.

Donors who are concerned with the allocation of their gifts after their death would form or support a foundation. There are considerable transactions costs in establishing a family foundation, but by organizing the foundation as a nonprofit and constituting the foundation's initial board of directors, bylaw, and rules for selecting successor boards, the donor can reduce agency problems while retaining flexibility to deal with emerging needs. Community foundations present much lower transactions costs for each donor. However, allocations are made by a board that represents the community of donors and so correspond less well to the preferences of individual donors.

Overall, does the presence of passthrough organizations increase or decrease total donations? The answer depends upon the size of opposing forces and the details of donor-option plan implementation. All else equal, donations may go up because the donor incurs lower transactions costs and knows that a more informed allocation will be made if he delegates decisionmaking to a UFO. Donations may go up or down depending on whether donors believe that contract failure is, on balance, reduced by UFO membership.

Bilodeau and Slivinski (1997) focused on another factor—the imperfect match between donor and UFO preferences. A donor who cared only about, say, allocations to diabetes research would be most distressed to learn that only 1% of UFO funds will be granted to this cause. This fixed-percentage allocation rule means that this donor would have to give \$100 to purchase \$1 of his desired public good. However, this donor also gets to enjoy donations by other donors, who may not care about diabetes but nonetheless find 1% of their donation spent on this cause. Donors recognize the "I'll give to your charity while you'll give to mine" nature of the transaction. Weighing these two opposing forces, Bilodeau and Slivinski (1997) show that if there are two public goods that are substitutes for each other, donations to a combined fund would be lower than donations to two standalone charities.

The nature of UFO membership decisions insures that most donors will be comfortable with the passthrough's allocations (Rose-Ackerman, 1980). Organizations will not be allowed to join unless incumbents expect that the resulting increment in donations to the combined campaign will exceed the new member's grant. Organizations will not seek to join unless the anticipated UFO grant exceeds the net amount they could raise via an independent campaign. Thus, at every stage of enlargement from one member to a mature organization, total net donations must be higher with the UFO than without. It also means that the set of members will enjoy consensus support among UFO donors. Allocations to controversial causes would not lead to a large increase in campaign proceeds, so that agencies supporting such causes would not be offered terms of entry they would willingly accept. This means that UFOs, like governments, are best at meeting consensus needs.

Although comfortable with UFO allocations, most donors would prefer an allocation that more closely approximates their own preferences, and donor option plans seem to address this need. However, given the choice, many donors do not specify how their gifts should be allocated across member agencies. Bilodeau (1992) argues that this is because donors recognize that their designation may not affect the ultimate pattern of spending. Any specification not in accord with the UFO's preferences can be undone through a reallocation of grants made from the fund's discretionary resources, provided there are sufficient undesignated donations. In turn, donors will provide unrestricted funds because they recognize that designation would be useless, and donor cynicism becomes self-fulfilling. Bilodeau and Slivinski (1997) show how this problem can be solved. If the UFO credibly commits to allocate a fixed share of unrestricted funds to each member agency regardless of donor designations, donor designations become effective. Thus assured, total donations go up, so that it is not surprising that Rose-Ackerman (1982) found that United Ways do, in fact, tend to allocate incremental discretionary funds in fixed proportions. The UFO obtains more donations, but need not compromise its goals regarding the final allocation of its discretionary plus donor-designated funds because it can plan its fixed share rule to undo any designations that would follow.

UFOs are often criticized for supporting only traditional and safe causes like disaster relief and youth services. United Way, for example, rarely if ever admits agencies that provide abortion services, AIDS/HIV education, or environmental advocacy. However, this seems like a natural function of the organizational form—were United Way to fund these services, youth service agencies and the like might find it advantageous to quit.

Heterogeneous demands are well accommodated by nonmember nonprofits, and if they want the transactions-cost efficiencies resulting from the UFO form, they can form an "alternative fund" such as a united arts fund (supporting only agencies that provide high culture) or a "green fund" (supporting environmental activist groups).

Even so, because employers are willing to offer only a limited number of payroll deduction options, United Way enjoys a near monopoly on workplace solicitation. Donor option plans often allow donors to specify that all or part of their gift will go to a nonmember agency, after a service fee is deducted by the UFO. The service fee is usually specified as a percentage of the designated gift, with some United Way local affiliates charging a rate designed to recoup no more than processing costs and others taking advantage of their monopoly position. Either way, this sort of donor option allows some advantages of united fundraising to be shared with nonprofits that support nontraditional or controversial causes without endangering the overall success of the campaign.

4.8. *Internal agency problems*

Some authors (those in the "property rights school," as defined in Steinberg, 1987, and discussed below) emphasize that the attenuated property rights of nonprofit owners (who cannot receive the financial residuals generated by their decisions) lead to a variety of inefficiencies. The board of directors and the top managers cannot receive, in monetary form, a share of the value they generate, so they may instead choose a compensation mix that emphasizes perks such as overly large offices in magnificent headquarter buildings, attractive rather than productive subordinates, and frequent conferences in exotic locations. This is inefficient because the cost of such perks is generally higher than the cost of purely monetary compensation that yields the same utility to the manager (Frech, 1976). In any case, because it is hard to structure non-monetary perks in ways that mimic profit-sharing, nonprofit owners will not look hard for ways to cut costs, monitor employee productivity, better meet customer needs, or otherwise seek efficiency. Further, there is no market for control of nonprofit organizations, so well-meaning but incompetent managers are not pushed out by attentive stockholders (Alchian and Demsetz, 1972; Frech, 1980). The only check on such inefficiencies is the necessity to avoid bankruptcy. Thus, the property rights school predicts that nonprofits will have higher costs than similar for-profits. Further, if nonprofit organizations are given competitive advantages such as tax exemption, this raises the ceiling on survivable inefficiency. Thus, the nonprofit cost disadvantage is exactly equal to any competitive advantage conveyed by public policies that favor the sector (e.g., Blair et al., 1975).

These arguments are, at best, exaggerated when applied to commercial nonprofits, and in any case neglect the public goods nature of nonprofit outputs. As we already pointed out, nondistribution of profits solves a particular agency problem between the donor and the recipient organization. As Thompson (1980, p. 134) put it, reduced efficiency owing to attenuated property rights "is often overshadowed by the increased efficiency in satisfying the customers that their contributions are being put to good use." More fundamentally, if employees view nonprofit outputs as an end in itself, rather than a means to the end of claims on financial residuals, they have every incentive to work efficiently. If the chance to contribute, through one's job, to a public good is a utility-relevant job attribute, then public good provision becomes an automatically-shared stimulus to efficiency. Thus, Slivinski (2002) shows that by using a combination of public goods and private goods that is legal under any interpretation of the nondistribution constraint, there exists a compensation scheme that induces optimal effort from each team member. This scheme requires knowledge of only observable team output, is budget-balancing, and renegotiation proof. Monetary payments to team members will be lower than those required for efficient production in for-profit teams, and the compensation mix is skewed more toward public goods (similar conclusions are reached in Schlesinger, 1985; Francois, 2001; and Handy and Katz, 1998).

Regardless of whether charitable output *per se* affects managerial utility, a variety of resource dependencies will force the manager to care about aspects of efficiency. First, Preston (1988) shows that managers who care about donations because they finance the managerial compensation package would be forced to provide public goods. In her model, donors are aware of the public-good content in an organization's output mix, and, if the organization is nonprofit, provide donations in proportion to this public-good content. More specifically, she considers a model in which potential outputs are arrayed by the ratio of public to private benefits, and shows that the equilibrium product spectrum with both for-profit and nonprofit firms Pareto-dominates the for-profit only equilibrium. Rose-Ackerman (1981, 1987) shows how government and foundation grants provide incentives that can move managerial decisions closer (in some cases) or farther away (in others) from donor ideals. Grønbjerg (1993) shows that government grants and contracts stipulate detailed reporting and audit requirements and force the organization to employ credentialed professionals. United Ways also hold member agencies accountable.

The internal efficiency of for-profit firms is monitored by stockholders who have limited interactions with their agents. In contrast, volunteer board members and line workers are likely to care passionately about the organizational mission and are uniquely situated to observe inefficiencies on a daily basis. Volunteers are not silenced by the threat of job loss, and are likely to leave if they are not satisfied by what they learn of the management of the organization. Volunteers are also financial donors, so when they learn of inefficiencies, the impact of their exit is multiplied (Mueller, 1975; Schiff, 1990). Volunteer exit also serves as a signal to other principals.

Handy (1995) models both the passive and active oversight roles played by nonprofit board members. When prominent citizens are willing to lend their good names to an organization, they put up their own reputation as collateral. As she explains, "...if Prince Philip endorses the World Wildlife Fund by being a trustee of that nonprofit, a donor can reasonably assume that the organization must be reputable: Prince Philip has too much to lose by being associated with a shady organization. ...In this way, trustees passively legitimize nonprofits." (p. 294). She demonstrates the tradeoff between active and passive legitimation—if an organization asks too much of its board members, nominees will be unwilling to serve. She then characterizes the determinants of board membership and the optimal mix of active and passive members.

Finally, competition serves as a check on inefficiency, even when the organizations involved are providing public goods. Although Bilodeau and Slivinski (1997) show that if entry is costly and there are no economies or diseconomies of scale, then at most one nonprofit would form to provide each public good, this market is still contestable. If the holder of the monopoly public-good niche were to depart too drastically from efficiency, another entrepreneur would enter and take over that place.

Like most questions in economics, the importance of internal agency problems in nonprofit organizations is ultimately an empirical question. Ostrower and Stone (2006) summarize a variety of empirical studies of the activities undertaken by nonprofit boards and the impact of boards on organizational performance. Not surprisingly, they find a mixed picture, in which boards are more effective in some environments, in some industries, and using some governance rules than in others. Several studies report on the use of performance-based pay for nonprofit executives (Oster, 1998; Roomkin and Weisbrod, 1999; Ehrenberg et al., 2000; Ballou and Weisbrod, 2003). They find limited use of these practices, with a variety of financial and mission-related triggers.

There are many studies that attempt to compare the productive efficiency of nonprofit versus for-profit organizations (e.g., Weisbrod, 1998; Schlesinger and Gray, 2006), finding mixed results and suggesting that the direction and size of any efficiency difference depends upon industry, level of competition, and other factors. However, huge methodological challenges remain, so it is unclear how persuasive this body of literature is, especially for the purposes needed here. Most available studies assess the costs of private goods produced by commercial nonprofits, which is not the focus of the present paper. The omission of public goods sometimes leads to misleading conclusions even about private good efficiency. For example, some studies conclude that nonprofit hospitals are inefficient because they maintain too many vacant beds. However, Holtmann (1983) contends that excess capacity in health care is a public good, allowing the system to avoid stock-outs during epidemics and natural disasters, and that nonprofits choose to provide this public good as part of their mission. Similarly, nonprofits that incorporate serving the disabled in their mission might employ their beneficiaries and so appear, in a simplistic study, to suffer from inefficient use of labor. When the focus is on donative nonprofits, the problem is even worse as there may be no for-profit providers to compare nonprofit costs with.

4.9. The long run

Economists have not written much about the long-run equilibrium of a market populated by donative nonprofits. Most existing literature concerns the long-run mixture of for-profit and nonprofit organizations in commercial markets and the survival of behavioral distinctions between the two sectors (e.g., Schiff, 1986; Lakdawalla and Philipson, 1998; Schiff and Weisbrod, 1991; Hirth, 1999). The only paper to really focus on donative nonprofits is Rose-Ackerman (1982), who models the market structure as monopolistically competitive. In her model, there is a continuum of public goods and distributions of consumer preferences over those goods. Donations to each organization come partly at the expense of neighboring organizations. Donors are unaware of the existence of any particular nonprofit organization (and so unaware of their opportunity to donate to the public good it provides) unless solicited, and solicitation is costly. Public goods are financed by the difference between donations received and solicitation costs. Making the admittedly extreme assumption of free entry, that a new nonprofit organization will enter at a particular point on the product spectrum whenever net donations are positive, she comes to the conclusion that charities will enter until fundraising costs approach 100% of revenue for all public goods. Thus, fundraising suffers from a commons externality, and this becomes fatal when there is free entry.

Rose-Ackerman's conclusion is robust. She shows that there will be excessive fundraising even if all donors care about high fundraising costs. Steinberg (1993a) argues, without formally modeling the point, that the conclusion is also robust to special privileges offered to nonprofit organizations but not their for-profit competitors (chiefly tax exemption), earnings from commercial ventures, and provision of volunteer labor. In order for nonprofits to provide public goods in the long run, there must be some "cushion"—a competitive advantage that is not eroded by entry. Expenditure on public goods is limited, in the long run, to the size of this cushion.

Thus, the received literature, scanty and incomplete as it is, suggests that nonprofits will not provide public goods in the long run unless there are barriers to entry or entrepreneurial scarcity. Two barriers arise naturally—economies of scale or scope leading to natural monopoly, and transactions costs of entry (as detailed in Ben-Ner and Van Hoomissen, 1991). Others result from public policies such as licensing of day-care centers or certificate-of-need approval for new health facilities. Bilodeau and Slivinski (1998) detail a possible third barrier, as founding entrepreneurs would, even absent transactions costs, prefer to remain contributors at large.

There is some evidence that competition affects nonprofit provision of public goods. First, anecdotally, many fundraisers report that it has become progressively more difficult to raise money as competition for the charitable dollar has grown. Feigenbaum (1987) finds that competition among health research charities increases the ratio of fundraising costs to gross receipts. Second, a variety of studies, mostly regarding nonprofit hospitals, find that the level of competition affects public good provision (e.g., Frank et al., 1990; Schlesinger et al., 1997; Wolff and Schlesinger, 1998).

The commons externality has implications for regulatory policies. Eckel and Steinberg (1991, 1993) provide a model in which nonprofit organizations produce both public goods and private perks in accord with the preferences of the founding entrepreneur. They finance these two outputs through sales of a service and charitable donations. They show that the traditional deadweight loss due to monopoly should be balanced against nonprofit correction of another market failure. Nonprofits sometimes devote their monopoly rents to the provision of public goods that are underprovided by other institutions. Thus, depending upon entrepreneurial preferences, it is possible that the traditional welfare ranking can be reversed, with nonprofit monopoly superior to duopoly and competition. The commons externality further complicates matters, so that any logically-possible welfare ordering is consistent with the model under reasonable parameter values. Thus, it might be that duopoly is best, perfect competition second-best, and monopoly last. They suggest that current antitrust laws, which make little distinction between nonprofit and for-profit combinations in restraint of trade, need to be carefully rethought (see also Steinberg, 1993b; Carlton et al., 1995).

In another paper, Steinberg (1997) examines whether the traditional approach of competitive bidding ought to be employed when government contracts with nonprofit organizations for the provision of social services. The paper mostly concerns commercial nonprofits, but there are some implications for nonprofit public goods provision. First, competitive bidding leaves little surplus for the nonprofit to devote to public goods production. Perhaps this is irrelevant, as the government has other ways to foster public goods production either internally or externally, but without additional formal analysis, we cannot ascertain whether, say, monopoly rents are a better way to finance public goods than coercive taxation. Second, multi-source bidding, employed to protect the government from post-contract opportunism, may worsen the commons externality.

5. Modeling nonprofit behaviors

Here we discuss specific behaviors of nonprofit organizations. First, we discuss fundraising—why it affects giving, why particular practices are employed, the decision to contract with external organizations to conduct campaigns, and the endogenous determination of expenditure levels. Next we discuss price and non-price allocation mechanisms—how nonprofit pricing, use of waiting lists, use of eligibility requirements, and quality dilution may differ from that of for-profits. Then we discuss the use of labor—paid and volunteered—by donative nonprofits. Finally, we discuss nonprofit use of capital and whether there are market failures that cause excessive capital accumulation, inadequate capital for growth, or misallocation of capital within nonprofit organizations.

5.1. Fundraising

Other chapters in this volume model aspects of the donor decision, but do not focus on why decisions may depend upon the solicitation process chosen by the nonprofit. Charities invest substantial resources finding, persuading, and cultivating donors (more than $2 billion per year in the U.S.A., according to Kelley, 1997), none of which would be necessary if donations could be entirely explained as an equilibrium of some game involving only potential donors. Models of fundraising's effect on giving parallel models of advertising's effect on purchasing. Fundraising is either assumed to affect donor preferences, give donors information (or reduce the cost of information that donors would otherwise seek), or to signal characteristics of the soliciting organization. However, there is one difference—unlike purchasers, who consider their response to products and advertisements without regard to the decisions of other purchasers, donors must also consider the response of other donors when deciding how to respond to solicitation.

In this section we examine various models of why donors respond to solicitation expenditures and practices. In particular, we see if there are economic ways to rationalize the institutions and beliefs of fundraising professionals about the conduct of campaigns. Several aspects of campaigning practice are puzzling. Often, particularly for capital campaigns, there are two campaign phases. Before the campaign is announced publicly, quiet attempts are made to secure commitments from a few major donors. This quiet phase continues until a large fraction of the ultimate campaign goal is secured, and then the public phase begins with an announcement of the campaign goal, the amount secured in the quiet phase through "leadership gifts," the identity of the leaders, and a broad-based call for additional gifts. No matter whether the campaign is divided into quiet and public phases, charities periodically announce a running total of how much has been collected. These two facts are surprising to economists in light of Varian's (Varian, 1994) result that in a two-stage (leader/follower) voluntary contributions game, less is contributed when donations are made sequentially rather than simultaneously.

Second, many campaigns use "giving clubs," where the identities of donors who make large gifts are identified and publicized by the nonprofit. The exact dollar amounts given are not revealed, but categories of largesse are reported for each major donor (e.g., "Patron—those making a gift exceeding $1 million; Benefactor—those making a gift exceeding $500,000; Golden Key Club Member—those making a gift exceeding $100,000; Angel—those making a gift exceeding $1000"). If announcement of donations is useful, why is it done in this way?

Third, some, but not all charities, act as if it is important to keep fundraising costs, as a percentage of contributions received, as low as possible. Charities advertise their low fundraising cost ratios to donors, and where there is discretion under accounting procedures, report expenditures in ways that minimize their apparent cost ratios. This accords with the intuition of many economists that the cost ratio has something to do with the relative efficiency of alternative recipients, but formal modeling suggests that this intuition is wrong.

Finally, published ethical codes prohibit fundraising professionals from working for a payment that is contingent on the results of the campaign (e.g., Association of Fundraising Professionals, 2001). This is puzzling to economists who believe that incentive payments can cure problems of agency.

5.1.1. Reduced form approaches

Most of the earlier papers take the "donations production function" or "donations cost function" as a primitive, asserting that there exists a stable and exploitable relationship between solicitation expenditures of various types and aggregate funds raised, possibly depending upon other aspects of nonprofit behavior (e.g., Boyle and Jacobs, 1978).

The production function shows the level of donations resulting from every possible combination of expenditures on various fundraising techniques, such as direct mail, telemarketing, foundation grant-seeking, and the like (Steinberg, 1985). The cost function is derived from the production function in the usual way (by equating the marginal donations resulting from incremental spending on each non-corner fundraising technique). The rule for calculating optimal fundraising expenditures is then fairly standard, except for one complication resulting from our uncertainty as to the organizational objective function.

Steinberg (1986b), building on Tullock's (Tullock, 1966) suggestion, considers two polar cases that he calls "service maximization" and "budget maximization." The service maximizer cares about the net proceeds derived from a campaign (donations minus solicitation expenditures), because these resources can support charitable activities, whereas the budget maximizer cares about the gross proceeds because any resources received by the organization support the power and prestige of those in control. He then constructs a family of objective functions consisting of the convex combination of these polar cases:

$$\Psi = \alpha(C(F) - F) + (1 - \alpha)C(F)$$

where: C denotes contributions received, F denotes solicitation expenditures, and α is a parameter between zero and one that defines objective functions within this family. When $\alpha = 1$, the organization is a service maximizer. When $\alpha = 0$, the organization is a budget maximizer.

Then, fundraising is optimal with respect to any objective function within this family if expenditures are such that $dC/dF = \alpha$.

In application, several complications apply. First, current expenditures, especially those devoted to "prospecting" (looking for likely future donors), affect the entire sequence of future donations. The optimization rule applies to the present value of the induced stream of future changes resulting from current expenditures. Second, organizations often use non-priced resources (volunteers and gifts in-kind) to conduct their campaigns. Efficiency requires that these resources be counted in the fundraising total at their opportunity costs to the charity. This can be either the value of volunteers in their next best use at the organization or the cost of replacing volunteers with paid labor, depending on what we wish to assume about the internal efficiency of resource allocation. Third, solicitation expenditures may produce incremental gifts in other forms (volunteer labor, gifts in kind, or matching grants) that should be valued at the amount of monetary donations the organization would willingly substitute for them. Finally, campaigns may jointly produce incremental donations that can be devoted to charitable outputs and the outputs themselves. Thus, a fundraising campaign by an advocacy organization can be successful even if it raises no money, provided the campaign literature affects the policy positions of those solicited. An organization whose purpose is to foster the early detection and treatment of cancer accomplishes its mission directly by including the "seven deadly warning signs" in its mailings. Side effects of campaigns on charitable missions can be positive or negative—those receiving literature from a cause they do not support may be galvanized into action to support the organization's rivals. These side-effects should all be valued at the charity's willingness-to-pay for the incremental accomplishment of mission (or willingness-to-pay to avoid the deleterious effect of fundraising on mission).

Several papers assert that donors dislike fundraising expenditures by charities they support and attempt to build this into the cost function. Thus, Rose-Ackerman (1982) and Weisbrod and Dominguez (1986) assume that donors view fundraising cost ratios (F/C) as a constant. Because part of their donation "leaks out" to fundraising expenditures, a higher cost ratio is equivalent to an increase in the "price of giving," the amount the donor must give to achieve a \$1 increase in charitable spending on mission. In particular, and neglecting additional factors detailed by the authors, the price of giving is $1/[1-(F/C)]$. Steinberg (1986a) criticizes this approach, noting that charities that optimize any objective function in the family specified above will not wish to hold their cost ratio constant; rather, they will hold F constant in response to marginal donations from a "small" donor. Thus, for small donors to optimizing charities, the price of giving is identically \$1, and variations in fundraising cost ratios reveal the relative popularity, rather than the relative efficiency, of alternative charities.

Perhaps donors "should" ignore fundraising cost ratios, as Steinberg argues but perhaps they do not. Rose-Ackerman's argument has considerable intuitive appeal, and charities like to advertise their low cost-ratios, so ultimately the matter must be resolved empirically. Here, results are mixed. Steinberg (1986a) uses a panel of U.S. nonprofit organizations and finds that although F is a highly significant determinant of giving, various measures related to F/C have small coefficients that are not statistically significant. Weisbrod and Dominguez (1986) and Okten and Weisbrod (2000), using similar panels, found the opposite to be true. A series of papers using progressively more sophisticated econometric techniques on a panel of U.K. charities found mixed results (Posnett and Sandler, 1989; Khanna et al., 1995; Khanna and Sandler, 2000). Thus, at this time, the matter remains unresolved.

The cost function is generally used in empirical studies that either provide guidance to organizations that wish to maximize their service (Boyle and Jacobs, 1978; Boyle et al., 1979; Jacobs and Lee, 1979; Weinberg, 1980; Steinberg, 1983; Luksetich et al., 1986; Weisbrod and Dominguez, 1986; Sargeant and Kähler, 1999) or reveal the underlying objective functions of organizations presumed to optimize within the family specified above (Steinberg, 1986b; Posnett and Sandler, 1989; Khanna et al., 1995; Khanna and Sandler, 2000). As a reduced form for empirical work, this approach is probably valid, but for deeper insights into the fundraising process, we need to specify the underlying utility functions of donors in order to account for interdependencies and perform welfare analysis.

5.1.2. *Structural models*

Rose-Ackerman (1982) provides the first model of fundraising derived from assertions about the utility functions of donors. In her model, donors have prespecified preferences over alternative charities that might exist, but are unaware of the existence of any particular charity until they receive that charity's solicitation letter. Donor utility is discontinuous in giving. Below some threshold amount, gifts produce no marginal utility. At the threshold, the donor believes he or she has "bought in" to the entire range of services provided by that charity, so marginal utility jumps to a positive level. Above the threshold, donors obtain marginal utility from incremental organizational expenditures resulting from their gift.

Fundraising expenditures consist of the cost of preparing and mailing solicitation letters. Solicitation by any one charity increases the expenditures by other charities required to raise a given level of donations, and in the free-entry limit, aggregate net donations per charity (donations minus solicitation costs) tend to zero. This provides a social-welfare rationale for united fundraising campaigns, restrictions on entry, or other anticompetitive policies.

Slivinski and Steinberg (1998) assume that communications received from charities provide direct utility to donors. Solicitation is a good complementary to "warm glow," and so those solicited will reduce their free-riding and contribute more to charity. In this way, they get at the essence of models that assume solicitation alters consumer preferences without creating the sort of havoc for welfare analysis that endogenous preference assumptions usually create. This work remains in progress, but progress to date suggests that the approach can be fruitful in (a) validating the reduced forms used in empirical work; (b) showing the irrelevance of fundraising cost ratios in greater generality; (c) analyzing the decision between in-house fundraising and contracting out; and (d) analyzing the design of contracts with external fundraisers.

Glazer and Konrad (1996) view giving as a form of conspicuous consumption in a competition for social status. Unlike private-goods consumption (which is, in addition, hard to observe at a distance) and income, large donations are a socially-commendable way to signal one's wealth. Fundraising professionals publicize these large donations, making donations more valuable to the donors as a signal of wealth and hence increasing equilibrium donations. Harbaugh (1998a) carries the analysis further. His donors compete for prestige with their gifts, regardless of whether that competition reveals the distribution of wealth. He formally models how a fundraiser can exploit this prestige competition by setting appropriate minimum donations for each category in a giving club. Harbaugh (1998b) estimates that between 20 and 25% of alumni gifts to a specific law school are motivated by prestige competition.

Vesterlund (2003) uses a standard model for pure public goods with one twist—the value of the public good produced by a particular charity is known by the fundraiser but not by donors. Potential donors can find out the quality of the charity through further investigation, but this investigation is costly. If a donor investigates and finds out that the charity is of high quality, she will want to convince other donors of that fact to increase provision for the public good she values. The manager of fundraising is also a player in the game she models, choosing to announce or not the donations of first-mover donors. The announcement strategy is known by potential donors before they decide whether to investigate further. Donors then choose whether to investigate and how much to give, conditional on the results of that investigation. Finally, other donors condition their gifts on any beliefs generated by the announcement (or not) of the size of the gift made by the first donor.

She then characterizes the perfect Bayesian equilibria that arise for differing costs of investigation. For an interesting range of parameter values, there is a hybrid equilibrium, where fundraisers at high-quality charities commit to announcing the first donation and fundraisers at low-quality charities pursue a mixed strategy. A separating equilibrium emerges from the actions of the first donor, who will investigate and if she finds quality to be high, make a sufficiently high donation to send an unambiguous signal to other donors. Thus, neither the initial uncertainty about quality nor the sequential nature of giving causes donations to be less than they would be in the standard simultaneous game (with complete information). The most surprising conclusion is that the total level of giving would exceed that generated by the standard simultaneous game. This is because the first donor recognizes that she will not get others to donate to a high-quality charity unless her gift is sufficiently large to provide an unambiguous signal that the first donor conducted the costly investigation. In conclusion, this model rationalizes the announcement of the first donation and shows how, sometimes, announcements can reduce equilibrium free-riding. Andreoni (2003) extends these results. Bac and Bag (2003) also discuss the role of information in fundraising.

Romano and Yildirim (2001) obtain similar conclusions from a very different model. Rather than build uncertainty into the standard model, they provide a more general utility function that can reverse Varian's (Varian, 1994) conclusion. Their specification of utility incorporates, as special cases, the standard model, the warm-glow (act of giving) motivation, snob effects (utility derived from giving more than others), and bandwagon effects (where giving by others is a complement to the value of own giving). They show that for some special cases of this utility function, Varian is right but for others (e.g., warm glow with upward-sloping reaction functions due to specified factors) he gets it backwards. They extend their results to n-player games and games with endogenous timing, and generally show the possibility that announcements of the first donation or of running totals of donations can increase the total amount given.

Andreoni (1998) views fundraising as spending to implement an economic mechanism that solves one problem with the voluntary contribution mechanism when nonconvexity is present. This nonconvexity can be due to fixed costs or increasing returns to scale (common in "capital campaigns") or to bandwagon effects (if donors obtain more warm glow when they support a successful campaign). In the convex case, there is, in general, a unique Nash equilibrium with positive donations; nonconvexity creates a second Nash equilibrium in which aggregate donations are zero. Alternative mechanisms can be adopted to eliminate the zero equilibrium, but he assumes that the transactions cost required to carry out these mechanisms grows with the size of the population covered. The role of the fundraiser is to select a subset of donors, the "leaders," implement a mechanism applied only to the leaders, and then collect donations from the leaders and from a subsequent simultaneous voluntary contribution game played by the "followers." To summarize, fundraising expenditures serve only to implement a mechanism that eliminates an inferior equilibrium. The remaining equilibrium is suboptimal (in the Samuelsonian sense) as there is still free-riding, but it is better for the charity than the eliminated equilibrium. Thus, he provides an economic rationale for leadership gifts. He also shows that government grants, financed by lump-sum taxes, can eliminate the zero equilibrium without incurring the transaction costs of the leadership mechanism. Perhaps this explains why some charities do not use leadership gifts.

Morelli and Vesterlund (2000) also model fundraising as the implementation of a mechanism, although in their case they do not detail any fundraising costs. As in Vesterlund (2003), the manager of fundraising is an active player and a first mover. However, here the manager chooses a threshold expenditure level on the public good provided by the charity (the 'provision point'), promising to provide that good if and only if contributions exceed that threshold. For varying assumptions about what the manager can credibly commit to, they analyze first the case of the fundraising manager that wishes to maximize total contributions (a plausible assumption given the career paths of many fundraisers) and then the case of a donor/manager (say the chair of the charity's board of directors). In the first case, equilibrium donations will exceed the Pareto-optimal level, and the threshold will be set to make every donor pivotal. This contrasts with the standard model, in which donations are sub-optimal and only the wealthiest few donate in the limit as the population grows. Donor/managers face a continuum of equilibria around their preferred threshold level, and so equilibrium predictions are less clear for the second case, but the set of equilibria contains a Pareto-efficient one.

5.1.3. Contracts with fundraising professionals

As noted above, many trade associations for fundraisers eschew the use of incentive contracts in their codes of professional ethics, declaring that "16. Members shall not accept compensation that is based on a percentage of charitable contributions, nor shall they accept finders' fees. 17. Members may accept performance-based compensation, such as bonuses, provided such bonuses ... are not based on a percentage of charitable contributions." (Association of Fundraising Professionals, 2001; most other such associations have similar language in their codes). Although some professional fundraisers do work on contingency (either because they are not members of the societies that incorporate the restriction in their ethical code or because they disobey the code), those that obey the codes are in the majority and continue to thrive. Steinberg (1986c, 1990) argues that this is because contracts with external fundraisers have effects on third parties (donors) which the principal (the charity) must consider. In particular, a commitment to give, say 50% of funds raised to the solicitor implies that a donor would have to give $2 for the charity to receive $1 in added resources. Thus, the contractual contingency creates an increase in the effective price to the donor of the charity's output. In contrast, a fixed fee contract would leave the price of giving unaffected, even if it absorbed 50% of the funds ultimately raised. Contingent contracts are only optimal if the added donations resulting from inducing the fundraiser (agent) to work harder exceeded the loss in donations due to the price increase.

Unfortunately, Steinberg's model made very restrictive assumptions, a problem that will perhaps be remedied in ongoing work related to Slivinski and Steinberg (1998). Regardless, Greenlee and Gordon (1998) tested the proposition, using a unique data set consisting of the universe of contracts between nonprofits and professional fundraisers filed in Pennsylvania between 1991 and 1996. They found that solicitors who are paid a fixed fee received greater donations and returned a larger portion of those donations to the charities they worked for.

5.1.4. Endogenous solicitation

If the goal of fundraising is to maximize resources available for the charitable mission, it is often quite sensible to regard solicitation expenditures as exogenous. If, say, government grants and contracts received by an organization were cut, that organization would have no scope to replace those revenues if fundraising had been optimal before the decrease. To a first approximation, this logic is akin to that applied to a profit-maximizing firm, which would not choose to increase its price to make up for an increase in fixed costs. However, researchers have relaxed that approximation in two ways. First, they have explored whether there are revenue interactions such that, in terms of the reduced form, the shape and location of the donations cost function would be affected by revenues from other sources. Here, the net-revenue-maximizing expenditure on fundraising would change, as would resulting donations. Second, they have explored objective functions governing fundraising that, like utility functions, result in income effects on fundraising effort. The matter is important because the effectiveness of grants, commercial income, or any other non-donated source of income depends on whether *net* donations are affected. If, for example, a marginal dollar in government grants caused gross donations to fall by only ten cents, we would want to know whether the organization chose to hold fundraising constant (in which case there was minimal crowding out) or to increase fundraising by ninety cents (in which case the marginal dollar was completely crowded out).

Revenues might affect the donations cost function for many reasons. First, in pure-public-goods or warm-glow models, other revenues would crowd-out donations. Rose-Ackerman (1981) details six reasons why the opposite effect could sometimes be expected, with grants leading to increased donations. First, government grants often come with strings attached that change the nature of charitable output. If the strings, representing a democratic consensus, brought the charitable output into closer alignment with donor wishes, donations would increase. Second, government grants sometimes have matching requirements that would reduce the effective donor-price of giving. Third, grants generally require that the organization become more professionally-managed, and donors might take that as a sign that their donations would be more efficiently spent. Fourth, grants might fund charitable outputs that are complementary to the outputs donors wish to fund (for example, the grant might build the museum, making contributions of artwork more worthwhile). Fifth, there may be increasing returns to scale in the production of the public good. Adapting all these results to the present question, however, is tricky as there are several alternative ways to graft a role for fundraising in these various models and researchers have not yet explored all the alternatives. Would crowding out result in a fixed (shift in the intercept) or variable (shift in the slope) effect on the donations cost function, and if variable, would it increase or decrease the slopes associated with various levels of fundraising expenditures? Would donors regard the government grants as a lead gift in the sense of Vesterlund (2003)? If so, a cutback in grants would reduce the fixed revenues from fundraising, but researchers have not explored the effect on the variable revenues. The models of Rose-Ackerman (1982), Glazer and Konrad (1996), Harbaugh (1998a), Slivinski and Steinberg (1998), Andreoni (1998), and Romano and Yildirim (2001) may also have something to say on these effects, but again, the analysis has not yet been conducted.

Other models explore organizational preferences or strategic reactions to changes in other revenues. Rose-Ackerman (1987) assumes that nonprofit managers have a preferred "ideology," that is, location on a one-dimensional quality spectrum, and that donors have other preferred ideologies along that spectrum. The managers select their equilibrium ideology strategically, compromising their most preferred point to become more attractive to donors and hence provide a larger quantity of output. In this setting, even lump sum government grants have an effect, as managers react to the income provided by the grant by compromising less on ideology.

Straub (2000) presents a more complete model in which fundraising expenditures reduce donor transactions costs and grant matching requirements cause both fundraising expenditures and contributions received at any given level of expenditures to change. Andreoni and Payne (2003) provide the first set of results that fully endogenize fundraising's reaction to government grants, drawing from both donor and organizational behaviors. Like Rose-Ackerman (1982), donors have a latent desire to give that is activated when they learn, through solicitation, that some charity is closer to their preferred quality level than those they had previously known about. Fundraising costs vary with the share of the population who are informed of the charity's existence. Unlike Rose-Ackerman (1987), the quality level offered by each charity is exogenously fixed. Finally, they assume that charities dislike solicitation, balancing their distaste for the activity against their need for donated resources. The authors characterize Nash equilibrium with two types of donors and two charities and show how it is perturbed by exogenous shifts in lump-sum government grants to one of those charities.

First, they suppose that either both the pure-public-goods and warm-glow motivations are operative, or that only the former is operative but that some costs of the government grant are borne by non-donors. Then, the standard result—partial crowding out—applies if we hold fundraising expenditures by both organizations constant. In turn, because donations to the grant recipient at each level of fundraising expenditure would be lower (continuing to hold fundraising expenditure by the other nonprofit constant), the recipient will optimally inform a smaller share of the population of its existence and fundraising expenditure will decrease. Finally, the competing charity will spend more on solicitation in Nash equilibrium, causing a further reduction in donations to the grant recipient. In total, fundraising and donations both fall at the recipient organization, but net expenditures (grant plus donations minus fundraising costs) rise. Next, they suppose that there is no public-goods motivation, and therefore no crowding-out to worry about. Then, government grants cause a reduction in fundraising through an income effect on organizational utility.

Turning to empirical work, there are few results to draw on. Schiff and Weisbrod (1991, p. 628) report on "regression results, not reported here" that show that revenues from commercial activities had a negative but insignificant effect on solicitation expenditures. Andreoni and Payne (2003) show that government grants appear to cause substantial and significant reductions in fundraising by arts and social service organizations when the endogeneity of grants is accounted for. Two other papers estimate the returns to fundraising while correcting for its possible endogeneity without reporting the detailed behavioral determinants of fundraising expenditures (Okten and Weisbrod, 2000; Straub, 2000).

5.2. *Pricing and non-price rationing*

How, if at all, does nonprofit pricing behavior differ from that of for-profit organizations? How do nonprofits use waiting lists, quality dilution, eligibility requirements, and other non-price mechanisms to allocate their services and does this allocation differ from for-profits? These are questions that are just being asked, and many intriguing possibilities have not been followed up in the literature. Thus, we can only provide a set of conjectures, largely based on Steinberg and Weisbrod (1998) and the sources cited therein. Sometimes there is every reason to expect that nonprofit pricing, or at least the rules characterizing nonprofit pricing, will be the same as that of for-profits. At other times, one suspects there are differences, subtle and pronounced, our second topic. We conclude this subsection by reporting on the scanty available empirical evidence.

If output markets are perfectly competitive with free entry, nonprofits are forced to use the same pricing rules as for-profits to survive, for even nonprofits need to break even. Donations, tax and regulatory preferences, or consumer preference to buy from a nonprofit organization (which allows nonprofits to charge a higher price than their for-profit competitors) may provide a "cushion" that allows nonprofits to depart from for-profit behaviors in general and pricing and rationing behaviors specifically. Tax and regulatory preferences lead to lower costs and hence allow the nonprofit to charge a lower price, consumer preference for nonprofits allow the nonprofit to charge a higher price, and either increases potential profits and hence potential cross-subsidization of other prices. However, free entry of competitors in the fundraising market and of for-profits-in-disguise (profit distributors who evade regulation and claim nonprofit status to obtain these cushions) would reduce or eliminate these cushions and force survivors to price like profit maximizers (Steinberg, 1987, 1993a).

When nonprofits engage in commercial activities in order to generate profits to support their principal (noncommercial) mission, they should use the same pricing and rationing rules as for-profits. Thus, if price discrimination is infeasible, they should pick quantities that equate marginal revenues and costs, and if price discrimination is feasible, they should charge each customer willing to pay marginal cost his or her reservation price. The only complication here is that noncommercial revenues may be affected by pricing behavior, a theme best developed (but still at the informal level) in Kingma's (Kingma, 1995) paper. Donors may care about whether the nonprofit engages in commercial activities at all, but not about the extent of those activities. This concern could arise if donors felt that the commercial activity would contribute to the erosion of the charity's concern with its core mission. Plausibly, this is an inframarginal effect that would reduce the profit resulting directly or indirectly from the commercial activity, and so enters the organization's pricing decision the same way as an increase in fixed costs—that is, not at all.

Alternatively, donors may care about the profits generated from sales. For example, in the pure-public-goods model, profits would partly crowd out donations (profits from nondonors would increase donor income, explaining why crowdout would not be total (Bilodeau, 2000)). This would operate like a pure profits tax to reduce nonprofit income from sales without affecting either the profit maximization rule or the profit-maximizing price. Alternatively, it could lead the nonprofit to charge a different price to donors (who would pay marginal costs) and nondonors (who would pay the profit maximizing price), particularly if commercial activities are taxed (Bilodeau, 2000). Finally, donors could care about price or quantity per se, and then the analysis would parallel that of multiproduct monopolies with demand-side interdependencies. Again, the rule for profit maximization is unchanged, but now the shape and location of the marginal revenue function would be altered so that the privately optimal price would change.

As noted earlier, the nondistribution constraint frees nonprofit organizations from the dictates of the market for control, and so it is reasonable to consider a range of activities, commercial or otherwise, for which the organizational goal is not profit maximization. Pricing can depart from the for-profit norm in a variety of ways, not all of which are socially beneficial as (Steinberg and Weisbrod, 1998, pp. 76–77) point out:

> Favoritism, nepotism, kickbacks, self-dealing, and other abusive power relationships can govern nonprofit allocation, particularly when allocation criteria require subjective judgments by the nonprofit employee. There is more scope for such abuse in the nonprofit sector because nonprofits are not subject to financially-motivated takeover bids that limit abuse among for-profits. On the other hand, insofar as nonprofit managers and board members are dedicated to the organizational social mission, this provides an internal check on abuse (Handy, 1995).

Usually, however, we suspect something better. Sliding scale fees and charitable provision to at least some clients may represent a concern for distributional equity (Steinberg and Weisbrod, 2002). Cross-subsidization may represent a desire to fix market failures (Eckel and Steinberg, 1993) or increase provision of a merit good or a good with positive externalities (Bilodeau and Steinberg, 1997). Tables 5 and 6, drawn from

Table 5
Nonprofit use of allocation mechanisms

Allocation mechanism	Examples	Hypotheses about nonprofit departures from profit-maximization
Price		
Uniform pricing		Nonprofits and for-profits use uniform prices identically for those outputs unrelated to the nonprofit mission (except disfavored activities)
Sliding-scale fees (interpersonal price discrimination)	Day care Mental health care Professional-society dues Net-of-financial-aid tuition	Nonprofits are more likely to price discriminate and to choose a lowest price that is below the marginal cost of serving their customers
Voluntary price discrimination (in that eligibility for particular prices cannot be verified by the seller)	Supporting-member dues Donations to arts organizations National Public Radio Volunteering	Nonprofits use extensively. The practice is not generally feasible for for-profits (except for cases where the volunteer can control, at least in part, who benefits from her contribution, as in for-profit day care)
Intertemporal price discrimination	Free-entrance days	Nonprofits are more likely to use this for those who will never be profitable to serve
Non-cash payments	Habitat For Humanity pricing (fees plus 'sweat equity')	Nonprofits may require partial payment in the form of labor or in-kind. For-profits stick to cash
Non-price		
Waiting lists	Day care Nursing homes Colleges and universities	Nonprofits are more likely to use waiting lists. For-profits are more likely to react to persistent excess demand by expanding capacity or increasing price
Eligibility requirements	University admissions ('merit') Fraternal societies Religious organizations Work-shelters for the disabled Food pantries	Nonprofits are more likely to: (1) Use requirements poorly or negatively correlated with willingness-to-pay (2) Restrict eligibility to those who cannot pay For-profits are more likely to: (1) Use requirements positively correlated with willingness-to-pay (2) Use eligibility requirements to establish a niche market

(*continued on next page*)

Table 5
(*Continued*)

Allocation mechanism	Examples	Hypotheses about nonprofit departures from profit-maximization
Externally-imposed eligibility requirements	To meet government contracting requirements To conform with tax and regulatory requirements	Nonprofits are more likely to construe requirements broadly for unprofitable clients and narrowly for profitable clients
Quality dilution and opportunistic quality sharing	Soup kitchens Homeless shelters Museums and zoos (congestion) Worker training	Nonprofits are more likely to hold excess capacity in order to avoid quality dilution For-profits are more likely to dilute quality in cases of contract failure
Product bundling	Museums Colleges and universities	Nonprofits are more likely to bundle 'merit goods' in pursuit of paternalistic objectives For-profits are more likely to bundle in pursuit of profit
Recruiting target populations	Hospital location School field-trips to museums	Nonprofits are more likely to target mission-related populations regardless of expected future profitability

Steinberg and Weisbrod (1998) summarize some conjectured nonprofit uses of allocation mechanisms and the effects of that use.

James (1983) presents a simple but very useful model of nonprofit cross-subsidization, in which some nonprofit outputs are "overpriced" in order to reduce the price of other outputs while remaining solvent. She considers a multiproduct nonprofit organization governed by a utility function that regards outputs as "favored," "neutral," or "disfavored" in that utility is increasing, unchanged, or decreasing in the respective quantities of outputs. For example, a university may regard faculty research and number of doctoral students as favored outputs, education of undergraduates as a neutral output, and executive education programs as a disfavored output. She distinguishes fixed from variable revenues associated with each activity by whether they vary with the scale of that activity. Thus, capital gains are fixed revenues, sales of goods and services variable revenues, and donations a mixture of the two. She then explores the comparative statics of cross-subsidization, concluding: (1) at the optimum, marginal revenue will exceed marginal costs for disfavored activities, equal marginal costs for neutral activities, and be less than marginal costs for favored activities. (2) An increase in fixed revenues or a decrease in fixed costs will have income effects, reducing disfavored activities and increasing favored ones. (3) An increase in the variable revenue function or decrease in the variable cost function associated with a favored activity will have both income and

Table 6
Effects of nonprofit distributional objectives

Effect of allocation mechanism	Hypotheses about differing effects of nonprofit and profit-maximizing behavior
Dividing total surplus	
Between consumers and producers	For-profits maximize producer surplus. Consumer surplus is provided only insofar as it enhances producer surplus. Nonprofits are more likely to expand consumer surplus at the expense of producer (or even total) surplus
Among consumers	For-profits do not care except insofar as the distribution of consumer surplus affects producer surplus. Nonprofits are more likely to consider fairness and distributional justice in the design of their allocation, cost-sharing, and pricing mechanisms
Allocating risks	For-profits bear risk only when there is a compensating increase in return. Nonprofits are more likely to bear the largest feasible share of risk, regardless of compensating financial returns, in order to insure that their clients are not harmed
Screening	For-profits use mechanisms designed to uncover those with highest ability and willingness to pay. Nonprofits are more likely to use mechanisms designed to uncover those with greatest 'need' (as in addictions treatment or child-abuse prevention), those who are most worthy (say, because they seem pious), or those with high willingness but not ability to pay For-profit mechanisms are also designed to deter those who would be most costly to serve (cream-skimming). Nonprofit mechanisms are less likely to deter high-cost clients. On the other hand, nonprofits are more likely to use exclusionary screens for non-cost reasons (for example, to deter those who are poorly motivated)
Providing a signal of trustworthiness	
To consumers and clients	Nonprofits are more likely to use waiting lists and highly-selective eligibility requirements to signal their quality. For-profits are more likely to use high prices to signal quality
To donors and grantmakers	Nonprofit use of fees depends upon the preferences of major funders regarding provision of seed money vs. operating support
Providing an incentive to economize on resource consumption	Nonprofits are less likely to use high prices and more likely to use non-price mechanisms to provide incentives for consumers to economize on the use of nonprofit outputs. Nonprofits will often use token fees to signal the importance of economizing

substitution effects that increase that activity. (4) An increase in the variable revenue or decrease in the variable cost function associated with a disfavored activity will have countervailing income and substitution effects so that the net impact on the scale of the disfavored activity is ambiguous. This model has been applied to the analysis of commercial activities unrelated to the charity's core mission (Schiff and Weisbrod, 1991, who regard commercial activities as disfavored or neutral) and to nonprofit savings behavior (Tuckman and Chang, 1992, who regard savings as a favored activity).

Kingma (1993) considers a nonprofit organization that "invests" in fundraising, grant-seeking, and commercial activities out of concern with both the return and the risk of these revenue sources. Drawing heavily from elementary finance, he concludes that the optimal nonprofit revenue "portfolio" depends upon the mean returns, variances, and covariances of the respective revenue sources.

Most existing empirical work attempts to estimate revenue interactions. For example, Jacobs and Wilder (1984) find that an increase in donations to Red Cross chapters results in a decrease in the price of blood products. Kingma (1995) finds that Red Cross health and safety training classes have large negative impacts on donations, and that an exogenous increase in donations appears to reduce commercial profits. Zhang (2000) finds that an increase in tuition and fees at research universities appears to cause an increase in donations. Others who examine interrelationships between commercial activities, government grants and contracts, and donations include Schiff and Weisbrod (1991), Wong et al. (1998), Segal and Weisbrod (1998), Payne (1998), Hughes and Luksetich (1999), Okten and Weisbrod (2000), Brooks (2000), and Payne (2001). Two papers by Weisbrod (1988, 1998) find that nonprofit nursing homes and facilities for the mentally handicapped are more likely to employ waiting lists than are corresponding for-profit facilities.

5.3. Labor

Nonprofit use of labor differs from that of for-profits for a variety of reasons, surveyed in Leete (2006). Four issues are particularly relevant for donative nonprofits. First, workers who value playing a role in public good provision will choose the nonprofit sector and will work for lower total compensation than similarly qualified workers in the for-profit sector (Hansmann, 1980; Handy and Katz, 1998). Note that it does not suffice for workers to care about the level of public goods, because those goods can be enjoyed whether or not they work for the nonprofit firm. Rather, they must enjoy playing a personal role in determining that those goods are provided. This personal role is played by, say, a nonprofit CEO but not by the janitorial staff. Thus, it is not surprising that empirical evidence is mixed about whether salaries at nonprofit organizations are lower, *ceteris paribus*, among line workers (e.g., Preston, 1989; Ruhm and Borkoski, 2000; Leete, 2001) but workers in key managerial positions in nonprofit hospitals do receive lower total compensation (base salary plus bonuses) (Roomkin and Weisbrod, 1999; Ballou and Weisbrod, 2003) and nonprofit managerial salaries are generally lower than those for comparable individuals employed in the for-profit sector (Preston, 1989; Frank, 1996), although Leete (2001) presents some contrary data.

Second, nonprofit labor demand may depend systematically upon different factors than for-profit labor demand. Freeman (1979) makes the not very convincing argument that nonprofit labor demand is more elastic than that of for-profit demanders because he assumes that nonprofits must have zero profits in each period. Others look at a preference for specific types of labor (e.g., the disabled) or to pay a living wage as part of the charitable mission (e.g., Feldstein, 1971). Finally, some assume that nonprofits are willing to pay a higher-than-market wage due to attenuated property rights (e.g., Borjas et al., 1983).

Third, nonprofits receive donations in the form of time (volunteering) and money. Why donations should come in this form is a bit of a puzzle. After all, there is no market matching mechanism, like there is in the paid labor market, to assure that volunteers are highly productive in their assigned tasks. Further, while monetary donations can be used to purchase productive labor, time donations cannot easily be converted into other, more productive inputs. (Schiff, 1990; Duncan, 1999). Thus, we have the puzzling situation in which doctors, lawyers, and other donors with high levels of education and wages volunteer to perform tasks that require skills similar to those of the organization's less-educated and lower-paid workers (Brown, 1999). Why do these people spend their time volunteering, instead of generating more income from their paid labor and donating some to the organization? The answer is that like monetary donations, time donations provide a variety of both private and public benefits to the volunteer.

Schiff (1990) draws five reasons for volunteering from the literature, developing models of each. First, as a form of donation, volunteering allows one to increment total provision of a public good. Second, as an active and participatory way of generating public goods, volunteering is a source of warm glow, in Andreoni's (Andreoni, 1989) terminology. Third, because time donations are on-site, they allow the donor to learn more about the quality and efficiency of the recipient organization, and hence better allocate his time and monetary donations in the future. Fourth, time donations allow one to develop and/or signal one's own human capital, and so are an investment for those new to the labor market or with interrupted market careers. Finally, time donations (particularly in the form of service on the nonprofit board or coaching your children's team) allow one to direct nonprofit outputs in preferred directions.

Volunteers are more willing to offer their services to nonprofits than for-profits (Wolff et al., 1993; Rose-Ackerman, 1996), but there is some volunteering for government agencies (chiefly schools) and even for-profit firms (chiefly nursing homes and hospitals or volunteering in the form of a limited-duration internship). This is perfectly consistent with the mixed public/private models of volunteering suggested by Schiff (1990) and others. Volunteers who seek to add to the provision of public goods restrict their time donations to organizations governed by the nondistribution constraint. Those motivated by private benefits are less concerned with the nonprofit status of the organization, and offer their services to any sector. Either of these motivations would also explain time donations to for-profit firms if the donor is performing tasks that the for-profit firm would otherwise not perform.

Volunteer labor supply is generated by models similar to the mixed public/private models used to rationalize donations of money, so that similar variables should be employed to explain both. At a minimum, it is desirable to estimate volunteer labor supply and monetary donations as jointly dependent on the wage rate (or other measure of the opportunity cost of time), tax variables (which affect the relative prices of the two forms of donating), and government spending on related public goods. This approach has been taken in the work of Schiff (1990), Brown and Lankford (1992), Day and Devlin (1996), and Andreoni et al. (1996). Some have gone even farther, suggesting that leisure demand (paid labor supply) should constitute an additional equation in the system, or that household paid and volunteer labor should be separately estimated for husband and wife (Segal, 1992; Carlin, 2001).

Some studies find positive relationships between earnings or wages and volunteering (Freeman, 1997; Day and Devlin, 1998; Wilson, 2000; Carlin, 2001), others find no relationship (Brown and Lankford, 1992) or the negative relationship predicted to stem from the opportunity cost of time (Menchik and Weisbrod, 1987; Andreoni et al., 1996). These disparate results likely reflect the multiplicity of motives, making results particularly sensitive to the characteristics of the population being sampled and the set of control variables (Leete, 2006, provides a more detailed and nuanced assessment of these studies; see also Govekar and Govekar, 2002).

The empirical relationship between time and money donations is especially interesting. Duncan (1999) develops the implications of assuming that the two are perfect substitutes. Under this assumption, other empirical studies are misspecified, and instead of estimating a system of equations, one should estimate an equation in which the dependent variable is total donations (money plus the monetary value of volunteering). He finds that one cannot reject the hypothesis (predicted by pure public good models) that crowding out is 100%. In contrast studies that estimate separate equations for time and money gifts generally find that the two are complements (Menchik and Weisbrod, 1987; Brown and Lankford, 1992; Carlin, 2001). This implies, for example, that some tax policies that encourage giving of money also encourage giving of time through cross-price effects.

Finally, although volunteer labor is freely offered, there are costs to the employing organization so that one would want to model volunteer labor demand as well as its supply. The costs of using volunteers include recruitment costs (analogous to fundraising costs), training costs, supervision costs, and the costs of goods and services used to retain experienced volunteers (plaques of appreciation, mileage reimbursement, conference fees). Volunteer labor demand would then depend inversely on these costs and positively or negatively with the wage rate for paid labor depending on whether paid and volunteer labor are substitutes or complements, respectively. A theoretical model consistent with these themes is presented in Smith and Steinberg (1990), but we have found no published estimates of the parameters of volunteer labor demand. Brudney and Duncombe (1992) calculate the effect of alternative assumptions on the optimal mixture of volunteer and paid labor in the firefighting industry. Emanuele (1997) presents indirect evidence in favor of a volunteer demand curve, finding that nonprofits who view paid and volunteer labor as substitutes (or complements) in 1982 continue to view them the same way in 1984.

5.4. Capital

The literature on nonprofit use of capital is small and divided on the question of whether there is too much capital or too little capital available to nonprofit organizations. Some papers worry that capital may get trapped in the nonprofit sector whatever its productivity elsewhere (e.g., Clotfelter, 1988–1989; Hansmann, 1989; Tuckman and Chang, 1993; Goodspeed and Kenyon, 1994); others worry about the high cost of capital to organizations that cannot issue economically-meaningful shares of stock (e.g., Hansmann, 1981b). We are aware of no literature at this time that treats the subject comprehensively, examining all the possible market failures that could lead to inefficient allocation of capital across the sectors or within the nonprofit sector.

Four sources of market failure have been claimed in various articles. First, the tax laws often treat nonprofit organizations differently from for-profit organizations. For example, each of the 11 countries surveyed by Weisbrod (1991) exempt nonprofit corporations from the corporate income tax or its equivalent for at least some of their activities. The incidence of the corporate income tax is controversial and varies according to the details of tax practice, but to the extent that the burden falls on capital, the cost of capital is made higher for taxable entities and lower for tax-exempts. This causes a misallocation of capital toward the nonprofit sector even when it would be more productively employed elsewhere. The problem is formally quite similar to that analyzed by Gravelle and Kotlikoff (1989), who look at the exemption of for-profit proprietorships and partnerships, but not corporations, from the corporate income tax.

Hansmann (1981b) argues that exemption of nonprofits from the corporate income tax is a crude corrective for the higher cost of capital nonprofits face because they are wholly debt-financed. However, he does not formally prove that the higher cost of capital for nonprofits is a market failure; it may be part of the efficient solution to contract failure. Goodspeed and Kenyon (1994) argue that nonprofits have several other advantages in acquiring capital (including access to tax-exempt bonds issued on their behalf and receipt of donations) and that tax exemption carries things too far. Steinberg (1991) argues, without any formal analysis, that the first-best solution would be to eliminate distortionary taxes on capital, and that if we must use a distortionary capital tax, the second-best solution may well be to exempt some capital from that tax despite the cross-sectoral distortions this would cause.

Second, donors place perpetual restrictions on their gifts, for example, requiring that the recipient institutions maintain the corpus of the gift and spend only dividends and interest. By itself, this may cause no restrictions on the organization's allocation of capital except in corner solutions, because the nonprofit board is free to create quasi-endowments (funds restricted by a reversible board decision, rather than a legal document) or to reduce its savings from other sources of revenue to maintain the desired level of capital. However, donor restrictions may also apply to the form in which the capital is held (for example, as a piece of artwork that must be maintained forever by the nonprofit) or to the uses to which the dividends and interest can be put (for example, to seek a cure for smallpox), and as conditions change following the death of the donor, these restrictions can cause inefficiency.[3] In common law countries, these restrictions can be eased under the legal doctrine of *cy pres*, but this requires costly and uncertain court action. Thus, we have the spectacle of the New-York Historical Society, with several billion dollars in assets and a much smaller annual budget but nonetheless near bankruptcy (Guthrie, 1996) because it can neither sell nor properly preserve the donated artifacts it so foolishly accepted. Legal scholars refer to the lasting control of donors long after the situation that prompted the restrictions have changed as the "dead hand." Economic scholars have not surrounded the concept with enough structure to determine whether such restrictions are *ex ante* efficient, although they are clearly inefficient *ex post*.

Third, the absence of property rights to financial residuals reduces the incentive to allocate capital efficiently within their organization and across time. Capital can be allocated to mission-related activities or managerial perquisites regardless of market rates of return. For example, Tuckman and Chang (1993) argue that nonprofit managers and board members derive particular satisfaction from accumulating wealth because it provides an objective measure of success that carries prestige among their social peers in business, unlike the fuzzy measures of accomplishment of the organization's mission. Hansmann et al. (2003) argue that nonprofits invest their surplus in overcapacity, and present evidence that nonprofit hospitals are less likely than for-profit hospitals to exit in times of declining demand. They suggest that this slowness of exit is evidence of inefficiency, but neither their model nor their empirical results suffice to establish this result.

Hansmann (1990) provides extensive evidence of large accumulations of capital in the higher education industry. For example, Harvard University's endowment and quasi-endowment totaled $4.2 billion in 1988, enough to pay the tuition for all its students in perpetuity. Interestingly, in this same year, Harvard obtained a $300 million bond issue, a peculiarity resulting from details of the tax law rather than irrational behavior. Hansmann analyzes the rules used by universities to decide how much they can spend from endowment each year, where the most liberal commonly-used rule allows them to spend an amount equal to the long-run average real rate of return. This rule, designed to perpetuate the value of the endowment, is too conservative for this purpose because universities expect additional donations to the corpus in the future. He develops an admittedly simple model of intertemporal efficiency, and shows that even if one spends the real rate of return plus the anticipated real rate of new donations, it is extremely hard to justify this rule on efficiency grounds.

Finally, Tuckman and Chang (1993) argue that the accumulation of capital may represent a form of contract failure, where donors who want their donations spent for current

[3] In an 1880 essay, Kenny (1880) argued "that whilst charity tends to do good, perpetual charities tend to do evil. Too often, misdirected by their Founder or misconducted by their administrators, they bless neither him that gives nor him that takes" (p. 3) and was saddened by "the inevitable tendency of endowed charities to be either neglected or perverted as time runs on. Hence it is utterly inexpedient to narrow their resources during their youth, for the purpose of augmenting their superfluities in their decrepitude." (p. 89).

purposes are misled. As an empirical matter, we suspect this market failure is unimportant, because donors are often willing to delegate the decision on timing of expenditure, donors have the right to attach legally-binding stipulations on how their contribution is to be spent, and if the marginal rate of return on investments available to the nonprofit exceeds that available to the donor (because of nonprofit tax exemption), the increase in value of eventual expenditures would more than compensate the donor for the discounted loss in utility.

Various countries regulate the accumulation of capital by nonprofit organizations. The U.S. requires "private foundations" to expend approximately 5% of the value of their capital each year, but does not regulate university endowments. Germany and Canada require all their nonprofits to make minimum annual expenditures. Serious analysis of these, and other proposed limitations on capital accumulation has just begun (Tuckman and Chang, 1993).

6. Conclusion

Nonprofit organizations do many things. In this chapter, we stress their role in facilitating the combination of donations necessary to finance a public good. We then show why someone would start such an organization, why it would be organized as a nonprofit-distributing corporation, and how the organization would behave subsequently. We have, at this time, the beginnings of a comprehensive theory of the role and functioning of donative nonprofit organizations. This is a new and burgeoning field and much research remains to be done before we can claim to fully understand donative nonprofit organizations.

References

AAFRC Trust for Philanthropy (2003). Giving USA 2003. Author, Indianapolis, IN.

Alchian, A., Demsetz, H. (1972). "Production, information costs, and economic organization". American Economic Review 62, 777–795.

Andreoni, J. (1989). "Giving with impure altruism: applications to charity and Ricardian equivalence". Journal of Political Economy 97, 1447–1458.

Andreoni, J. (1998). "Toward a theory of charitable fundraising". Journal of Political Economy 106, 1186–1213.

Andreoni, J. (2003). "Leadership giving in charitable fund-raising". Working paper available at http://www.ssc.wisc.edu/~andreoni/WorkingPapers.

Andreoni, J., Payne, A.A. (2003). "Do government grants to private charities crowd out giving or fundraising?". American Economic Review 93 (3), 792–812.

Andreoni, J., Gale, W., Scholz, J.K. (1996). "Charitable contributions of time and money". Working paper, University of Wisconsin Dept. of Economics, Madison, WI.

Arrow, K. (1974). The Limits of Organization. W.W. Norton and Co, New York.

Association of Fundraising Professionals (2001). "AFP code of ethical principles and standards of professional practice, statement of ethical principles", amended October 1999. Available through http://www.afpnet.org.

Australian Bureau of Statistics (2002). Non-Profit Institutions Satellite Account, Australian National Accounts, 1999–2000. Author, Canberra, AU.
Bac, M., Bag, P.K. (2003). "Strategic information revelation in fundraising". Journal of Public Economics 87, 659–679.
Ballou, J., Weisbrod, B.A. (2003). "Managerial rewards and the behavior of for-profit, governmental and nonprofit organizations: evidence from the hospital industry". Journal of Public Economics 87 (9–10), 1895–1920.
Ben-Ner, A. (1986). "Nonprofit organizations: why do they exist in market economies?". In: Rose-Ackerman, S. (Ed.), The Economics of Nonprofit Institutions: Studies in Structure and Policy. Oxford University Press, New York.
Ben-Ner, A., Jones, D. (1995). "Employee participation, ownership, and productivity: a theoretical framework". Industrial Relations 34 (4), 532–554.
Ben-Ner, A., Van Hoomissen, T. (1991). "Nonprofits in the mixed economy: a demand and supply analysis". Annals of Public and Cooperative Economics 62, 519–550.
Bergstrom, T., Blume, L., Varian, H. (1986). "On the private provision of public goods". Journal of Public Economics 29, 25–49.
Besley, T., Ghatak, M. (2001). "Government versus private ownership of public goods". Quarterly Journal of Economics 116 (4), 1343–1372.
Bilodeau, M. (1992). "Voluntary contributions to united charities". Journal of Public Economics 48, 119–133.
Bilodeau, M. (2000). "Profitable nonprofit firms". IUPUI Dept. of Economics Working Paper, Indianapolis, IN.
Bilodeau, M., Slivinski, A. (1996a). "Toilet cleaning and department chairing: volunteering a public service". Journal of Public Economics 59, 299–308.
Bilodeau, M., Slivinski, A. (1996b). "Volunteering nonprofit entrepreneurial services". Journal of Economic Behavior and Organization 31, 117–127.
Bilodeau, M., Slivinski, A. (1997). "Rival charities". Journal of Public Economics 66, 449–467.
Bilodeau, M., Slivinski, A. (1998). "Rational nonprofit entrepreneurship". Journal of Economics and Management Strategy 7, 551–571.
Bilodeau, M., Steinberg, R. (1997). "Ransom of the opera". IUPUI Department of Economics Working Paper, Indianapolis, IN.
Blair, R., Ginsburg, P.B., Vogel, R.J. (1975). "Blue cross–blue shield administration costs: a study of nonprofit health insurers". Economic Inquiry 13, 55–70.
Borjas, G.J., Frech III, H.E., Ginsburg, P.B. (1983). "Property rights and wages: the case of nursing homes". Journal of Human Resources 17, 231–246.
Boyle, S.E., Jacobs, P. (1978). "The economics of charitable fund raising". Philanthropy Monthly May, 21–27.
Boyle, S.E., Jacobs, P., Reingen, P. (1979). "How you can raise your fund raising productivity". National Society of Fund Raising Executives Journal IV (1), 4–6.
Brooks, A.C. (2000). "Is there a dark side to government support for nonprofits?". Public Administration Review 60, 211–218.
Brown, E. (1999). "Assessing the value of volunteer activity". Nonprofit and Voluntary Sector Quarterly 28, 3–17.
Brown, E., Lankford, R.H. (1992). "Gifts of money and gifts of time: estimating the effects of tax prices and available time". Journal of Public Economics 47, 321–341.
Brudney, J.L., Duncombe, W.D. (1992). "An economic evaluation of paid, volunteer, and mixed staffing options for public services". Public Administration Review 52, 474–481.
Carlin, P.S. (2001). "Evidence on the volunteer labor supply of married women". Southern Economic Journal 67, 801–824.
Carlton, D.W., Bamberger, G.E., Epstein, R.J. (1995). "Antitrust and higher education: was there a conspiracy to restrict financial aid?". The Rand Journal of Economics 26, 131–147.
Chang, C.F., Tuckman, H.P. (1990). "Why do nonprofit managers accumulate surpluses and how much do they accumulate?". Nonprofit Management and Leadership 1, 117–135.

Chillemi, O., Gui, B. (1991). "Uninformed customers and nonprofit organization: modelling 'contract failure' theory". Economics Letters 35, 5–8.

Clarkson, K. (1972). "Some implications of property rights in hospital management". Journal of Law and Economics 15, 363–385.

Clotfelter, C.T. (1988–1989). "Tax-induced distortions in the voluntary sector". Case Western Reserve Law Review 39, 663–704.

CNSP (2003). Johns Hopkins Comparative Nonprofit Sector Project, Phase II, 2003. Tables found on the web site www.jhu.edu/~cnp released April 15, 2003.

Coase, R.H. (1937). "The nature of the firm". Economica 4 (16), 386–405.

Day, K.M., Devlin, R.A. (1996). "Volunteerism and crowding out: Canadian econometric evidence". Canadian Journal of Economics 29 (1), 37–53.

Day, K.M., Devlin, R.A. (1998). "The payoff to work without pay: volunteer work as an investment in human capital". Canadian Journal of Economics 31, 1179–1191.

Duncan, B. (1999). "Modeling charitable contributions of time and money". Journal of Public Economics 72 (2), 213–242.

Easley, D., O'Hara, M. (1983). "The economic role of the nonprofit firm". Bell Journal of Economics 14, 531–538.

Eckel, C.C., Steinberg, R. (1991). "Cooperation meets collusion: antitrust and the nonprofit sector". IUPUI Department of Economics Working Paper, Indianapolis, IN.

Eckel, C.C., Steinberg, R. (1993). "Competition, performance, and public policy towards nonprofits". In: Hammack, D., Young, D. (Eds.), Nonprofit Organizations in a Market Economy. Jossey-Bass, Inc., San Francisco.

Ehrenberg, R., Cheslock, J., Epifantseva, J. (2000). "Paying our presidents: what do trustees value?". NBER Working Paper 7886, Cambridge, MA.

Emanuele (1997). "Volunteer and paid labor: substitutes in production?". In: ARNOVA Conference Proceedings. Association for Research on Nonprofit Organizations and Voluntary Action, Indianapolis, IN.

Feigenbaum, S. (1987). "Competition and performance in the nonprofit sector: the case of US medical research charities". The Journal of Industrial Economics 35 (3), 241–253.

Feldstein, M. (1971). "Hospital cost inflation: a study in nonprofit price dynamics". American Economic Review 61, 853–872.

Ferris, J.M., Graddy, E. (1995). Hospital industry dynamics and the nonprofit role in health care. Independent Sector Research Forum Working Papers. Independent Sector, Washington, DC.

Francois, P. (2001). "Employee care and the role of nonprofit organizations". Journal of Institutional and Theoretical Economics 157, 443–464.

Frank, R.G., Salkever, D.S., Mitchell, J. (1990). "Market forces and the public good: competition among hospitals and provision of indigent care". In: Scheffler, R., Rossiter, L. (Eds.), Advances in Health Economics and Health Services Research. JAI Press, Greenwich, CT, pp. 159–184.

Frank, R.H. (1996). "What price the high moral ground?". Southern Economic Journal 63 (1), 1–17.

Frech III, H.E. (1976). "The property rights theory of the firm: empirical results from a natural experiment". Journal of Political Economy 84, 143–152.

Frech III, H.E. (1980). "Health insurance: private, mutual, or government". In: Clarkson, K., Martin, D. (Eds.), The Economics of Nonproprietary Organizations. JAI Press, Greenwhich, CT.

Freeman, R.B. (1979). "The job market for college faculty". In: Lewis, D., Becker Jr., W. (Eds.), Academic Rewards in Higher Education. Ballinger, New York, pp. 63–103.

Freeman, R.B. (1997). "Working for nothing: the supply of volunteer labor". Journal of Labor Economics 15, S140–S166.

Gassler, R.S. (1989). "The economics of the nonprofit motive: a suggested formulation of objectives and constraints for firms and nonprofit enterprises". Vesalius College Working Paper, Vrije Universiteit Brussel, Brussels, Belgium.

Gassler, R.S. (1998). "The theory of political and social economics: beyond the neoclassical perspective". The Journal of Interdisciplinary Economics 9, 93–124.

Glazer, A., Konrad, K.A. (1996). "A signalling explanation for private charity". American Economic Review 86 (4), 1019–1028.
Glaeser, E., Schleifer, A. (2001). "Not-for-profit entrepreneurs". Journal of Public Economics 81, 99–116.
Goddeeris, J.H., Weisbrod, B.A. (1998). "Conversion from nonprofit to for-profit legal status: why does it happen and should anyone care?". In: Weisbrod, B.A. (Ed.), To Profit or Not To Profit: The Commercial Transformation of the Nonprofit Sector. Cambridge University Press, New York.
Goodspeed, T., Kenyon, D. (1994). "The nonprofit sector's capital constraint: does it provide a rationale for the tax-exemption granted to nonprofit firms?". Public Finance Quarterly, 22.
Govekar, P.L., Govekar, M.A. (2002). "Using economic theory and research to better understand volunteer behavior". Nonprofit Management and Leadership 13, 33–48.
Gravelle, J.G., Kotlikoff, L.J. (1989). "The incidence and efficiency costs of corporate taxation when corporate and noncorporate firms produce the same good". Journal of Political Economy 97, 749–780.
Greenlee, J., Gordon, T. (1998). "The impact of professional solicitors on fund raising in charitable organizations". Nonprofit and Voluntary Sector Quarterly 27 (3), 277–299.
Grønbjerg, K. (1993). Understanding Nonprofit Funding. Jossey-Bass, Inc., San Francisco.
Grønbjerg, K. (1994). "The NTEE: human service and regional applications". Voluntas 5, 301–328.
Gui, B. (1990). "Nonprofit organizations and product quality under asymmetric information", Dept. of Economics and Statistics Working Paper, Trieste University, Trieste, Italy.
Guthrie, K.M. (1996). The New-York Historical Society: Lessons from One Nonprofit's Long Struggle for Survival. Jossey-Bass, Inc., San Francisco.
Handy, F. (1995). "Reputation as collateral: an economic analysis of the role of trustees of nonprofits". Nonprofit and Voluntary Sector Quarterly 24 (4), 293–306.
Handy, F. (1997). "Co-existence of nonprofits, for-profits and public sector institutions". Annals of Public and Cooperative Economics 68, 201–224.
Handy, F. (2000). "How we beg: the analysis of direct mail appeals". Nonprofit and Voluntary Sector Quarterly 29 (3), 439–454.
Handy, F., Katz, E. (1998). "The wage differential between nonprofit institutions and corporations: getting more by paying less?". Journal of Comparative Economics 26, 246–261.
Hansmann, H. (1980). "The role of nonprofit enterprise". Yale Law Journal 89, 835–901.
Hansmann, H. (1981a). "Nonprofit enterprise in the performing arts". Bell Journal of Economics 12, 341–361.
Hansmann, H. (1981b). "The rationale for exempting nonprofit corporations from the corporate income tax". Yale Law Journal.
Hansmann, H. (1987). "Economic theories of nonprofit organization". In: Powell, W.W. (Ed.), The Nonprofit Sector: A Research Handbook. Yale University Press, New Haven, CT.
Hansmann, H. (1989). "Unfair competition and the unrelated business income tax". Virginia Law Review 75, 605–635.
Hansmann, H. (1990). "Why do universities have endowments?". Journal of Legal Studies 29, 3–42.
Hansmann, H., Kessler, D., McClellan, M. (2003). "Ownership form and trapped capital in the hospital business". In: Glaeser, E.L. (Ed.), The Governance of Not-for-Profit Firms. University of Chicago Press, Chicago. Chapter 1.
Harbaugh, W. (1998a). "What do donations buy? A model of philanthropy and tithing based on prestige and warm glow". Journal of Public Economics 67, 269–284.
Harbaugh, W. (1998b). "The prestige motive for making charitable transfers". American Economic Review 88, 277–282.
Hirth, R.A. (1999). "Consumer information and competition between nonprofit and for-profit nursing homes". Journal of Health Economics 18, 219–240.
Holtmann, A.G. (1983). "A theory of non-profit firms". Economica 50, 439–449.
Hughes, P.N., Luksetich, W.A. (1999). "The relationship among funding sources for art and history museums". Nonprofit Management and Leadership 10, 21–38.
Jacobs, P., Lee, R.Y. (1979). "Public broadcasting fund raising". Philanthropy Monthly September, 20–23.
Jacobs, P., Wilder, R.P. (1984). "Pricing behavior of non-profit agencies: the case of blood products". Journal of Health Economics 3, 49–61.

James, E. (1983). "How nonprofits grow: a model". Journal of Policy Analysis and Management 2, 350–366.

Kaplan, G.E. (1999). "The non-distribution constraint: fact or fiction in higher education?". Paper presented at the 28th annual ARNOVA (Association for Research on Nonprofit Organizations and Voluntary Action) Conference, Arlington, VA.

Kelley, K.S. (1997). "From motivation to mutual understanding: shifting the domain of donor research". In: Burlingame, D. (Ed.), Critical Issues in Fundraising. Wiley, New York.

Kenny, C.S. (1880). The True Principles of Legislation with Regard to Property Given for Charitable or Other Public Causes.

Khanna, J., Sandler, T. (2000). "Partners in giving: the crowding-in effects of UK government grants". European Economic Review 44, 1543–1556.

Khanna, J., Posnett, J., Sandler, T. (1995). "Charity donations in the UK: new evidence based on panel data". Journal of Public Economics 56, 257–272.

Kingma, B.R. (1993). "Portfolio theory and nonprofit financial stability". Nonprofit and Voluntary Sector Quarterly 22, 105–120.

Kingma, B.R. (1995). "Do profits "crowd out" donations, or vice versa? The impact of revenues from sales on donations to local chapters of the American Red Cross". Nonprofit Management and Leadership 6, 21–38.

Koebel, C.T., Dyck, R., Steinberg, R. (1998). "Public-private partnerships for affordable housing: definitions and applications in an international perspective". In: Koebel, C.T. (Ed.), Shelter and Society: Theory, Research, and Policy for Nonprofit Housing. SUNY Press, Albany, pp. 39–70.

Krashinsky, M. (1986). "Transactions costs and a theory of the nonprofit organization". In: Rose-Ackerman, S. (Ed.), The Economics of Nonprofit Institutions. Yale University Press, New Haven, pp. 114–132.

Lakdawalla, D., Philipson, T. (1998). "Nonprofit production and competition". NBER Working Paper 6377, Cambridge, MA.

Leete, L. (2001). "Whither the nonprofit wage differential? Estimates from the 1990 census". Journal of Labor Economics 19 (1).

Leete, L. (2006). "The nonprofit labor force". In: Powell, W.W., Steinberg, R. (Eds.), The Nonprofit Sector: A Research Handbook. 2nd edn. Yale University Press, New Haven. In press.

Legoretta, J.M., Young, D.R. (1986). "Why organizations turn nonprofit: lessons from case studies". In: Rose-Ackerman, S. (Ed.), The Economics of Nonprofit Institutions: Studies in Structure and Policy. Oxford University Press, New York.

Luksetich, W., Jacobs, P., Lange, M. (1986). "Productivity in museum fund raising: an economic analysis". Philanthropy Monthly, 20–23.

Menchik, P., Weisbrod, B. (1987). "Volunteer labor supply". Journal of Public Economics 32, 159–183.

Morelli, M., Vesterlund, L. (2000). "Provision point mechanism: a case of over provision of public goods", Working Paper, Dept. of Economics, Iowa State University, Ames, Iowa.

Mueller, M.W. (1975). "Economic determinants of volunteer work by women". SIGNS: Journal of Women and Culture in Society 1, 325–338.

Okten, C., Weisbrod, B. (2000). "Determinants of donations in private nonprofit markets". Journal of Public Economics 75, 255–272.

Oster, Sh.M. (1996). "Nonprofit organizations and their local affiliates: a study in organizational forms". Journal of Economic Behavior and Organization 30 (1), 83–95.

Oster, Sh. (1998). "Executive compensation in the nonprofit sector". Nonprofit Management and Leadership 8 (3), 207–222.

Ostrower, F., Stone, M.M. (2006). "Governance: research trends, gaps, and future prospects". In: Powell, W.W., Steinberg, R. (Eds.), The Nonprofit Sector: A Research Handbook. 2nd edn. Yale University Press, New Haven. In press.

Payne, A.A. (1998). "Does the government crowd-out private donations? New evidence from a sample of non-profit firms". Journal of Public Economics 69, 323–345.

Payne, A.A. (2001). "Measuring the effect of federal research funding on private donations at research universities: is federal research funding more than a substitute for private donations?". International Tax and Public Finance 8 (5–6), 731–751.

Payton, R.L. (1988). Philanthropy: Voluntary Action for the Public Good. American Council on Education/Macmillan Publishing Co, New York.
Posnett, J., Sandler, T. (1986). "Joint supply and the finance of charitable activity". Public Finance Quarterly 14 (2), 209–222.
Posnett, J., Sandler, T. (1988). "Transfers, transaction costs and charitable intermediaries". International Review of Law and Economics 8, 145–160.
Posnett, J., Sandler, T. (1989). "Demand for charity donations in private non-profit markets: the case of the U.K.". Journal of Public Economics 40, 187–200.
Preston, A.E. (1988). "The nonprofit firm: a potential solution to inherent market failures". Economic Inquiry 26, 493–506.
Preston, A.E. (1989). "The nonprofit worker in a for-profit world". Journal of Labor Economics 7, 438–463.
Preston, A.E. (1992). "Entrepreneurial self-selection into the nonprofit sector: effects on motivations and efficiency". W. Averell Harriman School for Management and Policy Working Paper, SUNY at Stony Brook, Stony Brook, NY.
Rawls, J.R., Ullrich, R., Nelson Jr., O. (1975). "A comparison of managers entering or reentering the profit and nonprofit sectors". Academy of Mangement Journal 18, 616–623.
Romano, R., Yildirim, H. (2001). "Why charities announce donations: a positive perspective". Journal of Public Economics 81, 423–447.
Roomkin, M., Weisbrod, B. (1999). "Managerial compensation in incentives in for-profit and nonprofit hospitals". Journal of Law, Economics and Organizations 15 (3), 750–781.
Rose-Ackerman, S. (1980). "United charities: an economic analysis". Public Policy 28, 323–348.
Rose-Ackerman, S. (1981). "Do government grants to charity reduce private donations?". In: White, M. (Ed.), Nonprofit Firms in a Three-Sector Economy. The Urban Institute, Washingon, DC.
Rose-Ackerman, S. (1982). "Charitable giving and "excessive" fundraising". Quarterly Journal of Economics 97, 195–212.
Rose-Ackerman, S. (1987). "Ideals versus dollars: donors, charity managers, and government grants". Journal of Political Economy 95, 810–823.
Rose-Ackerman, S. (1996). "Altruism, nonprofits, and economic theory". Journal of Economic Literature, 36.
Ruhm, Ch.J., Borkoski, C. (2000). "Compensation in the nonprofit sector", National Bureau of Economic Research Working Paper 7562, Cambridge, MA.
Salamon, L., Anheier, H.K. (1992). "In search of the nonprofit sector: the question of definitions". Voluntas 3, 125–152.
Salamon, L.M., Anheier, H.K., Sokolowski, W., Associates (1996). The Emerging Sector: A Statistical Supplement (1990 data). Center for Civil Society Studies, Johns Hopkins Institute for Policy Studies, Baltimore.
Salamon, L.M., Anheier, H.K., List, R., Toepler, S., Sokolowski, S.W., Associates (1999). Global Civil Society: Dimensions of the Nonprofit Sector. Center for Civil Society Studies, Johns Hopkins Institute for Policy Studies, Baltimore.
Sansing, R.C. (2000). "Joint ventures between non-profit and for-profit organizations". Journal of the American Taxation Association 22, 76–88.
Sargeant, A., Kähler, J. (1999). "Returns on fundraising expenditures in the voluntary sector". Nonprofit Management and Leadership 10, 5–20.
Schiff, J. (1986). "Expansion, entry and exit in the nonprofit sector: the long and the short run of it", Program on Nonprofit Organizations, Working Paper no. 111, Yale U.
Schiff, J. (1990). Charitable Giving and Government Policy: An Economic Analysis. Greenwood Press, Inc., Westport, CT.
Schiff, J., Weisbrod, B. (1991). "Competition between for-profit and nonprofit organizations in commercial markets". Annals of Public and Cooperative Economics 62 (4), 619–640.
Schlesinger, M. (1985). "Economic models of nonprofit organizations: a reappraisal of the property rights approach", Working Paper, JFK School, Harvard U.
Schlesinger, M., Dorwart, R.A., Hoover, C., Epstein, S. (1997). "Competition and access to hospital services: evidence from psychiatric hospitals". Medical Care 35 (9), 974–992.

Schlesinger, M., Gray, B. (2006). "Health care: burgeoning research, shifting expectations and persisting puzzles". In: Powell, W.W., Steinberg, R. (Eds.), The Nonprofit Sector: A Research Handbook. 2nd edn. Yale University Press, New Haven. In press.

Segal, L.M. (1992). "Volunteering family style", Paper presented at the 1992 annual conference of the Association for Research on Nonprofit Organizations and Voluntary Action.

Segal, L.M., Weisbrod, B.A. (1998). "Interdependence of commercial and donative revenues". In: Weisbrod, B.A. (Ed.), To Profit or Not To Profit: The Commercial Transformation of the Nonprofit Sector. Cambridge University Press, New York.

Slivinski, A. (2002). "Team incentives and organizational form". Journal of Public Economic Theory 4 (2), 185–206.

Slivinski, A., Steinberg, R. (1998). "Soliciting the warm glow: an economic model of fundraising", Working Paper, Dept. of Economics, University of Western Ontario, London, CA.

Smith, D.H. (1997). "The rest of the nonprofit sector: grassroots associations as the dark matter ignored in prevailing "flat earth" maps of the sector". Nonprofit and Voluntary Sector Quarterly 26, 114–131.

Smith, S.R., Lipsky, M. (1993). Nonprofits for Hire: The Welfare State in the Age of Contracting. Harvard University Press, Cambridge, MA.

Smith III, W.T., Steinberg, R. (1990). "The minimum wage and volunteering", Working Paper.

Spiegel, M. (1995). "Charity without altruism". Economic Inquiry 33, 625–639.

Steinberg, R. (1983). "Economic and empiric analysis of fund raising behavior by nonprofit firms", PONPO Working Paper No. 76, Program on Nonprofit Organizations, Yale University, New Haven.

Steinberg, R. (1985). "Optimal funds raising by nonprofit firms". In: Hodgkinson, V., Sumariwalla, R. (Eds.), Giving and Volunteering: New Frontiers of Knowledge. Independent Sector and United Way of America, Washington, DC.

Steinberg, R. (1986a). "Should donors care about fund raising?". In: Rose-Ackerman, S. (Ed.), The Economics of Nonprofit Institutions: Studies in Structure and Policy. Oxford University Press, New York.

Steinberg, R. (1986b). "The revealed objective functions of nonprofit firms". Rand Journal of Economics 17 (4), 508–526.

Steinberg, R. (1986c). "Optimal contracts need not be contingent: the case of nonprofit firms". In: Hyman, D., Parkum, K. (Eds.), Models of Health and Human Services in the Nonprofit Sector. Association of Voluntary Action Scholars, Harrisburg, PA.

Steinberg, R. (1987). "Nonprofits and the market". In: Powell, W.W. (Ed.), The Nonprofit Sector: A Research Handbook. Yale University Press, New Haven.

Steinberg, R. (1990). "Profits and incentive compensation in nonprofit firms". In: Nonprofit Management and Leadership, vol. 1, pp. 137–151.

Steinberg, R. (1991). ""Unfair" competition by nonprofits and tax policy". National Tax Journal 44, 351–364.

Steinberg, R. (1993a). "Public policy and the performance of nonprofit organizations: a general framework". Nonprofit and Voluntary Sector Quarterly 22 (1), 13–32.

Steinberg, R. (1993b). "How should antitrust laws apply to nonprofit organizations?". In: Young, D.R., Hollister, R.M., Hodgkinson, V.A., Associates (Eds.), Governing, Leading, and Managing Nonprofit Organizations. Jossey-Bass, Inc., San Francisco, pp. 279–305.

Steinberg, R. (1997). "Competition in contracted markets". In: Perri, Kendall, J. (Eds.), The Contract Culture in Public Services. Ashgate Publishing Co., Brookfield, VT, pp. 161–180.

Steinberg, R., Eckel, C.C. (1994). "Tax policy and the objectives of nonprofit organizations in a mixed-sector duopoly". Indiana University Center on Philanthropy Working Paper, Indianapolis, IN.

Steinberg, R., Weisbrod, B.A. (1998). "Pricing and rationing by nonprofit organizations with distributional objectives". In: Weisbrod, B.A. (Ed.), To Profit or Not to Profit: The Commercial Transformation of the Nonprofit Sector. Cambridge University Press, New York, pp. 65–82.

Steinberg, R., Weisbrod, B. (2002). "Give it away or make them pay? Price discrimination by nonprofit organizations with distributional objectives", IUPUI Dept. of Economics Working Paper, Indianapolis, IN.

Straub, J. (2000). "Fundraising and government crowd-out of private donations to public radio: an empirical study", Working Paper, Texas A&M University.

Thompson, E.A. (1980). "Charity and nonprofit organizations". In: Clarkson, K., Martin, D. (Eds.), The Economics of Non-Proprietary Organizations. JAI Press, Greenwich, CT, pp. 125–138.
Tuckman, H.P., Chang, C.F. (1992). "Nonprofit equity: a behavioral model and its policy implications". Journal of Policy Analysis and Management 11 (1), 76–87.
Tuckman, H.P., Chang, C.F. (1993). "Accumulating financial surpluses in nonprofit organizations". In: Young, D.R., Hollister, R.M., Hodgkinson, V.A., Associates (Eds.), Governing, Leading, and Managing Nonprofit Organizations: New Insights from Research and Practice. Jossey-Bass, San Francisco, pp. 253–278.
Tullock, G. (1966). "Information without profit". Papers on Non-Market Decision Making 1, 141–159.
Varian, H. (1994). "Sequential contributions to public goods". Journal of Public Economics 53, 165–183.
Vesterlund, L. (2003). "The informational value of sequential fundraising". Journal of Public Economics 87, 627–657.
Wedig, G. (1994). "Risk, leverage, donations and dividends-in-kind: a theory of nonprofit financial behavior". International Review of Economics and Finance 3, 257–278.
Weinberg, Ch.B. (1980). "Marketing mix decision rules for nonprofit organizations". Research in Marketing 3, 191–234.
Weisbrod, B. (1975). "Toward a theory of the voluntary nonprofit sector in a three-sector economy". In: Phelps, E.S. (Ed.), Altruism, Morality, and Economic Theory. Russell Sage Foundation, New York.
Weisbrod, B. (1988). The Nonprofit Economy. Harvard University Press, Cambridge, MA.
Weisbrod, B. (1991). "Tax policy toward nonprofit organizations: an eleven-country survey". (With the assistance of Elizabeth Mausser.) Voluntas 2, 3–25.
Weisbrod, B. (1998). "Institutional form and organizational behavior". In: Powell, W., Clemens, E. (Eds.), Private Action and the Public Good. Yale University Press, New Haven.
Weisbrod, B., Dominguez, N. (1986). "Demand for collective goods in private nonprofit markets: can fund raising expenditures help overcome free-rider behavior?". Journal of Public Economics 30, 83–95.
Wilson, J. (2000). "Volunteering". Annual Review of Sociology 26, 215–240.
Wolff, N., Schlesinger, M. (1998). "Ownership, competition and access to health care". Nonprofit and Voluntary Sector Quarterly 27 (2), 203–236.
Wolff, N., Weisbrod, B., Bird, E. (1993). "The supply of volunteer labor: the case of hospitals". Nonprofit Management and Leadership 4 (1), 23–46.
Wong, Ch.M., Chua, V.C.H., Vasoo, S. (1998). "Contributions to charitable organizations in a developing country: the case of Singapore". International Journal of Social Economics 25, 25–42.
Wright, J., Rotz, J.H. (1992). "Reasonable compensation", The Tax Exempt Organizations IRS Technical Training Program Manual, Calendar 1992, Fiscal 1993.
Yildirim, E. (2000). "Financing universities in Turkey". Unpublished term paper, available from the authors of this chapter.
Young, D.R. (1983). If Not For Profit, For What?. Lexington Books, Lexington, MA.
Young, D.R. (1989). "Local autonomy in a franchise age: structural change in national voluntary associations". Nonprofit and Voluntary Sector Quarterly 18, 101–117.
Zhang, Ch.Z. (2000). "How does government funding affect private donations to research universities". Unpublished M.A. thesis in Economics, IUPUI.

Chapter 20

THE ECONOMICS OF ORGAN TRANSPLANTATION

EMANUEL D. THORNE

Department of Economics, Brooklyn College of the City University of New York, Brooklyn, NY 11210, USA
e-mail: ethorne@brooklyn.cuny.edu

Contents

Handbook of the Economics of Giving, Altruism and Reciprocity, Volume 2
Edited by Serge-Christophe Kolm and Jean Mercier Ythier

DOI: 10.1016/S1574-0714(06)02020-3

Abstract

In the U.S. and Europe, a ban on a market in human organs has been in place since 1984. The system of organ procurement, therefore, relies on altruistic donation from stranger to stranger. The principle intellectual and policy issues surrounding organ procurement concern the question of whether, in banning the market to further ethical objectives, efficiency must inevitably be sacrificed. In the 1970s, Titmuss questioned whether a market could supply high quality blood in sufficient quantity, and this issue attracted the attention of some of the best minds in economics, such as Arrow and Solow. Since then, a large-scale industry relying on human tissue as a basic resource has emerged. In 2000, nearly 50 000 organs were transplanted. Remarkably, all of them were procured without providing financial incentives to suppliers. Despite the large number of donations, many more are needed. Today, more than 95 000 people are waiting for kidneys alone, and it is estimated that, in 2001, over 6000 Americans died waiting for an organ. Many believe that a market in organs would yield a greater supply and they hold the policy of banning an organ market responsible for the current tragic shortages. This chapter reviews the economic theory and evidence regarding market bans and considers them in the context of organ procurement.

Keywords

market-inalienability, organ transplants, organ procurement, altruism, common-property

JEL classification: D23, D64, H42, I18

1. Introduction

Jeremy Bentham (1831), in an essay entitled "Of What Use is a Dead Man to the Living?," argued in favor of legalizing autopsies because of the usefulness of human bodies to research. Indeed, Bentham invited his friends to observe the dissection of his own body upon his death. He thought, moreover, that men of exceptional quality could by their very presence inspire future generations of thinkers. In that spirit, each year since Bentham's death in 1832, the trustees of University College London have brought out his preserved body during their annual deliberations.

Were he alive today, Bentham would find that modern advances in biotechnology have made human beings—living and dead—useful to each other in ways he probably never imagined. Transplants of human hearts, livers, kidneys, blood, corneas, skin and bones are now commonplace, and new uses for human body parts are proposed almost daily. If therapies based on transplants of fetal tissue or stem cells prove successful in treating such diseases as Parkinson's, diabetes, and Alzheimer's, then several million more could benefit. Beyond these developments in transplantation is the increasing use by biotechnology companies of human tissue to develop commercial products. In short, it is fair to say, a large-scale production system involving physicians, hospitals, and pharmaceutical companies is emerging, and this industry relies on human tissue as a basic resource.

Aside from blood, of which more that 12 million units are collected annually in the U.S. for transfusion, the use of human organs for transplantation is most advanced. In 2000 alone, in North America, Europe and Australia, 41 974 organs from 14 178 dead individuals were transplanted; an additional 8025 kidneys were transplanted from living persons (see Table 1). At an estimated average cost of $200 000 per transplant, the cost of these transplantation procedures can be estimated roughly to amount to nearly $10 billion per year.

The entire transplant industry of physicians, hospitals, pharmaceutical companies rests on the supply organs. Remarkably, the nearly 50 000 organs transplanted in 2000 were procured without financial incentives to suppliers, as payment for organs was outlawed in the U.S. in 1984 and in Europe shortly thereafter.[1]

The major intellectual and policy issues surrounding organ procurement center on the ban on markets in organs. At the deepest level, the debate about organ markets is a manifestation of the larger debate concerning the appropriate domain of the market—a debate over the competing values of freedom, human rights and the commodification of human beings, economic justice, and, of course, efficiency in the alleviation of human suffering. Economists have joined this debate by examining possible market failures in organ markets.

At a policy level, many of those opposed to a market fear that a market would lead to exploitation of the poor, perhaps even to people being hijacked, and their organs forcibly

[1] The U.S. enacted the National Organ Transplant Act in 1984 which banned sales of human organs. Sales of other tissues such as blood was not banned.

Table 1
Organ donation in 1999–2000

Country	1999			2000					
	Population (millions)	Cadaveric donors		Cadaveric donors		Kidneys			Total organs
		Number	Per mill	Number	Per mil	Cadaveric	Living	Wait list	
Austria	8.1	202	25.0	191	23.6	362	52	715	685
Bel&Lux	10.5	241	23.0	229	21.8	452	13	819	821
Croatia	4.7	23	4.9	32	6.8	61	7	802	97
Czech.R	10.3	164	15.9	172	16.7	310	18	742	465
Denmark	5.4	76	14.2	70	13.1	121	41	525	254
Estonia	1.5	8	5.3	14	9.3	30	1	35	32
Finland	5.2	85	16.5	88	17.1	165	3	268	226
France	59.9	970	16.2	1066	17.8	1921	101	5124	3365
Germany	82.1	1039	12.7	1073	13.1	1964	382	9547	3867
Greece	10.0	45	4.5	32	3.2	74	89	1125	186
Hungary	10.3	119	11.6	137	13.3	259	9	1024	303
Italy	57.6	788	13.7	988	17.1	1447	99	7597	2782
Malta				6		11	0		15
Netherlands	16.0	165	10.3	187	11.7	337	163	1281	697
Norway	4.4	69	15.5	65	14.6	125	86	160	304
Poland	38.5	314	8.1	450	11.7	843	36	1531	1129
Portugal	10.0	190	19.1	202	20.3	359	6		571
Romania	22.1			21	1.0	40	126	1188	181
Spain	39.7	1334	33.6	1335	33.7	1893	31	4014	3422
Sweden	8.9	108	12.1	108	12.1	188	119	560	461
Switzerland	7.0	101	14.4	95	13.6	156	79	429	399
Turkey	65.0	60	0.9	89	1.4	162	329		625
UK+Ireland	62.9	816	13.0	847	13.5	1448	347		2894
U.S.A.	255.0	5788	22.7	6081	23.8	8859	5293	52 216	23 608
Canada	30.5	430	14.1	420	13.8	661	397	3014	1800
Australia	19.0	164	8.6	180	9.5	328	198	1595	810
Total	844.4	13 299	15.7	14 178	16.8	22 576	8025	94 311	49 999

Source: Spanish Transplant Society (ONT), http://www.msc.es/ont/ing/data/lastdata.htm

taken to supply the market. This fear has, so far, not been borne out. However, despite the large number of organs procured from donation, many who need organ transplants are nonetheless unable to get them because the supply of donated organs is not sufficient. Indeed as shown in Table 1, in 2000, more than 95 000 people were on waiting lists for kidneys alone. With regard to the U.S., the United Network for Organ Sharing (2002) estimated that, in 2001, more than 6000 Americans died while waiting for an organ. The desperate need for lifesaving transplants has spurred worrisome developments. To illustrate:

- Increasingly, kidneys are being procured from living donors, putting those donors at risk to their health to the point of death;[2]
- The practice of "organ swapping" is gaining adherents;[3]
- Proposals to enlarge the definition of death are under consideration;[4]
- Some fear that death might be hastened to make needed organs available;[5]
- It has been alleged that in China prisoners are being executed for their organs;[6]
- Black markets and organ trafficking have been documented.[7]

In the debate among economists over the market ban, many angles have been articulated. First, arguing from ethics and political philosophy, many economists have opposed restrictions on organ markets citing reasons of personal liberty and efficiency (see e.g., Epstein, 1994). Second, economists have long debated the efficiency of relying on altruism; this debate has been especially pointed in the context of human blood and organs. Third, still others have tried to justify restrictions on alienability in cases of market failure, which has led to a hunt for efficiency-related reasons to ban a market in human organs. This search for efficiency-based reasons to justify the ban on a market in human organs has preoccupied some of our finest economists. Although a case can be made that a market would encourage murder (a major market failure), as we will see, the search for more conventional types of market failure has, by and large, not succeeded.

Fourth, if there is no inefficiency to markets in human organs, what happens when markets are banned? Are we doomed to inefficiency? How much inefficiency does our ethics cause us? To get at those questions we must base our model of altruistic supply

[2] A recent significant study by Goyal et al. (2002) reported that 96 percent of suppliers of living kidneys in India "reported a deterioration in their health status after nephrectomy," (page 1589).

[3] See, for example, Okie (2001) and Menikoff (1999).

[4] See Childress (1993) and Kennedy Institute of Ethics [Entire] (1993) for a thoughtful discussion of the definition of death.

[5] See Weiss (1997) for a description of the dilemmas facing hospitals and organs procurers as they try to increase the supply of organs by maintaining the viability of the donor without hastening the donor's death.

[6] See, for example, Smith (2001) who reports that "a former Chinese Army doctor told a United States Congressional committee this week that he had helped harvest organs from executed prisoners and had even removed skin from a man who had not yet died."

[7] See Sipress (2001) who reports that "the Bush administration has criticized some of America's closest allies, including Israel, Saudi Arabia and South Korea, for failing to make a serious attempt to prevent trafficking of women and children for prostitution and other forms of forced labor". See also Rothman (1998) and Scheper-Hughes (1990, 1996, 1998).

of organs on a close examination of how the non-market system of procuring human organs works. Fifth, while the debate over an organ market has been heated, it has been largely theoretical. What empirical evidence can we bring to bear on the question of how to increase supply? Sixth, what can economics offer to further ethical objectives? Seventh, given the interdependent globalized world we live in today, how will trade in human organs evolve among countries whose values are different? And what role is there for the creation of international public goods by means of international regulation?

The chief aim of this chapter is to review the economic theory and evidence regarding market bans as it pertains to human organs whose supply society wishes to encourage. Section 2 discusses the controversy over justifications for the market ban, and, in particular, looks at the search for market failures. For those who find no market failure, or for whom any market failure is not a sufficient basis for a market ban, the argument that market bans reduce supply is compelling. Sections 3 and 4 evaluate this claim by examining two theoretical economic models of a ban on a market in organs. Section 3 presents the conventional model that implies that a market ban must, of necessity, cause a reduction in supply. Section 4 presents a model that shows, surprisingly, that, as a theoretical matter, the supply of donated organs might exceed market supply and argues that further empirical work is needed to settle the question.

The appropriate question for economists may be not whether to ban markets, but rather, how economics might help if, for non-economic ethical reasons, a society desires to ban a market. Are there ways to understand market bans that might improve their functioning? This is the subject of section 5, where I review the facts of the non-market organ procurement system.

Finally, in section 6, after some concluding remarks about the implications of all this for understanding production in a non-market setting, I will make a few remarks about the future, especially the increasing globalization of human tissue, and the harmonization of regulatory schemes. This raises questions concerning races to the bottom, desirable and undesirable trade, and whether markets overseas crowd out domestic donated supply.

2. Why is there a ban on an organ market?

Societies have long regulated many ethically questionable activities by banning markets. Today, the United States bans markets in elephant tusks, endangered species, slaves, human organs, babies, sex, forms of child labor, and certain hazardous activities. But whereas some market bans—such as those covering elephant tusks and endangered species—were enacted to prohibit trade altogether, the bans on markets in children, sexual favors, and human organs are characterized by a desire that supply flourish, but strictly on a donative, noncommercial basis. Because the human organ transplantation industry is of large scale, the procurement of donated organs serves as an excellent case-study of the effect of banning a market, and the discussion worked out in terms of the organ transplantation industry in the following pages is applicable to a larger domain of ethically problematic activities that society regulates by banning markets.[8]

What thinking underlies the ban on a market in organs, and other markets more generally? One line of thought focuses on the question of whether altruism or concern for others exist, and if such phenomena exist, whether relying on the altruistic motive is more or less efficient than relying on self-interest. Section 2.1 will discuss these issues as they have played out in the realm of blood and organ markets. The other basis for banning markets in blood and organs is market failure, and section 2.2 reviews the attempts to find such a market failure.

The proper domain of the market is, of course, of great and longstanding concern to economists. Some economists have opposed all restrictions on alienability, citing reasons of personal liberty and efficiency (see Epstein, 1985; Landes and Posner, 1978). Others have agreed to some restrictions on markets on the non-consequentialist grounds that people have a "right not to act out of desperation" (Okun, 1975, p. 19)). Still others justify restrictions on alienability in cases of market failure (see Calabresi and Melamed, 1972; Rose-Ackerman, 1985).[9]

What economists agree on nearly universally is that the ban on an organ market must necessarily cause shortages and other inefficiencies (see Kessel, 1974; Epstein, 1994; Pindyck and Rubinfeld, 1989; Barney and Reynolds, 1989; Kaserman and Barnett, 1991, 2002).

2.1. *The efficiency of relying on altruism*

The role and efficiency of self-interest and altruism that have been of long interest to economists are well discussed in this volume in the papers by Kolm and Bardsley and Sugden. The issue of defining altruism and the questions that follow such as, does altruism exist, how to model altruism in a utility framework, is utility commensurable or is it a vector, is altruism rational only in non utility frameworks, all have relevance to assessing the wisdom of the ban on markets in organs.

Two additions to the vast literature on the efficiency of self-interest and altruism are Collard's (Collard, 1978) *Altruism and Economy: A Study in Non-selfish Economics* and Hamish's (Hamish, 1992) *Rationality and the Market for Human Blood*. Each of these authors offers a theoretical model that demonstrates that it might be better to rely on voluntary donation than on the market to obtain whole blood.[10] And of course, there is the work of economists who continue to argue the inefficiency of gift-giving.[11]

[8] Following Radin (1987), I will characterize goods to which individuals have all property rights except the right to alienate through sale "market-inalienable."

[9] Kanbur (2001) tries to understand why some markets evoke such "popular, discomfort and even outrage" that society bans them.

[10] See also Frey (1997) and Frey and Oberholzer-Gee (1997).

[11] See, for example, Waldfogel (1993) who found that gift giving is welfare-reducing and Solnick and Hemenway (1996) who found that it is welfare improving. Also Kaserman and Barnett (2002) who argue strenuously for the inefficiency of organ gift-giving.

2.2. *Reliance on altruism as a fix for market failures—broadly and narrowly*

The second area of economic interest has been the search for market failures. The most well-known work in this area is that of Richard Titmuss, which generated a large discussion among economists of the caliber of Arrow, Solow, Tullock and others. So let us briefly review Titmuss' arguments.

The modern debate over markets in human tissue began with Titmuss (1971), who argued that an altruistic blood procurement system was not only more ethical than a market, but also more efficient. He found the basis for this claim of efficiency in comparisons of blood quality under the two systems: Titmuss presented evidence suggesting that a commercial system subjected both recipients and donors to unnecessary risks. He reported studies that showed that hepatitis rates from blood transfusions were much lower when the blood was donated rather than purchased. One might infer that, in the absence of effective tests for diseases like hepatitis, donated blood is of better quality because donors who are not paid for their blood have no incentive to conceal their illnesses. An appeal to altruism may also tend to attract people with healthier habits. Furthermore, offering financial incentives for blood could cause those in need of money to take unnecessary risks. They might, for example, supply too frequently, thereby endangering their own health.

Titmuss' book attracted the attention of many important social scientists, including several then-future Nobel prize winning economists.

Robert Solow (1971) found Titmuss's book to be "a devastating and unanswerable indictment of the American system as inferior to the British in efficiency, morality, and attractiveness" (p. 1696). Indeed, Solow felt that the benefit of Titmuss's work was such that "[e]ven if Titmuss fails to produce a convincing explanation of the success of the British system and the failure of the American, the facts themselves pose more of a challenge to 'economists' than to him" (p. 1705).

Arrow (1972) considered Titmuss's evidence to be a "powerful indictment of the efficiency of blood-giving in the United States" (p. 352). Arrow noted that the basic problem associated with procuring blood had parallels in the trade of other commodities and services in which the buyer is not in a position to know what he is buying, whereas the seller knows what he is selling. The market for used cars is a good example. In cases characterized by this type of asymmetry of information, "[s]ome alternative system for determining quality and providing assurance to buyers is needed." Where the price system breaks down, "ethical behavior can be regarded as a socially desirable institution which facilitates the achievement of economic efficiency."

However, Arrow and Titmuss disagreed fundamentally over how individuals respond when markets are introduced. Titmuss believed that the price incentives offered by markets would drive out altruism and cause donative supply to wither. For example, if organs came to be viewed generally as a commodity, and if some families refused to treat their loved ones' organs in this fashion, they might choose neither to donate nor to sell the organs. In short, Titmuss believed that either a market *or* donation is possible, but not both, and that the introduction of a market would deny people "the right to give."

Arrow found this argument of Titmuss'wanting on theoretical and empirical grounds. Arrow could "find no evidence for the existence" of such a phenomenon, and he stated that, "[i]n any case[,] the empirical evidence can only be made meaningful with at least a minimum of theoretical analysis." Arrow queried, "Why should it be that the creation of a market in blood would decrease the altruism embodied in giving blood? I do not find any clear answer in Titmuss" (Arrow, 1972, p. 350).[12]

Arrow's statement is consistent with the view that altruism is a limited resource that must be rationed. According to this view, altruistic and non-altruistic individuals respond to different incentives, and, furthermore, the ability to substitute the utility of selling for that of donating is small, perhaps zero. Altruistic individuals supply when sufficiently exhorted; non-altruistic individuals supply when offered a satisfactory financial incentive. Neither responds to the other's incentives. For Arrow, therefore, the introduction of a market elicits new supply from non-altruists, all the while leaving the donative supply from altruists unchanged. Likewise, reducing efforts to gain donations does not increase market supply.

Arrow's view on altruism reflects the general economists view that is nicely reflected in Dennis Robertson's (Robertson, 1956, p. 147) answer to the question: What Do Economists Economize? His answer was "love," by which, Solow (1971) explains, "[Robertson] meant that altruism is a scarce resource, and the business of economists is to find institutional arrangements that will accomplish society's purposes without depending too much on disinterested kindness" (p. 1706).

This discussion took place largely in the 1970's and early 1980's and in the context of blood procurement. In the main, today, the issue appears largely settled for economists. The quality issue seems of little concern to those who favor markets in human organs, nor are there other obvious market failures.[13] As a result, since the US banned the sale of human organs in 1984 the lines in the debate over commercialism are more clearly drawn: Those who favor a market in human organs argue primarily on efficiency grounds, contending that payments to donors would elicit greater supply, thereby reducing shortages; those who oppose a market argue on grounds of ethical principle rather than efficiency.

What's the basis for the nearly universally agreed on contention that market bans must necessarily cause shortages and other inefficiencies? In section 3 I present the price-control model of market-inalienability that leads to this result.

[12] For a response to Arrow, see Collard (1978, p. 147–150) who offers a simple model of voluntary donation that is consistent with rational economic behavior and with Titmuss's concern for the larger issues in blood donation.

[13] The quality issue may not be as settled as some believe. McNeil (2003) recently reported in the New York Times that a parasitic infection common in Latin America is threatening the United States blood supply. The infection, Chagas disease, while still rare in the United States, will kill 10 to 30 percent of those infected. There is no effective treatment for the disease and there will be no test for it in donated blood until 2005 at the earliest.

3. The conventional economic analysis of the effect of banning a market

3.1. The model

Economists have analyzed market bans using the standard price-control model with the banned good's price set at zero. This model implies unequivocally that market-inalienable goods and services will be in short supply.[14] The model's demonstration of welfare losses to banning markets depends critically on the following assumptions:

(a) The quality of goods procured is the same whether the goods are sold or donated;
(b) Altruists will continue to donate after a market is introduced;
(c) When markets are banned, not only is the cost of the good zero, but no other costs are required to procure the donated good;
(d) Nothing can be done to increase supply when markets are banned.

Figure 1 shows Pindyck and Rubinfeld's (Pindyck and Rubinfeld, 1989) analysis of the current organ procurement system.[15] The supply of cadaveric kidneys under the current donative system is shown as S_{DON} and is fixed at 8000. Market supply, S_{MKT}, is shown to rise with price, intersecting demand to the right of 8000 kidneys. A command system that made all organs the property of the state could procure all medically suitable organs, S_{COM}, the number of which is variously estimated at about 32 000 kidneys per year (Task Force on Organ Transplantation, 1986).

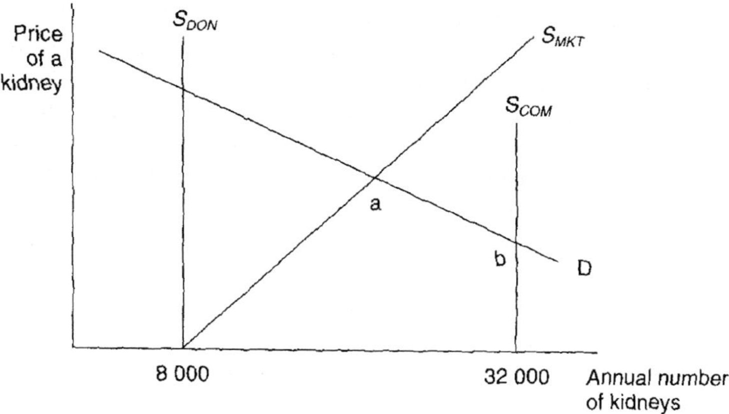

Figure 1. The price-control model with fixed donative supply. Source: Pindyck and Rubinfeld (1989).

[14] Technically, there is no shortage if the demand curve intercepts the X-axis at a quantity lower than that of the supply intercept.

[15] Barney and Reynolds (1989) and Kaserman and Barnett (1991) present more complex models that incorporate the derived demand for physician services and kidneys. The implications of their analyses are similar to those of Pindyck and Rubinfeld's simpler model; the critique presented in this chapter is equally applicable to the more complex models.

The model implies that a market in organs would ease shortages by increasing the quantity supplied. In addition, absent a market, a welfare loss might occur if, in order to obtain a share of the fixed supply, consumers engage in activities that they would not undertake in the absence of price controls. For example, waiting in a queue to establish a property right to a price-controlled good like gasoline dissipates its value. That is, the procurement effort associated with waiting in line for gasoline does not increase the *total* supply of the fuel; the activity merely *allocates* a fixed supply and, therefore, from a social perspective, might be viewed as wasteful. If, when markets are banned, procurers engage in activities that would be unnecessary in a market, then a similar welfare loss will occur as the good's rent is dissipated.

To summarize, the economic basis for opposing a ban on a market is that it may cause a variety of inefficiencies, including (i) shortages and (ii) a dissipation of the rents that otherwise would accrue to the owners. Some also oppose the ban on the basis that it may result in a redistribution of some of the good's rent from suppliers to consumers or intermediaries (Thorne, 1990).

3.2. Critiques of the conventional model

Each of the four assumptions of the above model is debatable. First, the concern that markets will endanger quality, originally raised by Titmuss and later supported by Arrow, remains: For example, for technical reasons, it is still difficult or impossible to test donors for conditions such as HIV. Second, altruistic donors may withdraw their supply when markets are introduced. If altruists do withdraw their supply, then the market supply curve in Figure 1 will shift left.[16]

But most open to challenge are assumptions (c) and (d) and their implications. The conventional price-control analysis ignores efforts, other than raising price, that are undertaken to elicit supply. It assumes that people simply line up to donate and that the cost of procuring the donated good is zero. The analysis presumes that people either are or are not altruistic, and that public education efforts to inform them of the need for the donated good or to exhort them to donate are unnecessary. According to this view, a system reliant on donation resembles either an authoritarian system in which people are required to donate at zero price, or a culture in which donation expresses social mores.

The fact is, to secure donations of organs, procurers must urge, coax, cajole, and otherwise exhort next-of-kin of potential donors to donate and hospital staff and physicians to refer potential donors. These donations do not come without cost. After examining the process of procuring market-inalienable goods in the following section, I argue that the activities of urging, pleading, coaxing, and cajoling ought to be viewed as a production process that is an alternative to the market.

[16] Even if altruists withdrew their supply upon the introduction of a market, the resultant welfare loss would be less than the welfare loss under a market ban.

4. Procuring market-inalienable organs by exhorting donors

4.1. *The exhortation effort model*

Thorne (1998a, 1998b) offers a model of market-inalienable procurement that attempts to capture the essentials of the non-market procurement. He introduces the term "exhortation" to describe the non-price efforts used to secure market-inalienable goods and services. Exhortation includes efforts to inform and persuade all participants in the donative system who cannot be paid for what they supply. In the case of organs, exhortation includes efforts by procurement organizations to get next-of-kin to donate organs, and also efforts directed at physicians and hospital staff to identify, without remuneration, potential donors.

Clearly, markets and command systems also rely on exhortation in the form of advertising, social marketing, and public education. In fact, exhortation is often used to secure what can be neither bought nor commanded, such as loyalty, friendship, devotion, and even love. A wonderful illustration of the need for exhortation (or intimidation), even in the face of apparently complete property rights, is given by Barzel (1997) in his explanation of how it was possible for slaves in the antebellum South to accumulate assets with which to buy their freedom.[17] Even under command systems, exhortation in the form of moral suasion is very much a feature of organization.[18]

The donative system's reliance on exhortation is especially striking in that it is the *sole* means of procuring market-inalienable goods. Moreover, for some market-inalienable goods, possibly including organs, the number of goods an agency procures

[17] The puzzle is: How could a slave have obtained the assets with which to buy his freedom when the slaveowner had complete property rights both to the slave and to any assets the slave could accumulate? Barzel's answer is that the slaveowner still had to spend money to enforce his property right over the slave. That is, the owner had to hire a guard to exhort (i.e., intimidate) the slave. This "transaction" cost drove a wedge between what the slave could have earned had he been able to work for himself and his net value to the owner. Barzel argues that "[t]he need for supervision and the desire to economize on its cost made ownership of slaves less than fully delineated" and that "[s]laves were able to capture some of these undelineated rights—in this case rights to themselves" (Barzel, 1997, p. 110). Because estimation of a slave's potential output was subject to error, and because setting production quotas too high would destroy the slave, it was in the slaveowner's self-interest to set quotas below what a slave could actually produce. Barzel suggests that it was also in the slaveowner's self-interest to permit slaves to own and accumulate some of the excess production above the quota. Thus, "partly due to skills in feigning inability, on the one hand, and to activities such as fishing, on the other, as well as the luck of having errors made in their favor," some slaves were eventually able to buy their own contracts. Barzel concludes that wherever there are transactions costs, "rights to assets will never be perfectly delineated."

[18] For a description of Stakhanovism, a 1930s program in the Soviet Union which was aimed at achieving increased worker productivity through exhortation, see Siegelbaum (1988). In the 1960s and 1970s, a great debate took place in the socialist world over the efficiency of providing "moral incentives" to workers (Bernardo, 1971). Moral incentives are a type of exhortation to be contrasted with material incentives and command. In Cuba, for example, Che Guevara argued that the use of moral incentives could be a partial substitute for intense central planning. Similar attempts were made in China and North Korea. For a comparison of the effectiveness of social marketing campaigns and regulation (i.e., exhortation versus command), see Adler and Pittle (1984).

will be directly related to the effort it expends on exhortation (Thorne, 1996). Thorne views the costly exhortation activities used by procurement agencies to secure supply as a production technique that is an alternative to expropriating or paying donors directly. Thorne argues that the price control model in Figure 1 depicts donative supply, S_{DON}, as fixed, and thus fails to reflect the cost of the effort to procure donations when a market is banned.

To depict donative supply more realistically, Thorne modifies the price control model in Figure 2 to show donative supply, S_{DON}, rising with expenditures on procurement effort.[19] While the relative positions and shapes of S_{DON} and S_{MKT} shown in Figure 2 are drawn for illustrative purposes only and are in fact unknown, the essential point is that the supply of donations is shown to increase with increased expenditure (unlike S_{DON} in Figure 1).[20]

The effect of banning a market, then, depends on two supply curves that are *both rising* in response to increasing expenditures: the donative supply responding to increased exhortation effort and the market supply responding to rising price. Which scenario garners the most organs for a given expenditure (i.e., which is the rightmost supply curve) becomes an empirical issue.

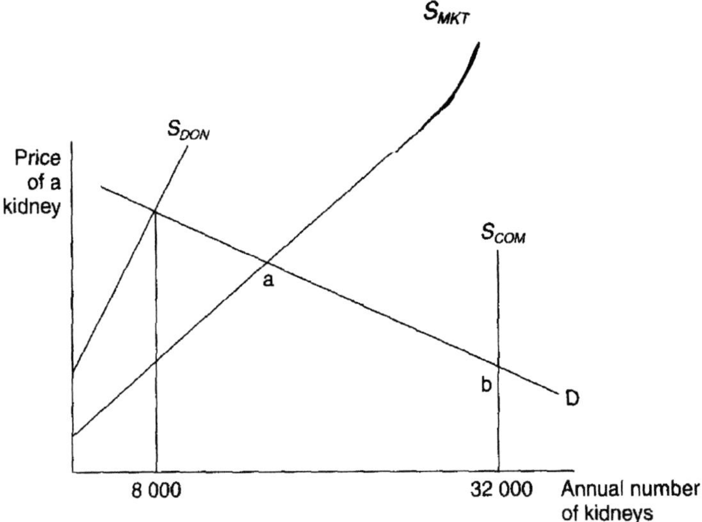

Figure 2. The price-control model with variable donative supply.

[19] Note that in this figure and in all figures describing exhortation, the price on the y-axis should not be interpreted as the dollar value of the benefits to the supplier but, rather, as the amount the procurer must expend to get the supply and the amount demanders are willing to pay.

[20] S_{DON} and S_{MKT} are both shown in Figure 2 as intersecting the y-axis above the origin on the assumption that there is some minimal disutility to supplying an organ that must be overcome either by price or exhortation.

Organs belong to a class of goods that differ from conventional goods in that people respond to campaigns exhorting them to donate when markets are banned. As indicated in section 2.1, the conventional view of what happens when the price of a good like gasoline is fixed below market equilibrium is that competition for the good encourages consumers to undertake wasteful activities, such as queuing, which activities would be unnecessary in a market. However, the "wasteful" activity undertaken by demanders of organs includes exhorting suppliers to donate. Whereas exhorting suppliers to donate a good like gasoline is not likely to yield much success, individuals do respond to pleas for donations of human organs. Thus, exhorting suppliers to donate a market-inalienable good like an organ may not merely redistribute supply; it may also *enlarge* supply, even beyond what a market would generate.

All else being equal, exhortation will produce a supply that exceeds the market supply when the marginal cost to procurers of the supply garnered by exhortation is lower than the marginal cost of market-generated supply. How can this happen? Part of the answer lies in what motivates donors to respond to exhortation campaigns. Donors respond to exhortation for reasons that may include a sense of duty, responsibility, love, and other psychological rewards. Exhortation by procurers can be thought to supply these donors with information. Because information elicits supply, the number of organs supplied under a market ban should depend on the level of effort expended on exhortation.

Another part of the answer depends on the behavior of procurers designed to appeal to these motives. The focus here is not on the efficiency of donor *motives* (i.e., altruism versus self-interest) but rather on the efficiency of the *actions* of procurers that appeal to these motives (i.e., exhortation versus payments).

The nature of the donative system and its reliance on exhortation is complex, but for the purposes of this theoretical Essay it is sufficient to accept that: (1) Exhortation is an important feature of the donative system; (2) Considerable sums of money are spent exhorting people to give; and (3) For some goods and services, people respond to exhortation by donating. Whatever the motive for donation, exhortation elicits supply, and there is no theoretical basis for asserting that the supply generated by exhortation must be smaller than market supply.[21]

4.1.1. Equilibrium supply under a market ban

The price-control model predicts unequivocally that a market ban will cause a shortage of organs and a dissipation of rents. By contrast, in the modified price-control model that incorporates the features of a donative system, a market ban does not necessarily decrease supply. Whether equilibrium in the latter will reflect a greater or lesser supply

[21] For donors who donate because exhortation provides them with utility that they could have purchased, the marginal cost of procurement by exhortation must exceed the market cost. But the supply curve for donation will be the average cost of exhortation, because market-inalienable goods are common property. Thus, even if the marginal cost of exhortation exceeds the market cost, the average cost of exhortation could still be lower than the market cost.

depends on several features of the industry's structure, including the cost of paying suppliers in relation to the cost of exhorting them to donate, the nonprofit/for-profit status of the procuring organizations, and the objectives of these organizations. Perhaps most importantly, the equilibrium supply of organs will depend on how the market and donative sectors interact—that is, on whether the existence of a market will drive out donations.

The price-control model presented earlier assumes that people would continue to donate if a market in organs emerged. According to that model, newly-permitted payments for organs would serve to elicit a supply over and above the donated supply, thereby increasing the aggregate supply. Regardless of how one conceives of donor behavior, there are conditions under which a market ban might, *as a theoretical matter*, enlarge supply.

Consider the Titmuss scenario that introducing a market will cause donations to wither. The Titmuss scenario assumes that the introduction of a market will cause donations to wither completely. According to this view, all individuals who supply when exhorted would prefer not to sell at any price. Thus aggregate supply is *either* the market supply *or* the exhortation supply.

At present, organ procurement takes place through government-designated nonprofit organizations, each of which, in effect, owns the sole franchise to procure in its region. In this case, where an agency is the sole owner in its region but must compete with other regional sole owners, each agency will produce at the private property equilibrium. Thus, if the marginal cost of exhortation (MC^1_{EXH} in Figure 3) is *greater* than the marginal cost of market supply (MC_{MKT} in Figure 3), the equilibrium supply of organs under exhortation (Point 1) will be smaller than the market supply (Point 2). However, if the marginal cost of exhortation (MC^2_{EXH} in Figure 3) is *less* than the marginal cost of market supply, the equilibrium supply of organs under exhortation (Point 3) will be greater than the market supply. If each nonprofit agency chooses to maximize its output instead of its surplus, then it will exhort at Point 4 in Figure 3, where AC^1_{EXH}, the average cost corresponding to MC^1_{EXH}, intersects demand. If it uses donated funds in its procurement efforts, then equilibrium will be to the right of Point 4.[22]

A similar analysis will explain Arrow's view that introducing a market will not affect donations. The following assumptions are consistent with Arrow's critique of Titmuss: (1) Individuals who supply when exhorted would not respond to financial incentives, and individuals who supply when offered a satisfactory financial incentive would not respond to exhortation; (2) Markets would elicit new supply, leaving the exhortation supply unchanged; and (3) Reducing exhortation effort would not increase market supply, and banning a market would not increase donations.

The analysis presented here and in the previous subsection shows that if the marginal cost of market procurement is greater than or equal to the marginal cost of exhortation (or, in some cases, the average cost of exhortation), then conditions exist under which

[22] The same result can be found in the case in which a single nonprofit agency is the sole owner in *every* region and has, therefore, a procurement monopoly.

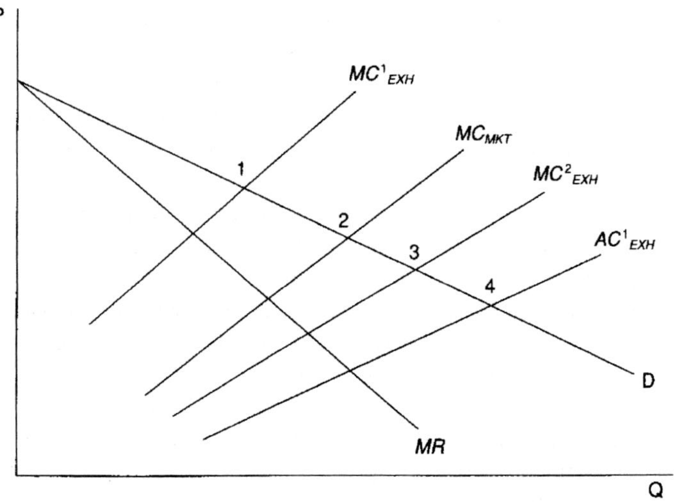

Figure 3. The equilibrium supply of organs (Titmuss).

a market ban need not reduce supply (at least theoretically). On the other hand, if both the marginal and average costs of exhortation exceed the marginal cost of procurement under a market, then the model suggests that a market ban will reduce supply.

As the next part demonstrates, an additional complication of the donative system's reliance on exhortation is the fact that market-inalienable goods are in essential ways common property, making the exhortation of donors much like "fishing" from a common pool. As will be seen, the appropriate supply of exhorted market-inalienable goods is the supply from the commons.

4.2. *The common property nature of human organs*

Finally, having shown that supply elicited by exhortation can exceed market supply, Thorne goes on to argue that, because of the attributes of market-inalienability, exhortation-generated supply might be even further enlarged because market-inalienable goods are fundamentally like common property. Exhorting donations of market-inalienable goods is analogous to fishing in common property waters.

4.2.1. *Market-inalienable goods as common property*

When man-made restrictions on property rights limit the right to *sell* a good but do not assign the rights to the economic value that the resource can earn, then a mixture of private and common property rights obtains. While individuals are unable to sell market-inalienable goods, they are free to donate such goods, and, if they choose to donate, they can also choose the recipient of the donation.

A market-inalienable good like a human organ is not naturally a common-property good because completely defined property rights could be established without difficulty. Unlike with common-property goods such as fish, air, and minerals, no technical difficulties impede barring free riders from enjoying the use of human organs, nor is the organ's use characterized by indivisibilities. In short, market-inalienable goods could be treated as private goods in the United States.

However, because the rights to the economic value of market-inalienable goods are unassigned, banning a market makes market-inalienable goods common property in a fundamental way. Because a market-inalienable good (and its economic value) will belong not to the owner but to the party to whom the good is donated, the good appears as common property from the perspective of those who want it. Someone who wants the market-inalienable good will engage in activities to obtain it that are remarkably similar to the activities of someone "fishing" in common property waters. A fisherman will invest his labor and capital to catch a fish by dangling a worm before it. If the fisherman is successful, the fish itself is free to him even though the fishing effort may have been costly. Likewise, someone wishing to obtain a market-inalienable good has every incentive to engage in costly exhortation/"fishing" activities that, if successful, will yield him the good for free. In short, by leaving the rights to a good's economic value unassigned, banning a market in that good allows everyone access to its free value and, in effect, creates a man-made common property resource.[23]

This notion that banning a market creates, in effect, a common property resource is an extension of Cheung's (Cheung, 1974) insight that whenever a price is fixed below the market price, a common-property rent (non-exclusive income, in his terminology) is created. It would appear, then, that private property, price control, market-inalienability, and common property really comprise varying degrees of property rights to a resource. Between private property goods at one end of the property rights spectrum and common property goods at the other are partial price-control and market-inalienable goods.[24]

[23] The class of goods and services that may be considered to have common-property attributes because they are market-inalienable is, in fact, quite broad. The property rights to those goods and services may be restricted in ways that make them either wholly or partially market-inalienable. Sexual favors and basketball talent are both illustrations of market-inalienable resources in that the resource's owner has only a limited right to transact. Our sexual rights are limited by legislation that bans prostitution. Similarly, a talented amateur basketball player's rights are limited by the arrangement among colleges that permits only "donations" of talent, not sales. While in neither of these two cases can the owner legally be forced to supply the resource for free, the owner does not have the right to sell the valuable service. In both cases, the owner retains the right to give the resource away. More importantly, anyone who wants the resource from the owner must exhort the owner to get it.

[24] Exhorting a donation of a partially or wholly market-inalienable good is different from exhorting a donation of a good that is completely private. With a private good, people can choose not only to whom to donate, but whether to donate at all. Norman Shore has brought to my attention an interesting class of goods that regulation makes into common property when such regulation requires that the goods be donated but does not specify the recipient of the donation. In such circumstances, people cannot keep the goods, because they must donate; their options are limited to the "to whom to give" question. A tax system, for example, creates

The effort expended to establish a property right by waiting in a queue is seen by Barzel as the source of the dissipation of the value of a price-controlled good like gasoline.[25] Barzel's analysis of the dissipation of the price-controlled good's rent is an application and extension of Cheung's insight into the common property nature of this rent. From the perspective of Barzel, Cheung, and others writing about dissipation by rationing-by-waiting, or rent-seeking, the dissipation of producer surplus by these efforts does not increase supply. All that rent-seeking accomplishes is the dissipation of the rent through activities that merely allocate a fixed supply. However, proceeding from Barzel's and Cheung's analyses of partial price controls, I argue here that exhortation-type rent-seeking need not dissipate producer surplus if, by these efforts, supply is increased.

4.2.2. The general common property problem

As property rights to the commons are undefined and access to it is non-exclusive, ownership of the commons' resources is governed by the rule of capture. Under this rule, parties have exclusive rights to the resources that they manage to procure, resources that are free to them.[26]

Open access to a common property, such as the ocean, causes a well-analyzed congestion externality, first described by Scott Gordon (1954).[27] The externality can be

goods with common property attributes much like market-inalienable goods. An early instance is given in *The Bible* when God requires a tithe to be paid to the Levites (Numbers 18:21). God does not specify to which Levite the tithe must be paid (e.g., the neighborhood Levite), so the tax apparently can be paid to the Levite of one's choice. While the economic value of the tax no longer belongs to the taxpayer, it does not belong to a particular Levite until the tithe is handed over to him. Until then, it belongs to no one. The fact that the tithe is unassigned could lead Levites to dissipate its value by making expenditures to exhort taxpayers to tithe to them. In our day, a similar dissipation of grants from charitable foundations may occur. To maintain their favorable tax status, private charitable foundations are required by the I.R.S. to disburse their funds (I.R.C. § 4942 (1994)). In effect, as with the tithe to the Levites, the foundations no longer have a right to the money—only the right to direct it. And as long as the funds are unassigned, potential grantees have every incentive to engage in activities that have the effect of dissipating the grants such as exhortation.

[25] More generally, Barzel argues:

> A commodity announced to be free is effectively placed in the public domain and is of no value until ownership is established. Establishing ownership requires that an individual fulfill certain criteria; in the example here, the criterion is to spend five minutes in the queue. Acquisition of the commodity consumes real resources over and above the resources used in production. In this example, ownership is established over one already produced unit of the commodity. Methods differ from case to case, but whatever the method by which rights are acquired, it may generally be stated that resources must be spent to gain possession of commodities in the public domain, and that individual maximization applies here no less than to conventional exchange (Barzel, 1997, p. 18).

[26] The term "free" is used to indicate that the resource itself has no cost. Naturally, costs may be incurred in capturing a free resource.

[27] For a clear treatment of the common property externality, see Cornes and Sandler (1986).

modeled in a simple static one-period model in which each fisherman's cost function depends not only on his level of production, but also on the aggregate level of production of the others fishing in the ocean. With average cost depending on aggregate ocean output, the marginal fishing of one fisherman imposes additional costs on all infra-marginal fishing.[28] This simple example illustrates why common property resources are used inefficiently. Individuals know that what they do not extract will be extracted by rivals, so they have little incentive to forego current extraction in favor of future extraction. In addition, individuals have little incentive to coordinate their efforts, as is true where traditional public goods are concerned. Consequently, people underinvest in renewing the resource and in developing information that would benefit all producers.

To apply this analysis to the procurement of human organs, consider the agencies that procure and distribute the organs—the middlemen in the transplantation process. Suppose the organ procurement industry consists of a given number of profit-maximizing organ procurers, each with free access to a common-property "fishing ground" containing an exogenously fixed number of individuals capable of supplying organs. Each organ procurer combines a common-property resource—the organ—with its labor—exhortation—to produce a transplantable organ as output. With the size of the potential pool of organs fixed at S (the number of brain-dead cadavers, or the size of the population if we were to allow live donation), the total number of organs procured by all the organ procurers, Q, depends on the size of the total procurement effort, E, and on S.

[28] The essence of a common property good can be appreciated by comparing it to a private good. Consider the economics of harvesting fish in a privately owned lake. The owner of a lake wishes to hire labor to fish and is willing to pay them the prevailing wage, say, the wage paid by McDonald's. If the owner expects the value of the fish caught by the first fisherman to exceed the wage, the lake owner will hire him. The owner will pocket the difference between the wage he paid the fisherman and the value of his catch. The value of the fish caught by the next fisherman to be hired will be less than the value of the first angler's catch because of congestion in the lake. However, as long as the value of the fish caught by each additional fisherman exceeds the wage he is paid, the owner will hire the additional fisherman. When the value of the fish caught by the nth fisherman drops below the wage he is paid, the owner of the lake will stop hiring. This is the optimal level of fishing. Any additional fishing would be inefficient because the fisherman could produce greater value at an activity other than fishing. At the optimal level of fishing, the excess of the value of output over wage costs is the profit earned by the owner of the lake. This profit is the value of the fish. Suppose now that the lake is made *common* property and that everyone has free access to the fish in it. If the existing fishermen can somehow collude and keep new workers from entering the fishing grounds, then they will continue to fish at the same level they did when the lake was private property—which has already been shown to be the efficient level. The fishermen will now pocket the profit that the owner received when the lake was private, increasing their earnings above the prevailing wage they earned when the lake was private. If there is open access to the lake, however, the higher earnings available to fishermen will attract workers who, in alternative work, can earn only the prevailing wage. If new entrants cannot be denied free access to the lake, then more fishermen will fish, which will result in inefficient overfishing (in comparison to the private property case). Once again, this inefficiency results from fishing at a level at which the value of the fishermen's catch is less than the prevailing wage that McDonald's might pay them. When there is unlimited free access to the lake, we have the common property problem with its well-known associated "tragedy." The lake is overfished; that is, it is fished beyond the level it would be if the lake were privately owned. This overfishing is financed by the value of the fish, which, in the private property case, was profit earned by the lake's owner.

The aggregate production function is $Q = Q(E, S)$. Let Q_E and Q_S represent the derivatives with respect to E and S, and Q_{EE} the second derivative with respect to E; we expect $Q_E > 0$, $Q_S > 0$, and $Q_{EE} < 0$.

The common property externality is introduced by allowing procurer i's cost to depend on aggregate procurement by the others in the region as well as on its own procurement, q^i.

If the cost function for the representative agency takes the form

$$C_i(q^i, Q, S) = q^i A(Q, S) \tag{1}$$

where $A(Q, S)$ is the unit or average cost function for each firm in the region, then the well-known equilibrium condition is

$$P = (1/n)MC + [(n-1)/n]AC \tag{2}$$

where P is the exogenously determined price of output,[29] and MC and AC are the industry marginal and average costs of exhortation, respectively.[30]

[29] While there might not be a market price for the market-inalienable good if procurers are not allowed to sell the good, procurers will at least be able to charge a reasonable fee reflecting their expenses. Moreover, a market-inalienable good like a human organ is an input into a process that results in a final good—a transplanted organ—for which there may be no limitation on price. Thus, for this thought experiment, the price P can be viewed either as a procurer's allowable reimbursable expenses or as that part of the price of the final good that reflects the value added by the market-inalienable good.

[30] Organ procurer i's problem is to maximize his profit, B_i, with respect to q^i

$$\text{Maximize } B_i = q^i[P - A(Q, S)], \tag{3}$$

where $q^i \geq 0$ and $Q = \sum q^j \leq S$ for $j = 1$ to n. The procurement agency's optimal quantity of procurement must satisfy the first-order condition

$$\mathrm{d}B_i/\mathrm{d}q^i = 0 = P - q^i A_Q(Q, S) - A(Q, S). \tag{4}$$

Equation (4) can be rewritten as

$$P = q^i A_Q(Q, S) + A(Q, S). \tag{5}$$

Because agency i's costs depend on aggregate procurement in that region, Q, the extent of the externality depends on the number of agencies involved. Since all agencies are assumed to be identical with the same unit cost function, then $q^i = Q/n$ for all i. Equation (5) can be rewritten to show how the externality varies with n:

$$P = (Q/n)A_Q(Q, S) + A(Q, S) \tag{6}$$

or

$$P = (1/n)[A(Q, S) + QA_Q(Q, S)] + [(n-1)/n]A(Q, S). \tag{7}$$

For the industry as a whole, the cost function is

$$C(Q, S) = QA(Q, S), \tag{8}$$

Equation (2) shows that the equilibrium price of output, P, is the weighted sum of the marginal and average costs of total regional procurement. In the case of a sole organ procurer,[31] $n = 1$, so the second term of Equation (2) is zero, and the quantity of organs procured is such that the price of output equals the sole procurer's marginal cost of procuring organs. This is Point A in Figure 5. As the number of organ procurers grows large, however, the weight of the first term approaches zero while that of the second term approaches one. In the extreme, as n becomes very large, procurement efforts will increase until the average cost of output for all procurers in the region equals the output price of an organ. This is Point B in Figure 5.

When the resource is held in common, the entire rent that would accrue to the owners of the resource if it were privately held is dissipated by inefficient overproduction at a level at which marginal cost exceeds the price of output. This is the standard result for common property resources.[32]

If a region contains many competing organ procurers, then, because of the common property feature of market-inalienable goods, the supply of each procurer will be represented by the average cost of exhortation. If there is competition in each region, then the aggregate market supply from all regions will be the sum of each competitor's average cost curve. Market equilibrium occurs at Point A in Figure 6.

If, instead of many competitors in a region, there is only a single exhorter—the sole owner—then the region's supply will be represented by the sole owner's marginal cost of exhortation. If there is a sole owner in each region, then the aggregate supply will be the sum of each sole owner's marginal cost curve. If sole owners compete with other sole owners in other regions, then market equilibrium will occur at Point B in Figure 6. This is the competitive equilibrium for private property. However, if there is one monopolist who is the sole owner in each region, then market equilibrium will occur at Point C in Figure 6.

In sum, theory suggests and experience confirms that common property will be overfished, depleting both current and future stocks. While the commons of human tissue

and the industry's marginal cost, MC, is

$$MC = \mathrm{d}C/\mathrm{d}Q = QA_Q(Q, S) + A(Q, S). \tag{9}$$

Rewriting Equation (7) as a function of MC and average cost, AC, yields the common-property equilibrium condition:

$$P = (1/n)MC + [(n-1)/n]AC. \tag{10}$$

[31] Although the sole supplier is the only supplier from this region (or lake), he is one of many suppliers to the market and is, therefore, still a price taker and not a monopolist.

[32] It is noteworthy that rent dissipation in the common property model is due solely to congestion in the commons. If competitors in the commons were to use intimidation or other forms of destructive competition to enforce a property right, such as cutting each other's fishing lines, then such activities would raise average costs for each competitor. The aggregate market supply curve from all commons would in that instance lie above the congestion-externality only supply curve.

under a market ban may also be "overfished," as in the standard model of the commons, the welfare implications of such a circumstance defy the standard view. By encouraging the procurement of tissue that otherwise would be discarded, treating human tissue as common property may actually *increase* its supply, if inefficiently.

4.2.3. Equilibrium supply of common property market-inalienable goods

To observe the effect on equilibrium supply of reflecting average cost rather than marginal cost in the supply curve of the market-inalienable good, one must again consider how the market and donative sectors interact.

4.2.3.1. Introducing a market will cause donations to wither (Titmuss) Significantly, when many nonprofit procurers are competing in each region and the organs' rents are treated as common property, equilibrium supply will be determined by the intersection of demand and the *average* cost of exhortation. Thus, nonprofit competitors, whether they are surplus-maximizers or output-maximizers, will behave like for-profit competitors. The equilibrium supply of organs under exhortation will occur where demand equals the average cost of exhortation (Point 7 in Figure 3 where AC^1_{EXH}, the average cost corresponding to MC^1_{EXH}, intersects demand). Supply at this equilibrium will be greater than the market supply as long as the average cost of exhortation is lower than the marginal cost of the market (as depicted in Figure 3). This result will hold even if the marginal cost of exhortation exceeds that of the market.

4.2.3.2. Introducing a market will not affect donations (Arrow) If the entire industry is competitive (no sole owners in the donative sector), then the supply curve in the donative sector, because of competition for common property rents, will be the exhortation average cost curve. Let the term "total supply curve" ("*TSC*") refer to the horizontal sum of the market marginal cost curve and the exhortation average cost curve. The *TSC* in Figure 4 is shown to be to the right of *MC*. Equilibrium occurs at Point B where the *TSC* intersects the demand curve. If Point B is above the kink, then introducing markets

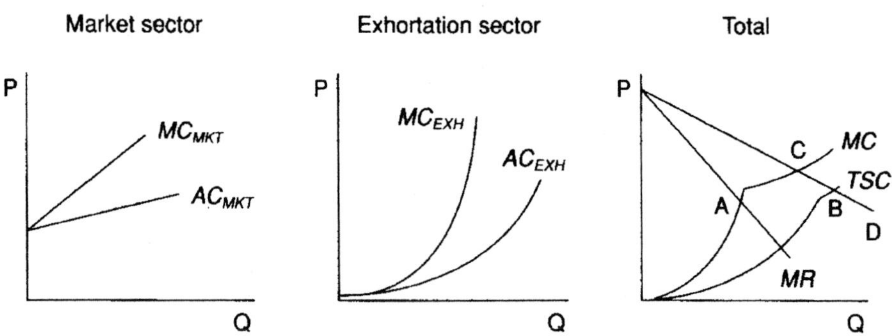

Figure 4. The equilibrium supply of organs (Arrow).

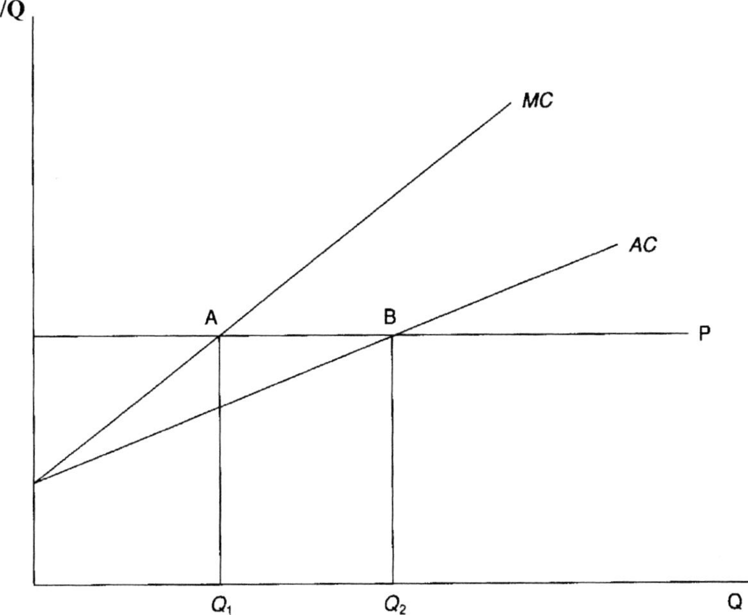

Figure 5. Equilibrium when price elasticity of demand of organs is infinite.

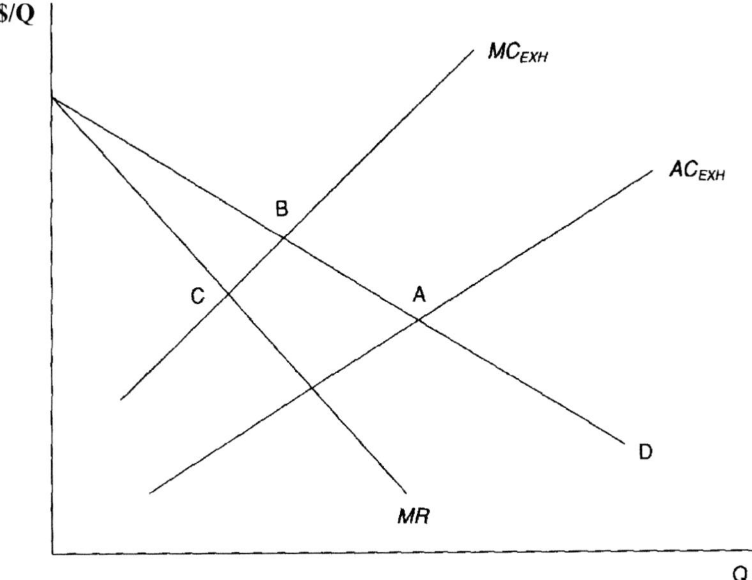

Figure 6. Equilibrium when price elasticity of demand for organs is finite.

will increase supply. If Point B is below the kink, then introducing markets will not affect equilibrium supply.

The relationship between the marginal and average costs of exhortation and the market cost is unknown. Which model of the interaction between the market and donative sectors most accurately reflects the effect of the introduction of a market is likewise unknown. While it is impossible to know (in the absence of a market) what the market price would have been, the cost of organs under the donative system does not seem prohibitive; on the contrary, it is relatively low.[33] But if exhortation is a cheap means of procuring organs, if greater effort yields more organs, and if the effect of making organs common property is to provide incentives to *over*-exhort people to donate, how are the apparent shortages in organs to be understood?

There is, in fact, no over-exhortation of common-property organs because regulatory policy grants regional monopolistic franchises to procurement organizations. Consequently, property rights to the organs that are potentially available in each region are assigned. But why is there *under*-exhortation of organs?

5. Why the organ shortage?

What are the obstacles to procuring a greater supply of market-inalienable goods and more fully exploiting the donative system's efficiency? As we will see, some of the obstacles may lie in the reliance on exhortation to secure organs and in difficulties associated with the organization of organ procurement by non-profit organizations. Also, the government may inadvertently be retarding the supply of organs. Before turning to these "non-market failures" let us look at the worldwide experience with donation.

What we can learn from the more successful organ procurement operations about the obstacles to effectively exploiting the possibilities to increased procurement under a market ban?

5.1. Spain's extraordinary success

Begin by looking at Table 1, which shows the most recent experience of the major transplanting countries. In 2000, the most recent year for which comprehensive data were available, 844.4 million people in North America, Europe and Australia provided 14 178 cadaveric donors. As a proportion of the population, the customary measure of effectiveness of organ procurement programs, the rate of donation per million population for this group of countries was 16.8. The variation in donation rates is quite striking, ranging from a low of 1.4 donors per million for Turkey to a high of 33.7 for Spain.

To appreciate Spain's remarkable accomplishment, consider that its rate of 33.7 donors per million is

[33] Elsewhere (Thorne, 1996) I have examined the cost of efforts to procure market-inalienable organs and found this cost to have been approximately $1650 per organ in 1990.

- double the overall average of 16.8,
- nearly double the rate of its neighbor, France (17.8),
- almost triple the rate of Germany (12.7),
- forty percent higher than the U.S. (23.8), whose rate comes closest to it.

Nor is Spain's achievement a one-year phenomenon. While other countries have stagnated in their procurement activities, Spain has continued to improve its efforts and widen its lead. Figure 7 shows the experience of several countries during the decade of the 90's. Despite already having the highest rate of 21.5 donors per million in 1991–93, Spain managed to increase its rate by 57 percent to 33.7 in 2000, while procurement in almost all other countries plateaued, or even declined.

Why the wide disparity between European countries? And, most especially, what accounts for Spain's unequaled success?

No adequate cultural, religious, or political explanations for Spain's exceptional success have been put forth. In general, countries have reacted to the data with stunned disbelief. Typical is a June 2000 Canadian study that claimed that Canada's low donation rate (13.8 donors per million in 2000) is not due to Canadians' stinginess with their organs. Rather, the report asserts, it is because Canadians wear seat belts, get good health care and can settle a squabble without gunfire. The report on organ donation claims to dispel the notion that Canadians are selfish, arguing instead, that they simply are not dying or killing each other at the rate of Spaniards or Americans. To wit:

> Organs once plucked from those who died in automobile accidents, or from aneurysm and stroke victims, are no longer available in the numbers they once

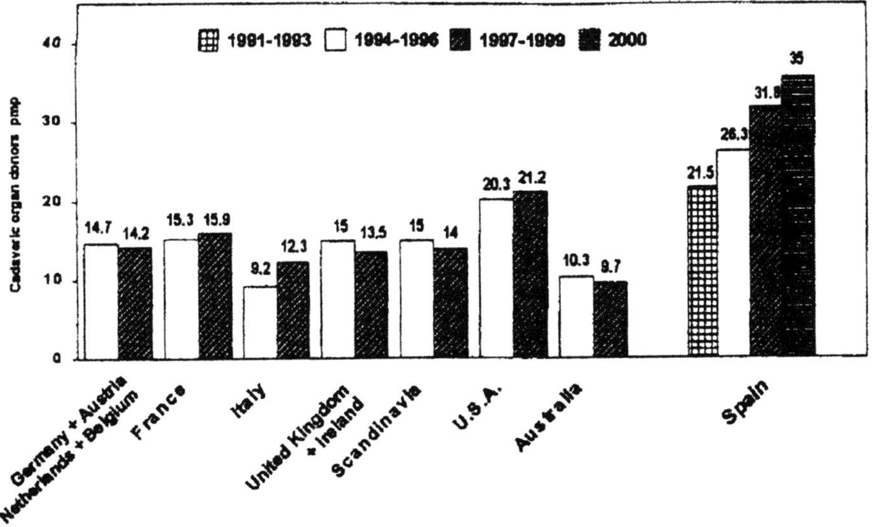

Figure 7. Cadaveric organ donor index per million population (pmp) 1991–2000. Lopez-Navidad and F. Caballero (2001).

were, due in part to tough laws against drinking and driving, to air bags in automobiles, and to Canadians' willingness to seek treatment for high blood pressure. In fact, Canada's death rate due to automobile accidents is roughly 50 per cent of what it is in Spain and the U.S. And when it comes to deaths from gunshot wounds, the Americans are way ahead, with a rate 3.5 times that of Canada. Canadians also less likely than Spaniards to die of cerebrovascular disease, such as stroke and aneurism, due to early and better care.[34]

There have been many attempts to understand Spain's success.[35] One notable attempt is in a detailed paper by Lopez-Navidad and Caballero (2001), two Spanish transplant surgeons, who describe the entire procurement process and try to account for the successes of the Spanish procurement system.[36] They conclude that:

> There are no substantially significant differences between Spain and these countries (Europe) in the level of culture of the population, in the attitude and general feelings of the population toward organ donation in the usual procedures for donation authorization by the family of the deceased potential donor, express written authorization, index of family refusal of donation in the corresponding interview, hospital infrastructures and quality, need to perform transplantations, provision of transplantation programme, or desire to perform transplants.
>
> The sole and major difference between Spain and all the other western countries which determines the spectacular distance in the cadaveric donor index per million population is the *organizational system for cadaver organ procurement for transplantation* (Emphasis added).

Wide disparity in procurement success is also found in the U.S. Table 2 shows the experience of the 34 of the Organ Procurement Organizations in the U.S. in 1990–2000. Donor to Population Rates in 2000, for example vary from a low of 15.7 to a high of 40.8. As we ask in the case of Europe, what might account for the variation? For the differences within the U.S. it is very hard to posit culture or different degrees of altruism.

Thorne (1996) tried to explain the variation in donor population rates across the U.S., not by "the level of culture of the population" or "the attitude and general feelings of the population toward organ donation," but rather by variations in the level of effort expended to achieve donations. Thorne (1996) reports that, on average, exhortation costs amounted to only $1650 per organ in 1990. Operating without offering market incentives to organ donors, the organ transplant industry now procures and transplants about 16 000 organs annually at a cost of more than $3 billion. The $25 to $30 million annual cost of procuring donations is a strikingly small fraction of the total cost of organ transplants. Also, increased expenditures appear to be associated with an increased

[34] Baxter and Smerdon (2000).

[35] See Caballero et al. (1999); Norberg et al. (2000); Fleischhauer et al. (2000).

[36] See Lopez-Navidad and Caballero (2001).

Table 2
U.S. organ procurement 1991–2000 by organ procurement agency

Organ procurement agency	Population (in millions)	Donor/population rate			
		1991–93	1994–96	1997–99	2000
Alabama Regional Organ Bank	4.10	22.1	25.3	24.4	30.7
Arkansas Regional Organ Recovery	2.10	18.4	17.8	17.8	15.7
California Transplant Donor Network	9.00	20.7	21.9	22.2	21.1
Carolina Organ Procurement Agency	3.20	24.7	31.3	32.6	37.2
Colorado Organ Recovery System, Inc.	3.70	18.7	22.8	23.5	23.2
Golden State Regional OPA	1.60	24.0	23.5	28.1	26.9
Hawaii OPO	1.10	15.5	11.2	14.5	26.4
Indiana Organ Procurement Organize	4.70	17.2	19.9	19.2	17.7
Intermountain Organ Recovery Syst	2.10	26.5	24.4	24.9	27.6
Kentucky Organ Donor Affiliates	3.70	20.9	22.8	25.3	22.7
Life Connection of NW Ohio	2.60	16.5	18.6	21.0	18.1
Lifelink of Georgia	4.20	18.3	25.3	42.3	40.7
Lifebanc	4.00	19.6	21.4	19.3	20.8
Lifeline of Ohio Organ Proc., Inc.	2.60	25.4	27.6	27.2	31.2
Lifelink of Florida	2.50	34.3	35.5	40.7	40.8
Lifelink of Southwest Florida	0.90	25.9	31.1	32.2	38.9
Lifesource Upper Midwest	5.80	22.1	25.8	27.2	27.8
Louisiana Organ Procurement Agency	4.40	21.0	23.3	19.9	22.7
Maryland Organ Procurement Center	3.10	21.0	21.6	21.2	26.8
Midwest Organ Bank	4.70	19.5	20.9	23.4	23.4
Mid-America Transplant	4.10	21.4	25.3	27.5	26.8
Nebraska Organ Retrieval System, Inc.	1.60	22.5	21.3	19.4	20.0
Nevada Donor Organ Recovery Serv	1.20	20.6	18.1	26.9	25.8
New England Organ Bank	11.50	14.9	15.6	16.2	15.5
New Jersey O & T Sharing Network	6.00	14.9	18.9	20.3	24.2
New Mexico Donor Program	1.40	27.4	28.1	17.1	21.4
Ohio Valley Organ Procurement Cen	2.10	20.0	21.9	21.3	22.4
Oklahoma Organ Sharing Network	2.00	24.2	35.2	32.7	33.5
Regional Organ Bank of Illinois	11.10	16.1	22.1	22.4	25.8
Southwest Organ Bank	6.60	22.4	25.2	26.0	23.9
Tennessee Donor Services	3.30	20.5	25.1	28.2	33.0
University of Miami OPO/HCL	4.00	22.6	29.2	32.3	26.3
Washington Regional Transplant	3.30	21.8	24.2	22.4	24.8
Total	128.30	20.1	23.0	24.1	25.0

Sources: United Network for Organ Sharing (2002) and Thorne (1996).
Notes: (1) Population is for 1990. Any population change between 1990–2000 will not alter results. (2) The Organ Procurement Organizations in this sample are those for which till data for till years was available.

yield of organs. This relationship can be seen in two ways. First, a 50 percent increase in the aggregate real cost of acquiring organs between 1988 and 1990 was associated with a 13 percent rise in the total number of kidneys procured. Furthermore, a cross-sectional analysis of organ procurement organizations showed that those organizations that engaged in greater procurement effort attracted more donors. In short, procuring organs by donation appears to be cheap, and organ shortages may be due to inadequate effort rather than to the inefficiency of appeals to donor altruism.

Why should there be too little effort to procure organs? Thorne (1998a, 1998b) explores several of the following reasons.

5.2. *Relying on exhortation*

Perhaps the most significant obstacles consist in the difficulties associated with relying on exhortation as a means of procurement. First, exhorting donations shares with advertising the difficulty of relating the level of effort to outcome. This is captured by the anecdote of the advertiser who says, "I waste half my advertising budget. I just don't know which half." The difficulty in measuring the effectiveness of effort could mistakenly lead to less effort than warranted.

Second, a procurement agency that exhorts people to donate market-inalienable goods may view its efforts as increasing total procurement rather than its particular share of the total. The inability to exclude free riders—an attribute of a public good—would tend to reduce exhortation from its efficient level. Furthermore, it is unclear whether an Organ Procurement Organization's (OPO) efforts directed at physicians and hospital personnel to refer patients to them is an effective means to garner referrals. With regard to the difficulty of getting physicians to inform the OPO of a donor, Shumway (1993) says that "... the doctors attending the brain-dead individuals don't want to bother. When the patient is finally brain-dead, the last thing they want to do is call an organ donation center and do more work to give away organs of the person they were trying to save."

A feature that distinguishes the organ commons from the fish commons is the fact that hospitals, unlike fishers, cannot be paid for their value they add to their "catch." Suppose that some fishers were to specialize in locating the fish. When they find some fish, they call in others who catch the fish. The fish catchers can pay the locators (or vice versa); thus, only the fish need to be "exhorted." In the organ case, both the "fish" (potential donors) and the locators (the hospitals) need to be exhorted, complicating both the analysis and the regulation.

Quite possibly, exhorting family members to donate is cost-effective because families view donation as somehow redeeming the deaths of their loved ones. But physicians and hospital staff may view involvement with donation as a bothersome task that subjects them to malpractice litigation and distracts them from attending to their living patients. If so, then exhorting these "locaters" to refer patients may not be cost-effective. Accordingly, organ procurement under a donative system might be inadequate, but not because altruism on the part of organ donors is an insufficient motivator for supply. Rather, the system's inefficiency may be due to a failure of organization; that is, the systems' failure to provide effective incentives to other integral actors in procurement, such as the hospital staff and physicians.

5.3. Organs are procured by nonprofit organizations

The procurement and distribution of blood and other tissues by the human tissue industry is dominated by nonprofit organizations. Nonprofits are suited to this role because both organ donors and recipients prefer to deal with them. Organ recipients prefer nonprofits because they want high quality disease-free organs and nonprofits are thought to provide superior quality. Organ donors prefer nonprofits because anonymous altruism (i.e., altruism by a stranger to a stranger) is subject to a market failure, as donors do not know and are not in contact with the recipients of their donations. Donors, therefore, need trustworthy agents. In addition, nonprofits dominate the human tissue industry because of the questionable ability of forprofit firms to persuade suppliers to donate an organ that the forprofit intends to re-sell.

In theory, nonprofits are in a position to use the surpluses they generate to supply more organs than their forprofit counterparts. They might also use their surpluses to supply a higher quality organ, charge less for the organs they supply, or finance other worthy activities. Nonprofits might, furthermore, supplement their revenues from organ sales with donated funds if they are able to fund-raise. In that case, they might even be willing to take losses.

But nonprofits also face conditions that would tend to reduce their supply of organs.

5.4. Problems with nonprofits

Nonprofits might underexhort for several reasons. First, nonprofit procurement organizations might not exhort efficiently because profits are an important motivator of management efficiency and because the profit motive is a powerful incentive for ensuring that firms enter an industry and expand when the demand for the industry's product increases. Furthermore, the attempts by nonprofit organizations to grow to achieve economies of scale often fail because mergers and acquisitions cannot take place through market mechanisms.

Second, if the nonprofit is a monopolist, it may prefer to seek donations at a lower level of output that would allow it to retain a monopoly surplus, which, under the best of circumstances, it would use to further other worthy objectives of the organization. The American Red Cross could, for example, use surpluses to finance disaster relief.

Third, nonprofits may be severely limited in their ability to raise capital since they are unable to sell equity shares, and must rely largely upon donations, retained earnings and debt for capital financing. Thus, they may be incapable of financing an efficient level of exhortation.

5.5. Government oversight

The effectiveness of exhortation is so little understood that the federal agency in charge of organ procurement, the Health Care Financing Administration, puts considerable pressure on OPOs to spend less on exhortation-related activities! Thus, not only is there a lack of support for additional procurement effort, but, current pressures from the Federal Government are actually in the direction of reduced effort, an approach likely to result in false efficiencies. The Inspector General of the Department of Health and Human Services and Aetna, the insurance company responsible for overseeing financial aspects of the government program, have repeatedly denounced the rise in organ acquisition costs and called for reductions. A report by the Inspector General of the department of health and Human services (Office of the Inspector General, 1987, p. 13) laments the fact that "kidney acquisition costs continue to be reimbursed by Medicare on a 'reasonable cost' basis," and says that "... quite clearly, a substantial portion of the Medicare funds spent on kidney acquisition are being spent unnecessarily."[37]

6. What to do about the organ shortage

6.1. Market-like schemes

In the absence of a market failure, many economists have concluded there is nothing left but to argue in favor of overturning the legislation that banned a market in organs.[38] Since an organ market is presently banned and it seems unlikely that the ban will overturned soon, some economists have offered market-like schemes that may appear not to be markets:

- insurance proposals,[39]
- label payments for organs as "rewarded gifts,"[40]
- provide payments in the guise of death benefits,[41]
- organ swapping.

As argued earlier in section 3, proponents of market and market-like schemes appear to assume either that altruism is fixed in supply (see model depicted in Figure 1) or, to use the language of the exhortation model of Figure 2, that the cost of appealing to altruistic motivations is very high. If the variation observed in Table 2 in procurement is due to differences in culture, values or altruism, we might say that countries have different exhortation curves. Alternatively, differences in culture, values or altruism might be

[37] Congressman Ernest Istook Jr., (R-Okla), recently inserted into a spending bill a provision prohibiting the Department of Health and Human Services from enforcing recent regulations intended to increase organ donations. The HHS rule issued requires hospitals to report all deaths to local organizations that specialize in donations. Rep. Istook argues that it is insensitive to approach grieving families about donation (Meckler, 1998).

[38] See Kaserman and Barnett (2002), Epstein (1994). See also Tanner (2002) describing the American Medical Association's call for research into whether financial payments would boost the nation's critical shortage of transplant organs.

[39] See Hansmann (1989).

[40] See Daar (1992) for a strong argument in favor of rewarded gifting.

[41] See Peters (1991).

minor, i.e., they all have same exhortation curve, and differences in procurement levels might be due to different levels of exhortation effort. Or, perhaps, some of both.[42]

At any rate, whether due to a shift in the exhortation curve, or to a movement along it, the U.S. managed to increase donors by 50 percent between 1988 and 2001.

Year	Donors
1988	4080
2001	6082

Source: United Network for Organ Sharing, http://www.unos.org.

6.2. *A proposal to allow a secondary market between the nonprofit procurers and hospitals*

This examination of the donative system for procuring organs has revealed that a system relying on the procurement of common property organs by exhortation by nonprofit organizations may obtain organs at a cost that is low, perhaps even lower than the market cost. It has also been shown that significant obstacles may exist to effective exploitation of the donative system's potential efficiencies.

For a donative system to be effective, regulation that bans the market must also address the obstacles to sufficient and effective exhortation mentioned earlier. These obstacles were identified as arising from (1) the nature of exhortation, (2) the fact that the market-inalienable good's rent is common property, and (3) the characteristics of the nonprofit organizations that procure market-inalienable goods. How the interplay of these elements affects the efficiency of the donative system depends on the nature of the market-inalienable good and the condition of supply and demand. Consequently, the regulation of each type of good should reflect its specific features.

In general, regulation banning a market should assign the good's rent to some party, unless the inefficiency of leaving it as common property will result in a greater supply or lower cost, or yield some other benefit. One way of assigning rights to other factors in the commons—such as fish in the ocean or broadcast frequencies in the air—is by auctioning licenses that grant exclusive rights to these resources. If people are unlikely to donate to forprofit firms, then auctioning licenses that would permit such firms to solicit donations may not be practical.

The government could grant designated nonprofits monopolistic rights to exhort in specific regions. This is, in effect, how the government currently regulates procurement of organs. While granting local monopolies would eliminate any overexhortation

[42] There has been considerable effort in the U.S. into trying to increase procurement by understanding what kind of effort works (e.g., Ozcan, 1999). See Beasley et al. (1997) describing the efforts of the Partnership for Organ Donation to get hospitals to focus on identifying and managing potential donors.

problems, the problem the current organ procurement system appears to face is under-exhortation.

Alternatively, the regulation banning a market might not assign property rights at all; this is the case with regard to babies offered for adoption and tissue used to produce pharmaceuticals. Competition that dissipates the common property rent can be expected to result from this approach. This dissipation of common property rent will also occur when a market is legal but it is common practice is to avoid a market, as with blood procurement. Although there is no regulation banning a market in blood, nearly all blood procured for transfusion is donated. If more of the market-inalienable good can be procured by not assigning property rights, even if such procurement is inefficient, government may still intentionally and knowingly make good common property.

No matter how the market-inalienable good is regulated, as long as its economic value influences expenditures on procurement or the party to whom it is allocated, some notion of commodification must be introduced, perhaps indirectly. How might "indirect commodification" work in the human organ arena? Some have suggested that, in lieu of paying for organs, the donated organs be treated as "rewarded gifts" with donors being compensated for the inconvenience, hospitalization, and loss of income necessitated by the donations. Others have devised sophisticated schemes whereby donors might receive tax breaks, or payments from insurance companies, for the right to their organs upon their death. And others have proposed to pay families of brain-dead cadavers a $1000 "death benefit" for their loved ones' organs. These schemes will likely elicit supply because they offer an incentive, but they are limited by their inability to ensure that the payments made to donors will elicit the optimum supply. Furthermore, the payments are not sufficiently indirect to appear as anything but payments.

Another alternative would be to assign the economic value of the organ, by law, to those regional nonprofit organizations currently designated as franchises by the organ procurement system. Under this alternative, these nonprofit franchises would be permitted complete property rights to the organ they manage to procure. The nonprofits would distribute the organ and be allowed and encouraged to charge the full value of the organ to intermediaries such as transplant surgeons, hospitals, or pharmaceutical companies. In effect, a market in organs would exist, but it would function at a later stage in the production process. Rather than charging a price based on cost plus administration, each nonprofit would charge the market price that reflects what the donor would have received had a market existed. Recipients of the organ would pay what the market price would have been.

Some nonprofits would use their surplus to finance additional exhortation of potential suppliers. Others would use the surplus to further worthy programs such as public education to increase donation. The regulators would monitor and publicize the activities of the nonprofits to assure that the surpluses are used in desirable ways, and not dissipated. Properly administered, this system would keep middlemen from appropriating the value of the organ, and would also promote productive efforts to procure the property rights to the free organs.

However, as Barzel (1997) has argued, even legal assignment of complete property rights to nonprofits may still leave the property right not fully delineated. Consequently, assignment of the property right to the economic value of the organ may still not eliminate the leverage of other parties involved in procuring organs as they seek to obtain a share of the organ's rent. Specifically, with regard to organ procurement, the procurement organizations are unable to approach the families of potential donors without first being informed of their existence by physicians and hospital personnel. The cooperation of physicians and hospital personnel is thus essential to the success of the donative system. But physicians and hospital personnel may not be easily moved to cooperate. For them, the act of donation may not have the significance that it may have for the donating families. Indeed, the most effective solution may be to allow these providers to receive a finder's fee, all the while continuing the ban on an organ market. Under current interpretation of the law, however, no such payment ("finder's fee") is permitted. Instead, in 1990, Medicare required that providers inform the procurement organizations when potential donors arrive at their facilities. Therefore, additional administrative measures may be required to enforce this policy.

The problem of balancing the need for markets against the aversion to commodification is not an unusual one; societies are often confronted with the need to govern in the face of commitments to contradictory principles. To mediate these conflicts, "legal fictions"[43] are sometimes created that appear to support both contradictory principles by adhering to the letter of one while eviscerating its spirit, and the letter as well as the spirit of the other. A cynic might view legal fictions as devices that hypocritically disguise the inconsistency and are effective only because what they are being deployed to do is not transparent. However one views legal fictions, they can be useful. Indeed, we might seek to resolve the dilemma of how to procure and allocate market-inalienable goods in an economically rational manner, without at the same time commodifying and exploiting human beings, by the deliberate use of legal fictions.

The proposal offered here to maintain a donative system while implementing markets at a step once-removed, to balance the competing need for markets against the aversion to commodification, is but one of a class of solutions of this type of legal fiction. Together with the proposed measures to overcome the obstacles to sufficient and effective exhortation, these measures might help the donative system achieve its potential efficiencies.

7. Conclusion

This chapter has investigated the arrangements people make in the face of a market ban—an extreme form of market failure. Two representative models have been reviewed. One, based on the standard price control model and the assumption that individuals act only out of narrow self-interest, concludes that the ban on organ markets

[43] See Fuller (1967).

is inherently unable to generate a sufficient supply of organs. The other, a model of altruism in which.exhortation effort designed to appeal to motives such as the redemption of death by donating the gift of life, provides a model of market-inalienability that provides a theoretical basis for a viable and possibly efficient alternative to a market.

Some of the implications of the alternative model are: (1) organs may be cheaper to procure by non-markets than markets by appealing to motives other than narrow self-interest, (2) failure to secure a greater supply may be due not to insufficient altruism, as claimed by market proponents, but instead be due to a failure to exploit the non-markets efficiencies, and (3) altruism does not come cheap, and even though organs are a free resource, there are still costs of extraction.[44]

The debate over the consequences of market-inalienability has been highly ideological, with little appeal to empirical evidence. Thus, the task now is to develop empirical approaches that might test the models. As a policy matter, it would be important to know how the Spanish in Europe and the successful organ procurement organizations in the United States achieve their results. If the rest of Europe raised donor rates to that of Spain, and the organ procurement in the U.S. matched that of the best organizations, the number of organs would more than double. This increase would provide organs sufficient to prevent deaths while waiting and would begin to reduce the numbers on waiting lists.

The human organ and tissue industry is increasingly becoming a global enterprise involving trade between countries with differing economic systems, definitions of death, and values related to the body. Thus, it may become important to understand how such trade will evolve, what problems the international trading system will face, and what national and international regulation (or guidelines or treaties) might foster the beneficial uses of the human body while deterring the evils also possible. Finally, we may be spared all this work should there be positive developments in xenotransplantation and or artificial body parts.[45] At which point, should we be so fortunate, we can take organ transplantation off the agenda of a conference on altruism.

References

Adler, R.S., Pittle, R.D. (1984). "Cajolery or command: are education campaigns an adequate substitute for regulation?". Yale Journal on Regulation 1, 159–193.

Arrow, K.J. (1972). "Gifts and exchanges". Philosophy and Public Affairs 1 (4).

Barney Jr., L.D., Reynolds, R.L. (1989). "An economic analysis of transplant organs". Atlantic Economic Journal 17, 12–20.

Barzel, Y. (1997). Economic Analysis of Property Rights, 2nd edn.

[44] Ineffective organ procurement programs such as President Bush's declaration of "National Organ and Tissue Donor Awareness Week" (see Bush, 2001) illustrates the attempt to avoid spending the money that might make the donative system. A serious program would spend some serious money.

[45] See Niklason and Langer (2001).

Baxter, D., Smerdon, J. (2000). "Donation Matters: Demographic and Organ Transplantation in Canada 2000–2040", Report by Urban Futures Institute, Vancouver, BC.

Beasley, C.L., Capossela, C.L., Brigham, L.E., et al. (1997). "The impact of a comprehensive hospital-focused intervention to increase organ donation". Journal of Transplant Coordination 7 (1), 6–13.

Bentham, J. (1831). Of What Use is a Dead Man to the Living.

Bernardo, R.M. (1971). The Theory of Moral Incentives in Cuba.

Bush, G.W. (2001). Proclamation of National Organ and Tissue Donor Awareness Week, April 4.

Caballero, F., Lopez-Navidad, A., Leal, J., Garcia-Sousa, S., Soriano, J.A., Domingo, P. (1999). "The cultural level of cadaveric potential organ donor relatives determines the rate of consent for donation". Transplantation Proceedings 31, 2601.

Calabresi, G., Melamed, A.D. (1972). "Property rules, liability rules, and inalienability: one view of the cathedral". Harvard Law Review 85.

Cheung, S. (1974). "A theory of price control". Journal of Law & Economics 17, 53–71.

Childress, J.F. (1993). "Non-heart-beating donors of organs: are the distinctions between direct and indirect effects and between killing and letting die relevant and helpful". Kennedy Institute of Ethics Journal 3 (2), 203–216.

Collard, D. (1978). Altruism and Economy: A Study in Non-Selfish Economics.

Cornes, R., Sandler, T. (1986). The Theory of Externalities, Public Goods, and Club Goods.

Daar, N.S. (1992). "Rewarded gifting". Transplantation Proceedings 24, 2207–2211.

Epstein, R. (1985). "Why restrain alienation?". Columbia Law Review 85, 970–990.

Epstein, R. (1994). "Organ transplantation: or, altruism run amuck", Univ. of Chicago, Occasional Papers from the Law School No. 31.

Fleischhauer, K., Hermeren, G., Holm, S., Honnefelder, L., Kimura, R., Quintana, O., Serrao, D., Wolfbran (2000). "Comparative report on transplantation and relevant ethical problems in five European Countries, and some Reflections on Japan". Transplant International 13 (4), 266–275.

Frey, B.S. (1997). Not for the Money: An Economic Theory of Personal Motivation. Elgar.

Frey, B.S., Oberholzer-Gee, F. (1997). "The cost of price incentives: an empirical analysis of motivation crowding out". American Economic Review, September.

Fuller, L. (1967). Legal Fictions.

Gordon, H.S. (1954). "The economic theory of a common property resource: the fishery". Journal of Political Economy 17, 121–142.

Goyal, M., Mehta, R.L., Schneiderman, L.J., Sehgal, A.R. (2002). "Economic and health consequences of selling a kidney in India". Journal of the American Medical Association 288 (13). October 2.

Hamish, S. (1992). "Rationality and the market for blood". Journal of Economic Behavior and Organization 19, 125–143.

Hansmann, H.B. (1989). "The ethics and economics of prohibiting markets for organs". Journal of Health Politics, Policy, and Law 14 (1).

Kaserman, D.L., Barnett, A.H. (1991). "An economic analysis of transplant organs: a comment and extension". Atlantic Economic Journal 19, 57–63.

Kaserman, D.L., Barnett, A.H. (2002). The U.S. Organ Procurement System: A Prescription for Reform. American Enterprise Institute for Public Policy Research.

Kanbur, R. (2001). "On Obnoxious Markets", Unpublished Paper, Cornel University, http://www.people.cornel.edu/pages/sk145.

Kennedy Institute of Ethics [Entire] (1993). 3 (2).

Kessel, R.A. (1974). "Transfused blood, serum hepatitis, and the Coase theorem". Journal of Law & Economics 17, 265–289.

Landes, E.M., Posner, R.A. (1978). "The economics of the baby shortage". Journal of Legal Studies 7, 323–348.

Lopez-Navidad, A., Caballero, F. (2001). "For a rational approach to the critical points of the cadaveric donation process". Transplantation Proceedings 33, 795.

McNeil, D.G. (2003). "Rare infection threatens to spread in blood supply", New York Times, November 18.

Meckler, L. (1998). "Organ donation effort meets with opposition", The Associated Press, July 18.
Menikoff, J.A. (1999). "Organ swapping". Hastings Center Report 29 (6).
Niklason, L., Langer, R. (2001). "Prospects for organ and tissue replacement". Journal of the American Medical Association 285 (5), 573–576. February 7.
Norberg, U., Soderlind, K., Franzén, L., Loven, C., Strandelius, E., Wolfbrand, A. (2000). "A modified "Spanish model" for organ donation in the region of southeast Sweden". Transplantation Proceedings 32, 72–74.
Office of the Inspector General (1987). Organ Acquisition Costs: An Overview. Department of Health and Human Services, Office of Analysis and Inspections.
Okie, S. (2001). "Organ exchanges push boundaries: new tactics to attract living donors raise issues of ethics and altruism", The Washington Post, June 9, P A01.
Okun, A.O. (1975). Equity and Efficiency. The Great Tradeoff.
Ozcan, Y. (1999). "Benchmarking organ procurement organizations: a national study", Health Services Research, October.
Peters, T. (1991). "Life or death: the issue of payment in cadaveric organ donation". Journal of the American Medical Association 265 (10). March 13.
Pindyck, R.S., Rubinfeld, D.L. (1989). Microeconomics.
Radin, M.J. (1987). "Market-inalienability". Harvard Law Review 100 (8), 1849–1937.
Robertson, D.H. (1956). "What does the economist economize?". In: Economic Commentaries.
Rose-Ackerman, S. (1985). "Inalienability and the theory of property rights". Columbia Law Review 85, 931–969.
Rothman, D.J. (1998). "The international organ traffic", The New York Review of Books, March 26.
Scheper-Hughes, N. (1990). "Theft of life", Society.
Scheper-Hughes, N. (1996). "Theft of life: the globalization of organ stealing rumors". Anthropology Today 12 (3). June 3–11.
Scheper-Hughes, N. (1998). "Organ trade: the new cannibalism". The New Internationalist, April 14–17.
Shumway, N. (1993). "Quoted in: Parents Find Solace in Donating Organs". E. Rosenthal. N.Y. Times, May 11.
Siegelbaum, L.H. (1988). "Stakhanovism and the Politics of Productivity in the U.S.S.R., 1935–1941".
Sipress, A. (2001). "U.S. Faults Some Allies On Human Trafficking". The Washington Post, July 13.
Smith, C. (2001). "Doctor says he took transplant organs from executed Chinese prisoners". New York Times, November 11.
Solnick, Hemenway (1996). "The Deadweight Loss of Christmas". American Economic Review, December.
Solow, R.M. (1971). "Blood and thunder". Yale Law Journal 80, 1696–1711.
Tanner, L. (2002). "AMA Votes on Organ Donation Payments", Associated Press, June 18.
Task Force on Organ Transplantation, U.S. Dept. of Health and Human Services (1986). Organ Transplantation: Issues and Recommendations 35.
Thorne, E.D. (1990). "Tissue transplants: the dilemma of the body's growing value". Public Interest, 37–48.
Thorne, E.D. (1996). "The cost of procuring market-inalienable human organs". Journal of Regulatory Economics 10, 191–200.
Thorne, E.D. (1998a). "When private parts are made public goods: the economics of market-inalienability". Yale Journal on Regulation 15, 149–175.
Thorne, E.D. (1998b). "The shortage in market-inalienable human organs: a consideration of "non-market" failures". The American Journal of Economics and Sociology 56, 247–260.
Titmuss, R. (1971). The Gift Relationship: From Human Blood to Social Policy.
United Network for Organ Sharing (2002). http://www.ustransplant.org/nat-center-summ.html.
Waldfogel (1993). "The deadweight loss of Christmas". American Economic Review, December.
Weiss, R. (1997). "Organ demand forces dilemmas". The Washington Post, p. A01, November 24.

Chapter 21

ALTRUISM, RECIPROCITY AND COOPERATION IN THE WORKPLACE

JULIO J. ROTEMBERG*

Harvard Business School

Contents

* I am grateful to Rawi Abdelal, Ramon Casadesus-Masanell, Tiziana Casciaro, Rafael Di Tella, Monica Higgins, Christina Fong, Rakesh Khurana, Joshua Margolis, Jean Mercier Ythier and Nitin Nohria for helpful comments and conversations and to the Harvard Business School's Division of Research for research support.

Handbook of the Economics of Giving, Altruism and Reciprocity, Volume 2
Edited by Serge-Christophe Kolm and Jean Mercier Ythier

DOI: 10.1016/S1574-0714(06)02021-5

Abstract

This paper surveys economic models where cooperation arises in the workplace because individuals' utility functions involve a concern for others (altruism) or a desire to respond to like with like (reciprocity). It also discusses empirical evidence which bears on the relevance of these theories. The paper considers separately the feelings employees have for their employers or their supervisors, those that employees have for others that occupy similar positions as themselves and the feelings of supervisors towards their subordinates. Altruism appears to play a role in the last two settings while reciprocity seems useful to explain the way employees react to employer actions which the employees regard as unfair.

Keywords

cooperation, altruism, reciprocity, labor relations, field studies

JEL classification: J530, L230, M540

1. Introduction

Capitalist workplaces produce goods that are ultimately sold for money. There is thus no doubt that financial incentives play a role in ensuring the exertion of those who spend their time in these workplaces. The result is that economists have devoted most of their effort to understanding the role of these financial incentives and have devoted less effort to the other factors that might also affect the output of capitalist enterprises. In this survey, I focus on two alternate motivations, namely those that flow from feelings of altruism and those that flow from the desire to behave in a "reciprocal" fashion (that is to respond to like with like).

This survey consists of a discussion of the (mostly theoretical) economic literature that is directed at the role these factors can play in the workplace while also commenting on the pertinent empirical evidence. While Fehr (2006) discusses the extensive experimental evidence, much of which simulates workplace environments, I focus exclusively on field observations. This empirical evidence is drawn from the field of "Organizational Behavior," a field that includes a vast array of papers suggesting that financial considerations are not sufficient for understanding what goes on inside capitalist enterprises. It is worth stressing, however, that this literature does not suggest that altruism and reciprocity are the only non-financial sources of effort in the workplace. At the same time, many of the papers that I regard as bearing on the relevance of altruism and reciprocity are not written with this particular focus in mind. Lastly, some of the relevant papers are themselves associated with large literatures that discuss related findings. As a result of these considerations, my survey of the empirical work that bears on altruism and reciprocity in the workplace is not at all exhaustive. Its aim, rather, is two-fold. First, it tries to show that empirical observations regarding conduct in organization do provide evidence for the importance of altruism and reciprocity. Second, it seeks to provide references that will help economists explore the parts of the field of Organizational Behavior that are most relevant to the question at hand.

Altruism matters in the workplace insofar people's actions at work depend on feelings of benevolence towards employers, co-workers or customers. People might work hard, for example, because they enjoy vicariously the benefits this gives to others that they care for. Reciprocity would matter instead if the actions of employers, co-workers or customers make people feel a loss in utility of they did not respond with "similar" actions. People might work hard, for example, because they would feel it would be unfair to others to do otherwise. Both altruism and reciprocity require that an individual's utility depend on more than his own material payoffs. An individual's utility depends on another's material payoffs in the case of altruism whereas, in the case of reciprocity, it depends on the extent to which the individual feels he is responding appropriately to the actions of another.

It is worth stressing, however, that altruism would serve little purpose while reciprocity would be hard to imagine if contracts were complete. A complete contract can be interpreted as telling the agent exactly what he is expected to do in each state of nature while also specifying the payment that attends the performance of these actions.

The idea behind such a contract is that it makes the actions of each agent completely predictable. Given this, the sentiments provoked by the actual or imagined actions of others are probably of little relevance. Similarly, once the contracts are signed, having individuals care about others is of little use since the actions are essentially pre-determined. It is worth stressing, however, that the economics literature abounds with incomplete contract models and, in these settings, altruism and reciprocity could easily play a role.

While I focus on altruism and reciprocity, I also consider other modifications of individual utility functions which have been shown to lead to cooperation in workplace settings. Akerlof (1983) modifies utility functions so that they include loyalty. Kandel and Lazear (1992) let utility be reduced by "peer pressure" which is triggered when an individual fails to act according to the wishes of his co-workers. They call these losses in utility "shame" in the case where the observable outcome of an agent's actions is below par and "guilt" in the case where nothing is observable but the agent feels bad when his unobservable action is unhelpful to the group. Along similar lines, Casadesus-Masanell (2004) models employees as choosing "norms" and "ethical standards". In his model, norms are expectations about the outcome of a relationship and employees feel shame when subsequent outcomes differ from the norm. By contrast, "ethical standards" are goals the employee has about his own actions and the employee feels guilt when his subsequent actions fall below this goal.

A unifying theme of this survey is that I focus on individual utility functions which do not depend exclusively on the individual's material payoffs. Rather, they depend also on the payoffs of others or on the way the individual's actions are related to the actions of others. This means that I do not discuss at length the extensive literature where individuals care only about their material payoffs but cooperation arises in equilibrium because the interactions are repeated. It is worth noting that cooperation is sustained in model of repeated interactions by a kind of behavior that is similar to reciprocity: individuals who deviate from the cooperative equilibrium expect to be punished. Wherever it seems possible to do so, I discuss the empirical features of cooperation in organizations that seem more consistent with the feelings I consider here than with equilibria in simple repeated game models. For example, repeated-game models differ from the ones I consider here in that the latter can easily lead to cooperation even in the last period of a relationship; and such cooperation is routinely observed in organizations.

This survey is organized as follows. First, section 2 considers models and evidence relating to the feeling employees have for their employers. Then, in section 3, I consider interactions between people who occupy similar positions in an organizational hierarchy while I turn my attention to feelings of supervisors for their subordinates in section 4. Section 5 concludes.

2. Workers cooperating with employers

I start my discussion of altruism and reciprocity in organizations by focusing on situations where a principal (firm owner) hires an agent (worker). In the simplest model of this sort, the agent chooses an action—usually called effort—such that an increase in effort is beneficial to the firm but costly to the worker. The firm's relevant action is how much it pays the worker, and here too an increase in this payment is bad for the person choosing the action (here the firm) while being good for the worker. A contract is sufficiently complete that the first best is achievable if the agent's payment depends on his action. At the opposite extreme one can consider a setting where contracts are so incomplete that the payment is completely independent of the actions of the worker.

If one ignores the timing of these various actions, the structure of this game is similar to that of the prisoners' dilemma. To see this, suppose that a worker can make only two levels of effort, high and low. Effort costs the worker disutility (in units of income) of c^i while it provides income to the firm of y^i where the superscript i denotes effort and equals either H or L. I suppose without loss of generality that $y^H > y^L$ and let the firm pay a wage equal to either w^H or w^L so both players can either play H or L. The payoff matrix is then

		Firm: L	Firm: H
Worker	L	$w^L - c^L, y^L - w^L$	$w^H - c^L, y^L - w^H$
	H	$w^L - c^H, y^H - w^L$	$w^H - c^H, y^H - w^H$

(1)

If the wages w^H and w^L split evenly the surplus generated by high and low effort respectively so that $2w^H = y^H + c^H$ and $2w^L = y^L + c^L$, this payoff matrix becomes

		Firm: L	Firm: H
Worker	L	A, A	$A + \frac{(y^H - y^L) + (c^H - c^L)}{2}, A - \frac{(y^H - y^L) + (c^H - c^L)}{2}$
	H	$A - (c^H - c^L), A + (y^H - y^L)$	$A + \frac{(y^H - y^L) - (c^H - c^L)}{2}, A + \frac{(y^H - y^L) - (c^H - c^L)}{2}$

where $A = \frac{y^L - c^L}{2}$. If $y^H - c^H > y^L - c^L$ and $c^H > c^L$, this is essentially identical to a prisoner's dilemma because, starting from a situation where the worker exerts high effort and the firm pays a high wage, each agent would benefit by playing L instead even though both payers are worse off at $\{L, L\}$ than at $\{H, H\}$.

The isomorphism of the normal form of this game with a prisoners' dilemma may not be all that helpful when thinking about the relationship between a firm and its employees. The reason is that firms and workers cannot usefully be thought of choosing wages and effort simultaneously. If firms choose their wages in advance and $c^H > c^L$, workers play a "one-sided" prisoners' dilemma game. Without repetition, and without the sentiments that I focus on, the outcome then involves low worker effort.

2.1. Reciprocity and the gift-exchange model

I now discuss two types of sentiments that can alleviate the problems posed when contracts are so incomplete that the employment relation leads to low effort. The first is closely related to Adams' (Adams, 1965) "exchange theory", though it was introduced into economics by Akerlof (1982). Akerlof supposes that workers' collective norms about the effort they should make are increasing in their wage and that individual workers suffer when their individual effort deviates from the collective norm. A more direct way of thinking about this effect, which is close to Adams (1965), is to suppose that workers feel psychological distress when they give back something whose value they perceive as different from the value of what they receive. They thus adjust what they give so that it corresponds as closely as possible to the value of what they receive.

Rabin (1993) proposes a formal model of reciprocity that can be applied to games in normal form. This model is based on three ingredients. The first is the extent to which the first agent feels that the second agent has been "kind" to him (and vice versa). Rabin (1993) assumes that this equals the difference between the payoffs that the first expects to receive from the second and the payoffs that it would "equitable" for the second to give to the first. The second ingredient is the definition of these equitable payoffs. He supposes that these are the average of the highest and the lowest payoffs the second agent can give to the first under the assumption that the player acts efficiently. Last, there is the utility each agent actually maximizes. This is supposed to be the sum of his material payoffs and the product of his own kindness times the kindness he expects to receive from the other agent. Thus, if the first agent expects the second to give the first a payoff that is higher than the "equitable" payoff, the first agent seeks to raise the second agent's payoff above that agent's equitable payoff. One important property of the model to which I return below is that the agent maximizes a utility function in which only the payoff-relevant actions of the other play a role. By contrast, the intentions behind the other's actions do not matter directly.

The Rabin (1993) model of reciprocity can be extended to cover dynamic games, as shown by Falk and Fiscbacher (2000) and Dufwenberg and Kirchsteiger (2004). Thus, suppose the firm moves first and pays the workers a wage of w^H which splits the surplus that results from high worker effort. If the worker cares only about income and effort while $c^H > c^L$, he would exert low effort. Alternatively, the considerations above could lead the workers to feel malaise if their effort was low so that one would have to subtract m from their payoff with effort equal to L. If $m > c^H - c^L$, the workers exert high effort, thereby making the decision to pay high wages rational to begin with. It is worth emphasizing that firms might be able to activate similar psychological mechanisms of loyalty using non-wage components of compensation. A firm might, for example foster these feelings of reciprocity by having a policy of not firing workers in downturns. From a firm's point of view, one big advantage of using reciprocity to achieve good outcomes is that reciprocity could be the result of a company-wide policy. It need not depend on taking actions that are tailored to each worker in particular.

The key question surrounding this kind of reciprocity is whether firms who do good deeds of this sort actually reap the rewards promised by the theory. Akerlof (1982) based his model on the observations by Homans (1962) of 10 women who carried out a simple clerical task called "cash-posting" which involved the processing of individual cards. Their employer required that, on average, these employees process at least 300 cards per hour. All 10 employees did more than this minimum amount of work, with some employees processing over 400 cards per hour. Akerlof (1982) points out that this is incompatible with effort minimization under the assumption that an increase in the number of processed cards requires more effort. He goes on to suggest that Homans' (Homans, 1962) observations of high output motivate his theory. An attractive aspect of Homans' setting is that it rules out several alternative explanations for high effort. For example, these workers were not motivated by expectations that their future income would vary with their current effort. The only promotion available to these workers was to a job with the same pay and more responsibilities, so that such promotions were sometimes turned down. In addition, many of these employees expected to leave their current job relatively soon because the company forced these women to retire when they married.

However, these observations have an alternative explanation, though this explanation may seem inconsistent with the standard economic assumption that people always seek to minimize their effort. This alternative is that, once workers are on the job, the disutility of effort is not minimized when doing no work but is minimized instead when carrying out a certain positive level of activity. In terms of my notation, this means that $c^H < c^L$, at least for those workers for whom Homans (1962) observed a relatively high rate of output. This point of view is not necessarily incompatible with the neoclassical theory of labor supply since workers might still prefer to spend time at home rather than at work. They might also prefer being idle while chatting with companions rather than working even when they are in the workplace, but their dislike of rebukes might stop them from engaging in such a completely "unproductive" activity. Homans (1962, p. 89) reports some evidence for this alternate viewpoint. He describes one worker by saying: "For me, she simply had a high activity rate: she had the highest output among the posters, and she also talked more than anyone else in the room... [She] never ... gave the slightest appearance of making an effort to work fast and she herself felt that if she concentrated she did not do so well."

This evidence still leaves open the question of whether, in actual firms, employers can get employees to make an extra effort (as opposed to that which is the result of their natural metabolic rate coupled with the presence of supervisors) by being extra nice.[1] One kind of evidence that might bear on this issue involves the analysis of variations in performance and job satisfaction across individual employees. In other words, one can ask employees whether they are satisfied with their jobs and study whether this answer

[1] An extensive experimental literature exists on this topic. This evidence is critically discussed in Goodman and Friedman (1971).

is correlated with supervisory ratings of performance. It seems reasonable to believe that employees differ in the extent to which they regard their employer as generous and it is equally reasonable to think that those who are more satisfied with their jobs ought to, on average, view their employer as more generous. Thus, a simple theory of reciprocity would lead one to expect higher performance, on average, from more satisfied employees. According to Lawler (1973) the extensive literature on this relationship has uncovered only a weak positive correlation between satisfaction and performance. Lawler (1973) suggests, in addition, that this relation is more likely to be due to the effect of performance on satisfaction rather than the reverse.

An alternative approach for gauging whether grateful employees work harder involves looking at organizations as a whole. The advantage of this approach is that the variation in actual management practice across organizations ought to lead to a larger variation in the extent to which employees feel well-treated. The disadvantage is that the variation in performance measures across organizations are due to a multitude of causes. Still, the qualitative evidence amassed by Kunda (1992) from a firm that has actively tried to manage its "corporate culture" by being nice to its employees seems relevant.

Both the managers and the engineers at the firm he calls "Tech" talked often about loyalty to the company. In an address to the employees, the Chief Executive Officer (CEO) that Kunda (1992) calls Sam Miller said "We hired consultants to examine things. They came back and said: 'We found trust, openness and cooperativeness, little selfishness.' Those were the words I wanted to hear." (Kunda, 1992, p. 114). A manager is quoted as saying "Maybe I've swallowed slogans, the party line, the whole 'Sam Miller do what's right' thing. But I do believe that Tech does what's right. We don't lay off, even though some people deserve to be laid off. So you feel loyalty back. Sam Miller believes in 'taking care of your people' and he gets paid back with loyalty. They've never done wrong by me" (Kunda, 1992, p. 173–174).

What is certain is that engineers and managers worked extremely hard at this company, with many blaming divorce and alcoholism on "burnout" caused by overwork. However, hard work was common also in high-technology companies that did not offer the job security of Tech. A Tech manager told Kunda "Loyalty—they make a big deal of that—is old school. What is important is work. Some people feel a sense of belonging, but in my case it is not strong" (Kunda, 1992, p. 182). And a more cynical view was also heard by Kunda. "Techies. We're all Techies. The whole goddam industry. It's a type of individual who is aggressive and involved, looks loyal, puts in a lot of time, but underneath the surface is self-serving and owes allegiance only to himself. They are mobile and choose the projects as they see fit."

What remains unclear, then, is the extent to which the effort of the employees at Tech was due to the Tech "culture," the nature of the work or the financial incentives faced by its employees. Comparative data on effort at firms that did and those that did not offer job security would seem necessary to settle this question. It is also somewhat unclear whether Tech reduced the incidence of quits by offering guaranteed employment. However, even data demonstrating the existence of lower quits at Tech would not establish an independent role for employee feelings of loyalty. The no-layoff policy obviously has value to the employees and thus makes jobs at Tech more attractive relative to those at companies that do not have this policy.

When $c^H < c^L$ so that workers prefer to exert effort H, a different version of the gift-exchange model can be operative. This is that workers will actually make an effort to reduce their output rate—and thereby hurt their employers—if they are upset at their employers for any reason. In terms of the payoff matrix above, this result would obtain if the employee lost m when exerting effort H if the firm paid him w^L. If $m > c^L - c^H$, this would lead the worker to make effort L whenever the firm pays a low wage (or does something else that the worker deems unjust). The parameter m can be thought of as the psychological benefit of "evening the score" or of "venting one's spite". The evidence surveyed in Fehr (2006) concerning responders' behavior in ultimatum games when they are offered shares of the pie that they regard as unfair is consistent with this behavior. The evidence for this set of attitudes in natural workplace settings seems strong as well.

To start, it is worth returning to the cash-posters example of Homans (1962). He reports that, at the time of his study, "No group norm put a ceiling on output. A couple of years before, when relations between the posters and a former division head were strained, there may have been some restriction [that led each worker to curtail output]". This suggests that, indeed, workers will go through extra trouble to lower output when they are unhappy.

More direct evidence for this is provided in Lord and Hohenfeld (1979). They consider a group of 23 baseball players who "played out their option" in 1976 and only got jobs as free agents either in the middle of the 1976 season or at the beginning of the 1977 season. Contract rules allowed club owners to cut the wages of these players in 1976 by up to 20% and a vast majority of these players did indeed see substantial pay cuts in that season. These players were largely "stars" whose batting performance before 1976 was substantially above that of their teammates. In 1976, however, their performance deteriorated substantially, only to recover after they signed up anew as free agents (with substantial salary increases). One extremely attractive feature of this evidence is that one would expect the labor market incentives of these players to favor an improvement in performance since these players were effectively looking for a job.

Along similar lines, Bewley (1999) interviewed a large number of firms and found that the principal reason firms were reluctant to cut wages in a recession was that "pay cuts hurt morale and demotivate workers" (p. 174). Interestingly, the experience of the relatively small number of managers that did cut wages was more mixed, and I return to this below. Leaving this aside for a moment, the rigidity of wages that motivated this study suggests that reciprocity does not involve locally smooth responses to the actions of others. In particular, the firms' tendency to keep wages constant would be rational if the loss in productivity induced by a small wage cut exceeds the gain in productivity that follows a small wage increase. In the Rabin (1993) framework, such a local nonlinearity might require a different functional form than the one he uses. In particular, wage rigidity might be due either to strong nonlinearities in the way the marginal utility of effort depends on the "perceived kindness" of the employer or in nonlinearities in the way the wage affects the perceived kindness of the employer.

A somewhat different kind of evidence that workers respond negatively to wage reductions has been uncovered in studying employee theft. Compelling evidence that wage reductions lead to increases in such theft comes from Greenberg (1990), who studied three plants belonging to the same company.[2] In two of these plants, a 15% pay cut was instituted for 10 weeks while pay was left unchanged in the third. Consistent with the idea that effort would fall in the plants with reduced wages, employee theft increased in the two plants with wage reductions. Before the experiment, and after wages were brought back to their previous level in the two plants with wage cuts, these plants had fairly low level of theft (or "shrinkage").

One potential economic explanation for this finding is that employees in the plants with lower wages felt they had less to lose from getting caught. This would fit the with efficiency wage model of Shapiro and Stiglitz (1984).[3] Greenberg (1993) offers evidence which is both unexpected from the point of view of the Shapiro–Stiglitz (Shapiro and Stiglitz, 1984) model and which suggests a somewhat different view of what prompts workers to be mad at their employers. In one of the plants where wages were cut, management expressed a great deal of regret and explained the need for wage cuts as a necessary response to reductions in demand. In the other, the explanations were cursory and the apologies perfunctory. If employee theft depended only on the wage itself, the two kinds of discourse would presumably have led to the same increase in theft. Instead, theft increased from about 3% to about 8% in the plant where the explanations were cursory while it only increased to about 4% in the plant were the explanations were elaborate. This fits with a common view among students of "organizational justice" (see Lind and Tyler, 1988, for example) that employees care at least as much about "procedural justice" than they do about receiving good outcomes (or "distributive justice"). Greenberg (1993) also contains evidence for this proposition from the behavior of quits. Over 25% of workers resigned in response to the pay cut in the plant with the perfunctory explanation while only 2% did so in the plant where the explanations were elaborate. The quit rate was negligible in the control group.[4]

According to Lind and Tyler (1988, p. 191–201), who develop the ideas in Thibaut and Walker (1975), employees regard organizations as having fair procedures if the organizations satisfy two key criteria. The first is that the organization gives the employee

[2] Analoui and Kakabadse (1991) provide different kinds of evidence for the view that theft involves reciprocation for ill-treatment. They say (Analoui and Kakabadse, 1991, p. 57) "Pilferage was thus often resorted as a means to get even with employers". In one example they give, a barmaid stole from a customer after her boss forbade her from going home early enough to catch a bus and thereby forced her to take a taxi.

[3] See also Bowles and Gintis (1992).

[4] In a different study using similar methods, Schaubroeck et al. (1994) ensured that some employees working at a firm that had instituted pay cuts were given elaborate explanations for this pay cut while others were not. In this study, the effect of giving explanations appears to be more muted.

"voice," i.e., an opportunity to state their side of the case.[5] The second is that the organization treats employees with respect, and in particular that it explains its acts in ways that makes individual employees feel that the organization values them as persons even if, for example, it no longer needs their services.[6]

Indeed, the most compelling evidence for the importance of procedural justice in organizations comes from actions taken by workers after they are dismissed from their jobs. Lind et al. (2000) interviewed 996 individuals who had been let go of their jobs and asked them whether they either had initiated a wrongful termination lawsuit or were intending to file such a suit. They then fitted statistical models that explained these dichotomous variables with standard economic variables such as the individual's subjective assessment of his likelihood of winning the suit and the amount the individual expected to collect if he won. As additional explanators, they added variables intended to capture the extent to which these employees felt that their employer had treated them fairly at the time of termination. These latter variables were strongly correlated with both the initiation of lawsuits and the intention to sue in the future, even after controlling for the expected payoffs of these lawsuits. As expected from the previous discussion, the variables measuring the extent to which these individuals thought employers had been fair at termination had a great deal to do with the explanations employers gave at that time. They were also correlated with the extent to which the previous employer sought to help the individual find a new job.

One attractive feature of these observations is that they do not seem easily explainable by repeated game models where agents care only about their material payoffs. If these lawsuits directly increase the material payoffs of terminated employees, all of them should pursue them. If they do not, it is not clear why concerns with future material payoffs should lead employees to sue their ex-employers. A model with reputations might be built that can account for these facts, but the idea that people seek revenge when they feel they have been treated badly seems more straightforward.

The response of workers to what they perceive as violations of procedural fairness raises questions about the underlying sources of "reciprocity." The simplest perspective on reciprocity is, as in Adams (1965), that workers respond to the tangible benefits they receive from their employers. The extent to which explanations for bad outcomes provide tangible benefits seems questionable, however. Giving people an opportunity to

[5] The organization's problem is in some sense the opposite of the one emphasized by Hirschman (1970). He focuses on the undersupply of "voice" to the organization when people have the "exit" option. Here, the organization gets into difficulties when it fails to listen to the "voice" that workers actually want to use. Because firms do sometimes get into these difficulties, it seems reasonable to conclude that listening to this "voice" has costs. A component of these costs that may be related to altruism is the emotional cost of interacting with unhappy employees.

[6] One way to give employees voice and respect is to have fair formal procedures, and this is the reason the term "procedural" justice is used in the literature. As emphasized by Bies (2001), however, voice and respect can also be given by individual supervisors, and he seeks to distinguish this "interactional" justice from that which is due to formal procedures. While I do not distinguish between the two, Bies (2001) argues that these two types of justice do not have identical effects.

express their point of view might well be a tangible benefit, but not of the type typically considered by economists, who might well question the idea that people are willing to pay to say something to someone who is not even their friend.

It is not immediately clear how the actions involved in procedural justice are payoff relevant in the way that is required to affect workers' reactions in the Rabin (1993) model. It may be possible to modify this model so that the explanations for bad outcomes help workers determine the payoffs that are "equitable, and thus give them information about the variables in their own utility function. However, this would require that the information provided by management be "hard." Moreover, it seems even harder to imagine how this model could be modified to explain why worker's reactions depend on whether they have been given an opportunity to express their point of view. The problem, again, is determining how this opportunity makes workers better off if they are not in fact able to affect the firm's decision.

An alternative viewpoint is that explanations, displays of employer contrition and willingness to listen to the worker's point of view, provide the worker with evidence about the favorable intentions of the employer. From this point of view, workers care not only about what they receive from employers but also about the extent to which employers are benevolent. If the employer is seen as benevolent, the worker is less inclined to respond to bad outcomes with revenge.[7]

In any event, workers' concerns with procedural justice might also account for some of the contradictory findings of Bewley (1999). While managers felt that cutting wages would reduce morale and productivity, the experience of the relatively small number of managers who cut wages (mostly as a result of financial distress) was mixed. Of those who did cut wages, 19% did not experience a fall in morale while 31% did not experience a fall in productivity (p. 203). However, productivity and morale fell much more sharply among those firms that cut wages in booms than it did among those who so in recessions. This suggests that workers see wage declines in booms as less fair. It may also be the case that those firms that experiences the smallest drops in morale and productivity were those that were able to convince their workers that these wage cuts were truly necessary for the firm to survive.

Low effort, turnover and theft do not exhaust the repertoire of reactions by workers who feel that their employer has treated them badly. Two additional reactions have been documented in the industrial relations literature. Sometimes, workers collectively refuse to work (or "strike") while demanding that their working conditions be changed. In other cases, workers demand that their employer bargain over working conditions with representatives of the workers' choosing. Even when such demands are not accompanied by strikes, the threat of a strike can be a potent argument for this type of negotiation. There are, of course, numerous and complex determinants of union militancy and I do not attempt a survey of this issue here. For the moment, what is worth stressing is that

[7] For a different perspective on what leads people to see themselves as victims of injustice, see Folger and Cropanzano (2001).

numerous observers have pointed out that sudden deteriorations of the terms of employment from the point of view of workers are often associated with increases in strike activity and union activism.

An interesting example of this is provided by Fantasia (1988, p. 82–93). He reports on the wildcat strike that took place in October 1975 at the Taylor Casting Company in response to the firing of a worker, who had been caught sleeping on the job. Partially because this worker was well liked (so that altruism may have played a role) and partially because the workers felt that the firm had not followed the proper procedure in firing the worker (so that procedural justice may have been important as well), the workers reacted by ceasing to work in a way that clearly ran counter to their labor contract.

Gouldner (1954, 1965) describes a strike that developed in response to a more widespread loss to workers. He considers workers at a gypsum plant who, initially, felt well treated by their employer even though wages were relatively low. As one worker describes the setting (Gouldner, 1954, p. 46) "This place is really tops. There is nobody coming around pushing you all the time." At a certain point, the firm changed a key manager and the new manager enforced rules more strictly and demanded more reports. As Gouldner (1954, p. 63) put it, "A college educated authority conscious, rule-oriented, personnel and safety manager was substituted for an informal 'lenient' man who has little taste for 'paper work'." The workers were unhappy with this change. The result was a successful series of strikes that included demands for both higher wages and specific union rights (Gouldner, 1965, p. 119–120).

Worker reactions to deteriorations in the terms of employment can also take forms that are even more costly to employers. In particular, angry workers can resort to sabotage. Jermier (1988) discusses several historical instances of this, the most contemporary one being the reaction of employees at General Motors' Lordstown plant to a rationalization plan that involved increased automation, some layoffs and an increase in the pace of production from 60 to about 100 cars an hour. Workers complained vocally that "pride in workmanship" was impossible under the new plant and sabotage increased significantly.

2.2. Individuals who subscribe to high-effort norms

So far, I have considered workers who respond to the actions of their employer. I now turn to workers who cooperate independently of these actions. As pointed out by Akerlof (1983) these workers can still earn high wages in equilibrium, as employers compete for their services. As Akerlof (1983) shows, workers thus have something to gain by putting themselves through a "loyalty filter" that leads them to work hard for their employer. The is closely related to Frank's (Frank, 1987) idea that individuals with "a conscience" can do better in the marketplace than selfish individuals as long as individuals with a conscience recognize each other. In both cases, workers receive high rewards as a result of being unable to maximize their personal gain *ex post* so that they work hard without supervision or explicit incentives for effort. In Akerlof's (Akerlof, 1983) model this requires an *ex ante* investment, like attending the proper schools, and then leads to offers of high wages. In Frank's (Frank, 1987) model, the transformation takes place in the genes and the reward comes because the worker ends up paired with a firm that is also reluctant to take advantage of the worker. One weakness of these models is that they require the transformed individuals to exert high effort regardless of the circumstances they face. Instead, as I pointed out, it appears that worker cooperation depends on the setting. While he does not focus on workers, Uzzi (1997) presents even more striking evidence against the idea that high effort is purely a function of individual characteristics. The people he considers carry out effort well beyond what is contractually required for some counterparties while they do not do so for others.

In Akerlof (1983), a worker with a high-effort norm gets his reward in advance whereas he only gets rewarded in my version of Frank's (Frank, 1987) model if he works for an employer who has a norm of paying high wages. Casadesus-Masanell (2004) shows that a worker with a high-effort norm can be rewarded *ex post* by a profit maximizing employer in such a way that he benefits from acquiring the high-effort norm *ex ante*. The Casadesus-Masanell (2004) model is similar to Rotemberg (1994) in that a worker can change his tastes *ex ante* so that he no longer maximizes his material payoffs *ex post*. The logic behind doing this is that the equilibrium that results after this change in preferences is better for the worker in the sense of leading to a higher level of utility using the original preferences or "material" payoffs. Naturally, this can only be beneficial to workers if someone else changes their actions as a result of the change in worker preferences.

Casadesus-Masanell (2004) focuses on a risk averse worker whose material payoffs U depend only on income and effort. To simplify, suppose that there are two levels of effort e^L and e^H and that, when income is held constant, $U(e^L) > U(e^H)$ while e^H leads to substantially higher profits. The only contractible way of inducing effort, however, is to make compensation depend linearly on an indicator variable x, which is random but rises with effort. There then exists a minimum slope of compensation with respect to x, call it α^H which makes the worker prefer e^H to e^L. The worker has a reservation level of utility $\bar{U}$ and the firm can also make a payment that is independent of x, which I label w. There then exists some level of this fixed payment w^H such that the utility the worker receives from α^H, w^H and e^H, which I write as $U(\alpha^H, w^H, e^H)$ equals $\bar{U}$. Alternatively, the firm can induce an effort equal to e^L by providing a fixed payment of w^L and setting the slope of compensation with respect to x equal to zero. The minimum level of w^L that keeps the worker at the firm ensures that $U(0, w^L, e^L)$ equals $\bar{U}$ as well. If e^H leads to profits that are sufficiently higher than e^L and the worker is not too risk averse, the firm prefers the set of compensation parameters that induces e^H to those that induce e^L.

Now suppose that, before the firm sets its compensation parameters, the worker can transform himself so that he suffers psychological losses when his level of effort differs from some benchmark (or norm) $\bar{e}$. Thus, Casadesus-Masanell (2004) supposes that his utility after this transformation is $U - V(|e - \bar{e}|)$ where e represents his level of effort and V is a strictly increasing function with a global minimum of zero at zero. Suppose that $\bar{e}$ is chosen so that it is closer to e^H than to e^L. Then, the minimum slope of compensation that leads a worker with this transformed utility to pick e^H, α^V, is necessarily smaller than α^H. The reason, quite simply, is that the worker now has something of a preference for e^H so a smaller incentive is needed for the worker to exert himself. Assuming the worker still has access to an outside option where his overall utility is $\bar{U}$, the fixed payment w^V that keeps this worker at the firm must now satisfy

$$U(\alpha^V, w^V, e^H) - V(|e^H - \bar{e}|) = \bar{U}$$

It follows that, if e^H is different from $\bar{e}$, so the worker suffers some guilt when he makes an effort e^H, $U(\alpha^V, w^V, e^H)$ exceeds $U(\alpha^H, w^H, e^H)$. Casadesus-Masanell (2004) interprets this to mean that, in some *ex ante* sense, the worker is better off with these transformed preferences and these new compensation parameters. The firm, too, can be better off because it gains from the lower value of α^V and this gain can easily offset any excess of w^V over w^H (which is not actually necessary for the model). As long as the firm benefits, it hires the worker with the transformed preferences.

In this setting, the worker only benefits from the acquisition of high-effort norms if the violation of this norm leads to psychological costs *ex post* which the worker ignores *ex ante*. Then, the income the worker receives to compensate him for the psychological cost is perceived as a net addition to welfare. An alternative viewpoint, however, is that the psychological distress caused by guilt is sufficiently serious that the worker ought to worry about it in advance.

2.3. *Altruism from the worker to his employer*

I now consider situations where the worker feels altruistic towards his employer. Altruism involves the ability to experience vicariously what others are experiencing so that the altruist's utility depends on that of someone else's. Psychologists like Lewicki and Bunker (1996) see this as involving the identification of one person with another. A central issue with respect to these feelings is what brings them about. It is often suggested that altruism is more likely to arise when the person experiencing altruism is physically close to the person who he identifies with. This raises the question whether the combination of proximity and frequent interaction are sufficient for altruism to develop or whether more is needed. My reading of the scattered empirical evidence on this subject is that proximity is by no means sufficient for altruism. For example, Burt and Knez (1996) asked a set of managers to identify the business contact that they saw, in effect, as most selfish and untrustworthy. Only about 11% of the respondents named someone they saw no more often than monthly, about 5% named someone they saw weekly and about 3% named someone they saw daily. Thus, even this extremely imperfect indicator of altruism is related to the frequency of interaction. However, the finding also suggests that quite frequent interactions on the job can be associated with extreme lack of altruism.

In any event, the role of proximity in facilitating altruism suggests that altruism may be bought, at least to some extent. The employment relation generally gives the employer the right to determine where the worker locates. Thus, an employer may obtain valuable services by hiring a worker and placing the worker near people that would benefit from the worker's altruism.

Barkema (1995) suggests that the proximity of managers to their CEOs may generate warm feelings from the former to the latter, though his evidence is fairly indirect. His empirical study focuses on the number of hours worked by a sample of Dutch managers. His sample of top managers include some that report to a CEO (and are thus expected to feel some altruism towards him), others that report to a board of directors and others that report to a parent company. The idea behind his study is that those managers who are close to CEOs but also subject to formal evaluation procedures will work less hard than those who are subject to less formal procedures because these procedures interfere with managerial altruism. In his study, the correlations between the number of hours worked and both the frequency and degree of structure of performance evaluations are negative when the manager reports to a CEO, and positive otherwise. Similarly the size of the bonus paid to the manager is negatively correlated with hours worked when the manager reports to a CEO and positive otherwise. Barkema (1995) interprets this as suggesting that bonuses are less effective at increasing hours when managers report to a CEO because such bonuses run counter the warm relationship that would otherwise prevail. This evidence is suggestive, though managers who report to CEO's differ from the other managers in his sample also in the sense that they occupy a rather different position in the hierarchy. This means that they might, for example, be unable to perform effectively their tasks unless they coordinate frequently with their CEO's and this might account both for their shorter hours and their more intense performance evaluations. In addition, their bonuses may be perks that attend their closeness to their CEOs. While alternative interpretations of this sort cannot be ruled out, Barkema's (Barkema, 1995) evidence certainly does suggest that CEO's have other methods of controlling managerial hours of work than bonuses and performance reviews.

Barkema's (Barkema, 1995) study is closely related to an issue that has been emphasized by Frey (1993) and Kreps (1997), namely that employee trust and loyalty towards the firm may be reduced by the use of explicit incentives that tie compensation to measures of output.[8] Kreps (1997) rationalizes this by imagining that employees fit their relationships with their employers into predefined "archetypes." If they see the this relationship as being similar to the reciprocal exchanges that take place inside a family, they work hard out of loyalty. A firm that offers explicit incentives may then change the way its employees see their relationship with the firm. In particular, they may come to see this as a more self-interested market mediated relation and reduce their effort. Group incentives, or payments that depend on the way the firm as a whole is doing may,

[8] Frey and Goette (1999) provide evidence they see as supporting the proposition that explicit incentives crowd out intrinsic ones. They show that, cross-sectionally, Swiss residents who receive small total monthly payments for volunteering spend fewer hours volunteering than either those that get paid nothing or those that get paid larger monthly sums. It remains possible that this study picks up cross-sectional differences in the desire to volunteer, however.

by contrast, be seen as more consistent with the sort of sharing that takes place inside families and thus be less destructive of employee effort.

Nagel (1975) points out that there is a different employment relation where employers definitely hope that employees will become altruistic towards them, or at least towards their family members. This situation arises when an employer hires someone to perform personal services such as child-care services. Such services have much more value if the employee genuinely cares for the child. What the employer is then hiring is the tendency of the employee to feel benevolence towards the someone the employer designates. It would be good to have more empirical evidence on the extent to which this automatic mechanism is operative in practice.

In other professions, employers appear to work hard to enhance the positive attitudes of employees towards the employer's customers. Airlines, for example, appear to spend considerable resources training their flight attendants so they will be helpful to passengers (Hochschild, 1983) and Disneyland spends considerable time training the ride operators that interact with customers (Van Maanen and Kunda, 1989). Hochschild (1983) reports that flight attendants are trained to change the emotions they feel when passengers lash out angrily. Using techniques that Hochschild (1983) labels "deep acting", they are told to try to see such "irates" as people to whom something has happened that calls for pity. Benevolence is thus induced by pretending that the passenger is deserving of benevolent treatment. Hochschild (1983, p. 183) suggests that this acting has important effects on the psyche of stewardesses in that it actually prevents them from feeling other emotions.[9] She also suggests that flight attendants have trouble doing their jobs if they simply fake their feelings for passengers.[10]

I now turn from benevolence towards customers to benevolence towards the employers themselves. Among employees of publicly held corporations employee expressions of altruism for managers and firm owners are relatively rare. Indeed, Homans (1950) suggests that people rarely have altruistic feelings for individuals who have direct authority over their actions. What may allow altruism to flourish in the "caring" professions in this regard is that the person entrusted to the caregiver is extremely dependent on the caregiver's actions. In more typical employment relations, the effect on the employer's utility of different employee actions is probably lower, and this may explain why employees obtain less vicarious utility when they make their employers happy.

A second reason why, compared to caregivers, typical employees do not feel much altruism for their supervisors and employers may be that caregivers are given more autonomy in determining their actions. This fits with the reason Homans (1950) gives for

[9] Hochschild (1983, p. 183) quotes a therapist who treats flight attendants and claims that many have difficulties in their relationships with men that are due to their job. Some of these difficulties may be due to the background that many flight attendants have in common, however. Indeed, the therapist quoted by Hochschild (1983) attributes these difficulties to a combination of innate characteristics of stewardesses and to their jobs.

[10] The general question of whether emotions in the workplace can be faked is clearly important. Casciaro (2001) provides evidence that people are at least somewhat able to detect whether other people like them. She shows a strong positive correlation between the extent to which one person (alter) expresses liking for another (ego) and the extent to which ego believes that he is liked by alter.

the relative lack of friendliness of subordinates for their supervisors. He attributes it to the fact that, when they give orders, supervisors initiate interactions and that friendliness in repeated interactions arises only "when no one originates the interaction with much greater frequency than the others" (p. 234). This interpretation suggests that friendship would be restored if the subordinate frequently asked questions of his supervisor because this would reestablish the balance in the frequency with which the two agents initiate interactions. A source of doubt about Homans' (Homans, 1950) interpretation is that cases where the supervisor feels friendly towards his subordinates but not vice-versa do not appear to be unusual. This suggests that there is something about the ability of the supervisor to give orders that mutes altruism from the subordinate to the supervisor. As Scott (1994) puts in his discussion of three somewhat unsuccessful attempts at reforming labor practices in Britain: "Management's willingness to issue direct instructions rather than allow workers to reach their own decisions may have inhibited the chances of self-discipline developing in the longer term" (p. 143–144).

Further indirect evidence for the view that there are difficulties associated with the arousal of altruism from employee to employer that such altruism is relatively common between contractors and those they provide services for. Uzzi (1997), for example, shows that altruism is ubiquitous between New York based "manufacturers" of clothing and the independent contractors who actually produce the clothing with the specifications and the cloth provided by the "manufacturers". Uzzi's evidence for altruism is strong. He reports, for example, a manufacturer who warned some of his contractors that he was moving to Asia even if this meant that the contractors thereby lost all incentive to provide him with high quality services. The manufacturer explained his actions by saying that this would help the contractors plan for the loss of his business. Moreover, much of the language used by the people Uzzi (1997) interviewed when discussing why they trust one another has a strong emotional component. One manager told Uzzi (1997, p. 43) "[trust] is a personal feeling" while another said "Trust means he's not going to find a way to take advantage of me. You are not selfish for your own self. The partnership [between firms] comes first."

These observations suggest that there may be cases where altruism flourishes more easily when the person who is supposed to provide services for another owns his own firm rather than being the other's employee. This could, in turn, imply that one reason not to vertically integrate with a supplier is to obtain better services as a result of the supplier's altruism. This is how Dore (1983) and Lorenz (1988) explain the success of non-integrated firms against integrated incumbents in the Japanese textile and the French engineering industries respectively.

I now discuss a theoretical model based on Rotemberg (2002) which has implications of this sort. The model hinges on the idea due to Simon (1951) that firms can force workers to be more productive than contractors because they can give orders to the former. This means that the firm loses less when it replaces an altruistic worker with a selfish one than when it replaces an altruistic contractor with a selfish one. As a result, workers may not get compensated for their altruism as much as contractors even if the outcome with worker altruism is more efficient.

To see this formally, consider a manufacturer who wishes to obtain a unit of output which he resells at a price of z. The timing of decisions is as follows. First, the manufacturer decides whether he is integrated or not. Second, a single worker (in the integrated case) or a single contractor (in the non-integrated one) decide whether to become altruistic towards the manufacturer. Becoming altruistic has a cost g and this cost has several possible interpretations. The first is that one must spend resources to convince someone of one's altruistic feelings, as in Camerer (1988).[11] The second is that there is a limit to the number of individuals one can feel altruistic towards, so that g represents the cost of foregoing an altruistic relation with someone else.

Third, the worker (or contractor) bargain with the firm over the size of a single payment, which is not allowed to depend on the quality of the good that is produced. Then the worker or contractor produce the good and the manufacturer sells it. The resale price z, depends on the effort of the worker or contractor. This resale price is z_0 when either selfish workers or contractors exert the effort e_0, which is the effort that they prefer. A key difference between hiring a worker and a contractor is that the firm is able to give certain kinds of orders to the worker, but not to the contractor. Thus, the firm can ask the worker to exert effort equal to e_1 which leads to a value of z equal to z_1. Naturally, $e_1 > e_0$ and $z_1 > z_0$ for otherwise the firm would either not want or not need to compel the effort e_1.

There also exists another level of effort e_2 which leads to an even higher value of z, z_2 but that the firm cannot compel the worker to exert effort e_2. To prevent the firm from obtaining this level of effort without altruism, one must also rule out contracts where the firm pays a higher wage (or price to the contractor) if it receives a unit of output whose value is higher. Imagine, then, that the only payment made by the firm to either the worker or the contractor is a fixed payment that is negotiated in advance.

There is a large pool of non-altruistic potential contractors and an equally large pool of non-altruistic potential workers. Each of these has a reservation value of r for the amount of time that it takes to produce a unit of output. In addition, any worker or contractor incurs a disutility equivalent to δ_i units of income if he exerts effort equal to e_i for i equals 1 or 2.

Suppose first that the initial contractor has decided to remain selfish. Nash bargaining between this contractor and the firm then implies that the contractor earns his reservation wage r and the manufacturer receives a good of value z_0. Now consider the integrated firm with a selfish worker. The quality of its output is independent of whether the firm keeps the original worker or not; the firm obtains a good with resale value z^1 in either case. Assuming Nash bargaining over the wage before the firm forces the worker to exert effort of e_1, the wage offered to the inside worker is his reservation wage, namely $r + \delta_1$. The worker accepts no less because he knows the firm will insist on an effort of e_1 and he gets no more because the firm can obtain this outcome from any of the

[11] Carmichael and MacLeod (1997) also considers settings where a cost must be spend initially to demonstrate cooperative intent, even though this model does not explicitly involve altruism.

other available workers. This means that, with selfish workers and contractors, the firm integrates if $z_1 - z_0 > \delta_1$ and uses an independent contractor otherwise.

Now consider what happens if the initial worker or contractor becomes altruistic towards the manufacturer. After spending g, the individual maximizes *ex post* a utility function that gives weight λ to the payoffs of the firm itself. Thus, an altruistic individual maximizes his own utility plus λ times the utility of the firm reseller.

Suppose that $\lambda(z_2 - z_1) > (\delta_2 - \delta_1)$ and $\lambda(z_2 - z_0) > \delta_2$ so a worker or contractor who is altruistic towards the firm makes an effort equal to e_2 since λ times the gain to the employer exceed the personal cost of carrying out this effort. Suppose further that the wages and contractor payments are determined by Nash bargaining so that the surplus that results from altruism is equally shared between the firm and its supplier.

Consider first the non-integrated firm. If it reaches agreement with the altruistic contractor, it earns $z_2 - p^c$ where p^c is what this contractor receives while it earns $z_0 - r$ if it fails to reach an agreement. Similarly, the contractor earns $p^c - \delta_2 - r$ if he reaches an agreement and earns zero on net otherwise. Thus, Nash bargaining leads to a value of p^c equal to

$$p^c = r + \frac{z_2 - z_0 + \delta_2}{2}$$

This means that the contractor benefits by spending g and becoming altruistic if $p^c - r - \delta_2$ exceeds g or if

$$z_2 - \delta_2 - z_0 > 2g \tag{2}$$

Total firm profits with an altruistic contractor π^c are $z_2 - p^c$, or

$$\pi^c = \frac{z_2 - \delta_2 + z_0}{2} - r$$

Now consider the integrated firm. If it reaches agreement with the altruistic worker it earns $z_2 - p^w$ where p^w is what the worker receives while it earns $z_1 - \delta_1 - r$ otherwise. The worker earns $p^w - \delta_2 - r$ if he reaches agreement while he again earns zero on net if he earns his reservation wage elsewhere. Thus, p^w satisfies

$$p^w = r + \frac{z_2 - z_1 + \delta_2 + \delta_1}{2}$$

and profits with an altruistic worker are

$$\pi^w = \frac{z_2 - \delta_2 + z_1 - \delta_1}{2} - r$$

The worker benefits from becoming altruistic if $p^w - r - \delta_2$ exceeds g or if

$$z_2 - \delta_2 - (z_1 - \delta_1) > 2g \tag{3}$$

If $z_1 - \delta_1 > z_0$, condition (3) is more stringent than condition (2). This means that, if (2) is satisfied while (3) is not, the firm has a choice between an altruistic contractor and a selfish worker. Profits with the former are larger if π^c exceeds $z_1 - \delta_1 - r$ or

$$z_2 - z_0 - \delta_2 > 2(z_1 - z_0 - \delta_1) \tag{4}$$

This implies that, if $z_1 - z_0 - \delta_1 > 0$ and $z_2 - \delta_2$ is high enough to satisfy (2) and (4) but not high enough to satisfy (3), the existence of endogenous altruism modifies the optimal level of integration. It would be optimal to be integrated without altruism but it would be more desirable to conduct business across firm boundaries otherwise.

The analysis above has demonstrated that, under certain conditions, business friendships are more likely to arise across firm boundaries than within firms. At the same time, it would seem that the analysis above abstracts from an additional consideration that further limits the viability of altruism from a worker towards his employer. While altruism can be directed at both institutions and individuals, the latter is a common phenomenon. In the case of outside contractors, the provision of high quality by an outside contractor seems consistent with altruism by the contractor for the individual in the organization as long as this individual negotiates the order and also benefits from the success of the product that uses the purchased input. The same might be true for a worker. However, worker altruism for an individual within the organization can be deleterious in a way that contractor altruism cannot. In particular a worker that cares for his or her supervisor can often take actions within the firm that make the boss look good at the expense of other employees. Such a course of action is much less open to outside contractors. This means that firms will be reluctant to raise wages of altruistic employees to the extent implied by the model (because the value to the firm from having such employees is lower) whereas they will be less reluctant to raise p^c to the extent implied by the model. This reinforces the conclusion that workers have less to gain from their altruism towards their supervisors than do contractors for their altruism towards their outside customers.

3. Workers cooperating with each other

Perhaps the most important reasons why production takes place inside "workplaces" is because different employees working in the same place are extremely interdependent. Thus, much of the cooperation that takes place in the workplace takes place among workers at the same level within the firm's hierarchy. Some of this cooperation is simply mandated. Individuals with relatively high positions in the hierarchy simply order their subordinates to take actions that depend on what others around them are doing. Indeed, one can imagine a great deal of coordination between employees resulting from a set of commands that take the form of "if you see a, you must do b." If the set of orders that supervisors can give is incomplete, however, it is up to the employees themselves to decide how much to cooperate for either the benefit or the detriment of the firm.

I consider first some theoretical models where altruism and reciprocity lead workers to cooperate with each other. It follows fairly naturally from these models that the conditions under which this cooperation arises need not be ones where this cooperation helps the employer. I then discuss how empirical observations bear on these theories.

3.1. Theory

Endogenous altruism can easily provide a rationale for cooperation among employees occupying the same position in a firm's hierarchy. To discuss this issue, it is worth reviewing briefly the conditions under which altruism arises in the model of Rotemberg (1994). In that model, two individuals each choose simultaneously the extent to which they wish to be altruistic towards the other. Then, in a second stage, they play a simultaneous move game in which the payoff to each depends on their own and the other's actions. The result of this two-stage interaction is that individuals who choose their altruism parameters to maximize the material payoffs from the second stage game become altruistic in equilibrium if their actions are strategic complements (after they have been normalized so that an increase in each individual's actions benefits the other). Strategic complementarity means that each individual increases his own action if he expects the other to do the same. Altruism from one individual to another commits the altruistic individual to increase his action, since this benefits the other. With strategic complementarity, this increases the other's action, thereby benefiting the individual who becomes altruistic.

In the prisoner's dilemma case where the payoffs are

		Column C	Column D
Row	C	$1, 1$	$-\ell, 1+g$
	D	$1+g, -\ell$	$0,0$

there is strategic complementarity so that altruism can arise endogenously if $\ell > g$. In this case, the benefit from playing D rather than playing C is higher when the other player plays D (where it equals ℓ) than when the other player plays C (where it equals g). In the game between the worker and the firm described by the normal form in (1), the actions of the two players are neither strategic substitutes nor complements. The benefit of making a low effort or giving a low wage are the same whether the other agent plays either L or H. Thus, this particular reason from altruism is absent from the relation between workers and their employers. By contrast, there are a number of interactions among workers that lead to strategic complementarity between their actions.

The simplest arises in the case of team production where output q depends on the costly effort e_1 and e_2 of two workers with $q = f(e_1, e_2)$, $\frac{\partial f}{\partial e_1}, \frac{\partial f}{\partial e_2}, \frac{\partial^2 f}{\partial e_1 \partial e_2} > 0$ and a "team incentive" where the payment to each worker is based on q. For a variety of reasons, these incentive payments are typically set so that the derivative of each individual's payment with respect of q is less than one. The result is that, as pointed out by Holmstrom (1982), these team incentives induce inefficiently low effort. With a slope of individual payments with respect to q equal to α and letting each individual's cost of effort be given by $c(e_i)$, selfish individuals set their effort to satisfy

$$\alpha \frac{\partial f}{\partial e_i} = c'$$

Efficiency requires that this equation hold with $\alpha = 1$. Thus, as long as $c'' > 0$ effort is below the first best level. Because $\frac{\partial^2 f}{\partial e_1 \partial e_2} > 0$, an increase in e_j raises the left hand side of this expression and, as a result, it raises the effort e_i. Thus, the two actions are strategically complementary and altruism can arise in equilibrium. This can also been seen directly by looking at the consequences of altruism.

If individual i is altruistic so that he maximizes a utility function that is the sum of his own material payoffs and λ_i times the gain he confers to the other, his optimal effort satisfies

$$\alpha\left(\frac{\partial f}{\partial e_i} + \lambda_i \frac{\partial f^2}{\partial e_1 \partial e_2}\right) = c'$$

Given the conditions I imposed on f, the left hand side is increasing in λ_i so that effort increases with λ_i. At the same time, as I argued above, the left hand side of this equation is increasing in e_j when λ_i equals zero. This means that, when λ_2 is equal to zero, the first worker benefits from acquiring a small positive level of λ_1. By doing so, he essentially commits himself to raising e_1 slightly, which has only second order costs for the agent. At the same time, this level of altruism leads the second agent to raise e_2 slightly, and this benefits the first agent to first order. So, each agent benefits from a small degree of altruism and altruism emerges in equilibrium. The result is an amelioration of the free rider problem faced by the team.

Two alternative ways of reducing this free rider problem are discussed in Kandel and Lazear (1992). The first is where the workers have a norm for effort which makes them feel guilt when their effort is below the average of that of other workers. This creates an incentive to increase effort because a worker that increases his own effort raises the "norm" and thus indirectly raises the effort of others. One interpretation for this mechanism is that it involves a kind of reciprocity where workers react to other worker's high effort by increasing their own.

This mechanism for increasing cooperation is similar to that in the dynamic model of Rob and Zemsky (2002). They suppose that effort e equals the sum of "cooperative effort" e_C and "individual effort e_I. They let individual utility be given by

$$U = W - C(e) - (h - e_C)g$$

where W is the wage worker's wage, $C(e)$ is increasing in e and h represents the "ideal" level of cooperative effort. The existence of a positive h might be attributable to altruism or to a positive disposition. The focus of their analysis, however, is the variable g, which gives the intensity with which people would like to set e_C equal to h. They suppose that g is a linear increasing function of the previous period's average value of

e_C across all the individuals that work on the same team.[12] In their setting, firms can give incentives for increasing e_I. Firms that refrain from doing so encourage "collective effort" indirectly and can end up with a cooperative "corporate culture". They show that, under certain conditions, firms that start out with a high value of g keep incentives low-powered so that g remains high while firms whose initial g is low prefer to provide high-powered incentives and thereby reduce g.

The second mechanism considered by Kandel and Lazear (1992) is one where workers directly take some other action, which they call "monitoring." This action has the effect of reducing other workers' net marginal disutility of effort. Workers in a team have an incentive to take these actions because they increase their own reward. This action can be thought of as an investment in a technology that leads workers to react negatively to their peer's low effort. In this interpretation, the action Kandel and Lazear (1992) call "monitoring" is closely linked to reciprocity.

This second mechanism for inducing cooperation has some features in common with the one considered in Bowles and Gintis (1992). They assume that workers' utility functions are such that they gain utility when they catch and discipline a shirking member of their team. Bowles and Gintis (1992) assume that this gain can exceed the cost of monitoring fellow members.[13] They then show that there are equilibria where some team members cheat by providing low effort while other team members monitor and catch the cheaters with positive probability. These equilibria exhibit higher effort, and thus more cooperation, than equilibria where everyone simply carries out low effort.

The examples I have just discussed are ones where altruism and reciprocity among workers increase firm profits. However, there are many settings where firms do not gain from the resulting cooperation of workers. Suppose, for example, that two workers are engaged in a tournament where, as in Lazear and Rosen (1981), the worker whose individual output is highest receives W_1 while the other receives W_2. Suppose individual output equals $e + \epsilon$ where e represents individual effort that costs the individual $C(e)$ and ϵ is a random variable whose c.d.f. is $F(\epsilon)$ and whose realization is independent across individuals. The payoff to worker i is then

$$W_2 + (W_1 - W_2)F(e_i - e_j) - C(e_i)$$

[12] It is interesting to compare this setup with Casadesus-Masanell (2004). In Casadesus-Masanell (2004), the worker chooses a parameter that plays a role very similar to h. If workers are only acting reciprocally with respect to the actions of other workers it does not make much sense for them to pick the parameter h at a level beyond the effort e_C that they intend to make. For this reason, the Rob and Zemsky (2002) approach of keeping h exogenous at a high level while making g respond to the actions of others is appealing even if it leaves the determination of h outside the model. On the other hand, an attractive feature of Casadesus-Masanell's (2004) model is that it can explain why h is chosen to be above e_C.

[13] This ensures that monitoring is individually rational. By contrast, Dow and Dong (1993) only let members choose between cooperating fully and exerting no effort at all. This makes it possible for monitoring to take place in the Dow and Dong (1993) model even though they assume that individuals care only about their own material payoffs and that the only reward to catching a deviating member is that the deviating member's wage is split among the remaining members.

where the subscript j represents the other employee. At a symmetric equilibrium, the two levels of effort are strategic complements if $F'' > 0$, they are strategic substitutes if $F'' < 0$ and are strategically unrelated if $F'' = 0$. When they are complements, altruism tends to arise endogenously and the result is that both employees curtail their effort levels and thereby undermine the basis for the tournament.

It follows for the above analysis that, comparing situations where a worker's wage depends positively on other employees' effort (as in the case of group incentives) and situations where it depends negatively (as in tournaments), firms might have more to gain from worker cohesion in the former. Indeed, if α is low in the case of group incentives considered above so that the firm keeps a large fraction of any increase in q that results from worker effort, the firm's gain from workers' cohesion can be quite high. The relevant question for the firm is then how it can raise intra-employee altruism. One lever that firms have at their disposal for doing so is to give employees opportunities to socialize with each other. One interesting aspect of this lever is that giving employees time to socialize on the job takes away from the time that employees devote to production. It might therefore be thought that socializing by employees on the job reduces profits unless employees are willing to accept lower wages in exchange for being allowed to engage in this activity. However, if employee altruism is important to the firm, this activity might also be profitable to the firm directly. I illustrate the effect of socializing on altruism with a variant of a model presented in Rotemberg (1994).

Imagine that there are two employees labelled 1 and 2 and that allowing employees to socialize allows them to confide in each other. At least in the case where agent 1 likes agent 2, receiving agent 2's confidence gives agent 1 an increase in utility that is equivalent to z units of income. These confidences cost v to agent 2. However, the confidences also give agent 1 the opportunity to react in a way that is desirable from the point of view of agent 2. Such reactions have a cost of i for agent 1 but a much larger benefit of f for agent 2. Indeed, f is so large that $f - v$ is positive. The payoff matrix that relates to 2's confidences is thus

		2	
		Confide	Don't
1	React well	$z - i,\ f - v$	$--,\ --$
	Don't	$z,\ -v$	$0, 0$

If agent 1 is selfish, he does not react well and agent 2 never confides. If $z - i$ is positive, this means that agent 1 gains by acquiring an altruism parameter equal to i/f, which I have assumed to be small. Agent 2 then knows that agent 1 will react well and confides in agent 1. A parallel argument applies to confidences by agent 1, so bilateral altruism arises in equilibrium. Note that the above argument suggests that socialization only leads to altruism if agent 1 actually enjoys the confidences of agent 2, which may well require that agent 1 like agent 2 to begin with. In this sense, liking and altruism are closely linked, at least if agents are given an opportunity to interact with one another.

3.2. Evidence

Individuals differ in the extent to which they help others at work. This has led Organ (1988) to propose a way of measuring the extent to which employees perform beyond the employer's requirements. His proposed measure of "organizational citizenship behavior" (OCB) of an individual is obtained by asking questions to the individual's supervisor. These questions fall into five categories: *altruism* meaning the extent to which the subordinate helps others, *courtesy* meaning the measure of respect he accords others, *conscientiousness* meaning the extent to which he works beyond what is required, *civic virtue* meaning his contributions to the political life of the organization and *sportsmanship* meaning the extent to which he expresses a positive attitude about the job. While this measure combines different types of behavior, subsequent studies have also looked at measures such as altruism in isolation. One important conclusion from these studies is that, indeed, employees do help each other at times.

This still leaves the question of what motivates this helping. Some of this helping takes an almost *quid pro quo* form. One nice example of this is given by Altheide et al. (1978, p. 113). They describe an incident in which a clerk gave another employee inappropriate discounts for the purchase of equipment and said "I might need your help later in getting something for myself." This behavior might be due to reciprocity, though it might be explicable in a repeated game setting where each employee fears that others will withdraw cooperation if he withdraws his own. In any event, this explicit *tit for tat* represents only a small part of the cooperation observed in organizations.

One type of helping that has received a great deal of attention in the Organizational Behavior literature is *mentoring* where one manager helps a subordinate with his career (see Kram, 1988, for a classic treatment). The extent to which one must appeal to selflessness to explain mentoring is unclear, however. In fact, this activity might well be rewarded by the firm itself since many firms have formal "mentoring programs." On the other hand, if mentoring is due either to the pleasure experienced from helping or to the expectation of later receiving benefits from the person being mentored, altruism or reciprocity play a role in the relationship.

One employee role whose rewards appears to be exclusively the result of the act of helping itself is described in Bacharach et al. (2000). They describe the actions of a group of flight attendants who volunteer as support providers in a peer-assistance program. As they say, all these providers can expect in return is to sometimes "receive a sense of gratification from his or her impact on the recipient" (p. 705). The effect on the recipients can be dramatic because many of the recipients suffer from substance abuse and need help to remain in treatment.

Altruism probably plays an equally important role in the friendships that people form in the workplace. These friendships appear to be important to the employees themselves.[14] Morse and Weiss (1955) explored why 80% of their sample of workers said

[14] Ibarra (1992) shows that friendship networks tend to be more segregated by sex than "instrumental" networks, i.e., the networks of relations people have on the job for to help each other professionally. Still, for both men and women, members of an individual's personal network typically played more than one role.

they would continue working even if they "inherited enough money to live comfortably without working." Their exploration involved the question "Suppose you didn't work, what would you miss most?." 31% of their sample answered "The people I know at or through work, the friends, contacts." This suggests that interpersonal relationships are indeed important in workplace settings.

At the other extreme from evidence about individuals lies evidence about organizations as a whole. A problem that arises when discussing large organizations is that the sheer variety of relationships makes it hard to ascertain what is "typical" about the psychological ties between individuals. Still, some firms place great stress on these ties and one company that became famous for this is Southwest Airlines, where employees routinely hugged each other in the hallways.[15] Oliva and Gittell (2002) quote a senior manager describing the unwritten rules at Southwest "You have to be compassionate to internal and external customers. You have to have a positive attitude. ... You have to have a great sense of humor." And indeed, O'Reilly and Pfeffer (1995) report that "employees routinely help each other out" (p. 11) and that they go to great lengths to help customers.

O'Reilly and Pfeffer (1995) also suggest that ties between employees contributed to productivity, particularly by shortening the amount of time it took to get a plane back in the air after it landed. The question of how Southwest managed to maintain this culture that differed dramatically from those of its competitors appears to be extremely difficult. It is not even obvious that Southwest's CEO knew the elements involved when he said "My biggest concern is that somehow, through maladroitness, through inattention, through misunderstanding, we lose the esprit de corps, the culture, the spirit. If we lose that, we will have lost our most valuable asset."[16]

Some of Southwest's culture may have been due to its beginnings as an embattled company. Though such a beginning is hardly unique, this may fit with the Rob and Zemsky (2002) model in which firms which start out with a cohesive culture choose low powered incentives so that this culture is maintained—or even enhanced. One difficulty with interpreting the evidence along these lines is that it is not clear that Southwest's competitors provided more individualistic incentives to their employees than did Southwest.

As discussed by O'Reilly and Pfeffer (1995) and Oliva and Gittell (2002), Southwest did seem to be unique in other ways. It had more supervisors than other airlines, though these helped their subordinates as needed. It encouraged an atmosphere of "fun" and spent considerable resources on parties and celebrations. It also hired "for attitude" rather than "for skills." A newspaper story illustrated this by describing group interviews where each applicant had to talk about him or herself for five minutes. Apparently, the applicants who cheered the speaker tended to be hired while those that worked on their own presentation tended to be passed over.[17] It thus appears that Southwest both

[15] See Boston Globe 5/11/200.

[16] Fortune, 11/01/1999.

[17] See Boston Globe 5/11/2000.

promoted altruism through the activities that employees carried out together while also trying to select altruistic individuals.

There are limits to the extent one can generalize about companies taken as a whole. An advantage of studying smaller groups is that one can describe more accurately the ties among individuals. The best known study of this sort is still the analysis by Roethlisberger and Dickson (1939) of observations and experiments that they carried out at the Hawthorne plant belonging to Western Electric. One of these experiments shows that, as suggested by the endogenous altruism model discussed above, the firm gained more from simultaneously offering employees some weak group incentives together with the opportunity to socialize than it gained by offering only one of these in isolation. In particular, productivity increased substantially in the "relay assembly room experiment" when a relatively small group of workers was compensated as a function of group output and was also given "rest pauses" that led the workers to become friends. These workers had originally worked together with a much larger group of workers and had been given a payment that depended on the output of this larger group. To see whether incentives alone where responsible for the increased output in the relay assembly room experiment, Roethlisberger and Dickson (1939) selected a different group of workers from the larger group and changed their compensation so it came to depend on the output of the smaller group. This new group was not given increased opportunities to socialize and their output rose only modestly.

Lastly, Roethlisberger and Dickson (1939) tried to test whether "rest pauses" alone caused increases in productivity. It was not practical to give individual incentives to workers performing the task of the relay assembly room experiment so this experiment was carried out with workers who performed a different task. In the mica splicing room experiment a group of workers originally paid on the basis of individual piecework was gathered in a room and given opportunities to socialize. Not only were output increases small and transitory, but esprit de corps did not develop. This last observation is also consistent with the model above because, in that model, both group incentives and the opportunity to socialize contribute to the generation of altruism so that one of these ingredients alone may not be enough in practice.

Rather than measuring altruism, or helping, directly, some studies measure the extent to which individuals are friends, and this variable is likely to be linked to altruism. Certainly, Roethlisberger and Dickson (Roethlisberger and Dickson, 1939, p. 506–507) show that there is strong correlation between friendship and helping behavior on the job. Pairs of workers that Roethlisberger and Dickson (1939) identified as being friends were more likely to be involved in helping relations than were other pairs. Another related variable that is often measured in empirical studies is the extent to which workers like one another. As argued above, there are good theoretical reasons to imagine that liking and altruism are linked so that people who like one another will choose to become altruistic towards one another.

An aggregate measure of the extent to which individuals in a group like other group members is often called group cohesiveness, and it seems reasonable to treat this variable as a measure of the extent to which people in a group feel benevolence towards one another. An extensive empirical literature has studied whether, in particular settings, groups that were more cohesive were more productive than less productive groups. Stodgill (1972) surveys this literature and shows that its results are contradictory. The two variables are positively correlated in some in some settings, while they are negatively correlated in others.[18]

This can be read as saying that the empirical relationship between intra-worker altruism and productivity is ambiguous. While this is consistent with the model above, it hardly provides strong support for the model. Of more interest in this respect are the studies that have looked at particular instances of cohesiveness in organizations.

One setting that was quite common in the past involved setting individual piece rates that were changed from time to time as a function of both the earnings of workers and the results of "time-motion" studies. In these settings, workers tended to suspect that increases in productivity would be followed by reductions in the piece rate. In Roethlisberger and Dickson's (Roethlisberger and Dickson, 1939, p. 418) observations of the bank wiring room, one worker they call W_5 says "The fellows who loaf along are liked better than anyone else... I think a lot of them have the idea that if you work fast the rate will be cut. That means they would work faster for the same money." It was also common for workers to put pressure on each other to keep their productivity low for this reason.[19]

Some of the relationships in this room were quite friendly, though some were not, and indeed the most socially isolated worker, whom they call W_2, worker consistently put out the largest volume of work (Roethlisberger and Dickson, 1939, p. 434 and 519). As W_2 put it "They don't like me to turn out so much, but I turn it out anyway". While social isolation was not sufficient to reduce W_2's output, other methods proved effective in the case of other workers. For example, Roethlisberger and Dickson (1939, p. 423) report an incident where W_8 struck (or "binged") W_6 and this did indeed lead W_6 to stop working.

These observations suggest that reciprocity, by itself, seems unable to lead work-groups to cooperate. Rather, it seems that some feelings of benevolence are required as well since some workers will simply not submit to the threats of co-worker sanctions. The simple threat of revenge is not enough to achieve cooperation, perhaps because people like W_2 would not be happy with their self-image if they saw themselves as submitting to these threats.

The model above can account for the appearance of altruism together with output restrictions in this setting. To see this, suppose that two workers can either produce high or low output. Starting from a position where both employees have low output, a worker

[18] For a recent example, the Wall Street Journal of 12/1/2000 reported on a Gallup study of 400 companies which found that workplaces with high productivity, customer satisfaction and profitability tended to be ones where individual employees reported having a best friend present.

[19] Frank (1991) offers a different rationale for the ostracism to which "rate-busters" are subject. He sees this as being the result of the fact that employees care about their relative compensation so that they dislike having other employees earn more than they do. While I was unable to find quotes from workers testifying as to the veracity of this explanation, this may simply reflect a weakness of the evidence on the subject.

that increases his output rate increases the odds that the piece rate will be reduced so the other worker's expected losses equal ℓ. For himself, however, he gains $g - \ell$, which could be positive even if ℓ is positive as well. If both workers increase their output rate, they each gain $g - \ell'$ where $\ell' > \ell$ because the piece rate is more likely to be reduced if both workers have high output. Thus, the matrix of payoffs can be written as

		2	
		Low output	High output
1	Low output	$0, 0$	$-\ell, g - \ell$
	High output	$g - \ell, -\ell$	$g - \ell', g - \ell'$

If $g - \ell$ and $g - \ell' + \ell$ are both positive, this has a prisoner's dilemma structure and both workers choose to produce high output if they are selfish. The former are the benefits of defecting by producing high output when the other worker is expected to make a low effort while the latter are the benefits of producing high output when the other worker is already doing so. Thus, the two actions are strategically complementary if $g - \ell' + \ell > g - \ell$ or $\ell > \ell'/2$. In this case an altruistic equilibrium with low output can exist.

Until now, my discussion of altruism and reciprocity among employees was unrelated to my discussion of the feelings of employees about their supervisors. Empirically, these feelings do appear to be linked, at least if one looks across employees working in individual organizations. As discussed above, the literature on OCB has collected measures of "citizenship" for individual employees by interviewing their supervisors. They have matched these with interviews of the employees themselves in an effort to understand the correlation between the answers given by supervisors and subordinates. A recurrent finding in this literature is that measures of OCB are positively associated with measures of the extent to which employees regard their employers as procedurally fair (see, for example, Moorman et al., 1998 and the references cited therein). This points to the possibility that employee cooperation with each other is associated with the extent to which employees feel positively about their employer as a whole.

4. Altruism towards subordinates

In this last section, I consider reasons why supervisors might feel altruism towards subordinates even when such feelings are not reciprocated. This absence of reciprocation distinguishes the phenomena I consider here from the cooperation between managers and workers I considered in section 1. One way of thinking about the relationships I consider here is that they have a paternalistic component, as in Becker's (Becker, 1991) model of the family, which features one-sided altruism from parent to child.[20]

[20] See the chapter by Laferrere and Wolff in this volume for a discussion.

A very interesting set of observations that suggests this one-way altruism is relevant in workplaces is provided by Crozier (1964). He observed a set of workers engaged in a clerical task. The task was carried out by four employees, one of which was the "leader" in the sense that she set the pace even though she had no authority over wages or promotions. In general, the employees in this setting had little affection for one another. Crozier (1964, p. 65) says: "only 20% feel positively about their workmates as potential friends." Insofar as friendly feelings existed, they flowed from the team leaders to the other employees. Crozier (1964, p. 36) writes: "The middle class girls who made positive comments about their workmates as possible friends were team leaders (half of them) and a few senior employees from the special workroom."

As in Rotemberg (1994), it is possible to rationalize this pattern of liking with a model of endogenous altruism. The idea behind the model is that a leader can benefit from altruism towards a subordinate if this altruism leads the subordinate to become more compliant because he believes that the leader takes into account the subordinate's desires.[21] Consider the following example drawn from Rotemberg (1994). The leader makes its decision first and must choose between S and F (which stand for slow and fast). Once the leader decides, the follower chooses between s or f knowing the leader's decision. The payoff from the couple $\{S, s\}$ is zero for both players. The payoffs from other combinations of actions depends on the state of nature. In particular, there are two possible configurations of payoffs which are equally likely *ex ante* and are given by

$$\begin{array}{c} \\ s \\ f \end{array}\begin{array}{c} \begin{array}{cc} S & F \end{array} \\ \begin{bmatrix} 0,0 & 0,-c \\ -c,0 & b,b \end{bmatrix} \end{array}, \qquad \begin{array}{c} \\ s \\ f \end{array}\begin{array}{c} \begin{array}{cc} S & F \end{array} \\ \begin{bmatrix} 0,0 & 0,-c \\ -c,0 & -c,d \end{bmatrix} \end{array}, \tag{5}$$

where b, c and d are all positive. The difference between the configuration on the left and that on the right is that, in the former, both workers gain from moving fast whereas only the leader gains in the latter. Suppose that the leader knows which of the two games is being played but the follower does not. If $c > b$, the only selfish equilibrium involves $\{S, s\}$ for both games. The reason is that the leader always plays F if he expects the follower to follow with f. The result is that the follower's expected payoff from following F with f equals $\frac{b-c}{2}$, which is negative. Thus, the followers plays s in response to F. The leader is thus better off playing S at all times and the only equilibrium is $\{S, s\}$.

On the other hand, if $d < c$, there is an equilibrium where the leader becomes altruistic. To see this suppose the leader picks an altruism parameter just over d/c and

[21] Tyler and Degoey (1996) present evidence that is somewhat consistent with the existence of a link between compliance and leader altruism. Their evidence is drawn from a phone interview of 409 Chicago workers who were asked whether they were willing to accept the decisions made by a supervisor. These workers were more willing to accept these decisions the more they trusted their supervisor, even after controlling for whether past decisions by the supervisor had been favorable to them. Among the questions they used to evaluate whether the supervisor was trustworthy were questions such as "How hard did your supervisor try to be fair to you?" Even a strong positive answer to this question does not necessarily imply that the supervisor is altruistic, though explaining such an answer with altruism has the advantage of being extremely simple.

consider an equilibrium where the leader picks F in the game on the left and S in the game on the right. The follower gains by following F with f and following S with s. On the other hand, the leader now has nothing to gain by deviating. Playing F on the game in the right gives the leader direct benefits but his vicarious losses are sufficient to offset these gains.

The essence of this example is that, while the leader always likes the follower to work hard by playing f, there are occasions where this benefits the follower and there are other occasions where this hurts the follower a great deal. The result is that some altruism from the leader to the follower assuages the follower's fears from playing f whenever the leader asks him to. Thus altruism begets trust.

This structure is somewhat special so that many theoretical models of supervisor-subordinate relationships do not lead to endogenous altruism by the supervisor. Rotemberg (1994) shows this is the case, for example, in the case of a supervisor who must declare which of two subordinates has scored highest in a tournament. Favoritism to an employee then simply reduces both employees' effort.

On the other hand, the above example is not the only model of supervisor-subordinate interaction that leads to endogenous altruism. A slightly different reason for altruism arises when the subordinate must take actions before the supervisor and where a selfish supervisor's actions are *ex post* inefficient because they put too much weight on the cost of transferring resources to the subordinate.[22] The commitment provided by altruism can solve this *ex post* problem and thereby improve investment *ex ante*.

A simple example of this is provided in Rotemberg and Saloner (1993). They consider a situation where an employee who exerts effort that costs him e yields a project whose payoff to the supervisor is z if the project is implemented at cost k. The payoff z is known after the employee makes his effort but, before he makes the effort, all that is known about z is that it has a c.d.f. $F(z)$. Rotemberg and Saloner (1993) consider a special contracting situation where the only incentive payment available for the employee is a payment of r when his project is implemented. There are a number of ways of justifying this restriction, including that r involves the non-pecuniary benefits of managing a project, that it includes the rewards that the external labor market confers to employees that become more visible in the firm and that the there is an implicit contract policed by co-workers which ensure that individuals whose project is implemented obtain a lump-sum payment.

With a selfish principal, the firm implements an employee's project only when $z-k \geq r$ even though it is efficient to implement all projects in which $z - k \geq 0$. At the same time, the employee only makes the effort if he gets a sufficient payoff from doing so. With a selfish principal, in particular, employee effort requires that

$$e \leq r[1 - F(r + k)]$$

[22] Al-Najjar and Casadesus-Masanell (2001) obtain a similar role for what they call "trustworthiness" of the principal in a setting where the *ex post* action is a simple transfer (which is never inefficient) but where a trustworthy principal makes a payment that justifies the agent's *ex ante* effort.

Increasing r thus has ambiguous effects on effort. It raises the amount the employee receives every time his project is implemented but it reduces the frequency with which such implementation takes place. This means that this type of incentive scheme can unravel completely so that no effort takes place in equilibrium even though effort is worthwhile. To see this, consider the first best. This involves the implementation of projects with $z \geq k$ so that implementation takes place with probability $1 - F(k)$ and effort is socially valuable if

$$e \leq \int_k (z - k) dF(z)$$

Returning now to equilibrium allocations, the lowest possible value of r that leads to employee effort is e. Thus, the first best cannot be obtained if $F(e + k) > F(k)$ so that the distribution F has positive support between k and $k + r$. Moreover, in this case, raising r above e may not lead to the provision of effort either because increases in r reduce the frequency with which the employee is paid and this require further increases in r.

Suppose that, instead, the individual deciding whether to implement the employee's project feels altruistic towards the employee. In particular, let his utility gain from employee payoffs equal λ times his utility gain from the firm's profits. The supervisor then implements the employee's project whenever $z - k \geq (1 - \lambda)r$ so the first best obtains when $\lambda = 1$. Even with a level of altruism short of this level, implementation is more frequent with $\lambda > 0$ than with a selfish supervisor. This is both desirable *ex post* and makes it easier to motivate the employee *ex ante*.

In structure, this model is similar to Becker (1991). As in Becker (1991), the selfish actor (here the employee) carries out a socially worthwhile action because this increases the transfer he receives from the altruist (here the employer). One relatively small difference between the two models is that, here, the transfer is not a unilateral action. Instead, the transfer is contractually tied to a decision which increases the altruist's revenue. Thus, the present model is one where even quite modest degrees of employer altruism can improve the actions of the employee.

5. Conclusions

Cooperation is so important for the production of goods and services that firms use all possible tools at their disposal to achieve such cooperation. The simplest of these is to design jobs so that the actions of each are easy to specify and so that each job involves activities that are complementary to those of the other jobs in the same firm. The firm then achieves a form of cooperation by the simple expedient of paying individuals to carry out particular tasks.

In this survey I have considered two mechanisms that rely on psychological motives for cooperation that are somewhat less straightforward than the desire to receive a salary. While these psychological motives can lead to cooperation in the workplace, they can also lead employees to take actions against shareholders. Thus, firms may not always be able to harness these motives to increase profits.

The motives I considered are the vicarious enjoyment of the utility that others derive from one's good deeds (or altruism) and the increase in utility one gets by responding in kind to the good—or bad—deeds of others (or the desire for reciprocity). These motives form the core of this handbook and are obviously related. People who feel altruistic towards one another will presumably do things for each other continuously so that their benevolent acts would seem hard to distinguish from those of reciprocators.

There are two situations where these psychological motives would appear to have different implications. Suppose that two agents have a relationship where they are both doing things for each other and one of them suddenly does something that the other regards as bad. A reciprocator would respond in kind while there may well be some pressure on the altruist to do otherwise. A second difference between altruism and reciprocity is that the former is consistent with one individual doing things for another even if he expects nothing in return.

Some observations from workplace settings suggests that such one-sided altruism is present. Some employees, for example, help co-workers more than they could possibly be helped in return. In addition, one observes supervisors who express warm feelings towards subordinates that are not reciprocated. This last observation is consistent with a theory of endogenous altruism where the supervisor becomes altruistic in order to obtain the trust of his subordinate. There is also some additional indirect support for the theory of endogenous altruism I have outlined. In particular, it appears that providing people with the opportunity to socialize increases cooperation under certain circumstances, as the model predicts. On the other hand, the help provided by peer-support providers, for example, seems much more similar to situations where people help strangers in need.

The existence of altruism and friendship ties among employees does not rule out the possibility that reciprocity also plays a role in the cooperation among employees. However, there is some evidence that where friendship is wholly absent, the credible threat of reprisals is not sufficient to get all employees to cooperate with one another. In particular, some individuals appear willing to remain "outsiders" even if they are punished for doing so.

On the other hand, some employees make explicit "deals" with each other where they give something with the explicit expectation of getting something back in the future. Since these deals are not enforceable in court the psychological force behind reciprocity, namely that the individual who receives first would feel guilty if he did not return the favor, might play a role. However, this behavior seems explicable also by supposing that the initial recipient does not want to develop a reputation for failing to come through on explicit "deals".

Reciprocity seems to play a clearer role in the feelings that employees have towards their employers although there is little evidence that reciprocity leads workers to work hard when their employers treat them particularly well. On the other hand, there is abundant evidence that workers who feel betrayed by their employer take actions that cause their employer harm. Morale does seem to suffer when wages are cut or employees are fired in ways that are regarded as "unfair". And, this loss in morale leads employees to withhold their cooperation in a variety of ways, including by increasing their theft from their employers.

What is perhaps most interesting is that violations of procedural justice appear to irk workers just as much if not more than reductions in workers' material outcomes. It remains an open question whether this can easily be reconciled with formal economic models of reciprocity. One possible way of interpreting the negative reactions of workers to what they see as lapses in procedural justice is that they react badly to situations where they feel that employers have insufficient altruism. What renders this story plausible is that an individual with even a small level of benevolence would give explanations for bad outcomes and would grant aggrieved parties the opportunity to present their point of view. This still leaves the question of why workers should care so much about the altruism of their employers. While by no means settling this question, I have presented both some models and some evidence suggesting that employer altruism can be good not just for the workers but also for the employers themselves.

References

Adams, J.S. (1965). "Inequity in social exchange". In: Berkowitz, L. (Ed.), Advances in Experimental Social Psychology, vol. 2. Academic Press, New York.

Akerlof, G. (1982). "Labor contracts as partial gift exchange". Quarterly Journal of Economics 97, 543–569.

Akerlof, G. (1983). "Loyalty filters". American Economic Review 73, 54–63.

Al-Najjar, N.I., Casadesus-Masanell, R. (2001). "Trust and discretion in agency contracts", mimeo.

Altheide, D.L., Adler, P.A., Altheide, D.A. (1978). "The social meaning of employee theft". In: Johnson, J.M., Douglas, S.D. (Eds.), Crime at the Top: Deviance in Business and the Professions. J.D. Lippincott, Philadelphia.

Analoui, F., Kakabadse, A. (1991). Sabotage. Mercury, London.

Bacharach, S.B., Bamberger, P., McKinney, V. (2000). "Boundary management tactics and logics of action: the case of peer-support providers". Administrative Science Quarterly 45, 704–736.

Barkema, H.G. (1995). "Do job executives work harder when they are monitored". Kyklos 48, 19–42.

Becker, G.S. (1991). Treatise on the Family. Harvard University Press, Cambridge, MA.

Bewley, T.F. (1999). Why Wages don't Fall during a Recession. Harvard University Press, Cambridge, MA.

Bies, R.J. (2001). "Interactional (in)justice: the sacred and the profane". In: Greenberg, J., Cropanzano, R. (Eds.), Advances in Organizational Justice. Stanford University Press, Stanford.

Bowles, S., Gintis, H. (1992). "Power and wealth in a competitive capitalist economy". Philosophy & Public Affairs 21, 324–353. Fall.

Burt, R.S., Knez, M. (1996). "Trust and third-party gossip". In: Kramner, R.M., Tyler, T.R. (Eds.), Trust in Organizations. Sage, Thousand Oaks.

Camerer, C. (1988). "Gifts as economic signals and social symbols". American Journal of Sociology 94 (Suppl.), S180–S214.

Carmichael, H.L., MacLeod, W.B. (1997). "Gift giving and the evolution of cooperation". International Economic Review 38, 485–509.

Casadesus-Masanell, R. (2004). "Trust in agency". Journal of Economics & Management Strategy 13, 375–404.

Casciaro, T. (2001). "Structure and Perception of interpersonal affect, and the formation of work networks", mimeo.

Crozier, M. (1964). The Bureaucratic Phenomenon. University of Chicago Press, Chicago.

Dong, X., Dow, G.K. (1993). "Monitoring costs in Chinese agricultural teams". Journal of Political Economy 101, 539–553.

Dore, R. (1983). "Goodwill and the spirit of market capitalism". British Journal of Sociology 34, 459–482.

Dufwenberg, M., Kirchsteiger, G. (2004). "A theory of sequential reciprocity". Games and Economic Behavior 47, 268–298.

Falk, A., Fiscbacher, U. (2000). "A theory of reciprocity". Institute for Empirical Economics, University of Zurich, Working Paper.

Fantasia, R. (1988). Cultures of Solidarity. University of California Press, Berkeley.

Fehr, E. (2006). "The economics of reciprocity: experimental evidence", this volume.

Folger, R., Cropanzano, R. (2001). "Fairness theory: justice as accountability". In: Greenberg, J., Cropanzano, R. (Eds.), Advances in Organizational Justice. Stanford University Press, Stanford.

Frank, R.H. (1987). "If homo economicus could choose his own utility function, would he want one with a conscience?". American Economic Review 77, 593–604.

Frank, R.H. (1991). "Social forces in the workplace". In: Koford, K.J., Miller, J.B. (Eds.), Social Norms and Economic Institutions. The University of Michigan Press, Ann Arbor.

Frey, B.S. (1993). "Does monitoring increase work effort: the rivalry with trust and loyalty". Economic Inquiry 31 (4), 663–670.

Frey, B.S., Goette L. (1999). "Does pay motivate volunteers", Institute for Empirical Economics, University of Zurich Working Paper.

Gouldner, A.W. (1954). Patterns of Industrial Bureaucracy. The Free Press, New York.

Gouldner, A.W. (1965). Wildcat Strike. Harper and Row, New York.

Goodman, P.S., Friedman, A. (1971). "An examination of Adam's theory of equity". Administrative Science Quarterly 16, 271–288.

Greenberg, J. (1990). "Employee theft as a reaction to underpayment inequity: the hidden cost of pay cuts". Journal of Applied Psychology 75, 561–568.

Greenberg, J. (1993). "The social side of fairness: interpersonal classes of organizational justice". In: Cropanzano, R. (Ed.), Justice in the Workplace. Erlbaum, Hillsdale, NJ.

Hirschman, A.O. (1970). Exit, Voice and Loyalty. Harvard University Press, Cambridge, MA.

Hochschild, A.R. (1983). The Managed Heart: Commercialization of Human Feeling. University of California Press, Berkeley.

Holmstrom, B. (1982). "Moral hazard in teams". Bell Journal of Economics 13, 324–340.

Homans, G.C. (1950). The Human Group. Harcourt, New York.

Homans, G.C. (1962). Sentiments & Activities; Essays in Social Science. Free Press of Glencoe, New York.

Ibarra, H. (1992). "Homophily and differential returns: sex differences in network structure and access in an advertizing firm". Administrative Science Quarterly 37, 422.

Jermier, J.M. (1988). "Sabotage at work: The rational view". In: Bacharach, S.B., DiTomaso, N. (Eds.), Research in the Sociology of Organizations, vol. 6. JAI Press, London, pp. 101–134.

Kandel, E., Lazear, E.P. (1992). "Peer pressure and partnerships". Journal of Political Economy 100, 801–817.

Kreps, D. (1997). "Intrinsic motivation and extrinsic incentives". American Economic Review Papers and Proceedings 87, 359–364.

Kunda, G. (1992). Engineering Culture: Control and Commitment in a High-Tech Corporation. Temple University Press, Philadelphia.

Kram, K.E. (1988). Mentoring at Work: Developmental Relationships in Organizational Life. University Press of America, Lanham, MD.

Lawler, E.E. III (1973). Motivation in Work Organizations. Wadsworth.

Lazear, E.P., Rosen, S. (1981). "Rank-order tournaments as optimum labor contracts". Journal of Political Economy 89, 841–864.

Lewicki, R., Bunker, B.B. (1996). "Developing and maintaining trust in working relationships". In: Kramner, R.M., Tyler, T.R. (Eds.), Trust in Organizations. Sage, Thousand Oaks.

Lind, E.A., Tyler, T.R. (1988). The Social Psychology of Procedural Justice. Plenum Press, New York.

Lind, E.A., Greenberg, J., Scott, K.S., Welchans, Th.D. (2000). "The winding road from employee to complainant: situational and psychological determinants of wrongful-termination claims". Administrative Science Quarterly 45, 557–590.
Lorenz, E.H. (1988). "Neither friends nor strangers: informal networks of subcontracting in French industry". In: Gambetta, D. (Ed.), Trust: Making and Breaking Cooperative Relations. Basil Blackwell, New York.
Lord, R.G., Hohenfeld, J.A. (1979). "Longitudinal field assessment of equity effects on the performance of major league baseball players". Journal of Applied Psychology 64, 19–26.
Moorman, R.H., Blakely, G.L., Niehoff, B.P. (1998). "Does perceived organizational support mediate the relationship between procedural justice and organizational citizenship behavior?". Academy of Management Journal 41, 351–357.
Nagle, Th. (1975). "Comment". In: Phelps, E.S. (Ed.), Altruism, Morality and Economic Theory. Russell Sage, New York.
Morse, N.C., Weiss, R.S. (1955). "The function and meaning of work and the job". American Sociological Review 20, 191–198.
Oliva, R., Gittell, J.H. (2002). "Southwest airlines in Baltimore". Harvard Business School Case 9-602-156, June.
O'Reilly, Ch., Pfeffer, J. (1995). "Southwest airlines: using human resources for competitive advantage (A)". Stanford Graduate School of Business Case HR-1A.
Organ, D.W. (1988). Organizational Citizenship Behavior. Lexington, Lexington, MA.
Rabin, M. (1993). "Incorporating fairness into game theory and economics". American Economic Review 83, 1281–1302.
Rob, R., Zemsky, P. (2002). "Social capital, corporate culture, and incentive intensity". Rand Journal of Economics 33, 243–257.
Roethlisberger, F.J., Dickson, W.J. (1939). Management and the Worker; an Account of a Research Program Conducted by the Western Electric Company. Hawthorne Works, Chicago. Harvard University Press, Cambridge, MA.
Rotemberg, J.J. (1994). "Human relations in the workplace". Journal of Political Economy 102, 684–718.
Rotemberg, J.J. (2002). "Endogenous altruism in buyer–seller relations and its implications for vertical integration", mimeo.
Rotemberg, J.J., Saloner, G. (1993). "Leadership style and incentives". Management Science 39, 1299–1318.
Schaubroeck, J., May, D.R., Brown, F.W. (1994). "Procedural justice explanations and employee reactions to economic hardship: a field experiment". Journal of Applied Psychology 79, 455–460.
Scott, A. (1994). Willing Slaves? British Workers under Human Resource Management. Cambridge University Press, Cambridge, UK.
Shapiro, C., Stiglitz, J.E. (1984). "Equilibrium unemployment as a worker disciplining device". American Economic Review 74, 433–444.
Simon, H. (1951). "A formal theory model of the employment relationship". Econometrica 19, 293–305.
Stodgill, R.M. (1972). "Group productivity, drive and cohesiveness". Organizational Behavior and Human Performance 8, 26–43.
Thibaut, J.W., Walker, L. (1975). Procedural Justice: A Psychological Analysis. Erlbaum, Hillsdale, NJ.
Tyler, T.R., Degoey, P. (1996). "Trust in organizational authorities: the influence of motive attributions on the willingness to accept decisions". In: Kramer, R.M., Tyler, T.R. (Eds.), Trust in Organizations: Frontiers of Theory and Research. Sage, Thousand Oaks, CA.
Uzzi, B. (1997). "Social structure and competition in interfirm networks: the paradox of embeddedness". Administrative Science Quarterly 42, 35–67.
Van Maanen, J., Kunda, G. (1989). "Real feelings: emotional expression and organizational culture". Research on Organizational Behavior 11, 43–103.

Chapter 22

RECIPROCITY, ALTRUISM, AND COOPERATIVE PRODUCTION

LOUIS PUTTERMAN

Contents

Handbook of the Economics of Giving, Altruism and Reciprocity, Volume 2
Edited by Serge-Christophe Kolm and Jean Mercier Ythier

DOI: 10.1016/S1574-0714(06)02022-7

Abstract

Economists believe that a problem of team production results from the desirability of production in (sometimes large) groups, the difficulty of rewarding individual group members based on their (difficult or impossible to measure) individual contributions, and the presumed interest of each individual in avoiding effort and earning more, without regard to the outcomes of others. Although a possible response is to expend resources on monitoring each worker and paying accordingly, there are indications that this may be a less cost-effective approach than is drawing upon workers' propensities to reciprocate the trust and liberality of an employer by providing more effort, and to engage in mutual monitoring, social sanctioning of free riders, and emulation of others' efforts, when faced with group-based incentives. The large literature on incentives in producer cooperatives that sprang up during the 1960s through the 1980s predates economists' recent work on reciprocity, but it did concern itself with the interdependence of choices and it included remarks about mutual monitoring. This chapter considers the roles that altruism and reciprocity might play in cooperatives, and it discusses the recent, largely experimental literature on reciprocity and other social preferences, considering its relevance to cooperatives and to incentives in teams more generally.

Keywords

labor managed firms, producer cooperatives, work incentives, reciprocity, altruism

JEL classification: D23, D64, H41, J54, P13, P32

Introduction

Seldom is anything produced in the modern world without engaging the efforts of many different individuals. The type of enterprise we call a producers' cooperative, workers' enterprise, or labor-managed firm arises when such individuals, working as a team, are also in ultimate control of their enterprise, with their earnings being a direct function of its net revenue or profit. Producers' cooperatives exist in many countries, although it is fair to say that with few exceptions they are more important as a conceptual alternative to the more common capitalist enterprise than as the basis of a large sector of the economy in their own right. The more common form of joint production in which many hands participate, but under the control of capital suppliers or managers responsible to them, could also be described as cooperative.[1] Such a firm, while conventional, shares some features of the cooperative problem because fully individualized incentives are usually difficult to create, and often undesirable. This chapter will focus primarily on cooperative enterprises in the narrower sense, but will treat cooperation more broadly where natural extensions suggest themselves.

Because the very term "cooperative" implies that the workers (or firms) involved must help one another if they are to do their jobs well, one might expect the study of cooperation in the workplace to be an area in which unselfish motives would have one of their most important applications in economic analysis. From the ascent of neoclassical economics until recent years, however, the preponderance of analyses of work were like other parts of economics in assuming that agents acted only in their self-interest. More surprisingly, perhaps, the same statement applies with equal force to the economics of producers' cooperatives, which flowered between the late 1960s and the mid-1980s, again before the growth in respectability of a more behavioral brand of economic analysis. This chapter's discussion of cooperatives, reciprocity, and altruism, has thus only a limited literature on which to draw directly. In significant part, it must be constructed by means of an attempt to "connect the dots" between the copious literature on incentives and cooperatives, on the one hand, and the recently growing literature on reciprocity and altruism, on the other.[2]

1. Group production, incentive problems, and the social element in their resolution

Since earliest times, human beings have wrested a living from nature in a cooperative manner. Men hunted and fished in groups, and even the gathering of plant foods often

[1] Karl Marx (1967 [1867]), e.g., denoted all factory production as cooperative, despite assuming ownership and control by a capital provider.

[2] The word "cooperatives" has been used just as often to discuss firms owned and controlled by buyers of a good or goods, or organizations created by independent producers to purchase their (e.g., agricultural) products from them at an advantageous price. Writing on these last two kinds of organizations has been rather separate from that on cooperation in the workplace, however, and because the author's expertise is restricted to work in the latter area, very little will be said about buyers' and sellers' cooperatives in this chapter.

depended importantly on the sharing of information about the locations of promising stands (Smith, 1975; Boyd and Richerson, 1985; Diamond, 1997; Hibbs and Olsson, 2004). The survival strategy of the human species was from the first a social one.

Agriculture has in some times and places offered a partial exception to this rule. Although in some settings the joint management of irrigation works was crucial to agriculture's feasibility—a fact that helps to explain the rise, e.g. in Egypt, of large-scale political entities that could oversee their management—the farm work itself could often be handled by the household, which did not require for the completion of its tasks the cooperation of others.[3] Modern industry put an end to such productive self-sufficiency for most. Due to the existence of economies of scale, automobiles, refrigerators, VCRs and computer chips cannot be fabricated efficiently by the family. Even in the delivery of services like transportation, communications, retail sales, hotel accommodations and food services, there are scale economies causing the family-based establishment to play a limited role in today's industrialized economies.

At the heart of the economics of group production lies the conundrum that many hands working together can achieve far higher average productivity than can few hands working alone, but once the individual becomes only one worker in a larger group, she faces the temptation to work with less energy and care than when producing for her own gain. This occurs because it tends to be costly, if not impossible, to ascertain the contribution of each individual to the group's output. But unless the individual's reward is closely tied to her productive effort, the calculus of self-interest dictates some substitution of leisure for work (Alchian and Demsetz, 1972).

Economists have suggested various ways of addressing this problem. If the individual's effort is easier to monitor than is his output, perhaps because no discrete product can be associated with that worker on his own, then a supervisor should check this effort until the marginal benefit of monitoring, in the form of improved incentives, equals the marginal cost of the monitoring, in the form of supervisory pay or the opportunity cost of the supervisor's time. Given that monitoring is not infinite, some slacking will continue under this best feasible solution. This in itself is perhaps not so special a problem. It is committing the "Nirvana fallacy," argue Jensen and Meckling (1976), to think that agency costs are any more avoidable than are the opportunity costs of ordinary factors of production. However, the monitoring solution of the work effort problem does create a second-order problem of "who will monitor the monitor?", a problem that might lead to an infinite regress of monitors of monitors. It is as a response to that problem, Alchian and Demsetz (1972) suggested, that the ultimate monitor of the other agents tends, at

[3] It's interesting in this context to note that even in small scale family farming, the practice of mutual aid among households has often been common. Although economies of scale might be obtainable in such tasks as rice transplanting, where seedlings are passed along a line of workers from seedbed to field, it is possible to argue that in many cases people worked in supra-family groups mainly for the sociability of it, working and singing together and celebrating afterwards in group parties as much to motivate one another to keep on with the work as for any technological benefit from cooperation.

least in smaller firms, to be the enterprise's residual claimant and owner. Ordinary workers, then, are paid by wages that reflect their specific levels of productivity, and do not share in enterprise profits. For Alchian and Demsetz, this analysis of the team effort problem provided the central explanation of why firms have capitalist owners.[4]

Although capitalist firms in which workers are paid by wages rather than profit-shares are indeed the norm in modern economies, there are problems with Alchian and Demsetz's argument, some of which have been widely noted. A key empirical problem is that profit-sharing by workers has become a popular element of the compensation package in the industrial world's larger firms, and there is little to suggest that the practice dampens workers' incentives to work hard. On the contrary, most studies conclude that in conventionally owned firms, profit-sharing is associated either with no systematic change or with higher productivity, stronger work incentives, and a reduced need for costly supervision (Blinder, 1990; Kruse, 1993). Strong work incentives are also commonly heralded features of worker-owned enterprises, like the once-numerous plywood cooperatives of the U.S. Pacific Northwest (Craig and Pencavel, 1995), in which workers share in claims on profits. This leads Dow and Putterman (2000) and Dow (2003) to conclude that the reason why worker ownership is not more common is unlikely to be found in the domain of work incentives.

A number of influential economists writing on the economics of the workplace note that a better grasp of its dynamics may require some understanding of social elements and, thus, of preferences over and above those of strict material self-interest. Alchian and Demsetz themselves argued that monitoring costs could be reduced through the promotion of team spirit. Williamson et al. (1975) suggested that considerations of "atmosphere" needed to be weighed against the benefits of close monitoring of employee performance. Kandel and Lazear (1992) showed that workers might be moved to work harder if they care about their standing in the eyes of fellow workers, and thus respond to the non-material "social pressure" that is likely to be aimed at free-riders when the earnings of each depend on the productivity of all. Social relations in the workplace are also studied by Rotemberg (1994) and Spagnolo (1999); see Rotemberg's chapter in this volume.

[4] Efficiency wage models, such as Shapiro and Stiglitz (1984) or the "contested exchange" variant due to Bowles and Gintis (1990), also assign a key role to monitoring, but they treat monitoring as an ordinary input that can be purchased by the firm, or they assume that it is present without analyzing how it is elicited. Holmström (1982) provided a formal proof that profit-sharing cannot generate efficient work incentives given self-interested workers in a one-shot interaction. He showed that the incentive problem could be solved by having a "budget-breaking" principal contract to pay each worker only when aggregate output is consistent with all having provided their socially optimal effort levels. Although his budget-breaker solution involved no monitoring, it did involve an asymmetric relationship between a central residual claimant and workers who would receive a fixed amount, if anything. For this reason Holmström, like Alchian and Demsetz, saw his analysis as providing a reason why workers don't share the residual in most firms. But his model has been criticized on theoretical grounds (see Eswaran and Kotwal, 1984; MacLeod, 1986), and its relative inapplicability to matters of practical work organization is generally conceded.

Baker et al. (1988) expressed puzzlement at the ubiquity of concern about "pay equity" which, they believed, tends to narrow pay differentials within enterprises relative to what productivity differences would dictate. A possible explanation had been provided by Akerlof (1982), who showed that it could be profitable for employers to respond to worker concerns about equity, if workers are sufficiently concerned about each others' welfare to respond to employer deference on the matter by reciprocating that gift with their own gift of greater effort.

Baker et al. also puzzled over the popularity of profit-sharing, which ought not to be effective in view of the free-riding prediction of economic theory. A partial response is Weitzman and Kruse's (Weitzman and Kruse, 1990) argument that a high effort, mutual monitoring equilibrium is in principle sustainable if interactions are ongoing and discount rates not too steep. But as Weitzman and Kruse note, even when cooperation is an equilibrium of the repeated game to which the incentive problem corresponds, it is only one of many possible equilibria. They suggest that one may have to invoke cultural norms, or company culture, to explain why a cooperative equilibrium emerges in one enterprise but not in another under structurally similar conditions.

In section 3, we will discuss social preferences, and the recent evidence of their importance that comes from experimental economics. First, however, we survey attempts to analyze the incentive problems of cooperative firms in particular, a literature which, as mentioned, remained grounded in the assumption of a *Homo economicus*.

2. Incentives, effort interdependence, and interdependence of rewards in cooperatives

Adam Smith and Karl Marx, while deeply concerned with self-interest and rationality, were also fully aware of the social nature of the human animal. To Smith (Smith, 1971 [1789]), our concern with how we are viewed by others is as powerful a motive as is our material self-interest. Marx supposed that the mere act of working side by side boosted the productive energies of people working in teams. Although great economists from J.S. Mill to Pareto, Edgeworth and Pigou continued to view individuals as having concerns beyond simple self-interest, Mill's fiction of the "economic man" and Edgeworth's dictum (Edgeworth, 1881) that "The first principle of Economics is that every agent is actuated only by self-interest" became ever more dominant in the neoclassical school of economics during the period spanning the 1940s to the 1980s. Only toward the end of the 20th Century did neoclassicism become sufficiently self-confident, did its research address so many diverse topics, and were so many anomalies encountered, that social aspects of behavior, and preferences other than self-interest, began to resurface in papers published in the most influential peer-reviewed journals. Still unsolved riddles about work organization were one source of the revived interest in social aspects of economic behavior. The introduction of the scientific method of experimentation into economics was another. That biology, using game theoretic models much like those popular in economics, had in the meantime offered possible explanations of how reciprocity could have emerged from natural selection, also encouraged cross-disciplinary conversation.

The specialized technical literature on cooperatives, however, sprang up under neoclassical auspices before social preferences had returned to good odor in the economics discipline. While noting the early interest in cooperatives by Marx, Mill, Walras and others as well as some early proto-theoretical contributions by Beatrice and Sidney Webb (Webb and Webb, 1920), Mikhail Tugan-Baranovsky (1921), and others, this new literature first set out on tracks parallel to the neoclassical theory of the firm. The first contributions to this literature, indeed, explored comparative statics at the firm level without focusing on work incentives as such (Ward, 1958; Domar, 1966; Vanek, 1970 [excepting one chapter]). The amount of work effort was assumed given by the number of workers, which was a choice variable to the firm. Reciprocity, altruism, and other "non-standard" motivations played no part.[5]

The Soviet and Chinese collective farms were probably the first "cooperative"-like enterprises to inspire analyses of effort choice by individuals.[6] Some early collective farm models treated labor supply as an aggregate determined by the farm manager, ignoring effort variation of the worker on the job. But because poor motivation was widely supposed to plague collective farm systems, other authors were soon analyzing the choice of effort by the individual collective farmer. Two possible causes of incentive problems assumed prominence from the outset. First, whereas agriculture in the countries involved had originally been a family concern, collectivization amalgamated the fields of many peasants, severing the direct link between individuals' efforts and the produce of particular plots within the village fields. If it was difficult to determine what any individual farmer had contributed to the farm's success, it would be difficult to link rewards with contributions. Second, the collective paid the worker a portion of its net produce and cash earnings rather than a fixed wage per unit of time or a piece rate per task completed. Although the worker's portion was linked to the number of labor days that he or she supplied, the compensation to be expected for each day worked could not be known in advance, or at least could not be known without some estimate of the

[5] An exception is found in parts of Vanek's book which explored "special dimensions" of the problem; but for the most part, his analysis was conventional and helped to spur dozens of further analyses of the "labor managed firm" in various time frames and market structures. Another exception, the consideration of altruism by Sen (1966), is discussed below.

[6] Although not true cooperatives because of their involuntary character and the ubiquity of commands by state authorities, these farms (but not the state farms or *sovkhozy* that also existed, especially in the Soviet Union) were nominally cooperatives or collectives, and they shared with *bona fide* cooperative enterprises the crucial feature that earnings were based on a division of revenue among the working members. The farms were of considerable empirical importance since they counted among their members tens of millions of Soviet and hundreds of millions of Chinese farmers, because they played a critical role in those countries' strategies for economic development, and because weakness of their agricultural sectors was an Achilles' heal of both countries' economies during the era of command planning.

amount of work to be supplied by others. Thus, work was being performed for uncertain payment.

Unfortunately, neither the effort measurement nor the pay uncertainty problem could be satisfactorily captured by the simpler theoretical models then common, and initial modeling results were thus somewhat paradoxical. To begin with, the nub of the incentive problem caused by pooling labor and land and blurring the link between individual effort and individual marginal product is a matter of imperfect information. However, imperfect information was originally assumed away in the models. Second, the uncertainty surrounding the value of the labor day derived from many sources, including uncertainties about weather and pests, uncertainty about farm prices, and uncertainty about the effort levels of co-workers on the collective farm. But more importantly, modeling the effects of uncertainty required incorporating risk-aversion, which some early modelers were loathe to do. Without explicitly incorporating imperfect information and risk-aversion into their models, it was difficult for the earlier modelers to capture their intuitions about collective incentive problems formally. In fact, the initial literature produced the unexpected result that the incentive to work in a collective farm might not after all be inefficiently weak, but rather might be excessively strong, leading to inefficient *overwork*.

To see why, suppose that each worker selects an effort level so as to maximize own utility, modeled conventionally as a function of income and effort (labor, or negative leisure) only ($U = f(y, l)$). Each worker supplies units of homogeneous effort to the coop, whose output is a well-defined function of the sum of the effort units supplied and of some non-labor inputs. The value of this output net of the cost of the other inputs is divided among the members in proportion to the effort that each supplies. Hence, the individual receives $(l_i/L)R$, where l_i is the individual's effort, L is the total effort, and $R = g(L, X)$ is the coop's net revenue, X being all other inputs. To select l_i so as to maximize utility, taking the efforts of others as given, the individual has to set the value of his marginal rate of substitution between effort and income equal to the marginal effect of his effort upon his payment of $(l_i/L)R$. The first order condition for utility maximization is

$$U_l/U_y = (l_i/L)R_l + (1 - l_i/L)(R/L) \tag{1}$$

where R_l is the marginal value product of labor and R/L is the value of the average product of labor, net of nonlabor input costs. The right hand side, which can be called the *marginal income yield of effort*, is thus a weighted average of the value of the marginal product of labor, and the value of the average product, R/L. Given the weights on marginal and average product (i.e., l_i/L and $(1 - l_i/L)$, respectively), it followed that in even a moderately large collective farm in which one worker's share of the total labor is small, the marginal income yield would approximate the *average* product. Now, since the socially efficient criterion for the choice of effort is that the marginal rate of substitution (MRS) should equal the value of the *marginal* product of labor, the equation of the MRS with the *average* product of labor, in a cooperative, suggests an inherent inefficiency. Rather than the result which had been expected, that of an *inadequate* incentive to effort, however, the model suggested that a cooperative's (collective farm's) incentives led members to *overwork* themselves. This is because the average product of labor tends to exceed the marginal product unless labor is relatively scarce.[7]

Although the collective farm models treated individuals as self-interested utility maximizers, they came tantalizingly close to the consideration of reciprocity in a certain respect. To form an estimate of the effect of effort on payment, in the models, the worker must know not only her own effort choice, but also the choices of the other workers (which together determine the values of the marginal and average product of labor). In their discussions of this problem, Bradley (1971, 1973), Cameron (1973a, 1973b), Bonin (1977), Chinn (1979) and Israelsen (1980) all noted that the individual might usefully form a conjecture about the effect of raising or lowering her personal effort upon the effort choices of others in the group. With the addition of such a conjecture, equation (1) becomes

$$U_l/U_y = (l_i/L)(\partial L/\partial l_i)R_l + (1 - [(l_i/L)(\partial L/\partial l_i)])(R/L) \tag{2}$$

If a member expects an increase in his own effort to be met by a proportionate rise in the effort of every other member, then $(\partial L/\partial l_i) = L/l_i$, and the right hand side of (2) becomes simply R_l, the value of the marginal product of labor. Expectations of emulation could thus solve the problem of non-optimal incentives. Thus Chinn, thinking of the rhetoric of Maoist China's Dazhai model, suggested that a positive interdependence between one workers' efforts and those of fellow workers could arise through "social cohesion."

Influenced by the Chinese case, some collective farm models also allowed that the farm's revenue might not all be distributed in proportion to work done, but might partly be distributed based on need, modeled simply as an equal distribution. Now, the less were distribution based on work done, the less incentive would the individual who cared only about own income and leisure have to provide effort, assuming the effort choices of different individuals were treated as independent of one another (that is, returning to the simpler assumption that $\partial L/\partial l_i = \partial l_i/\partial l_i = 1$). Formally, with equal distribution, equation (1) becomes

$$U_l/U_y = (1/N)R_l \tag{3}$$

where N is the number of members in the cooperative. The fact that the right hand side of (3) is only one Nth that of the optimal value, R_l, implies a serious disincentive to labor. As Amartya Sen (1966) noted, however, this could come in handy insofar as (1) implies that with payments proportionate to work, labor would be *over*supplied. If a cooperative wanted work incentives to be efficient, it could find a mix of "distribution according to work" and (by assumption, equal) "distribution according to needs" that

[7] Models of work incentives in labor-managed firms and collective farms are reviewed on pp. 36–54 of Bonin and Putterman (1987).

would get the weights on average and marginal product just right on the margin.[8] A mixed distribution system seemed indeed to be practiced in China's rural production teams, where cash earnings tended to be paid out in proportion to workpoints, but grain was often divided based on per capita needs.

Suppose, however, that rather than assuming workers to have treated one anothers' effort levels as given, they were assumed to have made optimistic assumptions about effort interdependence. In that case, distributing equally might not be useful only as a way of diluting incentives; it might be a viable way of distributing earnings in its own right. With a conjecture of complete emulation by others ($\partial L/\partial l_i = L/l_i$) and assuming members were identical in their preferences (so that $L/l_i = N$), the RHS of (3) (the marginal income yield of labor) becomes

$$\partial(R/N)/\partial l_i = (1/N)\partial R/\partial l_i = (1/N)(\partial R/\partial L)(\partial L/\partial l_i) = (1/N)R_l(N) \tag{4}$$

changing (3) to

$$U_l/U_y = R_l \tag{5}$$

which is the condition for socially optimal effort. This point was made by Chinn (1979) with reference to "emulation" or "cohesion" in a Chinese agricultural production team, and similar observations were made by Putterman (1983) and by Guttman and Schnytzer (1989) with regard to the Israeli *kibbutz*.

The last paper is based upon the model of Guttman (1978), in which individuals can pre-commit to matching the voluntary contributions of others to a public good. Guttman and Schnytzer compared the implications of such matching behavior in a collective farm or *kolkhoz*, where revenue is divided in proportion to effort, and in a *kibbutz*, where it is divided equally. Whereas matching behavior led to an optimal effort equilibrium in the *kibbutz*, in their model, it transformed the overwork outcome predicted when the *kolkhoz*'s 'distribution-according-to-work' formula operates without matching into a problem of effort undersupply,[9] assuming that there is no problem of observing individuals' efforts and matching rates. This, they proposed, might explain why *kibbutzim* were more successful economically than *kolkhozy*, even though one might have predicted the opposite based on the fact that *kibbutzim* unlike *kolkhozy* used no individually differentiated material incentives.

[8] When payment is a weighted average of one's work-proportionate share and of one's per capita share, the marginal return to effort is, as in (1), a weighted average of the value of the average product of labor and the value of the marginal product of labor. However, the weight on the average product is smaller the more is distributed equally. Since the average product is assumed to be above the marginal product, the trick is to raise the proportion distributed according to needs by just enough to lower the weighted average until it equals the value of the marginal product. Assuming $l_i/L \approx 1/N$, the requirement is that the proportion distributed equally should be equal to one minus the ratio of the marginal to the average product. See Sen (1966) and Putterman (1981).

[9] The intuition is that because *kolkhoz* members would compete to increase their relative shares of the labor and hence income, matching would become "a *threat*—'if you work harder, I'll work harder, so let's both of us work less!' " (Guttman and Schnytzer, 1989, p. 694; emphasis in original).

All of these results of high effort in collective or communal farms, and of more efficient effort without individual incentives, were clearly at odds with the belief, held by many observers, that deficient incentives typified such institutions. When China's production teams began experimenting with the contracting out of fields and quotas to individual households at the end of the 1970s, and when the result of this, of farm price increases, and of lifted restrictions on crop marketing and sideline activities, was a sharp increase in farm output, the conventional wisdom that communal production generates poor incentives received a powerful boost. In theoretical discussions, the possibility of high positive interdependence of effort choices began to be discounted, at least for those cases in which communal institutions had been foisted upon a population from above. A link between effort and pay was once again considered critical. And the main deficiency of this link in a collective farm was argued to be that only the number of hours or days worked, but not the amount of effective effort, could be measured with any accuracy (Lin, 1988, 1992; Liu, 1991). If an hour worked diligently and an hour spent idling in the field were both credited the same work point, then putative "distribution according to work," with first order condition (1), became "distribution according to needs," with first order condition (3), by default.

Theory does not automatically establish that poor observability or monitoring must lead to a low effort equilibrium. Suppose, for example, that each member's effort is measured with an unbiased error ε, so that the individual in a non-egalitarian cooperative is paid $(\ell_i/L)R$, where $\ell_i = l_i + \varepsilon$. It seems natural to depict an improvement in monitoring as a decline in the variance of ε. Yet it does not in general hold that as that variance goes down, the privately optimal effort level will go up (Putterman and Skillman, 1988; Bonin and Putterman, 1993). Intuitively, risk aversion can cause the individual to cut back on effort when a smaller level of effort can assure a desired level of income with greater certainty because monitoring has reduced the variance of the error term in ℓ_i. Still, one can find alternative specifications that support the conventional intuition. For example, if the amount of monitoring determines the probability that a given worker's effort will be perfectly observed, and if the worker receives $(l_i/L)R$ if observed and $(1/N)R$ if not observed, then a worker faces incentives that are a weighted average of the marginal income yields in (1) and (3), with (1) getting greater weight as monitoring improves. More effort is likely to be elicited when there is more monitoring, given this depiction of the matter (see again the references just cited).

Since theories assuming payment proportionate to effort predict effort oversupply, but the comparison of collective and non-collective agricultures indicate that effort was a problem in collectives, the case for the view that tying rewards to effort has been a problem at least in those cooperative-like organizations seems strong. For grain and other basic crops, family farms are far more common than cooperatives as well as wage-hiring plantations, around the world.[10]

[10] This conclusion about family farms is reached by Binswanger and Rosenzweig (1986) and Binswanger et al. (1993) among others. Whether monitoring was a problem on Chinese production teams due to insur-

3. Altruism and reciprocity

Unlike most of his contemporaries, Amartya Sen found it unnatural to visit the question of agricultural cooperatives without considering how the peasants' concerns for one another might affect matters. Sen included in his (Sen, 1966) model a parameter of "sympathy," being the weight that an individual cooperative member places on the utility of fellow members as part of his own objective function. When sympathy is zero, the result under egalitarian distribution is severely sub-optimal effort provision, when N is large (see also Holmström, 1982). But when the individual puts the same weight on the utility of others as on his own personal utility, incentives under egalitarian distribution are perfectly efficient. This is quite intuitive, for in this case, the individual weighs on the side of the benefit from effort not only his own $1/N$ share of the value of his marginal product, but also the $1/N$ shares of each of the other $(N-1)$ members, adding up to the full value of marginal product.[11]

While so high a level of altruism as to put equal weight on each other as on oneself seems unlikely to be sustained in a community of significant size, any degree of positive interdependence among members' utilities helps to reduce free-riding incentives. If the cooperative practices strictly equal distribution for ideological reasons or because individual inputs are simply unobservable, or if it practices any form of profit-sharing in which individual shares are fixed in advance, a degree of altruism or sympathy would help to raise incentives, although these would remain suboptimal unless the high level that Sen called "complete sympathy" obtained.

For the case of mixed systems of payment-by-work and equal sharing, however, Sen obtained a result that might seem counter-intuitive. Suppose that accurate observations of individual's labor contributions are available and that sharing output in proportion to inputs is the main payment scheme, as in (1). Suppose, further, that the marginal product of labor is expected to lie below the average product, so that the right hand side of (1) implies that work incentives are excessive. Diluting incentives by means of some equal sharing is then desirable, as discussed in the last section. It might seem that the degree of sympathy (altruism) should therefore be considered, since the more sympathy there is among the members, the less weight might need to be placed on "distribution according to work" to get the incentives right. But Sen demonstrated that, in his model at least, this is not the case. So long as sympathy is not complete (i.e., $\Sigma a_{ij} < N-1$),

mountable problems of observability or due to ideological opposition to individualized incentives (Putterman, 1988), and whether monitoring was in fact a serious problem in the teams (Putterman, 1991; Dong and Dow, 1993) remain subjects of debate.

[11] Formally, Sen, much like Pareto (1913) (see Kolm, 2000), defined agent i's maximand to be $W^i = U^i + \Sigma a_{ij} U^j$, where $0 \leq a_{ij} \leq 1$ is the weight worker i assigns to worker j's utility and where the summation is taken over all workers $j \neq i$. When i's income from the cooperative is $R(1/N)$, as it is with equal distribution, the first order condition for effort choice becomes $U_l^i = U_y^i(1/N)R_l + \Sigma a_{ij} U_y^j(1/N)R_l$. If $a_{ij} = 1$, all j, and if members have the same marginal utility from income, so that $U_y^i = U_y^j$, all j, then this simplifies to equation (5).

the optimal proportions in which work-linked distribution and equal sharing should be mixed are *not* a function of the degree of sympathy. They are given, instead, by the relationship between labor's marginal product and its average product net of nonlabor input costs, irrespective of sympathy.

Although voluntary contributions to the provision of such a public good may be motivated to some degree by altruism, an alternative form of interdependent preference seems likely to play an even more important role in group behavior. This is reciprocity. Positive reciprocity, the tendency to provide a gift or perform a favor in return for a similar act on another's part, has long been studied by sociologists and anthropologists (for references, see Kolm, 2000), but until recently received limited attention from economists. In remedying this inattention, economists such as Fehr and Gächter (2000b) and Hoffman et al. (1998) have given as much emphasis to the negative as to the positive side of reciprocity, identifying as a preference for recipcrocity both the desire to benefit others seen as benefiting one and the desire to harm others seen as harming one.

Reciprocity appears to work as much via the emotions as by way of its effect on rational calculations, and interest in the relationship between the emotions and moral behavior dates back to Darwin (1965 [1872]). In the late 20th Century, biologically-based students of social behavior beginning with Trivers (1971) have argued that evolution selected for reciprocity in certain species, including humans. The criterion of natural selection, according to much of contemporary evolutionary theory, is what is called "the inclusive fitness of the genes," that is, the ability of a gene to project itself as numerously as possible into future generations, irrespective of the survival of specific copies of the gene in individual organisms. According to Trivers, there are often situations in which one individual can bestow a large fitness advantage on another at a small fitness cost to itself—consider a hunter who has gorged himself on part of a large animal carcass who can return to camp and feed famished band members or consume by himself only a little more of the remaining meat before rot sets in. If the hunter bestows the favor now and if there is a sufficient likelihood that he will be repaid when the roles are reversed, then it is beneficial to both his and the others' genes that he do so.

Reciprocity is thought especially likely to flourish among human beings who have ongoing interactions with one another and who can remember one another's past behaviors, for then there is an incentive to invest in a reputation for being a reciprocator, and the whole group benefits from ongoing mutual assistance. Because there is still an individual incentive to defect in many instances for one time gain, however, it has been argued that reciprocity should be understood not as a strictly rational, self-interested solution for each individual social encounter, but as an inclination that is partly hard-wired by evolution and partly helped along by socialization and continuing social pressures. The individual wants not only to be well thought of, but also to think well of himself, and in a society in which norms of reciprocity have firm hold, there will be many situations in which he can seize personal advantage only at the expense of his self-image as "a good person." Quite possibly human beings would be unable to cooperate in many circumstances, and would thus forego many advantages, were they really the "rational economic men" of once-standard neoclassical theory. Thankfully, many would say, evolution has put in them traits that do better than individual rationality.[12]

4. Some evidence from experimental economics

The voluntary contribution mechanism (VCM) studied by Isaac and Walker (1988a, 1988b) among others (for reviews of the literature, see Davis and Holt (1993) and Ledyard (1995)) captures the main features of a workplace with profit-sharing. The VCM is a linear public goods game having the properties of an n-person prisoners' dilemma game, but with a multi-valued choice set for each player. Each of several individuals is endowed with a certain amount of money—for our purposes representing a capacity to provide work effort—that they are to allocate between an individual account, which accrues to them directly (for our purposes, shirking on the job), and a group account (for our purposes, working for the cooperative), which is scaled up (there are economies of team production) and divided equally (profit-sharing). For instance, if there are four group members and the scaling factor is 2, each one gets $0.50 = ([\$1 \times 2]/4)$ for every dollar put into the group account. Thus, if each member's endowment is \$10 and all four members put their \$10 in the group account, each earns \$20. If all put all ten dollars in their personal accounts, each earns \$10. If three put ten dollars in the group account and one puts ten dollars in his personal account, the latter earns \$25 and the former each earn \$15. Thus, each has an incentive to free ride so as to earn \$25 rather than \$20, but if all act on this incentive, each earns only \$10. These incentives mirror perfectly those in a cooperative enterprise with profit-sharing.

As is well known, standard economic theory predicts universal defection (contributing nothing) when the actors are strictly self-interested and the game is one-shot or repeated with known end-point. But in experimental enactments, subjects typically put an average of about 60% of their endowments into the group account in a one-shot game or in the first period of a finitely repeated game. With repetition, contributions tend to fall, suggesting movement toward the predicted equilibrium with learning. But several findings suggest that "learning the correct behavior" is not the main explanation for the trend. First, subjects return to higher contributions when there is a break and the game is restarted (Andreoni and Miller, 1993). Second, when high contributors are matched with other high contributors, their contributions show little or no tendency to decline with repetition (Gunnthorsdottir et al., 2002; Page et al., 2005). Third, when subjects are permitted to communicate with one another before making their decisions, they often achieve very high levels of cooperation, even without any way to enforce agreements

[12] A highly readable introduction to evolutionary psychology for the layman will be found in Wright (1994). Recent research by economists and anthropologists, with far-ranging references to the literature, is presented in Gintis et al. (2005).

(Isaac and Walker, 1988b; Sally, 1995; Brosig et al., 2003; Bochet et al., 2006;) and in at least one study, without even face-to-face contact (see the chat room treatment in Bochet et al., 2006). Fourth, when an extra stage is added to the game, in which subjects can reduce one another's earnings after learning of their contribution decisions, many sacrifice earnings to punish low contributors, and contributions tend to rise or to be sustained, rather than to fall, during further repetitions (Carpenter, 2000; Fehr and Gächter, 2000a, 2000b 2002; Sefton et al., 2002; Ertan et al., 2005; Page et al., 2005; Bochet et al., 2006). These findings suggest that rather than reflecting learning by sets of more or less homogeneous self-interested players, the declining trend in the standard repeated VCM experiment may be the result of interactions between subjects with different tastes (for instance, for reciprocity) and beliefs. This situation is better described by a Bayesian model with possible heterogeneity of agent types (Kreps et al., 1982) than by the standard iterated dominance solution with universally payoff-maximizing agents.

Suppose, for simplicity, that the subjects can be categorized according to one or another of two types: strict pay-off maximizers, who care only about their own earnings, and reciprocators, who prefer to forego the gains from free riding as long as they expect others also to do so. Suppose, further, that in addition to their differentiation by preference, subjects also vary in their beliefs about the number of reciprocators in their subject pool, and in their guesses about others' beliefs about this matter. Some assume that reciprocators are few if any and that few if any subjects believe reciprocators to be common; others believe that reciprocators may be common and that others are likely to share this belief. Finally, suppose that all reciprocators have optimistic beliefs about the frequency of reciprocators and about others' beliefs about that frequency, while non-reciprocators are divided in their beliefs. Then in the standard repeated VCM reciprocators who believe their type to be common may initially contribute much or all of their endowment to the group project, hoping for indications that others are like themselves. A second group, consisting of payoff-maximizers who believe that the reciprocator type, or at least the belief in the numerousness of this type, is common, will feign cooperation in the early periods of a repeated VCM, since they too are better off in a group that sustains cooperation until some later point, when they can benefit from defecting. Finally, there will be a third group, the payoff-maximizers who believe that the belief that everyone maximizes their payoff is widely shared. These individuals will not bother to feign cooperativeness even in a repeated game, but will contribute little or nothing from the outset. If the three types of players are roughly equal in number, contributions will start out at a fairly high level thanks to the reciprocators and those feigning reciprocity. But the reciprocators have no way to induce the skeptical payoff maximizers to raise their contributions and no way to punish free-riding or to defend themselves against it other than by reducing their own contributions. As a result, having seen free-riding by about 1-in-3 group members, the reciprocators, and those who mimic their behavior, will reduce their contributions, and group average contributions will steadily fall.[13] Restarting the interaction with a new subject group raises

[13] The situation is complicated by the fact that contributions to the public good by reciprocators and those feigning reciprocity in the early periods can alter the beliefs of skeptical payoff maximizers, because their

contributions back toward the initial level because reciprocators and strategic-minded payoff-maximizers who have reasonably optimistic prior expectations about the pervasiveness of reciprocity and about the belief that others are reciprocators will begin again with the hope that fellow group members are mainly reciprocators. Of course, a richer and more complicated pattern of behavior will occur in a more realistic model where beliefs and degree of reciprocity take on more gradations, and where beliefs are gradually updated in response to observed choices.

The otherwise anomalous findings about homogeneous subject assignment and communication can now be explained as well. With respect to homogeneous assignments, when reciprocator types are put in groups with other reciprocators, as in Gunnthorsdottir et al. (2002), their initial willingness to contribute is validated by seeing others do the same, so they continue to make large contributions to the group account, perhaps without any decline over time.[14] With regard to communication, when even randomly selected subjects communicate prior to decision-making,[15] they may be able to increase their confidence in their beliefs about the types of their fellow subjects. If more skeptical members become convinced that the others are reciprocators or will at least take cooperation as a sign that future cooperation is forthcoming, they may make higher contributions at the outset, and fulfillment of optimistic beliefs may then be self-sustaining.[16]

actions might be interpreted by the skeptics as evidence that many others believe cooperation to be possible. These actions imply that the initial beliefs of the skeptics (that nearly everyone assumes all are payoff maximizers) were wrong. This helps to explain why some low contributors actually raise their contributions in the early periods.

[14] A complicating factor is that if the subjects are grouped together on the basis of their contributions, rather than of type information obtained by other means, then true reciprocators will be assigned to the same groups as will payoff-maximizers feigning reciprocity. Once the latter decide that the time has arrived to defect, cooperation will collapse. Even more complicating is the fact that subjects may have different degrees of reciprocity and different beliefs about others' reciprocities and beliefs. For example, two individuals who are equally inclined towards conditional cooperation may make different initial decisions because of different prior beliefs about the likelihood that others will reciprocate. One of the reciprocators may cautiously test the waters by first contributing only half of the endowment, due to uncertainty that others will contribute, while another, more optimistic about others, puts in his whole endowment. If they are placed in the same group, the low contribution of the first person may lower the optimism of the second, and vice versa. If they are grouped by their initial contributions, as in Gunnthorsdottir et al., they are likely to be placed in different groups, have their expectations validated, and thus continue to behave differently as the game is repeated. Differences in initial beliefs, rather than in degree of reciprocity, may thus lead to what look like persistent differences in degree of reciprocity.

[15] Note that all of the experiments involving communication that have been referred to are ones in which subjects are randomly assigned to groups.

[16] Bochet et al. (2006) point out that a second "non-standard" preference may be equally as important here as is reciprocity: people may get disutility from going back on a promise that they have expressly given to others. If the material reward from lying is not very high, they may therefore choose to keep their word. Part of what subjects are assessing during the communication phase of such experiments, then, is whether the other subjects are people who are unlikely to break their word (who derive disutility from lying). Sally (1995), whose meta-analysis of the literature shows communication to be the most powerful means of inducing cooperation, goes so far as to suggest that "messages have no significance beyond their ability to convey promises."

To explain the findings about punishment, we need again to consider the full definition of reciprocity. As mentioned, Fehr and Gächter (2000b), Hoffman et al. (1998), and the literatures of evolutionary psychology and sociobiology see reciprocity as including both positive and negative dimensions.[17] The positive side of reciprocity, as we've seen, is a conditional willingness to reciprocate cooperative behavior by others. The negative side is an inclination to punish, even at cost to oneself, exploitative behavior or violation of the norms of reciprocity by others. This tendency to punish can dramatically alter game-theoretic predictions, and it makes a big difference in practice as seen in laboratory experiments. It must be emphasized that the tendency involves not merely punishing in a manner calculated to bring benefits to oneself in future interactions—although such benefits may help to stabilize or reinforce the behavior. People with a genuine taste for reciprocity will punish cheaters even in a one-shot situation, and sometimes they will incur costs to punish individuals who have exploited third parties, even if those actions brought no harm to the punisher himself.[18] In the presence of other individuals inclined towards both positive and negative reciprocity, individuals with no taste for reciprocity may nevertheless find it in their interest to act like positive reciprocators, for instance contributing to a public good so as to avoid punishment. How free riding on punishment itself (letting others incur the cost of punishing) is avoided, and how a tendency by some to punish even without benefit to themselves could have evolved within the human genetic or cultural make-up, are problems beyond the scope of the present paper.[19]

We can now offer an explanation for the results found in VCM experiments in which subjects have the opportunity to reduce one another's earnings at some cost after learning about contributions to the group account. To a reciprocator, the cooperative thing to do is for all group members to play their part in increasing one another's earnings by contributing to the public good. A subject who enjoys the earnings generated by the contributions of others without contributing himself is exploiting or cheating the others, and the reciprocator's utility will rise if she reduces this subject's earnings, even if her own earnings decline in the process. When the cost to the punisher is less than the cost to the person punished, as in most of the experiments described, the impulse of negative reciprocity does not need to be too strong in order for punishments to be elicited in the

[17] See also Ben-Ner and Putterman (2000).

[18] One-shot play is examined in the "perfect strangers" treatment in Fehr and Gächter (2000a). Last-period punishment is as common as punishment in other periods, in the repeated play experiments cited. Falk et al. (2005) attempt to estimate the proportion of punishment attributable to strategic considerations versus that due to the emotions or other nonstrategic factors, and find that the latter factors dominate. Punishment of those exploiting third parties is seen in an experiment by Carpenter and Matthews (2002) where two groups engage in separate public goods games but the members of each group have opportunities to impose costly punishment on members of the other group. Carpenter and Matthews find that there is enough punishment of outgroup members so that contributions approach the efficient level more fully in their treatment with both own and other-group punishment than in the treatment with own group punishment alone.

[19] An interesting discussion providing one point of entry into the literature is found in Henrich (2004).

face of free riding. Self-interested subjects who anticipate that there may be reciprocators in their group may accordingly raise their contributions so as to avoid punishment, even before they see evidence that punishment takes place (see the anticipation effects in Fehr and Gächter, 2000a, 2000b and Page et al., 2005). When free riders are actually punished, their contributions go up further and high contributions are sustained.

One concern raised by the collective action experiments in which punishment opportunities exist is that because punishment is costly, the rise in contributions which results from the presence of punishment may not be paralleled by a rise in subjects' earnings and social efficiency. In most of the experiments cited above, earnings indeed are no higher in treatments with punishment than without, although contributions are significantly higher with punishment.[20] This suggests that the social gains of negative reciprocity are small, if present at all. There is reason to believe that negative reciprocity is more beneficial in the real world than in these experiments, however. There are many different ways to punish a cheater. A verbal reprimand or the temporary reduction of social regard or shunning may suffice to change a free rider's behavior, as demonstrated in an experiment by Masclet et al. (2003).[21] Social sanctions, rather than fines, are probably the main mechanism through which the inclination to punish comes into play in the workplace.

Another way that efficiency may be enhanced in practice is by controlling the membership of cooperating groups. An experiment by Page et al. (2005) indicates that reciprocators achieve substantially higher levels of cooperation, and earnings, when they get to pick whom they interact with. Cooperative types are rewarded with an increased chance of playing with cooperative partners. The mechanism also elicits more cooperation from payoff maximizers who recognize the benefits of getting into cooperative groups.[22] Another experiment, by Cinyabuguma et al. (2005) indicates that cooperation can be dramatically increased by introducing the threat that non-cooperators will be expelled from the group—a threat that plays a central role in Bowles and Gintis's (Bowles and Gintis, 2004) theoretical model of the evolution of reciprocity.[23]

One factor that reduces the efficiencies of groups playing VCM games with punishment opportunities is that some subjects, contrary to the simple theory, also punish *high*

[20] In Fehr and Gächter (2000a), earnings are at first higher without punishment than with punishment, but this situation is eventually reversed with repetition. Nonetheless, independent calculations with their data show that earnings are lower overall when punishment is permitted.

[21] Gächter and Fehr (1999) also find that opportunities to express verbal approval or disapproval lead to higher contributions provided that subjects are able to establish social familiarity before anonymous decision-making begins.

[22] Since the majority are found to contribute to the public good in the known last period, with the number contributing varying predictably with the level of cooperation in each group during earlier periods, the authors conclude that most individuals in their subject pool have conditionally cooperative preferences. Note that in Page et al. (2005), two subjects are most likely to be grouped together if each ranks the other highly as a prospective partner. The grouping procedure is thus based on mutual, and not merely one-way, attraction. A different and less efficient result is attained by Erhart and Keser (1999), who allowed subjects to move from group to group based on unilateral expressions of preference.

[23] See also Hirshleifer and Rasmussen (1989).

contributors when permitted to. They may do this out of resentment at the moral behavior of the high contributors, to strike back at those they believe are punishing them, or to lower the earnings of others relative to their own earnings. It is thus of interest to know whether groups can act to lessen or eliminate the incidence of these perverse, anti-social punishments. Ertan et al. (2005) gave subjects the opportunity to rule out punishment of high or of low contributors, or both, by majority vote. In their main treatment, they found that each of 20 subject groups (with four subjects each) ruled out punishment of higher-than-average contributors in every one of the three opportunities each group was given to vote on the matter, and that groups which chose to allow punishment of low contributors achieved significantly higher earnings than in either play without punishment or play with unrestricted punishment. In a second treatment with five votes per session, another 20 groups also uniformly voted against letting individuals punish high contributors. Formal decisions over when punishment may be invoked can only occur in special circumstances. Perhaps the evolution of social equilibria in which pro-social punishments are favorably regarded and rewarded while anti-social punishments are frowned upon and punished can achieve a similar end.[24]

5. From laboratory results to the cooperative workplace

If the kinds of experiments just discussed successfully capture features of the incentive problems facing producers' cooperatives (as well as the workers in other settings in which reward depends partly on group behavior), we should expect to see many parallels between the experimental results, on the one hand, and the stylized facts in the literature on cooperatives, on the other. This is indeed the case.

Profit-sharing is widely reported to lead to mutual monitoring of workers by their fellow workers (Blinder, 1990). Peer pressure—described, for example, by Kandel and Lazear (1992) for conventional firms and by Lin (1988) for Chinese production teams—is a ubiquitous feature of cooperatives. By many accounts (for example, Barkai, 1977), it was an effective disciplinary tool in the highly egalitarian *kibbutzim*. The forces giving rise to mutual monitoring and peer pressure may be much the same as those exhibited

[24] To investigate this, Cinyabuguma et al. (2006) conducted voluntary contribution experiments with punishment stages like those discussed above, to which they added a third stage in which subjects can punish one another's choices about punishment itself. Subjects were shown the amount of punishment each had given to high contributors and the amount that each had given to low contributors to the group account at the original punishment stage, and were offered the opportunity to assign costly punishment in conjunction with this information only. Those who perversely punished high contributors in the original punishment stage tended to be punished in turn in this third stage. However, "pro-social" punishers of low contributors at the original punishment stage were just as frequently punished, almost always by low contributors. This suggests the strength of the motive of "getting even" and the difficulty of establishing cooperative equilibria without communication or group decision-making mechanisms.

in the cooperation and punishment experiments of Fehr and Gächter and others, i.e. the inclination to monitor and punish cheating which is associated with reciprocity.[25]

A common finding in the literature on firm organization is that participatory decision-making at the shop floor level enhances the effects of profit-sharing (Blinder, 1990). This effect probably stems from multiple causes, including the eliciting of workers' insights and the building of a sense of "ownership" over what is to be implemented. But an additional benefit of getting workers together to discuss the tasks facing them may be that communication fosters commitment to team goals, which may be effective for much the same reason as is communication in VCM experiments. The small size of agricultural production teams in China between 1962 and 1982, permitting face-to-face discussion and mutual monitoring, helped food production to keep pace with the addition of more than 340 million to the country's population in those decades. Although later shown to be far from the sector's production possibility frontier, the teams performed much better than the gigantic communes which they succeeded,[26] making the best of an environment of extractive pricing, irrational production targets, and official antipathy to the use of material incentives.

One of the most important mechanisms making cooperation sustainable may be the ability of an organization to choose its members, and the abilities of individuals to decide what groups they enter or exit. Individuals deciding on which group to join and groups evaluating prospective members would both be expected to look for evidence of cooperativeness, making it pay to invest in a reputation for this, as in the experiments of Page et al. (2005). The viability of true cooperatives is almost certainly helped by the fact that membership is voluntary and candidates for membership usually go through a probationary period and must be approved by the incumbent members (or their manager agents) before joining, thus permitting both self- and community selection against opportunistic types. Such mechanisms would be useless if all agents were of the same type, as presumed in some neoclassical models.

Whereas some Chinese agricultural cooperatives may have functioned well during the brief period (1952–55) in which membership was voluntary, making membership mandatory and universal, so that every resident of a village was automatically a member, deprived these units of an effective way to demand standards of behavior, i.e. the ability to threaten slackers with expulsion.[27] Often severely constrained, too, in their abilities to differentiate pay according to performance and to otherwise penalize free

[25] The tendency to be on the look-out for cheaters is emphasized by the evolutionary psychologists Cosmides and Tooby (1992).

[26] Communes of 5000 or more households were the production and accounting units in Chinese agriculture during 1958–1960. Although the communes continued to exist as administrative, service, and industrial organizations, production teams averaging 30 households took over responsibility for farming and distributed the revenue and produce from farming from 1962 until the "de-collectivization" of the early 1980s.

[27] Whereas Lin (1990) argues that it is the energetic worker's ability to threaten to quit which motivated fellow workers to pull their weight when membership in the agricultural cooperatives was voluntary in the mid-1950s, the rights to expel and to refuse admission to known slackers may have been at least as important in practice.

riders, China's agricultural production teams provide one of the best real-world analogues to groups in repeated VCM experiments which lack such mechanisms as targeted sanctions, endogenous group formation, or the right to expel unwanted members. The standard outcome of decaying cooperation in experimental groups is suggestive of why China's farm output rose by a large margin when families returned to separately farm land allocated to them by their villages, although improved external conditions were also a contributing factor (Putterman, 1993).

6. Reciprocity and cooperation in other settings

Reciprocity may play a part in generating higher effort levels in conventional firms as well as in cooperatives. Here, it may be helpful to think in terms of the reciprocity between employer and employee, on the one hand, and of that among employees, on the other. The first suggests that employees will reciprocate a generous wage and benefit package by providing a gift of non-contractable effort. The degree of the employer's generosity is measured by the difference between the value of the wage package and the worker's expected utility in her next best opportunity, possibly a lottery including unemployment. Akerlof's (Akerlof, 1982) depiction of such an interaction as a "gift exchange," one of the first attempts to formalize the sociological concept of reciprocity in an economic model, has been followed by a number of supportive experimental studies, including Fehr et al. (1997). A slightly different formalization was provided by Leibenstein (1982), who modeled worker-employer interaction as a prisoners' dilemma game with the employer as one player and the workers as the other. Leibenstein suggested that cooperative norms—perhaps akin to the idea of reciprocity—could make better treatment of workers, by the firm, and a higher effort response, by workers, a sustainable equilibrium.

The second kind of reciprocity, that between worker and worker, may help to explain why free-riding is not the usual result of profit-sharing. Recall that the choice of effort levels under profit-sharing can be viewed as an N-person repeated prisoners' dilemma game. Assuming a low probability of termination and a sufficiently mild time discount, cooperation at first-best effort levels is one of an infinite number of equilibria, sustainable by the threat of universal low effort following any defection. The fact that such an equilibrium Pareto-dominates the alternatives does not assure its selection, but Weitzman and Kruse (1990) argue, in a manner similar to Leibenstein, that normative and cultural factors might help solve the coordination problem. Reciprocity itself may be seen as one such norm, perhaps a particularly privileged one to which innate predisposition also lends support.

A problem resembling that of producers' cooperatives is cooperative effort to use sustainably a common resource, such as a fishery, a forest, or an irrigation system. While the construction and maintenance of an irrigation system or work on reforestation are public goods amenable to the same analysis as cooperative production, a different problem arises with respect to the use of such resources. Here, it is not underprovision but rather excessive exploitation of the resource that is the negative consequence of strictly self-interested choices. Elinor Ostrom and others (see for example Ostrom et al., 1992, 1994) have studied such problems extensively at the theoretical level, in the field, and in the laboratory, and their findings and explanatory frameworks closely parallel those of Fehr, Gächter, and the related public goods literature cited earlier. In the experimental lab, subjects who are denied opportunities to communicate or to discipline one another, tend to overexploit a common pool resource, although not always as severely as predicted by theory. However, communication eliminates most of the inefficiency, and subjects do avail themselves of opportunities to impose costly sanctions on over-users of the resource, the combination of communication and sanctioning being especially efficient. Through on-going communication and the possibility of social sanctions, real-world communities sometimes manage a common pool resource successfully, as well—so much so that a leading undergraduate textbook on economic development (Perkins et al., 2001) now recognizes that private and individual ownership is not the only conceivable response to the warning sounded in Garret Hardin's "Tragedy of the Commons" (Hardin, 1968).[28]

Reciprocity is undoubtedly at work in other forms of cooperative organization as well. A consumer cooperative that not only gives discounts on purchases by its members, but also pays out an end-of-year dividend from profits earned, may adopt this practice mainly for accounting convenience. However, the delayed exchange of cash reward for patronage might also be viewed as a gift exchange that helps to engender loyalty and a favorable orientation toward the organization. The same applies to systems of delayed second payments used by farmers' cooperatives.

In the small borrower groups that form the basis for loans made by the Grameen Bank and similar micro-credit institutions, both positive and negative reciprocity may have parts to play. The shared fate of group members, in terms of future credit access, encourages them to help one another where feasible so as to increase the likelihood of repayment. The certainty that social retribution will follow negligent failure to repay on the part of individual members may be underpinned by negative reciprocity as much as by rational self-interest. The social desire to remain in the good graces of one's neighbors gives the potential penalties their bite, thus helping to deter defaults that are within the control of individual members.

7. Conclusion

Economic analysis of the cooperative workplace has mostly followed the standard neoclassical approach of assuming self-interested agents concerned only with their own material pay-offs and effort. Early in the development of the literature, the possibility that effort choices might be interdependent was introduced into many analyses, but

[28] An example of the work on which this conclusion is based is Ostrom (1990).

what preferences might account for such interdependence was left largely unexplored. The recent economic literature on reciprocity provides a way of filling in this gap. The effort choices of members of cooperative enterprises are likely to be linked in part due to the common (but not uniformly strong) human propensity to attempt cooperation with those who offer cooperation, and to retaliate against those who exploit one's own good acts.

The growing experimental literature on reciprocity illuminates well-known results regarding the economic performance of cooperatives. In the absence of self-selection into a cooperative organization and of the right of the incumbent members to expel unwanted entrants and sanction free-riders, it is difficult if not impossible to control the tendency towards free-riding that is observed in repeated voluntary contribution experiments (although predictions of universal free-riding are born out fully in neither laboratory nor field). Participatory communication, the ability to evaluate the character ("type") of potential entrants, the right to expel free-riders, and the possibility of social and other sanctions, all foster high contribution or high effort outcomes in both laboratory and field.

Those seeking to understand why some cooperatives have succeeded and others failed might benefit from studying the roles of reciprocity and other social preferences in the dynamics of these organizations. This chapter has attempted to draw connecting lines between literatures on incentive problems in cooperatives, and on reciprocity in public goods settings, which have developed on separate tracks, with little or no explicit contact. Future research on cooperatives that is conducted by researchers with not only a strong command of the general techniques of economic analysis but also a full appreciation of the emerging literature on reciprocity and social preferences, will be breaking new ground and might therefore reap an unexpected harvest.

References

Akerlof, G. (1982). "Labor contracts as partial gift exchange". Quarterly Journal of Economics 47 (4), 543–569.

Alchian, A., Demsetz, H. (1972). "Production, information costs and economic organization". American Economic Review 62, 777–795.

Andreoni, J., Miller, J.H. (1993). "Rational cooperation in the finitely repeated prisoner's dilemma: experimental evidence". Economic Journal 103, 570–585.

Baker, G., Jensen, M., Murphy, K. (1988). "Compensation and incentives: practice vs. theory". Journal of Finance 43, 593–616.

Barkai, H. (1977). Growth Patterns of the Kibbutz Economy. North-Holland, New York.

Ben-Ner, A., Putterman, L. (2000). "On some implications of evolutionary psychology for the study of preferences and institutions". Journal of Economic Behavior and Organization 43, 91–99.

Binswanger, H., Rosenzweig, M. (1986). "Behavioral and material determinants of production relations in agriculture". Journal of Development Studies 22 (3), 503–539.

Binswanger, H., Deininger, K., Feder, G. (1993). "Agricultural land relations in the developing world". American Journal of Agricultural Economics 75 (5), 1242–1248.

Blinder, A. (Ed.) (1990). Paying for Productivity: A Look at the Evidence. Brookings Institution, Washington.

Bochet, O., Page, T., Putterman, L. (2006). "Communication and punishment in voluntary contribution experiments". Journal of Economic Behavior and Organization. In press.
Bonin, J. (1977). "Work incentives and uncertainty on a collective farm". Journal of Comparative Economics 1, 77–97.
Bonin, J., Putterman, L. (1987). Economics of Cooperation and the Labor-Managed Economy. Fundamentals of Pure and Applied Economics, vol. 14. Harwood Academic Publishers, London.
Bonin, J., Putterman, L. (1993). "Incentives and monitoring in cooperatives with labor-proportionate sharing schemes". Journal of Comparative Economics 17, 663–686.
Bowles, S., Gintis, H. (1990). Contested exchange: new microfoundations for the political economy of capitalism. Politics and Society 18 (2), 165–222.
Bowles, S., Gintis, H. (2004). The evolution of strong reciprocity: cooperation in heterogeneous populations. Theoretical Population Biology 65, 17–28.
Boyd, R., Richerson, P. (1985). Culture and the Evolutionary Process. University of Chicago Press, Chicago.
Bradley, M. (1971). "Incentives and labor supply on Soviet collective farms". Canadian Journal of Economics 4, 342–352.
Bradley, M. (1973). "Incentives and labor supply on Soviet collective farms: reply". Canadian Journal of Economics 6, 438–443.
Brosig, J., Ockenfels, A., Weimann, J. (2003). "Why does communication enhance cooperation?". German Economic Review 4, 217–242.
Cameron, N. (1973a). "Incentives and labor supply in cooperative enterprises". Canadian Journal of Economics 6, 16–23.
Cameron, N. (1973b). "Incentives and labor supply on Soviet collective farms: rejoinder". Canadian Journal of Economics 6, 442–445.
Carpenter, J. (2000). "Mutual monitoring in teams: the role of monitoring group size, second-order free-riding, or coordination", paper presented at a meeting of the Economic Science Association, New York, June.
Carpenter, J., Matthews, P. (2002). "Social reciprocity", unpublished paper. Middlebury College.
Chinn, D. (1979). "Team cohesion and collective-labor supply in Chinese agriculture". Journal of Comparative Economics 3, 375–394.
Cinyabuguma, M., Page, T., Putterman, L. (2005). "Cooperation under the threat of expulsion in a public goods experiment". Journal of Public Economics 89, 1421–1435.
Cinyabuguma, M., Page, T., Putterman, L. (2006). "Can second-order punishment deter perverse punishment?". Experimental Economics. In press.
Cosmides, L., Tooby, J. (1992). "Cognitive adaptations for social exchange". In: Barkow, Cosmides, Tooby (Eds.), pp. 163–228.
Craig, B., Pencavel, J. (1995). "Participation and productivity: a comparison of worker cooperatives and conventional firms in the plywood industry". In: Brookings Papers on Economic Activity: Microeconomics, pp. 121–174.
Darwin, Ch. (1965 [1872]). The Expression of the Emotions in Man and Animals. University of Chicago Press, Chicago.
Davis, D.D., Holt, Ch.A. (1993). Experimental Economics. Princeton University Press, Princeton.
Diamond, J. (1997). Guns, Germs and Steel: The Fates of Human Societies. Norton, New York.
Domar, E. (1966). "The Soviet collective farm as a producers' cooperative". American Economic Review 56, 734–757.
Dong, X.-Y., Dow, G. (1993). "Monitoring costs in Chinese agricultural teams". Journal of Political Economy 101 (3), 539–553.
Dow, G. (2003). Governing the Firm: Economic Theory and Workers' Control. Cambridge University Press, New York.
Dow, G., Putterman, L. (2000). "Why capital suppliers (usually) hire workers: what we know, and what we need to know". Journal of Economic Behavior and Organization 43, 319–336.
Edgeworth, F.Y. (1881). Mathematical Psychics; an Essay on the Application of Mathematics to the Moral Sciences. C.K. Paul, London.

Ehrhart, K.-M., Keser, C. (1999). "Mobility and cooperation: on the run". Working Paper 99s-24, CIRANO, Montreal.

Ertan, A., Page, T., Putterman, L. (2005). "Can endogenously chosen institutions mitigate the free-rider problem and reduce perverse punishment?". Working Paper 2005-13, Department of Economics, Brown University.

Eswaran, M., Kotwal, A. (1984). "The moral hazard of budget-breaking". Rand Journal of Economics 15 (4), 578–581.

Falk, A., Fehr, E., Fischbacher, U. (2005). "Driving forces behind informal sanctions". Econometrica 73, 2017.

Fehr, E., Gächter, S. (2000a). "Cooperation and punishment". American Economic Review 90, 980–994.

Fehr, E., Gächter, S. (2000b). "Fairness and retaliation: the economics of reciprocity". Journal of Economic Perspectives 14 (3), 159–181.

Fehr, E., Gächter, S. (2002). "Altruistic punishment in humans". Nature 415, 137–140.

Fehr, E., Gächter, S., Kirchsteiger, G. (1997). "Reciprocity as a contract enforcement device: experimental evidence". Econometrica 65 (4), 833–860.

Gächter, S., Fehr, E. (1999). "Collective action as a social exchange". Journal of Economic Behavior and Organization 39, 341–369.

Gintis, H., Bowles, S., Boyd, E., Fehr, R. (Eds.) (2005). Moral Sentiments and Material Interests: The Foundations of Cooperation in Economic Life. MIT Press, Cambridge, MA.

Gunnthorsdottir, A., Houser, D., McCabe, K., Ameden, H. (2002). "Disposition, history and contributions in a public goods experiment", unpublished manuscript. Department of Economics and Economic Science Laboratory, University of Arizona.

Guttman, J. (1978). "Understanding collective action: matching behavior". American Economic Review 68, 251–255.

Guttman, J., Schnytzer, A. (1989). "Strategic work interactions and the *Kibbutz–Kolkhoz* paradox". Economic Journal 99 (397), 686–699.

Hardin, G. (1968). "The tragedy of the commons". Science 162, 1243–1248.

Henrich, J. (2004). "Cultural group selection, co-evolutionary processes and large-scale cooperation". Journal of Economic Behavior and Organization 53 (1), 3–35.

Hibbs, D.A., Olsson, O. (2004). "Geography, biogeography, and why some countries are rich and others are poor". Proceedings of the National Academy of Sciences 101, 3715–3720.

Hirshleifer, D., Rasmussen, E. (1989). "Cooperation in a repeated prisoners dilemma with ostracism". Journal of Economic Behavior and Organization 12 (1), 87–106.

Hoffman, E., McCabe, K., Smith, V. (1998). "Behavioral foundations of reciprocity: experimental economics and evolutionary psychology". Economic Inquiry 36, 335–352.

Holmström, B. (1982). "Moral hazard in teams". Bell Journal of Economics 13, 324–340.

Isaac, R.M., Walker, J. (1988a). "Group size effects in public goods provision: the voluntary contribution mechanism". Quarterly Journal of Economics 103 (1), 179–199.

Isaac, R.M., Walker, J.M. (1988b). "Communication and free-riding behavior: the voluntary contributions mechanism". Economic Inquiry 26, 585–608.

Israelsen, L.D. (1980). "Collectives, communes, and incentives". Journal of Comparative Economics 4, 99–124.

Jensen, M., Meckling, W. (1976). "Theory of the firm: managerial behavior, agency costs and ownership structure". Journal of Financial Economics 3, 305–360.

Kandel, E., Lazear, E. (1992). "Peer pressure and partnerships". Journal of Political Economy 100, 801–817.

Kolm, S.-Ch. (2000). "Introduction: the economics of reciprocity, giving and altruism". In: Gérard-Varet, L.-A., Kolm, S.-Ch., Mercier-Ythier, J. (Eds.), The Economics of Reciprocity, Giving and Altruism. MacMillan, London.

Kreps, D., Milgrom, P., Roberts, J., Wilson, R. (1982). "Rational cooperation in finitely repeated prisoners' dilemma". Journal of Economic Theory 27, 245–252.

Kruse, D. (1993). Profit Sharing: Does It Make a Difference?. Upjohn Institute for Employment Research, Kalamazoo, MI.

Ledyard, J. (1995). "Public goods: a survey of experimental research". In: Kagel, J., Roth, A. (Eds.), Handbook of Experimental Economics. Princeton University Press, Princeton, pp. 111–194.

Leibenstein, H. (1982). "The prisoners' dilemma in the invisible hand". American Economic Review 72, 92–97.

Lin, J.Y. (1988). "The household responsibility system in China's agricultural reform: a theoretical and empirical study". Economic Development and Cultural Change 36 (Supplement), 199–234.

Lin, J.Y. (1990). "Collectivization and China's agricultural crisis in 1959–1961". Journal of Political Economy 98, 1228–1252.

Lin, J.Y. (1992). "Rural reforms and agricultural growth in China". American Economic Review 82, 34–51.

Liu, M. (1991). "Intersectoral labor allocation on China's communes: a temporal-priority analysis". Journal of Comparative Economics 15, 602–626.

MacLeod, B. (1986). "Behavior and the organization of the firm". Queen's Institute for Economic Research, Discussion Paper: 648.

Marx, K. (1967 [1867]). Capital: A Critique of Political Economy. The Process of Capitalist Production, vol. I. International Publishers, New York.

Masclet, D., Noussair, Ch., Tucker, S., Villeval, M.-C. (2003). "Monetary and non-monetary punishment in the voluntary contributions mechanism". American Economic Review 93 (1), 366–380.

Ostrom, E. (1990). Governing the Commons: The Evolution of Institutions for Collective Action. Cambridge University Press, New York.

Ostrom, E., Walker, J., Gardner, R. (1992). "Covenants with and without a sword: self governance is possible". American Political Science Review 86 (2), 404–416.

Ostrom, E., Gardner, R., Walker, J. (1994). Rules, Games, and Common-Pool Resources. University of Michigan Press, Ann Arbor.

Page, T., Putterman, L., Unel, B. (2005). "Voluntary association in public goods experiments: reciprocity, mimicry, and efficiency". Economic Journal 115, 1032–1053.

Pareto, V. (1913). "Il massimo di utilita per una colletivita". Gionale Degli Economisti 3, 337–341.

Perkins, D., Radelet, S., Snodgrass, D., Gillis, M. (2001). Economics of Development, 5th edn. W.W. Norton, New York.

Putterman, L. (1981). "On optimality in collective institutional choice". Journal of Comparative Economics 5, 392–402.

Putterman, L. (1983). "Incentives and the Kibbutz: toward an economics of communal work motivation". Zeitschrift fur Nationalokonomie 43, 157–188.

Putterman, L. (1988). "Group farming and work incentives in collective-era China". Modern China 14, 419–450.

Putterman, L. (1991). "Does poor supervisability undermine teamwork? Evidence from an unexpected source". American Economic Review 81 (4), 996–1001.

Putterman, L. (1993). Continuity and Change in China's Rural Development: Collective and Reform Eras in Perspective. Oxford University Press, New York.

Putterman, L., Skillman, G. Jr. (1988). "The incentive effects of monitoring under alternative compensation schemes". International Journal of Industrial Organization 6, 109–119.

Rotemberg, J. (1994). "Human relations in the workplace". Journal of Political Economy 102 (4), 684–717.

Sally, D. (1995). "Conversation and cooperation in social dilemmas: a meta-analysis of experiments from 1958 to 1992". Rationality and Society 7 (1), 58–92.

Sefton, M., Shupp, R., Walker, J. (2002). "The effect of rewards and sanctions in provision of public goods", Working Paper. Indiana University.

Sen, A. (1966). "Labor allocation in a cooperative enterprise". Review of Economic Studies 33, 361–371.

Shapiro, C., Stiglitz, J. (1984). "Equilibrium unemployment as a worker discipline device". American Economic Review 74, 433–444.

Smith, A. (1971 [1789]). The Theory of Moral Sentiments. Garland, New York.

Smith, V. (1975). "The economics of the primitive hunter culture, pleistocene extinctions, and the rise of agriculture". Journal of Political Economy 84 (4), 727–756.

Spagnolo, G. (1999). "Social relations and cooperation in organizations". Journal of Economic Behavior and Organization 38 (1), 1–25.

Trivers, R. (1971). "The evolution of reciprocal altruism". Quarterly Review of Biology 46, 35–56.

Tugan-Baranovsky, M. (1921). Sotsialnyia Osnovy Kooperatsii. Slowo Verlagsgesellschaft, Berlin.

Vanek, J. (1970). The General Theory of Labor-Managed Market Economies. Cornell University Press, Ithaca.

Ward, B. (1958). "The firm in illyria: market syndicalism". American Economic Review 68, 566–589.

Webb, S., Webb, B. (1920). A Constitution for the Socialist Commonwealth of Great Britain. Longmans, Green, London.

Weitzman, M., Kruse, D. (1990). "Profit-sharing and productivity". In: Blinder, A. (Ed.), Paying for Productivity: A Look at the Evidence. The Brookings Institution, Washington.

Williamson, O., Wachter, M., Harris, J. (1975). "Understanding the employment relation: the analysis of idiosyncratic exchange". Bell Journal of Economics 6, 250–278.

Wright, R. (1994). The Moral Animal Why We Are the Way We Are The New Science of Evolutionary Psychology. Pantheon, New York.

PART 4

THE POLITICAL ECONOMY OF VOLUNTARY TRANSFERS

Chapter 23

STRONG RECIPROCITY AND THE WELFARE STATE

CHRISTINA M. FONG

Carnegie Mellon University

SAMUEL BOWLES

University of Siena and Santa Fe Institute

HERBERT GINTIS*

Santa Fe Institute and Columbia University

Contents

* We would like to thank Rachel Locke for research assistance, Chris Boehm, Rob Boyd, Josh Cohen, Steve Farkas, Ernst Fehr, Marc Fleurbaey, Nancy Folbre, Martin Gilens, Kristin Hawkes, Serge Kolm, Larry Mead, Julio Rotemberg, Juliette Rouchier, Robert Shapiro, Elisabeth Wood and Erik Wright for helpful comments, and the John D. and Catherine T. MacArthur Foundation, the Behavioral Sciences Program of the Santa Fe Institute, and the Russell Sage Foundation for financial support.

Handbook of the Economics of Giving, Altruism and Reciprocity, Volume 2
Edited by Serge-Christophe Kolm and Jean Mercier Ythier

DOI: 10.1016/S1574-0714(06)02023-9

Abstract

We explore the contribution of reciprocity and other non selfish motives to the political viability of the modern welfare state. In the advanced economies, a substantial fraction of total income is regularly transferred from the better off to the less well off, with the approval of the electorate. Economists have for the most part misunderstood this process due to their endorsement of an empirically implausible theory of selfish human motivation. Drawing on anthropological, experimental, public opinion survey and other data we develop an alternative behavioral explanation for economic reasoning about sharing and insurance. In this alternative view, reciprocity motives are necessary for understanding support for and opposition to the welfare state. Modern citizens willingly share with those who uphold societal norms about what constitutes morally worthy behavior, while frequently seeking to punish those who transgress those norms, even when these actions are individually costly and yield no individual material benefit.

Keywords

fairness, reciprocity, distributive justice, equity, redistribution, welfare states

JEL classification: D63, H50

> A man ought to be a friend to his friend and repay gift with gift. People should meet smiles with smiles and lies with treachery.
>
> The Edda, a 13th century collection of Norse epic verse (Edda, 1923).

1. Introduction

The modern welfare state is a remarkable human achievement. In the advanced economies, a substantial fraction of total income is regularly transferred from the better off to the less well off, and the governments that preside over these transfers are regularly endorsed by publics (Atkinson, 1999). The modern welfare state is thus the most significant case in human history of a voluntary egalitarian redistribution of income among total strangers. What accounts for its popular support?

We suggest below that a compelling case can be made that people support the welfare state because it conforms to a behavioral schema which we call *strong reciprocity*. Strong reciprocity is *a propensity to cooperate and share with others similarly disposed, even at personal cost, and a willingness to punish those who violate cooperative and other social norms, even when punishing is personally costly and cannot be expected to entail net personal gains in the future.*[1] Economists have for the most part offered an alternative, empirically implausible, theory of self-regarding human motivation to explain who votes for redistribution. The most widely accepted model of the demand for redistribution in economics is the *median voter model*, which holds that each voter desires a personal wealth-maximizing level of redistribution. Under appropriate assumptions, it follows that the redistribution implemented by a government elected under a majority rule system is that preferred by the median-income voter. Because the distribution of income is generally skewed to the right (there are a few very rich individuals), the median voter is poorer than the mean voter and will therefore demand a positive level of redistribution.

An important implication of this model is that demand for redistribution decreases as personal income increases (Roberts, 1977). But personal income is a surprisingly poor predictor of support for redistribution (Gilens, 1999; Fong, 2001). A large fraction of the poor oppose income redistribution and a large fraction of the rich support it. Among respondents of a nationally representative American survey (Gallup-Organization, 1998) who have annual household incomes of at least $150 000 and expect their lives to improve in the next five years, 24 percent respond that the government should "redistribute wealth by heavy taxes on the rich," and 67 percent respond that the "government in

[1] Strong reciprocity goes beyond self-interested forms of cooperation, which include tit-for-tat and what biologists call *reciprocal altruism* (Trivers, 1971). Strong reciprocity is closer to the concept of reciprocity in Kolm (1984, 2000), who pioneered the analysis of reciprocity in economic theory. However, we treat reciprocity as a characteristic of the individual rather than as a relationship among individuals, and we include both rewarding and punishing as reciprocal behaviors, whereas Kolm stresses mutual gift-giving.

Washington DC should make every possible effort to improve the social and economic position of the poor." Equally striking is the fact that among those with annual family incomes of less than \$10 000 who did not expect to be better off in five years, 32 percent report that the government should *not* redistribute wealth by heavy taxes on the rich, and 23 percent say that the poor should help themselves rather than having the government "make every possible effort to improve the ... position of the poor."[2]

Thus, while self-interest is an important human motive, and income does explain some of the variance in redistributive attitudes, other motives appear to be at work. Abundant evidence from across the social sciences—much of it focusing on the United States with similar findings in smaller quantities from other countries around the world—has shown that when people blame the poor for their poverty, they support less redistribution than when they believe that the poor are poor through no fault of their own. That is, generosity toward the poor is conditional on the belief that the poor work hard (Williamson, 1974; Heclo, 1986; Farkas and Robinson, 1996; Gilens, 1999; Miller, 1999). For instance, in a 1972 sample of white women in Boston the perceived work ethic of the poor was a far better predictor of support for aid to the poor than one's family income, religion, education, and a host of other demographic and social background variables (Williamson, 1974). Indeed in predicting support for such aid, the addition of a single variable measuring beliefs about work motivation tripled the explanatory power of all the above background variables together. Moffitt et al. (1998) were among the first economists to report findings on this relationship. They used the General Social Survey, a large nationally representative data set with observations in nearly every year since 1972 to show that those who believe that people get ahead by "lucky breaks or help from others" rather than hard work prefer more spending on welfare. Fong (2001) used nationally representative data from a 1998 Gallup Social Audit to show that the effects of beliefs about the causes of income on demands for redistribution are surprisingly large and cannot be explained by missing measures of self-interest. Alesina et al. (2001) have reported related findings from the World Values Survey on the attitudes of Americans and Europeans. Americans have much stronger beliefs that poverty is caused by laziness; sixty percent of Americans say the poor are lazy, compared to just 27% of Europeans. The authors argue that this could be an important explanation for the small size of the American welfare state compared to the average European welfare state..

Our interpretation of these findings is that people are willing to help the poor, but they withdraw support when they perceive that the poor may cheat or fail to cooperate by not trying hard enough to be self-sufficient and morally upstanding. Within economics, our view is most similar to the taxpayer resentment view of the demand for redistribution modeled by Besley and Coate (1992), and the effect of reciprocity sentiments on redistributive public finance by Serge Kolm (1984).[3]

[2] The numbers of observations for these questions were 78 and 79 for the poor group and 294 and 281 for the rich group. Gilens (1999) makes similar observations using earlier data.

[3] See Moffitt (1983) for an early model of welfare stigma. See also Lindbeck et al. (1999) for related work that addresses the role of work norms in redistributive politics and treats such norms as endogenous to the provision of government transfers.

Our view is also consistent with interpretations by Heclo (1986) and Gilens (1999), who cite evidence that Americans support a wide array of benefits for the poor and are primarily opposed to "welfare," presumably because "welfare" refers to means-tested cash assistance, which may be perceived as a program that benefits able-bodied adults who choose to have children out of wedlock and prefer not to work. Our interpretation is also compatible with equity theory and attribution theory. According to equity theory, people should receive resources from a system that are proportional to their contributions (Walster et al., 1978; Deutsch, 1985; Miller, 1999). Attribution theorists argue that people are less likely to help someone if they determine that the person is individually responsible for his or her outcome (Skitka and Tetlock, 1993; Weiner, 1995).

Economists have been skeptical of non-selfish models for several reasons. First, there could be unmeasured self-interest variables that explain the support for redistribution. In particular, those with low-mean, high-variance incomes may be more likely to think that poverty is due to bad luck and also more likely to demand redistribution out of self-interest for insurance against a low income. We soundly reject this hypothesis in section 4.

Second, people who think that effort plays a major role in income generation may be concerned about the incentive effects of taxation or transfers rather than the "worthiness" of recipients (Piketty, 1995). We do have two pieces of evidence, however, that incentive costs cannot fully explain attitudes towards redistribution. One is that, were incentive costs of taxation the problem, those who believe that effort is important should support less government spending in general. Yet, as we show in section 4, the belief that effort is important to getting ahead in life is negatively correlated with support for redistribution and positively correlated with support for military spending. Another is that, as we report in section 3, subjects in a behavioral experiment on charitable giving to welfare recipients gave significantly more money when they were randomly paired with a welfare recipient who said she would like to work than when randomly paired with a welfare recipient who said she would not like to work. There were no disincentive costs in this experiment, so some other interpretation is necessary.

This experimental result also addresses a third concern that economists have raised: people who do not want to give to the poor may say that the poor are lazy to justify their selfishness. This cannot explain why randomly assigned treatment conditions in the charity experiment just described had significant effects on giving to welfare recipients.

Concern about the "undeserving poor" is pronounced in the U.S., but is far from absent in Europe. In Figure 1 we show that in twelve European countries, those who say that poverty is the result of the laziness support less government redistribution and are less concerned about unemployment, poverty, and inequality than those who do not. The data are from a Eurobarometer survey conducted in 1989 (Reif and Melich, 1993), representative of the population aged fifteen and over in the twelve European Union countries of that time. Of the data set's 11 819 respondents, we use the 8239 who answered all of the questions included in our analysis. Our dependent variable is the sum of responses to four questions about the importance of fighting unemployment (1) and poverty (2), the importance of reducing differences between regions within the country

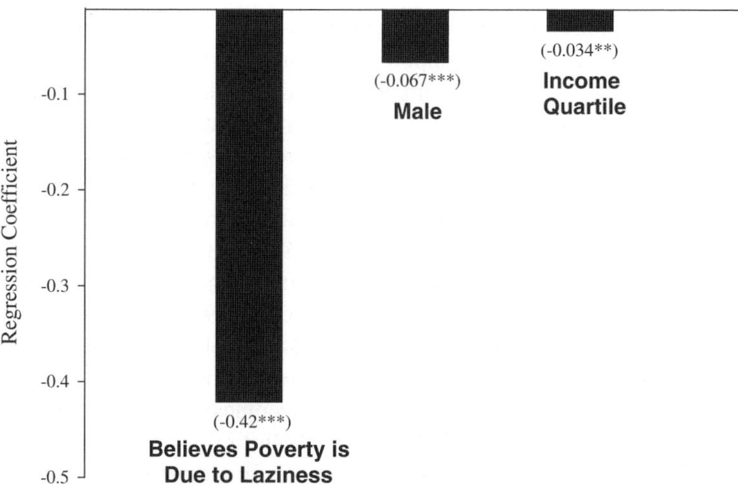

Figure 1. Explaining concern about poverty using data from twelve European countries. Bars represent ordinary least squares coefficients (value of the estimated coefficient is in parentheses) predicting concern about poverty. The dependent variable is standardized so that the estimated coefficient represents the effect of the variable indicated on concern about poverty measured in standard deviation units. The equation also includes: age and country dummy variables. Significance levels are based on robust standard errors that allow for clustered errors within countries. This regression uses sample weights, although the results are not sensitive to them. There are 8239 observations, $R^2 = 0.161$. ***Significant at the 1% level. **Significant at the 5% level.

by helping regions that are less developed or in difficulties (3), and whether the public authorities in the country do all that they should for poor people (4). The measure increases in concern about poverty, unemployment, and inequality and the belief that the public authorities do not "do enough for poor people." For simplicity, we refer to this composite measure as "concern about poverty." Our independent variable of primary interest is the belief that poverty is caused by laziness rather than being caused by bad luck, injustice, or no reason at all, or that poverty is inevitable.[4] The other variables included in the regression are family income quartiles, sex and age. Note that item (4) in our dependent variable is explicitly country specific. Cross-country comparisons of a question like this are of little value because people in a country with a generous redistribution system may care very much about poverty but believe that their own government is doing a good job of addressing it. The other three items used to construct our dependent measure are subject to the same concern, albeit to a lesser extent. To account for

[4] The exact wording of this questions is: "Why, in your opinion, are there people who live in need? Here are four opinions, which is the closest to yours? 1. Because they have been unlucky; 2. Because of laziness and lack of willpower; 3. Because there is much injustice in our society; 4. It is an inevitable part of modern progress; 5. None of these." Our dummy variable is one for respondents who answered "Because of laziness and lack of willpower," and zero for respondents who gave one of the other four responses.

the effects of unmeasured differences between countries, we use fixed effects to allow for country differences in mean responses.

The results, presented in Figure 1, show that those who say that poverty is caused by laziness are less concerned about poverty than the rest of the respondents by 0.42 standard deviations. In contrast, family income has a very modest effect.[5] The differences in concern about poverty between the richest and poorest quartiles is less than a quarter as great as the difference between those who think that poverty is due to laziness and those who do not. The respondent's sex has a significant effect on concern about poverty independently of income and the other regressors, with men being less concerned than women.

We do not doubt that self-regarding motives often underpin apparently generous actions. Rather, we suggest that they do not always do so. Understanding egalitarian politics today requires a reconsideration of *Homo economicus*, the unremittingly self-regarding actor of economic theory. We do not wish to replace the textbook self-regarding actor, however, with an equally one-dimensional altruistic actor willing to make unconditional, personally costly, contributions to the less well off. Rather, we believe that strong reciprocity, which involves *conditional* cooperation and punishment, better explains the motivations behind support for the welfare state.

As we will see, all three of our *persona—Homo economicus*, the strong reciprocator, and even the pure altruist—are represented in most groups of any size. For this reason, egalitarian policy-making, no less than the grand projects of constitutional design, risks irrelevance if it ignores the irreducible heterogeneity of human motivations. The problem of institutional design is not, as the classical economists thought, that uniformly self-regarding individuals be induced to interact in ways producing desirable aggregate outcomes, but rather that a mix of motives—self-regarding, reciprocal, and altruistic—interact in ways that prevent the self-regarding from exploiting the generous and hence unraveling cooperation when it is beneficial.

In the next section, we explain how individually costly but socially beneficial traits such as strong reciprocity can evolve in competition with self-regarding traits, when it might be expected that they would be eliminated by Darwinian competition.

2. The origins of strong reciprocity

Both historical and experimental evidence suggest that support for redistribution is often based on strong reciprocity motives. Consider first the historical evidence. In his *Injustice: the Social Bases of Obedience and Revolt*, Barrington Moore, Jr., (Moore, 1978)

[5] These results do not depend on the particular sample and specification that we present. In all specifications, the effect of moving up to the next income quartile is an order of magnitude smaller than the effect of believing that poverty exists because the poor are lazy. When the question about whether or not the public authorities are doing enough for the poor was omitted from our composite measure of concern about poverty, the effect of income was not even significant, regardless of whether other demographic variables were included in the regression, while the effect of beliefs that the poor are lazy remained large and highly significant.

sought to discern if there might be common motivational bases—"general conceptions of unfair and unjust behavior" (21)—for the moral outrage fueling struggles for justice that have recurred throughout human history. "There are grounds," he concludes from his wide-ranging investigation,

> for suspecting that the welter of moral codes may conceal a certain unity of original form ... a general ground plan, a conception of what social relationships ought to be. It is a conception that by no means excludes hierarchy and authority, where exceptional qualities and defects can be the source of enormous admiration and awe. At the same time, it is one where services and favors, trust and affection, in the course of mutual exchanges, are ideally expected to find some rough balancing out (4–5, 509).

Moore termed the general ground plan he uncovered "the concept of reciprocity—or better, mutual obligation, a term that does not imply equality of burdens or obligations ..." (506). In like manner James Scott (1976) analyzed agrarian revolts, identifying violations of the "norm of reciprocity" as one the essential triggers of insurrectionary motivations.

The experimental evidence reported below, as well as casual observation of everyday life, ethnographic and paleoanthropological accounts of hunter-gatherer foraging bands from the late Pleistocene to the present and historical narratives of collective struggles have combined to convince us that strong reciprocity is a powerful and ubiquitous motive. But we hesitate to revise *Homo economicus* by elevating the individually costly sharing and punishment of norm violators characteristic of the strong reciprocator to a privileged place in the repertoire of human behaviors until we have addressed an evolutionary puzzle. We are more prone to believe and to generalize from the experimental and historical evidence we introduce in this chapter if we can explain how strong reciprocity motives might have evolved despite the costs these motives seemingly impose on those bearing them.

Strong reciprocity supports the adherence to norms within groups and some of these norms—requiring work towards common ends, sharing, and monogamy for example—are beneficial to most group members (Boyd et al., 2003; Bowles and Gintis, 2004a). Where reciprocity motives embrace the individually costly enforcement of these group-beneficial norms, strong reciprocity may evolve because the strong reciprocator will be disproportionately likely to be in groups that have effective norm adherence, and hence to enjoy the group benefits of these norms. By contrast, where reciprocity motivates the individually costly enforcement of norms that on average confer little benefit on group members, or inflict group costs, of course reciprocity is unlikely to evolve.

Strong reciprocity thus allows groups to engage in common practices without the resort to costly and often ineffective hierarchical authority, and thereby vastly increases the repertoire of social experiments capable of diffusing through cultural and genetic competition. The relevant traits may be transmitted genetically and proliferate under the influence of natural selection, or they may be transmitted culturally through learning from elders and age mates and proliferate because successful groups tend to absorb failing groups, or to be emulated by them. We think it likely that both genetic and cultural transmission is involved. The 50–100 000 years in which anatomically modern humans lived primarily in foraging bands constitutes a sufficiently long time period, and a favorable social and physical ecology, for the evolution of the combination of norm enforcement and sharing that we term strong reciprocity (Gintis, 2000; Bowles et al., 2003). We survey related evolutionary models in Bowles and Gintis (2004b).

3. Experimental evidence

Behavioral experiments with human subjects provide overwhelming evidence against *Homo economicus*. Our first piece of evidence comes from the commonly observed rejection of substantial positive offers in ultimatum games. Experimental protocols differ, but the general structure of the ultimatum game is simple. Subjects are paired, one is the responder, the other the proposer. The proposer is provisionally awarded an amount ('the pie'—typically $10) to be divided between proposer and responder. The proposer offers a certain portion of the pie to the responder. If the responder accepts, the responder gets the proposed portion, and the proposer keeps the rest. If the responder rejects the offer both get nothing.[6] In experiments conducted in the United States, Slovakia, Japan, Israel, Slovenia, Germany, Russia, and Indonesia the vast majority of proposers offer between 40% and 50% of the pie, and offers lower than 30% of the pie are often rejected (Fehr and Schmidt, 1999). These results have occurred in experiments with stakes as high as three months' earnings (Cameron, 1999).

When asked why they offer more than one cent, proposers commonly say that they are afraid that respondents will consider low offers unfair and reject them as a way to punish proposers' unwillingness to share. When respondents reject offers, they give virtually the same reasons for their actions. The proposers' actions might be explained by prudent self-interest, but the respondents' cannot. Because these behaviors occur in single-shot interactions and on the last round of multi-round interactions, they cannot be accounted for by the responder's attempt to modify subsequent behavior of the proposer. Punishment *per se* is the most likely motive. As evidence for this interpretation, we note that the rejection of positive offers is substantially less when the game is altered so that rejection does not punish the proposer (Abbink et al., 1996). Moreover the fact that offers generated by a computer rather than another person are significantly less likely to be rejected (Blount, 1995). This suggests that those rejecting low offers at a cost to themselves are reacting to violations of fairness norms rather than simply rejecting disadvantageous offers.

Punishment is triggered by responders' beliefs about the *intentions* of the proposer. This is shown clearly in an ultimatum game experiment in which the proposer has only two choices: either offer two (and hence keep eight) or make an alternative offer that

[6] See Güth et al. (1982), Camerer and Thaler (1995) and Roth (1995).

varies across treatments in a way that allows the experimenters to test the effects of reciprocity and inequity aversion on rejection rates (Falk et al., 2002). The alternative offers in four treatments are five for the proposer and five for the responder (5/5), another is eight for the proposer and two for the responder (8/2), a third is 2 for the proposer and 8 the responder (2/8), and finally, 10 for the proposer and 0 for the responder (10/0). Using the 5/5 alternative, the rejection rate of the 8/2 offer is 44.4%, significantly higher than the rejection rates in each of the other three treatments. The most plausible interpretation of these results is that choosing a low offer when a fair one was possible suggests self-regarding intentions on the part of the proposer, which the responder often chooses to punish by rejecting the offer.[7]

Our second piece of evidence comes from the simplest, but still quite revealing, laboratory experiment: the *dictator game*. In this game, one of two players, the "proposer," is given a sum of money (typically $10), is asked to choose any part of the sum to give to the second player (the two players are mutually anonymous), and is permitted to keep the rest. *Homo economicus* gives nothing in this situation, whereas in actual experimental situations, a majority of proposers give positive amounts, typically ranging from 20% to 60% of the total (Forsythe et al., 1994).

Using dictator games, researchers have shown that people are more generous to worthy recipients and bargaining partners. For example, Eckel and Grossman (1996) found that subjects in dictator games gave roughly three times as much when the recipient was the American Red Cross than when it was an anonymous subject. More recently, Fong (2003) conducted charity games (n-donor dictator games) in which several dictators were paired with a single real-life welfare recipient. The treatment conditions were randomly assigned and differed according to whether the welfare recipient expressed strong or weak work preferences on a survey that she completed. Dictators read the welfare recipients' surveys just prior to making their offers. Dictators who were randomly assigned to welfare recipients who expressed strong work preferences gave significantly more than dictators who expressed weak work preferences. These experiments provide evidence for our view that strong reciprocity is a common motivation.

Additional evidence for strong reciprocity comes from n-player public goods experiments. The following is a common variant. Ten players are given $1 in each of ten rounds. On each round, each player can contribute any portion of the $1 (anonymously) to a "common pool." The experimenter divides the amount in the common pool by two, and gives *each* player that much money. If all ten players are cooperative, on each round each puts $1 in the pool, the experimenter divides the $10 in the pool by two, and gives each player $5. After ten rounds of this, each subject has $50. By being self-regarding, however, each player can do better as long as the others are cooperating. By keeping the $1, the player ends up with "his" $10, plus receives $45 as his share of the pool, for

[7] This experiment also found that 9% of 8/2 offers were rejected when the alternative offer was 10/0, indicating that some responders reject unequal outcomes at personal cost, even when the proposer is in no sense responsible for the unequal situation.

a total of \$55. If all behave this way, however, each receives only \$10. Thus this is an "iterated prisoner's dilemma" in which self-regarding players contribute nothing.

In fact, however, only a small fraction of players contribute nothing to the common pool. Rather, in the early stages of the game, people generally contribute half their money to the pool. In the later stages of the game, contributions decay until at the end, they are contributing very little. Proponents of the *Homo economicus* model initially suggested that the reason for decay of public contribution is that participants really do not understand the game at first, and as they begin to learn it, they begin to realize the superiority of the free-riding strategy. However, there is considerable evidence that this interpretation is incorrect. For instance, Andreoni (1988) finds that when the whole process is repeated with the same subjects, the initial levels of cooperation are restored, but once again cooperation decays as the game progresses.

Andreoni (1995) suggests an explanation for the decay of cooperation quite suggestive of strong reciprocity: public-spirited contributors want to retaliate against free-riders and the only way available to them in the game is by not contributing themselves. Indeed, if players are permitted to retaliate directly against non-contributors, but at a cost to themselves, they do so (Fehr and Gächter, 2000a, 2000b, 2002). In this situation, contributions rise in subsequent rounds to near the maximal level. Moreover punishment levels are undiminished in the final rounds, suggesting that disciplining norm violators is an end in itself and hence will be exhibited even when there is no prospect of modifying the subsequent behavior of the shirker or potential future shirkers.

Such experiments show that agents are willing to incur a cost to punish those whom they perceive to have treated them, or a group to which they belong, badly.[8] Also in everyday life, we see people consumed with the desire for revenge against those who have harmed them or their families, even where no material gain can be expected (Boehm, 1984; Nisbett and Cohen, 1996).

Another result that is consistent with reciprocity is that cooperating and punishing behavior are very sensitive to the situation framing the interaction. In early research on what is known as *inequality aversion*, Loewenstein et al. (1989) found that distributional preferences are sensitive to social context. They asked subjects to imagine themselves in various hypothetical situations. In one, the subject and another college student share the gains and losses from a jointly produced product. In another, the subject and a neighbor the split the profit from selling a vacant lot between their homes. In a third, the subject is a customer dividing the proceeds from an expired rebate, or the cost of repairs, with a salesperson. They found, first, that subjects care about relative payoffs even more than they care about their absolute payoffs. Second, controlling for the subjects' own payoffs, earning less than the other person had a strong negative effect on utility in all situations and relationship types. However, an effect on utility of earning *more* than the

[8] See Ostrom et al. (1992) on common pool resources, Fehr et al. (1997) on efficiency wages, and Fehr and Gächter (2000a) and Bowles et al. (2001) on public goods. Coleman (1988) develops the parallel point that free riding in social networks can be avoided if network members provide positive rewards for cooperating.

other person (referred to as advantageous inequality) was also present, and depended on the relationship and the situation. Subjects disliked advantageous inequality if the relationship was friendly. However, if the relationship was unfriendly, advantageous inequality had little effect on their satisfaction level. Interestingly, they found that subjects preferred advantageous inequality in the customer/salesperson scenario, but disliked it in the other two scenarios (producing a product and splitting the proceeds from an empty lot).

Although there may be many additional factors contributing to the context dependence of behavior, the finding that subjects are more adverse to advantageous inequality (or, equivalently, desire higher relative payoffs for the other subject) in friendly relationships than in unfriendly relationships is fully consistent with our interpretation of reciprocity. In another example, fraternity brothers at University of California, Los Angeles were asked to rank outcomes in a prisoner's dilemma situation given that they were interacting with a fellow fraternity brother, a member of another (unnamed) fraternity, a non-fraternity student at University of California, Los Angeles, a student from the nearby rival University of Southern California and an officer from the University of California, Los Angeles Police Department. They showed a strong preference for mutual cooperation over defection against one's partner when playing with fraternity brothers, with the rankings reversing with increasing social distance—they were as willing to exploit the University of Southern California students as the University of California, Los Angeles police (Kollock, 1997)!

4. Survey evidence

These results support our interpretation of attitudinal survey results, which show that people support more government redistribution to the poor if they think that poverty is caused by bad luck rather than laziness. Our interpretation of this is that because of strong reciprocity, people wish to help those who try to make it on their own, but for reasons beyond their own control, cannot. People wish to punish, or withhold assistance to, those who are able but unwilling to work hard. However, there are several alternative explanations of the effect of beliefs about the worthiness of the poor that are consistent with pure self-interest. In this section, we test these alternative explanations and find that self-interest alone cannot explain the relationship between beliefs about the worthiness of the poor and support for redistribution. These results are based on Fong (2001).

We use the 1998 Gallup Poll Social Audit Survey, "Haves and Have-Nots: Perceptions of Fairness and Opportunity," a randomly selected national sample of 5001 respondents. In each test, we use the set of all individuals who responded to all of the questions used in the regression, unless noted otherwise.[9]

[9] We drop non-responses and "don't know" responses. Another option would be to include "don't know" as a valid response. However, how and why people develop well-defined preferences and beliefs is beyond the scope of this chapter. We focus on why people oppose or support income redistribution given that their beliefs and preferences are well defined.

Relative to other commonly used surveys, the Gallup survey has a large sample size for a large number of questions on inequality and distribution. The sample size permits running regressions with full controls on narrow segments of the sample, namely, high income and low income sub-samples. There is a large number of self-interest measures that include not only the usual objective socioeconomic variables, but also subjective measures of economic well-being and future expectations. These may widen the net intended to capture self-interest.

To construct our dependent variable, we added the responses to the five questions below, signing the responses so that the measure increases in support for redistribution.

1. People feel differently about how far a government should go. Here is a phrase which some people believe in and some don't. Do you think our government should or should not redistribute wealth by heavy taxes on the rich? (response categories: should, should not).
2. Some people feel that the government in Washington, DC should make every possible effort to improve the social and economic position of the poor. Others feel that the government should not make any special effort to help the poor, because they should help themselves. How do you feel about this? (response categories: government should help the poor, the poor should help themselves).
3. Which one of the following groups do you think has the greatest responsibility for helping the poor: churches, private charities, the government, the families and relatives of poor people, the poor themselves, or someone else? (response categories: groups other than the poor, the poor themselves).
4. Do you feel that the distribution of money and wealth in this country today is fair, or do you feel that the money and wealth in this country should be more evenly distributed among a larger percentage of the people? (response categories: distribution is fair, should be more evenly distributed).
5. Do you think that the fact that some people in the United States are rich and others are poor (1) represents a problem that needs to be fixed or (2) Is an acceptable part of our economic system? (response categories: problem, acceptable).

Two sets of measures of the causes of income are used in this study. The first contains two questions concerning the importance of effort and luck in causing wealth and poverty, and one question on whether or not there is plenty of opportunity to work hard and get ahead in America today. The second set is a series of questions about the importance of various factors, including race and sex, for getting ahead in life (see Appendix A for wording of the questions).

Self-interest is measured by annual pre-tax household income and other variables likely to predict current and future tax obligations and current and future reliance on social insurance or redistribution programs. In Figures 2 and 3 we control for self-interest by including in the regressions income, race, sex, education, age, and the frequency with which respondents worry about meeting family expenses.[10]

[10] There are several additional questions that might capture self-interest that are excluded from the model presented here. See Fong (2001) for a discussion and analysis of these variables.

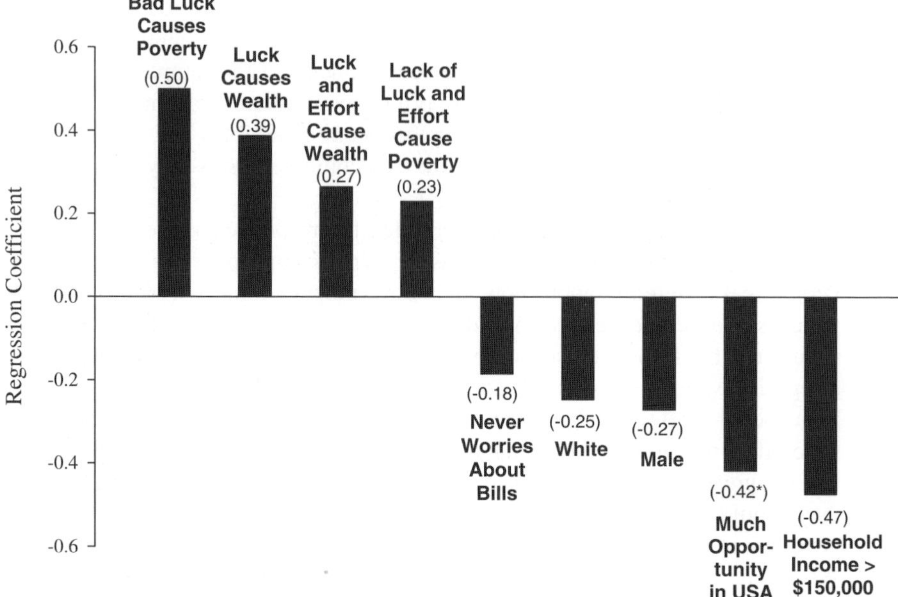

Figure 2. Determinants of the support for redistribution. Bars represent ordinary least squares coefficients (value of the estimated coefficient is in parentheses) predicting support for redistribution. The dependent variable is standardized so that the estimated coefficient represents the effect of the variable indicated on concern about poverty measured in standard deviation units. The equation also includes: seven additional income dummies, age, a dummy for attended college, and dummies for "worries about bills most of the time," "worries about bills some of the time." The omitted category for household income is less than \$10 000 per year. The omitted categories for causes of poverty and wealth are "lack of effort" and "strong effort" respectively. To simplify the presentation of race effects, we use the sample of white and black respondents only. The omitted category for "worries about bills" is "all of the time." There are 3417 observations. $R^2 = 0.260$. This regression uses sample weights, although the results are not sensitive to them. We use robust standard errors. All coefficients are significant at the 1% level.

In Figure 2 we present results from an ordinary least squares regression that predicts support for redistribution using two sets of variables: beliefs about the causes of wealth and poverty and the measures of self-interest. To facilitate interpreting the coefficients, we have standardized the dependent variable to have a zero mean and a standard deviation of one. The interpretation is as follows: those who say that bad luck alone causes poverty are 0.50 standard deviations higher in their support for redistribution than those who think lack of effort alone causes poverty. Those who think that good luck alone causes wealth are 0.39 standard deviations higher on the support for redistribution scale than those who think effort alone causes wealth, and people who respond that there is plenty of opportunity in the United States to get ahead scored 0.42 standard deviations lower in support for redistribution than people who do not think there is plenty of opportunity.

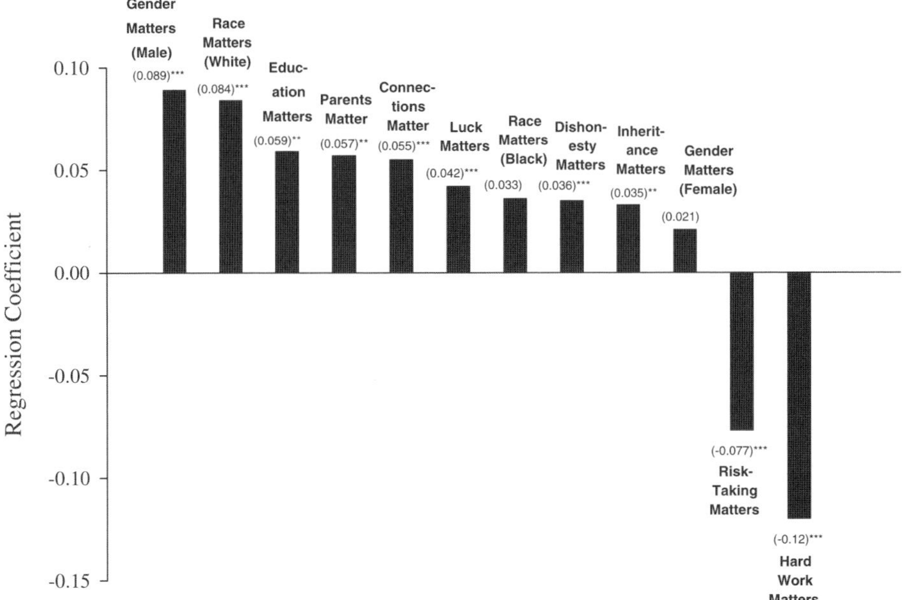

Figure 3. Effects on the support for redistribution of beliefs about the importance of various factors in getting ahead in life. Bars represent ordinary least squares coefficients (value of the estimated coefficient is in parentheses) predicting support for redistribution. The dependent variable is standardized. Independent variables are the respondent's belief in the importance of the factor shown to getting ahead in life (see Appendix for exact wording). The coefficients are the estimated effects of a one point increase in the response scale for a given belief on standard deviations of support for redistribution. Regressions also include all of the self-interest measures included in Figure 2, $R^2 = 0.184$. The number of observations is 3437. This regression uses sample weights, although the results are not sensitive to them. ***Significant at the 1% level. **Significant at the 5% level.

Measures of self-interest also have significant effects in the expected direction on support for redistribution. Those who are in the highest income category (annual household income greater than \$150 000) scored 0.47 standard deviations lower on support for redistribution than those in the lowest income category (income less than \$10 000). Those who almost never worry about bills are significantly less supportive of redistribution than those who worry all of the time. The self-interest variables are jointly significant at the one percent level.

The effect of being white is large and highly significant, and the effect of being male is even larger. At first glance, this may appear to contradict an empirical regularity that among the socioeconomic variables, race has one of the largest and most reliable effects while sex does not. However, if we omit the beliefs variables, the magnitude of the effects of race and sex increase and become roughly equivalent in size. This is consistent with the argument, put forth by Gilens (1999), that the effect of race is mediated by beliefs about the characteristics of the poor, especially poor blacks.

If we take the view that all of the socioeconomic variables together capture self-interest, then the effect of self-interest appears considerably larger than if we simply consider the size of the coefficient on income. Using ordered probit to estimate similar equations, (Fong, 2001) has estimated the sizes of the effects of the independent variables on the probabilities of scoring in each of the six categories of the support for redistribution scale. In an equation that controls for both beliefs about the causes of wealth and poverty and a large number of objective and subjective measures of and proxies for self-interest, the effect of being in the least privileged category (non-white, female, single, union member, part-time worker, no college education, in lowest income category, household size greater than four, and almost always worries about bills) as opposed to the most privileged are similar in size to the effects of believing that luck alone causes wealth and poverty as opposed to believing that effort alone causes wealth and poverty.

Could our results be driven by missing self-interest variables? People who believe that poverty is caused by bad luck or circumstances beyond individual control may be those who have low-mean, high-variance incomes. Such individuals may have higher expectations of needing government assistance in the future, and therefore demand more redistribution purely out of self-interest. For similar reasons, those who believe that the poor are lazy may simply be people who have higher-mean, lower-variance incomes and therefore less self-interest in redistribution. If this is true, then the effect of these beliefs on redistributive policy preferences may have nothing to do with the psychology of holding the poor accountable and blaming them for their outcomes. It would simply be the case that beliefs about the causes of income are correlated with a person's financial position which in turn determines his or her demand for redistribution.

If the beliefs about the causes of poverty and wealth operate through self-interest, then they should have no effect among people at the top and bottom of the distribution of income who expect to remain there. Those who do not expect to benefit should demand no redistribution at all, regardless of their beliefs about the causes of income, while those who expect to benefit should register the highest degree of support for redistribution regardless of their beliefs about the causes of income. To test whether this is the case, we use sub-samples of (1) individuals with household incomes over \$75 000 per year who expect to be better off in five years than they are today, and who worry about bills less often than "all of the time"; (2) individuals with household incomes under \$10 000 per year; and (3) individuals with household incomes under \$30,000 per year who do not expect to be better off in five years than they are today, and who worry about bills more often than "almost never."

In all of these sub-samples, a quite inclusive set of measures capturing self-interest is jointly insignificant. That is, we cannot reject the hypothesis that every single socioeconomic variable has a coefficient of zero. Yet, the beliefs about roles of luck, effort, and opportunity in generating life outcomes were jointly significant for all three sub-samples, and in most cases were individually significant in the expected directions as well.[11] Thus, among those who are poor and do not expect their lives to improve, those who believe that lack of effort causes poverty oppose redistribution. Analogously, support for redistribution is high among those securely well off respondents who believe that poverty is the result of back luck.

In another test of self-interest, we use questions on the respondents' views on the importance of various factors, including a person's race and sex, to getting ahead in life. Figure 3 presents an ordinary least squares regression of support for redistribution on the importance of various determinants of success, controlling for the same socioeconomic variables included in the regression presented in Figure 2. Beliefs that "willingness to take risks" and "hard work and initiative" explain "why some people get ahead and succeed in life and others do not" have highly significant negative effects on support for redistribution. Beliefs that education, people's parents, connections, good luck, dishonesty, and inherited money explain why some people get ahead have significant positive effects on support for redistribution. In addition, beliefs that a person's sex is important to getting ahead have significant positive effects on support for redistribution for men, while the effect of this belief for women is also positive but smaller and insignificant. Beliefs that a person's race is important to getting ahead in life have significant positive effects for whites, while the effect of these beliefs for blacks is positive but smaller and insignificant.

If people think that a person's race and sex are important to getting ahead in life, then effects of these beliefs on self-interested demand for redistribution should operate in opposite directions for those who expect to benefit and those who expect to lose from racial or gender discrimination.[12] In other words, whites who think race is important to getting ahead will expect to be economically advantaged and would have fewer self-interested reasons to support redistribution than whites who think that race does not matter. Similar reasoning holds for men who think a person's sex is important to getting ahead in life.

However, using an alternative form of the same regression presented in Figure 3, we find that the effect of believing that a person's sex is important to getting ahead in life is significantly more positive for men than it is for women. This interaction effect is significant at the one-percent level (unreported). As we have seen, this is inconsistent with self-interest, because men and whites with these beliefs would expect to benefit from discrimination and hence have less likelihood of benefiting from redistributive programs.

Concerns about the incentive effects of taxation are a final mechanism through which self-interest might cause beliefs that the poor are lazy and the rich industrious to decrease the demand for redistribution. When earned income is more sensitive to work effort, taxation may cause greater effort disincentives and reduce aggregate income. If

[11] Space limitations prevent us from presenting these results here. However, the finding using ordered probit are presented in Fong (2001).

[12] We assume that people agree on which group benefits and which loses when they believe that a person's race or sex is important to getting ahead.

so, then beliefs about the roles of effort, luck, and opportunity in generating income may affect the level of support for redistribution through concerns about incentive costs of redistribution (Piketty, 1995). This type of incentive concern should not apply only to redistribution, but to any tax-funded expenditure, including expenditures such as national defense. According to this tax-cost hypothesis, if beliefs that income is caused by factors under individual control decrease demand for redistribution, then they should decrease demand for other kinds of tax funded expenditures, including defense spending, as well. But there is no evidence that tax cost concerns adversely affect the demand for public expenditures. Using the 1990 General Social Survey, we estimate ordered probit regressions predicting support for spending on welfare, national defense, halting the rising crime rate, and dealing with drug addiction, respectively.[13] The independent variables are beliefs that the poor are poor because of lack of effort, and five demographic variables (income, education, race, sex, and age). In the samples reported above, the belief that the lack of effort causes poverty has a highly significant negative effect on support for redistribution. However, these same beliefs have no effect on support for spending on crime or drug addiction, and they have a significant positive effect on support for spending on defense. If these beliefs simply measure tax cost concerns, then their effect on support for all of these expenditure items should have been negative.

However, even more convincing evidence on this point comes from the experiment including actual welfare recipients described above. There were no disincentive costs at all in this experiment. Yet, student subjects gave more to the welfare recipients with the stronger work commitments. These results lend strong support to previously made hypotheses about well known patterns in survey data. Heclo (1986) reports that 81% percent of survey respondents favor public funding for child care if the mother is a widow who is trying to support three children while only 15% favor public such funding when the mother has never married and is not interested in working. Heclo also reports the results of a survey in which the wording of a question about support for public redistribution was manipulated so that some subjects were asked about spending on "welfare" while others were asked about spending on "assistance for the poor," or "caring for the poor." In that experiment, 41% of respondents stated that there is too much spending on welfare and 25% stated that there is too little. By contrast, only 11% and 7% of the respondents said that there is too much spending on assistance for and caring for the poor, respectively, and 64% and 69% said that there is too little spending on assistance for and caring for the poor, respectively. In a similar vein, Page and Shapiro (1992) report that support for social security spending has been very high and stable over time, while support for spending on welfare has been consistently low. The interpretation commonly given for findings such as these is that people are less generous to recipients who they think are not working when they could and should be, or who are otherwise considered to be in questionable moral standing (Heclo, 1986; Gilens, 1999). We have shown that these findings cannot be explained away by a fuller and more rigorous account of self-interest.

[13] The sample size in these regressions ranges from 584 to 594.

5. Strong reciprocity and the welfare state: unhappy marriage?

The following generalizations sum up the relevance of the experimental, survey, and other data to the problem of designing and sustaining programs to promote economic security and eliminate poverty. First, people exhibit significant levels of generosity, even towards strangers. Second, beliefs about the causes of high and low incomes matter. Third, people contribute to public goods and cooperate to collective endeavors, and consider it unfair to free-ride on the contributions and efforts of others. Fourth, people punish free riders at substantial costs to themselves, even when they cannot reasonably expect future personal gain therefrom.

It would not be difficult to design a system of income security and economic opportunity that would tap rather than offend the motivations expressed in these four generalizations. Such a system would be generous towards the poor, rewarding those who perform socially valued work and who seek to improve their chances of engaging in such work, as well as to those who are poor through accidents not of their own making, such as illness and job displacement.

While strong reciprocity may support egalitarianism, it may also help explain opposition to welfare state policies in some of the advanced market economies in the past decades. Specifically, in light of the empirical regularities outlined above, we suspect the following to be true as well: egalitarian policies that reward people independent only of whether and how much they contribute to society are considered unfair and are not supported, even if the intended recipients are otherwise worthy of support, and even if the incidence of non-contribution in the target population is rather low. This would explain the opposition to many welfare measures for the poor, particularly since such measures are thought to have promoted various social pathologies. At the same time it explains the continuing support for social security and Medicare in the United States, since the public perception is that the recipients are "deserving" and the policies are thought not to support what are considered anti-social behaviors. Results from public goods experiments are also consistent with the notion that tax resistance by the non-wealthy may stem from their perception that the well-to-do are not paying their fair share.

A striking fact about the decline in the support for the former Aid to Families with Dependent Children, Food Stamps, and other means-tested social support programs in the United States, however, is that overwhelming majorities oppose the *status quo*, whatever their income, race, or personal history with such programs. This pattern of public sentiment, we think, can be accounted for in terms of the principle of strong reciprocity.

We rely mainly on two studies. The first, Farkas and Robinson (1996), analyze data collected in late 1995 by Public Agenda, a nonprofit, nonpartisan research organization. The authors conducted eight focus groups around the country, then did a national survey, involving half-hour interviews, of 1000 randomly selected Americans, plus a national oversample of 200 African-Americans. The second, political scientist Martin Gilens'

Why Americans Hate Welfare, is an analysis and review of several polls executed during the 1990's and earlier by various news organizations.[14]

In the Public Agenda survey 63% of respondents thought the welfare system should be eliminated or "fundamentally overhauled" while another 34% thought it should be "adjusted somewhat." Only 3% approved of the system as is (p. 9). Even among respondents from households receiving welfare only 9% expressed basic approval of the system, while 42% wanted a fundamental overhaul and an additional 46% wanted some adjustments.

The cost of welfare programs cannot explain this opposition. While people generally overstate the share of the Federal budget devoted to welfare (p. 9), this cannot account for the observed opposition.[15] Farkas and Robinson note that

> By more than four to one (65% to 14%), Americans say the most upsetting thing about welfare is that "it encourages people to adopt the wrong lifestyle and values," not that "it costs too much tax money."... Of nine possible reforms presented to respondents—ranging from requiring job training to paying surprise visits to make sure recipients deserve benefits—reducing benefits ranked last in popularity (Table 4).

The cost, apparently, is not the problem. In focus groups:

> Participants invariably dismissed arguments about the limited financial costs of welfare in almost derisive terms as irrelevant and beside the point (p. 9, 10).

Nor can the perception of fraud account for this opposition. It is true that 64% of respondents (and 66% of respondents on welfare) believe welfare fraud is a serious problem. However most do not consider it more serious than in other government programs, and only 35% of survey respondents would be more "comfortable with welfare" if fraud were eliminated (p. 11, 12).

In commenting on this fact Martin Gilens (1999): 1, 2 observes that "Politics is often viewed, by élites at least, as a process centered on the question 'who gets what.' For ordinary Americans, however, politics is more often about 'who *deserves* what' and the welfare state is no exception." In the Public Agenda study, respondents overwhelmingly consider welfare to be unfair to working people and addictive to recipients. By a more than five to one margin (69% to 13% overall, and 64% to 11% for people receiving welfare), respondents say that recipients abuse the system—for instance by not looking for work—rather than actually cheating the system—e.g., by collecting multiple benefits (p. 12). Moreover, 68% think (59% of welfare recipients) that welfare is "passed on from generation to generation, creating a permanent underclass." In the same vein, 70%

[14] A third study by Weaver et al. (1995), drawing in addition on NORC and General Social Survey data, comes to broadly similar conclusions.

[15] As a general rule non-experts vastly overstate the share of the tax revenues devoted to things of which they disapprove, whether it be foreign aid, welfare, aids research, or military expenditure—the opposition is generally the cause of the exaggeration, not *vice-versa*.

(71% of welfare recipients) say welfare makes it "financially better for people to stay on welfare than to get a job," 57% (62% of welfare recipients) think welfare encourages "people to be lazy" and 60% (64% of welfare recipients) say the welfare system "encourages people to have kids out of wedlock" (p. 14, 15). Note that the welfare recipients and other citizens hold similar views in this respect.

That the respondents are correct in thinking that the welfare state cause these behaviors is beside the point. Whether or not, for example, welfare *causes* out of wedlock births, for example, or fosters an unwillingness to work, citizens object that the system provides financial support for those who undertake these socially disapproved behaviors. Their desire is to bear witness against the behavior and to disassociate themselves from it, whether or not their actions can change it.

Racial stereotyping and opposition to welfare are closely associated. The public agenda survey shows that whites are much more likely than African Americans to attribute negative attributes to welfare recipients, and much more likely to blame an individual's poverty on lack of effort. The survey data show, writes Gilens, that

> For most white Americans, race-based opposition to welfare is not fed by ill-will toward blacks, nor is it based on whites' desire to maintain their economic advantages over African Americans. Instead race-based opposition to welfare stems from the specific perception that, as a group, African Americans are not committed to the work ethic.

There is some evidence that people are more tolerant of redistributions within ethnic and racial categories than between. Erzo Luttmer (2001) found for a U.S. sample that individuals are more opposed to welfare if they live in neighborhoods where a higher percentage of welfare recipients is of a different race. Luttmer's findings are consistent with our reciprocity interpretation of redistributive politics, in light of the evidence that when people identify with a social group, they are more likely to blame outgroup members for their bad outcomes and behaviors and to give them little credit for their good outcomes and behaviors (Brewer and Miller, 1996). However, the salience of race in Luttmer's U.S. Data may be not be as pronounced in other cultural contexts, since the characteristics that determine who are "insiders" and who are "outsiders" is culturally specific.

Taking account of the *fact* that many Americans see the current welfare system as a violation of deeply held reciprocity norms does not require that policy makers adopt punitive measures and stingy budgets for the poor. Indeed the public strongly supports income support measures when asked in ways that make clear the deserving nature of the poor: a 1995 NYT/CBS poll, for instance, found that twice as many agreed as disagreed that "it is the responsibility of the government to take care of people who can't take care of themselves."

6. Conclusion

Like Petr Kropotkin (1989 [1903]) a century ago, we find compelling evidence—both evolutionary and contemporary—for the force of human behavioral predispositions to act both generously and reciprocally rather than self-interestedly in many social situations. While many economists have failed to appreciate the practical importance of these predispositions in policy matters, their salience was not missed by Frederick Hayek (1978): 18, 20

> ... [The] demand for a just distribution ... is ... an atavism, based on primordial emotions. And it is these widely prevalent feelings to which prophets, (and) moral philosophers ... appeal by their plans for the deliberate creation of a new type of society.

If we are right, economists have misunderstood both the support for the welfare state and the revolt against welfare (where it has occurred), attributing the latter to selfishness by the electorate rather than the failure of many programs to tap powerful commitments to fairness and generosity and the fact that some programs appear to violate deeply held reciprocity norms. Egalitarians have been successful in appealing to the more elevated human motives precisely when they have shown that dominant institutions violate norms of reciprocity, and may be replaced by institutions more consistent with these norms.

To mobilize rather than offend reciprocal values, policies should recognize that there is substantial support for generosity towards the less well off as long as they have provided or tried to provide a *quid pro quo* and are in good standing. The task of politically viable egalitarian policy design might thus begin by identifying those behaviors that entitle an individual to reciprocation. Among these in the U.S. today would be saving when one's income allows and working hard and taking risks in both productive endeavors and schooling. Persistent poverty is often the result of low returns to these socially admired behaviors: low wages for hard work, a low rate of return on savings, costly access to credit for those wishing to engage in uncertain entrepreneurial activities, and educational environments so adverse as to frustrate even the most diligent student. Policies designed to raise the returns to these activities when undertaken by the less well off would garner widespread support. A second principle of reciprocity-based policy design should be to insure individuals against the vagaries of bad luck without insuring them against the consequences of their own their actions, particularly when these actions violate widely held social norms against such things as illicit drug use or child bearing in the absence of reasonable guarantees of adequate parenting.

Many traditional projects of egalitarians, such as land reform and employee ownership of their workplaces are strongly consistent with reciprocity norms, as they make people the owners not only of the fruits of their labors, but more broadly of the consequences of their actions (Bowles and Gintis, 1998, 1999 provide overviews based on contemporary principal-agent models). The same may be said of more conventional initiatives such as improved educational opportunity and policies to support home ownership. There is good evidence, for example, that home ownership promotes active participation in local politics and a willingness to discipline personally those engaging in antisocial behaviors in the neighborhood (Sampson et al., 1997). An expansion of subsidies designed to promote employment and increase earnings among the poor, suggested by Edmund Phelps (1997), would tap powerful reciprocity motives. Similarly, social insurance programs might be reformulated along lines suggested by John Roemer (1993) to protect individuals from risks over which they have no control, while not indemnifying people against the results of their own choices, other than providing a minimal floor to living standards. In this manner, for example, families could be protected against regional fluctuations in home values—the main form of wealth for most people—as Robert Shiller (1993) has shown. Other forms of insurance could partially protect workers from shifts in demand for their services induced by global economic changes.

An egalitarian society can be built on the basis of these and other policies consistent with strong reciprocity, along with a guarantee of an acceptable minimal living standard consistent with the widely documented motives of basic needs generosity. But if we are correct, economic analysis will be an inadequate guide to policy making in the area unless it revises its foundational assumptions concerning human motivation.

Appendix A

Plenty of opportunity in the U.S.: Some people say that there's not much opportunity in America today that the average person doesn't have much chance to really get ahead. Others say there's plenty of opportunity and anyone who works hard can go as far as they want. Which one comes closer to the way you feel about this? (1) Not much opportunity (2) Plenty of opportunity.

Causes of poverty: Just in your opinion, which is more often to blame if a person is poor—lack of effort on his or her part, or circumstances beyond his or her control? (1) Lack of effort (2) Both (3) Luck or circumstances beyond his/her control.

Causes of wealth: Just in your opinion, which is more often to blame if a person is rich—strong effort on his or her part, or circumstances beyond his or her control? (1) Strong effort (2) Both (3) Luck or circumstances beyond his/her control.

Determinants of Success: I am going to read several reasons why some people get ahead and succeed in life and others do not. Using a one-to-five scale, where "1" means not at all important and "5" means extremely important, please tell me how important it is as a reason for a person's success. You can choose any number from one to five.
A: How important is willingness to take risks
B: How important is money inherited from families
C: How important is hard work and initiative
D: How important is ability or talent that a person is born with
E: How important is dishonesty and willingness to take what they can get
F: How important is [sic] good luck, being in the right place at the right time

G: How important is parents and the family environment they grow up in
H: How important is physical appearance and good looks
I: How important is [sic] connections and knowing the right people
J: How important is being a member of a particular race or ethnic group
K: How important is getting the right education or training
L: How important is a person's gender, that is whether they are male or female?

References

Abbink, K., Bolton, G.E., Sadrieh, A., Tang, F.-F. (1996). "Adaptive learning versus punishment in ultimatum bargaining". Discussion Paper No B0-381, University of Bonn.
Alesina, A., Glaeser, E., Sacerdote, B. (2001). "Why doesn't the United States have a European-style welfare state?". Brookings Papers on Economic Activity 2, 187–278.
Andreoni, J. (1988). "Why free ride? Strategies and learning in public good experiments". Journal of Public Economics 37, 291–304.
Andreoni, J. (1995). "Cooperation in Public goods experiments: kindness or confusion". American Economic Review 85 (4), 891–904.
Atkinson, A.B. (1999). The Economic Consequences of Rolling Back the Welfare State. MIT Press, Cambridge.
Besley, T., Coate, S. (1992). "Understanding welfare stigma: taxpayer resentment and statistical discrimination". Journal of Public Economics 48 (1), 165–183.
Blount, S. (1995). "When social outcomes aren't fair: the effect of causal attributions on preferences". Organizational Behavior & Human Decision Processes 63 (2), 131–144.
Boehm, Ch. (1984). Blood Revenge: The Enactment and Management of Conflict in Montenegro and Other Tribal Societies. University of Pennsylvania Press, Philadelphia, PA.
Bowles, S., Gintis, H. (1998). "Schooling, skills and earnings: a principal-agent approach". In: Arrow, K., Bowles, S., Durlauf, S. (Eds.), Meritocracy and Economic Inequality. Princeton University Press, Princeton, NJ.
Bowles, S., Gintis, H. (1999). "Recasting Egalitarianism: New Rules for Markets, States, and Communities". In: Wright, E.O. (Ed.). Verso, London.
Bowles, S., Gintis, H. (2004). "The evolution of strong reciprocity: cooperation in heterogeneous populations". Theoretical Population Biology 65, 17–28.
Bowles, S., Gintis, H. (2004). "The origins of human cooperation". In: Hammerstein, P. (Ed.), Genetic and Cultural Origins of Cooperation. MIT Press, Cambridge, MA.
Bowles, S., Carptenter, J., Gintis, H. (2001). "Mutual monitoring in teams: the importance of shame and punishment", University of Massachusetts.
Bowles, S., Choi, J.-K., Hopfensitz, A. (2003). "The co-evolution of individual behaviors and social institutions". Journal of Theoretical Biology 223, 135–147.
Boyd, R., Gintis, H., Bowles, S., Richerson, P.J. (2003). "Evolution of altruistic punishment". Proceedings of the National Academy of Sciences 100 (6), 3531–3535.
Brewer, M.B., Miller, N. (1996). Intergroup Relations. Brooks/Cole Publishing Company, Pacific Grove, CA.
Camerer, C., Thaler, R. (1995). "Ultimatums, dictators, and manners". Journal of Economic Perspectives 9 (2), 209–219.
Cameron, L.A. (1999). "Raising the stakes in the ultimatum game: experimental evidence from Indonesia". Economic Inquiry 37 (1), 47–59.
Coleman, J.S. (1988). "Free riders and zealots: the role of social networks". Sociological Theory 6, 52–57.
Deutsch, M. (1985). Distributive Justice. Yale University Press, New Haven.
Eckel, C., Grossman, Ph. (1996). "Altruism in anonymous dictator games". Games and Economic Behavior 16, 181–191.

Edda (1923). "Havamal". In: Clarke, D.E.M. (Ed.), The Havamal, with Selections from other Poems in the Edda. Cambridge University Press, Cambridge.
Falk, A., Fehr, E., Fischbacher, U. (2002). "Testing theories of fairness and reciprocity-intentions matter," University of Zurich.
Farkas, S., Robinson, J. (1996). The Values we Live By: What Americans Want from Welfare Reform. Public Agenda, New York.
Fehr, E., Schmidt, K.M. (1999). "A theory of fairness, competition, and cooperation". Quarterly Journal of Economics 114, 817–868.
Fehr, E., Gächter, S. (2000). "Cooperation and punishment". American Economic Review 90 (4), 980–994.
Fehr, E., Gächter, S. (2000). "Fairness and retaliation: the economics of reciprocity". Journal of Economic Perspectives 14 (3), 159–181.
Fehr, E., Gächter, S. (2002). "Altruistic punishment in humans". Nature 415, 137–140.
Fehr, E., Gächter, S., Kirchsteiger, G. (1997). "Reciprocity as a contract enforcement device: experimental evidence". Econometrica 65 (4), 833–860.
Fong, Ch.M. (2001). "Social preferences, self-interest, and the demand for redistribution". Journal of Public Economics 82 (2), 225–246.
Fong, Ch.M. (2003). "Empathic responsiveness: evidence from a randomized experiment on giving to welfare recipients," Carnegie-Mellon University.
Forsythe, R., Horowitz, J., Savin, N.E., Sefton, M. (1994). "Replicability, fairness and pay in experiments with simple bargaining games". Games and Economic Behavior 6 (3), 347–369.
Gallup Organization (1998). Haves and Have-Nots: Perceptions of Fairness and Opportunity. Gallup.
Gilens, M. (1999). Why Americans Hate Welfare. University of Chicago Press.
Gintis, H. (2000). "Strong reciprocity and human sociality". Journal of Theoretical Biology 206, 169–179.
Güth, W., Schmittberger, R., Schwarz, B. (1982). "An experimental analysis of ultimatum bargaining". Journal of Economic Behavior and Organization 3, 367–388.
Hayek, F. (1978). The Three Sources of Human Values. London School of Economics, London.
Heclo, H. (1986). "The political foundations of antipoverty policy". In: Danziger, Sh.H., Weinberg, D.H. (Eds.), Fighting Poverty: What Works and What Doesn't. Harvard University Press, Cambridge, pp. 312–341.
Kollock, P. (1997). "Transforming social dilemmas: group identity and cooperation". In: Danielson, P. (Ed.), Modeling Rational and Moral Agents. Oxford University Press, Oxford.
Kolm, S.-Ch. (1984). La Bonne Economie: La Réciprocité Générale. Presses Universitaires de France, Paris.
Kolm, S.-Ch. (2000). "The logic of good social relations". Public and Cooperative Economics 71 (2), 171–189.
Kropotkin, P. (1989 [1903]). "Mutual Aid: A Factor in Evolution". Black Rose Books, New York.
Lindbeck, A., Nyberg, S., Weibull, J. (1999). "Social norms and economic incentives in the welfare state". Quarterly Journal of Economics 114, 1–35.
Loewenstein, G.F., Thompson, L., Bazerman, M.H. (1989). "Social utility and decision making in interpersonal contexts". Journal of Personality and Social Psychology 57 (3), 426–441.
Luttmer, E.F.P. (2001). "Group loyalty and the taste for redistribution". Journal of Political Economy 109 (3), 500–528.
Miller, D. (1999). Principles of Social Justice. Harvard University Press, Cambridge, MA.
Moffitt, R. (1983). "An economic model of welfare stigma". American Economic Review 73, 1023–1035.
Moffitt, R., Ribar, D., Wilhelm, M. (1998). "Decline of welfare benefits in the US: the role of wage inequality". Journal of Public Economics 68 (3), 421–452.
Moore, Jr., B. (1978). Injustice: The Social Bases of Obedience and Revolt. M.E. Sharpe, White Plains.
Nisbett, R.E., Cohen, D. (1996). Culture of Honor: The Psychology of Violence in the South. Westview Press, Boulder.
Ostrom, E., Walker, J., Gardner, R. (1992). "Covenants with and without a sword: self-governance is possible". American Political Science Review 86 (2), 404–417.
Page, B., Shapiro, R. (1992). Robert The Rational Public: Fifty Years of Trends in American's Policy Preferences. University of Chicago Press, Chicago and London.

Phelps, E.S. (1997). Rewarding Work: How to Restore Participation and Self-support to Free Enterprise. Harvard University Press, Cambridge, MA.

Piketty, Th. (1995). "Social mobility and redistributive politics". Quarterly Journal of Economics CX (3), 551–584.

Reif, K., Melich, A. (1993). "Euro-Barometer 31A: European Elections, 1989: Post-Election Survey, June–July 1989". In: ICPSR (Ed.), Inter-university Consortium for Political and Social Research, Ann Arbor, MI. Conducted by Faits et Opinions, Paris. [Computer File].

Roberts, K. (1977). "Voting over income tax schedules". Journal of Public Economics 8, 329–340.

Roemer, J. (1993). "A pragmatic theory of responsibility for the egalitarian planner". Philosophy and Public Affairs 22, 146–166.

Roth, A. (1995). "Bargaining experiments". In: Kagel, J., Roth, A. (Eds.), The Handbook of Experimental Economics. Princeton University Press, Princeton, NJ.

Sampson, R.J., Raudenbush, S.W., Earls, F. (1997). "Neighborhoods and violent crime: a multilevel study of collective efficacy". Science 277, 918–924.

Scott, J.C. (1976). The Moral Economy of the Peasant: Rebellion and Subsistence in Southeast Asia. Yale University Press, New Haven, CT.

Shiller, R.J. (1993). Macro Markets: Creating Institutions for Managing Society's Largest Economic Risks. Clarendon Press, Oxford.

Skitka, L., Tetlock, Ph. (1993). "Providing public assistance: cognitive and motivational processes underlying liberal and conservative policy preferences". Journal of Personality and Social Psychology 65 (6), 1205–1223.

Trivers, R.L. (1971). "The evolution of reciprocal altruism". Quarterly Review of Biology 46, 35–57.

Walster, E.G., Walster, W., Berscheid, E. (1978). Equity, Theory and Research. Allyn and Bacon, Boston.

Weaver, R.K., Shapiro, R.Y., Jacobs, L.R. (1995). "Poll trends: welfare". Public Opinion Quarterly 39, 606–627.

Weiner, B. (1995). Judgments of Responsibility: A Foundation for a Theory of Social Conduct. The Guilford Press, New York and London.

Williamson, J.B. (1974). "Beliefs about the motivation of the poor and attitudes toward poverty policy". Social Problems 21 (5), 734–747.

Chapter 24

SELFISHNESS, ALTRUISM AND NORMATIVE PRINCIPLES IN THE ECONOMIC ANALYSIS OF SOCIAL TRANSFERS*

DIDIER BLANCHET

Département des Etudes Economiques d'Ensemble, Institut National de la Statistique et des Etudes Economiques, France
e-mail: didier.blanchet@insee.fr

MARC FLEURBAEY

CNRS-CERSES, University of Paris 5 and IDEP

Contents

* We thank Serge-Christophe Kolm, Jean Mercier-Ythier, Pierre Pestieau for their comments on a first version of this paper, as well as other participants to the Marseille Conference, January 23–26, 2002. Errors remain ours.

Handbook of the Economics of Giving, Altruism and Reciprocity, Volume 2
Edited by Serge-Christophe Kolm and Jean Mercier Ythier

DOI: 10.1016/S1574-0714(06)02024-0

Abstract

This chapter examines the role of altruistic motives in the economic analysis of public social transfers, both from a positive and from a normative point of view.

The positive question is to know whether we can fully neglect altruistic considerations to explain the development or sustainability of these transfers. Such is the implicit ambition of efficiency theories of the Welfare State. However, while these theories may be suited for explaining the development of public insurance or life-cycle transfers, they rapidly reach their limits when we try to explain more redistributive dimensions of social transfers. At the other extreme, descriptions of social transfers as systems of extended insurance (behind the veil of ignorance) implicitly do as if individuals were ready to completely abstract from their real world situations, and this can be analyzed as an extreme form of altruism.

Actual motivations for support of social transfers certainly lay somewhere in between, i.e., a mix of well-understood selfishness and partial altruism. This explains why these systems can redistribute more than explained by pure efficiency motives, but less than what would be predicted under the extended insurance hypothesis. One additional limit to redistribution is the fact that even very altruistic agents can deliberately reduce its scope because of its potential disincentive effects.

The second part of the chapter examines normative considerations which seem relevant to the evaluation of systems of social transfers. In particular, the idea of extended insurance has paradoxical implications in some circumstances, because of its structural similarity to utilitarianism. Therefore it appears useful to look for other normative theories, such as inequality-averse social welfare functions or fairness criteria. It is shown how both approaches can be useful in the study of second-best solutions under incentive constraints. The chapter ends with a critical examination of the incorporation of individuals' altruistic feelings in social welfare functions.

Keywords

altruism, welfare, redistribution, social insurance, social welfare functions, fairness

JEL classification: D30, D63, D71, D80, D91, H21, H51, H53, H55, I18, I30

1. Introduction

Systems of social transfers (ST), including social insurance (SI) and public assistance (PA), have reached a high level of development in most industrialized countries. A standard typology distinguishes three basic functions for such institutions (Barr, 1992): interpersonal redistribution (equalization of resources between individuals), life-cycle transfers or intrapersonal redistribution (equalization of resources over the life cycle) and insurance, i.e., redistribution across states of nature offering protection against various risks of life. These three broad categories include protection against health risks, against handicap, against risks of unemployment, poverty and/or income loss, and the financing of retirement. The scope is therefore quite large. For centuries, such protections had been provided—when they were—either by self-insurance, by intra-familial solidarity or through private or public charity. But collective systems of ST, in their various forms, have progressively emerged, over the last century, as the major tools for providing such services in developed countries.

At first sight, the economic analysis of such institutions is a field where considerations of altruism or at least solidarity motives should play a major role. This would be at least the spontaneous conviction of a non-economist. But a major part of the economic literature dealing with questions of development and sustainability of the welfare state has instead tried to develop theories which strictly conform to the assumption of selfish behavior: this is for instance the case of efficiency or interest group theories of the welfare state (Mulligan and Sala-I-Martin, 1999a, 1999b).

This observation will provide the point of departure of this paper. The question will be to examine how far these theories can actually go without relying on the assumption that there exists some form of solidarity or altruism. The general answer will be that, in fact, the two approaches do not have to be opposed but must rather be considered in continuity. The analysis of social transfers is precisely one field where this continuity and complementarity between selfish and altruistic motives finds strong illustrations. For instance, mutual insurance can, initially, correspond to a pure Pareto-improving exchange between selfish agents, but it will also create a form of solidarity or lead to the emergence of altruistic attitudes which, in turn, will reinforce the long term sustainability of this mutual insurance.

It must be added that such a complementarity or continuity matters not only for positive but also for normative analysis. The importance of thinking about rules for the optimal forms of social transfers increases if the existence of altruistic motives widens the scope for practically implementing these transfers in the real world. Normative and positive dimensions of the economic analysis of ST are, in fact, closely intertwined, and this is the reason why this normative dimension will be also explored in this chapter.

These ideas will be developed in four steps.

After this introduction, section 2 will first examine the core of efficiency arguments in favor of part of existing social transfers. These arguments show what features of social insurance can be interpreted as positive-sum games which increase long run *ex ante* well-being for all participants. These arguments are essentially based on the observation of market failures in the private provision of insurance, due to informational problems. Such arguments can be used both to defend social insurance strictly speaking and the public management of pension benefits.

Section 3 will then examine the redistributive features of existing ST systems. A close inspection shows that part of these redistributive features do not correspond to real redistribution, but still bear strong resemblance with insurance transfers and/or life-cycle transfers. Such forms of redistribution are still amenable to analyses in terms of efficiency. But this becomes progressively harder as we continuously move towards forms of redistribution which are increasingly remote from insurance or life-cycle motives. There exists, therefore, a large set of social transfers which are not amenable to the analyses of section 2.

Of course, the existence of some of these transfers can still be compatible with selfishness if we assume that the implementation of ST systems is the result of political processes that do not require unanimity. This is the approach of politico-economic models which have been mobilized by a number of authors to explain the development of ST and/or the welfare state, and which will be shortly reviewed in the last subsection of section 3. But these models suffer from two main limits. They do not provide us with arguments for considering that these transfers are "fair." These transfers will often remain below what seems to be recommended by reasonable normative principles, or they can as well, in some other instances, go beyond the warranted levels. Second, one can argue that the representation of the voter as only guided by a very limited conception of self-interest is misguiding and fails to account for many aspects of electoral or collective behavior.

Section 4 will then examine one possible way to go beyond this selfishness hypothesis, which directly relies upon the ambiguity of the distinction between redistribution and insurance stressed in section 4. This is the notion of extended or fundamental insurance, i.e., an insurance contracted "under the veil of ignorance," before knowing the position the individual is going to have in the society and during his entire life cycle. The notion of extended insurance can be used both as a normative tool for discussing the optimal level of insurance and as one formalization of altruism, referring to the ability to completely abstract oneself from one's current position in the society, in order to encompass all situations where one could have found oneself, in other states of the nature.

Moving the cursor that far toward extreme altruism, however, is not more realistic than remaining stuck into the assumption of pure self-interest. Real world altruism leads to levels of redistribution intermediate between the total or inexistent redistributions implied by these two equally extreme assumptions. Two factors can be considered to explain this intermediate situation: one is the fact that altruism is intrinsically limited; the other is the fact that agents internalize, in their altruistic choices, the incentive constraints to which redistribution or insurance policies are confronted. The first assumption is natural but its discussion is essentially an empirical topic and does not fall within the scope of this paper. The second one deserves longer developments. This assumption is equivalent to assuming that the altruistic individual more or less mimics the choices which would be made by a policy maker planning for second best solutions to the redistributive problem. The link or complementarity with the assumption that altruism is only partial is interesting to develop: apparent differences in the level of altruism can either correspond to intrinsic differences in tastes, or to different perceptions or beliefs about the magnitude of these incentive problems. The lower degree of altruism toward more distant groups or individuals may also result from our decreasing confidence in an efficient monitoring of incentive problems for these more distant individuals.

Analyzing these redistribution/efficiency trade-offs could be made, in fact, under various representations of first best redistributions. The fact that section 4 essentially insists on the extended insurance approach reflects the fact that it is the most widely used for the analysis of optimal ST systems. The reason for this preference is the continuity it offers with efficiency arguments of the standard insurance framework of section 1 (optimality is equivalent to efficiency "behind the veil of ignorance"), and the fact that it is directly related to a still widely used approach of normative economics, i.e., utilitarianism or Harsanyism. All this allows a direct transposition of analytical tools developed in these two frameworks.

The analytical attractiveness of the extended insurance, however, should not conceal its limits, which are shared with utilitarian theories of social choice. The purpose of section 5, essentially normative, will be to list these limits, and to examine how other existing strands of the literature on social choice try to overcome these limits.

Three words of warning should be given at last to delineate more precisely the scope of this paper. Its emphasis is on the selfishness/altruism alternative. The intermediate domain of "reciprocity" will not be developed explicitly, but the reader will easily find how additional arguments of reciprocity could fit in our general line of argumentation. See the chapter by Bowles, Fong and Gintis for specific developments on this dimension of reciprocity. This paper also supplements ours through its strong emphasis on empirical evidence in favor of the role of reciprocity/altruism in explaining individual or collective support for social transfers. Second, concerning the specific domain of public intergenerational transfers, our treatment of selfish/altruistic factors will not be exhaustive: the reader is referred to other chapters of this volume, in particular those by Cigno and by Michel, Thibault and Vidal. The first one deals more completely with the question of sustainability of public intergenerational transfers with or without altruism (a question that we will only briefly consider in our section 3.4). The second one discusses a connected topic, namely, how the existence of social security and the presence of intergenerational altruism interact to determine savings and economic growth. A large literature has been devoted to it since Barro (1974). Although this question concerns a link between altruism and social security, it will not be considered at all in the present chapter, since it is more a question about *consequences* of social security than a question about the role played by altruism among *causes* of social security.

2. Social transfers for selfish agents: core arguments of efficiency theories of the welfare state

Among the three functions of ST listed in the introduction, two emerge for which efficiency justifications are *a priori* available and whose existence could in principle be explained without resorting to the assumption of altruism. One is the "insurance" function strictly speaking, i.e., redistribution across states of the nature which increases everyone's *ex ante* utility by reducing uncertainty concerning future outcomes. The second one is what is sometimes labelled "intrapersonal redistribution," i.e., transfers aiming at smoothing income levels over the life cycle, whose impact is also to increase lifetime utility, under standard assumptions concerning intertemporal preferences. This section will basically insist on these two components, and examine how efficiency theories show the Pareto improving properties of ST along these two dimensions. This issue is not restricted to the question of knowing whether these dimensions of ST improve well-being when compared with a situation where no insurance or no life-cycle income smoothing exists at all. If this were the question, the answer would be trivial. The problem is to show that such collective systems are also Pareto superior to market solutions which would try to fulfil the same objectives: it is therefore a problem of identifying market failures in the private provision of these two services.

2.1. *Inefficiencies in the private provision of insurance*

Showing the efficiency enhancing properties of social insurance over the private provision of insurance by the market needs recalling how such a private market operates. We shall do so using the standard presentation of this market.[1]

Let us start with the representation of the demand side of the market. In the simplest case, individuals are supposed to be equally exposed at a period t to a given risk with probability p, and it is assumed that the consequences of this risk can be assimilated to an income loss of D. If we assume a VNM utility function $V = E(u(c))$ where c is consumption, $u(.)$ is a concave and strictly increasing function, and $E(.)$ the expected value operator, and if we assume that R is the level of income when the risk is not realised, then the expected utility for the individual is:

$$V_0 = pu(R - D) + (1 - p)u(R). \tag{1}$$

Insurance consists in offering a compensation q to those individuals for which the loss D will occur, financed by a global premium π paid whatever the state of the nature. The new expected utility becomes:

$$V_1 = pu(R - D + q - \pi) + (1 - p)u(R - \pi). \tag{2}$$

[1] This presentation and its further developments follow the one by Henriet and Rochet (1991).

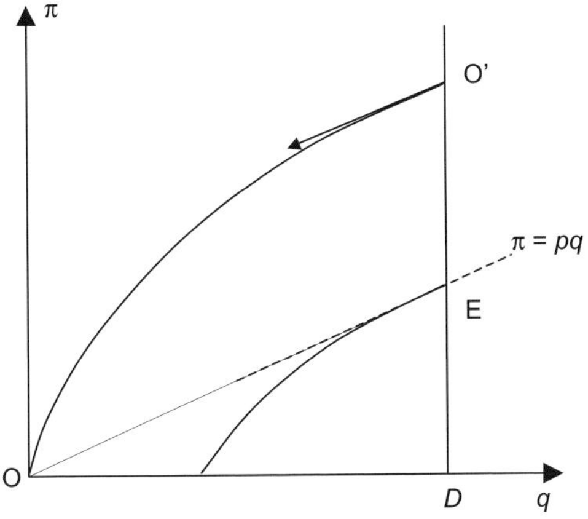

Figure 1.

Associated indifference curves are represented on Figure 1. Utility V_1 increases when we move downwards or to the right of the graph, and the indifference curves have the property that they all have the same slope of p at points of full insurance, i.e., points on the vertical line $q = D$. This results from writing that the total derivative of V_1 with respect to q and π is identically equal to zero along an indifference curve, which implies:

$$\frac{\mathrm{d}\pi}{\mathrm{d}q} = -\frac{\partial V_1/\partial q}{\partial V_1/\partial \pi} = \frac{pu'(R-\pi+q-D)}{pu'(R-\pi+q-D)+(1-p)u'(R-\pi)}, \tag{3}$$

whence, $\mathrm{d}\pi/\mathrm{d}q = p$ for $q = D$. Point O corresponds to the utility level which is reached without insurance. All points below the OO′ curve are therefore utility improving for the individual.

Let's now turn to the supply side of the market. Any firm offering an insurance contract (q, π) with $\pi \geq pq$ will make a non-negative profit. The corresponding points which are also attractive for consumers are those belonging to the area between the indifference curve OO′ and the line $\pi = pq$ which is the line of actuarial neutrality, i.e., the line where premiums paid are just equal to the expected level of compensation received.

On this basis, it is easy to show that the point $E = (D, pD)$ of full insurance (complete coverage of income loss D), with actuarial neutrality, should, in an ideal world, correspond to a competitive equilibrium. All insurance companies should concentrate their offers on this kind of contract since all other contracts are either unsustainable for them (if they are below the OE line) or less attractive for consumers (if they are on or above the OE line). In this simple case, there are no arguments in favour of SI, since the market works and is efficient. The efficiency arguments in favour of SI will come from the relaxation of some of the assumptions which have been implicitly made for constructing this ideal case.

One of these assumptions plays a central role, and most of the explanations of market failure in insurance markets can be more or less directly interpreted as resulting from its relaxation. It is the assumption of a perfect *ex ante* knowledge of p and D by the insurer, which is necessary for exactly positioning himself on the optimal contract at point E. In the real world, this knowledge is far from perfect and even very imperfect for many reasons. It is the case if (a) the risk is hard to quantify even at the macro level, if (b) p and/or D are dependent at the micro level on unobserved characteristics of individuals, or if (c) exposure to risk or the amount of necessary compensation are dependent on unobserved actions by individuals.

One or the other of these conditions can be sufficient to explain market failure in the provision of insurance, which will either result in situations of under-insurance (less than full coverage, with various possible restrictions limiting access to insurance), or in insurance premiums far higher than requested by actuarial neutrality, or in no insurance at all, if obstacles to a good functioning of the insurance market are so high that they dissuade any insurer from entering the market. We shall not recall here the formal justifications for all these kinds of market failures. We shall recall instead their transposition to many concrete problems of private insurance provision calling for public intervention.

Case (a) relates to the impossibility of providing insurance against macro-economic risks. If the average probability of the risk cannot be evaluated ex ante, it means that there is uncertainty about the frequency of the risk even at this macro level, and this is equivalent to the existence of a macro risk which cannot be diversified by the market. This kind of explanation is frequently used to explain the absence of private coverage against unemployment risk. But it can also be used to explain part of the hesitation of private insurers to offer protection against long term risks whose future evolution is difficult to anticipate. For instance, uncertainty about the future evolution of the average prevalence of handicap at old ages and about the future evolution of the costs of long term care is a familiar explanation for the low level of supply of private coverage against this risk. When such a coverage is offered, it is limited by strong restrictions (for instance in terms of indexation of benefits) which practically reduces the interest of such a coverage.

Case (b) includes all situations of adverse selection whose destabilizing properties for insurance markets are known since Rotschild and Stiglitz (1976). Unobservable inter-individual heterogeneity expose insurers to a risk of excess burden in case their insured population includes an excessive share of high risk individuals, or of individuals for whom the cost of providing coverage will be higher than the average. One possibility for them is to try to sort out these individuals by indirect means. The two main possibilities are to try to identify high risk individuals on the basis of their past record, or to propose separating contracts, i.e., couples of high price/full coverage contracts and low price/partial coverage contracts parameterised to be respectively attractive for high and low-risk individuals. But these tools are only imperfect. They will generally result in imperfect coverage even for good risks, and using such contracts may lead to phenomena of destructive competition where the competition for attracting the good risks prevents convergence toward any stable and sustainable market equilibrium.

Case (c) corresponds to the situation of moral hazard. The existence of coverage will in turn modify values of p and/or D, either because it lowers motivation to prevent risk occurrence (*ex ante* moral hazard, e.g., less effort against the risk of losing one's job) or because it increases the cost of providing compensation after the risk has realized (*ex post* moral hazard, for instance choosing more expensive treatments for a given pathology, or increasing the duration of the unemployment period if covered by generous benefits once one has lost his former job). This problem has points in common both with situations (a) and (b). Similarities with the consequences of adverse selection occur because inter-individual heterogeneity has the same consequences whatever the underlying causes, i.e., whether individual characteristics are beyond the control of individuals, or depend on voluntary actions and attitudes. Similarity with (a) appears because the existence of moral hazard means that the cost of coverage cannot be considered as an exogenous parameter even at the macro level. It will depend on the aggregate reaction of individuals to the introduction of coverage, which is not known when the insurance contact is set in. These similarities lead to similar results, that is, reluctance of private insurers to offer insurance against risks that they believe to be highly sensitive to individual behaviour, either at the micro and the macro level.

One last limit in the market provision of insurance, and not a minor one, can be added, namely, the existence of large operating costs for insurers, including costs of attracting and keeping customers, which can be fairly large. These operating costs are necessarily charged on the insured under the form of an extra premium implying that firms will, even under perfect information, not be able to position themselves on point E, but on a point E' lying somewhere between E and O', which will provide less utility to the insured than point E.

What are the solutions offered by social insurance to these various limits of private insurance? All these solutions derive from the fact that this insurance can be mandatory. This result in a monopolistic situation the consequences of which are the following:

- Obligation exempts the social insurer from the necessity of sorting out indirectly unobservable good and bad risks. In fact, since it is competition which, under adverse selection, is destabilizing for the private market, it is quite natural that the suppression of competition allowed by social insurance solves the problem.
- Obligation makes it easier for the private insurer to adapt *ex post* the cost of insurance to unexpected changes of average p or D, whether they result from exogenous changes or from endogenous evolutions of behaviours by the insured.
- Obligation also eliminates one part of operating costs: the costs of prospecting potential consumers. This lowers the individual cost of insurance (as long as this effect is not offset by increases in other operating costs, induced by the removal of competitive pressure).

All these elements, since they allow the public provision of larger amounts of insurance at lower costs than what is done by the market, lead to Pareto improvements, in the sense of an *ex ante* increase of utility for all individuals. Undoubtedly, such improvements are not only desirable, but should be spontaneously supported by a community of selfish agents.

2.2. *Inefficiencies in the private management of life-cycle transfers*

The analysis of the Pareto-improving properties of public intergenerational transfers has much in common with the analysis of Pareto-improving features of public insurance.

There is, first, a similarity between the formal representation of *ex ante* utility in the VNM framework and the representation of lifetime utility in a life-cycle framework. Assume for simplicity that individuals live two periods of equal length: active life with resources R, and retirement with no primary resources. Assuming an additive and separable utility function over the life cycle, we have, without social security, a life-cycle utility level:

$$V_0 = u(R) + u(0). \tag{4}$$

Improving this utility level will be possible if some transfers are organized between the two periods of life. This can be done in two ways. The first one is through private savings on capital markets, with or without the intermediation of private institutions such as pension funds of insurance companies. The second one is through social insurance, which can rely on two techniques: funding through the accumulation of reserves, and pay-as-you-go (PAYG) financing, i.e., direct transfers from workers to retired people.

The incidence of the two techniques can be analysed rapidly. Consider funding with a rate of return on investment equal to r. In that case, a savings rate of $1/(2+r)$ at the first period yields resources of $Rr/(2+r)$ at the second period. Lifetime utility becomes

$$V_1 = 2u(R(1+r)/(2+r)). \tag{5}$$

This utility level, for $r \geq 0$, is higher than or equal to $2u(R/2)$ and therefore higher than V_0, under standard concavity assumptions on u.

Under PAYG, an assumption has to be made about the demographic structure of the population. Assuming that the population growth rate is n, the contribution rate which equalizes income at the two successive periods of life is $1/(2+n)$, and the resulting lifetime utility is[2]:

$$V_1' = 2u(R(1+n)/(2+n)). \tag{6}$$

This presentation offers a first possibility for Pareto-improving outcomes with public pension schemes. If $r > n$, then a public PAYG scheme will do worse than fully funded private schemes, and no efficiency gain can result from the public provision of pension. But if r happened to be lower than n there would be room for a first form of Pareto improvement. This situation corresponds, in growth models, to the so-called

[2] If there is technical progress, n has to be replaced by $n+g$, where g is the productivity growth rate, without changing the following arguments.

situation of dynamic inefficiency with over-accumulation of capital compared to the "golden rule" accumulation rate which maximizes consumption per capita in the long run. Such a situation of over-accumulation could prevail if pension financing only relied on private savings. This was the efficiency justification offered by Samuelson (1975) for at least one component of public social security in the financing of retirement income.

However, the current tendency is to minimize this first argument considering that real world conditions are generally quite far from this risk of inefficient over-accumulation. Stronger efficiency arguments in favour of public schemes can rather be obtained if we mix life-cycle considerations with insurance motives, including considerations of uncertainty on n and r, or other elements of macro or micro uncertainty concerning life-cycle planning. For instance, the return on investment is uncertain both at the macro and the micro-level. It can change due to adverse macroeconomic shocks, and it is uncertain at the micro level due to the impossibility for individuals of realizing full arbitrages between the many potential savings instruments. And the length of the second period of life is not fixed and certain. It is uncertain, both at a macro level (life expectancy changes from one generation to the next) and at a micro level (it differs across individuals). Retirement financing must include insurance against these various categories of risk.

Private pension plans can, of course, offer some partial answers to these difficulties, but with the same limits as those detected for the simple basic insurance problem of section 1, amplified by the fact that the risks to be insured are long term risks. More precisely:

- Individual coverage against individual longevity risk is possible and proposed in life insurance contracts, but suffers from problems of adverse selection which empirically limit the development of private annuities (Eckstein et al., 1985). And no private coverage is available against the macro risk of an increasing average longevity.
- Micro financial risks are partly managed by financial intermediaries, but these cannot offer full protection against risk of bankruptcy, and cannot offer protection, *a fortiori*, against macro risks concerning real rates of return, which are not diversifiable, one important component of these macro risks being inflation (Bodie, 1990).

Against these two limits in the private provision of life-cycle resource smoothing, Pareto superiority of public pension schemes can result once again from their larger possibilities of mutualisation both between and within cohorts, offering larger coverage of micro and macro risks faced over these life cycles and more specifically during their second half. Once again, these possibilities are in the *ex ante* interest of all members of these successive cohorts. The implementation of public social security schemes offering these possibilities should be supported without the assumption of intra or inter-generational altruism.

3. Redistributive transfers under selfishness

All the previous considerations are of an evident importance. Stressing that one part of ST systems can be justified by efficiency or well-understood selfishness is a useful task. It offers a good defense against naïve proposals aiming at dismantling large parts of ST on the basis of ill-conceived selfishness. Many proposals to go back to pure market solutions in the provision of old age support or insurance generally overlook the limits of the private provision of such services and dismiss the fact that such changes could finally result in a Pareto deterioration.

However, efficiency theories, at first sight, generally fail to explain an important part of transfers performed by social insurance systems, which corresponds to the third component of ST mentioned in the introduction, i.e., redistribution. In this section we shall recall the main forms of redistributions performed by ST, examining to what extent they can remain justified on efficiency grounds and/or be kept compatible with an assumption of pure individual selfishness. Actually, Pareto improvement is not a necessary condition for sustainability under selfishness. Redistributive social transfers can remain compatible with self-interest if sustained by adequate political equilibrium, and this possibility must be explored before invoking the assumption of altruism.

3.1. Redistributive features of ST

The formal presentation of insurance and life-cycle motives has shown that these two motives necessarily imply some forms of redistributions, between the lucky and the unlucky after the realization of the risk in the first case, or between age groups at a given point in time, under PAYG, in the second one. But, conveniently consolidated, these transfers remain neutral and should not imply any true *ex ante* redistribution. In the case of insurance, this occurs if the premium respects the condition of actuarial neutrality, i.e., the identity between the premium and the expected levels of benefits $\pi = pq$ (up to a marginal difference corresponding to operating costs). In the case of life-time transfers an equivalent identity can be stated between premiums paid and benefits received at all ages, assuming a convenient choice of the actualisation rate. If the system is operating under pure PAYG rules, then the contribution $\pi = R/(2+n)$ at working age and the benefit $b = R(1+n)/(2+n)$ when retired satisfy the identity $-\pi + b/(1+n) = 0$ which corresponds to a simple form of intertemporal actuarial neutrality with a discount rate of n.

Now, real world ST systems present many deviations from these rules. We can list the most important ones. Let us start with cases of deviations from actuarial neutrality in the first sense of the term.

At a given point in time, individuals have different degrees of exposure to health risks. The destabilizing consequences of such heterogeneity for the private provision of insurance have been mentioned above. Public systems solve this problem by pooling high and bad risks. They are forced to do so when the degree of exposure to risk is an unobservable characteristic. But they generally pool as well between groups when exposure to risk is observable, albeit risk differentiation and strict actuarial neutrality would, in this case, be possible. In both cases, this pooling will result in redistribution, implicit in the first case or explicit in the second one. If λ and $1-\lambda$ are the respective shares of the two groups in the population, then the average premium paid under full insurance by members of the two groups will be $[\lambda p_H + (1-\lambda) p_L]D$. This implies that, compared to the non-redistributive actuarial fees, the group of low risk individuals will pay an extra cost of $\lambda(p_H - p_L)D$ for its health insurance while the group of high risk individuals will benefit from a subsidy of $(1-\lambda)(p_H - p_L)D$. The same kind of transfer will occur if contribution rates for unemployment insurance are not differentiated across sectors or social groups with different rates of exposure to unemployment, and so on.

A second common form of redistribution directly derives from this principle of non differentiation. One simple group of observable factors of differential exposure to risk are demographic factors such as gender and age. Non differentiated contributions between men and women and between age groups are therefore at the origin of significant redistributions across gender and age groups.

A third dimension of redistribution performed by ST systems is horizontal redistribution between households of different sizes. For instance, health expenditures by children can be reimbursed by social insurance at no extra cost for their parents. This can be considered as one form of intergenerational redistribution, with children benefiting from health coverage without contributing, but can be better considered as an implicit redistribution from households with no or few children to households with many children.

The last form of redistribution, and probably the one which deviates the most significantly from the commonsense definition of insurance is the vertical redistribution between income groups due to the fact that contributions are generally proportional to or increasing with income. As long as these contributions are used to finance benefits which are themselves proportional to income, such as sickness leave benefits or unemployment benefits proportional to foregone wages, this remains neutral. But this will not be the case if contributions to health insurance, for instance, are proportional to income. Admittedly, a positive correlation can be observed between income or social status and health consumption, due to a larger concern of high income people for their health, and this will mitigate somewhat the amount of vertical redistribution across income groups performed by such systems. But the compensation will be generally partial, since the income elasticity of health expenditures is generally lower than one. This form of vertical redistribution will be still higher when health expenditures are directly financed through income taxes which are progressive, instead of linear. Vertical redistribution is also predominant in the case of public assistance, the benefits of which, whatever their nature (minimum income, housing allowances, free medical services or other forms of in-kind benefits) are by construction limited to low income groups and financed, too, through progressive fiscal contributions. Vertical redistribution can also be implicit and result indirectly from the pooling mechanism, when exposure to risk is negatively rather than positively linked to income, as it is generally the case for unemployment insurance.

Similar analyses can be performed about redistributive properties of public pension schemes. Intertemporal actuarial neutrality will not be satisfied:

- If pension premiums are not differentiated across groups with different life expectancies, such as men and women, social groups (in this latter case it should be noted that redistribution should rather be labelled anti-redistribution, since longer life expectancies are generally associated with higher than with lower income).
- If the link is broken between contributions and the level of pensions. This can occur for instance if contributions are proportional to income while benefits are regressive with income, or if we have a system of completely flat benefits financed by proportional contributions on wages or through a proportional or progressive income tax.
- If benefits are provided irrespectively of past contribution efforts. Some examples of benefits independent of past contributions are additional entitlements linked to the fact of having raised children, or rules warranting a minimum level of pension even for individuals with very low past contributions records. This implies a form of redistribution from people with long contributions records to people with short contributions records, such as housewives or people with irregular careers.

Redistribution will also take place between cohorts, especially during the early stages of development of a PAYG pension system. The rate of return of n (or $n + g$, with technical progress), is only a long term rate of return, once contributions to the system are definitely fixed from one cohort to the next. But contributions rates generally change over time. The main beneficiaries of this redistribution are the first cohort of retirees covered by the PAYG system who, contrarily to what happens when a funded system is set up, receive benefits without having had to contribute during their active lives, since their parents were not covered by this PAYG system. For these cohorts, the PAYG system is equivalent to a free lunch, and the rate of return on their contributions is, formally, equal to infinity.

3.2. *Forms of redistribution that remain amenable to efficiency arguments*

The working of ST systems therefore entails large amounts of redistributions. Can some of these redistributions still be justified by efficiency arguments, warranting unanimous support by a community of selfish agents? The answer can remain positive up to a certain point. There are two possibilities.

First, a non neutral transfer can still be considered profitable for an apparent "loser" if there is no alternative to get an equivalent amount of insurance at a lower cost. When market failure is such that private insurance is not available, or incomplete or only available at a high price, then a redistributive social insurance can remain preferable even to those individuals who are taxed more than the actuarial equivalent of their benefits.

Figure 2 illustrates this point. It is the adaptation of Figure 1 to the case where two classes of risk coexist. The actuarially neutral contract for low risks (probability p_L) are those on the lower line, while the actuarially neutral contracts for high risks (probability p_H) are on the higher line. The pooling contract generally proposed by social insurance, with $\pi = [\lambda p_H + (1 - \lambda) p_L]q$, entails redistribution from the low risk to the bad risk, implying a loss for the former category.

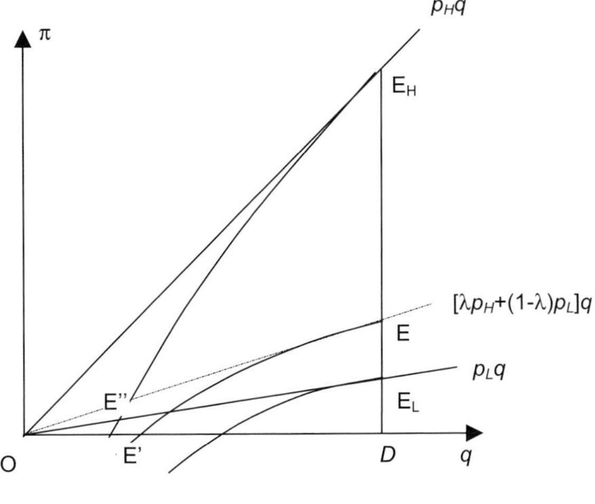

Figure 2.

Even in this case, the "loser" can remain a "winner" as long as market solutions are unable to provide any insurance contract below the E′E curve. One case is the one where market equilibrium can only sustain the set of separating contracts (E″, E_H), or the case when private contracts charge an extra-premium which makes them remain more expensive than the pooling equilibrium E.

A second idea is that apparent non neutrality can be the result of a higher order insurance contract, i.e., one covering "the risk of becoming a bad risk." This implies shifting from a two to a three period framework. In a first stage, neither the insurer nor the individuals are informed about individuals' degree of exposure to the risk; in a second stage, the quality of bad risk or good risk starts being revealed; finally, in a third stage the risk is realized. In the first stage, pooling contracts imply no detectable redistribution. Redistribution starts being apparent at the second stage, and fully takes place at the last stage, both within and between groups. Since pooling reduces uncertainty for all agents in the first stage, whatever their future quality, it can still be considered as Pareto improving from this point of view.

This is no more than expressing the relative nature of redistribution and actuarial neutrality which appears as soon as we try to combine the two dimensions of insurance and intertemporal transfers. Some transfers which appear as redistribution when measured as deviations from the instantaneous rule of actuarial neutrality formulated for pure insurance problems do not appear as such when consolidated over several periods of time and a fortiori when consolidated over the entire life-cycle. Conversely, deviations from the rule of equivalence between contributions and benefits over the life cycle, used to measure redistribution within pension schemes, cannot be interpreted as redistribution anymore if they can be interpreted as a result of insurance against the risk of shifting from one to the other group.

3.3. Forms of redistribution that are not amenable to efficiency arguments

We can precisely build upon the relativity of these concepts of redistribution and actuarial neutrality to examine more systematically what are the limits to the interpretation of social transfers as pareto-improving devices. In an intertemporal framework, the condition of actuarial neutrality can be written:

$$0 = \sum_{a=u}^{v} \frac{E_u(b_a) - E_u(\pi_a)}{(1+r)^{a-u}}, \tag{7}$$

where $E_u(\pi_a)$ and $E_u(b_a)$ are respectively the expectations of contributions paid and benefits received at age a, evaluated at an initial age of u, i.e., conditional upon all the information concerning the individual which is available at age u, summed until a limit age of v, and discounted at rate r.

This shows how the evaluation of actuarial neutrality strongly depends on many parameters: the list of benefits and contributions taken into account in the analysis, the discount rate, and the initial age u which is used as a point of departure for discounting. Let us assume that we adopt a global view of ST transfers, meaning that all kinds of potential net exchanges between the individual and the ST system are taken into account. Assume also that these transfers are considered for the maximum possible duration of life and that, finally, an appropriate discount rate has been chosen. There remains the crucial point of choosing the age u which is taken as a point of departure for summing and discounting net transfers. Modifying this age influences the result for two reasons:

- because the magnitude and net direction of transfers change with age;
- because the passage of time brings additional information about the degree of exposition of the individual to various risks so that $E_u(\pi_a)$ and $E_u(b_a)$ depend not only on a but also on u.

As a consequence, there is no intrinsic definition of the distinction between insurance and redistribution. It depends on a number of conventions. This relativity certainly explains why, despite the popularity of this distinction, there are only few empirical attempts to quantify the respective shares of the two categories in actual systems of social transfers.[3] From our positive point of view, its importance is to show the need to refine the simple analysis above of pareto-improving properties of insurance or life-cycle transfers that has been presented above. Attitudes in front of these transfers, in fact, are expected to depend both on positions within the society and within one's life cycle.

At early stages of the life cycle, perspectives are open and individuals may have little information about their future earning capacity and/or their future degree of exposure to various risks such as health risks. At such a stage, many apparent redistributive features of ST should be interpreted by the individual as offering life-cycle insurance against an uncertain future. On the other hand, at these young ages, such a perception can be

[3] See however Burkhauser and Warlick (1981) or Börsch-Supan and Reil-Held (2001).

counterbalanced by the fact that many of these risks can be underestimated or undervalued by the individuals. This can be due either to a high value of the discount rate, or to a downward bias on the estimation of expected benefits. These counterbalancing factors will limit the willingness of selfish young adults to freely accept social insurance: even if well understood selfishness should induce them to accept these redistributions for efficiency motives, they may not be inclined to do so.

At intermediate ages, the evolution is ambiguous. The individual may feel progressively more concerned by some risks (such as health risks), and more willing to consider a generous and non discriminating coverage of these risks as a form of insurance from which he or she can eventually benefit. On the other hand, the fact that he or she has a better information concerning his earning ability or the risk of seeing this earning ability increase or decrease may make him more reluctant, if this earnings ability is high, and if he or she is guided by purely selfish motives, to accept large vertical redistributions as forms of income insurance.

At higher ages, the individual becomes more and more dependant on ST or welfare, due to the increasing benefits derived from pensions and health insurance. This renders selfish individuals increasingly supportive of these two components of ST. But, if they remain guided by selfish motives, they should become conversely less supportive of components of ST aiming at covering risks whose realization is essentially behind them.

This analysis suggests that the frontier of transfers that will be considered as welfare improving by selfish agents is in fact a moving one, strongly dependent of the position both within the society and within the life-cycle. The consequence for a strict application of efficiency theories of the welfare state is rather destructive: the subset of transfers which, at a given point in time, will be considered as welfare improving for all coexisting agents will be, in fact, rather limited. Outside the coverage of risks to which anybody feels immediately exposed with a significant probability, the main candidates for a direct unanimous support are transfers occurring rather late over the life-cycle, assuming that younger age groups are sufficiently non myopic to value them positively—and sufficiently confident in their durability.

3.4. Redistribution that can be explained by political processes[4]

This does not imply that we need to jump at once to the introduction of altruistic considerations for the explanation of existing redistributions. Some forms of non-Pareto improving redistributions can still be stable and collectively accepted by a community of selfish agents, because unanimity is not a necessary condition for this support. It is the purpose of politico-economic models to examine alternative conditions on collective decision processes which can guarantee stability for such forms of redistribution. Initially developed for examining the stability of income redistribution, these models have found some applications to questions more directly connected to social insurance.

[4] This section owes much to Casamatta (1999).

This subsection will shortly review this literature, whose contribution is important but which, in turn, will appear to remain fragile as long as it is not supplemented by the incorporation of one or another form of altruistic behavior or by the assumption that individual judgments about social insurance are also under the influence of individual norms going beyond pure self interest.

Let us start by recalling the problem in the simple case of pure income redistribution and where redistribution takes the form of a linear tax financing a uniform benefit b. If R is labor income before tax, the net tax takes the form

$$T(R) = tR - b. \tag{8}$$

A balanced budget implies $b = tR_m$, where R_m denotes average income. The problem is therefore the one-dimensional problem of collectively choosing the tax level t. This problem has a unique solution under a majority rule for all choices among pairs if preferences over t are unimodal, i.e., if values of t can be ordered in such a way that, for every agent i, there is unique level t_i^{opt} maximizing individual utility and such that utility declines when we progressively move away from this ideal point t_i^{opt} either to the left or to the right.

In this situation, the median voter theorem states that it is the median value of the distribution of t_i^{opt} among individuals which will be supported in a collectivity where decisions are taken under a simple majority rule. It is generally the case that t_i^{opt} will be monotonically and decreasingly related to individual productivity, so that the collective choice will conform to preferences of the individual with the median level of productivity.

In the simplest but very theoretical case where no disincentive effect would be associated to this form of linear taxation, the preferred value of t_i^{opt} is 1 for individuals with below average productivity and 0 for individuals with above average productivity. If median productivity is below average productivity, and this is generally the case, it is therefore a total redistribution which would be supported by the political process. In the more realistic case where a disincentive effect is associated with taxation, we have a Laffer curve effect, i.e., a hump-shaped relation between b and t. In that case the preferred value of t_i^{opt} is lower than 1, so that the political process will support some amount of incomplete redistribution. The median voter will vote for rate t which maximizes:

$$(1 - t)R + b(t), \tag{9}$$

where R is his own level of before tax income under the chosen taxation profile, after taking into account this individual's own arbitrage in terms of labor supply or effort.

Similar forms of reasoning can be and have been applied to questions more directly linked to the organization of social insurance (Epple and Romano, 1996). One simple transcription concerns health insurance, where b can be identified to the level of publicly financed health expenditures per capita. Political support can be guaranteed for a system where these expenditures are financed by contributions proportional to wages rather than by "actuarially neutral" contributions proportional to intensity of exposure to health risk. The analysis can be refined by taking into account the fact that b is not only a cash transfer, but corresponds to the provision of an insurance service which cannot be provided at all by any other mean, in case of complete market failure for the private provision. One point to be noted here is that the median voter, in that case, is no more necessarily the one with the median level of productivity. This can be the case if the demand for b increases with income (this median voter may even opt for an amount of insurance higher than the one desired by people with lower income).

If there is no market failure, or if this failure is only partial and only implies an extra-premium for the market provision of the same service, the analysis must be refined, and median voter models remain useful for that. The availability of the same service on the market under quasi-actuarial premiums will lower the amount of publicly financed health expenditure desired by high income groups. One particular and interesting implication concerns the fact that targeted systems, i.e., very redistributive systems where benefits are only directed towards very low income people can leave them worse-off than the less redistributive systems where the proportional tax finances a universal benefit. This will happen if these targeted benefits do not cover the median voter, in which case his preferred level of t and b will be zero.

Other applications of median voter models concern the case of pensions. This research strand was inaugurated by Browning (1975). In fact, the specific contribution of this paper was not specifically to show how the median voter hypothesis can explain the support for ascending intergenerational transfers, it was rather to show how this median voter hypothesis can account for an overprovision of such transfers. The idea is a simple one: preferences for a large amount of transfers are increasing with age: the closer the perspective of retirement, the higher is the relative weight given by the individual to large pension benefits compared to contributions, since the number of remaining years over which such contributions will be due to the pension system decreases. At the limit, the preferred contribution rate to the pension system for an individual on the verge of retirement or already retired is hundred per cent. Because of this positive relationship between age t_i^{opt}, the median voter is therefore an individual of median age, and even if he is working and not retired, his preferred contribution rate will be higher than the one chosen by the individual at the start of adult life, supposed to be more representative of the optimal allocation of resources over the entire life-cycle.

This very simple model has been extended to describe voting procedures over pension systems mixing the two dimensions of intergenerational and intragenerational vertical redistribution. In this class of models, coalitions can form between low or medium-pay workers and retired people for a system which is generous along these two dimensions (Casamatta et al., 2000a).

What conclusions can be drawn from this literature? It proposes interesting insights into factors allowing a strong stability for some forms of non Pareto improving redistributions, but remains unsatisfactory in many respects.

First, it is well known that unimodality of preferences does not hold anymore when we abandon the assumption of linear taxation profiles (even this linearity assumption, in fact, is not always sufficient to warrant unimodality). If unimodality does not hold, then we go back to the standard Arrovian case where no natural and unique winner exists in the collective decision process, and other assumptions have to be made to solve this problem, none of them being fully satisfactory.

Second and more crucial to our analysis, the representation of selfish voters seems to strongly violate simple empirical observations. The Browning model can be taken as an extreme but very illustrative example of these limits. First the assumption of pensioners opting for confiscatory levies on younger age groups seems naturally counterfactual. Of course, we can consider that pensioners are limited, in their choices, by their consciousness of Laffer curve effects due to excessive taxation. This should prevent them from imposing extreme tax levels over subsequent generations. But supposing that such strategic considerations are the only limit to their greediness still appears a poor stylization of real individual motives. Second, there is a symmetrical problem on the side of younger age groups, as soon as we consider problems of temporal consistency in collective choices. If collective decisions are not definitive but regularly submitted to new votes, then the selfish voter of median age should rather opt for a zero-transfer, since he has no reason to believe that the transfer he will have voted for will be confirmed by the next consultation. The natural equilibrium with selfish agents and repeated vote is an equilibrium without social security, rather than with excess social security. Cooperative intergenerational equilibria can still exist, if we assume that voting at a given point in time depends on the past history of votes. Individuals can vote for a positive transfer if they anticipate that such a vote will encourage the next generations to vote for the same level of transfer (Hammond, 1975; Cooley and Soares, 1999). But such equilibria are not renegotiation-proof (Persson and Tabellini, 1999) and can always be disrupted in favor of the autarkic equilibrium without intergenerational transfers. They obviously remain fragile, and this calls for the additional cement of one or another form of altruism, or of norms concerning "fair" levels of support for older generations.

4. Social transfers under altruism I: intra and intergenerational altruism as support for extended insurance

What are the principles that can be used to define "fair" levels of redistribution, and what are the forms of altruistic behavior we can rely on to explain or expect the actual implementation of these fair redistributions? This section will first focus on one way to tackle the *normative* part of this question, which is the notion of extended insurance. It deserves particular emphasis because of its conceptual filiation with the notions of simple or standard insurance which have been seen above to be at the core of efficiency theories of ST. And it is by reference to this approach that we will examine the contributions of altruistic behavior to the implementation of real world solidarities: these real world solidarities can be considered as offering a level of coverage intermediate between the pure Pareto improving insurance of efficiency theories and this notion of extended insurance. This normative concept of extended insurance, however, raises itself some problems, but their examination will be delayed until section 5.

4.1. A normative benchmark: redistribution as extended insurance

In section 3.2, it was shown how moving the time of insurance coverage backward increases the scope of redistribution. One application of this idea is to start insurance at birth, so as to cover all risks that unfold during life. But even this comprehensive insurance can be viewed as rather limited, since it cannot cover individual characteristics which are already known at birth, such as the family of birth, the environment, the observable part of the individual genetic endowment (sex, basic physical characteristics).

Now, the distribution of such characteristics across individuals is just as arbitrary as the allocation of random factors and accidents which later affect their lifetime. It is commonly described as the "birth lottery," and this phrase conveys the similarity with ordinary risks perfectly well.

A natural idea, along this vein, is to extend the scope of insurance to cover the risks inherent in the birth lottery. Once it is accepted that no one deserves the characteristics inherited at birth, and the social advantages they confer, any more than the consequences of later accidents in life, it is indeed a small step. If a well-off individual accepts to pay for a redistribution scheme that might have been in her interest when considering taking an insurance at birth, she should almost as easily accept to pay in the name of an insurance she might have taken *before* birth, under a "veil of ignorance" hiding her characteristics.

This idea of individuals considering what they would have done under ignorance of who they are has a long history and has been given a first systematic formulation by Harsanyi (1953). His main inspiration was not the extension of insurance, and was essentially related to the principle of impartiality and the definition of ethical preferences for an observer of social situations. Harsanyi observed that if an individual chooses the optimal allocation under ignorance of who she is, by relying on expected utility, her decision criterion is formally equivalent to the utilitarian criterion of average utility. If c_i denotes her consumption if she happens to be individual i (for $i = 1, \ldots, n$), her decision criterion will be

$$(1/n)u(c_1) + \cdots + (1/n)u(c_n) \tag{10}$$

and maximizing this is equivalent to maximizing the average utility as measured by function u.

In addition, a well-known consequence of utilitarianism is that, with a unique function u for all individuals, as above, and if the total consumption $c_1 + \cdots + c_n$ is fixed, then the optimal allocation equalizes marginal utility, and therefore consumption, across individuals, a result which can be related to the full insurance result obtained for actuarially neutral insurance.

The more specific idea of covering birth characteristics by insurance was later developed by Dworkin (1981), who coined the expression "hypothetical insurance," and Kolm (1985), who called it "fundamental insurance." In their view, this comprehensive kind of insurance not only permits to justify more ambitious forms of redistribution.

It seems that it can also provide indications about the size of transfers. What advantaged individuals pay, as a tax or social contribution, should correspond to the insurance premium, and what disadvantaged individuals receive, as a benefit, should be roughly equal to the indemnity relative to their particular condition. Actuarial neutrality of the insurance provided to the population simply corresponds, for the redistributive agency mimicking the hypothetical insurer, to balancing the budget of transfers. Then, if damage in birth characteristics can be measured in terms of financial loss as above, a balanced redistributive agency should fully insure individuals, implying a full neutralization of the consequences of the birth lottery. This result is nothing more, actually, than the equalization result obtained with utilitarianism.[5]

4.2. Altruism and support for partial extensions of insurance

This concept of extended insurance has been frequently used as a normative tool for the exploration of some of the redistributive dimensions of social insurance listed above, including intergenerational redistribution (Smith, 1982; Gordon and Varian, 1988). The analogy or continuity between insurance and income redistribution that it suggests has been also mobilized in the analysis of taxation (Varian, 1980).

The way we have introduced this notion of extended insurance suggests a direct link to the idea of altruism. One possible way to formalize altruism—among others—is to consider it as an expression of the ability of individual i to imagine himself in the place of individual j, and therefore to approach the original position. The link with the motivations for insurance in the VNM framework is immediate. I accept to pay for insurance *ex ante* in proportion to my capacity to imagine myself, tomorrow in such or such situation; I accept to pay for redistribution today in proportion to my capacity to imagine that I could have been, today, in such or such situation which is different from my current situation.

Now, this does not mean that actual altruism will lead to the full redistribution or full equalization of economic situations between individuals. Empirical observation shows that it does not go that far, and the positive question is to explain why. Two complementary explanations can be provided. One explanation is that this altruism is only partial and confined to limited groups of peers or closely related individuals. The second is that even fully altruistic agents will opt for limited redistribution or partially extended insurance if they know (or believe) that redistribution or insurance lead to disincentive or moral hazard effects. These problems of moral hazard have already been mentioned as limiting the scope for the private provision of insurance. Contrary to other causes of under-provision of insurance by private markets, they do not disappear under collectively managed social insurance, and apply to extended insurance as well.

We shall examine these two limits to altruism in turn. The first one, in fact, is rather trivial and does not deserve a long theoretical examination. The fact that altruism is

[5] On some differences between Kolm's fundamental insurance, Dworkin's hypothetical insurance, Harsanyism and utilitarianism, see Kolm (1996, 1998).

more likely to be observed towards peers or individuals to whom one is closely tied provides a simple explanation to the fact that non-market solidarities are more traditionally observed within the family, within closed social groups such as professions or local collectivities. In the family case, the border is, incidentally, difficult to draw between altruism as an expression of empathy (I easily imagine myself in the place of my kin), or altruism resulting from a direct concern for my kin's well being.

A priori, altruism toward peers is the most relevant for explaining actual forms taken by social insurance systems, at least in those Bismarckian countries where the primary organization of ST has been based on socio-professional membership. The link between family solidarity and the Welfare State looks less obvious, since the introduction of the Welfare State has rather corresponded to extensions of solidarity beyond the traditional family circle. This implicitly suggests that this form of altruism, which remains of course fundamental in the explanation of private intergenerational transfers, plays a much minor role in the explanation of support for collective social insurance. But this conclusion would be hasty, as one can also argue that family solidarity plays a large role in explaining support for collective redistributions. A mix of well-understood selfishness and family solidarity can and should be mobilized for explaining the rather strong support which exists in favor of collective intergenerational transfers.

The reason is that agents whose altruism is limited to the family should be inclined to support social programs in which they have no direct private interest but which are of potential interest for other members of their families. This solution is preferable for them to manifesting this altruism through direct transfers within the family, precisely because such transfers provide very limited means of risk pooling. For instance, individuals who are themselves insulated from unemployment risk (civil servants, pensioners) can nevertheless prefer large public programs for the unemployed rather than facing the risk of directly endorsing support for unemployed members of their families. Adult children can prefer a collective financing of pensions or of old age dependency, even if their intergenerational altruism is only directed toward their own parents and not to the entireness of older generations. The reason for this is that this collective support can offer a better protection to these parents than the one they can individually offer. For instance, this can explain the large amount of redistribution directed toward the first generation of retired people when a PAYG pension system is set up. Hansson and Stuart (1989) propose a model which builds upon altruism toward the first generation of pensioners and altruism of all subsequent generations of workers toward their parents to explain a phenomenon of permanent lock-in in a PAYG system even when this system is less efficient in the long run than the fully funded one.[6] Intergenerational altruism is also introduced in a model of politico-economic equilibrium by Tabellini (2000), to jointly explain intra and intergenerational redistribution by the pension system.

Incidentally, family solidarity probably plays a role in explaining the fact that there is little contestation on redistributions between genders generated by social insurance and

[6] See also Lindbeck and Weibull (1988), for a parallel argument.

social security: these redistributions remain actuarially neutral for the dominant model of the altruistically linked couple.

On the other hand, the relatively low level of vertical mobility from one generation to the next generally implies that family solidarity will not constitute a sufficient motive for supporting large vertical redistributions. This provides a first explanation for a lower collective support for this vertical redistribution than for other forms of redistribution provided by the welfare state.

But an additional explanation of this specific point can be provided by the second factor suggested above, the role of incentive or moral hazard problems.

4.3. Extended insurance and altruism under incentive constraints

Even for a fully altruistic individual with extreme risk aversion placing himself behind the veil of ignorance, full coverage of all risks likely to occur over one's existence, including the one of being born with low abilities or social capital, is not the optimal solution, as soon as this redistribution or this coverage are likely to affect behavior in a way or another. This includes disincentive effects—such as the incidence of redistribution on effort or labor supply—as well as moral hazard effects—modifications of behavior toward risk once redistribution or insurance have been set up. These disincentive effects create, for the benevolent individual, a form of Samaritan's dilemma (Buchanan, 1975): opting for a maximal amount of redistribution could end up leaving every one worse off, whereas maintaining appropriate incentive levels requires a limited redistribution. "Rational" altruism should lead to the second option.

Formal representations of this optimal choice are well known. Figure 3 gives the usual graphical representation for the maximization of a collective or expected utility

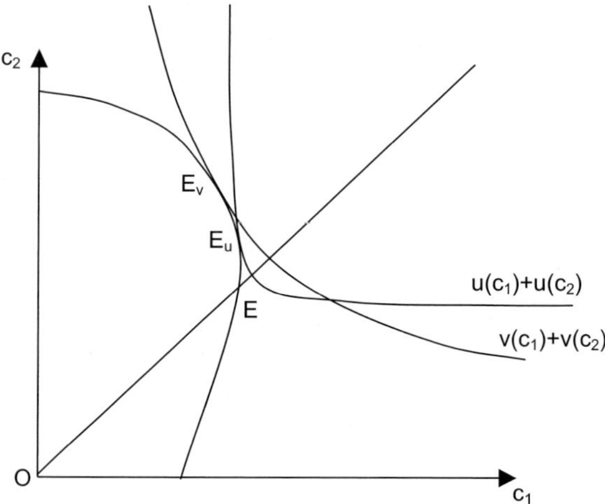

Figure 3.

function such as (10) if there is an incentive effect implying a contraction of total production $c_1 + c_2$ when the allocation of this total production between individuals 1 and 2 becomes increasingly equal. Maximization of the expected utilities behind the veil of ignorance (i.e., before the individual knows whether he will be of type 1 or of type 2), or equivalently of the aggregate ex post utility leads to optimal points such as E_v or E_u, whose positions depend on the exact shape of individual utilities, and which will be increasingly close to the point of full equality E when risk aversion or aversion for inequality increase, but which will never attain point E, even in the extreme "Rawlsian" case of the degenerate maximin utility $\min\{c_1, c_2\}$ corresponding to the limit value, for $\gamma \to \infty$ of the sum of individual utilities of the form $c_i^{1-\gamma}/(1-\gamma)$.

A parallel result can be formulated in the framework of section 3.2, assuming for instance that the fact of belonging to the classes of "good" or "bad" risks depends upon an unobserved effort taking two modalities, $e = 1$ for which $p(e) = p_L$ and $e = 0$ for which $p(e) = p_H$, with a cost of effort $c(e) = c$, which enters additively in the VNM utility function.[7] This function becomes, for a level of effort e:

$$V = p(e)u(R - \pi + q - D) + (1 - p(e))u(R - \pi) - c(e). \tag{11}$$

Equation (12) immediately shows that, under full insurance, the individual is never motivated to provide a prevention effort, since V collapses to:

$$V = u(R - \pi) - c(e), \tag{12}$$

which is monotonically decreasing in e. We will have therefore, in equilibrium, $p = p_H$, which will be a Pareto-dominated equilibrium, if the gain of collectively shifting to $p = p_b$ exceeds the sum of individual costs $c(e)$. This coordination problem, which occurs when effort is not observable, can be solved only through an under-provision of insurance. Incentive problems, here again, imply less than full insurance.

How can these ideas be mobilized more precisely to explain differences in support for various components of ST? The point is that the lower the suspicion of disincentive or moral hazard effects, the larger the collective support for redistribution from altruistic agents.

- Redistribution along dimensions of heterogeneity which are completely independent of individual behavior does not raise such problems, and altruistic agents will then be naturally ready to accept large redistributions. This includes redistribution across age groups, gender, but also across health status, as long as one is considered as being not or little responsible for this health status.
- Redistribution along the income dimension, on the other hand, is considered more likely to produce negative effects on total output, and will be more limited. This is not to say that agents consider that income is only the result of individual effort and that, for this reason, income redistribution should be avoided. This means that,

[7] This is only the case of *ex ante* moral hazard (modification of behavior before the realization of the risk). *Ex post* moral hazard (different behavior after realization of the risk) raises similar problems.

concerning income levels, the relative roles played by fatality or social determinism on the one side and individual effort on the other side are more balanced and/or less easy to sort out, since there are limited possibilities for the observation of individual abilities, and this pleads in favor of a more limited compensation of these forms of inequalities than of forms of inequalities due to health or age.

Piketty (1995) develops such explanation of the limited amount of income redistribution by insisting on the fact that this incorporation of incentive constraints in individual attitudes toward redistribution levels reflects beliefs at least as much as objective empirical observation of these disincentive effects, and that changes in levels of protection or political conflict over the desirable amount of redistribution will reflect changes or diversity of such beliefs.

Some other refinements of this approach could also be considered. The following question, in particular, must be raised. If agents are altruistic, this should, in principle, also preserve them from opportunistic behaviors which are at the root of disincentive or moral hazard problems. Altruism should both imply generous transfers from the better-off and a parsimonious reliance on these transfers by the least well-off. To our knowledge, such a track has not been followed much in the literature. Lindbeck's (Lindbeck, 1995a, 1995b, 1999) observations on the hazardous dynamics of the welfare state are however close to this point, the suggestion being the existence of two potential equilibria for the welfare state. The first would combine generosity (altruism) and responsibility, with a high protection but a take-up of benefits auto-limited to those who really deserve it. The second one would combine abuse by an increasing population of beneficiaries, leading to a reduced average generosity. Lindbeck suggests that the second state would be unfortunately more stable than the first one. When an increasing proportion of people adopt an opportunistic behavior, the remaining part of the population is increasingly induced to adopt the same behavior. Another possibility, closer to Piketty's approach, could be to consider that the existence of these two equilibria can be the source of a political cycle implying alternative phases of development or retrenchment of the welfare state.

Last, it must be recalled that disincentives or moral hazard effects can, in some instances, present some positive externalities, a point developed for instance by Sinn (1995): unemployment insurance or redistribution can stimulate growth through greater risk taking or by encouraging sectorial mobility, the negative effect of pensions on labor supply can also be beneficial, in some contexts (Sala-I-Martin, 1996). But this implies support for these systems both by the altruistic and selfish agents, so that we are brought back to the efficiency approach.

5. Social transfers under altruism II: other normative principles for a well-defined altruism?

The link between fundamental insurance and utilitarianism which has been stressed in the previous section has been commented by several authors, including Roemer (1985), who pointed out that their nice equality results in simple cases are accompanied by less nice consequences in slightly different contexts. This last section will first review objections to these two twin concepts, and, then, propose a brief survey of other potential approaches to the design of optimal redistributions.

The orientation of this last section, therefore, will be definitely normative. But this closer inspection of normative questions remains strongly linked with the general topic of altruism and its role in the analysis of ST. A thorough study of normative concepts is indeed of interest to the altruistic observer who wants to assess the quality of various distributions of resources and it may influence the political debate, between altruistic agents, about the choice of institutions for the redistributive system. In particular, it may help these altruistic individuals to give a precise political shape to their a priori vague benevolent feelings toward their fellow citizens. Contrary to ordinary tastes, which are, according to the consumer sovereignty principle, supposedly indisputable, altruistic feelings can be submitted to rational analysis and related to fundamental ethical principles. If an altruist individual feels that she wants the best for her country or for the planet, this just begs the question of what "the best" is. A normative theory of the just distribution of resources is therefore useful at the very basic level of preference formation.

5.1. Some pitfalls of fundamental insurance

There are limits to the appealing notion of hypothetical or fundamental insurance discussed and applied in section 4. In order to introduce the issues, let us first come back to Harsanyi's impartial observer argument. If individuals in the population have different utility functions u_i, then the observer should probably reckon that if she happens to be individual i, she will not only have consumption i, but also other characteristics, those of individual i, which will make her enjoy this consumption with utility function u_i. Harsanyi's analysis was actually presented in this fuller form, and the impartial observer's criterion should be

$$(1/n)u_1(c_1) + \cdots + (1/n)u_n(c_n), \tag{13}$$

which again corresponds to the utilitarian criterion for this population.

But utilitarianism in this broader form does no longer entail egalitarianism in resources. If total consumption is fixed, the optimal allocation will still equalize marginal utilities

$$u_i'(c_i) = u_j' c_j), \tag{14}$$

but this will no longer equalize consumptions. It will not even equalize *levels* of utilities. And this, as emphasized by Sen (1973), may be quite disturbing.

Sen's example is depicted on Figure 4. It shows the utilities of two individuals, 1 and 2, as a function of their consumption. Individual 1 is an ordinary individual, while individual is identical to 1 except for a particular handicap which makes him less happy. If one wanted to equalize utility levels across these two individuals, one should obviously

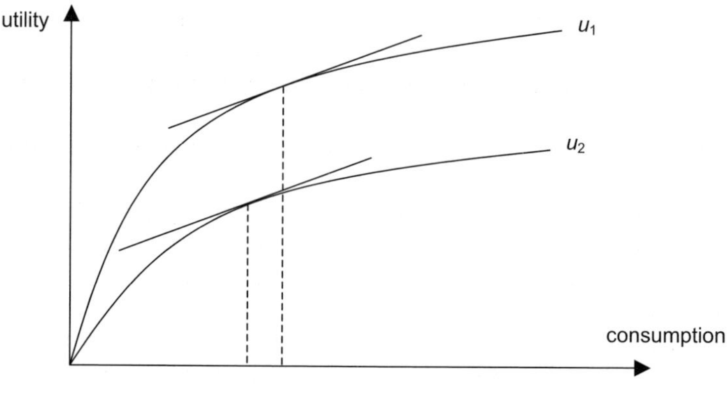

Figure 4.

give more resources to individual 2, and it is quite intuitive that the handicapped individual should receive more. But this is not the outcome if one tries instead to equalize marginal utilities. As illustrated on the figure, equality of marginal utility requires giving more resources to individual 1, because she enjoys consumption more, and this not only goes against the intuitive direction of transfer, it also widens the utility gap between the two individuals. As is now well understood, the root of this problem is simply that the utilitarian criterion displays no aversion to inequality of utilities. The fact that an individual has a lower utility level is in itself no reason to transfer any resources to him, under application of the utilitarian rule. Only marginal utilities matter for this criterion, which is a very serious drawback.

This drawback, unfortunately, affects fundamental insurance as well. What may happen with birth characteristics, more than with ordinary damages of life, is that they modify the utility function itself. The expected utility criterion, on which individual insurance decisions are based, is then applied to *state-dependent* VNM functions. Suppose that a particular damage in birth characteristics does not only imply a financial loss of D, but also transforms the utility function from u to v, with $v(c) < u(c)$ and $v'(c) < u'(c)$ for all $c > 0$.

In absence of insurance, the expected utility is equal to

$$V_0 = pv(R - D) + (1 - p)u(R), \tag{15}$$

while the possibility to obtain an indemnity q at the cost of a premium π transforms it into

$$V_1 = pv(R - D + q - \pi) + (1 - p)u(R - \pi). \tag{16}$$

If the insurance is actuarially neutral, one has $\pi = pq$, and then the optimal allocation of resources across states of nature for the individual is such that marginal utilities are equal. But this requires that the consumption is inferior in case of damage:

$$R - D + q - \pi < R - \pi, \tag{17}$$

implying $q < D$. In the particular case when the financial loss D is null, and the damage has a pure utility impact ($v \neq u$), this inequality requires $q < 0$, which means that the individual would like to take a counter-insurance, that is, to insure against the absence of damage!

One may accept that an individual decides to buy little insurance against a damage which reduces his marginal utility, and this may, in addition to myopia and other psychological phenomena, partly explain some of the apparently insufficient insurance that individuals spontaneously take in general. The problem with fundamental insurance is that this same fact is applied to different individuals. Under fundamental insurance, it should entail that individuals with unfavorable birth characteristics ought to receive little help, or would even be taxed in favor of more advantaged individuals.

As analyzed by Roemer (1985), related problems occur when birth characteristics do not affect individual utilities, but affect their productivities, and therefore their wages on the labor market. As it may also happen with the utilitarian criterion (Mirrless, 1974), the paradoxical consequence is then that, in a first-best situation, the fundamental insurance market will lead to an allocation in which the more talented individuals will end up worse-off than the less talented individuals.

These difficulties, similar for utilitarianism and for fundamental insurance, can be traced to a common feature. These approaches fail to take account of the separateness of persons, as was argued by Rawls (1971) against utilitarianism. In the case of fundamental insurance, one may criticize the fact that transfers between different persons are adjudicated on the basis of transfers between states of nature by one and the same person. It is hard to accept the fundamental insurance line of reasoning according to which, when an individual is ready to sacrifice his own welfare in an uncertain future state of nature, this justifies sacrificing a subpopulation which is existing for sure and is suffering already.

As argued by Kolm (1996), this critical argument can actually be extended to all theories of distributive justice based on veil-of-ignorance schemes, including Rawls' theory. Transforming issues of interpersonal transfers into issues of intrapersonal allocation dilutes the importance of the special care and respect that different persons deserve to be granted.

It is worth noting here that less dramatic but somehow related difficulties occur with any system of insurance, not only with fundamental insurance. When making insurance decisions separately, individuals shape the distribution of resources in the various possible states of nature, without taking account of the consequences their decisions have on ex post inequalities.[8] As an illustration, consider the choice between prevention and rescue policies in health care. A given amount of resources might be saved for one of two uses. Either they are spent for a prevention campaign that reduces the probability of a bad health condition from p to $p' < p$. Or they are spent on cure treatments for those who are hit by the condition, and raise their utility level from u_w to $u_m > u_w$.

[8] This issue has been discussed in particular by Broome (1991).

Suppose that u_g is the utility of those in good health. The two policies might ex ante be equivalent for all individuals, if they happened to yield equal expected utilities:

$$p' u_w + (1 - p') u_g = p u_m + (1 - p) u_g. \tag{18}$$

But the ex post distributions, which are known for sure at the social level, are quite different. With the prevention policy, a small minority p' of the population will be in the harsh condition u_w, whereas with the rescue policy, a larger proportion of the population will be in the milder condition u_m. Even if all individuals are ex ante indifferent, one may reasonably contradict the Pareto criterion and express a strict preference, at the social level, for one policy over the other. It may even be sensible to go against unanimous *strict preferences* of the population. Suppose the population slightly but strictly prefers the prevention policy ex ante. It would not be necessarily unreasonable to go against such preferences in order to avoid sacrificing the small minority which will be hit by the condition anyway. The main lesson here is that the Pareto criterion cannot be applied to *ex ante* expected utilities as unquestionably as to ordinary preferences under certainty.[9]

5.2. Social welfare with an egalitarian flavor

If fundamental insurance or traditional utilitarianism are not reliable ethical criteria for the assessment of redistributive institutions, one has to look for better alternatives. A very natural alternative is offered by inequality-averse generalizations of utilitarianism. While utilitarianism focuses on the simple sum of utilities

$$u_1 + \cdots + u_n, \tag{19}$$

generalized forms rely on transformations of utilities

$$\varphi(u_1) + \cdots + \varphi(u_n). \tag{20}$$

If the transformation φ is strictly concave, this introduces an aversion to inequality of utilities. Such inequality-aversion may alleviate the kind of problem illustrated on Figure 4 above, by giving priority to agents with low utility.[10]

One important problem in the application of any of these SWFs is how to measure individual utilities in an appropriate way. One should distinguish between a pragmatic and an ethical part of this problem. The pragmatic part is that the measurement of individual utilities has to be precise enough so that they may serve as a meaningful input in the SWFs. The ethical part has to do with the choice of an ethically relevant concept of well-being. The issue of measuring individual well-being in a relevant way

[9] For further elaborations on this topic, see Hammond (1982) and Ben Porath et al. (1997).

[10] The literature on such inequality-averse social welfare functions (SWFs) is immense, and useful surveys have been written by d'Aspremont (1985), Sen (1986), Bossert and Weymark (2000), among many others. On the related topic of the measurement of inequality, see Lambert (1989) or Silber (1999).

actually belongs to the realm of political philosophy more than economics. One interesting development in political philosophy deserves to be mentioned here. Rawls (1971), Dworkin (1981) and Sen (1979), in particular, have similarly argued that the traditional utilitarian focus on subjective satisfaction, with which economists are familiar, was questionable. Roughly speaking, their argument is that social justice implies a division of labor between social institutions and individual initiative. The former should only provide resources and background conditions on which the latter may be exercised in order to lead to eventual individual achievements.

Rawls and Dworkin proposed to define justice in terms of equality of resources, leaving it to individuals to make use of those resources as a function of their personal preferences and goals in life. This approach considers that individuals should be held responsible for their preferences, even though they have not controlled their formation. In particular, one argument is that it would incongruous for an individual to ask for an additional share of resources on the ground that he has more ambitious goals requiring more expenses to be achieved similarly as others. Authors such as Arneson (1989) and Cohen (1989) have objected that individuals should be held responsible only for their genuine choices, and that expensive preferences as such may justify help if their formation was not under the control of the individual. These authors' theories are then formulated in terms of equality of opportunities.

The main upshot of such theories is that inequalities may be legitimate when they are traceable to the exercise of individual responsibility. These abstract considerations thus have echoes in more concrete debates about the sustainability of the welfare state. The recent mood that bends toward screening the "deserving poor" from the rest of the needy seems to receive support from political philosophy.

Part of this convergence is perfectly unquestionable. Incentive compatibility in and of itself requires letting individuals suffer at least part of the consequences of their choices. A redistribution system which equalizes individual achievements without taking account of the possibility for individuals to exploit it in order to obtain the same benefits as others without exerting any effort would simply not be viable. As a simple example, consider a problem similar to that illustrated on Figure 4. Two individuals have different utilities u_1 and u_2, and one considers helping the worst-off. But suppose that utility functions are not observable directly. Incentive compatibility requires respecting the self-selection constraints

$$u_i(c_i) \geq u_i(c_j) \quad \text{for } i, j = 1, 2. \tag{21}$$

If consumption is one-dimensional, this simply requires $c_1 = c_2$, which means that the worst-off cannot benefit from any transfer, and has to suffer the consequences of his lower utility. If he can rightly be considered responsible for this less favorable utility function, then ethics and incentive-compatibility have the same consequences and support equality of resources. This is an example in terms of adverse selection, but moral hazard problems are even more prone to such a convergence, since individual choice plays a direct role there. If, for instance, individuals can affect the cost of curing a disease, then incentive compatibility may require letting them bear part of the cost, and ethics may also declare that this is justified.

This convergence, however, is obtained only when the set of unobservable characteristics and individual decisions coincides with the set of characteristics and decisions for which individuals are responsible. If individuals are not deemed responsible for some of those characteristics and decisions, then incentive compatibility prevents some desirable redistribution. The converse situation is less problematic. If some responsibility-laden characteristics or decisions are nonetheless observable, it is still perfectly feasible for the redistributive institutions to ignore those variables and let individuals suffer the related consequences. Physical ugliness is a well known example of an observed characteristic which does not elicit much social help, in spite of its documented consequences over success in social relations and professional careers.[11]

But, more generally, one should be very careful when invoking individual responsibility.[12] The boundary between resources and preferences (in Rawls' and Dworkin's theories), or between opportunities and effort (in other theories), is very thin, and its location is uncertain. For instance, an individual who forms the goal of becoming a manual worker may just adapt to his apparent lack of intellectual ability, and forgo valuable possibilities that a more voluntary system of education would have permitted. Similarly, an individual who, in spite of apparent good conditions, falls into alcoholism and fails in her career may be the victim of a hidden trauma. Therefore, invoking responsibility may too hastily justify cutting welfare programs, when it is decided, on more or less arbitrary or ideological grounds, that some subpopulations do not deserve to be helped any more. Notice that it may also happen, on the contrary, that theories of responsibility push us back toward a welfarist kind of satisfaction catering. If, for instance, it is declared that every macroscopic phenomenon is causally determined, and that, as a consequence, no one is ever responsible for her decisions or characteristics, then equality of opportunity should boil down to equality of full outcomes.

5.3. *Equity criteria in search of second-best applications*

Theories of justice in terms of equality of resources have a feature which should be attractive to economists. They justify disregarding individual subjective utility, and focusing at most on individual preferences in the process of evaluating resources. Indeed, since individuals are responsible for their ambitions, an individual with a normal share of resources (including personal characteristics ranked among internal resources) but a low utility because of excessive ambitions has no claim on social help.

Assessing social states of affairs on the basis of individual preferences only, and ignoring utilities, was the goal of New Welfare Economics and was passed on to the theory

[11] Theories of equality of resources or opportunities would likely advocate some help in this case. The fact that help is not organized is probably due to social conventions, and also to the fact that an official recognition of ugliness would be considered a lack of respect.

[12] For criticisms and alternative proposals, see e.g., Fleurbaey (1995, 2001) and Anderson (1999).

of social choice, as posited by Arrow (1951). It was also the aim of the theory of equity or fairness, whose foundational stone was Kolm's book *Justice et équité* (Kolm, 1972).[13] The theory of social choice has been producing mainly negative results for decades, because of its focus on Arrow's impossibility theorem, whose validity in many contexts has been thoroughly checked. In contrast, the theory of equity has developed a number of interesting concepts and solutions. Two main concepts of equity, or fairness, have been put forth. The first one is the no-envy criterion, which refers to situations where one agent would rather consume another agent's bundle. Let $>_i$ (resp. $\geq_i, \sim_i$) denotes agent i's strict preferences (resp. weak preferences, indifference). Agent i is said to envy agent j when $c_j >_i c_i$. An allocation is envy-free[14] whenever for all i, j, $c_i \geq_i c_j$. The second concept is that of egalitarian-equivalence, which refers to a situation in which all agents are indifferent between their current bundle and one particular bundle. That is, for every i, $c_i \sim_i c^*$ (or, more generally, $c_i \sim_i c_i^*$, where c_i^* is i's best choice in an option set C^*). Other concepts of fairness include the right for everyone to be at least as well-off as at an equal-split allocation of the available resources; the solidarity of all agents with respect to changes in the environment (resources, population size, preferences), implying that agents not directly involved in the change should be affected all positively or all negatively.

The theory of equity, in contrast to the theory of social choice, has many positive results, including axiomatic characterizations of solutions such as the Walrasian allocations with equal budgets (i.e., competitive equilibria in which all agents have equal endowments). But most of its results deal with the problem of first-best allocation in rather simple models, and have little relevance for the design of second-best institutions of ST and PA. This is why second-best issues are usually tackled with more traditional SWFs.

One way to make fairness concepts relevant to second-best issues would be to extend the solutions, which are defined in terms of subsets of first-best allocations, into full-fledged rankings of all allocations. With a social ranking of all allocations, the selection of second-best allocations would then be just a matter of maximizing the social ranking under the incentive compatibility constraints which make the second-best context differ from the first-best context.

But this direction is usually considered to be a blind alley, because of Arrow's impossibility theorem. The positive results of the theory of fairness are indeed commonly attributed to the fact that, contrary to Arrovian social choice, it does not seek to define full-fledged rankings, but only to determine the first-best selection.[15] This view, albeit widespread, is nonetheless incorrect. From a purely formal standpoint, a selection of a subset does define a complete preorder over all allocations. This preorder is coarse

[13] Extensive surveys of the last two theories are available in Arrow et al. (1997).

[14] The relation between this concept and the psychological feeling of "envy" is a debated topic. Notice that no consumption externality is assumed here, individual preferences bear only on personal bundles.

[15] This explanation is endorsed by Sen (1986) and by Moulin and Thomson (1996).

and has only two equivalence classes (the selected subset and the rest), but it is a pre-order, i.e., a reflexive and transitive binary relation. The important consequence of this observation is that the Arrovian theory of social choice and the theory of fairness actually do essentially the same exercise, namely, defining a social ranking on the basis of individual preferences. The positive results of the theory of fairness should not be sought in its supposedly different goal, but are mainly due to the fact that it relies on more information about individual preferences than Arrow allowed in the conditions of his theorem.[16] Arrow, in his famous axiom of Independence of Irrelevant Alternatives, required the comparison of two allocations to rely only upon the individual pairwise preferences over these two allocations. This extremely demanding restriction makes it impossible, for instance, to check whether an individual envies another, or is indifferent between her bundle and a benchmark c^*. The fairness concepts require more information in order to assess whether an allocation is acceptable or not.

On the basis of these remarks, one may ask whether the kind of information about individual preferences that is used in the theory of fairness would be enough to define fine-grained (and not only "full-fledged") rankings of all allocations. The answer is definitely positive, according to Fleurbaey and Maniquet (1996), who give examples of such rankings and provide a general method to transform a first-best solution into a fine-grained ranking. Such rankings may then be used in the analysis of income redistribution and ST.[17]

5.4. *Altruistic preferences and social welfare*

It has been argued above that theories of social welfare may be helpful for altruists who are looking for a well-founded formulation of their altruism, but one may ask if, conversely, the degree and direction of altruism in a given society should influence the definition of social welfare. Should a more altruistic population, for instance, lead to more egalitarian social preferences?

As a preliminary remark, it must be said that even for a purely selfish population, it makes sense to define social welfare, equity criteria, and the like. Even when individuals ignore issues of justice and only seek their own advantage, an outside or ideal observer may still make judgments about the ethical value of the arrangements made by the population. Therefore, it is out of question to define social welfare entirely and exclusively as a function of altruistic feelings.

But this reservation does not preclude adjusting some features of social preferences to the degree of altruism exhibited by the population. A pragmatic argument suggests that this is inevitable. Many details of the allocation of resources are decided by individuals in small-scale decisions that belong entirely to their private sphere. Christmas

[16] See Fleurbaey and Maniquet (1996) and Fleurbaey et al. (2005) for details on this point.

[17] For applications of this approach to income redistribution, see Fleurbaey and Maniquet (2002, 2006) and Fleurbaey (2003). Fleurbaey (2005) makes an application to health insurance.

gifts, for instance, alter the allocation of resources. It would seem very strange to have social preferences declaring these transfers undesirable, and advocating public policies designed to counter, in some way or other, the consequences of those transfers. In other words, the importance of the basic freedom of giving apparently constrains the formulation of social preferences.

The introduction of altruism in social preferences has, however, mostly been considered from a different perspective. In a welfarist approach to social preferences, individual well-being is viewed as a measure of subjective satisfaction, and subjective satisfaction normally includes the satisfaction of altruistic desires. But this seems to raise several problems.

Consider two individuals, Ann and Bob. Suppose that Ann is altruistic while Bob is purely selfish. Let u_A, u_B denote the personal part of their utility, and U_A denote Ann's overall utility. Ann's altruism means that her overall utility is a function of both u_A and u_B:

$$U_A = f(u_A, u_B), \tag{22}$$

which means that social welfare applied to the two individuals utilities would have u_B appear twice:

$$W(U_A, u_B) = W(f(u_A, u_B), u_B). \tag{23}$$

This introduces some partiality of social preferences in favor of Bob. It may look strange that social preferences seemingly reward the selfish and penalize the altruist.

It must noted, however, that the degree to which social preferences are distorted in favor of Bob depends on the shape of the functions f and W. The usual analysis of this "double-counting" problem is based on the utilitarian criterion. Suppose

$$f(u_A, u_B) = u_A + u_B \tag{24}$$

and

$$W(U_A, u_B) = U_A + u_B. \tag{25}$$

Then, indeed, one obtains

$$W(U_A, u_B) = u_A + 2u_B, \tag{26}$$

implying that Bob is given twice as great a weight as Ann. But if instead one had a different kind of altruism, in conformity with an egalitarian ethics:

$$f(u_A, u_B) = \min\{u_A, u_B\} \tag{27}$$

and

$$W(U_A, u_B) = \min\{U_A, u_B\}, \tag{28}$$

one would eventually have

$$W(U_A, u_B) = \min\{u_A, u_B\}. \tag{29}$$

In this case, no distorsion in favor of Bob is created by Ann's altruism.

Should altruism be left to create partiality in social preferences, when this occurs as in the utilitarian example above? This question may be embedded in the broader question of the role of moral, political and more generally "non-personal" preferences. The idea that sadist or malevolent preferences could distort a social welfare function in favor of the individuals endowed with anti-social preferences has been used in particular as an argument against welfarism (Sen, 1979). The standard response of welfarists, such as Goodin (1986) and Harsanyi (1982), is that anti-social preferences should be removed from consideration, by "laundering" preferences and removing those unrespectable features. But it is not obvious that altruistic preferences should be given a different treatment, since they also lead to rewarding the selfish, which is not much more acceptable than rewarding the sadist.

A slightly different, but related difficulty with the incorporation of altruistic preferences is the following. Suppose that Ann, in the first example above, adopts utilitarian personal preferences out of a commitment for utilitarianism in general. Then she would prefer the social welfare function *not* to take account of this, because social preferences biased in favor of Bob would then contradict Ann's utilitarian views. Ann would certainly prefer that social decisions conform to an impartial version of utilitarianism, as in her own altruistic preferences. In other words, the same concern for impartiality that may motivate altruism in individual preferences seems to justify disregarding altruistic preferences in the computation of social welfare.

Other approaches to social justice, such as Rawls' theory, do not take account of non-personal preferences at all for more basic reasons. The idea, in such theories, is that social justice does not have to do with the distribution of satisfaction, be it selfish or altruistic, but only with the allocation of resources. Whether, with fair endowments of resources, individuals decide to pursue altruistic or more down-to-earth goals is, then, their own responsibility. The final allocation of resources will be influenced by altruism, but fairness of initial endowments is all that matters.

6. Conclusion

Theories of ST based on the assumption of self interest are not incorrect or useless, but remain incomplete. The economic analysis of ST has to walk on two legs: self-interest and altruism. The systems which will be the most stable are generally those which rely on these two elements.

This should allow breaking the exclusive focus on efficiency justifications to social insurance, which has characterized most of the existing literature to date, and calls therefore for renewed efforts on normative bases for the design of ST and PA. Most of the literature which tried to address these questions, for practical reasons, has been based on simple utilitarian criteria, or their transcription in terms of "extended insurance," including the basic textbook version of the Rawlsian approach—the maximin—as a limit case of fundamental insurance with extreme risk aversion. But these approaches are not without flaws and some of their conclusions may be questioned. Shifting to altruistically based theories of the welfare state should stimulate the exploration of practical consequences of alternative normative criteria: a flavor of tracks opened by these alternative approaches has been proposed in the last section of this chapter. Some further research undoubtedly needs to be done along these dimensions, in parallel with the incorporation of elements of altruism in positive models of the welfare state and in parallel with empirical research on the strength of these altruistic motives.

References

Anderson, E. (1999). "What is the point of equality?". Ethics 109, 287–337.
Arneson, R.J. (1989). "Equality and equal opportunity for welfare". Philosophical Studies 56, 77–93.
Arrow, K.J. (1951). Social Choice and Individual Values. John Wiley, New York.
Arrow, K.J., Sen, A.K., Suzumura, K. (Eds.) (1997). Social Choice Re-examined. Macmillan and St. Martin's Press, London and New York.
d'Aspremont, C. (1985). "Axioms for social welfare orderings". In: Hurwicz, L., Schmeidler, D., Sonnenschein, H. (Eds.), Social Goals and Social Organization. Cambridge University Press, Cambridge.
Barr, N. (1992). "Economic theory and the welfare state: a survey and interpretation". Journal of Economic Literature 30, 741–803.
Barro, R.J. (1974). "Are government bonds net wealth?". Journal of Political Economy 82, 1095–1117.
Ben Porath, E., Gilboa, I., Schmeidler, D. (1997). "On the measurement of inequality under uncertainty". Journal of Economic Theory 75, 194–204.
Bodie, Z. (1990). "Pensions as retirement income insurance". Journal of Economic Literature 28 (1), 28–49.
Börsch-Supan, A., Reil-Held, A. (2001). "How much is transfer and how much is insurance in a pay-as-you-go system? The German case". Scandinavian Journal of Economics 103 (3), 505–524.
Bossert, W., Weymark, J. (2000). "Utility in social choice". In: Barbera, S., Hammond, P.J., Seidl, C. (Eds.), Handbook of Utility Theory, vol. 2. Kluwer, Dordrecht, forthcoming.
Broome, J. (1991). Weighing Goods. Basil Blackwell, Oxford.
Browning, E.K. (1975). "Why the social insurance budget is too large in a democracy". Economic Inquiry 13, 373–388.
Buchanan, J. (1975). "The Samaritan's dilemna". In: Phelps, E.S. (Ed.), Altruism, Morality and Economic Theory. Russel Sage Foundation, New York.
Burkhauser, R., Warlick, J. (1981). "Disentalgling the annuity from the redistriutive aspects of social security in the United States". Review of Income and Wealth 27, 401–421.
Casamatta G. (1999). "L'économie politique de la protection sociale et de la redistribution". PhD Thesis, University of Toulouse.
Casamatta, G., Cremer, H., Pestieau, P. (2000a). "The political economy of social security". The Scandinavian Journal of Economics 3, 102.
Cohen, G.A. (1989). "On the currency of egalitarian justice". Ethics 99, 906–944.
Cooley, T.F., Soares, J. (1999). "A positive theory of social security based on reputation". Journal of Political Economy 107, 135–160.
Dworkin, R. (1981). "What is equality? Part 2: Equality of resources". Philosophy & Public Affairs 10, 283–345.
Epple, D., Romano, R. (1996). "Public provision of private goods". Journal of Political Economy 104, 57–84.
Eckstein, Z., Eichenbaum, M., Peled, D. (1985). "Uncertain lifetimes and the welfare enhancing properties of annuity markets and social security". Journal of Public Economics 26, 303–326.
Fleurbaey, M. (1995). "Equal opportunity or equal social outcome?". Economics & Philosophy 11, 25–55.
Fleurbaey, M. (2001). "Egalitarian opportunities". Law and Philosophy 20, 499–530.
Fleurbaey, M. (2003). "Social welfare, priority to the worst-off and the dimensions of individual well-being". In: Farina, F., Savaglio, E. (Eds.), Inequality and Economic Integration. Routledge, London, in press.

Fleurbaey, M. (2005). "Health, wealth and fairness". Journal of Public Economic Theory 7, 253–284.
Fleurbaey, M., Maniquet, F. (1996). "Utilitarianism versus fairness in welfare economics". In: Salles, M., Weymark, J.A. (Eds.), Justice, Political Liberalism and Utilitarianism: Themes from Harsanyi and Rawls. Cambridge University Press, Cambridge.
Fleurbaey, M., Maniquet, F. (2002). "Help the low-skilled or let the hardworking thrive? A study of fairness in optimal income taxation". Univ. of Namur and Univ. of Pau, mimeo.
Fleurbaey, M., Maniquet, F. (2006). "Fair income tax". Review of Economic Studies 73, 55–83.
Fleurbaey, M., Tadenuma, K., Suzumura, K. (2005). "The informational basis of the theory of fair allocation". Social Choice and Welfare 24, 311–342.
Goodin, R. (1986). "Laundering preferences". In: Elster, J., Hylland, A. (Eds.), Foundations of Social Choice Theory. Cambridge University Press, Cambridge.
Gordon, R., Varian, H. (1988). "Intergenerational risk sharing". Journal of Public Economics 37, 185–202.
Hammond, P.J. (1975). "Charity: altruism or cooperative egoism?". In: Phelps, E.S. (Ed.), Altruism, Morality and Economic Theory. Russel Sage Foundation, New York.
Hammond, P.J. (1982). "Utilitarianism, uncertainty and information". In: Sen, A.K., Williams, B. (Eds.), Utilitarianism and Beyond. Cambridge University Press, Cambridge.
Hansson, I., Stuart, C. (1989). "Social security as trade among living generations". American Economic Review 79 (5), 1182–1195.
Harsanyi, J.C. (1953). "Cardinal utility in welfare economics and in the theory of risk-taking". Journal of Political Economy 63, 434–435.
Harsanyi, J.C. (1982). "Morality and the theory of rational behaviour". In: Sen, A.K., Williams, B. (Eds.), Utilitarianism and Beyond. Cambridge University Press and Editions de la MSH, Cambridge and Paris.
Henriet, D., Rochet, J.C. (1991). Microéconomie de l'assurance. Economica, Paris.
Kolm, S.C. (1972). Justice et équité. Editions du CNRS, Paris.
Kolm, S.C. (1985). Le contrat social liberal. PUF, Paris.
Kolm, S.C. (1996). Modern Theories of Justice. MIT Press, Cambridge, MA.
Kolm, S.C. (1998). "Chance and justice: social policies and the Harsanyi-Vickrey-Rawls problem". European Economic Review 42, 1393–1416.
Lambert, P.J. (1989). The Distribution and Redistribution of Income: A Mathematical Analysis. Blackwell, Oxford.
Lindbeck, A. (1995a). "Welfare state disincentives with endogenous habits and norms". Scandinavian Journal of Economics 97, 477–494.
Lindbeck, A. (1995b). "Hazardous welfare state dynamics". American Economic Review 85 (2), 9–15.
Lindbeck, A. (1999). "Social norms and economic incentives in the welfare state". Quarterly Journal of Economics 114, 1–35.
Lindbeck, A., Weibull, J.W. (1988). "Altruism and time consistency: the economics of *fait accompli*". Journal of Political Economy 96, 1165–1182.
Mirrless, J.A. (1974). "Notes on welfare economics, information and uncertainty". In: Balch, M.S., McFadden, D., Wu, S.Y. (Eds.), Essays on Economic Behaviour under Uncertainty. North-Holland, Amsterdam.
Moulin, H., Thomson, W. (1996). "Axiomatic analysis of resource allocation problems". In: Arrow, K.J., Sen, A.K., Suzumura, K. (Eds.), Social Choice Re-examined, vol. 1. IEA Conference Volume. Macmillan, London.
Mulligan C.B., Sala-I-Martin X. (1999a). "Social security in theory and practice (I): facts and political theories". NBER working paper 7118.
Mulligan C.B., Sala-I-Martin X. (1999b). "Social security in theory and practice (II): efficiency theories, narrative theories and implications for reform". NBER working paper 7119.
Persson, T., Tabellini, G. (1999). "Political economics and public finance". In: Auerbach, A., Feldstein, M. (Eds.), Handbook of Public Economics. North Holland, Amsterdam.
Piketty, T. (1995). "Social mobility and redistributive politics". Quarterly Journal of Economics 110, 551–584.
Rawls, J. (1971). A Theory of Justice. Harvard University Press, Cambridge, MA.

Roemer, J.E. (1985). "Equality of talent". Economics and Philosophy 1, 151–187.
Rotschild, R.S., Stiglitz, J.E. (1976). "Equilibrium in competitive insurance market". Quarterly Journal of Economics 11, 629–649.
Sala-I-Martin, X. (1996). "A positive theory of social security". Journal of Economic Growth 1 (2), 277–304.
Samuelson, P.A. (1975). "Optimum social security in a life-cycle growth model". International Economic Review 16, 539–544.
Sen, A.K. (1973). On Economic Inequality. Clarendon Press, Oxford.
Sen, A.K. (1979). "Utilitarianism and welfarism". Journal of Philosophy 76, 463–489.
Sen, A.K. (1986). "Social choice theory". In: Arrow, K.J., Intriligator, M.D. (Eds.), Handbook of Mathematical Economics, vol. 3. North-Holland, Amsterdam.
Silber, J. (Ed.) (1999). Handbook of Income Inequality Measurement. Kluwer, Dordrecht.
Sinn, H.W. (1995). "A theory of the welfare state". The Scandinavian Journal of Economics 97, 495–526.
Smith, A. (1982). "Intergenerational transfers as social insurance". Journal of Public Economics 19, 97–106.
Tabellini, G. (2000). "A positive theory of social security". The Scandinavian Journal of Economics 102 (3), 523–545.
Varian, H. (1980). "Redistributive taxation as social insurance". Journal of Public Economics 14, 46–68.

Chapter 25

THE POLITICAL ECONOMY OF INTERGENERATIONAL COOPERATION

ALESSANDRO CIGNO*

University of Florence, CESifo, CHILD and IZA

Contents

* The author is grateful to Dan Anderberg, Simone Bertoli, Michele Boldrin, Alex Kemnitz, Serge Kolm, Lex Meijdam and Jean Mercier-Ythier for valuable comments. Remaining errors and shortcomings are the author's responsibility.

Handbook of the Economics of Giving, Altruism and Reciprocity, Volume 2
Edited by Serge-Christophe Kolm and Jean Mercier Ythier

DOI: 10.1016/S1574-0714(06)02025-2

Abstract

This chapter examines the scope for mutually beneficial intergenerational cooperation, and looks at various attempts to theoretically explain the emergence of norms and institutions that facilitate this cooperation. The contributions reviewed come from branches of economics as far apart as household economics and political economy, and encompass both the normative and the positive branch of public economics. Section 2 establishes a normative framework. Sections 3 and 4 examine the properties of the *laissez-faire* solution in a pure market economy, and in one where reproductive decisions and intra-family transfers are constrained by self-enforcing family constitutions. Section 5 introduces the state, and shows that first and second-best policy include a pension and a child benefit scheme. Section 6 rexamines the same issues in the presence of educational investment. Section 7 introduces uncertainty and asymmetrical information, and shows that second-best public transfers to families are conditional on number of children, and on some measure of the children's success in adult life. Section 8 looks at the possibility that intergenerational redistribution might be supported by some kind of political equilibrium. One type of model looks at the possibility of a self-enforcing constitution governing intergenerational transfers at societal rather than family level. Another type of model looks for voting equilibria in direct, and in representative democracies.

Keywords

intergenerational cooperation, family, fertility, saving, private transfers, education, child benefits, pensions, self-enforcing constitutions, direct democracy, representative democracy

JEL classification: D7, D82, D91, H2, H5, H31, I2, J1

1. Introduction

> "Let us assume that men enter the labor market at about the age of twenty. They work for forty-five years or so and then live for fifteen years in retirement. Naturally, men will want to consume less than they produce in their working years so that they can consume something in the years when they produce nothing. ...
> If there were only Robinson Crusoe, he would hope to put by some durable goods which could be drawn on in his old age. He would, so to speak, want to trade with Mother Nature current consumption goods in return for future consumption goods. ...
> For the present purpose, I shall make the extreme assumption that nothing will keep at all. Thus no intertemporal trade with Nature is possible. If Crusoe were alone, he would obviously die at the beginning of his retirement years.
> But we live in a world where new generations are always coming along. ... [C]annot men during their productive years give up some of their product to bribe other men to support them in their retirement years?" (Samuelson, 1958)

The answer to Paul Samuelson's question is clearly "yes, if there are ways of ensuring that the bribed person will deliver his side of the deal when the time comes". Samuelson's own solution to this enforcement problem is what he calls "social contrivances": contract law and its associated legal enforcement apparatus, money that "gives workers of one epoch a claim on workers of a later epoch" (Samuelson, 1958). But what about the very young? They need support too, indeed more than the old because, unlike them, they have not had an earlier phase of life in which to put by durable goods. Therefore, if anyone is willing to be "bribed", it is precisely them. The problem is that Samuelson's contrivances are not much help here. In most legal systems, minors are not allowed to enter into binding commercial agreements (and babies could not anyway). Why is there no mention of them in Samuelson's analysis? As Martin Shubik perceptively put it,

> "... Samuelson's model is implicitly a three period model where he dropped the first period by the assumption that child support was to be purely instinctive and hence not in the analysis" (Shubik, 1981).

The same implicit assumption underlies much of the subsequent literature on the subject, including some of the articles referred to in this chapter. The basis for making such an assumption, one may suppose, is that successful animal species are genetically programmed to care for their offspring. But is that enough? The existence of laws and social norms deputed to ensure that children get adequate support suggests that it may not. This does not necessarily mean that parents do not care about their children, but it does imply that externalities, or some other kind of coordination failure, could be responsible for at least some of the parents giving their children less than is socially desirable. Even Gary Becker, the economist most closely identified with the view that parental transfers to children are gifts, uses the argument that parents may underinvest in their children to explain public intervention.

> "State intervention in the provision of education and other human capital could raise investments in children to the efficient level. ... The compulsory schooling laws in the United States that began in the 1880s ... tended to have this effect. A state usually set minimum requirements at a level that was already exceeded by all but the poorest families in the state. These laws raised the schooling of poor children but did not tend to affect the schooling of other children" (Becker and Murphy, 1988).

The aim of this chapter is to examine the scope for mutually beneficial intergenerational cooperation, and theoretically explain the emergence of certain norms and institutions (hence the *political economy* label) as a rational response to the coordination problems we have just outlined. The contributions on which we draw come from several branches of economics, as far apart as household economics and the constitutional department of political economy, and encompassing both the normative and the positive branch of public economics. Pooling the work of authors with very different intellectual traditions faces special difficulties, in that each sub-literature approaches the point at issue from its own distinctive point of view, and makes the simplifying assumptions that appear most appropriate from that particular perspective. As mere juxtaposition would have served little purpose, what we have attempted is a systematic re-exposition of the entire subject area within a coherent framework.[1]

A cost of this expositional strategy is that the basic assumptions made have to be the lowest common denominator of those typical of the different modelling traditions. A good part of the formal analysis will be based on the hypothesis that individuals are not altruistic, and that utility depends only on the consumption of market goods (essentially money); leisure is not mentioned explicitly. The latter could be interpreted as literally meaning that free time is not a good, or that the utility function is weakly separable. If the second interpretation is followed, consumption includes the consumption-equivalent of the utility of leisure, costs include opportunity-costs, and income is to be interpreted as full income. The assumption that people derive utility also from the consumption or well-being of others is common in household economics, but unusual in other branches of economics.[2] The same may be said of the hypothesis that utility depends also on the personal services of specified individuals. We shall look first for the possibility of cooperation between generations of selfish individuals deriving utility from money only, then ask whether altruism, or the existence of personal services for which the market does not provide a perfect substitute, make things any easier.

Another cost of spreading the net so wide is that important contributions where the primary focus in not on intergenerational cooperation will have to be excluded. Except

[1] Many of the authors cited will feel that some part or other of this chapter "sounds like, but is not quite" what they wrote.

[2] Robertson (1956) warns economists that love or altruism is a scarce good, on which they should economize. Indeed, there is little empirical evidence that individual actions are *systematically* driven by such sentiments.

where *intra*-generational heterogeneity impinges very directly on *inter*-generational matters, as in some voting models, we deal with intra-generational diversity parenthetically. Perhaps less justifiably, we do not go into the important issue of intergenerational risk sharing.[3]

A good part of the analysis refers to a small open economy. The motivation is not so much realism, as expositional convenience. In a small open economy without restrictions on international capital flows, the rate of interest is in fact exogenous, and capital accumulation is independent of domestic saving. By uncoupling intergenerational cooperation from capital accumulation, the small open economy assumption allows us to reproduce the results of the greater part of the literature on private intergenerational transfers that takes factor prices as given. The closed economy assumption will be used only where factor price endogeneity is crucial to the argument.

Wherever practical,[4] we treat fertility as endogenous. The reason for this assumption is not only that the empirical evidence strongly supports it. There is also a theoretical motivation, namely that giving present adults the power to influence the number of partners to any future intergenerational agreement makes it more likely that an agreement will be reached. Except in section 7, where we deal with hidden actions, we shall reason *as if* parents could decide how many children to have. In reality, parents can only condition (by frequency of intercourse and contraceptive practice) the probability of an extra birth. Like most things in life, completed fertility is thus the result of a combination of chance and deliberate action. The cost of making the simplifying assumption that parents can actually choose fertility is that policy prescriptions take an unpleasant totalitarian tone ("thou shalt have n children, or else ..."), but that is only a theoretical artefact. When it is recognized that parents can only choose the fertility conditioning variable, not the actual outcome, the policy takes the more acceptable form of an incentive (or disincentive) to have children. Again for the sake of simplicity, we shall assume parthenogenesis (for coherence, rather than political correctness, we shall thus use the feminine gender). Allowing for sexual reproduction would complicate the analysis considerably without throwing any extra light on the points at issue.

Throughout the exposition, we take the life-cycle to consist of three periods, labelled $i = 0, 1, 2$. A person is said to be young in period 0, adult in period 1, old in period 2. Adults are able to produce income, and to reproduce; the young and the old can do neither. Each adult is endowed with a certain earning capacity, and with the potential to have children (up to an unspecified physiological maximum, generally assumed to be inconsequential) by bearing a fixed cost per birth, p. This cost includes the child's subsistence consumption in period 0 (above-subsistence consumption is a choice variable), as well as all the expenditures and opportunity costs associated with childbearing. We

[3] Barro (1979), and Gordon and Varian (1988) show that public debt may permit risk sharing between generations; Gale (1991), Thogersen (1998) and Wagener (2003) show the same to be true of pay-as-you-go pension systems.

[4] When educational investment is brought into the picture, or in dealing with voting models, endogenous fertility makes things too complicated.

adopt the convention of calling t the generation that enters period 1 of its life at date t. As individuals are active in that period only, this has the expositional advantage of making the date of the action coincide with the generational label of the actor.

2. A normative benchmark

Before embarking on an analysis of the institutions that might make it possible for members of a generation to cooperate with members of another generation, it is useful to establish a normative benchmark against which to measure the performance of any such arrangement. In this section, we approach the issue under the assumption that capital is the only durable good, and that all members of the same generation are the same (these assumptions will be relaxed in later sections).

Let the lifetime utility of each member of generation t be given by

$$U^t = u_0(c_0^t) + u_1(c_1^t) + u_2(c_2^t), \tag{1}$$

where c_i^t denotes consumption in the i-th period of life ($i = 0, 1, 2$) of a member of generation t. The function $u_i(.)$ is assumed to be concave, with $u_i(0) = 0$, and $u_i'(0) = \infty$.

Income (output net of capital depreciation) is determined by

$$y^t = f(k^t), \tag{2}$$

where k^t, y^t and n^t denote, respectively, the capital, income and number of children of each member of generation t (or, equivalently, capital, income and fertility per adult at date t), and $f(.)$ is the per-adult production function. Assuming a small open economy, and perfect capital mobility, the interest rate, $r^t - 1$, is exogenously given.

The resource constraint for any date t may be written as

$$k^t - r^t d^t + f(k^t) = \frac{c_2^{t-1}}{n^{t-1}} + c_1^t + \left(p + c_0^{t+1} + \frac{k^{t+1} - d^{t+1}}{r^t}\right)n^t, \tag{3}$$

where d^t is per-adult foreign debt, and n^t the fertility rate, at date t. As already mentioned, p is a positive constant, representing the unavoidable part of the cost of a child. Since this constant will include the subsistence part of a young child's consumption, the variable c_0^{t+1} is to be interpreted as the above-subsistence consumption of a child born at t.[5]

Suppose that social welfare is measured by

$$W^0 = \sum_{t=0}^{\infty} (\delta)^t U^t, \quad 0 < \delta \leq 1. \tag{4}$$

[5] We could similarly introduce constants representing subsistence consumption in periods 1 and 2 of a person's life, and define c_i^t as above-subsistence consumption in the i-th period of life by a person born at $t - 1$, but that would serve no useful purpose.

If δ is equal to unity, society is concerned with the average utility of its present and future members as suggested by John Stuart Mill. By extension, we shall then call (4) the Millian welfare function, and the $(c_i^t, n^t)_{t=1,2\ldots}$ sequence that maximizes it, subject to (3) for each t,[6] the Millian optimum.

Given (c_0^0, d^0, k^0), a Millian optimum satisfies

$$f'(k^t) = r^t - 1, \tag{5}$$

$$\frac{u_0'(c_0^{t+1})}{u_1'(c_1^{t+1})} = r^t = \frac{u_1'(c_1^t)}{u_2'(c_2^t)} \tag{6}$$

and

$$\frac{u_2'(c_2^t)}{u_1'(c_1^t)} \frac{c_2^t}{n^t} = p + c_0^{t+1} + \frac{k^{t+1} - d^{t+1}}{r^t}, \tag{7}$$

for every $t \geq 0$.

The first of these conditions, (5), determines k^t as a function of r^t.[7] The second one, (6), equates the marginal rate of substitution of present for future consumption of children and adults to each other, and to the current interest factor. The third one, (7), equates the social benefit of adding another person to generation $t+1$ to the social cost. The former is the adult consumption equivalent of the contribution that a member of generation $t+1$ will make to the old-age consumption of current adults, $\frac{u_2'(c_2^t)}{u_1'(c_1^t)} \frac{c_2^t}{n^t}$. The latter is the sum of the expenditure required to bring a child into the world and provide for her consumption at date t, $(p + c_0^{t+1})$, and of the cost of endowing the future adult with net assets $(k^{t+1} - d^{t+1})$ at date $t+1$.

Notice that (5)–(6) are the necessary conditions for a Pareto-optimal allocation of consumption across generations of *given* size. If the population profile were exogenously given, and given that all members of the same generation are assumed to be the same, Pareto and Millian optimum would coincide. Since fertility is endogenous, however, there is an efficient allocation for each possible population profile. Out of all these profiles and associated consumption allocations, society favours the one that satisfies (7).

Alternatively, suppose that social welfare is measured by

$$W^0 = \sum_{t=0}^{\infty} (\delta)^t N^t U^t, \quad 0 < \delta \leq 1, \tag{8}$$

[6] There is also the constraint that, for each t, n^t cannot be less than zero, or greater than a certain physiological maximum. In reality, these restrictions may well be binding for some women, but average fertility is always inside the limits. Since, in our analysis, all women are the same, we follow the common pratice of assuming that these restrictions are not binding at the optimum.

[7] This implies that any gap between domestic investment and domestic saving is filled by a change in the foreign debt.

where

$$N^t \equiv \prod_{j=0}^{t} n^{j-1} \tag{9}$$

is the number of persons in generation t. If $\delta = 1$, society is concerned with the sum of the utilities of its present and future members as suggested by Jeremy Bentham. Stretching things a bit, we shall then call the $(c_i^t, n^t)_{t=1,2...}$ sequence that maximizes (8), subject to (3) for each t, the Benthamite optimum.

Given (c_0^0, d^0, k^0), a Benthamite optimum satisfies (5)–(6) like a Millian optimum, but the fertility condition is now

$$\frac{\delta W^{t+1}}{u_1'(c_1^t)} + \frac{u_2'(c_2^t)}{u_1'(c_1^t)} \frac{c_2^t}{n^t} = p + c_0^{t+1} + \frac{k^{t+1} - d^{t+1}}{r^t} \tag{10}$$

for every $t \geq 0$. Compared with (7), the social benefit of adding a person to generation $t+1$ has an extra term, $\frac{\delta W^{t+1}}{u_1'(c_1^t)}$, representing the adult consumption equivalent for a member of generation t of the value that society attaches to an extra member of generation $t+1$ *per se* (that is to say, irrespective of the effect that this person will have on the consumption of existing members of society).

In the positive analysis of fertility behaviour, it is often assumed that parents are altruistic, in the sense that they derive direct utility from the consumption or utility of each of their children. That is the case in most of Gary Becker's contributions to the field. In a number of other studies (e.g., Kollmann, 1997), it is assumed that parents derive utility only from the number of children. As an alternative to (1), let us then assume that the utility of each member of generation 0 is given by

$$U^t = u_0(c_0^t) + u_1(c_1^t) + u_2(c_2^t) + \beta n^t U^{t+1}, \quad 0 < \beta \leq 1, \tag{11}$$

where β is a measure of parental altruism (in some formulations, this is assumed to be a decreasing function of n^t).

This implies that a person's utility is ultimately a function of the fertility and lifetime consumption of all her descendents.[8] In particular, the utility of a member of generation 0 is given by

$$U^0 = u_0(c_0^0) + u_1(c_1^0) + u_2(c_2^0) + \sum_{t=1}^{\infty} (\beta)^t N^t U^t, \tag{12}$$

where $N^t \equiv \prod_{j=1}^{t} n$ is the number of this person's adult descendents at date t. Since (12) is effectively a Benthamite welfare function, it would make little sense to define social welfare as the sum or the mean of the maximands of successive generations.

[8] That would not be the case, notice, if parents derived utility from the consumption, rather than the utility, of their children. For an analysis of that case, see Kolmar (1997).

Having assumed that all individuals are the same, it seems more natural to postulate that δ is equal to the common β, and thus to identify W^t with U^t. The conditions for a social optimum are then (5)–(6) and (10).

Positive economists generally regard social optimality as a tall order, and limit themselves to looking for the possibility of a Pareto optimum. The latter, however, applies only to a world without endogenous fertility, because the Paretian criterion allows us to compare only allocations to a given set of individuals. It cannot be applied to a situation where the number of future adults is determined or conditioned by actions taken by current adults. To deal with such a situation, Baland and Robinson (2002) propose a *quasi*-Paretian criterion according to which an allocation $\mathbf{x}$ is deemed preferable to an allocation $\mathbf{y}$ if the utility of the parent, and the average utility of the children, is higher in $\mathbf{x}$ than in $\mathbf{y}$. The reference to an *average* level of utility leaves the door open for the possibility that the number of children associated with $\mathbf{x}$ is different from the number associated with $\mathbf{y}$. It thus allows us to make comparisons across different population profiles. A necessary condition for efficiency in the Baland–Robinson sense is that the marginal rate of substitution of present for future consumption is the same for the parent's and the children's generation.

3. The market

Are there institutions that can generate a (Millian or Benthamite) social optimum, or at least allocate resources efficiently? In the present section, we assume that individual decisions are coordinated by competitive markets. In later ones, we shall look at the role of the family, and of the state.

At any date t, income per adult, y^t, is determined by (2), and the stock of capital per adult, k^t, satisfies (5). Given the stock of assets per adult,

$$a^t = k^t - d^t, \tag{13}$$

y^t includes earnings equal to

$$w^t = y^t - (r^t - 1)a^t. \tag{14}$$

3.1. A life-cycle model

Standard life-cycle theory assumes that everyone is out for himself. The young support themselves by borrowing. Adults save for their own old age. The old live off their savings. The population profile is exogenous. Consider a simple Modigliani-like economy where each member of generation t chooses her consumption stream (c_0^t, c_1^t, c_2^t) so as to maximize the utility function (1), subject to the lifetime budget constraint

$$c_0^t r^{t-1} + c_1^t - w^t + \frac{c_2^t}{r^t} = a^t. \tag{15}$$

The solution will satisfy

$$\frac{u_0'(c_0^t)}{u_1'(c_1^t)} = r^{t-1} \quad \text{and} \quad \frac{u_1'(c_1^t)}{u_2'(c_2^t)} = r^t. \tag{16}$$

Since this is true for every t, (16) implies (6). The market equilibrium is then a Pareto optimum conditional on the exogenously given population profile. In reality, however, credit may be rationed. Where adults are concerned, this may reflect an adverse selection problem (Stiglitz and Weiss, 1981). Where the young are concerned, there is also the problem that minors cannot enter into legally binding agreements. If credit is rationed for anybody, (16), hence (6) does not hold, and the equilibrium is not a Pareto optimum.

If fertility is a choice variable, there is a further and much bigger problem. Since a child costs her parent at least p, but yields no benefit, fertility will be zero. The economy will then vanish with generation 0. This is a rather extreme instance of a population externality. Atomistic agents ignore the social benefit—the difference between the left-hand side and the last two right-hand-side terms of either (7) or (10)—of putting an extra person into the world. Further externalities emerge if we drop the small closed economy assumption, or allow for non-reproducible resource constraints.[9]

3.2. A dynastic model

One way to make fertility choice compatible with a pure market economy and, at the same time, get round the problem that the young cannot support themselves by borrowing from the market, is to assume, like Becker and Barro (1988), that adults get direct utility not only from their own lifetime consumption, but also from the utility of each of their children ("descending altruism"). In this model, each dynasty behaves like an infinite-lived individual, and the actions of this myriad of synthetic individuals are coordinated by the market just like those of ordinary mortals in life-cycle theory.

At date 0, a^0 is given, and c_0^0 a bygone. Each current adult then chooses the dynastic plan $(c_1^t, c_2^t, n^t, c_0^{t+1}, a^{t+1})_{t=0,1\ldots}$ that maximizes (11), subject to the dynastic budget constraint,

$$\sum_{t=1}^{\infty}\left((p + c_0^t)r^{t-1} + c_1^t - w^t + \frac{c_2^t}{r^t}\right)\frac{N^t}{R^t} \leq a^0 + w^0 - c_1^0 - \frac{c_2^0}{r^0}, \tag{17}$$

where $R^t \equiv \prod_{j=1}^{t} r^{j-1}$ is the capitalization factor from date 0 to date t, and to two further restrictions for every $t \geq 0$.

The first of these additional restrictions,

$$a^{t+1} \equiv \frac{[a^t + w^t - c_1^t - (p + c_0^{t+1})n^t]r^t - c_2^t}{n^t} \geq 0, \tag{18}$$

[9] See, for example, Eckstein and Wolpin (1985), Michel and Pestieau (1993), Razin and Sadka (1995).

says that an elderly parent cannot make negative transfers to her adult children. This follows from (a) the assumption that people are altruistic towards their children, but not towards their parents, and (b) the legal principle that a person is not obliged to inherit her parent's debts. The second one,

$$s^t \equiv a^t + w^t - c_1^t - (p + c_0^{t+1})n^t \geq -b^t, \tag{19}$$

says that an adult and her young children are jointly allowed to borrow no more than a certain amount b^t.

The founder of the dynasty can directly implement only the first tranche, $(c_1^0, c_2^0, n^0, c_0^1, a^1)$, of the dynastic plan. Once the first tranche is implemented, however, what is left of the plan is optimal also for each of the founder's n^0 children, who will thus carry out the second tranche, $(c_1^1, c_2^1, n^1, c_0^2, a^2)$, and so on.

Becker and Barro (1988) take it for granted that neither (18) nor (19) will ever be binding. Under this assumption, the dynastic plan satisfies (6) and

$$\frac{\beta}{\lambda} U^{t+1} = p + c_0^{t+1} + \frac{a^{t+1}}{r^t}, \tag{20}$$

where $\lambda = u_1'(c_1^t)$ is the Lagrange multiplier of (17), for every $t \geq 0$. The market equilibrium is efficient in the Baland–Robinson sense. Even assuming (see section 2) that δ is equal to the common value of β, so that W^t coincides with U^t, however, the allocation is not socially optimal. Comparing (20) with (10), it is in fact clear that atomistic parents do not take account of the contribution to aggregate production, represented by the second left-hand-side term of (10), that an extra child would make at date $t + 1$. There is thus a positive population externality. Fertility (hence, population size at each $t > 0$) is too low for each $t \geq 0$.

If either (18) or (19) is binding for any t, the allocation is not even efficient in the Baland–Robinson sense. The former is intuited in Becker and Murphy (1988), where it is pointed out that "operative bequests" are necessary for an efficient allocation of consumption.[10] Baland and Robinson (2002) show that, if either of the said constraints is binding, fertility will be inefficiently high, and youthful consumption inefficiently low. The argument goes as follows.

Suppose that children (i) are born in (rapid) sequence, and (ii) once born, are treated the same. This allows us to, so to speak, step in the middle of a person's reproductive career, and enquire whether the children born until then could successfully bribe their parent not to have any more. That is obviously not possible if the allocation is efficient. But, suppose that the nonnegative-transfer constraint is binding. Instead of (6),

[10] What those authors had in mind, however, is the standard Pareto criterion, which cannot be applied in an endogenous fertility context. The terminology reflects the assumption in the Becker–Barro model that elderly parents do not make *inter-vivos* transfers to adult children. If they make any transfers, therefore, it will be in the form of bequest.

the allocation will then satisfy

$$\frac{u_0'(c_0^{t+1})}{u_1'(c_1^{t+1})} = \left(1 + \frac{\mu^t}{\lambda} r^t\right) r^t > r^t = \frac{u_1'(c_1^t)}{u_2'(c_2^t)}, \tag{21}$$

where μ^t is the Lagrange multiplier of (18). As the children value their current consumption, at the margin, more than the parent values hers, there is then scope for mutually beneficial exchange. The problem is that the exchange will not go through, because young children cannot credibly commit to reimburse their parent when they become adults.

The issue can be illustrated with the help of Figure 1. The horizontal axis measures a child's current (youthful) consumption, the vertical axis her future (adult) consumption. The convex-to-the-origin curves are the child's indifference curves. If (17) were the only constraint, the parent would maximize her utility by procuring n^A births, and

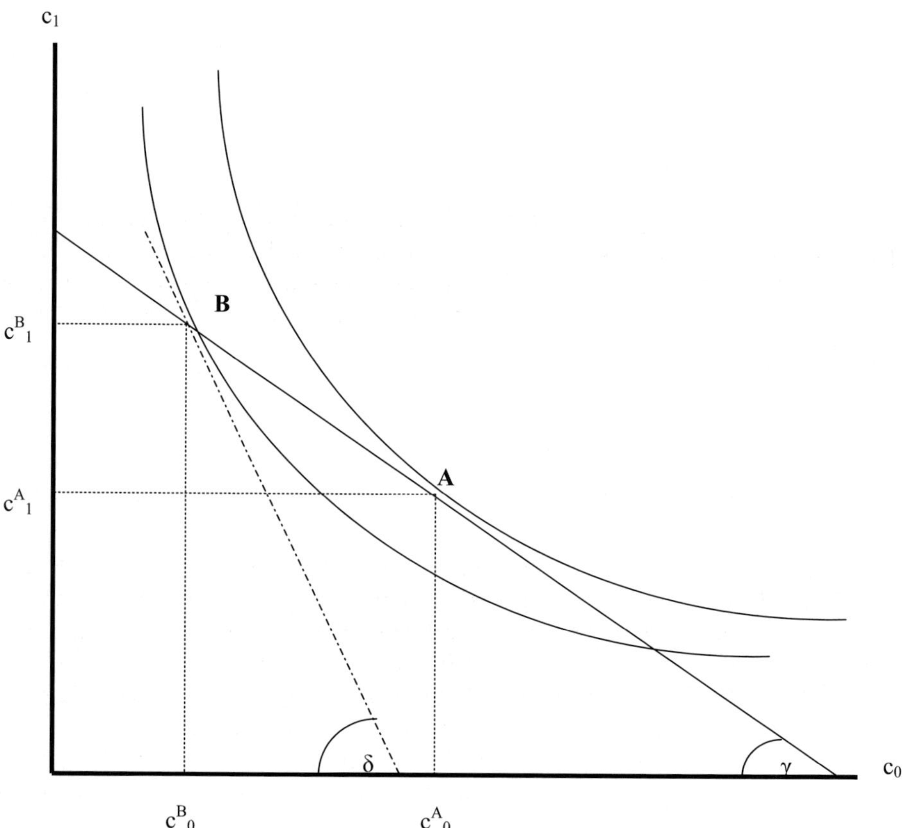

Figure 1. The dynastic model with nonnegative-transfers and credit-rationing constraints.

allocating the resources under her control so that each of her children consumes c_0^A now, and c_1^A as an adult. But, suppose that any level of adult consumption lower than c_1^B implies a negative transfer (e.g., a negative bequest). As c_1^A violates (18), and given that (c_0^A, c_1^B) costs more than (c_0^A, c_1^A), the parent will then reduce the current consumption of each child to c_0^B, and recover *some* of the utility loss by having more than n^A children, say n^B.[11] Clearly, (n^B, c_0^B, c_1^B) gives the parent, and each of her children, lower utility than (n^A, c_0^A, c_1^A).

Now, suppose that n^A children are already born. Each of these children would be willing to trade $(c_1^B - c_1^A)$ of adult consumption for $(c_0^A - c_0^B)$ units of current consumption. If they could credibly commit to pay $(c_1^B - c_1^A)$ next period, their parent would accept the trade, because this would allow her to carry out the preferred plan (n^A, c_0^A, c_1^A). As there is no way of holding a young child to her word, however, the parent can do no better than have another $(n^B - n^A)$ children, and deploy the resources under her control so that each child consumes (c_0^B, c_1^B). By the Baland–Robinson definition, the final fertility level n^B is inefficiently high.

A similar argument applies if the borrowing constraint (19) is binding. Instead of (6), the allocation then satisfies

$$\frac{u_0'(c_0^{t+1})}{u_1'(c_1^{t+1})} = \left(1 + \frac{\upsilon^t}{\lambda}\right) r^t = \frac{u_1'(c_1^t)}{u_2'(c_2^t)}, \tag{22}$$

where υ^t is the Lagrange multiplier of (19). In this case, the parent and the children place the same marginal value on current consumption, but this common value is greater than the interest factor. Rather than insufficient commitment, the problem is now that neither party can borrow as much as would be required for an efficient allocation of resources.

4. The family

In the real world, individuals interact not only through the market, but also through lower-level organizations such as families, clubs, and interest groups. In particular, decisions regarding fertility and the intergenerational allocation of resources tend to be coordinated by families. In game-theoretical language, any such organization is a *coalition*, a subset of the population whose members are better off re-distributing their endowments among themselves, rather than going to the market.

Intendedly, Becker and Barro (1988) is about the family, but the model is rigged-up in such a way, that no member of the family has any reason to dissent from the parent's decisions. As already pointed out, the family thus operates *as if* it consisted of just one infinite-lived individual. The same may be said of much of Gary Becker's contributions

[11] In Gary Becker's language, she will substitute quantity for quality of children.

to the subject, epitomized by his "rotten kid theorem" (Becker, 1974). In essence, there is always a member of the family who, by virtue of (a) having the well-being of other members at heart, and (b) controlling a sufficiently large part of family resources to be in a position to make gifts (bequests in the model with Barro), can effectively decide how much each member will consume, subject only to the constraints imposed by the market.

An early attempt at giving the family a distinctive role, additional and in some sense alternative to that of the market, is Neher (1971). Elaborating on an idea of Leibenstein (1960), that the demand for children may be derived from that for old-age support (the so-called "old-age security motive"), Philip Neher imagines a situation were property rights are vested in families, rather than individuals, and family income is distributed according to a "... *share alike ethic* whereby all members of the family have equal claim to the product whether they work or not." Thus conceived, a family creates opportunities (of free-riding!), and places restrictions on individual behaviour, that would not be there if individuals interacted only through the market. In such a situation, fertility turns out to be higher than it would be if adults could individually accumulate assets, and higher also than the social optimum. The rules governing Neher's family are arbitrarily given. We now look in somewhat greater detail at a model where the rules are endogenously determined.

A useful way of characterizing an organization is to describe its fundamental rules, its *constitution*. Economic theory tells us that it may be in the interest of every member of a community to agree first on a constitution, allowing them to safely renounce the dominant strategy in a prisoner's dilemma type of situation, and then optimize individually subject to that constitution (Buchanan, 1987). Although originally conceived with reference to city or nation states, the constitution concept can be applied also to smaller groupings, such as families. Cigno (1993) puts forward the idea of a "family constitution", and establishes conditions under which this is self-enforcing in the sense that it is in the best interest of every family member to obey it, and have it obeyed. Cigno (2006) identifies circumstances in which a constitution is self-enforcing also in the stronger sense that, once established, it is renegotiation-proof. Statistical testing does not appear to reject the hypothesis that behaviour is constrained by such constitutions.[12] This approach provides an analytical basis for Leibenstein's original intuition that selfish adults have children in order to secure old-age support.

4.1. *Self-enforcing family constitutions*

Suppose that people are self-interested, so that the lifetime utility of each person is given by (1). If a cooperative agreement will stick under such unpromising conditions, all the more it will if people love their parent and children. At any given date, a family consists of individuals at different points of the life-cycle. Age differences are important,

[12] See Cigno et al. (2007).

because they provide an opportunity for mutually beneficial deals between members of the same family.[13] Let a family constitution be defined as a set of (unwritten, typically unspoken) rules prescribing, for each date t, the minimum amount of income, z^t, that each adult must transfer to each of her children (if she has any), and the minimum amount of income, x^t, that she must transfer to her parent, subject to the *pro viso* that nothing is due to a parent who did not herself obey the rules. The last clause makes it in every adult's interest to punish transgressors. That is important, because only an adult can punish another adult. Neither children nor old people have the means to do so.

It is sometimes claimed, especially in the household and development economics literatures, that mutually beneficial transactions not possible at the market level may come-off at the family or local community level. The argument is that proximity helps overcome the adverse selection and moral hazard problems associated with anonymous exchange. The possible objection, that informal transactions between relatives or neighbours cannot be enforced in a court of law, is typically brushed aside by implicitly or explicitly assuming that tightly-knit communities have extra-legal means, like ostracism (or downright illegal ones, like physical force), of deterring defection. No such assumption is required to justify the family constitution story. The clause that makes it in the interest of every adult family member to punish a disobedient parent turns an informational advantage (a person presumably knows the history of *her own* family) into an enforcement advantage.

The existence of a family constitution faces each adult with a choice of two strategies: *comply* with the constitution (cooperate), or *go it alone* in the market (defect). Since children cost their parents something (at least p), but will only bring a return if the constitution is complied with, it is clear that a go-it-aloner will not have children. It is also clear that a complier will not transfer her parent and children more than the minimum required by the constitution. For reasons that will become clear in a moment, compliers have no interest in lending to the capital market (and are not allowed to borrow from the market against their constitutional entitlements).

Suppose that the interest rate, hence the stock of capital and the wage rate, are constant over time, $x^t = x$ and $z^t = z$ for all t. That is a convenient simplification, but there is no conceptual difficulty in dealing with changing environments, hence with family constitutions that prescribe generation-specific (and, if the state of the world is uncertain, state-conditional) payments. Dispensing with time superscripts, and using s to denote the amount lent to the market in period 1, the pay-off to going it alone is then

$$v(r, w) = \max_s u_1(w - s) + u_2(rs). \tag{23}$$

For any given (r, w), the choice of s satisfies

$$\frac{u_1'(w - s)}{u_2'(rs)} = r. \tag{24}$$

[13] Such opportunities arise also from differences of sex and other personal characteristics, but we assume these differences away to concentrate on intergenerational relations.

The effects of changes in r or w on the pay-off of this strategy are

$$v_w = u_1'(w - s), \qquad v_r = s u_2'(rs). \tag{25}$$

The pay-off to complying, provided that the agent's children also comply, is

$$v^*(w, x, z) = \max_n u_1(w - x - (p + z)n) + u_2(xn). \tag{26}$$

For any given (x, w, z), the choice of n satisfies

$$\frac{u_1'(w - x - (p + z)n)}{u_2'(xn)} = \frac{x}{p + z}. \tag{27}$$

The effects of changes in x, w or z on the pay-off of this strategy are

$$v_x^* = -u_1'(w - x - (p + z)n) + n u_2'(xn), \tag{28}$$

$$v_w^* = u_1'(w - x - (p + z)n), \tag{29}$$

$$v_z^* = -n u_1'(w - x - (p + z)n). \tag{30}$$

If

$$v^*(w, x, z) \geq v(r, w), \tag{31}$$

complying is the best response to everyone else doing the same. The set of "comply" strategies (one for each member of each generation of the same family) is thus a Nash equilibrium. Since complying implies threatening one's own parent of punishment if she does not comply too, and the threat is credible because carrying it out is in the interest of the person making it, the equilibrium is sub-game perfect. In equilibrium, the threat is never carried out because every member of the family complies.

For a complier, having a child is a form of investment, costing $p + z$ in the current period, and yielding, in equilibrium, x in the next. The marginal return on this investment is thus $x/(p + z)$. In order to qualify for this return, however, the complier must pay a fixed amount x to her parent. A necessary condition for (31) to be true is then that the marginal return to investing in children is strictly larger than the return to buying conventional assets,

$$\frac{x}{p + z} > r. \tag{32}$$

Were that not so, there is in fact no way that an agent could recover the fixed cost of complying. Given (32), a complier will not save.[14] We can then think of the amount

[14] Strictly speaking, that is true only if the physiological ceiling on fertility is not binding. Were it binding, the agent could not procure as many children (acquire as many entitlements to future transfers) as she would like, and would then find it optimal to top-up her stock of domestic credits with market assets; in other words, save (Cigno and Rosati, 2000). Allowing for this possibility complicates the analysis without bringing any additional insight.

x that a complier pays to her parent as an entrance fee, entitling members to earn a marginal return higher than r.

While making it disadvantageous for compliers to lend to the market, (32) makes it advantageous for them to borrow from the market in order to finance additional births. But there are limits to this arbitrage operation. First, fertility cannot increase without bound because it will eventually hit its physiological ceiling. Second, there is no legal mechanism through which entitlements arising from an informal family arrangement can be transferred to a third party. Since an entitlement that cannot be legally transferred to a third party cannot be used as collateral to obtain credit from the market, we assume that compliers cannot borrow from the market at all (but nothing of substance changes if we allow them to borrow up to some positive amount, smaller than nz).

Figure 2 illustrates the properties of the set of constitutions that can be supported by a sub-game perfect Nash equilibrium. The set consists of all the (z, x) pairs that satisfy (31). Any of these constitutions would secure transfers from adult children to elderly parents. Since young children have no income, and cannot thus make transfers to their parents, z cannot be negative. It could be zero, however, because the decision makers are adults, who have already received z from their own parents. They would thus be happy to subscribe to a constitution that did not oblige them to *make* transfers to their children in the current period. By contrast, x must be positive, because the decision makers would not countenance a constitution that did not entitle them to *receive* transfers from their children in the next period. Therefore, all points in the set satisfy $z \geq 0$, and $x > 0$. The slope of the line segment joining $(-p, 0)$ to any point in the set

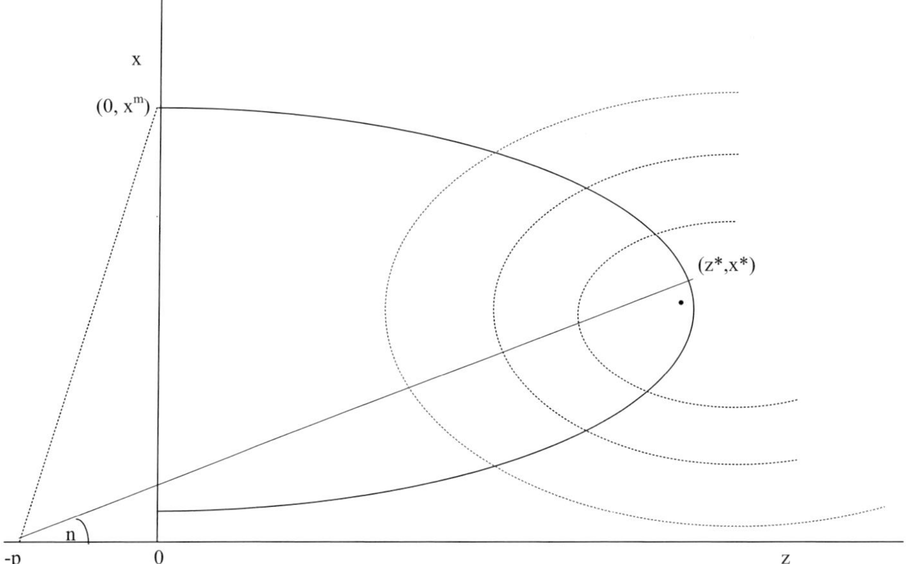

Figure 2. The Nash-frontier and the self-enforcing family constitution.

is the marginal return to children implied by the constitution represented by that point. The constitution $(0, x^m)$ yields the highest marginal return compatible with a sub-game perfect Nash equilibrium.

The boundary of the set (the heavy curve in Figure 2) is the locus of the (z, x) pairs that make (31) into an equation. The slope of this boundary is given by

$$\frac{dz}{dx} = \frac{(p+z)n - x}{nx}. \tag{33}$$

Since

$$\frac{d^2 z}{d(x)^2} = -\frac{p+z}{(x)^2} \tag{34}$$

is negative, z is maximized at the point, shown in Figure 2 as (z^*, x^*), where

$$\frac{x}{p+z} = n. \tag{35}$$

Therefore, the marginal return to children implied by the constitution (z^*, x^*) is equal to the number of children that a complier would choose given that constitution.

Given that v_r is positive in view of (25), a rise in r will shift the boundary inwards. Intuitively, that is because the lowest rate of return to children that makes complying with the constitution at least as attractive as going it alone in the market increases with the market rate of interest. By contrast, a rise in w shifts the boundary outwards. Although v_w and v_w^* are both positive in view of (25) and (29), the latter is in fact larger than the former. The reason is simply that, in view of (32), compliers have lower current consumption, and consequently higher marginal utility of the same, than go-it-aloners. While an exogenous rise in the interest rate would make the set of sustainable constitutions smaller, an exogenous rise in the wage rate would thus make it larger. For w/r sufficiently low, the set will be empty. An interesting implication of these results is that a rise in the interest rate would result in lower aggregate fertility. Neher, mentioned earlier, reached the same conclusion by a different route.

We have assumed that compliers are always credit rationed (or they would have the maximum number of children that nature permits), but we have not imposed a similar restriction on go-it-aloners. If we do, that will reduce the pay-off to going it alone, and enlarge the set of sustainable family constitutions. Generalized credit rationing has thus the same effect as an increase in w/r.[15] The opposite is true of financial market developments allowing wider strata of society to engage in credit and insurance operations.[16]

[15] Using Italian survey data, Cigno et al. (2007) find that credit rationing increases the probability of making voluntary transfers to one's own children.

[16] Evidence that financial market development crowds-out intra-family arrangements is reported in Cigno and Rosati (1992) for a developed country, in Foster and Rosenzweig (2000) for a developing one.

4.2. Picking a constitution

Given that an infinite number of (z, x) pairs may satisfy (31), and that an infinite number of constitutions might thus be sustained by a sub-game perfect Nash equilibrium, which will prevail? Cigno (1993) suggests that the family founder will choose the constitution which suits her best. Since the founder is a selfish adult, she will obviously favour the one that prescribes the largest sustainable transfer to the old, and zero transfers (on top of the subsistence minimum included in p) to children. In Figure 2, this constitution is represented by point $(0, x^m)$.[17] Cigno (2006) offers an alternative selection criterion, akin to the renegotiation-proofness concept of Bernheim and Ray (1989), and Maskin and Farrell (1989).[18]

At any date t, any adult member of any existing family is at liberty to propose a new constitution (in other words, to found a new family). Will her children take any notice? Not if (i) the old constitution satisfies (31), and (ii) no other constitution satisfying (31) makes generations $t, t+1, t+2, \ldots$ better-off. In other words, a constitution is renegotiation-proof if, in addition to being a sub-game perfect Nash equilibrium, it is not Pareto-dominated by any other constitution which is itself a sub-game perfect Nash equilibrium.

If the existing constitution is undominated, the only way a person can offer her children a better deal, and not loose in the bargain, is by paying her parent *less* than the existing constitution requires—in other words, by defaulting on the existing constitution. But that would make her liable to punishment at the hands of her own children. The latter would in fact be better-off abiding by the existing constitution, which entitles them to pay nothing to their parent, than acquiescing to the proposed new one.[19] Once established, a constitution satisfying the double requirement of being a sub-game perfect Nash equilibrium, and undominated by any other constitution which is itself a sub-game perfect Nash equilibrium, is thus renegotiation-proof.

Let us characterize such a constitution. At any given date, the adults of the day are only interested in adult and old-age consumption, but their children are interested also in youthful consumption. A family constitution is then renegotiation-proof if it maximizes the lifetime utility of the representative individual (generation),

$$U(x, z, w) = u_0(z) + u_1(w - x - (p + z)n) + u_2(xn), \tag{36}$$

subject to (31).

[17] Provided, of course, that the associated n does not violate the physiological ceiling on fertility. If it does, the founder will pick the constitution that makes it optimal for each family member to choose n just equal to that maximum.

[18] In the latter two articles, however, the players are assumed to be always the same. In the present overlapping-generations context, by contrast, the players change at each round.

[19] Anderberg and Balestrino (2003) point out that this corresponds to the weak notion of renegotiation-proofness (*internal consistency*). The strong notion (*external consistency*) requires an equilibrium to be undominated by any weakly renegotiation-proof equilibrium.

If the constraint is not binding, the renegotiation-proof constitution satisfies

$$\frac{u_0'(z)}{u_1'(w-x-(p+z)n)}=n=\frac{u_1'(w-x-(p+z)n)}{u_2'(xn)} \tag{37}$$

and (35). It thus equalizes the parent and the children's marginal rate of substitution of present for future consumption. In this case, the point representing the renegotiation-proof constitution could be located anywhere inside the Nash frontier.

If (31) is binding, a renegotiation-proof constitution satisfies

$$\frac{u_0'(z)}{u_1'(w-x-(p+z)n)}=(1+\lambda)n, \tag{38}$$

where λ is the Lagrange-multiplier of (31),

$$\frac{u_1'(w-x-(p+z)n)}{u_2'(xn)}=n \tag{39}$$

and (35). At the margin, the children then value their current consumption more than the parent values hers. In this case, the renegotiation-proof constitution is represented by a point on the Nash frontier. Since the only point of the frontier satisfying (35) is (x^*, z^*), the renegotiation-proof constitution is the one that maximizes transfers to the young.

In Figure 2, the broken curves, with slope $(u_0' - u_1'n)/(-u_1' + u_2'n)$, are the contours of $U(.,.,w)$. The picture is drawn under the assumption that U happens to reach a maximum (represented by a large dot) just inside the Nash frontier, close to (z^*, x^*). Since the Nash frontier shifts inwards as the interest rate rises relative to the wage rate, the probability of such a solution increases with r/w. Notice that $(0, x^m)$, the constitution favoured by the family founder, could never be renegotiation-proof.

Since the return to money spent on children is greater than the return to saving in view of (32), the allocation brought about by a renegotiation-proof constitution cannot be a social optimum. Even in the case where (31) is not binding, and the marginal rates of substitution are thus equalized, the common value of these marginal rates is in fact higher than the interest factor. Therefore, (6) is not satisfied. In the case where (31) is binding, the children's marginal rate of substitution of present for future consumption is larger than the parent's. Fertility is thus inefficiently high in the Baland–Robinson sense (see, again, Figure 1), but the allocation nonetheless preferred by the adults of the day to anything the market could achieve.

If all agents are the same as we have assumed so far, everybody behaves the same. Then, either everybody complies with a family constitution, the same for all families, or nobody does. In the second case, nobody has children. In the first, nobody saves. This unrealistic feature of the model disappears if we allow for heterogeneity. If agents are different, some of them may in fact comply and have children, others may go it alone and save. The aggregate fertility rate will then be at most equal to the number of children per complier, and not necessarily higher than r.

4.3. Uncertainty and the demand for attention

If we drop the assumption that the future is known with certainty, we must allow for the possibility that a constitution prescribing a fixed payment to elderly parents and young children might one day become unenforceable. For example, it could happen that, for reasons beyond her control (bad luck, low talent, ill health, premature death), an adult will not be able to comply. It is also possible that a change of policy, or a rise in the internationally determined interest rate, will alter the economic environment in such a way that it is no longer in an adult's interest to comply. That could be avoided by making the constitutional prescriptions conditional on the state of the world. Intra-family arrangements would then allow risks to be shared between generations as in Di Tella and MacCullogh (2002). Realistically assuming that drawing up a fully contingent constitution is prohibitively costly, family constitutions might then rely on simple rules, of the kind that a child is excused from making a fixed transfer to her parent if, through no fault of her own, her own income falls below a certain level. As shown in Rosati (1996), it may then be worthwhile for a risk-averse complier to do some precautionary saving, in addition to having children.[20] Therefore, it is not necessarily true that, if all agents are the same, either the saving rate or the fertility rate is zero.

Many theories of household behaviour, including the basic family constitution model, assume that all goods other than children can be bought from the market. That is the same as assuming that the market supplies perfect substitutes for the personal services of the agent's own parent or children. What if the services supplied by the market substitute for those offered by one's own parent or children ("attention") at a diminishing marginal rate? Cox (1987), and Cox and Jakubson (1995) hypothesize intra-family exchanges of money for attention. But, the family is not a competitive market. Suppose, for example, that an elderly parent does not regard the assistance of a professional helper as a perfect substitute for the attention of her own children, but her grown-up children are indifferent between hiring themselves out to the market, or to their own parent. The children could then collude to raise the price of attention to such a level, that the parent is indifferent between buying from them, or from the market. The entire surplus produced by the exchange would then be appropriated by the children.

An example of opposite sign is provided by Bernheim et al. (1985), who argue that parents make bequests in order to get cut-price attention from their children.[21] The idea is that a parent can write a conditional testament (in effects, offer her children a contract) whereby she commits to leave her entire estate to the child who gives her the most attention, on condition that this attention does not fall below a certain minimum (in which case the money would go to someone other than the children, say a charity). By dangling this all-or-nothing offer—so the argument goes—the parent can extract from

[20] Provided that risks are either uncorrelated or negatively correlated, that will remain true even if the return on capital is uncertain too.

[21] The argument is further developed in Cremer et al. (1992); see section 6.

her children the entire surplus generated by the exchange. To this it may be objected, however, that children can counter the parent's move by drawing up a perfectly legal contract among themselves, whereby they agree that (a) only one of them will give the parent any attention (the minimum stated in the testament), and (b) the child receiving the estate will keep back just enough of it as is necessary to compensate her for the attention given to the parent, and share the rest equally with her siblings.[22]

Exploitation on either side can be avoided, if attention giving is incorporated in the family constitution. Cigno and Rosati (2000) re-formulate the constitution story to the effect that each adult is required to transfer a certain level of utility, rather than income, to her elderly parent and young children. Permitting compliers to choose the combination of money and personal services with which to discharge their family duties minimizes the cost of complying. It also raises the level of utility that a self-enforcing constitution can require agents to give their parent and children. Extending the model in this way makes it more likely that an intra-family scheme can offer a higher return (now in money-equivalent, rather than actual money terms) than the market, and thus that a self-enforcing family constitution exists. It also helps to explain why, in developed countries, intra-family money transfers go mostly to the young, while the old get mostly attention. Having relatively large pensions or accumulated savings, many old persons can in fact be expected to value personal services without perfect market substitutes far more than money.

4.4. Altruism in a family constitution context

What if individuals are altruistic towards other members of their family? Cigno (2006) examines the constitutional implications of descending altruism *à la* Barro–Becker. Under that assumption, compliers and go-it-aloners alike may save, have children, and make transfers. If parents are rich and generous enough to make each of their adult children transfers (say bequests) at least equal to the minimum that each child is constitutionally obliged to give them, the element of threat implied by the comply strategy disappears, and the constitution cannot be a subgame-perfect Nash equilibrium. That apart, however, descending altruism makes remarkably little difference.

Let us now consider the possibility that altruism flows upwards, as well as downwards. The most optimistic assumption is that all members of the same dynasty unanimously maximize (12). As every member of the same dynasty solves the same optimization problem, there is then no call for a family constitution to coordinate individual decisions. If credit is not rationed (and given that there are no nonnegative-transfer constraints, because grown-up children are happy to subsidize elderly parents), the solution is in that case a Benthamite social optimum. A less optimistic assumption is that the utility functions of different generations are symmetrical, rather identical.

To keep things simple, suppose that, at date 0, there is one adult with an exogenously given number of children, n. Suppose that this person will have no grandchildren, so the

[22] The point was originally made in Cigno (1991).

story ends with generation 1. The parent would like to maximize

$$U^0 = u_1(c_1^0) + u_2(c_2^0) + \gamma n[u_0(c_0^1) + u_1(c_1^1) + u_2(c_2^1)], \quad 0 < \gamma \leq 1, \tag{40}$$

subject only to the dynastic budget constraint,

$$c_1^0 + (p + c_0^1)n + \frac{c_2^0 + c_1^1 n}{r^0} + \frac{c_2^1 n}{r^0 r^1} \leq w^0 + \frac{w^1 n}{r^0}. \tag{41}$$

Each of her children would like to maximize

$$U^1 = u_0(c_0^1) + u_1(c_1^1) + u_2(c_2^1) + \frac{\gamma}{n}[u_1(c_1^0) + u_2(c_2^0)], \quad 0 < \gamma \leq 1 \tag{42}$$

subject to the same budget constraint. If $\gamma = 1$, we are back to the unanimity case. If $\gamma < 1$, however, there is a conflict of interests between the two generations (and, since there are no rotten kids,[23] the eponymous theorem does not apply). Stark (1993) models this situation as a non-cooperative game, and finds that the solution is generally inefficient. If the story literally ends at date 1, that is all there is to say. If the story goes on, however, a self-enforcing family constitution may exist, and everything we said about the descending altruism case will apply here too.

Which of these assumptions is the right one? Arguably none. Love for one's parent or children (the Latin *pietas*, not to be confused with *amor*, sexual love) develops with acquaintance. Psychologists talk of "bonding", ethologists of "imprinting".[24] In Becker and Murphy (1988) and elsewhere in Gary Becker's writings, the process of getting to love a parent or child is compared with that of becoming addicted to the consumption of certain substances. Making somebody's utility or consumption an argument in someone else's utility function does not capture this. Let us then consider the following alternative.

A childless adult is looking for the best way of providing for her own old age. Assuming that a self-enforcing constitution exists, she will have children. If she has grown to love her own parent, she will give the latter more than the minimum prescribed by the constitution. Once her children are born, she may get to love them too, and give them more than the constitution prescribes. In turn, her children may learn to love her, and give her more than the constitution prescribes. If the same happens at every step, each member of the dynasty will consume more than z when she is young, and more than nx when she is old.

It may happen, however, that some member of some generation, a black sheep (or, if you prefer, a rotten kid), will not get to love her parent or children. In the absence of a self-enforcing constitution, this black sheep would give nothing to her parent or

[23] Since children love their parent, *albeit* less than they love themselves, the utility of the former is not entirely contained in that of the latter.

[24] Something similar happens also outside the family. Experimental economists report that players behave differently in artificial game situations if they have had the opportunity to become acquainted beforehand, than if they go in cold.

children. In the presence of a self-enforcing constitution, by contrast, it will be in her interest to pay her parent and children the minimum that the constitution prescribes. In the same way as legal sanctions and a police apparatus are needed to deter malfeasance even in a generally law abiding society, so a self-enforcing constitution is needed as a defence against the possible appearance of a black sheep even in a mostly loving family. It is then an empirical question whether the constitution "bites" often enough to have a statistically significant effect on behaviour.[25]

Since complying is the dominant strategy, the argument goes through irrespective of whether the agent attaches a positive probability to the event that she will get to love her children once they are born, or is taken entirely by surprise. What we are proposing, therefore, is not a veil-of-ignorance argument (Rawls, 1971). According to the latter, the agent favours a redistributive policy because she is not sure whether she will be among the benefactors, or among the beneficiaries. Here, by contrast, an adult knows full well that adhering to a constitution will make her a benefactor in the current period, and a beneficiary in the next. The only thing she is not sure about is whether any member of the family, herself included, will give more than is strictly required by the constitution.

5. The state

We have seen that a *laissez-faire* equilibrium need not be a social optimum, and may not even be efficient. Can the state succeed where the market and the family fail? In this section, we look for ways in which the shortcomings of *laissez-faire* equilibria can be remedied by deliberate policy, under the assumption that the government (i) can costlessly observe parental actions, and (ii) does not have to account to an electorate for its policies. The problem of hidden parental actions will be dealt with in section 7, that of political acceptability in section 8.

Suppose that all individuals are the same, that r (hence, w) is constant, that individual behaviour is observable, and that the market is the only spontaneous coordination mechanism available. Under these assumptions, Groezen et al. (2003) show that a Millian social optimum can be implemented by introducing, side by side, a pay-as-you-go pension scheme and a system of child benefits, each financed by a lump-sum tax on adults. Analogous results are obtained by Peters (1995), and Kolmar (1997). Groezen et al. assume that people derive utility not only from their own consumption, but also from the number of children.[26] The argument, however, has more general validity. We adapt their analysis to the case where people derive utility from consumption only.

[25] For Italy, Cigno et al. (2007) estimate that up to 60 percent of voluntary transfers can be attributed to the effect of family constitutions.

[26] What they actually say is that an adult derives utility from having children only if she can give her a certain level of consumption. As this is a constant, included in the fixed cost of procuring a child, p, that is the same as saying that parents do not derive utility from their children's c_0.

Let η be a lump-sum benefit payable to each old person, and θ a lump-sum contribution payable by each adult. Assuming that the scheme must break even,

$$\eta = \theta n, \tag{43}$$

the policy imposes a life-cycle reallocation, but not an intergenerational transfer. Similarly, let φ be the benefit payable to adults for each child they have, and τ a lump-sum tax, payable by each adult. Assuming that it, too, must break even,

$$\varphi n = \tau, \tag{44}$$

this scheme does not impose an intergenerational transfer, but does re-distribute in favour of adults with children.

Let an asterisk denote the socially optimal value of a variable. The government can implement the social optimum by setting $\eta = c_2^*$, $\theta = \frac{c_2^*}{n^*}$, $\varphi = p + c_0^*$, and offering each adult j the following "forcing contract":[27]

$$\begin{array}{ll} \tau^j = (p + c_0^*)n^* & \text{if } n^j = n^* \text{ and } c_0^j = c_0^* \\ \tau^j = \tau' > (p + c_0^*)n^* & \text{otherwise} \end{array}. \tag{45}$$

The agent has then two alternatives: *either* procure n^* births, spend $p+c_0^*$ for each child that is born, and save nothing; *or* have no children, and save some positive amount, s^j. Given (1), the pay-off to the first course of action is

$$u_1(w - \theta) + u_2(\eta). \tag{46}$$

The pay-off to the second is

$$\max_s u_1(w - \theta - \tau' - s^i) + u_2(\eta + rs^i). \tag{47}$$

By setting τ' sufficiently large,[28] the government can induce j to choose the first alternative. Then, $n^j = n^*$, and $c_i^j = c_i^*$ $(i = 0, 1, 2)$ for every j. The policy looks remarkably like a family constitution, but with an important difference. Since the government, unlike the family, has the power to coerce, the former does not need to distort individual incentives in order to persuade people to comply. Combined with lack of uncertainty and informational asymmetries, that is what permits the government to achieve a first best.

[27] The expression comes from the principal-agent literature, and applies to any situation where the agent's actions are observable by the principal. As pointed out in the Introduction, a forcing contract applied to the number of children has an unpleasant ring about it, but this is purely a consequence of the simplifying assumption that parents control the number of births, and that the action of procuring a certain number of children thus coincides with its visible outcome; more about this in section 7.

[28] Alternatively, the government could threaten the agent with a drastically reduced pension. The important point to be noted is that it costs the government nothing to enforce the socially optimal plan.

Groezen et al. (2003) make the point that, without a child benefit scheme by its side, a pay-as-you-go pension scheme would create a positive population externality, because atomistic agents do not take into account that an extra birth increases social welfare by relaxing (43). We might then be tempted to regard φ as a Pigovian subsidy, but that would not be right. The policy maker does not in fact pay child benefits to induce agents to choose the right level of fertility, because that is costlessly achieved by threatening them with a sufficiently high penalty if they do otherwise. This unpleasant implication of first-best policy is an unavoidable implication of the fact that the number of children is observable, and of the assumption that parents can produce children by *fiat*. It will only go away when we allow for a random factor in realized fertility (see section 7). Under present assumptions, child benefits serve only to refund agents of the optimal cost of raising the optimal number of children, and thus to allow the parents themselves to buy the socially optimal level of consumption.

In real life agents are differentiated by a number of personal characteristics (earning capacity, cost of raising children, etc.). For a first best, public transfers would then need to be personalized. If some of these characteristics are private information, all that can be achieved is a second best. Provided the government has statistical information on the frequency distribution of these characteristics, it can induce agents to reveal their characteristics by offering them a menu of fiscal treatments, one for each type of agent. This approach involves distorting the decisions of the type more benignly treated by the fisc in order to deter mimicking. Since the number of children is a choice variable, however, the mimicker must procure the same number of children as the mimicked.[29] Mimicking is thus more difficult, and the distortion required to deter it smaller, than it would be if fertility were exogenous.[30]

Let us now bring family constitutions back into the picture. If the market provided perfect substitutes for attention, it is clear that these domestic arrangements would be wiped out by the policy we have just described. The same would be true if attention could be costlessly monitored by the public authorities, because the amount of attention due from each agent could then be specified in the forcing contract. But that would be stretching credibility too far. If we realistically assume that no public authority can enforce attention at zero cost, a first best would be out of reach, and family constitutions securing the delivery of attention to both the young and the old might then survive in the folds of second-best policy, even if individual actions and characteristics were observable. We shall come back to this issue, and to the one concerning the enforceability of optimal fertility control, in section 7.

[29] See Balestrino et al. (2002).

[30] Alternatively, if the self-revelation game is too costly to administrate, it may be preferable for the government to give up the idea of discovering who is who, and take the linear taxation route instead. Since the number of children is easily observable, however, the information conveyed by this variable should in any case be exploited to improve the design of the second-best policy. See Cigno and Pettini (2003).

6. Education

Reflecting a growing interest in human capital as the mainspring of economic growth, numerous papers on intergenerational transfers, including Cremer et al. (1992), Docquier and Michel (1999), Kaganovich and Zilcha (1999), Pecchenino and Utendorf (1999), Kemnitz (2000), Boldrin and Montes (2002), and Anderberg and Balestrino (2003), focus on children's education, rather than consumption. The basic questions asked in this sub-literature are analogous to those posed in earlier sections. What is the socially optimal level of transfers from parents to young children (this time in the form of education), and from children to elderly parents? Is *laissez faire* efficient? What can be done if it is not?

To compensate for the complication that education is a factor in the production of human capital, and that human capital is in turn an input into the production of income, contributors to the field make a number of simplifying assumptions. A common one is to treat fertility as exogenous. This is generally justified by saying that education decisions are taken when a child is already born, but is not legitimate in a dynamic analysis, where fertility choice and educational decisions should be linked by backward induction. Further simplifications include disregarding the above-subsistence consumption of the young ($c_0 = 0$), and assuming that the only effect of education is to increase future earning capacity. With the exception of Pecchenino and Utendorf, the authors mentioned assume that agents are moved by self-interest. With the exception of Cremer et al., who introduce filial attention in the utility function of the parents, they also assume that utility depends only on market goods (or that these are perfect substitutes for attention).

6.1. Market equilibrium and education policy

Taking the lowest common denominator of the various contributions, we write the life objective of each member of generation t as

$$U^t = u_1(c_1^t) + u_2(c_2^t). \tag{48}$$

The income produced by an adult at date t is given by

$$y^t = f(h^t, k^t), \tag{49}$$

where $f(.)$ is a constant-returns-to-scale production function with the usual properties, h^t is the stock of human capital, and k^t the stock of capital, all in per-adult terms. The stock of human capital is similarly determined by

$$h^t = g(e^t, \xi), \tag{50}$$

where $g(.)$ is another per-adult production function, with properties analogous to those of $f(.)$. Here, e^t denotes the (cost of the) education that a member of generation t received at date $t - 1$, and ξ is a parameter representing the endowment of human capital with which a person is born ("native talent").

The interest rate is still exogenous, but this does not pin down the capital/labour ratio as in the one-asset model of earlier sections, because it is now possible to substitute capital with human capital in the production of income. Given constant returns to scale, however, the asset mix and the price of human capital are determined by the rate of interest. The resource constraint is now

$$f(g(e^t,\xi),k^t) - r^t d^t = \frac{c_2^{t-1}}{n^{t-1}} + c_1^t + \left(p + e^{t+1} + \frac{k^{t+1} - d^{t+1}}{r^t}\right)n^t. \tag{51}$$

The first-order conditions for maximizing social welfare,[31] subject to (51), are

$$\frac{u_1'(c_1^t)}{u_2'(c_2^t)} = r^t \tag{52}$$

and

$$f_h(h^t,k^t)g_e(e^t,\xi) = r^t = 1 + f_k(h^t,k^t). \tag{53}$$

The latter is a portfolio condition, stating that the rate of return to education must equal the rate of return to capital.[32] Since fertility is exogenous (and all members of the same generations are the same), the first-order conditions for a social optimum coincide with those for a Pareto optimum.

Is market equilibrium efficient? Boldrin and Montes (2002) address the question under the assumption that markets are competitive, and that people can take their own lifetime decisions right from the moment they are born as in the Modigliani-like model discussed in section 3.1.[33] There is thus no need for parents (loving or otherwise) to buy goods on their children's behalf.

In the absence of credit rationing, a person born at date $t-1$ chooses (e^t, c_1^t, c_2^t) to maximize (48), subject only to the lifetime budget constraint

$$(p + e^t)r^t + c_1^t + \frac{c_2^t}{r^t} = h^t\omega^t, \tag{54}$$

where ω^t is the return to human capital at date t. The wage rate is now $h^t\omega^t$.[34] Given (50), this person borrows from the capital market, in period 0, to the point where the marginal return to education equals the return to capital,

$$\omega^t g_e(e^t,\xi) = r^t. \tag{55}$$

[31] With exogenous fertility, it does not matter whether the social welfare function is of the Benthamite, or the Millian variety.

[32] Like Boldrin and Montes, we are implicitly assuming that the young cannot save, and adults cannot be educated. Without this simplification, the timing of investment would have to be endogenously determined.

[33] They also assume a closed economy. As this complicates matters, but makes no difference to the points of concern here, we stick to our small-open-economy assumption.

[34] Boldrin and Montes assume that p is equal to zero (it costs nothing to have a child, and the young live on air). We retain the assumption that p is positive.

In period 1, the same person lends to the capital market to the point where (52) is satisfied.

A firm equates the marginal product of capital to the interest rate,

$$f_k(h^t, k^t) = r^t - 1 \tag{56}$$

and the marginal product of human capital to its price,

$$f_h(h^t, k^t) = \omega^t. \tag{57}$$

In view of (55), (52)–(53) is then satisfied. As in the simple life-cycle model of subsection 3.1, if everyone is free to borrow or lend any amount at the given interest rate, market coordination is thus enough to ensure that individual decisions allocate consumption efficiently.

As in section 3, however, we must allow for the possibility that the young cannot borrow from the market enough to finance the efficient level of educational investment. If that is the case, the economy will produce too little human capital. The policy remedy offered by Boldrin and Montes is analogous to that discussed in section 5, namely a lump-sum transfer φ to every young person, and a lump-sum transfer η to every old person, each financed by a specific lump-sum tax (respectively, $\tau = \varphi n$ and $\theta = \eta n$) payable by every current adult. The only difference is that φ is now to be interpreted as an educational grant, rather than a child benefit. Setting η equal to the optimal c_2, and φ equal to the optimal e,[35] will yield the social optimum. As fertility is now exogenous, there is no need for a forcing contract to get parents to deliver the right number of children.

If parents are altruistic as in Pecchenino and Utendorf (1999), there is the complication that public transfers may crowd out voluntary provision for education. We shall see in the next subsection that the same is true if parental choice is conditioned by the existence of self-enforcing family constitutions.

6.2. *Families again*

Instead of going straight for corrective policy, Anderberg and Balestrino (2003) look first for the possibility of an intra-family solution to the rationing problem faced by the young. The agent is again the parent, rather than the child. As in the model of section 4, they start by asking whether a family constitution (they call it a "family norm") involving transfers to children and to the old could be self-enforcing. Then, they check whether it is efficient (as fertility is now exogenous, the standard Pareto criterion can be applied). Adults are again faced with the alternative of either complying with a family constitution, or going it alone in the market. Again, the constitution prescribes the amount x that each adult must pay to her elderly parent, and the amount z that she must

[35] Recall that, by assumption, the government can observe and thus make sure that parents use φ for their children's education, and not for their own consumption.

pay to each of her young children (in addition to bearing the fixed per-child cost p). The difference is that z now pays for the child's education, rather than consumption, and that n is now assumed to be exogenous as in the model of the last subsection. Utility is given by (48).

The first step is again to characterize the set of constitutions that can be sustained by a sub-game perfect Nash equilibrium. The pay-off to going it alone in the market is again (23). Since n is exogenous, however, the pay-off to complying is simply[36]

$$v^*(w, x, z) = u_1(w - x - nz) + u_2(nx). \tag{58}$$

There is thus no reason why the marginal rate of substitution of adult for old-age consumption should equal the marginal return to money spent on children as in the endogenous fertility case. The necessary and sufficient condition for a constitution to be a sub-game perfect Nash equilibrium is again (31)

$$v^*(w, x, z) \geq v(r, w). \tag{59}$$

As the marginal return on the resources invested in children is now x/z, rather than $x/(p + z)$, however, (31) now implies

$$\frac{x}{z} > r,$$

rather than (32).

The boundary of the set of sustainable constitutions has again the shape depicted in Figure 2, but with a crucial difference. What is now equated to the number of children at the point where z reaches a maximum is the marginal rate of substitution of adult for old-age consumption, rather than the marginal return on children as in the endogenous fertility case,

$$\frac{u_1'(w - x - (p + z)n)}{u_2'(nx)} = n. \tag{60}$$

Once again, a constitution is renegotiation-proof if it is not Pareto-dominated by any other constitution that is itself a Nash equilibrium. It will thus maximize

$$U(x, z) = u_1(g(z, \xi)\omega - x - (p + z)n) + u_2(nx), \tag{61}$$

subject to (31). The solution satisfies (60), and

$$g_e(z, \xi)\omega = (1 + \upsilon)n, \tag{62}$$

where υ is the Lagrange-multiplier of (31). This tells us that the marginal return to education will be equal to n if the Nash constraint is not binding ($\upsilon = 0$), greater than

[36] With the number of children given, a person deciding to comply has nothing more to choose. Anderberg and Balestrino introduce a further element of choice by putting leisure in the utility function. As the utility function is assumed to be separable in consumption and leisure, however, this has no implications for the rest of the analysis.

n if it is binding ($\upsilon > 0$). In the first case, the point representing the constitution could be anywhere inside the Nash frontier. In the second, it is at (z^*, x^*), because that is the only point of the Nash frontier satisfying (60). In either case, there is nothing to ensure that the allocation is efficient. There is then scope for an education policy.

A very different kind of family is that described in Cremer et al. (1992). As in Bernheim et al. (1985), discussed at the end of subsection 4.4, it is assumed that parents use the promise of a bequest to extract attention from their children at rock-bottom price. But the question is now whether investing in the children's education will raise the amount of filial attention that parents get in return, sufficiently to induce the latter to invest the efficient amount. In the absence of corrective policy, the answer is no. Conveniently assuming that the exogenously given n equals the exogenously given r as in the Anderberg–Balestrino model, the authors show that an efficient equilibrium can again be induced by a judicious combination of public education and public pensions.

7. Uncertainty and hidden actions

In this section we examine the implications of dropping some of the more unrealistic assumptions made up to now. One is that domestic activities are costlessly observable by the government. Another is that a person's earning capacity is either exogenous, or depends only on education. Yet another is that parents can directly choose how many children to have. Let us start by supposing that a child's chances of success in life depend not only on actions taken by their parents, as we assumed in the last section, but also on chance, and that some parental actions are not observable by the government.

In the context of section 6, for example, we could re-interpret e as the vector of, broadly defined, educational activities carried out by the child's own parents. While school fees and some domestic expenditures are easily observable, some other domestic expenditures, and the time that parents spend with their children, may be impossible (or very costly) for the government to monitor. That would not make a difference if the unobservable actions could be inferred from the observation of h. It will make a difference, however, if we realistically assume that h depends not only on e, but also on luck, for in that case e will not be inferable from h. The same may be said about fertility decisions, if we realistically recognize that parents cannot directly choose n. The latter will then depend on an unobservable parental action (frequency of intercourse, contraceptive practice), denoted by b, and on random factors. An implication of all this is that the policy optimization takes the form of an agency problem, with the government in the role of principal, and parents in that of agents. Another is that the normative benchmark developed in section 2 can no longer be applied.

In section 2, we assumed that the government's objective ought to be that of maximizing social welfare, defined as a weighted mean or sum of the utilities of present and future individuals. The equivalent of that, in a situation where the size and characteristics of future generations are uncertain, would be to maximize the expectation of the social welfare over all possible states of the world. But that would contradict the methodological individualism principle that welfare assessments must be based on judgements made by a given set of individuals. Since the individuals that exist in a state of the world may be different from those that exist in another, maximizing expected social welfare could in fact involve averaging judgements made by *alternative* sets of individuals (Broome, 1993).

The implication is that policy can be judged only by its effects on the well-being of existing individuals. This is not a licence to exploit future generations, but does imply that the well-being of potential persons is taken in consideration only insofar and inasmuch as it contributes to the well-being of actual persons. Like so many economic propositions, this may be hard to swallow for many decent people, who regard it as their moral duty to do what they think is good for future generations. But that is precisely the point: moral individuals can only do what *they* think is good for people yet to come.[37] There is thus no conflict between the proposition that people, or some of them, are concerned with the well-being of potential persons, and the proposition that welfare judgements can only be based on the preferences of actual persons.

Cigno et al. (2003) assume that adults can directly choose n, but treat h as a random variable with given density conditional on e. In Cigno and Luporini (2006), n is treated as a random variable too, with given density conditional on b. The gain from relaxing the assumption that children can be produced by *fiat* is not only greater realism. It also gets rid of the unpalatable implication that the government can implement a social optimum by threatening to punish parents who have the wrong number of children (see section 5). Both the policy optimization and the decision problem of each agent have a dynamic programming structure, and are solved by backward induction. We shall draw on both papers to characterize the second-best policy under the simplifying assumption that existing adults are *ex-ante* identical.[38]

7.1. Parents as government agents

Given the tax system and the interest rate structure, the present value of a person's lifetime tax payments is a monotone function of earnings, hence as good a measure as any of a person's human capital at the start of adult life. Let us then measure the stock of human capital that a child born at date t will have at date $t+1$, h^{t+1}, as the present value (at date t) of the taxes that the future adult will pay at $t+1$. Let us assume that the adults living at date t derive utility from the present value, denoted by C^t, of their own consumption over what is left of their life. Possibly, they will derive utility also from n^t and h^{t+1}—either for altruistic reasons, or because a self-enforcing family constitution

[37] Doing that requires people to guess what future people will be like. Especially where their own children are concerned, many tend to see these potential persons as projections of themselves, and to impute them their own preferences and values.

[38] Cigno and Luporini (2006) allow for differences in parental ability to influence their children's future earning ability, but we shall not go into that here.

entitles them to receive transfers from their grown-up children conditionally on h^{t+1} (see subsections 4.1 and 6.2).

Continue to assume that human capital is determined by (50) as in section 6. Now, however, we take ξ to be a random variable with given density. We may interpret ξ again as native talent or, more generally, as luck (regarding not only natural ability, but also the fortuitous events that contribute to a person's success in the market place). Then h itself is a random variable, with probability density $\phi(h, e)$ derived, via (50), from that of ξ. As e is interpreted as educational investment, the higher the value of this variable, the better the chances that the future adult will have a high h.[39]

Although identical *ex ante*, agents are different *ex post* because of the random nature of n and x. Dispensing with time superscripts, because we are looking at the decisions of just one generation, the utility of agent j may now be written as

$$u_j = u(C_j + v(h_j)n_j), \tag{63}$$

where $u(.)$ is increasing and concave. We may interpret $v(h_j)$ either as the money-equivalent of the pleasure that j derives from her child's success, or as the actual money transfers that the constitution entitles her to receive, in old age, from a child with human capital h_j. The function $v(.)$ will be increasing and concave too.

The household budget constraint is

$$C_j = w + Y(n_j) + [y(h_j, n_j) - c(e_j) - p]n_j, \tag{64}$$

where w represents the agent's own income (net of taxes, and exclusive of transfers), Y is a government subsidy payable to parents when n_j is known, and possibly conditional on it,[40] y is a per-child government subsidy payable to parents when h_j is known, possibly conditional on it and on n_j,[41] $c(e_j)$ is the per-child cost of the action e_j, and p has the usual interpretation. Since $c(e_j)$ includes the opportunity-cost of the fixed household resources used by the action e_j, the function $c(.)$ may be taken to be increasing and convex (increasing marginal cost of e_j).[42]

Agent j decides first how much to invest in each child she might have, taking into account the way in which this decision will affect the probability distribution of h_j. She

[39] In more technical language, for any $e_2 > e_1$, the cumulative distribution corresponding to $\phi(., e_2)$ first-order stochastically dominates the one corresponding to $\phi(., e_1)$.

[40] As agents are *ex-ante* identical, the reward for choosing the right level of reproductive activity b_j, Y, cannot depend on anything other than the outcome of that activity, n_j.

[41] At the stage when they decide their educational investments, e_j, parents are differerentiated by number of children. Therefore, the φ payable to agent j may depend on the realized value of n_j, as well as on the outcome of the educational investment, h_j.

[42] If the resources used by this action include the agent's own time, w is to be interpreted as full income. If $v(h_j)$ is interpreted as future transfers from j's child, but this informal credit cannot be borrowed against (see subsection 4.1), the budget constraint remains (64), but w is then to be interpreted as net of any transfers due to j's parent, and $c(e_j)$ as net of any transfers due to each of j's children.

thus chooses e_j to maximize her utility expectation over all possible realizations of h_j,

$$U_j = \int u_j \phi(h_j, e_j) dh_j, \tag{65}$$

where u_j is determined by (63)–(64), taking n_j as a parameter. Assuming that agents are too many to collude, j takes government policy, represented by $Y(n_j)$ and $y(., n_j)$, as given. The first-order condition,

$$-c' n_j \int u'_j \phi dh_j + \int u_j \phi_{e_j} dh_j = 0, \tag{66}$$

tells us that j will raise e_j to the point where the expected marginal cost equals the expected marginal benefit. Notice that, if j gets neither pleasure nor money from h_j, $v(h_j) \equiv 0$, the benefit of e_j can come only through y. She will then choose e_j positive only if y is increasing in h_j.

The decision we have just examined associates a value of e_j with each possible realization of n_j. Armed with that information, j will then choose b, taking into account the effect that this will have on the probability distribution of n_j. In recognition of the fact that n_j can only take values 0, 1, 2, ..., we write its density in the discrete form $\pi(n_j, b)$. The agent will then choose b to maximize her expectation of U_j over all possible realizations of n_j and h_j,

$$E(U_j) = \sum_{n_j} \pi(n_j, b) \int u_j \phi(h_j, e_j) dh_j. \tag{67}$$

Let b be so defined that, the higher the value of this variable, the greater the chances of having many children. Since b carries no direct cost (it has only an expected indirect cost, via its expected effect on n_j), the first-order condition is

$$\sum_{n_j} \pi_b(n_j, b) \int u_j \phi(h_j, e_j) dh_j = 0, \tag{68}$$

meaning that the agent will increase b to the point where its expected marginal utility is equal to zero. Since u_j is increasing in Y, it is clear that, the larger this subsidy for any given n_j, the higher b.

7.2. *The government as principal*

Since the government acts on behalf of current adults, and adults are ex-ante identical, we may assume that the principal's objective is the same as that of the agents, namely to make the expected value of (63) as large as possible given (64).[43] But the government's choice of policy is subject also to an intergenerational budget constraint. Since

[43] If $v(h)$ is interpreted as money forthcoming to parents under a self-enforcing family constitution, this raises the question whether such informal arrangements will survive government intervention. Without rehearsing

the number of agents (hence the number of future tax payers) is "large", the government does not face uncertainty over its current transfer expenditure, and future tax revenue. We may then write this budget constraint in expected value terms.

At the stage where n_j is known, and $Y(n_j)$ consequently given, the government budget constraint is

$$\sum_j n_j \int (h_j - y(h_j, n_j))\phi(h_j, e_j)dh_j = \sum_j Y(n_j), \tag{69}$$

implying that the government can finance its transfers to current adults with the taxes paid by future adults.[44] But why should the government do that? Comparison of (69) with (64) makes it clear that j has no reason to take into account the effect of her own choice of e_j on the government budget constraint. There is thus an externality. A justification for the policy is then that, by promising to pay j at least part of the expected h_j, the government is in effect reducing this externality. Another justification is that, not facing any risk, the government can raise social welfare by insuring parents with a direct interest in their children's future against the risk that their children have low human capital.

At this stage of the game, the government chooses the payment schedule $y(.,.)$ that maximizes the sum of the objective functions of its agents,[45]

$$W = \sum_j U_j, \tag{70}$$

subject to its budget constraint (69), and to the incentive-compatibility constraints (66).[46] The fertility vector, $\mathbf{n}$, and the vector of per-adult transfers, $\boldsymbol{y}$, are taken as parameters.

The first-order conditions of this policy optimization tell us that, for each possible realization of h_j, y_j must satisfy

$$(u'_j - \lambda)y_j + \mu_j(-n_j c' u''_j \phi + u'_j \phi_{e_j}) = 0, \tag{71}$$

where λ is the Lagrange multiplier of (69) (the marginal social utility of tax revenue), and μ_j the Lagrange multiplier of (66) (the marginal social utility of relaxing the jth incentive-compatibility constraint).

the arguments used in the last two sections, it is clear that first-best (full-information) policy will wipe out any such arrangement. The interpretation of $v(h)$ as actual money is tenable only in a second-best (asymmetric information) setting, because families have an informational advantage over any public authority, that may ensure the survival of informal intra-family arrangements in the face of government policy. Di Tella and MacCullogh (2002) use this argument in relation to the mutual insurance role of families.

[44] At this stage, the taxes paid by current adults have already been used to finance transfers to their parents.

[45] Since the number of agents is given, it makes no difference whether we average or add-up. There is thus no conflict between the two versions of utilitarianism (see section 2).

[46] Standard restrictions on the distribution functions ensure that an agent's first-order condition can be used as an incentive-compatibility constraint.

If the government could observe educational investments, the incentive compatibility constraints would not be binding ($\mu_j = 0$ for all j),[47] and (71) would reduce to $u'_j = \lambda$ for all j. A first best could then be implemented by choosing the payment schedule $y(.,.)$ so that

$$y(h_j, n_j) + v(h_j) = \text{const.} \tag{72}$$

What this means is that, if the principal could observe how much money and time parents dedicate to their children's education, it would (i) order parents to undertake the socially optimal level of educational investment (the forcing contract idea), and (ii) assure them a given level of utility irrespective of how many children they happen to have, and how well each of these children will do in the future.[48] If parents have no interest in their children's future achievements ($v \equiv 0$), this implies that $y_h = 0$.[49] By contrast, if parents have a direct interest in their children's achievements ($v' > 0$), the government must fully insure parents against the risk that their children will meet with bad luck. In that case, the less the child achieves, the more the parent must be subsidized, $y_h < 0$.

Since educational investments are not fully observable, however, there is a moral hazard problem. The guarantee of full compensation would induce parents to underinvest in their children's education. The government will then borrow against the tax payments it expects to receive in the future from today's children in order to give parents the incentive to spend more for their children's education. The outcome is a second best. Let us see what we can say about the shape of the second-best $y(.,.)$.

Since μ_j is now positive, it is convenient to re-write (71) as

$$\frac{\lambda}{u'_j} = 1 + (\alpha n_j c' + \beta)\mu_j, \tag{73}$$

where $\alpha \equiv -u''_j/u'_j$ is the Arrow–Pratt measure of absolute risk aversion, assumed constant. The term $\beta \equiv \phi_{e_j}/\phi$ is a close relative of the likelihood ratio, assumed increasing in h_j. It is clear from (73) that, in second best, utilities will not be equalized as in first best. It is also clear that the optimal subsidy to j depends on n_j. Since u'_j is decreasing, and μ_j increasing in n_j,[50] agents with more children will be offered a larger transfer for the same amount of human capital ($y_n > 0$). Using standard arguments, it can also be shown that

$$y_h = \frac{\beta'}{\frac{\lambda}{\mu_j}\frac{\alpha n_j}{u'_j}} - v'. \tag{74}$$

[47] If e_j is observable, j can be forced to invest the optimal amount. There is thus no externality.

[48] Thogersen (1998) and Wagener (2003) show that a pay-as-you-go pension system does that under certain conditions.

[49] There is then no real need to use this policy instrument, η is enough.

[50] An increase in the number of children increases the marginal utility of income, and tightens the incentive-compatibility constraint.

If parents have no direct interest in their children's achievements ($\upsilon \equiv 0$), (74) tells us that the amount transferred must increase with the quantity of human capital per child, $y_h > 0$. In other words, parents are rewarded for having clever children, even though that is only partly their doing. That may not be the optimal policy, however, if parents have a direct interest in their children's future ($\upsilon' > 0$). Since υ' is decreasing in h_j, the transfer schedule is in that case likely to be U-shaped—decreasing in the child's human capital at low levels of h_j, where insurance considerations are paramount, increasing at high levels of h_j, where incentive considerations predominate. That provides a rationale for the common practice of subsidizing both the parents of handicapped or educationally subnormal children, and those of highly talented ones.

Let us now take a step back to the stage where n_j is still a random variable, conditional on j's choice of reproductive behaviour. Having already associated a function $y(.,.)$ with each possible combination of $\mathbf{n}$ and $\boldsymbol{Y}$, the government's problem is now to choose the payment schedule $Y(.)$. Since the logical structure of this stage of the policy optimization is analogous to the previous one, we shall simply summarize the procedure, and enunciate the main results. The government's objective is now to maximize the expectation of (70) over all possible realizations of $\mathbf{n}$. Its budget constraint differs from (69) only in that n_j is now a random variable with discrete density conditional on b_j. The incentive-compatibility constraint is now (68), the same for all j.

The first-order condition on the choice of $\mathbf{Y}(.)$ (i.e., of a value of $\mathbf{Y}$ for each possible realization of $\mathbf{n}$) may be written as

$$\frac{\upsilon}{\int u'\phi dh} = 1 + \gamma\psi, \tag{75}$$

where υ is the Lagrange multiplier associated with the government budget constraint, and γ the Lagrange multiplier of (68). The analogue of β, $\psi \equiv \pi_b/\pi$, is an increasing function of n_j.

Let us again start by considering the first-best situation, where individual actions are observable. As this implies that the incentive-compatibility constraints are not binding at any stage of the policy optimization problem ($\gamma = 0,\ \mu_j = 0$), (75) reduces to

$$u' = \upsilon. \tag{76}$$

The first-best policy is then to (i) order each agent to undertake the optimal level of reproductive activity, and (ii) use Y to provide parents with full insurance against the risk of getting too many, or too few, children.

Let us now come to the second-best situation, where individual actions are not observable. In this case, agents cannot be offered an unconditional subsidy, because that would tempt them to choose too low a level of b (a moral hazard problem). As (68) is now binding, γ is positive. Since ψ is an increasing function of n_j, and does not depend on any other variable, the same must be true of Y. Therefore, $Y' > 0$. It can be shown that the second-best b is larger than the one any agent would have chosen in the absence of policy (recall that reproductive activity has no immediate cost, but will have one if children are born). This means that there is a positive population externality. Since the second-best policy equates the expected net external benefit of b to the cost for the government of providing each agent with the incentive to choose a higher b, Y is a Pigovian subsidy. The reader will recall that the same could not be said of child benefits, in subsection 3.1, because the number of children was then assumed to be deterministically chosen, and agents could thus be ordered to choose the right n.

It comes natural to interpret the subsidy conditional on realized fertility as child benefits, $\varphi_j = Y'(n_j)$. The per-child subsidy conditional on realized human capital lends itself to two alternative interpretations. To the extent that scholastic performance is a predictor of future tax paying capacity, we may interpret $y(h_j, n_j)$ as a scholarship, conditional on "merit" (school record), and adjusted for "need" (family size). Since tax paying capacity can be gaged with any accuracy only when a person is well into middle age, and her parent on the point of retirement, it seems more natural, however, to interpret $\eta_j = y(h_j, n_j)n_j$ as a pension entitlement conditional on the number and contributive capacity of the pensioner's children. Notice that this policy gives adults an incentive to have children and invest in their education. It thus differs from a conventional pay-as-you-go scheme, where the contributions paid by current adults go into a common pool, and there is thus no incentive for adults to produce high earners.[51]

8. Political acceptability

We now address the question whether a system of public transfers can be implemented in a democratic society. Browning (1975) makes the fundamental point that, since children do not vote, direct democracy produces a pension system that is larger than the one which would maximize the lifetime utility of the representative agent. This argument is further developed in a long series of public choice papers, including Boadway and Wildasin (1989), Hansson and Stuart (1989), Tabellini (1991), Verbon (1993), Peters (1995), Meijdam and Verbon (1996), Kolmar (1997), Grossman and Helpman (1998), Boldrin and Rustichini (2000), Conde-Ruiz and Galasso (2000), and Kemnitz (2000) among others. See Breyer (1994) for an early survey.

A somewhat smaller number of contributions, beginning with Shubik (1981) and including, among others, Kotlikoff et al. (1986), Kotlikoff (1988), Esteban and Sakovics (1993), and Caillaud and Cohen (2000), attempt to explain public intergenerational transfers as the outcome of some kind of constitutional arrangement. These constitutional political economy papers pose, at the level of society, the same sort of questions that the papers examined in section 4 and subsection 6.2 pose at the level of the family. Although the idea of a constitution comes from politics, the kind of unspoken agreement these authors are looking for is in fact closer in spirit to a family constitution, than to a political constitution in the usual sense. To avoid confusion, we shall thus refer to such an arrangement as a "social compact", rather than a constitution.

[51] Indeed, if contributions increase with earnings as is normally the case, there is an incentive to have fewer children, and spend as little time as possible with each of them.

The contributions to this sub-literature share a number of common assumptions. The first is that fertility is exogenous. The second is that (with rare exceptions such as Hansson and Stuart, who postulate altruism towards the old) agents are self-interested. The third is that, with the notable exception of Shubik's pioneering work, people are either born adult,[52] or do not eat when young. Transfers to the young come into the picture only insofar as they serve to pay for education, and inasmuch as education raises future productivity.

The last assumption is difficult to justify. Even assuming (unrealistically) that they do not require material or personal assistance from their own or anyone else's children, the old still need adults around to transform any capital stock they may have accumulated into consumption goods. Therefore, current adults may be expected to have a keen interest in the survival, hence in the consumption, of those who are currently young. Future productivity should be only a second-order consideration. Why are the young ignored then? As Martin Shubik noted with reference to Samuelson (1958),[53] there is an implicit assumption that parents will instinctively provide for the survival of their offspring. Either that, one might add, or political agreement on legislation obliging parents to care for their children is reached as a matter of course. But neither of these assumptions is sufficient to ensure that the young will receive the efficient level of support.

8.1. A social compact?

We now look for the possibility that intergenerational cooperation might be the result of some kind of constitution-like social agreement. Esteban and Sakovics (1993) examine a number of stylized institutions that redistribute intergenerationally, and explain their emergence as the outcome of some kind of either cooperative or non cooperative game between generations. Rather than looking for a self-enforcing mechanism, these authors rely on the build-up of trust to make the agreement stick. By contrast, Caillaud and Cohen (2000) search for the society-wide equivalent of a self-enforcing family constitution.

The framework is highly simplified. Adults produce but do not consume,[54] and the old consume but do not produce, a perishable consumption good. Production per adult at date t is determined by

$$y^t = k^t l^t, \tag{77}$$

where l^t is the labour supplied by an adult at date t, and k^t is now interpreted as the state of knowledge (but could just as well be the stock of capital) at that same date. The time-path of k is exogenous (but nothing of substance changes if it is endogenized).

[52] Significantly, working-age individuals are in fact referred to as "the young". For coherence with the terminological conventions of this chapter, we promote them to the rank of adults.

[53] The actual quotation is in section 1.

[54] A more palatable way of putting this would be to say that, in period 1 (as in period 0), consumption is a constant, normalized to zero.

Population is also exogenous, and taken to be constant. The lifetime utility of a member of generation t is determined by

$$U^t = -v(k^t, l^t) + c_2^t, \tag{78}$$

where $v(k^t, .)$ is a convex loss function, measuring the disutility (given the current state of knowledge, k^t) of supplying l^t units of labour in period 1 for a member of generation t.

A Pareto-optimal l^t maximizes (78), subject to (77). The market alone will not yield such an outcome. Since people care only about their own consumption, generation t will in fact produce goods only if this induces generation $t+1$ to do the same. In the absence of a mechanism ensuring that, nobody produces anything;[55] consequently, nobody grows to be old. We are back to Samuelson (1958).

The way out proposed by Caillaud and Cohen is analogous to Cigno (1993, 2006), examined in section 4. They look for a "standard of behaviour" thus conceived, that any "generation should not be in a position such that it would prefer to erase the past, name itself generation [0] and reinitialize the strategy profile that was followed up to this date, rather than continue to abide by the current strategy profile" (Caillaud and Cohen, 2000). As in subsection 4.2, an undominated allocation of consumption meets this criterion, and is thus renegotiation-proof. Alternative approaches, such as the one proposed by Kotlikoff et al. (1986), who view the constitution as an asset that the old would like to sell to the adult generation, do not pin down a unique standard of behaviour.

A problem with this transposition of the constitution idea from the family level to society at large is that a single defector cannot be punished without also punishing the whole generation to which the defector belongs. While a family constitution entitles an adult to punish her own parent (not the entire category) if the latter misbehaved, the standard of behaviour proposed by Caillaud and Cohen does in fact entitle a generation to collectively punish all members of the previous generation (e.g., by stopping pension payments) if just one of them misbehaved. That makes the threat less than credible. Furthermore, for the argument to go through, it is required that each adult know not only how her own parent, but also how every other member of her parent's generation behaved. This imposes an unrealistically heavy informational requirement on the scheme.

These problems go away if adults are altruistically inclined towards the old, as assumed in an earlier contribution by Veall (1986). Altruism, however, is a stronger assumption to make at the level of the whole of society, than in a family context. If we think of altruistic behaviour as a product of acquaintance (see subsection 4.3), and society is not just the population of a little village, but an entire nation a lifetime will not be enough for anyone to get to know and love every other member of society.

[55] Had we not put period-1 consumption to zero, we could have said that adults deploy the amount of labour, and produce the amount of goods, that just meets their own immediate consumption requirements.

8.2. Direct democracy

Browning's seminal contribution assumes direct democracy. Taken literally, this means that citizens are able to vote on every single policy. That is unusual in real life, but some political constitutions do contemplate referenda on a range of specified issues. Others allow only consultative referenda, but the outcome of these consultations heavily conditions the decisions of parliament. Direct democracy gives current voters the power to condition future voting because it creates vested interests. Suppose, for example, that a pay-as-you-go pension system is voted in at date t. At date $t+1$, part of the electorate (the old of the day) will have a vested interest in keeping the system going. The same may be said about a vote, at date $t+1$, on whether to honour the public debt issued on the strength of a vote at date t.

We now examine a number of contributions that exploit the dynamic interdependence of single-issue political consultations under the assumption of rational expectations. As these papers look for conditions such that a decision is not overturned (at least not immediately) by a subsequent vote, the research agenda is not very different from that of the "constitutional" models looked at in subsection 8.1. The crucial difference is that the generation or generations who introduce the policy have now a first-mover advantage on subsequent generations. Constitutions are designed to prevent exactly that!

An equilibrium is defined as a sequence of policy decisions and market prices such that, at each date, (i) markets clear, (ii) the utility of each agent is at a maximum given the policy and the prices, and (iii) the policy is weakly preferred to any other by a majority of current voters. The last restriction plays a role analogous to that of renegotiation-proofness in a constitutional model. The rational expectations assumption bites more deeply here than in an ordinary market equilibrium model, because it implies an understanding on the part of all voters not only of the general equilibrium effects of the policy they are called to vote upon, but also of the way in which the policy will condition future voting behaviour.

8.2.1. Voting over pensions

Boldrin and Rustichini (2000) are interested in the possibility that a pay-as-you-go pension system brought in by referendum at a certain date will never be revoked, or will at least survive the generations that voted it in. The set-up is similar to that of section 3, except that fertility is now exogenous, and the economy is assumed to be closed. The latter is essential, because the argument now rests crucially on the general-equilibrium effects that the policy is expected to have on factor prices. At each date t, adult and old citizens are called to vote on a policy that taxes each adult $\theta^t = \tau^t w^t$ $(0 \leq \tau^t < 1)$, and pays each old person $\eta^{t-1} = n^{t-1}\theta^t$.[56] The vote is essentially about the value of τ^t

[56] Recall that n^{t-1} is the fertility rate of generation $t-1$, an thus the ratio of tax payers to pensioners at date t.

($\tau^t = 0$ means that the policy is rejected). Clearly, the old will favour as large a τ^t as possible. Adults may face a trade-off. On the one hand, any τ^t greater than zero reduces their current consumption; on the other, the policy could offer a higher return than the market ($\frac{\eta^t}{\theta^t} > r^t$).

Given k^t and τ^t, and the expectations held by current adults about η^t (the actual one will depend on n^t and τ^{t+1}), market competition determines factor prices, and the amount saved by each adult, at date t. A vote at date t in favour of introducing, or maintaining, a pay-as-you-go pension system would influence the amount collectively saved by generation t, hence the capital stock, and factor prices, at date $t+1$. Therefore, the outcome of the vote taken at t creates facts on the ground, that will condition future voting behaviour. Under particular functional assumptions (not dissimilar from those of Caillaud and Cohen, examined in the last subsection), Boldrin and Rustichini establish conditions on technology and individual preferences, such that a sequence of tax rates $(\tau^0, \tau^1, \tau^2, \ldots)$ is a subgame-perfect Nash equilibrium.

Boldrin and Rustichini find that there may be equilibria where the pension system is not brought in until a certain date, but it is then kept forever. The opposite case, where the system is abandoned after a certain date, is not admissible in a growing economy. If n is always greater than 1, there are always more adult than old voters. Were it known in advance that generation t would vote against the system at date t, generation $t-1$ would vote against it at $t-1$, otherwise it would find itself financing the pensions of generation $t-2$ for no good reason. Since the same applies to generations $t-2$, $t-3$, $\ldots$, a pay-as-you-go pension system can exist only if everyone believes that it will go on forever.[57] Suppose, however, that a sudden drop in the population growth rate will some day make the pay-as-you-go pension system unsustainable as a sub-game perfect Nash equilibrium. If the agents know that this will happen, but are not sure when, they may take the risk of voting for the maintenance of the pay-as-you-go system one period more.[58]

It is interesting to compare this way of dealing with the issue with that of Caillaud and Cohen, examined in the last subsection. There, many alternative standards of behaviour could be sustained as sub-game perfect Nash equilibria, but only one was renegotiation-proof. Here, if an economic-political equilibrium exists, it may be unique (in the examples provided by Boldrin and Rustichini, there is only one stable equilibrium). In contrast with a renegotiation-proof standard of behaviour, however, the economic-political equilibrium brought about by a sequence of plebiscites need not be efficient.

8.2.2. *Voting over the public debt*

At various stages of this chapter, we have come across the result that allowing for either altruism or intra-generational heterogeneity facilitates intergenerational cooperation.

[57] The same is of course of the family constitutions examined in sections 4 and 6, and of the standard of behaviour discussed earlier in this section.

[58] Boldrin and Rustichini show this to be the case under certain functional assumptions.

Tabellini (1991) assumes both intragenerational heterogeneity, and (bilateral) altruism, but the result is an increase in the first-mover advantage of earlier generations. It would thus appear that, in the absence of a constitution at some level, altruism or intragenerational heterogeneity bring about exploitation of future generations, rather than mutually beneficial cooperation.

The policy under consideration is now government debt, rather than a pay-as-you-go pension system as in Boldrin and Rustichini, just examined. The latter also implies a public debt, because it commits a generation to make a net transfer to the previous one; it, too, can be repudiated just like and explicit debt. But the creditors of a pension system are the old of the land, not just those of them who chose to buy government bonds. Tabellini looks for conditions such that the public debt issued at a certain date will not be repudiated at the next. The amount of debt to be issued, and the subsequent decision whether or not to honour it, are the subject of referendum. As usual, only adults and the old can vote.

At date 0, there is a certain number of adults, each of whom begets an exogenously given number of children, n. At date 1, those children will be adults, and their parents will be old. In order to end the story there, it is assumed that generation 1 does not have children, and will not live to be old. Apart from this (and from the common assumption that the young live on air), the utility functions of parents and children are, respectively, (40) and (42) as in the bilateral altruism model of subsection 3.2. Therefore, parents may choose to make gifts to their children, and children to their parents (but things are so arranged that, in equilibrium, neither of them will).

Intragenerational heterogeneity is introduced by assuming that, in periods 1 and 2 of her life, each agent j receives a_i^j $(i = 1, 2)$ units of a perishable good. The cumulative distribution of this endowment is common knowledge, but the actual a^j is known only to j. In other words, individual wealth is not observable. Each member of generation t $(t = 0, 1)$ produces w^t units of the good in period 1 of her life. Unlike initial endowments, w^t is the same for all j (but may vary endogenously with t). This assumption is intended to capture the empirical regularity that income is generally less unequally distributed than wealth.

Let us now describe the political process. At date 0, the government submits to referendum a policy proposal that would pay every current adult a lump sum $g \geq 0$, and finance these transfers by issuing bonds. The vote is about the value of g ($g = 0$ means that no debt is issued, and no public transfer is consequently made). Since there are no old people yet, only adults vote. Once the vote is taken, each adult decides how much to save; adult j saves s^j. Assuming that there is no store of value other public debt, saving means buying government bonds. Notice that, as adults have different wealth endowments, they may save different amounts.

At date 1, the electorate is called upon to decide whether to honour or repudiate the debt. If it is decided that the debt should be honoured, the government will have to recover the cost by taxing current incomes and bond holdings. Since inherited wealth is not observable, bond holdings can be taxed only at a flat rate, denoted by θ. Since w is the same for all adults, the income tax rate, τ, is also the same for everybody. If it is decided that the debt should be repudiated, there is no need to raise taxes, but bonds become worthless. The vote is about the values of θ and τ ($0 \le \theta \le 1, 0 \le \tau < 1$). Whichever policy emerges from the polls, it will redistribute not only between, but also within generations.

On the assumption that $n > 1$, at date 1, there are more adult than old voters. Therefore, the old alone could not push through a resolution in favour of honouring the debt. Furthermore, it is not in the interest of all the old that the debt should be honoured, because some of them do not hold bonds, but all have children. If the debt is honoured, any bonds held by the former will in fact have a positive redemption value, but the latter will have to pay tax on their incomes. Therefore, families without savings are unambiguously in favour of repudiating the debt (i.e., of expropriating the rich), but families with savings face a trade-off. Assuming single-peaked preferences, the outcome of the vote is determined by the "median voter" who, in the present context, is a kind of synthetic family, consisting of an old person m, holding a share $\frac{s^m}{g}$ of the outstanding debt, and an adult (not m's own child) whose parent holds a share $\frac{s^m}{\gamma^2 g}$; $\frac{s^m}{g}$ is so determined that, in the economic-political equilibrium, the two members of this synthetic family vote in exactly the same way.

Under certain functional and other restrictions, Tabellini shows that a majority comprised of both adult and old voters may favour honouring the debt ($\theta, \tau > 0$). A necessary condition for this to happen is that

$$\frac{s^m}{g} \ge \gamma u_1'(c_1^1), \tag{79}$$

where adult consumption, c_1^1, is the same for every member of generation 1 because of the functional and distributional assumptions made. In equilibrium,

$$c_1^1 = w^1 - (r-1)\frac{g}{n}, \tag{80}$$

where r is the net redemption value of a government bond ($r - 1$ is the implicit rate of return on a bond after paying the tax θ).

The properties of the politically viable set are illustrated in Figure 3. The abscissa measures the size of the outstanding debt. The ordinate shows the values of the left and right-hand sides of (79). The graph of $\gamma u_1'(c_1^1)$ is upward-sloping and convex, because the income tax rate must obviously increase with the size of the debt (hence, c_1^1 decreases, and u_1' increases, as g goes up). Since the number of bonds held by the median voter increases with the overall size of the debt, but not necessarily in the same proportion, the graph of s^m/g may slope up or down. A plausible hypothesis is that the curve will be upward-sloping at low levels of g, downward-sloping at high ones.[59] The politically viable set is represented by the segment $g'g''$.

[59] Tabellini shows this to be the case under certain special assumptions, including a uniform distribution of wealth endowments.

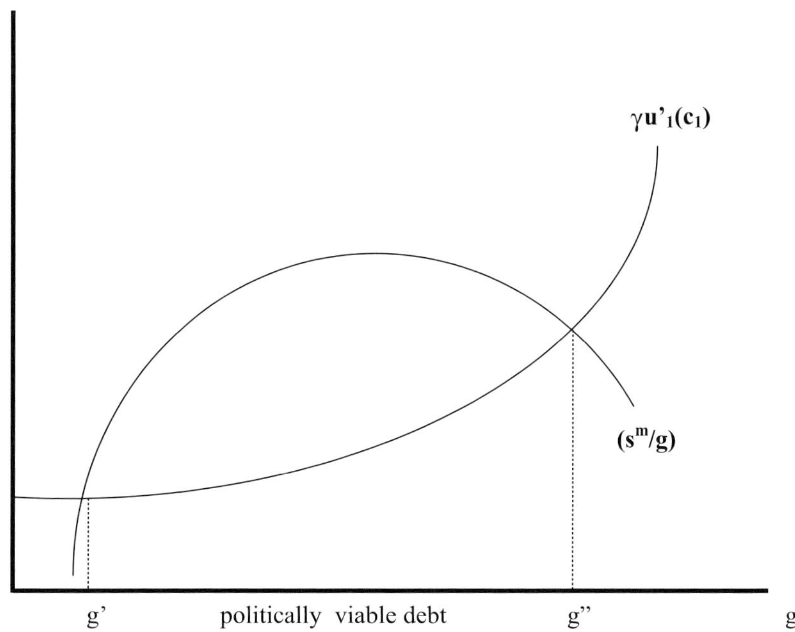

Figure 3. The set of politically viable public debt levels.

If the politically viable set is non-empty as illustrated, generation 0 will vote, at date 0, in favour of a public transfer to themselves, confident in the knowledge that the resulting debt will fall partly on generation 1. Clearly, these voters will favour the largest sustainable debt, g''. Such a policy would not have been passed if generation 1 could have voted at date 0. In the absence of a constitution preventing generation 0 from exploiting their first-mover advantage, however, generation 0 will vote to change the economic environment in such a way, that it is then in the interest of a sufficient number of members of generation 1 to vote, at the next referendum, in favour of honouring the debt. This underlines the difference between a sequential voting model, such as this, or the one of the last sub-subsection, and a "constitutional" model where the ground rules are laid down before anyone has a chance to change things to her advantage.

In contrast with the model of the last sub-subsection, a pay-as-you-go pension system would not be politically viable in the present context. Since generation 1 does not have children, and knows that it will not live to be old, its members would in fact oppose being taxed to give generation 0 a pension (being altruistic towards *their* parents, however, they may give *them* gifts);[60] but this result is contrived. If generation 1 did not die

[60] Being altruistic towards *their* parents, however, the may give them gifts.

prematurely, and were followed by a generation 2, a generation 3, etc., a pay-as-you-go pension system might be sustainable.[61] It is more interesting to note that, in the Tabellini model, generation 0 can change the landscape for generation 1 not only via factor price changes as in Boldrin and Montes, but also via changes in the personal distribution of wealth. That is possible because Tabellini allows for the initial distribution of wealth to be unequal, and assumes bilateral altruism. The first assumption uncouples the fate of individual agents from that of the rest of their generation, the second ties it to that of their ascendants and descendents. Without these two assumptions, debt-financing would not be politically viable.

8.3. Representative democracy

We have already noted that, in real life, "government by the people" usually means representative democracy. In such a system, policies are decided upon by the government, or by the parliamentary majority that supports it. Since governments are voted-in on the basis of broad, often vaguely worded, electoral programmes, that gives the executive a certain latitude over which measures actually to implement. It also leaves the government open to pressure by interest groups (which, in our context, reflect age groups). While direct democracy models predict the behaviour of voters, representative democracy models thus predict essentially the behaviour of politicians.

There are two ways, respectively inspired by Becker (1983) and Coughlin (1986), of modelling the political process in a representative democracy. Becker makes the relative political weight of each interest group a function of its relative expenditure on lobbying. Coughlin shows that maximizing the probability of re-election in a two-party system tantamounts to maximizing the sum of the objective functions of the voters.[62] The public choice literature on intergenerational transfers draws on both these considerations by expressing the government's objective (some authors call it "target", others "political support") function, at any date t, as a weighted sum of the utilities of generations t and $t-1$. This differs from a conventional social welfare function in that the relative weight of each generation depends on its ability to exert political influence, rather than on ethical considerations. As only electors count, the young have zero political weight. Their consumption or utility would enter the objective function of the government if it were an argument in the utility function of their respective parents, but it is assumed that it is not.

With the exception of Hansson and Stuart (1989), who implicitly *assume* the existence of a constitution by imposing that each generation has the right to block any new legislation that would leave it worse-off, the assumption commonly made in representative democracy models is that any decision taken by a parliament can be reversed by

[61] Conde-Ruiz and Galasso (2000) find precisely that.

[62] Coughlin et al. (1990) nuance this by introducing ideological bias in favour of one or the other party, and show that more ideologically homogeneous groups are more successful in influencing government policy than less homogeneous ones.

the next. Again with the exception of Hansson and Stuart, who postulate ascending altruism, another common assumption is that individuals, and the governments they elect, are self-interested. In the models we shall examine in some detail, adult individuals maximize the utility they get from their own consumption over what is left of their life cycle. The government maximizes the probability of its own re-election. At any given date, adults decide how much to save, taking current and future taxes and benefits as given.

As in the last subsection, the economic-political equilibrium is modelled as a sequence of non-cooperative games. At each date, the government chooses current taxes and benefits, taking current saving decisions, and future taxes and benefits as given (in comparison with the direct democracy models, the sequence of economic and political decisions is thus reversed). Since future taxes and benefits will be decided by the future governments, the current Nash equilibrium is conditioned by political expectations. Boadway and Wildasin (1989) assume arbitrary expectations about future political decisions; the papers examined below impose rational ones.

8.3.1. Lobbying for pensions

Meijdam and Verbon (1996) postulate a closed economy, such that the interest rate is endogenous. Their motivation for making this assumption is to rule out corner solutions with either zero private saving, or zero public pensions.[63] At any date t, adults choose (c_1^t, c_2^t, s^t) so as to maximize (48), subject to

$$c_1^t = w^t - \theta^t - s^t \tag{81}$$

and

$$c_2^t = s^t r^t + \eta^{t+1}, \tag{82}$$

taking the current pension contribution, θ^t, and the future pension benefit, η^{t+1}, as given. As usual, the first-order condition yields (16). Having conveniently assumed that the young live on air, this ensures that consumption is efficiently allocated over the life-cycle of each generation. The old have no allocative decision to take. Given the current pension benefit, η^t, their consumption at date t is determined by past saving decisions,

$$c_2^{t-1} = s^{t-1} r^{t-1} + \eta^t. \tag{83}$$

Since k^t is pre-determined by s^{t-1}, the private sector of the economy is closed using (2), (5) and (14).

Taking s^t and η^{t+1} as given, today's government chooses θ^t and η^t so as to maximize its objective function,

$$W^t = n^{t-1}\left[u_1\left(c_1^t\right) + u_2\left(c_2^t\right)\right] + \rho^t u_2\left(c_2^{t-1}\right), \tag{84}$$

[63] As noted in section 5, that could have also been taken care of by allowing for intragenerational heterogeneity, or introducing uncertainty.

where ρ^t denotes the relative political weight of the old, subject to (81)–(83), and to the pay-as-you-go constraint,

$$\eta^t = \theta^t n^{t-1}. \tag{85}$$

Political weight could simply reflect numerical strength, in which case $\rho^t = 1$ for all t. More generally, however, it may reflect ability to coordinate, and thus to exert political influence by lobbying.

As the authors themselves point out, the larger a group, the more costly it is for its members to coordinate their lobbying activities. From the argument that political weight may differ from numerical strength as a result of lobbying, it then follows that the political weight of the old could *increase* with the relative numerical strength of adults.[64] Casual observation does indeed suggest that an increase in the dependency ratio (the number of old people per adult) raises public concern for the welfare of the working generations, not of the retired. Nonetheless, Meijdam and Verbon assume that the relative political weight of the old increases with their numbers, $\rho^t = \rho(n^{t-1})$, $\rho'(.) < 0$.

The first-order conditions yield

$$\frac{u_1'(y^t - \theta^t - s^t)}{u_2'(s^{t-1}r^{t-1} + n^{t-1}\theta^t)} = \rho^t. \tag{86}$$

If a Nash equilibrium exists, the value of θ^t that solves (86) maximizes the government's chances of re-election. Therefore, a sequence of voting equilibria *may* support transfers to the old. Will it allocate consumption efficiently?[65] In general it will not, because there is nothing to ensure that public transfers satisfy (6). In view of (16), however, (86) implies $r^t = \rho(n^{t-1})$ for all t. If the exogenously given rate of population growth is constant over time ($n^t = n$ for all t), the political process then yields a steady state characterized by

$$r = \rho(n). \tag{87}$$

If it so happens, but it would only be chance, that $\rho(n) = \frac{n}{\delta}$, (6) is satisfied, and consumption is then efficiently allocated across generations.

8.3.2. Lobbying for pensions and education subsidies

Finding that, if pensions are the only item on the agenda, the political process may not deliver a system of intergenerational transfers should not have come as a surprise. Given a capital market, or the possibility of directly accumulating a durable good, adults can in

64 This line of reasoning is followed in Kemnitz (2000), to be considered next.

65 Such a question is not in the public choice spirit. Indeed, it is not addressed in Meijdam and Verbon (1996); we have a stab at it exploiting the analogies with Meijdam and Verbon (1997).

fact do without a public pension system, because they can save for old age. Intergenerational transfers are strictly needed only by the young, who cannot support themselves in other ways. We also know since section 5 that, if the young are allowed in the picture, a pension system on its own is not enough to allocate consumption efficiently.

Konrad (1995) argues that the old have an interest in paying for public education, because this will shift the Laffer curve. A similar line is taken by Kemnitz (2000). Since education increases future per-capita income, educational grants make it possible to increase pension benefits (of interest to adults, as well as to the old) without increasing taxes. *Mutatis mutandis*, these two papers present similarities with the Cremer et al. (1992) model, reviewed in subsection 6.2, where parents strategically choose how much to spend for their children's education with an eye to how this will raise their pay-off in the subsequent bequests-for-attention game. There, however, the game is restricted to members of the same family. Here, it involves the entire polity.

Let φ be again the amount that the government pays to parents for each of their children, and τ the lump-sum tax imposed on each adult to finance the scheme. As in section 6, we interpret φ as an educational grant (again, children eat nothing), and assume that parents can be forced to choose $e = \varphi$.[66] A pension system paying η to every old person, and charging θ to every adult, is also in place. Of course, either of these schemes could be inactive (θ or τ could be zero). Human capital is still determined by (50). Following Kemnitz, however, we now assume that $\xi^t = h^{t-1}$ stands for the parent's stock of human capital, rather than for the child's own native talent. Therefore, parents have a tutorial role.

Beside putting education on the political agenda, Kemnitz introduces uncertainty about survival into old age. Assuming a perfect annuity market,[67] and denoting by π the probability that an adult will live to be old, a unit of money saved by an adult at date t is now worth r^t/π, rather than simply r^t, a period later. Since uncertainty leaves scope for an equilibrium with both saving and public transfers even if the interest rate is exogenous, there is no need to assume a closed economy just to get that result. A small open economy assumption is thus assumed.

In contrast with Meijdam and Verbon, the political weight of each age group explicitly depends, *à la* Becker, on how much the group spends to influence government policy. Therefore, political weight is now truly endogenous. As all persons of the same age look the same, there is not a problem of preference aggregation, decisions are unanimous. Since political weight benefits all members of the group equally, however, there is still a free-riding problem (political weight is a kind of local public good). To get round this, Kemnitz assumes that "influence expenditure" serves to pay not only for lobbying, but also for maintaining group discipline. As the cost of maintaining discipline increases with numbers (like Coase's transaction costs), the amount of political influence bought by a unit of money decreases as the size of the group increases.

[66] What to do when e is not observable was discussed in section 7.

[67] Without it, there would be precautionary saving (to guard against the risk of having to support oneself in old age), and involuntary bequests *à la* Modigliani.

Being uncertain whether they will still be alive at $t+1$, adults at date t choose $(c_1^t, c_2^t, s^t, x_1^t, x_2^t)$ so as to maximize the expectation of (48),[68]

$$E(U^t) = u_1(c_1^t) + \pi u_2(c_2^t), \tag{88}$$

subject to

$$c_1^t = (w^t - \theta^t - \tau^t)h^t - x_1^t - s^t \tag{89}$$

and

$$c_2^t = \frac{s^t r^t}{\pi} + \eta^{t+1} - x_2^t, \tag{90}$$

where x_i^t is "influence" expenditure in period i $(i = 1, 2)$. As in section 6, w^t is interpreted as the rate of return to human capital at date t. The wage rate is again given by $h^t w^t$, but h^t is now entirely determined by past education policies, rather than private decisions. The private sector of the economy is closed by the factor pricing equations, (56) and (57).

The government's objective is

$$W^t = n^{t-1} E(U^t) + \pi \rho^t u_2(s^{t-1} r^{t-1} + \eta^t - x_2^{t-1}), \tag{91}$$

where $E(U^t)$ is given by (88)–(90). This differs from (84), not only because survival into old age is now uncertain, but also because the relative political weight of the old is now a function of "influence" expenditures, as well as of numbers,

$$\rho^t = \rho\left(\frac{x_2^{t-1}}{x_1^t}, \frac{n^{t-1}}{\pi}\right). \tag{92}$$

The temporary economic-political equilibrium is again the solution of a non-cooperative game, where voters choose saving and expenditures, and the government chooses the policy. Under certain functional restrictions, Kemnitz demonstrates that a sub-game perfect Nash equilibrium exists. There is again no guarantee that the intergenerational transfers resulting from a sequence of such equilibria is efficient.

9. Conclusion

We begun this chapter by asking whether intergenerational cooperation (a) is socially desirable, (b) will be realized by spontaneous agreement at some level. The answer to (a) is obviously yes, the answer to (b) is problematic. The literature reviewed in this chapter shows that an economy consisting of selfish individuals coordinated only by the market would vanish with the first generation, because the market does not provide such individuals with the incentive to have children. An economy consisting of altruistic

[68] Kemnitz uses a log-linear utility function to get explicit results.

individuals coordinated only by the market may deliver an optimal population profile, and allocate consumption efficiently given that profile, but the conditions are rather strong. One is that parents are rich and generous enough to make positive transfers to their grown-up children. The other is that credit is not rationed.

In the absence of altruism (but its presence does no harm), cooperative behaviour at the level of the family may be generated by a self-enforcing constitution, such that it is in the interest of each family member to comply with it, and punish anyone who does not. For it to be credible, such an arrangement must be renegotiation-proof, otherwise any generation could set itself up as a constitutional assembly, and modify the arrangement to its own advantage. A distinctive feature of these intra-family arrangements is that they guarantee support for both the old and the young, but efficiency is not guaranteed. The idea can be transposed from the level of the family to that of society, but enforcement becomes more and more problematic as the reference population gets larger.

We also enquired whether there are policies that—in conjunction with, or as an alternative to, the market and the family—would be capable of delivering a social optimum. Assuming that the government is driven by ethical considerations, and does not have to answer to any constituency (the "benevolent dictator" paradigm), the literature reviewed shows that both the first and the second best policy include public transfers to the old and to the young, interpretable as pensions and child benefits (or educational subsidies). The optimal policy reproduces, at societal level, the workings of a family constitution. If informational asymmetries put the first best out of the government's reach, family arrangements may survive in the folds of second-best policy.

In the absence of a benevolent dictator, intergenerational redistribution requires some kind of political equilibrium. Economic-political models are of two kinds. Some assume direct democracy, in which case they predict the behaviour of voters (essentially of the median one). Others assume representative democracy, in which case they predict the behaviour of politicians. Under direct democracy, a durable equilibrium supporting a system of mandatory intergenerational transfers (such as an unfunded pension system, or public debt) can come about only if it creates vested interests. Any such system will inevitably favour the generation or generations that voted for it in the first instance, at the expense of the generations that come later. Rather than of intergenerational cooperation, we should thus be talking of *fait accompli*.

Representative democracy weakens the link between policy and electorate. Policies affecting the intergenerational distribution of resources reflect the relative political weight of different age groups, rather than any ethical consideration. As in a direct democracy, the young do not count. Their interests are taken into account by policy only insofar as they coincide with those of their own parents, or with those of the generation to which their parents belong. If education enhances a person's future tax paying capacity, a policy involving transfers to the young in the form of educational subsidies may be favoured by adult voters, because it will help pay for their pensions. Without a society-wide constitutional arrangement governing transfers between generations, however, intergenerational efficiency and social optimality are again unlikely.

References

Anderberg, D., Balestrino, A. (2003). "Self-enforcing transfers and the provision of education". Economica 70, 55–71.

Baland, J.M., Robinson, A. (2002). "Rotten parents". Journal of Public Economics 84, 341–356.

Balestrino, A., Cigno, A., Pettini, A. (2002). "Endogenous fertility and the design of family taxation". International Tax and Public Finance 9, 175–193.

Barro, R. (1979). "On the determination of the public debt". Journal of Political Economy 87, 940–971.

Becker, G.S. (1974). "A theory of social interactions". Journal of Political Economy 82, 1063–1093.

Becker, G.S. (1983). "A theory of competition among pressure groups for political influence". Quarterly Journal of Economics 98, 371–400.

Becker, G.S., Barro, R.J. (1988). "A reformulation of the economic theory of fertility". Quarterly Journal of Economics 103, 1–25.

Becker, G.S., Murphy, K.M. (1988). "The family and the state". Journal of Law and Economics 31, 1–18.

Bernheim, B.D., Ray, D. (1989). "Collective dynamic consistency in repeated games". Games and Economic Behavior 1, 295–326.

Bernheim, B.D., Schleifer, A., Summers, L.H. (1985). "The strategic bequest motive". Journal of Political Economy 93, 1045–1076.

Boadway, R.W., Wildasin, D. (1989). "A median voter model of social security". International Economic Review 30, 307–328.

Boldrin, M., Montes A. (2002). "The intergenerational state: education and pensions". CEPR W. P. 3275.

Boldrin, M., Rustichini, A. (2000). "Equilibria with social security". Review of Economic Dynamics 4, 41–78.

Breyer, F. (1994). "The political economy of intergenerational redistribution". European Journal of Political Economy 10, 61–84.

Broome, J. (1993). "The value of living". Recherches Economiques de Louvain 58, 125–142.

Browning, E.K. (1975). "Why the social security budget is too large in a democratic society". Economic Enquiry 13, 373–388.

Buchanan, J. (1987). "Constitutional economics". In: The New Palgrave: A Dictionary of Economics. MacMillan, London.

Caillaud, B., Cohen, D. (2000). "Intergenerational transfers and common values in a society". European Economic Review 44, 1091–1103.

Cigno, A. (1991). Economics of the Family. Clarendon Press and Oxford University Press, Oxford and New York.

Cigno, A. (1993). "Intergenerational transfers without altruism: family, market and state". European Journal of Political Economy 9, 505–518.

Cigno, A. (2006). "A constitutional theory of the family". Journal of Population Economics 19, 264–283.

Cigno, A., Giannelli, G.C., Rosati, F.C., Vuri, D. (2007). "Is there such a thing as a family constitution? A test based on credit rationing". Review of Economics of the Household, in press.

Cigno, A., Luporini, A. (2006). "Optimal policy towards families with different amounts of social capital, in the presence of asymmetric information and stochastic fertility". In: Cigno, A., Pestieau, P., Rees, R. (Eds.), Taxation and the Family. MIT Press, Cambridge, MA.

Cigno, A., Luporini, A., Pettini, A. (2003). "Transfers to families with children as a principal-agent problem". Journal of Public Economics 87, 1165–1177.

Cigno, A., Pettini, A. (2003). "Taxing family size and subsidizing child-specific commodities?". Journal of Public Economics 87, 75–90.

Cigno, A., Rosati, F.C. (1992). "The effects of financial markets and social security on saving and fertility behaviour in Italy". Journal of Population Economics 5, 319–341.

Cigno, A., Rosati, F.C. (2000). "Mutual interest, self-enforcing constitutions and apparent generosity". In: Gérard-Varet, L.A., Kolm, S.C., Mercier-Ythier, J. (Eds.), The Economics of Reciprocity, Giving and Altruism. MacMillan and St. Martin's Press, London and New York.

Coughlin, P. (1986). "Elections and income redistribution". Public Choice 50, 27–91.
Coughlin, P., Mueller, D., Murrell, P. (1990). "Electoral politics, interest groups, and the size of government". Economic Enquiry 28, 682–705.
Conde-Ruiz, J.I. Galasso, V. (2000). "Positive arithmetic of the welfare state", mimeo.
Cox, D. (1987). "Motives for private income transfers". Journal of Political Economy 95, 508–546.
Cox, D., Jakubson, G. (1995). "The connection between public transfers and private interfamily transfers". Journal of Public Economics 36, 1–16.
Cremer, H., Kessler, D., Pestieau, P. (1992). "Intergenerational transfers within the family". European Economic Review 36, 1–16.
Di Tella, R., MacCullogh, R. (2002). "Informal family insurance and the design of the welfare state". Economic Journal 112, 481–503.
Docquier, F., Michel, P. (1999). "Education subsidies, social security and growth: the implications of a demographic shock". Scandinavian Journal of Economics 101, 425–440.
Eckstein, Z., Wolpin, K.I. (1985). "Endogenous fertility and optimum population size". Journal of Public Economics 27, 93–106.
Esteban, J.M., Sakovics, J. (1993). "Intertemporal transfer institutions". Journal of Economic Theory 61, 189–205.
Foster, A.D., Rosenzweig, M.R. (2000). "Financial intermediation, transfers, and commitment: do banks crowd out private insurance arrangements in low-income rural areas?". In: Mason, A., Tapinos, G. (Eds.), Sharing the Wealth: Intergenerational Economic Relations and Demographic Change. Oxford University Press, New York and Oxford.
Gale, D. (1991). "The efficient design of public debt". In: Dornbusch, R., Draghi, M. (Eds.), Public Debt Management: Theory and History. Cambridge University Press, Cambridge, MA.
Gordon, R., Varian, H. (1988). "Intergenerational risk sharing". Journal of Public Economics 37, 185–202.
Groezen, B., van Leers, T., Meijdam, L. (2003). "Social security and endogenous fertility: pensions and child allowances as Siamese twins". Journal of Public Economics 87, 233–251.
Grossman, G.M., Helpman, E. (1998). "Intergenerational redistribution with short-lived governments". Economic Journal 108, 1299–1328.
Hansson, I., Stuart, C. (1989). "Social security as trade among living generations". American Economic Review 79, 1182–1195.
Kaganovich, M., Zilcha, M. (1999). "Education, social security and growth". Journal of Public Economics 71, 289–309.
Kemnitz, A. (2000). "Social security, public education and growth in a representative democracy". Journal of Population Economics 13, 443–462.
Kollmann, R. (1997). "Endogenous fertility in a model with non-dynastic parental altruism". Journal of Population Economics 10, 87–95.
Kolmar, M. (1997). "Intergenerational redistribution in a small open economy with endogenous fertility". Journal of Population Economics 10, 335–356.
Konrad, K.A. (1995). "Social capital and strategic inter-vivos transfers of social capital". Journal of Population Economics 8, 315–326.
Kotlikoff, L.J. (1988). "Intergenerational transfers and saving". Journal of Economic Perspectives 2, 41–58.
Kotlikoff, L.J., Persson, T., Svensson, L. (1986). "Social contracts as assets: a possible solution to the time-consistency problem". American Economic Review 78, 662–677.
Leibenstein, H. (1960). Economic Backwardness and Economic Growth. Wiley, New York.
Maskin, E., Farrell, J. (1989). "Renegotiation in repeated games". Games and Economic Behavior 1, 327–360.
Meijdam, L., Verbon, H.A.A. (1996). "Aging and political decision making on public pensions". Journal of Population Economics 9, 141–158.
Meijdam, L., Verbon, H.A.A. (1997). "Aging and public pensions in an overlapping generations model". Oxford Economic Papers 49, 29–42.
Michel, Ph., Pestieau, P. (1993). "Population growth and optimality. When does serendipity hold?". Journal of Population Economics 6, 353–362.

Neher, P.A. (1971). "Peasants, procreation and pensions". American Economic Review 61, 380–389.
Pecchenino, R.A., Utendorf, K.R. (1999). "Social security, social welfare and the aging population". Journal of Population Economics 12, 607–623.
Peters, W. (1995). "Public pensions, family allowances and endogenous demographic change". Journal of Population Economics 8, 161–183.
Rawls, J. (1971). A Theory of Justice. Belknap, Cambridge, MA.
Razin, A., Sadka, E. (1995). Population Economics. MIT Press, Cambridge, MA.
Robertson, D.H. (1956). "What does the economist maximize?". In: Robertson, D.H. (Ed.), Economic Commentaries. Staples, London.
Rosati, F.C. (1996). "Social security in a non-altruistic model with uncertainty and endogenous fertility". Journal of Public Economics 60, 283–294.
Samuelson, P.A. (1958). "An exact consumption–loan model with or without the social contrivance of money". Journal of Political Economy 66, 467–482.
Shubik, M. (1981). "Society, land, love or money". Journal of Economic Behavior and Organization 6, 359–385.
Stiglitz, J.E., Weiss, A. (1981). "Credit rationing in markets with imperfect information". American Economic Review 71, 393–410.
Stark, O. (1993). "Nonmarket transfers and altruism". European Economic Review 37, 1413–1424.
Tabellini, G. (1991). "The politics of intergenerational redistribution". Journal of Political Economy 99, 335–357.
Thogersen, O. (1998). "A note on intergenerational risk sharing and the design of pay-as-you-go pension programs". Journal of Population Economics 11, 373–378.
Veall, M.R. (1986). "Public pensions as optimal social contracts". Journal of Public Economics 31, 237–251.
Verbon, H.A.A. (1993). "Public pensions: the role of public choice and expectations". Journal of Population Economics 6, 123–135.
Wagener, A. (2003). "Pensions as a portfolio problem: fixed contribution rates vs. fixed replacement rates reconsidered". Journal of Population Economics 16, 111–134.

Chapter 26

THE ECONOMICS OF INTERNATIONAL AID

RAVI KANBUR

Cornell University, Ithaca, NY, USA
e-mail: sk145@cornell.edu

Contents

Handbook of the Economics of Giving, Altruism and Reciprocity, Volume 2
Edited by Serge-Christophe Kolm and Jean Mercier Ythier

DOI: 10.1016/S1574-0714(06)02026-4

Abstract

This paper presents an overview of the economics of international aid, highlighting the historical literature and the contemporary debates. It reviews the "trade-theoretic" and the "contract-theoretic" analytical literature, and the empirical and institutional literature. It demonstrates a great degree of continuity in the policy concerns of the aid discourse in the twentieth century, and shows how the theoretical, empirical and institutional literature has evolved to address specific policy concerns of each period.

Keywords

development aid, trade theory, contract theory, international institutions, conditionality

JEL classification: F35, O19, O20

1. Introduction

> "[T]he decade of the 1990s was marked by a strong and lingering case of 'aid fatigue' influenced by the rising fear that foreign assistance was generating aid dependency relationships in poor countries. The issue of the effectiveness of aid conditionality was also critically debated." (Thorbecke, 2000, p. 47).

> "Foreign aid programmes for providing economic assistance to less developed countries have fallen on hard times. The nominal amounts of aid pledged by developed areas have recently been falling and the real values of economic assistance have fallen even further. This is due in part to the diversion of attention of the donor countries to other foreign policy issues. It is due partly to their increased pre-occupation with their own domestic problems. There has, however, also been a growing disenchantment with the potential for development in the poor countries and also with the role which foreign aid can play in development. Optimistic expectations of rapid growth in less developed countries have given way to skeptical evaluations of their actual performance. The contribution of foreign aid to development has also been evaluated more skeptically and its possible disincentive effects are now emphasized." (Bhagwati and Eckhaus, 1970, p. 7).

> "The foreign aid program, as an instrument of United States foreign policy, is now ten years old. To it has been committed upwards of 70 billion dollars, a sum representing around 25 percent of the national debt, and the annual appropriations have been a major factor in the recurring budgetary deficits of the federal government. Despite this massive effort, its success is questionable... In consequence, the Administration's budget for foreign aid has met increasing criticism. Congressional support, at one time overwhelming, has steadily diminished. Disclosures by investigating committees of waste and extravagance in the administration of the program have added distrust, and it is not surprising that the whole concept of foreign aid has aroused anxiety among the electorate." (Groseclose, 1958, p. 25).

International aid, or development assistance, is defined by the OECD to "include grants and loans to developing countries and territories which are: (i) undertaken by the official sector of the donor country, (ii) with the promotion of economic development and welfare in the recipient country as the main objective and (iii) at concessional financial terms (i.e. if a loan, have a grant element of at least 25 percent)" (Hjertholm and White, 2000, p. 100).[1] Whatever the definition, it might surprise the reader to see the similarity in the three assessments given above of international aid, or "foreign aid," over a period spanning four decades. But ever since its modern inception after the Second

[1] While this definition is generally accepted, there are of course many nuances to these criteria, and analysts do deviate from them as they need to. Thus Krueger et al. (1989) include in their definition the non-concessional loans by the World Bank, and some include loans from the IMF (concessional or not) also in this category.

World War, international aid has raised a number of constant themes in the policy arena, in particular its underlying rationale and its actual effectiveness in aiding development in recipient countries. Moreover, international aid looms larger in public discourse than its magnitude would seem to justify. An indication of this is that polls in rich countries often show people to believe foreign aid to be several multiples of its actual level.[2]

Associated with these policy themes have been a number of recurring analytical issues that essentially boil down to two basic questions:

(i) What does a transfer of resources do to the well being of donor and recipient?

(ii) How can and should resource transfer be conditioned to enhance the objective function of donor and recipient?

These two questions run through this overview of the economics of international aid. The paper will consider the history of aid and aid making institutions (section 2), the theoretical analysis of aid (section 3) and, the empirical analysis of the impact of aid (section 4); section 5 concludes.

2. The history of aid

2.1. *The origins of modern aid*

There is no doubt some evidence of international aid in antiquity. But in the modern era the issue of aid began to surface in the 19th and early 20th centuries as the western powers considered their colonies and other poor countries. In Britain the Colonial Development Act of 1929 was the culmination of a long process of moving from laissez faire in the economic operation of the colonies to assistance, but it was of a restrictive kind:

> "From about the turn of the century, the UK Government began to take a slightly more active interest in colonial economies, and a variety of committees studied education, the use of natural resources, and similar topics in selected colonies... In 1929, for the first time, provision was made for assisting colonial governments to develop their economies by means of grants and loans for what is now called 'infrastructure'; for improving transport, research, power and water supplies, land surveys, and so on. Education was excluded, and a strong subsidiary aim of the new Colonial Development Act of 1929 was to promote employment in Britain by stimulating the colonial economies and their demand for British exports. Funds therefore had to be spent on British products as far as possible." (Little and Clifford, 1965, p. 31).

[2] Raffer and Singer (1996) refer to US polls showing that people believe the share of development assistance in the federal budget to be of the order of 15 percent, when the actual figure is less than 1 percent.

The 1940 and 1945 Colonial Development and Welfare Acts went further and included education, and also allowed recurrent costs to be paid for under the provisions of the acts, and the 1948 Overseas Resources Development Act, the last in this sequence, set up the Colonial Development Corporation.

It is interesting to see that "tied aid" was already a key feature of British development assistance right from the beginning. The same is true of American aid in the 1930's and 1940's to Latin American countries, made under the "Good Neighbor Policy" of the Roosevelt Administration. In fact, such assistance goes back to the 19th century (Mikesell, 1968). As early as 1812 Congress passed an Act for the Relief of the Citizens of Venezuela, and from the late 19th century onwards food surpluses began to be deployed for tied aid (Hjertholm and White, 2000). In their fascinating account of US technical assistance overseas, Curti and Birr (1954, pp. 41–42) trace the following story a few years after Commodore Perry's fateful arrival in Japan:

> "When the new Meiji government undertook the colonization of the northern island of Yezo, or Hokkaido, it turned to the United States for technical aid... [T]he government, late in 1870, sent General Kuroda Kiyotak to America instructed to choose a chief advisor in agriculture... When Kuroda sought the counsel of President Grant on personnel, he was referred to Horace Capron, Commissioner of Agriculture... Capron outlined his terms. Kuroda met them... He was to have his expenses paid to and from Japan and to be given a house, guards, and servants—and to get $10 000 a year. This was a handsome salary for an American public official and considerably more than that of the prime minister of Japan."

To those familiar with the current state of technical assistance aid, it will indeed seem like very little has changed!

But the real expansion and crystallization of an aid doctrine, in the US but also elsewhere, came in the aftermath of the Second World War. Table 1, reproduced from Hjertholm and White (2000), provides a useful overview of the evolution of the history of aid in the post-war period. By common consent there were two major events in the evolution of aid in the 1940's. The Marshall Plan symbolized bilateral assistance, from the United States to countries of Europe. The setting up of the United Nations, and the Bretton Woods conference that set up the World Bank and the International Monetary Fund (IMF), represented the multilateral tendency in development assistance. The issues raised in the1940's during the setting up and operation of these initiatives are still present with us today—indeed, one often hears the call that what Africa needs is a "New Marshall Plan."

Of course, for both the Marshall Plan and the World Bank, the objective was reconstruction of a war-ravaged Europe, not the development of the non-industrialized world. But attention began to turn to the developing countries very soon after. President Harry Truman's inaugural address of 1949 contained the famous Point Four Program, with the objective of "making the benefits of our scientific advances and industrial progress available for the improvement and growth of underdeveloped areas." The Act for International development of 1950 followed up by establishing "the policy of the United

Table 1
Schematic overview of main developments in the history of foreign aid

	Dominant or rising institutions	Donor ideology	Donor focus	Types of aid
1940s	Marshall Plan and UN system (including World Bank)	Planning	Reconstruction	Marshall Plan was largely programme aid
1950s	United States, with Soviet Union gaining importance from 1956	Anti-communist, but with role for the state	Community development movement	Food aid and projects
1960s	Establishment of bilateral programmes	As for the 1950s, with support for state in productive sectors	Productive sectors (e.g. support to the green revolution) and infrastructure	Bilaterals gave technical assistance (TA) and budget support; multilaterals supported projects
1970s	Expansion of multilaterals (especially World Bank, IMF and Arab-funded agencies)	Continued support for state activities in productive activities and meeting basic needs	Poverty, taken as agriculture and basic needs (social sectors)	Fall in food aid and start of import support
1980s	Rise of NGOs from mid-1980s	Market-based adjustment (rolling back the state)	Macroeconomic reform	Financial programme aid and debt relief
1990s	Eastern Europe and FSU become recipients rather than donors; emergence of corresponding institutions	Move back to the state toward end of the decade	Poverty and then governance (environment and gender passed more quickly)	Move toward sector support at end of the decade

Note: Entries are main features or main changes, there are of course exceptions. Source: Reproduced from Hjertholm and White (2000), p. 81, Table 3.1.

States to aid the efforts of the peoples of economically underdeveloped areas to develop their resources and improve their living conditions." (Quoted in Ohlin, 1966, p. 25). The modern era of international aid was thus launched with great ceremony more than half a century ago. How did it evolve?

2.2. *Evolution of the aid doctrine before and after the cold war*

As the large and still growing literature on aid has documented, the history of development assistance since the second world war has been determined by two key factors—the evolution of geopolitics, and the evolution of development thinking. The central geopolitical factor determining aid was the cold war in the first 40 years, and its absence since then. But the evolution of development thinking has been more complex and non-linear in nature.

While the need for foreign aid as a moral obligation of the rich to the poor was ever present in the discourse of the 1940's and 1950's it is now widely accepted that the main ultimate objective of western aid during the cold war was to stop developing countries going over to "the other side". Of course, that was the objective of aid from the Soviet bloc as well. Indeed, some of the analytical critiques of aid in the 1950s stemmed from a perceived disconnect between this objective and the modalities of aid. As Milton Friedman (1958, pp. 63, 77–78) observed at the time:

> "Foreign economic aid is widely regarded as a weapon in the ideological war in which the United States is now involved. Its assigned role is to help win over to our side those uncommitted nations that are also underdeveloped and poor... The objectives of foreign economic aid are commendable. The means are, however, inappropriate to the objectives... The proponents of foreign aid have unwittingly adopted a basic premise of the Communist ideology that foreign aid is intended to combat. They have accepted the view that centralized and comprehensive economic planning and control by government is an essential prerequisite for economic development... An effective program must be based on our ideology, not on the ideology we are fighting." (Friedman, 1958, pp. 63, 77–78)

Another influential economist at that time, Ian Little, wrote:

> "We believe that we—the West—should be interested in the development of most underdeveloped countries which aspire to a neutral or Western-committed existence, and as much interested in the neutrals as the committed. Our interest derives from the probability that some considerable economic progress has become essential to the continued long term existence of governments, or succeeding governments, which are likely to preserve neutrality or remain favorable to the West... The anti-communist objective which aid is given in the above account is nothing to be ashamed of. We, after all, believe that Communism is a major menace to the ideals in which we believe." (Little and Clifford, 1965, pp. 115–116).

While the cold war positions above are perhaps unusual in their clarity and openness, there is no question that these were the views held by western policy makers throughout the cold war period, and indeed by many economists of a less conservative outlook. But what is interesting in both Friedman's and Little and Clifford's statements is the central role they place on the role of economic development—for them, then, the real question was the conditions under which aid actually led to development. This cannot of course be disentangled from the debates on development doctrine. Economists could, and did, differ in their views of what caused development, and therefore what role aid should play in it.

In fact, of course, Friedman's views on the inefficacy of central planning etc were in the minority at that time. This was the time of Rosenstein-Rodan (1943, 1961) and the "big-push", of Rostow (1960) and the "stages of economic growth", and of Chenery and Bruno (1962) and the "two-gap model". In their different ways, these authors and their followers argued that the main constraint to economic development was capital accumulation, and supplementing domestic savings was the role of aid. At the same time, as even the very term "big-push" signified, there were sufficiently strong market failures and externalities that the government and central planning had to play a key role in managing the investment and aid process in the recipient country. It was believed that "infant industries" needed to be protected from external competition in the early stages. These doctrines were amply illustrated in the India's first and second five year plans—even the phrase "five year plan" has a period feel to it. Thus throughout the 1950's and 1960's western aid was helping to finance these plans, with the objective of keeping India out of the clutches of communism, based on an argument that economic development was what would keep developing countries in the western camp, and the further argument that aid for centrally guided capital accumulation would help economic development.

During the 1960's and 1970's, bilateral assistance expanded, as did the assistance from multilateral organizations, particularly the World Bank. Since resources for the reconstruction of Europe and Japan were largely not needed by the 1960's, the attention of the multilaterals turned increasingly to developing countries. The "soft loan" window of the World Bank (the International Development Association—IDA) was opened, and Regional Development Banks were started in Asia, Africa and Latin America. These new multilateral arrangements reflected a general sense that "consortia" of donors would overcome the coordination and other problems of a multitude of individual aid programs (Rosenstein-Rodan, 1968).

In keeping with the development doctrine there was support for state led initiatives, but the doctrine itself evolved during this period. Instead of just focusing on growth of overall national income, the attention shifted to poverty and the social sectors. The experience of fast growing countries like Brazil, where inequality increased so fast that poverty gains from growth were eroded, brought a note of caution to the earlier growth through capital investment optimism (Fishlow, 1972). Under the catch all heading of a "basic needs" strategy, the development doctrine moved to emphasize direct beneficial outcomes for the poor, as opposed to the "trickle down" from general growth. India's five year plans reflected the change. And the aid doctrine itself moved, still within the overall policy framework of combating Communism, to stressing poverty reduction with a focus on agriculture and the social sectors like education and health. The World Bank's President, Robert McNamara, called for change to the strategy. With the World Bank's growing influence in aid, and backed up by other UN agencies, this became the new orthodoxy of the development doctrine and the aid doctrine.

Throughout the 1950's, the 1960's and the 1970's, through the different development and aid doctrines, one issue was constantly alluded to and criticized by both left and right in the west. This was the practice of tied aid, a practice with a tradition going back to the earliest origins of aid, where the recipient country was given the money conditional on spending it on the products of the donor country. Economic analysts pointed to the inefficiency of this method of transferring resources (Bhagwati, 1970). Other analysts focused on the issue of transferring agricultural surpluses in the west, particularly US surpluses as the result of farm price supports, as aid to recipient countries. Apart from perpetuating the inefficiency of domestic policy in the donor country, it was argued that such "food aid" actually harmed the recipient countries by hitting their agricultural production (Schultz, 1960). Relatedly, there was discussion of aid for specific projects versus overall budgetary support for the country—so called "program support" (Singer, 1965). Once this issue had been broached then the question of conditionality could not be far behind. A project has its own implicit conditionality—the money only flows as the project is completed. But with overall budgetary support it is the broad policies of the country that have to be conditioned on. As we shall see, program support conditioned on policy was about to become prominent in aid debates.

The 1980's were a turbulent decade for the development doctrine and the aid doctrine. They were introduced by the OPEC oil shocks of 1973 and 1979, and ended with the fall of the Berlin wall and the effective collapse of the Soviet bloc and hence the end of the cold war. In many ways the decade represents the peak of the cold war, albeit in its final stages. This was also the decade in which electorates in the North moved towards conservative administrations such as those of Ronald Reagan in the US, Margaret Thatcher in the UK and Helmut Kohl in Germany. With this background, there was a decided move away from the statist approach of the earlier aid doctrine towards supporting market based routes to development. The statist and inward looking "import substitution" strategies of the earlier era came under attack from policy makers and analysts alike, and the financial crises of the late 1970's and early 1980's, in the wake of global economic instability, provided the leverage for those who could finance or refinance developing country debts. The era of "structural adjustment" was upon us.

Analytical criticism of the statist and inward looking development strategies of the 1960s and 1970s had been building for some time. Scholars such as Ian Little, Anne Krueger, Jagdish Bhagwati and Bela Balassa had been building up a case for openness throughout the 1970's in particular. A good summary of this line of thought is provided in Krueger (1978). Anne Krueger became Vice President and Chief Economist of the World Bank in the early 1980's, replacing Hollis Chenery. The change was symbolic and substantive. Since the 1980's the World Bank has remained a staunch supporter of free trade arguments. It is not surprising that in the 1980s the development doctrine and the aid doctrine melded into one. Overall country policy was regarded to be the key determinant of development, market oriented policies were regarded to be the best. Thus the 1980s saw the peak of the "structural adjustment" aid doctrine where transfers were made increasingly in the form of budget support, conditioned on policy reform that conformed to the tenets of the "Washington Consensus." (For a history of this term, see Williamson, 1999).

The Latin American debt crisis of the early 1980's was very much a part of the development and aid discourse in the 1980's. Support for debt relief, or in the aftermath of debt default, was conditioned on policy reform. The same was true for Africa. These conditions, and their supposed outcomes, led to a massive debate, with civil society becoming vocal and involved at the highest policy making levels. Some of these argued for "adjustment with a human face" (Cornia et al., 1987), while others argued that the aid and development doctrine of the 1980's was solely in the interests of the creditors of the North and should be rejected. They called for outright debt cancellation or major debt relief. These interventions undoubtedly altered the terms of the debate as the 1990s rolled around.

The 1990's are perhaps too recent to get a clear view of the evolution of the aid and development doctrine. But there are some clear difference between the first half and the second half of the decade. In the early part of the decade the 1980's doctrine continued to hold sway, especially as concerned to the transition of the formerly communist economies of Eastern Europe and the successor states of the Soviet Union. It was held by many in official circles that a rapid transition was best, and the term "shock therapy" was coined in this context. But by the second half of the decade the disastrous consequences of the transition in many countries ("more shock than therapy") could no longer be ignored, and a reassessment started (Stiglitz, 2000).

Apart from the transition to market economies of the formerly centrally planned economies, the major event of the decade of the 1990s was the East Asian financial crisis in 1997, and the subsequent crises in Latin America and in Russia, with considerable spillover effects to most poor economies. Many critics pinned the crisis on too rapid a liberalization of capital accounts, itself thought to be the result of the over-confidence in market forces that ruled in the 1980s and in the first half of the 1990s (Sakakibara, 2001). Increasingly, the international financial institutions, the World Bank and particularly the IMF, were held to be responsible directly or indirectly as conduits of the policies of the rich countries. Partly as a result of the strong criticisms of the market based approaches of the 1980's and the early 1990's, the development doctrine in the 1990's moved back to emphasizing poverty reduction as the ultimate objective of development, and supporting specific interventions to this end. The World Bank's two World Development Reports of 1990 and 2000/2001 are illustrative of this shift in the aid agencies, and this takes us right up to the current state of the aid and development debate (World Bank, 1990, 2000).

The current state of the aid discourse, in the first years of the 21st century, reflects its evolution over the last fifty years or more. It also reflects the current state of the development doctrine. This doctrine appears to be at a high state of synthesis, with most of the elements of the previous debates being present (Kanbur and Vines, 2000). While there is no strong move to return to the highly statist and inward looking regimes of the 1950's through the 1970's, the "market fundamentalism" zeal of the 1980s and early 1990s has been tempered considerably (Kanbur, 2001). The role of government is more clearly recognized, as is the importance of accountability of these governments. Overall macroeconomic policy is important (although there continue to be debates on exchange rate regimes or on trade liberalization), but specific interventions to help the poor benefit from overall policy and growth are very much on the agenda. Thus intrahousehold and gender issues are emphasized, as are environmental degradation and its effects on the poor. The role of institutions, national and global, in determining the outcomes of policy is thought to be central. One factor that is emphasized more strongly than ever before is global interdependence and the need for strong management of international spillovers, be they through infectious diseases, civil war, or financial contagion.

The aid debate similarly has a rich set of issues that engage it. Some of these are very familiar from the earliest period of the origins of aid, and from how the doctrine has evolved since then. What benefits does aid confer on the donors? Do transfers actually benefit economic development and welfare in recipient countries? What sort of conditioning of transfers can improve the performance of aid in helping economic development in and welfare in poor countries? But some new issues, such as the role of aid in supplying various "international public goods" have also appeared on the horizon. The analysis underlying these and related questions will be reviewed in the sections that follow.

3. The theory of aid

3.1. Unconditional international transfers

The policy debates on aid are influenced by, and in turn influence, the theoretical analysis of transfers between countries. There are two broad strands of the theory. One considers the consequences of unconditional transfers, and is trade-theoretic in construct. The other focuses on conditional transfers, and is contract-theoretic in nature. Each of these will be discussed in turn.

Start from the general equilibrium of a standard neo-classical competitive model, and consider a comparative static transfer of endowment from one agent (the donor) to another agent (the recipient). What will be the consequences for the welfare of the donor and of the recipient? If the transfer is small enough that it does not disturb the equilibrium prices, and there are no distortions so that we really are in classically first best competitive market framework, then the result is clear. The transfer makes the donor worse off and the recipient better off. Clearly, the recipient prefers the transfer. The theoretical question, however, is why the donor should ever make such a transfer?

There are several ways to address this question. One is to say that the donor has no choice. The donor is told to make this transfer by a "world government" and that is that. But this is unsatisfactory since international transfers are voluntary, thinking of each country as an agent. When can a transfer be to the advantage of the donor? One answer is that the donor has the interests of the recipient at heart and the wellbeing of the recipient enters the utility function of the donor. Such consumption externalities violate the basic assumptions of the standard model, but they are well recognized in economics, and can indeed provide an argument as to why a donor might wish to make a transfer[3].

[3] Many of the chapters in this volume are focused precisely on a detailed analysis such motives as pure altruism. We accept such motives as part of the rationale for aid, but we do not analyze them any further.

There may be economies of scale in making transfers, making it efficient for individuals in a country to band together and for the country as a whole to make the transfer. We can then construct an argument for the sort of aid system we have, of government-to-government transfers:

> "It is clearly wrong in most people's judgment that most people in the rich countries should be able to lead lives of considerable luxury whilst a thousand million people—a quarter of the world's population—do not even get enough food to eat. But individual taxpayers in these countries, because of selfishness or ignorance, may not recognize this moral imperative; if they recognize it they may not know what they can do about it as individuals; if they do know what they can do, namely give to voluntary agencies, they may be reluctant to give unless assured that others will also contribute their share. Lacking an assurance, they look to governments to provide on an international basis, through aid, the same functions of income redistribution which they supply on a national basis through the progressive income tax and the various institutions of social security."[4] (Mosley, 1987, p. 3).

However, opening up such departures from the standard competitive equilibrium naturally leads to considerations of other departures as well. What if the terms of trade are not given but could change as the result of a transfer between donor and recipient? Changing terms of trade as the result of a transfer will still leave the donor worse off and the recipient better off if there are no other distortions and the donor and the recipient are the only two agents in the model, provided certain standard stability assumptions are satisfied. But when there are more than two parties both donor and recipient can be made better off when the post transfer equilibrium terms of trade are different, even if there are no other distortions. The classic contribution is that of Gale (1974), and this led to a large literature and generalizations (see Bhagwati et al., 1983, and Kemp and Kojima, 1985).

Once the standard competitive model is abandoned, then other channels emerge for a benefit to the donor of the transfer. If, for example, the rate of return to capital is higher in the recipient country than in the donor country, the donor can charge an interest higher than the domestic rate but lower than the recipient rate. This is concessional lending from the point of view of the recipient, but a good proposition from the point of view of the donor. Similarly, if the marginal propensity to consume is higher in the recipient country in a situation of generalized deficient aggregative demand, on Keynesian grounds one can make a case that it would be in the donor's interest to make a transfer to the recipient (Mosley, 1987). The Keynesian argument illustrates the spillovers from recipient to the donor that go beyond the simple "warm glow" of altruism. In an interdependent world, it is argued that negative outcomes in one country quickly spillover to others. Thus rich countries have an interest in assuring that these negative outcomes do not happen. These cross-border externalities will be taken up in a later section.

[4] The focus of this paper is solely on official, government-to-government transfers. Transfers through non-governmental organizations are not discussed here.

Thinking of a donor country as many agents can motivate aid as the national coordination of individual giving. But the many agents scenario also opens up other aspects of political economy, namely the tying of aid. Clearly, the tying of aid reduces the value of the transfer to the recipient. If this value to the recipient is the reason for giving, why would we ever observe the practice of aid tying? The answer is that some agents in the country benefit directly from aid tying. It is, in fact, a way of redistributing income within the donor country, if aid is raised from general taxation but spent, effectively, on purchasing the output of a particular sector or a particular area:

> "Northern politicians openly stress employment effects of ODA to their own constituencies. The Federal republic of Germany (FRG) even introduced a law demanding that employment effects in Germany must be proved for each German project... Commercial pressures on aid are not new but—as the DAC itself acknowledges—they 'have been growing in recent years'. In defence against Republican plans to slash aid substantially, US-AID 'distributed fat folders of documents showing that nearly 80 percent of its budget is recycled to the United States' (*Time*, 29 May 1995)." (Raffer and Singer, 1996, p. 6).

Added to the above cases is the disposal of farm surplus in the US and in Europe, which arises from policies to protect farm income, as foreign aid (Schultz, 1960). While there has been a considerable amount of analytical work on the consequences of such disposal or tying of aid for the recipient countries, and there is a basic understanding that it is driven by the donor's domestic political economy, there is little recent analysis of such tying using the methods and models of the new political economy literature (for a recent survey, see Barrett, 2002).

So much for the benefits to the donor. But does the transfer actually benefit the recipient? The theoretical literature delivers a highly ambiguous answer, except in the special case where there are no terms of trade effects and no distortions anywhere, in which case the recipient does indeed benefit. But if terms of trade change and there are more than two agents, there are conditions under which the recipient can in fact be made worse off because of the general equilibrium repercussions of the transfer. In general, these terms of trade arguments, while theoretically plausible, seem a little stretched when one considers that the flow of aid, around $100 billion a year, is dwarfed by global trade flows. It is unlikely that such a small tail can wag the global terms of trade significantly.

However, while the total flow of aid is small compared to global trade flows, it can be large for individual recipient countries. If there are distortions in the recipient country itself, then an inflow of capital could end up leading to immiserization. This argument is made for projects by Bauer (1971, pp. 99–100):

> "[It] is by no means unusual for projects to absorb domestic inputs of greater value than the net output, especially when the cost of administering the projects and the explicit or implicit obligation to maintain and replace fixed assets originally donated is also considered. Large losses in activities and projects financed by aid have been reported in many poor countries."

The key here is the value of domestic inputs absorbed relative to the net output, measured at shadow prices. A more general form of this argument is made in trade theory (Brecher and Bhagwati, 1982). The basic intuition can be stated quite simply. Suppose the inflow of capital changes domestic demand patterns in such a way that production shifts towards a sector that is distorted. Then the social value of national output could fall even though total resources have gone up.

There are many specific cases of this general phenomenon, including the famous "Dutch disease" syndrome that arises upon the discovery of a natural resource. The argument here is that the increased wealth is spent partly on non-tradable goods. The domestic production pattern is then changed in this direction. If we further postulate that the non-tradable sectors are less capable of undergoing productivity increases (because, among other reasons, they are less exposed to competition and influences from abroad), then the detrimental effects are clear. Indeed, some authors have analyzed the effects of aid precisely in terms of the Dutch disease (Younger, 1992).

This distortion induced immiserization is most easily amenable to trade theoretic economic analysis. There is another line of argument that is more suitable for a political economy treatment. This is that aid does not just flow neutrally into the recipient economy as postulated in trade models. Rather, it flows to the government of the recipient country, and as such is controlled and disposed of by the elites:

> "While the former Zaire's Mobutu Sese Seko was reportedly amassing one of the world's largest fortunes personal fortunes (invested, naturally, outside his own country), decades of large-scale foreign assistance left not a trace of progress. Zaire (now the Democratic republic of Congo) is just one of several examples where a steady flow of aid ignored, if not encouraged, incompetence, corruption, and misguided policies." (World Bank, 1998, p. 1).

The combination of policy based distortions that might lead to aid becoming immiserizing, and worries about misuse of aid by local elites, leads naturally to the argument that if the flow of aid could be conditioned on these things being put right, then gains to the recipient could be better ensured.

3.2. Conditionality

The case for conditionality is well stated by Little and Clifford (1965). Addressing the motivation for aid based on redistribution from rich to poor, they argue as follows:

> " The weakness of such arguments is that they assume that if income is redistributed from rich to poor countries, redistribution of income from rich to poor people—which is the only morally desirable form of redistribution—will automatically be achieved. This assumption is far from justified, unless steps are taken to ensure that governments receiving aid use it in certain clearly specified ways. The right of a poor country's government to receive aid must depend on this condition. If the strings attached to the use of money within developing countries were, in

> part at least, development strings... [this] would, we think, be considerably more appealing to the electorates of donor countries, to whom many stories of the luxurious living of minorities in the underdeveloped countries would filter back." (Little and Clifford, 1965, pp. 93–94).

It is not surprising that conditionality has been an ongoing theme in the aid discourse ever since the beginning. Of course, when aid is given for strategic reasons—to induce a country's government to vote with the West in the United Nations during the cold war, for example—the conditionality is self-evident. But when the ostensible purpose of aid is to help economic development and especially the welfare of the poor, the issue of conditionality is considerably more delicate, as we shall see.

The basic idea behind conditionality is straightforward. All of the discussion in the previous section assumes that the transfer takes place unconditionally. The responses of the two agents follow the transfer of resources, and are undertaken in unconstrained manner. Suppose now that instead of just the transfer of resources, there is a simultaneous undertaking of some other action or set of actions, (typically by the recipient but it could in general include actions by the donor). If a "world government" had the choice, it would always avail itself of the broader set of instruments, since a subset of the available instruments would still be unconditional aid. It is easy to see that with the right broadening, some of the seemingly perverse effects of transfers could be mitigated. For example, suppose that it was production distortions that led to the immiserizing effects of incoming transfers. Then transfers combined with, or conditional on, removing those production distortions would obviously make the recipient better off.

Conditionality is also important when we move from a "world government" view of international aid to a more direct "principal-agent" framework, where the donor is the principal and the recipient is the agent. In this framework it is assumed that the donor will only make the transfer of resources if it improves the donor's objective function. However, in addition, if the donor can make the transfer conditional on further action by the recipient, these actions can be chosen judiciously to make the donor even better off and perhaps, relatedly, the recipient better off as well. Thus, in the example given above, if the donor can insist that the recipient remove certain distortions, the transfer would make the recipient better off and then, since it is assumed the donor values this, the donor is made better off as well. On this line of argument, conditionality again simply expands the instrument set and cannot make the donor worse off—it will also make the recipient better off and thus, since it is assumed that this is what the donor wants, the donor is better off as well.

The above line of argument has been explored at length in the aid literature (see, for example, Mosley et al., 1995; Murshed and Sen, 1995; Hopkins et al., 1997; Killick, 1997; White and Morrissey, 1997; Adam and O'Connell, 1999; Kanbur, 2000; and Svensson, 2000, 2003). It is also central in the literature on debt relief and cancellation, where it is argued that making the cancellation conditional on adoption of good policies increases the value of the relief (see, for example, Sachs, 1989, 1990; Iqbal and Kanbur, 1997). The basic contract-theoretic answer seems straightforward—just apply the conditionality that ensures that the poor in the recipient country will be better off with the transfer. But there are at least two problems, which belie the clear-cut conclusions above. First, which conditionality to apply, to ensure that the poor do indeed benefit? Here we come up against the state of the development doctrine. As we saw in section 2, this has cycled from one view to another. In the 1950's the conditionality would have been, indeed was, to have large-scale industrial development plans and inward looking import substitution strategies. In the 1960's and 1970's this would have remained intact, but additional conditionality would have been introduced to ensure adequate expansion of the social sectors and of agriculture, especially small-farmer agriculture. In the 1980's the conditionality swung to insist on "market-friendly" reforms, including opening up the economy to imports and foreign direct investment, privatization of state owned enterprises, opening up of the international capital account, and maintaining fiscal balance through austerity in public expenditures. In the 1990s the debate focuses on which of these elements could form part of a successful development strategy, which would include a broader set of conditions, for example on public expenditure restructuring, governance, etc.

But there is a second problem that is in many ways deeper. It is that conditionality simply does not seem to work. It is indeed part of many aid agreements. It is not met, but the aid flows anyway. The interesting point about the Mobutu Sese Seko case quoted in the previous section is that it happened despite the fact that the World Bank and the IMF had strongly conditioned assistance programs. Using data from 200 structural adjustment programs, Svensson (2003, p. 3) finds "no link between a country's reform effort, or fulfillment of 'conditionality', and the disbursement rate" of aid funds. The World Bank's own internal evaluations find a similar disconnect between disbursement and conditionality fulfillment (World Bank, 1992a). Why does this happen? The following account from Kanbur (2000) provides some hints:

> ". . . in 1992 Ghana consummated its transition to democracy and, in the process, the government gave in to pressures to grant enormous pay increases to civil servants and the military. In late 1992, in advance of the elections, an 80% across the board pay increase, backdated, was announced. As a result, the budgetary conditionality in the World Bank's then current Structural Adjustment Credit was violated, and the impending tranche release was suspended. Through its own tranche, and through co-financing tied to it, the World Bank found itself holding up as much as one eighth of the annual import bill of the country.
>
> One would think that holding one eighth of the annual import bill of a poor cash strapped economy would give enormous leverage to the World Bank and the donors to dictate terms to the Ghanaians. In fact, as the representative of the World Bank on the ground, I came under pressure from several sources, some of them quite surprising, to release the tranche with minimal attention to conditionality. There was a steady stream of private sector representatives, domestic and foreign, arguing for release of the tranche both because of fears of what macroeoconomic disruption would do to the business climate in general, and also because some of them had specific contracts with the government which were unlikely to be paid on time if the government did not in turn get the money from the World Bank and other donors.

> Next in line, were the bilateral donors—even those who had tied themselves to the presumably greater discipline of the World Bank by co-financing. Some of these had "fiscal year" concerns—they feared the consequences within their agencies of not releasing the funds in the fiscal year for which they were slated. Others worried about a melt down of the economy if the tranche was not released. Yet others found their projects slowing up because government counterpart funds were not available, and many project agreements stipulate that donor money flows in a fixed relationship to government contributions. Rather like private sector contractors, these aid agency personnel were dependent upon the government releasing enough resources for the success of their specific projects, and this money would not come, or not come soon enough, if the tranche release was delayed. I include in this list of donors the World Bank itself—implementation of old projects, and development of new ones, would be severely affected so long as the impasse lasted." (Kanbur, 2000, pp. 414–415).

This account highlights the many different dimensions of why conditionality fails. Some of these are similar to the reasons for tied aid discussed earlier. The steady flow of aid is a source of income to many interest groups in the donor country. Their dominant concern is their income, not necessarily the wellbeing of the aid recipients. If conditionality is violated, the short term interest of these groups is for the aid to flow in any case (at least, that part of the aid which flows back to them). What this suggests is a more complicated game than the simple principal-agent framework that rationalizes conditionality. There is now (at least) a triadic relationship between (say) the company in the donor country which depends on contract payments from the developing country, the developing country government, and the donor government or agency. Such a model is developed by Villanger (2002). Another line of argument focuses on the incentives facing bureaucrats in aid agencies:

> "Both donor and recipient have incentive systems which reward reaching a high volume of resource transfer, measured in relation to a predefined ceiling... In many administrations, both bilateral and multilateral, the emphasis is on disbursements and country allocations. Non-disbursed amounts will be noted by executive boards or parliamentary committees and may result in reduced allocation for the next fiscal year... results are measured against volume figures, with no regards for the quality... besides, when the time has come to evaluate the actual outcome, most of those responsible for the project on both sides will have been transferred." (Gus Edgren, former Chief Economist of the Swedish aid agency, quoted in Svensson, 2003, p. 381).

At the same time as these "selfish" interests, there is a real "Samaritan's dilemma" even for those whose objectives really are to help the recipient. Enforcing conditionality will inflict short term pain on the very people the aid is meant to help. Of course such "tough love" may be best in the long run, but this does not mitigate the short term temptation to overlook the violation of conditionality (this argument is developed in a different context, by Coate and Morris, 1995).

Most analytical modeling of the problems of conditionality focuses on the problem of time inconsistency. Thus, for example, Svensson (2000) models the game between donor and recipients as follows. In the first period, recipients choose a set of actions ("reform"). In the second period these actions interact with the state of nature to produce outcomes with uncertainty. Given these outcomes, in the second stage the donor allocated aid funds. If there was a "commitment technology" such that the donor could stick to a disbursement rule conditional on reform actions, even though disbursement takes place in the second period, then it can be shown that the reform effort is greater than the case where there is no aid. But when such commitment is not possible, and aid disbursement can be decided after the state of the world is declared in the second stage of the game, then the incentives to reform are reduced, leading to a worse outcome for all concerned. Such outcomes are very familiar from the literature on time inconsistency in macroeconomic policy, and the aid conditionality literature is a development of the policy commitment literature in general (Coate and Morris, 1999; Drazen, 2000). Indeed, some authors have taken the failure of conditionality seriously enough that they have begun to analyze aid allocations when aid can only be unconditional, in the manner of the earlier trade theoretic literature, explicitly eschewing the assumption in the contract-theoretic literature that recipient government policy can in fact be changed by conditionality (Kanbur and Tuomala, 2001).

4. Empirical and institutional analysis of aid

Given the great ideological divides in development doctrines and in aid policy, and given the ambiguities in the theoretical analysis of the impact of aid, it is not surprising that the empirical literature on aid evaluation—assessing "aid effectiveness"—has taken on special significance. This has been the case throughout its fifty-year history. Apart from ongoing evaluations within each agency (the World Bank's Operations Evaluation Department produces an Annual Review of Development Effectiveness, and most other agencies produce similar assessments of their own operations), there are some periods when assessing aid effectiveness becomes particularly intensive. These coincide with cycles of doubt on the efficacy of aid as an instrument of foreign policy or as an instrument of economic development:

> "... [It] was not until 1956–7, after a series of foreign policy set-backs and the appearance of the Soviet Union in the foreign aid field, that the United States foreign aid programme was suddenly subjected to the most intensive study and publicity it had yet received. Reports were prepared by a Presidential Committee of Citizen Advisers, by the International Development Advisory Aboard appointed under the Point Four programme..., and by a Special Committee to Study Foreign Aid set up by the Senate. The Special Committee contracted for eleven studies on different aspects of the foreign aid programme by private research organizations and also dispatched ten individuals to survey foreign aid programmes in different parts of the world." (Ohlin, 1966, pp. 26–27).

In fact, the quote from Ohlin is itself taken from a retrospective on aid done by the OECD ten years after the major US effort. Such evaluations continued over the next two decades. In the mid 1980s a major evaluation was commissioned by the international community. Its findings were published under the title "Does Aid Work?" (Cassen, 1986). The answer given there can be summarized as "by and large, yes." In the early 1990's much discussion was occasioned by a World Bank report (the "Wapenhans report", World Bank, 1992b) that questioned the success of many of its own projects. Another major study at the end of the decade (World Bank, 1998) questioned the efficacy of aid disbursed into poor policy environments. And Tarp (2000) maintains the tradition of assessments of aid by collections of analysts. So where does all this evaluation leave us?

4.1. Development impact of aid

Throughout the assessments of aid that have been carried out over the last few decades, there seems to have emerged a "micro-macro" paradox. This is that micro level evaluations of specific projects give a much better picture than do macro level assessments of the impact of aid on economic development, specifically on growth. It is easy to see how such a disconnect could arise in principle. For example, if there are distortionary policies in place and projects are evaluated taking these as given, each project in isolation could be assessed positively while the overall impact could be negative. Of course, this problem could be overcome if the projects are evaluated at "shadow prices" that take account of the macro level distortions, but this is not actually done (see Little and Mirrlees, 1990). In any event, it is the overall impact of aid on economic development that should be our concern, not the success of this or that project. For this reason, this section will focus on the macro analysis of the impact of aid, primarily on economic growth.

Hansen and Tarp (2000) review 131 cross-country regressions of the impact of aid on growth, from a thirty year period starting in the late 1960's to the late 1990's. They divide the studies into three "generations." Corresponding to the development and aid doctrine at the time, the first generation of studies focused on the impact of foreign aid on domestic savings and investment. The early optimism (e.g. Rosenstein-Rodan, 1961) of a one for one link between aid and investment was challenged by authors such as Griffin and Enos (1970). Indeed, Griffin and Enos (1970) found a negative association between aid and growth, and put this down to a negative relationship between aid and savings, which had also been found in other studies. Papanek (1972) and Newlyn (1973) were among those who in turn challenged the overly pessimistic conclusions drawn from these studies. While it was true that aid did not increase recipient savings and investment one for one, so long as there was some increase then the net effect would be to increase total investment. Based on their comprehensive survey of studies over thirty years, Hansen and Tarp (2000, pp. 109–110) concur:

> "Neither extreme view of the aid-savings-growth link is valid. There is no evidence for a positive impact, and in only one study does aid lead to lower total savings.

> The overwhelming evidence from these studies is that aid leads to an increase in total savings, although not by as much as the aid flow. Given the underlying Harrod-Domar growth model, the implication is that aid spurs growth."

But this well established relationship between aid and total savings then raises another question—has aid in fact led to increased growth? Mosley et al. (1987, 1992) are among a number of "second-generation studies" that find no significant relationship between aid and growth. However, as Hansen and Tarp (2000) point out, in these studies the effect of savings on growth is insignificant as well. They argue that among reduced-from regression studies, in those that the identifying assumption (that savings impacts growth positively) holds, the vast majority do in fact find that aid does benefit growth as well.

The last five years have produced a "third generation" of studies that are more sophisticated in that they attempt to take into account the endogeneity of aid and also the policy and institutional environment in the recipient country. The key paper is that by Burnside and Dollar (2000). Although published in 2000 the paper was first circulated as a World Bank discussion paper in 1997 and immediately made an impact because of a novel claim. Although the simple correlation of aid and growth in the data may be zero, this was confounding two types of countries, those with "good" policies and those whose policies were "bad". In fact the impact of aid on growth was positive in good policy environments, identified as a significant and positive coefficient on an "aid $\times$ policy" interaction term in a growth regression, after taking into account the endogeneity of policy and aid. In fact, Burnside and Dollar (2000) find that there is no effect of aid on policy, but there is a positive effect of aid on growth when the policy environment is "right". The first of these findings has been little noticed, but it is clearly an indictment of policy conditionality. The inference, rather, is that countries choose their policies because of domestic reasons uninfluenced by aid. But if this internal process does lead to good policies, then aid will have a positive impact on growth.

The Burnside and Dollar (2000) findings underpin the World Bank's (World Bank, 1998) report on aid, where the implication was drawn that there should be aid selectivity. Aid should flow to those countries that have good policies rather than, as seems to be the case, a system where aid allocation takes place on other criteria altogether, like former colonial ties or political allegiance of the regime during the cold war era (Alesina and Dollar, 2000). These findings have in turn sparked a debate on selectivity, where for many people simply abandoning the poor in bad policy regimes seems too harsh a policy. One compromise is that official aid should cease in such situations, but unofficial aid, through non-governmental organizations, should continue.

However, the Burnside and Dollar (2000) findings have been questioned by Hansen and Tarp (2000), who argue that not taking into account non-linearities in the aid-growth relationship may bias results. They find that once a quadratic term in aid is introduced into the standard regressions, the coefficients show a diminishing marginal growth return to aid, but the "aid $\times$ policy" interaction term becomes insignificant. This result survives taking into account the endogeneity of aid through instrumental variables estimation. The general point is that non-linearities have to be addressed carefully in this empirical literature, to make sure that spurious relationships are not being picked up as proxies for underlying non-linearities. Even more recently, Easterly et al., 2003 have questioned the robustness of the Burnside and Dollar (2000) findings to the use of more up to date data.

4.2. Aid dependence

The macro-econometric investigation of aid-growth regressions will no doubt continue into the next century. There are sufficient issues of data (how exactly is "aid" defined?), of econometrics (how can the truly independent effects of aid be identified from a mix of interdependent relationships?) and of development doctrine (what is "good policy"?) to keep the debate alive. But parallel to the econometric literature is a literature that looks at how the "aid business" works in practice, and lays much of the blame for the failure of aid on institutional features. Many in this literature charge that the system creates a syndrome of "aid dependency" that perpetuates itself and undermines the development effort.

Nowhere is the phenomenon more discussed than in the area of "technical assistance." This is assistance provided by donor country professionals in a wide variety of fields, financed by the aid budget of rich countries. It is, in effect, a form of tied aid—giving assistance in the form of the time of a professional, or giving financial assistance with the condition that it be used to purchase the expertise of a donor country national. Review upon review of technical assistance (see, for example, Berg, 1993) has highlighted its ineffectiveness. Chief among these is the fact that the incentives in the system are all geared towards continuing the technical assistance rather than local capacity building. For the expatriates, the continuation provides a source of income. For the hard pressed local officials in the recipient country, it provides short term assistance that they can use. Thus the form of the assistance turns out to be not one that builds local capacity to carry on, but that keeps the need unsatisfied.

Related to the technical assistance issue is that the aid flows, and the mechanisms donors adopt to track and monitor them, are very intensive in terms of recipient capacity. Each donor agency has its own reporting system. In a typical African country, there can be upwards of 20 aid agencies from different countries and multilateral agencies. The hard-pressed civil servants spend much of their time managing the paper flow. At the political level, ministers have to spend a considerable amount of time in turn meeting with donor delegations. But perhaps as important than the sheer time use is that these senior technocrats and politicians become oriented towards convincing the aid agencies to keep the aid flow going, rather than towards listening to the domestic population and the local development agenda.

A key problem that the above fragmentation of the aid flows between myriad donors is that of lack of coordination, which interacts badly with tied aid. Thus there can be equipment of incompatible specifications supplied by different donors for a water supply project. Or there can be "experts" from different aid agencies giving different advice—and this can cause real difficulty if it crystallizes into inconsistent conditionality. The lead given to the IMF on macroeconomic conditionality, and to the World Bank on sectoral and microeconomic conditionality, was a response by the donor community to such potential inconsistency. But this leads to another problem—a donor cartel behind a particular aid doctrine which suppresses innovation. The design question is how to balance the twin extremes of fragmentation and a donors' cartel. Relatedly, there is the question of the enormous burden on domestic capacity of managing the aid relationship, and the fact that as a result of this relationship the projects and programs tend to reflect donor views more than recipient priorities.

It is to address these sorts of issues that Kanbur et al. (1999) have put forward the concept of the "common pool". The objectives are (i) to reduce day-to-day donor interference in the management of the aid program, (ii) reduce fragmentation within and across projects and policies, (iii) improve "ownership" of the development strategy by the domestic political economy of the recipient country, and (iv) still give donors the right to modulate their funding based on recipient characteristics. The concept works as follows. Aid flows support the overall program of the government, rather than this or that project. After a period of dialogue, with the donors but more importantly with its own population, the government puts forward an overall program of expenditures, with alternative scenarios based on different levels of aid flows. The donors look at this, and put into a common pool resources that will finance the overall program along with domestic and other resources. At no time is a particular part of the program identified with a particular donor. All aspects of aid are folded into this structure.

The theory and practice of this common pool framework needs to be worked out more fully. How exactly are the different donor preferences and aid doctrines "aggregated" through this mechanism? Will there not be free rider problems through the common pool? And what exactly is the nature of the game between recipient and donors in this framework? In fact, these questions apply equally well to another major institutional question in the aid debate—the balance between bilateral and multilateral assistance. The issue is as old as aid itself (see Rosenstein-Rodan, 1968). One of the strongest arguments for moving to multilateralism was to reduce the influence of vested interest in each donor country. The idea is that when faced with a demand from a domestic constituency to skew aid away from a generally accepted development doctrine, the government could use the fact of an international agreement as a check. In effect, through the multilateral agreement they would tie their own hands. But what if the domestic constituencies could lobby their government to in turn lobby the multilateral agency? This clearly happens (see the quote above from Kanbur, 2000). Yet there is very little economic analysis of this type of problem (for a start in this direction, see Villanger, 2002).

4.3. *International public goods and aid*

An emerging policy and institutional issue, requiring analytical foundations, is that of cross-border externalities and international public goods, and the role of aid from rich to poor countries in addressing these problems. This discourse has brought together two venerable literatures in economics—that on aid and transfers, and that on externalities and public goods, the latter being suitably "internationalized" by interpreting agents as nations rather than individuals.

A cross-border externality occurs when events and developments in one country, whether policy induced or exogenous, spill over into other countries and have consequences that are not mediated by classically competitive markets. Thus technical progress that makes the exports of one country cheaper and thereby benefits another country through a decline in the price of its imports, is not an externality. But there are many other cases where such an externality occurs. Civil war in one country can lead to an influx of refugees to a neighboring country. Carbon emissions from the industry of one country can pollute the global atmosphere. Underground water extraction by one country for its agriculture lowers the amount available for another country sharing the same water table. Poor control of infectious diseases in one country leads to spillover effects in other countries. Financial contagion, as the name suggests, spreads from one country to another. These are all examples of negative externalities from one country to another. Competitive markets will see an oversupply of these activities, because in such markets no single agent will take account of the negative spillovers for other agents. Managing this inefficiency requires mechanisms of coordination between agents.

A pure public good is defined as one whose benefits are non-rival and non-excludable across agents. By non-rival is meant that consumption by one agent does not diminish the consumption of another. By non-excludable is meant that no agent can be excluded from enjoying the benefits of such a good. It is well known that such goods will be undersupplied by competitive markets because of the free rider problem—no single agent will take into account the positive benefits to other agents of supplying this good.

Notice first of all that if there is an international mechanism of coordination that addresses cross-border negative externalities, then this mechanism is an international public good—by definition, its benefits are non-rival and non-excludable for those agents being coordinated. However, in addition to such coordination mechanisms there are other examples of international public goods. Basic medical research in one country can benefit citizens of another as the knowledge spreads. An international institution that allows economies of scale and scope in a particular activity to be reaped conveys benefits to all member countries in non-rival and non-excludable fashion.

What, then, is the connection between the undersupply of international public goods and development assistance? Recall that the latter is a transfer from wealthier countries, intended to benefit poorer countries. In section 2 we focused on the case where the transfer is made directly to the poorer country, unconditionally or conditionally. However, if international public goods are undersupplied, and if increasing this supply would benefit poorer countries, then international public goods of this type would be legitimate targets of development assistance funds. But such transfers will typically not be from a rich to a poor country directly. Rather, they will finance the public good. For example, they could finance basic research in the rich country, the results of which will then be made available to the poorer countries. Or they could finance a coordination mechanism which resolves a cross-border negative externality among a group of poor countries. Or they could finance a coordination mechanism that cuts across rich and poor countries, thereby benefiting poor countries. Let us take each of these three types of international public goods in turn (the topic of international public goods and development assistance is taken up in greater detail in Sandler, 1998; Kanbur et al., 1999; Kaul et al., 1999; Gerrard et al., 2001; Sagasti and Bezanson, 2001; Arce and Sandler, 2002; Ferroni and Mody, 2002; Kanbur, 2002, 2003, 2004).

Basic research into tropical agriculture or medicine that is undertaken in rich countries clearly helps poor countries, provided its findings are made widely available. Having the activity take place in the donor countries avoids the problems of conditionality discussed in section 2, since the interaction between donor and recipient is minimized, but it is not without problems of is own. The general problem is common to all issues of basic research, and resides in the tension between the generally greater efficiency of the private sector in conducting research, and the need to make the output of the research available as a public good. A recent attempt to resolve this tension is seen in the proposed Vaccine Purchase Fund (VPF). With this arrangement, private companies are guaranteed purchases of the vaccine, provided it is developed to a certain pre-specified standard. Thus aid resources are used not in direct support of poor countries, but in creating a demand for basic research into their problems. If the institutional arrangements can ensure adequate input of poor countries into defining the problems, this seems like an attractive mechanism to be explored.

Consider a cross-border externality problem that cuts across a number of contiguous countries in Africa. There are many examples of these: including water rights, infectious diseases, forest cover, transportation between inland areas and coastal ports. By definition, the response to these problems will be inadequate without coordination, since no single country will fully take into account the benefits of a coordination mechanism. Such a coordination mechanism will be beneficial to the poor countries, but it is not costless. There will be the costs of the actual act of coordination, and the costs of possible compensation that might need to be paid to individual countries who may lose in the short term, if it proves impossible to convince the gainers to provide the compensation (if there are no gainers at all from the coordination mechanism, or if the gains do not exceed the losses, the mechanism is not worth pursuing). If these costs are not met, the coordination will not take place and the poor countries will be worse off. Hence, the financing of such activities is a prime candidate for the use of aid resources.

Finally, consider a cross-border externality that cuts across developed and developing countries. Coordination of global carbon emissions, mechanisms to control financial contagion, or the coordination and channeling of bilateral aid through international institutions to reap the benefits of economies of scale and scope, are all examples of this type of international public good. Since these mechanism involve both rich and poor countries, and since the objective of aid is (or should be) to help poor countries, the central question to be asked in these sorts of arrangements goes beyond the efficiency of the arrangement, in the sense of having a positive gain overall, but is rather about how much of the gain accrues to poorer countries. An arrangement which leads to gains for the rich countries and losses for the poor would still be efficient in the standard economic sense if the gains outweighed the losses, but would not have claim on aid resources, unless the aid was effectively compensation from the rich to the poor for the losses they suffer as a result of the coordination mechanism. Hence the issue turns on the precise nature of the coordination mechanism, particularly its distributional consequences.

The above arguments have strong implications for international institutions, who are increasingly putting themselves forward as the suppliers of international public goods of different types. For the first category of international public goods, there is a strong argument for international institutions to play a convening role in developing instruments such as the Vaccine Purchase Fund, and to help finance them. For the second category, there remains the issue of the comparative advantage of global versus regional institutions in financing and managing coordination mechanisms across closely contiguous countries within a region such as Africa, and there remain questions about the development of new transfer instruments, going beyond the clearly inadequate sovereign loan instruments of the World Bank and the Regional Development Banks, to address these multi country problems. For the third category of international public goods, which cross rich and poor countries, and include the international institutions themselves as international public goods, there is the central issue of how to ensure appropriate governance mechanisms so that the benefits are sufficiently skewed in favor of poor countries, and hence aid resources can reasonably be justified in financing their supply. Each of these policy issues leads to a detailed discussion and debate, as reported in the papers listed above.

5. Conclusion

As the quotes at the start of this paper make abundantly clear, the fundamental policy issues in aid have remained unchanged for half a century. The search has been for mechanisms of transfer from rich to poor countries that benefit the poor countries while meeting a host of other objectives and constraints. The competing objectives in the past have included shoring up support from poor countries in the geopolitics of the cold war. While the cold war has ended, other emerging trends in geopolitics, for example the "war on terror", mean that rich countries will always need allies among poorer nations, and transfer of resources will be one way to achieve this.

Of course, as in the past, there is a strong strand in the policy discourse that at least some geopolitical alignment is to be had through encouraging development in poor nations, which then leads to the ongoing debate about the effectiveness of aid in promoting development. Closely entwined with effectiveness of aid is the effectiveness of conditionality, where the policy discourse seems to have come full circle. Attempts at intensifying the conditionality of aid in the 1980s are now recognized to have failed, and there is growing acceptance that while aid effectiveness is clearly helped by appropriate domestic policies in recipient countries, ensuring these policies by the carrot of aid flow and the stick of aid withdrawl does not seem to have been possible. The domestic political economy is too strong to be influenced by aid flows, at least in anything beyond the very short run. These fundamental concerns are equally present in the current debate on use of aid resources to provide debt relief to poor countries.

Where then does this leave the current policy thrusts on the uses of aid resources? First, there is a growing consensus that official assistance should only flow to those countries that are likely to use it well, as judged by their policies and institutions. Second, aid can assist in the domestic dialogue on these policies and institutions, but it cannot make them come about through conditionality. Third, in view of the experience with country-specific aid, and in view of the emerging problems of cross-border externalities, there should be some orientation of aid resources towards the supply of international public goods. Fourth, there is considerable discussion on the many and varied mechanisms of aid delivery, bilateral and multilateral, and how, if at all they should and can be rationalized. Indeed, some have argued that aid should flow not through official channels at all, but should use non-governmental organizations, and the allocation mechanisms should be more market oriented.[5]

As shown in this paper, the policy conjuncture has influenced developments in the economic analysis of aid. In the middle of the twentieth century the focus was on a "trade-theoretic" analysis of the welfare effects of transfers on donors and recipients. Tied aid, a feature of aid since its modern emergence in the late19th and early 20th centuries, was subjected to carefully theoretical scrutiny, and was criticized by mainstream economists as an inefficient transfer mechanism, whatever its political economy rationale. Empirical work focused on whether transfers did in fact improve the situation of the recipient in the terms of investment and growth. With the emergence of policy conditionality in the latter part of the 20th century, a "contract-theoretic" analysis developed to explain why such conditionality was superior to unconditional transfers, and to analyze different types of conditionality. Principal-agent models were used to good effect in illuminating the basic considerations. Corresponding to these theoretical developments, empirical work focused on what combination of aid flows and policies was best for development. Most recently, the upsurge of policy interest in international public goods has led to a spate of analytical contributions at the intersection of two great literatures in economics—that on aid and transfers and that on externalities and public goods. This literature has illuminated the subtleties of the arguments for using aid resources to finance international public goods, and, treating aid delivery institutions as public goods, has begun the discussion of a rational arrangement of the functions of these institutions.

If the historical evolution of the aid literature experience is anything to go by, it is unlikely that a survey of international aid in ten years time will have entirely and dramatically new policy issues from the ones highlighted here. The fundamental themes will recur, perhaps modified somewhat by context. But analysis will not doubt advance,

[5] Such an argument is made recently by Easterly (2002).

as it has done at every stage in the last century, by trying to provide a framework for answering the specific questions raised by the policy discourse.

References

Adam, C.S., O'Connell, S.A. (1999). "Aid, taxation and development in Sub-Saharan Africa". Economics and Politics 11 (3), 225–254.

Alesina, A., Dollar, D. (2000). "Who gives aid to whom and why?". Journal of Economic Growth 5, 33–64.

Arce, M.D.G., Sandler, T. (2002). Regional Public Goods: Typologies. Provision, Financing and Development Assistance. Almkvist and Wiksell International, Stockholm.

Barrett, C. (2002). "Food security and food assistance programs". In: Gardner, B., Rausser, G. (Eds.), Handbook of Agricultural Economics. Elsevier Science B.V.

Bauer, P. (1971). Dissent on Development: Studies and Debates in Developmental Economics. Weidenfeld and Nicholson, London.

Berg, E.J. (1993). Rethinking Technical Cooperation—Reforms for Capacity Building in Africa, UNDP, 92-1-126022-1.

Bhagwati, J. (1970). "The tying of aid". In: Bhagwati, J., Eckhaus, R. (Eds.), Foreign Aid. Penguin, Harmondsworth, pp. 235–293.

Bhagwati, J., Brecher, R., Hatta, T. (1983). "The generalized theory of transfers and welfare: bilateral transfers in a multilateral world". American Economic Review 73 (4), 606–618.

Bhagwati, J., Eckhaus, R. (1970). "Introduction". In: Bhagwati, J., Eckhaus, R. (Eds.), Foreign Aid. Penguin, Harmondsworth, pp. 7–18.

Brecher, R.A., Bhagwati, J. (1982). "Immiserizing transfers from abroad". Journal of International Economics 13, 353–364.

Burnside, C., Dollar, D. (2000). Aid, policies and growth. American Economic Review 90 (4), 847–868.

Cassen, R. (1986). Does Aid Work? Report of the Independent Consultants' Study of Aid-Effectiveness. Oxford University Press, Oxford.

Chenery, H.B., Bruno, M. (1962). "Development alternative in an open economy: the case of Israel". Economic Journal 77 (285), 79–103.

Coate, S., Morris, S. (1995). "Altruism, the Samaritan's dilemma, and government transfer policy". American Economic Review 85 (1), 46–57.

Coate, S., Morris, S. (1999). "Policy persistence". American Economic Review 89 (5), 1327–1336.

Cornia, G., Jolly, R., Stewart, F. (1987). Adjustment with a Human Face: Protecting the Vulnerable and Promoting Growth. Clarendon Press, Oxford.

Curti, M., Birr, K. (1954). Prelude to Point Four: American Technical Missions Overseas, 1838–1938. University of Wisconsin Press, Madison.

Drazen, A. (2000). Political Economy in Macroeconomics. Princeton University Press.

Easterly, W. (2002). "The cartel of good intentions: the problem bureaucracy in foreign aid". Journal of Policy Reform 5 (4), 223–250.

Easterly, W., Levine, R., Roodman, D. (2003). "New data, new doubts: a comment on Burnside and Dollar's 'Aid, Policies and Growth (2000)' ". Processed. Department of Economics, New York University.

Ferroni, M., Mody, A. (Eds.) (2002). International Public Goods: Incentives, Measurement and Financing. Kluwer Academic Publishers, Norwell, MA.

Fishlow, A. (1972). "Brazilian size distribution of income". American Economic Review 62, 391–402.

Friedman, M. (1958). "Foreign economic aid: means and objectives". In: Bhagwati, J., Eckhaus, R. (Eds.), Foreign Aid. Penguin, Harmondsworth.

Gale, D. (1974). "Exchange equilibrium and coalitions: an example". Journal of Mathematical Economics 1, 63–66.

Gerrard, Ch.D., Ferroni, M., Mody, A. (Eds.) (2001). Global Public Policies and Programs: Implications for Financing and Evaluation. The World Bank, Washington DC.

Griffin, K., Enos, J. (1970). "Foreign assistance: objectives and consequences". Economic Development and Cultural Change 18 (3), 313–327.
Groseclose, E. (1958). "Diplomacy or altruism?". In: Wiggins, J.W., Schoeck, H. (Eds.), Foreign Aid Reexamined: A Critical Appraisal. Public Affairs Press, Washington, DC.
Hansen, H., Tarp, F. (2000). "Aid effectiveness disputed". In: Tarp, F. (Ed.), Foreign Aid and Development. Routledge, London and New York, pp. 103–128.
Hjertholm, P., White, H. (2000). "Foreign aid in historical perspective: background and trends". In: Tarp, F. (Ed.), Foreign Aid and Development. Routledge, London and New York, pp. 80–102.
Hopkins, R., Powell, A., Roy, A., Gilbert, C. (1997). "The world bank and conditionality". Journal of International Development 9 (4), 507–516.
Iqbal, Z., Kanbur, R. (Eds.) (1997). External Finance for low Income Countries. IMF Institute, Washington, DC.
Kanbur, R. (2000). "Aid, conditionality and debt in Africa". In: Tarp, F. (Ed.), Foreign Aid and Development. Routledge, London and New York, pp. 409–422.
Kanbur, R. (2001). "Economic policy, distribution and poverty: the nature of disagreements". World Development 29 (6), 1083–1094.
Kanbur, R. (2002). "Conceptualizing RFI's versus GFI's", Paper presented to the IADB/ADB conference on Regional Public Goods and Regional Development Assistance, Washington, DC, November 6–7.
Kanbur, R. (2003). "International financial institutions and international public goods: operational implications for the World Bank". In: Buira, A. (Ed.), Challenges to the World Bank and IMF. Anthem Press.
Kanbur, R. (2004). "Cross-border externalities and international public goods: implications for aid agencies". In: Beneria, L., Bisnath, S. (Eds.), Global Tensions: Challenges and Opportunities in the World Economy. Routledge, London.
Kanbur, R., Sandler, T., Morrison, K. (1999). "The Future of Development Assistance: Common Pools and International Public Goods". Johns Hopkins Press for the Overseas Development Council, Washington, DC.
Kanbur, R., Tuomala, M. (2001). "Incentives, inequality and the allocation of aid when conditionality doesn't work: an optimal nonlinear taxation approach", Cornell University, Department of Applied Economics and Management, Working Paper 2001-11.
Kanbur, R., Vines, D. (2000). "The World Bank and poverty reduction: past, present and future". In: Gilbert, C., Vines, D. (Eds.), The World Bank: Structure and Policies. Cambridge University Press.
Kaul, I., Grunberg, I., Stern, M.A. (Eds.) (1999). Global Public Goods: International Cooperation in the 21st Century. Oxford University Press, New York.
Kemp, M., Kojima, S. (1985). "The welfare economics of foreign aid". In: Feiwel, G. (Ed.), Issues in Contemporary Microeconomics and Welfare. State University of New York Press, Albany, pp. 470–483.
Killick, T. (1997). "Principals, agents and the failings of conditionality". Journal of International Development 9 (4), 483–495.
Krueger, A. (1978). Foreign Trade Regimes and Economic development: Liberalization Attempts and Consequences. Ballinger for National Bureau of Economic Research, Cambridge, MA.
Krueger, A., Michalopoulos, C., Ruttan, V. (1989). Aid and Development. John Hopkins University Press, Baltimore.
Little, I.M.D., Clifford, J.M. (1965). "International Aid". George Allen and Unwin Ltd, London.
Little, I.M.D., Mirrlees, J.A. (1990). "Project appraisal and planning twenty years on". In: Fischer, S., de Tray, D., Shah, S. (Eds.), Proceedings of the World Bank Annual Conference on Development Economics, 1990. The World Bank, Washington, DC, pp. 351–382.
Mikesell, R. (1968). Economics of Foreign Aid. Weidenfeld and Nicholson, London.
Mosley, P. (1987). Overseas Aid—Its Defense and Reform. Wheatsheaf Books, Brighton.
Mosley, P., Harrigan, J., Toye, J. (1995). "Aid and Power, vol. 1", 2nd edn. Routledge, London.
Mosley, P., Hudson, J., Horrell, S. (1987). "Aid, the public sector and the market in developing countries". Economic Journal 97 (387), 616–641.
Mosley, P., Hudson, J., Horrell, S. (1992). "Aid, the public sector and the market in developing countries: a return to the scene of the crime". Journal of International Development 4 (2), 139–150.

Murshed, M., Sen, S. (1995). "Aid conditionality and military expenditure reduction in developing countries: models of asymmetric information". Economic Journal 105, 498–509.
Newlyn, W. (1973). "The effect of aid and other resource transfers on savings and growth in less developed countries: a comment". Economic Journal 83 (331), 867–869.
Ohlin, G. (1966). "The evolution of aid doctrine". In: Foreign Aid Policies Reconsidered. OECD, pp. 13–54. Reprinted in: Bhagwati, J., Eckhaus, R. (Eds.), Foreign Aid. Penguin, Harmondsworth, 1970, pp. 21–62.
Papanek, G.F. (1972). "The effect of aid and other resource transfers on savings and growth in less developed countries". Economic Journal 82 (327), 934–950.
Raffer, K., Singer, H.W. (1996). The Foreign Aid Business: Economic Assistance and development Cooperation. Edward Elgar, Cheltenham, UK.
Rosenstein-Rodan, P.N. (1943). "Problems of industrialization in Southern and Eastern Europe". Economic Journal 53 (210), 202–211.
Rosenstein-Rodan, P.N. (1961). "International aid for underdeveloped countries". Review of Economics and Statistics 63 (2), 107–138.
Rosenstein-Rodan, P.N. (1968). "The consortia technique". International Organization 22 (1), 223–230.
Rostow, W.W. (1960). The Stages of Economic Growth. Cambridge University Press.
Sachs, J.D. (Ed.) (1989). Developing Country Debt and Economic Performance. University of Chicago Press, Chicago.
Sachs, J.D. (1990). "A strategy for efficient debt reduction". Journal of Economic Perspectives 4, 19–30.
Sagasti, F., Bezanson, K. (2001). Financing and Providing Global Public Goods: Expectations and Prospects. Fritzes Kundservice, Stockholm.
Sakakibara, E. (2001). "The East Asian crisis: two years later". In: Proceedings of the Annual World Bank Conference on Development Economics, 2000. The World Bank, Washington, DC, pp. 243–255.
Sandler, T. (1998). "Global and regional public goods: a prognosis for collective action". Fiscal Studies 19 (3), 221–247.
Schultz, T.W. (1960). "Value of U.S. farm surpluses to underdeveloped countries". Journal of Farm Economics 42, 1019–1030.
Singer, H.W. (1965). "External aid: for plans or projects?". Economic Journal 75, 539–545.
Stiglitz, J. (2000). "Whither reform? Ten years of the transition". In: Proceedings of the Annual World Bank Conference on Development Economics, 1999. The World Bank, Washington, DC, pp. 27–56.
Svensson, J. (2000). "When is foreign aid policy credible? Aid dependence and conditionality". Journal of Development Economics 61, 61–84.
Svensson, J. (2003). "Why conditional aid does not work and what can be done about it". Journal of Development Economics 70 (2), 381–402.
Tarp, F. (Ed.) (2000). Foreign Aid and Development. Routledge, London and New York.
Thorbecke, E. (2000). "The development doctrine and foreign aid 1950–2000". In: Tarp, F. (Ed.), Foreign Aid and Development. Routledge, London and New York, pp. 17–47.
Villanger, E. (2002). "Company influence on foreign aid disbursement: is conditionality credible when donors are selfish?". Processed. Department of Economics. Norwegian School of Economics and Business Administration.
White, H., Morrissey, O. (1997). "Conditionality when donor and recipient preferences vary". Journal of International Development 9 (4), 497–505.
Williamson, J. (1999). "What should the World Bank think about the Washington Consensus?". http://www.iie.com/publications/papers/williamson0799.htm, accessed November 10, 2003.
World Bank (1990). World Development Report 1990: Poverty. Oxford University Press for the World Bank, New York.
World Bank (1992a). World Bank Structural and Sectoral Adjustment Operations: the Second OED Review. Operations Evaluation Department report 10870. World Bank, Washington, DC.
World Bank (1992b). Effective Implementation: Key to Development Impact. Report of the World Bank's Management Task Force. Washington, DC.
World Bank (1998). Assessing Aid: What Works, What Doesn't, and Why. Oxford University Press, New York.

World Bank (2000). World Development Report 2000/2001: Attacking Poverty. Oxford University Press for the World Bank, New York.

Younger, S. (1992). "Aid and the Dutch disease: macroeconomic management when everybody loves you". World Development 20 (11), 1587–1597.

AUTHOR INDEX OF VOLUME 2

n indicates citation in a footnote.

SUBJECT INDEX OF VOLUME 2